Fundamentals of Advanced Accounting

Ninth Edition

Joe B. Hoyle

Associate Professor of Accounting
Accounting Teaching Fellow
Robins School of Business
University of Richmond

Thomas F. Schaefer

Professor Emeritus of Accountancy
Mendoza College of Business
University of Notre Dame

Timothy S. Doupnik

Distinguished Professor Emeritus of Accounting
Darla Moore School of Business
University of South Carolina

Mc
Graw
Hill

FUNDAMENTALS OF ADVANCED ACCOUNTING

Published by McGraw Hill LLC, 1325 Avenue of the Americas, New York, NY 10019. Copyright ©2024 by McGraw Hill LLC. All rights reserved. Printed in the United States of America. No part of this publication may be reproduced or distributed in any form or by any means, or stored in a database or retrieval system, without the prior written consent of McGraw Hill LLC, including, but not limited to, in any network or other electronic storage or transmission, or broadcast for distance learning.

Some ancillaries, including electronic and print components, may not be available to customers outside the United States.

This book is printed on acid-free paper.

1 2 3 4 5 6 7 8 9 LWI 28 27 26 25 24 23

ISBN 978-1-266-26853-3
MHID 1-266-26853-7

Cover Image: *Shutterstock / Mehaniq*

mheducation.com/highered

To our families

The real purpose of books is to trap the mind into doing its own thinking.

—Christopher Morley

About the Authors

Courtesy of Joe B. Hoyle

Joe B. Hoyle, *University of Richmond*

Joe B. Hoyle is an associate professor of accounting at the Robins School of Business at the University of Richmond. He is also an Accounting Teaching Fellow. In 2015, he was the first recipient of the J. Michael and Mary Anne Cook Prize for undergraduate teaching. The Cook Prize is awarded by the American Accounting Association and "is the foremost recognition of an individual who consistently demonstrates the attributes of a superior teacher in the discipline of accounting." In 2019, former students raised money to create an Accounting Teaching Fellowship, which will be renamed the "Joe Hoyle Accounting Teaching Fellowship" on his eventual retirement. He has authored a book of essays titled *Tips and Thoughts on Improving the Teaching Process in College,* which is available at https://facultystaff.richmond .edu/~jhoyle/documents/book-teaching-x.doc.pdf. His blog, *Teaching—Getting the Most from Your Students,* at http://joehoyle-teaching.blogspot.com/ was named the Accounting Education Innovation of the Year for 2013 by the American Accounting Association.

Courtesy of Thomas F. Schaefer

Thomas F. Schaefer, *University of Notre Dame*

Thomas F. Schaefer is a professor emeritus of accountancy at the University of Notre Dame. He has written a number of articles for scholarly journals such as the *Accounting Review, Journal of Accounting Research, Journal of Accounting & Economics, Accounting Horizons,* and others. His primary teaching and research interests are in financial accounting and reporting. Tom is a past president of the American Accounting Association's Accounting Program Leadership Group. He received the 2007 Joseph A. Silvoso Faculty Merit Award from the Federation of Schools of Accountancy and the 2013 Notre Dame Master of Science in Accountancy Dincolo Outstanding Professor Award.

Courtesy of Timothy S. Doupnik

Timothy S. Doupnik, *University of South Carolina*

Timothy S. Doupnik is a distinguished professor emeritus of accounting at the University of South Carolina. His primary teaching interests are in financial and international accounting. Tim has published extensively in the area of international accounting in journals such as the *Accounting Review; Accounting, Organizations, and Society; Abacus; International Journal of Accounting;* and *Journal of International Business Studies.* Tim is a past president of the American Accounting Association's (AAA) International Accounting Section and a recipient of the section's Outstanding International Accounting Educator Award. He is a coauthor of the paper that received the AAA's Notable Contribution to the Auditing Literature Award in 2019.

Overall—this edition of the text provides relevant and up-to-date accounting standards references to the Financial Accounting Standards Board (FASB) *Accounting Standards Codification®* **(ASC). We've also added new Hint Videos, Integrated Excel problems, and Data Analytics materials available only in Connect!**

Chapter Changes for *Fundamentals of Advanced Accounting,* 9th Edition:

Chapter 1

- Updated real-world references and examples.
- Revised several end-of-chapter problems.

Chapter 2

- Three new business combinations are discussed in terms of motivations to combine Goodyear Tire and Rubber-Cooper Tire and Rubber, Google-Fitbit, and Uber-Postmates.
- Updated real-world references and examples.
- Revised several end-of-chapter problems and added three new business combination cases.

Chapter 3

- Added a special *On the Horizon* discussion titled "FASB Considers Goodwill Amortization."
- Updated real-world references and examples.
- Revised several end-of-chapter problems. In particular, previous asset allocations to customer-related items in acquisitions were changed to other intangible asset categories in light of proposed FASB action.
- Updated and revised end-of-chapter impairment analysis case.

Chapter 4

- Updated real-world references and examples.
- Revised end-of-chapter problems and cases.

- Revised and streamlined the "Does GAAP Undervalue Post-Control Stock Acquisitions?" *discussion question.*
- Revised several end-of-chapter problems (including the conversion of eight multiple choice questions to open-ended problems).
- Included a new step-acquisition case and an updated Costco noncontrolling interest case.

Chapter 5

- Revised end-of-chapter problems including the conversion of six multiple-choice questions to open-ended problems.
- Included a new end-of-chapter problem that focuses on intra-entity transfers (inventory and equipment) for a 100 percent-owned subsidiary.

Chapter 6

- Updated real-world references and examples.
- Revised, clarified, and simplified the section on consolidated earnings per share (EPS). The EPS example now includes only the effect of subsidiary convertible bonds for consideration of the subsidiary's effect on diluted EPS. The example is not only simplified but provides improved alignment with end-of-chapter problems.
- Revised end-of-chapter problems including the conversion of three multiple-choice questions to open-ended problems.

Chapter 7

- Replaced one of the real-world example companies used in the "Introduction" to demonstrate the significance of export sales and foreign currency hedging for some entities.

- Updated real-world references including excerpts from annual reports.
- Changed the exchange rate in the fictitious International Company illustration included in "Derivatives Accounting" to be more consistent with the current U.S. dollar/Mexican peso exchange rate.
- Added a discussion question "Is Bitcoin a Foreign Currency?"
- Changed several multiple-choice format problems at the end of the chapter to a requirement format.
- Added several new multiple-choice format problems to replace those converted to a requirement format.
- Changed hypothetical company names in several end-of-chapter problems to provide more diversity.
- Made a variety of changes to the historical exchange rates internet case, including changing the company name, locations of customers, and so on.

Chapter 8

- Replaced merger-and-acquisition bullet items at the beginning of this chapter with updated information from a different set of companies.
- Updated information about countries currently meeting the definition of highly inflationary economy.
- Updated real-world references, including examples of company practices and excerpts from annual reports.
- Rephrased most bullet items in the section "*International Accounting Standard 21—The Effects of Changes in Foreign Exchange Rates.*"
- Deleted a quote related to determining the functional currency in "Comparison of the Results from Applying the Two Different Methods."
- Converted several multiple-choice format problems at the end of the chapter to a requirement format.
- Added one new multiple-choice problem.
- Changed fictitious company names in several problems and cases to increase diversity.

Chapter 9

- Updated real-world references.
- Revised end-of-chapter problems, including the conversion of six multiple-choice questions to open-ended problems.

Chapter 10

- Changed the names of fictitious partners in several illustrations, discussion questions, and end-of-chapter problems and cases to add diversity.
- Converted several multiple-choice format problems to a requirement format.

Chapter 11

- Updated numerous references to the financial statements of a wide variety of state and local governments such as the City of Houston, the City of Dallas, the City of Greensboro, and the City of Las Vegas. This information helps students to see real-world examples of financial reporting in its current form.
- Updated all references from the old terminology (Comprehensive Annual Financial Report) to the new terminology (Annual Comprehensive Financial Report).

Chapter 12

- Provided discussion of GASB's current project to update the financial reporting model for state and local governments.
- Updated references to the financial statements of state and local governments such as the City of Los Angeles, the City of Buffalo, the City of Atlanta, the City of Detroit, and the City of Boston.
- Created a completely new illustration of the financial statements for a public college or university to help students better understand the meaning and structure of the reporting process.

The approach used by Hoyle, Schaefer, and Doupnik allows students to think critically about accounting, just as they will in their careers and as they prepare for the CPA exam. Read on to understand how students will succeed as accounting majors and as future CPAs by using *Fundamentals of Advanced Accounting,* 9e.

Thinking Critically

With this text, students gain a well-balanced appreciation of the accounting profession. As *Fundamentals of Advanced Accounting,* 9e, introduces them to the field's many aspects, it often focuses on past controversies and present resolutions. The text shows the development of financial reporting as a product of intense and considered debate that continues today and will in the future.

Readability

The writing style of the previous editions has been highly praised. **Students easily comprehend** chapter concepts because of the conversational tone used throughout the book. The authors have made every effort to ensure that the writing style remains engaging, lively, and consistent.

Real-World Examples

Students are better able to relate what they learn to what they will encounter in the business world after reading these frequent examples. Quotations, articles, and illustrations from *Forbes,* the *Wall Street Journal, Time,* and *Bloomberg BusinessWeek* are incorporated throughout the text. Data have been pulled from business, not-for-profit, and government financial statements as well as official pronouncements.

Discussion Questions

This feature **facilitates student understanding** of the underlying accounting principles at work in particular reporting situations. Similar to mini cases, these questions help explain the issues at hand in practical terms. Many times, these cases are designed to demonstrate to students why a topic is problematic and worth considering.

McGraw Hill and UWorld are dedicated to supporting every accounting student along their journey, ultimately helping them achieve career success in the accounting profession.

In partnership with UWorld, a global leader in education technology, we provide students a smooth transition from the accounting classroom to successful completion of the CPA Exam. While many aspiring accountants wait until they have completed their academic studies to begin preparing for the CPA Exam, research shows that those who become familiar with exam content earlier in the process have a stronger chance of successfully passing. Accordingly, students using these McGraw Hill materials will have access to the highest quality CPA Exam task-based simulations from UWorld, with expert-written explanations and solutions. All questions are either directly from the AICPA or are modeled on AICPA questions that appear in the exam.

For more information about the full UWorld CPA Review program, exam requirements, and exam content, visit https://accounting.uworld.com/cpa-review/partner/university/.

End-of-Chapter Materials

As in previous editions, the end-of-chapter material remains a strength of the text. The sheer number of questions, problems, and Connect assignments test and, therefore, **expand the students' knowledge** of chapter concepts.

"Develop Your Skills" asks questions that address the four skills students need to master to pass the CPA exam: Research, Analysis, Spreadsheet, and Communication. An icon indicates when these skills are tested.

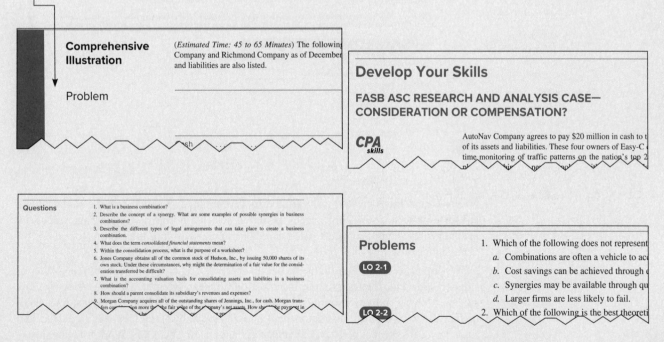

The 9th edition of *Fundamentals of Advanced Accounting* has a full Connect package, with the following features available for instructors and students.

- **SmartBook**® is the market-leading adaptive study resource that is proven to strengthen memory recall, increase retention, and boost grades. SmartBook 2.0 identifies and closes knowledge gaps through a continually adapting reading and questioning experience that helps students master the key concepts in the chapter. SmartBook 2.0 is the latest version of SmartBook, with key updates to: improve accessibility, provide mobile functionality, allow a more granular level of content selection, and provide the ability to assign Recharge activities.

- The **end-of-chapter content** in Connect provides a robust offering of review and question material designed to aid and assess the student's retention of chapter content. The end-of-chapter content is composed of both static and algorithmic versions of the problems in each chapter, which are designed to challenge students using McGraw Hill Education's state-of-the-art online homework technology. Connect helps students learn more efficiently by providing feedback and practice material when and where they need it. Connect grades homework automatically, and students benefit from the immediate feedback that they receive, particularly on any questions they may have missed.

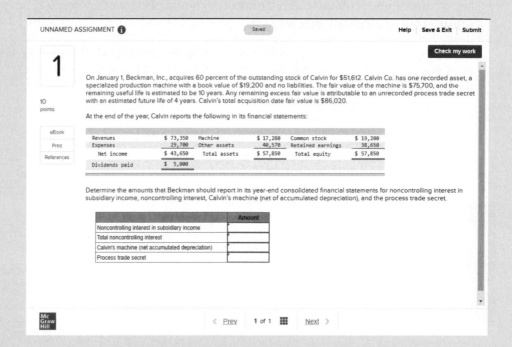

- NEW! **Hint Videos** created and narrated by text author Joe Hoyle provide students with guidance on to how to approach key points of selected problems. These Hint videos are available only within Connect. The instructor can chose to turn the Hint feature on or off via assignment settings.

- NEW! **Integrated Excel** assignments pair the power of Microsoft Excel with the power of Connect. A seamless integration of Excel within Connect, Integrated Excel questions allow students to work in live, auto-graded Excel spreadsheets—no additional logins, no need to upload or download files. Instructors can choose to grade by formula or solution value, and students receive instant cell-level feedback via integrated Check My Work functionality.

- NEW! **Applying Tableau** data analytics assignments are available only in Connect. (Tableau software is free to students and instructors). These assignments provide students with an Excel data file and detailed instructions that walk through the necessary steps and functions of creating a Tableau dashboard.

- The **Test Bank** for each chapter has been updated to stay current with new and revised chapter material, with all questions available for assignment through Connect. Instructors can also create tests and quizzes with Test Builder, a cloud-based tool available within Connect that formats tests for printing or for administering within an LMS.

- The **Instructor and Student Resources** have been updated and are available in the Connect Instructor Resources page. Available resources include Instructor and Solutions Manuals and PowerPoint presentations. All applicable Student Resources will be available in a convenient file that can be distributed to students for classes either directly, through Connect, or via courseware.

Acknowledgments

We could not produce a textbook of the quality and scope of *Fundamentals of Advanced Accounting* without the help of a great number of people. Special thanks go to the following:

- Gregory Schaefer for his Chapter 2 descriptions of recent business combinations.
- Additionally, we would like to thank John Abernathy of Kennesaw State University, for updating and revising the PowerPoint presentations; Robert J. Knisley of Wheaton College and Dwayne Powell of Arkansas State University for contributing to the Integrated Excel Exercises; Eric Weinstein of SUNY Suffolk for contributing to the Data Analytics materials; Stacie Hughes for updating the test bank; Mark McCarthy of East Carolina University and Beth Kobylarz of Accuracy Counts for checking the text, Solutions Manual, and test bank for accuracy; Barbara Gershman of Northern Virginia Community College for checking the PowerPoints, and Beth Kobylarz and Teri Zuccaro for their Connect accuracy reviews.

We also want to thank the many people who completed questionnaires and reviewed the book. Our sincerest thanks to them all:

John Abernathy, *Kennesaw State University*
Lisa Busto, *Harper College*
Kevin Cabe, *Indiana Wesleyan University*
Jason Chen, *Central Connecticut State University*
Michael Cohen, *Rutgers University—Newark*
Lorraine Contri, *Kean University*
Martha Owens Cranford, *Rowan Cabarrus Community College*
Hong Kim Duong, *Old Dominion University*
Zev Fried, *Fairleigh Dickinson University*
Marina Grau, *Houston Community College*
Thomas P. Hayes, Jr., *University of Arkansas*
Shuoyuan He, *Tulane University*
Barry Hettler, *Ohio University*
Yongtao Hong, *North Dakota State University*
Stacie Hughes, *Athens State University*
Marianne James, *California State University, Los Angeles*
Sehan Kim, *University of Houston—Clear Lake*
Laura Lee, *Saint Mary's University—Minnesota*
Lisa Ludlum, *Western Illinois University*
Steven Mezzio, *Pace University*

Daniel Neely, *University of Wisconsin—Milwaukee*
Matthew Njoku, *Central Piedmont Community College*
Peggy O'Kelly, *Northeastern University*
Luis Plascencia, *Harold Washington College*
Philip Slater, *Forsyth Technical Community College*
Hakjoon Song, *California State University, Dominguez Hills*
Vernon Stanger, *Trine University*
Cindy Steward, *University of Illinois at Urbana—Champaign*
Andrea Still, *Indiana University*
William D. Stout, *University of Louisville*
Inho Suk, *SUNY—Buffalo*
Ian A. Van Deventer, *Spalding University*
Cammy Wayne, *Harper College*
James Webb, *University of California—Berkeley*
Arthur Wharton, *Virginia State University*
Jan Williams, *University of Baltimore*
Hannah Wong, *William Paterson University*
Sung Wook Yoon, *California State University, Northridge*
Nancy Yuen, *Saint Mary's College of California*
Kathy Zolton, *University of Texas at Dallas*

We also pass along a word of thanks to all the people at McGraw Hill Education who participated in the creation of this edition. In particular, Sherry Kane, Content Project Manager; Rachel Hirschfield, Manufacturing Project Manager; Christina Sanders, Lead Product Developer; Rachel Hinton, Assessment Product Developer; Stephanie DeRosa, Associate Portfolio Manager; Becky Olson, Director; Brian Nacik, Lead Assessment Content Project Manager; and, Harper Christopher, Marketing Manager, all contributed significantly to the project, and we appreciate their efforts.

Instructors
Student Success Starts with You

Tools to enhance your unique voice

Want to build your own course? No problem. Prefer to use an OLC-aligned, prebuilt course? Easy. Want to make changes throughout the semester? Sure. And you'll save time with Connect's auto-grading, too.

65%
Less Time Grading

Laptop: Getty Images; Woman/dog: George Doyle/Getty Images

A unique path for each student

In Connect, instructors can assign an adaptive reading experience with SmartBook® 2.0. Rooted in advanced learning science principles, SmartBook 2.0 delivers each student a personalized experience, focusing students on their learning gaps, ensuring that the time they spend studying is time well-spent. **mheducation.com/highered/connect/smartbook**

Affordable solutions, added value

Make technology work for you with LMS integration for single sign-on access, mobile access to the digital textbook, and reports to quickly show you how each of your students is doing. And with our Inclusive Access program, you can provide all these tools at the lowest available market price to your students. Ask your McGraw Hill representative for more information.

Solutions for your challenges

A product isn't a solution. Real solutions are affordable, reliable, and come with training and ongoing support when you need it and how you want it. Visit **supportateverystep.com** for videos and resources both you and your students can use throughout the term.

Students
Get Learning that Fits You

Effective tools for efficient studying

Connect is designed to help you be more productive with simple, flexible, intuitive tools that maximize your study time and meet your individual learning needs. Get learning that works for you with Connect.

Study anytime, anywhere

Download the free ReadAnywhere® app and access your online eBook, SmartBook® 2.0, or Adaptive Learning Assignments when it's convenient, even if you're offline. And since the app automatically syncs with your Connect account, all of your work is available every time you open it. Find out more at **mheducation.com/readanywhere**

"I really liked this app—it made it easy to study when you don't have your text-book in front of you."

- Jordan Cunningham, Eastern Washington University

iPhone: Getty Images

Everything you need in one place

Your Connect course has everything you need—whether reading your digital eBook or completing assignments for class, Connect makes it easy to get your work done.

Learning for everyone

McGraw Hill works directly with Accessibility Services Departments and faculty to meet the learning needs of all students. Please contact your Accessibility Services Office and ask them to email accessibility@mheducation.com, or visit **mheducation.com/about/accessibility** for more information.

Brief Contents

Contents

The Equity Method of Accounting for Investments

T he first several chapters of this text present the accounting and reporting for investment activities of businesses. The focus is on investments when one firm possesses either significant influence or control over another through ownership of voting shares. When one firm owns enough voting shares to be able to affect the decisions of another, accounting for the investment can become challenging and complex. The source of such complexities typically stems from the fact that transactions among the firms affiliated through ownership cannot be considered independent, arm's-length transactions. As in many matters relating to financial reporting, we look to transactions with *outside parties* to provide a basis for accounting valuation. When firms are affiliated through a common set of owners, measurements that recognize the relationships among the firms help provide objectivity in financial reporting.

Why Do Business Firms Invest in the Equity Shares of Other Business Firms?

We frequently see businesses buying equity shares (e.g., common stock) of other businesses. To understand the accounting for equity share acquisitions, it's helpful to understand two fundamental motivations for such investments. First, firms may temporarily invest in another firm's equity shares simply to earn a return on otherwise idle cash. Companies such as Microsoft, Google, and Starbucks each have large amounts of short-term investments in marketable equity securities that can produce both dividend income and share value appreciation.

Second, in sufficient quantity, equity shares can provide a powerful business tool to investors. Equity share ownership typically provides voting privileges to elect members to a firm's board of directors. Boards of directors are the highest authority in the management of a corporation. They make strategic decisions regarding how the firm will conduct its business. Boards set company policies and hire (and fire) management. Thus, the ability to vote for directors can be a powerful tool to influence the decisions of an investee corporation. Consequently, many firms will buy sufficient voting shares to enable the election of their representatives to another firm's board of directors. The range of ownership may result in the ability to influence the investee through the election of a single director all the way to complete control.

By exercising their voting rights over the investee, an investor firm can wield power over the strategic direction of the investee in ways that align with its own operating and financial interests. For example, an investee may be considering inventory purchases or sale contracts with several outside firms. An investor firm, through its designated members on the investee

Learning Objectives

After studying this chapter, you should be able to:

LO 1-1 Describe motivations for a firm to gain significant influence over another firm.

LO 1-2 Describe in general the various methods of accounting for an investment in equity shares of another company.

LO 1-3 Identify the sole criterion for applying the equity method of accounting and know the guidelines to assess whether the criterion is met.

LO 1-4 Describe the financial reporting for equity method investments and prepare basic equity method journal entries for an investor.

LO 1-5 Allocate the cost of an equity method investment and compute amortization expense to match revenues recognized from the investment to the excess of investor cost over investee book value.

LO 1-6 Understand the financial reporting consequences for:
a. A change to the equity method.
b. Investee's other comprehensive income.
c. Investee losses.
d. Sales of equity method investments.

LO 1-7 Describe the rationale and computations to defer the investor's share of gross profits on intra-entity inventory sales until the goods are either consumed by the owner or sold to outside parties.

LO 1-8 Explain the rationale and reporting implications of fair-value accounting for investments otherwise accounted for by the equity method.

LO 1-1

Describe motivations for a firm to gain significant influence over another firm.

board of directors, possesses the power to influence the selection of the outside firm—including the investor firm itself. Other examples abound, including cooperation between the investor and investee on research, technology, product development, licensing, advertising, distribution, market expansion, etc. Thus, we see businesses acquiring the equity shares of other businesses throughout the economy.

The Reporting of Investments in Corporate Equity Securities

In its 2021 annual report, The Coca-Cola Company describes its 28 percent investment in Coca-Cola FEMSA, a Mexican bottling company with operations throughout much of Latin America. The Coca-Cola Company uses the equity method to account for several of its bottling company investments, including Coca-Cola FEMSA. The annual report states:

> We use the equity method to account for investments in companies, if our investment provides us with the ability to exercise significant influence over operating and financial policies of the investee. Our consolidated net income includes our Company's proportionate share of the net income or loss of these companies.
>
> Our judgment regarding the level of influence over each equity method investment includes considering key factors such as our ownership interest, representation on the board of directors, participation in policy-making decisions and material intercompany transactions.

Such information is hardly unusual in the business world; corporate investors frequently acquire ownership shares of both domestic and foreign businesses. These investments can range from the purchase of a few shares to the acquisition of 100 percent control. Although purchases of corporate equity securities (such as the ones made by Coca-Cola) are not uncommon, they pose a considerable number of financial reporting issues because a close relationship has been established without the investor gaining actual control. These issues are currently addressed by the *equity method.* This chapter deals with accounting for stock investments that fall under the application of this method.

Generally accepted accounting principles (GAAP) recognize four different approaches to the financial reporting of investments in corporate equity securities:

LO 1-2

Describe in general the various methods of accounting for an investment in equity shares of another company.

1. Fair-value method.
2. Cost method for equity securities without readily determinable fair values.
3. Consolidation of financial statements.
4. Equity method.

The financial statement reporting for a particular investment depends primarily on the degree of influence that the investor (stockholder) has over the investee, a factor most often indicated by the relative size of ownership.[1] Because voting power typically accompanies ownership of equity shares, influence increases with the relative size of ownership. The resulting influence can be very little, a significant amount, or, in some cases, complete control.

Fair-Value Method

In many instances, an investor possesses only a small percentage of an investee company's outstanding stock, perhaps only a few shares. Because of the limited level of ownership, the investor cannot expect to significantly affect the investee's operations or decision making. These shares are bought in anticipation of cash dividends or appreciation of stock market values. Such investments are recorded at cost and periodically adjusted to fair value according to the Financial Accounting Standards Board (FASB) *Accounting Standards Codification®* (ASC) Topic 321, "Investments—Equity Securities."

---

[1] The relative size of ownership is most often the key factor in assessing one company's degree of influence over another. However, as discussed later in this chapter, other factors (e.g., contractual relationships between firms) can also provide influence or control over firms, regardless of the percentage of shares owned.

Fair value is defined by the ASC (Master Glossary) as the "price that would be received to sell an asset or paid to transfer a liability in an orderly transaction between market participants at the measurement date." For most investments in equity securities, quoted stock market prices represent fair values.

Because a full coverage of limited ownership investments in equity securities is presented in intermediate accounting textbooks, only the following basic principles of the fair value method are noted here:

- Initial investments in equity securities are recorded at cost and subsequently adjusted to fair value if fair value is readily determinable (typically by reference to market value); otherwise, the investment remains at cost.
- Changes in the fair values of equity securities during a reporting period are recognized as income.[2]
- Dividends declared on the equity securities are recognized as income.

The preceding procedures are followed for equity security investments (with readily determinable fair values) when the owner possesses neither significant influence nor control.

Cost Method (Investments in Equity Securities without Readily Determinable Fair Values)

When the fair value of an investment in equity securities is not readily determinable, and the investment provides neither significant influence nor control, the investment may be measured at cost. Such investments sometimes can be found in ownership shares of firms that are not publicly traded or experience only infrequent trades.

Investments in equity securities that employ the cost method often continue to be reported at their original cost over time.[3] Income from cost method equity investments usually consists of the investor's share of dividends declared by the investee. However, despite its emphasis on cost measurements, GAAP allows for two fair-value assessments that may affect cost method amounts reported on the balance sheet and the income statement.

- First, cost method equity investments periodically must be assessed for impairment to determine if the fair value of the investment is less than its carrying amount. The ASC allows a qualitative assessment to determine if impairment is likely.[4] Because the fair value of a cost method equity investment is not readily available (by definition), if impairment is deemed likely, an entity must estimate a fair value for the investment to measure the amount (if any) of the impairment loss.
- Second, ASC (321-10-35-2) allows for recognition of "observable price changes in orderly transactions for the identical or a similar investment of the same issuer." Any unrealized holding gains (or losses) from these observable price changes are included in earnings with a corresponding adjustment to the investment account. So even if equity shares are only infrequently traded (and thus fair value is not readily determinable), such trades can provide a basis for financial statement recognition under the cost method for equity investments.

Consolidation of Financial Statements

Many corporate investors acquire enough shares to gain actual control over an investee's operations. In financial accounting, such control may be achieved when a stockholder

---

[2] ASC 320, *Investments—Debt and Equity Securities,* requires equity investments (except those accounted for under the equity method of accounting or those that result in consolidation of the investee) to be measured at fair value with changes in fair value recognized in net income, unless fair values are not readily determinable.

[3] Dividends received in excess of earnings subsequent to the date of investment are considered returns of the investment and are recorded as reductions of cost of the investment.

[4] Impairment indicators include assessments of earnings performance, economic environment, going-concern ability, etc. If the qualitative assessment does not indicate impairment, no further testing is required. If an equity security without a readily determinable fair value is impaired, the investor recognizes the difference between the investment's fair value and carrying amount as an impairment loss in net income (ASC 321-10-35-3).

accumulates more than 50 percent of an organization's outstanding voting stock. At that point, rather than simply influencing the investee's decisions, the investor often can direct the entire decision-making process. A review of the financial statements of America's largest organizations indicates that legal control of one or more subsidiary companies is an almost universal practice. PepsiCo, Inc., as just one example, holds a majority interest in the voting stock of literally hundreds of corporations.

Investor control over an investee presents a special accounting challenge. Normally, when a majority of voting stock is held, the investor–investee relationship is so closely connected that the two corporations are viewed as a single entity for reporting purposes.[5] Consequently, an entirely different set of accounting procedures is applicable. Control generally requires the consolidation of the accounting information produced by the individual companies. Thus, a single set of financial statements is created for external reporting purposes with all assets, liabilities, revenues, and expenses brought together. The various procedures applied within this consolidation process are examined in subsequent chapters of this textbook.

The FASB ASC Section 810-10-05 on variable interest entities expands the use of consolidated financial statements to include entities that are financially controlled through special contractual arrangements rather than through voting stock interests. Prior to the accounting requirements for variable interest entities, many firms (e.g., Enron) avoided consolidation of entities that they owned little or no voting stock in but otherwise controlled through special contracts. These entities were frequently referred to as special purpose entities (SPEs) and provided vehicles for some firms to keep large amounts of assets and liabilities off their consolidated financial statements. Accounting for these entities is discussed in Chapters 2 and 6.

Equity Method

Another investment relationship is appropriately accounted for using the equity method. In many investments, although control is not achieved, the degree of ownership indicates the ability of the investor to exercise *significant influence* over the investee. If an investor holds between 20 and 50 percent of the voting stock of the investee, significant influence is normally assumed and the equity method is applied. For example, Berkshire Hathaway notes in its 2021 annual report that it owns 26.5 percent of the outstanding shares of The Kraft Heinz Company common stock, which is accounted for under the equity method. Undoubtedly, through its ownership, Berkshire Hathaway can influence Kraft Heinz's decisions and operations.

To provide objective reporting for investments with significant influence, FASB ASC Topic 323, "Investments—Equity Method and Joint Ventures," describes the use of the equity method. The equity method employs the accrual basis for recognizing the investor's share of investee income. Accordingly, the investor recognizes income as it is earned by the investee. As noted in FASB ASC (para. 323-10-05-5), because of its significant influence over the investee, the investor

> has a degree of responsibility for the return on its investment and it is appropriate to include in the results of operations of the investor its share of earnings or losses of the investee.

Furthermore, under the equity method, the investor records its share of investee dividends declared as a decrease in the investment account, not as income.

In today's business world, many corporations hold significant ownership interests in other companies without having actual control. The Coca-Cola Company, for example, owns between 20 and 50 percent of several bottling companies, both domestic and international. Many other equity method investments represent joint ventures in which two or more companies form a new enterprise to carry out a specified operating purpose. For example, Boeing and Lockheed Martin formed a joint venture named United Launch Alliance that manufactures and operates rocket vehicles for both scientific and national security purposes. Each partner owns 50 percent of the joint venture. For each of these investments, the investors do not possess absolute control because they hold less than a majority of the voting stock. Thus, the preparation of consolidated financial statements is inappropriate. However, the large percentage of ownership indicates that each investor possesses some ability to affect the investee's decision-making process.

---

[5] As discussed in Chapter 2, ownership of a majority voting interest in an investee does not always lead to consolidated financial statements.

[?] **Discussion Question**

DID THE COST METHOD INVITE EARNINGS MANIPULATION?

Prior to GAAP for equity method investments, firms used the cost method to account for their unconsolidated investments in common stock regardless of the presence of significant influence. Under the cost method, when the investee declares a dividend, the investor records "dividend income." The investment account typically remains at its original cost—hence the term *cost method.*

Many firms' compensation plans reward managers based on reported annual income. How might the use of the cost method of accounting for significant influence investments have resulted in unintended wealth transfers from owners to managers? Do the equity or fair-value methods provide similar incentives?

Finally, as discussed at the end of this chapter, firms may elect a fair-value option in their financial reporting for certain financial assets and financial liabilities. Among the qualifying financial assets for fair-value reporting are significant influence investments otherwise accounted for by the equity method.

Application of the Equity Method

An understanding of the equity method is best gained by initially examining the FASB's treatment of two questions:

1. What factors indicate when the equity method should be used for an investment in another entity's ownership securities?
2. How should the investor report this investment, and the income generated by it, to reflect the relationship between the two entities?

LO 1-3

Identify the sole criterion for applying the equity method of accounting and know the guidelines to assess whether the criterion is met.

Criterion for Utilizing the Equity Method

The rationale underlying the equity method is that an investor begins to gain the ability to influence the decision-making process of an investee as the level of ownership rises. According to FASB ASC Topic 323 on equity method investments, achieving this "ability to exercise significant influence over operating and financial policies of an investee even though the investor holds 50 percent or less of the common stock" is the sole criterion for requiring application of the equity method (FASB ASC [para. 323-10-15-3]).

Clearly, a term such as *the ability to exercise significant influence* is nebulous and subject to a variety of judgments and interpretations in practice. At what point does the acquisition of one additional share of stock give an owner the ability to exercise significant influence? This decision becomes even more difficult in that only the *ability* to exercise significant influence need be present. There is no requirement that any actual influence must ever be applied.

FASB ASC Topic 323 provides guidance to the accountant by listing several conditions that indicate the presence of this degree of influence:

- Investor representation on the board of directors of the investee.
- Investor participation in the policy-making process of the investee.
- Material intra-entity transactions.

- Interchange of managerial personnel.
- Technological dependency.
- Extent of ownership by the investor in relation to the size and concentration of other ownership interests in the investee.

No single one of these guides should be used exclusively in assessing the applicability of the equity method. Instead, all are evaluated together to determine the presence or absence of the sole criterion: the ability to exercise significant influence over the investee.

These guidelines alone do not eliminate the leeway available to each investor when deciding whether the use of the equity method is appropriate. To provide a degree of consistency in applying this standard, the FASB provides a general ownership test: *If an investor holds between 20 and 50 percent of the voting stock of the investee, significant influence is normally assumed, and the equity method is applied.*

> An investment (direct or indirect) of 20 percent or more of the voting stock of an investee shall lead to a presumption that in the absence of predominant evidence to the contrary an investor has the ability to exercise significant influence over an investee. Conversely, an investment of less than 20 percent of the voting stock of an investee shall lead to a presumption that an investor does not have the ability to exercise significant influence unless such ability can be demonstrated.[6]

Limitations of Equity Method Applicability

At first, the 20 to 50 percent rule may appear to be an arbitrarily chosen boundary range established merely to provide a consistent method of reporting for investments. However, the essential criterion is still the ability to significantly influence (but not control) the investee, rather than 20 to 50 percent ownership. If the absence of this ability is proven (or control exists), the equity method should not be applied, regardless of the percentage of shares held.

For example, the equity method is not appropriate for investments that demonstrate any of the following characteristics, regardless of the investor's degree of ownership:[7]

- An agreement exists between investor and investee by which the investor surrenders significant rights as a shareholder.
- A concentration of ownership operates the investee without regard for the views of the investor.
- The investor attempts but fails to obtain representation on the investee's board of directors.

In each of these situations, because the investor is unable to exercise significant influence over its investee, the equity method is not applied.

Alternatively, if an entity can exercise *control* over its investee, regardless of its ownership level, consolidation (rather than the equity method) is appropriate. FASB ASC (para. 810-10-05-8) limits the use of the equity method by expanding the definition of a controlling financial interest and addresses situations in which financial control exists absent majority ownership interest. In these situations, control is achieved through contractual and other arrangements called *variable interests.*

To illustrate, one firm may create a separate legal entity in which it holds less than 50 percent of the voting interests but nonetheless controls that entity through governance document provisions and/or contracts that specify decision-making power and the distribution of profits and losses. Entities controlled in this fashion are typically designated as *variable interest entities,* and their sponsoring firm may be required to include them in consolidated financial reports despite the fact that ownership is less than 50 percent. For example, the Walt Disney Company reclassified several former equity method investees as variable interest entities and now consolidates these investments.[8]

---

[6] FASB ASC (para. 323-10-15-8).

[7] FASB ASC (para. 323-10-15-10). This paragraph deals specifically with limits to using the equity method for investments in which the owner holds 20 to 50 percent of the outstanding shares.

[8] Chapters 2 and 6 provide further discussions of variable interest entities.

Extensions of Equity Method Applicability

For some investments that either fall short of or exceed 20 to 50 percent ownership, the equity method is nonetheless appropriately used for financial reporting. As an example, The Coca-Cola Company owns a 19 percent investment in Monster Beverage Corporation. Coca-Cola noted in its financial statements following its Monster Beverage investment that "Based on our equity ownership percentage, the significance that our expanded distribution and coordination agreements have on Monster's operations, and our representation on Monster's Board of Directors, the Company is accounting for its interest in Monster as an equity method investment."

Conditions can also exist where the equity method is appropriate despite a majority ownership interest. In some instances, rights granted to noncontrolling shareholders restrict the powers of the majority shareholder. Such rights may include approval over compensation, hiring, termination, and other critical operating and capital spending decisions of an entity. If the noncontrolling rights are so restrictive as to call into question whether control rests with the majority owner, the equity method is employed for financial reporting rather than consolidation. For example, prior to its acquisition of BellSouth, AT&T, Inc., stated in its financial reports, "we account for our 60 percent economic investment in Cingular under the equity method of accounting because we share control equally with our 40 percent partner BellSouth."

To summarize, the following table indicates the method of accounting that is typically applicable to various stock investments:

Criterion	Normal Ownership Level	Applicable Accounting Method
Inability to significantly influence	Less than 20%	Fair value or cost method
Ability to significantly influence	20%–50%	Equity method or fair value
Control through voting interests	More than 50%	Consolidated financial statements
Control through variable interests (governance documents, contracts)	Primary beneficiary status (no ownership required)	Consolidated financial statements

LO 1-4

Describe the financial reporting for equity method investments and prepare basic equity method journal entries for an investor.

Accounting for an Investment—The Equity Method

Now that the criteria leading to the application of the equity method have been identified, a review of its reporting procedures is appropriate. Knowledge of this accounting process is especially important to users of the investor's financial statements because the equity method affects both the timing of income recognition and the carrying amount of the investment account.

In applying the equity method, the accounting objective is to report the investment and investment income to reflect the close relationship between the investor and investee. After recording the cost of the acquisition, two equity method entries periodically record the investment's impact:

1. The investor's investment account *increases as the investee recognizes and reports income.* Also, the investor recognizes investment income using the accrual method—that is, in the same period as reported by the investee in its financial statements. If an investee reports income of $100,000, a 30 percent owner should immediately increase its own income by $30,000. This earnings accrual reflects the essence of the equity method by emphasizing the connection between the two companies; as the owners' equity of the investee increases through the earnings process, the investment account also increases. Although the investor initially records the acquisition at cost, upward adjustments in the asset balance are recorded as soon as the investee makes a profit. The investor reduces the investment account if the investee reports a loss.

2. The investor decreases its investment account for its share of investee cash dividends. When the investee declares a cash dividend, its owners' equity decreases. The investor mirrors this change by recording a reduction in the carrying amount of the investment rather than recognizing the dividend as revenue. Furthermore, because the investor recognizes income when the investee recognizes it, double counting would occur if the investor also recorded its share of subsequent investee dividends as revenue. Importantly, a cash dividend declaration is not an appropriate point for income recognition. As stated in FASB ASC (para. 323-10-35-4),

> Under the equity method, an investor shall recognize its share of the earnings or losses of an investee in the periods for which they are reported by the investee in its financial statements rather than in the period in which an investee declares a dividend.

Because the investor can influence their timing, investee dividends cannot objectively measure income generated from the investment.

Application of Equity Method	
Investee Event	**Investor Accounting**
Income is recognized.	Proportionate share of income is recognized.
Dividends are declared.	Investor's share of investee dividends reduce the investment account.

Application of the equity method thus causes the investment account on the investor's balance sheet to vary directly with changes in the investee's equity.

In contrast, the fair-value method reports investments at fair value if it is readily determinable. Also, income is recognized both from changes in fair value and upon receipt of dividends. Consequently, financial reports can vary depending on whether the equity method or fair-value method is appropriate.

To illustrate, assume that Big Company purchased a 20 percent interest in Little Company on January 1, 2023, for $210,000. Little then reports net income of $200,000, $300,000, and $400,000, respectively, in the next three years while declaring dividends of $50,000, $100,000, and $200,000. The fair values of Big's investment in Little, as determined by market prices, were $245,000, $282,000, and $325,000 at the end of 2023, 2024, and 2025, respectively.

Exhibit 1.1 compares the accounting for Big's investment in Little across the two methods. The fair-value method carries the investment at its market values, presumed to be readily available in this example. Income is recognized both through changes in Little's fair value and as Little declares dividends.

EXHIBIT 1.1 Comparison of Fair-Value Method (ASC 321) and Equity Method (ASC 323)

Year	Income of Little Company	Dividends Declared by Little Company	Accounting by Big Company When Influence Is Not Significant (fair-value method)			Accounting by Big Company When Influence Is Significant (equity method)	
			Dividend Income	**Fair-Value Change to Income**	**Carrying Amount of Investment**	**Equity in Investee Income***	**Carrying Amount of Investment†**
2023	$200,000	$ 50,000	$ 10,000	$ 35,000	$245,000	$ 40,000	$240,000
2024	300,000	100,000	20,000	37,000	282,000	60,000	280,000
2025	400,000	200,000	40,000	43,000	325,000	80,000	320,000
Total income recognized			$ 70,000	$115,000		$180,000	

*Equity in investee income is 20 percent of the current year income reported by Little Company. For simplicity, we assume that Little's assets and liabilities have book values that approximate fair values at the acquisition date and Big's cost is proportionate to Little's book value.

†The carrying amount of an investment under the equity method is the original cost plus income recognized less dividends. For 2023, as an example, the $240,000 reported balance is the $210,000 cost plus $40,000 equity income less $10,000 in dividends.

In contrast, under the equity method, Big recognizes income as it is recorded by Little. As shown in Exhibit 1.1, Big recognizes $180,000 in income over the three years, and the carrying amount of the investment is adjusted upward to $320,000. Dividends from Little are not an appropriate measure of income because of the assumed significant influence over the investee. Big's ability to influence Little's decisions applies to the timing of dividend distributions. Therefore, dividends from Little do not objectively measure Big's income from its investment in Little. As Little records income, however, under the equity method Big recognizes its share (20 percent) of the income and increases the investment account. Thus, the equity method reflects the accrual model: The investor recognizes income as it is recognized by the investee, not when the investee declares a cash dividend.

Exhibit 1.1 shows that the carrying amount of the investment fluctuates each year under the equity method. This recording parallels the changes occurring in the net asset figures reported by the investee. If the owners' equity of the investee rises through income, an increase is made in the investment account; decreases such as losses and dividends cause reductions to be recorded. Thus, the equity method conveys information that describes the relationship created by the investor's ability to significantly influence the investee.

Equity Method Accounting Procedures

Once guidelines for the application of the equity method have been established, the mechanical process necessary for recording basic transactions is straightforward. The investor accrues its percentage of the earnings reported by the investee each period. Investee dividend declarations reduce the investment balance to reflect the decrease in the investee's book value.[9]

Referring again to the information presented in Exhibit 1.1, Little Company reported a net income of $200,000 during 2023 and declared and paid cash dividends of $50,000. These figures indicate that Little's net assets have increased by $150,000 during the year. Therefore, in its financial records, Big Company records the following journal entries to apply the equity method:

Investment in Little Company	40,000	
Equity in Investee Income		40,000
To accrue earnings of a 20 percent–owned investee ($200,000 × 20%).		
Dividend Receivable	10,000	
Investment in Little Company		10,000
To record a dividend declaration by Little Company ($50,000 × 20%).		
Cash	10,000	
Dividend Receivable		10,000
To record collection of the cash dividend.		

In the first entry, Big accrues income based on the investee's reported earnings. The second entry reflects the dividend declaration and the related reduction in Little's net assets followed then by the cash collection. The $30,000 net increment recorded here in Big's investment account ($40,000 − $10,000) represents 20 percent of the $150,000 increase in Little's book value that occurred during the year.

Excess of Investment Cost over Book Value Acquired

LO 1-5

Allocate the cost of an equity method investment and compute amortization expense to match revenues recognized from the investment to the excess of investor cost over investee book value.

After the basic concepts and procedures of the equity method are mastered, more complex accounting issues can be introduced. Surely one of the most common problems encountered in applying the equity method occurs when the investment cost exceeds the proportionate book value of the investee company.[10]

---

[9] In this text, the terms *book value* and *carrying amount* are used synonymously. Each refers to either an account balance, an amount appearing in a financial statement, or the amount of net assets (stockholders' equity) of a business entity.

[10] Although encountered less frequently, investments can be purchased at a cost that is less than the underlying book value of the investee. Accounting for this possibility is explored in later chapters.

Discussion Question

DOES THE EQUITY METHOD REALLY APPLY HERE?

Abraham, Inc., a New Jersey corporation, operates 57 bakeries throughout the northeastern section of the United States. In the past, its founder, James Abraham, owned all the company's outstanding common stock. However, during the early part of this year, the corporation suffered a severe cash flow problem brought on by rapid expansion. To avoid bankruptcy, Abraham sought additional investment capital from a friend, Dennis Bostitch, who owns Highland Laboratories. Subsequently, Highland paid $700,000 cash to Abraham, Inc., to acquire enough newly issued shares of common stock for a one-third ownership interest.

At the end of this year, the accountants for Highland Laboratories are discussing the proper method of reporting this investment. One argues for maintaining the asset at its original cost: "This purchase is no more than a loan to bail out the bakeries. Mr. Abraham will continue to run the organization with little or no attention paid to us. After all, what does anyone in our company know about baking bread? I would be surprised if Abraham does not reacquire these shares as soon as the bakery business is profitable again."

One of the other accountants disagrees, stating that the equity method is appropriate. "I realize that our company is not capable of running a bakery. However, the official rules state that we must have only the *ability* to exert significant influence. With one-third of the common stock in our possession, we certainly have that ability. Whether we use it or not, this ability means that we are required to apply the equity method."

How should Highland Laboratories account for its investment in Abraham, Inc.?

Unless the investor acquires its ownership at the time of the investee's conception, paying an amount equal to book value is rare. A number of possible reasons exist for a difference between the book value of a company and its fair value as reflected by the price of its stock. A company's fair value at any time is based on a multitude of factors such as company profitability, the introduction of a new product, expected dividend payments, projected operating results, and general economic conditions. Furthermore, stock prices are based, at least partially, on the perceived worth of a company's net assets, amounts that often vary dramatically from underlying book values. Many asset and liability accounts shown on a balance sheet tend to measure historical costs rather than current value. In addition, these reported figures are affected by the specific accounting methods adopted by a company. Inventory costing methods such as LIFO and FIFO, for example, obviously lead to different book values as does each of the acceptable depreciation methods.

If an investment is acquired at a price in excess of the investee's book value, logical reasons should explain the additional cost incurred by the investor. The source of the excess of cost over book value is important. Income recognition requires matching the income generated from the investment with its cost. Excess costs allocated to fixed assets will likely be expensed over longer periods than costs allocated to inventory. In applying the equity method, the cause of such an excess payment can be divided into two general categories:

1. Specifically identifiable investee assets and liabilities can have fair values that differ from their present book values. The excess payment can be identified directly with individual accounts such as inventory, equipment, franchise rights, and so on.
2. The investor may pay an extra amount because it expects future benefits to accrue from the investment. Such benefits could be anticipated as the result of factors such as the estimated profitability of the investee or the expected relationship between the two companies. When

the additional payment cannot be attributed to any specifically identifiable investee asset or liability, the investor recognizes an intangible asset called *goodwill.* For example, eBay, Inc., once disclosed in its annual report that goodwill related to its equity method investments was approximately $27.4 million.

As an illustration, assume that Grande Company is negotiating the acquisition of 30 percent of the outstanding shares of Chico Company. Chico's balance sheet reports assets of $500,000 and liabilities of $300,000 for a net book value of $200,000. After investigation, Grande determines that Chico's equipment is undervalued in the company's financial records by $60,000. One of its patents is also undervalued, but only by $40,000. By adding these valuation adjustments to Chico's book value, Grande arrives at an estimated $300,000 worth for the company's net assets. Based on this computation, Grande offers $90,000 for a 30 percent share of the investee's outstanding stock.

Book value of Chico Company [assets – liabilities (or stockholders' equity)]	$200,000
Undervaluation of equipment...	60,000
Undervaluation of patent..	40,000
Value of net assets...	$300,000
Percentage acquired	30%
Purchase price...	$ 90,000

Although Grande's purchase price is in excess of the proportionate share of Chico's book value, this additional amount can be attributed to two specific accounts: Equipment and Patents. No part of the extra payment is traceable to any other projected future benefit. Thus, the cost of Grande's investment is allocated as follows:

Payment by investor...		$90,000
Percentage of book value acquired ($200,000 × 30%)		60,000
Payment in excess of book value		30,000
Excess payment identified with specific assets:		
Equipment ($60,000 undervaluation × 30%).........................	$18,000	
Patent ($40,000 undervaluation × 30%)............................	12,000	30,000
Excess payment not identified with specific assets—goodwill..........		$ –0–

Of the $30,000 excess payment made by the investor, $18,000 is assigned to the equipment whereas $12,000 is traced to a patent and its undervaluation. No amount of the purchase price is allocated to goodwill.

To take this example one step further, assume that Chico's owners reject Grande's proposed $90,000 price. They believe that the value of the company as a going concern is higher than the fair value of its net assets. Because the management of Grande believes that valuable synergies will be created through this purchase, the bid price is raised to $125,000 and accepted. This new acquisition price is allocated as follows:

Payment by investor...		$125,000
Percentage of book value acquired ($200,000 × 30%)		60,000
Payment in excess of book value		65,000
Excess payment identified with specific assets:		
Equipment ($60,000 undervaluation × 30%).........................	$18,000	
Patent ($40,000 undervaluation × 30%)............................	12,000	30,000
Excess payment not identified with specific assets—goodwill........		$ 35,000

As this example indicates, *any extra payment that cannot be attributed to a specific asset or liability is assigned to the intangible asset goodwill.* Although the actual purchase price can be computed by a number of different techniques or simply result from negotiations, goodwill is always the excess amount not allocated to identifiable asset or liability accounts.

Under the equity method, the investor enters total cost in a single investment account regardless of the allocation of any excess purchase price. If all parties accept Grande's bid of $125,000, the acquisition is initially recorded at that amount despite the internal assignments made to equipment, patents, and goodwill. The entire $125,000 was paid to acquire this investment, and it is recorded as such.

The Amortization Process

In the preceding transaction, the extra payment over Grande's book value was made for specific identifiable assets (equipment and patents), and goodwill. Even though the actual dollar amounts are recorded within the investment account, a definite historical cost can be attributed to these assets. With a cost to the investor as well as a specified life, the payment relating to each asset (except land, goodwill, and other indefinite life intangibles) should be amortized over an appropriate time period. However, certain intangibles such as goodwill, some trademarks. and some licenses are considered to have indefinite lives and thus are not subject to amortization.[11]

Goodwill associated with equity method investments, for the most part, is measured in the same manner as goodwill arising from a business combination (see Chapters 2 through 6). One difference is that goodwill arising from a business combination is subject to annual impairment reviews, whereas goodwill implicit in equity method investments is not. Equity method investments are tested in their entirety for permanent declines in value.[12]

To show the amortization process for definite-lived assets, we continue with our Grande and Chico example. Assume that the equipment has a 10-year remaining life, the patent a 5-year life, and the goodwill an indefinite life. If the straight-line method is used with no salvage value, *the investor's cost* should be amortized initially as follows:[13]

Account	Cost Assigned	Remaining Useful Life	Annual Amortization
Equipment	$18,000	10 years	$1,800
Patent	12,000	5 years	2,400
Goodwill	35,000	Indefinite	–0–
Annual expense (for five years until patent cost is completely amortized)			$4,200

In recording this annual expense, Grande reduces the investment balance in the same way it would amortize the cost of any other asset that had a limited life. Therefore, at the end of the first year of holding the investment, the investor records the following journal entry under the equity method:

Equity in Investee Income	4,200	
Investment in Chico Company		4,200
To record amortization of excess payment allocated to equipment and patent.		

Because this amortization relates to investee assets, the investor does not establish a specific expense account. Instead, as in the previous entry, the expense is recognized by decreasing the the investor's equity income accruing from the investee company.

To illustrate this entire process, assume that Tall Company purchases 20 percent of Short Company for $200,000. Tall can exercise significant influence over the investee; thus, the equity method is appropriately applied. The acquisition is made on January 1, 2023, when

---

[11] Other intangibles (such as certain licenses, trademarks, etc.) also can be considered to have indefinite lives and thus are not amortized unless and until their lives are determined to be limited. Further discussion of intangibles with indefinite lives appears in Chapter 3.

[12] Because equity method goodwill is not separable from the related investment, goodwill should not be separately tested for impairment. See also FASB ASC (para. 350-20-35-59).

[13] Unless otherwise stated, all amortization computations are based on the straight-line method with no salvage value.

Short holds net assets with a book value of $700,000. Tall believes that the investee's building (10-year remaining life) is undervalued within the financial records by $80,000 and equipment with a 5-year remaining life is undervalued by $120,000. Any goodwill established by this purchase is considered to have an indefinite life. During 2023, Short reports a net income of $150,000 and at year-end declares a cash dividend of $60,000.

Tall's three basic journal entries for 2023 pose little problem:

January 1, 2023		
Investment in Short Company.	200,000	
Cash		200,000
To record acquisition of 20 percent of the outstanding shares of Short Company.		

December 31, 2023		
Investment in Short Company.	30,000	
Equity in Investee Income.		30,000
To accrue 20 percent of the 2023 reported earnings of investee ($150,000 × 20%).		
Dividend Receivable	12,000	
Investment in Short Company		12,000
To record a dividend declaration by Short Company ($60,000 × 20%).		

An allocation of Tall's $200,000 purchase price must be made to determine whether an additional adjusting entry is necessary to recognize annual amortization associated with the extra payment:

Payment by investor.		$200,000
Percentage of 1/1/23 book value ($700,000 × 20%)		140,000
Payment in excess of book value.		60,000
Excess payment identified with specific assets:		
Building ($80,000 × 20%)	$16,000	
Equipment ($120,000 × 20%)	24,000	40,000
Excess payment not identified with specific assets—goodwill		$ 20,000

As can be seen, $16,000 of the purchase price is assigned to a building and $24,000 to equipment, with the remaining $20,000 attributed to goodwill. For each asset with a definite useful life, periodic amortization is required.

Asset	Attributed Cost	Remaining Useful Life	Annual Amortization
Building	$16,000	10 years	$1,600
Equipment	24,000	5 years	4,800
Goodwill	20,000	Indefinite	–0–
Total for 2023			$6,400

At the end of 2023, Tall must also record the following adjustment in connection with these cost allocations:

Equity in Investee Income	6,400	
Investment in Short Company		6,400
To record 2023 amortization of excess payment allocated to building ($1,600) and equipment ($4,800).		

Although these entries are shown separately here for better explanation, Tall would probably net the income accrual for the year ($30,000) and the amortization ($6,400) to create a single entry increasing the investment and recognizing equity income of $23,600. Thus, the first-year return on Tall Company's beginning investment balance (defined as equity earnings/beginning investment balance) is equal to 11.80 percent ($23,600/$200,000).

International Accounting Standard 28—Investments in Associates

The International Accounting Standards Board (IASB), similar to the FASB, recognizes the need to take into account the significant influence that can occur when one firm holds a certain amount of voting shares of another. The IASB defines significant influence as the power to participate in the financial and operating policy decisions of the investee, but it is not control or joint control over those policies. The following describes the basics of the equity method in International Accounting Standard (IAS) 28:

> If an investor holds, directly or indirectly (e.g., through subsidiaries), 20 percent or more of the voting power of the investee, it is presumed that the investor has significant influence, unless it can be clearly demonstrated that this is not the case. Conversely, if the investor holds, directly or indirectly (e.g., through subsidiaries), less than 20 per cent of the voting power of the investee, it is presumed that the investor does not have significant influence, unless such influence can be clearly demonstrated. A substantial or majority ownership by another investor does not necessarily preclude an investor from having significant influence.
>
> Under the equity method, the investment in an associate is initially recognised at cost and the carrying amount is increased or decreased to recognise the investor's share of the profit or loss of the investee after the date of acquisition. The investor's share of the profit or loss of the investee is recognised in the investor's profit or loss. Distributions received from an investee reduce the carrying amount of the investment.[14]

As seen from the above IAS 28 excerpt, the equity method concepts and applications described are virtually identical to those prescribed by the FASB ASC. Nonetheless, some differences do exist. First, as described later in this chapter, the FASB allows a fair-value reporting option for investments that otherwise are accounted for under the equity method. IAS 28, however, does not provide for a fair-value reporting option. Second, if the investee employs accounting policies that differ from those of the investor, IAS 28 requires the financial statements of the investee to be adjusted to reflect the investor's accounting policies for the purpose of applying the equity method. U.S. GAAP does not have a similar conformity requirement.

Equity Method—Additional Issues

The previous sections on equity income accruals and excess cost amortizations provide the basics for applying the equity method. However, several other nonroutine issues can arise during the life of an equity method investment. More specifically, special procedures are required in accounting for each of the following:

1. Reporting a change to the equity method.
2. Reporting investee income from sources other than continuing operations.
3. Reporting investee losses.
4. Reporting the sale of an equity investment.

Reporting a Change to the Equity Method

LO 1-6a

Understand the financial reporting consequences for a change to the equity method.

In many instances, an investor's ability to significantly influence an investee is not achieved through a single stock acquisition. The investor could possess only a minor ownership for some years before purchasing enough additional shares to require conversion to the equity method. Before the investor achieves significant influence, any investment should be reported by either the fair-value method or, if the investment fair value is not readily determinable, the cost method. After the investment reaches the point at which the equity method becomes

---

[14] International Accounting Standards Board, IAS 28, "Investments in Associates," Technical Summary, www.iasb.org.

applicable, a technical question arises about the appropriate means of changing from one method to the other.[15]

FASB ASC (para. 323-10-35-33) addresses the issue of how to account for an investment in the common stock of an investee that, through additional stock acquisition or other means (e.g., increased degree of influence, reduction of investee's outstanding stock, etc.) becomes qualified for use of the equity method.

> If an investment qualifies for use of the equity method . . . , the investor shall add the cost of acquiring the additional interest in the investee (if any) to the current basis of the investor's previously held interest and adopt the equity method of accounting as of the date the investment becomes qualified for equity method accounting.

Thus, the FASB requires a prospective approach by requiring that the cost of any new share acquired simply be added to the current investment carrying amount. By mandating prospective treatment, the FASB avoids the complexity of restating prior period amounts.[16]

To illustrate, assume that on January 1, 2023, Alpha Company exchanges $84,000 for a 10 percent ownership in Bailey Company. At the time of the transaction, officials of Alpha do not believe that their company gained the ability to exert significant influence over Bailey. Alpha properly accounts for the investment using the fair-value method and recognizes in net income its 10 percent ownership share of changes in Bailey's fair value. The fair and book values of Bailey's common stock appear in the following table:

Date	Fair Value	Book Value
January 1, 2023	$840,000	$670,000
December 31, 2023	890,000	715,000

At the end of 2023, Alpha recognizes the increase in its 10 percent share of Bailey's fair value and increases its investment account to $89,000. Because the fair-value method is used to account for the investment, Bailey's $670,000 book value balance at January 1, 2023, does not affect Alpha's accounting.

Then, on January 1, 2024, Alpha purchases an additional 30 percent of Bailey's outstanding voting stock for $267,000 and achieves the ability to significantly influence the investee's decision making. Alpha will now apply the equity method to account for its investment in Bailey. To bring about the prospective change to the equity method, Alpha prepares the following journal entry on January 1, 2024:

Investment in Bailey Company	267,000	
Cash		267,000
To record an additional 30 percent investment in Bailey Company.		

On January 1, 2024, Bailey's carrying amounts for its assets and liabilities equaled their fair values except for a patent, which was undervalued by $175,000 and had a 10-year remaining useful life.

To determine the proper amount of excess fair-value amortization required in applying the equity method, Alpha prepares an investment allocation schedule. The fair value of Alpha's total (40 percent) investment serves as the valuation basis for the allocation schedule as of January 1, 2024, the date Alpha achieves the ability to exercise significant influence over Bailey. The following is the January 1, 2024, investment allocation schedule:

---

[15] A switch to the equity method also can be required if the investee purchases a portion of its own shares as treasury stock. This transaction can increase the investor's percentage of outstanding stock.

[16] Prior to 2017, the FASB required a retrospective adjustment to an investor's previous ownership shares upon achieving significant influence over an investee.

Investment Fair Value Allocation Schedule
Investment in Bailey Company
January 1, 2024

Current fair value of initial 10 percent ownership of Bailey	$ 89,000
Payment for additional 30 percent investment in Bailey	267,000
Total fair value of 40 percent investment in Bailey	356,000
Alpha's share of Bailey's book value (40% × $715,000)	286,000
Investment fair value in excess of Bailey's book value	70,000
Excess fair value attributable to Bailey's patent (40% × $175,000)	70,000
	$ –0–

We next assume that Bailey reports net income of $130,000 and declares and pays a $50,000 dividend at the end of 2024. Accordingly, Alpha applies the equity method and records the following three journal entries at the end of 2024:

Investment in Bailey Company.	45,000	
Equity in Investee Income.		45,000
To accrue 40 percent of the year 2024 income reported by Bailey Company ($130,000 × 40%) – $7,000 excess patent amortization (10-year remaining life).		
Dividend Receivable	20,000	
Investment in Bailey Company.		20,000
To record the 2024 dividend declaration by Bailey Company ($50,000 × 40%).		
Cash	20,000	
Dividend Receivable		20,000
To record collection of the cash dividend.		

LO 1-6b

Understand the financial reporting consequences for investee's other comprehensive income.

Reporting Investee's Other Comprehensive Income and Irregular Items

In many cases, reported net income and dividends sufficiently capture changes in an investee's owners' equity. By recording its share of investee income and dividends, an investor company typically ensures its investment account reflects its share of the underlying investee equity. However, when an investee company's activities require recognition of other comprehensive income (OCI), its owners' equity (and net assets) will reflect changes not captured in its reported net income.[17]

Equity method accounting requires that the investor record its share of investee OCI, which then is included in its balance sheet as Accumulated Other Comprehensive Income (AOCI). As noted by The Coca-Cola Company in its 2021 annual 10-K report,

> AOCI attributable to shareowners of The Coca-Cola Company is separately presented on our consolidated balance sheets as a component of The Coca-Cola Company's shareowners' equity, which also includes our proportionate share of equity method investees' AOCI.

Included in AOCI are items such as accumulated derivative net gains and losses, foreign currency translation adjustments, and certain pension adjustments.

To examine this issue, assume that Charles Company applies the equity method in accounting for its 30 percent investment in the voting stock of Norris Company. No excess amortization resulted from this investment. In 2023, Norris reports net income of $500,000. Norris also reports $80,000 in OCI from pension and other postretirement adjustments. Charles Company accrues earnings of $150,000 based on 30 percent of the $500,000 net figure. However, for proper financial reporting, Charles must recognize an increase in its Investment in

---

[17] OCI is defined as revenues, expenses, gains, and losses that under generally accepted accounting principles are included in comprehensive income but excluded from net income. OCI is accumulated and reported in stockholders' equity.

Norris account for its 30 percent share of its investee's OCI. This treatment is intended, once again, to mirror the close relationship between the two companies.

The journal entry by Charles Company to record its equity interest in the income and OCI of Norris follows:

Investment in Norris Company...	174,000	
Equity in Investee Income..		150,000
Other Comprehensive Income of Investee		24,000
To accrue the investee's operating income and other comprehensive income from equity investment.		

OCI thus represents a source of change in investee company net assets that is recognized under the equity method. In the preceding example, Charles Company includes $24,000 of other comprehensive income in its balance sheet AOCI total.

Other equity method recognition issues arise for irregular items traditionally included within net income. For example, an investee may report income (loss) from discontinued operations as components of its current net income. In such cases, the equity method requires the investor to record and report its share of these items in recognizing equity earnings of the investee.

LO 1-6c

Understand the financial reporting consequences for investee losses.

Reporting Investee Losses

Although most of the previous illustrations are based on the recording of profits, accounting for losses incurred by the investee is handled in a similar manner. The investor recognizes the appropriate percentage of each loss and reduces the carrying amount of the investment account. Even though these procedures are consistent with the concept of the equity method, they fail to take into account all possible loss situations.

Impairments of Equity Method Investments

Investments can suffer permanent losses in fair value that are not evident through equity method accounting. Such declines can be caused by the loss of major customers, changes in economic conditions, loss of a significant patent or other legal right, damage to the company's reputation, and the like. Permanent reductions in fair value resulting from such adverse events might not be reported immediately by the investor through the normal equity entries discussed previously. The FASB ASC (para. 323-10-35-32) provides the following guidance:

> A loss in value of an investment which is other than a temporary decline shall be recognized. Evidence of a loss in value might include, but would not necessarily be limited to, absence of an ability to recover the carrying amount of the investment or inability of the investee to sustain an earnings capacity that would justify the carrying amount of the investment.

Thus, when a permanent decline in an equity method investment's value occurs, the investor must recognize an impairment loss and reduce the asset to fair value.

However, this loss must be permanent before such recognition becomes necessary. Under the equity method, a temporary drop in the fair value of an investment is simply ignored.

The Coca-Cola Company, for example, noted the following in its 2021 10-Q report (3rd quarter):

> The Company recognized an other-than-temporary impairment charge of $38 million related to one of our equity method investees in Latin America, primarily driven by revised projections of future operating results.

Investment Reduced to Zero

Through the recognition of reported losses as well as any permanent drops in fair value, the investment account can eventually be reduced to a zero balance. This condition is most likely to occur if the investee has suffered extreme losses or if the original purchase was made at a low, bargain price. Regardless of the reason, the carrying amount of the investment account is sometimes eliminated in total.

When an investment account is reduced to zero, the investor should discontinue using the equity method rather than establish a negative balance. The investment retains a zero balance until subsequent investee profits eliminate all unrecognized losses. Once the original cost of the investment has been eliminated, no additional losses can accrue to the investor (since the entire cost has been written off).

For example, Switch, Inc., a technology infrastructure company, explains in its 2020 annual 10-K report that

> The Company discontinues applying the equity method of accounting when the investment is reduced to zero. If the investee subsequently reports net income or other comprehensive income, the Company resumes applying the equity method of accounting only after its share of unrecognized net income and other comprehensive income, respectively, equals the share of losses not recognized during the period the equity method of accounting was suspended.

Reporting the Sale of an Equity Investment

LO 1-6d

Understand the financial reporting consequences for sales of equity method investments.

At any time, the investor can choose to sell part or all of its holdings in the investee company. If a sale occurs, the equity method continues to be applied until the transaction date, thus establishing an appropriate carrying amount for the investment. The investor then reduces this balance by the percentage of shares sold.

As an example, assume that Top Company owns 40 percent of the 100,000 outstanding shares of Bottom Company, an investment accounted for by the equity method. Any excess investment cost over Top's share of Bottom's book value is considered goodwill. Although these 40,000 shares were acquired some years ago for $200,000, application of the equity method has increased the asset balance to $320,000 as of January 1, 2024. On July 1, 2024, Top elects to sell 10,000 of these shares (one-fourth of its investment) for $110,000 in cash, thereby reducing ownership in Bottom from 40 percent to 30 percent. Bottom Company reports net income of $70,000 during the first six months of 2024 and declares and pays cash dividends of $30,000.

Top, as the investor, initially makes the following journal entries on July 1, 2024, to accrue the proper income and establish the correct investment balance:

Investment in Bottom Company..	28,000	
Equity in Investee Income...		28,000
To accrue equity income for first six months of 2024 ($70,000 × 40%).		
Dividend Receivable	12,000	
Investment in Bottom Company....................................		12,000
To record a cash dividend declaration by Bottom Company ($30,000 × 40%).		
Cash	12,000	
Dividend Receivable		12,000
To record collection of the cash dividend.		

These two entries increase the carrying amount of Top's investment by $16,000, creating a balance of $336,000 as of July 1, 2024. The sale of one-fourth of these shares can then be recorded as follows:

Cash	110,000	
Investment in Bottom Company....................................		84,000
Gain on Sale of Investment..		26,000
To record sale of one-fourth of investment in Bottom Company (¼ × $336,000 = $84,000).		

After the sale is completed, Top continues to apply the equity method to this investment based on 30 percent ownership rather than 40 percent. However, if the sale had been of sufficient magnitude to cause Top to lose its ability to exercise significant influence over Bottom, the equity method would cease to be applicable. For example, if Top Company's holdings were reduced from 40 percent to 15 percent, the equity method might no longer be appropriate after the sale. The remaining shares held by the investor are reported according to the fair-value method, with the remaining book value becoming the new *cost* figure for the investment rather than the amount originally paid.

If an investor is required to change from the equity method to the fair-value method, no retrospective adjustment is made. As previously demonstrated, a change to the equity method is also treated prospectively.

LO 1-7

Describe the rationale and computations to defer the investor's share of gross profits on intra-entity inventory sales until the goods are either consumed by the owner or sold to outside parties.

Deferral of Intra-Entity Gross Profits in Inventory[18]

Many equity acquisitions establish ties between companies to facilitate the direct purchase and sale of inventory items. For example, The Coca-Cola Company recently disclosed net sales in excess of $13 billion to its equity method investees. The significant influence relationship between an investor and investee in many ways creates its own entity that works to achieve business objectives. Thus, we use the term *intra-entity* to describe sales between an investor and its equity method investee.

Intra-entity sales require special accounting to ensure proper timing for profit recognition. A fundamental accounting concept is that an entity cannot recognize profits through activities with itself. For example, when an investor company sells inventory to its 40 percent-owned investee at a profit, 40 percent of this sale effectively is with itself. Consequently, the investor company delays 40 percent of the gross profit recognition until the inventory is sold to an independent party or is consumed.[19]

Thus, in the presence of significant influence, the amount of profit deferred is limited to the investor's ownership share of the investee. In applying the equity method, the investor therefore defers only its share of the profit from intra-entity sales until the buyer's ultimate disposition of the goods. When the inventory is eventually consumed within operations or resold to an unrelated party, the investor recognizes the remaining gross profit. Accounting for both the profit deferral and subsequent recognition takes place through adjustments to the "Equity in Investee Income" and "Investment" accounts.

Intra-entity inventory sales are identified as either *downstream* or *upstream*. *Downstream sales* refer to the investor's sale of an item to the investee. Conversely, an *upstream sale* describes one that the investee makes to the investor (see Exhibit 1.2). *Although the direction of intra-entity sales does not affect reported equity method balances for investments when significant influence exists, it has definite consequences when financial control requires the consolidation of financial statements, as discussed in Chapter 5.* Therefore, these two types of intra-entity sales are examined separately, even at this introductory stage.

Downstream Sales of Inventory

Assume that Major Company owns a 40 percent share of Minor Company and accounts for this investment through the equity

EXHIBIT 1.2 Downstream and Upstream Sales

Downstream sale

Investor → Investee

Upstream sale

Investor ← Investee

---

[18] Intra-entity transfers can involve the sale of items other than inventory. The intra-entity transfer of depreciable fixed assets and land is discussed in a later chapter.

[19] When inventory is consumed—for example, in a manufacturing process—sales of the resulting production are assumed to generate revenues from outside, unrelated parties.

method. In 2024, Major sells inventory to Minor at a price of $50,000. This figure includes a gross profit of 30 percent, or $15,000. By the end of 2024, Minor has sold $40,000 worth of these goods to outside parties while retaining $10,000 in inventory for sale during the subsequent year.

The investor has made downstream sales to the investee. In applying the equity method, recognition of the related profit must be delayed until the buyer disposes of these goods. Although total intra-entity inventory sales amounted to $50,000 in 2024, $40,000 of this merchandise has already been resold to outsiders, thereby justifying the normal reporting of profits. For the $10,000 still in the investee's inventory, the investor delays gross profit recognition. In computing equity income, the investor's portion of the intra-entity profit must be deferred until Minor disposes of the goods.

The gross profit on the original intra-entity sale was 30 percent of the sale price; therefore, Major's profit associated with these remaining items is $3,000 ($10,000 × 30%). *However, because only 40 percent of the investee's stock is held, just $1,200 ($3,000 × 40%) of this profit is deferred.* Major's ownership percentage reflects the intra-entity portion of the profit. The total $3,000 gross profit within the ending inventory balance is not the amount deferred. Rather, 40 percent of that gross profit is viewed as the currently deferred figure.

Remaining Ending Inventory	Gross Profit Percentage	Gross Profit in Ending Inventory	Investor Ownership Percentage	Deferred Intra-Entity Gross Profit
$10,000	30%	$3,000	40%	$1,200

After calculating the appropriate deferral, the investor decreases current equity income by $1,200 to reflect the deferred portion of the intra-entity profit. This procedure temporarily removes this portion of the profit from the investor's books in 2024 until the investee disposes of the inventory in 2025. Major accomplishes the actual deferral through the following year-end journal entry:

Intra-Entity Gross Profit Deferral		
Equity in Investee Income	1,200	
Investment in Minor Company		1,200
To defer gross profit on sale of inventory to Minor Company.		

In the subsequent year, when this inventory is eventually consumed by Minor or sold to unrelated parties, the deferral is no longer needed. Because a sale to an outside party has now occurred, Major should recognize the $1,200. By merely reversing the preceding deferral entry, the accountant succeeds in moving the investor's profit into the appropriate time period. Recognition shifts from the year of inventory transfer to the year in which the sale to customers outside of the affiliated entity takes place.

Subsequent Recognition of Intra-Entity Gross Profit		
Investment in Minor Company	1,200	
Equity in Investee Income		1,200
To recognize income on intra-entity sale that now can be recognized after sales to outsiders.		

Upstream Sales of Inventory

Unlike consolidated financial statements (see Chapter 5), the equity method reports upstream sales of inventory in the same manner as downstream sales. Hence, the investor's share of gross profits remaining in ending inventory is deferred until the items are used or sold to unrelated parties. To illustrate, assume that Major Company once again owns 40 percent of Minor Company. During the current year, Minor sells merchandise costing $40,000 to Major for $60,000. At the end of the fiscal period, Major still retains $15,000 of these goods. Minor reports net income of $120,000 for the year.

To reflect the basic accrual of the investee's earnings, Major records the following journal entry at the end of this year:

Income Accrual		
Investment in Minor Company	48,000	
Equity in Investee Income		48,000
To accrue income from 40 percent–owned investee ($120,000 × 40%).		

The amount of the deferred intra-entity gross profit remaining at year-end is computed using the 33⅓ gross profit percentage of the sales price ($20,000/$60,000):

Remaining Ending Inventory	Gross Profit Percentage	Gross Profit in Ending Inventory	Investor Ownership Percentage	Deferred Intra-Entity Gross Profit
$15,000	33⅓%	$5,000	40%	$2,000

Based on this calculation, a second entry is required of the investor at year-end. Once again, a deferral of the gross profit created by the intra-entity sale is necessary for proper timing of income recognition. *Under the equity method for investments with significant influence, the direction of the sale between the investor and investee (upstream or downstream) has no effect on the final amounts reported in the financial statements.*

Intra-Entity Gross Profit Deferral		
Equity in Investee Income	2,000	
Investment in Minor Company		2,000
To defer recognition of intra-entity gross profit until inventory is used or sold to unrelated parties.		

After the adjustment, Major, the investor, reports earnings from this equity investment of $46,000 ($48,000 − $2,000). The income accrual is reduced because the investor defers its portion of the intra-entity gross profit. In an upstream sale, the investor's own inventory account contains the deferred gross profit. The previous entry, though, defers recognition of this profit by decreasing Major's investment account rather than the inventory balance. An alternative treatment would be the direct reduction of the investor's inventory balance as a means of accounting for this deferred amount. Although this alternative is acceptable, decreasing the investment account remains the traditional approach for deferring gross profits, even for upstream sales.

When the investor eventually consumes or sells the $15,000 in merchandise, the preceding journal entry is reversed as shown below. In this way, the effects of the inventory transfer are reported in the proper accounting period when sales to an outside party allow the recognition of the previously deferred intra-entity gross profit via the Equity in Investee Income account.

Subsequent Recognition of Intra-Entity Gross Profit		
Investment in Minor Company	2,000	
Equity in Investee Income..		2,000
To recognize income on intra-entity sale that now can be recognized after sales to outsiders.		

Whether upstream or downstream, the investor's sales and purchases are still reported as if the transactions were conducted with outside parties. Only the investor's share of the gross profit is deferred, and that amount is adjusted solely through the equity income account. Furthermore, because the companies are not consolidated, the investee's reported balances are not altered at all to reflect the nature of these sales/purchases. Obviously, readers of the financial statements need to be made aware of the inclusion of these amounts in the income statement. Thus, reporting companies must disclose certain information about related-party transactions. These disclosures include the nature of the relationship, a description of the transactions, the dollar amounts of the transactions, and amounts due to or from any related parties at year-end.

Financial Reporting Effects and Equity Method Criticisms

Equity Method Reporting Effects

It is important to realize that business decisions, including equity investments, typically involve the assessment of a wide range of consequences. For example, managers frequently are very interested in how financial statements report the effects of their decisions. This attention to financial reporting effects of business decisions arises because measurements of financial performance often affect the following:

- The firm's ability to raise capital.
- Managerial compensation.
- The ability to meet debt covenants and future interest rates.
- Managers' reputations.

Managers are also keenly aware that measures of earnings per share can strongly affect investors' perceptions of the underlying value of their firms' publicly traded stock. Consequently, prior to making investment decisions, firms will study and assess the prospective effects of applying the equity method on the income reported in financial statements. Additionally, such analyses of prospective reported income effects can influence firms regarding the degree of influence they wish to have, or even on the decision of whether to invest. For example, managers could have a required projected rate of return on an initial investment. In such cases, an analysis of projected income will be made to assist in setting an offer price.

For example, Investmor Co. is examining a potential 25 percent equity investment in Marco, Inc., that will provide a significant level of influence. Marco projects an annual income of $300,000 for the near future. Marco's book value is $450,000, and it has an unrecorded newly developed technology appraised at $200,000 with an estimated useful life of 10 years. In considering offer prices for the 25 percent investment in Marco, Investmor projects equity earnings as follows:

Projected income (25% × $300,000)	$75,000
Excess unpatented technology amortization [(25% × $200,000) ÷ 10 years].........	(5,000)
Annual expected equity in Marco earnings..................................	$70,000

Investmor's required first-year rate of return (before tax) on these types of investments is 20 percent. Therefore, to meet the first-year rate of return requirement involves a maximum price of $350,000 ($70,000 ÷ 20% = $350,000). If the shares are publicly traded (leaving the firm a "price taker"), such income projections can assist the company in making a recommendation to wait for share prices to move to make the investment attractive.

Criticisms of the Equity Method

Over the past several decades, thousands of business firms have accounted for their investments using the equity method. Recently, however, the equity method has come under criticism for the following:

- Emphasizing the 20–50 percent of voting stock in determining significant influence versus control.
- Allowing off-balance-sheet financing.
- Potentially biasing performance ratios.

The guidelines for the equity method suggest that a 20–50 percent ownership of voting shares indicates significant influence that falls short of control. But can one firm exert "control" over another firm absent an interest of more than 50 percent? Clearly, if one firm controls another, consolidation is the appropriate financial reporting technique. However, over the years, firms have learned ways to control other firms despite owning less than 50 percent of voting shares. For example, contracts across companies can limit one firm's ability to act without permission of the other. Such contractual control can be seen in debt arrangements, long-term sales and purchase agreements, and agreements concerning board membership. As a result, control is exerted through a variety of contractual arrangements. For financial reporting purposes, however, if ownership is 50 percent or less, a firm can argue that control technically does not exist.

In contrast to consolidated financial reports, when applying the equity method, the investee's assets and liabilities are not combined with the investor's amounts. Instead, the investor's balance sheet reports a single amount for the investment, and the income statement reports a single amount for its equity in the earnings of the investee. If consolidated, the assets, liabilities, revenues, and expenses of the investee are combined and reported in the body of the investor's financial statements.

Thus, for those companies wishing to actively manage their reported balance sheet numbers, the equity method provides an effective means. By keeping its ownership of voting shares less than 50 percent, a company can technically meet the rules for applying the equity method for its investments and at the same time report investee assets and liabilities "off balance sheet." As a result, relative to consolidation, a firm employing the equity method will report smaller values for assets and liabilities. Consequently, higher rates of return for its assets and sales, as well as lower debt-to-equity ratios, could result.

On the surface, it appears that firms can avoid balance sheet disclosure of debts by maintaining investments at less than 50 percent ownership. However, the equity method requires summarized information as to assets, liabilities, and results of operations of the investees to be presented in the notes or in separate statements. Therefore, supplementary information could be available under the equity method that would not be separately identified in consolidation. Nonetheless, some companies have contractual provisions (e.g., debt covenants, managerial compensation agreements) based on ratios in the main body of the financial statements. Meeting the provisions of such contracts could provide managers strong incentives to maintain technical eligibility to use the equity method rather than full consolidation.

LO 1-8

Explain the rationale and reporting implications of fair-value accounting for investments otherwise accounted for by the equity method.

Fair-Value Reporting for Equity Method Investments

Financial reporting standards allow a fair-value option under which an entity may irrevocably elect fair value as the initial and subsequent measurement attribute for certain financial assets and financial liabilities. Under the fair-value option, changes in the fair value of the elected financial items are included in earnings. Among the many financial assets available for the fair-value option were investments otherwise accounted for under the equity method.

For example, Citigroup has reported at fair value certain of its investments that previously were reported using the equity method. In its 2021 annual report, Citigroup noted that "Certain investments that would otherwise have been accounted for using the equity method are carried at fair value with changes in fair value recognized in earnings, since the Company elected to apply fair value accounting." Many other firms, however, have been reluctant to elect the fair-value option for their equity method investments.

Firms using fair-value accounting simply report the investment's fair value as an asset and changes in fair value as earnings. As such, firms neither compute excess cost amortizations nor adjust earnings for intra-entity profits. Dividends from an investee are included in earnings under the fair-value option. Because dividends typically reduce an investment's fair value, an increase in earnings from investee dividends would be offset by a decrease in earnings from the decline in an investment's fair value.

To illustrate, on January 1, 2023, Westwind Co. pays $722,000 in exchange for 40,000 common shares of Armco, Inc., which has 100,000 common shares outstanding, the majority of which continue to trade on the New York Stock Exchange. During the next two years, Armco reports the following information:

Year	Net Income	Cash Dividends	Common Shares Total Fair Value at December 31
2023	$158,000	$25,000	$1,900,000
2024	125,000	25,000	1,870,000

Westwind elects to use fair-value accounting and accordingly makes the following journal entries for its investment in Armco over the next two years.

2023

Investment in Armco, Inc.	722,000	
Cash		722,000
To record Westwind's initial 40 percent investment in Armco, Inc.		
Cash	10,000	
Dividend Income*		10,000
To recognize 2023 dividends received (40%) as Investment income.		
Investment in Armco, Inc.	38,000	
Investment Income		38,000
To recognize Westwind's 40 percent of the 2023 change in Armco's fair value [($1,900,000 × 40%) − $722,000].		

2024

Cash	10,000	
Dividend Income*		10,000
To recognize 2024 dividends received (40%) as investment income.		
Investment Loss	12,000	
Investment in Armco, Inc.		12,000
To recognize Westwind's 40 percent of the 2024 change in Armco's fair value [40% × ($1,870,000 − $1,900,000)].		

*This example assumes dividend declaration and payment occur at the same time.

In its December 31, 2024, balance sheet, Westwind thus reports its Investment in Armco account at $748,000, equal to 40 percent of Armco's total fair value (or $722,000 initial cost adjusted for 2023–2024 fair value changes of $38,000 less $12,000).

In addition to the increasing emphasis on fair values in financial reporting, the fair-value option also was motivated by a perceived need for consistency across various balance sheet items. In particular, the fair-value option is designed to limit volatility in earnings that occurs when some financial items are measured using cost-based attributes and others at fair value.

As FASB ASC (para. 825-10-10-1) observes, the objective of the fair-value option is

> to improve financial reporting by providing entities with the opportunity to mitigate volatility in reported earnings caused by measuring related assets and liabilities differently without having to apply complex hedge accounting provisions.

Thus, the fair-value option is designed to match asset valuation with fair-value reporting requirements for many liabilities.

Summary

1. The equity method of accounting for an investment reflects the close relationship that could exist between an investor and an investee. More specifically, this approach is available when the owner achieves the ability to apply significant influence to the investee's operating and financial decisions. Significant influence is presumed to exist at the 20 to 50 percent ownership level. However, the accountant must evaluate each situation, regardless of the percentage of ownership, to determine whether this ability is actually present.

2. To mirror the relationship between the companies, the equity method requires the investor to accrue income when the investee reports it in its financial statements. In recording this profit or loss, the investor separately reports items such as other comprehensive income and discontinued operations, to highlight their special nature. Dividend declarations decrease the owners' equity of the investee company; therefore, the investor reduces the investment account for its share of investee dividends.

3. When acquiring capital stock, an investor often pays an amount that exceeds the investee company's underlying book value. For accounting purposes, such excess payments must be either identified with specific assets and liabilities (such as land or buildings) or allocated to an intangible asset referred to as *goodwill*. The investor then amortizes each assigned cost (except for any amount attributed to land, goodwill, or other indefinite life assets) over the expected useful lives of the assets and liabilities. This amortization affects the amount of equity income recognized by the investor.

4. If the investor sells the entire investment or any portion of it, the equity method is applied until the date of disposal. A gain or loss is computed based on the adjusted book value at that time. Remaining shares are accounted for by means of either the equity method or the fair-value method, depending on the investor's subsequent ability to significantly influence the investee.

5. Inventory (or other assets) can be transferred between investor and investee. Because of the relationship between the two companies, the equity income accrual should be reduced to defer the portion of any gross profit included on these intra-entity sales until the items are either sold to outsiders or consumed. Thus, the amount of intra-entity gross profit in ending inventory decreases the amount of equity income recognized by the investor in the current period although this effect is subsequently reversed.

6. Firms may elect to report significant influence investments at fair value with changes in fair value as earnings. Under the fair-value option, firms simply report the investment's fair value as an asset and changes in fair value as earnings.

Comprehensive Illustration

(*Estimated Time: 30 to 50 Minutes*) Every chapter in this textbook concludes with an illustration designed to assist students in tying together the essential elements of the material presented. After a careful reading of each chapter, attempt to work through the comprehensive problem. Then review the solution that follows the problem, noting the handling of each significant accounting issue.

Problem

Part A

On January 1, 2022, Red Hawk Company pays $70,000 for a 10 percent interest in Wolf Company's common stock. Because market quotes for Wolf's stock are readily available on a continuing basis, the investment account has been appropriately maintained at fair value.

On January 1, 2023, Red Hawk acquires an additional 20 percent of Wolf Company for $176,000. This second purchase provides Red Hawk the ability to exert significant influence over Wolf, and Red Hawk will now apply the equity method. At the time of this transaction, Wolf had a January 1, 2023, book value of $650,000 although Wolf's equipment with a four-year remaining life was undervalued by $80,000 relative to its fair value.

During these two years, Wolf reported the following operational results (cash dividends are declared and paid in July each year):

Year	Net Income	Cash Dividends	Fair Value at January 1
2022	$210,000	$110,000	$700,000
2023	270,000	110,000	880,000

Required

a. What income did Red Hawk originally report for 2022 in connection with this investment?

b. On comparative financial statements for 2022 and 2023, what figures should Red Hawk report in connection with this investment?

Part B (Continuation of Part A)

In 2024, Wolf Company reports $400,000 in income and $60,000 in other comprehensive income from foreign currency translation adjustments. The company declares and pays a $120,000 cash dividend. During this fiscal year, Red Hawk sells inventory costing $80,000 to Wolf for $100,000. Wolf continues to hold 50 percent of this merchandise at the end of 2024. Red Hawk maintains 30 percent ownership of Wolf throughout the period.

Required

Prepare all necessary journal entries for Red Hawk for the year 2024.

Solution

Part A

a. Red Hawk Company accounts for its investment in Wolf Company at fair value during 2022. Because Red Hawk held only 10 percent of the outstanding shares, significant influence apparently was absent. Because stock quotes were readily available, the investment was periodically updated to fair value. Therefore, the investor recorded both dividends and changes in fair value in its 2022 financial statements as follows:

Dividend income (10% × $110,000)	$11,000
Increase in fair value [10% × ($880,000 − $700,000)]	18,000
Total income recognized from investment in Wolf in 2022	$29,000

b. Changes to the equity method are accounted for prospectively. Therefore, in comparative statements, Red Hawk's 2022 income from its investment in Wolf is $29,000, as reflected in the fair value method shown in part (a).

Red Hawk's 2023 financial statements will reflect the equity method as a result of the January 1, 2023, share purchase that resulted in significant influence. To determine the 2023 equity method income, Red Hawk first evaluates its combined investments in Wolf to assess whether either goodwill or incremental asset values need to be reflected within the equity method procedures.

Fair Value Allocation of 30 Percent Ownership of Wolf Company on January 1, 2023	
Fair value of initial 10 percent purchase at January 1, 2023	$ 88,000
Payment for 20 percent investment at January 1, 2023	176,000
Fair value of 30 percent ownership	264,000
Book value acquired ($650,000 × 30%)	195,000
Fair value in excess of book value	69,000
Excess fair value identified with specific assets:	
Equipment ($80,000 × 30%)	24,000
Excess fair value not identified with specific assets—goodwill	$ 45,000

In allocating Wolf's January 1, 2023, fair value, $24,000 of the payment is attributable to the undervalued equipment with $45,000 assigned to goodwill. Because the equipment now has only a four-year remaining life, annual amortization of $6,000 is appropriate ($24,000/4).

Financial Reporting—2023

Equity in Investee Income (income statement)	
Income reported by Wolf	$270,000
Red Hawk's ownership	30%
Red Hawk's share of Wolf's reported income	$ 81,000
Less: Amortization expense:	
Equipment ($24,000/4 years)	(6,000)
Equity in investee income—2023	$ 75,000
Investment in Wolf (balance sheet)	
Fair value—1/1/23 (above)	$264,000
Equity in investee income (above)	75,000
Less: Investee dividends ($110,000 × 30%)	(33,000)
Investment in Wolf—12/31/23	$306,000

Part B

In July 2024, Wolf declares and pays a $36,000 cash dividend to Red Hawk (30% × $120,000). According to the equity method, this dividend reduces the carrying amount of the investment account:

Dividend Receivable	36,000	
Investment in Wolf Company		36,000
To record the 2024 cash dividend declaration by Wolf Company.		
Cash	36,000	
Dividend Receivable		36,000
To record collection of the cash dividend.		

Red Hawk records no other journal entries in connection with this investment until the end of 2024. At that time, the annual accrual of income as well as the adjustment to record amortization is made (see Part A for computation of expense). The investee's net income is reported separately from its other comprehensive income.

Investment in Wolf Company	138,000	
Equity in Investee Income		120,000
Investee Other Comprehensive Income		18,000
To recognize reported income of investee based on a 30 percent ownership level of $400,000 net income and $60,000 other comprehensive income.		
Equity in Investee Income	6,000	
Investment in Wolf Company		6,000
To record annual amortization on excess payment made in relation to equipment ($24,000/4 years).		

Red Hawk needs to make only one other equity entry during 2024. Intra-entity sales have occurred, and Wolf continues to hold a portion of the inventory. Therefore, the investor's share of gross profit must be deferred. The gross profit rate from the sale was 20 percent ($20,000/$100,000). Because the investee still possesses $50,000 of this merchandise, the related gross profit is $10,000 ($50,000 × 20%). However, Red Hawk owns only 30 percent of Wolf's outstanding stock; thus, the intra-entity gross profit in inventory at year-end is $3,000 ($10,000 × 30%). That amount must be deferred until Wolf either consumes the inventory or sells it to unrelated parties.

Equity in Investee Company	3,000	
Investment in Wolf Company		3,000
To defer the investor's share of intra-entity gross profit in ending inventory.		

Questions

1. What advantages does a company achieve when it possesses significant influence over another company through voting stock ownership?

2. A company acquires a rather large investment in another corporation. What criteria determine whether the investor should apply the equity method of accounting to this investment?

3. What accounting treatments are appropriate for investments in equity securities without readily determinable fair values?

4. What indicates an investor's ability to significantly influence the decision-making process of an investee?

5. Why does the equity method record dividends from an investee as a reduction in the investment account, not as dividend income?

6. Jones Company owns a 25 percent interest in shares of Sandridge Company common stock. Under what circumstances might Jones decide that the equity method would not be appropriate to account for this investment?

7. Smith, Inc., has maintained an ownership interest in Watts Corporation for a number of years. This investment has been accounted for using the equity method. What transactions or events create changes in the Investment in Watts Corporation account as recorded by Smith?

8. Although the equity method is a generally accepted accounting principle (GAAP), recognition of equity income has been criticized. What theoretical problems can opponents of the equity method identify? What managerial incentives exist that could influence a firm's percentage ownership interest in another firm?

9. Because of the acquisition of additional investee shares, an investor will now change from the fair-value method to the equity method. Which procedures are applied to accomplish this accounting change?

10. Riggins Company accounts for its investment in Bostic Company using the equity method. During the past fiscal year, Bostic reported other comprehensive income from translation adjustments related to its foreign investments. How would this other comprehensive income affect the investor's financial records?

11. During the current year, Davis Company's common stock suffers a permanent drop in market value. In the past, Davis has made a significant portion of its sales to one customer. This buyer recently announced its decision to make no further purchases from Davis Company, an action that led to the loss of market value. Hawkins, Inc., owns 35 percent of the outstanding shares of Davis, an investment that is recorded according to the equity method. How would the loss in value affect this investor's financial reporting?

12. Wilson Company acquired 40 percent of Andrews Company at a bargain price because of losses expected to result from Andrews's failure in marketing several new products. Wilson paid only $100,000, although Andrews's corresponding book value was much higher. In the first year after acquisition, Andrews lost $300,000. In applying the equity method, how should Wilson account for this loss?

13. In a stock acquisition accounted for by the equity method, a portion of the purchase price often is attributed to goodwill or to specific assets or liabilities. How are these amounts determined at acquisition? How are these amounts accounted for in subsequent periods?

14. Princeton Company holds a 40 percent interest in shares of Yale Company common stock. On June 19 of the current year, Princeton sells part of this investment. What accounting should Princeton make on June 19? What accounting will Princeton make for the remainder of the current year?

15. What is the difference between downstream and upstream sales? How does this difference affect application of the equity method?

16. How is the investor's share of gross profit on intra-entity sales calculated? Under the equity method, how does the deferral of gross profit affect the recognition of equity income?

17. How are intra-entity transfers reported in an investee's separate financial statements if the investor is using the equity method?

18. What is the fair-value option for reporting equity method investments? How do the equity method and fair-value accounting differ in recognizing income from an investee?

Problems

LO 1-4

1. When an investor uses the equity method to account for investments in common stock, the investor's share of cash dividends from the investee should be recorded as
   a. A deduction from the investor's share of the investee's profits.
   b. Dividend income.
   c. A deduction from the stockholders' equity account, Dividends to Stockholders.
   d. A deduction from the investment account.
   (AICPA adapted)

LO 1-2

2. The equity method tends to be most appropriate if
   a. An investment represents 50 percent or more of the voting stock of an investee.
   b. An investment enables the investor to influence the operating and financial decisions of the investee.
   c. Majority ownership of the investee is concentrated among a small group of shareholders who operate the investee without regard to the views of the investor.
   d. The investor is unable to obtain representation on the investee's board of directors.

LO 1-6a

3. Hawkins Company has owned 10 percent of Larker, Inc., for the past several years. This ownership did not allow Hawkins to have significant influence over Larker. Recently, Hawkins acquired an additional 30 percent of Larker and now will use the equity method. How will the investor report this change?
   a. A cumulative effect of an accounting change is shown in the current income statement.
   b. A retrospective adjustment is made to restate all prior years presented using the equity method.
   c. No change is recorded; the equity method is used from the date of the new acquisition.
   d. Hawkins will report the change as a component of accumulated other comprehensive income.

LO 1-8

4. Under fair-value accounting for an equity investment, which of the following affects the income the investor recognizes from its ownership of the investee?
   a. The investee's reported income adjusted for excess cost over book value amortizations
   b. Changes in the fair value of the investor's ownership shares of the investee
   c. Intra-entity profits from upstream sales
   d. Other comprehensive income reported by the investee

LO 1-6c

5. When an equity method investment account is reduced to a zero balance
   a. The investor should establish a negative investment account balance for any future losses reported by the investee.
   b. The investor should discontinue using the equity method until the investee begins paying dividends.
   c. Future losses are reported as unusual items in the investor's income statement.
   d. The investment retains a zero balance until subsequent investee profits eliminate all unrecognized losses.

LO 1-4

6. On January 1, Belleville Company paid $2,295,000 to acquire 90,000 shares of O'Fallon's voting common stock, which represents a 30 percent investment. No allocations to goodwill or other specific accounts were made. Significant influence over O'Fallon is achieved by this acquisition, and so Belleville applies the equity method. O'Fallon declared a $1 per share dividend during the year and reported net income of $750,000. What is the balance in the Investment in O'Fallon account found in Belleville's financial records as of December 31?
   a. $2,295,000
   b. $2,430,000
   c. $2,520,000
   d. $2,610,000

LO 1-4, 1-5

7. In January 2023, Domingo, Inc., acquired 20 percent of the outstanding common stock of Martes, Inc., for $700,000. This investment gave Domingo the ability to exercise significant influence over Martes, whose balance sheet on that date showed total assets of $3,900,000 with liabilities of $900,000. Any excess of cost over book value of the investment was attributed to a patent having a remaining useful life of 10 years.
   In 2023, Martes reported net income of $170,000. In 2024, Martes reported net income of $210,000. Dividends of $70,000 were declared in each of these two years. What is the equity method balance of Domingo's Investment in Martes, Inc., at December 31, 2024?
   a. $728,000
   b. $748,000
   c. $756,000
   d. $776,000

LO 1-4, 1-5

8. Franklin purchases 40 percent of Johnson Company on January 1 for $500,000. Although Franklin did not use it, this acquisition gave Franklin the ability to apply significant influence to Johnson's operating and financing policies. Johnson reports assets on that date of $1,400,000 with liabilities of $500,000. One building with a 7-year remaining life is undervalued on Johnson's books by $140,000. Also, Johnson's book value for its trademark (10-year remaining life) is undervalued by $210,000. During the year, Johnson reports net income of $90,000 while declaring dividends of $30,000. What is the Investment in Johnson Company balance (equity method) in Franklin's financial records as of December 31?

    a. $504,000
    b. $507,600
    c. $513,900
    d. $516,000

LO 1-4, 1-5

9. Max Company reports net income of $140,000 each year and declares an annual cash dividend of $50,000. The company holds net assets of $1,200,000 on January 1, 2023. On that date, Eden Company purchases 40 percent of Max's outstanding common stock for $600,000, which gives it the ability to significantly influence Max. At the purchase date, the excess of Eden's cost over its proportionate share of Max's book value was assigned to an indefinite-lived asset. On December 31, 2025, what is the Investment in Max Company balance (equity method) in Eden's financial records?

    a. $600,000
    b. $660,000
    c. $690,000
    d. $708,000

LO 1-7

10. Perez, Inc., applies the equity method for its 25 percent investment in Senior, Inc. During 2024, Perez sold goods with a 40 percent gross profit to Senior, which sold all of these goods in 2024. How should Perez report the effect of the intra-entity sale on its 2024 income statement?

    a. Sales and cost of goods sold should be reduced by the amount of intra-entity sales.
    b. Sales and cost of goods sold should be reduced by 25 percent of the amount of intra-entity sales.
    c. Investment income should be reduced by 25 percent of the gross profit on the amount of intra-entity sales.
    d. No adjustment is necessary.

LO 1-7

11. Jubilee, Inc., owns 35 percent of JPW Company and applies the equity method. During the current year, Jubilee buys inventory costing $60,000 and then sells it to JPW for $75,000. At the end of the year, JPW still holds only $30,000 of merchandise. What amount of gross profit must Jubilee defer in reporting this investment using the equity method?

    a. $2,100
    b. $2,625
    c. $6,000
    d. $10,500

LO 1-4, 1-5, 1-7

12. Alex, Inc., buys 40 percent of Steinbart Company on January 1, 2023, for $530,000. The equity method of accounting is to be used. Steinbart's net assets on that date were $1.2 million. Any excess of cost over book value is attributable to a trade name with a 20-year remaining life. Steinbart immediately begins supplying inventory to Alex as follows:

Year	Cost to Steinbart	Transfer Price	Amount Held by Alex at Year-End (at transfer price)
2023	$70,000	$100,000	$25,000
2024	96,000	150,000	45,000

Inventory held at the end of one year by Alex is sold at the beginning of the next.

Steinbart reports net income of $80,000 in 2023 and $110,000 in 2024 and declares $30,000 in dividends each year. What is the equity income in Steinbart to be reported by Alex in 2024?

    a. $34,050
    b. $38,020
    c. $46,230
    d. $51,450

LO 1-4, 1-5

13. On January 3, 2024, Matteson Corporation acquired 40 percent of the outstanding common stock of O'Toole Company for $1,160,000. This acquisition gave Matteson the ability to exercise significant influence over the investee. The book value of the acquired shares was $820,000. Any excess cost over the underlying book value was assigned to a copyright that was undervalued on its balance sheet. This copyright has a remaining useful life of 10 years. For the year ended December 31, 2024, O'Toole reported net income of $260,000 and declared cash dividends of $50,000. On December 31, 2024, what should Matteson report as its investment in O'Toole under the equity method?

LO 1-4

14. On January 1, 2024, Kroll Corporation paid $2,290,000 for 35 percent of the outstanding voting stock of Sharon, Inc., and appropriately applied the equity method for its investment. Any excess of cost over Sharon's book value was attributed to an indefinite-lived asset. During 2024, Sharon reports $720,000 in net income and a $100,000 other comprehensive income loss. Steel also declares and pays $20,000 in dividends.

    a. What amount should Kroll report as its Investment in Sharon on its December 31, 2024, balance sheet?

    b. What amount should Kroll report as Equity in Earnings of Sharon on its 2024 income statement?

LO 1-4, 1-5

15. On January 1, 2023, Ridge Road Company acquired 20 percent of the voting shares of Sauk Trail, Inc., for $2,700,000 in cash. Both companies provide commercial internet support services but serve markets in different industries. Ridge Road made the investment to gain access to Sauk Trail's board of directors and thus facilitate future cooperative agreements between the two firms. Ridge Road quickly obtained several seats on Sauk Trail's board, which gave it the ability to significantly influence Sauk Trail's operating and investing activities.

    The January 1, 2023, carrying amounts and corresponding fair values for Sauk Trail's assets and liabilities follow:

	Carrying Amount	Fair Value
Cash and Receivables	$ 110,000	$ 110,000
Computing Equipment	5,000,000	5,700,000
Patented Technology	100,000	4,000,000
Trademark	150,000	2,000,000
Liabilities	(185,000)	(185,000)

Also, as of January 1, 2023, Sauk Trail's computing equipment had a seven-year remaining estimated useful life. The patented technology was estimated to have a three-year remaining useful life. The trademark's useful life was considered indefinite. Ridge Road attributed to goodwill any unidentified excess cost.

During the next two years, Sauk Trail reported the following net income and dividends:

	Net Income	Dividends Declared
2023	$1,800,000	$150,000
2024	1,985,000	160,000

    a. How much of Ridge Road's $2,700,000 payment for Sauk Trail is attributable to goodwill?

    b. What amount should Ridge Road report for its equity in Sauk Trail's earnings on its income statements for 2023 and 2024?

    c. What amount should Ridge Road report for its investment in Sauk Trail on its balance sheets at the end of 2023 and 2024?

LO 1-4, 1-5, 1-8

16. On January 1, 2023, Bertrand, Inc., paid $60,000 for a 40 percent interest in Chestnut Corporation's common stock. This investee had assets with a book value of $200,000 and liabilities of $75,000. A patent held by Chestnut having a $5,000 book value was actually worth $20,000. This patent had a six-year remaining life. Any further excess cost associated with this acquisition was attributed to an indefinite-lived asset. During 2023, Chestnut earned income of $30,000 and declared and paid dividends of $10,000. In 2024, it had income of $50,000 and dividends of $15,000. During 2024, the fair value of Bertrand's investment in Chestnut had risen from $68,000 to $75,000.

    a. Assuming Bertrand uses the equity method, what balance should appear in the Investment in Chestnut account as of December 31, 2024?

    b. Assuming Bertrand uses fair-value accounting, what income from the investment in Chestnut should be reported for 2024?

LO 1-4, 1-7

17. On January 1, 2024, Alamar Corporation acquired a 40 percent interest in Burks, Inc., for $210,000. On that date, Burks's balance sheet disclosed net assets with both a fair and book value of $360,000. During 2024, Burks reported net income of $80,000 and declared and paid cash dividends of $25,000. Alamar sold inventory costing $30,000 to Burks during 2024 for $40,000. Burks used all of this merchandise in its operations during 2024. Prepare all of Alamar's 2024 journal entries to apply the equity method to this investment.

LO 1-2, 1-3, 1-4, 1-5, 1-6a

18. Milani, Inc., acquired 10 percent of Seida Corporation on January 1, 2023, for $190,000 and appropriately accounted for the investment using the fair-value method. On January 1, 2024, Milani purchased an additional 30 percent of Seida for $600,000 that resulted in significant influence over Seida. On that date, the fair value of Seida's common stock was $2,000,000 in total. Seida's January 1, 2024, book value equaled $1,850,000, although land was undervalued by $120,000. Any additional excess fair value over Seida's book value was attributable to a trademark with an eight-year remaining life. During 2024, Seida reported income of $300,000 and declared and paid dividends of $110,000. Prepare the 2024 journal entries for Milani related to its investment in Seida.

LO 1-7

19. Camille, Inc., sold $120,000 in inventory to Eckerle Company during 2023 for $200,000. Eckerle resold $85,000 of this merchandise in 2023 with the remainder to be disposed of during 2024. Assuming that Camille owns 30 percent of Eckerle and applies the equity method, what journal entry is recorded at the end of 2023 to defer the intra-entity gross profit?

LO 1-4, 1-5, 1-7

20. BuyCo, Inc., holds 25 percent of the outstanding shares of Marqueen Company and appropriately applies the equity method of accounting. Excess cost amortization (related to a patent) associated with this investment amounts to $10,000 per year. For 2023, Marqueen reported earnings of $100,000 and declares cash dividends of $30,000. During that year, Marqueen acquired inventory for $50,000, which it then sold to BuyCo for $80,000. At the end of 2023, BuyCo continued to hold merchandise with a transfer price of $32,000.

    a. What Equity in Investee Income should BuyCo report for 2023?

    b. How will the intra-entity transfer affect BuyCo's reporting in 2024?

    c. If BuyCo had sold the inventory to Marqueen, how would the answers to parts (a) and (b) have changed?

LO 1-2, 1-3, 1-4, 1-5, 1-6a

21. On January 1, 2022, Halstead, Inc., purchased 75,000 shares of Sedgwick Company common stock for $1,480,000, giving Halstead 25 percent ownership and the ability to apply significant influence over Sedgwick. Any excess of cost over book value acquired was attributed solely to goodwill.

    Sedgwick reports net income and dividends as follows. These amounts are assumed to have occurred evenly throughout these years. Dividends are declared and paid in the same period.

	Net Income	Annual Cash Dividends (paid quarterly)
2022	$340,000	$120,000
2023	480,000	140,000
2024	600,000	160,000

    On July 1, 2024, Halstead sells 12,000 shares of this investment for $25 per share, thus reducing its interest from 25 to 21 percent, but maintaining its significant influence.

    Determine the amounts that would appear on Halstead's 2024 income statement relating to its ownership and partial sale of its investment in Sedgwick's common stock.

LO 1-2, 1-3, 1-4, 1-5, 1-6d

22. Eileen, Inc., purchased 10 percent of Bravo Corporation on January 1, 2023, for $345,000 and accounted for the investment using the fair-value method. Eileen acquires an additional 15 percent of Bravo on January 1, 2024, for $585,000. The equity method of accounting is now appropriate for this investment. No intra-entity sales have occurred.

    a. How does Eileen determine the income to be reported in 2023 in connection with its ownership of Bravo?

    b. What factors should have influenced Eileen in its decision to apply the equity method in 2024?

    c. What factors could have prevented Eileen from adopting the equity method after this second purchase?

    d. What is the objective of the equity method of accounting?

    e. What criticisms have been leveled at the equity method?

    f. In Eileen's 2024 income statement, how is the income from its investment in Bravo determined? Why is this accounting appropriate?

    g. How is the allocation of Eileen's acquisition made?

    h. If Bravo declares a cash dividend in 2024, what impact does it have on Eileen's financial records under the equity method? Why is this accounting appropriate?

    i. Assume the January 1, 2024 fair value of Eileen's original 10 percent investment in Bravo equals $390,000. On financial statements for 2024, how should Eileen determine the balance of its Investment in Bravo account?

LO 1-4, 1-7

23. Parrot Corporation holds a 42 percent ownership of Sunrise, Inc., and applies the equity method to account for its investment. Parrot assigned the entire original excess purchase price over book value to goodwill. During 2023, the two companies made intra-entity inventory transfers. A portion of this merchandise was not resold until 2024. During 2024, additional transfers were made.

    a. What is the difference between upstream transfers and downstream transfers?

    b. How does the direction of an intra-entity transfer (upstream versus downstream) affect the application of the equity method?

    c. How is the intra-entity gross profit deferral computed in applying the equity method?

    d. How should Parrot compute the amount of equity income to be recognized in 2023? What entry is made to record this income?

    e. How should Parrot compute the amount of equity income to be recognized in 2024?

    f. If none of the transferred inventory had remained at the end of 2023, how would these transfers have affected the application of the equity method?

    g. How do these intra-entity transfers affect Sunrise's financial reporting?

LO 1-2, 1-6d

24. Several years ago, Einstein, Inc., bought 40 percent of the outstanding voting stock of Brooks Company. The equity method is appropriately applied. On August 1 of the current year, Einstein sold a portion of these shares.

    a. How does Einstein compute the book value of this investment on August 1 to determine its gain or loss on the sale?

    b. How should Einstein account for this investment after August 1?

    c. If Einstein retains only a 2 percent interest in Brooks so that it holds virtually no influence over Brooks, what figures appear in the investor's income statement for the current year?

    d. If Einstein retains only a 2 percent interest in Brooks so that virtually no influence is held, does the investor have to retroactively adjust any previously reported figures?

LO 1-4, 1-5, 1-7

25. Matthew, Inc., owns 30 percent of the outstanding stock of Lindman Company and has the ability to significantly influence the investee's operations and decision making. On January 1, 2024, the balance in the Investment in Lindman account is $335,000. Amortization associated with this acquisition is $9,000 per year. In 2024, Lindman earns an income of $90,000 and declares cash dividends of $30,000. Previously, in 2023, Lindman had sold inventory costing $24,000 to Matthew for $40,000. Matthew consumed all but 25 percent of this merchandise during 2023 and used the rest during 2024. Lindman sold additional inventory costing $28,000 to Matthew for $50,000 in 2024. Matthew did not consume 40 percent of these 2024 purchases from Lindman until 2025.

    a. What amount of equity method income would Matthew recognize in 2024 from its ownership interest in Lindman?

    b. What is the equity method balance in the Investment in Lindman account at the end of 2024?

LO 1-2, 1-4, 1-5

26. On December 31, 2022, Akron, Inc., purchased 5 percent of Zip Company's common shares on the open market in exchange for $16,000. On December 31, 2023, Akron, Inc., acquires an additional 25 percent of Zip Company's outstanding common stock for $95,000. During the next two years, the following information is available for Zip Company:

	Income	Dividends Declared	Common Stock Fair Value (12/31)
2022			$320,000
2023	$75,000	$ 7,000	380,000
2024	88,000	15,000	480,000

At December 31, 2023, Zip reports a net book value of $290,000. Akron attributed any excess of its 30 percent share of Zip's fair over book value to its share of Zip's franchise agreements. The franchise agreements had a remaining life of 10 years at December 31, 2023.

a. Assume Akron applies the equity method to its Investment in Zip account:

   1. What amount of equity income should Akron report for 2024?

   2. On Akron's December 31, 2024, balance sheet, what amount is reported for the Investment in Zip account?

b. Assume Akron uses fair-value accounting for its Investment in Zip account:

   1. What amount of income from its investment in Zip should Akron report for 2024?

   2. On Akron's December 31, 2024, balance sheet, what amount is reported for the Investment in Zip account?

LO 1-4, 1-5, 1-6d, 1-7

27. Belden, Inc., acquires 30 percent of the outstanding voting shares of Sheffield, Inc., on January 1, 2023, for $312,000, which gives Belden the ability to significantly influence Sheffield. Sheffield has a net book value of $800,000 at January 1, 2023. Sheffield's asset and liability accounts showed carrying amounts considered equal to fair values, except for a copyright whose value accounted for Belden's excess cost over book value in its 30 percent purchase. The copyright had a remaining life of 16 years at January 1, 2023. No goodwill resulted from Belden's share purchase.

   Sheffield reported net income of $180,000 in 2023 and $230,000 of net income during 2024. Dividends of $70,000 and $80,000 are declared and paid in 2023 and 2024, respectively. Belden uses the equity method.

a. On its 2024 comparative income statements, how much income would Belden report for 2023 and 2024 in connection with the company's investment in Sheffield?

b. If Belden sells its entire investment in Sheffield on January 1, 2025, for $400,000 cash, what is the impact on Belden's income?

c. Assume that Belden sells inventory to Sheffield during 2023 and 2024 as follows:

Year	Cost to Belden	Price to Sheffield	Year-End Balance (at transfer price)
2023	$30,000	$50,000	$20,000 (sold in following year)
2024	33,000	60,000	40,000 (sold in following year)

What amount of equity income should Belden recognize for the year 2024?

LO 1-4, 1-5, 1-6b, 1-7

28. Harper, Inc., acquires 40 percent of the outstanding voting stock of Kinman Company on January 1, 2023, for $210,000 in cash. The book value of Kinman's net assets on that date was $400,000, although one of the company's buildings, with a $60,000 carrying amount, was actually worth $100,000. This building had a 10-year remaining life. Kinman owned a royalty agreement with a 20-year remaining life that was undervalued by $85,000.

   Kinman sold inventory with an original cost of $60,000 to Harper during 2023 at a price of $90,000. Harper still held $15,000 (transfer price) of this amount in inventory as of December 31, 2023. These goods are to be sold to outside parties during 2024.

   Kinman reported a $40,000 net loss and a $20,000 other comprehensive loss for 2023. The company still manages to declare and pay a $10,000 cash dividend during the year.

   During 2024, Kinman reported a $40,000 net income and declared and paid a cash dividend of $12,000. It made additional inventory sales of $80,000 to Harper during the period. The original cost of the merchandise was $50,000. All but 30 percent of this inventory had been resold to outside parties by the end of the 2024 fiscal year.

   Prepare all journal entries for Harper for 2023 and 2024 in connection with this investment. Assume that the equity method is applied.

LO 1-4, 1-5, 1-6b, 1-7

29. On January 1, 2024, Pine Company owns 40 percent (40,000 shares) of Seacrest, Inc., which it purchased several years ago for $182,000. Since the date of acquisition, the equity method has been properly applied, and the carrying amount of the investment account as of January 1, 2024,

is $293,600. Excess patent cost amortization of $12,000 is still being recognized each year. During 2024, Seacrest reports net income of $342,000 and a $120,000 other comprehensive loss, both incurred uniformly throughout the year. No dividends were declared during the year. Pine sold 8,000 shares of Seacrest on August 1, 2024, for $93,000 in cash. However, Pine retains the ability to significantly influence the investee.

During the last quarter of 2023, Pine sold $50,000 in inventory (which it had originally purchased for only $30,000) to Seacrest. At the end of that fiscal year, Seacrest's inventory retained $10,000 (at sales price) of this merchandise, which was subsequently sold in the first quarter of 2024.

On Pine's financial statements for the year ended December 31, 2024, what income effects would be reported from its ownership in Seacrest?

LO 1-4, 1-5, 1-7

30. On July 1, 2022, Burrough Company acquired 88,000 of the outstanding shares of Carter Company for $13 per share. This acquisition gave Burrough a 25 percent ownership of Carter and allowed Burrough to significantly influence the investee's decisions.

    As of July 1, 2022, the investee had assets with a book value of $3 million and liabilities of $74,400. At the time, Carter held equipment appraised at $364,000 more than book value; it was considered to have a seven-year remaining life with no salvage value. Carter also held a copyright with a five-year remaining life on its books that was undervalued by $972,000. Any remaining excess cost was attributable to an indefinite-lived trademark. Depreciation and amortization are computed using the straight-line method. Burrough applies the equity method for its investment in Carter.

    Carter's policy is to declare and pay a $1 per share cash dividend every April 1 and October 1. Carter's income, earned evenly throughout each year, was $598,000 in 2022, $639,600 in 2023, and $692,400 in 2024.

    In addition, Burrough sold inventory costing $91,200 to Carter for $152,000 during 2023. Carter resold $92,000 of this inventory during 2023 and the remaining $60,000 during 2024.

    a. Determine the equity income to be recognized by Burrough during each of these years.

    b. Compute Burrough's investment in Carter Company's balance as of December 31, 2024.

LO 1-2, 1-3, 1-4, 1-5, 1-6d

31. On January 1, 2023, Fisher Corporation purchased 40 percent (80,000 shares) of the common stock of Bowden, Inc., for $982,000 in cash and began to use the equity method for the investment. The price paid represented a $60,000 payment in excess of the book value of Fisher's share of Bowden's underlying net assets. Fisher was willing to make this extra payment because of a recently developed patent held by Bowden with a 15-year remaining life. All other assets were considered appropriately valued on Bowden's books.

    Bowden declares and pays a $100,000 cash dividend to its stockholders each year on September 15. Bowden reported net income of $400,000 in 2023 and $380,000 in 2024. Each income figure was earned evenly throughout its respective years.

    On July 1, 2024, Fisher sold 10 percent (20,000 shares) of Bowden's outstanding shares for $330,000 in cash. Although it sold this interest, Fisher maintained the ability to significantly influence Bowden's decision-making process.

    Prepare the journal entries for Fisher for the years of 2023 and 2024.

LO 1-4, 1-5, 1-7

32. On January 1, 2023, Stream Company acquired 30 percent of the outstanding voting shares of Q-Video, Inc., for $770,000. Q-Video manufactures specialty cables for computer monitors. On that date, Q-Video reported assets and liabilities with book values of $1.9 million and $700,000, respectively. A customer list compiled by Q-Video had an appraised value of $300,000, although it was not recorded on its books. The expected remaining life of the customer list was five years with straight-line amortization deemed appropriate. Any remaining excess cost was not identifiable with any particular asset and thus was considered goodwill.

    Q-Video generated net income of $250,000 in 2023 and a net loss of $100,000 in 2024. In each of these two years, Q-Video declared and paid a cash dividend of $15,000 to its stockholders.

    During 2023, Q-Video sold inventory that had an original cost of $100,000 to Stream for $160,000. Of this balance, $80,000 was resold to outsiders during 2023, and the remainder was sold during 2024. In 2024, Q-Video sold inventory to Stream for $175,000. This inventory had cost only $140,000. Stream resold $100,000 of the inventory during 2024 and the rest during 2025.

    For 2023 and then for 2024, compute the amount that Stream should report as income from its investment in Q-Video in its external financial statements under the equity method.

Develop Your Skills

DATA ANALYSIS CASE 1: DETERMINE MAXIMUM INVESTMENT PRICE

CPA
skills

On January 1, 2024, Delta Co. is considering purchasing a 40 percent ownership interest in Omega Co., a privately held enterprise, for $700,000. Omega predicts its profit will be $185,000 in 2024, projects a 10 percent annual increase in profits in each of the next four years, and expects to pay a steady annual dividend of $30,000 for the foreseeable future. Because Omega has on its books a patent that is undervalued by $375,000, Delta realizes that it will have an additional amortization expense of $15,000 per year over the next 10 years—the patent's estimated remaining useful life. Any remaining excess paid by Delta over Omega's fair value was attributable to indefinite-lived intangible assets. All of Omega's other assets and liabilities have book values that approximate market values. Delta uses the equity method for its investment in Omega.

Required

1. Using an Excel spreadsheet, set the following values in cells:
   - Delta's cost of investment in Omega.
   - Percentage acquired.
   - First-year Omega reported income.
   - Projected growth rate in income.
   - Omega annual dividends.
   - Annual excess patent amortization.
2. Referring to the values in (1), prepare the following schedules using columns for the years 2024 through 2028.
   - Delta's equity in Omega earnings with rows showing these:
     - Delta's share of Omega reported income.
     - Amortization expense.
     - Delta's equity in Omega earnings.
   - Delta's investment in Omega balance with rows showing the following:
     - Beginning balance.
     - Equity earnings.
     - Dividends.
     - Ending balance.
   - Return on beginning investment balance = Equity earnings/Beginning investment balance in each year.
3. Given the preceding values, compute the average of the projected returns on beginning investment balances for the first five years of Delta's investment in Omega. What is the maximum Delta can pay for Omega if it wishes to earn at least a 10 percent average return on beginning investment balance over the next five years? (*Hint:* Under Excel's Tools tab, select the Goal Seek capability to produce a 10 percent average return on beginning investment balance by changing the cell that contains Delta's cost of investment in Omega. Excel's Solver should produce an exact answer while Goal Seek should produce a close approximation. You may need to first add in the Solver capability in Excel under Tools>Excel Add-ins.)

DATA ANALYSIS CASE 2: COMPUTE EQUITABLE TRANSFER PRICE

On January 1, Intergen, Inc., invests $200,000 for a 40 percent interest in Ryan, a new joint venture with two other partners, each investing $150,000 for 30 percent interest. Intergen plans to sell all of its production to Ryan, which will resell the inventory to retail outlets. The equity partners agree that Ryan will buy inventory only from Intergen. Also, Intergen plans to use the equity method for financial reporting.

During the year, Intergen expects to incur costs of $850,000 to produce goods with a final retail market value of $1,200,000. Ryan projects that, during this year, it will resell three-fourths of these goods for $900,000. It should sell the remainder in the following year.

The equity partners plan a meeting to set the price Intergen will charge Ryan for its production. One partner suggests a transfer price of $1,025,000 but is unsure whether it will result in an equitable return across the equity holders. Importantly, Intergen agrees that its total rate of return (including its own operations and its investment in Ryan) should be equal to that of the other investors' return on their investments in Ryan. All agree that Intergen's value including its investment in Ryan is $1,000,000.

Required

1. Create an Excel spreadsheet analysis showing the following:
   - Projected income statements for Intergen and Ryan. Formulate the statements to do the following:
     - Link Ryan's cost of goods sold to Intergen's sales (use a starting value of $1,025,000 for Intergen's sales).
     - Link Intergen's equity in Ryan's earnings to Ryan's net income (adjusted for Intergen's gross profit rate × Ryan's ending inventory × 40 percent ownership percentage).
     - Be able to change Intergen's sales and see the effects throughout the income statements of Ryan and Intergen. Note that the cost of goods sold for Intergen is fixed.
   - The rate of return for the two 30 percent equity partners on their investment in Ryan.
   - The total rate of return for Intergen based on its $1,000,000 value.
2. What transfer price will provide an equal rate of return for each of the investors in the first year of operation? (*Hint:* Under Excel's Tools tab, select Goal Seek to produce a zero difference in rates of return across the equity partners by changing the cell that contains Intergen's sales. Excel's Solver add-in will work as well.)

RESEARCH AND DISCUSSION CASE

Access a recent copy of The Coca-Cola Company's SEC 10-K filing at www.coca-cola.com and address the following:

1. What companies does Coca-Cola describe as significant equity method investments? How do these investments help Coca-Cola?
2. What criteria does Coca-Cola use in choosing to apply the equity method for these investments?
3. How does Coca-Cola describe its application of the equity method?
4. What amount of equity income did Coca-Cola report?
5. Coca-Cola discloses the fair values of its publicly traded bottlers accounted for as equity method investments. List the carrying amounts and fair values for these equity method investments that have publicly traded data. Discuss the relevance of each of these two values.

RESEARCH AND ANALYSIS CASE—IMPAIRMENT

Wolf Pack Transport Co. has a 25 percent equity investment in Maggie Valley Depot (MVD), Inc., which owns and operates a warehousing facility used for the collection and redistribution of various consumer goods. Wolf Pack paid $1,685,000 for its 25 percent interest in MVD several years ago, including a $300,000 allocation for goodwill as the only excess cost over book value acquired. Wolf Pack Transport has since appropriately applied the equity method to account for the investment. In its most recent balance sheet, because of recognized profits in excess of dividends since the acquisition, Wolf Pack reported a $2,350,000 amount for its Investment in Maggie Valley Depot, Inc., account.

However, competition in the transit warehousing industry has increased in the past 12 months. In the same area as the MVD facility, a competitor company opened two additional warehouses that are much more conveniently located near a major interstate highway. MVD's revenues declined 30 percent as customers shifted their business to the competitor's facilities and the prices for warehouse services declined. The market value of Wolf Pack's stock ownership in MVD fell to $1,700,000 from a high last year of $2,500,000. MVD's management is currently debating ways to respond to these events but has yet to formulate a firm plan.

Required

1. What guidance does the FASB ASC provide for equity method investment losses in value?
2. Should Wolf Pack recognize the decline in the value of its holdings in MVD in its current year financial statements?
3. Should Wolf Pack test for impairment of the value it had initially assigned to goodwill?

RESEARCH CASE—NONCONTROLLING SHAREHOLDER RIGHTS

Consolidated financial reporting is appropriate when one entity has a controlling financial interest in another entity. The usual condition for a controlling financial interest is ownership of a majority voting interest. But in some circumstances, control does not rest with the majority owner—especially when noncontrolling owners are contractually provided with approval or veto rights that can restrict the actions of the majority owner. In these cases, the majority owner employs the equity method rather than consolidation.

Required

Address the following by searching the FASB ASC Topic 810 on consolidation.

1. What are protective noncontrolling rights?

2. What are substantive participating noncontrolling rights?

3. What noncontrolling rights overcome the presumption that all majority-owned investees should be consolidated?

4. Zee Company buys 60 percent of the voting stock of Bee Company with the remaining 40 percent noncontrolling interest held by Bee's former owners, who negotiated the following noncontrolling rights:

   • Any new debt above $1,000,000 must be approved by the 40 percent noncontrolling shareholders.

   • Any dividends or other cash distributions to owners in excess of customary historical amounts must be approved by the 40 percent noncontrolling shareholders.

   According to the FASB ASC, what are the issues in determining whether Zee should consolidate Bee or report its investment in Bee under the equity method?

Consolidation of Financial Information

Financial statements published and distributed to owners, creditors, and other interested parties appear to report the operations and financial position of a single company. In reality, these statements frequently represent a number of separate organizations tied together through common control (a *business combination*). When financial statements represent more than one corporation, we refer to them as *consolidated financial statements*.

Consolidated financial statements are typical in today's business world. Most major organizations, and many smaller ones, hold control over an array of organizations. For example, over the past two decades, Cisco Systems, Inc., reported more than 100 business acquisitions that now are consolidated in its financial reports. PepsiCo, Inc., as another example, annually consolidates data from a multitude of companies into a single set of financial statements. By gaining control over these companies (often known as *subsidiaries*)—which include Frito-Lay, Naked Juice, Quaker Oats, South Beach Beverage, and Tropicana Products—PepsiCo (the *parent*) forms a single business combination and single reporting entity.

The consolidation of financial information as exemplified by Cisco Systems and PepsiCo is one of the most complex procedures in all of accounting. Comprehending this process completely requires understanding the theoretical logic that underlies the creation of a business combination. Furthermore, a variety of procedural steps must be mastered to ensure that proper accounting is achieved for this single reporting entity. The following coverage introduces both of these aspects of the consolidation process.

The FASB *Accounting Standards Codification*® (ASC) contains the current accounting standards for business combinations under the following topics:

- "Business Combinations" (Topic 805).
- "Consolidation" (Topic 810).

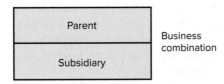

The ASC "Business Combinations" topic provides guidance on the accounting and reporting for business combinations using the *acquisition method*. The acquisition method embraces a *fair-value* measurement attribute. Adoption of this attribute reflects the FASB's increasing emphasis on fair value for measuring and assessing business activity. In the past, financial reporting standards embraced the cost principle to measure and report the financial

Learning Objectives

After studying this chapter, you should be able to:

LO 2-1 Discuss the motives for business combinations.

LO 2-2 Recognize when consolidation of financial information into a single set of statements is necessary.

LO 2-3 Define the term *business combination* and differentiate across various forms of business combinations.

LO 2-4 Describe the valuation principles of the acquisition method.

LO 2-5 Determine the total fair value of the consideration transferred for an acquisition, and allocate that fair value to specific subsidiary assets acquired (including goodwill) and liabilities assumed or to a gain on bargain purchase.

LO 2-6 Prepare the journal entry to
   a. consolidate the accounts of a subsidiary if dissolution takes place.
   b. record the various related costs involved in a business combination.
   c. record a business combination when the acquired firm retains its separate existence.

LO 2-7 Prepare a worksheet to consolidate the accounts of two companies that form a business combination in the absence of dissolution.

LO 2-8 Describe the accounting treatment for the various intangible assets often acquired in a business combination.

LO 2-9 Appendix 2A: Identify the general characteristics of the legacy purchase and pooling of interest methods of accounting for past business combinations. Understand the effects that persist today in financial statements from the use of these legacy methods.

LO 2-10 Appendix 2B: Explain the rationale and procedures underlying a subsidiary's election to adopt pushdown accounting.

effects of business combinations. This fundamental change from a cost-based to a fair-value model has transformed the way we account for and report business combinations in our society.

The ASC "Consolidation" topic provides guidance on circumstances that require a firm to prepare consolidated financial reports and various other related reporting issues. Basically, consolidated financial reports must be prepared whenever one firm has a controlling financial interest in another. Although ownership of a majority voting interest is the usual condition for a controlling financial interest, the power to control may also exist with a smaller percentage of ownership through governance contracts, leases, or agreements with other stockholders.[1]

In this chapter, we first present expansion through corporate takeovers and present an overview of the consolidation process. Then we present the specifics of the acquisition method of accounting for business combinations where the acquirer obtains complete ownership of another firm. Later, beginning in Chapter 4, we introduce coverage of acquisitions with less than complete ownership.

Financial reporting for business combinations has experienced many changes over the past decade. Prior to the acquisition method requirement, accounting standards allowed either the purchase method or the earlier pooling of interests method of accounting for business combinations. Neither of these methods is now permitted for reporting the formation of new business combinations. However, because of the prospective application of the acquisition method beginning in 2009, legacy effects of these methods remain in many of today's financial statements. Therefore, an appendix to this chapter provides a review of the purchase method and pooling of interests method.

Expansion through Corporate Takeovers

Reasons for Firms to Combine

A frequent economic phenomenon is the combining of two or more businesses into a single entity under common management and control. During recent decades, the United States and the rest of the world have experienced an enormous number of corporate mergers and takeovers, transactions in which one company gains control over another. According to Refinitiv, the volume of mergers and acquisitions globally in 2021 stood at $5.8 trillion, its highest level ever. Of these deals, more than $2.5 trillion involved a U.S. firm. As indicated by Exhibit 2.1, the magnitude of recent combinations continues to be large.

As with any other economic activity, business combinations can be part of an overall managerial strategy to maximize shareholder value. Shareholders—the owners of the firm—hire managers to direct resources so that the firm's value grows over time. In this way, owners receive a return on their investment. Successful firms receive substantial benefits through enhanced share value. Importantly, the managers of successful firms also receive substantial benefits in salaries, especially if their compensation contracts are partly based on stock market performance of the firm's shares.

If the goal of business activity is to maximize the firm's value, in what ways do business combinations help achieve that goal? Clearly, the business community is moving rapidly toward business combinations as a strategy for growth and competitiveness. Size and scale are obviously becoming critical as firms compete in today's markets. Importantly, valuable synergies often accompany business combinations.

If large firms can be more efficient in delivering goods and services, they gain a competitive advantage and become more profitable for the owners. Increases in scale can produce larger profits from enhanced sales volume despite smaller (more competitive) profit margins. When two firms integrate successive stages of production and distribution of products, coordinating raw material purchases, manufacturing, and delivery, substantial savings can result.

---

[1] We discuss entities controlled through contractual means (known as variable interest entities) in Chapter 6.

EXHIBIT 2.1   Recent Notable Business Combinations

Acquirer	Target	Deal Value
S&P Global	IHS Markit (United Kingdom)	$ 44.0B
T-Mobile	Sprint	$ 40.8B
Analog Devices	Maxim Integrated Products	$ 27.9B
Salesforce.com	Slack Technologies	$ 27.7B
Microsoft	Nuance	$ 20.0B
Intuit	Mailchimp	$ 12.0B
Merck & Company	Acceleron Pharma	$ 11.5B
Nvidia	Mellanox	$ 7.0B
Johnson & Johnson	Momenta Pharmaceuticals	$ 6.5B
Verizon Communications	Tracfone Wireless	$ 6.2B
Cisco	Acacia Communications	$ 4.5B
Uber Technologies	Postmates	$ 3.9B
Goodyear Tire & Rubber Company	Cooper Tire & Rubber Company	$ 3.1B
Google	Fitbit	$ 2.1B
Costco Wholesale Corp.	Innovel Solutions	$ 1.0B
Peloton Interactive	Precor	$412.0M

As an example, Oracle's acquisition of Sun Microsystems creates synergies by enabling Oracle to integrate its software product lines with Sun's hardware specifications. The acquisition further allows Oracle to offer complete systems made of chips, computers, storage devices, and software with an aim toward increased efficiency and quality.[2] Other cost savings resulting from elimination of redundant processes, such as data processing and marketing, can make a single entity more profitable than the separate parent and subsidiary had been in the past. Such synergies often accompany business combinations.

Although no two business combinations are exactly alike, many share one or more of the following characteristics that potentially enhance profitability:

- Vertical integration of one firm's output and another firm's distribution or further processing.
- Cost savings through elimination of duplicate facilities and staff.
- Quick entry for new and existing products into domestic and foreign markets.
- Economies of scale allowing greater efficiency and negotiating power.
- The ability to access financing at more attractive rates. As firm size increases, negotiating power with financial institutions can increase also.
- Diversification of business risk.

Business combinations also occur because many firms seek the continuous expansion of their organizations, often into diversified areas. Acquiring control over a vast network of different businesses has been a strategy utilized by a number of companies (sometimes known as *conglomerates*) for decades. Entry into new industries is immediately available to the parent without having to construct facilities, develop products, train management, or create market recognition. Many corporations have successfully employed this strategy to produce huge, highly profitable organizations. Unfortunately, others discovered that the task of managing a widely diverse group of businesses can be a costly learning experience. Even combinations that are designed to take advantage of operating synergies and cost savings will fail if the integration is not managed carefully.

Overall, the primary motivations for many business combinations can be traced to an increasingly competitive environment. Three recent business combinations provide interesting examples of distinct motivations to combine: Goodyear Tire & Rubber and Cooper Tire & Rubber, Google and Fitbit, and Uber and Postmates. Each is discussed briefly in turn.

[2] Ben Worthen, Cari Tuna, and Justin Scheck, "Companies More Prone to Go 'Vertical,'" *Wall Street Journal*, November 30, 2009.

Goodyear Tire & Rubber and Cooper Tire & Rubber

On June 7, 2021, The Goodyear Tire & Rubber Company announced that it had completed its acquisition of Cooper Tire & Rubber Company for total consideration of $3.097 billion. Goodyear acquired 100% of Cooper's outstanding shares of common stock. The consideration paid included both cash and shares of Goodyear common stock. The acquisition positions Goodyear as the largest U.S.-based tire manufacturer. The acquisition was the largest in the tire industry since the Michelin-Uniroyal Goodrich and Bridgestone-Firestone mergers of the 1980s.

According to Richard Kramer, Goodyear chairman and CEO, "The combination strengthens Goodyear's ability to serve more consumers globally and provides increased scale to support greater investments in new mobility and fleet solutions."[3] By acquiring Cooper, Goodyear enhances its market power through greater size and scale. The acquisition enables Goodyear to increase marketing of both company's products through a combined global retail distribution system. For example, in China alone, the combination nearly doubles Goodyear's presence. Moreover, cost synergies will likely be realized through savings at the corporate level as well as operating synergies.[4]

Intangible assets represented much of the value paid for Cooper. According to Goodyear's June 30, 2021, 10-Q report, included in the $3.097 billion purchase price was $1.086 billion for identifiable intangibles including trade names (the large majority of which are considered indefinite-lived), customer relationships, and noncompete agreements. An additional $475 million was allocated to goodwill. As expected, the acquisition of a manufacturing entity resulted in substantial purchase price allocations to accounts receivable, inventories, and property plant and equipment.

Google and Fitbit

On January 14, 2021, the technology company Google announced that it had completed its $2.1 billion acquisition of Fitbit, a producer of wireless-enabled wearable fitness monitors. The deal was subject to extensive regulatory scrutiny both in the United States and abroad, prompted by concerns of safeguarding consumers' privacy. In response, Google made a series of binding commitments to maintain data privacy and separation between Fitbit users' health data and Google advertisements.[5]

The Fitbit acquisition creates a platform for Google to leverage its technology capabilities in the health care field. Given Google's size and scale, it makes sense for it to work with premier companies in health care, like Fitbit. Google is all about data processing, and fittingly, Fitbit monitors and measures data on an individual's health, converts the data into useful metrics, and communicates the metrics to the wearer. As observed by Google's senior vice president, devices and services, "We're confident the combination of Fitbit's leading technology, product expertise and health and wellness innovation with the best of Google's AI (artificial intelligence), software and hardware will drive more competition in wearables and make the next generation of devices better and more affordable."[6]

Moreover, Fitbit brings to the deal working partnerships with health insurance companies and direct corporate wellness programming. Google stands to benefit from Fitbit's experience in partnering with corporate, government, and other health care entities.[7] Clearly, Google expects significant synergies from the combination. According to Alphabet's (Google's parent company) September 30, 2021, 10-Q report, of the $2.1 billion acquisition price, $1.2 billion was allocated to goodwill. The report states that the goodwill is "primarily attributable to synergies expected to arise after the acquisition."

[3] Press Release, "Goodyear Completes Acquisition of Cooper," Goodyear, June 7, 2021.

[4] Ibid.

[5] Heather Landi, "Google Closes $2.1B Acquisition of Fitbit as Justice Department Probe Continues," Fierce Healthcare, January 14, 2021.

[6] Rick Osterloh, "Google Completes Fitbit Acquisition," Google blog post, January 14, 2021.

[7] Patrick Lucas Austin, "The Real Reason Google is Buying Fitbit," *Time Magazine,* November 4, 2019.

Uber and Postmates

On December 1, 2020, Uber Technologies, a mobility service provider, announced that it had completed the acquisition of Postmates, Inc., a food-delivery service, in an all-stock transaction valued at $3.9 billion. Uber offers technology applications that support ride services, restaurant and grocer deliveries, and other sales with delivery service providers. According to Uber's 2020 10-K report, the "acquisition brings together our global Mobility and Delivery platform with Postmates' distinctive delivery business in the United States." The Uber Eats platform and Postmates will integrate their services positioning Uber as the second-largest food delivery provider in the United States. Although Uber Eats and Postmates will remain separate entities with their own apps and marketplaces, they will eventually combine their delivery and merchant networks.[8]

The Postmates acquisition provides Uber with additional size and scale in the delivery market space that includes competitors such as DoorDash, GrubHub, Deliveroo, Just Eat Takeaway, and many other firms. In both the delivery and ride share markets, Uber has repeatedly turned to business combinations to fuel its growth and competitive position. As noted in its 2020 10-K report, during 2020 alone, Uber has also acquired Careem (Dubai), Cornershop (Mexico and Chile), and Routematch (United States and Australia).

The Postmates acquisition price was largely attributed to intangibles. Of the $4.33 billion fair value assigned to Postmates's assets, $3.15 billion was recognized as goodwill along with $1.02 billion allocated to other intangible assets including relationships with merchants (e.g., restaurants), fleet (Postmates couriers), and consumers. Developed technology, trade names, and in-process research and development were also recognized as intangible assets in the acquisition.

LO 2-2

Recognize when consolidation of financial information into a single set of statements is necessary.

Business Combinations, Control, and Consolidated Financial Reporting

The consolidation of financial information into a single set of statements becomes necessary when the business combination of two or more companies creates a single economic entity. As stated in FASB ASC (810-10-10-1): "There is a presumption that consolidated financial statements are more meaningful than separate financial statements and that they are usually necessary for a fair presentation when one of the entities in the consolidated group directly or indirectly has a controlling financial interest in the other entities."

Thus, in producing financial statements for external distribution, the reporting entity transcends the boundaries of incorporation to encompass (i.e., consolidate) all companies for which control is present. Even though the various companies may retain their legal identities as separate corporations, the resulting information is more meaningful to outside parties when consolidated into a single set of financial statements.

To explain the process of preparing consolidated financial statements for a business combination, we address three questions:

1. How is a business combination formed?
2. What constitutes a controlling financial interest?
3. How is the consolidation process carried out?

LO 2-3

Define the term *business combination* and differentiate across various forms of business combinations.

Business Combinations—Creating a Single Economic Entity

A business combination refers to a transaction or other event in which an acquirer obtains control over one or more businesses.

Business combinations are formed by a wide variety of transactions or events with various formats. For example, each of the following is identified as a business combination although it differs widely in legal form. In every case, two or more enterprises are united into a single economic entity so that consolidated financial statements are required.

---

[8] Joe Guszkowski, "Uber Eats Completes Postmates Acquisition," *Restaurant Business,* November 30, 2020.

Mergers

- One company obtains the assets, and often the liabilities, of another company in exchange for cash, other assets, liabilities, stock, or a combination of these. The second organization normally dissolves itself as a legal corporation. Thus, only the acquiring company remains in existence, having absorbed the acquired net assets directly into its own operations. Any business combination in which only one of the original companies continues to exist is referred to in legal terms as a *statutory merger.*

- One company obtains all of the capital stock of another in exchange for cash, other assets, liabilities, stock, or a combination of these. After gaining control, the acquiring company can decide to transfer all assets and liabilities to its own financial records with the second company being dissolved as a separate corporation.[9] The business combination is, once again, a statutory merger because only one of the companies maintains legal existence. This merger, however, is achieved by obtaining equity securities rather than by buying the target company's assets. Because stock is obtained, the acquiring company must gain 100 percent control of all shares before legally dissolving the subsidiary.

Consolidations

Two or more companies transfer either their assets or their capital stock to a newly formed corporation. Both original companies are dissolved, leaving only the new organization in existence. A business combination achieved in this manner is a *statutory consolidation.* The use here of the term *consolidation* should not be confused with the accounting meaning of that same word. In accounting, *consolidation* refers to the mechanical process of bringing together the financial records of two or more organizations to form a single set of statements. A statutory consolidation denotes a specific type of business combination that has united two or more existing companies under the ownership of a newly created company.

Investments in Subsidiaries

One company achieves legal control over another by acquiring a majority of voting stock. *Although control is present, no dissolution takes place; each company remains in existence as an incorporated operation.* Whole Foods Market, as an example, continues to retain its legal status as a limited liability company after being acquired by Amazon. Separate incorporation is frequently preferred to take full advantage of any intangible benefits accruing to the acquired company as a going concern. Better utilization of such factors as licenses, trade names, employee loyalty, and the company's reputation can be possible when the subsidiary maintains its own legal identity. Moreover, maintaining an independent information system for a subsidiary often enhances its market value for an eventual sale or initial public offering as a stand-alone entity.

Because the asset and liability account balances are not physically combined as in statutory mergers and consolidations, each company continues to maintain an independent accounting system. To reflect the combination, the acquiring company enters the takeover transaction into its own records by establishing a single investment asset account. However, the newly acquired subsidiary omits any recording of this event; its stock is simply transferred to the parent from the subsidiary's shareholders. Thus, the subsidiary's financial records are not directly affected by a takeover.

Investments in Variable Interest Entities

A final vehicle for control of another business entity does not involve a majority voting stock interest or direct ownership of assets. Control of a variable interest entity (VIE) by design often does not rest with its equity holders. Instead, control is exercised through contractual arrangements with a sponsoring firm that, although it technically may not own the VIE, becomes its "primary beneficiary" with rights to its residual profits. These contracts can take the form of leases, participation rights, guarantees, or other interests. Past use of VIEs was criticized because these structures provided sponsoring firms with off-balance sheet financing and

---

[9] Although the acquired company has been legally dissolved, it frequently continues to operate as a separate division within the surviving company's organization.

EXHIBIT 2.2 **Business Combinations**

Type of Combination	Action of Acquiring Company	Action of Acquired Company
Merger through asset acquisition.	Acquires assets and often liabilities.	Dissolves and goes out of business.
Merger through capital stock acquisition.	Acquires all stock and then transfers assets and liabilities to its own books.	Dissolves as a separate corporation, often remaining as a division of the acquiring company.
Consolidation through capital stock or asset acquisition.	Newly created entity receives assets or capital stock of original companies.	Original companies may dissolve while remaining as separate divisions of newly created company.
Investment in subsidiary—acquisition of more than 50 percent of the voting stock.	Acquires stock that is recorded as an investment; controls decision making of acquired company.	Remains in existence as legal corporation, although now a subsidiary of the acquiring company.
Control through ownership of variable interests (see Chapter 6). Risks and rewards often flow to a sponsoring firm that may or may not hold equity shares.	Establishes contractual control over a variable interest entity to engage in a specific activity.	Remains in existence as a separate legal entity—often a trust or partnership.

sometimes questionable profits on sales to their VIEs. Prior to 2004, many sponsors of VIEs did not technically meet the definition of a controlling financial interest (i.e., majority voting stock ownership) and thus did not consolidate their VIEs. Current GAAP, however, expands the notion of control and thus requires consolidation of VIEs by their primary beneficiary.

As you can see, business combinations are created in many distinct forms. The specific format is a critical factor in the subsequent consolidation of financial information. Exhibit 2.2 provides an overview of the various combinations.

Control—An Elusive Quality

The definition of control is central to determining when two or more entities become one economic entity and therefore one reporting entity. Control of one firm by another is most often achieved through the acquisition of voting shares. The ASC (810-10-15-8) describes control as follows:

> The usual condition for a controlling financial interest is ownership of a majority voting interest, and, therefore, as a general rule ownership by one reporting entity, directly or indirectly, of more than 50 percent of the outstanding voting shares of another entity is a condition pointing toward consolidation.

By exercising majority voting power, one firm can literally dictate the financing and operating activities of another firm. Accordingly, U.S. GAAP traditionally has pointed to a majority voting share ownership as a controlling financial interest that requires consolidation.

Notably, the power to control may also exist with less than 50 percent of the outstanding shares of another entity. The ASC (810-10-15-8) goes on to observe that

> The power to control may also exist with a lesser percentage of ownership, for example, by contract, lease, agreement with other stockholders, or by court decree.

Therefore, despite possessing less than 50 percent of the subsidiary's voting stock, one ownership group can enter into contractual arrangement with other ownership groups that provide control.

Alternatively, majority ownership does not always indicate an exclusive ability for one entity to exercise control over another. According to the FASB ASC Glossary, control can also be defined as

> The direct or indirect ability to determine the direction of management and policies through ownership, contract, or otherwise.

This description recognizes the complex profit-sharing agreements that sometimes accompany economic resource sharing. To reduce their risk, several parties may participate in directing the activities of another entity. For example, a parent with majority ownership may grant certain decision rights to noncontrolling shareholders in exchange for economic support. Such noncontrolling participation rights may be powerful enough to prevent the majority owners from controlling the entity.

As the complexity of ownership arrangements increases, defining when one firm controls another remains a continuing challenge for financial reporting standard setters. Nonetheless, the primary way U.S. firms exercise control remains through the acquisition of a majority of another firm's voting shares. Consequently, in this text, we largely focus on control relationships established through voting interests. In Chapter 6, however, we expand our coverage to include the consolidation of firms where control is exercised through variable interests.

Consolidation of Financial Information

When one company gains control over another, a business combination is established. Financial data gathered from the individual companies are then brought together to form a single set of consolidated statements. Although this process can be complicated, the objectives of a consolidation are straightforward to report the financial position, results of operations, and cash flows for the combined entity. As a part of this process, reciprocal accounts and intra-entity transactions must be adjusted or eliminated to ensure that all reported balances truly represent the single entity.

Applicable consolidation procedures vary significantly depending on the legal format employed in creating a business combination. *For a statutory merger or a statutory consolidation, when the acquired company (or companies) is (are) legally dissolved, only one accounting consolidation ever occurs.* On the date of the combination, the surviving company simply records the various account balances from each of the dissolving companies. Because the accounts are brought together permanently in this manner, no further consolidation procedures are necessary. After the balances have been transferred to the survivor, the financial records of the acquired companies are closed out as part of the dissolution.

Conversely, in a combination when all companies retain incorporation, a different set of consolidation procedures is appropriate. Because the companies preserve their legal identities, each continues to maintain its own independent accounting records. *Thus, no permanent consolidation of the account balances is ever made. Rather, the consolidation process must be carried out anew each time the reporting entity prepares financial statements for external reporting purposes.*

When separate recordkeeping is maintained, the accountant faces a unique problem: The financial information must be brought together periodically without disturbing the accounting systems of the individual companies. Because these consolidations are produced outside the financial records, worksheets traditionally are used to expedite the process. Worksheets are a part of neither company's accounting records nor the resulting financial statements. Instead, they are an efficient structure for organizing and adjusting the information used to prepare externally reported consolidated statements.

Consequently, the legal characteristics of a business combination have a significant impact on the approach taken to the consolidation process:

What is to be consolidated?

- If dissolution takes place, appropriate account balances are physically consolidated in the surviving company's financial records.
- If separate incorporation is maintained, only the financial statement information (not the actual records) is consolidated.

When does the consolidation of financial information take place?

- If dissolution takes place, a permanent consolidation of financial information occurs at the date of the combination.
- If separate incorporation is maintained, the financial information consolidation process is carried out at regular intervals whenever financial statements are to be prepared.

How are the accounting records affected?

- If dissolution takes place, the surviving company's accounts are adjusted to include appropriate balances of the dissolved company. The dissolved company's records are closed out.
- If separate incorporation is maintained, each company continues to retain its own records. Using worksheets facilitates the periodic consolidation process without disturbing the individual accounting systems.

Financial Reporting for Business Combinations

LO 2-4

Describe the valuation principles of the acquisition method.

The Acquisition Method

Regardless of whether the acquired firm maintains its separate incorporation or dissolution takes place, current standards require the acquisition method to account for business combinations.[10] Applying the acquisition method involves recognizing and measuring

- The consideration transferred for the acquired business and any noncontrolling interest.
- The separately identified assets acquired and liabilities assumed.
- Goodwill, or a gain from a bargain purchase.

Fair value is the measurement attribute used to recognize these and other aspects of a business combination. Therefore, prior to examining specific applications of the acquisition method, we present a brief discussion of the fair-value concept as applied to business combinations.

Consideration Transferred for the Acquired Business

The fair value of the consideration transferred to acquire a business from its former owners is the starting point in valuing and recording a business combination. In describing the acquisition method, the FASB ASC states:

> The consideration transferred in a business combination shall be measured at fair value, which shall be calculated as the sum of the acquisition-date fair values of the assets transferred by the acquirer, the liabilities incurred by the acquirer to former owners of the acquiree, and the equity interests issued by the acquirer. (ASC 805-30-30-7)

The acquisition method thus embraces the fair value of the consideration transferred in measuring the acquirer's interest in the acquired business.[11] Fair value is defined as the price that would be received to sell an asset or paid to transfer a liability in an orderly transaction between market participants at the measurement date. Thus, market values are often the best source of evidence of the fair value of consideration transferred in a business combination. Items of consideration transferred can include cash, securities (either stocks or debt), and other property or obligations.

Contingent Consideration: An Additional Element of Consideration Transferred

Contingent consideration, when present in a business combination, is an additional element of consideration transferred. Contingent consideration can be useful in negotiations when two parties disagree with each other's estimates of future cash flows for the target firm or when valuation uncertainty is high.[12] Acquisition agreements often contain provisions to pay

---

[10] To qualify for the acquisition method, an acquired entity must first meet the definition of a *business*. According to ASC 805, a business must include an input and a substantive process that together significantly contribute to the ability to create output. Thus, if only a single asset (or group of similar assets) is acquired, the assets do not represent a business.

[11] An occasional exception occurs in a bargain purchase in which the fair value of the net assets acquired serves as the valuation basis for the acquired firm. Other exceptions include situations in which control is achieved without a transfer of consideration, or determination of the fair value of the consideration transferred is less reliable than other measures of the business fair value.

[12] Matthew D. Cain, David J. Denis, and Diane K. Denis, "Earnouts: A Study of Financial Contracting in Acquisition Agreements," *Journal of Accounting and Economics* 51 (2011), pp. 151–70.

former owners (typically cash or additional shares of the acquirer's stock) upon achievement of specified future performance measures. Such agreements are frequently referred to as *earnouts*.

Contingent consideration frequently involves potential cash payments to the acquired firm's former owners and accordingly are recorded at acquisition-date fair value on the records of the acquiring firm. For example, in 2021, Verizon Communications (Verizon) acquired Tracfone, Inc., a provider of prepaid and value mobile services. Included in its consideration transferred was contingent consideration. As part of the agreement, the sellers of Tracfone were able to earn additional contingent consideration of up to $650 million if certain performance measures are achieved along with other commercial arrangements. Because the achievement of the performance measures and other commercial arrangements was uncertain, Verizon estimated the fair value of the contingent consideration at $542 million at the acquisition date.[13] The acquisition method treats contingent consideration obligations as a negotiated component of the fair value of the consideration transferred. Verizon estimated the fair value of contingent future payments using probability assessments of discounted future cash flows and accordingly recorded a $542 million contingent liability.

Regardless of the elements that constitute the consideration transferred, the parent's financial statements must now incorporate its newly acquired ownership interest in a controlled entity. In this chapter and in Chapter 3, we focus exclusively on combinations that result in complete ownership by the acquirer (i.e., no noncontrolling interest in the acquired firm). As described in Chapter 4, in a less-than-100-percent acquisition, the noncontrolling interest also is measured initially at its fair value. Then, the combined fair values of the parent's consideration transferred and the noncontrolling interest comprise the valuation basis for the acquired firm in consolidated financial reports.

Assets Acquired and Liabilities Assumed

A fundamental principle of the acquisition method is that an acquirer must identify the assets acquired and the liabilities assumed in the business combination. Further, once these have been identified, the acquirer measures the assets acquired and the liabilities assumed at their acquisition-date fair values, with only a few exceptions.[14] As demonstrated in subsequent examples, the principle of recognizing and measuring assets acquired and liabilities assumed at fair value applies across all business combinations.

Fair value, as defined by GAAP, is the price that would be received from selling an asset or paid for transferring a liability in an orderly transaction between market participants at the measurement date. However, determining the acquisition-date fair values of the individual assets acquired and liabilities assumed can prove challenging.[15] The ASC (820-10-35-28) points to three sets of valuation techniques typically employed: the market approach, the income approach, and the cost approach.

Market Approach

The market approach estimates fair values using other market transactions involving similar assets or liabilities. In a business combination, assets acquired such as marketable securities and some tangible assets may have established markets that can provide comparable market values for estimating fair values. Similarly, the fair values of many liabilities assumed can be determined by reference to market trades for similar debt instruments.

Income Approach

The income approach relies on multi-period estimates of future cash flows projected to be generated by an asset. These projected cash flows are then discounted at a required rate of return

---

[13] Verizon Communications, Inc., Annual Report Form 10-K, filed February 11, 2022.

[14] Exceptions to the fair-value measurement principle include deferred taxes, certain employee benefits, indemnification assets, reacquired rights, share-based awards, and assets held for sale.

[15] Identifying and measuring the acquired firm's financial statement items can take some time. ASC (805-10-25-14) allows an acquirer to adjust the provisional amounts recognized for a business combination up to a year after the acquisition date.

that reflects the time value of money and the risk associated with realizing the future estimated cash flows. The multi-period income approach is often useful for obtaining fair-value estimates of intangible assets and acquired in-process research and development.

Cost Approach

The cost approach estimates fair values by reference to the current cost of replacing an asset with another of comparable economic utility. Used assets can present a particular valuation challenge if active markets only exist for newer versions of the asset. Thus, the cost to replace a particular asset reflects both its estimated replacement cost and the effects of obsolescence. In this sense, obsolescence is meant to capture economic declines in value including both technological obsolescence and physical deterioration. The cost approach is widely used to estimate fair values for many tangible assets acquired in business combinations such as property, plant, and equipment.

Goodwill, and Gains on Bargain Purchases

In a business combination, the parent must account for both the consideration transferred and the individual amounts of the identified assets acquired and liabilities assumed at their acquisition-date fair values. However, in many cases, the respective collective amounts of these two values will differ. Current GAAP accounting for the difference requires one of two outcomes—in one, the acquirer recognizes an asset (goodwill); in the other, a gain.

When the consideration transferred exceeds the acquisition-date net amount of the identified assets acquired and the liabilities assumed, the acquirer recognizes the asset goodwill for the excess.[16] Goodwill is defined as an asset representing the future economic benefits arising in a business combination that are not individually identified and separately recognized. Goodwill often embodies the expected synergies that the acquirer expects to achieve through control of the acquired firm's assets. Goodwill may also capture nonrecognized intangibles of the acquired firm such as employee expertise.

Conversely, if the collective fair value of the net identified assets acquired and liabilities assumed exceeds the consideration transferred, the acquirer recognizes a "gain on bargain purchase." In such cases, the fair value of the net assets acquired replaces the consideration transferred as the valuation basis for the acquired firm. Bargain purchases can result from business divestitures forced by regulatory agencies or other types of distress sales. Before recognizing a gain on bargain purchase, however, the acquirer must reassess whether it has correctly identified and measured all of the acquired assets and liabilities. Illustrations and further discussions of goodwill and of bargain purchase gains follow in the next section.

LO 2-5

Determine the total fair value of the consideration transferred for an acquisition, and allocate that fair value to specific subsidiary assets acquired (including goodwill) and liabilities assumed or to a gain on bargain purchase.

Procedures for Consolidating Financial Information

To demonstrate an application of the acquisition method, assume BigNet Company specializes in communications equipment and business software that provide web-based applications for retail companies. BigNet seeks to expand its operations and plans to acquire Smallport on December 31. Smallport Company owns computers, telecommunications equipment, and software that customize website billing and ordering systems for their clients. BigNet hopes to expand Smallport's client base, utilize its recently developed software, and create other synergies by combining with Smallport.

Exhibit 2.3 lists the December 31 account balances for both BigNet and Smallport. In addition, the estimated fair values of Smallport's assets and liabilities are shown. Although Smallport's computers and equipment have a $400,000 book value, their current fair value is $600,000. Smallport's software has only a $100,000 value on its books; the internal development costs were primarily expensed. The software's observable fair value, however, is

---

[16] Assuming a 100 percent acquisition. For combinations with less than complete ownership, goodwill is computed as the excess of the consideration transferred plus the acquisition-date fair value of the noncontrolling interest over the collective fair values of the net identified assets acquired and liabilities assumed.

EXHIBIT 2.3 **Basic Consolidation Information**

	BigNet Company Book Values December 31	Smallport Company Book Values December 31	Fair Values December 31
Current assets	$ 1,100,000	$ 300,000	$ 300,000
Computers and equipment (net).	1,300,000	400,000	600,000
Capitalized software (net)	500,000	100,000	1,200,000
Trademarks	–0–	–0–	700,000
Notes payable	(300,000)	(200,000)	(250,000)
Net assets	**$2,600,000**	**$600,000**	**$2,550,000**
Common stock—$10 par value	$ (1,600,000)		
Common stock—$5 par value		$(100,000)	
Additional paid-in capital.	(40,000)	(20,000)	
Retained earnings, 1/1.	(870,000)	(370,000)	
Dividends declared.	110,000	10,000	
Revenues	(1,000,000)	(500,000)	
Expenses	800,000	380,000	
Owners' equity 12/31	**$(2,600,000)**	**$(600,000)**	
Retained earnings, 12/31	(960,000)*	(480,000)*	

*Retained earnings balance after closing out revenues, expenses, and dividends.
Note: Parentheses indicate a credit balance.

$1,200,000. Similarly, although not reflected in its financial records, Smallport has several internally developed trademarks. BigNet estimates the fair value of the trademarks at $700,000. Smallport also has a $200,000 note payable incurred to help finance the software development. Because interest rates are currently low, this liability (incurred at a higher rate of interest) has a present value of $250,000.

Smallport's net assets (total assets less total liabilities) have a book value of $600,000 but a fair value of $2,550,000. Fair values for only the assets and liabilities are appraised here; the capital stock, retained earnings, dividend, revenue, and expense accounts represent historical measurements rather than any type of future values. Although these equity and income accounts can give some indication of the organization's overall worth, they are not property and thus not transferred in the combination.

Legal as well as accounting distinctions divide business combinations into several separate categories. To facilitate the introduction of consolidation accounting, we present the various procedures utilized in this process according to the following sequence:

1. Acquisition method when dissolution takes place.
2. Acquisition method when separate incorporation is maintained.

Acquisition Method When Dissolution Takes Place

When the acquired firm's legal status is dissolved in a business combination, the continuing firm takes direct ownership of the former firm's assets and assumes its liabilities. Thus, the continuing firm will prepare a journal entry to record

- The fair value of the consideration transferred by the acquiring firm to the former owners of the acquiree, and
- The identified assets acquired and liabilities assumed at their individual fair values.

However, the entry to record the combination further depends on the relation between the consideration transferred and the net amount of the fair values assigned to the identified assets acquired and liabilities assumed. Therefore, we initially provide three illustrations that demonstrate the procedures to record a business combination, each with different amounts of consideration transferred relative to the acquired asset and liability fair values. Each example assumes a merger takes place, and, therefore, the acquired firm is dissolved. In each situation, the consideration transferred is compared to the fair value of the net identifiable assets acquired and liabilities assumed to determine if goodwill or a bargain purchase gain should be recorded.

Consideration Transferred Equals Net Fair Values of Identified Assets Acquired and Liabilities Assumed

Assume that after negotiations with the owners of Smallport, BigNet agrees to pay cash of $550,000 and to issue 20,000 previously unissued shares of its $10 par value common stock (currently selling for $100 per share) for all of Smallport's assets and liabilities. Following the acquisition, Smallport then dissolves itself as a legal entity. The consideration transferred from BigNet to Smallport is computed as follows and, in this case, exactly equals the collective fair values of Smallport's assets less liabilities:

Cash payment	$ 550,000
Common stock issued by BigNet ($100 × 20,000 shares)	2,000,000
Total consideration transferred	$2,550,000
Fair value of Smallport's net identifiable assets	$2,550,000

The $2,550,000 fair value of the consideration transferred by BigNet represents the fair value of the acquired Smallport business and serves as the basis for recording the combination in total.

BigNet also must record all of Smallport's identified assets and liabilities at their *individual* fair values. These two valuations present no difficulties because BigNet's consideration transferred exactly equals the $2,550,000 collective net fair values of the individual assets and liabilities acquired as shown in Exhibit 2.3.

Because Smallport Company will be dissolved, BigNet (the surviving company) enters a journal entry in its financial records to record the combination. BigNet has directly acquired the assets and assumed the liabilities of Smallport. Under the acquisition method, BigNet records Smallport's assets and liabilities at fair value ignoring original book values. Revenue, expense, dividend, and equity accounts cannot be transferred to a parent and are not included in recording the business combination.

Acquisition Method: Consideration Transferred Equals Net Identified Asset Fair Values—Subsidiary Dissolved

LO 2-6a

Prepare the journal entry to consolidate the accounts of a subsidiary if dissolution takes place.

BigNet Company's Financial Records—December 31		
Current Assets.	300,000	
Computers and Equipment.	600,000	
Capitalized Software	1,200,000	
Trademarks	700,000	
Notes Payable.		250,000
Cash (paid by BigNet)		550,000
Common Stock (20,000 shares issued by BigNet at $10 par value)		200,000
Additional Paid-In Capital		1,800,000
To record acquisition of Smallport Company. Assets acquired and liabilities assumed are recorded at fair value.		

BigNet's financial records now show $1,900,000 in the Computers and Equipment account ($1,300,000 former balance + $600,000 acquired), $1,700,000 in Capitalized Software ($500,000 + $1,200,000), and so forth. Note that the trademarks, despite being unrecorded on Smallport's books, are nonetheless identified and recognized on BigNet's financial records as part of the assets acquired in the combination. These items have been added into BigNet's balances (see Exhibit 2.3) at their fair values. Conversely, BigNet's revenue balance continues to report the company's own $1,000,000 with expenses remaining at $800,000 and dividends of $110,000. Under the acquisition method, only the subsidiary's revenues, expenses, dividends, and equity transactions that occur subsequent to the takeover affect the business combination.

Consideration Transferred Exceeds Net Amount of Fair Values of Identified Assets Acquired and Liabilities Assumed

In this next illustration, BigNet transfers to the owners of Smallport consideration of $1,000,000 in cash plus 20,000 shares of common stock with a fair value of $100 per share in exchange for ownership of the company. The consideration transferred from BigNet to Smallport is now computed as follows and results in an excess amount exchanged over the fair value of the net assets acquired:

Cash payment	$1,000,000
Common stock issued by BigNet ($100 × 20,000 shares)	2,000,000
Total consideration transferred	$3,000,000
Fair value of Smallport's net identifiable assets	$2,550,000
Goodwill	$ 450,000

As presented in the preceding calculation, when the consideration transferred in an acquisition exceeds total net fair value of the identified assets and liabilities, the excess ($450,000 in this case) is allocated to an unidentifiable asset known as goodwill.[17] Unlike other assets, we consider goodwill as unidentifiable because we presume it emerges from several other assets acting together to produce an expectation of enhanced profitability. Goodwill essentially captures all sources of profitability beyond what can be expected from simply summing the fair values of the acquired firm's assets and liabilities.

The resulting consideration paid is $450,000 more than the $2,550,000 fair value of Smallport's net identifiable assets and is assigned to the unidentifiable asset Goodwill.

Several factors may have affected BigNet's $3,000,000 acquisition offer. First, BigNet may expect its assets to act in concert with those of Smallport, thus creating synergies that will produce profits beyond the total expected for the separate companies. In our earlier examples, Google, Uber, and Goodyear all clearly anticipated substantial synergies from their acquisitions. Other factors such as Smallport's history of profitability, its reputation, the quality of its personnel, and the current economic condition of the industry in which it operates may also affect the acquisition offer. In general, if a target company is projected to generate unusually high profits relative to its asset base, acquirers frequently are willing to pay a premium price.

Acquisition Method: Consideration Transferred Exceeds Net Identified Asset Fair Values—Subsidiary Dissolved

Returning to BigNet's $3,000,000 consideration, $450,000 is in excess of the fair value of Smallport's net assets. Thus, goodwill of that amount is entered into BigNet's accounting system along with the fair value of each individual asset and liability. BigNet makes the following journal entry at the date of acquisition:

BigNet Company's Financial Records—December 31

Current Assets	300,000	
Computers and Equipment	600,000	
Capitalized Software	1,200,000	
Trademarks	700,000	
Goodwill	450,000	
Notes Payable		250,000
Cash (paid by BigNet)		1,000,000
Common Stock (20,000 shares issued by BigNet at $10 par value)		200,000
Additional Paid-In Capital		1,800,000

To record acquisition of Smallport Company. Assets acquired and liabilities assumed are recorded at individual fair values with excess fair value attributed to goodwill.

[17] In business combinations, such excess payments are not unusual and can be quite large. When Oracle acquired PeopleSoft, it initially assigned $4.5 billion of its $11 billion purchase price to the fair value of the acquired identified net assets. It assigned the remaining $6.5 billion to goodwill.

Once again, BigNet's financial records now show $1,900,000 in the Computers and Equipment account ($1,300,000 former balance + $600,000 acquired), $1,700,000 in Capitalized Software ($500,000 + $1,200,000), and so forth. As the only change, BigNet records goodwill of $450,000 for the excess consideration paid over the net identified asset fair values.[18]

Bargain Purchase—Consideration Transferred Is Less Than Net Amount of Fair Values of Identified Assets Acquired and Liabilities Assumed

Occasionally, the fair value of the consideration transferred by the acquirer is less than the fair value received in an acquisition. Such bargain purchases typically are considered anomalous. Businesses generally do not sell assets or businesses at prices below their fair values. Nonetheless, bargain purchases do occur—most often in forced or distressed sales.

For example, Rite-Aid Corporation's acquisition of Bartell Drug Company, a Seattle-area drug store chain, resulted in a $47.7 million "bargain purchase" gain. As Rite-Aid reported in their 2021 annual 10-K report (amount shown in thousands):

> The Acquisition resulted in a bargain purchase gain of $47,705 primarily due to fair value adjustments related to prescription files and the tradename compared to book values. The Company believes that the bargain purchase gain was primarily the result of the decision by the Bartell stockholders to sell their interests as Bartell had been experiencing increasing borrowings under its credit agreements to meet its operating needs and increasing net losses. . . With the Company's existing infrastructure, scale and expertise, the Company believes that it has access to the necessary synergies to allow necessary operational improvements to be implemented more efficiently than the seller was capable of.

This gain treatment is consistent with the view that the acquiring firm is immediately better off by the amount that the fair value acquired in the business combination exceeds the consideration transferred.

To demonstrate accounting for a bargain purchase, our third illustration begins with BigNet transferring consideration of $2,000,000 to the owners of Smallport in exchange for their business. BigNet conveys no cash and issues 20,000 shares of $10 par common stock that has a $100 per share fair value. The consideration transferred from BigNet to Smallport is now computed as follows and results in a gain on bargain purchase:

Cash payment	$ –0–
Common stock issued by BigNet ($100 × 20,000 shares)	2,000,000
Total consideration transferred	$2,000,000
Fair value of Smallport's identifiable net assets	$2,550,000
Gain on bargain purchase	$ 550,000

In accounting for this acquisition, at least two competing fair values are present. First, the $2,000,000 consideration transferred for Smallport represents a negotiated transaction value for the business. Second, the net amount of fair values individually assigned to the identified assets acquired and liabilities assumed produces $2,550,000. Additionally, based on expected synergies with Smallport, BigNet's management may believe that the fair value of the business exceeds the net asset fair value. Nonetheless, because the consideration transferred is less than the net asset fair value, a bargain purchase has occurred.

The acquisition method records the identified assets acquired and liabilities assumed at their individual fair values. In a bargain purchase situation, this net asset fair value effectively replaces the consideration transferred as the acquired firm's valuation basis for financial reporting. The consideration transferred serves as the acquired firm's valuation basis only if the consideration equals or exceeds the net amount of fair values for the assets acquired and liabilities assumed (as in the first two examples). In this case, however, the $2,000,000

---

[18] As discussed in Chapter 3, the assets and liabilities (including goodwill) acquired in a business combination are assigned to reporting units of the combined entity. A reporting unit is simply a line of business (often a segment) in which an acquired asset or liability will be employed. The objective of assigning acquired assets and liabilities to reporting units is to facilitate periodic goodwill impairment testing.

consideration paid is less than the $2,550,000 net asset fair value, indicating a bargain purchase. Thus, the $2,550,000 net asset fair value serves as the valuation basis for the combination. A $550,000 *gain on bargain purchase* results because the $2,550,000 recorded value is accompanied by a payment of only $2,000,000. The acquirer recognizes this gain on its income statement in the period the acquisition takes place.

Acquisition Method: Consideration Transferred Is Less Than Net Identified Asset Fair Values—Subsidiary Dissolved

BigNet Company's Financial Records—December 31		
Current Assets	300,000	
Computers and Equipment	600,000	
Capitalized Software	1,200,000	
Trademarks	700,000	
Notes Payable		250,000
Common Stock (20,000 shares issued by BigNet at $10 par value)		200,000
Additional Paid-In Capital		1,800,000
Gain on Bargain Purchase		550,000
To record acquisition of Smallport Company. Assets acquired and liabilities assumed are each recorded at fair value. Excess net asset fair value is attributed to a gain on bargain purchase.		

A consequence of implementing a fair-value concept to acquisition accounting is the recognition of an unrealized gain on the bargain purchase. A criticism of the gain recognition is that the acquirer recognizes profit from a buying activity that occurs prior to traditional accrual measures of earned income (i.e., selling activity). Nonetheless, an exception to the general rule of recording business acquisitions at fair value of the consideration transferred occurs in the rare circumstance of a bargain purchase. Thus, in a bargain purchase, the fair values of the assets received and all liabilities assumed in a business combination are considered more relevant for asset valuation than the consideration transferred.

Summary: Acquisition Method When Dissolution Takes Place

When the acquired firm is dissolved in a business combination, the acquiring firm prepares a journal entry to record the combination on its books. The fair value of the consideration transferred by the acquiring firm provides the starting point for recording the acquisition. With few exceptions, the separately identified assets acquired and liabilities assumed are recorded at their individual fair values. Goodwill is recognized if the fair value of the consideration transferred exceeds the net identified asset fair value. If the net identified asset fair value of the business acquired exceeds the consideration transferred, a gain on a bargain purchase is recognized and reported in current income of the combined entity. Exhibit 2.4 summarizes possible allocations using the acquisition method.

EXHIBIT 2.4 Valuation Bases—The Acquisition Method

Valuation Basis for Acquired Business	Acquisition Accounting
Consideration transferred equals the fair values of net identified assets acquired.	Identified assets acquired and liabilities assumed are recorded at their fair values.
Consideration transferred is greater than the fair values of net identified assets acquired.	Identified assets acquired and liabilities assumed are recorded at their fair values. The excess consideration transferred over the net identified asset fair value is recorded as goodwill.
Bargain purchase—consideration transferred is less than the fair values of net identified assets acquired. **The total of the individual fair values of the net identified assets acquired** becomes the acquired business valuation basis.	Identified assets acquired and liabilities assumed are recorded at their fair values. The excess amount of net identified asset fair value over the consideration transferred is recorded as a gain on bargain purchase.

Types of Combination Costs	Acquisition Accounting
Direct combination costs (e.g., accounting, legal, investment banking, appraisal fees, etc.)	Expense as incurred
Indirect combination costs (e.g., internal costs such as allocated secretarial or managerial time)	Expense as incurred
Amounts incurred to register and issue securities	Reduce the value assigned to the fair value of the securities issued (typically a debit to additional paid-in capital)

EXHIBIT 2.5 Acquisition Method—Accounting for Costs Frequently Associated with Business Combinations

LO 2-6b

Prepare the journal entry to record the various related costs involved in a business combination.

Related Costs of Business Combinations

Three additional categories of costs typically accompany business combinations, regardless of whether dissolution takes place. First, firms often engage attorneys, accountants, investment bankers, and other professionals for combination-related services. The acquisition method does not consider such expenditures as part of the fair value received by the acquirer. Therefore, professional service fees are expensed in the period incurred. The second category concerns an acquiring firm's internal costs. Examples include secretarial and management time allocated to the acquisition activity. Such indirect costs are reported as current-year expenses, too. Finally, amounts incurred to register and issue securities in connection with a business combination simply reduce the otherwise determinable fair value of those securities. Exhibit 2.5 summarizes the three categories of related payments that accompany a business combination and their respective accounting treatments.

To illustrate the accounting treatment of these costs that frequently accompany business combinations, assume the following in connection with BigNet's acquisition of Smallport.

- BigNet pays an additional $100,000 in accounting and attorney fees.
- Internal secretarial and administrative costs of $75,000 are indirectly attributable to BigNet's combination with Smallport.
- Costs to register and issue BigNet's securities issued in the combination total $20,000.

Following the acquisition method, regardless of whether dissolution occurs or separate incorporation is maintained, BigNet would record these transactions as follows:

BigNet Company's Financial Records		
Professional Services Expense	100,000	
Cash		100,000
To record as expenses of the current period any direct combination costs.		
Salaries and Administrative Expenses	75,000	
Accounts Payable (or Cash)		75,000
To record as expenses of the current period any indirect combination costs.		
Additional Paid-In Capital	20,000	
Cash		20,000
To record costs to register and issue stock in connection with the Smallport acquisition.		

The Acquisition Method When Separate Incorporation Is Maintained

When each company retains separate incorporation in a business combination, many aspects of the consolidation process are identical to those demonstrated in the previous section. Fair value, for example, remains the basis for initially consolidating the subsidiary's assets and liabilities. Also, the acquiring firm records a journal entry on its books reflecting the investment and the consideration transferred in the combination.

However, several significant differences are evident in combinations in which each company remains a legally incorporated separate entity. Most noticeably, the consolidation of the financial information is only simulated; the acquiring company does not physically record the acquired assets and liabilities. *Because dissolution does not occur, each company maintains independent recordkeeping.* To facilitate the preparation of consolidated financial statements, a worksheet and consolidation entries are employed using data gathered from these separate companies.

A worksheet provides the structure for generating financial reports for the single economic entity. An integral part of this process employs consolidation worksheet entries that either adjust or eliminate various account balances of the parent and subsidiary. These adjustments and eliminations are entered on the worksheet to produce consolidated statements as if the financial records had been physically combined. *Because no actual union occurs, neither company ever records consolidation worksheet entries in its journals.* Instead, these adjustments and eliminations appear solely on the worksheet to derive consolidated balances for financial reporting purposes.

Example (Includes Stock Issue, Related Combination Costs, and Contingent Consideration)

To illustrate the worksheet mechanics, we again use the Exhibit 2.3 example of BigNet and Smallport. We also include combination costs and contingent consideration. Assume that BigNet acquires Smallport Company on December 31 by issuing 26,000 shares of $10 par value common stock valued at $100 per share (or $2,600,000 in total). BigNet pays fees of $40,000 to a third party for its assistance in arranging the transaction.

Then, to settle a difference of opinion regarding Smallport's fair value, BigNet promises to pay an additional $83,200 to the former owners if Smallport's earnings exceed $300,000 during the next annual period. BigNet estimates a 25 percent probability that the $83,200 contingent payment will be required. A discount rate of 4 percent (to represent the time value of money) yields an expected present value of $20,000 for the contingent liability ($83,200 × 25% × 0.961538). The fair-value approach of the acquisition method views such contingent payments as part of the consideration transferred. According to this view, contingencies have value to those who receive the consideration and represent measurable obligations of the acquirer.[19] Therefore, the fair value of the consideration transferred in this example consists of the following two elements:

Fair value of securities issued by BigNet	$2,600,000
Fair value of contingent performance liability	20,000
Total fair value of consideration transferred	$2,620,000

To facilitate a possible future spin-off, BigNet maintains Smallport as a separate corporation with its independent accounting information system intact. Therefore, whenever financial statements for the combined entity are prepared, BigNet utilizes a worksheet in simulating the consolidation of these two companies.

Although the assets and liabilities are not transferred, BigNet must still record the consideration provided to Smallport's owners. When the subsidiary remains separate, the parent establishes an investment account that initially reflects the acquired firm's acquisition-date fair value. Because Smallport maintains its separate identity, BigNet prepares the following journal entries on its books to record the business combination.

LO 2-6c

Prepare the journal entry to record a business combination when the acquired firm retains its separate existence.

Acquisition Method—Subsidiary Is Not Dissolved

BigNet Company's Financial Records—December 31		
Investment in Smallport Company (consideration transferred).	2,620,000	
Contingent Performance Liability.		20,000
Common Stock (26,000 shares issued by BigNet at $10 par value)		260,000
Additional Paid-In Capital (value of shares in excess of par value).		2,340,000
To record acquisition of Smallport Company, which maintains its separate legal identity.		
Professional Services Expense	40,000	
Cash (paid for third-party fees).		40,000
To record combination costs.		

LO 2-7

Prepare a worksheet to consolidate the accounts of two companies that form a business combination in the absence of dissolution.

As Exhibit 2.6 demonstrates, a worksheet can be prepared on the date of acquisition to arrive at consolidated totals for this combination. The entire process consists of six steps.

[19] The ASC (805-30-35-1) notes several reasons for contingent consideration including meeting an earnings target, reaching a specified share price, or reaching a milestone on a research and development project.

EXHIBIT 2.6   Acquisition Method—Date of Acquisition

Accounts	BigNet	Smallport	Consolidation Entries Debits	Consolidation Entries Credits	Consolidated Totals
Income Statement					
Revenues	(1,000,000)				(1,000,000)
Expenses	840,000*				840,000
Net income	(160,000)				(160,000)
Statement of Retained Earnings					
Retained earnings, 1/1	(870,000)				(870,000)
Net income (above)	(160,000)*				(160,000)
Dividends declared	110,000				110,000
Retained earnings, 12/31	(920,000)				(920,000)
Balance Sheet					
Current assets	1,060,000*	300,000			1,360,000
Investment in Smallport Company	2,620,000*	–0–		(S) 600,000	–0–
				(A) 2,020,000	
Computers and equipment	1,300,000	400,000	(A) 200,000		1,900,000
Capitalized software	500,000	100,000	(A) 1,100,000		1,700,000
Trademarks	–0–	–0–	(A) 700,000		700,000
Goodwill	–0–	–0–	(A) 70,000		70,000
Total assets	5,480,000	800,000			5,730,000
Notes payable	(300,000)	(200,000)		(A) 50,000	(550,000)
Contingent performance liability	(20,000)*				(20,000)
Common stock	(1,860,000)*	(100,000)	(S) 100,000		(1,860,000)
Additional paid-in capital	(2,380,000)*	(20,000)	(S) 20,000		(2,380,000)
Retained earnings, 12/31 (above)	(920,000)	(480,000)	(S) 480,000		(920,000)
Total liabilities and equities	(5,480,000)	(800,000)	2,670,000	2,670,000	(5,730,000)

Note: Parentheses indicate a credit balance.
*Balances have been adjusted for consideration transferred and payment of direct acquisition costs. Also note follow-through effects to net income and retained earnings from the expensing of the direct acquisition costs.
(S) Elimination of Smallport's stockholders' equity accounts as of December 31 and book value portion of the investment account.
(A) Allocation of BigNet's consideration fair value in excess of book value.

Step 1

Prior to constructing a worksheet, the parent prepares a formal allocation of the acquisition-date fair value similar to the equity method procedures presented in Chapter 1.[20] Thus, the following schedule is appropriate for BigNet's acquisition of Smallport:

Acquisition-Date Fair-Value Allocation Schedule

Fair value of consideration transferred by BigNet		$2,620,000
Book value of Smallport (see Exhibit 2.3).		600,000
Excess of fair value over book value.		$2,020,000
Allocations made to specific accounts based on acquisition-date fair and book value differences (see Exhibit 2.3):		
Computers and equipment ($600,000 – $400,000).	$ 200,000	
Capitalized software ($1,200,000 – $100,000).	1,100,000	
Trademarks ($700,000 – 0).	700,000	
Notes payable ($250,000 – $200,000).	(50,000)	1,950,000
Excess fair value not identified with specific items—Goodwill		$ 70,000

---

[20] This allocation procedure is helpful but not critical if dissolution occurs. The asset and liability accounts are simply added directly into the parent's books at their acquisition-date fair value with any excess assigned to goodwill, as shown in the previous sections of this chapter.

Note that this schedule initially subtracts Smallport's acquisition-date book value. The resulting $2,020,000 difference represents the total amount needed on the Exhibit 2.6 worksheet to adjust Smallport's individual assets and liabilities from book value to fair value (and to recognize goodwill). Next, the schedule shows how this $2,020,000 total is allocated to adjust each individual item to fair value. The fair-value allocation schedule thus effectively serves as a convenient supporting schedule for the Exhibit 2.6 worksheet and is routinely prepared for every consolidation.

No part of the $2,020,000 excess fair value is attributed to the current assets because their book values equal their fair values. The Notes Payable account shows a negative allocation because the debt's present value exceeds its book value. An increase in debt decreases the fair value of the company's net assets.

Step 2

The consolidation process begins with preparing the first two columns of the worksheet (see Exhibit 2.6) containing the separate companies' acquisition-date book value financial figures (see Exhibit 2.3). BigNet's accounts have been adjusted for the journal entries recorded earlier for the investment and the combination costs. As another preliminary step, Smallport's revenue, expense, and dividend accounts have been closed into its Retained Earnings account. The subsidiary's operations prior to the December 31 takeover have no direct bearing on the operating results of the business combination. These activities occurred before Smallport was acquired; thus, the new owner should not include any precombination subsidiary revenues or expenses in the consolidated statements.

Step 3

Consolidation Entry S eliminates Smallport's stockholders' equity accounts (S is a reference to beginning subsidiary stockholders' equity) as follows:

Consolidation Entry S

Common Stock (Smallport Company)...................................	100,000	
Additional Paid-In Capital (Smallport Company)	20,000	
Retained Earnings (Smallport Company).	480,000	
Investment in Smallport Company.....................................		600,000

Consolidation Entry S is a worksheet entry and accordingly does not affect the financial records of either company. The subsidiary balances (Common Stock, Additional Paid-In Capital, and Retained Earnings) represent ownership interests that are now held by the parent—thus, they are not represented as equity in the parent's consolidated balance sheet. Moreover, by removing these account balances on the worksheet, only Smallport's assets and liabilities remain to be combined with the parent company figures.

Consolidation Entry S also removes the $600,000 component of the parent's Investment in Smallport Company account balance that equates to the book value of the subsidiary's net assets. For external reporting purposes, BigNet should include each of Smallport's assets and liabilities rather than a single investment balance. In effect, this portion of the parent's Investment in Smallport Company account balance is eliminated and replaced by the specific subsidiary assets and liabilities that are already listed in the second column of the worksheet.

Step 4

Consolidation Entry A removes the $2,020,000 excess payment in the Investment in Smallport Company and assigns it to the specific accounts indicated by the fair-value allocation schedule as follows:

Consolidation Entry A

Computers and Equipment...	200,000	
Capitalized Software	1,100,000	
Trademarks	700,000	
Goodwill	70,000	
Note Payable..		50,000
Investment in Smallport Company............................		2,020,000

Consequently, Computers and Equipment is increased by $200,000 to agree with Smallport's fair value: $1,100,000 is attributed to Capitalized Software, $700,000 to Trademarks, and $50,000 to Notes Payable. The unidentified excess of $70,000 is allocated to Goodwill. This entry for the consolidation worksheet is labeled Entry A to indicate that it represents the allocations made in connection with Smallport's acquisition-date fair value.

Consolidation Entry A also completes the Investment in Smallport Company account balance elimination on the worksheet. The investment remains on BigNet's books, but it does not appear on the consolidated balance sheet. Instead the investment account is replaced on the worksheet with Smallport's actual assets and liabilities as shown in Step 5.

Step 5

All accounts are extended into the Consolidated Totals column. For accounts such as Current Assets, this process simply adds Smallport and BigNet book values. However, when applicable, this extension also includes any allocations to establish the acquisition-date fair values of Smallport's assets and liabilities. Computers and Equipment, for example, is increased by $200,000. By increasing the subsidiary's book value to fair value, the reported balances are the same as in the previous examples when dissolution occurred. The use of a worksheet does not alter the consolidated figures but only the method of deriving those numbers.

Step 6

We subtract consolidated expenses from revenues to arrive at a $160,000 net income. Note that because this is an acquisition-date worksheet, we consolidate no amounts for Smallport's revenues and expenses. Having just been acquired, Smallport has not yet earned any income for BigNet owners. Consolidated revenues, expenses, and net income are identical to BigNet's balances. Subsequent to acquisition, of course, Smallport's revenue and expense accounts will be consolidated with BigNet's (coverage of this topic begins in Chapter 3).

Worksheet Mechanics

In general, totals (such as net income and ending retained earnings) are not directly consolidated across on the worksheet. Rather, the components (such as revenues and expenses) are extended across and then combined vertically to derive the appropriate figure. Net income is then carried down on the worksheet to the statement of retained earnings and used (along with beginning retained earnings and dividends) to compute the December 31 retained earnings balance. In the same manner, ending retained earnings of $920,000 is entered into the balance sheet to arrive at total liabilities and equities of $5,730,000, a number that reconciles with the total of consolidated assets.

Although it remains on BigNet's books, the Investment in Smallport account is eliminated entirely in consolidation. On the worksheet, the investment account is effectively replaced with the acquisition-date fair values of Smallport's assets and liabilities along with goodwill created by the combination.

The balances in the final column of Exhibit 2.6 are used to prepare consolidated financial statements for the business combination of BigNet Company and Smallport Company. The worksheet entries serve as a catalyst to bring together the two independent sets of financial information. The actual accounting records of both BigNet and Smallport remain unaltered by this consolidation process.

Bargain Purchase of a Separately Incorporated Subsidiary

Finally, although not addressed directly by the preceding example, bargain purchase gains can also occur in acquisitions of separately incorporated subsidiaries. If the consideration transferred is less than the fair value of a newly acquired subsidiary's identifiable net assets, then the parent records a bargain purchase gain on its books as part of the investment journal entry. The bargain purchase gain then appears on the the consolidated income statement for the reporting period that contains the acquisition date.

LO 2-8

Describe the accounting treatment for the various intangible assets often acquired in a business combination.

Acquisition-Date Fair-Value Allocations—Additional Issues

Intangibles

An important element of acquisition accounting is the acquirer's recognition and measurement of the assets acquired and liabilities assumed in the combination. In particular, the advent of the information age brings new measurement challenges for a host of intangible assets that provide value in generating future cash flows. Intangible assets often comprise the largest proportion of an acquired firm. For example, when AT&T acquired AT&T Broadband, it allocated approximately $19 billion of the $52 billion purchase price to franchise costs. These franchise costs form an intangible asset representing the value attributed to agreements with local authorities that allow access to homes.

Intangible assets include both current and noncurrent assets (not including financial instruments) that lack physical substance. In determining whether to recognize an intangible asset in a business combination, two specific criteria are essential.

1. Does the intangible asset arise from contractual or other legal rights?
2. Is the intangible asset capable of being sold or otherwise separated from the acquired enterprise?

Intangibles arising from contractual or legal rights are commonplace in business combinations. Often identified among the assets acquired are trademarks, patents, copyrights, franchise agreements, and a number of other intangibles that derive their value from governmental protection (or other contractual agreements) that allow a firm exclusive use of the asset. Most intangible assets recognized in business combinations meet the contractual-legal criterion.

Also seen in business combinations are intangible assets meeting the separability criterion. An acquired intangible asset is recognized if it is capable of being separated or divided from the acquiree and sold, transferred, licensed, rented, or exchanged individually or together with a related contract, identifiable asset, or liability. The acquirer is not required to have the intention to sell, license, or otherwise exchange the intangible in order to meet the separability criterion. For example, an acquiree may have developed internally a valuable customer list or other noncontractual customer relationships. Although the value of these items may not have arisen from a specific legal right, they nonetheless convey benefits to the acquirer that may be separable through sale, license, or exchange.

Exhibit 2.7 provides an extensive listing of intangible assets with indications of whether they typically meet the contractual-legal or separability criteria.

The FASB (Exposure Draft, *Business Combinations and Intangible Assets,* para. 271) recognized the inherent difficulties in estimating the separate fair values of many intangibles and stated that

difficulties may arise in assigning the acquisition cost to individual intangible assets acquired in a basket purchase such as a business combination. Measuring some of those assets is less difficult than measuring other assets, particularly if they are exchangeable and traded regularly in the marketplace. . . . Nonetheless, even those assets that cannot be measured on that basis may have cash flow streams directly or indirectly associated with them that can be used as the basis for measuring them. While the resulting measures may lack the precision of other measures, they provide information that is more representationally faithful than would be the case if those assets were simply subsumed into goodwill on the grounds of measurement difficulties.

Undoubtedly, as our knowledge economy continues its rapid growth, asset allocations to items such as those identified in Exhibit 2.7 are expected to be frequent.

EXHIBIT 2.7 **Illustrative Examples of Intangible Assets That Meet the Criteria for Recognition Separately from Goodwill (FASB ASC paragraphs 805-20-55-11 through 45)**

The following are examples of intangible assets that meet the criteria for recognition as an asset apart from goodwill. The following illustrative list is not intended to be all-inclusive; thus, an acquired intangible asset could meet the recognition criteria of this statement but not be included on that list. Assets designated by the symbol (c) are those that would generally be recognized separately from goodwill because they meet the contractual-legal criterion. Assets designated by the symbol (s) do not arise from contractual or other legal rights but should nonetheless be recognized separately from goodwill because they meet the separability criterion. The determination of whether a specific acquired intangible asset meets the criteria in this statement for recognition apart from goodwill should be based on the facts and circumstances of each individual business combination.*

Marketing-Related Intangible Assets

1. Trademarks, trade names.[c]
2. Service marks, collective marks, certification marks.[c]
3. Trade dress (unique color, shape, or package design).[c]
4. Newspaper mastheads.[c]
5. Internet domain names.[c]
6. Noncompetition agreements.[c]

Customer-Related Intangible Assets

1. Customer lists.[s]
2. Order or production backlog.[c]
3. Customer contracts and related customer relationships.[c]
4. Noncontractual customer relationships.[s]

Artistic-Related Intangible Assets

1. Plays, operas, and ballets.[c]
2. Books, magazines, newspapers, and other literary works.[c]
3. Musical works such as compositions, song lyrics, and advertising jingles.[c]
4. Pictures and photographs.[c]
5. Video and audiovisual material, including motion pictures, music videos, and television programs.[c]

Contract-Based Intangible Assets

1. Licensing, royalty, standstill agreements.[c]
2. Advertising, construction, management, service, or supply contracts.[c]
3. Lease agreements.[c]
4. Construction permits.[c]
5. Franchise agreements.[c]
6. Operating and broadcast rights.[c]
7. Use rights such as landing, drilling, water, air, mineral, timber cutting, and route authorities.[c]
8. Servicing contracts such as mortgage servicing contracts.[c]
9. Employment contracts.[c]

Technology-Based Intangible Assets

1. Patented technology.[c]
2. Computer software and mask works.[c]
3. Unpatented technology.[s]
4. Databases, including title plants.[s]
5. Trade secrets, including secret formulas, processes, and recipes.[c]

*The intangible assets designated by the symbol (c) also could meet the separability criterion. However, separability is not a necessary condition for an asset to meet the contractual-legal criterion.

Preexisting Goodwill on Acquired Firm's Books

In our examples of business combinations so far, the assets acquired and liabilities assumed have all been specifically identifiable (e.g., current assets, capitalized software, computers and equipment, customer contracts, and notes payable). However, in many cases, an acquired firm has an unidentifiable asset (i.e., goodwill recorded on its books in connection with a previous business combination of its own). A question arises as to the parent's treatment of this preexisting goodwill on the newly acquired subsidiary's books.

By its very nature, such preexisting goodwill is not considered identifiable by the parent. Therefore, in calculating the new goodwill acquired in the combination, the new owner simply excludes the carrying amount of any preexisting goodwill from the subsidiary's acquisition-date net assets. In a merger situation, the acquiring firm simply records any new goodwill (along with the identifiable assets and liabilities acquired) and ignores the acquired firm's preexisting goodwill.

In the case of an acquisition where the subsidiary continues its separate legal existence, the preexisting subsidiary goodwill must be eliminated on the consolidated worksheet. The parent company effectively reallocates any preexisting subsidiary goodwill via a credit in consolidation worksheet Entry A. This worksheet credit to the subsidiary's goodwill balance is then offset by worksheet entries to identifiable assets and liabilities, followed by a debit to the new goodwill from the combination.

For example, assume Pride Company acquires Stone Company for cash consideration and will maintain Stone as a wholly owned subsidiary. Stone has previously recognized $5,000 goodwill on its books. Also assume that Stone has a trademark undervalued by $4,000 on its books and Pride will recognize new goodwill of $3,000 from the acquisition. Consolidation worksheet entry A would then be prepared as follows:

Consolidation Entry A		
Goodwill (new)	3,000	
Trademark	4,000	
Goodwill (previous subsidiary amount)		5,000
Investment in Stone		2,000

Note that the subsidiary's precombination goodwill balance is eliminated in consolidation Entry A in formulating an acquisition-date consolidated balance sheet. The logic is that the parent's consideration transferred is first allocated to the subsidiary's identifiable assets and liabilities. Only if an excess amount remains after recognizing the fair values of the net identified assets is any goodwill recognized. Thus, in all business combinations, only goodwill reflected in the current acquisition is brought forward in the consolidated entity's financial reports.

Acquired In-Process Research and Development

The negotiations for a business combination begin with the identification of the tangible and intangible assets acquired and liabilities assumed by the acquirer. The fair values of the acquired individual assets and liabilities then provide the basis for financial statement valuations. Many firms—especially those in pharmaceutical and high-tech industries—have allocated significant portions of acquired businesses to in-process research and development (IPR&D).

Current accounting standards require that acquired IPR&D be measured at acquisition-date fair value and recognized in consolidated financial statements as an asset. However, this was not always the case. Past standards required immediate expense treatment for acquired IPR&D. Nonetheless, arguments about the future economic benefits of IPR&D ultimately persuaded the FASB to require asset recognition. For example, in commenting on the nature of IPR&D as an asset, Pfizer in an October 28, 2005, comment letter to the FASB observed that

> board members know that companies frame business strategies around IPR&D, negotiate for it, pay for it, fair value it, and nurture it and they view those seemingly rational actions as inconsistent with the notion that IPR&D has no probable future economic benefit.

Asset recognition for acquired IPR&D is now standard even though benefits must be estimated and may be uncertain. To illustrate, when ARCA Biopharma acquired a significant in-process research and development asset through a merger with Nuvelo, Inc., it disclosed the following in its financial statements:

> A valuation firm was engaged to assist ARCA in determining the estimated fair values of these (IPR&D) assets as of the acquisition date. Discounted cash flow models are typically used in these valuations, and the models require the use of significant estimates and assumptions including but not limited to:
>
> - Projecting regulatory approvals.
> - Estimating future cash flows from product sales resulting from completed products and in-process projects.
> - Developing appropriate discount rates and probability rates by project.

The IPR&D asset is initially considered an indefinite-lived intangible asset and is not subject to amortization. IPR&D is then tested for impairment annually or more frequently if events or changes in circumstances indicate that the asset might be impaired.

Recognizing acquired IPR&D as an asset is clearly consistent with the FASB's fair-value approach to acquisition accounting. Similar to costs that result in goodwill and other internally generated intangibles (e.g., customer lists, trade names, etc.), IPR&D costs are expensed as incurred in ongoing business activities. However, a business combination is considered a significant recognition event for which all fair values transferred in the transaction should be fully accounted for, including any values assigned to IPR&D. Moreover, because the acquirer paid for the IPR&D, an expectation of future economic benefit is assumed, and, therefore, the amount is recognized as an asset.

To illustrate further, assume that ClearTone Company pays $2,300,000 in cash for all assets and liabilities of Newave, Inc., in a merger transaction. ClearTone manufactures components for cell phones. The primary motivation for the acquisition is a particularly attractive research and development project under way at Newave that will extend a cell phone's battery life by up to 50 percent. ClearTone hopes to combine the new technology with its manufacturing process and projects a resulting substantial revenue increase. ClearTone is optimistic that Newave will finish the project in the next two years. At the acquisition date, ClearTone prepares the following schedule that recognizes the items of value it expects to receive from the Newave acquisition:

Consideration transferred		$2,300,000
Receivables	$ 55,000	
Patents	220,000	
In-process research and development	1,900,000	
Accounts payable	(175,000)	
Fair value of identified net assets acquired		2,000,000
Goodwill		$ 300,000

ClearTone records the transaction as follows:

Receivables	55,000	
Patents	220,000	
Research and Development Asset	1,900,000	
Goodwill	300,000	
Accounts Payable		175,000
Cash		2,300,000

Research and development expenditures incurred subsequent to the date of acquisition will continue to be expensed. Acquired IPR&D assets initially should be considered indefinite-lived until the project is completed or abandoned. As with other indefinite-lived intangible assets, an acquired IPR&D asset is tested for impairment and is not amortized until its useful life is determined to be no longer indefinite.

Convergence between U.S. and International Accounting Standards

The FASB ASC Topics "Business Combinations" (805) and "Consolidation" (810) represent outcomes of a joint project between the FASB and the International Accounting Standards Board (IASB). The primary objective of the project was stated as follows:

> to develop a single high-quality standard for business combinations that can be used for both domestic and cross-border financial reporting. The goal is to develop a standard that includes a common set of principles and related guidance that produces decision-useful information and minimizes exceptions to those principles. The standard should improve the completeness, relevance, and comparability of financial information about business combinations. . . .[21]

The IASB subsequently issued International Financial Reporting Standard 3 (*IFRS 3*) Revised (effective July 2009), which along with FASB ASC Topics 805, "Business Combinations," and 810, "Consolidation," effectively converged the accounting for business combinations internationally. The two standards are identical in most important aspects of accounting for business combinations although differences can result in noncontrolling interest valuation and some other limited applications.[22] The joint project on business combinations represents one of the first successful implementations of the agreement between the two standard-setting groups to coordinate efforts on future work with the goal of developing high-quality comparable standards for both domestic and cross-border financial accounting.

Summary

1. Consolidation of financial information is required for external reporting purposes when one organization gains control of another, thus forming a single economic entity. In many combinations, all but one of the companies is dissolved as a separate legal corporation. Therefore, the consolidation process is carried out fully at the date of acquisition to bring together all accounts into a single set of financial records. In other combinations, the companies retain their identities as separate enterprises and continue to maintain their own separate accounting systems. For these cases, consolidation is a periodic process necessary whenever the parent produces external financial statements. This periodic procedure is frequently accomplished through the use of a worksheet and consolidation entries.

[21] FASB Project Updates: Business Combinations: Applying the Acquisition Method—Joint Project of the IASB and FASB: October 25, 2007.

[22] Chapter 4 of this text provides further discussion of noncontrolling interest accounting differences across U.S. GAAP and IFRS. Other differences are presented in chapters where the applicable topics are covered.

Discussion Question

WHAT IF AN ACQUIRED ENTITY IS NOT A BUSINESS?

To qualify for the acquisition method (ASC 805), the acquired entity must meet the definition of a *business*. Otherwise the transaction is accounted for as an *asset acquisition*.

When substantially all of the fair value of gross assets acquired is concentrated in a single asset (or a group of similar assets), the assets acquired would not represent a business. To be considered a business, an acquisition must include an input and a substantive process that together significantly contribute to the ability to create outputs.

Asset acquisitions are measured and reported based on cost and reflect the following:

- No goodwill (or gain on bargain purchase)—excess consideration transferred is reallocated to identifiable assets based on relative fair values.
- Transaction costs (expensed in a business combination) are capitalized in an asset acquisition).
- In-process research and development (capitalized in a business combination) are expensed in an asset acquisition).
- Contingent consideration (capitalized at acquisition-date fair value in a business combination) is recognized in an asset acquisition when it is probable that a liability has been incurred and the amount can be reasonably estimated.

For example, when Travere Pharmaceuticals, Inc., acquired Orphan Technologies, the acquisition was reported in Travere's 10-K as follows:

> On November 12, 2020, the Company completed the acquisition of Orphan Technologies Limited ("Orphan"), including Orphan's rare metabolic disorder drug OT-58. . . . The Company has applied the principles of ASC 805 in determining the proper accounting treatment for the acquisition. Substantially all of the value of the assets acquired is concentrated within OT-58, and as of the acquisition date, the Company does not anticipate any economic benefit to be derived from OT-58 other than the primary indication. Accordingly, the transaction is treated as an asset acquisition with amounts charged to expense for the acquired IPR&D on the date of acquisition.

Also, because Orphan Technologies was not considered a business, Travere did not recognize in its financial statements the fair values of the contingent consideration elements at the acquisition date.

What potential accounting complexities (and costs) does a company avoid when it acquires another company that does not qualify as a business?

2. Current financial reporting standards require the acquisition method in accounting for business combinations. Under the acquisition method, the fair value of the consideration transferred provides the starting point for valuing the acquired firm. The fair value of the consideration transferred by the acquirer includes the fair value of any contingent consideration. The acquired company assets and liabilities are consolidated at their individual acquisition-date fair values. Direct combination costs are expensed as incurred because they are not part of the acquired business fair value. Also, the fair value of all acquired in-process research and

development is recognized as an asset in business combinations and is subject to subsequent impairment reviews.

3. If the consideration transferred for an acquired firm exceeds the total fair value of the acquired firm's net assets, the residual amount is recognized in the consolidated financial statements as goodwill, an intangible asset. When a bargain purchase occurs, individual assets and liabilities acquired continue to be recorded at their fair values, and a gain on bargain purchase is recognized.

4. Particular attention should be given to the recognition of intangible assets in business combinations. An intangible asset must be recognized in an acquiring firm's financial statements if the asset arises from a legal or contractual right (e.g., trademarks, copyrights, artistic materials, royalty agreements). If the intangible asset does not represent a legal or contractual right, the intangible will still be recognized if it is capable of being separated from the firm (e.g., unpatented technology, databases).

Comprehensive Illustration

Problem

(*Estimated Time: 45 to 65 Minutes*) The following are the preacquisition account balances of Miller Company and Richmond Company as of December 31. The fair values of Richmond Company's assets and liabilities are also listed.

	Miller Company Book Values 12/31	Richmond Company Book Values 12/31	Richmond Company Fair Values 12/31
Cash	$ 600,000	$ 200,000	$ 200,000
Receivables	900,000	300,000	290,000
Inventory	1,100,000	600,000	820,000
Buildings and equipment (net)	9,000,000	800,000	900,000
Unpatented technology	–0–	–0–	500,000
In-process research and development	–0–	–0–	100,000
Accounts payable	(400,000)	(200,000)	(200,000)
Notes payable	(3,400,000)	(1,100,000)	(1,100,000)
Totals	$ 7,800,000	$ 600,000	$1,510,000
Common stock—$20 par value	$(2,000,000)		
Common stock—$5 par value		$ (220,000)	
Additional paid-in capital	(900,000)	(100,000)	
Retained earnings, 1/1	(2,300,000)	(130,000)	
Revenues	(6,000,000)	(900,000)	
Expenses	3,400,000	750,000	
Totals	$(7,800,000)	$ (600,000)	

Note: Parentheses indicate a credit balance.

Additional Information (not reflected in the preceding figures)

- On December 31, Miller issues 50,000 shares of its $20 par value common stock for all of the outstanding shares of Richmond Company.
- As part of the acquisition agreement, Miller agrees to pay the former owners of Richmond $250,000 if certain profit projections are realized over the next three years. Miller calculates the acquisition-date fair value of this contingency at $100,000.
- In creating this combination, Miller pays $10,000 in stock issue costs and $20,000 in accounting and legal fees.

Required

a. Miller's stock has a fair value of $32 per share. Using the acquisition method:
   1. Prepare the necessary journal entries if Miller dissolves Richmond so it is no longer a separate legal entity.

2. Assume instead that Richmond will retain separate legal incorporation and maintain its own accounting systems. Prepare a worksheet to consolidate the accounts of the two companies.

b. If Miller's stock has a fair value of $26 per share, describe how the consolidated balances would differ from the results in requirement part (a).

Solution

a. 1. In a business combination, the accountant first determines the total fair value of the consideration transferred. Because Miller's stock is valued at $32 per share, the 50,000 issued shares are worth $1,600,000 in total. Included in the consideration transferred is the $100,000 acquisition-date fair value of the contingent performance obligation.

This $1,700,000 total fair value is compared to the $1,510,000 fair value of Richmond's assets and liabilities (including the fair value of IPR&D). Miller recognizes the $190,000 excess fair value ($1,700,000 − $1,510,000) as goodwill. Because dissolution occurs, Miller records on its books the individual fair values of Richmond's identifiable assets and liabilities with the excess recorded as goodwill.

The $10,000 stock issue cost reduces Additional Paid-In Capital. The $20,000 direct combination costs (accounting and legal fees) are expensed when incurred.

Miller Company's Financial Records—December 31

Cash	200,000	
Receivables	290,000	
Inventory	820,000	
Buildings and Equipment	900,000	
Unpatented Technology	500,000	
Research and Development Asset	100,000	
Goodwill	190,000	
Accounts Payable		200,000
Notes Payable		1,100,000
Contingent Performance Obligation		100,000
Common Stock (Miller) (par value)		1,000,000
Additional Paid-In Capital (fair value in excess of par value)		600,000
To record acquisition of Richmond Company.		
Professional Services Expense	20,000	
Cash (paid for combination costs)		20,000
To record legal and accounting fees related to the combination.		
Additional Paid-In Capital	10,000	
Cash (stock issuance costs)		10,000
To record payment of stock issuance costs.		

2. Under this scenario, the acquisition fair value is equal to that computed in part (a1).

50,000 shares of stock at $32.00 each	$1,600,000
Contingent performance obligation	100,000
Acquisition-date fair value of consideration transferred	$1,700,000

Because the subsidiary is maintaining separate incorporation, Miller establishes an investment account to reflect the $1,700,000 acquisition consideration:

Miller's Financial Records—December 31

Investment in Richmond Company	1,700,000	
Contingent Performance Obligation		100,000
Common Stock (Miller) (par value)		1,000,000
Additional Paid-In Capital (fair value in excess of par value)		600,000
To record investment in Richmond Company.		
Professional Services Expense	20,000	
Cash (paid for combination costs)		20,000
To record legal and accounting fees related to the combination.		
Additional Paid-In Capital	10,000	
Cash (stock issuance costs)		10,000
To record payment of stock issuance costs.		

Because Richmond maintains separate incorporation and its own accounting system, Miller prepares a worksheet for consolidation. To prepare the worksheet, Miller first allocates Richmond's fair value to assets acquired and liabilities assumed based on their individual fair values:

Fair value of consideration transferred by Miller....................	$1,700,000
Book value of Richmond	600,000
Excess fair value over book value................................	$1,100,000

Allocations are made to specific accounts based on differences in fair values and book values:

Receivables ($290,000 − $300,000).........................	$ (10,000)	
Inventory ($820,000 − $600,000)............................	220,000	
Buildings and equipment ($900,000 − $800,000)..............	100,000	
Unpatented technology ($500,000 − 0)	500,000	
In-process research and development.......................	100,000	910,000
Goodwill		$190,000

The following steps produce the consolidated financial statements total in Exhibit 2.8.

EXHIBIT 2.8   Comprehensive Illustration—Solution—Acquisition Method

MILLER COMPANY AND RICHMOND COMPANY
Consolidation Worksheet
For Period Ending December 31

Accounts	Miller Company	Richmond Company	Consolidation Entries Debit	Consolidation Entries Credit	Consolidated Totals
Income Statement					
Revenues	(6,000,000)				(6,000,000)
Expenses	3,420,000*				3,420,000*
Net income	(2,580,000)				(2,580,000)
Statement of Retained Earnings					
Retained earnings, 1/1	(2,300,000)				(2,300,000)
Net income (above)	(2,580,000)				(2,580,000)
Retained earnings, 12/31	(4,880,000)				(4,880,000)
Balance Sheet					
Cash	570,000*	200,000			770,000
Receivables	900,000	300,000		(A) 10,000	1,190,000
Inventory	1,100,000	600,000	(A) 220,000		1,920,000
Investment in Richmond Company	1,700,000*	–0–		(A) 1,100,000	–0–
				(S) 600,000	
Buildings and equipment (net)	9,000,000	800,000	(A) 100,000		9,900,000
Goodwill	–0–	–0–	(A) 190,000		190,000
Unpatented technology	–0–	–0–	(A) 500,000		500,000
Research and development asset	–0–	–0–	(A) 100,000		100,000
Total assets	13,270,000	1,900,000			14,570,000
Accounts payable	(400,000)	(200,000)			(600,000)
Notes payable	(3,400,000)	(1,100,000)			(4,500,000)
Contingent performance obligation	(100,000)*	–0–			(100,000)
Common stock	(3,000,000)*	(220,000)	(S) 220,000		(3,000,000)
Additional paid-in capital	(1,490,000)*	(100,000)	(S) 100,000		(1,490,000)
Retained earnings, 12/31 (above)	(4,880,000)*	(280,000)†	(S) 280,000		(4,880,000)
Total liabilities and equities	(13,270,000)	(1,900,000)	1,710,000	1,710,000	(14,570,000)

Note: Parentheses indicate a credit balance.
*Balances have been adjusted for issuance of stock, payment of combination expenses, and recognition of contingent performance obligation.
†Beginning retained earnings plus revenues minus expenses.

- Miller's balances have been updated on this worksheet to include the effects of both the newly issued shares of stock, the recognition of the contingent performance liability, and the combination expenses.
- Richmond's revenue and expense accounts have been closed to Retained Earnings. The acquisition method consolidates only postacquisition revenues and expenses.
- Worksheet Entry S eliminates the $600,000 book value component of the Investment in Richmond Company account along with the subsidiary's stockholders' equity accounts.
- Entry A adjusts all of Richmond's assets and liabilities to fair value based on the allocations determined earlier.

b. If the fair value of Miller's stock is $26.00 per share, then the fair value of the consideration transferred in the Richmond acquisition is recomputed as follows:

Fair value of shares issued ($26 × 50,000 shares)	$1,300,000
Fair value of contingent consideration	100,000
Total consideration transferred at fair value	$1,400,000

Because the consideration transferred is $110,000 less than the $1,510,000 fair value of the net assets received in the acquisition, a bargain purchase has occurred. In this situation, Miller continues to recognize each of the separately identified assets acquired and liabilities assumed at their fair values. Resulting differences in the consolidated balances relative to the requirement part (*a*) solution are as follows:

- The $110,000 excess fair value recognized over the consideration transferred is recognized as a "gain on bargain purchase."
- Consolidated net income increases by the $110,000 gain to $2,690,000.
- No goodwill is recognized.
- Miller's additional paid-in capital decreases by $300,000 to $1,190,000.
- Consolidated retained earnings increase by the $110,000 gain to $4,990,000.

Also, because of the bargain purchase, the "Investment in Richmond Company" account balance on Miller's separate financial statements shows the $1,510,000 fair value of the net identified assets received. This valuation measure is an exception to the general rule of using the consideration transferred to provide the valuation basis for the acquired firm.

Appendix A

LO 2-9

Identify the general characteristics of the legacy purchase and pooling of interests methods of accounting for past business combinations. Understand the effects that persist today in financial statements from the use of these legacy methods.

Legacy Methods of Accounting for Business Combinations

The acquisition method provides the accounting for business combinations occurring in 2009 and thereafter. However, for decades, business combinations were accounted for using either the **purchase** or **pooling of interests** method. From 2002 through 2008, the purchase method was used exclusively for business combinations. Prior to 2002, financial reporting standards allowed two alternatives: the purchase method and the pooling of interests method. Because the FASB required prospective application of the acquisition method for 2009 and beyond, the purchase and pooling of interests methods continue to provide the basis for financial reporting for pre-2009 business combinations and thus will remain relevant for many years. Literally tens of thousands of past business combinations will continue to be reported in future statements under one of these legacy methods.

The following sections describe the purchase and pooling of interests methods along with comparisons to the acquisition method.

The Purchase Method: An Application of the Cost Principle

A basic principle of the purchase method was to record a business combination at the cost to the new owners. For example, several years ago MGM Grand, Inc., acquired Mirage Resorts, Inc., for approximately $6.4 billion. This purchase price continued to serve as the valuation basis for Mirage Resorts's assets and liabilities in the preparation of MGM Grand's consolidated financial statements.

Several elements of the purchase method reflect a strict application of the cost principle. The following items represent examples of how the cost-based purchase method differs from the fair value–based acquisition method.

- Acquisition date allocations (including bargain purchases).
- Direct combination costs.
- Contingent consideration.
- In-process research and development.

We next briefly discuss the accounting treatment for these items across the current and previous financial reporting regimes.

Purchase-Date Cost Allocations (Including Bargain Purchases)

In pre-2009 business combinations, the application of the cost principle often was complicated because literally hundreds of separate assets and liabilities were acquired. Accordingly, for asset valuation and future income determination, firms needed a basis to allocate the total cost among the various assets and liabilities received in the bargained exchange. Similar to the acquisition method, the purchase method based its cost allocations on the combination-date fair values of the acquired assets and liabilities. Also closely related to the acquisition method procedures, any excess of cost over the sum of the net identified asset fair values was attributed to goodwill.

But the purchase method stands in marked contrast to the acquisition method in bargain purchase situations. Under the purchase method, a bargain purchase occurred when the sum of the individual fair values of the acquired net assets exceeded the purchase cost. To record a bargain purchase at cost, however, the purchase method required that certain long-term assets be recorded at amounts below their assessed fair values.

For example, assume Adams Co. paid $520,000 for Brook Co. in 2008. Brook has the following assets with appraised fair values:

Accounts receivable	$ 15,000
Land	200,000
Building	400,000
Accounts payable	(5,000)
Total net fair value	$610,000

However, to record the combination at its $520,000 cost, Adams cannot use all of the fair values. The purchase method solution was to require that Adams reduce the valuation assigned to the acquired long-term assets (land and building) proportionately by $90,000 ($610,000 − $520,000). The total fair value of the long-term assets, in this case $600,000, provided the basis for allocating the reduction. Thus, Adams would reduce the acquired land by $(2/6 \times \$90,000) = \$30,000$ and the building by $(4/6 \times \$90,000) = \$60,000$. Adams's journal entry to record the combination using the purchase method would then be as follows:

Accounts Receivable	15,000	
Land ($200,000 − $30,000)	170,000	
Building ($400,000 − $60,000)	340,000	
Accounts Payable		5,000
Cash		520,000

Note that current assets and liabilities did not share in the proportionate reduction to cost. Long-term assets were subject to the reduction because their fair-value estimates were considered less reliable than current items and liabilities. Finally, in rare situations, firms recognized an extraordinary gain on a purchase, but only in the very unusual case that the long-term assets were reduced to a zero valuation.

In contrast, the acquisition method embraces the fair-value concept and discards the consideration transferred as a valuation basis for the business acquired in a bargain purchase. Instead, the acquirer measures and recognizes the fair values of each of the assets acquired and liabilities assumed at the date of combination, regardless of the consideration transferred in the transaction. As a result, (1) no assets are recorded at amounts below their assessed fair values, as is the case with bargain purchases accounted for by the purchase method, and (2) a gain on bargain purchase is recognized at the acquisition date.

Direct Combination Costs

Almost all business combinations employ professional services to assist in various phases of the transaction. Examples include target identification, due diligence regarding the value of an acquisition, financing, tax planning, and preparation of formal legal documents. Prior to 2009, under the purchase method, the investment cost basis included direct combination costs. In contrast, the acquisition method considers these costs as payments for services received, not part of the fair value exchanged for the business. Thus, under the acquisition method, direct combination costs are expensed as incurred.

Contingent Consideration

Often business combination negotiations result in agreements to provide additional payments to former owners if they meet specified future performance measures. The purchase method accounted for such contingent consideration obligations as postcombination adjustments to the purchase cost (or stockholders' equity if the contingency involved the parent's equity share value) upon resolution of the contingency. The acquisition method treats contingent consideration obligations as a negotiated component of the fair value of the consideration transferred, consistent with the fair-value measurement attribute.

In-Process Research and Development (IPR&D)

Prior to 2009, financial reporting standards required the immediate expensing of acquired IPR&D if the project had not yet reached technological feasibility and the assets had no future alternative uses. Expensing acquired IPR&D was consistent with the accounting treatment for a firm's ongoing research and development costs.

The acquisition method, however, requires tangible and intangible assets acquired in a business combination to be used in a particular research and development activity, including those that may have no alternative future use, to be recognized and measured at fair value at the acquisition date. These capitalized research and development costs are reported as intangible assets with indefinite lives subject to periodic impairment reviews. Moreover, because the acquirer identified and paid for the IPR&D, the acquisition method assumes an expectation of future economic benefit and therefore recognizes an asset.

The Pooling of Interests Method: Continuity of Previous Ownership

Historically, former owners of separate firms would agree to combine for their mutual benefit and continue as owners of a combined firm. It was asserted that the assets and liabilities of the former firms were never really bought or sold; former owners merely exchanged ownership shares to become joint owners of the combined firm. Combinations characterized by exchange of voting shares and continuation of previous ownership became known as pooling of interests. Rather than an exchange transaction with one ownership group replacing another, a pooling of interests was characterized by a continuity of ownership interests before and after the business combination. Prior to its elimination, this method was applied to a significant number of business combinations.[23] To reflect the continuity of ownership, two important steps characterized the pooling of interests method:

1. The book values of the assets and liabilities of both companies became the book values reported by the combined entity.
2. The revenue and expense accounts were combined retrospectively as well as prospectively. The idea of continuity of ownership gave support for the recognition of income accruing to the owners both before and after the combination.

Therefore, in a pooling, reported income was typically higher than under the contemporaneous purchase accounting. Under pooling, not only did the firms retrospectively combine incomes, but also the smaller asset bases resulted in smaller depreciation and amortization expenses. Because net income reported in financial statements often is used in a variety of contracts, including managerial compensation, managers considered the pooling method an attractive alternative to purchase accounting.

Prior to 2002, accounting and reporting standards allowed both the purchase and the pooling of interest methods for business combinations. However, standard setters established strict criteria for use of the pooling method. The criteria were designed to prevent managers from engaging in purchase transactions and then reporting them as poolings of interests. Business combinations that failed to meet the pooling criteria had to be accounted for by the purchase method.

These criteria had two overriding objectives. First, to ensure the complete fusion of the two organizations, one company had to obtain substantially all (90 percent or more) of the voting stock of the other. The second general objective of these criteria was to prevent purchase combinations from being disguised as poolings. Past experience had shown that combination transactions were frequently manipulated so that they would qualify for pooling of interests treatment (usually to increase reported earnings). However, subsequent events, often involving cash being paid or received by the parties, revealed the true nature of the combination: One company was purchasing the other in a bargained exchange. A number of qualifying criteria for pooling of interests treatment were designed to stop this practice.

---

[23] Past prominent business combinations accounted for by the pooling of interests method include Exxon-Mobil, Pfizer-Warner Lambert, Yahoo!-Broadcast.com, and Pepsi-Quaker Oats, among thousands of others.

EXHIBIT 2.9
Precombination
Information for Baker
Company

January 1	Book Values	Fair Values
Current assets	$ 30,000	$ 30,000
Internet domain name	160,000	300,000
Licensing agreements	–0–	500,000
In-process research and development	–0–	200,000
Notes payable	(25,000)	(25,000)
Total net assets	$165,000	$1,005,000

Note: Parentheses indicate a credit balance.

Comparisons across the Pooling of Interests, Purchase, and Acquisition Methods

To illustrate some of the differences across the purchase, pooling of interests, and acquisition methods, assume that on January 1, Archer, Inc., acquired Baker Company in exchange for 10,000 shares of its $1.00 par common stock having a fair value of $1,200,000 in a transaction structured as a merger. In connection with the acquisition, Archer paid $25,000 in legal and accounting fees. Also, Archer agreed to pay the former owners additional cash consideration contingent upon the completion of Baker's existing contracts at specified profit margins. The current fair value of the contingent obligation was estimated to be $150,000. Exhibit 2.9 provides Baker's combination-date book values and fair values.

Purchase Method Applied

Archer's valuation basis for its purchase of Baker is computed and allocated as follows:

Fair value of shares issued		$1,200,000
Direct combination costs (legal and accounting fees)		25,000
Cost of the Baker purchase		$1,225,000
Cost allocation:		
Current assets	$ 30,000	
Internet domain name	300,000	
Licensing agreements	500,000	
Research and development expense	200,000	
Notes payable	(25,000)	
Total net fair value of items acquired		1,005,000
Goodwill		$ 220,000

Note the following characteristics of the purchase method from the above schedule.

- The valuation basis is cost and includes direct combination costs but excludes the contingent consideration.
- The cost is allocated to the assets acquired and liabilities assumed based on their individual fair values (unless a bargain purchase occurs and then the long-term items may be recorded as amounts less than their fair values).
- Goodwill is the excess of cost over the fair values of the net assets purchased.
- Acquired in-process research and development is expensed immediately at the purchase date.

Pooling of Interests Method Applied

Because a purchase sale was deemed not to occur, the pooling method relied on previously recorded values reflecting a continuation of previous ownership. Thus, the following asset would be recorded by Archer in a business combination accounted for as a pooling of interests.

	Values Assigned
Current assets	$ 30,000
Internet domain name	160,000
Licensing agreements	–0–
In-process research and development	–0–
Notes payable	(25,000)
Total value assigned within the combination	$165,000

Note the following characteristics of the pooling of interests method from the preceding schedule:

- Because a pooling of interests was predicated on a continuity of ownership, the accounting incorporated a continuation of previous book values and ignored fair values exchanged in a business combination.
- Previously unrecognized (typically internally developed) intangibles continue to be reported at a zero-value postcombination.
- Because the pooling of interests method values an acquired firm at its previously recorded book value, no new amount for goodwill was ever recorded in a pooling.

Acquisition Method Applied

According to the acquisition method, Archer's valuation basis for its acquisition of Baker is computed as follows:

Fair value of shares issued		$1,200,000
Fair value of contingent performance obligation		150,000
Total consideration transferred for the Baker acquisition		$1,350,000
Cost allocation:		
Current assets	$ 30,000	
Internet domain name	300,000	
Licensing agreements	500,000	
Research and development asset	200,000	
Notes payable	(25,000)	
Total net fair value of items acquired		1,005,000
Goodwill		$ 345,000

Note the following characteristics of the acquisition method from the preceding schedule:

- The valuation basis is fair value of consideration transferred and includes the contingent consideration but excludes direct combination costs.
- The assets acquired and liabilities assumed are recorded at their individual fair values.
- Goodwill is the excess of the consideration transferred over the fair values of the net assets acquired.
- Acquired in-process research and development is recognized as an asset.
- Professional service fees to help accomplish the acquisition are expensed.

The following table compares the amounts from Baker that Archer would include in its combination-date consolidated financial statements under the pooling of interests method, the purchase method, and the acquisition method.

	Values Incorporated in Archer's Consolidated Balance Sheet Resulting from the Baker Transaction		
	Pooling of Interests Method	Purchase Method	Acquisition Method
Current assets	$ 30,000	$ 30,000	$ 30,000
Internet domain name	160,000	300,000	300,000
Licensing agreements	–0–	500,000	500,000
In-process research and development asset*	–0–	–0–	200,000
Goodwill	–0–	220,000	345,000
Notes payable	(25,000)	(25,000)	(25,000)
Contingent performance obligation	–0–	–0–	(150,000)
Total net assets recognized by Archer	$165,000	$1,025,000	$1,200,000

*Acquired in-process research and development was expensed under the purchase method and not recognized at all under the pooling of interests method.

Several comparisons should be noted across these methods of accounting for business combinations:

- In consolidating Baker's assets and liabilities, the purchase and acquisition methods record fair values. In contrast, the pooling method uses previous book values and ignores fair values. Consequently, although a fair value of $1,350,000 is exchanged, only a net value of $165,000 (assets less liabilities) is reported in the pooling.

- The pooling method, as reflected in the preceding example, typically shows smaller asset values and consequently lowers future depreciation and amortization expenses. Thus, higher future net income was usually reported under the pooling method compared to similar situations that employed the purchase method.

- Under pooling, financial ratios such as Net Income/Total Assets were dramatically inflated. Not only was this ratio's denominator understated through failure to recognize internally developed assets acquired (and fair values in general), but the numerator was overstated through smaller depreciation and amortization expenses.

- Although not shown, the pooling method retrospectively combined the acquired firm's revenues, expenses, dividends, and retained earnings. The purchase and acquisition methods incorporate only postcombination values for these operational items. Also all costs of the combination (direct and indirect acquisition costs and stock issue costs) were expensed in the period of combination under the pooling of interests method.

- Finally, with adoption of the acquisition method, the FASB has moved clearly in the direction of increased management accountability for the fair values of all assets acquired and liabilities assumed in a business combination.

Appendix B

LO 2-10

Explain the rationale and procedures underlying a subsidiary's election to adopt pushdown accounting.

Pushdown Accounting

In the analysis of business combinations to this point, discussion has focused on (1) the recording of the combination by the parent company and (2) required consolidation procedures. An additional reporting issue, however, arises concerning the separate postacquisition financial statements of subsidiary companies.

This issue has become especially significant in recent years because of business acquisitions by private-equity firms. An organization, for example, might acquire a company, work to improve its business model, and subsequently offer the shares back to the public in hopes of making a large profit. What valuation basis should be used in reporting the subsidiary's financial statements that accompany the initial public offering? In other situations, a subsidiary company may need to provide its own separate financial statements in connection with a new public debt issue. Should the subsidiary's financial statements utilize the new basis of accounting that the parent company established in the acquisition or continue its financial statement carrying amounts established prior to the acquisition?

To illustrate, assume that Strand Company owns one asset: a production machine with a carrying amount of $200,000 but a fair value of $900,000. Parker Corporation pays exactly $900,000 in cash to acquire Strand. Consolidation offers no real problem here: The machine will be reported by the business combination at $900,000.

However, if Strand continues to issue separate financial statements (for example, to its creditors or potential stockholders), should the machine be reported at $200,000 or $900,000? If adjusted, should the $700,000 increase be reported as a gain by the subsidiary or as an addition to contributed capital? Should depreciation be based on $200,000 or $900,000? If the subsidiary is to be viewed as a new entity with a new basis for its assets and liabilities, should Retained Earnings be returned to zero? If the parent acquires only 51 percent of Strand, does that change the answers to the previous questions?

Proponents of pushdown accounting argue that a change in ownership creates a new basis for subsidiary assets and liabilities. An unadjusted balance ($200,000 in the preceding illustration) is a cost figure applicable to previous stockholders. That amount is no longer relevant information. Rather, according to this argument, the fair value at the date control of the company changes is now relevant, a figure best reflected by the consideration transferred to acquire the subsidiary. Balance sheet accounts should be reported at the asset's acquisition-date fair value ($900,000 in the illustration) rather than the cost incurred by the previous owners of the company. Moreover, the subsidiary can now recognize any previously unrecognized intangible assets as valued by its new owner concurrently with the acquisition.

External Reporting Option for Pushdown Accounting

To address the valuation issues for a subsidiary's separately issued financial statements, the FASB issued Accounting Standards Update (ASU) No. 2014-17, *Business Combinations: Pushdown Accounting* in November 2014. The ASU does not require pushdown accounting, but instead provides an option to apply pushdown accounting following a business combination in which the acquirer obtains control of an acquired entity and the acquired entity maintains separate incorporation. A newly acquired entity (e.g., subsidiary firm) may elect the option to apply pushdown accounting in the reporting period immediately following the acquisition.[24] Alternatively, a newly acquired company may simply choose to continue using its previous accounting valuations in separately issued financial statements.

When an acquired entity elects to apply pushdown accounting, it reflects in its financial statements the valuations for the individual assets and liabilities used by the parent in allocating the consideration transferred in the acquisition. Thus, the parent's acquisition-date valuations for its newly acquired subsidiary are "pushed down" to the subsidiary's financial statements.

As discussed next, the FASB (ASC 805-50-30) provides particular guidance for three accounting issues: goodwill, bargain purchase gains, and acquisition-related liabilities. We then discuss other accounting issues including acquisition-date retained earnings and other owners' equity effects.

Goodwill

When an entity elects pushdown accounting, any goodwill recognized in the combination is reported in the acquired entity's separate financial statements.

Bargain Purchase Gains

An exception to pushdown accounting's general rule of using the parent's valuations for the subsidiary's separate financial statement occurs for bargain purchases. Recall that when the fair values assigned to the subsidiary's collective net assets exceed the parent's consideration transferred, the parent recognizes a bargain purchase gain on its income statement. In this case, however, pushdown accounting requires that the acquired entity not recognize the gain in its income statement, but instead as an adjustment to its additional paid-in capital. The reflection of the bargain purchase gain in additional paid-in capital prevents income recognition by both the acquirer and the acquiree for the same event.

Acquisition-Related Liabilities

When acquisition-related liabilities arise, pushdown accounting recognizes only the debt that the acquired firm must recognize under other generally accepted accounting principles. Thus, if an acquired firm is either jointly or severally liable for repayment of the debt, such debt is pushed down to its separate financial statements, possibly including debt incurred by the acquirer.

Acquisition-Date Subsidiary Retained Earnings

After recognizing the new basis for its assets and liabilities, the acquired firm must then report the effects of the acquisition in its owners' equity section. Because pushdown accounting treats the acquired firm as a new reporting entity, the acquired firm reports zero acquisition-date retained earnings. The elimination of acquisition-date subsidiary retained earnings is consistent with consolidated financial reporting.

Additional Paid-In Capital from Pushdown Accounting

The overall effect of the combined pushdown accounting adjustments to the previous carrying amounts of the subsidiary's assets and liabilities then is reported as an adjustment to the subsidiary's additional paid-in capital attributable to the common shareholders. For example, a subsidiary may report "Additional paid-in capital from pushdown accounting" in its separate balance sheet. The total effect in the additional paid-in capital from pushdown accounting results from both the elimination of acquisition-date retained earnings and the revaluation of the acquired firm's assets and liabilities to the parent's basis.

Example: Pushdown Accounting

To illustrate an application of pushdown accounting, we use the Exhibit 2.3 BigNet and Smallport Company example presented previously in this chapter. If Smallport Company applies pushdown accounting, its acquisition-date separately reported balance sheet would appear as presented in Exhibit 2.10.

---

[24] The acquired entity can also elect to apply pushdown accounting in periods subsequent to the acquisition, but must report the election as a retrospective change in accounting principle (ASC Topic 250, Accounting Changes and Error Corrections). Once made, the decision to apply pushdown accounting to a specific change-in-control event is irrevocable.

EXHIBIT 2.10
Pushdown Accounting—Date of Acquisition

Smallport Company Balance Sheet at January 1

Current assets	$ 300,000
Computers and equipment	600,000
Capitalized software	1,200,000
Customer contracts	700,000
Goodwill	70,000
Total assets	$ 2,870,000
Liabilities	$ (250,000)
Common stock	(100,000)
Additional paid-in capital excess over par	(20,000)
Additional paid-in capital from pushdown accounting	(2,500,000)
Retained earnings, 1/1	–0–
Total liabilities and equities	$ 2,870,000

Note that the values for each asset and liability in Smallport's separate balance sheet are identical to those reported in BigNet's consolidated acquisition-date balance sheet.

Internal Reporting

Pushdown accounting has several advantages for internal reporting. For example, it simplifies the consolidation process. If the subsidiary enters the acquisition-date fair value allocations into its records, worksheet Entry A (to recognize the allocations originating from the fair-value adjustments) is not needed. Amortizations of the excess fair-value allocation (see Chapter 3) would be incorporated in subsequent periods as well.

Despite some simplifications to the consolidation process, pushdown accounting does not address the many issues in preparing consolidated financial statements that appear in subsequent chapters of this text. Therefore, it remains to be seen how many acquired companies will choose to elect pushdown accounting. For newly acquired subsidiaries that expect to issue new debt or eventually undergo an initial public offering, fair values may provide investors with a better understanding of the company.

In summary, pushdown accounting provides a newly acquired subsidiary the option to revalue its assets and liabilities to acquisition-date fair values in its separately reported financial statements. This valuation option may be useful when the parent expects to offer the subsidiary shares to the public following a period of planned improvements. Other benefits from pushdown accounting may arise when the subsidiary plans to issue debt and needs its separate financial statements to incorporate acquisition-date fair values and previously unrecognized intangibles in their stand-alone financial reports.

Questions

1. What is a business combination?
2. Describe the concept of a synergy. What are some examples of possible synergies in business combinations?
3. Describe the different types of legal arrangements that can take place to create a business combination.
4. What does the term *consolidated financial statements* mean?
5. Within the consolidation process, what is the purpose of a worksheet?
6. Jones Company obtains all of the common stock of Hudson, Inc., by issuing 50,000 shares of its own stock. Under these circumstances, why might the determination of a fair value for the consideration transferred be difficult?
7. What is the accounting valuation basis for consolidating assets and liabilities in a business combination?
8. How should a parent consolidate its subsidiary's revenues and expenses?
9. Morgan Company acquires all of the outstanding shares of Jennings, Inc., for cash. Morgan transfers consideration more than the fair value of the company's net assets. How should the payment in excess of fair value be accounted for in the consolidation process?
10. Catron Corporation is having liquidity problems, and as a result, it sells all of its outstanding stock to Lambert, Inc., for cash. Because of Catron's problems, Lambert is able to acquire this stock at less than the fair value of the company's net assets. How is this reduction in price accounted for within the consolidation process?

11. Sloane, Inc., issues 25,000 shares of its own common stock in exchange for all of the outstanding shares of Benjamin Company. Benjamin will remain a separately incorporated operation. How does Sloane record the issuance of these shares?

12. To obtain all of the stock of Molly, Inc., Harrison Corporation issued its own common stock. Harrison had to pay $98,000 to lawyers, accountants, and a stock brokerage firm in connection with services rendered during the creation of this business combination. In addition, Harrison paid $56,000 in costs associated with the stock issuance. How will these two costs be recorded?

Problems

LO 2-1

1. Which of the following does not represent a primary motivation for business combinations?
   a. Combinations are often a vehicle to accelerate growth and competitiveness.
   b. Cost savings can be achieved through elimination of duplicate facilities and staff.
   c. Synergies may be available through quick entry for new and existing products into markets.
   d. Larger firms are less likely to fail.

LO 2-2

2. Which of the following is the best theoretical justification for consolidated financial statements?
   a. In form, the companies are one entity; in substance, they are separate.
   b. In form, the companies are separate; in substance, they are one entity.
   c. In form and substance, the companies are one entity.
   d. In form and substance, the companies are separate. (AICPA)

LO 2-3

3. What is a statutory merger?
   a. A merger approved by the Securities and Exchange Commission
   b. An acquisition involving the purchase of both stock and assets
   c. A takeover completed within one year of the initial tender offer
   d. A business combination in which only one company continues to exist as a legal entity

LO 2-4

4. What is goodwill?
   a. An intangible asset representing the excess of consideration transferred over the collective fair values of the net identifiable assets acquired in a business combination
   b. An expense that an acquiring firm recognizes for the excess of consideration transferred over the collective fair values of the net identifiable assets acquired in a business combination
   c. A concept representing synergies resulting from a business combination but not recognized for financial reporting purposes
   d. An internally developed intangible asset that is recognized on a business firm's balance sheet as the business generates profits in excess of a normal rate of return on its identifiable net assets

LO 2-4

5. FASB ASC 805, "Business Combinations," provides principles for allocating the fair value of an acquired business. When the collective fair values of the separately identified assets acquired and liabilities assumed exceed the fair value of the consideration transferred, the difference should be
   a. Recognized as an ordinary gain from a bargain purchase.
   b. Treated as negative goodwill to be amortized over the period benefited, not to exceed 40 years.
   c. Treated as goodwill and tested for impairment on an annual basis.
   d. Applied pro rata to reduce, but not below zero, the amounts initially assigned to specific noncurrent assets of the acquired firm.

LO 2-8

6. What is the appropriate accounting treatment for the value assigned to in-process research and development acquired in a business combination?
   a. Expense upon acquisition.
   b. Capitalize as an asset.
   c. Expense if there is no alternative use for the assets used in the research and development and technological feasibility has yet to be reached.
   d. Expense until future economic benefits become certain and then capitalize as an asset.

LO 2-8

7. Consolidated financial statements are typically prepared when one company has
   a. Accounted for its investment in another company by the equity method.
   b. Dividend income from another company.
   c. Significant influence over the operating and financial policies of another company.
   d. Control over another company.

LO 2-4

8. When does gain recognition accompany a business combination?

    a. When a bargain purchase occurs

    b. In a combination created in the middle of a fiscal year

    c. In an acquisition when the value of all assets and liabilities cannot be determined

    d. When the amount of a bargain purchase exceeds the value of the applicable noncurrent assets (other than certain exceptions) held by the acquired company

LO 2-6b

9. According to the acquisition method of accounting for business combinations, costs paid to attorneys and accountants for services in arranging a merger should be

    a. Capitalized as part of the overall fair value acquired in the merger.

    b. Recorded as an expense in the period the merger takes place.

    c. Included in recognized goodwill.

    d. Written off over a five-year maximum useful life.

LO 2-4

10. When negotiating a business acquisition, buyers sometimes agree to pay extra amounts to sellers in the future if performance metrics are achieved over specified time horizons. How should buyers account for such contingent consideration in recording an acquisition?

    a. The amount ultimately paid under the contingent consideration agreement is added to goodwill when and if the performance metrics are met.

    b. The fair value of the contingent consideration is expensed immediately at acquisition date.

    c. The fair value of the contingent consideration is included in the overall fair value of the consideration transferred.

    d. The fair value of the contingent consideration is recorded as a reduction of the otherwise determinable fair value of the acquired firm.

LO 2-5

11. An acquired firm's financial records sometimes show goodwill from previous business combinations. How does a parent company account for the preexisting goodwill of its newly acquired subsidiary?

    a. The parent tests the preexisting goodwill for impairment before recording the goodwill as part of the acquisition.

    b. The parent includes the preexisting goodwill as an identified intangible asset acquired.

    c. The parent ignores preexisting subsidiary goodwill and allocates the subsidiary's fair value among the separately identifiable assets acquired and liabilities assumed.

    d. Preexisting goodwill is excluded from the identifiable assets acquired unless the subsidiary can demonstrate its continuing value.

LO 2-5

12. On June 1, Cline Co. paid $800,000 cash for all of the issued and outstanding common stock of Renn Corp. The carrying amounts for Renn's assets and liabilities on June 1 follow:

Cash	$150,000
Accounts receivable	180,000
Capitalized software costs	320,000
Goodwill	100,000
Liabilities	(130,000)
Net assets	$620,000

On June 1, Renn's accounts receivable had a fair value of $140,000. Additionally, Renn's in-process research and development was estimated to have a fair value of $200,000. All other items were stated at their fair values. On Cline's June 1 consolidated balance sheet, how much is reported for goodwill?

    a. $320,000

    b. $120,000

    c. $80,000

    d. $20,000

Problems 13 and 14 relate to the following:

On May 1, Donovan Company reported the following account balances:

Current assets	$ 90,000
Buildings & equipment (net)	220,000
Total assets	$310,000
Liabilities	$ 60,000
Common stock	150,000
Retained earnings	100,000
Total liabilities and equities	$310,000

On May 1, Beasley paid $400,000 in stock (fair value) for all of the assets and liabilities of Donovan, which will cease to exist as a separate entity. In connection with the merger, Beasley incurred $15,000 in accounts payable for legal and accounting fees.

Beasley also agreed to pay $75,000 to the former owners of Donovan contingent on meeting certain revenue goals during the following year. Beasley estimated the present value of its probability adjusted expected payment for the contingency at $20,000. In determining its offer, Beasley noted the following:

- Donovan holds a building with a fair value $30,000 more than its book value.
- Donovan has developed unpatented technology appraised at $25,000, although is it not recorded in its financial records.
- Donovan has a research and development activity in process with an appraised fair value of $45,000. The project has not yet reached technological feasibility.
- Book values for Donovan's current assets and liabilities approximate fair values.

LO 2-4, 2-5

13. What should Beasley record as total liabilities incurred or assumed in connection with the Donovan merger?
    a. $15,000
    b. $75,000
    c. $95,000
    d. $150,000

LO 2-5, 2-8

14. How much should Beasley record as total assets acquired in the Donovan merger?
    a. $400,000
    b. $420,000
    c. $410,000
    d. $480,000

Problems 15 through 18 are based on the following information:

On July 1, TruData Company issues 10,000 shares of its common stock with a $5 par value and a $40 fair value in exchange for all of Webstat Company's outstanding voting shares. Webstat's precombination book and fair values are shown along with book values for TruData's accounts as follows:

	TruData Book Values	Webstat Book Values	Webstat Fair Values
Revenues (1/1 to 7/1)	$(250,000)	$(130,000)	
Expenses (1/1 to 7/1)	170,000	80,000	
Retained earnings, 1/1	(130,000)	(150,000)	
Cash and receivables	140,000	60,000	$ 60,000
Inventory	190,000	145,000	175,000
Patented technology (net)	230,000	180,000	200,000
Land	400,000	200,000	225,000
Buildings and equipment (net)	100,000	75,000	75,000
Liabilities	(540,000)	(360,000)	(350,000)
Common stock	(300,000)	(70,000)	
Additional paid-in capital	(10,000)	(30,000)	

LO 2-5

15. On its acquisition-date consolidated balance sheet, what amount should TruData report as goodwill?
    a. –0–
    b. $15,000
    c. $35,000
    d. $100,000

LO 2-5

16. On its acquisition-date consolidated balance sheet, what amount should TruData report as patented technology (net)?
    a. $200,000
    b. $230,000
    c. $410,000
    d. $430,000

LO 2-5, 2-7

17. On its acquisition-date consolidated balance sheet, what amount should TruData report as common stock?
    a. $70,000
    b. $300,000
    c. $350,000
    d. $370,000

LO 2-5, 2-7

18. On its acquisition-date consolidated balance sheet, what amount should TruData report as retained earnings as of July 1?
    a. $130,000
    b. $210,000
    c. $260,000
    d. $510,000

Problems 19 and 20 are based on the following information. The separate condensed balance sheets of Patrick Corporation and its wholly owned subsidiary, Sean Corporation, are as follows:

BALANCE SHEETS
December 31, 2023

	Patrick	Sean
Cash	$ 80,000	$ 60,000
Accounts receivable (net)	140,000	25,000
Inventories	90,000	50,000
Plant and equipment (net)	625,000	280,000
Investment in Sean	460,000	
Total assets	$1,395,000	$415,000
Accounts payable	$ 160,000	$ 95,000
Long-term debt	110,000	30,000
Common stock ($10 par)	340,000	50,000
Additional paid-in capital		10,000
Retained earnings	785,000	230,000
Total liabilities and shareholders' equity	$1,395,000	$415,000

Additional Information:

- On December 31, 2023, Patrick acquired 100 percent of Sean's voting stock in exchange for $460,000.
- At the acquisition date, the fair values of Sean's assets and liabilities equaled their carrying amounts, respectively, except that the fair value of certain items in Sean's inventory were $25,000 more than their carrying amounts.

LO 2-4, 2-5

19. In the December 31, 2023, consolidated balance sheet of Patrick and its subsidiary, what amount of total assets should be reported?
    a. $1,375,000
    b. $1,395,000
    c. $1,520,000
    d. $1,980,000

LO 2-4, 2-5

20. In the December 31, 2023, consolidated balance sheet of Patrick and its subsidiary, what amount of total stockholders' equity should be reported?

    a. $1,100,000
    b. $1,125,000
    c. $1,150,000
    d. $1,355,000

LO 2-5, 2-6b

21. Peak issues 51,000 new shares of its common stock valued at $3 per share for all of the outstanding stock of Scene. Peak also incurred attorney costs of $10,000 related to the combination. Prior to these transactions, Peak, Inc., and Scene Corporation had the following stockholders' equity figures:

	Peak	Scene
Common stock ($1 par value)	$180,000	$ 45,000
Additional paid-in capital	90,000	20,000
Retained earnings	300,000	110,000

Immediately following the business combination, what totals would appear on a consolidated balance sheet for Additional Paid-In Capital and Retained Earnings, respectively?

    a. $104,000 and $300,000
    b. $110,000 and $400,000
    c. $192,000 and $290,000
    d. $212,000 and $410,000

LO 2-8

22. Prospect Co. merges with Stuyvesant, Inc., and acquires several different categories of intangible assets including trademarks, copyrights on artistic materials, agreements to receive royalties on leased intellectual property, and unpatented technology.

    a. Describe the criteria for determining whether an intangible asset acquired in a business combination should be separately recognized apart from goodwill.

    b. For each of the acquired intangibles listed, identify which recognition criteria (separability and contractual-legal) may or may not apply in recognizing the intangible on the acquiring firm's financial statements.

LO 2-6a, 2-6b

23. The following book and fair values were available for Beech Company as of June 1:

	Book Value	Fair Value
Inventory	$ 630,000	$600,000
Land	750,000	990,000
Buildings	1,700,000	2,000,000
Trademarks	–0–	800,000
Accounts payable	(80,000)	(80,000)
Common stock	(2,000,000)	
Additional paid-in capital	(500,000)	
Retained earnings, 1/1	(360,000)	
Revenues	(420,000)	
Expenses	280,000	

Alder Company pays $3,900,000 cash and issues 20,000 shares of its $2 par value common stock (fair value of $50 per share) for all of Beech's common stock in a merger, after which Beech will cease to exist as a separate entity. Stock issue costs amount to $25,000, and Alder pays $42,000 for legal fees to complete the transaction. Prepare Alder's journal entries to record its acquisition of Beech.

LO 2-6a, 2-6b, 2-8

24. Use the same facts as in Problem 23, but assume instead that Alder pays cash of $4,200,000 to acquire Beech. No stock is issued. Prepare Alder's journal entries to record its acquisition of Beech.

LO 2-4, 2-5, 2-6a, 2-6b, 2-6c

25. Following are preacquisition financial balances for Padre Company and Sol Company as of December 31. Also included are fair values for Sol Company accounts.

	Padre Company Book Values 12/31	Sol Company Book Values 12/31	Sol Company Fair Values 12/31
Cash	$400,000	$120,000	$120,000
Receivables	220,000	300,000	300,000
Inventory	410,000	210,000	260,000
Land	600,000	130,000	110,000
Building and equipment (net)	600,000	270,000	330,000
Franchise agreements	220,000	190,000	220,000
Accounts payable	(300,000)	(120,000)	(120,000)
Accrued expenses	(90,000)	(30,000)	(30,000)
Long-term liabilities	(900,000)	(510,000)	(510,000)
Common stock—$20 par value	(660,000)		
Common stock—$5 par value		(210,000)	
Additional paid-in capital	(70,000)	(90,000)	
Retained earnings, 1/1	(390,000)	(240,000)	
Revenues	(960,000)	(330,000)	
Expenses	920,000	310,000	

Note: Parentheses indicate a credit balance.

On December 31, Padre acquires Sol's outstanding stock by paying $360,000 in cash and issuing 10,000 shares of its own common stock with a fair value of $40 per share. Padre paid legal and accounting fees of $20,000 as well as $5,000 in stock issuance costs.

Determine the value that would be shown in Padre's consolidated financial statements for each of the accounts listed:

Accounts	
Inventory	Revenues
Land	Additional paid-in capital
Buildings and equipment	Expenses
Franchise agreements	Retained earnings, 1/1
Goodwill	Retained earnings, 12/31

LO 2-5, 2-6a, 2-6b, 2-8

26. On May 1, Soriano Co. reported the following account balances along with their estimated fair values:

	Carrying Amount	Fair Value
Receivables	$ 90,000	$ 90,000
Inventory	75,000	75,000
Copyrights	125,000	480,000
Patented technology	825,000	700,000
Total assets	$1,115,000	$1,345,000
Current liabilities	$ 160,000	$ 160,000
Long-term liabilities	645,000	635,000
Common stock	100,000	
Retained earnings	210,000	
Total liabilities and equities	$1,115,000	

On that day, Zambrano paid cash to acquire all of the assets and liabilities of Soriano, which will cease to exist as a separate entity. To facilitate the merger, Zambrano also paid $100,000 to an investment banking firm.

The following information was also available:

- Zambrano further agreed to pay an extra $70,000 to the former owners of Soriano only if they meet certain revenue goals during the next two years. Zambrano estimated the present value of its probability adjusted expected payment for this contingency at $35,000.

- Soriano has a research and development project in process with an appraised value of $200,000. However, the project has not yet reached technological feasibility, and the project's assets have no alternative future use.

Prepare Zambrano's journal entries to record the Soriano acquisition assuming its initial cash payment to the former owners was

a. $700,000.

b. $800,000.

LO 2-4, 2-5, 2-6b, 2-7

27. On June 30, 2023, Wisconsin, Inc., issued $300,000 in debt and 15,000 new shares of its $10 par value stock to Badger Company owners in exchange for all of the outstanding shares of that company. Wisconsin shares had a fair value of $40 per share. Prior to the combination, the financial statements for Wisconsin and Badger for the six-month period ending June 30, 2023, were as follows (credit balances in parentheses):

	Wisconsin	Badger
Revenues	$ (900,000)	$ (300,000)
Expenses	660,000	200,000
Net income	$ (240,000)	$ (100,000)
Retained earnings, 1/1	$ (800,000)	$ (200,000)
Net income	(240,000)	(100,000)
Dividends declared	90,000	–0–
Retained earnings, 6/30	$ (950,000)	$ (300,000)
Cash	$ 80,000	$ 110,000
Receivables and inventory	400,000	170,000
Patented technology (net)	900,000	300,000
Equipment (net)	700,000	600,000
Total assets	$ 2,080,000	$ 1,180,000
Liabilities	$ (500,000)	$ (410,000)
Common stock	(360,000)	(200,000)
Additional paid-in capital	(270,000)	(270,000)
Retained earnings	(950,000)	(300,000)
Total liabilities and equities	$(2,080,000)	$(1,180,000)

Wisconsin also paid $30,000 to a broker for arranging the transaction. In addition, Wisconsin paid $40,000 in stock issuance costs. Badger's equipment was actually worth $700,000, but its patented technology was valued at only $280,000.

What are the consolidated balances for the following accounts?

a. Net income

b. Retained earnings, 1/1/23

c. Patented technology

d. Goodwill

e. Liabilities

f. Common stock

g. Additional paid-in capital

LO 2-4, 2-7

28. On January 1, 2024, Casey Corporation exchanged $3,300,000 cash for 100 percent of the outstanding voting stock of Kennedy Corporation. Casey plans to maintain Kennedy as a wholly owned subsidiary with separate legal status and accounting information systems.

At the acquisition date, Casey prepared the following fair-value allocation schedule:

Fair value of Kennedy (consideration transferred)		$3,300,000
Carrying amount acquired		2,600,000
Excess fair value		$ 700,000
to buildings (undervalued)	$ 382,000	
to licensing agreements (overvalued)	(108,000)	274,000
to goodwill (indefinite life)		$ 426,000

Immediately after closing the transaction, Casey and Kennedy prepared the following postacquisition balance sheets from their separate financial records (credit balances in parentheses).

Accounts	Casey	Kennedy
Cash	$ 457,000	$ 172,500
Accounts receivable	1,655,000	347,000
Inventory	1,310,000	263,500
Investment in Kennedy	3,300,000	–0–
Buildings (net)	6,315,000	2,090,000
Licensing agreements	–0–	3,070,000
Goodwill	347,000	–0–
Total assets	$13,384,000	$5,943,000
Accounts payable	$ (394,000)	$ (393,000)
Long-term debt	(3,990,000)	(2,950,000)
Common stock	(3,000,000)	(1,000,000)
Additional paid-in capital	–0–	(500,000)
Retained earnings	(6,000,000)	(1,100,000)
Total liabilities and equities	$(13,384,000)	$(5,943,000)

Prepare an acquisition-date consolidated balance sheet for Casey Corporation and its subsidiary Kennedy Corporation.

LO 2-4, 2-5, 2-6b, 2-6c, 2-7

29. On January 1, 2024, Presidio Company acquired 100 percent of the outstanding common stock of Mason Company. To acquire these shares, Presidio issued to the owners of Mason $200,000 in long-term liabilities and 20,000 shares of common stock having a par value of $1 per share but a fair value of $10 per share. Presidio paid $30,000 to accountants, lawyers, and brokers for assistance in the acquisition and another $12,000 in connection with stock issuance costs.

Prior to these transactions, the balance sheets for the two companies were as follows:

	Presidio Company	Mason Company
Cash	$ 60,000	$ 20,000
Receivables	270,000	90,000
Inventory	360,000	140,000
Land	200,000	180,000
Buildings (net)	420,000	220,000
Equipment (net)	160,000	50,000
Accounts payable	(150,000)	(40,000)
Long-term liabilities	(430,000)	(200,000)
Common stock—$1 par value	(110,000)	
Common stock—$20 par value		(120,000)
Additional paid-in capital	(360,000)	–0–
Retained earnings, 1/1/24	(420,000)	(340,000)

Note: Parentheses indicate a credit balance.

Presidio's appraisal of Mason's fair values deemed three accounts to be undervalued: Inventory by $5,000, Land by $20,000, and Buildings by $30,000. Presidio plans to maintain Mason's separate legal identity and to operate Mason as a wholly owned subsidiary.

a. Prepare Presidio's journal entries to record its acquisition of Mason, related professional fees paid, and stock acquisition costs.

b. Separately determine each individual amount that Presidio Company would report in its consolidated balance sheet following the acquisition of Mason. Include in Presidio's retained earnings any adjustments to income accounts from part (a).

c. To verify the answers found in part (b), adjust Presidio's column of accounts for the journal entries in part (a) and then prepare a worksheet to consolidate the balance sheets of these two companies at the acquisition date.

LO 2-4, 2-5, 2-7, 2-8

30. Pratt Company acquired all of the outstanding shares of Spider, Inc., on December 31, 2024, for $495,000 cash. Pratt will operate Spider as a wholly owned subsidiary with a separate legal and accounting identity. Although many of Spider's book values approximate fair values, several of its accounts have fair values that differ from book values. In addition, Spider has internally developed assets that remain unrecorded on its books. In deriving the acquisition price, Pratt assessed Spider's fair and book value differences as follows:

	Book Values	Fair Values
Computer software	$ 20,000	$ 70,000
Equipment	40,000	30,000
Client contracts	–0–	100,000
In-process research and development	–0–	40,000
Notes payable	(60,000)	(65,000)

At December 31, 2024, the following financial information is available for consolidation (credit balances in parentheses):

	Pratt	Spider
Cash	$ 36,000	$ 18,000
Receivables	116,000	52,000
Inventory	140,000	90,000
Investment in Spider	495,000	–0–
Computer software	210,000	20,000
Buildings (net)	595,000	130,000
Equipment (net)	308,000	40,000
Client contracts	–0–	–0–
Goodwill	–0–	–0–
Total assets	$1,900,000	$350,000
Accounts payable	$ (88,000)	$ (25,000)
Notes payable	(510,000)	(60,000)
Common stock	(380,000)	(100,000)
Additional paid-in capital	(170,000)	(25,000)
Retained earnings	(752,000)	(140,000)
Total liabilities and equities	$(1,900,000)	$(350,000)

Prepare a consolidated balance sheet for Pratt and Spider as of December 31, 2024.

LO 2-4, 2-5, 2-6a

31. Allerton Company acquires all of Deluxe Company's assets and liabilities for cash on January 1, 2024, and subsequently formally dissolves Deluxe. At the acquisition date, the following book and fair values were available for the Deluxe Company accounts:

	Book Values	Fair Values
Current assets	$ 60,000	$ 60,000
Building	90,000	50,000
Land	10,000	20,000
Trademark	–0–	30,000
Goodwill	15,000	?
Liabilities	(40,000)	(40,000)
Common stock	(100,000)	
Retained earnings	(35,000)	

Prepare Allerton's journal entry to record its acquisition of Deluxe in its accounting records assuming the following cash exchange amounts:

a. $145,000.

b. $110,000.

LO 2-4, 2-5, 2-6a, 2-6b

32. On June 30, 2024, Sundown Company reported the following account balances:

Receivables	$ 83,900	Current liabilities	$ (12,900)
Inventory	70,250	Long-term liabilities	(54,250)
Buildings (net)	78,900	Common stock	(90,000)
Equipment (net)	24,100	Retained earnings	(100,000)
Total assets	$257,150	Total liabilities and equities	$(257,150)

On June 30, 2024, Pelcore Company paid $310,800 cash for all assets and liabilities of Sundown, which will cease to exist as a separate entity. In connection with the acquisition, Pelcore paid $15,100 in legal fees. Pelcore also agreed to pay $55,600 to the former owners of Sundown contingent on meeting certain revenue goals during 2025. Pelcore estimated the present value of its probability adjusted expected payment for the contingency at $17,900.

In determining its offer, Pelcore noted the following pertaining to Sundown:

- It holds a building with a fair value $43,100 more than its book value.
- It has developed a database appraised at $25,200, although it is not recorded in its financial records.
- It has research and development activity in process with an appraised fair value of $36,400. However, the project has not yet reached technological feasibility, and the assets used in the activity have no alternative future use.
- Book values for the receivables, inventory, equipment, and liabilities approximate fair values.

Prepare Pelcore's accounting entries to record the combination with Sundown.

LO 2-4, 2-5, 2-8, 2-6b

33. Sandstone Corporation has the following account balances and respective fair values on June 30:

	Book Values	Fair Values
Receivables	$ 80,000	$ 80,000
Patented technology	100,000	700,000
Computer software	–0–	500,000
In-process research and development	–0–	300,000
Liabilities	(400,000)	(400,000)
Common stock	(100,000)	
Additional paid-in capital	(300,000)	
Retained earnings deficit, 1/1	700,000	
Revenues	(300,000)	
Expenses	220,000	

Patriot, Inc., obtained all of the outstanding shares of Sandstone on June 30 by issuing 20,000 shares of common stock having a $1 par value but a $75 fair value. Patriot incurred $10,000 in stock issuance costs and paid $75,000 to an investment banking firm for its assistance in arranging the combination. In negotiating the final terms of the deal, Patriot also agrees to pay $100,000 to Sandstone's former owners if it achieves certain revenue goals in the next two years. Patriot estimates the probability adjusted present value of this contingent performance obligation at $30,000.

a. What is the fair value of the consideration transferred in this combination?

b. How should the stock issuance costs appear in Patriot's postcombination financial statements?

c. How should Patriot account for the fee paid to the investment bank?

d. How does the issuance of these shares affect the stockholders' equity accounts of Patriot, the parent?

e. How is the fair value of the consideration transferred in the combination allocated among the assets acquired and the liabilities assumed?

f. What is the effect of Sandstone's revenues and expenses on consolidated totals? Why?

g. What is the effect of Sandstone's Common Stock and Additional Paid-In Capital balances on consolidated totals?

h. If Patriot's stock had been worth only $50 per share rather than $75, how would the consolidation of Sandstone's assets and liabilities have been affected?

LO 2-4, 2-5, 2-6a, 2-6b, 2-6c, 2-7, 2-8

34. On January 1, NewTune Company exchanges 15,000 shares of its common stock for all of the outstanding shares of On-the-Go, Inc. Each of NewTune's shares has a $4 par value and a $50 fair value. The fair value of the stock exchanged in the acquisition was considered equal to On-the-Go's fair value. NewTune also paid $25,000 in stock registration and issuance costs in connection with the merger. Several of On-the-Go's accounts' fair values differ from their book values on this date (credit balances in parentheses):

	Book Values	Fair Values
Receivables	$65,000	$ 63,000
Trademarks	95,000	225,000
Record music catalog	60,000	180,000
In-process research and development	–0–	200,000
Notes payable	(50,000)	(45,000)

Precombination book values for the two companies are as follows:

	NewTune	On-the-Go
Cash	$ 60,000	$ 29,000
Receivables	150,000	65,000
Trademarks	400,000	95,000
Record music catalog	840,000	60,000
Equipment (net)	320,000	105,000
Totals	$ 1,770,000	$ 354,000
Accounts payable	$ (110,000)	$ (34,000)
Notes payable	(370,000)	(50,000)
Common stock	(400,000)	(50,000)
Additional paid-in capital	(30,000)	(30,000)
Retained earnings	(860,000)	(190,000)
Totals	$(1,770,000)	$(354,000)

a. Assume that this combination is a statutory merger so that On-the-Go's accounts will be transferred to the records of NewTune. On-the-Go will be dissolved and will no longer exist as a legal entity. Prepare a postcombination balance sheet for NewTune as of the acquisition date.

b. Assume that no dissolution takes place in connection with this combination. Rather, both companies retain their separate legal identities. Prepare a worksheet to consolidate the two companies as of the combination date.

c. How do the balance sheet accounts compare across parts (a) and (b)?

LO 2-4, 2-5, 2-6b, 2-6c, 2-7

35. On December 31, Pacifica, Inc., acquired 100 percent of the voting stock of Seguros Company. Pacifica will maintain Seguros as a wholly owned subsidiary with its own legal and accounting identity. The consideration transferred to the owner of Seguros included 50,000 newly issued Pacifica common shares ($20 market value, $5 par value) and an agreement to pay an additional $130,000 cash if Seguros meets certain project completion goals by December 31 of the following year. Pacifica estimates a 50 percent probability that Seguros will be successful in meeting these goals and uses a 4 percent discount rate to represent the time value of money.

Immediately prior to the acquisition, the following data for both firms were available:

	Pacifica	Seguros Book Values	Seguros Fair Values
Revenues	$(1,200,000)		
Expenses	875,000		
Net income	$ (325,000)		
Retained earnings, 1/1	$ (950,000)		
Net income	(325,000)		
Dividends declared	90,000		
Retained earnings, 12/31	$(1,185,000)		

(*continued*)

(*continued*)

	Pacifica	Seguros Book Values	Seguros Fair Values
Cash	$ 110,000	$ 85,000	$ 85,000
Receivables and inventory	750,000	190,000	180,000
Property, plant, and equipment	1,400,000	450,000	600,000
Trademarks	300,000	160,000	200,000
Total assets	$ 2,560,000	$ 885,000	
Liabilities	$ (500,000)	$ (180,000)	$ (180,000)
Common stock	(400,000)	(200,000)	
Additional paid-in capital	(475,000)	(70,000)	
Retained earnings	(1,185,000)	(435,000)	
Total liabilities and equities	$ (2,560,000)	$ (885,000)	

In addition, Pacifica assessed a research and development project under way at Seguros to have a fair value of $100,000. Although not yet recorded on its books, Pacifica paid legal fees of $15,000 in connection with the acquisition and $9,000 in stock issue costs.

Prepare the following:

a. Pacifica's journal entries to record the consideration transferred to the former owners of Seguros, the direct combination costs, and the stock issue and registration costs. (Use a 0.961538 present value factor where applicable.)

b. A postacquisition column of accounts for Pacifica.

c. A worksheet to produce a consolidated balance sheet as of the acquisition date.

LO 2-4, 2-7, 2-8

36. On January 1, 2024, James Corporation exchanged $3,050,000 cash for 100 percent of the outstanding voting stock of Johnson Corporation. James plans to maintain Johnson as a wholly owned subsidiary with separate legal status and accounting information systems.

At the acquisition date, James prepared the following fair-value allocation schedule:

Consideration transferred for Johnson Corporation		$3,050,000
Johnson's carrying amount	$2,300,000	
Less: Johnson's preexisting goodwill........................	(75,000)	
Identifiable net assets carrying amount		2,225,000
Excess consideration transferred over carrying amount		$ 825,000
of identifiable net assets		
to Johnson's patents (undervalued)		800,000
to new goodwill from Johnson acquisition (indefinite life) ...		$ 25,000

Immediately after closing the transaction, James and Johnson prepared the following postacquisition balance sheets from their separate financial records.

Accounts	James	Johnson
Cash	$ 245,000	$ 110,000
Accounts receivable	1,830,000	360,000
Inventory	3,500,000	280,000
Investment in Johnson	3,050,000	–0–
Patents	7,000,000	1,000,000
Trademarks	–0–	3,200,000
Goodwill	150,000	75,000
Total assets	$ 15,775,000	$ 5,025,000
Accounts payable	$ (100,000)	$ (515,000)
Long-term debt	(4,300,000)	(2,210,000)
Common stock	(5,000,000)	(1,000,000)
Additional paid-in capital	–0–	(200,000)
Retained earnings	(6,375,000)	(1,100,000)
Total liabilities and equities	$ (15,775,000)	$ (5,025,000)

Prepare an acquisition-date consolidated balance sheet for James Corporation and its subsidiary Johnson Corporation.

Appendix 2A Problems

LO 2-9

37. In a pre-2009 business combination, Acme Company acquired all of Brem Company's assets and liabilities for cash. After the combination, Acme formally dissolved Brem. At the acquisition date, the following book and fair values were available for the Brem Company accounts:

	Book Values	Fair Values
Current assets	$ 80,000	$ 80,000
Equipment	120,000	180,000
Trademark	–0–	320,000
Liabilities	(55,000)	(55,000)
Common stock	(100,000)	
Retained earnings	(45,000)	

In addition, Acme paid an investment bank $25,000 cash for assistance in arranging the combination.

a. Using the legacy purchase method for pre-2009 business combinations, prepare Acme's entry to record its acquisition of Brem in its accounting records assuming the following cash amounts were paid to the former owners of Brem:

1. $610,000.
2. $425,000.

b. How would these journal entries change if the acquisition occurred post-2009 and therefore Acme applied the acquisition method?

LO 2-9

38. On February 1, Piscina Corporation completed a combination with Swimwear Company. At that date, Swimwear's account balances were as follows:

	Book Values	Fair Values
Inventory	$ 600,000	$ 650,000
Land	450,000	750,000
Buildings	900,000	1,000,000
Unpatented technology	–0–	1,500,000
Common stock ($10 par value)	(750,000)	
Retained earnings, 1/1	(1,100,000)	
Revenues	(600,000)	
Expenses	500,000	

Piscina issued 30,000 shares of its common stock with a par value of $25 and a fair value of $150 per share to the owners of Swimwear for all of their Swimwear shares. Upon completion of the combination, Swimwear Company was formally dissolved.

Prior to 2002, business combinations were accounted for using either purchase or pooling of interests accounting. The two methods often produced substantially different financial statement effects. For this scenario,

a. What are the respective consolidated values for Swimwear's assets under the pooling method and the purchase method?

b. Under each of the following methods, how would Piscina account for Swimwear's current year, but prior to acquisition, revenues, and expenses?
   • Pooling of interests method
   • Purchase method

c. Explain the alternative impact of pooling versus purchase accounting on performance ratios such as return on assets and earnings per share in periods subsequent to the combination.

Appendix 2B Problems

LO 2-10

39. What is pushdown accounting?

   a. A requirement that a subsidiary must use the same accounting principles as a parent company

   b. Inventory transfers made from a parent company to a subsidiary

   c. A subsidiary's recording of the fair-value allocations as well as subsequent amortization

   d. The adjustments required for consolidation when a parent has applied the equity method of accounting for internal reporting purposes

LO 2-10

40. On May 1, Burns Corporation acquired 100 percent of the outstanding ownership shares of Quigley Corporation in exchange for $710,000 cash. At the acquisition date, Quigley's book and fair values were as follows:

	Book Values	Fair Values
Cash	$ 95,000	$ 95,000
Receivables	200,000	200,000
Inventory	210,000	260,000
Land	130,000	110,000
Building and equipment (net)	270,000	330,000
Patented technology	–0–	220,000
Total assets	$905,000	$1,215,000
Accounts payable	$120,000	$ 120,000
Long-term liabilities	510,000	510,000
Common stock ($5 par value)	210,000	
Additional paid-in capital	90,000	
Retained earnings	(25,000)	
Total liabilities and stockholders equity	$905,000	

Burns directs Quigley to seek additional financing for expansion through a new long-term debt issue. Consequently, Quigley will issue a set of financial statements separate from that of its new parent to support its request for debt and accompanying regulatory filings. Quigley elects to apply pushdown accounting in order to show recent fair valuations for its assets.

Prepare a separate acquisition-date balance sheet for Quigley Corporation using pushdown accounting.

Develop Your Skills

FASB ASC RESEARCH AND ANALYSIS CASE— CONSIDERATION OR COMPENSATION?

CPA *skills*

AutoNav Company agrees to pay $20 million in cash to the four former owners of Easy-C, Inc., for all of its assets and liabilities. These four owners of Easy-C developed and patented a technology for real-time monitoring of traffic patterns on the nation's top 200 frequently congested highways. AutoNav plans to combine the new technology with its existing global positioning systems and projects a resulting substantial revenue increase.

As part of the acquisition contract, AutoNav also agrees to pay additional amounts to the former owners upon achievement of certain financial goals. AutoNav will pay $8 million to the four former owners of Easy-C if revenues from the combined system exceed $100 million over the next three years. AutoNav estimates this contingent payment to have a probability adjusted present value of $4 million.

The four former owners have also been offered employment contracts with AutoNav to help with system integration and performance enhancement issues. The employment contracts are silent as to service periods, have nominal salaries similar to those of equivalent employees, and specify a profit-sharing component over the next three years (if the employees remain with the company) that AutoNav estimates to have a current fair value of $2 million. The four former owners of Easy-C say they will stay on as employees of AutoNav for at least three years to help achieve the desired financial goals.

Should AutoNav account for the contingent payments promised to the former owners of Easy-C as consideration transferred in the acquisition or as compensation expense to employees?

ASC RESEARCH CASE—DEFENSIVE INTANGIBLE ASSET

ComWire Company manufactures wireless transponders for satellite applications. ComWire has recently acquired Martin Company, which is primarily known for its software communications development but also manufactures a specialty transponder under the trade name "M-Tech" that competes with one of ComWire's products. ComWire will now discontinue M-Tech and projects that its own product line will see a market share increase. Nonetheless, ComWire's management will maintain the rights to the M-Tech trade name as a defensive intangible asset to prevent its use by competitors, despite the fact that its highest and best use would be to sell the trade name. ComWire estimates that the trade name has an internal value of $1.5 million but, if sold, would yield $2 million.

Answer the following with supporting citations from the FASB ASC:

a. How does the FASB ASC Glossary define a defensive intangible asset?

b. According to ASC Topic 805, "Business Combinations," what is the measurement principle that an acquirer should follow in recording identifiable assets acquired in a business combination?

c. According to ASC Topic 820, "Fair Value Measurement," what value premise (in-use or in-exchange) should ComWire assign to the M-Tech trade name in its consolidated financial statements?

d. According to ASC Topic 350, "General Intangibles Other Than Goodwill," how should ComWire determine the estimated useful life of its defensive intangible asset?

RESEARCH CASE—PELOTON'S ACQUISITION OF PRECOR

On April 1, 2021, Peloton Interactive (Peloton) acquired Precor, Inc. Access Peloton's 2021 financial statements and media reports near the time of the acquisition, and answer the following questions:

1. Why did Peloton acquire Precor?

2. How did Peloton account for the Precor acquisition?

3. What amount of goodwill did Peloton recognize in the combination? Prepare a schedule that computes the goodwill recognized in the acquisition as the difference between the consideration transferred for Precor and the fair values of the individually identified assets and liabilities acquired.

4. What were the acquisition-related costs Peloton incurred regarding the combination, and how were these costs accounted for?

5. How did Peloton report the Precor acquisition in its 2021 statement of cash flows?

RESEARCH CASE—ANALOG DEVICES'S ACQUISITION OF MAXIM INTEGRATED PRODUCTS

On August 26, 2021, Analog Devices, Inc. (Analog), announced it had acquired all of the outstanding stock of Maxim Integrated Products, Inc. (Maxim), in exchange for $29.9 billion primarily in stock to the stockholders of Maxim. Referring to Analog's 2021 financial statements and any media coverage, answer the following questions regarding the Maxim acquisition:

1. Why did Analog acquire Maxim?

2. What was the composition of the consideration transferred in the combination?

3. Analog included precombination service compensation (for acquisition-related equity awards) in the total consideration transferred. What support is provided for this treatment in the *Accounting Standards Codification*® (see ASC 805-30-30, paragraphs 9-13)?

4. What allocations did Analog make to the assets acquired and liabilities assumed in the acquisition? Provide a calculation showing how Analog determined the amount allocated to goodwill.

5. How will Analog account for the intangible assets acquired in the Maxim combination?

RESEARCH CASE—ANIKA THERAPEUTIC'S ACQUISITIONS OF PARCUS MEDICAL AND ARTHROSURFACE

Anika Therapeutics, Inc. (Anika), develops and manufactures products that help physicians treat patients with osteoarthritis and other joint issues. In 2020, Anika acquired Parcus Medical (Parcus) and Arthrosurface companies. Parcus is a sport medicine company focused on patient solutions for surgical repair and reconstruction of ligaments and tendons, while Arthrosurface specializes in joint surface and preservation solutions. Anika acquired each of these two companies in exchange for cash and contingent consideration. Referring to Anika's 2020 annual report, answer the following question regarding these acquisitions.

1. What is the maximum contingent payment amount to the former owners of Parcus Medical and Arthrosurface? What events determine whether the contingent payments will be paid?

2. What value for the contingent payments was included in the total for consideration transferred? How was this value determined?

3. Where were the contingent payments shown in Anika's 2020 consolidated balance sheet?

4. Identify and discuss some possible motivations to explain why Anika, Parcus Medical, and Arthrosurface agreed to contingent payments as part of the total consideration transferred in the acquisitions.

Consolidations— Subsequent to the Date of Acquisition

In 2017, Amazon.com, Inc., acquired all of the outstanding stock of Whole Foods Market, Inc., an upscale grocery store chain. Although this transaction involved well-known companies, it was not unique; mergers and acquisitions have long been common in the business world.

Amazon.com's current financial statements indicate that Whole Foods Market remains a component of this economic entity. However, Whole Foods Market, Inc., continues as a separate legally incorporated concern long after its acquisition. As discussed in Chapter 2, a parent will often maintain separate legal status for a subsidiary corporation to better utilize its inherent value as a going concern.

For external reporting purposes, maintenance of incorporation creates an ongoing challenge for the accountant. In each subsequent period, consolidation must be simulated anew through the use of a worksheet and consolidation entries. Thus, for many years, the financial data for Amazon.com and Whole Foods Market (along with dozens of other subsidiaries) have been brought together periodically to provide figures for the financial statements that represent this business combination.

As also discussed in Chapter 2, the acquisition method governs the way we initially record a business combination. In periods subsequent to acquisition, the fair-value bases (established at the acquisition date) for subsidiary assets acquired and liabilities assumed will be amortized (or tested for possible impairment) for proper income recognition. Additionally, some combinations require accounting for the eventual disposition of contingent consideration, which is typically resolved with the passage of time.

In the next several sections of this chapter, we present the procedures to prepare consolidated financial statements in the years subsequent to acquisition. We start by analyzing the relation between the parent's internal accounting method for its subsidiary investment and the adjustments required in consolidation. We also examine the specific procedures for amortizing the acquisition-date fair-value adjustments to the subsidiary's assets and liabilities. We then cover testing for goodwill impairment and postacquisition accounting for contingent consideration. Finally, an appendix presents the alternative goodwill model available as a reporting option for private companies.

Learning Objectives

After studying this chapter, you should be able to:

LO 3-1 Recognize the complexities in preparing consolidated financial reports that emerge from the passage of time.

LO 3-2 Identify and describe the various methods a parent company may select for its Investment in Subsidiary account in its internal records.

LO 3-3 Prepare consolidated financial statements subsequent to acquisition when the parent has applied in its internal records:

   a. The equity method.

   b. The initial value method.

   c. The partial equity method.

LO 3-4 Understand that a parent's internal accounting method for its subsidiary investments has no effect on the resulting consolidated financial statements.

LO 3-5 Discuss the rationale for the goodwill impairment testing approach.

LO 3-6 Describe the procedures for conducting a goodwill impairment test.

LO 3-7 Describe the rationale and procedures for impairment testing for intangible assets other than goodwill.

LO 3-8 Understand the accounting and reporting for contingent consideration subsequent to a business acquisition.

LO 3-9 Appendix: Describe the alternative accounting treatments for goodwill and other intangible assets available for business combinations by private companies.

LO 3-1

Recognize the complexities in preparing consolidated financial reports that emerge from the passage of time.

Consolidation—The Effects Created by the Passage of Time

In Chapter 2, consolidation accounting is analyzed at the date that a combination is created. The present chapter carries this process one step further by examining the consolidation procedures that must be followed in subsequent periods whenever separate incorporation of the subsidiary is maintained.

Despite complexities created by the passage of time, the basic objective of all consolidations remains the same: to combine asset, liability, revenue, expense, and equity accounts of a parent and its subsidiaries. From a mechanical perspective, a worksheet and consolidation entries continue to provide structure for the production of a single set of financial statements for the combined business entity.

Consolidated Net Income Determination

Subsequent to an acquisition, the parent company reports its net income on a consolidated basis. Consolidated income determination involves first combining the separately recorded revenues and expenses of the parent with those of the subsidiary on a consolidated worksheet. Because of separate recordkeeping systems, however, the subsidiary's expenses typically are based on their original book values and not the acquisition-date values the parent must recognize. Consequently, adjustments are made that reflect the amortization of the excess of the parent's consideration transferred over the subsidiary book value. Additionally, the effects of any intra-entity transactions are removed.

Over time the parent, in its own financial records, recognizes income from its subsidiary. Consequently, as part of the consolidation process, it is necessary to remove that income figure each period so that (1) the subsidiary's revenues and expenses can separately be included when creating an income statement for the combined business entity, and (2) to avoid double-counting the subsidiary's income.

The Parent's Choice of Investment Accounting

The time factor introduces other complications into the consolidation process as well. For internal recordkeeping purposes, the parent must select and apply an accounting method to monitor the relationship between the two companies. The investment balance recorded by the parent varies over time as a result of the method chosen, as does the income subsequently recognized. These differences affect the periodic consolidation process but not the figures to be reported by the combined entity. Regardless of the amount, the parent's investment account is eliminated (brought to a zero balance) on the worksheet so that the subsidiary's actual assets and liabilities can be consolidated.

LO 3-2

Identify and describe the various methods a parent company may select for its Investment in Subsidiary account in its internal records.

Investment Accounting by the Acquiring Company

For a parent company's external financial reporting, consolidation of a subsidiary becomes necessary whenever control exists. For internal recordkeeping, though, the parent has a choice for monitoring the activities of its subsidiaries. Although several variations occur in practice, three methods have emerged as the most prominent: the **equity method,** the **initial value method,**[1] and the **partial equity method.**

At the acquisition date, each investment accounting method (equity, initial value, and partial equity) begins with an identical value recorded in an investment account. Typically the fair value of the consideration transferred by the parent will serve as the recorded valuation basis

---

[1] The initial value method is sometimes referred to as the cost method.

on the parent's books.[2] Subsequent to the acquisition date, however, the three methods produce different amounts on the parent company's accounting records for the following:

- Investment in subsidiary
- Income recognized from the subsidiary's activities
- Retained earnings

Importantly, the selection of a particular method does not affect the totals ultimately reported for the combined companies. Nonetheless, the parent's choice of an internal accounting method does lead to distinct procedures for consolidating financial information from the separate organizations.

Internal Investment Accounting Alternatives—The Equity Method, Initial Value Method, and Partial Equity Method

The internal reporting philosophy of the acquiring company often determines the accounting method choice for its subsidiary investment. Depending on the measures a company uses to assess the ongoing performances of its subsidiaries, parent companies may choose their own preferred internal reporting method. Regardless of this choice, however, the investment balance will be eliminated in preparing consolidated financial statements for external reporting.

The Equity Method

The equity method embraces full accrual accounting in maintaining the parent's investment in subsidiary account and related income over time. Under the equity method, the parent company accrues its share of subsidiary income in the same period when the subsidiary earns it. To match the additional fair values recorded in the combination against income, amortization expense stemming from the acquisition-date excess fair-value allocations is recognized through periodic adjusting entries. Unrealized gross profits on intra-entity transactions are deferred; subsidiary dividends serve to reduce the investment account balance. As discussed in Chapter 1, the equity method creates a parallel between the parent's investment accounts and changes in the underlying equity of the acquired company.[3]

When the parent has complete ownership, equity method earnings from the subsidiary, combined with the parent's other income sources, create a total income figure reflective of the entire combined business entity. Consequently, the equity method often is referred to as a single-line consolidation. The equity method is especially popular in companies where management periodically (e.g., monthly or quarterly) measures each subsidiary's profitability using accrual-based income figures.

The Initial Value Method

Under the initial value method, the investment balance remains on the parent's financial records at the initial fair value assigned at the acquisition date. In contrast to the equity method, the initial value method does not recognize income as it is earned by the subsidiary. Instead, the parent recognizes dividend income from its share of any subsidiary dividends when declared. Because little time typically elapses between dividend declaration and cash distribution, the initial value method frequently reflects the cash basis for income recognition.

A parent might select the initial value method because it does not require an accrual-based income measure of subsidiary performance. For example, the parent may wish to assess subsidiary performance on its ability to generate cash flows, on revenues generated, or some other nonincome basis. Also, some firms may find the initial value method's ease of application attractive. Because the investment account is eliminated in consolidation, and the actual

---

[2] In the unusual case of a bargain purchase, the valuation basis for the investment account is the fair value of the net amount of the assets acquired and liabilities assumed.

[3] In Chapter 1, the equity method was introduced in connection with the external reporting of investments in which the owner held the ability to apply significant influence over the investee (usually by possessing 20 to 50 percent of the company's voting stock). Here, the equity method is utilized for the internal reporting of the parent for investments in which control is maintained. Although the accounting procedures are similar, the reason for using the equity method is different.

Discussion Question

HOW DOES A COMPANY REALLY DECIDE WHICH INVESTMENT METHOD TO APPLY?

Pilgrim Products, Inc., buys a controlling interest in the common stock of Crestwood Corporation. Shortly after the acquisition, a meeting of Pilgrim's accounting department is convened to discuss the internal reporting procedures required by the ownership of this subsidiary. Each member of the staff has a definite opinion as to whether the equity method, initial value method, or partial equity method should be adopted. To resolve this issue, Pilgrim's chief financial officer outlines several of her concerns about the decision.

I already understand how each method works. I know the general advantages and disadvantages of all three. I realize, for example, that the equity method provides more detailed information, whereas the initial value method is much easier to apply. What I need to know are the factors specific to our situation that should be considered in deciding which method to adopt. I must make a recommendation to the president on this matter, and he will want firm reasons for my favoring a particular approach. I don't want us to select a method and then find out in six months that the information is not adequate for our needs or that the cost of adapting our system to monitor Crestwood outweighs the benefits derived from the data.

What are the factors that Pilgrim's officials should evaluate when making this decision?

subsidiary revenues and expenses are eventually combined, firms may avoid the complexity of the equity method unless they need the specific information provided by the equity income measure for internal decision making.

The Partial Equity Method

A third method available to the acquiring company is a partial application of the equity method. Similar to the equity method, the parent company accrues its share of subsidiary income in the same period when the subsidiary earns it. Also, like the equity method, subsidiary dividends declared reduce the investment balance. However, no other equity adjustments (e.g., amortizations or deferrals of unrealized gross profits) are recorded. Thus, in many cases, income from applying the partial equity method, along with the parent's other income, approximates consolidated net income but without the effort associated with a full application of the equity method.

Moreover, some parent companies rely on internally designed performance measures (rather than GAAP net income) to evaluate subsidiary management or to make resource allocation decisions. For such companies, a full equity method application may be unnecessary for internal purposes. In these cases, the partial equity method, although only approximating the GAAP net income measure, may be sufficient for decision making.

Summary of Internal Investment Accounting Methods

Exhibit 3.1 summarizes the three internal accounting techniques. Importantly, the method the acquiring company adopts affects only its separate financial records and has no impact on the subsidiary's balances. Regardless of the parent's choice of internally accounting for its subsidiary, the particular method selected (i.e., initial value, equity, or partial equity) has no effect on the amounts ultimately reported on consolidated financial statements to external users.

EXHIBIT 3.1 **Internal Reporting of Investment Accounts by Acquiring Company**

Method	Investment Account	Income Account	Advantages
Equity	Continually adjusted to reflect current owner's equity of acquired company.	Income accrued as earned; amortizations and other adjustments are recognized.	Acquiring company totals give a true representation of consolidation figures.
Initial value	Remains at acquisition-date value assigned.	Dividends declared recorded as Dividend Income.	It is easy to apply; it often reflects cash flows from the subsidiary.
Partial equity	Adjusted only for accrued income and dividends declared by the acquired company.	Income accrued as earned; no other adjustments recognized.	It usually gives balances approximating consolidation figures, but it is easier to apply than the equity method.

Because specific worksheet procedures differ depending on the investment method utilized by the parent, the consolidation process subsequent to the date of combination will be introduced twice. First, we review consolidations in which the acquiring company uses the equity method. Then we redevelop all procedures when the investment is recorded by one of the alternative methods.

LO 3-3a

Prepare consolidated financial statements subsequent to acquisition when the parent has applied **the equity method** in its internal records.

Subsequent Consolidation—Investment Recorded by the Equity Method

Acquisition Made during the Current Year

As a basis for this illustration, assume that Parrot Company obtains all of the outstanding common stock of Sun Company on January 1, 2023. Parrot acquires this stock for $800,000 in cash.

The book values as well as the appraised fair values of Sun's accounts follow:

	Book Values 1/1/23	Fair Values 1/1/23	Difference
Current assets	$ 320,000	$320,000	$ –0–
Trademarks (indefinite life).	200,000	220,000	+ 20,000
Patented technology 10-year remaining life)	320,000	450,000	+130,000
Equipment (5-year remaining life).	180,000	150,000	(30,000)
Liabilities	(420,000)	(420,000)	–0–
Net book value.	$600,000	$720,000	$120,000
Common stock—$40 par value.	$(200,000)		
Additional paid-in capital	(20,000)		
Retained earnings, 1/1/23	(380,000)		

Parrot considers the economic life of Sun's trademarks as extending beyond the foreseeable future and thus having an indefinite life. Such assets are not amortized but are subject to periodic impairment testing.[4] For the definite-lived assets acquired in the combination (patented technology and equipment), we assume that straight-line amortization and depreciation with no salvage value is appropriate.[5]

Parrot paid $800,000 cash to acquire Sun Company, clear evidence of the fair value of the consideration transferred. This $800,000 consideration transferred becomes the acquisition-date subsidiary valuation basis for consolidated reporting purposes. As shown in Exhibit 3.2, after recognizing Sun's overall $600,000 book value, Parrot makes individual allocations

---

[4] In other cases, trademarks can have a definite life and thus would be subject to regular amortization.
[5] Unless otherwise stated, all amortization and depreciation expense computations in this textbook are based on the straight-line method with no salvage value.

totaling $200,000 to adjust Sun's accounts from their book values to their acquisition-date collective $800,000 net fair value. Because the total net fair value of Sun's *identifiable* assets and liabilities was only $720,000, Parrot recognizes *goodwill* of $80,000 for consolidation purposes.

Note that the Exhibit 3.2 adjustments to patented technology and equipment represent valuations associated with a definite life. As discussed in Chapter 1, under the equity method Parrot must amortize each allocation over its expected life. The expense recognition necessitated by this fair-value allocation is calculated in Exhibit 3.3.

Two aspects of this amortization schedule warrant further explanation. First, we use the term *amortization* in a generic sense to include both the amortization of definite-lived intangibles and depreciation of tangible assets. Second, the acquisition-date fair value of Sun's equipment is $30,000 *less* than its book value. Therefore, instead of attributing an additional amount to this asset, the $30,000 allocation actually reflects a fair-value reduction. As such, the amortization shown in Exhibit 3.3 relating to Equipment is not an additional expense but instead is an expense reduction.

Having determined the allocation of the acquisition-date fair value in the previous example as well as the associated amortization, the parent's separate recordkeeping for its first year of Sun Company ownership can be constructed. Assume that Sun earns income of $100,000 during the year, declares a $40,000 cash dividend on August 1, and pays the dividend on August 8.

In this first illustration, Parrot has adopted the equity method. Apparently, this company believes that the information derived from using the equity method is useful in its evaluation of Sun.

EXHIBIT 3.2
Excess Fair-Value Allocation

PARROT COMPANY
100 Percent Acquisition of Sun Company
Allocation of Acquisition-Date Subsidiary Fair Value
January 1, 2023

Sun Company fair value (consideration transferred by Parrot Company)		$800,000
Book value of Sun Company:		
Common stock	$200,000	
Additional paid-in capital	20,000	
Retained earnings, 1/1/23	380,000	(600,000)
Excess of fair value over book value		200,000
Allocation to specific accounts based on fair values:		
Trademarks	$ 20,000	
Patented technology	130,000	
Equipment (overvalued)	(30,000)	120,000
Excess fair value not identified with specific accounts—goodwill		$ 80,000

EXHIBIT 3.3
Annual Excess Amortization

PARROT COMPANY
100 Percent Acquisition of Sun Company
Excess Amortization Schedule—Allocation of Acquisition-Date Fair Values

Account	Allocation	Remaining Useful Life	Annual Excess Amortizations
Trademarks	$ 20,000	Indefinite	$ –0–
Patented technology	130,000	10 years	13,000
Equipment	(30,000)	5 years	(6,000)
Goodwill*	80,000	Indefinite	–0–
			$ 7,000†

*As discussed in this chapter, the FASB is considering a requirement to amortize goodwill as a definite-lived asset.
†Total excess amortizations will be $7,000 annually for five years until the equipment allocation is fully removed. At the end of each asset's life, future amortizations will change.

Application of the Equity Method

	Parrot's Financial Records		
1/1/23	Investment in Sun Company.............................	800,000	
	Cash		800,000
	To record the acquisition of Sun Company.		
8/1/23	Dividend Receivable	40,000	
	Investment in Sun Company.......................		40,000
	To record cash dividend declaration from subsidiary.		
8/8/23	Cash	40,000	
	Dividend Receivable		40,000
	To record receipt of the subsidiary cash dividend.		
12/31/23	Investment in Sun Company.........................	100,000	
	Equity in Subsidiary Earnings		100,000
	To accrue income earned by 100 percent owned subsidiary.		
12/31/23	Equity in Subsidiary Earnings	7,000	
	Investment in Sun Company.......................		7,000
	To recognize amortizations on allocations made in acquisition of subsidiary (see Exhibit 3.3).		

Parrot's application of the equity method, as shown in this series of entries, causes the Investment in Sun Company account balance to rise from $800,000 to $853,000 ($800,000 − $40,000 + $100,000 − $7,000). During the same period, the parent recognizes a $93,000 equity income figure (the $100,000 earnings accrual less the $7,000 excess amortization expenses).

The consolidation procedures for Parrot and Sun one year after the date of acquisition are illustrated next. For this purpose, Exhibit 3.4 presents the separate 2023 financial statements for these two companies. Parrot recorded both investment-related accounts (the $853,000 asset balance and the $93,000 income accrual) based on applying the equity method.

EXHIBIT 3.4
Separate Records—Equity Method Applied

PARROT COMPANY AND SUN COMPANY
Financial Statements
For Year Ending December 31, 2023

	Parrot Company	Sun Company
Income Statement		
Revenues	$(1,500,000)	$ (400,000)
Cost of goods sold	700,000	232,000
Amortization expense	120,000	32,000
Depreciation expense	80,000	36,000
Equity in subsidiary earnings.....................	(93,000)	–0–
Net income	$ (693,000)	$ (100,000)
Statement of Retained Earnings		
Retained earnings, 1/1/23	$ (840,000)	$ (380,000)
Net income (above)................................	(693,000)	(100,000)
Dividends declared*	120,000	40,000
Retained earnings, 12/31/23	$(1,413,000)	$ (440,000)
Balance Sheet		
Current assets....................................	$ 1,040,000	$ 400,000
Investment in Sun Company (at equity)............	853,000	–0–
Trademarks	600,000	200,000
Patented technology	370,000	288,000
Equipment (net)...................................	250,000	220,000
Total assets...................................	$ 3,113,000	$ 1,108,000
Liabilities	$ (980,000)	$ (448,000)
Common stock	(600,000)	(200,000)
Additional paid-in capital.........................	(120,000)	(20,000)
Retained earnings, 12/31/23 (above)	(1,413,000)	(440,000)
Total liabilities and equity......................	$(3,113,000)	$(1,108,000)

Note: Parentheses indicate a credit balance.
*Dividends declared, whether currently paid or not, provide the appropriate amount to include in a statement of retained earnings. To help keep the number of worksheet rows (i.e., dividends payable and receivable) at a minimum, throughout this text we assume that dividends are declared and paid in the same period.

Determination of Consolidated Totals

Before becoming immersed in the mechanical aspects of a consolidation, the objective of this process should be understood. As indicated in Chapter 2, in the preparation of consolidated financial reports, the subsidiary's revenue, expense, asset, and liability accounts are added to the parent company balances. Within this procedure, several important guidelines must be followed:

- Sun's assets and liabilities are adjusted to reflect their acquisition-date fair-value allocations.
- Because of the passage of time, the income effects (e.g., amortizations) of these allocations must also be recognized within the consolidation process.
- Any reciprocal or intra-entity[6] accounts must be offset. If, for example, one of the companies owes money to the other, the receivable and the payable balances have no connection with an outside party. Thus, when the companies are viewed as a single consolidated entity, the receivable and the payable represent intra-entity balances that should be eliminated for external reporting purposes.

The consolidation of the two sets of financial information in Exhibit 3.4 is a relatively uncomplicated task and can even be carried out without the use of a worksheet. Understanding the origin of each reported figure is the first step in gaining a knowledge of this process.

- *Revenues* = $1,900,000. The revenues of the parent and the subsidiary are added together.
- *Cost of goods sold* = $932,000. The cost of goods sold of the parent and subsidiary are added together.
- *Amortization expense* = $165,000. The balances of the parent and of the subsidiary are combined along with the $13,000 additional amortization from the recognition of the excess fair value over book value attributed to the subsidiary's patented technology, as shown in Exhibit 3.3.
- *Depreciation expense* = $110,000. The depreciation expenses of the parent and subsidiary are added together along with the $6,000 reduction in equipment depreciation, as indicated in Exhibit 3.3.
- *Equity in subsidiary earnings* = –0–. The investment income recorded by the parent is eliminated and replaced by adding across the subsidiary's revenues and expenses to the consolidated totals.
- *Net income* = $693,000. Consolidated revenues less consolidated expenses.
- *Retained earnings, 1/1/23* = $840,000. The parent figure only. This acquisition-date parent's balance has yet to be affected by any equity method adjustments.
- *Dividends declared* = $120,000. The parent company balance only because the subsidiary's dividends are attributable intra-entity to the parent, not to an outside party.
- *Retained earnings, 12/31/23* = $1,413,000. Consolidated retained earnings as of the beginning of the year plus consolidated net income less consolidated dividends declared.
- *Current assets* = $1,440,000. The parent's book value plus the subsidiary's book value.
- *Investment in Sun Company* = –0–. The asset recorded by the parent is eliminated and replaced by adding the subsidiary's assets and liabilities across to the consolidated totals.
- *Trademarks* = $820,000. The parent's book value plus the subsidiary's book value plus the $20,000 acquisition-date fair-value allocation. Note that the trademark has an indefinite life and therefore is not amortized.
- *Patented technology* = $775,000. The parent's book value plus the subsidiary's book value plus the $130,000 acquisition-date fair-value allocation less current year amortization of $13,000.

[6] The FASB *Accounting Standards Codification*® (ASC) uses the term *intra-entity* to describe transfers of assets across business entities affiliated though common stock ownership or other control mechanisms. The phrase indicates that although such transfers occur across separate legal entities, they are nonetheless made within a commonly controlled entity. Prior to the use of the term *intra-entity,* such amounts were routinely referred to as intercompany balances.

- *Equipment* = $446,000. The parent's book value plus the subsidiary's book value less the $30,000 fair-value reduction allocation plus the current-year expense reduction of $6,000.
- *Goodwill* = $80,000. The residual allocation is shown in Exhibit 3.2. Note that goodwill is considered to have an indefinite life and thus is not amortized.
- *Total assets* = $3,561,000. A vertical summation of consolidated assets.
- *Liabilities* = $1,428,000. The parent's book value plus the subsidiary's book value.
- *Common stock* = $600,000. The parent's book value. Subsidiary shares owned by the parent are treated as if they are no longer outstanding.
- *Additional paid-in capital* = $120,000. The parent's book value. Subsidiary shares owned by the parent are treated as if they are no longer outstanding.
- *Retained earnings, 12/31/23* = $1,413,000. Computed previously.
- *Total liabilities and equities* = $3,561,000. A vertical summation of consolidated liabilities and equities.

Consolidation Worksheet

Although the consolidated figures to be reported can be computed as just shown, accountants normally prefer to use a worksheet. A worksheet provides an organized structure for this process, a benefit that becomes especially important in consolidating complex combinations.

For Parrot and Sun, only five consolidation entries are needed to arrive at the same figures previously derived for this business combination. As discussed in Chapter 2, *worksheet entries are the catalyst for developing totals to be reported by the entity but are not physically recorded in the individual account balances of either company.*

Consolidation Entry S

Common Stock (Sun Company)	200,000	
Additional Paid-In Capital (Sun Company)	20,000	
Retained Earnings, 1/1/23 (Sun Company)	380,000	
Investment in Sun Company		600,000

As shown in Exhibit 3.2, Parrot's $800,000 Investment account balance at January 1, 2023, reflects two components: (1) a $600,000 amount equal to Sun's book value and (2) a $200,000 figure attributed to the acquisition-date difference between the book value and fair value of Sun's assets and liabilities (with a residual allocation made to goodwill). Entry S removes the $600,000 component of the Investment in Sun Company account, which is then replaced by adding the *book values* of each subsidiary asset and liability across to the consolidated figures. A second worksheet entry (Entry **A**) eliminates the remaining $200,000 portion of the January 1, 2023, Investment in Sun account and replaces it with the specific acquisition-date excess fair over book-value allocations along with any goodwill. Importantly, worksheet entries **S** and **A** are part of the sequence of worksheet adjustments that bring the investment account to zero.

Entry **S** also removes Sun's stockholders' equity accounts as of the beginning of the year. Because consolidated statements are prepared for the parent company owners, the subsidiary equity accounts are not relevant to the business combination and should be eliminated for consolidation purposes. The elimination is made through this entry because the equity accounts and the $600,000 component of the investment account represent reciprocal balances: Both provide a measure of Sun's book value as of January 1, 2023.

Before moving to the next consolidation entry, a clarification point should be made. In actual practice, worksheet entries are usually identified numerically. However, as in the previous chapter, the label "Entry **S**" used in this example refers to the elimination of Sun's beginning Stockholders' Equity. As a reminder of the purpose being served, all worksheet entries are identified in a similar fashion. Thus, throughout this textbook, "Entry **S**" always refers to the removal of the subsidiary's beginning stockholders' equity balances for the year against the book-value portion of the investment account.

Consolidation Entry A

Trademarks	20,000	
Patented Technology...	130,000	
Goodwill	80,000	
Equipment		30,000
Investment in Sun Company.....................................		200,000

Consolidation Entry **A** adjusts the subsidiary balances from their book values to acquisition-date fair values (see Exhibit 3.2) and includes goodwill created by the acquisition. This entry is labeled "Entry **A**" to indicate that it represents the **A**llocations made in connection with the excess of the subsidiary's fair values over its book values. Sun's accounts are adjusted collectively by the $200,000 excess of Sun's $800,000 acquisition-date fair value over its $600,000 book value.

Consolidation Entry I

Equity in Subsidiary Earnings	93,000	
Investment in Sun Company.....................................		93,000

"Entry **I**" (for **I**ncome) removes from the worksheet the subsidiary income recognized by Parrot during the year. For reporting purposes, we must add the subsidiary's individual revenue and expense accounts (and the current excess amortization expenses) to the parent's respective amounts to arrive at consolidated totals. Worksheet Entry **I** thus effectively removes the one-line Equity in Subsidiary Earnings, which is then replaced with the addition of the subsidiary's separate revenues and expenses (already listed on the worksheet in the subsidiary's balances). The $93,000 figure eliminated here represents the $100,000 income accrual recognized by Parrot, reduced by the $7,000 in excess amortizations. Observe that the entry originally recorded by the parent is simply reversed on the worksheet to remove its impact.

Consolidation Entry D

Investment in Sun Company..	40,000	
Dividends Declared		40,000

The dividends declared by the subsidiary during the year also must be eliminated from the consolidated totals. The entire $40,000 dividend goes to the parent, which from the viewpoint of the consolidated entity is simply an intra-entity transfer. The dividend declaration did not affect any outside party. Therefore, "Entry **D**" (for **D**ividends) is designed to offset the impact of this transaction by removing the subsidiary's Dividends Declared account. Because the equity method has been applied, Parrot originally recorded these dividends as a decrease in the Investment in Sun Company account. To eliminate the impact of this reduction, the investment account is increased.

Consolidation Entry E

Amortization Expense	13,000	
Equipment	6,000	
Patented Technology		13,000
Depreciation Expense...		6,000

This final worksheet entry recognizes the current year's excess amortization expenses relating to the adjustments of Sun's assets to acquisition-date fair values. Because the equity method amortization was eliminated within Entry **I**, "Entry **E**" (for **E**xpense) now enters on the worksheet the current-year expense attributed to each of the specific account allocations (see Exhibit 3.3). Note that we adjust depreciation expense for the tangible asset *equipment* and we adjust amortization expense for the intangible asset *patented technology*. As mentioned earlier, we refer to the adjustments to all expenses resulting from excess acquisition-date fair-value allocations collectively as *excess amortization expenses*.

Thus, the worksheet entries necessary for consolidation when the parent has applied the equity method are as follows:

Entry S—Eliminates the subsidiary's stockholders' equity accounts as of the beginning of the current year along with the equivalent book-value component within the parent's investment account.

Entry A—Recognizes the unamortized allocations as of the beginning of the current year associated with the original adjustments to fair value.

Entry I—Eliminates the impact of intra-entity subsidiary income accrued by the parent.

Entry D—Eliminates the impact of intra-entity subsidiary dividends.

Entry E—Recognizes excess amortization expenses for the current period on the allocations from the original adjustments to fair value.

Exhibit 3.5 provides a complete presentation of the December 31, 2023, consolidation worksheet for Parrot Company and Sun Company. The series of entries just described

EXHIBIT 3.5 Consolidation Worksheet—Equity Method Applied

PARROT COMPANY AND SUN COMPANY
Consolidation Worksheet
Investment: Equity Method **For Year Ending December 31, 2023**

Accounts	Parrot Company	Sun Company	Consolidation Entries Debit	Consolidation Entries Credit	Consolidated Totals
Income Statement					
Revenues	(1,500,000)	(400,000)			(1,900,000)
Cost of goods sold	700,000	232,000			932,000
Amortization expense	120,000	32,000	(E) 13,000		165,000
Depreciation expense	80,000	36,000		(E) 6,000	110,000
Equity in subsidiary earnings	(93,000)	–0–	(I) 93,000		–0–
Net income	(693,000)	(100,000)			(693,000)
Statement of Retained Earnings					
Retained earnings, 1/1/23	(840,000)	(380,000)	(S) 380,000		(840,000)
Net income (above)	(693,000)	(100,000)			(693,000)
Dividends declared	120,000	40,000		(D) 40,000	120,000
Retained earnings, 12/31/23	(1,413,000)	(440,000)			(1,413,000)
Balance Sheet					
Current assets	1,040,000	400,000			1,440,000
Investment in Sun Company	853,000	–0–	(D) 40,000	(S) 600,000 (A) 200,000 (I) 93,000	–0–
Trademarks	600,000	200,000	(A) 20,000		820,000
Patented technology	370,000	288,000	(A) 130,000	(E) 13,000	775,000
Equipment (net)	250,000	220,000	(E) 6,000	(A) 30,000	446,000
Goodwill	–0–	–0–	(A) 80,000		80,000
Total assets	3,113,000	1,108,000			3,561,000
Liabilities	(980,000)	(448,000)			(1,428,000)
Common stock	(600,000)	(200,000)	(S) 200,000		(600,000)
Additional paid-in capital	(120,000)	(20,000)	(S) 20,000		(120,000)
Retained earnings, 12/31/23 (above)	(1,413,000)	(440,000)			(1,413,000)
Total liabilities and equities	(3,113,000)	(1,108,000)	982,000	982,000	(3,561,000)

Note: Parentheses indicate a credit balance.
Consolidation entries:
(S) Elimination of Sun's stockholders' equity January 1 balances and the book-value portion of the investment account.
(A) Allocation of Sun's acquisition-date excess fair values over book values.
(I) Elimination of parent's equity in subsidiary earnings accrual.
(D) Elimination of intra-entity dividends.
(E) Recognition of current-year excess fair-value amortization and depreciation expenses.

brings together the separate financial statements of these two organizations. Note that the consolidated totals are the same as those computed previously for this combination.

Observe that Parrot separately reports net income of $693,000 as well as ending retained earnings of $1,413,000, figures that are identical to the totals generated for the consolidated entity. However, subsidiary income earned after the date of acquisition is to be *added* to that of the parent. Thus, a question arises in this example as to why the parent company figures alone equal the consolidated balances of both operations.

In reality, Sun's income for this period is contained in both Parrot's reported balances and the consolidated totals. Through the application of the equity method, the current-year earnings of the subsidiary have already been accrued by Parrot along with the appropriate amortization expense. *The parent's Equity in Subsidiary Earnings account is, therefore, an accurate representation of Sun's effect on consolidated net income.* If the equity method is employed properly, the worksheet process simply replaces this single $93,000 balance with the specific revenue and expense accounts that it represents. *Consequently, when the parent employs the equity method, its net income and retained earnings mirror consolidated totals.*

Consolidation Subsequent to Year of Acquisition—Equity Method

In many ways, every consolidation of Parrot and Sun prepared after the date of acquisition incorporates the same basic procedures outlined in the previous section. However, the continual financial evolution undergone by the companies prohibits an exact repetition of the consolidation entries demonstrated in Exhibit 3.5.

As a basis for analyzing the procedural changes necessitated by the passage of time, assume that Parrot Company continues to hold its ownership of Sun Company as of December 31, 2026. This date was selected at random; any date subsequent to 2023 would serve equally well to illustrate this process. As an additional factor, assume that Sun now has a $40,000 liability that is payable to Parrot.

For this consolidation, assume that the January 1, 2026, Sun Company's Retained Earnings balance has risen to $600,000. Because that account had a reported total of only $380,000 on January 1, 2023, Sun's book value apparently has increased by $220,000 during the 2023–2025 period. Although knowledge of individual operating figures in the past is not required, Sun's reported totals help to clarify the consolidation procedures.

Year	Sun Company Net Income	Dividends Declared	Increase in Book Value	Ending Retained Earnings
2023	$100,000	$ 40,000	$ 60,000	$440,000
2024	140,000	50,000	90,000	530,000
2025	90,000	20,000	70,000	600,000
	$330,000	$110,000	$220,000	

For 2026, the current year, we assume that Sun reports net income of $160,000 and declares and pays cash dividends of $70,000. Because it applies the equity method, Parrot recognizes earnings of $160,000. Furthermore, as shown in Exhibit 3.3, amortization expense of $7,000 applies to 2026 and must also be recorded by the parent. Consequently, Parrot reports an Equity in Subsidiary Earnings balance for the year of $153,000 ($160,000 − $7,000).

Although this income figure can be reconstructed with little difficulty, the current balance in the Investment in Sun Company account is more complicated. Over the years, the initial $800,000 acquisition price has been subjected to adjustments for

1. The annual accrual of Sun's income.
2. The receipt of dividends from Sun.
3. The recognition of annual excess amortization expenses.

EXHIBIT 3.6
Investment Account under
Equity Method

PARROT COMPANY Investment in Sun Company Account As of December 31, 2026 Equity Method Applied		
Fair value of consideration transferred at date of acquisition		$ 800,000
Entries recorded in prior years:		
Accrual of Sun Company's income		
2023	$100,000	
2024	140,000	
2025	90,000	330,000
Sun Company—Dividends declared		
2023	$ (40,000)	
2024	(50,000)	
2025	(20,000)	(110,000)
Excess amortization expenses		
2023	$ (7,000)	
2024	(7,000)	
2025	(7,000)	(21,000)
Entries recorded in current year—2026		
Accrual of Sun Company's income	$160,000	
Sun Company—Dividends declared	(70,000)	
Excess amortization expenses	(7,000)	83,000
Investment in Sun Company, 12/31/26		$1,082,000

Exhibit 3.6 analyzes these changes and shows the components of the Investment in Sun Company account balance as of December 31, 2026.

Following the construction of the Investment in Sun Company account, the consolidation worksheet developed in Exhibit 3.7 should be easier to understand. Current figures for both companies appear in the first two columns. The parent's investment balance and equity income accrual as well as Sun's income and stockholders' equity accounts correspond to the information given previously. Worksheet entries (lettered to agree with the previous illustration) are then utilized to consolidate all balances.

Several steps are necessary to arrive at these reported totals. The subsidiary's assets, liabilities, revenues, and expenses are added to those same accounts of the parent. The unamortized portion of the original acquisition-date fair-value allocations are included along with current excess amortization expenses. The investment and equity income balances are both eliminated as are the subsidiary's stockholders' equity accounts. Intra-entity dividends are removed as are the existing receivable and payable balances between the two companies.

Consolidation Entry S

Once again, this first consolidation entry offsets reciprocal amounts representing the subsidiary's book value as of the beginning of the current year. Sun's January 1, 2026, stockholders' equity accounts are eliminated against the book-value portion of the parent's investment account. Here, though, the amount eliminated is $820,000 rather than the $600,000 shown in Exhibit 3.5 for 2023. Both balances have changed during the 2023–2025 period. Sun's operations caused a $220,000 increase in retained earnings. Parrot's application of the equity method created a parallel effect on its Investment in Sun Company account (the income accrual of $330,000 less dividends collected of $110,000).

Although Sun's Retained Earnings balance is removed in this entry, the income this company earned since the acquisition date is still included in the consolidated figures. Parrot accrues these profits annually through application of the equity method. Thus, elimination of the subsidiary's entire Retained Earnings is necessary; a portion was earned prior to the acquisition, and the remainder has already been recorded by the parent.

Entry **S** removes these balances as of the first day of 2026 rather than at the end of the year. The consolidation process is made a bit simpler by segregating the effect of preceding

EXHIBIT 3.7 Consolidation Worksheet Subsequent to Year of Acquisition—Equity Method Applied

			Consolidation Entries		
	PARROT COMPANY AND SUN COMPANY Consolidation Worksheet				
Investment: Equity Method	For Year Ending December 31, 2026				
Accounts	**Parrot Company**	**Sun Company**	**Debit**	**Credit**	**Consolidation Totals**
Income Statement					
Revenues	(2,100,000)	(600,000)			(2,700,000)
Cost of goods sold	1,000,000	380,000			1,380,000
Amortization expense	200,000	20,000	(E) 13,000		233,000
Depreciation expense	100,000	40,000		(E) 6,000	134,000
Equity in subsidiary earnings	(153,000)	–0–	(I) 153,000		–0–
Net income	(953,000)	(160,000)			(953,000)
Statement of Retained Earnings					
Retained earnings, 1/1/26	(2,044,000)	(600,000)	(S) 600,000		(2,044,000)
Net income (above)	(953,000)	(160,000)			(953,000)
Dividends declared	420,000	70,000		(D) 70,000	420,000
Retained earnings, 12/31/26	(2,577,000)	(690,000)			(2,577,000)
Balance Sheet					
Current assets	1,705,000	500,000		(P) 40,000	2,165,000
Investment in Sun Company	1,082,000	–0–	(D) 70,000	(S) 820,000	–0–
				(A) 179,000	
				(I) 153,000	
Trademarks	600,000	240,000	(A) 20,000		860,000
Patented technology	540,000	420,000	(A) 91,000	(E) 13,000	1,038,000
Equipment (net)	420,000	210,000	(E) 6,000	(A) 12,000	624,000
Goodwill	–0–	–0–	(A) 80,000		80,000
Total assets	4,347,000	1,370,000			4,767,000
Liabilities	(1,050,000)	(460,000)	(P) 40,000		(1,470,000)
Common stock	(600,000)	(200,000)	(S) 200,000		(600,000)
Additional paid-in capital	(120,000)	(20,000)	(S) 20,000		(120,000)
Retained earnings, 12/31/26 (above)	(2,577,000)	(690,000)			(2,577,000)
Total liabilities and equities	(4,347,000)	(1,370,000)	1,293,000	1,293,000	(4,767,000)

Note: Parentheses indicate a credit balance.
Consolidation entries:
  (S) Elimination of Sun's stockholders' equity January 1 balances and the book-value portion of the investment account.
  (A) Allocation of Sun's acquisition-date excess fair values over book values, unamortized balance as of beginning of year.
  (I) Elimination of parent's equity in subsidiary earnings accrual.
  (D) Elimination of intra-entity dividends.
  (E) Recognition of current-year excess fair-value amortization and depreciation expenses.
  (P) Elimination of intra-entity receivable/payable.

operations from the transactions of the current year. Thus, *all worksheet entries relate specifically to either the previous years (S and A) or the current period (I, D, E, and P).*

Consolidation Entry A

In the initial consolidation (2023), fair-value allocations amounting to $200,000 were entered, but these balances have now undergone three years of amortization. As computed in Exhibit 3.8, expenses for these prior years totaled $21,000, leaving a balance of $179,000. Allocation of this amount to the individual accounts is also determined in Exhibit 3.8 and reflected in worksheet Entry **A.** As with Entry **S,** these balances are calculated as of January 1, 2026, and replaced by current-year expenses, as shown in Entry **E.**

Consolidation Entry I

As before, this entry eliminates the equity income recorded currently by Parrot ($153,000) in connection with its ownership of Sun. The subsidiary's revenue and expense accounts are left intact so they can be included in the consolidated figures.

EXHIBIT 3.8
Excess Amortizations Relating to Individual Accounts as of January 1, 2026

Accounts	Original Allocation	Annual Excess Amortizations			Balance 1/1/26
		2023	2024	2025	
Trademarks	$ 20,000	$ –0–	$ –0–	$ –0–	$ 20,000
Patented technology	130,000	13,000	13,000	13,000	91,000
Equipment	(30,000)	(6,000)	(6,000)	(6,000)	(12,000)
Goodwill	80,000	–0–	–0–	–0–	80,000
	$200,000	$ 7,000	$7,000	$7,000	$179,000
			$21,000		

Consolidation Entry D

This worksheet entry offsets the $70,000 intra-entity dividends (from Sun to Parrot) during the current period.

Consolidation Entry E

Excess amortization expenses relating to acquisition-date fair-value adjustments are individually recorded for the current period.

Before progressing to the final worksheet entry, note the close similarity of these entries with the five entries incorporated in the 2023 consolidation (Exhibit 3.5). Except for the numerical changes created by the passage of time, the entries are identical.

Consolidation Entry P

This last entry (labeled "Entry **P**" because it eliminates an intra-entity **P**ayable) introduces a new element to the consolidation process. As noted earlier, intra-entity reciprocal accounts do not relate to outside parties. Therefore, Sun's $40,000 payable and Parrot's $40,000 receivable must be removed on the worksheet because the companies are being reported as a single entity.

In reviewing Exhibit 3.7, note several aspects of the consolidation process:

- The stockholders' equity accounts of the subsidiary are removed.
- The Investment in Sun Company and the Equity in Subsidiary Earnings are both removed.
- The parent's Retained Earnings balance is not adjusted. Because the parent applies the equity method, this account should be correct.
- The acquisition-date fair-value adjustments to the subsidiary's assets are recognized but only after adjustment for prior periods' annual excess amortization expenses.
- Intra-entity balances such as dividends and receivables/payables are offset.

Subsequent Consolidations—Investment Recorded Using Initial Value or Partial Equity Method

As discussed at the beginning of this chapter, the parent company may opt to use the initial value method or the partial equity method for internal recordkeeping for its subsidiary investment rather than the equity method. Application of either alternative changes the balances recorded by the parent over time and, thus, the procedures followed in preparing consolidation worksheets. *Nonetheless, the parent's choice of either the initial value method or the partial equity method does not affect any of the final consolidated figures to be reported.*

As demonstrated in the previous section, when a company utilizes the equity method, the consolidated worksheet eliminates all reciprocal accounts, assigns unamortized fair-value allocations to specific accounts, and records amortization expense for the current year. Application of either the initial value method or the partial equity method has no effect on these basic worksheet processes. For this reason, many of the consolidation entries remain the same regardless of the parent's investment accounting method.

In reality, just three of the parent's accounts actually vary because of the method applied:

- The investment in subsidiary account.

- The income recognized from the subsidiary.
- The parent's retained earnings (in periods after the initial year of the combination).

Only the differences found in these balances of the parent affect the consolidation process. Thus, any time after the acquisition date, accounting for these three balances is of special importance.

Acquisition Made during the Current Year

To illustrate the modifications required by the adoption of an alternative investment accounting method, the consolidation of Parrot and Sun as of December 31, 2023, is reconstructed. Only one differing factor is introduced: the method by which Parrot accounts for its investment. Exhibit 3.9 presents the 2023 consolidation based on Parrot's use of the **initial value method.** Exhibit 3.10 demonstrates this same process, assuming that the parent applied the **partial equity method.** Each consolidation entry on these worksheets is labeled to correspond with the 2023 consolidation in which the parent used the equity method (Exhibit 3.5). Differences with the equity method (both for the parent company records and the consolidation entries) are highlighted on each of the worksheets.

EXHIBIT 3.9   Consolidation Worksheet—Initial Value Method Applied

	PARROT COMPANY AND SUN COMPANY					
	Consolidation Worksheet					
Investment: Initial Value Method	For Year Ending December 31, 2023					
Accounts	**Parrot Company**	**Sun Company**	**Consolidation Entries**		**consolidation Totals**	
			Debit	**Credit**		
Income Statement						
Revenues	(1,500,000)	(400,000)			(1,900,000)	
Cost of goods sold	700,000	232,000			932,000	
Amortization expense	120,000	32,000	(E) 13,000		165,000	
Depreciation expense	80,000	36,000		(E) 6,000	110,000	
Dividend income	(40,000)*	–0–	(I) 40,000*		–0–	
Net income	(640,000)	(100,000)			(693,000)	
Statement of Retained Earnings						
Retained earnings, 1/1/23	(840,000)	(380,000)	(S) 380,000		(840,000)	
Net income (above)	(640,000)	(100,000)			(693,000)	
Dividends declared	120,000	40,000		(I) 40,000*	120,000	
Retained earnings, 12/31/23	(1,360,000)	(440,000)			(1,413,000)	
Balance Sheet						
Current assets	1,040,000	400,000			1,440,000	
Investment in Sun Company	800,000*	–0–		(S) 600,000	–0–	
				(A) 200,000		
Trademarks	600,000	200,000	(A) 20,000		820,000	
Patented technology	370,000	288,000	(A) 130,000	(E) 13,000	775,000	
Equipment (net)	250,000	220,000	(E) 6,000	(A) 30,000	446,000	
Goodwill	–0–	–0–	(A) 80,000		80,000	
Total assets	3,060,000	1,108,000			3,561,000	
Liabilities	(980,000)	(448,000)			(1,428,000)	
Common stock	(600,000)	(200,000)	(S) 200,000		(600,000)	
Additional paid-in capital	(120,000)	(20,000)	(S) 20,000		(120,000)	
Retained earnings, 12/31/23 (above)	(1,360,000)	(440,000)			(1,413,000)	
Total liabilities and equities	(3,060,000)	(1,108,000)	889,000	889,000	(3,561,000)	

Note: Parentheses indicate a credit balance.
*Boxed items highlight differences with consolidation in Exhibit 3.5.
Consolidation entries:
   (S) Elimination of Sun's stockholders' equity January 1 balances and the book-value portion of the investment account.
   (A) Allocation of Sun's acquisition-date excess fair values over book values.
   (I) Elimination of intra-entity dividend income and dividends declared by Sun.
   (E) Recognition of current-year excess fair-value amortization and depreciation expenses.
Note: Consolidation entry (D) is unnecessary when the parent applies the initial value method. Entry (I) eliminates intra-entity dividend effects.

EXHIBIT 3.10 **Consolidation Worksheet—Partial Equity Method Applied**

PARROT COMPANY AND SUN COMPANY
Consolidation Worksheet

Investment: Partial Equity Method   **For Year Ending December 31, 2023**

Accounts	Parrot Company	Sun Company	Consolidation Entries Debit	Consolidation Entries Credit	Consolidation Totals
Income Statement					
Revenues	(1,500,000)	(400,000)			(1,900,000)
Cost of goods sold	700,000	232,000			932,000
Amortization expense	120,000	32,000	(E) 13,000		165,000
Depreciation expense	80,000	36,000		(E) 6,000	110,000
Equity in subsidiary earnings	(100,000)*	–0–	(I) 100,000 *		–0–
Net income	(700,000)	(100,000)			(693,000)
Statement of Retained Earnings					
Retained earnings, 1/1/23	(840,000)	(380,000)	(S) 380,000		(840,000)
Net income (above)	(700,000)	(100,000)			(693,000)
Dividends declared	120,000	40,000		(D) 40,000	120,000
Retained earnings, 12/31/23	(1,420,000)	(440,000)			(1,413,000)
Balance Sheet					
Current assets	1,040,000	400,000			1,440,000
Investment in Sun Company	860,000 *	–0–	(D) 40,000	(S) 600,000	–0–
				(A) 200,000	
				(I) 100,000 *	
Trademarks	600,000	200,000	(A) 20,000		820,000
Patented technology	370,000	288,000	(A) 130,000	(E) 13,000	775,000
Equipment (net)	250,000	220,000	(E) 6,000	(A) 30,000	446,000
Goodwill	–0–	–0–	(A) 80,000		80,000
Total assets	3,120,000	1,108,000			3,561,000
Liabilities	(980,000)	(448,000)			(1,428,000)
Common stock	(600,000)	(200,000)	(S) 200,000		(600,000)
Additional paid-in capital	(120,000)	(20,000)	(S) 20,000		(120,000)
Retained earnings, 12/31/23 (above)	(1,420,000)	(440,000)			(1,413,000)
Total liabilities and equities	(3,120,000)	(1,108,000)	989,000	989,000	(3,561,000)

Note: Parentheses indicate a credit balance.
*Boxed items highlight differences with consolidation in Exhibit 3.5.
Consolidation entries:
   (S) Elimination of Sun's stockholders' equity January 1 balances and the book-value portion of the investment account.
   (A) Allocation of Sun's acquisition-date excess fair values over book values.
   (I) Elimination of parent's equity in subsidiary earnings accrual.
   (D) Elimination of intra-entity dividends.
   (E) Recognition of current-year excess fair-value amortization and depreciation expenses.

LO 3-3b

Prepare consolidated financial statements subsequent to acquisition when the parent has applied **the initial value method** in its internal records.

Initial Value Method Applied—2023 Consolidation

Although the initial value method theoretically stands in marked contrast to the equity method, few reporting differences actually exist. In the year of acquisition, Parrot's income and investment accounts relating to the subsidiary are the only accounts affected.

Under the initial value method, income recognition in 2023 is limited to the $40,000 dividend received by the parent; no equity income accrual is made. At the same time, the investment account retains its $800,000 initial value. Unlike the equity method, no adjustments are recorded in the parent's investment account in connection with the current-year operations, subsidiary dividends, or amortization of any fair-value allocations.

After the composition of the dividend income and investment accounts has been established, worksheet entries can be used to produce the consolidated figures found in Exhibit 3.9 as of December 31, 2023.

Consolidation Entry S

As with the previous Entry **S** in Exhibit 3.5, the $600,000 component of the investment account is eliminated against the beginning stockholders' equity account of the subsidiary. Both are equivalent to Sun's net assets at January 1, 2023, and are, therefore, reciprocal balances that must be offset. This entry is not affected by the accounting method in use.

Consolidation Entry A

Sun's $200,000 excess acquisition-date fair value over book value is allocated to Sun's assets and liabilities based on their fair values at the date of acquisition. The $80,000 residual is attributed to goodwill. This procedure is identical to the corresponding entry in Exhibit 3.5 in which the equity method was applied.

Consolidation Entry I

Under the initial value method, the parent records dividends declared by the subsidiary as income. Entry **I** removes this Dividend Income account along with Sun's Dividends Declared. From a consolidated perspective, these two $40,000 balances represent an intra-entity transfer that had no financial impact outside of the entity. In contrast to the equity method, Parrot has not accrued subsidiary income, nor has amortization been recorded; thus, no further income elimination is needed.

Dividend Income..	40,000	
Dividends Declared..		40,000
To eliminate intra-entity income.		

Consolidation Entry D

When the initial value method is applied, the parent records intra-entity dividends as income. Because these dividends were already removed from the consolidated totals by Entry **I,** no separate Entry **D** is required.

Consolidation Entry E

Regardless of the parent's method of accounting for its subsidiary investment, the reporting entity must recognize excess amortizations for the current year in connection with the original fair-value allocations. Thus, Entry **E** serves to bring the current-year expenses into the consolidated financial statements.

Consequently, using the initial value method rather than the equity method changes only Entries **I** and **D** in the year of acquisition. Despite the change in methods, reported figures are still derived by (1) eliminating all reciprocals, (2) allocating the excess portion of the acquisition-date fair values, and (3) recording amortizations on these allocations. As indicated previously, the consolidated totals appearing in Exhibit 3.9 are identical to the figures produced previously in Exhibit 3.5. Although the income and the investment accounts on the parent company's separate statements vary, the consolidated balances are not affected.

One significant difference between the initial value method and equity method does exist: The parent's separate statements do not reflect consolidated income totals when the initial value method is used. Because equity adjustments (such as excess amortizations) are not recorded, neither Parrot's reported net income of $640,000 nor its retained earnings of $1,360,000 provide an accurate portrayal of consolidated figures.

LO 3-3c

Prepare consolidated financial statements subsequent to acquisition when the parent has applied **the partial equity method** in its internal records.

Partial Equity Method Applied—2023 Consolidation

Exhibit 3.10 presents a worksheet to consolidate Parrot and Sun for 2023 (the year of acquisition) based on the assumption that Parrot applied the partial equity method in accounting for its subsidiary investment. Again, the only changes from previous examples are found in (1) the parent's separate records for this investment and its related income and (2) worksheet Entries **I** and **D.**

As discussed earlier, under the partial equity approach, the parent's recordkeeping is limited to two periodic journal entries: the annual accrual of subsidiary income and the recognition

EXHIBIT 3.11   **Comparisons of Parrot Company Journal Entries across Initial Value and Partial Equity Methods**

Parrot Company Books Initial Value Method 2023		Parrot Company Books Partial Equity Method 2023	
Dividend Receivable.................. 40,000		Dividend Receivable................... 40,000	
Dividend Income.................	40,000	Investment in Sun	
Subsidiary dividends declared.		Company.......................	40,000
		Subsidiary dividends declared.	
Cash 40,000		Cash 40,000	
Dividend Receivable.............	40,000	Dividend Receivable..............	40,000
To record the receipt of the cash		To record the receipt of the cash	
dividend.		dividend.	
		Investment in Sun Company 100,000	
		Equity in Subsidiary Earnings......	100,000
		Accrual of subsidiary income.	

of dividends. Hence, within the parent's records, only a few differences exist when the partial equity method is applied rather than the initial value method. Exhibit 3.11 shows the journal entries recorded by Parrot in connection with Sun's 2023 operations to illustrate both of these approaches to accounting for the parent's subsidiary investment.

As seen in Exhibit 3.11, by applying the partial equity method, the investment account on the parent's pre-consolidation balance sheet rises to $860,000 by the end of 2023. This total is composed of the original $800,000 acquisition-date fair value for Sun adjusted for the $100,000 income recognition and the $40,000 cash dividend. The same $100,000 equity income figure appears within the parent's separate pre-consolidation income statement. These two balances are appropriately found in Parrot's records in Exhibit 3.10.

Because of differences in income recognition and the effects of subsidiary dividends when the parent employs the partial equity method, Entries **I** and **D** again differ on the worksheet. The $100,000 partial equity method income is eliminated (Entry **I**) by reversing the parent's entry. Removing this accrual allows the individual revenue and expense accounts of the subsidiary to be reported without double-counting. The $40,000 intra-entity dividend must also be removed (Entry **D**). The Dividends Declared account is simply brought to zero on the worksheet. However, note that Entry **D** increases the Investment in Sun balance. As part of the investment elimination sequence, this increase offsets the reduction in the Investment in Sun account recorded when the parent recognized the subsidiary dividend. All other consolidation entries (Entries **S, A,** and **E**) are the same for all three methods.

Comparisons across Internal Investment Methods

LO 3-4

Understand that a parent's internal accounting method for its subsidiary investments has no effect on the resulting consolidated financial statements.

Consolidated financial worksheets have now been completed when the parent uses the equity, initial value, and partial equity methods. At this point, it is instructive to compare the final consolidated balances in Exhibits 3.5, 3.9, and 3.10. Note the identical final consolidated column balances across the three internal methods of investment accounting. Thus, the parent's internal investment method choice has no effect on the resulting consolidated financial statements.

Consolidation Subsequent to Year of Acquisition—Initial Value and Partial Equity Methods

By again incorporating the December 31, 2026, financial data for Parrot and Sun (presented in Exhibit 3.7), consolidation procedures for the initial value method and the partial equity method are examined for years subsequent to the date of acquisition. *In both cases, establishment of an appropriate beginning retained earnings figure becomes a significant goal of the consolidation.*

Conversion of the Parent's Retained Earnings to a Full-Accrual (Equity) Basis

Consolidated financial statements require a *full accrual-based measurement of both income and retained earnings.* The initial value method, however, recognizes income when the subsidiary declares a dividend, thus ignoring when the underlying income was earned. The partial equity method only partially accrues subsidiary income. Thus, neither provides a full accrual-based measure of the subsidiary activities on the parent's income. As a result, over time the parent's retained earnings account fails to show a full accrual-based amount. Therefore, new worksheet adjustments are required to convert the parent's beginning-of-the-year retained earnings balance to a full-accrual basis. These adjustments are made to *beginning-of-the-year retained earnings* because current-year earnings are readily converted to full-accrual basis by simply combining current-year revenue and expenses. The resulting current-year combined income figure is then added to the adjusted beginning-of-the-year retained earnings to arrive at a full-accrual ending retained earnings balance.

This concern was not faced previously when the equity method was adopted. Under that approach, the parent's Retained Earnings account balance already reflects a full-accrual basis so that no adjustment is necessary. In the earlier illustration, the $330,000 income accrual for the 2023–2025 period as well as the $21,000 amortization expense was recognized by the parent in applying the equity method (see Exhibit 3.6). Recorded in this manner, these two balances form a permanent part of Parrot's retained earnings and are included automatically in the consolidated total. Consequently, if the equity method is applied, the process is simplified; no worksheet entries are needed to adjust the parent's Retained Earnings account to record subsidiary operations or amortization for past years.

Conversely, if a method other than the equity method is used, a worksheet change must be made to the parent's beginning Retained Earnings account (in every subsequent year) to equate this balance with a full-accrual amount. To quantify this adjustment, the parent's recognized income for these past three years under each method is first determined (Exhibit 3.12). For consolidation purposes, the beginning Retained Earnings account must then be increased or decreased to create the same effect as the equity method.

Initial Value Method Applied—Subsequent Consolidation

As shown in Exhibit 3.12, if Parrot applied the initial value method during the 2023–2025 period, it recognizes $199,000 less income than under the equity method ($309,000 − $110,000). Two items cause this difference. First, Parrot has not accrued the $220,000 increase in the subsidiary's book value across the periods prior to the current year. Although the $110,000 in dividends was recorded as income, the parent never recognized the remainder of the $330,000 earned by the subsidiary.[7] Second, no accounting has been made of the $21,000 excess amortization expenses. Thus, the parent's beginning Retained Earnings account is $199,000 ($220,000 − $21,000) below the appropriate consolidated total and must be adjusted.[8]

To simulate the equity method so that the parent's beginning Retained Earnings account reflects a full-accrual basis, this $199,000 increase is recorded through a worksheet entry. The initial value method figures reported by the parent effectively are converted into equity method balances.

EXHIBIT 3.12
Retained Earnings Differences

PARROT COMPANY AND SUN COMPANY Previous Years—2023–2025			
	Equity Method	Initial Value Method	Partial Equity Method
Equity accrual	$330,000	$ –0–	$330,000
Dividend income	–0–	110,000	–0–
Excess amortization expenses	(21,000)	–0–	–0–
Increase in parent's retained earnings	$309,000	$110,000	$330,000

[7] Two different calculations are available for determining the $220,000 in nonrecorded income for prior years: (1) subsidiary income less dividends declared and (2) the change in the subsidiary's book value as of the first day of the current year. The second method works only if the subsidiary has had no other equity transactions such as the issuance of new stock or the purchase of treasury shares. Unless otherwise stated, the assumption is made that no such transactions have occurred.

[8] Because neither the income in excess of dividends nor excess amortization is recorded by the parent under the initial value method, its beginning Retained Earnings account is $199,000 less than the $2,044,000 reported under the equity method (Exhibit 3.7). Thus, a $1,845,000 balance is shown in Exhibit 3.13 ($2,044,000 less $199,000). Conversely, if the partial equity method had been applied, Parrot's absence of amortization would cause the Retained Earnings account to be $21,000 higher than the figure derived by the equity method. For this reason, Exhibit 3.14 shows the parent with a beginning Retained Earnings account of $2,065,000 rather than $2,044,000.

Investment in Sun Company..	199,000	
Retained Earnings, 1/1/26 (Parrot Company)		199,000
To convert parent's beginning retained earnings from the initial value method to equity method.		

This adjustment is labeled Entry ***C.** The *C* refers to the **c**onversion being made to equity method (full-accrual) totals. The asterisk indicates that this equity simulation relates solely to transactions of prior periods. Thus, *Entry *C should be recorded before the other worksheet entries to align the beginning balances for the year.*

Exhibit 3.13 provides a complete presentation of the consolidation of Parrot and Sun as of December 31, 2026, based on the parent's application of the initial value method. After Entry ***C** has been recorded on the worksheet, the remainder of this consolidation follows the same pattern as previous examples. Sun's stockholders' equity accounts are eliminated (Entry **S**) while the

EXHIBIT 3.13 **Consolidation Worksheet Subsequent to Year of Acquisition—Initial Value Method Applied**

PARROT COMPANY AND SUN COMPANY
Consolidation Worksheet
Investment: Initial Value Method **For Year Ending December 31, 2026**

Accounts	Parrot Company	Sun Company	Consolidation Entries Debit	Consolidation Entries Credit	Consolidation Totals
Income Statement					
Revenues	(2,100,000)	(600,000)			(2,700,000)
Cost of goods sold	1,000,000	380,000			1,380,000
Amortization expense	200,000	20,000	(E) 13,000		233,000
Depreciation expense	100,000	40,000		(E) 6,000	134,000
Dividend income	(70,000)*	–0–	(I) 70,000*		–0–
Net income	(870,000)	(160,000)			(953,000)
Statement of Retained Earnings					
Retained earnings, 1/1/26					
Parrot Company	(1,845,000) †*			(*C) 199,000*	(2,044,000)
Sun Company		(600,000)	(S)600,000		–0–
Net income (above)	(870,000)	(160,000)			(953,000)
Dividends declared	420,000	70,000		(I) 70,000*	420,000
Retained earnings, 12/31/26	(2,295,000)	(690,000)			(2,577,000)
Balance Sheet					
Current assets	1,705,000	500,000		(P) 40,000	2,165,000
Investment in Sun Company	800,000*	–0–	(*C) 199,000	(S) 820,000	–0–
				(A) 179,000	
Trademarks	600,000	240,000	(A) 20,000		860,000
Patented technology	540,000	420,000	(A) 91,000	(E) 13,000	1,038,000
Equipment (net)	420,000	210,000	(E) 6,000	(A) 12,000	624,000
Goodwill	–0–	–0–	(A) 80,000		80,000
Total assets	4,065,000	1,370,000			4,767,000
Liabilities	(1,050,000)	(460,000)	(P) 40,000		(1,470,000)
Common stock	(600,000)	(200,000)	(S) 200,000		(600,000)
Additional paid-in capital	(120,000)	(20,000)	(S) 20,000		(120,000)
Retained earnings, 12/31/26 (above)	(2,295,000)	(690,000)			(2,577,000)
Total liabilities and equities	(4,065,000)	(1,370,000)	1,339,000	1,339,000	(4,767,000)

Note: Parentheses indicate a credit balance.
*Boxed items highlight differences with consolidation in Exhibit 3.7.
†See footnote 8.
Consolidation entries:
    (*C) To convert parent's beginning retained earnings to full accrual basis.
    (S) Elimination of Sun's stockholders' equity January 1 balances and the book-value portion of investment account.
    (A) Allocation of Sun's excess acquisition-date fair value over book value, unamortized balance as of beginning of year.
    (I) Elimination of intra-entity dividend income and dividends declared by Sun.
    (E) Recognition of current-year excess fair-value amortization and depreciation expenses.
    (P) Elimination of intra-entity receivable/payable.
Note: Consolidation entry (D) is not needed when the parent applies the initial value method because entry (I) eliminates the intra-entity dividend effects.

allocations stemming from the $800,000 initial fair value are recorded (Entry **A**) at their unamortized balances as of January 1, 2026 (see Exhibit 3.8). Intra-entity dividend income is removed (Entry **I**), and current-year excess amortization expenses are recognized (Entry **E**). To complete this process, the intra-entity receivable and payable of $40,000 are offset (Entry **P**).

In retrospect, the only new element introduced here is the adjustment of the parent's beginning Retained Earnings. For a consolidation produced after the initial year of acquisition, an Entry ***C** is required if the parent has not applied the equity method.

Partial Equity Method Applied—Subsequent Consolidation

Exhibit 3.14 demonstrates the worksheet consolidation of Parrot and Sun as of December 31, 2026, when the investment accounts have been recorded by the parent using the partial equity method.

EXHIBIT 3.14 **Consolidation Worksheet Subsequent to Year of Acquisition—Partial Equity Method Applied**

PARROT COMPANY AND SUN COMPANY
Consolidation Worksheet
For Year Ending December 31, 2026

Investment: Partial Equity Method

Accounts	Parrot Company	Sun Company	Consolidation Entries Debit	Consolidation Entries Credit	Consolidation Totals
Income Statement					
Revenues	(2,100,000)	(600,000)			(2,700,000)
Cost of goods sold	1,000,000	380,000			1,380,000
Amortization expense	200,000	20,000	(E) 13,000		233,000
Depreciation expense	100,000	40,000		(E) 6,000	134,000
Equity in subsidiary earnings	(160,000)*	–0–	(I) 160,000*		–0–
Net income	(960,000)	(160,000)			(953,000)
Statement of Retained Earnings					
Retained earnings, 1/1/26					
Parrot Company	(2,065,000) †*		(*C) 21,000*		(2,044,000)
Sun Company		(600,000)	(S) 600,000		–0–
Net income (above)	(960,000)	(160,000)			(953,000)
Dividends declared	420,000	70,000		(D) 70,000*	420,000
Retained earnings, 12/31/26	(2,605,000)	(690,000)			(2,577,000)
Balance Sheet					
Current assets	1,705,000	500,000		(P) 40,000	2,165,000
Investment in Sun Company	1,110,000*	–0–	(D) 70,000	(*C) 21,000*	–0–
				(S) 820,000	
				(A) 179,000	
				(I)160,000*	
Trademarks	600,000	240,000	(A) 20,000		860,000
Patented technology	540,000	420,000	(A) 91,000	(E) 13,000	1,038,000
Equipment (net)	420,000	210,000	(E) 6,000	(A) 12,000	624,000
Goodwill	–0–	–0–	(A) 80,000		80,000
Total assets	4,375,000	1,370,000			4,767,000
Liabilities	(1,050,000)	(460,000)	(P) 40,000		(1,470,000)
Common stock	(600,000)	(200,000)	(S) 200,000		(600,000)
Additional paid-in capital	(120,000)	(20,000)	(S) 20,000		(120,000)
Retained earnings, 12/31/26 (above)	(2,605,000)	(690,000)			(2,577,000)
Total liabilities and equities	(4,375,000)	(1,370,000)	1,321,000	1,321,000	(4,767,000)

Note: Parentheses indicate a credit balance.
*Boxed items highlight differences with consolidation in Exhibit 3.7.
†See footnote 8.
Consolidation entries:
　(*C) To convert parent's beginning retained earnings to full accrual basis.
　(S) Elimination of Sun's stockholders' equity January 1 balances and the book-value portion of investment account.
　(A) Allocation of Sun's excess acquisition-date fair over book value, unamortized balance as of beginning of year.
　(I) Elimination of parent's equity in subsidiary earnings accrual.
　(D) Elimination of intra-entity dividends.
　(E) Recognition of current-year excess fair-value amortization and depreciation expenses.
　(P) Elimination of intra-entity receivable/payable.

Discussion Question

In consolidation worksheet Entry *C, we adjust the parent's *beginning-of-the-year* retained earnings to a full-accrual basis. Why don't we adjust to the parent's *end-of-the-year* retained earnings balance using consolidation worksheet Entry *C?

Clearly, in a consolidated balance sheet, we wish to report the parent's end-of-period consolidated retained earnings at its full-accrual GAAP basis. To accomplish this goal, we utilize the following separate individual components of end-of-period retained earnings available on the worksheet.

> Beginning-of-the-year balance (after *C adjustment if parent does not employ equity method)
> + Net income (parent's share of consolidated net income adjusted to full accrual by combining revenues and expenses—including excess acquisition-date fair-value amortizations)
> − Dividends (parent's dividends)
> = End-of-the-year balance

The worksheet provides for the computation of current-year full-accrual consolidated net income via the income statement section. Dividends are already provided in the retained earnings section of the consolidated worksheet. The only component of the ending balance of retained earnings that requires a special adjustment (*C) is the beginning balance.

How does the consolidation worksheet entry *C differ when the parent uses the initial value method versus the partial equity method? Why is no *C adjustment needed when consolidated statements are prepared for the first fiscal year-end after the business combination?

This approach accrues subsidiary income each year but records no other equity adjustments. Therefore, as of December 31, 2026, Parrot's Investment in Sun Company account has a balance of $1,110,000:

Fair value of consideration transferred for Sun Company 1/1/23		$800,000
Sun Company's 2023–2025 increase in book value:		
Accrual of Sun Company's income	$330,000	
Sun Company's dividends	(110,000)	220,000
Sun Company's 2026 operations:		
Accrual of Sun Company's income	$160,000	
Sun Company's dividends	(70,000)	90,000
Investment in Sun Company, 12/31/26 (Partial equity method)		$1,110,000

As indicated here and in Exhibit 3.12, Parrot has recognized the yearly equity income accrual but not amortization. When the parent employs the partial equity method, the parent's beginning Retained Earnings account must be adjusted to include this expense. Therefore, Entry ***C** provides the three-year $21,000 amortization total to simulate the equity method and, hence, consolidated totals.

Consolidation Entry *C

Retained Earnings, 1/1/26 (Parrot Company)	21,000	
Investment in Sun Company.		21,000
To convert parent's beginning Retained Earnings from partial equity method to equity method by including excess amortizations.		

By recording Entry ***C** on the worksheet, all of the subsidiary's operational results for the 2023–2025 period are included in the consolidation. As shown in Exhibit 3.14, the remainder of the worksheet entries follow the same basic pattern as that illustrated previously for the year of acquisition (Exhibit 3.10).

Summary of Worksheet Procedures

Having three investment methods available to the parent means that three sets of entries must be understood to arrive at reported figures appropriate for a business combination. The process can initially seem to be a confusing overlap of procedures. However, at this point in the coverage, only three worksheet entries actually are affected by the choice of either the equity method, partial equity method, or initial value method: Entries ***C, I,** and **D.** Furthermore, accountants should never get so involved with a worksheet and its entries that they lose sight of the balances that this process is designed to calculate. Exhibit 3.15 provides a summary of the final consolidated totals and how they are calculated. These figures are never affected by the parent's choice of an accounting method.

After the appropriate balance for each account is understood, worksheet entries assist the accountant in deriving these figures. To help clarify the consolidation process required under each of the three accounting methods, Exhibit 3.16 describes the purpose of each worksheet entry: first during the year of acquisition and second for any period following the year of acquisition.

EXHIBIT 3.15
Consolidated Totals Subsequent to Acquisition*

Current revenues	Parent revenues are included. Subsidiary revenues are included but only for the period since the acquisition.
Current expenses	Parent expenses are included. Subsidiary expenses are included but only for the period since the acquisition. Amortization expenses of the excess fair-value allocations are included by recognition on the worksheet.
Investment (or dividend) income	Income recognized by parent is eliminated and effectively replaced by the subsidiary's revenues and expenses.
Retained earnings, beginning balance	Parent balance is included. The change in the subsidiary balance since acquisition is included either as a regular accrual by the parent or through a worksheet entry to increase parent balance. Past amortization expenses of the excess fair-value allocations are included either as a part of parent balance or through a worksheet entry.
Assets and liabilities	Parent balances are included. Subsidiary balances are included after adjusting for acquisition-date fair values less amortization to beginning of current period. Intra-entity receivable/payable balances are eliminated.
Goodwill	Original fair-value allocation is included unless reduced by impairment.
Investment in subsidiary	Asset account recorded by parent is eliminated on the worksheet so that the balance is not included in consolidated figures.
Capital stock and additional paid-in capital	Parent balances only are included although they will have been adjusted at acquisition date if stock was issued.

*The next few chapters discuss the necessity of altering some of these balances for consolidation purposes. Thus, this table is not definitive but is included only to provide a basic overview of the consolidation process as it has been described to this point.

EXHIBIT 3.16 Consolidation Worksheet Entries

Equity Method Applied	Initial Value Method Applied	Partial Equity Method Applied
Year of Acquisition		
Entry **S** — Beginning stockholders' equity of subsidiary is eliminated against book value portion of investment account.	Same as equity method.	Same as equity method.
Entry **A** — Excess fair value is allocated to assets and liabilities based on difference in book values and fair values; residual is assigned to goodwill.	Same as equity method.	Same as equity method.
Entry **I** — Equity income accrual (including amortization expense) is eliminated.	Dividend income is eliminated.	Equity income accrual is eliminated.
Entry **D** — Intra-entity dividends declared by subsidiary are eliminated.	No entry—intra-entity dividends are eliminated in Entry **I.**	Same as equity method.
Entry **E** — Current-year excess amortization expenses of fair-value allocations are recorded.	Same as equity method.	Same as equity method.
Entry **P** — Intra-entity payable/receivable balances are offset.	Same as equity method.	Same as equity method.
Entry ***C** — No entry—equity income for prior years has already been recognized along with amortization expenses.	Increase in subsidiary's book value during prior years and excess amortization expenses are recognized (conversion is made to equity method).	Excess amortization expenses for prior years are recognized (conversion is made to equity method).
Subsequent to Year of Acquisition		
Entry **S** — Same as initial year.	Same as initial year.	Same as initial year.
Entry **A** — Unamortized excess fair value at beginning of year is allocated to specific accounts and to goodwill.	Same as equity method.	Same as equity method.
Entry **I** — Same as initial year.	Same as initial year.	Same as initial year.
Entry **D** — Same as initial year.	Same as initial year.	Same as initial year.
Entry **E** — Same as initial year.	Same as initial year.	Same as initial year.
Entry **P** — Same as initial year.	Same as initial year.	Same as initial year.

Excess Fair Value Attributable to Subsidiary Long-Term Debt: Postacquisition Procedures

In the previous consolidation examples for Parrot and Sun Company, the acquisition-date excess fair values were attributed solely to long-term assets. Similarly, however, the acquisition-date fair value of subsidiary long-term debt may also differ from its carrying amount. Although the long-term debt adjustment to fair value is relatively straightforward, the adjustments to interest expense in periods subsequent to acquisition require additional analysis.

In subsequent periods, the acquisition-date fair-value adjustment to long-term debt is amortized to interest expense over the remaining life of the debt. When the acquisition-date fair value of subsidiary long-term debt exceeds its carrying amount on the subsidiary's books, the parent increases the value of the debt reported on its consolidated balance sheet (and vice versa). Consequently, when the parent reflects the increased value of the subsidiary's long-term debt valuation, it must reduce interest expense recognized on the consolidated income statement over the debt's remaining life. When the long-term debt valuation is decreased, interest expense increases.

Exhibit 3.17 summarizes the worksheet effects when acquisition-date long-term debt's carrying amount differs from its fair value.

EXHIBIT 3.17 Long-Term Debt: Consolidation Worksheet Adjustments

Long-Term Debt Valuation at Acquisition Date	Worksheet Adjustment to Long-Term Debt	Worksheet Adjustment to Interest Expense
Fair value > Carrying amount	Increase long-term debt to adjust to fair value (less previous periods interest amortization)	Debit Long-Term Debt and credit Interest Expense
Fair value < Carrying amount	Decrease long-term debt to adjust to fair value (less previous periods interest amortization)	Debit Interest Expense and credit Long-Term Debt

At first glance, it may seem counterintuitive that when long-term debt is ***increased,*** interest expense is ***decreased.*** Certainly for plant assets like equipment, when we increase their carrying amounts to acquisition-date fair values on the worksheet, we increase the related depreciation expense. Why do we seem to do the opposite for long-term liabilities?

The answer can be seen in the fact that even though the acquisition-date fair value of the subsidiary's long-term debt exceeds its carrying amount, the acquisition does not affect the subsidiary's contractual obligation for repaying the debt. The ultimate amount of debt to be repaid at maturity remains the same. For example, assume Pax Company acquires Sax Company on January 1, 2023. Exhibit 3.18 provides information about Sax Company's long-term debt.

By acquiring Sax, Pax has taken on (and effectively borrowed) $105,000 of fair-value debt but will only have to pay back $100,000 at the debt's maturity date. As shown in Exhibit 3.19, the additional $5,000 excess fair value over book value (that will not be repaid) is recognized as a reduction in overall interest expense, similar to amortizing a bond premium. Therefore, when consolidated statements are prepared, interest expense is reduced over the life of the long-term debt.

EXHIBIT 3.18
Acquisition-Date Long-Term Debt Valuation

	Long-Term Debt January 1, 2023	Long-Term Debt Maturity Value January 1, 2028
Fair value	$105,000	$100,000
Carrying amount	100,000	100,000

EXHIBIT 3.19
Worksheet Adjustments for Excess Acquisition-Date Fair Value Attributable to Subsidiary Long-Term Debt

December 31, 2023, Consolidation Worksheet		
Consolidation Entry A		
Investment in Sax Company	5,000	
Long-term debt		5,000
To adjust the subsidiary's long-term debt to acquisition-date fair value.		
Consolidation Entry E		
Long-term debt	1,000	
Interest expense		1,000
To recognize the reduction in current-year interest expense.		
December 31, 2024, Consolidation Worksheet		
Consolidation Entry A		
Investment in Sax Company	4,000	
Long-term debt		4,000
To adjust the subsidiary's long-term debt to unamortized balance as of the beginning of the year ($5,000 – $1,000 from year 2023).		
Consolidation Entry E		
Long-term debt	1,000	
Interest expense		1,000
To recognize the reduction in current-year interest expense.		

To complete this example, we assume the sole acquisition-date excess fair-value adjustment made by Pax Company is to long-term debt, and straight-line amortization is used for the interest adjustments.

Finally, the carrying amount of a subsidiary's long-term debt may exceed its fair value. In that case, a consolidation entry is required to decrease the long-term debt reported in the consolidated balance sheet. Then, in periods subsequent to acquisition, worksheet entries are also needed to increase the amount of interest expense to be recognized in the consolidated income statement.

Goodwill Impairment

LO 3-5

Discuss the rationale for the goodwill impairment testing approach.

FASB ASC Topic 350, "Intangibles—Goodwill and Other," provides accounting standards for determining, measuring, and reporting goodwill impairment losses. Because goodwill is considered to have an indefinite life, an impairment approach is used rather than amortization. The FASB reasoned that although goodwill can decrease over time, it does not do so in the "rational and systematic" manner that periodic amortization suggests. Only upon recognition of an impairment loss (or partial sale of a subsidiary) will goodwill decline from one period to the next. Goodwill impairment losses are reported as operating items in the consolidated income statement.

The notion of an indefinite life allows many firms to report over time the original amount of goodwill recognized in a business combination. However, goodwill can become impaired, requiring loss recognition and a reduction in the amount reported in the consolidated balance sheet. Evidence shows that goodwill impairment losses can be substantial. Exhibit 3.20 provides examples of some recent goodwill impairment losses. Unlike amortization, which periodically reduces asset values, impairment must first be revealed before a write-down is justified. Accounting standards therefore require periodic tests for goodwill impairment.

Goodwill impairment tests are performed at the reporting unit level within a combined entity. As discussed next, all assets acquired (including goodwill) and liabilities assumed in a business combination must be assigned to *reporting units* within a consolidated enterprise. The goodwill residing in each reporting unit is then separately subjected to periodic impairment reviews. Current financial reporting standards require, at a minimum, an annual assessment for potential goodwill impairment.

Because impairment testing procedures can be costly, the FASB provides firms the option to first conduct a *qualitative* analysis to assess whether further testing procedures are appropriate. If circumstances indicate a potential decline in the fair value of a reporting unit below its carrying amount, then a further test determines the existence of goodwill impairment. Our coverage of goodwill impairment addresses the following:

- The assignment of acquired goodwill to reporting units.
- The option to conduct an annual qualitative test for potential goodwill impairment.
- The goodwill impairment testing procedure.
- Comparison with international accounting standards.

EXHIBIT 3.20
Recent Goodwill
Impairments

Baker, Hughes Company	$14.8 billion
AT&T, Inc.	10.5 billion
The Procter & Gamble Company	6.8 billion
Lumen Technologies, Inc.	6.5 billion
Frontier Communications Corporation	5.7 billion
Coty, Inc.	3.0 billion
Dollar Tree, Inc.	2.7 billion
The Kraft Heinz Company	2.3 billion
Conduent, Inc.	2.0 billion
Sprint Corporation	2.0 billion

Assigning Goodwill to Reporting Units

Combined companies typically organize themselves into separate *units* along distinct operating lines. Each individual operating unit has responsibility for managing its assets and liabilities to earn profits for the combined entity. These operating units report information about their earnings activities to top management to support decision making. Such operating units are known as *reporting units.*

Following a business combination, the identifiable assets and liabilities acquired are assigned to the firm's reporting units based on where they will be employed. Any amount assigned to goodwill also is assigned to reporting units expected to benefit from the synergies of the combination. Thus, any individual reporting unit where goodwill resides is the appropriate level for goodwill impairment testing.

In practice, firms often assign goodwill to reporting units either at the level of a reporting segment—as described in ASC Topic 280, "Segment Reporting"—or at a lower level within a segment of a combined enterprise. Reporting units may thus include the following:

- A component of an operating segment at a level below that operating segment. Segment management should review and assess performance at this level. Also, the component should be a business in which discrete financial information is available and should differ economically from other components of the operating segment.
- The segments of an enterprise.
- The entire enterprise.

For example, AT&T, Inc., is a provider of communications and digital entertainment services. In its recent annual report, AT&T identified its principal operating segments (or one level below them) as reporting units:

> We test goodwill for impairment at a reporting unit level, which is deemed to be our principal operating segments or one level below. . . our Communications segment has three reporting units: Mobility, Business Wireline and Consumer Wireline. The reporting unit is deemed to be the operating segment for WarnerMedia and Latin America.

Goodwill impairment testing is performed at the reporting unit level, rather than collectively at the combined entity level. Separate testing of goodwill within individual reporting units prevents the masking of goodwill impairment in one reporting unit with contemporaneous increases in the value of goodwill in other reporting units.

Qualitative Assessment Option

LO 3-6

Describe the procedures for conducting a goodwill impairment test.

Because goodwill impairment tests require firms to calculate fair values for their reporting units each year, such a comprehensive measurement exercise can be costly. To help reduce costs, FASB ASC Topic 350 allows an entity the option to first assess qualitative factors to determine whether more rigorous testing for goodwill impairment is needed.[9] The qualitative approach assesses the *likelihood* that a reporting unit's fair value is less than its carrying amount. The more-likely-than-not threshold is defined as having a likelihood of more than 50 percent.

In assessing whether a reporting unit's fair value exceeds its carrying amount, a firm must examine all relevant facts and circumstances, including

- Macroeconomic conditions such as a deterioration in general economic conditions, limitations on accessing capital, fluctuations in foreign exchange rates, or other developments in equity and credit markets.
- Industry and market considerations such as a deterioration in the environment in which an entity operates, an increased competitive environment, a decline (both absolute and relative to its peers) in market-dependent multiples or metrics, a change in the market for an entity's products or services, or a regulatory or political development.

---

[9] An entity, on the basis of its discretion, may bypass the qualitative assessment for any reporting unit in any period and proceed directly to performing the quantitative impairment test. An entity may resume performing the qualitative assessment in any subsequent period (FASB ASC, para. 350-20-35-3B).

- Cost factors such as increases in raw materials, labor, or other costs that have a negative effect on earnings.
- Overall financial performance such as negative or declining cash flows or a decline in actual or planned revenue or earnings.
- Other relevant entity-specific events such as changes in management, key personnel, strategy, or customers; contemplation of bankruptcy; or litigation.
- Events affecting a reporting unit such as a change in the carrying amount of its net assets, a more-likely-than-not expectation of selling or disposing all or a portion of a reporting unit, the testing for recoverability of a significant asset group within a reporting unit, or recognition of a goodwill impairment loss in the financial statements of a subsidiary that is a component of a reporting unit.
- If applicable, a sustained decrease (both absolute and relative to its peers) in share price. (FASB ASC, para. 350-20-35-3C)

The underlying rationale for comparing a reporting unit's fair value and carrying amount is as follows. If a reporting unit's fair value is deemed greater than its carrying amount, then its collective net assets are maintaining their value. It then can be argued that a decline in any particular asset (i.e., goodwill) within the reporting unit is also unlikely, and no further impairment tests are necessary. On the other hand, if the relevant facts and circumstances listed earlier suggest that a reporting unit's fair value is likely less than its carrying amount, then a quantitative test for goodwill impairment is appropriate. Nonetheless, a qualitative assessment of a sufficient fair value for a reporting unit circumvents further goodwill impairment testing.

The FASB ASC (para. 350-20-35-28) requires an entity to assess its goodwill for impairment annually for each of its reporting units where goodwill resides. Moreover, more frequent impairment assessment is required if events or circumstances change that make it more likely than not that a reporting unit's fair value has fallen below its carrying amount.

Testing Goodwill for Impairment

In contrast to the qualitative assessment, goodwill impairment measurement relies on quantitative fair-value measures for reporting units as a whole as compared to their individually respective carrying amounts. If, after performing the qualitative assessment described earlier, an entity concludes that it is more likely than not that the fair value of a reporting unit is less than its carrying amount, then the entity is required to proceed to quantitative goodwill impairment testing.

Goodwill Impairment Test: Is the Carrying Amount of a Reporting Unit More Than Its Fair Value?

For impairment testing, the consolidated entity calculates fair values for each of its reporting units with allocated goodwill. Each reporting unit's fair value is then compared with its carrying amount (*including goodwill*).[10] If an individual reporting unit's fair value exceeds its carrying amount, its goodwill is not considered impaired—goodwill remains at its current carrying amount. Alternatively, if the fair value of a reporting unit has fallen below its carrying amount, then goodwill impairment is measured as the excess of the carrying amount over the fair value of the reporting unit, and a loss is recognized. The impairment loss equals the excess of the carrying amount of the reporting unit goodwill over its fair value. However, the impairment loss is limited to the carrying amount of goodwill.[11]

---

[10] A reporting unit's carrying amount simply consists of the net sum of the values of the assets and liabilities assigned to that reporting unit. When an acquired subsidiary is designated in its entirety as a reporting unit, and the parent employs the equity method, then the parent's investment in subsidiary account reflects that reporting unit's carrying amount.

[11] Prior to 2020, goodwill impairment standards relied on comparisons across goodwill's implied value and its carrying amount (known as Step 2 of the legacy ASC 350). The goodwill implied value computation required fair value determinations for each reporting unit's assets and liabilities and thus was considered costly. The new standard (ASU 2017-04) shown in this text simplifies goodwill impairment testing and is effective for fiscal years beginning after December 15, 2019, for public business entities with early adoption permitted.

Illustration—Accounting and Reporting for a Goodwill Impairment Loss

To illustrate the testing procedures for goodwill impairment, assume that on January 1, 2023, investors form ProCall Corporation to consolidate the telecommunications operations of DSM, Inc., and VisionTalk Company in a deal valued at $2.2 billion. ProCall organizes each former firm as an operating segment. Additionally, DSM comprises two divisions—DSM Wired and DSM Wireless—that, along with VisionTalk, are treated as independent reporting units for internal performance evaluation and management reviews. ProCall recognizes $215 million as goodwill at the merger date and allocates this entire amount to its reporting units as follows:

ProCall's Reporting Units	Goodwill Assigned at Acquisition Date
DSM Wired	$ 22,000,000
DSM Wireless	155,000,000
VisionTalk	38,000,000

In December 2023, ProCall performs a qualitative analysis for each of its three reporting units to assess potential goodwill impairment. Accordingly, ProCall examines the relevant events and circumstances that may affect the fair values of its reporting units. The analysis reveals that the fair value of each reporting unit likely exceeds its carrying amount—except for DSM Wireless, which has had difficulty realizing expected cost-saving synergies with VisionTalk.

Because the DSM Wireless reporting unit has failed the qualitative assessment for goodwill impairment, ProCall must now proceed to the quantitative goodwill impairment test. Consequently, ProCall computes the following December 31, 2023, amounts for its DSM Wireless reporting unit:

December 31, 2023	Fair Value	Carrying Amount
DSM Wireless reporting unit as a whole	$650,000,000	$720,000,000*

* Reporting unit's assets (including goodwill) – liabilities.

Then, to measure any goodwill impairment, ProCall compares the fair value of the DSM Wireless reporting unit to its carrying amount as follows:

DSM Wireless December 31, 2023, carrying amount before impairment	$720,000,000
DSM Wireless December 31, 2023, fair value	650,000,000
Goodwill impairment loss	$ 70,000,000

Thus, ProCall reports a $70,000,000 goodwill impairment loss as a separate line item in the operating section of its consolidated income statement. As of December 31, 2023, ProCall reports $85,000,000 of goodwill ($155,000,000 less $70,000,000 goodwill impairment loss) for its DSM Wireless reporting unit. Additional disclosures are required describing (1) the facts and circumstances leading to the impairment and (2) the method of determining the fair value of the associated reporting unit (e.g., market prices, comparable business, present-value technique, etc.). The reported amounts for the other assets and liabilities of DSM Wireless remain the same and are not changed based on the goodwill testing procedure.

The only exception to the previously mentioned impairment measurement occurs when the initially computed goodwill impairment loss exceeds the carrying amount of goodwill. In the ProCall example, the DSM reporting unit's goodwill carrying amount of $155,000,000 is sufficient to absorb the $70,000,000 impairment. However, if the reporting unit's goodwill carrying amount was less than $70,000,000, the goodwill impairment loss would be limited to the lower carrying amount. Thus, the impairment loss cannot exceed the carrying amount of any particular reporting unit's goodwill.

On the Horizon

FASB CONSIDERS GOODWILL AMORTIZATION, BUT RETAINS IMPAIRMENT-ONLY MODEL FOR POST-ACQUISITION GOODWILL

The Financial Accounting Standards Board (FASB) recently reexamined several key aspects of accounting for business combinations through its project, "Identifiable Intangible Assets and Subsequent Accounting for Goodwill." Although this project was ultimately removed from the FASB's agenda in 2022, the FASB had discussed whether the benefit of information under the impairment-only model for post-acquisition goodwill valuation was worth the cost of preparing and auditing that information.

The impairment-only model for post-acquisition goodwill valuation has come under criticism by both financial statement users and some standard setters. The requirement to annually test goodwill for impairment, despite several recent simplifications adopted by the FASB, is considered by some to be excessively costly. Moreover, the information provided by a goodwill impairment has been deemed by others as lacking timeliness. Also, many argued that our increasingly changing business environment undermines the notion of an indefinite life for goodwill.

To address these concerns the FASB considered a requirement that all business entities adopt an amortization-with-impairment model that would require companies to both amortize goodwill[12] and subject goodwill to impairment testing either periodically and/or based on a triggering event. In contrast to an impairment-only approach, amortization considers goodwill to have a definite life and allocates the cost of an acquisition to the periods that the entity realizes the benefits of the acquired goodwill. Moreover, as goodwill is amortized over time, its balance declines. As a result, both the need for goodwill testing and goodwill impairments would have become less likely.

Goodwill amortization is not without its critics. Some argue that making impairments less likely by reducing goodwill through amortization, information about management's acquisitions performance may be obscured. As observed by *CFO,*[13]

> Ultimately, there is no relevant information for investors in goodwill amortization. We call it the "zero-information approach." By contrast, when impairment is taken in a timely manner, it provides investors with insight regarding whether management's acquisitive activities were successful.

Perhaps because of these and similar criticisms, FASB decided to not require goodwill amortization at this time, and thus maintain the impairment-only model for post-acquisition goodwill valuation. Nonetheless, the FASB may revisit post-acquisition reporting for goodwill at any time.

Please consult the FASB website for further updates on accounting for goodwill.

Comparisons with International Accounting Standards

International Financial Reporting Standards (IFRS) and U.S. GAAP both require goodwill recognition in a business combination when the fair value of the consideration transferred exceeds the net fair values of the assets acquired and liabilities assumed. Subsequent to acquisition, both IFRS and U.S. GAAP require an assessment for goodwill impairment at least annually, and more frequently in the presence of indicators of possible impairment.

---

[12] The option to amortize goodwill over a 10-year period is already available to *private* companies (see the appendix to this chapter).

[13] Sandy Peters, "FASB Turns Up the Heat on Goodwill Impairment Testing," *CFO,* February 12, 2020.

Also, for both sets of standards, goodwill impairments, once recognized, are not recoverable. However, differences exist across the two sets of standards in the way goodwill impairment is tested for and recognized. In particular, goodwill allocation, impairment testing, and determination of the impairment loss differ across the two reporting regimes, as discussed next.

Goodwill Allocation

- *U.S. GAAP.* Goodwill acquired in a business combination is allocated to reporting units expected to benefit from the goodwill. Reporting units are operating segments or a business component one level below an operating segment.
- *IFRS.* International Accounting Standard *(IAS) 36* requires goodwill acquired in a business combination to be allocated to cash-generating units (CGU) or groups of CGUs that are expected to benefit from the synergies of the business combination. CGUs represent the lowest level within the entity at which the goodwill is monitored for internal management purposes and are not to be larger than an operating segment as determined in accordance with *IFRS 8,* "Operating Segments."

Impairment Testing

- *U.S. GAAP.* Firms have the option to perform a qualitative assessment to evaluate possible goodwill impairment based on a greater than 50 percent likelihood that a reporting unit's fair value is less than its carrying amount. If such a likelihood exists, then a reporting unit's total fair value is compared to its carrying amount. If the carrying amount exceeds fair value, a goodwill impairment loss is recognized for the difference, limited to the carrying amount of goodwill assigned to the reporting unit.
- *IFRS.* No similar qualitative assessment option for goodwill impairment (as in U.S. GAAP) exists under IFRS. Instead, a one-step approach compares the carrying amount (including goodwill) and *recoverable amounts* of each cash-generating unit where goodwill resides. The recoverable amount is the higher of fair value less cost to sell and value in use[14] of the cash-generating unit. If the carrying amount exceeds the recoverable amount of the cash-generating unit, then goodwill (and possibly other assets of the cash-generating unit) is considered impaired.

Determination of the Impairment Loss

- *U.S. GAAP.* Goodwill impairment is computed as the excess of a reporting unit's carrying amount over its fair value. Goodwill impairment is limited to its carrying amount for each reporting unit.
- *IFRS.* Any excess carrying amount over recoverable amount for a cash-generating unit is first assigned to reduce goodwill. If goodwill is reduced to zero, then the other assets of the cash-generating unit are reduced pro rata based on the carrying amounts of the cash-generating unit's assets.

LO 3-7

Describe the rationale and procedures for impairment testing for intangible assets other than goodwill.

Amortization and Impairment of Other Intangibles

As discussed in Chapter 2, the acquisition method governs how we initially consolidate the assets acquired and liabilities assumed in a business combination. Subsequent to acquisition, income determination becomes a regular part of the consolidation process. The fair-value bases (established at the acquisition date) for definite-lived subsidiary assets acquired and liabilities assumed will be amortized over their remaining lives for income recognition. For indefinite-lived assets (e.g., goodwill, certain other intangibles), an impairment model is used to assess whether asset write-downs are appropriate.

---

[14] IFRS defines value in use as the present value of future cash flows expected to be derived from an asset or a cash-generating unit.

Current accounting standards suggest categories of intangible assets for possible recognition when one business acquires another. Examples include internet domain names, patents, franchise agreements, databases, trademarks, lease agreements, licenses, and many others. All identified intangible assets should be amortized over their economic useful life unless such life is considered *indefinite*. The term *indefinite life* is defined as a life that extends beyond the foreseeable future. A recognized intangible asset with an indefinite life should not be amortized unless and until its life is determined to be finite. Importantly, *indefinite* does not mean "infinite." Also, the useful life of an intangible asset should not be considered indefinite because a precise finite life is not known.

For intangible assets with finite lives, the amortization method should reflect the pattern of decline in the economic usefulness of the asset. If no such pattern is apparent, the straight-line method of amortization should be used. The amount to be amortized should be the value assigned to the intangible asset less any residual value. In most cases, the residual value is presumed to be zero. However, that presumption can be overcome if the acquiring enterprise has a commitment from a third party to purchase the intangible at the end of its useful life or an observable market exists for the intangible asset.

The length of the amortization period for identifiable intangibles (i.e., those not included in goodwill) depends primarily on the assumed economic life of the asset. Factors that should be considered in determining the useful life of an intangible asset include

- Legal, regulatory, or contractual provisions.
- The effects of obsolescence, demand, competition, industry stability, rate of technological change, and expected changes in distribution channels.
- The enterprise's expected use of the intangible asset.
- The level of maintenance expenditure required to obtain the asset's expected future benefits.

Any recognized intangible assets considered to possess indefinite lives are not amortized but instead are assessed for impairment on an annual basis.[15] Similar to goodwill impairment assessment, an entity has the option to first perform qualitative assessments for its indefinite-lived intangibles to see if further quantitative tests are necessary. According to the FASB ASC (350-30-65-3), if an entity elects to perform a qualitative assessment, it examines events and circumstances to determine whether it is more likely than not (that is, a likelihood of more than 50 percent) that an indefinite-lived intangible asset is impaired. Qualitative factors include costs of using the intangible, legal and regulatory factors, industry and market considerations, and other. If the qualitative assessment indicates impairment is unlikely, no additional tests are needed.

If the qualitative assessment indicates that impairment is likely, the entity then must perform a quantitative test to determine if a loss has occurred. To test an indefinite-lived intangible asset for impairment, its carrying amount is compared to its fair value. If the fair value is less than the carrying amount, then the intangible asset is considered impaired and an impairment loss is recognized. The asset's carrying amount is reduced accordingly for the excess of its carrying amount over its fair value.

LO 3-8

Understand the accounting and reporting for contingent consideration subsequent to a business acquisition.

Contingent Consideration—Postcombination

As introduced in Chapter 2, contingency agreements frequently accompany business combinations. In many cases, the target firm asks for consideration based on projections of its future performance. The acquiring firm, however, may not share the projections and, thus, may be unwilling to pay now for uncertain future performance. To close the deal, future contingent payment agreements from the acquirer to the former owners of the target, also known as "earnouts," are common. Such contingent payments may be in the form of cash or the acquirer's equity shares—with each form requiring separate accounting in periods subsequent to a business combination.

---

[15] An entity has an unconditional option to bypass the qualitative assessment for any indefinite-lived intangible asset in any period and proceed directly to performing the quantitative impairment test.

For example, when The Coca-Cola Company acquired its controlling interest in fairlife, a provider of a variety of milk products, part of the negotiated terms of the deal involved contingent consideration. As stated in Coca-Cola's 2021 annual report

> Under the terms of the agreement, we are subject to making future milestone payments which are contingent on fairlife achieving certain financial targets through 2024 and, if achieved, are payable in 2021, 2023 and 2025 . . . we recorded a $270 million liability representing our best estimate of the fair value of this contingent consideration as of the acquisition date. . . . We are required to remeasure this liability to fair value quarterly with any changes in the fair value recorded in income until the final milestone payment is made

As seen in Coca-Cola's fairlife contingency, and discussed following, postcombination accounting for contingent consideration liabilities often involves both revaluation of the contingent liability and recognition of the related revaluation gain or loss. Alternatively, if the obligation for the contingent consideration is classified as equity, no revaluation takes place.

Accounting for Contingent Consideration in Periods Subsequent to a Business Combination

To illustrate the accounting for contingent consideration, assume that Prefab, Inc., acquires 100 percent of the voting stock of Steel Company on January 1, 2023, in exchange for the following:

- $850,000 market value of 10,000 shares of its $1 par common stock.
- A contingent payment of $35,000 cash if Steel's 2023 cash flow from operations exceeds $70,000.
- A contingent issuance of 1,000 shares of Prefab common stock if Steel's 2023 net income exceeds $100,000.

Under the acquisition method, each of the three elements of consideration represents a portion of the negotiated fair value of Steel and therefore must be included in the recorded value entered on Prefab's accounting records. For the cash contingency, Prefab estimates that there is a 75 percent chance that the $35,000 payment will be required. For the stock contingency, Prefab estimates a 21 percent probability that Steel will meet the $100,000 net income target. In the event of the contingent stock issue, Prefab and Steel agree that the 1,000 shares would have a likely $85,000 total future value. Prefab employs an interest rate of 5 percent to incorporate the time value of money.

To determine the fair values of the contingent consideration, Prefab computes the probability-adjusted present value of the expected payments as follows:

- *Cash contingency fair value* = $35,000 × 75% × [1/(1 + .05)] = $25,000
- *Stock contingency fair value* = $85,000 × 21% × [1/(1 + .05)] = $17,000

Prefab then records in its accounting records the acquisition of Steel as follows:

Investment in Steel	892,000	
Common Stock ($1 par)		10,000
Additional Paid-In Capital		840,000
Contingent Performance Obligation		25,000
Additional Paid-In Capital—Contingent Equity Outstanding		17,000
To record acquisition of Steel at fair value of consideration transferred including performance contingencies.		

Prefab, on its acquisition-date consolidated balance sheet, will report the contingent performance obligation under liabilities and the contingent stock payment as a component of stockholders' equity. Subsequent to acquisition, however, the accounting for contingent consideration differs depending on it balance sheet classification as a liability or equity. In each accounting period subsequent to acquisition,

- An obligation for contingent consideration classified as a **liability** is remeasured to current fair value. An increase (decrease) in the fair value of the contingent consideration obligation is recognized in each period's net income as a revaluation loss (gain).
- An obligation for contingent consideration classified as **equity** is not subsequently remeasured to fair value, consistent with other equity issues (e.g., common stock).

To continue the preceding example, assume that by the end of 2023 Steel exceeds the cash flow from operations threshold of $70,000, thus requiring an additional payment of $35,000 from Prefab. Also, Steel's 2023 net income was $117,000, triggering the payment of an additional 1,000 shares of Prefab common stock to the former owners of Steel. Prefab's recording of these events is as follows:

Prefab's Journal Entries—Both Year-End Cash and Stock Contingency Thresholds Are Met		
Loss from Revaluation of Contingent Performance Obligation	10,000	
Contingent Performance Obligation		10,000
To remeasure the contingent performance obligation to fair value.		
Contingent Performance Obligation	35,000	
Cash		35,000
To record cash payment required by original Steel acquisition contingency agreement.		
Additional Paid-In Capital—Contingent Equity Outstanding	17,000	
Common Stock ($1 par)		1,000
Additional Paid-In Capital		16,000
To record contingent stock issue required by original Steel acquisition contingency agreement.		

The loss from revaluation of the contingent performance obligation is reported in Prefab's consolidated income statement as a component of ordinary income. Regarding the additional required stock issue, note that Prefab's total paid-in capital (Common Stock plus APIC) remains unchanged from the total $867,000 recorded at the acquisition date. Contingent equity is not adjusted to fair value over time but remains at its originally recorded amount.

Alternatively, if Steel failed to meet both the $70,000 operating cash flow threshold and the $100,000 net income threshold, Prefab would record the following adjustments to its records:

Prefab's Journal Entries—Neither Year-End Cash nor Stock Contingency Thresholds Are Met		
Contingent Performance Obligation	25,000	
Gain from Revaluation of Contingent Performance Obligation		25,000
To record Steel's failure to meet performance threshold and remeasure the contingent performance obligation to zero.		
Additional Paid-In Capital—Contingent Equity Outstanding	17,000	
Additional Paid-In Capital—Contingent Equity Forfeited		17,000
To reclassify contingent stock issue as APIC—contingent equity forfeited. Steel did not meet performance threshold to qualify for additional stock issue.		

The preceding illustrations demonstrate that the initial fair value assigned to the acquired firm continues as the acquisition-date valuation for the business combination, regardless of whether the contingency thresholds are met or not.

Summary

1. The procedures used to consolidate financial information generated by the separate companies in a business combination are affected by both the passage of time and the method applied by the parent in accounting for the subsidiary. Thus, no single consolidation process that is applicable to all business combinations can be described.

2. The parent might elect to utilize the equity method to account for a subsidiary. As discussed in Chapter 1, the parent accrues income when earned by the subsidiary. The parent records dividend declarations by the subsidiary as reductions in the investment account. The effects of excess fair-value amortizations or any intra-entity transactions also are reflected within the parent's financial records. The equity method provides the parent with accurate information concerning the subsidiary's impact on consolidated totals; however, it is usually somewhat complicated to apply.

3. The initial value method and the partial equity method are two alternatives to the equity method. The initial value method recognizes only the subsidiary's dividends as income while the asset balance remains at the acquisition-date fair value. This approach is simple and typically reflects cash flows between the two companies. Under the partial equity method, the parent accrues the subsidiary's income as earned but does not record adjustments that might be required by excess fair-value amortizations or intra-entity transfers. The partial equity method is easier to apply than the equity method and, in many cases, the parent's income is a reasonable approximation of the consolidated total.

4. For a consolidation in any subsequent period, all reciprocal balances must be eliminated. Thus, the subsidiary's equity accounts, the parent's investment balance, intra-entity income, dividends, and liabilities are removed. In addition, the remaining unamortized portions of the fair-value allocations are recognized along with excess amortization expenses for the period. If the equity method has not been applied, the parent's beginning Retained Earnings account also must be adjusted for any previous income or excess amortizations that have not yet been recorded.

5. For each subsidiary acquisition, the parent must assign the acquired assets and liabilities (including goodwill) to individual reporting units of the combined entity. The reporting units should be at operating segment level or lower and serve as the basis for future assessments of fair value. Any value assigned to goodwill is not amortized but instead is tested annually for impairment. Firms have the option to perform a qualitative assessment to evaluate whether a reporting unit's fair value more likely than not exceeds its carrying amount. If the assessment shows excess fair value over carrying amount for the reporting unit, a firm can forgo further testing. Otherwise, if a reporting unit fails the qualitative test, the reporting unit's fair value is compared to its carrying amount. If the reporting unit's carrying amount exceeds its fair value, then a goodwill impairment loss is measured as the excess of a reporting unit's carrying amount over its fair value. A goodwill impairment loss is reported as an operating item in the consolidated income statement.

6. Subsequent to a business combination, any newly recognized subsidiary identifiable intangible assets (i.e., other than goodwill) considered to possess indefinite lives are not amortized but instead are assessed for impairment on an annual basis. Similar to goodwill impairment assessment, an entity has the option to first perform qualitative assessments for its indefinite-lived intangibles to see if further quantitative tests are necessary. For intangible assets with finite lives, amortization expense is recognized over the intangible asset's useful life. The amortization method should reflect the pattern of decline in the economic usefulness of the asset. If no such pattern is apparent, the straight-line method of amortization should be used.

7. The acquisition-date fair value assigned to a subsidiary can be based, at least in part, on the fair value of any contingent consideration. For contingent obligations that meet the definition of a liability, the obligation is adjusted for changes in fair value over time with corresponding recognition of gains or losses from the revaluation. For contingent obligations classified as equity, no remeasurement to fair value takes place. In either case, the initial value recognized in the combination does not change, regardless of whether the contingency is eventually paid or not.

Comprehensive Illustration

(*Estimated Time: 40 to 65 Minutes*) On January 1, 2022, Plush Company acquired all of Sofa Company's outstanding common stock for $842,000 in cash. As of that date, one of Sofa's buildings with a 12-year remaining life was undervalued on its financial records by $72,000. Equipment with a 10-year remaining life was undervalued, but only by $10,000. The book values of all of Sofa's other assets and liabilities were equal to their fair values at that time except for an unrecorded licensing agreement with an assessed value of $40,000 and a 20-year remaining useful life. Sofa's book value at the acquisition date was $720,000.

Problem

During 2022, Sofa reported net income of $100,000 and declared $30,000 in dividends. Earnings were $120,000 in 2023 with $20,000 in dividends declared by the subsidiary. As of December 31, 2024, the companies reported the following selected balances, which include all revenues and expenses for the year:

	Plush Company December 31, 2024		Sofa Company December 31, 2024	
	Debit	Credit	Debit	Credit
Buildings	$1,540,000		$460,000	
Cash and receivables ...	50,000		90,000	
Common stock		$ 900,000		$400,000
Dividends declared	70,000		10,000	
Equipment	280,000		200,000	
Cost of goods sold	500,000		120,000	
Depreciation expense ...	100,000		60,000	
Inventory	280,000		260,000	
Land	330,000		250,000	
Liabilities		480,000		260,000
Retained earnings, 1/1/24		1,360,000		490,000
Revenues		900,000		300,000

Required

a. If Plush applies the equity method, what is its investment account balance as of December 31, 2024?

b. If Plush applies the initial value method, what is its investment account balance as of December 31, 2024?

c. Regardless of the accounting method in use by Plush, what are the consolidated totals as of December 31, 2024, for each of the following accounts?

Buildings	Revenues
Equipment	Net Income
Land	Investment in Sofa
Depreciation Expense	Dividends Declared
Amortization Expense	Cost of Goods Sold

d. Prepare the worksheet entries required on December 31, 2024, to consolidate the financial records of these two companies. Assume that Plush applied the equity method to its investment account.

e. How would the worksheet entries in requirement part (d) be altered if Plush has used the initial value method?

Solution

a. To determine the investment balances under the equity method, four items must be determined: the initial value assigned, the income accrual, dividends, and amortization of excess acquisition-date fair value over book value. Although the first three are indicated in the problem, amortizations must be calculated separately.

An allocation of Sofa's acquisition-date fair values as well as the related amortization expense follows:

Fair value of consideration transferred by Plush Company	$842,000
Book value of Sofa Company, 1/1/22	(720,000)
Excess fair value over book value	$122,000

Adjustments to specific accounts based on fair values:

		Remaining Life (years)	Annual Amortization
Buildings	$ 72,000	12	$6,000
Equipment	10,000	10	1,000
Licensing agreement	40,000	20	2,000
Totals	$122,000		$9,000

Thus, if Plush adopts the equity method to account for this subsidiary, the Investment in Sofa account shows a December 31, 2024, balance of $1,095,000, computed as follows:

Initial value (fair value of consideration transferred by Plush) ...		$ 842,000
Sofa Company's 2022–2023 increase in book value (income less dividends)		170,000
Excess amortizations for 2022–2023 ($9,000 per year for two years)		(18,000)
Current-year recognition (2024):		
Equity income accrual (Sofa's revenues less its expenses)	$120,000	
Excess amortization expenses	(9,000)	
Dividends from Sofa	(10,000)	101,000
Investment in Sofa Company, 12/31/24		$1,095,000

The $120,000 income accrual and the $9,000 excess amortization expenses indicate that an Equity in Subsidiary Earnings balance of $111,000 appears in Plush's income statement for the current period.

b. If Plush Company applies the initial value method, the Investment in Sofa Company account permanently retains its original $842,000 balance, and the parent recognizes only the intra-entity dividend of $10,000 as income in 2024.

c. • The consolidated Buildings account as of December 31, 2024, has a balance of $2,054,000. Although the two book-value figures total only $2 million, a $72,000 allocation was made to this account based on fair value at the date of acquisition. Because this amount is being depreciated at the rate of $6,000 per year, the original allocation will have been reduced by $18,000 by the end of 2024, leaving only a $54,000 increase.

• On December 31, 2024, the consolidated Equipment account amounts to $487,000. The book values found in the financial records of Plush and Sofa provide a total of $480,000. Once again, the allocation ($10,000) established by the acquisition-date fair value must be included in the consolidated balance after being adjusted for three years of depreciation ($1,000 × 3 years, or $3,000).

• Land has a consolidated total of $580,000. Because the book value and fair value of Sofa's land were in agreement at the date of acquisition, no additional allocation was made to this account. Thus, the book values are simply added together to derive a consolidated figure.

• *Cost of goods sold* = $620,000. The cost of goods sold of the parent and subsidiary are added together.

• *Depreciation expense* = $167,000. The depreciation expenses of the parent and subsidiary are added together along with the $6,000 additional building depreciation and the $1,000 additional equipment depreciation as presented in the fair-value allocation schedule.

• *Amortization expense* = $2,000. An additional expense of $2,000 is recognized from the amortization of the licensing agreement acquired in the business combination.

• The Revenues account appears as $1.2 million in the consolidated income statement. None of the worksheet entries in this example affects the individual balances of either company. Consolidation results merely from the addition of the two book values.

• Net income for this business combination is $411,000: consolidated expenses of $789,000 subtracted from revenues of $1.2 million.

• The parent's Investment in Sofa account is removed entirely on the worksheet so that no balance is reported. For consolidation purposes, this account is always eliminated so that the individual assets and liabilities of the subsidiary can be included.

• Dividends declared for the consolidated entity should be reported as $70,000, the amount Plush distributed. Because Sofa's dividends are entirely intra-entity, they are deleted in arriving at consolidated figures.

d. Consolidation Entries Assuming Equity Method Used by Parent:

Entry S

Common Stock (Sofa Company)	400,000	
Retained Earnings, 1/1/24 (Sofa Company)	490,000	
Investment in Sofa Company		890,000
Elimination of subsidiary's beginning stockholders' equity accounts against book value portion of investment account.		

Entry A

Buildings	60,000	
Equipment	8,000	
Licensing Agreement	36,000	
Investment in Sofa Company		104,000

To recognize fair-value allocations to the subsidiary's assets in excess of book value. Balances represent original allocations less two years of amortization for the 2022–2023 period.

Entry I

Equity in Subsidiary Earnings	111,000	
Investment in Sofa Company		111,000

To eliminate parent's equity income accrual, balance is computed in requirement part (*a*).

Entry D

Investment in Sofa	10,000	
Dividends Declared		10,000

To eliminate intra-entity dividends from the subsidiary to the parent (and recorded as a reduction in the investment account because the equity method is in use).

Entry E

Depreciation Expense	7,000	
Amortization Expense	2,000	
Equipment		1,000
Buildings		6,000
Licensing Agreement		2,000

To recognize excess fair-value depreciation and amortization for 2024.

e. If Plush utilizes the initial value method rather than the equity method, three changes are required in the development of consolidation entries:

(1) An Entry ***C** is required to update the parent's beginning Retained Earnings account as if the equity method had been applied. Both an income accrual as well as excess amortizations for the prior two years must be recognized because these balances were not recorded by the parent.

Entry *C

Investment in Sofa Company	152,000	
Retained Earnings, 1/1/24 (Plush Company)		152,000

To convert to the equity method by accruing the net effect of the subsidiary's operations (income less dividends) for the prior two years ($170,000) along with excess amortization expenses ($18,000) for this same period.

(2) An alteration is needed in Entry **I** because, under the initial value method, only dividends are recorded by the parent as income.

Entry I

Dividend Income	10,000	
Dividends Declared		10,000

To eliminate intra-entity dividends recorded by parent as income.

(3) Finally, because the intra-entity dividends have been eliminated in Entry **I,** no separate Entry **D** is needed.

Appendix: Private Company Accounting for Business Combinations

LO 3-9

Describe the alternative accounting treatments for goodwill and other intangible assets available for business combinations by private companies.

External Reporting Option for Private Company Goodwill Accounting

In January 2014, the Financial Accounting Standards Board (FASB) approved an *Accounting Standards Update* (ASU 2014-02) to Topic 350, "Intangibles—Goodwill and Other, on Accounting for Goodwill." This ASU emerged as a consensus of the FASB's Private Company Council (PCC) and gives private companies an option to apply a simplified alternative to the more complex goodwill accounting model required of public companies. As discussed in this appendix, the new standard allows a private company both to amortize goodwill and to apply a simplified impairment test at either the reporting unit or entity level.

The private company standards apply only to businesses that do not meet the definition of a public business entity or a not-for-profit entity. In general, a business is a public entity if the Securities and Exchange Commission (or a foreign or other domestic regulatory agency) requires the business to furnish financial statements (ASU 2013-12). In this textbook, our focus is squarely on public business entities. Nonetheless, the goodwill accounting option for private companies provides an interesting alternative that the FASB may someday consider for public entities as well.[16]

The standard allows a private company to elect to amortize goodwill over a 10-year period.[17] The amortization process effectively treats goodwill as a definite-lived intangible asset. This approach, of course, stands in marked contrast to the goodwill accounting for public companies, which treats goodwill as an indefinite-lived asset, prohibits amortization, and requires annual impairment testing for goodwill. In justifying the differential treatment for private companies, the FASB reasoned that, based on research by the PCC, goodwill impairment tests provided

> limited decision-useful information because most users of private company financial statements generally disregard goodwill and goodwill impairment losses in their analysis of a private company's financial condition and operating performance. (ASU 2014-02, Summary)

Equally important, the PCC expressed concerns about the cost and complexity of goodwill impairment tests, especially for private companies. The cost and complexity arise in large part from the efforts required in determining fair values for a company's reporting units and their identifiable assets and liabilities.

In many cases, goodwill amortization will replace the need to periodically assess and, when deemed necessary, write-down goodwill through the recognition of impairment losses. Private companies who elect the alternative goodwill accounting, however, will still be required to test goodwill balances for impairment if a triggering event occurs (i.e., any event or change in circumstances that may have caused the fair value of the acquired entity—or the reporting unit—to fall below its carrying amount). However, no annual assessment for goodwill impairment is required.

Unlike public companies, a private company also has the option to designate and test goodwill for impairment either at the entity level or the reporting unit level—a policy election made at the adoption of the alternative goodwill method. Thus, the accounting for goodwill impairment is simplified by both the ability to assess goodwill at the entity level and the use of a single-step test that compares the fair value of the entity to its carrying amount. Similar to public companies, a private company may skip the qualitative assessment.

External Reporting Option for Private Company Accounting for Other Intangible Assets in a Business Combination

In addition to the private company separate guidance for goodwill, in December 2014, the FASB issued ASU 2014-18, "Accounting for Identifiable Intangible Assets in a Business Combination (a consensus of the Private Company Council)," an amendment of Business Combinations (Topic 805). The standard allows private companies an option to simplify their accounting by recognizing fewer intangible assets in future business combinations. Private companies can elect to (1) limit the customer-related intangibles it recognizes separately to those capable of being sold or licensed independently from the other assets of the business, and (2) avoid separate recognition of noncompetition agreements.

By limiting the separate recognition of customer-related intangibles (e.g., customer lists, customer relationships, commodity supply contracts, etc.) and noncompetition agreements, the value of these intangible assets is effectively subsumed into goodwill. As with other private company financial reporting options, the FASB cited cost/benefit considerations.

---

[16] In November 2014, the FASB directed its staff to extend its research on goodwill amortization to public companies, focusing on the most appropriate useful life if goodwill were amortized and simplifying the goodwill impairment test

[17] A less-than-10-year amortization period is available if it can be shown to be appropriate (ASC 350-20-35-63).

By providing an accounting alternative, this Update reduces the cost and complexity associated with the measurement of certain identifiable intangible assets without significantly diminishing decision-useful information to users of private company financial statements. (ASU 2014-18, Summary)

A private company may elect this alternative only if it also elects the private company goodwill accounting alternative, which includes goodwill amortization—thus ensuring that any non-recognized intangibles subsumed into goodwill are also subject to amortization. Companies that choose the goodwill accounting alternative, however, are not required to elect the intangible assets accounting alternative.

Questions

1. CCES Corporation acquires a controlling interest in Schmaling, Inc. CCES may utilize any one of three methods to internally account for this investment. Describe each of these methods, and indicate their advantages and disadvantages.

2. Maguire Company obtains 100 percent control over Williams Company. Several years after the takeover, consolidated financial statements are being produced. For each of the following accounts, briefly describe the values that should be included in consolidated totals.

   a. Equipment.
   b. Investment in Williams Company.
   c. Dividends Declared.
   d. Goodwill.
   e. Revenues.
   f. Expenses.
   g. Common Stock.
   h. Net Income.

3. When a parent company uses the equity method to account for an investment in a subsidiary, why do both the parent's Net Income and Retained Earnings account balances agree with the consolidated totals?

4. When a parent company uses the equity method to account for investment in a subsidiary, the amortization expense entry recorded during the year is eliminated on a consolidation worksheet as a component of Entry **I.** What is the necessity of removing this amortization?

5. When a parent company applies the initial value method or the partial equity method to an investment, a worksheet adjustment must be made to the parent's beginning Retained Earnings account (Entry ***C*)** in every period after the year of acquisition. What is the necessity for this entry? Why is no similar entry found when the parent utilizes the equity method?

6. Several years ago, Jenkins Company acquired a controlling interest in Lambert Company. Lambert recently borrowed $100,000 from Jenkins. In consolidating the financial records of these two companies, how will this debt be handled?

7. Benns adopts the equity method for its 100 percent investment in Waters. At the end of six years, Benns reports an investment in Waters of $920,000. What figures constitute this balance?

8. One company acquired another in a transaction in which $100,000 of the acquisition price is assigned to goodwill. Several years later, a worksheet is being produced to consolidate these two companies. How is the reported value of the goodwill determined at this date?

9. When should a parent consider recognizing an impairment loss for goodwill associated with a subsidiary? How should the loss be reported in the financial statements?

10. Reimers Company acquires Rollins Corporation on January 1, 2023. As part of the agreement, the parent states that an additional $100,000 cash payment to the former owners of Rollins will be made in 2024, if Rollins achieves certain income thresholds during the first two years following the acquisition. How should Reimers account for this contingency in its 2023 consolidated financial statements?

Problems

LO 3-2

1. A company acquires a subsidiary and will prepare consolidated financial statements for external reporting purposes. For internal reporting purposes, the company has decided to apply the initial value method. Why might the company have made this decision?

   a. It is a relatively easy method to apply.
   b. Operating results appearing on the parent's financial records reflect consolidated totals.
   c. GAAP now requires the use of this particular method for internal reporting purposes.
   d. Consolidation is not required when the parent uses the initial value method.

LO 3-2

2. A company acquires a subsidiary and will prepare consolidated financial statements for external reporting purposes. For internal reporting purposes, the company has decided to apply the equity method. Why might the company have made this decision?

   a. It is a relatively easy method to apply.

   b. Operating results appearing on the parent's financial records reflect consolidated totals.

   c. GAAP now requires the use of this particular method for internal reporting purposes.

   d. Consolidation is not required when the parent uses the equity method.

LO 3-4

3. On January 1, 2024, Jay Company acquired all the outstanding ownership shares of Zee Company. In assessing Zee's acquisition-date fair values, Jay concluded that the carrying value of Zee's long-term debt (eight-year remaining life) was less than its fair value by $20,000. At December 31, 2024, Zee Company's accounts show interest expense of $12,000 and long-term debt of $250,000. What amounts of interest expense and long-term debt should appear on the December 31, 2024, consolidated financial statements of Jay and its subsidiary Zee?

	Interest expense	Long-term debt
a.	$14,500	$270,000
b.	$14,500	$267,500
c.	$ 9,500	$270,000
d.	$ 9,500	$267,500

LO 3-5

4. When should a consolidated entity recognize a goodwill impairment loss?

   a. When the fair value of a reporting unit exceeds its respective carrying amount

   b. Whenever the entity's fair value declines significantly

   c. When the fair value of a reporting unit with goodwill falls below its carrying amount

   d. Annually on a systematic and rational basis

LO 3-1

5. Paar Corporation bought 100 percent of Kimmel, Inc., on January 1, 2021. On that date, Paar's equipment (10-year remaining life) has a book value of $420,000 but a fair value of $520,000. Kimmel has equipment (10-year remaining life) with a book value of $272,000 but a fair value of $400,000. Paar uses the equity method to record its investment in Kimmel. On December 31, 2023, Paar has equipment with a book value of $294,000 but a fair value of $445,200. Kimmel has equipment with a book value of $190,400 but a fair value of $357,000. What is the consolidated balance for the Equipment account as of December 31, 2023?

   a. $574,000

   b. $802,200

   c. $612,600

   d. $484,400

LO 3-4

6. How would the answer to Problem 5 change if the parent had applied the initial value method rather than the equity method?

   a. No effect: The method the parent uses is for internal reporting purposes only and has no impact on consolidated totals.

   b. The consolidated Equipment account would have a higher reported balance.

   c. The consolidated Equipment account would have a lower reported balance.

   d. The balance in the consolidated Equipment account cannot be determined for the initial value method using the information given.

LO 3-5

7. Goodwill recognized in a business combination must be allocated across a firm's identified reporting units. For a consolidated entity with multiple reporting units, when is goodwill considered to be impaired?

   a. When any individual reporting unit's carrying amount exceeds its fair value

   b. When any individual reporting unit's fair value exceeds its carrying amount

   c. When the sum of the carrying amounts of all reporting units within a business combination exceeds the sum of their respective fair values

   d. When the sum of the fair values of all reporting units within a business combination exceeds the sum of their respective carrying amounts

LO 3-7

8. If no legal, regulatory, contractual, competitive, economic, or other factors limit the life of an intangible asset, the asset's assigned value is allocated to expense over which of the following?

   a. 20 years

   b. 20 years with an annual impairment review

c. Infinitely

d. Indefinitely (no amortization) with an annual impairment review until its life becomes finite

LO 3-7

9. Camille, Inc., bought all outstanding shares of Jordan Corporation on January 1, 2022, for $700,000 in cash. This portion of the consideration transferred results in a fair-value allocation of $35,000 to equipment and goodwill of $88,000. At the acquisition date, Camille also agrees to pay Jordan's previous owners an additional $110,000 on January 1, 2024, if Jordan earns a 10 percent return on the fair value of its assets in 2022 and 2023. Jordan's profits exceed this threshold in both years. Which of the following is true?

a. The additional $110,000 payment is reported as an adjustment to the beginning balance of consolidated retained earnings.

b. The fair value of the expected contingent payment increases goodwill at the acquisition date.

c. Consolidated goodwill as of January 1, 2024, increases by $110,000.

d. The $110,000 is recorded as a revaluation gain in 2024.

Problems 10, 11, and 12 relate to the following:

On January 1, 2022, Palmcroft Co. acquired 100 percent of the outstanding voting shares of Salt River, Inc., for $600,000 cash. At January 1, 2022, Salt River's net assets had a total carrying amount of $420,000. Equipment (eight-year remaining life) was undervalued on Salt River's financial records by $80,000. Any remaining excess fair over book value was attributed to a database developed by Salt River (four-year remaining life), but not recorded on its books. Palmcroft applies the equity method to account for its investment in Salt River. Each year since the acquisition, Salt River has declared a $20,000 dividend. Salt River recorded net income of $70,000 in 2022 and $80,000 in 2023.

Selected account balances from the two companies' individual records were as follows:

	Palmcroft	Salt River
2024 Revenues	$498,000	$285,000
2024 Expenses	350,000	195,000
2024 Income from Salt River	55,000	
Retained earnings, 12/31/24	250,000	175,000

LO 3-3a

10. What is consolidated net income for Palmcroft and Salt River for 2024?

a. $148,000

b. $203,000

c. $228,000

d. $238,000

LO 3-3a

11. What is Palmcroft's consolidated retained earnings balance at December 31, 2024?

a. $250,000

b. $290,000

c. $330,000

d. $360,000

LO 3-3a

12. On its December 31, 2024, consolidated balance sheet, what amount should Palmcroft report for Salt River's database?

a. $10,000

b. $20,000

c. $25,000

d. $50,000

LO 3-7

13. SK Corporation acquired Neptune, Inc., on January 1, 2023, by issuing 125,000 shares of common stock with a $5 per share par value and a $30 market value. This transaction resulted in recognizing $95,000 of goodwill. SK also agreed to compensate Neptune's former owners with an additional 20,000 shares of SK's common stock if Neptune's 2023 cash flow from operations exceeds $600,000. On February 1, 2024, SK issues the additional 20,000 shares to Neptune's former owners to honor the contingent consideration agreement. Which of the following is true?

a. The fair value of the number of shares issued for the contingency increases the Goodwill account on February 1, 2024.

b. The parent's additional paid-in capital from the contingent equity recorded at the acquisition date is reclassified as a regular common stock issue on February 1, 2024.

c. All of the subsidiary's asset and liability accounts must be revalued for consolidation purposes based on their fair values as of February 1, 2024.

d. The additional shares are assumed to have been issued on January 1, 2023, so that a retrospective adjustment is required.

LO 3-3, 3-4

14. Herbert, Inc., acquired all of Rambis Company's outstanding stock on January 1, 2023, for $574,000 in cash. Annual excess amortization of $12,000 results from this transaction. On the date of the takeover, Herbert reported retained earnings of $400,000, and Rambis reported a $200,000 balance. Herbert reported internal net income of $40,000 in 2023 and $50,000 in 2024 and declared $10,000 in dividends each year. Rambis reported net income of $20,000 in 2023 and $30,000 in 2024 and declared $5,000 in dividends each year.

a. Assume that Herbert's internal net income figures do not include any income from the subsidiary.
   - If the parent uses the equity method, what is the amount reported as consolidated retained earnings on December 31, 2024?
   - Would the amount of consolidated retained earnings change if the parent had applied either the initial value or partial equity method for internal accounting purposes?

b. Under each of the following situations, what is the Investment in Rambis account balance on Herbert's books on January 1, 2024?
   - The parent uses the equity method.
   - The parent uses the partial equity method.
   - The parent uses the initial value method.

c. Under each of the following situations, what is Entry *C on a 2024 consolidation worksheet?
   - The parent uses the equity method.   0
   - The parent uses the partial equity method.   12,000
   - The parent uses the initial value method.   3,000

LO 3-3, 3-4

15. Parkovash, Inc., obtained 100 percent of Salerno Company's common stock on January 1, 2023, by issuing 9,000 shares of $10 par value common stock. Parkovash's shares had a $15 per share fair value. On that date, Salerno reported a net book value of $100,000. However, its equipment (with a 5-year remaining life) was undervalued by $5,000 in the company's accounting records. Also, Salerno had developed computer software with an assessed value of $30,000, although no value had been recorded on Salerno's books. The computer software had an estimated remaining useful life of 10 years.

The following balances come from the individual accounting records of these two companies as of December 31, 2023:

	Parkovash	Salerno
Revenues	$(600,000)	$(230,000)
Expenses	440,000	120,000
Investment income	Not given	–0–
Dividends declared	80,000	50,000

The following balances come from the individual accounting records of these two companies as of December 31, 2024:

	Parkovash	Salerno
Revenues	$(700,000)	$(280,000)
Expenses	460,000	150,000
Investment income	Not given	–0–
Dividends declared	90,000	40,000
Equipment	500,000	300,000

a. What balance does Parkovash's Investment in Salerno account show on December 31, 2024, when the equity method is applied?

b. What is the consolidated net income for the year ending December 31, 2024?

c. What is the consolidated equipment balance as of December 31, 2024? How would this answer be affected by the investment method applied by the parent?

d. If Parkovash has applied the initial value method to account for its investment, what adjustment is needed to the beginning of the Retained Earnings account on a December 31, 2024, consolidation worksheet? How would this answer change if the partial equity method had been in use? How would this answer change if the equity method had been in use?

LO 3-6

16. Arcadia, Inc., acquired 100 percent of the voting shares of Bruno Company on January 1, 2023. In exchange, Arcadia paid $198,000 in cash and issued 100,000 shares of its own $1 par value common stock. On this date, Arcadia's stock had a fair value of $15 per share. The combination is a statutory merger with Bruno subsequently dissolved as a legal corporation. Bruno's assets and liabilities are assigned to a new reporting unit.

The following shows fair values for the Bruno reporting unit for January 1, 2023, along with respective carrying amounts on December 31, 2024:

Bruno Reporting Unit	Fair Values 1/1/23	Carrying Amounts 12/31/24
Cash	$ 65,000	$ 40,000
Receivables	203,000	235,000
Inventory	275,000	250,000
Patents	531,000	550,000
Royalty agreements	580,000	450,000
Equipment (net)	215,000	335,000
Goodwill	?	400,000
Accounts payable	(111,000)	(275,000)
Long-term liabilities	(460,000)	(425,000)

a. Prepare Arcadia's journal entry to record the assets acquired and the liabilities assumed in the Bruno merger on January 1, 2023.

b. On December 31, 2024, Arcadia opts to forgo any goodwill impairment qualitative assessment and estimates that the total fair value of the entire Bruno reporting unit is $1,325,000. What amount of goodwill impairment, if any, should Arcadia recognize on its 2024 income statement?

LO 3-6

17. Apollo Co., a consolidated enterprise, conducted an impairment review for each of its reporting units. In its qualitative assessment, one particular reporting unit, Stande, emerged as a candidate for possible goodwill impairment. Stande had recognized net assets with carrying amounts totaling $1,094, including goodwill of $755. Stande's reporting unit fair value is assessed at $1,028 and includes two internally developed unrecognized intangible assets (a patent and a royalty agreement with fair values of $199 and $56, respectively). The following table summarizes current financial information for the Stande reporting unit:

	Carrying Amounts	Fair Values
Tangible assets, net	$ 84	$137
Recognized intangible assets, net	255	326
Goodwill	755	?
Unrecognized intangible assets	–0–	255

a. Determine the amount of any goodwill impairment for Apollo's Stande reporting unit.

b. After recognition of any goodwill impairment loss, what are the reported carrying amounts for the following assets of Apollo's reporting unit Stande?

- Tangible assets, net
- Goodwill
- Patent
- Royalty agreement

LO 3-6

18. Pelota Company recently acquired several businesses and recognized goodwill in each acquisition. Pelota allocated the resulting goodwill to its three reporting units: R-one, R-two, and R-three. Pelota opts to skip the qualitative assessment and therefore performs a quantitative goodwill impairment review annually.

In its current-year assessment of goodwill, Pelota provides the following individual asset and liability carrying amounts for each of its reporting units:

	Carrying Amounts		
	R-one	R-two	R-three
Tangible assets	$180,000	$200,000	$140,000
Trademark	170,000		
Computer software	90,000		
Unpatented technology		170,000	
Licenses		90,000	
Copyrights			50,000
Goodwill	120,000	150,000	90,000
Liabilities	(30,000)		

The total fair values for each reporting unit (including goodwill) are $510,000 for R-one, $580,000 for R-two, and $560,000 for R-three. To date, Pelota has reported no goodwill impairments.

How much goodwill impairment should Pelota report this year for each of its reporting units?

Problems 19 through 21 should be viewed as independent situations. They are based on the following data:

Chapman Company obtains 100 percent of Abernethy Company's stock on January 1, 2023. As of that date, Abernethy has the following trial balance:

	Debit	Credit
Accounts payable.		$ 50,000
Accounts receivable.	$ 40,000	
Additional paid-in capital		50,000
Buildings (net) (4-year remaining life)	120,000	
Cash and short-term investments	60,000	
Common stock		250,000
Equipment (net) (5-year remaining life)	200,000	
Inventory.	90,000	
Land.	80,000	
Long-term liabilities (mature 12/31/26).		150,000
Retained earnings, 1/1/23.		100,000
Supplies	10,000	
Totals.	$600,000	$600,000

During 2023, Abernethy reported net income of $80,000 while declaring and paying dividends of $10,000. During 2024, Abernethy reported net income of $110,000 while declaring and paying dividends of $30,000.

LO 3-3a

19. Assume that Chapman Company acquired Abernethy's common stock for $490,000 in cash. As of January 1, 2023, Abernethy's land had a fair value of $90,000, its buildings were valued at $160,000, and its equipment was appraised at $180,000. Chapman uses the equity method for this investment. Prepare consolidation worksheet entries for December 31, 2023, and December 31, 2024.

LO 3-3b

20. Assume that Chapman Company acquired Abernethy's common stock for $500,000 in cash. Assume that the equipment and long-term liabilities had fair values of $220,000 and $120,000, respectively, on the acquisition date. Chapman uses the initial value method to account for its investment. Prepare consolidation worksheet entries for December 31, 2023, and December 31, 2024.

LO 3-3c

21. Assume that Chapman Company acquired Abernethy's common stock by paying $520,000 in cash. All of Abernethy's accounts are estimated to have a fair value approximately equal to present book values. Chapman uses the partial equity method to account for its investment. Prepare the consolidation worksheet entries for December 31, 2023, and December 31, 2024.

LO 3-3a, 3-3b, 3-4

22. Adams, Inc., acquires Clay Corporation on January 1, 2023, in exchange for $510,000 cash. Immediately after the acquisition, the two companies have the following account balances. Clay's equipment (with a 5-year remaining life) is actually worth $440,000. Credit balances are indicated by parentheses.

	Adams	Clay
Current assets	$ 300,000	$ 220,000
Investment in Clay.	510,000	–0–
Equipment	600,000	390,000
Liabilities.	(200,000)	(160,000)
Common stock	(350,000)	(150,000)
Retained earnings, 1/1/23	(860,000)	(300,000)

In 2023, Clay earns a net income of $55,000 and declares and pays a $5,000 cash dividend. In 2023, Adams reports net income from its own operations (exclusive of any income from Clay) of $125,000 and declares no dividends. At the end of 2024, selected account balances for the two companies are as follows:

	Adams	Clay
Revenues	$(400,000)	$(240,000)
Expenses	290,000	180,000
Investment income	Not given	–0–
Retained earnings, 1/1/24.	Not given	(350,000)
Dividends declared.	–0–	8,000
Common stock	(350,000)	(150,000)
Current assets	580,000	262,000
Investment in Clay.	Not given	–0–
Equipment	520,000	420,000
Liabilities.	(152,000)	(130,000)

a. What are the December 31, 2024, Investment Income and Investment in Clay account balances assuming Adams uses the

- Equity method.
- Initial value method.

b. How does the parent's internal investment accounting method choice affect the amount reported for expenses in its December 31, 2024, consolidated income statement?

c. How does the parent's internal investment accounting method choice affect the amount reported for equipment in its December 31, 2024, consolidated balance sheet?

d. What is Adams's January 1, 2024, Retained Earnings account balance assuming Adams accounts for its investment in Clay using the

- Equity value method.
- Initial value method.

e. What worksheet adjustment to Adams's January 1, 2024, Retained Earnings account balance is required if Adams accounts for its investment in Clay using the initial value method?

f. Prepare the worksheet entry to eliminate Clay's stockholders' equity.

g. What is consolidated net income for 2024?

LO 3-1, 3-4

23. The following are selected account balances from Penske Company and Stanza Corporation as of December 31, 2024:

	Penske	Stanza
Revenues	$(700,000)	$ (400,000)
Cost of goods sold	250,000	100,000
Depreciation expense	150,000	200,000
Investment income	Not given	–0–
Dividends declared.	80,000	60,000
Retained earnings, 1/1/24.	(600,000)	(200,000)
Current assets	400,000	500,000
Copyrights	900,000	400,000
Royalty agreements	600,000	1,000,000
Investment in Stanza	Not given	–0–
Liabilities.	(500,000)	(1,380,000)
Common stock	(600,000) ($20 par)	(200,000) ($10 par)
Additional paid-in capital.	(150,000)	(80,000)

On January 1, 2024, Penske acquired all of Stanza's outstanding stock for $680,000 fair value in cash and common stock. Penske also paid $10,000 in stock issuance costs. At the date of acquisition, copyrights (with a six-year remaining life) have a $440,000 book value but a fair value of $560,000.

a. As of December 31, 2024, what is the consolidated copyrights balance?

b. For the year ending December 31, 2024, what is consolidated net income?

c. As of December 31, 2024, what is the consolidated retained earnings balance?

d. As of December 31, 2024, what is the consolidated balance to be reported for goodwill?

LO 3-2, 3-3, 3-4

24. Foxx Corporation acquired all of Greenburg Company's outstanding stock on January 1, 2022, for $600,000 cash. Greenburg's accounting records showed net assets on that date of $470,000, although equipment with a 10-year remaining life was undervalued on the records by $90,000.

Greenburg reports net income in 2022 of $90,000 and $100,000 in 2023. The subsidiary declared dividends of $20,000 in each of these two years.

Account balances for the year ending December 31, 2024, follow. Credit balances are indicated by parentheses.

	Foxx	Greenburg
Revenues	$ (800,000)	$ (600,000)
Cost of goods sold	100,000	150,000
Depreciation expense	300,000	350,000
Investment income	(20,000)	–0–
Net income	$ (420,000)	$ (100,000)
Retained earnings, 1/1/24	$(1,100,000)	$ (320,000)
Net income	(420,000)	(100,000)
Dividends declared	120,000	20,000
Retained earnings, 12/31/24	$(1,400,000)	$ (400,000)
Current assets	$ 300,000	$ 100,000
Investment in subsidiary	600,000	–0–
Equipment (net)	900,000	600,000
Buildings (net)	800,000	400,000
Land	600,000	100,000
Total assets	$ 3,200,000	$ 1,200,000
Liabilities	$ (900,000)	$ (500,000)
Common stock	(900,000)	(300,000)
Retained earnings	(1,400,000)	(400,000)
Total liabilities and equity	$(3,200,000)	$(1,200,000)

a. Determine the December 31, 2024, consolidated balance for each of the following accounts:

Depreciation Expense   Buildings
Dividends Declared   Goodwill
Revenues   Common Stock
Equipment

b. How does the parent's choice of an accounting method for its investment affect the balances computed in requirement part (a)?

c. Which method of accounting for this subsidiary is the parent actually using for internal reporting purposes?

d. If the parent company had used a different method of accounting for this investment, how could that method have been identified?

e. What would be Foxx's balance for retained earnings as of January 1, 2024, if each of the following methods had been in use?
- Initial value method
- Partial equity method
- Equity method

LO 3-1, 3-3a, 3-4

25. Allison Corporation acquired all of the outstanding voting stock of Mathias, Inc., on January 1, 2023, in exchange for $5,875,000 in cash. Allison intends to maintain Mathias as a wholly owned subsidiary. Both companies have December 31 fiscal year-ends. At the acquisition date, Mathias's stockholders' equity was $2,000,000 including retained earnings of $1,500,000.

At the acquisition date, Allison prepared the following fair-value allocation schedule for its newly acquired subsidiary:

Consideration transferred		$5,875,000
Mathias stockholders' equity		2,000,000
Excess fair over book value		$3,875,000
to unpatented technology (8-year remaining life)	$ 800,000	
to patents (10-year remaining life)	2,500,000	
to increase long-term debt (undervalued, 5-year remaining life)	(100,000)	3,200,000
Goodwill		$ 675,000

Postacquisition, Allison employs the equity method to account for its investment in Mathias. During the two years following the business combination, Mathias reports the following income and dividends:

	Income	Dividends
2023	$480,000	$25,000
2024	960,000	50,000

No asset impairments have occurred since the acquisition date.

Individual financial statements for each company as of December 31, 2024, follow. Parentheses indicate credit balances. Dividends declared were paid in the same period.

Income Statement	Allison	Mathias
Sales	$ (6,400,000)	$(3,900,000)
Cost of goods sold	4,500,000	2,500,000
Depreciation expense	875,000	277,000
Amortization expense	430,000	103,000
Interest expense	55,000	60,000
Equity earnings in Mathias	(630,000)	–0–
Net income	$ (1,170,000)	$ (960,000)
Statement of Retained Earnings		
Retained earnings, 1/1	$ (5,340,000)	$(1,955,000)
Net income (above)	(1,170,000)	(960,000)
Dividends declared	560,000	50,000
Retained earnings, 12/31	$ (5,950,000)	$(2,865,000)
Balance Sheet		
Cash	$ 75,000	$ 143,000
Accounts receivable	950,000	225,000
Inventories	1,700,000	785,000
Investment in Mathias	6,580,000	–0–
Equipment (net)	3,700,000	2,052,000
Patents	95,000	–0–
Unpatented technology	2,125,000	1,450,000
Goodwill	425,000	–0–
Total assets	$ 15,650,000	$ 4,655,000
Accounts payable	$ (500,000)	$ (90,000)
Long-term debt	(1,000,000)	(1,200,000)
Common stock	(8,200,000)	(500,000)
Retained earnings, 12/31	(5,950,000)	(2,865,000)
Total liabilities and equity	$(15,650,000)	$(4,655,000)

Required

a. Show how Allison determined its December 31, 2024, Investment in Mathias balance.

b. Prepare a worksheet to determine the consolidated values to be reported on Allison's financial statements.

26. On January 3, 2022, Persoff Corporation acquired all of the outstanding voting stock of Sea Cliff, Inc., in exchange for $6,000,000 in cash. Persoff elected to exercise control over Sea Cliff as a wholly owned subsidiary with an independent accounting system. Both companies have December 31 fiscal year-ends. At the acquisition date, Sea Cliff's stockholders' equity was $2,500,000 including retained earnings of $1,700,000.

Persoff pursued the acquisition, in part, to utilize Sea Cliff's technology and computer software. These items had fair values that differed from their values on Sea Cliff's books as follows:

Asset	Book Value	Fair Value	Remaining Useful Life
Patented technology	$140,000	$2,240,000	7 years
Computer software	$ 60,000	$1,260,000	12 years

Sea Cliff's remaining identifiable assets and liabilities had acquisition-date book values that closely approximated fair values. Since acquisition, no assets have been impaired. During the next three years, Sea Cliff reported the following income and dividends:

	Net Income	Dividends
2022	$900,000	$150,000
2023	940,000	150,000
2024	975,000	150,000

December 31, 2024, financial statements for each company follow. Parentheses indicate credit balances. Dividends declared were paid in the same period.

Income Statement	Persoff	Sea Cliff
Revenues	$ (2,720,000)	$(2,250,000)
Cost of goods sold	1,350,000	870,000
Depreciation expense	275,000	380,000
Amortization expense	370,000	25,000
Equity earnings in Sea Cliff	(575,000)	–0–
Net income	$ (1,300,000)	$ (975,000)
Statement of Retained Earnings		
Retained earnings, 1/1	$ (7,470,000)	$(3,240,000)
Net income (above)	(1,300,000)	(975,000)
Dividends declared	600,000	150,000
Retained earnings, 12/31	$ (8,170,000)	$(4,065,000)
Balance Sheet		
Current assets	$ 490,000	$ 375,000
Investment in Sea Cliff	7,165,000	–0–
Computer software	300,000	45,000
Patented technology	800,000	80,000
Goodwill	100,000	–0–
Equipment	1,835,000	4,500,000
Total assets	$ 10,690,000	$ 5,000,000
Liabilities	$ (520,000)	$ (135,000)
Common stock	(2,000,000)	(800,000)
Retained earnings, 12/31	(8,170,000)	(4,065,000)
Total liabilities and equity	$(10,690,000)	$(5,000,000)

a. Construct Persoff's acquisition-date fair-value allocation schedule for its investment in Sea Cliff.

b. Show how Persoff determined its Equity earnings in Sea Cliff balance for the year ended December 31, 2024.

c. Show how Persoff determined its December 31, 2024, Investment in Sea Cliff balance.

d. Prepare a worksheet to determine the consolidated values to be reported on Persoff's financial statements.

LO 3-1, 3-3a

27. On January 1, 2023, Palo Verde Corporation acquired 100 percent of the voting stock of Silverstone Corporation in exchange for $2,030,000 in cash and securities. On the acquisition date, Silverstone had the following balance sheet:

Cash	$ 23,000	Accounts payable	$1,050,000
Accounts receivable	97,000		
Inventory	140,000		
Equipment (net)	1,490,000	Common stock	800,000
Trademarks	850,000	Retained earnings	750,000
	$2,600,000		$2,600,000

At the acquisition date, the book values of Silverstone's assets and liabilities were generally equivalent to their fair values except for the following assets:

Asset	Book Value	Fair Value	Remaining Useful Life
Equipment	$1,490,000	$1,610,000	8 years
Royalty agreements	–0–	160,000	4 years
Trademarks	850,000	900,000	Indefinite

During the next two years, Silverstone has the following income and dividends in its own separately prepared financial reports to its parent.

	Net Income	Dividends
2023	$175,000	$25,000
2024	375,000	45,000

Dividends are declared and paid in the same period. The December 31, 2024, separate financial statements for each company follow. Parentheses indicate credit balances.

Income Statement	Palo Verde	Silverstone
Revenues	$ (4,200,000)	$(2,200,000)
Cost of goods sold	2,300,000	1,550,000
Depreciation expense	495,000	275,000
Amortization expense	105,000	–0–
Equity earnings in Silverstone	(320,000)	–0–
Net income	$ (1,620,000)	$ (375,000)

Statement of Retained Earnings		
Retained earnings, 1/1	$ (2,900,000)	$ (900,000)
Net income (above)	(1,620,000)	(375,000)
Dividends declared	150,000	45,000
Retained earnings, 12/31	$ (4,370,000)	$(1,230,000)

Balance Sheet		
Cash	$ 430,000	$ 35,000
Accounts receivable	693,000	75,000
Inventory	890,000	420,000
Investment in Silverstone	2,400,000	–0–
Equipment	6,000,000	1,400,000
Royalty agreements	115,000	–0–
Trademarks	2,500,000	850,000
Goodwill	172,000	–0–
Total assets	$ 13,200,000	$ 2,780,000
Accounts payable	$ (330,000)	$ (750,000)
Common stock	(8,500,000)	(800,000)
Retained earnings, 12/31	(4,370,000)	(1,230,000)
Total liabilities and equity	$(13,200,000)	$(2,780,000)

a. Prepare Palo Verde's acquisition-date fair-value allocation schedule for its investment in Silverstone.

b. Show how Palo Verde determined its December 31, 2024, Investment in Silverstone balance.

c. Prepare a worksheet to determine the balances for Palo Verde's December 31, 2024, consolidated financial statements.

LO 3-1, 3-3a

28. Kelsey Corporation acquired 100 percent of Snowdon Company's outstanding common stock on January 1 for $550,000 in cash. Snowdon reported net assets with a carrying amount of $350,000 at that time. Some of Snowdon's assets either were unrecorded (having been internally developed) or had fair values that differed from book values as follows:

	Book Values	Fair Values
Trademarks (indefinite life)	$ 60,000	$160,000
Software (5-year remaining life)	–0–	75,000
Equipment (10-year remaining life)	342,000	312,000

No impairment charges occurred during the year.

The following are financial statements at the end of the first year for these two companies prepared from their separately maintained accounting systems. Snowdon declared and paid dividends in the same period. Credit balances are indicated by parentheses.

	Kelsey	Snowdon
Revenues	$(1,125,000)	$(520,000)
Cost of goods sold	300,000	228,000
Depreciation expense	75,000	70,000
Amortization expense	25,000	–0–
Income from Snowdon	(210,000)	–0–
Net Income	$ (935,000)	$(222,000)
Retained earnings, 1/1	$ (700,000)	$(250,000)
Net Income	(935,000)	(222,000)
Dividends declared	142,000	80,000
Retained earnings, 12/31	$(1,493,000)	$(392,000)
Cash	$ 185,000	$ 105,000
Receivables	225,000	56,000
Inventory	175,000	135,000
Investment in Snowdon	680,000	–0–
Trademarks	474,000	60,000
Software	–0–	–0–
Equipment (net)	925,000	272,000
Goodwill	–0–	–0–
Total assets	$ 2,664,000	$ 628,000
Liabilities	$ (771,000)	$(136,000)
Common stock	(400,000)	(100,000)
Retained earnings, 12/31	(1,493,000)	(392,000)
Total liabilities and equity	$(2,664,000)	$(628,000)

a. Show how Kelsey computed the $210,000 Income from Snowdon balance. Discuss how you determined which accounting method Kelsey uses for its investment in Snowdon.

b. Without preparing a worksheet or consolidation entries, determine and explain the totals to be reported for this business combination for the year ending December 31.

c. Verify the totals determined in part (b) by producing a consolidation worksheet for Kelsey and Snowdon for the year ending December 31.

LO 3-1, 3-3a, 3-3b, 3-4

29. Following are separate financial statements of Michael Company and Aaron Company as of December 31, 2024 (credit balances indicated by parentheses). Michael acquired all of Aaron's outstanding voting stock on January 1, 2020, by issuing 20,000 shares of its own $1 par common stock. On the acquisition date, Michael Company's stock actively traded at $23.50 per share.

	Michael Company 12/31/24	Aaron Company 12/31/24
Revenues	$ (610,000)	$ (370,000)
Cost of goods sold	270,000	140,000
Amortization expense	115,000	80,000
Dividend income	(5,000)	–0–
Net income	$ (230,000)	$ (150,000)
Retained earnings, 1/1/24	$ (880,000)	$ (490,000)
Net income (above)	(230,000)	(150,000)
Dividends declared	90,000	5,000
Retained earnings, 12/31/24	$(1,020,000)	$ (635,000)
Cash	$ 110,000	$ 15,000
Receivables	380,000	220,000
Inventory	560,000	280,000
Investment in Aaron Company	470,000	–0–
Copyrights	460,000	340,000
Royalty agreements	920,000	380,000
Total assets	$ 2,900,000	$ 1,235,000
Liabilities	$ (780,000)	$ (470,000)
Preferred stock	(300,000)	–0–
Common stock	(500,000)	(100,000)
Additional paid-in capital	(300,000)	(30,000)
Retained earnings, 12/31/24	(1,020,000)	(635,000)
Total liabilities and equity	$(2,900,000)	$(1,235,000)

On the date of acquisition, Aaron reported retained earnings of $230,000 and a total book value of $360,000. At that time, its royalty agreements were undervalued by $60,000. This intangible was assumed to have a 6-year remaining life with no residual value. Additionally, Aaron owned a trademark with a fair value of $50,000 and a 10-year remaining life that was not reflected on its books. Aaron declared and paid dividends in the same period.

a. Using the preceding information, prepare a consolidation worksheet for these two companies as of December 31, 2024.

b. Instead of the initial value method, assume now that Michael applies the equity method to its Investment in Aaron account. What account balances would the parent's individual financial statements then show for the Equity in Subsidiary Earnings, Retained Earnings, and Investment in Aaron accounts?

c. Assuming that Michael applied the equity method to this investment, how would the consolidation entries differ on a December 31, 2024, worksheet?

d. Assuming that Michael applied the equity method to this investment, how would the December 31, 2024, reported consolidated balances differ?

LO 3-1, 3-3, 3-6

30. Giant acquired all of Small's common stock on January 1, 2020, in exchange for cash of $770,000. On that day, Small reported common stock of $170,000 and retained earnings of $400,000. At the acquisition date, $90,000 of the fair-value price was attributed to undervalued land while $50,000 was assigned to undervalued equipment having a 10-year remaining life. The $60,000 unallocated portion of the acquisition-date excess fair value over book value was viewed as goodwill. Over the next few years, Giant applied the equity method to the recording of this investment.

The following are individual financial statements for the year ending December 31, 2024. On that date, Small owes Giant $10,000. Small declared and paid dividends in the same period. Credits are indicated by parentheses.

a. How was the $135,000 Equity in Income of Small balance computed?

b. Without preparing a worksheet or consolidation entries, determine and explain the totals to be reported by this business combination for the year ending December 31, 2024.

c. Verify the amounts determined in part (b) by producing a consolidation worksheet for Giant and Small for the year ending December 31, 2024.

d. If Giant determined that the entire amount of goodwill from its investment in Small was impaired in 2024, how would the parent's accounts reflect the impairment loss? How would the worksheet process change? What impact does an impairment loss have on consolidated financial statements?

	Giant	Small
Revenues	$(1,175,000)	$ (360,000)
Cost of goods sold	550,000	90,000
Depreciation expense	172,000	130,000
Equity in income of Small	(135,000)	–0–
Net income	$ (588,000)	$ (140,000)
Retained earnings, 1/1/24	$(1,417,000)	$ (620,000)
Net income (above)	(588,000)	(140,000)
Dividends declared	310,000	110,000
Retained earnings, 12/31/24	$(1,695,000)	$ (650,000)
Current assets	$ 398,000	$ 318,000
Investment in Small	995,000	–0–
Land	440,000	165,000
Buildings (net)	304,000	419,000
Equipment (net)	648,000	286,000
Goodwill	–0–	–0–
Total assets	$ 2,785,000	$ 1,188,000
Liabilities	$ (840,000)	$ (368,000)
Common stock	(250,000)	(170,000)
Retained earnings (above)	(1,695,000)	(650,000)
Total liabilities and equity	$(2,785,000)	$ (1,188,000)

31. On January 1, 2023, Pinnacle Corporation exchanged $3,200,000 cash for 100 percent of the outstanding voting stock of Strata Corporation. On the acquisition date, Strata had the following balance sheet:

Cash	$ 122,000	Accounts payable	$ 375,000
Accounts receivable	283,000	Long-term debt	2,655,000
Inventory	350,000	Common stock	1,500,000
Buildings (net)	1,875,000	Retained earnings	1,100,000
Licensing agreements	3,000,000		$5,630,000
	$5,630,000		

Pinnacle prepared the following fair-value allocation:

Fair value of Strata (consideration transferred)		$3,200,000
Carrying amount acquired		2,600,000
Excess fair value		600,000
to buildings (undervalued)	$300,000	
to licensing agreements (overvalued)	(100,000)	200,000
to goodwill (indefinite life)		$ 400,000

At the acquisition date, Strata's buildings had a 10-year remaining life and its licensing agreements were due to expire in 5 years. On December 31, 2024, Strata's accounts payable included an $85,000 current liability owed to Pinnacle. Strata Corporation continues its separate legal existence as a wholly owned subsidiary of Pinnacle with independent accounting records. Pinnacle employs the initial value method in its internal accounting for its investment in Strata.

The separate financial statements for the two companies for the year ending December 31, 2024, follow. Credit balances are indicated by parentheses.

	Pinnacle	Strata
Sales	$ (7,000,000)	$(3,000,000)
Cost of goods sold	4,650,000	1,700,000
Interest expense	255,000	160,000
Depreciation expense	585,000	350,000
Amortization expense		600,000
Dividend income	(50,000)	
Net income	$ (1,560,000)	$ (190,000)
Retained earnings, 1/1/24	$ (5,000,000)	$(1,350,000)
Net income	(1,560,000)	(190,000)
Dividends declared	560,000	50,000
Retained earnings, 12/31/24	$ (6,000,000)	$(1,490,000)
Cash	$ 433,000	$ 165,000
Accounts receivable	1,210,000	200,000
Inventory	1,235,000	1,500,000
Investment in Strata	3,200,000	
Buildings (net)	5,572,000	2,040,000
Licensing agreements		1,800,000
Goodwill	350,000	
Total assets	$ 12,000,000	$ 5,705,000
Accounts payable	$ (300,000)	$ (715,000)
Long-term debt	(2,700,000)	(2,000,000)
Common stock	(3,000,000)	(1,500,000)
Retained earnings, 12/31/24	(6,000,000)	(1,490,000)
Total liabilities and OE	$(12,000,000)	$(5,705,000)

a. Prepare a worksheet to consolidate the financial information for these two companies.

b. Compute the following amounts that would appear on Pinnacle's 2024 separate (nonconsolidated) financial records if Pinnacle's investment accounting was based on the equity method.

- Subsidiary income.
- Retained earnings, 1/1/24.
- Investment in Strata.

c. What effect does the parent's internal investment accounting method have on its consolidated financial statements?

LO 3-1, 3-3, 3-4

32. The following are selected accounts and balances for Jonah Company and Hill, Inc., as of December 31, 2024. Several of Jonah's accounts have been omitted. Credit balances are indicated by parentheses. Dividends were declared and paid in the same period.

	Jonah	Hill
Revenues	$(600,000)	$(250,000)
Cost of goods sold	280,000	100,000
Depreciation expense	120,000	50,000
Investment income	Not given	NA
Retained earnings, 1/1/24	(900,000)	(600,000)
Dividends declared	130,000	40,000
Current assets	200,000	690,000
Land	300,000	90,000
Buildings (net)	500,000	140,000
Equipment (net)	200,000	250,000
Liabilities	(400,000)	(310,000)
Common stock	(300,000)	(40,000)
Additional paid-in capital	(50,000)	(160,000)

Assume that Jonah acquired Hill on January 1, 2020, by issuing 7,000 shares of common stock having a par value of $10 per share but a fair value of $100 each. On January 1, 2020, Hill's land was undervalued by $20,000, its buildings were overvalued by $30,000, and equipment was undervalued by $60,000. The buildings had a 10-year remaining life; the equipment had a 5-year remaining life. A proprietary database with an appraised value of $100,000 was developed internally by Hill and was estimated to have a 20-year remaining useful life.

a. Determine and explain the December 31, 2024, consolidated totals for the following accounts:

Revenues	Amortization Expense	Database
Cost of Goods Sold	Buildings	Common Stock
Depreciation Expense	Equipment	Additional Paid-In Capital

b. In requirement part (a), why can the consolidated totals be determined without knowing which method the parent used to account for the subsidiary?

c. If the parent uses the equity method, what consolidation entries would be used on a 2024 worksheet?

LO 3-3, 3-4, 3-6

33. On January 1, 2024, Brooks Corporation exchanged $1,183,000 fair-value consideration for all of the outstanding voting stock of Chandler, Inc. At the acquisition date, Chandler had a book value equal to $1,105,000. Chandler's individual assets and liabilities had fair values equal to their respective book values except for the patented technology account, which was undervalued by $204,000 with an estimated remaining life of six years. The Chandler acquisition was Brooks's only business combination for the year.

In case expected synergies did not materialize, Brooks Corporation wished to prepare for a potential future spin-off of Chandler, Inc. Therefore, Brooks had Chandler maintain its separate incorporation and independent accounting information system as elements of continuing value.

On December 31, 2024, each company submitted the following financial statements for consolidation. Dividends were declared and paid in the same period. Parentheses indicated credit balances.

	Brooks Corp.	Chandler Inc.
Income Statement		
Revenues	$ (640,000)	$ (587,000)
Cost of goods sold	255,000	203,000
Gain on bargain purchase	(126,000)	–0–
Depreciation and amortization	150,000	151,000
Equity earnings from Chandler	(199,000)	–0–
Net income	$ (560,000)	$ (233,000)
Statement of Retained Earnings		
Retained earnings, 1/1	$(1,835,000)	$ (805,000)
Net income (above)	(560,000)	(233,000)
Dividends declared	100,000	40,000
Retained earnings, 12/31	$(2,295,000)	$ (998,000)
Balance Sheet		
Current assets	$ 343,000	$ 432,000
Investment in Chandler	1,468,000	–0–
Trademarks	134,000	221,000
Patented technology	395,000	410,000
Equipment	693,000	341,000
Total assets	$ 3,033,000	$ 1,404,000
Liabilities	$ (203,000)	$ (106,000)
Common stock	(535,000)	(300,000)
Retained earnings, 12/31	(2,295,000)	(998,000)
Total liabilities and equity	$(3,033,000)	$(1,404,000)

a. Show how Brooks determined the following account balances:
  • Gain on bargain purchase.
  • Earnings from Chandler.
  • Investment in Chandler.

b. Prepare a December 31, 2024, consolidated worksheet for Brooks and Chandler.

LO 3-3a 3-3b, 3-8

34. Branson paid $465,000 cash for all of the outstanding common stock of Wolfpack, Inc., on January 1, 2023. On that date, the subsidiary had a book value of $340,000 (common stock of $200,000 and retained earnings of $140,000), although various unrecorded royalty agreements (10-year remaining life) were assessed at a $100,000 fair value. Any remaining excess fair value was considered goodwill.

In negotiating the acquisition price, Branson also promised to pay Wolfpack's former owners an additional $50,000 if Wolfpack's income exceeded $120,000 total over the first two years after the acquisition. At the acquisition date, Branson estimated the probability-adjusted present value of this contingent consideration at $35,000. On December 31, 2023, based on Wolfpack's earnings to date, Branson increased the value of the contingency to $40,000.

During the subsequent two years, Wolfpack reported the following amounts for income and dividends:

	Net Income	Dividends Declared
2023	$65,000	$25,000
2024	75,000	35,000

In keeping with the original acquisition agreement, on December 31, 2024, Branson paid the additional $50,000 performance fee to Wolfpack's previous owners.

Prepare each of the following:

a. Branson's entry to record the acquisition of the shares of its Wolfpack subsidiary.

b. Branson's entries at the end of 2023 and 2024 to adjust its contingent performance obligation for changes in fair value and the December 31, 2024, payment.

c. Consolidation worksheet entries as of December 31, 2024, assuming that Branson has applied the equity method.

d. Consolidation worksheet entries as of December 31, 2024, assuming that Branson has applied the initial value method.

LO 3-3

35. Allen Company acquired 100 percent of Bradford Company's voting stock on January 1, 2020, by issuing 10,000 shares of its $10 par value common stock (having a fair value of $14 per share). As of that date, Bradford had stockholders' equity totaling $105,000. Land shown on Bradford's accounting records was undervalued by $10,000. Equipment (with a 5-year remaining life) was undervalued by $5,000. A secret formula developed by Bradford was appraised at $20,000 with an estimated life of 20 years.

The following are the separate financial statements for the two companies for the year ending December 31, 2024. There were no intra-entity payables on that date. Credit balances are indicated by parentheses.

	Allen Company	Bradford Company
Revenues	$ (485,000)	$(190,000)
Cost of goods sold	160,000	70,000
Depreciation expense	130,000	52,000
Equity in subsidiary earnings	(66,000)	–0–
Net income	$ (261,000)	$ (68,000)
Retained earnings, 1/1/24	$ (659,000)	$ (98,000)
Net income (above)	(261,000)	(68,000)
Dividends declared	175,500	40,000
Retained earnings, 12/31/24	$ (744,500)	$(126,000)
Current assets	$ 268,000	$ 75,000
Investment in Bradford Company	216,000	–0–
Land	427,500	58,000
Buildings and equipment (net)	713,000	161,000
Total assets	$ 1,624,500	$ 294,000
Current liabilities	$ (190,000)	$(103,000)
Common stock	(600,000)	(60,000)
Additional paid-in capital	(90,000)	(5,000)
Retained earnings, 12/31/24	(744,500)	(126,000)
Total liabilities and equity	$(1,624,500)	$(294,000)

a. Explain how Allen derived the $66,000 balance in the Subsidiary Earnings account.

b. Prepare a worksheet to consolidate the financial information for these two companies.

36. Tyler Company acquired all of Jasmine Company's outstanding stock on January 1, 2022, for $206,000 in cash. Jasmine had a book value of only $140,000 on that date. However, equipment (having an 8-year remaining life) was undervalued by $54,400 on Jasmine's financial records. A building with a 20-year remaining life was overvalued by $10,000. Subsequent to the acquisition, Jasmine reported the following:

	Net Income	Dividends Declared
2022	$50,000	$10,000
2023	60,000	40,000
2024	30,000	20,000

In accounting for this investment, Tyler has used the equity method. Selected accounts taken from the financial records of these two companies as of December 31, 2024, follow:

	Tyler Company	Jasmine Company
Revenues—operating.	$(310,000)	$(104,000)
Expenses	198,000	74,000
Equipment (net)	320,000	50,000
Buildings (net)	220,000	68,000
Common stock	(290,000)	(50,000)
Retained earnings, 12/31/24	(410,000)	(160,000)

Determine and explain the following account balances as of December 31, 2024:

a. Investment in Jasmine Company (on Tyler's individual financial records).

b. Equity in Subsidiary Earnings (on Tyler's individual financial records).

c. Consolidated Net Income.

d. Consolidated Equipment (net).

e. Consolidated Buildings (net).

f. Consolidated Goodwill (net).

g. Consolidated Common Stock.

h. Consolidated Retained Earnings, 12/31/24.

37. On January 1, 2023, Procise Corporation acquired 100 percent of the outstanding voting stock of GaugeRite Corporation for $1,980,000 cash. On the acquisition date, GaugeRite had the following balance sheet:

Cash	$ 14,000	Accounts payable	$ 120,000
Accounts receivable	100,000	Long-term debt	930,000
Land	700,000	Common stock	1,000,000
Equipment (net)	1,886,000	Retained earnings	650,000
	$2,700,000		$2,700,000

At the acquisition date, the following allocation was prepared:

Fair value of consideration transferred		$1,980,000
Book value acquired		1,650,000
Excess fair value over book value		330,000
To in-process research and development	$44,000	
To equipment (8-year remaining life)	56,000	100,000
To goodwill		$ 230,000

Although at acquisition date Procise had expected $44,000 in future benefits from GaugeRite's in-process research and development project, by the end of 2023 it was apparent that the research project was a failure with no future economic benefits.

On December 31, 2024, Procise and GaugeRite submitted the following trial balances for consolidation. There were no intra-entity payables on that date.

	Procise	GaugeRite
Sales	$ (3,500,000)	$(1,000,000)
Cost of goods sold	1,600,000	630,000
Depreciation expense	350,000	130,000
Other operating expenses	190,000	30,000
Subsidiary income.	(203,000)	–0–
Net income.	$ (1,563,000)	$ (210,000)
Retained earnings 1/1/24	$ (3,000,000)	$ (800,000)
Net income.	(1,563,000)	(210,000)
Dividends declared.	200,000	25,000
Retained earnings 12/31/24	$ (4,363,000)	$ (985,000)
Cash	$ 228,000	$ 50,000
Accounts receivable.	840,000	155,000
Inventory.	900,000	580,000
Investment in GaugeRite	2,257,000	–0–
Land.	3,500,000	700,000
Equipment (net)	4,785,000	1,700,000
Goodwill	290,000	–0–
Total assets	$ 12,800,000	$ 3,185,000
Accounts payable	$ (193,000)	$ (400,000)
Long-term debt	(3,094,000)	(800,000)
Common stock	(5,150,000)	(1,000,000)
Retained earnings 12/31/24.	(4,363,000)	(985,000)
Total liabilities and equities.	$(12,800,000)	$(3,185,000)

a. Show how Procise derived its December 31, 2024, Investment in GaugeRite account balance.

b. Explain the treatment of the acquired in-process research and development.

c. Prepare a consolidated worksheet for Procise and GaugeRite as of December 31, 2024.

LO 3-4, 3-6

38. On January 1, Palisades, Inc., acquired 100 percent of Sherwood Company's common stock for a fair value of $120,000,000 in cash and stock. The carrying amounts of Sherwood's assets and liabilities equaled their fair values except for its equipment, which was undervalued by $500,000 and had a 10-year remaining life.

Palisades specializes in media distribution and viewed its acquisition of Sherwood as a strategic move into content ownership and creation. Palisades expected both cost and revenue synergies from controlling Sherwood's artistic content (a large library of classic movies) and its sports programming specialty video operation. Accordingly, Palisades allocated all of Sherwood's assets and liabilities (including all $50,000,000 of goodwill recognized in the acquisition) to a newly formed operating segment appropriately designated as a reporting unit.

However, Sherwood's assets have taken longer than anticipated to produce the expected synergies with Palisades's operations. Accordingly, Palisades reviewed events and circumstances and concluded that Sherwood's fair value was likely less than its carrying amount. At year-end, Palisades assessed the Sherwood reporting unit's fair value to $110,000,000.

At December 31, Palisades and Sherwood submitted the following balances for consolidation. There were no intra-entity payables on that date. Also, Palisades had not yet recorded any goodwill impairment.

	Palisades, Inc.	Sherwood Co.
Revenues	$(18,570,000)	$(12,000,000)
Operating expenses.	10,350,000	11,800,000
Equity in Sherwood's earnings	(150,000)	
Dividends declared.	300,000	80,000
Retained earnings, 1/1.	(52,000,000)	(2,000,000)

(continued)

(continued)

	Palisades, Inc.	Sherwood Co.
Cash	175,000	109,000
Receivables (net).	210,000	897,000
Investment in Sherwood	120,070,000	
Broadcast licenses	350,000	14,014,000
Movie library.	365,000	45,000,000
Equipment (net)	131,000,000	17,500,000
Current liabilities	(185,000)	(650,000)
Long-term debt	(21,915,000)	(7,250,000)
Common stock	(170,000,000)	(67,500,000)

a. What is the relevant test to determine whether goodwill is impaired?

b. How did Palisades determine Sherwood's December 31 carrying amount of $120,070,000?

c. At what amount should Palisades record an impairment loss for its Sherwood reporting unit for the year?

d. What is consolidated net income for the year?

e. What is the December 31 consolidated balance for goodwill?

f. Prepare a consolidated worksheet for Palisades and Sherwood (Palisades's trial balance should first be adjusted for any appropriate impairment loss).

Appendix Problems

LO 3-8

39. Briefly discuss the cost savings that may result from a private company electing to amortize goodwill as opposed to annual impairment testing.

LO 3-8

40. Angela Corporation (a private company) acquired all of the outstanding voting stock of Eddy Tech, Inc., on January 1, 2024, in exchange for $9,000,000 in cash. At the acquisition date, Eddy Tech's stockholders' equity was $7,200,000 including retained earnings of $3,000,000.

At the acquisition date, Angela prepared the following fair value allocation schedule for its newly acquired subsidiary:

Consideration transferred		$9,000,000
Eddy's stockholder's equity		7,200,000
Excess fair over book value		$1,800,000
to patented technology (5-year remaining life)	$150,000	
to trade names (indefinite remaining life)	500,000	
to equipment (8-year remaining life)	50,000	700,000
Goodwill		$1,100,000

At the end of 2024, Angela and Eddy Tech report the following amounts from their individually maintained account balances, before consideration of their parent–subsidiary relationship. Parentheses indicate a credit balance.

	Angela	Eddy Tech
Sales	$(7,850,000)	$(2,400,000)
Cost of goods sold	4,200,000	1,300,000
Depreciation expense	425,000	48,000
Amortization expense	250,000	12,000
Other operating expenses	75,000	53,750
Net income.	$(2,900,000)	$ (986,250)

Required

Prepare a 2024 consolidated income statement for Angela and its subsidiary Eddy Tech. Assume that Angela, as a private company, elects to amortize goodwill over a 10-year period.

Develop Your Skills

RESEARCH CASE

CPA
skills

Jonas Tech Corporation recently acquired Innovation Plus Company. The combined firm consists of three related businesses that will serve as reporting units. In connection with the acquisition, Jonas requests your help with the following asset valuation and allocation issues. Support your answers with references to FASB ASC as appropriate.

Jonas recognizes several identifiable intangibles from its acquisition of Innovation Plus. It expresses the desire to have these intangible assets written down to zero in the acquisition period.

The price Jonas paid for Innovation Plus indicates that it paid a large amount for goodwill. However, Jonas worries that any future goodwill impairment may send the wrong signal to its investors about the wisdom of the Innovation Plus acquisition. Jonas thus wishes to allocate the combined goodwill of all of its reporting units to one account called *Enterprise Goodwill.* In this way, Jonas hopes to minimize the possibility of goodwill impairment because a decline in goodwill in one business unit could be offset by an increase in the value of goodwill in another business unit.

Required

1. Advise Jonas on the acceptability of its suggested immediate write-off of its identifiable intangibles.
2. Indicate the relevant factors to consider in allocating the value assigned to identifiable intangibles acquired in a business combination to expense over time.
3. Advise Jonas on the acceptability of its suggested treatment of goodwill.
4. Indicate the relevant factors to consider in allocating goodwill across an enterprise's business units.

TAPESTRY, INC., IMPAIRMENT ANALYSIS CASE

In its fiscal year 2020, Tapestry, Inc., the company that makes Coach and Kate Spade bags as well as Stuart Weitzman, reported a $210.7 million charge for goodwill impairment. Referring to Tapestry's 2020 financial statements and any other information from the media, address the following:

1. Which of Tapestry's reporting units suffered a 2020 goodwill impairment? What other Tapestry intangible asset declined due to impairment in 2020?
2. What were the underlying business reasons that required Tapestry recorded a goodwill impairment in 2020?
3. How did Tapestry reflect the 2020 goodwill impairment in its income statement and cash flow statement?
4. Describe in your own words the goodwill impairment testing performed by Tapestry in 2020 and the consequent loss measurement.

FASB ASC AND IASB RESEARCH CASE

A vice president for operations at Poncho Platforms asks for your help on a financial reporting issue concerning goodwill. Two years ago, the company suffered a goodwill impairment loss for its Chip Integration reporting unit. Since that time, however, the Chip Integration unit has recovered nicely and its current cash flows (and projected cash flows) are at an all-time high. The vice president now asks whether the goodwill loss can be reversed given the reversal of fortunes for the Chip Integration reporting unit.

1. Is impairment of goodwill reversible under U.S. GAAP? How about under IFRS? (Refer to FASB Topic 350, "Intangibles—Goodwill and Other," and *IAS 36,* "Impairment of Assets.")
2. Are goodwill impairment testing procedures the same under IFRS and U.S. GAAP? If not, how is goodwill tested for impairment under IFRS? (Refer to *IAS 36,* "Impairment of Assets.")

EXCEL CASE 1

On January 1, 2023, Innovus, Inc., acquired 100 percent of the common stock of ChipTech Company for $670,000 in cash and other fair-value consideration. ChipTech's fair value was allocated among its net assets as follows:

Fair value of consideration transferred for ChipTech		$670,000
Book value of ChipTech:		
Common stock and additional paid-in capital (APIC)	$130,000	
Retained earnings	370,000	500,000
Excess fair value over book value to		170,000
Trademark (10-year remaining life)	$ 40,000	
Existing technology (5-year remaining life)	80,000	120,000
Goodwill		$ 50,000

The December 31, 2024, trial balances for the parent and subsidiary follow (there were no intra-entity payables on that date):

	Innovus	ChipTech
Revenues	$ (990,000)	$(210,000)
Cost of goods sold	500,000	90,000
Depreciation expense	100,000	5,000
Amortization expense	55,000	18,000
Dividend income	(40,000)	–0–
Net income	$ (375,000)	$ (97,000)
Retained earnings, 1/1/24	$(1,555,000)	$(450,000)
Net income	(375,000)	(97,000)
Dividends declared	250,000	40,000
Retained earnings, 12/31/24	$(1,680,000)	$(507,000)
Current assets	$ 960,000	$ 355,000
Investment in ChipTech	670,000	
Equipment (net)	765,000	225,000
Trademark	235,000	100,000
Existing technology	–0–	45,000
Goodwill	450,000	–0–
Total assets	$ 3,080,000	$ 725,000
Liabilities	$ (780,000)	(88,000)
Common stock	(500,000)	(100,000)
Additional paid-in capital	(120,000)	(30,000)
Retained earnings, 12/31/24	(1,680,000)	(507,000)
Total liabilities and equity	$(3,080,000)	$(725,000)

Required

a. Using Excel, compute consolidated balances for Innovus and ChipTech. Either use a worksheet approach or compute the balances directly.

b. Prepare a second spreadsheet that shows a 2024 impairment loss for the entire amount of goodwill from the ChipTech acquisition.

EXCEL CASE 2

On January 1, 2023, Hi-Speed.com acquired 100 percent of the common stock of Wi-Free Co. for cash of $730,000. The consideration transferred was allocated among Wi-Free's net assets as follows:

Wi-Free fair value (cash paid by Hi-Speed)		$730,000
Book value of Wi-Free:		
Common stock and additional paid-in capital (APIC)	$ 130,000	
Retained earnings	370,000	500,000
Excess fair value over book value to		230,000
In-process R&D	$ 75,000	
Computer software (overvalued)	(30,000)	
Internet domain name	120,000	165,000
Goodwill		$ 65,000

At the acquisition date, the computer software had a 4-year remaining life, and the internet domain name was estimated to have a 10-year remaining life. By the end of 2023, it became clear that the acquired in-process research and development would yield no economic benefits and Hi-Speed.com recognized an impairment loss. At December 31, 2024, Wi-Free's accounts payable included a $30,000 amount owed to Hi-Speed.

The December 31, 2024, trial balances for the parent and subsidiary follow:

	Hi-Speed.com	Wi-Free Co.
Revenues	$(1,100,000)	$(325,000)
Cost of goods sold	625,000	122,000
Depreciation expense	140,000	12,000
Amortization expense	50,000	11,000
Equity in subsidiary earnings	(175,500)	–0–
Net income	$ (460,500)	$(180,000)
Retained earnings, 1/1/24	$(1,552,500)	$(450,000)
Net income	(460,500)	(180,000)
Dividends declared	250,000	50,000
Retained earnings, 12/31/24	$(1,763,000)	$(580,000)
Current assets	$ 1,034,000	$ 345,000
Investment in Wi-Free	856,000	–0–
Equipment (net)	713,000	305,000
Computer software	650,000	130,000
Internet domain name	–0–	100,000
Goodwill	–0–	–0–
Total assets	$ 3,253,000	$ 880,000
Liabilities	$ (870,000)	$(170,000)
Common stock	(500,000)	(110,000)
Additional paid-in capital	(120,000)	(20,000)
Retained earnings, 12/31/24	(1,763,000)	(580,000)
Total liabilities and equity	$(3,253,000)	$(880,000)

Required

a. Using Excel, prepare calculations showing how Hi-Speed derived the $856,000 amount for its investment in Wi-Free.

b. Using Excel, compute consolidated balances for Hi-Speed and Wi-Free. Either use a worksheet approach or compute the balances directly.

Excel Spreadsheet Project

Alternative Investment Methods, Goodwill Impairment, and Consolidated Financial Statements

In this project, you are to provide an analysis of alternative accounting methods for controlling interest investments and subsequent effects on consolidated reporting using Excel. Modeling in Excel helps you quickly assess the impact of alternative accounting methods on consolidated financial reporting, and helps you develop a better understanding of accounting for combined reporting entities.

Consolidated Worksheet Preparation

You will be creating and entering formulas to complete four worksheets. The first objective is to demonstrate the effect of different methods of accounting for the investments (equity, initial value, and partial equity) on the parent company's trial balance and on the consolidated worksheet subsequent to acquisition. The second objective is to show the effect on consolidated balances and key financial ratios of recognizing a goodwill impairment loss.

The project requires preparation of the following four separate worksheets:

a. Consolidated information worksheet (follows).
b. Equity method consolidation worksheet.
c. Initial value method consolidation worksheet.
d. Partial equity method consolidation worksheet.

In formulating your solution, each worksheet should link directly to the first worksheet. Also, feel free to create supplemental schedules to enhance the capabilities of your worksheet.

Project Scenario

Pecos Company acquired 100 percent of Suaro's outstanding stock for $1,450,000 cash on January 1, 2023, when Suaro had the following balance sheet:

Assets		Liabilities and Equity	
Cash	$ 37,000	Liabilities	$(422,000)
Receivables	82,000		
Inventory	149,000	Common stock	(350,000)
Land	90,000	Retained earnings	(126,000)
Equipment (net)	225,000		
Software	315,000		
Total assets	$898,000	Total liabilities and equity	$(898,000)

At the acquisition date, the fair values of each identifiable asset and liability that differed from book value were as follows:

Land	$ 80,000	
Brand name	60,000	(indefinite life—unrecognized on Suaro's books)
Software	415,000	(2-year estimated remaining useful life)
In-process R&D	300,000	

Additional Information

- Although at acquisition date Pecos expected future benefits from Suaro's in-process research and development (R&D), by the end of 2023 it became clear that the research project was a failure with no future economic benefits.

- During 2023, Suaro earns $75,000 and pays no dividends.

- Selected amounts from Pecos's and Suaro's separate financial statements at December 31, 2024, are presented in the consolidated information worksheet. All consolidated worksheets are to be prepared as of December 31, 2024, two years subsequent to acquisition.

- Pecos's January 1, 2024, Retained Earnings balance—before any effect from Suaro's 2023 income—is $(930,000) (credit balance).

- Pecos has 500,000 common shares outstanding for EPS calculations and reported $2,943,100 for consolidated assets at the beginning of the period.

The following is the consolidated information worksheet:

	A	B	C	D
1	**December 31, 2024, trial balances**			
2				
3		**Pecos**	**Suaro**	
4	Revenues	$(1,052,000)	$(427,000)	
5	Operating expenses	821,000	262,000	
6	Goodwill impairment loss	?		
7	Income of Suaro	?		
8	Net income	?	$(165,000)	
9				
10	Retained earnings—Pecos 1/1/24	?		
11	Retained earnings—Suaro 1/1/24		(201,000)	
12	Net income (above)	?	(165,000)	
13	Dividends declared	200,000	35,000	
14	Retained earnings 12/31/24	?	$(331,000)	
15				
16	Cash	195,000	95,000	
17	Receivables	247,000	143,000	
18	Inventory	415,000	197,000	
19	Investment in Suaro	?		
20				
21				
22				
23	Land	341,000	85,000	
24	Equipment (net)	240,100	100,000	
25	Software		312,000	
26	Other intangibles	145,000		
27	Goodwill			
28	Total assets	?	$ 932,000	
29				
30	Liabilities	(1,537,100)	(251,000)	
31	Common stock	(500,000)	(350,000)	
32	Retained earnings (above)	?	(331,000)	
33	Total liabilities and equity	?	$(932,000)	
34				
35	Fair-value allocation schedule			
36	Price paid	1,450,000		
37	Book value	476,000		
38	Excess initial value	974,000	Amortizations	
39	to land	(10,000)	2020	2021
40	to brand name	60,000	?	?

(continued)

(continued)

	A	B	C	D
41	to software	100,000	?	?
42	to IPR&D	300,000	?	?
43	to goodwill	524,000	?	?
44				
45	Suaro's RE changes	Income	Dividends	
46	2023	75,000	0	
47	2024	165,000	35,000	

Project Requirements

Complete the four worksheets as follows:

1. Input the consolidated information worksheet provided and complete the fair-value allocation schedule by computing the excess amortizations for 2023 and 2024.

2. Using separate worksheets, prepare Pecos's trial balances for each of the indicated accounting methods (equity, initial value, and partial equity). Use only formulas for the Investment in Suaro, the Income of Suaro, and Retained Earnings accounts.

3. Using references to other cells only (either from the consolidated information worksheet or from the separate method sheets), prepare for each of the three consolidation worksheets:
   - Adjustments and eliminations.
   - Consolidated balances.

4. Calculate and present the effects of a 2024 total goodwill impairment loss on the following ratios for the consolidated entity:
   - Earnings per share (EPS).
   - Return on assets.
   - Return on equity.
   - Debt to equity.

   Your worksheets should have the capability to adjust immediately for the possibility that all acquisition goodwill can be considered impaired in 2024.

5. Prepare a report that describes and discusses the following worksheet results:
   a. The effects of alternative investment accounting methods on the parent's trial balances and the final consolidation figures.
   b. The relation between consolidated retained earnings and the parent's retained earnings under each of the three (equity, initial value, partial equity) investment accounting methods.
   c. The effect on EPS, return on assets, return on equity, and debt-to-equity ratios of the recognition that all acquisition-related goodwill is considered impaired in 2024.

Consolidated Financial Statements and Outside Ownership

Walmart, Inc. (Walmart), in its 2021 consolidated financial statements, includes the accounts of the company and all of its subsidiaries in which a controlling interest is maintained. For those consolidated subsidiaries where Walmart's ownership is less than 100 percent, the outside stockholders' interests are shown as *noncontrolling interests* in the stockholders' equity section of its consolidated balance sheet. On its consolidated income statement, Walmart also allocates a share of the consolidated net income and other comprehensive income to the noncontrolling interest.

A number of reasons exist for one company to hold less than 100 percent ownership of a subsidiary. The parent might not have had sufficient resources available to obtain all of the outstanding stock. As a second possibility, a few subsidiary stockholders may elect to retain their ownership, perhaps in hope of getting a better price at a later date.

Lack of total ownership is frequently encountered with foreign subsidiaries. The laws of some countries prohibit outsiders from maintaining complete control of domestic business enterprises. In other areas of the world, a parent can seek to establish better relations with a subsidiary's employees, customers, and local government by maintaining some percentage of native ownership.

LO 4-1

Understand that business combinations can occur with less than complete ownership.

Regardless of the reason for owning less than 100 percent, the parent consolidates the financial data of every subsidiary when control is present. As discussed in Chapter 2, *complete ownership is not a prerequisite for consolidation.* A single economic entity is formed whenever one company is able to control the decision-making process of another.

Although most parent companies own 100 percent of their subsidiaries, a significant number, such as Walmart, establish control with a lesser amount of stock. The remaining outside owners are collectively referred to as *a noncontrolling interest,* which replaces the traditional term *minority interest.*[1] The presence of these other stockholders poses a number of reporting questions for the accountant. Whenever less than 100 percent of a subsidiary's voting stock is held, how should the subsidiary's accounts be valued within consolidated financial statements? How should the presence of these additional owners be acknowledged?

[1] The term *minority interest* had been used almost universally to identify the presence of other outside owners. However, current GAAP refers to these outside owners as the noncontrolling interest. Because this term is more descriptive, it is used throughout this textbook.

Learning Objectives

After studying this chapter, you should be able to:

LO 4-1 Understand that business combinations can occur with less than complete ownership.

LO 4-2 Describe the concepts and valuation principles underlying the acquisition method of accounting for the noncontrolling interest.

LO 4-3 Allocate goodwill acquired in a business combination across the controlling and noncontrolling interests.

LO 4-4 Demonstrate the computation and allocation of consolidated net income in the presence of a noncontrolling interest.

LO 4-5 Identify and calculate the four noncontrolling interest figures that must be included within the consolidation process, and prepare a consolidation worksheet in the presence of a noncontrolling interest.

LO 4-6 Identify appropriate placements for the components of the noncontrolling interest in consolidated financial statements.

LO 4-7 Determine the effect on consolidated financial statements of a control premium paid by the parent.

LO 4-8 Understand the impact on consolidated financial statements of a midyear acquisition.

LO 4-9 Understand the impact on consolidated financial statements when a step acquisition has taken place.

LO 4-10 Record the sale of a subsidiary (or a portion of its shares).

159

LO 4-2

Describe the concepts and valuation principles underlying the acquisition method of accounting for the noncontrolling interest.

Consolidated Financial Reporting in the Presence of a Noncontrolling Interest

Noncontrolling Interest Defined

The authoritative accounting literature defines a noncontrolling interest as follows:

> The ownership interests in the subsidiary that are held by owners other than the parent is a non-controlling interest. The noncontrolling interest in a subsidiary is part of the equity of the consolidated group. (FASB ASC 810-10-45-15)

When a parent company acquires a controlling ownership interest with less than 100 percent of a subsidiary's voting shares, it must account for the noncontrolling shareholders' interest in its consolidated financial statements. The noncontrolling interest represents an additional set of owners who have legal claim to the subsidiary's net assets. Examples of companies with noncontrolling interests include the following:

Company	Recent Noncontrolling Interest Value
AT&T	$ 17.5 billion
Walmart	8.5 billion
Exxon Mobil	6.9 billion
General Motors	6.0 billion
Walt Disney	4.5 billion
Coca-Cola	1.9 billion
Verizon	1.4 billion
Costco	514.0 million

Exhibit 4.1 provides a framework for introducing several fundamental challenges in accounting and reporting for a noncontrolling interest. The issues focus on how the parent, in its consolidated financial statements, should

- Recognize the subsidiary's assets and liabilities.
- Assign values to the subsidiary's assets and liabilities.
- Value and disclose the presence of the other owners as the noncontrolling interest.

The acquisition method's solution to these challenges involves both the *economic unit concept* and the *fair-value* measurement attribute. First, the economic unit concept views the parent and subsidiary companies as a single economic unit for financial reporting purposes. Thus, a controlled company must always be consolidated as a whole regardless of the parent's level of ownership. As shown in Exhibit 4.1, when a parent controls a subsidiary through a 70 percent ownership, the parent must consolidate 100 percent of the subsidiary's (and the parent's) assets and liabilities in order to reflect the single economic unit. The consolidated balance sheet then provides an owners' equity amount for the noncontrolling owners' interest—a recognition that the parent does not own 100 percent of the subsidiary's assets and liabilities.

EXHIBIT 4.1
Noncontrolling Interest—Date of Acquisition

PARENT AND 70% OWNED SUBSIDIARY COMPANIES Consolidated Balance Sheet Date of Acquisition	
Parent's assets (100%) **Subsidiary's assets (100%)**	Parent's liabilities (100%) **Subsidiary's liabilities (100%)** Parent company owners' equity • 100% of parent's net assets • **70% of subsidiary's net assets** **Noncontrolling owners' interest** • **30% of subsidiary net assets**

The acquisition method also captures the subsidiary's acquisition-date fair values as the relevant measurement attribute for reporting the financial effects of the business combination—including the noncontrolling interest. Fair values also provide for managerial accountability to investors and creditors for assessing the success or failure of the combination. In contrast, the parent's assets and liabilities remain at their previous carrying amounts.

Control and Accountability

In acquiring a controlling interest, a parent company becomes responsible for managing all the subsidiary's assets and liabilities even though it may own only a partial interest. If a parent can control the business activities of its subsidiary, it directly follows that the parent is accountable to its investors and creditors for all of the subsidiary's assets, liabilities, and profits. To provide a complete picture of the acquired subsidiary requires fair-value measurements for both the subsidiary as a whole and its individual assets and liabilities. Thus, for business combinations involving less-than-100 percent ownership, the acquirer recognizes and measures the following at the acquisition date:

- All subsidiary identifiable assets and liabilities at their full fair values.[2]
- Noncontrolling interest at fair value.
- Goodwill or a gain from a bargain purchase.

In concluding that consolidated statements involving a noncontrolling interest should initially show all of the subsidiary's assets and liabilities at their full fair values, the 2005 FASB exposure draft Business Combinations (para. B23.a.) observed:

> The acquirer obtains control of the acquiree at the acquisition date and, therefore, becomes responsible and accountable for all of the acquiree's assets, liabilities, and activities, regardless of the percentage of its ownership in the investee.
>
> . . . an important purpose of financial statements is to provide users with relevant and reliable information about the performance of the entity and the resources under its control. That applies regardless of the extent of the ownership interest a parent holds in a particular subsidiary. The Boards concluded that measurement at fair value enables users to better assess the cash generating abilities of the identifiable net assets acquired in the business combination and the accountability of management for the resources entrusted to it.

To summarize, even though a company acquires less than 100 percent of another firm, financial reporting standards require the parent to include in its consolidated financial statements 100 percent of the assets acquired and liabilities assumed. At the acquisition date, the parent measures at fair value both the subsidiary as a whole and its identifiable assets and liabilities. Also, the parent recognizes the noncontrolling interest at its acquisition-date fair value. However, as discussed next, measuring the fair value of the noncontrolling interest presents some special challenges.

Subsidiary Acquisition-Date Fair Value in the Presence of a Noncontrolling Interest

When a parent company acquires a less-than-100 percent controlling interest in another firm, the acquisition method requires a determination of the acquisition-date fair value of the acquired firm for consolidated financial reporting. The total acquired firm fair value in the presence of a partial acquisition is the sum of the following two components at the acquisition date:

- The fair value of the controlling interest.
- The fair value of the noncontrolling interest.

The sum of these two components serves as the starting point for the parent in valuing and reporting the subsidiary acquisition. If the sum exceeds the collective fair values of the identifiable net assets acquired and liabilities assumed, then goodwill is recognized. Conversely, if the collective fair values of the identifiable net assets acquired and liabilities assumed exceed the total fair value, the acquirer recognizes a gain on bargain purchase.

Measurement of the acquisition-date **controlling interest** fair value remains straightforward in the vast majority of cases—the consideration transferred by the parent typically

---

[2] As noted in Chapter 2, exceptions to the fair-value measurement principle include deferred taxes, certain employee benefits, indemnification assets, reacquired rights, share-based awards, and assets held for sale.

Discussion Question

NONCONTROLLING INTEREST VALUATION

The FASB received numerous comment letters during its deliberations prior to adopting the current financial accounting standards on business combinations. Many of these letters addressed the FASB's proposed (and ultimately accepted) use of the economic unit concept as a valuation basis for less-than-100-percent acquisitions. A sampling of these letters includes the following observations:

Bob Laux, Microsoft: Microsoft agrees with the board that the principles underlying standards should strive to reflect the underlying economics of transactions and events. However, we do not believe the board's conclusion that recognizing the entire economic value of the acquiree, regardless of the ownership interest in the acquiree at the acquisition date, reflects the underlying economics.

Patricia A. Little, Ford Motor Company: We agree that recognizing 100 percent of the fair value of the acquiree is appropriate. We believe that this is crucial in erasing anomalies which were created when only the incremental ownership acquired was fair valued and the minority interest was reflected at its carryover basis.

Sharilyn Gasaway, Alltel Corporation: One of the underlying principles . . . is that the acquirer should measure and recognize the fair value of the acquiree as a whole. If 100 percent of the ownership interests are acquired, measuring and recognizing 100 percent of the fair value is both appropriate and informative. However, if less than 100 percent of the ownership interests are acquired, recognizing the fair value of 100 percent of the business acquired is not representative of the value actually acquired. In the instance in which certain minority owners retain their ownership interest, recognizing the fair value of the minority interest does not provide sufficient benefit to financial statement users to justify the additional cost incurred to calculate that fair value.

Pricewaterhouse Coopers: We agree that the noncontrolling interest should be recorded at its fair value when it is initially recorded in the consolidated financial statements. As such, when control is obtained in a single step, the acquirer would record 100 percent of the fair value of the assets acquired (including goodwill) and liabilities assumed.

Loretta Cangialosi, Pfizer: While we understand the motivation of the FASB to account for all elements of the acquisition transaction at fair value, we are deeply concerned about the practice issues that will result. The heavy reliance on expected value techniques, use of the hypothetical market participants, the lack of observable markets, and the obligation to affix values to "possible" and even "remote" scenarios, among other requirements, will all conspire to create a standard that will likely prove to be nonoperational, unauditable, representationally unfaithful, abuse-prone, costly, and of limited (and perhaps negative) shareholder value.

Do you think the FASB made the correct decision in requiring consolidated financial statements to recognize all of the subsidiary's assets and liabilities at fair value, regardless of the percentage ownership acquired by the parent?

provides the best evidence of fair value of the acquirer's interest. However, there is no parallel consideration transferred available to value the **noncontrolling interest** at the acquisition date. Therefore, the parent must employ other valuation techniques to estimate the fair value of the noncontrolling interest at the acquisition date. Often, a parent can rely on readily available market trading activity to provide a fair valuation for its subsidiary's noncontrolling interest. As seen in FASB ASC 805-20-30-7, the acquisition method

> requires the acquirer to measure a noncontrolling interest in the acquiree at its fair value at the acquisition date. An acquirer sometimes will be able to measure the acquisition-date fair value of a noncontrolling interest on the basis of a quoted price in an active market for the equity shares (that is, those not held by the acquirer).

However, in the absence of fair-value evidence based on market trades, firms must turn to less objective measures of noncontrolling interest fair value. FASB ASC 805-20-30-7 goes on to say that

> In other situations, however, a quoted price in an active market for the equity shares will not be available. In those situations, the acquirer would measure the fair value of the noncontrolling interest using another valuation technique.

For acquired firms that are not actively traded (e.g., private companies), noncontrolling interest fair-value measurements are frequently determined using significant inputs not observable in a market.[3] In such cases, valuation models based on subsidiary discounted cash flows or residual income projections may be employed to estimate the acquisition-date fair value of the noncontrolling interest.

For example, when Walmart, Inc., acquired 77 percent of FlipKart, an Indian e-commerce company for $16 billion, Walmart measured the acquisition-date fair value of the 23 percent noncontrolling interest at $4.9 billion. As noted in Walmart's 10-Q report at the time, the $4.9 billion noncontrolling interest measurement was determined using a projected income approach.

Control Premiums, Noncontrolling Interest Valuation, and Goodwill

Acquirers frequently pay a premium price per share to garner sufficient shares to ensure a controlling interest. Then, once enough shares are acquired to obtain control (and the percentage ownership desired), the remaining (noncontrolling interest) shares no longer provide the added benefit of transferring control to the new owner and, therefore, may sell at a price less than the shares that yielded control.

For example, when Expedia, Inc., acquired its 63 percent controlling interest in Trivago, the fair value of the noncontrolling interest excluded any control premium. In discussing the Trivago acquisition, Expedia's annual report noted

> The fair value of the 37% noncontrolling interest was estimated to be $344 million at the time of acquisition based on the fair value per share, excluding the control premium. The control premium was derived directly based on the additional consideration paid to certain shareholders in order to obtain control. The additional consideration was determined to be the best estimate to represent the control premium as it was a premium paid only to the controlling shareholders.

Control premiums are properly included in the fair value of the controlling interest, but as the Expedia–Trivago combination demonstrates, they sometimes do not affect the fair values of the remaining subsidiary shares. Therefore, separate independent valuations for the controlling and noncontrolling interests are often needed for measuring the total fair value of the subsidiary.

One important accounting and reporting effect of a control premium involves the goodwill acquired in the acquisition. When a parent company pays a control premium, the additional consideration transferred typically increases goodwill. However, because the noncontrolling interest shareholders did not pay a control premium, the incremental amount of goodwill is attributable to the parent.

To properly report ownership equity in consolidated financial statements, acquisition-date goodwill should be apportioned across the controlling and noncontrolling interests. As presented in the following section, the amount of goodwill attributable to the parent and noncontrolling interest depends on whether the parent has paid a control premium in the acquisition. If no control premium was paid, goodwill is allocated in proportion to the ownership percentages of the parent and noncontrolling interests. However, when a control premium is paid, the goodwill is allocated disproportionately to the parent, reflecting the extra price paid to extract synergies from the acquired firm.

Goodwill Allocation across Ownership Interests—Parent Pays No Control Premium

In some situations, the parent pays no control premium for an acquired firm. Such cases may include the acquisition of firms in distress or firms for which a sale to an acquirer presents an attractive option for current shareholders to maintain their value going forward. To illustrate,

LO 4-3

Allocate goodwill acquired in a business combination across the controlling and noncontrolling interests.

---

[3] Such determinations represent a level 3 fair-value measurement in the fair-value hierarchy as defined in ASC Topic 820, Fair Value Measurement.

assume Portage, Inc., pays $70 per share for 9,000 shares of Stone, Inc., representing a 90 percent equity interest. Also assume that the remaining 1,000 noncontrolling interest shares continue to trade at $70. The total fair value of Stone is then estimated at $700,000 as follows:

Fair value of controlling interest ($70 × 9,000 shares)	$630,000
Fair value of noncontrolling interest ($70 × 1,000 shares).	70,000
Acquisition-date fair value of Stone, Inc.	$700,000

At the acquisition date, Portage assessed the total fair value of Stone's identifiable net assets at $600,000. Therefore, we compute goodwill as the excess of the acquisition-date fair value of the firm as a whole over the sum of the fair values of the identifiable net assets as follows:

Acquisition-date fair value of Stone, Inc..	$700,000
Fair value of Stone's identifiable net assets.	600,000
Goodwill	$100,000

We then allocate goodwill across the controlling and noncontrolling interest based on the excess of their respective acquisition-date fair values and their proportionate share of the subsidiary's identifiable net assets as follows:

	90% Controlling Interest	10% Noncontrolling Interest	Total
Acquisition-date fair value of Stone, Inc. . . .	$630,000	$70,000	$700,000
Relative fair value of Stone's identifiable net assets (90% and 10%).	540,000	60,000	600,000
Goodwill	$ 90,000	$10,000	$100,000

Note that in this case, because the price per share paid by the parent equals the noncontrolling interest per share fair value, goodwill is recognized proportionately across the two ownership groups.

Goodwill Allocation across Ownership Interests—Parent Pays a Control Premium

In many situations, acquirers must bid up the price beyond current trading values to induce sufficient numbers of shareholder to sell. The incremental amount paid in a business combination above the preacquisition subsidiary value is referred to as a **control premium.** As observed in ASC 805-20-30-8,

> The fair values of the acquirer's interest in the acquiree and the noncontrolling interest on a per-share basis might differ. The main difference is likely to be the inclusion of a control premium in the per-share fair value of the acquirer's interest in the acquiree.

Such control premiums affect acquisition-date valuation and goodwill allocation across the controlling and noncontrolling interests. To illustrate, we now assume that Portage pays a control premium to acquire Stone. Although Stone's shares were trading at $70 per share, Portage ended up paying $675,000 (an average of $75 per share) to acquire 90 percent of the outstanding shares.[4] Thus, Portage paid a $45,000 control premium for its acquisition of 90 percent of Stone as follows:

Amount paid by Portage, Inc., for 90% of Stone, Inc. shares	$675,000
Preacquisition trading value of 90% Stone, Inc. shares	630,000
Control premium	$ 45,000

During the weeks following the acquisition, the 10 percent noncontrolling interest in Stone, Inc., continues to trade in a $69-to-$71 range.

In this case, the $75 average per share price paid by Portage ($675,000 ÷ 9,000 shares) does not appear representative of the fair value of all the shares of Stone, Inc. The fact that

---

[4] A more detailed analysis of the effect of a control premium on consolidated financial reporting is presented later in this chapter.

the noncontrolling interest shares continued to trade around $70 per share indicates a $70,000 fair value for the 1,000 shares not owned by Portage. Therefore, the noncontrolling interest valuation is best evidenced by the $70,000 traded fair value for 1,000 of Stone's shares, not the price paid by Portage.

The 9,000 shares acquired by Portage, though, have a fair value of $675,000 and incorporate the additional value Portage expects to extract with Stone beyond the per share preacquisition price. Thus, the fair value of Stone is measured as the sum of the respective fair values of the controlling and noncontrolling interests as follows:

Fair value of controlling interest ($75 × 9,000 shares)	$675,000
Fair value of noncontrolling interest ($70 × 1,000 shares)	70,000
Acquisition-date fair value of Stone, Inc.	$745,000

Next, we allocate the goodwill acquired in the Stone acquisition across the controlling and noncontrolling interests as follows:

	Controlling Interest	Noncontrolling Interest	Total
Acquisition-date fair value of Stone, Inc.	$675,000	$70,000	$745,000
Relative fair value of Stone's identifiable net assets (90% and 10% of $600,000)	540,000	60,000	600,000
Goodwill	$135,000	$10,000	$145,000

Observe in the schedule that the parent first allocates goodwill to its controlling interest for the excess of the fair value of the parent's equity interest over its share of the fair value of the identifiable net assets. In a similar fashion, the acquisition-date fair value of the noncontrolling interest is compared to its share of the fair value of the identifiable net assets. As a result, the previous goodwill allocation (~93 percent to the controlling interest and ~7 percent to the noncontrolling interest) is disproportionate to the 90 percent and 10 percent relative ownership interests.

Comparing the current case (control premium paid) with the previous case (no control premium paid) provides insight into the resulting goodwill allocation.

	No Control Premium	Control Premium	Difference
Price paid by Portage	$630,000	$675,000	+$45,000
Goodwill allocated to Portage	$ 90,000	$135,000	+$45,000

As seen in the preceding schedule, the entire incremental $45,000 paid by Portage as a control premium results in an extra $45,000 goodwill allocation to Portage. None of the incremental payment resulted in additional goodwill allocation to the noncontrolling interest, which remains at $10,000 in both cases.

In the unlikely event that the noncontrolling interest's proportionate share of the subsidiary's net asset fair values exceeds its total fair value, such an excess would serve to reduce the goodwill recognized by the parent and no goodwill would be allocated to the noncontrolling interest. Finally, if the total fair value of the acquired firm is less than the collective sum of its identifiable net assets, a *bargain purchase* occurs. In such rare combinations, the parent recognizes the entire gain on bargain purchase in current income. In no case is any amount of the gain allocated to the noncontrolling interest.

LO 4-4

Demonstrate the computation and allocation of consolidated net income in the presence of a noncontrolling interest.

Allocating Consolidated Net Income to the Parent and Noncontrolling Interest

Consolidated net income measures the results of operations for the combined entity. Reflecting the economic unit concept, consolidated net income includes 100 percent of the parent's net income and 100 percent of the subsidiary's net income, adjusted for excess acquisition-date fair value over book value amortizations. Once consolidated net income is determined, it is then allocated to the parent company and the noncontrolling interests. Because the noncontrolling interests' ownership pertains only to the subsidiary, their share of consolidated net income is limited to a share of the subsidiary's net income adjusted for acquisition-date excess fair-value amortizations.[5]

To illustrate, again assume that Portage acquires 90 percent of Stone, Inc. Further assume that current-year consolidated net income equals $108,000, including $10,000 of annual acquisition-date excess fair-value amortization. If Stone reports revenues of $280,000 and expenses of $160,000 based on its internal book values, then the noncontrolling interest share of Stone's income can be computed as follows:

Noncontrolling Interest in Subsidiary Stone Company Net Income	
Stone revenues	$280,000
Stone expenses	160,000
Stone net income	$120,000
Excess acquisition-date fair-value amortization	10,000
Stone net income adjusted for excess amortization	$110,000
Noncontrolling interest percentage	10%
Noncontrolling interest share of adjusted subsidiary net income	$ 11,000

The $11,000 noncontrolling interest share of adjusted subsidiary net income is equivalent to the noncontrolling interest share of consolidated net income. This figure is then simply subtracted from the combined entity's consolidated net income to derive the parent's interest in consolidated net income. Thus, the allocation is presented in Portage's consolidated financial statements as follows:

Consolidated Net Income Allocation	
Consolidated net income	$108,000
Less: Net income attributable to noncontrolling interest	11,000
Net income attributable to parent (controlling interest)	$ 97,000

Note that the noncontrolling shareholders' portion of consolidated net income is limited to their 10 percent share of the adjusted *subsidiary* income. These shareholders own a 10 percent interest in the subsidiary company but no ownership in the parent firm.[6]

LO 4-5

Identify and calculate the four noncontrolling interest figures that must be included within the consolidation process, and prepare a consolidation worksheet in the presence of a noncontrolling interest.

Partial Ownership Consolidations (Acquisition Method)

Having reviewed the basic concepts of accounting for a noncontrolling interest, we now concentrate on the mechanical aspects of the consolidation process when an outside ownership is present. Specifically, we examine consolidations for time periods subsequent to the date of acquisition to analyze the full range of accounting complexities created by a noncontrolling interest. This discussion centers on the acquisition method as required under generally accepted accounting principles.

The acquisition method focuses initially on incorporating in the consolidated financial statements 100 percent of the subsidiary's assets and liabilities at their acquisition-date fair values. Note that subsequent to acquisition, changes in current fair values for assets and liabilities are not recognized.[7] Instead, the subsidiary assets acquired and liabilities assumed are

---

[5] Adjusting the subsidiary net income for the excess fair-value amortizations recognizes that the noncontrolling interest represents equity in the subsidiary's net assets as remeasured to fair values on the acquisition date.

[6] In this text, we assume that the relative ownership percentages of the parent and noncontrolling interest represent an appropriate basis for allocating adjusted subsidiary net income across ownership groups.

[7] Exceptions common to all firms (whether subject to consolidation or not) include recognizing changing fair values for marketable equity securities and other financial instruments.

reflected in future consolidated financial statements using their acquisition-date fair values net of subsequent excess fair value amortizations (or possibly reduced for impairment).

The presence of a noncontrolling interest does not dramatically alter the consolidation procedures presented in Chapter 3. The unamortized balance of the acquisition-date fair-value allocation must still be computed and included within the consolidated totals. Excess fair-value amortization expenses of these allocations are recognized each year as appropriate. Reciprocal balances are eliminated. Beyond these basic steps, the measurement and recognition of four noncontrolling interest balances add a new dimension to the process of consolidating financial information. The parent company must determine and then enter each of these figures when constructing a worksheet:

- Noncontrolling interest in the subsidiary as of the beginning of the current year.
- Net income attributable to the noncontrolling interest.
- Subsidiary dividends attributable to the noncontrolling interest.
- Noncontrolling interest as of the end of the year (found by combining the three preceding balances).

We next illustrate the effects of a less-than-100-percent acquisition on the preparation of consolidated financial statements when no control premium was paid by the parent. Then, we provide an example characterized by an acquisition control premium.

Illustration—Partial Acquisition with No Control Premium

To illustrate, assume that King Company acquires 80 percent of Pawn Company's 100,000 outstanding voting shares on January 1, 2023, for $9.75 per share or a total of $780,000 cash consideration. Further assume that the 20 percent noncontrolling interest shares traded both before and after the acquisition date at an average of $9.75 per share. The total fair value of Pawn to be used initially in consolidation is

Consideration transferred by King ($9.75 × 80,000 shares)	$780,000
Noncontrolling interest fair value ($9.75 × 20,000 shares)	195,000
Pawn's acquisition-date fair value	$975,000

Thus, King did not pay a control premium to acquire its share of Pawn—both sets of shares have identical per share fair values.

Exhibit 4.2 presents the book value of Pawn's accounts as well as the fair value of each asset and liability on the acquisition date. Pawn's total fair value is attributed to Pawn's assets and liabilities, as shown in Exhibit 4.3. Annual amortization relating to these allocations also is included in this schedule. Although expense figures are computed for only the initial years, some amount of amortization is recognized in each of the 20 years following the acquisition (the life assumed for the patented technology).

EXHIBIT 4.2
Subsidiary Accounts—Date of Acquisition

PAWN COMPANY			
Account Balances			
January 1, 2023			
	Book Value	**Fair Value**	**Difference**
Current assets	$ 440,000	$440,000	$ –0–
Trademarks (indefinite life)	260,000	320,000	60,000
Patented technology (20-year remaining life) . . .	480,000	600,000	120,000
Equipment (10-year remaining life)	110,000	100,000	(10,000)
Long-term liabilities (8 years to maturity)	(550,000)	(510,000)	40,000
Net assets	$ 740,000	$950,000	$210,000
Common stock	$(230,000)		
Retained earnings, 1/1/23	(510,000)		

Note: Parentheses indicate a credit balance.

EXHIBIT 4.3   Excess Fair-Value Allocations

KING COMPANY AND 80% OWNED SUBSIDIARY PAWN COMPANY
Fair-Value Allocation and Amortization
January 1, 2023

	Allocation	Remaining Life (years)	Annual Excess Amortizations
Pawn's acquisition-date fair value (100%)	$975,000		
Pawn's acquisition-date book value (100%)	(740,000)		
Fair value in excess of book value	$235,000		
Adjustments (100%) to			
Trademarks	$ 60,000	indefinite	$ –0–
Patented technology	120,000	20	6,000
Equipment	(10,000)	10	(1,000)
Long-term liabilities (8 years to maturity)	40,000	8	5,000
Goodwill	$ 25,000	indefinite	$ –0–
Annual amortizations of excess fair value over book value			
(initial years)			$ 10,000

Goodwill Allocation to the Controlling and Noncontrolling Interests

	Controlling Interest	Noncontrolling Interest	Total
Fair value at acquisition date	$780,000	$195,000	$975,000
Relative fair value of Pawn's identifiable net assets			
(80% and 20%)	760,000	190,000	950,000
Goodwill	$ 20,000	$ 5,000	$ 25,000

Exhibit 4.3 shows first that all identifiable assets acquired and liabilities assumed are adjusted to their full individual fair values at the acquisition date. The noncontrolling interest will share proportionately in these fair-value adjustments. Exhibit 4.3 also shows that any excess fair value not attributable to Pawn's identifiable net assets is assigned to goodwill. Because the controlling and noncontrolling interests' acquisition-date fair values are identical at $9.75 per share, the resulting goodwill is allocated proportionately across these ownership interests.

Consolidated financial statements will be produced for the year ending December 31, 2024. This date is arbitrary. Any time period subsequent to 2023 could serve to demonstrate the applicable consolidation procedures. Having already calculated the acquisition-date fair-value allocations and related amortization, the accountant can construct a consolidation of these two companies along the lines demonstrated in Chapter 3. Only the presence of the 20 percent noncontrolling interest alters this process.

To complete the information needed for this combination, assume that Pawn Company reports the following changes in retained earnings since King's acquisition:

Current year (2024)	
Net income	$90,000
Less: Dividends declared	(50,000)
Increase in retained earnings	$40,000
Prior years (only 2023 in this illustration):	
Increase in retained earnings	$70,000

Assuming that King Company applies the equity method, the Investment in Pawn Company account as of December 31, 2024, can be constructed as shown in Exhibit 4.4. Note that the $852,000 balance is computed based on applying King's 80 percent ownership to Pawn's income (less amortization) and dividends. Although 100 percent of the subsidiary's assets,

EXHIBIT 4.4
Equity Method Investment Balance

KING COMPANY Investment in Pawn Company Equity Method December 31, 2024		
Acquisition price for 80% interest		$780,000
Prior year (2023):		
Increase in retained earnings (80% × $70,000)	$56,000	
Excess amortization expenses (80% × $10,000) (Exhibit 4.3)	(8,000)	48,000
Current year (2024):		
Income accrual (80% × $90,000)	72,000	
Excess amortization expense (80% × $10,000) (Exhibit 4.3)	(8,000)	
Equity in subsidiary earnings	64,000*	
Dividends from Pawn (80% × $50,000)	(40,000)	24,000
Balance, 12/31/24		$852,000

*This figure appears in King's 2024 income statement. See Exhibit 4.5.

liabilities, revenues, and expenses will be combined in consolidation, the internal accounting for King's investment in Pawn is based on its 80 percent ownership. This technique facilitates worksheet adjustments that allocate various amounts to the noncontrolling interest. Exhibit 4.5 presents the separate financial statements for these two companies as of December 31, 2024, and the year then ended, based on the information provided.

EXHIBIT 4.5
Separate Financial Records

KING COMPANY AND PAWN COMPANY Separate Financial Statements For December 31, 2024, and the Year Then Ended		
	King	**Pawn**
Revenues	$ (910,000)	$ (430,000)
Cost of goods sold	344,000	200,000
Depreciation expense	60,000	20,000
Amortization expense	100,000	75,000
Interest expense	70,000	45,000
Equity in subsidiary earnings (see Exhibit 4.4)	(64,000)	–0–
Net income	$ (400,000)	$ (90,000)
Retained earnings, 1/1	$ (860,000)	$ (580,000)
Net income (above)	(400,000)	(90,000)
Dividends declared	60,000	50,000
Retained earnings, 12/31	$(1,200,000)	$ (620,000)
Current assets	$ 726,000	$ 445,000
Trademarks	304,000	295,000
Patented technology	880,000	540,000
Equipment (net)	390,000	160,000
Investment in Pawn Company (see Exhibit 4.4)	852,000	–0–
Total assets	$ 3,152,000	$ 1,440,000
Long-term liabilities	$(1,082,000)	$ (590,000)
Common stock	(870,000)	(230,000)
Retained earnings, 12/31	(1,200,000)	(620,000)
Total liabilities and equities	$(3,152,000)	$(1,440,000)

Note: Parentheses indicate a credit balance.

Consolidated Totals

Although the inclusion of a 20 percent outside ownership complicates the consolidation process, the 2024 totals to be reported by this business combination can nonetheless be determined without the use of a worksheet:

- *Revenues* = $1,340,000. The revenues of the parent and the subsidiary are added together. The acquisition method includes the subsidiary's revenues in total although King owns only 80 percent of the stock.
- *Cost of Goods Sold* = $544,000. The parent and subsidiary balances are added together.
- *Depreciation Expense* = $79,000. The parent and subsidiary balances are added together along with the $1,000 reduction in equipment depreciation, as indicated in Exhibit 4.3.
- *Amortization Expense* = $181,000. The parent and subsidiary balances are added together along with the $6,000 additional patented technology amortization expense, as indicated in Exhibit 4.3.
- *Interest Expense* = $120,000. The parent and subsidiary balances are added along with an additional $5,000. Exhibit 4.3 shows Pawn's long-term debt reduced by $40,000 to fair value. Because the maturity value remains constant, the $40,000 represents a discount amortized to interest expense over the remaining eight-year life of the debt.
- *Equity in Subsidiary Earnings* = –0–. The parent's investment income is replaced with the subsidiary's separate revenues and expenses, which are then included in the consolidated totals.
- *Consolidated Net Income* = $416,000. The consolidated entity's total earnings before allocation to the controlling and noncontrolling ownership interests.
- *Net Income Attributable to Noncontrolling Interest* = $16,000. The outside owners are assigned 20 percent of Pawn's reported net income of $90,000 less $10,000 total excess fair-value amortization. The acquisition method shows this amount as an allocation of consolidated net income.
- *Net Income Attributable to King Company (Controlling Interest)* = $400,000. The acquisition method shows this amount as an allocation of consolidated net income.
- *Retained Earnings, 1/1* = $860,000. The parent company figure equals the consolidated total because the equity method was applied. If the initial value method or the partial equity method had been used, the parent's balance would require adjustment to include any unrecorded figures.
- *Dividends Declared* = $60,000. Only the parent company balance is reported. Eighty percent of the subsidiary's dividends are distributable to the parent and are thus eliminated. The remaining distribution goes to the outside owners and serves to reduce the noncontrolling interest balance.
- *Retained Earnings, 12/31* = $1,200,000. The balance is found by adding the controlling interest's share of consolidated net income to the beginning consolidated retained earnings balance and then subtracting the parent's dividends. Because the equity method is utilized, the parent company figure reflects the total for the business combination.
- *Current Assets* = $1,171,000. The parent's and subsidiary's balances are added.
- *Trademarks* = $659,000. The parent's balance is added to the subsidiary's balance plus the $60,000 allocation of the acquisition-date fair value (see Exhibit 4.3).
- *Patented Technology* = $1,528,000. The parent's balance is added to the subsidiary's balance plus the $120,000 excess fair-value allocation less two years' excess amortizations of $6,000 per year (see Exhibit 4.3).
- *Equipment* = $542,000. The parent's balance is added to the subsidiary's balance less the $10,000 acquisition-date fair-value reduction plus two years' expense reductions of $1,000 per year (see Exhibit 4.3).
- *Investment in Pawn Company* = –0–. The balance reported by the parent is eliminated so that the subsidiary's assets and liabilities can be included in the consolidated totals.
- *Goodwill* = $25,000. The total goodwill allocation shown in Exhibit 4.3 is reported.

- *Total Assets* = $3,925,000. This balance is a summation of the consolidated assets.
- *Long-Term Liabilities* = $1,642,000. The parent's balance is added to the subsidiary's balance less the $40,000 acquisition-date fair-value allocation net of two years' amortizations of $5,000 per year (see Exhibit 4.3).
- *Noncontrolling Interest in Subsidiary* = $213,000. The outside ownership is 20 percent of the subsidiary's year-end book value adjusted for any unamortized excess fair value attributed to the noncontrolling interest:

Noncontrolling interest in Pawn at 1/1		
20% of $810,000 beginning book value—common stock plus 1/1		
retained earnings		$162,000
20% of unamortized excess fair-value allocations as of 1/1		45,000
Noncontrolling interest in Pawn 1/1		$207,000
Net income attributable to noncontrolling interest (see page 170)		16,000
Dividends distributable to noncontrolling interest (20% of $50,000 total)		(10,000)
Noncontrolling interest in Pawn at 12/31		$213,000

- *Common Stock* = $870,000. Only the parent's balance is reported.
- *Retained Earnings, 12/31* = $1,200,000, as shown in Exhibit 4.5.
- *Total Liabilities and Equities* = $3,925,000. This total is a summation of consolidated liabilities, noncontrolling interest, and equities.

Alternative Calculation of Noncontrolling Interest at December 31, 2024

The acquisition method requires that the noncontrolling interest in the subsidiary's net assets be measured at fair value at the date of acquisition. Subsequent to acquisition, however, the noncontrolling interest value is adjusted for its share of subsidiary net income, excess fair-value amortizations, and dividends. The following schedule demonstrates how the noncontrolling interest's acquisition-date fair value is adjusted to show the ending consolidated balance sheet amount.

Fair value of 20% noncontrolling interest in Pawn at acquisition date		$195,000
20% of $70,000 change in Pawn's 2023 retained earnings	14,000	
20% of excess fair-value amortizations	(2,000)	12,000
2024 net income allocation [20% × ($90,000 − $10,000)]		16,000
2024 dividends (20% × $50,000)		(10,000)
Noncontrolling interest in Pawn at December 31, 2024		$213,000

As the schedule shows, the fair-value principle applies only to the initial noncontrolling interest valuation.

Worksheet Process—Acquisition Method

The consolidated totals for King and Pawn also can be determined by means of a worksheet, as shown in Exhibit 4.6. Comparing this example with Exhibit 3.7 in Chapter 3 indicates that the presence of a noncontrolling interest does not create a significant number of changes in the consolidation procedures.

    The worksheet still includes elimination of the subsidiary's stockholders' equity accounts (Entry **S**) although, as explained next, this entry is expanded to record the beginning noncontrolling interest for the year. The second worksheet entry (Entry **A**) recognizes the excess acquisition-date fair-value allocations at January 1 after one year of amortization with an additional adjustment to the beginning noncontrolling interest. Intra-entity income and dividends are removed also (Entries **I** and **D**) while current-year excess amortization expenses are recognized (Entry **E**). The differences from the Chapter 3 illustrations relate exclusively to

EXHIBIT 4.6   Noncontrolling Interest (No Control Premium) Illustrated

KING COMPANY AND PAWN COMPANY
Consolidation Worksheet
For Year Ending December 31, 2024

Investment: Equity Method   *Ownership: 80%*

Accounts	King Company*	Pawn Company*	Consolidation Entries Debit	Consolidation Entries Credit	Noncontrolling Interest	Consolidated Totals
Revenues	(910,000)	(430,000)				(1,340,000)
Cost of goods sold	344,000	200,000				544,000
Depreciation expense	60,000	20,000		(E) 1,000		79,000
Amortization expense	100,000	75,000	(E) 6,000			181,000
Interest expense	70,000	45,000	(E) 5,000			120,000
Equity in Pawn's earnings (see Exhibit 4.4)	(64,000)	–0–	(I) 64,000			–0–
Separate company net income	(400,000)	(90,000)				
Consolidated net income						(416,000)
Net income attributable to noncontrolling interest					(16,000)	16,000
Net income attributable to King Company						(400,000)
Retained earnings, 1/1	(860,000)	(580,000)	(S) 580,000			(860,000)
Net income (above)	(400,000)	(90,000)				(400,000)
Dividends declared	60,000	50,000		(D) 40,000	10,000 *reduce*	60,000
Retained earnings, 12/31	(1,200,000)	(620,000)				(1,200,000)
Current assets	726,000	445,000				1,171,000
Trademarks	304,000	295,000	(A) 60,000			659,000
Patented technology	880,000	540,000	(A) 114,000	(E) 6,000		1,528,000
Equipment (net)	390,000	160,000	(E) 1,000	(A) 9,000		542,000
Investment in Pawn Company (see Exhibit 4.4)	852,000	–0–	(D) 40,000	(S) 648,000 (A) 180,000 (I) 64,000		–0–
Goodwill	–0–	–0–	(A) 25,000			25,000
Total assets	3,152,000	1,440,000				3,925,000
Long-term liabilities	(1,082,000)	(590,000)	(A) 35,000	(E) 5,000		(1,642,000)
Common stock	(870,000)	(230,000)	(S) 230,000			(870,000)
Noncontrolling interest in Pawn, 1/1				(S) 162,000 (A) 45,000	(207,000)	
Noncontrolling interest in Pawn, 12/31					(213,000)	(213,000)
Retained earnings, 12/31	(1,200,000)	(620,000)				(1,200,000)
Total liabilities and equities	(3,152,000)	(1,440,000)	1,160,000	1,160,000		(3,925,000)

*See Exhibit 4.5.
Note: Parentheses indicate a credit balance.
Consolidation entries:
(S) Elimination of subsidiary's stockholders' equity along with recognition of January 1 noncontrolling interest.
(A) Allocation of subsidiary total fair value in excess of book value, unamortized balances as of January 1.
(I)   Elimination of intra-entity income (equity accrual less amortization expenses).
(D) Elimination of intra-entity dividends.
(E) Recognition of amortization expenses of fair-value allocations.

the recognition of the three components of the noncontrolling interest. In addition, *a separate Noncontrolling Interest column is added to the worksheet to accumulate these components to form the year-end figure to be reported on the consolidated balance sheet.*

Noncontrolling Interest—Beginning of Year   Under the acquisition method, the noncontrolling interest shares proportionately in the fair values of the subsidiary's identifiable net assets as adjusted for excess fair-value amortizations. On the consolidated worksheet, this total net fair value is represented by two components:

1. Pawn's stockholders' equity accounts (common stock and beginning retained earnings) indicate a January 1, 2024, book value of $810,000.
2. January 1, 2024, acquisition-date fair-value net of previous year's amortizations (in this case, 2023 only).

Therefore, the January 1, 2024, balance of the 20 percent outside ownership is computed as follows:

20% × $810,000 subsidiary book value at 1/1/24.	$162,000
20% × $225,000* unamortized excess fair-value allocation at 1/1/24	45,000
Noncontrolling interest in Pawn at 1/1/24	$207,000
*Acquisition-date excess fair over book value (Exhibit 4.3)	$235,000
Less: 2023 excess fair over book value amortization	(10,000)
Unamortized excess fair over book value amount at 1/1/24	$225,000

The $207,000 noncontrolling interest balance at 1/1/24 is recognized on the worksheet through Entry **S** ($162,000) and Entry **A** ($45,000):

Consolidation Entry S

Common Stock (Pawn)	230,000	
Retained Earnings, 1/1/24 (Pawn)	580,000	
Investment in Pawn Company (80%)		648,000
Noncontrolling Interest in Pawn Company, 1/1/24 (20%)		162,000
To eliminate beginning stockholders' equity accounts of subsidiary along with book-value portion of investment (equal to 80 percent ownership). Noncontrolling interest of 20 percent is also recognized.		

Consolidation Entry A

Trademarks	60,000	
Patented Technology	114,000	
Liabilities	35,000	
Goodwill	25,000	
Equipment		9,000
Investment in Pawn Company (80%)		180,000
Noncontrolling Interest in Pawn Company, 1/1/24 (20%)		45,000
To recognize unamortized excess fair value as of January 1, 2024, to Pawn's assets acquired and liabilities assumed in the combination. Also to allocate the unamortized fair value to the noncontrolling interest. Goodwill is attributable proportionately to controlling and noncontrolling interests.		

The total $207,000 balance assigned here to the outside owners at the beginning of the year is extended to the Noncontrolling Interest worksheet column (see Exhibit 4.6).

To complete the required worksheet adjustments, Entries **I, D,** and **E** are prepared as follows:

Consolidation Entry I

Equity in Pawn's Earnings	64,000	
Investment in Pawn Company		64,000
To eliminate intra-entity income accrual comprising subsidiary income less excess acquisition-date fair-value amortizations.		

Consolidation Entry D

Investment in Pawn Company	40,000	
Dividends Declared		40,000
To eliminate intra-entity dividends.		

Consolidation Entry E

Amortization Expense	6,000	
Interest Expense	5,000	
Equipment (net)	1,000	
Depreciation Expense		1,000
Patented Technology		6,000
Long-Term Liabilities		5,000
To recognize current-year excess fair-value amortizations.		

Noncontrolling Interest—Share of Current-Year Consolidated Net Income   Exhibit 4.6 shows the noncontrolling interest's share of current-year earnings is $16,000. The amount is based on the subsidiary's $90,000 net income (Pawn Company column) less excess acquisition-date fair-value amortizations. Thus, King assigns $16,000 to the outside owners computed as follows:

Net Income Attributable to Noncontrolling Interest	
Pawn Company net income	$90,000
Excess acquisition-date fair-value amortization	10,000
Net income adjusted for excess amortizations	$80,000
Noncontrolling interest percentage	20%
Net income attributable to noncontrolling interest in Pawn	$16,000

In effect, 100 percent of each subsidiary revenue and expense account (including excess acquisition-date fair-value amortizations) is consolidated with an accompanying 20 percent allocation to the noncontrolling interest. The 80 percent net effect corresponds to King's ownership.

Because $16,000 of consolidated net income accrues to the noncontrolling interest, this amount is added to the $207,000 beginning balance assigned (in Entries **S** and **A**) to these outside owners. The noncontrolling interest increases because the subsidiary generated a profit during the period.

Although we could record this allocation through an additional worksheet entry, the $16,000 is usually shown, as in Exhibit 4.6, by means of a columnar adjustment. The current-year accrual is simultaneously entered in the Income Statement section of the consolidated column as an allocation of consolidated net income and in the Noncontrolling Interest column as an increase. This procedure assigns a portion of the combined earnings to the outside owners rather than to the parent company owners.

Noncontrolling Interest—Dividends   The $40,000 dividend to the parent company is eliminated routinely through Entry **D,** but the remainder of Pawn's dividend went to the noncontrolling interest. The impact of the dividend (20 percent of the subsidiary's total) distributable to the other owners must be acknowledged. As shown in Exhibit 4.6, this remaining $10,000 is extended directly into the Noncontrolling Interest column on the worksheet as a reduction. It represents the decrease in the underlying claim of the outside ownership that resulted from the subsidiary's dividend declaration.

Noncontrolling Interest—End of Year   The ending assignment for these other owners is calculated by a summation of

Noncontrolling interest in Pawn beginning of year—credit balance	$207,000
Net income attributable to noncontrolling interest.....................	16,000
Less: Dividends to the outside owners................................	(10,000)
Noncontrolling interest in Pawn end of year—credit balance............	$213,000

The Noncontrolling Interest column on the worksheet in Exhibit 4.6 accumulates these figures. The $213,000 total is then transferred to the balance sheet, where it appears in the consolidated financial statements.

Consolidated Financial Statements

Having successfully consolidated the information for King and Pawn, the resulting financial statements for these two companies are produced in Exhibit 4.7. These figures are taken from the consolidation worksheet.

Exhibit 4.7 shows the consolidated income statement first. Consolidated net income is computed at the combined entity level as $416,000 and then allocated to the noncontrolling and controlling interests. The statement of changes in owners' equity provides details of the

EXHIBIT 4.7
Consolidated Statements with Noncontrolling Interest—Acquisition Method

KING COMPANY AND PAWN COMPANY
Consolidated Financial Statements
Income Statement
Year Ended December 31, 2024

Revenues	$1,340,000
Cost of goods sold	(544,000)
Depreciation expense	(79,000)
Amortization expense	(181,000)
Interest expense	(120,000)
Consolidated net income	$ 416,000
To noncontrolling interest	16,000
To King Company (controlling interest)	$ 400,000

Statement of Changes in Owners' Equity
Year Ended December 31, 2024

	King Company Owners		Noncontrolling Interest
	Retained Earnings	Common Stock	
Balance, January 1	$ 860,000	$870,000	$207,000
Net income	400,000		16,000
Less: Dividends	(60,000)		(10,000)
Balance, December 31	$1,200,000	$870,000	$213,000

Balance Sheet
At December 31, 2024

Assets	
Current assets	$1,171,000
Trademarks	659,000
Patented technology	1,528,000
Equipment (net)	542,000
Goodwill	25,000
Total assets	$3,925,000
Liabilities	
Long-term liabilities	$1,642,000
Owners' Equity	
Common stock—King Company	870,000
Noncontrolling interest in Pawn	213,000
Retained earnings	1,200,000
Total liabilities and owners' equity	$3,925,000

ownership changes for the year for both the controlling and noncontrolling interest shareholders. Finally, note the placement of the noncontrolling interest in the subsidiary's equity squarely in the consolidated owners' equity section.[8]

LO 4-7

Determine the effect on consolidated financial statements of a control premium paid by the parent.

Illustration—Partial Acquisition with Control Premium

To illustrate the valuation implications for an acquisition involving a control premium, again assume that King Company acquires 80 percent of Pawn Company's 100,000 outstanding voting shares on January 1, 2023. We also again assume that Pawn's shares traded before the acquisition date at an average of $9.75 per share. In this scenario, however, we assume that to acquire sufficient shares to gain control King pays a total of $880,000 cash consideration (an average price of $11 per share) for its 80 percent interest. King thus pays a $100,000 control premium to acquire Pawn ($880,000 less $9.75 × 80,000 shares). King anticipates that synergies with Pawn will create additional value for King's shareholders. Following the acquisition, the remaining 20 percent noncontrolling interest shares continue to trade at $9.75.

The total fair value of Pawn to be used initially in consolidation is thus computed as follows:

Consideration transferred by King ($11.00 × 80,000 shares)	$ 880,000
Noncontrolling interest fair value ($9.75 × 20,000 shares)	195,000
Pawn's total fair value at January 1, 2023	$1,075,000

In keeping with the acquisition method's requirement that identifiable assets acquired and liabilities assumed be adjusted to fair value, King allocates Pawn's total fair value as follows:

Fair value of Pawn at January 1, 2023		$1,075,000
Book value of Pawn at January 1, 2023		(740,000)
Fair value in excess of book value		$ 335,000
Adjustments to		
Trademarks	$ 60,000	
Patented technology	120,000	
Equipment	(10,000)	
Long-term liabilities	40,000	210,000
Goodwill		$ 125,000

Compared to the previous illustration with no control premium, note that the *identifiable* assets acquired and liabilities assumed are again adjusted to their full individual fair values at the acquisition date. Only the amount designated as goodwill is changed. Goodwill recognized is now $125,000—a $100,000 increase from $25,000 in the original fair-value allocation example as shown in Exhibit 4.3. In this case, King allocates $120,000 of the $125,000 total goodwill amount to its own interest as follows:

	Controlling Interest	Noncontrolling Interest	Total
Fair value at acquisition date	$880,000	$195,000	$1,075,000
Relative fair value of Pawn's identifiable			
net assets (80% and 20%)	760,000	190,000	950,000
Goodwill	$120,000	$ 5,000	$ 125,000

The initial acquisition-date fair value of $195,000 for the noncontrolling interest includes only a $5,000 goodwill allocation from the combination. Because the parent paid proportionately more for its share than the noncontrolling interest fair value, it receives a disproportionate amount of the combination goodwill.

---

[8] If appropriate, each component of other comprehensive income is allocated to the controlling and noncontrolling interests. The statement of changes in owners' equity would also provide an allocation of accumulated other comprehensive income elements across the controlling and noncontrolling interests.

To account for the disproportionate allocation of goodwill across the controlling and non-controlling interests, we separate the familiar consolidated worksheet entry **A** into two components labeled **A1** and **A2**. The **A1** worksheet entry allocates the excess acquisition-date fair value to the *identifiable* assets acquired and liabilities assumed (trademarks, patented technology, equipment, and liabilities). Note that the relative ownership percentages of the parent and noncontrolling interest (80 percent and 20 percent) provide the basis for allocating the $200,000 net identifiable asset adjustment to the parent's Investment account ($160,000) and the January 1, 2024, balance of the noncontrolling interest ($40,000).

Next, consolidated worksheet entry **A2** provides the recognition and allocation of the goodwill balance taking into account the differing per share prices of the parent's consideration transferred and the noncontrolling interest fair value. Note that the presence of a control premium affects primarily the parents' shares, and, thus, goodwill is disproportionately (relative to the ownership percentages) allocated to the controlling and noncontrolling interests. Exhibit 4.8 shows the consolidated worksheet for this extension to the King and Pawn example.

Consolidation Entry A1

Trademarks	60,000	
Patented Technology	114,000	
Liabilities	35,000	
Equipment		9,000
Investment in Pawn Company (80%)		160,000
Noncontrolling Interest in Pawn 1/1/24 (20%)		40,000

Consolidation Entry A2

Goodwill	125,000	
Investment in Pawn Company		120,000
Noncontrolling Interest in Pawn 1/1/24		5,000

The worksheet calculates the December 31, 2024, noncontrolling balance as follows:

Pawn January 1, 2024: 20% book value	$162,000
January 1, 2024: 20% excess fair-value allocation for Pawn's identifiable net assets ($200,000 × 20%) + $5,000 goodwill allocation	45,000
Noncontrolling interest at January 1, 2024	$207,000
2024 consolidated net income allocation	16,000
Noncontrolling interest share of Pawn dividends	(10,000)
Noncontrolling interest in Pawn, December 31, 2024	$213,000

Note that the $45,000 January 1, 2024, excess fair-value allocation to the noncontrolling interest includes the noncontrolling interest's full share of the amortized *identifiable* assets acquired and liabilities assumed in the combination but only $5,000 for goodwill. Because the parent King Company paid a $100,000 control premium (80,000 shares × $1.25), the additional $100,000 is allocated entirely to the controlling interest.

By comparing Exhibits 4.6 and 4.8, we can assess the effect of the separate acquisition-date valuations for the controlling and noncontrolling interests. As seen in the differences across Exhibits 4.6 and 4.8 calculated next, the presence of King's control premium affects the goodwill component in the consolidated financial statements and little else.

	Exhibit 4.6	Exhibit 4.8	Difference
On King's Separate Financial Statements			
Current assets	$ 726,000	$ 626,000	−$100,000
Investment in Pawn	852,000	952,000	+ 100,000
On the Consolidated Balances			
Current assets	1,171,000	1,071,000	− 100,000
Goodwill	25,000	125,000	+ 100,000

EXHIBIT 4.8   Noncontrolling Interest (Control Premium) Illustrated

KING COMPANY AND PAWN COMPANY
Consolidation Worksheet
For Year Ending December 31, 2024

Investment: Equity Method   *Ownership: 80%*

Accounts	King Company	Pawn Company	Consolidation Entries Debit	Consolidation Entries Credit	Noncontrolling Interest	Consolidated Totals
Revenues	(910,000)	(430,000)				(1,340,000)
Cost of goods sold	344,000	200,000				544,000
Depreciation expense	60,000	20,000		(E) 1,000		79,000
Amortization expense	100,000	75,000	(E) 6,000			181,000
Interest expense	70,000	45,000	(E) 5,000			120,000
Equity in Pawn's earnings	(64,000)	–0–	(I) 64,000			–0–
Separate company net income	(400,000)	(90,000)				
Consolidated net income						(416,000)
Net income attributable to noncontrolling interest					(16,000)	16,000
Net income attributable to King Company						(400,000)
Retained earnings, 1/1	(860,000)	(580,000)	(S) 580,000			(860,000)
Net income (above)	(400,000)	(90,000)				(400,000)
Dividends declared	60,000	50,000		(D) 40,000	10,000	60,000
Retained earnings, 12/31	(1,200,000)	(620,000)				(1,200,000)
Current assets	626,000	445,000				1,071,000
Trademarks	304,000	295,000	(A1) 60,000			659,000
Patented technology	880,000	540,000	(A1) 114,000	(E) 6,000		1,528,000
Equipment (net)	390,000	160,000	(E) 1,000	(A1) 9,000		542,000
Investment in Pawn Company	952,000	–0–	(D) 40,000	(S) 648,000		–0–
				(A1) 160,000		
				(A2) 120,000		
				(I) 64,000		
Goodwill	–0–	–0–	(A2) 125,000			125,000
Total assets	3,152,000	1,440,000				3,925,000
Long-term liabilities	(1,082,000)	(590,000)	(A1) 35,000	(E) 5,000		(1,642,000)
Common stock	(870,000)	(230,000)	(S) 230,000			(870,000)
Noncontrolling interest in Pawn 1/1				(S) 162,000		
				(A1) 40,000		
				(A2) 5,000	(207,000)	
Noncontrolling interest in Pawn 12/31					(213,000)	(213,000)
Retained earnings, 12/31	(1,200,000)	(620,000)				(1,200,000)
Total liabilities and equities	(3,152,000)	(1,440,000)	1,260,000	1,260,000		(3,925,000)

Note: Parentheses indicate a credit balance.
Consolidation entries:
(S)   Elimination of subsidiary's stockholders' equity along with recognition of January 1 noncontrolling interest.
(A1) Allocation of subsidiary identifiable net asset fair value in excess of book value, unamortized balances as of January 1.
(A2) Allocation of goodwill to parent and noncontrolling interest.
(I)   Elimination of intra-entity income (equity accrual less amortization expenses).
(D)   Elimination of intra-entity dividends.
(E)   Recognition of amortization expenses of fair-value allocations.

Because King paid an additional $100,000 for its 80 percent interest in Pawn, the initial value assigned to the Investment account increases, and current assets (i.e., additional cash paid for the acquisition) decrease by $100,000. The extra $100,000 then simply increases goodwill on the consolidated balance sheet. Note that the noncontrolling interest amount remains unchanged at $213,000 across Exhibits 4.6 and 4.8, consistent with the fact that its acquisition-date fair value was left unchanged at $195,000.

Effects Created by Alternative Investment Methods

In the King and Pawn illustrations, the parent uses the equity method and bases all worksheet entries on that approach. As discussed in Chapter 3, had King incorporated the initial value method or the partial equity method, a few specific changes in the consolidation process would be required although the reported figures would be identical.

Initial Value Method

The initial value method ignores two accrual-based adjustments. First, the parent recognizes dividend income rather than an equity income accrual. Thus, the parent does not accrue the percentage of the subsidiary's net income earned in past years in excess of dividends (the increase in subsidiary retained earnings). Second, the parent does not record amortization expense under the initial value method and therefore must include it in the consolidation process if proper totals are to be achieved. Because neither of these figures is recognized in applying the initial value method, an Entry *C is added to the worksheet to convert the previously recorded balances to the equity method. The parent's beginning Retained Earnings is affected by this adjustment as well as the Investment in Subsidiary account. The exact amount is computed as follows.

Conversion to Equity Method from Initial Value Method (Entry *C)

Combine:

1. The increase (since acquisition) in the subsidiary's retained earnings during past years (net income less dividends) times the parent's ownership percentage, and
2. The parent's percentage of total amortization expense for these same past years.

The parent's use of the initial value method requires an additional procedural change. Under this method, the parent recognizes income when its subsidiary declares a dividend. Entry (I) removes both intra-entity dividend income and subsidiary dividends to the parent. Thus, when the initial value method is used, Entry **D** is unnecessary.

Partial Equity Method

Again, an Entry *C is needed to convert the parent's retained earnings as of January 1 to the equity method. In this case, however, only the amortization expense for the prior years must be included. Recall that under the partial equity method, although the parent accrues its share of reported subsidiary income, it does not recognize any acquisition-date excess fair value amortization expenses.

LO 4-8

Understand the impact on consolidated financial statements of a midyear acquisition.

Revenue and Expense Reporting for Midyear Acquisitions

In virtually all of our previous examples, the parent gains control of the subsidiary on the first day of the fiscal year. How is the consolidation process affected if an acquisition occurs on a midyear (any other than the first day of the fiscal year) date?

When a company gains control at a midyear date, a few obvious changes are needed. The new parent must compute the subsidiary's book value as of that date to determine excess total fair value over book value allocations (e.g., intangibles). Excess amortization expenses as well as any equity accrual and dividend distributions are recognized for a period of less than a year. Finally, because only net income earned by the subsidiary after the acquisition date accrues to the new owners, it is appropriate to include only postacquisition revenues and expenses in consolidated totals.

Consolidating Postacquisition Subsidiary Revenue and Expenses

Following a midyear acquisition, a parent company excludes current-year subsidiary revenue and expense amounts that have accrued prior to the acquisition date from its consolidated totals. For example, when Comcast acquired AT&T Broadband, its December 31 year-end income statement included AT&T Broadband revenues and expenses only subsequent to the acquisition date. Comcast reported $8.1 billion in revenues that year. However, in a pro forma schedule, Comcast noted that had it included AT&T Broadband's revenues from January 1, total revenue for the year would have been $16.8 billion. However, because the $8.7 billion additional revenue ($16.8 billion − $8.1 billion) was not earned by Comcast owners, Comcast excluded this preacquisition revenue from its consolidated total.

To further illustrate the complexities of accounting for a midyear acquisition, assume that Tyler Company acquires 90 percent of Steven Company on July 1, 2024, for $900,000 and prepares the following fair-value allocation schedule:

Steven Company fair value, 7/1/24		$1,000,000
Steven Company book value, 7/1/24		
Common stock	$600,000	
Retained earnings, 7/1/24	200,000	800,000
Excess fair value over book value		$ 200,000
Adjust trademark to fair value (4-year remaining life)		200,000
Goodwill		$ –0–

The affiliates report the following 2024 income statement amounts from their own separate operations:

	Tyler	Steven
Revenues	$450,000	$300,000
Expenses	325,000	150,000
Dividends (declared quarterly)	100,000	20,000

Assuming that all revenues and expenses occurred evenly throughout the year, the December 31, 2024, consolidated income statement appears as follows:

TYLER COMPANY **Consolidated Income Statement** **For the Year Ended December 31, 2024**	
Revenues	$600,000
Expenses	425,000
Consolidated net income	$175,000
To noncontrolling interest	5,000
To Tyler Company (controlling interest)	$170,000

- *Revenues* = $600,000. Combined balances of $750,000 less $150,000 (½ of Steven's revenues).
- *Expenses* = $425,000. Combined balances of $475,000 less $75,000 (½ of Steven's expenses) plus $25,000 excess amortization ($200,000 ÷ 4 years × ½ year).
- *Net Income Attributable to Noncontrolling Interest* = $5,000. 10% × ($150,000 Steven's income − $50,000 excess amortization) × ½ year.

In this example, preacquisition subsidiary revenue and expense accounts are eliminated from the consolidated totals. Note also that by excluding 100 percent of the preacquisition income accounts from consolidation, the noncontrolling interest is viewed as coming into being as of the parent's acquisition date.[9]

---

[9] Current practice provides comparability across fiscal years through pro forma disclosures of various categories of revenue and expense as if the combination had occurred at the beginning of the reporting period. With the advent of modern information systems, separate cutoffs for revenues and expenses are readily available.

A midyear acquisition requires additional adjustments when preparing consolidation worksheets. The balances the subsidiary submits for consolidation typically include results for its entire fiscal period. Thus, in the December 31 financial statements, the book value of the firm acquired on a midyear date is reflected by a January 1 retained earnings balance plus revenues, expenses, and dividends from the beginning of the year to the acquisition date. To effectively eliminate subsidiary book value as of the acquisition date, Consolidation Entry **S** includes these items in addition to the other usual elements of book value (i.e., stock accounts). To illustrate, assuming that both affiliates submit fiscal year financial statements for consolidation, Tyler would make the following 2024 consolidation worksheet entry:

Consolidation Worksheet Entry S

Common Stock—Steven	600,000	
Retained Earnings—Steven (1/1/24)*	135,000	
Revenues	150,000	
Dividends Declared—Steven		10,000
Expenses		75,000
Noncontrolling Interest (7/1/24)		80,000
Investment in Steven		720,000

*To arrive at Steven's January 1 retained earning balance, we use the July 1 balance of $200,000 less income from the first six months of $75,000 (1/2 of $150,000 annual Steven income) plus $10,000 dividends declared.

Through Entry **S**, preacquisition subsidiary revenues, expenses, and dividends are effectively

- Included as part of the subsidiary book value elimination in the year of acquisition.
- Included as components of the beginning value of the noncontrolling interest.
- Excluded from the consolidated income statement and statement of retained earnings.

Acquisition Following an Equity Method Investment

In many cases, a parent company owns a noncontrolling equity interest in a firm prior to obtaining control. In such cases, as the preceding example demonstrates, the parent consolidates the postacquisition revenues and expenses of its new subsidiary. Because the parent owned an equity investment in the subsidiary prior to the control date, however, the parent reports on its income statement the "equity in earnings of the investee" that accrued up to the date control was obtained. In this case, in the year of acquisition, the consolidated income statement reports both combined revenues and expenses (postacquisition) of the subsidiary and equity method income (preacquisition).

In subsequent years, the need to separate pre- and postacquisition amounts is limited to ensuring that excess amortizations correctly reflect the midyear acquisition date. Finally, if the parent employs the initial value method of accounting for the investment in subsidiary on its books, the conversion to the equity method must also reflect only postacquisition amounts.

LO 4-9

Understand the impact on consolidated financial statements when a step acquisition has taken place.

Step Acquisitions

When Starbucks increased its percentage of ownership in its East China joint venture from 50 percent to 100 percent, it began consolidating its investment in East China. Prior to the acquisition of control through majority ownership, Starbucks accounted for its investment in East China using the equity method of accounting.

In all previous consolidation illustrations, control over a subsidiary was assumed to have been achieved through a single transaction. Obviously, Starbucks's takeover of East China shows that a combination can also result from a series of stock purchases. These step acquisitions further complicate the consolidation process. The financial information of the separate companies must still be brought together, but varying amounts of consideration have been transferred to former owners at several different dates. How do the initial acquisitions affect this process?

Control Achieved in Steps—Acquisition Method

A **step acquisition** occurs when control is achieved in a series of equity acquisitions, as opposed to a single transaction. As with all business combinations, the acquisition method measures the acquired firm (including the noncontrolling interest) at fair value at the date control is obtained. The acquisition of a controlling interest is considered an important economic, and therefore measurement, event. Consequently, the parent utilizes a single uniform valuation basis for all subsidiary assets acquired and liabilities assumed—fair value at the date control is obtained.

If the parent previously held a noncontrolling interest in the acquired firm, the parent remeasures that interest to fair value and recognizes a gain or loss. For example, when Coca-Cola increased its equity ownership in fairlife from 42.5 percent to 100 percent, it obtained control over fairlife, a producer of dairy products. To measure the subsidiary's acquisition-date fair value, Coca-Cola revalued its previously held 42.5 percent equity interest to fair value and recognized a $902 million gain. As a result, Coca-Cola increased its investment account for both the cash paid for the newly acquired shares and the increase in the fair value of its previously owned shares in fairlife.

Once control exists, if the parent acquires additional ownership shares in the subsidiary, no further remeasurement takes place. The parent simply accounts for the additional subsidiary shares acquired as an equity transaction—consistent with any transactions with other owners, as opposed to outsiders. Next, we present an example of consolidated reporting when the parent obtains a controlling interest in a series of steps. Then we present an example of a parent's post-control acquisition of its subsidiary's shares.

Example: Step Acquisition Resulting in Control—Acquisition Method

To illustrate, assume that Alta Company obtains control of Swan Company through two cash acquisitions. The details of each acquisition are provided in Exhibit 4.9. Assuming that Alta has gained the ability to significantly influence Swan's decision-making process, the first investment, for external reporting purposes, is accounted for by means of the equity method as discussed in Chapter 1. Thus, Alta must determine any allocations and amortization associated with its purchase price (see Exhibit 4.10). A royalty agreement with a 22-year estimated remaining life represented the initial excess payment.

Application of the equity method requires the accrual of investee income by the parent while any dividends from the investee are recorded as a decrease in the Investment account. Alta must also reduce both the income and asset balances in recognition of the annual $2,000 amortization indicated in Exhibit 4.10. Following the information provided in Exhibits 4.9 and 4.10, over the next two years, Alta Company's Investment in Swan account grows to $190,000:

Price paid for 30% investment in Swan—1/1/22	$164,000
Accrual of 2022 equity income ($60,000 × 30%)	18,000
Share of dividends 2022 ($20,000 × 30%)	(6,000)
Amortization for 2022	(2,000)
Accrual of 2023 equity income ($80,000 × 30%)	24,000
Share of dividends 2023 ($20,000 × 30%)	(6,000)
Amortization for 2023	(2,000)
Investment in Swan—1/1/24	$190,000

EXHIBIT 4.9
Consolidation Information for a Step Acquisition

ALTA COMPANY'S ACQUISITIONS OF SWAN COMPANY SHARES

	Consideration Transferred	Percentage Acquired	Swan Company (100%)	
			Book Value	Fair Value
January 1, 2022	$164,000	30%	$400,000	$546,667
January 1, 2024	350,000	50	500,000	700,000

Swan Company's Income and Dividends for 2022–2024

	Income	Dividends
2022	$ 60,000	$20,000
2023	80,000	20,000
2024	100,000	20,000

EXHIBIT 4.10
Allocation of First Noncontrolling Acquisition

ALTA COMPANY AND SWAN COMPANY	
Fair Value Allocation and Amortization	
January 1, 2022	
Fair value of consideration transferred.................	$164,000
Book value equivalent of Alta's ownership	
($400,000 × 30%).....................................	(120,000)
Royalty agreement......................................	$ 44,000
Assumed remaining life.................................	22 years
Annual amortization expense...........................	$ 2,000

On January 1, 2024, Alta's ownership is increased to 80 percent by the purchase of another 50 percent of Swan Company's outstanding common stock for $350,000. Although the equity method can still be utilized for internal reporting, this second acquisition necessitates the preparation of consolidated financial statements beginning in 2024. Alta now controls Swan; the two companies are viewed as a single economic entity for external reporting purposes.

Once Alta gains control over Swan on January 1, 2024, the acquisition method focuses exclusively on control-date fair values and considers any previous amounts recorded by the acquirer as irrelevant for future valuations. Thus, in a step acquisition, all previous values for the investment prior to the date control is obtained are remeasured to fair value on the date control is obtained.

We add the assumption that the $350,000 consideration transferred by Alta in its second acquisition of Swan represents the best available evidence for measuring the fair value of Swan Company at January 1, 2024. Therefore, an estimated fair value of $700,000 ($350,000 ÷ 50%) is assigned to Swan Company as of January 1, 2024, and provides the valuation basis for the assets acquired, the liabilities assumed, and the 20 percent noncontrolling interest. Exhibit 4.11 shows Alta's allocation of Swan's $700,000 acquisition-date fair value, first to the ownership interests and then to Swan's assets.

Note that the acquisition method views a multiple-step acquisition as essentially the same as a single-step acquisition. In the Alta Company and Swan Company example, once control is evident, the only relevant values in consolidating the accounts of Swan are fair values at January 1, 2024. A new basis of accountability arises for Swan Company on that single date because obtaining control of another firm is considered a significant remeasurement event.

EXHIBIT 4.11
Allocation of Acquisition-Date Fair Value

ALTA COMPANY AND SWAN COMPANY	
Swan Fair Value at Date Control Is Obtained	
January 1, 2024	
Fair value of 50% equity acquisition by Alta................	$350,000
Fair value of 30% equity already owned by Alta	210,000
Fair value of 20% noncontrolling interest	140,000
Total fair value assigned to Swan Company..............	$700,000
Excess Fair over Book Value Allocation and Amortization	
January 1, 2024	
Swan Company fair value	$700,000
Swan Company book value	(500,000)
Royalty agreements......................................	$200,000
Assumed remaining life	20 years
Annual amortization expense	$ 10,000

Previously owned noncontrolling blocks of stock are consequently revalued to fair value on the date control is obtained.

In revaluing a previous stock ownership in the acquired firm, the acquirer recognizes any resulting gain or loss in income. Therefore, on January 1, 2024, Alta increases the Investment in Swan account to $210,000 (30% × $700,000 fair value) and records the revaluation gain as follows:

Investment in Swan	20,000	
Gain on Revaluation of Swan		20,000

Fair value of Alta's 30% investment in Swan at 1/1/24 (30% × $700,000)...	$210,000
Book value of Alta's 30% investment in Swan at 1/1/24.............	190,000
Gain on revaluation of Swan to fair value........................	$ 20,000

Worksheet Consolidation for a Step Acquisition (Acquisition Method)

To continue the example, the amount in Alta Company's 80 percent Investment in Swan account is updated for 2024:

Investment in Swan (after revaluation on 1/1/24)	$210,000
January 1, 2024—Second acquisition price paid	350,000
Equity income accrual—2024 (80% × $100,000)	80,000
Amortization of royalty agreement (80% × $10,000)	(8,000)
Share of Swan dividends—2024 (80% × $20,000)	(16,000)
Investment in Swan—12/31/24	$616,000

The worksheet for consolidating Alta Company and Swan Company is shown in Exhibit 4.12. Observe that

- The consolidation worksheet entries are essentially the same as if Alta had acquired its entire 80 percent ownership on January 1, 2024.
- The noncontrolling interest is allocated 20 percent of the excess fair-value allocation from the royalty agreements.
- The noncontrolling interest is allocated 20 percent of Swan's 2024 income less its share of the excess amortization attributable to the royalty agreements.
- The gain on revaluation of Alta's initial investment in Swan is recognized as income of the current period.

Example: Step Acquisition Resulting after Control Is Obtained

The previous example demonstrates a step acquisition with control achieved with the most recent purchase. Post-control acquisitions by a parent of a subsidiary's stock, however, often continue as well. Recall that the acquisition method measures an acquired firm at its fair value on the date control is obtained.

A parent's subsequent subsidiary stock acquisitions do not affect these initially recognized fair values. For example, when Walmart increased its ownership in Walmart Chile from 75 percent to 100 percent, it did not change the valuation bases of Walmart Chile's assets. The acquisition of the 25 percent noncontrolling interest was treated as an equity transaction with a corresponding adjustment to additional paid-in capital. As the Walmart example shows, once the subsidiary's valuation basis is established as of the date control is obtained, as long as control is maintained, this valuation basis remains the same. Any further purchases (or sales) of the subsidiary's stock are treated as equity transactions.

EXHIBIT 4.12 Step Acquisition Illustrated

			Consolidation Entries		Noncontrolling	Consolidated
Investment: Equity Method		**ALTA COMPANY AND SWAN COMPANY** Consolidation Worksheet For Year Ending December 31, 2024				*Ownership: 80%*
Accounts	Alta Company	Swan Company	Debit	Credit	Noncontrolling Interest	Consolidated Totals
Income Statement						
Revenues	(600,000)	(260,000)				(860,000)
Expenses	425,000	160,000	(E) 10,000			595,000
Equity in subsidiary earnings	(72,000)	–0–	(I) 72,000			–0–
Gain on revaluation of Swan	(20,000)	–0–				(20,000)
Separate company net income	(267,000)	(100,000)				
Consolidated net income						(285,000)
Net income attributable to noncontrolling interest					(18,000)	18,000
Net income attributable to Alta Company						(267,000)
Statement of Retained Earnings						
Retained earnings, 1/1						
Alta Company	(758,000)					(758,000)
Swan Company		(230,000)	(S) 230,000			
Net income (above)	(267,000)	(100,000)				(267,000)
Dividends declared	125,000	20,000		(D) 16,000	4,000	125,000
Retained earnings, 12/31	(900,000)	(310,000)				(900,000)
Balance Sheet						
Current assets	509,000	280,000				789,000
Land	205,000	90,000				295,000
Buildings (net)	646,000	310,000				956,000
Investment in Swan Company	616,000	–0–	(D) 16,000	(A) 160,000 (S) 400,000 (I) 72,000		–0–
Royalty agreement	–0–	–0–	(A) 200,000	(E) 10,000		190,000
Total assets	1,976,000	680,000				2,230,000
Liabilities	(461,000)	(100,000)				(561,000)
Noncontrolling interest in Swan Company, 1/1	–0–	–0–		(S) 100,000 (A) 40,000	(140,000)	
Noncontrolling interest in Swan Company, 12/31	–0–	–0–			(154,000)	(154,000)
Common stock	(355,000)	(200,000)	(S) 200,000			(355,000)
Additional paid-in capital	(260,000)	(70,000)	(S) 70,000			(260,000)
Retained earnings, 12/31 (above)	(900,000)	(310,000)				(900,000)
Total liabilities and equities	(1,976,000)	(680,000)	798,000	798,000		(2,230,000)

Note: Parentheses indicate a credit balance.
Consolidation entries:
(S) Elimination of subsidiary's stockholders equity along with recognition of 1/1 noncontrolling interest.
(A) Allocation of subsidiary total fair value in excess of book value, unamortized balances as of 1/1.
(I) Elimination of intra-entity income (equity accrual less amortization expenses).
(D) Elimination of intra-entity dividends.
(E) Recognition of amortization expenses on fair-value allocations.

To illustrate a post-control step acquisition, assume that on January 1, 2023, Alameda Co. obtains 70 percent of Sunset, Inc., for $350,000 cash. We also assume that the $350,000 consideration paid represents the best available evidence for measuring the fair value of the noncontrolling interest. Therefore, Sunset Company's total fair value is assessed at $500,000 ($350,000 ÷ 70%). Sunset's January 1, 2023 book value was $400,000 with any excess acquisition-date fair over book value attributable to an indefinite-lived trademark. Then, on

Discussion Question

DOES GAAP UNDERVALUE POST-CONTROL STOCK ACQUISITIONS?

At a recent board of directors meeting, Margaret Liu, Chief Executive Officer of StepUp Corporation, discussed her company's post-control step acquisition in Escalator, Inc., as follows:

> Escalator provides an example of how accounting fails to capture the gap between book value and fair value. Let me explain. . .
>
> This year we purchased additional shares in our subsidiary Escalator, increasing our ownership to 90% (up from the 75% we acquired a few years ago). What I find puzzling is that the GAAP rules require us to report the current year's purchase not at what we paid, but at an amount based on the current book value of our original 75% purchase which is less than our purchase price. Our accountants tell me that if we didn't already own the original 75%, we would record the additional 15% investment at our $1.5 million cost.
>
> I'm further puzzled as to why our total investment in Escalator doesn't reflect current fair value. We recently paid $1.5 million for a 15% share, which implies a $10 million valuation. But the total amount of the Escalator investment on our books is $7 million. What sense does this make?*

How would you explain accounting valuations for post-control step acquisitions to the StepUp Corporation executives? Do you agree or disagree with GAAP treatment of reporting additional investments in subsidiaries when control has previously been established?

*Warren Buffet raised similar issues in Berkshire Hathaway's 2012 annual report.

January 1, 2024, when Sunset's book value has increased to $420,000, Alameda buys another 20 percent of Sunset for $95,000, bringing its total ownership to 90 percent. Under the acquisition method, the valuation basis for the subsidiary's net assets was established on January 1, 2023, the date Alameda obtained control. Subsequent transactions in the subsidiary's stock (purchases or sales) are now viewed as transactions in the combined entity's own stock. Therefore, when Alameda acquires additional shares post-control, it recognizes the difference between the fair value of the consideration transferred and the underlying subsidiary valuation as an adjustment to Additional Paid-In Capital.

The difference between the $95,000 price and the underlying consolidated subsidiary value is computed as follows:

1/1/24 price paid for 20% interest.		$95,000
Noncontrolling interest (NCI) acquired:		
Book value (20% of $420,000)	$84,000	
Trademark (20% of $100,000).	20,000	
Noncontrolling interest book value (20%) 1/1/24		104,000
Additional paid-in capital from 20% NCI acquisition.		$ 9,000

Alameda then prepares the following journal entry to record the acquisition of the 20 percent noncontrolling interest:

Investment in Sunset	104,000	
Cash		95,000
Additional Paid-In Capital		9,000

By purchasing 20 percent of Sunset for $95,000, the consolidated entity's owners have acquired a portion of their own firm at a price $9,000 less than consolidated book value. From a worksheet perspective, the $104,000 increase in the investment account simply replaces the 20 percent allocation to the noncontrolling interest. Note that the $95,000 exchanged for the 20 percent interest in Sunset's net assets does not affect consolidated asset valuation. The basis for the reported values in the consolidated financial statements was established on the date control was obtained.

LO 4-10

Record the sale of a subsidiary (or a portion of its shares).

Parent Company Sales of Subsidiary Stock—Acquisition Method

Frequently, a parent company will sell a portion or all of the shares it owns of a subsidiary. For example, when General Electric Company reported the sale of its NBC Universal business, it noted in its financial statements:

> We transferred the assets of the NBCU business and Comcast transferred certain of its assets to a newly formed entity, NBC Universal LLC (NBCU LLC). In connection with the transaction, we received $6,197 million in cash from Comcast and a 49% interest in NBCU LLC. Comcast holds the remaining 51% interest in NBCU LLC. We will account for our investment in NBCU LLC under the equity method. As a result of the transaction, we expect to recognize a small after-tax gain.

Importantly, the accounting effect from selling subsidiary shares depends on whether the parent continues to maintain control after the sale. If the sale of the parent's ownership interest results in the loss of control of a subsidiary as in the GE example, it recognizes any resulting gain or loss in consolidated net income.

If the parent sells some subsidiary shares but retains control, it recognizes no gains or losses on the sale. Under the acquisition method, as long as control remains with the parent, transactions in the stock of the subsidiary are considered to be transactions in the equity of the consolidated entity. Because such transactions are considered to occur with owners, the parent records any difference between proceeds of the sale and carrying amount as additional paid-in capital.

Sale of Subsidiary Shares with Control Maintained

To illustrate, assume Adams Company owns 100 percent of Smith Company's 25,000 voting shares and appropriately carries the investment on its books at January 1, 2024, at $750,000 using the equity method. Assuming Adams sells 5,000 shares to outside interests for $165,000 on January 1, 2024, the transaction is recorded as follows:

Cash	165,000	
Investment in Smith		150,000
Additional Paid-In Capital from Noncontrolling Interest Transaction		15,000
To record sale of 5,000 Smith shares to noncontrolling interest with excess of sale proceeds over carrying amount attributed to additional paid-in capital.		

The $15,000 "gain" on sale of the subsidiary shares is not recognized in income, but is reported as an increase in owners' equity. This equity treatment for the "gain" is consistent with the economic unit notion that as long as control is maintained, payments received from owners of the firm are considered contributions of capital. The ownership group of the consolidated entity specifically includes the noncontrolling interest. Therefore, the preceding treatment of sales to an ownership group is consistent with accounting for other stock transactions with owners (e.g., treasury stock transactions).

Sale of Subsidiary Shares with Control Lost

The loss of control of a subsidiary is a remeasurement event that can result in gain or loss recognition. The gain or loss is computed as the difference between the sale proceeds and the carrying amount of the shares sold. Using the Adams and Smith example, assume now that instead of selling 5,000 shares, Adams sells 20,000 of its shares in Smith to outside interests on January 1, 2024, and keeps the remaining 5,000 shares. Assuming sale proceeds of $675,000, we record the transaction as follows:

Cash	675,000	
Investment in Smith		600,000
Gain on Sale of Smith Investment		75,000
To record sale of 20,000 Smith shares, resulting in the loss of control over Smith Company.		

If the former parent retains any of its former subsidiary's shares, the retained investment should be remeasured to fair value on the date control is lost. Any resulting gain or loss from this remeasurement should be recognized in the parent's net income.

In our Adams and Smith example, Adams still retains 5,000 shares of Smith Company (25,000 original investment less 20,000 shares sold). Assuming further that the $675,000 sale price for the 20,000 shares sold represents a reasonable value for the remaining shares of $33.75, Adams's shares now have a fair value of $168,750 ($33.75 × 5,000 shares). Adams would thus record the revaluation of its retained 5,000 shares of Smith as follows:

Investment in Smith	18,750	
Gain on Revaluation of Retained Smith Shares to Fair Value		18,750
To record the revaluation of Smith shares to a $33.75 per share fair value from their previous equity method January 1, 2024, carrying amount of $30.00 per share.		

The preceding revaluation of retained shares reflects the view that the loss of control of a subsidiary is a significant economic event that changes the fundamental relationship between the former parent and subsidiary. Also, the fair value of the retained investment provides the users of the parent's financial statements with more relevant information about the investment.

Cost-Flow Assumptions

If it sells less than an entire investment, the parent must select an appropriate cost-flow assumption when it has made more than one purchase. In the sale of securities, the use of specific identification based on serial numbers is acceptable, although averaging or FIFO assumptions often are applied. Use of the averaging method is especially appealing because all shares are truly identical, creating little justification for identifying different cost figures with individual shares.

Accounting for Shares That Remain

If Adams sells only a portion of the investment, it also must determine the proper method of accounting for the shares that remain. Three possible scenarios are described as follows:

1. Adams could have so drastically reduced its interest that the parent no longer controls the subsidiary or even has the ability to significantly influence its decision making. For example, assume that Adams's ownership drops from 80 to 5 percent. In the current period prior to the sale, the 80 percent investment is reported by means of the equity method with the market-value method used for the 5 percent that remains thereafter. Consolidated financial statements are no longer applicable.

2. Adams could still apply significant influence over Smith's operations although it no longer maintains control. A drop in the level of ownership from 80 to 30 percent normally meets this condition. In this case, the parent utilizes the equity method for the entire year. Application is based on 80 percent until the time of sale and then on 30 percent for the remainder of the year. Again, consolidated statements cease to be appropriate because control has been lost.

3. The decrease in ownership could be relatively small so that the parent continues to maintain control over the subsidiary even after the sale. Adams's reduction of its ownership in Smith from 80 to 60 percent is an example of this situation. After the disposal, consolidated financial statements are still required, but the process is based on the *end-of-year ownership percentage*. Because only the retained shares (60 percent in this case) are consolidated, the parent must separately recognize any current-year income accruing to it from its terminated interest. Thus, Adams shows earnings on this portion of the investment (a 20 percent interest in Smith for the time during the year that it is held) in the consolidated income statement as a single-line item computed by means of the equity method.

Comparisons with International Accounting Standards

As observed in previous chapters of this text, the accounting and reporting standards for business combinations between U.S. and international standards have largely converged with FASB ASC Topic 805 and *IFRS 3R*— each of which carries the title "Business Combinations"—and ASC Topic 810: Consolidation. Each set of standards requires the acquisition method and embraces a fair-value model for the assets acquired and liabilities assumed in a business combination. Both sets of standards treat exchanges between the parent and the noncontrolling interest as equity transactions, unless control is lost. However, the accounting for the noncontrolling interest can diverge across the two reporting regimes.

- *U.S. GAAP.* In reporting the noncontrolling interest in consolidated financial statements, U.S. GAAP requires a fair-value measurement attribute, consistent with the overall valuation principles for business combinations. Thus, acquisition-date fair value provides a basis for reporting the noncontrolling interest, which is adjusted for its share of subsidiary income and dividends subsequent to acquisition.

- *IFRS.* In contrast, *IFRS 3R* allows an option for reporting the noncontrolling interest for each business combination. Under IFRS, the noncontrolling interest may be measured either at its acquisition-date fair value, which can include goodwill, or at a proportionate share of the acquiree's identifiable net asset fair value, which excludes goodwill. The IFRS proportionate-share option effectively assumes that any goodwill created through the business combination applies solely to the controlling interest.

Summary

1. A parent company need not acquire 100 percent of a subsidiary's stock to form a business combination. Only control over the decision-making process is necessary, a level that has historically been achieved by obtaining a majority of the voting shares. Ownership of any subsidiary stock that is retained by outside unrelated parties is collectively referred to as a noncontrolling interest.

2. A consolidation takes on an added degree of complexity when a noncontrolling interest is present. The noncontrolling interest represents a group of subsidiary owners, and their equity is recognized by the parent in its consolidated financial statements.

3. The valuation principle for the noncontrolling interest is acquisition-date fair value. The fair value of the noncontrolling interest is added to the consideration transferred by the parent to determine the acquisition-date fair value of the subsidiary. This fair value is then allocated to the subsidiary's assets acquired and liabilities assumed based on their individual fair values. At the acquisition date, each of the subsidiary's assets and liabilities is included in consolidation at its individual fair value regardless of the degree of parent ownership. Any remaining excess fair value beyond the total assigned to the identifiable net assets is recognized as goodwill.

4. The fair value of the noncontrolling interest is adjusted over time for subsidiary income (less excess fair-value amortization) and subsidiary dividends.

5. Consolidated goodwill is allocated across the controlling and noncontrolling interests based on the excess of their respective acquisition-date fair values less their percentage share of the identifiable subsidiary net asset fair value. The goodwill allocation, therefore, does not necessarily correspond proportionately to the ownership interest of the parent and the noncontrolling interest.

6. Four noncontrolling interest figures appear in the annual consolidation process. First, a beginning-of-the-year balance in the book value of the subsidiary's net assets is recognized on the worksheet (through Entry **S**) followed by the noncontrolling interest's share of the unamortized excess acquisition-date fair values of the subsidiary's assets and liabilities (including a separate amount for goodwill if appropriate). Next, the noncontrolling interest share of the subsidiary's net income for the period (recorded by a columnar entry) is recognized. Subsidiary dividends to these unrelated owners are entered as a reduction of the noncontrolling interest. The final balance for the year is found as a summation of the Noncontrolling Interest column and is presented on the consolidated balance sheet, within the Stockholders' Equity section.

7. When a midyear business acquisition occurs, consolidated revenues and expenses should not include the subsidiary's current year preacquisition revenues and expenses. Only postacquisition subsidiary revenues and expenses are consolidated.

8. A parent can obtain control of a subsidiary by means of several separate purchases occurring over time, a process often referred to as a step acquisition. Once control is achieved, the acquisition method requires that the parent adjust to fair value all prior investments in the acquired firm and recognize any gain or loss. The fair values of these prior investments, along with the consideration transferred in the current investment that gave the parent control and the noncontrolling interest fair value, all constitute the total fair value of the acquired company.

9. When a parent sells some of its ownership shares of a subsidiary, it must establish an appropriate investment account balance to ensure an accurate accounting. If the equity method has not been used, the parent's investment balance is adjusted to recognize any income or amortization previously omitted. The resulting balance is then compared to the amount received for the stock to arrive at either an adjustment to additional paid-in capital (control maintained) or a gain or loss (control lost). Any shares still held will subsequently be reported through either consolidation, the equity method, or the fair-value method, depending on the influence retained by the parent.

Comprehensive Illustration

(*Estimated Time: 60 to 75 Minutes*) On January 1, 2020, Father Company acquired an 80 percent interest in Sun Company for $425,000. The acquisition-date fair value of the 20 percent noncontrolling interest's ownership shares was $102,500. Also as of that date, Sun reported total stockholders' equity of $400,000: $100,000 in common stock and $300,000 in retained earnings. In setting the acquisition price, Father appraised four accounts at values different from the balances reported within Sun's financial records.

Problem

Buildings (8-year remaining life)	Undervalued by $20,000
Land	Undervalued by $50,000
Equipment (5-year remaining life)	Undervalued by $12,500
Royalty agreement (20-year remaining life)	Not recorded, valued at $30,000

As of December 31, 2024, the trial balances of these two companies are as follows:

	Father Company	Sun Company
Debits		
Current assets	$ 605,000	$ 280,000
Investment in Sun Company	425,000 *	–0–
Land	200,000	300,000
Buildings (net)	640,000	290,000
Equipment (net)	380,000	160,000
Expenses	550,000	190,000
Dividends declared	90,000	20,000
Total debits	$2,890,000	$1,240,000
Credits		
Liabilities	$ 910,000	$ 300,000
Common stock	480,000	100,000
Retained earnings, 1/1/24	704,000	480,000
Revenues	780,000	360,000
Dividend income	16,000	–0–
Total credits	$2,890,000	$1,240,000

[handwritten: Remove from assets + liabilities]

Included in these figures is a $20,000 payable that Sun owes to the parent company. No goodwill impairments have occurred since the Sun Company acquisition.

Required

a. Determine consolidated totals for Father Company and Sun Company for the year 2024.

b. Prepare worksheet entries to consolidate the trial balances of Father Company and Sun Company for the year 2024.

c. Assume instead that the acquisition-date fair value of the noncontrolling interest was $104,500. What balances in the December 31, 2024, consolidated statements would change?

Solution

a. The consolidation of Father Company and Sun Company begins with the allocation of the subsidiary's acquisition-date fair value, as shown in Exhibit 4.13. Because this consolidation is taking place after several years, the unamortized balances for the various allocations at the beginning of the current year also should be determined (see Exhibit 4.14).

Next, the parent's method of accounting for its subsidiary should be ascertained. The continuing presence of the original $425,000 acquisition price in the investment account indicates that Father is applying the initial value method. This same determination can be made from the Dividend Income account, which equals 80 percent of the subsidiary's dividends. Thus, Father's accounting records have ignored the increase in Sun's book value as well as the excess amortization expenses for the prior periods of ownership. These amounts have to be added to the parent's January 1, 2024, Retained Earnings account to arrive at the proper consolidated balance.

During the 2020–2023 period of ownership, Sun's Retained Earnings account increased by $180,000 ($480,000 − $300,000). Father's 80 percent interest necessitates an accrual of $144,000 ($180,000 × 80%) for these years. In addition, the acquisition-date fair-value allocations require the recognition of $20,800 in excess amortization expenses for this same period ($6,500 × 80% × 4 years). Thus, a net increase of $123,200 ($144,000 − $20,800) is needed to adjust the parent's beginning retained earnings balance to reflect the equity method.

Once the adjustment from the initial value method to the equity method is determined, the consolidated figures for 2024 can be calculated:

Current Assets = $865,000. The parent's book value is added to the subsidiary's book value. The $20,000 intra-entity balance is eliminated.

Investment in Sun Company = –0–. The intra-entity ownership is eliminated so that the subsidiary's specific assets and liabilities can be consolidated.

Land = $550,000. The parent's book value is added to the subsidiary's book value plus the $50,000 excess fair-value allocation (see Exhibit 4.13).

EXHIBIT 4.13
Excess Fair-Value Allocations

425,000 +102,500

FATHER COMPANY AND SUN COMPANY
Acquisition-Date Fair-Value Allocation and Amortization
2020–2023

	Allocation	Remaining Life (years)	Annual Excess Amortization
Acquisition-date fair value.............	$527,500		
Sun book value (100%)................	400,000		
Excess fair value......................	127,500		
Allocation to specific subsidiary accounts based on fair value:			
Buildings..........................	$ 20,000	8	$ 2,500
Land..............................	50,000	indefinite	–0–
Equipment........................	12,500	5	2,500
Royalty agreement.................	30,000	20	1,500
Goodwill...........................	$ 15,000		
Annual excess amortization expenses....			$ 6,500

Goodwill Allocation to the Controlling and Noncontrolling Interests

	Controlling Interest	Noncontrolling Interest	Total
Acquisition-date fair value..............	$425,000	$102,500	$527,500
Relative fair value of Sun's identifiable net assets (80% and 20%)............	410,000	102,500	512,500
Goodwill...........................	$ 15,000	$ –0–	$ 15,000

527500
−15000

EXHIBIT 4.14
Excess Fair-Value Allocation Balances

FATHER COMPANY AND SUN COMPANY
Unamortized Excess Fair-Value over Book-Value Allocation
Balances at January 1, 2024

Account	Excess Original Allocation	Excess Amortization 2020–2023	Balance 1/1/24
Buildings...........................	$ 20,000	$10,000	$ 10,000
Land...............................	50,000	–0–	50,000
Equipment..........................	12,500	10,000	2,500
Royalty agreement..................	30,000	6,000	24,000
Goodwill...........................	15,000	–0–	15,000
Total..........................	$127,500	$26,000	$101,500

Buildings (*net*) = $937,500. The parent's book value is added to the subsidiary's book value plus the $20,000 fair-value allocation (see Exhibit 4.14) and less five years of amortization (2020 through 2024).

Equipment (*net*) = $540,000. The parent's book value is added to the subsidiary's book value. The $12,500 fair-value allocation has been completely amortized after five years.

Royalty Agreement = $22,500. The original residual allocation from the acquisition-date fair value is recognized after taking into account five years of amortization (see Exhibit 4.13).

Goodwill = $15,000. Original acquisition-date value assigned.

Liabilities = $1,190,000. The parent's book value is added to the subsidiary's book value. The $20,000 intra-entity balance is eliminated.

Revenues = $1,140,000. The parent's book value is added to the subsidiary's book value.

Expenses = $746,500. The parent's book value is added to the subsidiary's book value plus current-year amortization expenses on the fair-value allocations (see Exhibit 4.13).

Consolidated Net Income = $393,500. The combined total of consolidated revenues and expenses.

> *Net Income Attributable to Noncontrolling Interest* = $32,700. The outside owners are assigned a 20 percent share of the subsidiary's net income less excess fair-value amortizations: 20% × ($170,000 − $6,500).

Net Income Attributable to Father Company = $360,800. Consolidated net income less the amount allocated to the noncontrolling interest.

Common Stock = $480,000. Only the parent company's balance is reported.

Retained Earnings, 1/1/24 = $827,200. Only the parent company's balance after a $123,200 increase to convert from the initial value method to the equity method.

Dividends Declared = $90,000. Only parent company dividends are consolidated. Subsidiary dividends distributable to the parent are eliminated; the remainder reduce the Noncontrolling Interest balance.

Retained Earnings 12/31/24 = $1,098,000. The parent's adjusted beginning balance of $827,200, plus $360,800 net income to the controlling interest, less $90,000 dividends declared by Father Company.

Dividend Income = –0–. The intra-entity dividend declarations are eliminated.

Noncontrolling Interest in Subsidiary, 12/31/24 = $162,000.

NCI in Sun's 1/1/24 book value (20% × $580,000)	$116,000
NCI in unamortized excess fair-value allocations (20% × $86,500)	17,300
January 1, 2024, NCI in Sun's fair value	133,300
NCI in Sun's net income [20% × ($360,000 − 196,500)]	32,700
NCI dividend share (20% × $20,000)	(4,000)
Noncontrolling interest in Sun Company, December 31, 2024	$162,000

b. Six worksheet entries are necessary to produce a consolidation worksheet for Father Company and Sun Company.

Entry *C

Investment in Sun Company	123,200	
Retained Earnings, 1/1/24 (parent)		123,200

This increment is required to adjust the parent's Retained Earnings from the initial value method to the equity method.
The amount is $144,000 (80% of the $180,000 increase in the subsidiary's book value during previous years) less $20,800 in excess amortization over this same 4-year period ($6,500 × 80% × 4 years).

Entry S

Common Stock (subsidiary)	100,000	
Retained Earnings, 1/1/24 (subsidiary)	480,000	
Investment in Sun Company (80%)		464,000
Noncontrolling Interest in Sun Company (20%)		116,000

To eliminate beginning stockholders' equity accounts of the subsidiary and recognize the beginning balance book value attributed to the outside owners (20%).

Entry A1 and A2 Combined

Buildings	10,000	
Land	50,000	
Equipment	2,500	
Royalty Agreement	24,000	
Goodwill	15,000	
Investment in Sun Company		84,200
Noncontrolling Interest in Sun Company		17,300

To recognize unamortized excess fair- over book-value allocations as of the first day of the current year (see Exhibit 4.14). All goodwill is attributable to the controlling interest.

Entry I

Dividend Income	16,000	
Dividends Declared		16,000

To eliminate intra-entity dividend declarations recorded by
parent (using the initial value method) as income.

Entry E

Depreciation Expense	5,000	
Amortization Expense	1,500	
Buildings		2,500
Equipment		2,500
Royalty Agreement		1,500

To recognize excess amortization expenses for the current year
(see Exhibit 4.13).

Entry P

Liabilities	20,000	
Current Assets		20,000

To eliminate the intra-entity receivable and payable.

c. If the acquisition-date fair value of the noncontrolling interest were $104,500, then Sun's fair value would increase by $2,000 to $529,500 and goodwill would increase by the same $2,000 to $17,000. The entire $2,000 increase in goodwill would be allocated to the noncontrolling interest as follows:

	Controlling Interest	Noncontrolling Interest	Total
Acquisition-date fair value................	$425,000	$104,500	$529,500
Relative fair value of Sun's identifiable net assets (80% and 20%)	410,000	102,500	512,500
Goodwill	$ 15,000	$ 2,000	$ 17,000

Therefore, the consolidated balance sheet would show goodwill at $17,000 (instead of $15,000), and the noncontrolling interest in Sun Company balance would show $164,000 (instead of $162,000).

Questions

1. What does the term *noncontrolling interest* mean?
2. Atwater Company acquires 80 percent of the outstanding voting stock of Belwood Company. On that date, Belwood possesses a building with a $160,000 book value but a $220,000 fair value. At what value would this building be consolidated?
3. What is a control premium and how does it affect consolidated financial statements?
4. Where should the noncontrolling interest's claims be reported in a set of consolidated financial statements?
5. How is the noncontrolling interest in a subsidiary company calculated as of the end of a reporting period?
6. December 31 consolidated financial statements are being prepared for Allsports Company and its new subsidiary acquired on July 1 of the current year. Should Allsports adjust its consolidated balances for the preacquisition subsidiary revenues and expenses?
7. Tree, Inc., has held a 10 percent interest in the stock of Limb Company for several years. Because of the level of ownership, this investment has been accounted for using the fair-value method. At the beginning of the current year, Tree acquires an additional 70 percent interest, which provides the company with control over Limb. In preparing consolidated financial statements for this business combination, how does Tree account for the previous 10 percent ownership interest?
8. Duke Corporation owns a 70 percent equity interest in Salem Company, a subsidiary corporation. During the current year, a portion of this stock is sold to an outside party. Before recording this transaction, Duke adjusts the book value of its investment account. What is the purpose of this adjustment?
9. In question (8), how would the parent record the sales transaction?
10. In question (8), how would Duke account for the remainder of its investment subsequent to the sale of this partial interest?

Problems

LO 4-1

1. What is a basic premise of the acquisition method regarding accounting for a noncontrolling interest?

    a. Consolidated financial statements should be primarily for the benefit of the parent company's stockholders.

    b. Consolidated financial statements should be produced only if both the parent and the subsidiary are in the same basic industry.

    c. A subsidiary is an indivisible part of a business combination and should be included in its entirety regardless of the degree of ownership.

    d. Consolidated financial statements should not report a noncontrolling interest balance because these outside owners do not hold stock in the parent company.

LO 4-2

2. Mittelstaedt, Inc., buys 60 percent of the outstanding stock of Sherry, Inc. Sherry owns a piece of land that cost $212,000 but had a fair value of $549,000 at the acquisition date. What value should be attributed to this land in a consolidated balance sheet at the date of takeover?

    a. $549,000

    b. $337,000

    c. $127,200

    d. $421,800

LO 4-2

3. Jordan, Inc., holds 75 percent of the outstanding stock of Paxson Corporation. Paxson currently owes Jordan $400,000 for inventory acquired over the past few months. In preparing consolidated financial statements, what amount of this debt should be eliminated?

    a. $ –0–

    b. $100,000

    c. $300,000

    d. $400,000

LO 4-2

4. On January 1, 2023, Grand Haven, Inc., reports net assets of $760,000 although equipment (with a four-year remaining life) having a book value of $440,000 is worth $500,000 and an unrecorded patent is valued at $45,000. Van Buren Corporation pays $692,000 on that date to acquire an 80 percent equity ownership in Grand Haven. If the patent has a remaining life of nine years, at what amount should the patent be reported on Van Buren's consolidated balance sheet at December 31, 2024?

    a. $28,000

    b. $35,000

    c. $36,000

    d. $40,000

LO 4-6

5. The noncontrolling interest represents an outside ownership in a subsidiary that is not attributable to the parent company. Where in the consolidated balance sheet is this outside ownership interest recognized?

    a. In the liability section.

    b. In a mezzanine section between liabilities and owners' equity.

    c. In the owners' equity section.

    d. The noncontrolling interest is not recognized in the consolidated balance sheet.

LO 4-4

6. On January 1, 2023, Chamberlain Corporation pays $388,000 for a 60 percent ownership in Neville. Annual excess fair-value amortization of $15,000 results from the acquisition. On December 31, 2024, Neville reports revenues of $400,000 and expenses of $300,000 and Chamberlain reports revenues of $700,000 and expenses of $400,000. The parent figures contain no income from the subsidiary. What is consolidated net income attributable to Chamberlain Corporation?

    a. $385,000

    b. $351,000

    c. $366,000

    d. $400,000

Problems 7 and 8 relate to the following:

On January 1, 2022, Pride Corporation purchased 90 percent of the outstanding voting shares of Star, Inc., for $540,000 cash. The acquisition-date fair value of the noncontrolling interest was $60,000. At January 1, 2022, Star's net assets had a total carrying amount of $420,000. Equipment (8-year remaining life) was undervalued on Star's financial records by $80,000. Any remaining excess fair value over book value was attributed to unpatented technology developed by Star (4-year remaining life), but not recorded on its books. Star recorded net income of $70,000 in 2022 and $80,000 in 2023. Each year since the acquisition, Star has declared a $20,000 dividend. At January 1, 2024, Pride's retained earnings show a $250,000 balance.

Selected account balances for the two companies from their separate operations were as follows:

	Pride	Star
2024 Revenues	$498,000	$285,000
2024 Expenses	350,000	195,000

LO 4-4

7. What is consolidated net income for 2024?
   a. $194,000
   b. $197,500
   c. $203,000
   d. $238,000

LO 4-4

8. Assuming that Pride, in its internal records, accounts for its investment in Star using the equity method, what amount of retained earnings would Pride report on its January 1, 2024, consolidated balance sheet?
   a. $250,000
   b. $286,000
   c. $315,000
   d. $360,000

LO 4-8

9. James Company acquired 85 percent of Mark-Right Company on April 1. On its December 31 consolidated income statement, how should James account for Mark-Right's revenues and expenses that occurred before April 1?
   a. Include 100 percent of Mark-Right's revenues and expenses and deduct the preacquisition portion as noncontrolling interest in net income.
   b. Exclude 100 percent of the preacquisition revenues and 100 percent of the preacquisition expenses from their respective consolidated totals.
   c. Exclude 15 percent of the preacquisition revenues and 15 percent of the preacquisition expenses from consolidated expenses.
   d. Deduct 15 percent of the net combined revenues and expenses relating to the preacquisition period from consolidated net income.

LO 4-9

10. Amie, Inc., has 100,000 shares of $2 par value stock outstanding. Prairie Corporation acquired 30,000 of Amie's shares on January 1, 2021, for $120,000 when Amie's net assets had a total fair value of $350,000. On July 1, 2024, Prairie bought an additional 60,000 shares of Amie from a single stockholder for $6 per share. Although Amie's shares were selling in the $5 range around July 1, 2024, Prairie forecasted that obtaining control of Amie would produce significant revenue synergies to justify the premium price paid. If Amie's identifiable net assets had a fair value of $500,000 at July 1, 2024, how much goodwill should Prairie report in its postcombination consolidated balance sheet?
    a. $60,000
    b. $90,000
    c. $100,000
    d. $ –0–

LO 4-9

11. A parent buys 32 percent of a subsidiary in one year and then buys an additional 40 percent in the next year. In a step acquisition of this type, the original 32 percent acquisition should be
    a. Maintained at its initial value.
    b. Adjusted to its equity method balance at the date of the second acquisition.
    c. Adjusted to fair value at the date of the second acquisition with any resulting gain or loss recognized.
    d. Adjusted to fair value at the date of the second acquisition with a resulting adjustment to additional paid-in capital.

LO 4-4, 4-8

12. On April 1, Pujols, Inc., exchanges $430,000 for 70 percent of the outstanding stock of Ramirez Corporation. The remaining 30 percent of the outstanding shares continued to trade at a collective fair value of $165,000. Ramirez's identifiable assets and liabilities each had book values that

equaled their fair values on April 1 for a net total of $500,000. During the remainder of the year, Ramirez generates revenues of $600,000 and expenses of $360,000 and declared no dividends. On a December 31 consolidated balance sheet, what amount should be reported as noncontrolling interest?

   a. $219,000

   b. $237,000

   c. $234,000

   d. $250,500

LO 4-10

13. McKinley, Inc., owns 100 percent of Jackson Company's 45,000 voting shares. On June 30, McKinley's internal accounting records show a $192,000 equity method balance for its investment in Jackson. McKinley sells 15,000 of its Jackson shares on the open market for $80,000 on June 30. How should McKinley record the excess of the sale proceeds over its carrying amount for the shares?

   a. Reduce goodwill by $64,000.

   b. Recognize a gain on sale for $16,000.

   c. Increase its additional paid-in capital by $16,000.

   d. Recognize a revaluation gain on its remaining shares of $48,000.

LO 4-2, 4-4, 4-5

14. On January 1, 2023, French Company acquired 60 percent of K-Tech Company for $300,000 when K-Tech's book value was $400,000. The fair value of the newly comprised 40 percent noncontrolling interest was assessed at $200,000. At the acquisition date, K-Tech's trademark (10-year remaining life) was undervalued in its financial records by $60,000. Also, patented technology (5-year remaining life) was undervalued by $40,000.

    In 2023, K-Tech reports $30,000 net income and declares no dividends. At the end of 2024, the two companies report the following figures (stockholders' equity accounts have been omitted):

	French Company Carrying Amounts	K-Tech Company Carrying Amounts	K-Tech Company Fair Values
Current assets	$ 620,000	$ 300,000	$ 320,000
Trademarks	260,000	200,000	280,000
Patented technology	410,000	150,000	190,000
Liabilities	(390,000)	(120,000)	(120,000)
Revenues	(900,000)	(400,000)	
Expenses	500,000	300,000	
Investment income	Not given		

   a. Compute the 2024 consolidated net income before allocation to the controlling and noncontrolling interests.

   b. In 2024, assuming K-Tech has declared no dividends, compute the noncontrolling interest's share of the subsidiary's income and the ending balance of the noncontrolling interest in the subsidiary.

   c. Compute the amount reported for trademarks in the 2024 consolidated balance sheet.

LO 4-2

15. On January 1, Park Corporation and Strand Corporation had condensed balance sheets as follows:

	Park	Strand
Current assets	$ 70,000	$20,000
Noncurrent assets	90,000	40,000
Total assets	$160,000	$60,000
Current liabilities	$ 30,000	$10,000
Long-term debt	50,000	–0–
Stockholders' equity	80,000	50,000
Total liabilities and equities	$160,000	$60,000

On January 2, Park borrowed $60,000 and used the proceeds to obtain 80 percent of the outstanding common shares of Strand. The acquisition price was considered proportionate to Strand's total fair value. The $60,000 debt is payable in 10 equal annual principal payments, plus interest, beginning December 31. The excess fair value of the investment over the underlying book value of the acquired net assets is allocated to inventory (60 percent) and to goodwill (40 percent). On a consolidated balance sheet as of January 2, calculate the amounts for each of the following:

a. Current assets

b. Noncurrent assets

c. Current liabilities

d. Noncurrent liabilities

e. Stockholders' equity
    (AICPA adapted)

LO 4-3, 4-4, 4-5

16. On January 1, 2024, Pasture Company acquires 80 percent of Spring Company for $1,712,000 in cash consideration. The remaining 20 percent noncontrolling interest shares had an acquisition-date estimated fair value of $428,000. Spring's acquisition-date total book value was $1,700,000.

    The fair value of Spring's recorded assets and liabilities equaled their carrying amounts. However, Spring had two unrecorded assets—a trademark with an indefinite life and estimated fair value of $245,000 and licensing agreements estimated to be worth $180,000 with 4-year remaining lives. Any remaining acquisition-date fair value in the Spring acquisition was considered goodwill.

    During 2024, Spring reported $172,000 net income and declared and paid dividends totaling $50,000. Also in 2024, Pasture reported $350,000 net income, but neither declared nor paid dividends.

    a. What amount should Pasture assign to the 20 percent noncontrolling interest of Spring at the acquisition date?

    b. How much of 2024 consolidated net income should be allocated to the noncontrolling interest?

    c. What amount of 2024 dividends should be allocated to the noncontrolling interest?

    d. What amount of noncontrolling interest should appear in the owners' equity section of Pasture's consolidated balance sheet at December 31, 2024?

LO 4-4, 4-5

17. On January 1, 2023, Harrison, Inc., acquired 90 percent of Starr Company in exchange for $1,125,000 fair-value consideration. The total fair value of Starr Company was assessed at $1,200,000. Harrison computed annual excess fair-value amortization of $8,000 based on the difference between Starr's total fair value and its underlying book value. The subsidiary reported net income of $70,000 in 2023 and $90,000 in 2024 with dividend declarations of $30,000 each year. Apart from its investment in Starr, Harrison had net income of $220,000 in 2023 and $260,000 in 2024.

    a. What is the consolidated net income in each of these two years?

    b. What is the balance of the noncontrolling interest in Starr at December 31, 2024?

LO 4-2, 4-4, 4-5

18. On January 1, 2024, Johnsonville Enterprises, Inc., acquired 80 percent of Stayer Company's outstanding common shares in exchange for $3,000,000 cash. The price paid for the 80 percent ownership interest was proportionately representative of the fair value of all of Stayer's shares.

    At acquisition date, Stayer's books showed assets of $4,200,000 and liabilities of $1,600,000. The recorded assets and liabilities had fair values equal to their individual book values except that a building (10-year remaining life) with book value of $195,000 had an appraised fair value of $345,000. Stayer's books showed a $175,500 carrying amount for this building at the end of 2024.

    Also, at acquisition date Stayer possessed unrecorded technology processes (zero book value) with an estimated fair value of $1,000,000 and a 20-year remaining life. For 2024, Johnsonville reported net income of $650,000 (before recognition of Stayer's income), and Stayer separately reported earnings of $350,000. During 2024, Johnsonville declared dividends of $85,000 and Stayer declared $50,000 in dividends.

    Compute the amounts that Johnsonville Enterprises should report in its December 31, 2024, consolidated financial statements for the following items:

    a. Stayer's building (net of accumulated depreciation)

    b. Stayer's technology processes (net of accumulated amortization)

    c. Net income attributable to the noncontrolling interest

    d. Net income attributable to controlling interest

    e. Noncontrolling interest in Stayer

LO 4-4, 4-5, 4-7

19. On January 1, Patterson Corporation acquired 80 percent of the 100,000 outstanding voting shares of Soriano, Inc., in exchange for $31.25 per share cash. The remaining 20 percent of Soriano's shares continued to trade for $30 both before and after Patterson's acquisition.

At January 1, Soriano's book and fair values were as follows:

	Book Values	Fair Values	Remaining Life
Current assets	$ 80,000	$ 80,000	
Buildings and equipment	1,250,000	1,000,000	5 years
Trademarks	700,000	900,000	10 years
Patented technology	940,000	2,000,000	4 years
	$2,970,000		
Current liabilities	$ 180,000	$ 180,000	
Long-term notes payable	1,500,000	1,500,000	
Common stock	50,000		
Additional paid-in capital	500,000		
Retained earnings	740,000		
	$2,970,000		

In addition, Patterson assigned a $600,000 value to certain unpatented technologies recently developed by Soriano. These technologies were estimated to have a 3-year remaining life.

During the year, Soriano declared a $30,000 dividend for its shareholders. The companies reported the following revenues and expenses from their separate operations for the year ending December 31.

	Patterson	Soriano
Revenues...............................	$3,000,000	$1,400,000
Expenses	1,750,000	600,000

a. What amount should Patterson recognize as the total value of the acquisition in its January 1 consolidated balance sheet?

b. What valuation principle should Patterson use to report each of Soriano's identifiable assets and liabilities in its January 1 consolidated balance sheet?

c. For years subsequent to acquisition, how will Soriano's identifiable assets and liabilities be valued in Patterson's consolidated financial statements?

d. How much goodwill resulted from Patterson's acquisition of Soriano?

e. What is the consolidated net income for the year and what amounts are allocated to the controlling and noncontrolling interests?

f. What is the noncontrolling interest amount reported in the December 31 consolidated balance sheet?

g. Assume instead that, based on its share prices, Soriano's January 1 total fair value was assessed at $2,250,000. How would the reported amounts for Soriano's net assets change on Patterson's acquisition-date consolidated balance sheet?

LO 4-9

20. On January 1, 2023, Palka, Inc., acquired 70 percent of the outstanding shares of Sellinger Company for $1,141,000 in cash. The price paid was proportionate to Sellinger's total fair value, although at the acquisition date, Sellinger had a total book value of $1,380,000. All assets acquired and liabilities assumed had fair values equal to book values except for a patent (6-year remaining life) that was undervalued on Sellinger's accounting records by $240,000. On January 1, 2024, Palka acquired an additional 25 percent common stock equity interest in Sellinger Company for $415,000 in cash. On its internal records, Palka uses the equity method to account for its shares of Sellinger.

During the two years following the acquisition, Sellinger reported the following net income and dividends:

	2023	2024
Net income	$340,000	$440,000
Dividends declared	150,000	180,000

a. Show Palka's journal entry to record its January 1, 2024, acquisition of an additional 25 percent ownership of Sellinger Company shares.

b. Prepare a schedule showing Palka's December 31, 2024, equity method balance for its Investment in Sellinger account.

LO 4-2, 4-7, 4-8

21. Parker, Inc., acquires 70 percent of Sawyer Company for $420,000. The remaining 30 percent of Sawyer's outstanding shares continue to trade at a collective value of $174,000. On the acquisition date, Sawyer has the following accounts:

	Book Value	Fair Value
Current assets	$ 210,000	$210,000
Land.	170,000	180,000
Buildings	300,000	330,000
Liabilities	(280,000)	(280,000)

The buildings have a 10-year remaining life. In addition, Sawyer holds a patent worth $140,000 that has a 5-year remaining life but is not recorded on its financial records. At the end of the year, the two companies report the following balances:

	Parker	Sawyer
Revenues	$(900,000)	$(600,000)
Expenses	600,000	400,000

a. Assume that the acquisition took place on January 1. What figures would appear in a consolidated income statement for this year?

b. Assume that the acquisition took place on April 1. Sawyer's revenues and expenses occurred uniformly throughout the year. What amounts would appear in a consolidated income statement for this year?

LO 4-2, 4-4, 4-5

22. On January 1, Beckman, Inc., acquires 60 percent of the outstanding stock of Calvin Co. for $36,000. Calvin has one recorded asset, a specialized production machine with a book value of $10,000 and no liabilities. The fair value of the machine is $50,000, and the remaining useful life is estimated to be 10 years. Any remaining excess fair value is attributable to an unrecorded process trade secret with an estimated future life of 4 years. Calvin's total acquisition-date fair value is $60,000.

At the end of the year, Calvin reports the following in its financial statements:

Revenues	$50,000	Machine	$ 9,000	Common stock	$10,000
Expenses	20,000	Other assets	26,000	Retained earnings	25,000
Net income	$30,000	Total assets	$35,000	Total equity	$35,000
Dividends declared	$ 5,000				

Determine the amounts that Beckman should report in its year-end consolidated financial statements for noncontrolling interest in subsidiary income, noncontrolling interest, Calvin's machine (net of accumulated depreciation), and the process trade secret.

LO 4-1, 4-5, 4-6

23. Plaza, Inc., acquires 80 percent of the outstanding common stock of Stanford Corporation on January 1, 2024, in exchange for $900,000 cash. At the acquisition date, Stanford's total fair value, including the noncontrolling interest, was assessed at $1,125,000. Also at the acquisition date, Stanford's book value was $690,000.

Several individual items on Stanford's financial records had fair values that differed from their book values as follows:

	Book Value	Fair Value
Trade names (indefinite life)	$360,000	$383,000
Property and equipment (net, 8-year remaining life)	290,000	330,000
Patent (14-year remaining life)	132,000	272,000

For internal reporting purposes, Plaza, Inc., employs the equity method to account for this investment. The following account balances are for the year ending December 31, 2024, for both companies:

	Plaza	Stanford
Revenues	$(1,400,000)	$ (825,000)
Cost of goods sold	774,000	395,750
Depreciation expense	328,000	36,250
Amortization expense	–0–	28,000
Equity in income of Stanford	(280,000)	–0–
Net income	$ (578,000)	$ (365,000)
Retained earnings, 1/1/24	$(1,275,000)	$ (530,000)
Net income	(578,000)	(365,000)
Dividends declared	300,000	50,000
Retained earnings, 12/31/24	$(1,553,000)	$ (845,000)
Current assets	$ 860,000	$ 432,250
Investment in Stanford	1,140,000	–0–
Trade names	240,000	360,000
Property and equipment (net)	1,030,000	253,750
Patents	–0–	104,000
Total assets	$ 3,270,000	$ 1,150,000
Accounts payable	$ (142,000)	$ (145,000)
Common stock	(300,000)	(120,000)
Additional paid-in capital	(1,275,000)	(40,000)
Retained earnings (above)	(1,553,000)	(845,000)
Total liabilities and equities	$(3,270,000)	$(1,150,000)

At year-end, there were no intra-entity receivables or payables.

Prepare a worksheet to consolidate the financial statements of Plaza, Inc., and its subsidiary Stanford.

LO 4-3, 4-5, 4-7

24. On January 1, 2022, Parflex Corporation exchanged $344,000 cash for 90 percent of Eagle Corporation's outstanding voting stock. Eagle's acquisition date balance sheet follows:

Cash and receivables	$ 15,000	Liabilities	$ 76,000
Inventory	35,000	Common stock	150,000
Property and equipment (net)	350,000	Retained earnings	174,000
	$400,000		$400,000

On January 1, 2022, Parflex prepared the following fair-value allocation schedule:

Consideration transferred by Parflex	$344,000
10% noncontrolling interest fair value	36,000
Fair value of Eagle	380,000
Book value of Eagle	324,000
Excess fair over book value	56,000
to equipment (undervalued, remaining life of 9 years)	18,000
to goodwill (indefinite life)	$ 38,000

The companies' financial statements for the year ending December 31, 2024, follow:

	Parflex	Eagle
Sales	$ (862,000)	$(366,000)
Cost of goods sold	515,000	209,000
Depreciation expense	191,200	67,000
Equity in Eagle's earnings	(79,200)	–0–
Separate company net income	$ (235,000)	$ (90,000)

(*continued*)

(*continued*)

	Parflex	Eagle
Retained earnings 1/1	$ (500,000)	$(278,000)
Net income	(235,000)	(90,000)
Dividends declared	130,000	27,000
Retained earnings 12/31	$ (605,000)	$(341,000)
Cash and receivables	$ 135,000	$ 82,000
Inventory	255,000	136,000
Investment in Eagle	488,900	–0–
Property and equipment (net)	964,000	328,000
Total assets	$ 1,842,900	$ 546,000
Liabilities	$ (722,900)	(55,000)
Common stock—Parflex	(515,000)	–0–
Common stock—Eagle	–0–	(150,000)
Retained earnings 12/31	(605,000)	(341,000)
Total liabilities and owners' equity	$(1,842,900)	$(546,000)

At year-end, there were no intra-entity receivables or payables.

a. Compute the goodwill allocation to the controlling and noncontrolling interest.

b. Show how Parflex determined its "Investment in Eagle" account balance.

c. Determine the amounts that should appear on Parflex's December 31, 2024, consolidated statement of financial position and its 2024 consolidated income statement.

LO 4-3, 4-5, 4-7

25. On January 1, 2023, Holland Corporation paid $8 per share to a group of Zeeland Corporation shareholders to acquire 60,000 shares of Zeeland's outstanding voting stock, representing a 60 percent ownership interest. The remaining 40,000 shares of Zeeland continued to trade in the market close to its recent average of $6.50 per share both before and after the acquisition by Holland. Zeeland's acquisition date balance sheet follows:

Current assets	$ 14,000	Liabilities	$212,000
Property and equipment (net)	268,000	Common stock	100,000
Patents	190,000	Retained earnings	160,000
	$472,000		$472,000

On January 1, 2023, Holland assessed the carrying amount of Zeeland's equipment (5-year remaining life) to be undervalued by $55,000. Holland also determined that Zeeland possessed unrecorded patents (10-year remaining life) worth $285,000. Zeeland's acquisition-date fair values for its current assets and liabilities were equal to their carrying amounts. Any remaining excess of Zeeland's acquisition-date fair value over its book value was attributed to goodwill.

The companies' financial statements for the year ending December 31, 2024, follow:

	Holland	Zeeland
Sales	$ (640,500)	$(428,500)
Cost of goods sold	325,000	200,000
Depreciation expense	80,000	34,000
Amortization expense	14,000	21,000
Other operating expenses	52,000	63,500
Equity in Zeeland earnings	(42,300)	–0–
Separate company net income	$ (211,800)	$(110,000)
Retained earnings 1/1	$ (820,200)	$(296,500)
Net income	(211,800)	(110,000)
Dividends declared	50,000	30,000
Retained earnings 12/31	$ (982,000)	$(376,500)

(*continued*)

(*continued*)

	Holland	Zeeland
Current assets	$ 125,000	$ 81,500
Investment in Zeeland	562,500	–0–
Property and equipment (net)	837,000	259,000
Patents	149,000	147,500
Total assets	$ 1,673,500	$ 488,000
Liabilities	$ (371,500)	$ (11,500)
Common stock—Holland	(320,000)	–0–
Common stock—Zeeland	–0–	(100,000)
Retained earnings 12/31	(982,000)	(376,500)
Total liabilities and owners equity	$(1,673,500)	$(488,000)

At year-end, there were no intra-entity receivables or payables.

a. Compute the amount of goodwill recognized in Holland's acquisition of Zeeland and the allocation of goodwill to the controlling and noncontrolling interest.

b. Show how Holland determined its December 31, 2024, Investment in Zeeland account balance.

c. Prepare a worksheet to determine the amounts that should appear on Holland's December 31, 2024, consolidated financial statements.

26. On January 1, 2024, Morey, Inc., exchanged $178,000 for 25 percent of Amsterdam Corporation. Morey appropriately applied the equity method to this investment. At January 1, the book values of Amsterdam's assets and liabilities approximated their fair values.

    On June 30, 2024, Morey paid $560,000 for an additional 70 percent of Amsterdam, thus increasing its overall ownership to 95 percent. The price paid for the 70 percent acquisition was proportionate to Amsterdam's total fair value. At June 30, the carrying amounts of Amsterdam's assets and liabilities approximated their fair values. Any remaining excess fair value was attributed to goodwill.

    Amsterdam reports the following amounts at December 31, 2024 (credit balances shown in parentheses):

Revenues	$ (210,000)
Expenses	140,000
Retained earnings, January 1	(200,000)
Dividends declared, October 1	20,000
Common stock	(500,000)

    Amsterdam's revenue and expenses were distributed evenly throughout the year, and no changes in Amsterdam's stock have occurred.

    Using the acquisition method, compute the following:

    a. The acquisition-date fair value of Amsterdam to be included in Morey's June 30 consolidated financial statements.

    b. The revaluation gain (or loss) reported by Morey for its 25 percent investment in Amsterdam on June 30.

    c. The amount of goodwill recognized by Morey on its December 31 balance sheet (assume no impairments have been recognized).

    d. The noncontrolling interest amount reported by Morey on its
    - June 30 consolidated balance sheet.
    - December 31 consolidated balance sheet.

27. Posada Company acquired 7,000 of the 10,000 outstanding shares of Sabathia Company on January 1, 2022, for $840,000. The subsidiary's total fair value was assessed at $1,200,000 although its book value on that date was $1,130,000. The $70,000 fair value in excess of Sabathia's book value was assigned to a patent with a 5-year remaining life.

    On January 1, 2024, Posada reported a $1,085,000 equity method balance in the Investment in Sabathia Company account. On October 1, 2024, Posada sells 1,000 shares of the investment for $191,000. During 2024, Sabathia reported net income of $120,000 and declared dividends of $40,000. These amounts are assumed to have occurred evenly throughout the year.

    a. How should Posada report the 2024 income that accrued to the 1,000 shares prior to their sale?

LO 4-8, 4-9

LO 4-10

b. What is the effect on Posada's financial statements from this sale of 1,000 shares?

c. How should Posada report in its financial statements the 6,000 shares of Sabathia it continues to hold?

LO 4-5

28. On January 1, 2022, Telconnect acquires 70 percent of Bandmor for $490,000 cash. The remaining 30 percent of Bandmor's shares continued to trade at a total value of $210,000. The new subsidiary reported common stock of $300,000 on that date, with retained earnings of $180,000. A patent was undervalued in the company's financial records by $30,000. This patent had a 5-year remaining life. Goodwill of $190,000 was recognized and allocated proportionately to the controlling and noncontrolling interests. Bandmor earns net income and declares cash dividends as follows:

Year	Net Income	Dividends
2022	$ 75,000	$39,000
2023	96,000	44,000
2024	110,000	60,000

On December 31, 2024, Telconnect owes $22,000 to Bandmor.

a. If Telconnect has applied the equity method, what consolidation entries are needed as of December 31, 2024?

b. If Telconnect has applied the initial value method, what Entry *C is needed for a 2024 consolidation?

c. If Telconnect has applied the partial equity method, what Entry *C is needed for a 2024 consolidation?

d. What noncontrolling interest balances will appear in consolidated financial statements for 2024?

LO 4-2, 4-3, 4-5

29. Miller Company acquired an 80 percent interest in Taylor Company on January 1, 2022. Miller paid $664,000 in cash to the owners of Taylor to acquire these shares. In addition, the remaining 20 percent of Taylor shares continued to trade at a total value of $166,000 both before and after Miller's acquisition.

On January 1, 2022, Taylor reported a book value of $600,000 (Common Stock = $300,000; Additional Paid-In Capital = $90,000; Retained Earnings = $210,000). Several of Taylor's buildings that had a remaining life of 20 years were undervalued by a total of $80,000.

During the next three years, Taylor reports income and declares dividends as follows:

Year	Net Income	Dividends
2022	$ 70,000	$10,000
2023	90,000	15,000
2024	100,000	20,000

Determine the appropriate answers for each of the following questions:

a. What amount of excess depreciation expense should be recognized in the consolidated financial statements for the initial years following this acquisition?

b. If a consolidated balance sheet is prepared as of January 1, 2022, what amount of goodwill should be recognized?

c. If a consolidation worksheet is prepared as of January 1, 2022, what Entry S and Entry A should be included?

d. On the separate financial records of the parent company, what amount of investment income would be reported for 2022 under each of the following accounting methods?

- The equity method
- The partial equity method
- The initial value method

e. On the parent company's separate financial records, what would be the December 31, 2024, balance for the Investment in Taylor Company account under each of the following accounting methods?

- The equity method
- The partial equity method
- The initial value method

f. As of December 31, 2023, Miller's Buildings account on its separate records has a balance of $800,000 and Taylor has a similar account with a $300,000 balance. What is the consolidated balance for the Buildings account?

g. What is the balance of consolidated goodwill as of December 31, 2024?

h. Assume that the parent company has been applying the equity method to this investment. On December 31, 2024, the separate financial statements for the two companies present the following information:

	Miller Company	Taylor Company
Common stock	$500,000	$300,000
Additional paid-in capital	280,000	90,000
Retained earnings, 12/31/21	620,000	425,000

What will be the consolidated balance of each of these accounts?

LO 4-1, 4-8

30. The following are several account balances taken from the records of Karson and Reilly as of December 31, 2024. A few asset accounts have been omitted here. All revenues, expenses, and dividend declarations occurred evenly throughout the year. Annual tests have indicated no goodwill impairment.

	Karson	Reilly
Sales	$ (800,000)	$(500,000)
Cost of goods sold	400,000	280,000
Operating expenses	200,000	100,000
Investment income	not given	–0–
Retained earnings, 1/1	(1,400,000)	(700,000)
Dividends declared	80,000	20,000
Trademarks	600,000	200,000
Royalty agreements	700,000	300,000
Licensing agreements	400,000	400,000
Liabilities	(500,000)	(200,000)
Common stock ($10 par value)	(400,000)	(100,000)
Additional paid-in capital	(500,000)	(600,000)

On July 1, 2024, Karson acquired 80 percent of Reilly for $1,330,000 cash consideration. In addition, Karson agreed to pay additional cash to the former owners of Reilly if certain performance measures are achieved after three years. Karson assessed a $30,000 fair value for the contingent performance obligation as of the acquisition date and as of December 31, 2024.

On July 1, 2024, Reilly's assets and liabilities had book values equal to their fair value except for some trademarks (with 5-year remaining lives) that were undervalued by $150,000. Karson estimated Reilly's total fair value at $1,700,000 on July 1, 2024.

For the following items, what balances would be reported on Karson's December 31, 2024, consolidated financial statements?

Sales	Consolidated Net Income
Expenses	Retained Earnings, 1/1
Noncontrolling Interest in Subsidiary's Net Income	Trademarks
	Goodwill

LO 4-5

31. Nascent, Inc., acquires 60 percent of Sea-Breeze Corporation for $414,000 cash on January 1, 2021. The remaining 40 percent of the Sea-Breeze shares traded near a total value of $276,000 both before and after the acquisition date. On January 1, 2021, Sea-Breeze had the following assets and liabilities:

	Book Value	Fair Value
Current assets	$ 150,000	$ 150,000
Land	200,000	200,000
Buildings (net) (6-year remaining life)	300,000	360,000
Equipment (net) (4-year remaining life)	300,000	280,000
Patent (10-year remaining life)	–0–	100,000
Liabilities	(400,000)	(400,000)

The companies' financial statements for the year ending December 31, 2024, follow:

	Nascent	Sea-Breeze
Revenues	$ (600,000)	$ (300,000)
Operating expenses.	410,000	210,000
Investment income	(42,000)	–0–
Net income.	$ (232,000)	$ (90,000)
Retained earnings, 1/1/24.	$ (700,000)	$ (300,000)
Net income.	(232,000)	(90,000)
Dividends declared.	92,000	70,000
Retained earnings, 12/31/24	$ (840,000)	$ (320,000)
Current assets	$ 330,000	$ 100,000
Land.	220,000	200,000
Buildings (net)	700,000	200,000
Equipment (net)	400,000	500,000
Investment in Sea-Breeze	414,000	–0–
Total assets	$ 2,064,000	$ 1,000,000
Liabilities.	$ (500,000)	$ (200,000)
Common stock	(724,000)	(480,000)
Retained earnings, 12/31/24	(840,000)	(320,000)
Total liabilities and equities.	$(2,064,000)	$(1,000,000)

Answer the following questions:

a. What account balances reveal that the parent has applied the initial value method?

b. What is the annual excess amortization initially recognized in connection with this acquisition?

c. If the parent had applied the equity method, what investment income would the parent have recorded in 2024?

d. What amount should the parent report as retained earnings in its January 1, 2024, consolidated balance sheet?

e. What is consolidated net income for 2024, and what amounts are attributable to the controlling and noncontrolling interests?

f. Within consolidated statements at January 1, 2021, what balance is included for the subsidiary's Buildings account?

g. What is the consolidated Buildings reported balance as of December 31, 2024?

LO 4-1, 4-5, 4-7

32. On January 1, 2023, Perlman Corporation exchanged $1,710,000 cash for 90 percent of the outstanding voting stock of Stein Company. The consideration transferred by Perlman provided a reasonable basis for assessing the total January 1, 2023, fair value of Stein Company. At the acquisition date, Stein reported the following owners' equity amounts in its balance sheet:

Common stock	$400,000
Additional paid-in capital	60,000
Retained earnings	265,000

In determining its acquisition offer, Perlman noted that the values for Stein's recorded assets and liabilities approximated their fair values. Perlman also observed that Stein had developed software internally with an assessed fair value of $800,000 that was not reflected on Stein's books. Perlman expected both cost and revenue synergies from the combination.

At the acquisition date, Perlman prepared the following fair-value allocation schedule:

Fair value of Stein Company	$1,900,000
Book value of Stein Company	725,000
Excess fair value	1,175,000
to software (10-year remaining life)	800,000
to goodwill	$ 375,000

At December 31, 2024, the two companies report the following balances:

	Perlman	Stein
Revenues	$(1,843,000)	$ (675,000)
Cost of goods sold	1,100,000	322,000
Depreciation expense	125,000	120,000
Amortization expense	275,000	11,000
Interest expense	27,500	7,000
Equity in income of Stein	(121,500)	–0–
Net income	$ (437,000)	$ (215,000)
Retained earnings, 1/1	$(2,625,000)	$ (395,000)
Net income	(437,000)	(215,000)
Dividends declared	350,000	25,000
Retained earnings, 12/31	$(2,712,000)	$ (585,000)
Current assets	$ 1,204,000	$ 430,000
Investment in Stein	1,854,000	–0–
Buildings and equipment	931,000	863,000
Copyrights	950,000	107,000
Total assets	$ 4,939,000	$ 1,400,000
Accounts payable	$ (485,000)	$ (200,000)
Notes payable	(542,000)	(155,000)
Common stock	(900,000)	(400,000)
Additional paid-in capital	(300,000)	(60,000)
Retained earnings, 12/31	(2,712,000)	(585,000)
Total liabilities and equities	$(4,939,000)	$(1,400,000)

At year-end, there were no intra-entity receivables or payables.

a. Determine the consolidated balances for this business combination as of December 31, 2024.

b. If instead the noncontrolling interest's acquisition-date fair value is assessed at $167,500, what changes would be evident in the consolidated statements?

LO 4-5, 4-6, 4-7

33. The Holtz Corporation acquired 80 percent of the 100,000 outstanding voting shares of Devine, Inc., for $7.20 per share on January 1, 2023. The remaining 20 percent of Devine's shares also traded actively at $7.20 per share before and after Holtz's acquisition. An appraisal made on that date determined that all book values appropriately reflected the fair values of Devine's underlying accounts except that a building with a 5-year future life was undervalued by $85,500 and a fully amortized trademark with an estimated 10-year remaining life had a $64,000 fair value. At the acquisition date, Devine reported common stock of $100,000 and a retained earnings balance of $226,500.

Following are the separate financial statements for the year ending December 31, 2024:

	Holtz Corporation	Devine, Inc.
Sales	$ (641,000)	$(399,000)
Cost of goods sold	198,000	176,000
Operating expenses	273,000	126,000
Dividend income	(16,000)	–0–
Net income	$ (186,000)	$ (97,000)
Retained earnings, 1/1/24	$ (762,000)	$(296,500)
Net income (above)	(186,000)	(97,000)
Dividends declared	70,000	20,000
Retained earnings, 12/31/24	$ (878,000)	$(373,500)
Current assets	$ 121,000	$ 120,500
Investment in Devine, Inc.	576,000	–0–
Buildings and equipment (net)	887,000	335,000
Trademarks	149,000	236,000
Total assets	$ 1,733,000	$ 691,500
Liabilities	$ (535,000)	$(218,000)
Common stock	(320,000)	(100,000)
Retained earnings, 12/31/24 (above)	(878,000)	(373,500)
Total liabilities and equities	$(1,733,000)	$(691,500)

At year-end, there were no intra-entity receivables or payables.

a. Prepare a worksheet to consolidate these two companies as of December 31, 2024.

b. Prepare a 2024 consolidated income statement for Holtz and Devine.

c. If instead the noncontrolling interest shares of Devine had traded for $4.76 surrounding Holtz's acquisition date, what is the impact on goodwill?

34. Padre, Inc., buys 80 percent of the outstanding common stock of Sierra Corporation on January 1, 2024, for $802,720 cash. At the acquisition date, Sierra's total fair value, including the noncontrolling interest, was assessed at $1,003,400, although Sierra's book value was only $690,000. Also, several individual items on Sierra's financial records had fair values that differed from their book values as follows:

	Book Value	Fair Value
Land	$ 65,000	$ 290,000
Buildings and equipment (10-year remaining life)	287,000	263,000
Copyright (20-year remaining life)	122,000	216,000
Notes payable (due in 8 years)	(176,000)	(157,600)

For internal reporting purposes, Padre, Inc., employs the equity method to account for this investment. The following account balances are for the year ending December 31, 2024, for both companies:

	Padre	Sierra
Revenues	$(1,394,980)	$ (684,900)
Cost of goods sold	774,000	432,000
Depreciation expense	274,000	11,600
Amortization expense	0	6,100
Interest expense	52,100	9,200
Equity in income of Sierra	(177,120)	–0–
Net income	$ (472,000)	$ (226,000)
Retained earnings, 1/1/24	$(1,275,000)	$ (530,000)
Net income	(472,000)	(226,000)
Dividends declared	260,000	65,000
Retained earnings, 12/31/24	$(1,487,000)	$ (691,000)
Current assets	$ 856,160	$ 764,700
Investment in Sierra	927,840	–0–
Land	360,000	65,000
Buildings and equipment (net)	909,000	275,400
Copyright	–0–	115,900
Total assets	$ 3,053,000	$ 1,221,000
Accounts payable	$ (275,000)	$ (194,000)
Notes payable	(541,000)	(176,000)
Common stock	(300,000)	(100,000)
Additional paid-in capital	(450,000)	(60,000)
Retained earnings (above)	(1,487,000)	(691,000)
Total liabilities and equities	$(3,053,000)	$(1,221,000)

At year-end, there were no intra-entity receivables or payables.

Prepare a worksheet to consolidate the financial statements of these two companies.

LO 4-1, 4-5

35. Adams Corporation acquired 90 percent of the outstanding voting shares of Barstow, Inc., on December 31, 2022. Adams paid a total of $603,000 in cash for these shares. The 10 percent non-controlling interest shares traded on a daily basis at fair value of $67,000 both before and after Adams's acquisition. On December 31, 2022, Barstow had the following account balances:

	Book Value	Fair Value
Current assets	$ 160,000	$160,000
Land	120,000	150,000
Buildings (10-year remaining life)	220,000	200,000
Equipment (5-year remaining life)	160,000	200,000
Patents (10-year remaining life)	–0–	50,000
Notes payable (due in 5 years)	(200,000)	(180,000)
Common stock	(180,000)	
Retained earnings, 12/31/22	(280,000)	

December 31, 2024, adjusted trial balances for the two companies follow:

	Adams Corporation	Barstow, Inc.
Debits		
Current assets	$ 610,000	$ 250,000
Land	380,000	150,000
Buildings	490,000	250,000
Equipment	873,000	150,000
Investment in Barstow, Inc.	702,000	–0–
Cost of goods sold	480,000	90,000
Depreciation expense	100,000	55,000
Interest expense	40,000	15,000
Dividends declared	110,000	70,000
Total debits	$3,785,000	$1,030,000
Credits		
Notes payable	$ 860,000	$ 230,000
Common stock	510,000	180,000
Retained earnings, 1/1/24	1,367,000	340,000
Revenues	940,000	280,000
Investment income	108,000	–0–
Total credits	$3,785,000	$1,030,000

At year-end, there were no intra-entity receivables or payables.

a. Prepare schedules for acquisition-date fair-value allocations and amortizations for Adams's investment in Barstow.

b. Determine Adams's method of accounting for its investment in Barstow. Support your answer with a numerical explanation.

c. Without using a worksheet or consolidation entries, determine the balances to be reported as of December 31, 2024, for this business combination.

d. To verify the figures determined in requirement part (c), prepare a consolidation worksheet for Adams Corporation and Barstow, Inc., as of December 31, 2024.

LO 4-1, 4-4, 4-8

36. Following are the individual financial statements for Gibson and Davis for the year ending December 31, 2024:

	Gibson	Davis
Sales	$ (600,000)	$ (300,000)
Cost of goods sold	300,000	140,000
Operating expenses	174,000	60,000
Dividend income	(24,000)	–0–
Net income	$ (150,000)	$ (100,000)
Retained earnings, 1/1/24	$ (700,000)	$ (400,000)
Net income	(150,0000)	(100,000)
Dividends declared	80,000	40,000
Retained earnings, 12/31/24	$ (770,000)	$ (460,000)
Cash and receivables	$ 248,000	$ 100,000
Inventory	500,000	190,000
Investment in Davis	528,000	–0–
Buildings (net)	524,000	600,000
Equipment (net)	400,000	400,000
Total assets	$ 2,200,000	$ 1,290,000
Liabilities	(800,000)	(490,000)
Common stock	(630,000)	(340,000)
Retained earnings, 12/31/24	(770,000)	(460,000)
Total liabilities and stockholders' equity	$(2,200,000)	$(1,290,000)

Gibson acquired 60 percent of Davis on April 1, 2024, for $528,000. On that date, equipment owned by Davis (with a 5-year remaining life) was overvalued by $30,000. Also on that date, the fair value of the 40 percent noncontrolling interest was $352,000. Davis earned income evenly during the year but declared the $40,000 dividend on November 1, 2024.

a. Prepare a consolidated income statement for the year ending December 31, 2024.

b. Determine the consolidated balance for each of the following accounts as of December 31, 2024:

Goodwill	Buildings (net)
Equipment (net)	Dividends Declared
Common Stock	

LO 4-2, 4-3, 4-6, 4-7, 4-8

37. On July 1, 2024, Truman Company acquired a 70 percent interest in Atlanta Company in exchange for consideration of $720,000 in cash and equity securities. The remaining 30 percent of Atlanta's shares traded closely near an average price that totaled $290,000 both before and after Truman's acquisition.

In reviewing its acquisition, Truman assigned a $100,000 fair value to a patent recently developed by Atlanta, even though it was not recorded within the financial records of the subsidiary. This patent is anticipated to have a remaining life of five years.

The following financial information is available for these two companies for 2024. In addition, the subsidiary's income was earned uniformly throughout the year. The subsidiary declared dividends quarterly.

	Truman	Atlanta
Revenues	$ (670,000)	$ (400,000)
Operating expenses	402,000	280,000
Income of subsidiary	(35,000)	–0–
Net income	$ (303,000)	$ (120,000)
Retained earnings, 1/1/24	$ (823,000)	$ (500,000)
Net income (above)	(303,000)	(120,000)
Dividends declared	145,000	80,000
Retained earnings, 12/31/24	$ (981,000)	$ (540,000)

(*continued*)

(continued)

	Truman	Atlanta
Current assets	$ 481,000	$ 390,000
Investment in Atlanta	727,000	–0–
Land	388,000	200,000
Buildings	701,000	630,000
Total assets	$ 2,297,000	$ 1,220,000
Liabilities	$ (816,000)	$ (360,000)
Common stock	(95,000)	(300,000)
Additional paid-in capital	(405,000)	(20,000)
Retained earnings, 12/31/24	(981,000)	(540,000)
Total liabilities and stockholders' equity	$(2,297,000)	$(1,220,000)

Answer each of the following:

a. How did Truman allocate Atlanta's acquisition-date fair value to the various assets acquired and liabilities assumed in the combination?

b. How did Truman allocate the goodwill from the acquisition across the controlling and noncontrolling interests?

c. How did Truman derive the Investment in Atlanta account balance at the end of 2024?

d. Prepare a worksheet to consolidate the financial statements of these two companies as of December 31, 2024. At year-end, there were no intra-entity receivables or payables.

LO 4-9

38. On January 1, 2023, Payne Company bought a 15 percent interest in Scout Company. The acquisition price of $184,500 reflected an assessment that all of Scout's accounts were fairly valued within the company's accounting records. During 2023, Scout reported net income of $100,000 and declared cash dividends of $30,000. Payne possessed the ability to significantly influence Scout's operations and, therefore, accounted for this investment using the equity method.

On January 1, 2024, Payne acquired an additional 80 percent interest in Scout and provided the following fair-value assessments of Scout's ownership components:

Consideration transferred by Payne for 80% interest	$1,400,000
Fair value of Payne's 15% previous ownership	262,500
Noncontrolling interest's 5% fair value	87,500
Total acquisition-date fair value for Scout Company	$1,750,000

Also, as of January 1, 2024, Payne assessed a $400,000 value to an unrecorded database internally developed by Scout. The database is anticipated to have a remaining life of four years. Scout's other assets and liabilities were judged to have fair values equal to their book values. Payne elects to continue applying the equity method to this investment for internal reporting purposes.

At December 31, 2024, the following financial information is available for consolidation:

	Payne Company	Scout Company
Revenues	$ (931,000)	$ (380,000)
Operating expenses	615,000	230,000
Equity earnings of Scout	(47,500)	–0–
Gain on revaluation of Investment in Scout to fair value	(67,500)	–0–
Net income	$ 431,000	$ 150,000
Retained earnings, January 1	$ (965,000)	$ (600,000)
Net income	(431,000)	(150,000)
Dividends declared	140,000	40,000
Retained earnings, December 31	$(1,256,000)	$ (710,000)

(continued)

(continued)

	Payne Company	Scout Company
Current assets	$ 288,000	$ 540,000
Investment in Scout (equity method)	1,672,000	–0–
Property, plant, and equipment	826,000	590,000
Patented technology	850,000	370,000
Database	–0–	–0–
Total assets	$ 3,636,000	$ 1,500,000
Liabilities	$(1,300,000)	$ (90,000)
Common stock	(900,000)	(500,000)
Additional paid-in capital	(180,000)	(200,000)
Retained earnings, December 31	(1,256,000)	(710,000)
Total liabilities and equities	$(3,636,000)	$(1,500,000)

a. How should Payne allocate Scout's total acquisition-date fair value (January 1, 2024) to the assets acquired and liabilities assumed for consolidation purposes?

b. Show how the following amounts on Payne's pre-consolidation 2024 statements were derived:

- Equity in earnings of Scout
- Gain on revaluation of Investment in Scout to fair value
- Investment in Scout

c. Prepare a worksheet to consolidate the financial statements of these two companies as of December 31, 2024.

At year-end, there were no intra-entity receivables or payables.

LO 4-9

39. On January 1, 2023, Bretz, Inc., acquired 60 percent of the outstanding shares of Keane Company for $573,000 in cash. The price paid was proportionate to Keane's total fair value although at the date of acquisition, Keane had a total book value of $810,000. All assets acquired and liabilities assumed had fair values equal to book values except for a copyright (six-year remaining life) that was undervalued in Keane's accounting records by $120,000. During 2023, Keane reported net income of $150,000 and declared cash dividends of $80,000. On January 1, 2024, Bretz bought an additional 30 percent interest in Keane for $300,000.

The following financial information is available for these two companies for 2024. Keane issued no additional capital stock during either 2023 or 2024. Also, at year-end, there were no intra-entity receivables or payables.

	Bretz, Inc.	Keane Company
Revenues	$ (402,000)	$ (300,000)
Operating expenses	200,000	120,000
Equity in Keane earnings	(144,000)	–0–
Net income	$ (346,000)	$ (180,000)
Retained earnings, 1/1	$ (797,000)	$ (500,000)
Net income (above)	(346,000)	(180,000)
Dividends declared	143,000	60,000
Retained earnings, 12/31	$(1,000,000)	$ (620,000)
Current assets	$ 224,000	$ 190,000
Investment in Keane Company	994,500	–0–
Trademarks	106,000	600,000
Copyrights	210,000	300,000
Equipment (net)	380,000	110,000
Total assets	$ 1,914,500	$ 1,200,000

(continued)

(continued)

Liabilities	$ (453,000)	$ (200,000)
Common stock	(400,000)	(300,000)
Additional paid-in capital	(60,000)	(80,000)
Additional paid-in capital—step acquisition	(1,500)	–0–
Retained earnings, 12/31	(1,000,000)	(620,000)
Total liabilities and equities	$(1,914,500)	$(1,200,000)

   a. Show the journal entry Bretz made to record its January 1, 2024, acquisition of an additional 30 percent of Keane Company shares.

   b. Prepare a schedule showing how Bretz determined the Investment in Keane Company balance as of December 31, 2024.

   c. Prepare a consolidated worksheet for Bretz, Inc., and Keane Company for December 31, 2024.

Develop Your Skills

RESEARCH CASE: U.S. STEEL'S STEP ACQUISITION OF BIG RIVER STEEL

Prior to 2021, United States Steel Corporation (U.S. Steel), a global steelmaker, had owned a 49.9 percent equity interest in Big River Steel Holdings LLC (Big River Steel). Big River Steel owns one of the largest electric arc furnace-oriented flat-rolled mills in North America. On January 15, 2021 U.S. Steel acquired the remaining ownership of Big River Steel, resulting in Big River Steel becoming a wholly owned subsidiary of U.S. Steel.

Access U.S. Steel's 2021 10-K annual report, and answer the following:

1. What amounts and components did U.S. Steel identify to determine the total consideration for the acquisition of Big River Steel? (*Hint:* Include $50 million for U.S Steel's assumption of liabilities in the purchase.)

2. Prepare a schedule that shows
   - total consideration transferred by U.S. Steel for Big River Steel from part 1 above.
   - total fair value of the *identifiable* assets acquired in the combination.
   - total fair value of the liabilities assumed in the combination.
   - shows the difference between the total consideration transferred and the net total of identifiable assets acquired (assets less liabilities) as goodwill.

3. Prior to its acquisition of control, how did U.S. Steel account for its 49.9 percent investment in Big River Steel and why?

4. Upon acquisition of its controlling interest on January 15, 2021, how did U.S. Steel account for the change in fair value of its original 49.9 percent ownership interest in Big River Steel? How was this amount reported in the consolidated financial statements?

RESEARCH CASE: COSTCO'S NONCONTROLLING INTERESTS

Costco Wholesale Corporation owns and operates membership warehouses in the United States, Canada, United Kingdom, Mexico, Japan, Korea, Australia, Spain, France, and Iceland. Costco also engages in retail operations through a majority-owned subsidiary in Taiwan. The outside equity interests (not owned by Costco) in the Taiwanese subsidiary are presented as noncontrolling interests in Costco's consolidated financial statements.

Access Costco's 2021 10-K annual report, and answer the following:

1. How does Costco present the noncontrolling interest in the following financial statements?
   - Consolidated Balance Sheet
   - Consolidated Income Statement
   - Consolidated Statement of Other Comprehensive Income
   - Consolidated Statement of Cash Flows

2. Explain how Costco's presentations of the noncontrolling interest reflect the acquisition method for consolidated financial reporting as a single economic entity.

BARDEEN ELECTRIC: FASB ASC AND IFRS RESEARCH CASE

On October 18, 2023, Armstrong Auto Corporation ("Armstrong") announced its plan to acquire 80 percent of the outstanding 500,000 shares of Bardeen Electric Corporation's ("Bardeen") common stock in a business combination following regulatory approval. Armstrong will account for the transaction in accordance with ASC 805, "Business Combinations."

On December 1, 2023, Armstrong purchased an 80 percent controlling interest in Bardeen's outstanding voting shares. On this date, Armstrong paid $40 million in cash and issued one million shares of Armstrong common stock to the selling shareholders of Bardeen. Armstrong's share price was $26 on the announcement date and $24 on the acquisition date.

Bardeen's remaining 100,000 shares of common stock had been purchased for $3,000,000 by a small number of original investors. These shares have never been actively traded. Using other valuation techniques (comparable firms, discounted cash flow analysis, etc.), Armstrong estimated the acquisition-date fair value of Bardeen's noncontrolling shares at $16,500,000.

The parties agreed that Armstrong would issue to the selling shareholders an additional 1 million shares contingent upon the achievement of certain performance goals during the first 24 months following the acquisition. The acquisition-date fair value of the contingent stock issue was estimated at $8 million.

Bardeen has a research and development (R&D) project underway to develop a superconductive electrical/magnetic application. Total costs incurred to date on the project equal $4,400,000. However, Armstrong estimates that the technology has a fair value of $11 million. Armstrong considers this R&D as in-process because it has not yet reached technological feasibility and additional R&D is needed to bring the project to completion. No assets have been recorded in Bardeen's financial records for the R&D costs to date.

Bardeen's other assets and liabilities (at fair value) include the following:

Cash	$ 425,000
Accounts receivable	788,000
Land	3,487,000
Building	16,300,000
Machinery	39,000,000
Patents	7,000,000
Accounts payable	(1,500,000)

Neither the receivables nor payables involve Armstrong.

Answer the following questions citing relevant support from the ASC and IFRS.

1. What is the total consideration transferred by Armstrong to acquire its 80 percent controlling interest in Bardeen?

2. What values should Armstrong assign to identifiable intangible assets as part of the acquisition accounting?

3. What is the acquisition-date value assigned to the 20 percent noncontrolling interest? What are the potential noncontrolling interest valuation alternatives available under IFRS?

4. Under U.S. GAAP, what amount should Armstrong recognize as goodwill from the Bardeen acquisition? What alternative goodwill valuations are allowed under IFRS?

Consolidated Financial Statements— Intra-Entity Asset Transactions

C hapter 1 analyzed the deferral and subsequent recognition of gross profits created by inventory transfers between two affiliated companies in connection with equity method accounting. The central theme of that discussion is that intra-entity[1] profits cannot be recognized until the goods are ultimately sold to an unrelated party or consumed in the production process. This same accounting logic applies to transactions between companies within a business combination. Such sales within a single economic entity create neither profits nor losses. In reference to this issue, FASB ASC 810-10-45-1 states,

> As consolidated financial statements are based on the assumption that they represent the financial position and operating results of a single economic entity, such statements shall not include gain or loss on transactions among the entities in the consolidated group. Accordingly, any intra-entity profit or loss on assets remaining within the consolidated group shall be eliminated; the concept usually applied for this purpose is gross profit or loss.

The elimination of the accounting effects created by intra-entity transfers is one of the most significant problems encountered in the consolidation process. Such transfers are especially common in companies organized as a vertically integrated chain of organizations. For example, after acquiring its bottling companies, PepsiCo noted,

> we acquired PBG and PAS to create a more fully integrated supply chain and go-to-market business model, improving the effectiveness and efficiency of the distribution of our brands and enhancing our revenue growth.

[1] The FASB *Accounting Standards Codification*® (ASC) uses the term *intra-entity* to describe transfers of assets across entities affiliated through common ownership or other control mechanisms. The term indicates that although such transfers occur across separate legal entities, they are nonetheless made within a consolidated entity. In addition to the term *intra-entity*, such transfers are routinely referred to as *intercompany*.

Learning Objectives

After studying this chapter, you should be able to:

LO 5-1 Understand why intra-entity asset transfers create accounting effects within the financial records of affiliated companies that must be eliminated or adjusted in preparing consolidated financial statements.

LO 5-2 Demonstrate the consolidation procedures to eliminate intra-entity sales and purchases balances.

LO 5-3 Explain why consolidated entities defer intra-entity gross profit in ending inventory and the consolidation procedures required to subsequently recognize profits.

LO 5-4 Understand that the consolidation process for inventory transfers is designed to defer the intra-entity gross profit remaining in ending inventory from the year of transfer into the year of disposal or consumption.

LO 5-5 Explain the difference between upstream and downstream intra-entity transfers and how each affects the computation of noncontrolling interest balances.

LO 5-6 Prepare the consolidation entry to defer any gain created by an intra-entity transfer of land from the accounting records of the year of transfer and subsequent years.

LO 5-7 Prepare the consolidation entries to remove the effects of upstream and downstream intra-entity fixed asset transfers across affiliated entities.

Entities such as PepsiCo can reduce their costs and increase revenues by developing affiliations in which one operation furnishes products to another.

Intra-entity asset transactions take several forms. In particular, inventory transfers are especially prevalent. However, the sale of land and depreciable assets also can occur between the parties within a combination. This chapter examines the consolidation procedures for each of these different types of intra-entity asset transfers.[2]

Intra-Entity Inventory Transfers

LO 5-1

Understand why intra-entity asset transfers create accounting effects within the financial records of affiliated companies that must be eliminated or adjusted in preparing consolidated financial statements.

As previous chapters discussed, companies that make up a business combination frequently retain their legal identities as separate operating centers and maintain their own recordkeeping. Thus, inventory sales between these companies trigger the independent accounting systems of both parties. The seller duly records revenue, and the buyer simultaneously enters the purchase into its accounts. For internal reporting purposes, recording an inventory transfer as a sale/purchase provides vital data to help measure the operational efficiency of each enterprise.[3]

Despite the internal information benefits of accounting for the transaction in this manner, from a consolidated perspective, neither a sale nor a purchase has occurred. *An intra-entity transfer is merely the internal movement of inventory, an event that creates no net change in the financial position of the business combination taken as a whole.* Thus, in producing consolidated financial statements, the recorded effects of these transfers are eliminated so that consolidated statements reflect only transactions (and thus profits) with outside parties. Worksheet entries serve this purpose; they adapt the financial information reported by the separate companies to the perspective of the consolidated enterprise. The entire impact of the intra-entity transfer must be identified and then removed. Deleting the effects of the actual transfer is described here first.

The Sales and Purchases Accounts

LO 5-2

Demonstrate the consolidation procedures to eliminate intra-entity sales and purchases balances.

To account for related companies as a single economic entity requires eliminating all intra-entity sales/purchases balances. For example, if Arlington Company makes an $80,000 inventory sale to Zirkin Company, an affiliated party within a business combination, both parties record the transfer in their internal records as a normal sale/purchase. The following consolidation worksheet entry is then necessary to remove the resulting balances from the externally reported figures. Cost of Goods Sold is reduced here under the assumption that the Purchases account usually is closed out prior to the consolidation process.

Consolidation Entry TI		
Sales	80,000	
Cost of Goods Sold (purchases component)		80,000
To eliminate effects of intra-entity transfer of inventory. (Labeled *TI* in reference to the transferred inventory.)		

In the preparation of consolidated financial statements, the preceding elimination must be made for all intra-entity inventory transfers. The total recorded (intra-entity) sales figure is deleted regardless of whether the transfer was downstream (from parent to subsidiary) or upstream (from subsidiary to parent). Furthermore, any gross profit included in the transfer price does not affect this sales/purchases elimination. Because the entire amount of the transfer occurred between related parties, the total effect must be removed in preparing the consolidated statements.

---

[2] In practice, the terms *intra-entity transaction* and *intra-entity transfer* are used interchangeably. Some argue that the use of the term *transaction* should be reserved for activities with entities outside the consolidated group.

[3] For all intra-entity transfers, the two parties involved view the events from different perspectives. Thus, the transfer is both a sale and a purchase, often creating both a receivable and a payable. To indicate the dual nature of such transfers, these accounts are indicated within this text as sales/purchases, receivables/payables, and so on.

Intra-Entity Gross Profit—Year of Transfer (Year 1)

Removal of the sale/purchase is often just the first in a series of consolidation entries necessitated by inventory transfers. Despite the previous elimination, gross profits in ending inventory created by such sales can still exist in the accounting records at year-end. These profits initially result when the merchandise is priced at more than historical cost. Actual transfer prices are established in several ways, including the normal sales price of the inventory, sales price less a specified discount, or at a predetermined markup above cost. For example, in past financial statements, Ford Motor Company explained that

> intercompany sales among geographic areas consist primarily of vehicles, parts, and components manufactured by the company and various subsidiaries and sold to different entities within the consolidated group; transfer prices for these transactions are established by agreement between the affected entities.

Regardless of the method used for this pricing decision, gross profits that remain in inventory at year-end as a result of intra-entity sales during the period must be removed in arriving at consolidated figures.

All Inventory Remains at Year-End

In the preceding illustration, assume that Arlington acquired or produced this inventory at a cost of $50,000 and then sold it to Zirkin, an affiliated party, at the indicated $80,000 price. From a consolidated perspective, the inventory still has a historical cost of only $50,000. However, Zirkin's records now reflect the inventory at the $80,000 transfer price. In addition, because of the markup, Arlington's records show a $30,000 gross profit from this intra-entity sale. However, because the transaction did not occur with an outside party, recognition of this profit is not appropriate for the combination as a whole.

Thus, although the Consolidation Entry **TI** shown earlier eliminated the sale/purchase figures, the $30,000 inflation created by the transfer price still exists in two areas of the individual statements:

- Ending inventory remains overstated by $30,000.
- Gross profit is artificially overstated by this same amount.

Correcting the ending inventory requires only reducing the asset. However, correcting gross profit requires a careful analysis of the effect of the intra-entity transfer on the Cost of Goods Sold account.

Cost of Goods Sold Computation
Beginning Inventory
+ Purchases
= Goods Available
− Ending Inventory
= **Cost of Goods Sold**

Note that the ending inventory total serves as a negative component within the Cost of Goods Sold computation; it represents the *cost* of inventory that was not sold. Thus, the $30,000 *overstatement* of Inventory *understates* Cost of Goods Sold. *Despite Entry* TI, *the inflated ending inventory figure causes Cost of Goods Sold to be too low and, thus, profits to be too high by $30,000.* For consolidation purposes, we increase Cost of Goods Sold by this amount through a worksheet adjustment that effectively removes the gross profit from consolidated net income.

Consequently, if all of the transferred inventory is retained by the business combination at the end of the year, the following worksheet entry also must be included to eliminate the effects of the seller's gross profit that remains within the buyer's ending inventory:

Reduces cogs

Consolidation Entry G—Year of Transfer (Year 1)		
All Inventory Remains		
Cost of Goods Sold (ending inventory component)	30,000	
Inventory (balance sheet account)		30,000
To remove gross profit in ending inventory created by intra-entity sales.		

? Discussion Question

EARNINGS MANAGEMENT

Enron Corporation experienced one of the most stunning and disastrous bankruptcies in U.S. history. The ensuing scandal surrounding Enron, to a large extent, stemmed from its creative and deceptive accounting practices.

For example, Enron's 2001 third-quarter 10-Q report disclosed the following activities with LJM2, a nonconsolidated special purpose entity (SPE) that was formed by Enron:

> In June 2000, LJM2 purchased dark fiber optic cable from Enron for a purchase price of $100 million. LJM2 paid Enron $30 million in cash and the balance in an interest-bearing note for $70 million. Enron recognized $67 million in pretax earnings in 2000 related to the asset sale. Pursuant to a marketing agreement with LJM2, Enron was compensated for marketing the fiber to others and providing operation and maintenance services to LJM2 with respect to the fiber. LJM2 sold a portion of the fiber to industry participants for $40 million, which resulted in Enron recognizing agency fee revenue of $20.3 million.

As investigations later discovered, Enron controlled LJM2 in many ways.

The FASB ASC now requires the consolidation of SPEs (as variable interest entities) that are essentially controlled by their primary beneficiary.

By selling goods to SPEs that it controlled but did not consolidate, did Enron overstate its earnings? What effect does consolidation have on the financial reporting for transactions between a firm and its controlled entities?

This entry (labeled **G** for gross profit) reduces the consolidated Inventory account to its original $50,000 historical cost. Furthermore, increasing Cost of Goods Sold by $30,000 effectively removes the intra-entity amount from recognized gross profit. Thus, this worksheet entry resolves both reporting problems created by the transfer price markup.

Only a Portion of Inventory Remains

Obviously, a company does not buy inventory to hold it indefinitely. It either uses the purchased inventory within the company's operations or resells it to unrelated, outside parties. Intra-entity profits ultimately are recognized by subsequently consuming or reselling these goods. However, the transferred inventory still held at year-end continues to be recorded in the separate accounts at a value more than the historical cost. For this reason, *the ending inventory intra-entity gross profit elimination (Entry* **G***) is based not on total intra-entity sales but only on the amount of transferred merchandise retained within the business at the end of the year.*

To illustrate, assume that Arlington transferred inventory costing $50,000 to Zirkin, a related company, for $80,000, thus recording a gross profit of $30,000. Assume further that by year-end, Zirkin has resold $60,000 of these goods to unrelated parties but retains the other $20,000 (for resale in the following year). From the viewpoint of the consolidated company, it has now completed the revenue recognition process on the $60,000 portion of the intra-entity sale and need not make an adjustment for consolidation purposes.

Nonetheless, any gross profit recorded in connection with the $20,000 in merchandise that remains is still a component within Zirkin's Inventory account. Because the gross profit rate was 37½ percent ($30,000 gross profit/$80,000 transfer price), this retained inventory is stated at a value $7,500 more than its original cost ($20,000 × 37½%). The required reduction (Entry **G**) is not the entire $30,000 shown previously, but only the $7,500 intra-entity gross profit that remains in ending inventory.

Consolidation Entry G—Year of Transfer (Year 1)		
25% of Inventory Remains (replaces previous entry)		
Cost of Goods Sold (ending inventory component)	7,500	
Inventory		7,500
To defer the intra-entity gross profit in ending inventory in year of transfer.		

LO 5-4

Understand that the consolidation process for inventory transfers is designed to defer the intra-entity gross profit in ending inventory from the year of transfer into the year of disposal or consumption.

Intra-Entity Gross Profit—Year Following Transfer (Year 2)

Whenever intra-entity profit is present in ending inventory, one further consolidation entry is eventually required. Although Entry **G** removes the gross profit from the *consolidated* inventory balances in the year of transfer, the $7,500 overstatement remains within the separate financial records of the buyer and seller. The effects of this deferred gross profit are carried into their beginning balances in the subsequent year. Hence, a worksheet adjustment is necessary in the period following the transfer. For consolidation purposes, the ending inventory portion of intra-entity gross profit must be adjusted in two successive years (from ending inventory in the year of transfer and from beginning inventory of the next period).

Referring again to Arlington's sale of inventory to Zirkin, the $7,500 intra-entity gross profit is still in Zirkin's Inventory account at the start of the subsequent year. Once again, the overstatement is removed within the consolidation process but this time from the beginning inventory balance (which appears in the financial statements only as a positive component of Cost of Goods Sold). This consolidation worksheet entry is labeled *G. The asterisk indicates that a previous-year transfer created the intra-entity gross profits.

Consolidation Entry *G—Year Following Transfer (Year 2)		
Retained Earnings (beginning balance of seller)	7,500	
Cost of Goods Sold (beginning inventory component)		7,500
To remove from retained earnings the gross profit in beginning inventory and to currently recognize the profit through a reduction in cost of goods sold.		

Reducing Cost of Goods Sold (beginning inventory) through Entry *G increases the gross profit reported for this second year. For consolidation purposes, the gross profit on the transfer is recognized in the period in which the items are actually sold to outside parties. As shown in the diagram below, Entry **G** initially deferred the $7,500 intra-entity gross profit in the year of transfer. Entry *G now increases consolidated net income (by decreasing Cost of Goods Sold) to reflect the sales activity with outside parties in the current year.

In Entry *G, removal of the $7,500 from beginning inventory (within Cost of Goods Sold) appropriately increases current net income and should not pose a significant conceptual problem. However, the rationale for decreasing the seller's beginning Retained Earnings deserves further explanation. This reduction removes the intra-entity gross profit in ending inventory (recognized by the seller in the year of transfer) so that the profit is reported in the period when a sale to an outside party takes place. Despite the consolidation entries in Year 1, the $7,500 gross profit remained on this company's separate books and was closed to Retained Earnings at the end of the period. Recall that consolidation entries are never posted to the individual affiliate's books. Therefore, from a consolidated view, the buyer's Cost of Goods Sold (through the

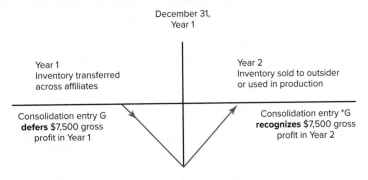

beginning inventory component) and the seller's Retained Earnings accounts as of the beginning of Year 2 contain the intra-entity profit and must both be reduced in Entry *G.[4]

Intra-Entity Beginning Inventory Profit Adjustment—Downstream Sales When Parent Uses Equity Method

The worksheet eliminations for intra-entity sales/purchases (Entry **TI**) and intra-entity gross profit in ending inventory (Entry **G**) are both standard, regardless of the circumstances of the consolidation. In contrast, for one specific situation, the consolidation entry to recognize intra-entity beginning inventory gross profit differs from the Entry *G just presented. If (1) the original transfer is downstream (intra-entity sales made by the parent), and (2) the parent applies the equity method for internal accounting purposes, then the **Investment in Subsidiary** account replaces the parent's beginning Retained Earnings in Consolidation Entry *G as follows:

Consolidation Entry *G—Year Following Transfer (Year 2) (replaces previous Entry *G for downstream transfers when the equity method is used)		
Investment in Subsidiary	7,500	
Cost of Goods Sold (beginning inventory component)		7,500
To recognize previously deferred intra-entity downstream inventory gross profit as part of current-year net income when the parent uses the equity method.		

Why debit the Investment in Subsidiary (and not the parent's beginning Retained Earnings) account in this situation? When the parent uses the equity method in its internal records, it recognizes beginning inventory gross profits on its books (and defers intra-entity ending inventory gross profits) as part of its equity income accruals. Therefore, through the application of the equity method, both the parent's net income and retained earnings appropriately reflect consolidated balances and require no adjustment.

At year-end, using the equity method, the parent increases its Investment in Subsidiary account for beginning inventory intra-entity gross profits. These same intra-entity profits were recorded as decreases to the Investment account in the prior year. Consolidation Entry **I**, however, removes the current-year equity income accruals from the Investment in Subsidiary account as part of the investment elimination sequence. With the equity income accrual removed, the beginning inventory intra-entity profit reappears as a credit to the Investment in Subsidiary account's beginning-of-the-year balance.

Following our example, Consolidation Entry *G is thus needed to transfer the original $7,500 Year 1 Investment in Subsidiary account credit to a Year 2 earnings credit (through Cost of Goods Sold). Consolidation Entry *G also ensures that the Investment in Subsidiary account is brought to a zero balance on the worksheet.[5]

To summarize, for **intra-entity beginning inventory profits resulting from downstream transfers when the parent applies the equity method:**

- The parent's beginning retained earnings reflect the consolidated balance from application of the equity method and need no adjustment.
- The parent's Investment in Subsidiary account as of the beginning of Year 2 contains a credit from the deferral of Year 1 intra-entity downstream profits.
- Worksheet Entry *G debits the Investment account and credits Cost of Goods Sold, effectively recognizing the profit in the year of sale to outsiders.

---

[4] For upstream intra-entity profit in beginning inventory, the subsidiary's retained earnings remain overstated and must be adjusted through Consolidation Entry *G.

[5] An acceptable alternative to recognizing intra-entity inventory profits in the subsidiary's beginning inventory (downstream sale) when the parent uses the equity method (*G) is as follows:

Equity in Subsidiary Earnings	7,500	
Cost of Goods Sold		7,500

In this case, Consolidation Entry I removes the remaining amount of the Equity in Subsidiary Earnings against the Investment in Subsidiary account. In either alternative adjustment for recognizing intra-entity inventory gross profits in beginning inventory, the final consolidated balances are exactly the same: Equity in Subsidiary Earnings = 0, Investment in Subsidiary = 0, and Cost of Goods Sold is reduced by $7,500.

EXHIBIT 5.1
Relationship between Gross Profit Rate and Markup on Cost

In determining appropriate amounts of intra-entity profits for deferral and subsequent recognition in consolidated financial reports, two alternative—but mathematically related—profit percentages are often seen. Recalling that Gross Profit = Sales − Cost of Goods Sold, then

$$\textbf{Gross profit rate (GPR)} = \frac{\text{Gross profit}}{\text{Sales}} = \frac{MC}{1 + MC}$$

$$\textbf{Markup on cost (MC)} = \frac{\text{Gross profit}}{\text{Cost of goods sold}} = \frac{GPR}{1 - GPR}$$

Example:	Sales (transfer price)	$1,000
	Cost of goods sold	800
	Gross profit	$ 200

Here the *GPR* = $200 ÷ $1,000 = 20%, and the *MC* = $200 ÷ $800 = 25%. In most intra-entity purchases and sales, the sales (transfer) price is known, and, therefore, the *GPR* is the simplest percentage to use to determine the amount of intra-entity profit.

$$\text{Intra-entity profit} = \text{Transfer price} \times GPR$$

Instead, if the markup on cost is available, it readily converts to a *GPR* by the preceding formula. In this case, 0.25 ÷ 1.25 = 20%.

Finally, various markup percentages determine the dollar values for intra-entity profit deferrals. Exhibit 5.1 shows formulas for both the gross profit rate and markup on cost and the relationship between the two.

Intra-Entity Gross Profit—Effect on Noncontrolling Interest

The worksheet entries just described appropriately account for the effects of intra-entity inventory transfers on business combinations. However, one question remains: What impact do these procedures have on the measurement of a noncontrolling interest? In regards to this issue, paragraph 810-10-45-18 of the FASB ASC states,

> The amount of intra-entity profit or loss to be eliminated in accordance with paragraph 810-10-45-1 is not affected by the existence of a noncontrolling interest. The complete elimination of the intra-entity income or loss is consistent with the underlying assumption that consolidated financial statements represent the financial position and operating results of a single economic entity. The elimination of the intra-entity income or loss may be allocated between the parent and noncontrolling interests.

The last sentence indicates that alternative approaches are available in computing the noncontrolling interest's share of a subsidiary's net income. According to this pronouncement, gross profits in inventory resulting from intra-entity transfers *may or may not* affect recognition of outside ownership. Because the amount attributed to a noncontrolling interest reduces consolidated net income, the handling of this issue can affect the reported profitability of a business combination.

To illustrate, assume that Large Company owns 70 percent of the voting stock of Small Company. To avoid extraneous complications, assume that no amortization expense resulted from this acquisition. Assume further that Large reports current net income (from its separate operations) of $500,000 while Small reports net income of $100,000. During the current period, intra-entity transfers of $200,000 occur with a total markup of $90,000. At the end of the year, a $40,000 intra-entity gross profit remains within the inventory accounts.

The consolidated net income prior to the reduction for the 30 percent noncontrolling interest is $560,000 computed as follows:

Net income reported by Large	$500,000
Net income reported by Small	100,000
Intra-entity ending inventory gross profit deferral	(40,000)
Consolidated net income	$560,000

The problem facing the accountant is the computation of the noncontrolling interest's share of Small's net income. Because of the flexibility allowed by the FASB ASC, this figure may be reported as either

- $30,000 (30 percent of Small's $100,000 net income), or
- $18,000 (30 percent of Small's $100,000 net income less $40,000 intra-entity gross profit in ending inventory).

To appropriately measure the noncontrolling interest income allocation, the direction of the intra-entity transfer must be considered. If a transfer is downstream (the parent sells inventory to the subsidiary), a logical view would seem to be that the intra-entity ending inventory gross profit deferral is attributable to the parent company. The parent made the original sale; therefore, the gross profit is included in its financial records. Because the subsidiary's net income is unaffected, little justification exists for adjusting the noncontrolling interest to reflect the deferral of the intra-entity gross profit. Consequently, in the example of Large and Small, if the transfers were downstream, the 30 percent noncontrolling interest would be $30,000 based on Small's reported net income of $100,000.

In contrast, when the subsidiary sells inventory to the parent (an upstream transfer), the subsidiary recognizes the entire gross profit in its financial records even though part of the gross profit is deferred from a consolidation perspective. A reasonable conclusion is that because the subsidiary created the gross profit, a portion of that profit is attributable to the noncontrolling interest.

In this textbook, the noncontrolling interest's share of consolidated net income is based on the reported net income of the subsidiary after adjusting for intra-entity gross profit in inventories from *upstream* sales. Returning to Large Company and Small Company, if the $40,000 intra-entity gross profit results from an upstream sale from subsidiary to parent, only $60,000 of Small's $100,000 net income should be recognized currently for consolidation purposes. The allocation to the noncontrolling interest is, therefore, reported as $18,000, or 30 percent of the $60,000 subsidiary net income after adjusting for the intra-entity profit remaining in ending inventory.

Although the noncontrolling interest figure is based here on the subsidiary's reported net income adjusted for the effects of upstream intra-entity transfers, GAAP, as quoted earlier, does not require this treatment. Giving effect to upstream transfers in this calculation but not to downstream transfers is simply an attempt to select the most logical approach among acceptable alternatives.[6]

Intra-Entity Inventory Transfers Summarized

To assist in overcoming the complications created by intra-entity transfers, we demonstrate the consolidation process in three different ways:

1. Before proceeding to a numerical example, we review the impact of intra-entity transfers on consolidated figures. Ultimately, the accountant must understand how the balances reported by a business combination are derived when intra-entity gross profit in inventory result from either upstream or downstream sales.

2. Next, two alternative consolidation worksheets are produced: one for downstream transfers and the other for upstream. The various consolidation procedures used in these worksheets are explained and analyzed.

3. Finally, several of the consolidation worksheet entries are shown side by side to illustrate the differences created by the direction of the transfers.

---

[6] The 100 percent allocation of downstream profits to the parent affects its application of the equity method. As seen later in this chapter, in applying the equity method, the parent removes 100 percent of intra-entity profits resulting from downstream sales from its investment and equity earnings accounts rather than its percentage ownership in the subsidiary.

The Development of Consolidated Totals

A summary of the effects of intra-entity inventory transfers on consolidated totals follows:

- *Revenues.* Parent and subsidiary balances are combined, but all intra-entity transfers are then removed.
- *Cost of Goods Sold.* Parent and subsidiary balances are combined, but all intra-entity transfers are removed. The resulting total is decreased by any intra-entity gross profit in beginning inventory (thus raising net income) and increased by any intra-entity gross profit in ending inventory (reducing net income).
- *Net Income Attributable to the Noncontrolling Interest.* The subsidiary's reported net income is adjusted for any excess acquisition-date fair-value amortizations and the effects of intra-entity gross profits in inventory from upstream transfers (but not downstream transfers) and then multiplied by the percentage of outside ownership.
- *Retained Earnings at the Beginning of the Year.* As discussed in previous chapters, if the equity method is applied, the parent's balance mirrors the consolidated total. When any other method is used, the parent's beginning Retained Earnings must be converted to the equity method by Entry *C. Accruals for this purpose must recognize (1) the effects on reported subsidiary net income of intra-entity gross profits in beginning inventory that arose from upstream sales in the prior year, and (2) prior years' excess acquisition-date fair-value amortizations.
- *Inventory.* Parent and subsidiary balances are combined. Any intra-entity gross profit remaining at the end of the current year is removed to adjust the reported balance to historical cost.
- *Noncontrolling Interest in Subsidiary at End of Year.* The final total begins with the noncontrolling interest at the beginning of the year. This figure is based on the subsidiary's book value on that date plus its share of any unamortized acquisition-date excess fair value less its share of gross profits in beginning inventory arising from prior year upstream sales. The beginning balance is updated by adding the portion of the subsidiary's net income assigned to these outside owners (as previously described) and subtracting the noncontrolling interest's share of subsidiary dividends.

Intra-Entity Inventory Transfers Illustrated: Parent Uses Equity Method

To examine the various consolidation procedures required by intra-entity inventory transfers, assume that Top Company acquires 80 percent of the voting stock of Bottom Company on January 1, 2023. The parent pays $400,000, and the acquisition-date fair value of the noncontrolling interest is $100,000. Top allocates the entire $50,000 excess fair value over book value to adjust a database owned by Bottom to fair value. The database has an estimated remaining life of 20 years. Top Company applies the equity method to its investment in Bottom.[7]

The subsidiary reports net income of $30,000 in 2023 and $70,000 in 2024, the current year. The subsidiary declares dividends of $20,000 in the first year and $50,000 in the second. After the takeover, intra-entity inventory transfers between the two companies occurred as shown in Exhibit 5.2. A $10,000 intra-entity receivable and payable also exists as of December 31, 2024.

EXHIBIT 5.2
Intra-Entity Transfers

	2023	2024
Transfer prices	$80,000	$100,000
Historical cost	60,000	70,000
Gross profit	$20,000	$ 30,000
Inventory remaining at year-end (at transfer price)	$16,000	$ 20,000
Gross profit percentage	25%	30%
Gross profit remaining in year-end inventory	$ 4,000	$ 6,000

[7] Later in this chapter, we extend the example to when the parent applies the initial value method.

The 2024 consolidation of Top and Bottom is presented twice. First, we assume the intra-entity transfers are downstream from parent to subsidiary. Second, consolidated figures are recomputed with the transfers being viewed as upstream. This distinction between upstream and downstream transfer becomes significant when the parent uses the equity method and in the presence of a noncontrolling interest.

Downstream Inventory Transfers: Parent Uses the Equity Method

To understand the consolidation procedures for intra-entity inventory transfers, it's useful first to analyze the parent's internal accounting for the investment. Under the equity method, the parent's investment-related accounts are subjected to (1) income accrual, (2) excess fair-over book-value amortization, (3) adjustments required by intra-entity gross profit in inventory, and (4) dividends. Exhibit 5.3 shows the changes to the Investment in Bottom Company from the acquisition date until the end of the current year (2024).

Note in particular the computations of Top's equity in earnings of Bottom Company in Exhibit 5.3. First, the calculations for equity method income are identical to those presented in Chapter 4, with the addition of an adjustment for intra-entity profits. Also observe that the $4,000 intra-entity profit deferred in 2023 is subsequently recognized in 2024. Thus, the $4,000 intra-entity profit is not eliminated but simply reallocated across time to the period when it is recognized by the consolidated entity. Next, observe that, because the inventory transfers are downstream from parent to subsidiary, 100 percent of the profit deferral and subsequent recognition is allocated to the parent's equity earnings and investment account. As a result, the intra-entity profit reallocation across time affects neither Bottom's net income nor the noncontrolling interest.

Exhibit 5.4 presents the worksheet to consolidate these two companies for the year ending December 31, 2024. Most of the worksheet entries found in Exhibit 5.4 are described and analyzed in previous chapters of this textbook. Thus, we examine only three of these entries in detail along with the computation of the net income attributable to the noncontrolling interest.

First, Consolidation Entry ***G** adjusts for the intra-entity gross profit carried over in the beginning inventory from the 2023 intra-entity downstream transfers.

EXHIBIT 5.3
Investment Balances—Equity Method—Downstream Sales

Investment in Bottom Company Analysis 1/1/23 to 12/31/24		
Consideration paid (fair value) 1/1/23		$400,000
Bottom Company reported net income for 2023	$30,000	
Database amortization	(2,500)	
Bottom Company adjusted 2023 net income	$27,500	
Top's ownership percentage	80%	
Top's share of Bottom Company's net income	$22,000	
Deferred profit from Top's 2023 downstream sales	(4,000)	
Equity in earnings of Bottom Company, 2023		$ 18,000
Top's share of Bottom Company dividends, 2023 (80%)		(16,000)
Balance 12/31/23		$402,000
Bottom Company reported net income for 2024	$70,000	
Database amortization	(2,500)	
Bottom Company adjusted 2024 net income	$67,500	
Top's ownership percentage	80%	
Top's share of Bottom Company's net income	$54,000	
Recognized profit from Top's 2023 downstream sales	4,000	
Deferred profit from Top's 2024 downstream sales	(6,000)	
Equity in earnings of Bottom Company, 2024		$ 52,000
Top's share of Bottom Company dividends, 2024 (80%)		(40,000)
Balance 12/31/24		$414,000

EXHIBIT 5.4 Downstream Inventory Transfers

			Consolidation Entries			
TOP COMPANY AND BOTTOM COMPANY Consolidation Worksheet						
Investment: Equity Method		For Year Ending December 31, 2024				***Ownership: 80%***
Accounts	**Top Company**	**Bottom Company**	**Debit**	**Credit**	**Noncontrolling Interest**	**Consolidated Totals**
Income Statement						
Sales	(600,000)	(300,000)	(TI) 100,000			(800,000)
Cost of goods sold	320,000	180,000	(G) 6,000	(*G) 4,000		402,000
				(TI) 100,000		
Operating expenses	170,000	50,000	(E) 2,500			222,500
Equity in earnings of Bottom Company	(52,000)		(I) 52,000†			–0–
Separate company net income	(162,000)	(70,000)				
Consolidated net income						(175,500)
Net income attributable to noncontrolling interest					(13,500)†	13,500
Net income to Top Company						(162,000)
Statement of Retained Earnings						
Retained earnings, 1/1/24						
Top Company	(652,000)					(652,000)
Bottom Company		(310,000)	(S) 310,000			
Net income (above)	(162,000)	(70,000)				(162,000)
Dividends declared	70,000	50,000		(D) 40,000	10,000	70,000
Retained earnings, 12/31/24	(744,000)	(330,000)				(744,000)
Balance Sheet						
Cash and receivables	280,000	120,000		(P) 10,000		390,000
Inventory	220,000	160,000		(G) 6,000		374,000
Investment in Bottom	414,000		(D) 40,000	(I) 52,000		–0–
			(*G) 4,000	(S) 368,000		
				(A) 38,000		
Land	410,000	200,000				610,000
Plant assets (net)	190,000	170,000				360,000
Database			(A) 47,500	(E) 2,500		45,000
Total assets	1,514,000	650,000				1,779,000
Liabilities	(340,000)	(170,000)	(P) 10,000			(500,000)
Noncontrolling interest in Bottom Company, 1/1/24				(S) 92,000		
				(A) 9,500	(101,500)	
Noncontrolling interest in Bottom Company, 12/31/24					(105,000)	(105,000)
Common stock	(430,000)	(150,000)	(S) 150,000			(430,000)
Retained earnings, 12/31/24 (above)	(744,000)	(330,000)				(744,000)
Total liabilities and equities	(1,514,000)	(650,000)	722,000	722,000		(1,779,000)

Note: Parentheses indicate a credit balance.

†Because intra-entity sales are made downstream (by the parent), the subsidiary's adjusted net income is the $70,000 reported less $2,500 excess amortization figure with a 20% allocation to the noncontrolling interest ($13,500).

‡Boxed items highlight differences with upstream transfers examined in Exhibit 5.6.

Consolidation entries:

(*G) Recognition of intra-entity beginning inventory gross profit in current-period consolidated net income. Downstream sales are attributed to parent.

(S) Elimination of subsidiary's stockholders' equity accounts along with recognition of the noncontrolling interest as of January 1.

(A) Allocation of excess fair value over subsidiary's book value, unamortized balance as of January 1.

(I) Elimination of intra-entity income remaining after *G elimination.

(D) Elimination of intra-entity dividend.

(E) Recognition of amortization expense for current year on excess fair value allocated to database.

(P) Elimination of intra-entity receivable/payable balances.

(TI) Elimination of intra-entity sales/purchases balances.

(G) Deferral of intra-entity ending inventory gross profit from current-period consolidated net income and removal of intra-entity gross profit from ending inventory.

Consolidation Entry *G

Investment in Bottom	4,000	
Cost of Goods Sold		4,000

To remove 2023 intra-entity gross profit in inventory from seller's beginning balance and recognize the gross profit in 2024 following sales to outsiders. Top uses the equity method, and intra-entity sales were downstream.

The gross profit rate (Exhibit 5.2) on these items was 25 percent ($20,000 gross profit/ $80,000 transfer price), indicating an intra-entity profit of $4,000 (25 percent of the remaining $16,000 in inventory). To recognize this gross profit in 2024, Entry *G reduces Cost of Goods Sold (or the beginning inventory component of that expense) by that amount. The reduction in Cost of Goods Sold creates an increase in current-year net income. From a consolidation perspective, the gross profit is correctly recognized in 2024 when the inventory is sold to an outside party. The debit to the Investment in Bottom account becomes part of the sequence of adjustments to bring that account to a zero balance in consolidation.

Consolidation Entry TI

Sales	100,000	
Cost of Goods Sold		100,000

To eliminate current-year intra-entity sales/purchases.

Entry **TI** eliminates the intra-entity sales/purchases for 2024. The entire $100,000 transfer recorded by the two parties during the current period is removed to arrive at consolidated figures for the business combination.

Consolidation Entry G

Cost of Goods Sold	6,000	
Inventory		6,000

To defer intra-entity gross profit in ending inventory.

Entry **G** defers the intra-entity gross profit remaining in ending inventory at the end of 2024. The $20,000 in transferred merchandise (Exhibit 5.2) that Bottom has not yet sold has a gross profit rate of 30 percent ($30,000 gross profit/$100,000 transfer price); thus, the intra-entity gross profit amounts to $6,000. On the worksheet, Entry **G** eliminates this over-statement in the Inventory asset balance as well as the ending inventory (credit) component of Cost of Goods Sold. Because the gross profit must be deferred, the increase in this expense appropriately decreases consolidated net income.

Net Income Attributable to the Noncontrolling Interest

In this first illustration, the intra-entity transfers are downstream. Thus, the deferred intra-entity gross profits are considered to relate solely to the parent company, creating no effect on the subsidiary or the outside ownership. For this reason, the noncontrolling interest's share of consolidated net income is unaffected by the downstream intra-entity profit deferral and subsequent recognition. Therefore, Top allocates $13,500 of Bottom's net income to the non-controlling interest computed as 20 percent of $67,500 ($70,000 reported net income less $2,500 current-year database excess fair-value amortization).

By including these entries along with the other routine worksheet eliminations and adjust-ments, the accounting information generated by Top and Bottom is brought together into a single set of consolidated financial statements. However, the effect of this process extends beyond the worksheet entries; it also affects reported net income. A $4,000 gross profit is removed on the worksheet from 2023 figures and subsequently recognized in 2024 (Entry *G). A $6,000 gross profit is deferred in a similar fashion from 2024 (Entry **G**) and subse-quently recognized in 2025. However, these changes do not affect the noncontrolling interest because the transfers were downstream.

Special Equity Method Procedures for Deferred Intra-Entity Profits from Downstream Transfers

Exhibit 5.3 presents the parent's equity method investment accounting procedures in the presence of deferred intra-entity gross profits resulting from downstream inventory transfers. This application of the equity method differs from that presented in Chapter 1 for a significant influence (typically 20 to 50 percent ownership) investment. For significant influence investments, an investor company defers intra-entity gross profits in inventory only to the extent of its percentage ownership, regardless of whether the profits resulted from upstream or downstream transfers. In contrast, Exhibit 5.3 shows a 100 percent deferral in 2023, with a subsequent 100 percent recognition in 2024, for intra-entity gross profits resulting from Top's inventory transfers to Bottom, its 80 percent–owned subsidiary.

Why the distinction? When control (rather than just significant influence) exists, 100 percent of all intra-entity gross profits are removed from consolidated net income regardless of the direction of the underlying sale.[8] The 100 percent intra-entity profit deferral on Top's books for downstream sales ensures that none of the deferral will be allocated to the noncontrolling interest. As discussed previously, when the parent is the seller in an intra-entity transfer, little justification exists to allocate a portion of the gross profit deferral to the noncontrolling interest. In contrast, for an upstream sale, the subsidiary recognizes the gross profit on its books. Because the noncontrolling interest owns a portion of the subsidiary (but not of the parent), partial allocation of intra-entity gross profit deferrals and subsequent recognition to the noncontrolling interest is appropriate when resulting from upstream sales.

Upstream Inventory Transfers: Parent Uses the Equity Method

A different set of consolidation procedures is necessary if the intra-entity transfers are upstream from Bottom to Top. As previously discussed, upstream gross profits are attributed to the subsidiary rather than to the parent company. Therefore, had these transfers been upstream, both the $4,000 beginning inventory gross profit recognition (Entry ***G**) and the $6,000 intra-entity gross profit deferral (Entry **G**) would be considered adjustments to Bottom's reported totals.

In contrast to the downstream example in Exhibit 5.3, Exhibit 5.5 includes the intra-entity profit deferral and subsequent recognition in the adjustments to Bottom's net income. Because the inventory transfers are upstream from subsidiary to parent, only 80 percent of the profit deferral and subsequent recognition is allocated to the parent's equity earnings and investment account. As a result, the intra-entity profit reallocation across time affects both the subsidiary's reported net income and the noncontrolling interest. Similar to the previous example, the $4,000 intra-entity profit is not eliminated, but simply reallocated across time to the period when it is recognized by the consolidated entity.

To illustrate the effects of upstream inventory transfers, in Exhibit 5.6 we consolidate the financial statements of Top and Bottom again. *The individual records of the two companies are changed from Exhibit 5.4 to reflect the parent's application of the equity method for upstream sales.* This change creates several important differences between Exhibits 5.4 and 5.6.

Because the intra-entity sales are upstream, the $4,000 beginning intra-entity gross profit (Entry ***G**) deferral no longer involves a debit to the parent's Investment in Bottom account. Recall that Top and Bottom, as separate legal entities, maintain independent accounting information systems. Thus, when it transferred inventory to Top in 2023, Bottom recorded the transfer as a regular sale even though the counter party (Top) is a member of the consolidated group. Because $16,000 of these transfers remain in Top's inventory, $4,000 of gross profit (25 percent) is deferred from a consolidated perspective as of January 1, 2024. Also from a consolidated standpoint, Bottom's January 1, 2024, Retained Earnings are overstated by the $4,000 gross profit from the 2023 intra-entity transfers. Thus, Exhibit 5.6 shows a worksheet

---

[8] When only significant influence is present, purchasing-related decisions are typically made in conjunction with the interests of other outside owners of the investee. Profits are partially deferred because sales are considered to be partially made to the other outside owners. When control is present, decision making usually rests exclusively with the majority owner, providing little basis for objective profit measurement in the presence of intra-entity sales.

EXHIBIT 5.5
Investment Balances—
Equity Method—Upstream
Sales

Investment in Bottom Company Analysis 1/1/23 to 12/31/24		
Consideration paid (fair value) 1/1/23		$400,000
Bottom Company reported net income for 2023	$30,000	
Database amortization	(2,500)	
Deferred profit from Bottom's 2023 upstream sales	(4,000)	
Bottom Company adjusted 2023 net income	$23,500	
Top's ownership percentage	80%	
Equity in earnings of Bottom Company, 2023		$ 18,800
Top's share of Bottom Company dividends, 2023 (80%)		(16,000)
Balance 12/31/23		$402,800
Bottom Company reported net income for 2024	$70,000	
Database amortization	(2,500)	
Recognized profit from Bottom's 2023 upstream sales	4,000	
Deferred profit from Bottom's 2024 upstream sales	(6,000)	
Bottom Company's adjusted 2024 net income	$65,500	
Top's ownership percentage	80%	
Equity in earnings of Bottom Company, 2024		$ 52,400
Top's share of Bottom Company dividends, 2024 (80%)		(40,000)
Balance 12/31/24		$415,200

adjustment that reduces Bottom's January 1, 2024, Retained Earnings balance. Similar to Exhibit 5.4, the credit to Cost of Goods Sold increases consolidated net income to recognize the profit in 2024 from sales to outsiders as follows:

Consolidation Entry *G

Retained earnings—Bottom	4,000	
Cost of Goods Sold		4,000

To remove 2023 intra-entity gross profit in inventory from seller's beginning balance and recognize the gross profit in 2024 following sales to outsiders. Top uses the equity method and intra-entity sales were upstream.

Following this adjustment, Bottom's beginning Retained Earnings on the worksheet becomes $306,000. Reassigning the $4,000 gross profit from 2023 into 2024 dictates the adjustment of the subsidiary's beginning Retained Earnings balance (as the seller of the goods) to $306,000 from the $310,000 found in the company's separate records on the worksheet.

Consolidation Entry **S** eliminates a portion of the parent's investment account and provides the initial noncontrolling interest balance. This worksheet entry also removes the stockholders' equity accounts of the subsidiary as of the beginning of the current year. Thus, the above $4,000 reduction in Bottom's January 1, 2024, Retained Earnings to defer the intra-entity gross profit affects Entry **S.** After posting Entry ***G,** only $306,000 remains as the subsidiary's January 1, 2024, Retained Earnings, which along with Bottom's common stock, is eliminated as follows:

Consolidation Entry S

Common Stock—Bottom	150,000	
Retained earnings—Bottom	306,000	
Investment in Bottom		364,800
Noncontrolling Interest		91,200

This combined equity elimination figure ($456,000) above forms the basis for the 20 percent noncontrolling interest ($91,200) and the elimination of the 80 percent parent company investment ($364,800).

In comparing the consolidated totals across Exhibits 5.4 and 5.6, note that consolidated net income, inventory, total assets, and total liabilities and equities are all identical. The sole

EXHIBIT 5.6 Upstream Inventory Transfers

Investment: Equity Method		**TOP COMPANY AND BOTTOM COMPANY** **Consolidation Worksheet** **For Year Ending December 31, 2024**				**Ownership: 80%**
Accounts	**Top Company**	**Bottom Company**	**Consolidation Entries**		**Noncontrolling Interest**	**Consolidated Totals**
			Debit	**Credit**		
Income Statement						
Sales	(600,000)	(300,000)	(TI) 100,000			(800,000)
Cost of goods sold	320,000	180,000	(G) 6,000	(*G) 4,000		402,000
				(TI) 100,000		
Operating expenses	170,000	50,000	(E) 2,500			222,500
Equity in earnings of Bottom	(52,400)		(I) 52,400‡			
Separate company net income	(162,400)	(70,000)				
Consolidated net income						(175,500)
Net income attributable to noncontrolling interest					(13,100)†	13,100
Net income to Top Company						(162,400)
Statement of Retained Earnings						
Retained earnings, 1/1/24						
Top Company	(652,800)					(652,800)
Bottom Company		(310,000)	(*G) 4,000			
			(S) 306,000			
Net income (above)	(162,400)	(70,000)				(162,400)
Dividends declared	70,000	50,000		(D) 40,000	10,000	70,000
Retained earnings, 12/31/24	(745,200)	(330,000)				(745,200)
Balance Sheet						
Cash and receivables	280,000	120,000		(P) 10,000		390,000
Inventory	220,000	160,000		(G) 6,000		374,000
Investment in Bottom	415,200		(D) 40,000	(I) 52,400		–0–
				(S) 364,800		
				(A) 38,000		
Land	410,000	200,000				610,000
Plant assets (net)	190,000	170,000				360,000
Database			(A) 47,500	(E) 2,500		45,000
Total assets	1,515,200	650,000				1,779,000
Liabilities	(340,000)	(170,000)	(P) 10,000			(500,000)
Noncontrolling interest in Bottom Company, 1/1/24				(S) 91,200		
				(A) 9,500	(100,700)	
Noncontrolling interest in Bottom Company, 12/31/24					(103,800)	(103,800)
Common stock	(430,000)	(150,000)	(S) 150,000			(430,000)
Retained earnings, 12/31/24 (above)	(745,200)	(330,000)				(745,200)
Total liabilities and equities	(1,515,200)	(650,000)	718,400	718,400		(1,779,000)

Note: Parentheses indicate a credit balance.

†Because intra-entity sales were upstream, the subsidiary's $70,000 net income is decreased for the $6,000 gross profit deferred into next year and increased for $4,000 gross profit deferred from the previous year. After further reduction for $2,500 excess amortization, the resulting $65,500 provides the noncontrolling interest with a $13,100 allocation (20%).

‡Boxed items highlight differences with downstream transfers examined in Exhibit 5.4.

Consolidation entries:

(*G) Recognition of intra-entity beginning inventory gross profit in current-period consolidated net income. Upstream sales are attributed to the subsidiary.

(S) Elimination of adjusted stockholders' equity accounts along with recognition of the noncontrolling interest as of January 1.

(A) Allocation of excess fair value over subsidiary's book value, unamortized balance as of January 1.

(I) Elimination of intra-entity income.

(D) Elimination of intra-entity dividends.

(E) Recognition of amortization expense for current year on database.

(P) Elimination of intra-entity receivable/payable balances.

(TI) Elimination of intra-entity sales/purchases balances.

(G) Deferral of intra-entity ending inventory gross profit from current-period consolidated net income and removal of intra-entity gross profit from ending inventory.

effect of the direction of the intra-entity inventory transfers (upstream or downstream) resides in the allocation of the temporary income effects of profit deferral and subsequent recognition to the controlling and noncontrolling interests.

Finally, to complete the consolidation, the noncontrolling interest's share of consolidated net income entered on the worksheet is $13,100, computed as follows:

Bottom reported net income, 2024	$70,000
Excess fair-value database amortization ($50,000/20 years)	(2,500)
2023 intra-entity gross profit recognized	4,000
2024 intra-entity gross profit deferred	(6,000)
Bottom 2024 net income adjusted	$65,500
Noncontrolling interest percentage	20%
Net income attributable to the noncontrolling interest, 2024	$13,100

Upstream transfers affect this computation although the downstream sales in the previous example did not. Thus, the noncontrolling interest balance reported previously in the income statement in Exhibit 5.4 differs from the allocation in Exhibit 5.6.

Consolidations—Downstream versus Upstream Transfers

To help clarify the effect of downstream and upstream transfers when the parent uses the equity method, we compare two of the worksheet entries in more detail:

Downstream Transfers			Upstream Transfers		
(Exhibit 5.4)			(Exhibit 5.6)		
Entry *G			**Entry *G**		
Investment in Bottom..................	4,000		Retained Earnings, 1/1/24—Bottom...........	4,000	
Cost of Goods Sold		4,000	Cost of Goods Sold		4,000

To remove 2023 intra-entity gross profit effect from seller's beginning balance and recognize the gross profit in 2024.			To remove 2023 intra-entity gross profit effect from seller's beginning balance and recognize the gross profit in 2024.		

Entry S			**Entry S**		
Common stock—Bottom	150,000		Common stock—Bottom	150,000	
Retained Earnings, 1/1/24—Bottom	310,000		Retaining Earnings, 1/1/24— Bottom (as adjusted)	306,000	
Investment in Bottom (80%)		368,000	Investment in Bottom (80%)...........		364,800
Noncontrolling interest—1/1/24 (20%)		92,000	Noncontrolling interest—1/1/24 (20%).................		91,200

To remove subsidiary's stockholders' equity accounts and portion of investment balance. Book value at beginning of year is appropriate.			To remove subsidiary's stockholders' equity accounts (as adjusted in Entry *G) and portion of investment balance. Adjusted book value at beginning of year is appropriate.		

Net Income Attributable to the Noncontrolling Interest = $13,500; 20% of Bottom's reported net income less excess database amortization.

Net Income Attributable to the Noncontrolling Interest = $13,100; 20% of Bottom's net income (after adjustment for intra-entity gross profit in inventory and excess database amortization).

Effects of Alternative Investment Methods on Consolidation

In Exhibits 5.3 through 5.6, the parent company utilized the equity method. When the parent uses either the initial value or the partial equity method, consolidation procedures normally continue to follow the same patterns analyzed in the previous chapters of this textbook. However, these alternative methods lack the full accrual properties of the equity method. Therefore, an additional worksheet adjustment (***C**) is needed to ensure the consolidated financial statements reflect a full accrual GAAP basis. As was the case previously, the worksheet adjustments depend on whether the intra-entity inventories result from downstream or upstream sales.

Using the same example, we now assume the parent applies the **initial value method.** Given that the subsidiary declares and pays dividends of $20,000 in 2023 and $50,000 in 2024, Top records dividend income of $16,000 ($20,000 × 80%) and $40,000 ($50,000 × 80%) during these two years.

Exhibits 5.7 and 5.8 present the worksheets to consolidate these two companies for the year ending December 31, 2024. As in the previous examples, most of the worksheet entries found in Exhibits 5.7 and 5.8 are described and analyzed in previous chapters of this textbook. Additionally, many of the worksheet entries required by intra-entity sales are identical to those used when the parent applies the equity method. Thus, only Consolidation Entries ***C** and ***G** are examined in detail separately for downstream intra-entity sales (Exhibit 5.7) and upstream intra-entity sales (Exhibit 5.8).

*Downstream Transfers—Consolidation Entries *C and *G: Parent Uses Initial Value Method*

Consolidation Entry ***C** is required in periods subsequent to acquisition whenever the parent does not apply the equity method. This adjustment converts the parent's beginning Retained Earnings to a full-accrual consolidated total. In the current illustration, Top did not accrue its portion of the 2023 increase in Bottom's book value [($30,000 net income less $20,000 in dividends) × 80%, or $8,000] or record the $2,000 amortization expense for this same period. Because the parent recognized neither number in its financial records, the worksheet process adjusts the parent's beginning retained earnings by $6,000 as follows:

Consolidation Entry *C		
Investment in Bottom	6,000	
Retained Earnings—Top		6,000
To convert Top's retained earnings to the accrual basis. Intra-entity sales were downstream and therefore do not affect the adjustment.		

The intra-entity inventory transfers do not affect this entry because they were downstream; the gross profits had no impact on the net income recognized by the subsidiary.

Under the initial value method, the parent makes no entries in its internal financial records to adjust for the intra-entity sales. Because in this case the sales are downstream, the parent's January 1, 2024, Retained Earnings will be overstated from a consolidated view by the intra-entity $4,000 gross profit in beginning inventory recognized from its 2023 intra-entity sales. Consolidation Entry ***G** corrects this overstatement and appropriately recognizes (through the credit to Cost of Goods Sold) the profit in the current year as follows:

Consolidation Entry *G		
Retained Earnings—Top	4,000	
Cost of Goods Sold		4,000
To remove 2023 intra-entity gross profit in inventory from seller's beginning balance and recognize the gross profit in 2024 following sales to outsiders. Top uses the initial value method and intra-entity sales were downstream.		

Note that the preceding Entry ***G** simply reassigns the intra-entity beginning inventory gross profit from downstream transfers to 2024 from 2023.

EXHIBIT 5.7　Downstream Inventory Transfers

TOP COMPANY AND BOTTOM COMPANY
Consolidation Worksheet
For Year Ending December 31, 2024

Investment: Initial Value Method　　　　　*Ownership: 80%*

Accounts	Top Company	Bottom Company	Consolidation Entries Debit	Consolidation Entries Credit	Noncontrolling Interest	Consolidated Totals
Income Statement						
Sales	(600,000)	(300,000)	(TI)100,000			(800,000)
Cost of goods sold	320,000	180,000	(G)　6,000	(*G)　4,000 (TI)100,000		402,000
Operating expenses	170,000	50,000	(E)　2,500			222,500
Dividend income	(40,000)		(I)　40,000			
Separate company net income	(150,000)	(70,000)				
Consolidated net income						(175,500)
Net income attributable to noncontrolling interest					(13,500)‡	13,500
Net income to Top Company						(162,000)
Statement of Retained Earnings						
Retained Earnings, 1/1/24						
Top Company	(650,000)		(*G)　4,000	(*C)　6,000		(652,000)
Bottom Company		(310,000)	(S) 310,000‡			
Net income (above)	(150,000)	(70,000)				(162,000)
Dividends declared	70,000	50,000		(I)　40,000	10,000	70,000
Retained earnings, 12/31/24	(730,000)	(330,000)				(744,000)
Balance Sheet						
Cash and receivables	280,000	120,000		(P)　10,000		390,000
Inventory	220,000	160,000		(G)　6,000		374,000
Investment in Bottom	400,000		(*C)　6,000	(S) 368,000 (A)　38,000		–0–
Land	410,000	200,000				610,000
Plant assets (net)	190,000	170,000				360,000
Database	–0–	–0–	(A)　47,500	(E)　2,500		45,000
Total assets	1,500,000	650,000				1,779,000
Liabilities	(340,000)	(170,000)	(P)　10,000			(500,000)
Noncontrolling interest in Bottom Company, 1/1/24				(S)　92,000 (A)　9,500	(101,500)	
Noncontrolling interest in Bottom Company, 12/31/24					105,000	(105,000)
Common stock	(430,000)	(150,000)	(S) 150,000			(430,000)
Retained earnings, 12/31/24 (above)	(730,000)	(330,000)				(744,000)
Total liabilities and equities	(1,500,000)	(650,000)	676,000	676,000		(1,779,000)

Note: Parentheses indicate a credit balance.

†Because intra-entity sales are made downstream (by the parent), the subsidiary's adjusted net income is the $70,000 reported figure less $2,500 excess amortization with a 20% allocation to the noncontrolling interest ($13,500).

‡Boxed items highlight differences with upstream transfers examined in Exhibit 5.8.

Consolidation entries:

(*G) Recognition of intra-entity beginning inventory gross profit in current-period consolidated net income. Downstream sales are attributed to the parent.

(*C) Recognition of increase in book value and amortization relating to ownership of subsidiary for year prior to the current year.

(S) Elimination of subsidiary's stockholders' equity accounts along with recognition of the noncontrolling interest as of January 1.

(A) Allocation of subsidiary's fair value in excess of book value, unamortized balance as of January 1.

(I) Elimination of intra-entity dividends recorded by parent as dividend income.

(E) Recognition of amortization expense for current year on database.

(P) Elimination of intra-entity receivable/payable balances.

(TI) Elimination of intra-entity sales/purchases balances.

(G) Deferral of intra-entity ending inventory gross profit from current-period consolidated net income and removal of intra-entity gross profit from ending inventory.

EXHIBIT 5.8   Upstream Inventory Transfers

			Consolidation Entries			
TOP COMPANY AND BOTTOM COMPANY Consolidation Worksheet *Investment: Initial Value Method* For Year Ending December 31, 2024 *Ownership: 80%*						
Accounts	**Top Company**	**Bottom Company**	**Debit**	**Credit**	**Noncontrolling Interest**	**Consolidated Totals**
Income Statement						
Sales	(600,000)	(300,000)	(TI) 100,000			(800,000)
Cost of goods sold	320,000	180,000	(G) 6,000	(*G) 4,000 (TI) 100,000		402,000
Operating expenses	170,000	50,000	(E) 2,500			222,500
Dividend income	(40,000)		(I) 40,000			
Separate company net income	(150,000)	(70,000)				
Consolidated net income						(175,500)
Net income attributable to noncontrolling interest					(13,100)[†]	13,100
Net income to Top Company						(162,400)
Statement of Retained Earnings						
Retained earnings, 1/1/24						
Top Company	(650,000)			(*C) 2,800		(652,800)
Bottom Company		(310,000)	(*G) 4,000 (S) 306,000 [‡]			
Net income (above)	(150,000)	(70,000)				(162,400)
Dividends declared	70,000	50,000		(I) 40,000	10,000	70,000
Retained earnings, 12/31/24	(730,000)	(330,000)				(745,200)
Balance Sheet						
Cash and receivables	280,000	120,000		(P) 10,000		390,000
Inventory	220,000	160,000		(G) 6,000		374,000
Investment in Bottom	400,000		(*C) 2,800	(S) 364,800 (A) 38,000		–0–
Land	410,000	200,000				610,000
Plant assets (net)	190,000	170,000				360,000
Database	–0–	–0–	(A) 47,500	(E) 2,500		45,000
Total assets	1,500,000	650,000				1,779,000
Liabilities	(340,000)	(170,000)	(P) 10,000			(500,000)
Noncontrolling interest in Bottom Company, 1/1/24				(S) 91,200 (A) 9,500	(100,700)	
Noncontrolling interest in Bottom Company, 12/31/24					(103,800)	(103,800)
Common stock	(430,000)	(150,000)	(S) 150,000			(430,000)
Retained earnings, 12/31/24 (above)	(730,000)	(330,000)				(745,200)
Total liabilities and equities	(1,500,000)	(650,000)	668,800	668,800		(1,779,000)

Note: Parentheses indicate a credit balance.

[†] Because intra-entity sales were upstream, the subsidiary's $70,000 net income is decreased for the $6,000 gross profit deferred into next year and increased for $4,000 gross profit deferred from the previous year. After further reduction for $2,500 excess amortization, the resulting $65,500 provides the noncontrolling interest with a $13,100 allocation (20%).

[‡] Boxed items highlight differences with downstream transfers examined in Exhibit 5.7.

Consolidation entries:

(*G) Recognition of intra-entity beginning inventory gross profit in current-period consolidated net income. Upstream sales are attributed to the subsidiary.

(*C) Recognition of increase in book value and amortization relating to ownership of subsidiary for year prior to the current year.

(S) Elimination of adjusted stockholders' equity accounts along with recognition of the noncontrolling interest as of January 1.

(A) Allocation of subsidiary's fair value in excess of book value, unamortized balance as of January 1.

(I) Elimination of intra-entity dividends recorded by parent as dividend income.

(E) Recognition of amortization expense for current year on fair value allocated to value of database.

(P) Elimination of intra-entity receivable/payable balances.

(TI) Elimination of intra-entity sales/purchases balances.

(G) Deferral of intra-entity ending inventory gross profit from current-period consolidated net income and removal of intra-entity gross profit from ending inventory.

? Discussion Question

WHAT PRICE SHOULD WE CHARGE OURSELVES?

Slagle Corporation is a large manufacturing organization. Over the past several years, it has obtained an important component used in its production process exclusively from Harrison, Inc., a relatively small company in Topeka, Kansas. Harrison charges $90 per unit for this part:

Variable cost per unit	$40
Fixed cost assigned per unit	30
Markup	20
Total price	$90

In hope of reducing manufacturing costs, Slagle purchases all of Harrison's outstanding common stock. This new subsidiary continues to sell merchandise to a number of outside customers as well as to Slagle. Thus, for internal reporting purposes, Slagle views Harrison as a separate profit center.

A controversy has now arisen among company officials about the amount that Harrison should charge Slagle for each component. The administrator in charge of the subsidiary wants to continue the $90 price. He believes this figure best reflects the division's profitability: "If we are to be judged by our profits, why should we be punished for selling to our own parent company? If that occurs, my figures will look better if I forget Slagle as a customer and try to market my goods solely to outsiders."

In contrast, the vice president in charge of Slagle's production wants the price set at variable cost, total cost, or some derivative of these numbers. "We bought Harrison to bring our costs down. It only makes sense to reduce the transfer price; otherwise the benefits of acquiring this subsidiary are not apparent. I pushed the company to buy Harrison; if our operating results are not improved, I will get the blame."

Will the decision about the transfer price affect consolidated net income? Which method would be easiest for the company's accountant to administer? As the company's accountant, what advice would you give to these officials?

Upstream Transfers—Consolidation Entries *C and *G: Parent Uses Initial Value Method

We now change the example by assuming the intra-entity transfers are upstream from Bottom to Top. In this case, the $4,000 intra-entity gross profit remaining in Top's 2023 ending inventory has been recorded by Bottom as part of its 2023 net income and retained earnings. Because $4,000 of Bottom's 2023 net income is deferred until 2024, the increase in the subsidiary's book value in the previous year is only $6,000 rather than $10,000 ($30,000 net income less $20,000 in dividends) as reported. Consequently, conversion to the equity method (Entry *C) requires an increase of just $2,800:

$6,000 net increase (after intra-entity profit deferral) in subsidiary's book value during 2023 × 80%	$ 4,800
2023 amortization expense (80% × $2,500)	(2,000)
Increase in parent's beginning retained earnings (Entry *C)	$ 2,800

In applying the initial value method in its financial records, the parent did not recognize the increase in subsidiary book value, excess fair-value amortization, or any effects from intra-entity transfers remaining in inventory. The worksheet process thus adjusts the parent's beginning retained earnings by $2,800, as shown here:

Consolidation Entry *C

Investment in Bottom	2,800	
Retained Earnings—Top		2,800

To convert Top's retained earnings to the accrual basis. Intra-entity sales were upstream.

In this case, the intra-entity inventory transfers affect Consolidation Entry *C because they were downstream; the gross profits directly affected the net income recognized by the subsidiary.

Using the initial value method, the parent makes no entries in its internal financial records to adjust for the intra-entity sales. Because in this case the sales are upstream, the subsidiary's January 1, 2024, Retained Earnings will be overstated from a consolidated view by the intra-entity gross profit in beginning inventory. Consolidation Entry *G corrects this overstatement and appropriately recognizes the profit in the current year as follows:

Consolidation Entry *G

Retained Earnings—Bottom	4,000	
Cost of Goods Sold		4,000

To remove 2023 intra-entity gross profit in inventory from seller's beginning balance and recognize the gross profit in 2024 following sales to outsiders. Top uses the initial value method and intra-entity sales were upstream.

Note again how the preceding Entry *G simply reassigns the intra-entity beginning inventory gross profit to 2024 from 2023.

Finally, if the parent had applied the **partial equity method** in its internal records, little would change in the consolidation processes previously described for the equity method. The primary change would involve inclusion of a Consolidation Entry *C. Because the parent would have recorded changes in reported subsidiary book value, the *C adjustment would be computed only for (1) previous years' excess fair over book value amortizations and (2) the immediate past year's intra-entity profit deferral.

LO 5-6

Prepare the consolidation entry to defer any gain created by an intra-entity transfer of land from the accounting records of the year of transfer and subsequent years.

Intra-Entity Land Transfers

Although not as prevalent as inventory transactions, intra-entity sales of other assets occur occasionally. The final two sections of this chapter examine the worksheet procedures that noninventory transfers necessitate. We first analyze land transactions and then discuss the effects created by the intra-entity sale of depreciable assets such as buildings and equipment.

Accounting for Land Transactions

The consolidation procedures necessitated by intra-entity land transfers partially parallel those for intra-entity inventory. As with inventory, the sale of land creates a series of effects on the individual records of the two companies. The worksheet process must then adjust the account balances to reflect the perspective of a single economic entity.

By reviewing the sequence of events occurring in an intra-entity land sale, the similarities to inventory transfers can be ascertained as well as the unique features of this transaction.

1. The original seller of the land reports a gain (losses are rare in intra-entity asset transfers), even though the transaction occurred between related parties. At the same time, the acquiring company capitalizes the inflated transfer price rather than the land's historical cost to the business combination.

2. The gain the seller recorded is closed into Retained Earnings at the end of the year. From a consolidated perspective, this account has been artificially increased by a related party. Thus, both the buyer's Land account and the seller's Retained Earnings account continue to contain the intra-entity gain.

3. The gain on the original transfer is recognized in consolidated net income only when the land is subsequently disposed of to an outside party. Therefore, appropriate

consolidation techniques must be designed to eliminate the intra-entity gain each period until the time of resale.

Clearly, two characteristics encountered in inventory transfers also exist in intra-entity land transactions: inflated book values and intra-entity gains subsequently culminated through sales to outside parties. Despite these similarities, significant differences exist. Because of the nature of the transaction, the individual companies do not use sales/purchases accounts when land is transferred. Instead, the seller establishes a separate gain account when it removes the land from its books. And because it's an intra-entity gain, the balance must be eliminated when preparing consolidated statements.

In addition, the subsequent resale of land to an outside party does not always occur in the year immediately following the transfer. Although inventory is normally disposed of within a relatively short time, the buyer often holds land for years, if not permanently. Thus, the overvalued Land account can remain on the acquiring company's books indefinitely. As long as the land is retained, the effects of the intra-entity gain (the equivalent of Entry *G in inventory transfers) must be eliminated for each subsequent consolidation. By repeating this worksheet entry every year, the consolidated financial statements properly state both the Land and the Retained Earnings accounts.

Eliminating Intra-Entity Gains—Land Transfers

To illustrate these worksheet procedures, assume that Hastings Company and Patrick Company are related parties. On July 1, 2024, Hastings sold land that originally cost $60,000 to Patrick at a $100,000 transfer price. The seller reports a $40,000 gain; the buyer records the land at the $100,000 acquisition price. At the end of this fiscal period, the intra-entity effect of this transaction must be eliminated for consolidation purposes:

Consolidation Entry TL (year of transfer)		
Gain on Sale of Land	40,000	
Land		40,000
To eliminate effects of intra-entity transfer of land. (Labeled **TL** in reference to the transferred land.)		

This worksheet entry eliminates the intra-entity gain from the 2024 consolidated statements and returns the land to its recorded value at date of transfer, for consolidated purposes. However, as with the transfer of inventory, the effects created by the original transaction remain in the financial records of the individual companies for as long as the property is held. The gain recorded by Hastings carries through to Retained Earnings while Patrick's Land account retains the inflated transfer price. *Therefore, for every subsequent consolidation until the land is eventually sold, the elimination process must be repeated.* Including the following entry on each subsequent worksheet removes the intra-entity gain from the asset and from the earnings reported by the combination:

Consolidation Entry *GL (every year following transfer)		
Retained Earnings (beginning balance of seller)	40,000	
Land		40,000
To eliminate effects of intra-entity transfer of land made in a previous year. (Labeled ***GL** in reference to the gain on a land transfer occurring in a prior year.)		

Note that the reduction in Retained Earnings is changed to an increase in the Investment in Subsidiary account when the original sale is downstream and the parent has applied the equity method. In that specific situation, equity method adjustments have already corrected the timing of the parent's intra-entity gain. Removing the gain has created a reduction in the Investment account that is appropriately allocated to the subsidiary's Land account on the worksheet. Conversely, if sales were upstream, the Retained Earnings of the seller (the subsidiary) continue to be overstated even if the parent applies the equity method.

One final consolidation concern exists in accounting for intra-entity transfers of land. If the property is ever sold to an outside party, the company making the sale records a gain or loss based on its recorded book value. However, this cost figure is actually the internal transfer price. The gain or loss being recognized is incorrect for consolidation purposes; it has not been computed by comparison to the land's historical cost. Again, the separate financial records fail to reflect the transaction from the perspective of the single economic entity.

Therefore, if the company eventually sells the land, it must recognize the gain deferred at the time of the original transfer. Gain recognition is appropriate once the property is sold to outsiders. On the worksheet, the gain is removed one last time from beginning Retained Earnings (or the investment account, if applicable). In this instance, though, the worksheet entry reclassifies the amount as a recognized gain. Thus, the gain recognition is reallocated from the year of transfer into the fiscal period in which the land is sold to the unrelated party.

Returning to the previous illustration, Hastings acquired land for $60,000 and sold it to Patrick, a related party, for $100,000. Consequently, the $40,000 intra-entity gain was eliminated on the consolidation worksheet in the year of transfer as well as in each succeeding period. However, if this land is subsequently sold to an outside party for $115,000, Patrick recognizes only a $15,000 gain. From the viewpoint of the business combination, the land (having been bought for $60,000) was actually sold at a $55,000 gain. To correct the reporting, the following consolidation entry must be made in the year that the property is sold to the unrelated party. This adjustment increases the $15,000 gain recorded by Patrick to the consolidated balance of $55,000:

Consolidation Entry *GL (year of sale to outside party)		
Retained Earnings (Hastings)	40,000	
Gain on Sale of Land		40,000
To remove intra-entity gain from year of transfer so that total profit can be recognized in the current period when land is sold to an outside party.		

As in the accounting for inventory transfers, the entire consolidation process demonstrated here accomplishes two major objectives:

1. It reports historical cost for the transferred land for as long as it remains within the business combination.
2. It defers income recognition until the land is sold to outside parties.

Recognizing the Effect on Noncontrolling Interest—Land Transfers

The preceding discussion of intra-entity land transfers ignores the possible presence of a noncontrolling interest. In constructing financial statements for an economic entity that includes outside ownership, the guidelines already established for inventory transfers remain applicable.

If the original sale was a *downstream* transaction, neither the annual deferral nor the eventual recognition of the intra-entity gain has any effect on the noncontrolling interest. The rationale for this treatment, as previously indicated, is that profits from downstream transfers relate solely to the parent company.

Conversely, if the transfer is made *upstream,* deferral and recognition of gains are attributed to the subsidiary and, hence, to the noncontrolling interest. As with inventory, all noncontrolling interest balances are computed on the reported earnings of the subsidiary after adjustment for any upstream transfers.

To reiterate, the accounting consequences stemming from land transfers are these:

1. In the year of transfer, any intra-entity gain is deferred, and the Land account is reduced to historical cost. When an upstream sale creates the gain, the amount also is excluded in calculating the noncontrolling interest's share of the subsidiary's net income for that year.
2. Each year thereafter, the intra-entity gain will be removed from the seller's beginning Retained Earnings. If the transfer was upstream, eliminating this earlier gain directly affects the balances recorded within both Entry *C (if conversion to the equity method is required) and Entry S. The additional equity accrual (Entry *C, if needed) as well as

the elimination of beginning Stockholders' Equity (Entry **S**) must be based on the newly adjusted balance in the subsidiary's Retained Earnings. This deferral process also has an impact on the noncontrolling interest's share of the subsidiary's net income, but only in the year of transfer and the eventual year of sale.

3. If the land is ever sold to an outside party, the original gain is recognized and reported in consolidated net income.

LO 5-7

Prepare the consolidation entries to remove the effects of upstream and downstream intra-entity fixed asset transfers across affiliated entities.

Intra-Entity Transfer of Depreciable Assets

Just as related parties can transfer inventory and land, the intra-entity sale of a host of other assets is possible. Equipment, patents, franchises, buildings, and other long-lived assets can be involved. Accounting for such intra-entity transactions resembles that demonstrated for land sales. However, the subsequent calculation of depreciation or amortization provides an added challenge in the development of consolidated financial statements.[9]

Deferral and Subsequent Recognition of Intra-Entity Gains

When faced with intra-entity sales of depreciable assets, financial reporting objectives remain unchanged: *defer intra-entity gains, reestablish historical cost balances, and recognize appropriate income within the consolidated financial statements.* More specifically, we defer gains created by intra-entity transfers until such time as the subsequent use or resale of the asset consummates the original transaction. For inventory sales, the culminating disposal normally occurs currently or in the year following the transfer. In contrast, transferred land may be kept indefinitely, thus deferring the recognition of the intra-entity profit indefinitely.

When depreciable asset sales occur across firms within a consolidated entity, the accounting effects for both the seller and buyer of the depreciable asset must be analyzed in preparing consolidated financial statements. For example, assume a parent company sells a delivery truck to its subsidiary at a transfer price in excess of the parent's carrying amount for the asset. In recording the sale, the parent recognizes a gain on its books. Clearly, this is an intra-entity gain that must be removed in consolidation.

In the subsidiary's financial records, the purchased truck is recorded at the transfer price and subsequently depreciated. However, because of the parent–subsidiary control relationship, no sale of the truck occurred with an outside entity. Consequently, from a consolidated reporting perspective, the carrying amount of the truck account becomes overstated and further results in overstated depreciation expense and accumulated depreciation. The resulting overstatements of the truck, depreciation expense, and accumulated depreciation must also be removed in consolidation.

However, as the subsidiary uses the truck to generate revenues over time, the decline in the truck's future economic benefit can be viewed as an indirect, gradual sale to outsiders. From a consolidated perspective, as the truck is consumed in producing revenues from outsiders, it becomes gradually "sold," and the intra-entity gain can be gradually recognized. Thus, for depreciable asset transfers, the ultimate recognition of any gain on sale typically occurs over a period of several years.

Because of the long-term nature of depreciable assets, so long as the entity owns the asset, the effects of an intra-entity transfer must be accounted for in preparing the consolidated entity's financial statements. In the year of the intra-entity fixed asset transfer, consolidation procedures to remove the intra-entity gain and its effects on the asset, depreciation expense, and accumulated depreciation are relatively straightforward. First, a worksheet entry eliminates the gain and returns the asset and accumulated depreciation accounts to their pre-transfer amounts. Then, a second worksheet entry accordingly reduces the overstated current year depreciation expense and related accumulated depreciation.

In years subsequent to the intra-entity asset transfer, we observe that the gain on sale recognized by the seller has now been closed to Retained Earnings. The overstated depreciation expense also has been closed to the Retained Earnings of the buyer. Consolidation worksheet entries thus

---

[9] To avoid redundancy within this analysis, all further references are made to depreciation expense alone, although this discussion is equally applicable to the amortization of intangible assets and the depletion of wasting assets.

reflect the net effect of the gain on sale and the overstated depreciation on the affiliate's separate accounting records. Next, we provide an illustration of the consolidated worksheet entries in the year of the intra-entity transfer followed by the year subsequent to the intra-entity transfer.

Depreciable Asset Intra-Entity Transfers Illustrated

To examine the consolidation procedures required by the intra-entity transfer of a depreciable asset, assume that Able Company sells equipment to Baker Company at the current market value of $90,000. Able originally acquired the equipment for $100,000 several years ago; since that time, it has recorded $40,000 in accumulated depreciation. The transfer is made on January 1, 2023, when the equipment has a 10-year remaining life.[10]

Year of Intra-Entity Transfer

The 2023 effects on the separate financial accounts of the two companies can be quickly enumerated:

1. Baker, as the buyer, enters the equipment into its records at the $90,000 transfer price. However, from a consolidated view, the asset has not been sold, and, therefore, the $60,000 book value ($100,000 cost less $40,000 accumulated depreciation) remains appropriate.
2. Able, as the seller, reports a $30,000 gain, although the consolidated entity has not yet sold the asset to outsiders. After preparation of the December 31, 2023, consolidated financial statements, Able then closes this gain to its Retained Earnings account.
3. Assuming application of the straight-line depreciation method with no salvage value, Baker records expense of $9,000 at the end of 2023 ($90,000 transfer price/10 years). The proper depreciation expense for consolidation, however, is based on the asset's carrying amount to the consolidated entity at the date of the intra-entity transfer. Consolidated depreciation expense for this asset would thus be $6,000 ($60,000 carrying amount/10 remaining years). This requires a $3,000 consolidated worksheet adjustment to depreciation expense.

To report these events as seen by the consolidated entity, we first acknowledge that an asset write-up cannot be recognized based on an intra-entity transfer. A consolidated worksheet entry must therefore return the asset to its pre-transfer carrying amount based on historical cost. Moreover, both the $30,000 intra-entity gain and the $3,000 overstatement in depreciation expense must be eliminated on the worksheet. The two consolidation entries for 2023 are shown:

Consolidation Entry TA (year of transfer)[11]		
Gain on Sale of Equipment	30,000	
Equipment	10,000	
Accumulated Depreciation		40,000
To remove intra-entity gain and return equipment accounts to balances based on original historical cost. (Labeled **TA** in reference to transferred asset.)		

Consolidation Entry ED (year of transfer)		
Accumulated Depreciation	3,000	
Depreciation Expense		3,000
To eliminate overstatement of depreciation expense caused by inflated transfer price. (Labeled **ED** in reference to excess depreciation.) *Entry must be repeated for all 10 years of the equipment's remaining life.*		

[10] Although this example assumes an intra-entity gain on sale, intra-entity losses may occur as well. If the loss cannot be attributed to an asset impairment, then parallel consolidation procedures to those provided in the example, reflecting a loss, would be appropriate.

[11] If the worksheet uses only one account for a net depreciated asset, this entry would have been

Gain on sale	30,000	
Equipment (net)		30,000
To reduce the $90,000 to original $60,000 book value at date of transfer rather than reinstating original balances.		

From the viewpoint of a single consolidated entity, these entries accomplish several objectives:

- Reinstate the asset's historical cost of $100,000.
- Return the January 1, 2023, book value to the appropriate $60,000 figure by recognizing accumulated depreciation of $40,000.
- Eliminate the $30,000 intra-entity gain recorded by Able so the amount does not appear in the consolidated income statement.
- Reduce depreciation for the year from $9,000 to $6,000, the appropriate expense based on pre-transfer carrying amount of the asset.
- Although the gain is eliminated, the credit to depreciation expense increases consolidated net income serving as a partial recognition of the gain for 2023.

Over the remaining life of the asset, consolidation entries serve to reallocate the gain from the year of transfer to each of the 10 years following the transfer as the asset is consumed in the production process. Recall that for intra-entity gross profit in ending inventory, the ultimate recognition of the profit deferral was achieved on the consolidated worksheet through a credit to *cost of goods sold.* In a parallel fashion, deferred intra-entity profits on depreciable asset transfers are achieved on the consolidated worksheet through a credit to *depreciation expense.*

In the year of the intra-entity depreciable asset transfer, the preceding consolidation entries **TA** and **ED** are applicable regardless of whether the transfer was upstream or downstream. They are likewise applicable regardless of whether the parent applies the equity method, initial value method, or partial equity method of accounting for its investment. As discussed subsequently, however, in the years following the intra-entity transfer, we make a slight modification to consolidation entry ***TA** for downstream transfers when the equity method is applied.

Years Following the Intra-Entity Transfer

Again, the preceding worksheet entries do not actually remove the effects of the intra-entity transfer from the individual records of these two organizations. Both the intra-entity gain and the excess depreciation expense remain on the separate books and are closed into Retained Earnings of the respective companies at year-end. Similarly, the Equipment account with the related Accumulated Depreciation continues to hold balances based on the transfer price, not historical cost. *Thus, for every subsequent period, the separately reported figures must be adjusted on the worksheet to present the consolidated totals from a single entity's perspective.*

To derive worksheet entries at any future point, the balances in the accounts of the individual companies must be ascertained and compared to the figures appropriate for the consolidated entity. As an illustration, the separate records of Able and Baker two years after the transfer (December 31, 2024) follow. Consolidated totals are calculated based on the original historical cost of $100,000 and accumulated depreciation of $40,000.

Account	Individual Records	Consolidated Perspective	Worksheet Adjustments
Equipment 12/31/24	$ 90,000	$ 100,000	$ 10,000
Accumulated Depreciation 12/31/24	(18,000)	(52,000)*	(34,000)
Depreciation Expense for 2024	9,000	6,000	(3,000)
1/1/24 Retained Earnings effect	(21,000)†	6,000	27,000

Note: Parentheses indicate a credit balance.
*Accumulated depreciation before transfer $(40,000) plus 2 years × $(6,000).
†Intra-entity transfer gain ($30,000) less one year's depreciation of $9,000.

Because the intra-entity transfer's effects remain in the separate financial records, the various accounts must be adjusted in each subsequent consolidation. Moreover, the amounts involved must be updated every period because of the continual impact of depreciation recorded by the buyer. Continuing our example, to adjust the individual figures to the consolidated totals derived previously, the 2024 worksheet includes the following entries:

Consolidation Entry *TA (year following transfer)

Equipment	10,000	
Retained Earnings, 1/1/24 (Able)	27,000	
Accumulated Depreciation		37,000

To return the Equipment account to original historical cost and adjust the 1/1/24 balances of Retained Earnings and Accumulated Depreciation.

Consolidation Entry ED (year following transfer)

Accumulated Depreciation	3,000	
Depreciation Expense		3,000

To remove excess depreciation expense on the intra-entity transfer price and adjust Accumulated Depreciation to its 12/31/24 consolidated balance.

Note that the $34,000 increase in 12/31/24 consolidated Accumulated Depreciation results from a $37,000 credit in Entry ***TA** and a $3,000 debit in Entry **ED.**

We observe that in consolidation entry ***TA,** $27,000 of the original intra-entity gain on sale is removed from Retained Earnings. Then, in consolidation entry **ED,** the $3,000 credit to Depreciation Expense serves to increase consolidated net income by $3,000. Essentially, the remaining intra-entity gain as of the beginning of the year is removed from Retained Earnings and partially recognized as a current-year increase in consolidated net income (via the decrease in depreciation expense).[12]

The ***TA** adjustment to the Equipment account remains constant over the life of the asset. However, the ***TA** adjustments to beginning Retained Earnings and Accumulated Depreciation vary with each succeeding consolidation. At December 31, 2023, the individual companies closed out both the intra-entity gain of $30,000 and $9,000 depreciation expense on their books. *Importantly, the $9,000 depreciation expense was overstated by $3,000 from a consolidated perspective.* Therefore, as reflected in Entry ***TA,** the beginning Retained Earnings account for the 2024 consolidation is overstated by a net amount of only $27,000 rather than $30,000. *Over the life of the asset, the intra-entity gain in consolidated retained earnings will be systematically reduced to zero as excess depreciation expense ($3,000) is closed out each year on the books of the company that possesses the asset.* Hence, on subsequent consolidation worksheets, the beginning Retained Earnings account decreases by this amount: $27,000 in 2024; $24,000 in 2025; $21,000 in the following period; and so on. This reduction continues until, at the end of 10 years, the intra-entity gain has been completely recognized in the consolidation process.

Similarly, the change in beginning Accumulated Depreciation varies with each succeeding consolidation. At December 31, 2023, the buyer recorded a $3,000 overstatement of depreciation expense and Accumulated Depreciation. Therefore, as reflected in Entry ***TA,** the Accumulated Depreciation account at the beginning of 2024 is undervalued by a net amount of only $37,000 rather than $40,000.

If this equipment is ever resold to an outside party, the remaining portion of the gain is immediately recognized by the consolidated entity. As in the previous discussion of land, the remaining intra-entity profit existing at the date of resale must be recognized on the consolidated income statement to arrive at the appropriate amount of gain or loss on the sale.

Years Following Downstream Intra-Entity Depreciable Asset Transfers—Parent Uses Equity Method

Consolidation entry ***TA** requires a slight modification when the intra-entity depreciable asset transfer is downstream and the parent uses the equity method. In applying the equity method, the parent adjusts its book income for both the original transfer gain and periodic depreciation expense adjustments. Thus, in downstream intra-entity transfers when the equity method

---

[12] Alternatively, because the straight-line method is used, the depreciation expense adjustment can also be computed as the original gain on sale divided by the remaining life of the transferred asset ($30,000/10 years).

is used, from a consolidated view, the parent's Retained Earnings balance has been already reduced for the gain. Therefore, continuing with the previous example, the following worksheet consolidation entries would be made for a downstream sale assuming that (1) Able is the parent and (2) Able has applied the equity method to account for its investment in Baker.

Consolidation Entry *TA (year following transfer)		
Equipment	10,000	
Investment in Baker	27,000	
Accumulated Depreciation		37,000

Consolidation Entry ED (year following transfer)		
Accumulated Depreciation	3,000	
Depreciation Expense		3,000

In Entry ***TA,** note that the Investment in Baker account replaces the parent's Retained Earnings. This temporary increase to the Investment account then effectively allocates the adjustments necessitated by the intra-entity transfer to the appropriate subsidiary Equipment and Accumulated Depreciation accounts.

Effect on Noncontrolling Interest—Depreciable Asset Transfers

Because of the lack of official guidance, no easy answer exists as to the assignment of any income effects created within the consolidation process. Consistent with the previous sections of this chapter, all income is assigned here to the original seller. In Entry ***TA,** for example, the beginning Retained Earnings account of Able (the seller) is reduced. Both the intra-entity gain on the transfer and the excess depreciation expense subsequently recognized are assigned to that party.

Thus, again, downstream sales are assumed to have no effect on any noncontrolling interest values. The parent rather than the subsidiary made the sale. Conversely, the impact on net income created by upstream sales must be considered in computing the balances attributed to these outside owners. Currently, this approach is one of many acceptable alternatives. However, in its future deliberations on consolidation policies and procedures, the FASB could mandate a specific allocation pattern.

Summary

1. The transfer of assets, especially inventory, between the members of a consolidated entity is a common practice. In producing consolidated financial statements, any effects on the separate accounting records created by such transfers must be removed because the transactions did not occur with an outside unrelated party.

2. Inventory transfers are the most prevalent form of intra-entity asset transaction. Despite being only a transfer, one company records a sale while the other reports a purchase. These balances are reciprocals that must be offset on the worksheet in the process of producing consolidated figures.

3. Additional accounting problems result if inventory is transferred at a markup. Any portion of the merchandise still held at year-end is valued at more than historical cost because of the inflation in price. Furthermore, the gross profit that the seller reports on these goods must be deferred from a consolidation perspective. Thus, this gross profit must be removed from the ending Inventory account, a figure that appears as an asset on the balance sheet and as a negative component within cost of goods sold.

4. Intra-entity inventory gross profits in ending inventory also create a consolidation problem in the year following the transfer. Within the separate accounting systems, the seller closes the gross profit to Retained Earnings. The buyer's ending Inventory balance becomes the next period's beginning balance (within Cost of Goods Sold). Therefore, the inflation must be removed again but this time in the subsequent year. The seller's beginning Retained Earnings is decreased to eliminate the intra-entity gross profit while Cost of Goods Sold is reduced to remove the overstatement from the beginning inventory component. However, when the parent applies the equity method and sales are downstream, the parent's Retained Earnings are correctly stated from a consolidated view. Therefore, in this case, the Investment in Subsidiary account is used in the beginning intra-entity inventory profit adjustment,

instead of the parent's Retained Earnings. Through this process, the intra-entity profit is deferred from the year of transfer so that recognition can be made at the point of disposal or consumption.

5. The deferral and subsequent recognition of intra-entity gross profits raise a question concerning the measurement of noncontrolling interest balances: Does the change in the period of recognition alter these calculations? Although the issue is currently under debate, no formal answer to this question is yet found in official accounting pronouncements. In this textbook, the deferral of profits from upstream transfers (from subsidiary to parent) is assumed to affect the noncontrolling interest, whereas downstream transactions (from parent to subsidiary) do not. When upstream transfers are involved, noncontrolling interest values are based on the gross profit recognized after adjustment for any intra-entity gross profit remaining in inventory.

6. Inventory is not the only asset that can be transferred between the members of a consolidated entity. For example, transfers of land sometimes occur. Again, if the transfer price exceeds original cost, the buyer's records state the asset at an inflated value while the seller recognizes an intra-entity gain. As with inventory, the consolidation process must return the asset's recorded balance to cost while deferring the gain. Repetition of this procedure is necessary in every consolidation for as long as the land remains within the consolidated entity.

7. The consolidation process required by the intra-entity transfer of depreciable assets differs somewhat from that demonstrated for inventory and land. The intra-entity gain created by the transaction must still be deferred along with an adjustment for the asset's overstatement. However, because of subsequent depreciation, these adjustments systematically change from period to period. Additionally, because the excess depreciation is closed annually to Retained Earnings, the overstatement of the equity account resulting from the intra-entity gain is constantly reduced. To produce consolidated figures at any point in time, the remaining overstatement in these figures (as well as in the current depreciation expense) must be determined and removed. Overall, the intra-entity gain is removed from the year of the depreciable asset transfer and subsequently recognized over the remaining life of the asset. Consolidation worksheet entries that serve to reduce depreciation expense become the vehicle for recognizing the annual portion of the intra-entity gain.

Comprehensive Illustration

Problem

(*Estimated Time: 45 to 65 Minutes*) On January 1, 2022, Pullman Company acquired 80 percent of Spencer Company for $594,000 in cash. Spencer's total book value on that date was $610,000, and the fair value of the noncontrolling interest was $148,500. The newly acquired subsidiary possessed patented technology (10-year remaining life) that, although unrecorded on Spencer's accounting records, had a fair value of $75,000. Any remaining excess acquisition-date fair value was attributed to a trademark with an indefinite life.

Pullman decided to acquire Spencer so that the subsidiary could furnish component parts for the parent's production process. During the ensuing years, Spencer sold inventory to Pullman as follows:

Year	Cost to Spencer Company	Transfer Price	Gross Profit Rate	Transferred Inventory Still Held at End of Year (at transfer price)
2022	$100,000	$140,000	28.6%	$20,000
2023	100,000	150,000	33.3	30,000
2024	120,000	160,000	25.0	68,000

Any transferred merchandise that Pullman retained at year-end was always put into production during the following period.

On January 1, 2023, Pullman sold Spencer several pieces of equipment that had a 10-year remaining life and were being depreciated on the straight-line method with no salvage value. This equipment was transferred at an $80,000 price, although it had an original $100,000 cost to Pullman and a $44,000 book value at the date of exchange.

On January 1, 2024, Pullman sold land to Spencer for $50,000, its fair value at that date. The original cost had been only $22,000. By the end of 2024, Spencer had made no payment for the land.

The following separate financial statements are for Pullman and Spencer as of December 31, 2024. Pullman has applied the equity method to account for this investment.

	Pullman Company	Spencer Company
Sales	$ (900,000)	$ (500,000)
Cost of goods sold	598,000	300,000
Operating expenses	210,000	80,000
Gain on sale of land	(28,000)	–0–
Equity in earnings of Spencer Company	(60,000)	–0–
Net income	$ (180,000)	$ (120,000)
Retained earnings, 1/1/24	$ (620,000)	$ (430,000)
Net income	(180,000)	(120,000)
Dividends declared	55,000	50,000
Retained earnings, 12/31/24	$ (745,000)	$ (500,000)
Cash and accounts receivable	$ 348,000	$ 410,000
Inventory	430,400	190,000
Investment in Spencer Company	737,600	–0–
Land	454,000	280,000
Equipment	270,000	190,000
Accumulated depreciation	(180,000)	(50,000)
Total assets	$ 2,060,000	$ 1,020,000
Liabilities	(715,000)	(120,000)
Common stock	(600,000)	(400,000)
Retained earnings, 12/31/24	(745,000)	(500,000)
Total liabilities and equities	$(2,060,000)	$(1,020,000)

Required

Answer the following questions:

a. By how much did Spencer's book value increase during the period from January 1, 2022, through December 31, 2023?

b. During the initial years after the takeover, what annual amortization expense was recognized in connection with the acquisition-date excess of fair value over book value?

c. What amount of intra-entity gross profit exists within the parent's inventory figures at the beginning and at the end of 2024?

d. Equipment has been transferred between the companies. What amount of additional depreciation is recognized in 2024 because of this transfer?

e. The parent reports Income of Spencer Company of $60,000 for 2024. How was this figure calculated?

f. Without using a worksheet, determine consolidated totals.

g. Prepare the December 31, 2024, worksheet entries required by the transfers of inventory, land, and equipment.

Solution

a. The subsidiary's acquisition-date book value is given as $610,000. At the beginning of 2024, the company's common stock and retained earnings total is $830,000 ($400,000 and $430,000, respectively). In the previous years, Spencer's book value has apparently increased by $220,000 ($830,000 – $610,000).

b. To determine amortization, an allocation of Spencer's acquisition-date fair value must first be made. The $75,000 allocation needed to show Spencer's patented technology at fair value leads to an additional annual expense of $7,500 for the initial years of the combination. The $57,500 assigned to the indefinite-lived trademark is not subject to amortization.

Acquisition-Date Fair-Value Allocation and Excess Amortization Schedule

Consideration paid by Pullman for 80% of Spencer	$594,000
Noncontrolling interest (20%) fair value	148,500
Spencer's fair value at acquisition date	$742,500
Book value of Spencer Company	(610,000)
Excess fair value over book value	$132,500

		Remaining Life (Years)	Annual Excess Amortizations	Excess Amortizations 2022–2024	Unamortized Balance, 12/31/24
Patented technology ...	$ 75,000	10	$7,500	$22,500	$52,500
Trademark	57,500	indefinite	–0–	–0–	57,500
Totals	$132,500		$7,500	$22,500	

c. From the inventory transferred to Pullman during 2023, $30,000 is still held at the beginning of 2024. This merchandise contains an intra-entity gross profit of $10,000 ($30,000 × 33.3% gross profit rate for that year). At year-end, $17,000 ($68,000 remaining inventory × 25% gross profit rate) remains as intra-entity gross profit in the ending inventory.

d. Additional 2024 depreciation on Spencer's books for the transferred equipment is $3,600. Equipment with a book value of $44,000 was transferred at a price of $80,000. The net of $36,000 to this asset's account balances would be written off over 10 years for an extra $3,600 per year recognized as part of the consolidation process.

e. According to the separate statements given, the subsidiary reports net income of $120,000. However, in determining the net income allocation between the parent and the noncontrolling interest, this reported figure must be adjusted for the effects of *any upstream transfers*. Because Spencer sold the inventory upstream to Pullman, the $10,000 gross profit deferred in requirement (c) from 2023 into the current period is attributed to the subsidiary (as the seller). Likewise, the $17,000 intra-entity gross profit at year-end is viewed as a reduction in Spencer's net income.

All other transfers are downstream and not considered to have an effect on the subsidiary. Therefore, the Equity in earnings of Spencer Company balance can be verified as follows:

Company's reported net income—2024	$120,000
Recognition of 2023 intra-entity gross profit	10,000
Deferral of 2024 intra-entity gross profit	(17,000)
Excess patented technology amortization expense—2024 (see requirement [b])	(7,500)
Recognized subsidiary net income from consolidated perspective	105,500
Parent's ownership percentage	80%
Equity income before downstream transfer effects	$ 84,400
Adjustments attributed to parent's ownership	
Deferral of intra-entity gain—land	(28,000)
Removal of excess depreciation (see requirement [d])	3,600
Equity in earnings of Spencer Company—2024	$ 60,000

f. Each of the 2024 consolidated totals for this business combination can be determined as follows:

Sales = $1,240,000. The parent's balance is added to the subsidiary's balance less the $160,000 in intra-entity transfers for the period.

Cost of Goods Sold = $745,000. The computation begins by adding the parent's balance to the subsidiary's balance less the $160,000 in intra-entity transfers for the period. The $10,000 intra-entity gross profit in inventory from the previous year is deducted to recognize this income currently. Next, the $17,000 ending intra-entity gross profit is added to cost of goods sold to defer the income until a later year when the goods are sold to an outside party.

Operating Expenses = $293,900. The parent's balance is added to the subsidiary's balance. Annual excess fair-value amortization of $7,500 (see requirement [b]) is also included. Excess depreciation of $3,600 resulting from the transfer of equipment (see requirement [e]) is removed.

Gain on Sale of Land = 0. This amount is eliminated for consolidation purposes because the transaction was intra-entity.

Equity in Earnings of Spencer Company = 0. The equity earnings figure is removed and replaced with the subsidiary's actual revenues and expenses in the consolidated financial statements.

Net Income Attributable to Noncontrolling Interest = $21,100. Requirement (e) shows the subsidiary's net income from a consolidated perspective as $105,500 after adjustments for intra-entity upstream gains and excess fair-value amortization. Because outsiders hold 20 percent of the subsidiary, a $21,100 allocation ($105,500 × 20%) is made.

⚹*Consolidated Net Income* = $201,100 computed as Sales less Cost of Goods Sold and Operating Expenses. The consolidated net income is then distributed: $21,100 to the noncontrolling interest and $180,000 to the parent company owners.

Retained Earnings, 1/1/24 = $620,000. The equity method has been applied; therefore, the parent's balance equals the consolidated total.

Dividends Declared = $55,000. Only the parent's dividends are shown in the consolidated statements. Distributions from the subsidiary to the parent are eliminated as intra-entity transfers. Any dividends distributable to the noncontrolling interest reduce the ending balance attributed to these outside owners.

Cash and Accounts Receivable = $708,000. The two balances are added after removal of the $50,000 intra-entity receivable created by the transfer of land.

Inventory = $603,400. The two balances are added after removal of the $17,000 ending intra-entity gross profit (see requirement [c]).

Investment in Spencer Company = 0. The investment balance is eliminated and replaced with actual assets and liabilities of the subsidiary.

Land = $706,000. The two balances are added. The $28,000 intra-entity gain created by the transfer is removed.

Equipment = $480,000. The two balances are added. Because of the intra-entity transfer, $20,000 must also be included to adjust the $80,000 transfer price to the original $100,000 cost of the asset.

Accumulated Depreciation = $278,800. The balances are combined and adjusted for $52,400 to reinstate the historical balance for the equipment transferred across affiliates ($56,000 written off at date of transfer less $3,600 for the previous year's depreciation on the intra-entity gain). Then, an additional $3,600 is removed for the current year's depreciation on the intra-entity gain.

Patented Technology = $52,500. The amount is from the original $75,000 acquisition-date excess fair-value allocation less three years' amortization at $7,500 per year.

Trademark = $57,500. The amount is from the original allocation of Spencer's acquisition-date fair value.

Total Assets = $2,328,600. This figure is a summation of the preceding consolidated assets.

Liabilities = $785,000. The two balances are added after removal of the $50,000 intra-entity payable created by the transfer of land.

Noncontrolling Interest in Subsidiary, 12/31/24 = $198,600. This figure is composed of several different balances:

Spencer 20% book value (adjusted for upstream intra-entity profits) at 1/1/24	$164,000
20% of 1/1/24 unamortized excess fair-value allocation for Spencer's net identifiable assets (20% × [$132,500 − $15,000])	23,500
Noncontrolling interest at 1/1/24	$187,500
2024 Spencer net income allocation	21,100
Noncontrolling interest share of Spencer dividends	(10,000)
December 31, 2024, balance	$198,600

Common Stock = $600,000. Only the parent company balance is reported within the consolidated statements.

⚹*Retained Earnings, 12/31/24* = $745,000. The retained earnings amount is found by adding the parent's (Pullman) share of consolidated net income to the beginning Retained Earnings balance and then subtracting the parent's dividends. All of these figures have been computed previously.

Total Liabilities and Equities = $2,328,600. This figure is the summation of all consolidated liabilities and equities.

g.

Consolidation Worksheet Entries to Adjust for Intra-Entity Transfers
December 31, 2024

Inventory

Entry *G

Retained Earnings, 1/1/24—Subsidiary	10,000	
Cost of Goods Sold		10,000

To remove 2023 intra-entity gross profit from beginning balances of the current year. Because transfers were upstream, retained earnings of the subsidiary (as the original seller) are reduced. Balance is computed in requirement (c).

Entry TI

Sales...	160,000	
Cost of Goods Sold		160,000

To eliminate current-year intra-entity transfer of inventory.

Entry G

Cost of Goods Sold	17,000	
Inventory		17,000

To remove 2024 intra-entity gross profit from ending accounts of the current year. Balance is computed in requirement (c).

Land

Entry TL

Gain on Sale of Land	28,000	
Land		28,000

To eliminate gross profit created on first day of current year by an intra-entity transfer of land.

Equipment

Entry *TA

Equipment	20,000	
Investment in Spencer Company	32,400	
Accumulated Depreciation		52,400

To remove remaining gain (as of January 1, 2024) created by intra-entity transfer of equipment and to adjust equipment and accumulated depreciation to historical cost figures.

Equipment is increased from the $80,000 transfer price to $100,000 cost.

Accumulated depreciation of $56,000 was eliminated at the time of transfer. Excess depreciation of $3,600 per year has been recorded for the prior year ($3,600); thus, the accumulated depreciation is now only $52,400 less than the cost-based figure.

The intra-entity gain on the transfer was $36,000 ($80,000 less $44,000). That figure has now been reduced by one year of excess depreciation ($3,600). Because the parent used the equity method and this transfer was downstream, the adjustment here is to the investment account rather than the parent's beginning Retained Earnings.

Entry ED

Accumulated Depreciation	3,600	
Operating Expenses (depreciation)		3,600

To eliminate the current-year overstatement of depreciation created by inflated transfer price.

Questions

1. Intra-entity transfers between the component companies of a business combination are quite common. Why do these intra-entity transactions occur so frequently?

2. Barker Company owns 80 percent of the outstanding voting stock of Walden Company. During the current year, intra-entity sales amount to $100,000. These transactions were made with a gross profit rate of 40 percent of the transfer price. In consolidating the two companies, what amount of these sales would be eliminated?

3. Padlock Corp. owns 90 percent of Safeco, Inc. During the year, Padlock sold 3,000 locking mechanisms to Safeco for $900,000. By the end of the year, Safeco had sold all but 500 of the locking mechanisms to outside parties. Padlock marks up the cost of its locking mechanisms by 60 percent in computing its sales price to affiliated and nonaffiliated customers. How much intra-entity profit remains in Safeco's inventory at year-end?

4. How are intra-entity inventory gross profits created, and what consolidation entries does the presence of these gross profits necessitate?

5. James, Inc., sells inventory to Matthews Company, a related party, at James's standard gross profit rate. At the current fiscal year-end, Matthews still holds some portion of this inventory. If consolidated financial statements are prepared, why are worksheet entries required in two different fiscal periods?

6. How do intra-entity profits present in any year affect the noncontrolling interest calculations?

7. A worksheet is being developed to consolidate Allegan, Inc., and Stark Company. These two organizations have made considerable intra-entity transactions. How would the consolidation process be affected if these transfers were downstream? How would consolidated financial statements be affected if these transfers were upstream?

8. King Company owns a 90 percent interest in the outstanding voting shares of Pawn Company. No excess fair-value amortization resulted from the acquisition. Pawn reports a net income of $110,000 for the current year. Intra-entity sales occur at regular intervals between the two companies. Intra-entity gross profits of $30,000 were present in the beginning inventory balances, whereas $60,000 in similar gross profits were recorded at year-end. What is the noncontrolling interest's share of consolidated net income?

9. When a subsidiary sells inventory to a parent, the intra-entity profit is removed from the subsidiary's net income for consolidation and reduces the income allocation to the noncontrolling interest. Is the profit permanently eliminated from the noncontrolling interest, or is it merely shifted from one period to the next? Explain.

10. The consolidation process applicable when intra-entity land transfers have occurred differs somewhat from that used for intra-entity inventory sales. What differences should be noted?

11. A subsidiary sells land to the parent company at a significant gain. The parent holds the land for two years and then sells it to an outside party, also for a gain. How does the business combination account for these events?

12. Why does an intra-entity sale of a depreciable asset (such as equipment or a building) require subsequent adjustments to depreciation expense within the consolidation process?

13. If a seller makes an intra-entity sale of a depreciable asset at a price above book value, the seller's beginning Retained Earnings is reduced when preparing each subsequent consolidation. Why does the amount of the adjustment change from year to year?

Problems

1. What is the primary reason we defer financial statement recognition of gross profits on intra-entity sales for goods that remain within the consolidated entity at year-end?
   a. Revenues and COGS must be recognized for all intra-entity sales regardless of whether the sales are upstream or downstream.
   b. Intra-entity sales result in gross profit overstatements regardless of amounts remaining in ending inventory.
   c. Gross profits must be deferred indefinitely because sales among affiliates always remain in the consolidated group.
   d. When intra-entity sales remain in ending inventory, control of the goods has not changed.

2. James Corporation owns 80 percent of Carl Corporation's common stock. During October, Carl sold merchandise to James for $250,000. At December 31, 40 percent of this merchandise remains in James's inventory. Gross profit percentages were 20 percent for James and 30 percent for Carl. The amount of intra-entity gross profit in inventory at December 31 that should be eliminated in the consolidation process is
   a. $24,000.
   b. $30,000.
   c. $20,000.
   d. $75,000.

LO 5-5

3. In computing the noncontrolling interest's share of consolidated net income, how should the subsidiary's net income be adjusted for intra-entity transfers?

   a. The subsidiary's reported net income is adjusted for the impact of upstream transfers prior to computing the noncontrolling interest's allocation.

   b. The subsidiary's reported net income is adjusted for the impact of all transfers prior to computing the noncontrolling interest's allocation.

   c. The subsidiary's reported net income is not adjusted for the impact of transfers prior to computing the noncontrolling interest's allocation.

   d. The subsidiary's reported net income is adjusted for the impact of downstream transfers prior to computing the noncontrolling interest's allocation.

LO 5-2, 5-3

Use the following information for Problems 4–6:

Alpha Company owns 80 percent of the voting stock of Beta Company. Alpha and Beta reported the following account information from their year-end separate financial records:

	Alpha	Beta
Inventory	$ 95,000	$ 88,000
Sales Revenue	800,000	300,000
Cost of Goods Sold	600,000	180,000

During the current year, Alpha sold inventory to Beta for $100,000. As of year-end, Beta had resold only 60 percent of these intra-entity purchases. Alpha sells inventory to Beta at the same markup it uses for all of its customers.

4. What is the total for consolidated sales revenue?

   a. $800,000
   b. $970,000
   c. $1,000,000
   d. $1,100,000

5. What is the total for consolidated inventory?

   a. $143,000
   b. $173,000
   c. $175,000
   d. $183,000

6. What is the total for consolidated cost of goods sold?

   a. $670,000
   b. $690,000
   c. $788,000
   d. $790,000

LO 5-2, 5-3

7. Parkette, Inc., acquired a 60 percent interest in Skybox Company several years ago. During 2023, Skybox sold inventory costing $160,000 to Parkette for $200,000. A total of 18 percent of this inventory was not sold to outsiders until 2024. During 2024, Skybox sold inventory costing $297,500 to Parkette for $350,000. A total of 30 percent of this inventory was not sold to outsiders until 2025. In 2024, Parkette reported cost of goods sold of $607,500 while Skybox reported $450,000. What is the consolidated cost of goods sold in 2024?

   a. $698,950
   b. $720,000
   c. $1,066,050
   d. $716,050

LO 5-3, 5-4, 5-5

8. Angela, Inc., holds a 90 percent interest in Corby Company. During 2023, Corby sold inventory costing $77,000 to Angela for $110,000. Of this inventory, $40,000 worth was not sold to outsiders until 2024. During 2024, Corby sold inventory costing $72,000 to Angela for $120,000. A total of $50,000 of this inventory was not sold to outsiders until 2025. In 2024, Angela reported separate net income of $150,000 while Corby's net income was $90,000 after excess amortizations. What is the noncontrolling interest in the 2024 income of the subsidiary?

   a. $8,000
   b. $8,200

c. $9,000

d. $9,800

LO 5-7

9. Dunn Corporation owns 100 percent of Grey Corporation's common stock. On January 2, 2023, Dunn sold to Grey for $40,000 machinery with a carrying amount of $30,000. Grey is depreciating the acquired machinery over a five-year remaining life by the straight-line method. The net adjustments to compute 2023 and 2024 consolidated net income would be an increase (decrease) of

2023	**2024**
a. $(8,000)	$2,000
b. $(8,000)	–0–
c. $(10,000)	$2,000
d. $(10,000)	–0–

(AICPA adapted)

LO 5-7

10. Thomson Corporation owns 70 percent of the outstanding stock of Stayer, Inc. On January 1, 2022, Thomson acquired a building with a 10-year life for $460,000. Thomson depreciated the building on the straight-line basis assuming no salvage value. On January 1, 2024, Thomson sold this building to Stayer for $430,400. At that time, the building had a remaining life of 8 years but still no expected salvage value. In preparing financial statements for 2024, how does this transfer affect the computation of consolidated net income?

a. Net income is reduced by $62,400.

b. Net income is reduced by $59,440.

c. Net income is reduced by $70,200.

d. Net income is reduced by $54,600.

LO 5-2, 5-3, 5-5, 5-7

11. On January 1, Jarel acquired 80 percent of the outstanding voting stock of Suarez for $260,000 cash consideration. The remaining 20 percent of Suarez had an acquisition-date fair value of $65,000. On January 1, Suarez possessed equipment (5-year remaining life) that was undervalued on its books by $25,000. Suarez also had developed several secret formulas that Jarel assessed at $50,000. These formulas, although not recorded on Suarez's financial records, were estimated to have a 20-year future life.

As of December 31, the financial statements appeared as follows:

	Jarel	**Suarez**
Revenues	$ (300,000)	$(200,000)
Cost of goods sold	140,000	80,000
Expenses	20,000	10,000
Net income	$ (140,000)	$(110,000)
Retained earnings, 1/1	$ (300,000)	$(150,000)
Net income	(140,000)	(110,000)
Dividends declared	–0–	–0–
Retained earnings, 12/31	$ (440,000)	$(260,000)
Cash and receivables	$ 210,000	$ 90,000
Inventory	150,000	110,000
Investment in Suarez	260,000	–0–
Equipment (net)	440,000	300,000
Total assets	$ 1,060,000	$ 500,000
Liabilities	$ (420,000)	$(140,000)
Common stock	(200,000)	(100,000)
Retained earnings, 12/31	(440,000)	(260,000)
Total liabilities and equities	$(1,060,000)	$(500,000)

Included in the preceding statements, Jarel sold inventory costing $80,000 to Suarez for $100,000. Of these goods, Suarez still owns 60 percent on December 31. Compute the following amounts for the December 31 consolidated financial statements for Jarel and Suarez.

a. Revenues

b. Cost of goods sold

c. Expenses

d. Noncontrolling interest appearing on the balance sheet

e. Equipment (net)

f. Inventory

LO 5-2, 5-3, 5-5

12. The following are several figures reported for Poyer and Sutter as of December 31, 2024:

	Poyer	Sutter
Inventory	$ 500,000	$300,000
Sales	1,000,000	800,000
Investment income	not given	
Cost of goods sold	500,000	400,000
Operating expenses	230,000	300,000

Poyer acquired 90 percent of Sutter in January 2023. In allocating the newly acquired subsidiary's fair value at the acquisition date, Poyer noted that Sutter had developed a unpatented technology worth $78,000 that was unrecorded on its accounting records and had a 4-year remaining life. Any remaining excess fair value over Sutter's book value was attributed to an indefinite-lived trademark. During 2024, Sutter sells inventory costing $130,000 to Poyer for $180,000. Of this amount, 10 percent remains unsold in Poyer's warehouse at year-end.

Determine balances for the following items that would appear on Poyer's consolidated financial statements for 2024:

a. Inventory

b. Sales

c. Cost of Goods Sold

d. Operating Expenses

e. Net Income Attributable to Noncontrolling Interest

LO 5-3, 5-4, 5-5

13. On January 1, 2023, Corgan Company acquired 80 percent of the outstanding voting stock of Smashing, Inc., for a total of $980,000 in cash and other consideration. At the acquisition date, Smashing had common stock of $700,000, retained earnings of $250,000, and a noncontrolling interest fair value of $245,000. Corgan attributed the excess of fair value over Smashing's book value to various covenants with a 20-year remaining life. Corgan uses the equity method to account for its investment in Smashing.

During the next two years, Smashing reported the following:

	Net Income	Dividends Declared	Inventory Purchases from Corgan
2023	$150,000	$35,000	$100,000
2024	130,000	45,000	120,000

Corgan sells inventory to Smashing using a 60 percent markup on cost. At the end of 2023 and 2024, 40 percent of the current year purchases remain in Smashing's inventory.

a. Compute the equity method balance in Corgan's Investment in Smashing, Inc., account as of December 31, 2024.

b. Prepare the worksheet adjustments for the December 31, 2024, consolidation of Corgan and Smashing.

LO 5-1, 5-3, 5-4, 5-5, 5-6, 5-7

14. Placid Lake Corporation acquired 80 percent of the outstanding voting stock of Scenic, Inc., on January 1, 2023, when Scenic had a net book value of $400,000. Any excess fair value was assigned to intangible assets and amortized at a rate of $5,000 per year.

Placid Lake's 2024 net income before consideration of its relationship with Scenic (and before adjustments for intra-entity sales) was $300,000. Scenic reported net income of $110,000. Placid Lake declared $100,000 in dividends during this period; Scenic paid $40,000. At the end of 2024, selected figures from the two companies' balance sheets were as follows:

	Placid Lake	Scenic
Inventory..	$140,000	$ 90,000
Land..	600,000	200,000
Equipment (net)................................	400,000	300,000

During 2023, intra-entity sales of $90,000 (original cost of $54,000) were made. Only 20 percent of this inventory was still held within the consolidated entity at the end of 2023. In 2024, $120,000 in intra-entity sales were made with an original cost of $66,000. Of this merchandise, 30 percent had not been resold to outside parties by the end of the year.

Each of the following questions should be considered as an independent situation for the year 2024.

a. What is consolidated net income for Placid Lake and its subsidiary?

b. If the intra-entity sales were upstream, how would consolidated net income be allocated to the controlling and noncontrolling interest?

c. If the intra-entity sales were downstream, how would consolidated net income be allocated to the controlling and noncontrolling interest?

d. What is the consolidated balance in the ending Inventory account?

e. Assume that no intra-entity inventory sales occurred between Placid Lake and Scenic. Instead, in 2023, Scenic sold land costing $30,000 to Placid Lake for $50,000. On the 2024 consolidated balance sheet, what value should be reported for land?

f. Assume that no intra-entity inventory or land sales occurred between Placid Lake and Scenic. Instead, on January 1, 2023, Scenic sold equipment (that originally cost $100,000 but had a $60,000 book value on that date) to Placid Lake for $80,000. At the time of sale, the equipment had a remaining useful life of five years. What worksheet entries are made for a December 31, 2024, consolidation of these two companies to eliminate the impact of the intra-entity transfer? For 2024, what is the noncontrolling interest's share of Scenic's net income?

LO 5-2, 5-3, 5-4, 5-5

15. On January 1, 2023, Doone Corporation acquired 60 percent of the outstanding voting stock of Rockne Company for $300,000 consideration. At the acquisition date, the fair value of the 40 percent non-controlling interest was $200,000, and Rockne's assets and liabilities had a collective net fair value of $500,000. Doone uses the equity method in its internal records to account for its investment in Rockne and there is no excess acquisition-date fair value amortization. Rockne reports net income of $160,000 in 2024. Since being acquired, Rockne has regularly supplied inventory to Doone at 25 percent more than cost. Sales to Doone amounted to $250,000 in 2023 and $300,000 in 2024. Approximately 30 percent of the inventory purchased during any one year is not used until the following year.

a. What is the noncontrolling interest's share of Rockne's 2024 income?

b. Prepare Doone's 2024 consolidation entries required by the intra-entity inventory transfers.

LO 5-3, 5-4, 5-5, 5-7

16. Protrade Corporation acquired 80 percent of the outstanding voting stock of Seacraft Company on January 1, 2023, for $612,000 in cash and other consideration. At the acquisition date, Protrade assessed Seacraft's identifiable assets and liabilities at a collective net fair value of $765,000, and the fair value of the 20 percent noncontrolling interest was $153,000. No excess fair value over book value amortization accompanied the acquisition.

The following selected account balances are from the individual financial records of these two companies as of December 31, 2024:

	Protrade	Seacraft
Sales	$880,000	$600,000
Cost of goods sold	410,000	317,000
Operating expenses	174,000	129,000
Retained earnings, 1/1/24	980,000	420,000
Inventory	370,000	144,000
Buildings (net)	382,000	181,000
Investment income	Not given	–0–

Each of the following problems is an independent situation:

a. Assume that Protrade sells Seacraft inventory at a markup equal to 60 percent of cost. Intra-entity transfers were $114,000 in 2023 and $134,000 in 2024. Of this inventory, Seacraft retained and then sold $52,000 of the 2023 transfers in 2024 and held $66,000 of the 2023 transfers until 2024.

Determine balances for the following items that would appear on consolidated financial statements for 2024:

Cost of Goods Sold
Inventory
Net Income Attributable to Noncontrolling Interest

b. Assume that Seacraft sells inventory to Protrade at a markup equal to 60 percent of cost. Intra-entity transfers were $74,000 in 2023 and $104,000 in 2024. Of this inventory, $45,000 of the 2023 transfers were retained and then sold by Protrade in 2024, whereas $59,000 of the 2024 transfers were held until 2025.

Determine balances for the following items that would appear on consolidated financial statements for 2024:

Cost of Goods Sold
Inventory
Net Income Attributable to Noncontrolling Interest

c. Protrade sells Seacraft a building on January 1, 2023, for $128,000, although its book value was only $74,000 on this date. The building had a 5-year remaining life and was to be depreciated using the straight-line method with no salvage value.

Determine balances for the following items that would appear on consolidated financial statements for 2024:

Buildings (net)
Operating Expenses
Net Income Attributable to Noncontrolling Interest

LO 5-3, 5-4, 5-5

17. Akron, Inc., owns all outstanding stock of Toledo Corporation. Amortization expense of $15,000 per year for patented technology resulted from the original acquisition. For 2024, the companies had the following account balances:

	Akron	Toledo
Sales	$1,100,000	$600,000
Cost of goods sold	500,000	400,000
Operating expenses	400,000	220,000
Investment income	Not given	–0–
Dividends declared	80,000	30,000

Intra-entity sales of $320,000 occurred during 2023 and again in 2024. This merchandise cost $240,000 each year. Of the total transfers, $70,000 was still held on December 31, 2023, with $50,000 unsold on December 31, 2024.

a. For consolidation purposes, does the direction of the transfers (upstream or downstream) affect the balances to be reported here?

b. Prepare a consolidated income statement for the year ending December 31, 2024.

LO 5-7

18. On January 1, 2023, QuickPort Company acquired 90 percent of the outstanding voting stock of NetSpeed, Inc., for $810,000 in cash and stock options. At the acquisition date, NetSpeed had common stock of $800,000 and Retained Earnings of $40,000. The acquisition-date fair value of the 10 percent noncontrolling interest was $90,000. QuickPort attributed the $60,000 excess of NetSpeed's fair value over book value to a database with a 5-year remaining life.

During the next two years, NetSpeed reported the following:

	Net Income	Dividends Declared
2023	$ 80,000	$8,000
2024	115,000	8,000

On July 1, 2023, QuickPort sold communication equipment to NetSpeed for $42,000. The equipment originally cost $48,000 and had accumulated depreciation of $9,000 and an estimated remaining life of three years at the date of the intra-entity transfer.

a. Compute the equity method balance in QuickPort's Investment in NetSpeed, Inc., account as of December 31, 2024.

b. Prepare the worksheet adjustments for the December 31, 2024, consolidation of QuickPort and NetSpeed.

LO 5-7

19. Padre holds 100 percent of the outstanding shares of Sonora. On January 1, 2022, Padre transferred equipment to Sonora for $95,000. The equipment had cost $130,000 originally but had a $50,000 book value and 5-year remaining life at the date of transfer. Depreciation expense is computed according to the straight-line method with no salvage value.

    Consolidated financial statements for 2024 currently are being prepared. What worksheet entries are needed in connection with the consolidation of this asset? Assume that the parent applies the partial equity method.

LO 5-7

20. On January 1, 2024, Ackerman sold equipment to Brannigan (a wholly owned subsidiary) for $200,000 in cash. The equipment had originally cost $180,000 but had a book value of only $110,000 when transferred. On that date, the equipment had a 5-year remaining life. Depreciation expense is computed using the straight-line method.

    Ackerman reported $300,000 in net income in 2024 (not including any investment income) while Brannigan reported $98,000. Ackerman attributed any excess acquisition-date fair value to Brannigan's unpatented technology, which was amortized at a rate of $4,000 per year.

    a. What is consolidated net income for 2024?

    b. What is the parent's share of consolidated net income for 2024 if Ackerman owns only 90 percent of Brannigan?

    c. What is the parent's share of consolidated net income for 2024 if Ackerman owns only 90 percent of Brannigan and the equipment transfer was upstream?

    d. What is the consolidated net income for 2025 if Ackerman reports $320,000 (does not include investment income) and Brannigan $108,000 in income? Assume that Brannigan is a wholly owned subsidiary and the equipment transfer was downstream.

LO 5-2, 5-3, 5-4, 5-7

21. Allison Corporation acquired 90 percent of Bretton on January 1, 2022. Of Bretton's total acquisition-date fair value, $60,000 was allocated to undervalued equipment (with a 10-year remaining life) and $80,000 was attributed to franchises (to be written off over a 20-year period).

    Since the takeover, Bretton has transferred inventory to its parent as follows:

Year	Cost	Transfer Price	Remaining at Year-End
2022	$45,000	$90,000	$30,000 (at transfer price)
2023	48,000	80,000	35,000 (at transfer price)
2024	69,000	92,000	50,000 (at transfer price)

    On January 1, 2023, Allison sold Bretton a building for $50,000 that had originally cost $70,000 but had only a $30,000 book value at the date of transfer. The building is estimated to have a five-year remaining life (straight-line depreciation is used with no salvage value).

    Selected figures from the December 31, 2024, trial balances of these two companies are as follows:

	Allison	Bretton
Sales	$700,000	$400,000
Cost of goods sold	440,000	220,000
Operating expenses	120,000	80,000
Investment income	Not given	–0–
Inventory	210,000	90,000
Equipment (net)	140,000	110,000
Buildings (net)	350,000	190,000

    Determine consolidated totals for each of these account balances.

LO 5-3, 5-4, 5-5, 5-7

22. On January 1, 2024, Sledge had common stock of $120,000 and retained earnings of $260,000. During that year, Sledge reported sales of $130,000, cost of goods sold of $70,000, and operating expenses of $40,000.

    On January 1, 2022, Percy, Inc., acquired 80 percent of Sledge's outstanding voting stock. At that date, $60,000 of the acquisition-date fair value was assigned to unrecorded contracts (with a 20-year life) and $20,000 to an undervalued building (with a 10-year remaining life).

    In 2023, Sledge sold inventory costing $9,000 to Percy for $15,000. Of this merchandise, Percy continued to hold $5,000 at year-end. During 2024, Sledge transferred inventory costing $11,000 to Percy for $20,000. Percy still held half of these items at year-end.

On January 1, 2023, Percy sold equipment to Sledge for $12,000. This asset originally cost $16,000 but had a January 1, 2023, book value of $9,000. At the time of transfer, the equipment's remaining life was estimated to be five years.

Percy has properly applied the equity method to the investment in Sledge.

a. Prepare worksheet entries to consolidate these two companies as of December 31, 2024.

b. Compute the net income attributable to the noncontrolling interest for 2024.

LO 5-1, 5-2, 5-3, 5-4, 5-5, 5-7 23. Pitino acquired 90 percent of Brey's outstanding shares on January 1, 2022, in exchange for $342,000 in cash. The subsidiary's stockholders' equity accounts totaled $326,000, and the noncontrolling interest had a fair value of $38,000 on that day. However, a building (with a 9-year remaining life) in Brey's accounting records was undervalued by $18,000. Pitino assigned the rest of the excess fair value over book value to Brey's patented technology (6-year remaining life).

Brey reported net income from its own operations of $64,000 in 2022 and $80,000 in 2023. Brey declared dividends of $19,000 in 2022 and $23,000 in 2023.

Brey sells inventory to Pitino as follows:

Year	Cost to Brey	Transfer Price to Pitino	Inventory Remaining at Year-End (at transfer price)
2022	$69,000	$115,000	$25,000
2023	81,000	135,000	37,500
2024	92,800	160,000	50,000

At December 31, 2024, Pitino owes Brey $16,000 for inventory acquired during the period.

The separate account balances for the two companies at December 31, 2024, and the year then ended follow. Credits are indicated by parentheses.

	Pitino	Brey
Sales revenues	$ (862,000)	$(366,000)
Cost of goods sold	515,000	209,000
Expenses	185,400	67,000
Equity in earnings of Brey	(68,400)	–0–
Net income	$ (230,000)	$ (90,000)
Retained earnings, 1/1/24	$ (488,000)	$(278,000)
Net income (above)	(230,000)	(90,000)
Dividends declared	136,000	27,000
Retained earnings, 12/31/24	$ (582,000)	$(341,000)
Cash and receivables	$ 146,000	$ 98,000
Inventory	255,000	136,000
Investment in Brey	450,000	–0–
Land, buildings, and equipment (net)	964,000	328,000
Total assets	$ 1,815,000	$ 562,000
Liabilities	$ (718,000)	$ (71,000)
Common stock	(515,000)	(150,000)
Retained earnings, 12/31/24	(582,000)	(341,000)
Total liabilities and equities	$(1,815,000)	$(562,000)

Answer each of the following questions:

a. What was the annual amortization resulting from the acquisition-date fair-value allocations?

b. Were the intra-entity transfers upstream or downstream?

c. What intra-entity gross profit in inventory existed as of January 1, 2024?

d. What intra-entity gross profit in inventory existed as of December 31, 2024?

e. What amounts make up the $68,400 Equity in Earnings of Brey account balance for 2024?

f. What is the net income attributable to the noncontrolling interest for 2024?

g. What amounts make up the $450,000 Investment in Brey account balance as of December 31, 2024?

h. Prepare the 2024 worksheet entry to eliminate the subsidiary's beginning owners' equity balances.

i. Without preparing a worksheet or consolidation entries, determine the consolidation balances for these two companies.

LO 5-2, 5-3, 5-4

24. ProForm acquired 70 percent of ClipRite on June 30, 2023, for $910,000 in cash. Based on Clip-Rite's acquisition-date fair value, an unrecorded intangible of $400,000 was recognized and is being amortized at the rate of $10,000 per year. No goodwill was recognized in the acquisition. The noncontrolling interest fair value was assessed at $390,000 at the acquisition date. The 2024 financial statements are as follows:

	ProForm	ClipRite
Sales	$ (800,000)	$ (600,000)
Cost of goods sold	535,000	400,000
Operating expenses	100,000	100,000
Dividend income	(35,000)	–0–
Net income	$ (200,000)	$ (100,000)
Retained earnings, 1/1/24	$(1,300,000)	$ (850,000)
Net income	(200,000)	(100,000)
Dividends declared	100,000	50,000
Retained earnings, 12/31/24	$(1,400,000)	$ (900,000)
Cash and receivables	$ 400,000	$ 300,000
Inventory	290,000	700,000
Investment in ClipRite	910,000	–0–
Fixed assets	1,000,000	600,000
Accumulated depreciation	(300,000)	(200,000)
Totals	$ 2,300,000	$ 1,400,000
Liabilities	$ (600,000)	$ (400,000)
Common stock	(300,000)	(100,000)
Retained earnings, 12/31/24	(1,400,000)	(900,000)
Totals	$(2,300,000)	$(1,400,000)

ProForm sold ClipRite inventory costing $72,000 during the last six months of 2023 for $120,000. At year-end, 30 percent remained. ProForm sold ClipRite inventory costing $200,000 during 2024 for $250,000. At year-end, 10 percent is left. With these facts, determine the consolidated balances for the following:

Sales
Cost of Goods Sold
Operating Expenses
Dividend Income
Net Income Attributable to Noncontrolling Interest
Inventory
Noncontrolling Interest in Subsidiary, 12/31/24

LO 5-2, 5-3, 5-4, 5-5

25. Compute the balances in Problem 24 again, assuming that all intra-entity transfers were made from ClipRite to ProForm.

LO 5-1, 5-2, 5-3, 5-4, 5-5, 5-6, 5-7

26. Following are financial statements for Moore Company and Kirby Company for 2024:

	Moore	Kirby
Sales	$ (800,000)	$ (600,000)
Cost of goods sold	500,000	400,000
Operating and interest expenses	100,000	160,000
Net income	$ (200,000)	$ (40,000)
Retained earnings, 1/1/24	$ (990,000)	$ (550,000)
Net income	(200,000)	(40,000)
Dividends declared	130,000	–0–
Retained earnings, 12/31/24	$(1,060,000)	$ (590,000)

(*continued*)

(*continued*)

	Moore	Kirby
Cash and receivables	$ 217,000	$ 180,000
Inventory	224,000	160,000
Investment in Kirby	657,000	–0–
Equipment (net)	600,000	420,000
Buildings	1,000,000	650,000
Accumulated depreciation—buildings	(100,000)	(200,000)
Other assets	200,000	100,000
Total assets	$ 2,798,000	$ 1,310,000
Liabilities	$(1,138,000)	$ (570,000)
Common stock	(600,000)	(150,000)
Retained earnings, 12/31/24	(1,060,000)	(590,000)
Total liabilities and equity	$(2,798,000)	$(1,310,000)

- Moore purchased 90 percent of Kirby on January 1, 2023, for $657,000 in cash. On that date, the 10 percent noncontrolling interest was assessed to have a $73,000 fair value. Also at the acquisition date, Kirby held equipment (4-year remaining life) undervalued in its financial records by $20,000 and interest-bearing liabilities (5-year remaining life) overvalued by $40,000. The rest of the excess fair over book value was assigned to previously unrecognized brand names and amortized over a 10-year life.
- During 2023, Kirby reported a net income of $80,000 and declared no dividends.
- Each year, Kirby sells Moore inventory at a 20 percent gross profit rate. Intra-entity sales were $145,000 in 2023 and $160,000 in 2024. On January 1, 2024, 30 percent of the 2023 transfers were still on hand, and on December 31, 2024, 40 percent of the 2024 transfers remained.
- Moore sold Kirby a building on January 2, 2023. It had cost Moore $100,000 but had $90,000 in accumulated depreciation at the time of this transfer. The price was $25,000 in cash. At that time, the building had a five-year remaining life.

Determine all consolidated balances either computationally or by using a worksheet.

LO 5-2, 5-3, 5-4, 5-5

27. On January 1, 2023, Pulaski, Inc., acquired a 60 percent interest in the common stock of Sheridan, Inc., for $372,000. Sheridan's book value on that date consisted of common stock of $100,000 and retained earnings of $220,000. Also, the acquisition-date fair value of the 40 percent noncontrolling interest was $248,000. The subsidiary held patents (with a 10-year remaining life) that were undervalued within the company's accounting records by $70,000 and also had unpatented technology (15-year estimated remaining life) undervalued by $45,000. Any remaining excess acquisition-date fair value was assigned to an indefinite-lived trade name. Since acquisition, Pulaski has applied the equity method to its Investment in Sheridan account. At year-end, there are no intra-entity payables or receivables.

Intra-entity inventory sales between the two companies have been made as follows:

Year	Cost to Pulaski	Transfer Price to Sheridan	Ending Balance (at transfer price)
2023	$120,000	$150,000	$50,000
2024	112,000	160,000	40,000

The individual financial statements for these two companies as of December 31, 2024, and the year then ended follow:

	Pulaski, Inc.	Sheridan, Inc.
Sales	$ (700,000)	$(335,000)
Cost of goods sold	460,000	205,000
Operating expenses	188,000	70,000
Equity in earnings in Sheridan	(28,000)	–0–
Net income	$ (80,000)	$ (60,000)

(*continued*)

(*continued*)

	Pulaski, Inc.	Sheridan, Inc.
Retained earnings, 1/1/24	$ (695,000)	$(280,000)
Net income	(80,000)	(60,000)
Dividends declared	45,000	15,000
Retained earnings, 12/31/24	$ (730,000)	$(325,000)
Cash and receivables	$ 248,000	$ 148,000
Inventory	233,000	129,000
Investment in Sheridan	411,000	–0–
Buildings (net)	308,000	202,000
Equipment (net)	220,000	86,000
Patents (net)	–0–	20,000
Total assets	$ 1,420,000	$ 585,000
Liabilities	$ (390,000)	$(160,000)
Common stock	(300,000)	(100,000)
Retained earnings, 12/31/24	(730,000)	(325,000)
Total liabilities and equities	$(1,420,000)	$(585,000)

a. Show how Pulaski determined the $411,000 Investment in Sheridan account balance. Assume that Pulaski defers 100 percent of downstream intra-entity profits against its share of Sheridan's income.

b. Prepare a consolidated worksheet to determine appropriate balances for external financial reporting as of December 31, 2024.

LO 5-2, 5-3, 5-4, 5-5

28. On January 1, 2022, Plymouth Corporation acquired 80 percent of the outstanding voting stock of Sander Company in exchange for $1,200,000 cash. At that time, although Sander's book value was $925,000, Plymouth assessed Sander's total business fair value at $1,500,000. Since that time, Sander has neither issued nor reacquired any shares of its own stock.

The book values of Sander's individual assets and liabilities approximated their acquisition-date fair values except for the patent account, which was undervalued by $350,000. The undervalued patents had a five-year remaining life at the acquisition date. Any remaining excess fair value was attributed to goodwill. No goodwill impairments have occurred.

Sander regularly sells inventory to Plymouth. The following are details of the intra-entity inventory sales for the past three years:

Year	Intra-Entity Sales	Intra-Entity Ending Inventory at Transfer Price	Gross Profit Rate on Intra-Entity Inventory Transfers
2022	$125,000	$ 80,000	25%
2023	220,000	125,000	28
2024	300,000	160,000	25

Separate financial statements for these two companies as of December 31, 2024, follow:

	Plymouth	Sander
Revenues	$(1,740,000)	$ (950,000)
Cost of goods sold	820,000	500,000
Depreciation expense	104,000	85,000
Amortization expense	220,000	120,000
Interest expense	20,000	15,000
Equity in earnings of Sander	(124,000)	–0–
Net income	$ (700,000)	$ (230,000)
Retained earnings, 1/1/24	$(2,800,000)	$ (345,000)
Net income	(700,000)	(230,000)
Dividends declared	200,000	25,000
Retained earnings, 12/31/24	$(3,300,000)	$ (550,000)

(*continued*)

(*continued*)

	Plymouth	Sander
Cash	$ 535,000	$ 115,000
Accounts receivable	575,000	215,000
Inventory	990,000	800,000
Investment in Sander	1,420,000	–0–
Buildings and equipment	1,025,000	863,000
Patents	950,000	107,000
Total assets	$ 5,495,000	$ 2,100,000
Accounts payable	$ (450,000)	$ (200,000)
Notes payable	(545,000)	(450,000)
Common stock	(900,000)	(800,000)
Additional paid-in capital	(300,000)	(100,000)
Retained earnings, 12/31/24	(3,300,000)	(550,000)
Total liabilities and stockholders' equity	$(5,495,000)	$(2,100,000)

a. Prepare a schedule that calculates the Equity in Earnings of Sander account balance.

b. Prepare a worksheet to arrive at consolidated figures for external reporting purposes. At year-end, there are no intra-entity payables or receivables.

LO 5-2, 5-3, 5-4, 5-5, 5-7

29. On January 1, 2022, Monica Company acquired 70 percent of Young Company's outstanding common stock for $665,000. The fair value of the noncontrolling interest at the acquisition date was $285,000. Young reported stockholders' equity accounts on that date as follows:

Common stock—$10 par value	$300,000
Additional paid-in capital	90,000
Retained earnings	410,000

In establishing the acquisition value, Monica appraised Young's assets and ascertained that the accounting records undervalued a building (with a 5-year remaining life) by $50,000. Any remaining excess acquisition-date fair value was allocated to a franchise agreement to be amortized over 10 years.

During the subsequent years, Young sold Monica inventory at a 30 percent gross profit rate. Monica consistently resold this merchandise in the year of acquisition or in the period immediately following. Transfers for the three years after this business combination was created amounted to the following:

Year	Transfer Price	Inventory Remaining at Year-End (at transfer price)
2022	$60,000	$10,000
2023	80,000	12,000
2024	90,000	18,000

In addition, Monica sold Young several pieces of fully depreciated equipment on January 1, 2023, for $36,000. The equipment had originally cost Monica $50,000. Young plans to depreciate these assets over a six-year period.

In 2024, Young earns a net income of $160,000 and declares and pays $50,000 in cash dividends. These figures increase the subsidiary's Retained Earnings to a $740,000 balance at the end of 2024. During this same year, Monica reported dividend income of $35,000 and an investment account containing the initial value balance of $665,000. No changes in Young's common stock accounts have occurred since Monica's acquisition.

Prepare the 2024 consolidation worksheet entries for Monica and Young. In addition, compute the net income attributable to the noncontrolling interest for 2024.

LO 5-2, 5-3, 5-4, 5-5, 5-7

30. Assume the same basic information as presented in Problem 29 except that Monica employs the equity method of accounting. Hence, it reports $102,740 investment income for 2024 with an Investment account balance of $826,220. Under these circumstances, prepare the worksheet entries required for the consolidation of Monica Company and Young Company.

LO 5-1, 5-2, 5-3, 5-4, 5-5, 5-6, 5-7

31. The individual financial statements for Abbey Company and Bellstar Company for the year ending December 31, 2024, follow. Abbey acquired a 60 percent interest in Bellstar on January 1, 2023, in exchange for various considerations totaling $570,000. At the acquisition date, the fair value of the noncontrolling interest was $380,000 and Bellstar's book value was $850,000. Bellstar had developed internally a trademark that was not recorded on its books but had an acquisition-date fair value of $100,000. This intangible asset is being amortized over 20 years. Abbey uses the partial equity method to account for its investment in Bellstar.

Abbey sold Bellstar land with a book value of $60,000 on January 2, 2023, for $100,000. Bellstar still holds this land at the end of the current year.

Bellstar regularly transfers inventory to Abbey. In 2023, it shipped inventory costing $100,000 to Abbey at a price of $150,000. During 2024, intra-entity shipments totaled $200,000, although the original cost to Bellstar was only $140,000. In each of these years, 20 percent of the merchandise was not resold to outside parties until the period following the transfer. Abbey owes Bellstar $40,000 at the end of 2024.

	Abbey Company	Bellstar Company
Sales	$ (800,000)	$ (500,000)
Cost of goods sold	500,000	300,000
Operating expenses	100,000	60,000
Equity in earnings of Bellstar	(84,000)	–0–
Net income	$ (284,000)	$ (140,000)
Retained earnings, 1/1/24	$(1,116,000)	$ (620,000)
Net income (above)	(284,000)	(140,000)
Dividends declared	115,000	60,000
Retained earnings, 12/31/24	$(1,285,000)	$ (700,000)
Cash	$ 177,000	$ 90,000
Accounts receivable	356,000	410,000
Inventory	440,000	320,000
Investment in Bellstar	726,000	–0–
Land	180,000	390,000
Buildings and equipment (net)	496,000	300,000
Total assets	$ 2,375,000	$ 1,510,000
Liabilities	$ (480,000)	$ (400,000)
Common stock	(610,000)	(320,000)
Additional paid-in capital	–0–	(90,000)
Retained earnings, 12/31/24	(1,285,000)	(700,000)
Total liabilities and equities	$(2,375,000)	$(1,510,000)

a. Prepare a worksheet to consolidate the separate 2024 financial statements for Abbey and Bellstar.

b. How would the consolidation entries in requirement (a) have differed if Abbey had sold a building on January 2, 2023, with a $60,000 book value (cost of $140,000) to Bellstar for $100,000 instead of land, as the problem reports? Assume that the building had a 10-year remaining life at the date of transfer.

LO 5-2, 5-3, 5-4, 5-6

32. On January 1, 2023, Panther, Inc., issued securities with a total fair value of $577,000 for 100 percent of Stark Corporation's outstanding ownership shares. Stark has long supplied inventory to Panther. The companies expect to achieve synergies with production scheduling and product development with this combination.

Although Stark's book value at the acquisition date was $300,000, the fair value of its trademarks was assessed to be $45,000 more than their carrying amounts. Additionally, Stark's patented technology was undervalued in its accounting records by $232,000. The trademarks were considered to have indefinite lives, and the estimated remaining life of the patented technology was eight years.

In 2023, Stark sold Panther inventory costing $75,000 for $125,000. As of December 31, 2023, Panther had resold 74 percent of this inventory. In 2024, Panther bought from Stark $140,000 of inventory that had an original cost of $70,000. At the end of 2024, Panther held $38,000 (transfer price) of inventory acquired from Stark, all from its 2024 purchases.

During 2024, Panther sold Stark a parcel of land for $88,000 and recorded a gain of $16,000 on the sale. Stark still owes Panther $62,000 (current liability) related to the land sale.

At the end of 2024, Panther and Stark prepared the following statements for consolidation.

	Panther, Inc.	Stark Corporation
Revenues	$ (710,000)	$(360,000)
Cost of goods sold	305,000	189,000
Other operating expenses	167,000	81,000
Gain on sale of land	(16,000)	–0–
Equity in Stark's earnings	(39,000)	–0–
Net income	$ (293,000)	$ (90,000)
Retained earnings, 1/1/24	$ (367,000)	$(292,000)
Net income	(293,000)	(90,000)
Dividends declared	80,000	25,000
Retained earnings, 12/31/24	$ (580,000)	$(357,000)
Cash and receivables	$ 102,000	$ 154,000
Inventory	311,000	110,000
Investment in Stark	691,000	–0–
Trademarks	–0–	58,000
Land, buildings, and equip. (net)	638,000	280,000
Patented technology	–0–	125,000
Total assets	$ 1,742,000	$ 727,000
Liabilities	$ (462,000)	$(220,000)
Common stock	(400,000)	(100,000)
Additional paid-in capital	(300,000)	(50,000)
Retained earnings, 12/31/24	(580,000)	(357,000)
Total liabilities and equity	$(1,742,000)	$(727,000)

a. Show how Panther computed its $39,000 equity in Stark's earnings balance.

b. Prepare a 2024 consolidated worksheet for Panther and Stark.

LO 5-2, 5-3, 5-4, 5-5

33. Kelly Company acquired 75 percent of Helton Company's outstanding voting shares on January 1, 2022, in exchange for $285,000 in cash. The subsidiary's stockholders' equity accounts totaled $326,000, and the noncontrolling interest had a fair value of $95,000 on that day. However, a building (with a 12-year remaining life) in Helton's accounting records was undervalued by $18,000. Kelly assigned the remaining excess fair over book value to Helton's patented technology (3-year remaining life).

Helton sold inventory to Kelly as follows:

Year	Cost to Helton	Transfer Price to Kelly	Inventory Held by Kelly at Year End (at transfer price)
2022	$69,000	$103,000	$18,000
2023	81,000	135,000	27,500
2024	40,000	100,000	50,000

Following are selected separate account balances for these two companies for the year ended December 31, 2024. Credit balances are indicated by parentheses.

	Kelly	Helton
Sales revenue	$ (962,000)	$ (466,000)
Cost of goods sold	515,000	210,000
Depreciation expense	81,100	32,500
Amortization expense	79,900	23,000
Other operating expenses	124,000	112,000
Equity in earnings of Helton	(42,000)	–0–
Net income	$ (204,000)	$ (88,500)

Prepare a consolidated income statement for Kelly Company and its subsidiary Helton for the year ended December 31, 2024. Include a proper title and line items allocating consolidated net income to the controlling and noncontrolling interests. Omit per share amounts.

LO 5-2, 5-7

34. On January 1, Paisley, Inc., paid $560,000 for all of Skyler Corporation's outstanding stock. At the acquisition date, the book values of Skyler's accounts equaled their respective fair values. Any excess fair value is assigned to an intangible asset and will be amortized over a 10-year period.

During the year, Skyler sold inventory costing $60,000 to Paisley for $90,000. All but $18,000 (measured at transfer price) of this merchandise has been resold to outsiders by the end of the year. At the end of the year, Paisley continues to owe Skyler for the last shipment of inventory priced at $28,000.

Also, on January 2, Paisley sold Skyler equipment for $20,000 although it had a carrying amount of only $12,000 (original cost of $30,000). Both companies depreciate such property according to the straight-line method with no salvage value. The remaining life at this date was four years.

The following financial statements are for each company for the year ending December 31 (credit balances indicated by parentheses). Determine consolidated financial totals for this business combination.

	Paisley, Inc.	Skyler Corporation
Sales	$ (800,000)	$(400,000)
Cost of goods sold	528,000	260,000
Expenses	180,000	130,000
Gain on sale of equipment	(8,000)	–0–
Net income.	$ (100,000)	$ (10,000)
Retained earnings, 1/1	$ (400,000)	$(150,000)
Net income	(100,000)	(10,000)
Dividends declared	60,000	–0–
Retained earnings, 12/31	$ (440,000)	$(160,000)
Cash	$ 30,000	$ 40,000
Accounts receivable	300,000	100,000
Inventory	260,000	180,000
Investment in Skyler Corporation	560,000	–0–
Land, buildings, and equipment	680,000	500,000
Accumulated depreciation	(180,000)	(90,000)
Total assets	$ 1,650,000	$ 730,000
Accounts payable	$ (140,000)	$ (90,000)
Long-term liabilities	(240,000)	(180,000)
Common stock	(620,000)	(300,000)
Additional paid-in capital	(210,000)	–0–
Retained earnings, 12/31	(440,000)	(160,000)
Total liabilities and equity	$(1,650,000)	$(730,000)

Develop Your Skills

EXCEL CASE

CPA *skills*

On January 1, 2023, PondBlue Company purchased 100 percent of the outstanding voting stock of SweetWater, Inc., for $1,000,000 in cash and other consideration. At the purchase date, SweetWater had common stock of $500,000 and retained earnings of $185,000. PondBlue attributed the excess of acquisition-date fair value over Stillwater's book value to a trade name with an estimated 25-year remaining useful life. PondBlue uses the equity method to account for its investment in SweetWater.

During the next two years, SweetWater reported the following:

	Income	Dividends Declared	Inventory Transfers to PondBlue at Transfer Price
2023	$78,000	$25,000	$190,000
2024	85,000	27,000	210,000

SweetWater sells inventory to PondBlue after a markup based on a gross profit rate. At the end of 2023 and 2024, 30 percent of the current-year purchases remain in PondBlue's inventory.

Required

Create an Excel spreadsheet that computes the following:

1. Equity method balance in PondBlue's Investment in SweetWater, Inc., account as of December 31, 2024.
2. Worksheet adjustments for the December 31, 2024, consolidation of PondBlue and SweetWater.

Formulate your solution so that SweetWater's gross profit rate on sales to James is treated as a variable.

ANALYSIS AND RESEARCH CASE: ACCOUNTING INFORMATION AND SALARY NEGOTIATIONS

The Reston Rockets Players' Association and Mr. Scorekeep, the CEO and majority owner of Reston Rockets Soccer, Inc., ask your help in resolving a salary dispute. Mr. Scorekeep presents the following income statement to the players' representatives.

RESTON ROCKETS SOCCER, INC.
Income Statement

Ticket revenues		$3,500,000
Stadium rent expense	$2,500,000	
Ticket expense	30,000	
Promotion expense	80,000	
Player salaries	700,000	
Staff salaries and miscellaneous	265,000	3,575,000
Net income (loss)		$ (75,000)

The players contend that their salaries are below market and a raise is warranted. Mr. Scorekeep argues that the Reston Rockets really lose money and, until ticket revenues increase, a salary hike is out of the question.

As part of your due diligence, you discover that Reston Rockets Soccer owns 85 percent of the voting stock in Rockets Stadium, Inc. This venue is specifically designed for soccer and is where the Rockets play their entire home game schedule.

However, Mr. Scorekeep does not wish to consider the profits of Rockets Stadium in the negotiations with the players. He claims that "the stadium is really a separate business entity that was purchased separately from the team and therefore does not concern the players. On top of that, we allocate all the ticket revenues to the team's income statement."

The Rockets Stadium income statement appears as follows:

ROCKETS STADIUM, INC.
Income Statement

Stadium rent revenue	$2,500,000	
Concession revenue	875,000	
Parking revenue	95,000	$3,470,000
Cost of goods sold	270,000	
Depreciation expense	190,000	
Grounds maintenance expense	410,000	
Staff salaries and miscellaneous	200,000	1,070,000
Net income (loss)		$2,400,000

Required

1. What advice would you provide the negotiating parties regarding the issue of considering the Rockets Stadium income statement in their discussions? What authoritative literature could you cite in supporting your advice?

2. What other pertinent information would you need to provide a specific recommendation regarding players' salaries?

Variable Interest Entities, Intra-Entity Debt, Consolidated Cash Flows, and Other Issues

The consolidation of financial information can be a highly complex process often encompassing a number of practical challenges. This chapter examines the procedures required by several additional issues:

- Variable interest entities.
- Intra-entity debt.
- Subsidiary preferred stock.
- The consolidated statement of cash flows.
- Computation of consolidated earnings per share.
- Subsidiary stock transactions.

Variable interest entities emerged over recent decades as a new type of business structure that provided effective control of one firm by another without overt ownership. In response to the evolving nature of control relationships among firms, the FASB expanded its definition of control beyond the long-standing criterion of a majority voting interest to include control exercised through variable interests. This topic and some of the more traditional advanced business combination subjects listed earlier provide for further exploration of the complexities faced by the financial reporting community in providing decision-useful information to users of consolidated financial reports.

Consolidation of Variable Interest Entities

Several decades ago, many firms began establishing separate business structures to help finance their operations at favorable rates. These structures became commonly known as *special-purpose entities* (SPEs), *special-purpose vehicles,* or *off-balance-sheet structures.* In this text, we refer to all such entities collectively as *variable interest entities,* or VIEs. Many firms routinely included their VIEs in their consolidated financial reports. However, others sought to avoid consolidation.

VIEs can help accomplish legitimate business purposes. Nonetheless, their use was widely criticized in the aftermath of Enron Corporation's 2001 collapse. Because many firms avoided consolidation and used VIEs

Learning Objectives

After studying this chapter, you should be able to:

LO 6-1   Describe a variable interest entity, a primary beneficiary, and the factors used to decide when a variable interest entity is subject to consolidation.

LO 6-2   Demonstrate the process to consolidate a primary beneficiary with a variable interest entity.

LO 6-3   Demonstrate the consolidation procedures to eliminate all intra-entity debt accounts and recognize any associated gain or loss created whenever one company acquires an affiliate's debt instrument from an outside party.

LO 6-4   Understand that subsidiary preferred stock not owned by the parent is a component of the noncontrolling interest and is initially measured at acquisition-date fair value.

LO 6-5   Prepare a consolidated statement of cash flows.

LO 6-6   Compute basic and diluted earnings per share for a business combination.

LO 6-7   Demonstrate the accounting effects of subsidiary stock transactions on the parent's financial records and consolidated financial statements.

for off-balance-sheet financing, such entities were often characterized as vehicles to hide debt and mislead investors. Other critics observed that firms with variable interests recorded questionable profits on sales to their VIEs that were not arm's-length transactions.[1] The FASB ASC "Variable Interest Entities" sections within the "Consolidations" topic were issued in response to such financial reporting abuses.

What Is a VIE?

A VIE can take the form of a trust, partnership, joint venture, or corporation, although sometimes it has neither independent management nor employees. Most are established for valid business purposes, and transactions involving VIEs have become widespread. Common examples of VIE activities include transfers of financial assets, leasing, hedging financial instruments, research and development, and other arrangements. An enterprise often creates a VIE to accomplish a well-defined and limited business activity and to provide low-cost financing.

Low-cost financing of asset purchases is frequently a benefit available through VIEs. Rather than engaging in the transaction directly, a business enterprise may establish a VIE to purchase and finance an asset acquisition. The VIE then leases the asset back to the business enterprise that established the VIE. This strategy saves the business enterprise money because the VIE is often eligible for a lower interest rate. This advantage is achieved for several reasons. First, the VIE typically operates with a very limited set of assets—in many cases, just one asset. By isolating an asset in a VIE, the asset's risk is isolated from the business enterprise's overall risk. Thus, the VIE creditors remain protected by the specific collateral in the asset. Second, the governing documents can strictly limit the actions of a VIE. These limits further protect lenders by preventing the VIE from engaging in any activities not specified in its agreements. As a major public accounting firm noted,

> The borrower/transferor gains access to a source of funds less expensive than would otherwise be available. This advantage derives from isolating the assets in an entity prohibited from undertaking any other business activity or taking on any additional debt, thereby creating a better security interest in the assets for the lender/investor.[2]

Because governing agreements limit activities and decision making in most VIEs, ownership of a VIE's common stock typically does not provide control of the VIE. In fact, the enterprise that created the VIE may own very little, if any, of the VIE's voting stock. Prior to current consolidation requirements for VIEs, many enterprises left such entities unconsolidated in their financial reports because technically they did not own a majority of the entity's voting stock. In utilizing the VIE as a conduit to provide financing, the related assets and debt were effectively removed from the enterprise's balance sheet.

In general, the party that primarily benefits (or risks losses) from the economic activities of the VIE and has the power to direct the VIE's activities is deemed to have a controlling financial interest in the VIE. We use the term **primary beneficiary** to designate the party with such financial control. The primary beneficiary (most often a business) typically exercises its financial control through governance documents or other contractual agreements that provide it with decision-making authority over the VIE. Once identified, the primary beneficiary must consolidate in its financial statements the VIE's assets, liabilities, revenues, expenses, and noncontrolling interest.

Characteristics of Variable Interest Entities

Similar to most business entities, VIEs generally have assets, liabilities, and investors with equity interests. Unlike most businesses, because a VIE's activities and decision making can be strictly limited, the role of the equity investors can be fairly minor. The VIE may have

---

[1] In its 2001 fourth-quarter 10-Q, Enron recorded earnings restatements of more than $400 million related to its failure to properly consolidate several of its SPEs (e.g., Chewco and LJM2). Enron also admitted an improper omission of $700 million of its SPE's debt. Within a month of the restatements, Enron filed for bankruptcy.

[2] KPMG, "Defining Issues: New Accounting for SPEs," March 1, 2002.

been created specifically by the primary beneficiary to provide it with low-cost financing. Thus, the equity investors may serve simply as a technical requirement to allow the VIE to function as a legal entity. Because they bear relatively low economic risk, equity investors may be provided only a small rate of return.

The small equity investments in a VIE normally are insufficient to induce lenders to provide financing for the VIE. As a result, another party (e.g., the primary beneficiary) must contribute substantial resources—often loans and/or guarantees—to enable the VIE to secure additional financing needed to accomplish its purpose. For example, the primary beneficiary may guarantee the VIE's debt, thus assuming the risk of default. Other contractual arrangements may limit returns to equity holders while participation rights or management fees provide increased profit potential and risks to the primary beneficiary. Risks and rewards such as these cause the primary beneficiary's economic interest to vary depending on the created entity's success—hence the term **variable interest entity.** In contrast to a traditional entity, a VIE's risks and rewards frequently are distributed not according to stock ownership but according to other variable interests. Exhibit 6.1 describes variable interests further and provides several examples.

Variable interests increase a firm's risk as the resources it provides (or guarantees) to the VIE increase. With increased risks come incentives to restrict the VIE's decision making. In fact, a firm with variable interests will regularly limit the equity investors' power through the VIE's governance documents. As noted by FASB ASC (810-10-05-13),

> If the total equity investment at risk is not sufficient to permit the legal entity to finance its activities, the parties providing the necessary additional subordinated financial support most likely will not permit an equity investor to make decisions that may be counter to their interests.

Although the equity investors are technically the owners of the VIE, in reality they may retain little of the traditional responsibilities, risks, and benefits of ownership. In fact, the equity investors sometimes cede financial control of the VIE to those with variable interests in exchange for a guaranteed rate of return. Alternatively, equity ownership is also a variable interest, and a minority equity holder may be the primary beneficiary and end up consolidating the VIE.

Consolidation of Variable Interest Entities

Prior to current financial reporting standards, assets, liabilities, and results of operations for VIEs and other entities frequently were not consolidated with those of the firm that controlled the entity. These firms invoked a reliance on voting interests, as opposed to variable interests,

EXHIBIT 6.1
Examples of Variable Interests

Variable interests in a variable interest entity are contractual, ownership, or other pecuniary interests in an entity that change with changes in the entity's net asset value. Variable interests absorb portions of a variable interest entity's expected losses if they occur or receive portions of the entity's expected residual returns if they occur.

The following are some examples of variable interests and the related potential losses or returns:

Variable interests	Potential losses or returns
• Participation rights.	• Entitles holder to portions of profits.
• Asset purchase options.	• Entitles holder to benefit from increases in asset fair values.
• Debt or guarantee of debt.	• If a VIE cannot repay liabilities, non-repayment of a loan or honoring a debt guarantee will produce a loss.
• Subordinated debt instruments.	• If a VIE's cash flow is insufficient to repay all senior debt, subordinated debt may be required to absorb the loss.
• Lease residual value guarantees.	• If leased asset declines below the residual value, honoring the guarantee will produce a loss.
• Common stock.	• Entitles holder to residual profits, losses, and dividends.
• Management fee contracts.	• Entitles primary beneficiary to receive payment (often variable) from providing management services.

to indicate a lack of a controlling financial interest. As legacy FASB standard *FIN 46R* observed,

> An enterprise's consolidated financial statements include subsidiaries in which the enterprise has a controlling financial interest. That requirement usually has been applied to subsidiaries in which an enterprise has a majority voting interest, but in many circumstances, the enterprise's consolidated financial statements do not include variable interest entities with which it has similar relationships. The voting interest approach is not effective in identifying controlling financial interests in entities that are not controllable through voting interests or in which the equity investors do not bear residual economic risk.[3]

Thus, a business enterprise is required to consolidate the assets and liabilities of a variable interest entity if it can exercise financial control through its role as a primary beneficiary. Variable interests often serve as the vehicle for a controlling financial interest, even in the absence of any equity investment whatsoever.

Business enterprises must first determine if they have a controlling financial interest in any affiliated entity by applying the variable interest model. Each enterprise involved with a VIE must evaluate whether it possesses a controlling financial interest and thus qualifies as the primary beneficiary of the VIE's activities. The VIE's primary beneficiary is then required to include the assets, liabilities, and results of the activities of the VIE in its consolidated financial statements. If the affiliated entity is not a VIE, then a voting interest model is utilized to assess whether financial control exists.

As noted by General Electric Company in a recent annual report:

> Our financial statements consolidate all of our affiliates—entities in which we have a controlling financial interest, most often because we hold a majority voting interest. To determine if we hold a controlling financial interest in an entity, we first evaluate if we are required to apply the variable interest entity (VIE) model to the entity, otherwise, the entity is evaluated under the voting interest model.
>
> Where we hold current or potential rights that give us the power to direct the activities of a VIE that most significantly impact the VIE's economic performance, combined with a variable interest that gives us the right to receive potentially significant benefits or the obligation to absorb potentially significant losses, we have a controlling financial interest in that VIE.

Identification of a Variable Interest Entity

An entity qualifies as a VIE if *either* of the following conditions exists:

- The total equity at risk is not sufficient to permit the entity to finance its activities without additional subordinated financial support provided by any parties, including equity holders. In most cases, if equity at risk is less than 10 percent of total assets, the risk is deemed insufficient.[4]
- The equity investors in the VIE, as a group, lack any one of the following three characteristics of a controlling financial interest:

  1. The power, through voting rights or similar rights, to direct the activities of an entity that most significantly impact the entity's economic performance.
  2. The obligation to absorb the expected losses of the entity (e.g., the primary beneficiary may guarantee a return to the equity investors).
  3. The right to receive the expected residual returns of the entity (e.g., the investors' return may be capped by the entity's governing documents or other arrangements with variable interest holders).

---

[3] (Summary, page 2) *FASB Interpretation No. 46R (FIN 46R),* "Consolidation of Variable Interest Entities," December 2003.

[4] Alternatively, a 10 percent or higher equity interest may also be insufficient. According to GAAP, "Some entities may require an equity investment greater than 10 percent of their assets to finance their activities, especially if they engage in high-risk activities, hold high-risk assets, or have exposure to risks that are not reflected in the reported amounts of the entities' assets or liabilities" (FASB ASC [para. 810-10-25-46]).

Identification of the Primary Beneficiary of the VIE

Once it is established that a firm has a relationship with a VIE, the firm must determine whether it qualifies as the VIE's primary beneficiary. According to FASB ASC (810-10-05-8A), an enterprise with a variable interest that provides it with a controlling financial interest in a variable interest entity is the primary beneficiary and will have both of the following characteristics:

- The power to direct the activities that most significantly impact the VIE's economic performance.
- The obligation to absorb losses of the VIE that could potentially be significant to the VIE or the right to receive benefits from the VIE that could potentially be significant to the VIE.

Note that these characteristics mirror those that the equity investors often lack in a VIE. Instead, the primary beneficiary will absorb a significant share of the VIE's losses or receive a significant share of the VIE's residual returns or both. The fact that the primary beneficiary may own no voting shares whatsoever becomes inconsequential because such shares do not effectively give the equity investors power to exercise control. Thus, a careful examination of the VIE's governing documents, contractual arrangements among parties involved, and who bears the risk is necessary to determine whether a reporting entity possesses control over a VIE.

The magnitude of the effect of consolidating an enterprise's VIEs can be large. For example, Walt Disney Company consolidates its Asian Theme Parks as variable interest entities. In its 2021 annual report, Disney states the following:

> The Company enters into relationships or investments with other entities that may be variable interest entities (VIE). A VIE is consolidated in the financial statements if the Company has the power to direct activities that most significantly impact the economic performance of the VIE and has the obligation to absorb losses or the right to receive benefits from the VIE that could potentially be significant (as defined by ASC 810-10-25-38) to the VIE. Hong Kong Disneyland Resort and Shanghai Disney Resort (collectively the Asia Theme Parks) are VIEs in which the Company has less than 50% equity ownership.

Because Disney has the ability to direct the day-to-day operations and to develop business strategies, and because it receives management fees, Disney consolidates the Asia Theme Parks in its financial statements. As a result of the 2021 consolidation of these VIEs, Disney's total assets increased by $7.5 billion while its total debt increased by $2.2 billion.

Example of a Primary Beneficiary and Consolidated Variable Interest Entity

Assume that Twin Peaks Electric Company seeks to acquire a generating plant for a negotiated price of $400 million from Ace Electric Company. Twin Peaks wishes to expand its market share and expects to be able to sell the electricity generated by the plant acquisition at a profit to its owners.

In reviewing financing alternatives, Twin Peaks observed that its general credit rating allowed for a 4 percent annual interest rate on a debt issue. Twin Peaks also explored the establishment of a separate legal entity whose sole purpose would be to own the electric generating plant and lease it back to Twin Peaks. Because the separate entity would isolate the electric generating plant from Twin Peaks's other risky assets and liabilities and provide specific collateral, an interest rate of 3 percent on the debt is available, producing before-tax savings of $4 million per year. To obtain the lower interest rate, however, Twin Peaks must guarantee the separate entity's debt. Twin Peaks must also maintain certain of its own predefined financial ratios and restrict the amount of additional debt it can assume.

To take advantage of the lower interest rate, on January 1, 2023, Twin Peaks establishes Power Finance Co., an entity designed solely to own, finance, and lease the electric generating plant to Twin Peaks. The documents governing the new entity specify the following:

- The sole purpose of Power Finance is to purchase the Ace electric generating plant, provide equity and debt financing, and lease the plant to Twin Peaks.
- An outside investor will provide $16 million in exchange for a 100 percent nonvoting equity interest in Power Finance.

- Power Finance will issue debt in exchange for $384 million. Because the $16 million equity investment by itself is insufficient to attract low-interest debt financing, Twin Peaks will guarantee the debt.

- Twin Peaks will lease the electric generating plant from Power Finance in exchange for payments of $12 million per year based on a 3 percent fixed interest rate for both the debt and equity investors for an initial lease term of five years.

- At the end of the five-year lease term (or any extension), Twin Peaks must do one of the following:

  - Renew the lease for five years, subject to the approval of the equity investor.

  - Purchase the electric generating plant for $400 million.

  - Sell the electric generating plant to an independent third party. If the proceeds of the sale are insufficient to repay the equity investor, Twin Peaks must make a payment of $16 million to the equity investor.

Once the purchase of the electric generating plant is complete and the equity and debt are issued, Power Finance Company reports the following balance sheet:

POWER FINANCE COMPANY
Balance Sheet
January 1, 2023

Electric Generating Plant	$400 million	Long-Term Debt	$384 million
		Owners' Equity	16 million
Total Assets	$400 million	Total Liabilities and OE	$400 million

Exhibit 6.2 shows the relationships between Twin Peaks, Power Finance, the electric generating plant, and the parties financing the asset purchase.

In evaluating whether Twin Peaks Electric Company must consolidate Power Finance Company, two conditions must be met. First, Power Finance must qualify as a VIE by either (1) an inability to secure financing without additional subordinated support or (2) a lack of either the risk of losses or entitlement to residual returns (or both). Second, Twin Peaks must qualify as the primary beneficiary of Power Finance.

EXHIBIT 6.2
Variable Interest Entity to Facilitate Financing

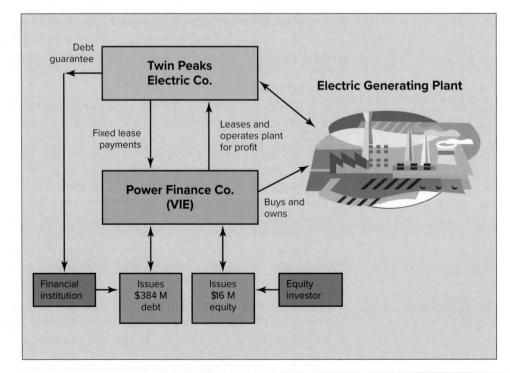

In assessing the first condition, several factors point to VIE status for Power Finance. Its owners' equity comprises only 4 percent of total assets, far short of the 10 percent benchmark. Moreover, Twin Peaks guarantees Power Finance's debt, suggesting insufficient equity to finance its operations without additional support. Finally, the equity investor appears to bear almost no risk with respect to the operations of the Ace electric plant. These characteristics indicate that Power Finance qualifies as a VIE.

In evaluating the second condition for consolidation, an assessment is made to determine whether Twin Peaks qualifies as Power Finance's primary beneficiary. Clearly, Twin Peaks has the power to direct Power Finance's activities. But to qualify for consolidation, Twin Peaks must also have the obligation to absorb losses or the right to receive returns from Power Finance—either of which could potentially be significant to Power Finance. But what possible losses or returns would accrue to Twin Peaks? What are Twin Peaks's variable interests that rise and fall with the fortunes of Power Finance?

As stated in the VIE agreement, Twin Peaks will pay a fixed fee to lease the electric generating plant. It will then operate the plant and sell the electric power in its markets. If the business plan is successful, Twin Peaks will enjoy residual profits from operating while Power Finance's equity investors receive the fixed fee. On the other hand, if prices for electricity fall, Twin Peaks may generate revenues insufficient to cover its lease payments while Power Finance's equity investors are protected from this risk. Moreover, if the plant's fair value increases significantly, Twin Peaks can exercise its option to purchase the plant at a fixed price and either resell it or keep it for its own future use. Alternatively, if Twin Peaks were to sell the plant at a loss, it must pay the equity investors all of their initial investment, furthering the loss to Twin Peaks. Each of these elements points to Twin Peaks as the primary beneficiary of its VIE through variable interests. As the primary beneficiary, Twin Peaks must consolidate the assets, liabilities, and results of operations of Power Finance with its own.

Procedures to Consolidate Variable Interest Entities

As Power Finance's balance sheet exemplifies, VIEs typically possess only a few assets and liabilities. Also, their business activities usually are strictly limited. Thus, the actual procedures to consolidate VIEs are relatively uncomplicated. Nonetheless, ASC (810-10-35-3) provides the following overall guidance:

> The principles of consolidated financial statements in this Topic apply to primary beneficiaries' accounting for consolidated variable interest entities (VIEs). After the initial measurement, the assets, liabilities, and noncontrolling interests of a consolidated VIE shall be accounted for in consolidated financial statements as if the VIE were consolidated based on voting interests . . . The consolidated entity shall follow the requirements for elimination of intra-entity balances and transactions and other matters . . . and existing practices for consolidated subsidiaries.

Initial Measurement Issues

As the ASC states, the financial reporting principles for consolidating variable interest entities require asset, liability, and noncontrolling interest valuations. These valuations initially, and with few exceptions, are based on fair values.

Recall that the acquisition method requires an allocation of the acquired business fair value based on the underlying fair values of its assets and liabilities. The fair-value principle applies to consolidating VIEs in the same manner as business combinations accomplished through voting interests. If the total business fair value of the VIE exceeds the collective fair values of its net assets, goodwill is recognized.[5] Conversely, if the collective fair values of the net assets exceed the total business fair value, then the primary beneficiary recognizes a gain on bargain purchase.

---

[5] The FASB in ASU 2017-01, *Business Combinations (Topic 805): Clarifying the Definition of a Business,* describes the requirement that a business include, at a minimum, an input and a substantive process that together significantly contribute to the ability to create outputs. If the activities of the VIE are so restricted that it does not qualify as a business, the excess fair value is recognized as an acquisition loss, as opposed to goodwill.

In the previous example, assuming that the debt and noncontrolling interests are stated at fair values, Twin Peaks simply includes in its consolidated balance sheet the Electric Generating Plant at $400 million, the Long-Term Debt at $384 million, and a noncontrolling interest of $16 million.

Consolidation of VIEs Subsequent to Initial Measurement

After the initial measurement, consolidations of VIEs with their primary beneficiaries should follow the same process as if the entity were consolidated based on voting interests. Importantly, all intra-entity transactions between the primary beneficiary and the VIE (including management fees, expenses, other sources of income or loss, and intra-entity inventory transfers, etc.) must be eliminated in consolidation. Finally, the VIE's income must be allocated among the parties involved (e.g., equity holders and the primary beneficiary). For a VIE, contractual arrangements, as opposed to ownership percentages, typically specify the distribution of its income. Therefore, a close examination of these contractual arrangements is needed to determine the appropriate allocation of VIE income to its equity owners and those holding variable interests.

LO 6-2

Demonstrate the process to consolidate a primary beneficiary with a variable interest entity.

Consolidation of a Primary Beneficiary and VIE Illustrated

The next example considers (1) the issues that arise when a primary beneficiary obtains control through variable interests of an existing business, and (2) financial reporting for a VIE in periods subsequent to obtaining control.

Assume that on January 1, 2024, Payton Corporation provides a $2,200,000 loan to Vicente, Inc., a business entity. The loan is due on January 1, 2029. Until receiving the loan from Payton, Vicente had been unable to secure the financing needed to continue its operations.

As part of the loan contract, Vicente agrees to provide the following to Payton during the next five years:

- 5 percent annual interest (market rate) on the $2,200,000 loan.
- Decision-making power over Vicente's operating and financing activities.
- An annual management fee equal to 10 percent of Vicente's sales.

At the end of the five-year agreement Payton has the option of either acquiring ownership of Vicente, Inc., for $500,000 or extending the original contract for an additional five years.

As a result of the agreement, Vicente is a variable interest entity, and Payton is its primary beneficiary. Upon consummation of the variable interest agreement, the companies' balance sheets appears as follows:

January 1, 2024	Payton	Vicente
Cash	$ 35,000	$ 2,308,000
Accounts receivable	33,000	145,000
Loan receivable from Vicente	2,200,000	–0–
Patented technology	–0–	9,000
Equipment (net)	2,245,000	400,000
Total assets	$ 4,513,000	$ 2,862,000
Accounts payable	$ (44,000)	$ (644,000)
Long-term debt	(955,000)	(2,200,000)
Common stock	(2,500,000)	(10,000)
Retained earnings, 1/1/24	(1,014,000)	(8,000)
Total liabilities and equity	$(4,513,000)	$(2,862,000)

At January 1, 2024, Payton estimated the fair value of Vicente's common stock at $143,000. The $125,000 difference between the fair value of the common stock and Vicente's book value ($143,000 − $18,000) was attributed entirely to the patented technology with a 10-year estimated remaining life.

Exhibit 6.3 shows the consolidation worksheet for Payton (the primary beneficiary) and Vicente (the variable interest entity) at January 1, 2024, the date Payton obtained financial control over Vicente.

EXHIBIT 6.3 Acquisition-Date Consolidation Worksheet—Primary Beneficiary and VIE

PAYTON AND VICENTE COMPANIES
Consolidation Worksheet
At January 1, 2024

Balance Sheet	Payton	Vicente	Consolidation Entries		Noncontrolling Interest	Consolidated Balance Sheet
Cash	35,000	2,308,000				2,343,000
Accounts receivable	33,000	145,000				178,000
Loan receivable from Vicente	2,200,000			(P)2,200,000		–0–
Patented technology		9,000	(A) 125,000			134,000
Equipment (net)	2,245,000	400,000				2,645,000
Total assets	4,513,000	2,862,000				5,300,000
Accounts payable	(44,000)	(644,000)				(688,000)
Long-term debt	(955,000)	(2,200,000)	(P)2,200,000			(955,000)
Common stock—Payton	(2,500,000)					(2,500,000)
Common stock—Vicente		(10,000)	(S) 10,000			
Retained earnings—Payton	(1,014,000)					(1,014,000)
Retained earning—Vicente		(8,000)	(S) 8,000			
Noncontrolling interest				(S) 18,000		
				(A) 125,000	(143,000)	(143,000)
Total liabilities and equity	(4,513,000)	(2,862,000)	2,343,000	2,343,000		(5,300,000)

Observe that in Exhibit 6.3,

- Consolidation Entry **S** eliminates the VIE's owners' equity account balances and recognizes the 100 percent equity ownership as a noncontrolling interest.
- Consolidation Entry **P** eliminates the intra-entity Long-Term Debt and Loan Receivable from Vicente.
- Consolidation Entry **A** allocates the excess fair over book value to Patented Technology with a corresponding increase in the noncontrolling interest.
- The noncontrolling interest appears in the consolidated balance sheet at its acquisition-date fair value of $143,000.

Consolidation of VIEs Subsequent to Initial Measurement

Following the first year of operations, Exhibit 6.4 shows the consolidation worksheet for December 31, 2024, at the end of the first year in which Payton obtained control of the variable interest entity. At the end of the year, Vicente paid

- A $5,000 dividend to its equity holders.
- The $40,000 management fee (10 percent of Vicente's sales) to Payton. The fee was recorded by Vicente as an other operating expense.
- The $110,000 interest due on the loan to Payton.

The following worksheet entries, as seen in Exhibit 6.4, are used to consolidate the financial statements of Payton Corporation and its VIE, Vicente, as of December 31, 2024:

Consolidation Entry S		
Retained earnings—Vicente 1/1/24	8,000	
Common stock—Valente.	10,000	
Noncontrolling interest		18,000
To eliminate the beginning stockholders' equity of the VIE and recognize the 100 percent equity ownership of the noncontrolling interest.		

EXHIBIT 6.4   Consolidation Worksheet for Primary Beneficiary and VIE (Post-Control)

PAYTON AND VICENTE COMPANIES
Consolidation Worksheet
For the year ended, December 31, 2024

Income Statement	Payton	Vicente	Consolidation Entries		Noncontrolling Interest	Consolidated
Sales	(932,000)	(400,000)				(1,332,000)
Management fee	(40,000)	–0–	(F) 40,000			
Cost of goods sold	530,000	175,000				705,000
Other operating expenses	122,000	95,000	(E) 12,500	(F) 40,000		189,500
Interest income	(110,000)	–0–	(IE) 110,000			–0–
Interest expense	33,000	110,000		(IE) 110,000		33,000
Net income	(397,000)	(20,000)				
Consolidated net income						(404,500)
to noncontrolling interest					(7,500)	7,500
to controlling interest						(397,000)
Statement of Retained Earnings						
Retained earnings, 1/1	(1,014,000)	(8,000)	(S) 8,000			(1,014,000)
Net income	(397,000)	(20,000)				(397,000)
Dividends declared	36,000	5,000			5,000	36,000
Retained earnings, 12/31	(1,375,000)	(23,000)				(1,375,000)
Balance Sheet						
Cash	214,000	8,800				222,800
Accounts receivable	258,000	71,500				329,500
Loan receivable from Vicente	2,200,000	–0–		(P) 2,200,000		–0–
Patented technology		7,200	(A) 125,000	(E) 12,500		119,700
Equipment (net)	2,528,000	2,250,000				4,778,000
Total assets	5,200,000	2,337,500				5,450,000
Accounts payable	(425,000)	(104,500)				(529,500)
Long-term debt	(900,000)	(2,200,000)	(P) 2,200,000			(900,000)
Common stock	(2,500,000)	(10,000)	(S) 10,000			(2,500,000)
Retained earnings, 12/31	(1,375,000)	(23,000)				(1,375,000)
				(A) 125,000		
				(S) 18,000	(143,000)	
Noncontrolling interest					(145,500)	(145,500)
Total liabilities and equities	(5,200,000)	(2,337,500)	2,505,500	2,505,500		(5,450,000)

Consolidation Entry A

Patented technology	125,000	
Noncontrolling interest		125,000

To allocate the excess fair value to patented technology and credit the noncontrolling interest as part of their fair valuation as of the date Payton obtained control.

Consolidation Entry P

Long-term debt	2,200,000	
Loan receivable from Vicente		2,200,000

To eliminate the long-term receivable and debt representing Payton's initial investment in Vicente.

Consolidation Entry E

Other operating expenses	12,500	
Patented technology		12,500

To amortize the excess fair value allocation to unpatented technology over its five-year remaining life.

Consolidation Entry IE

Interest income	110,000	
Interest expense.		110,000

To eliminate the intra-entity interest related to the loan from Payton to Vicente.

Consolidation Entry F

Management fee.	40,000	
Other operating expenses		40,000

To eliminate the intra-entity management fee.

Consolidation Entry F is a new worksheet entry introduced to eliminate the management fee. Such management fees are a common arrangement between variable interest entities and their primary beneficiaries and are routinely eliminated in consolidation. As ASC (810-10-35-3) observes

> Fees or other sources of income or expense between a primary beneficiary and a consolidated VIE shall be eliminated against the related expense or income of the VIE. The resulting effect of that elimination on the net income or expense of the VIE shall be attributed to the primary beneficiary (and not to noncontrolling interests) in the consolidated financial statements.

Both the $40,000 management fee and the $110,000 intra-entity loan interest, although eliminated in consolidation, continue to be allocated to the primary beneficiary because of the contractual arrangement with the VIE. Although the effect of Consolidation Entry F and Consolidation Entry IE eliminations is to increase the VIE's net income by $150,000, none of this increase is attributed to the noncontrolling interest.

In Exhibit 6.4, the $7,500 income allocation to the NCI is computed as all of Vicente's $20,000 net income less the $12,500 control-date excess fair value amortization attributed to Vicente's patented technology. The entire $7,500 is allocated to the noncontrolling interest because Payton, the primary beneficiary, holds no equity interest in Vicente, the VIE. Overall, as shown by Exhibit 6.4, consolidation of a VIE with its primary beneficiary follows a similar process as if the entity were consolidated based on voting interests.

Variable Interest Entity Disclosure Requirements

VIE disclosure requirements are designed to provide users of financial statements with more transparent information about an enterprise's involvement in a VIE. The enhanced disclosures are required for any enterprise that holds a variable interest in a VIE.

Included among the enhanced disclosures are requirements to show:

- The VIE's nature, purpose, size, and activities.
- The significant judgments and assumptions made by an enterprise in determining whether it must consolidate a VIE and/or disclose information about its involvement in a VIE.
- The nature of restrictions on a consolidated VIE's assets and on the settlement of its liabilities reported by an enterprise in its statement of financial position, including the carrying amounts of such assets and liabilities.
- The nature of, and changes in, the risks associated with an enterprise's involvement with the VIE.
- How an enterprise's involvement with the VIE affects the enterprise's financial position, financial performance, and cash flows.

Comparisons with International Accounting Standards

Under both U.S. GAAP and IFRS, a controlling financial interest is the critical concept in assessing whether an entity should be consolidated by a reporting enterprise. Nonetheless, the FASB and IASB so far have employed different criteria to determine the existence of control. IFRS employs a single consolidation model for all entities regardless of whether control is evidenced by voting interests or variable interests. In contrast, U.S. GAAP employs separate models for assessing control for variable interest entities and voting interest entities. As a result, current reporting standards differ across jurisdictions for enterprises seeking to determine whether to consolidate another entity.

The International Accounting Standards Board *IFRS 10,* "Consolidated Financial Statements" and *IFRS 12,* "Disclosure of Interests in Other Entities" cover situations where financial control exists either through a majority voting share or through other means. These standards define control to encompass all possible ways (voting power, contractual power, decision-making rights, etc.) in which one entity can exercise power over another. In particular, the criteria for assessing control are

- Power over an investee—does the reporting entity have the current ability to direct activities that significantly affect another entity's returns?
- Exposure to, or rights to, variable returns from involvement with another entity
- Linkage between power and returns—does the investor have the ability to affect its returns through its power?

These criteria recognize one entity can control another through its power to direct its operating and financing activities. For example, even with less than majority ownership, voting interests can provide an enterprise control if the nonowned shares are diffusely held and lack arrangements to act in a coordinated manner. Control can also be achieved through obtaining decision-making rights that relate to the relevant activities of an investee. Importantly, such decision-making rights can extend beyond merely voting rights. By establishing a broad concept of control as opposed to a bright-line rule (e.g., consolidate if an entity has majority voting rights or the majority of risks and rewards), the IASB seeks to avoid standards that create structuring opportunities to achieve a particular accounting outcome.[6]

IFRS 12 provides for enhanced disclosures about the relationship between a parent and the entities it controls. These disclosures focus on helping investors understand first why a parent controls (or does not control) another entity and the claims of the noncontrolling interest. Second, the disclosures are designed to help investors evaluate the risks assumed by the parent.[7]

Intra-Entity Debt Transactions

LO 6-3

Demonstrate the consolidation procedures to eliminate all intra-entity debt accounts and recognize any associated gain or loss created whenever one company acquires an affiliate's debt instrument from an outside party.

The previous chapter explored the consolidation procedures required by the intra-entity transfer of inventory, land, and depreciable assets. In preparing consolidated financial statements, all resulting gains were deferred until either the asset was sold to an outside party or consumed through use. Deferral was necessary because these gains, although legitimately recognized by the individual companies, were based on activities of the consolidated entity with itself. The separate financial information of each company was adjusted on the worksheet to be consistent with treating the related companies as a single economic concern.

This same objective applies in consolidating all other intra-entity activities: The financial statements must represent the business combination as one enterprise rather than as a group of independent organizations. Consequently, in designing consolidation procedures for

---

[6] Patrick Finnegan, Board Member of the IASB. "At Long-Last—A Single Model for Consolidation," IFRS Foundation, May 2011 perspectives.

[7] Ibid.

intra-entity transactions, we first isolate the effects recorded by the individual companies. After analyzing the impact of each action, worksheet entries recast these events from the vantage point of the business combination. Although this process involves a number of nuances and complexities, the desire for reporting financial information solely from the perspective of the consolidated entity remains constant.

We introduced the intra-entity sales of inventory, land, and depreciable assets together (in Chapter 5) because these transfers result in similar consolidation procedures. In each case, one of the affiliated companies recognizes a gain prior to the time the consolidated entity is entitled to recognize it. The worksheet entries required by these transactions simply realign the separate financial information to agree with the viewpoint of the business combination. The gain is removed, and the inflated asset value is reduced to historical cost.

The next section of this chapter examines the intra-entity acquisition of bonds and notes. Although accounting for the related companies as a single economic entity continues to be the central goal, the consolidation procedures applied to intra-entity debt transactions stand in marked contrast to the process utilized in Chapter 5 for asset transfers.

Before delving into this topic, note that *direct* loans used to transfer funds between affiliated companies create no unique consolidation problems. Regardless of whether bonds or notes generate such amounts, the resulting receivable/payable balances are necessarily identical. Because no money is owed to or from an outside party, these reciprocal accounts must be eliminated in each subsequent consolidation. A worksheet entry simply offsets the two corresponding balances. Furthermore, the interest revenue/expense accounts associated with direct loans also agree and are removed in the same fashion.

Acquisition of Affiliate's Debt from an Outside Party

The difficulties encountered in consolidating intra-entity liabilities relate to a specific type of transaction: the purchase of an affiliate's debt instrument from an outside third party. For example, a subsidiary may have issued bonds in the past that continue to be traded in the open market. If the parent then purchases all or a portion of these outstanding subsidiary bonds in the open market, from a consolidated view, the combined entity (parent and subsidiary) has reacquired its own bonds. Nonetheless, because the companies maintain independent accounting systems, the parent records an Investment in Bonds account as well as periodic interest income. The subsidiary shows the bonds as still outstanding and records periodic interest expense.

Although the individual companies continue to carry both the debt and the investment on their individual financial records, *from a consolidation viewpoint, this liability is effectively retired as of the debt reacquisition date.* From that date forward, the debt is no longer owed to a party outside the business combination. Subsequent interest payments are simply intra-entity cash transfers. To create consolidated statements, worksheet entries must be developed to adjust the various balances to report the debt's effective retirement.

Acquiring an affiliate's bond or note from an unrelated party poses no significant consolidation problems if the purchase price equals the corresponding carrying amount of the liability. Reciprocal balances within the individual records would always be identical in value and easily offset in each subsequent consolidation.

Realistically, though, such reciprocity rarely occurs when a debt instrument is purchased from a third party. A variety of economic factors typically produce a difference between the price paid for the investment and the carrying amount of the obligation. The debt is originally sold under market conditions at a particular time. Any premium or discount associated with this issuance is then amortized over the life of the bond, creating a continuous adjustment to its carrying amount. The acquisition of this instrument at a later date is made at a price influenced by current economic conditions, prevailing interest rates, and myriad other financial and market factors.

Therefore, the cost paid to purchase the debt could be either more or less than the carrying amount of the liability currently found within the issuing company's financial records. *To the business combination, this difference is a gain or loss because the acquisition effectively retires the bond; the debt is no longer owed to an outside party.* For external reporting purposes, this gain or loss must be recognized immediately by the consolidated entity.

Accounting for Intra-Entity Debt Transactions— Individual Financial Records

The following accounting problems emerge in consolidating intra-entity debt transactions:

1. Intra-entity investments in debt securities and related debt accounts must be eliminated in consolidation despite their differing balances.
2. Intra-entity interest revenue/expense (as well as any interest receivable/payable accounts) must be removed although these balances also fail to agree in amount.
3. The amortization process for discounts and premiums causes continual changes in each of the preceding accounts.
4. The business combination must recognize the gain or loss on the effective retirement of the debt, even though it is not recognized within the financial records of either company.

To illustrate, assume that Alpha Company possesses an 80 percent interest in the outstanding voting stock of Omega Company. On January 1, 2021, Omega issued $1 million in 10-year bonds paying cash interest of 9 percent annually. Because of market conditions prevailing on that date, Omega sold the debt for $938,555 to yield an effective interest rate of 10 percent per year. Shortly thereafter, the interest rate began to fall, and by January 1, 2023, Omega made the decision to retire this debt prematurely and refinance it at a currently lower rate. To carry out this plan, Alpha purchased all of these bonds in the open market on January 1, 2023, for $1,057,466. This price was based on an effective yield of 8 percent, which is assumed to be in line with the interest rates at the time.

Many reasons could exist for having Alpha, rather than Omega, reacquire this debt. For example, company cash levels at that date could necessitate Alpha's role as the purchasing agent. Also, contractual limitations could prohibit Omega from repurchasing its own bonds.

In accounting for this business combination, Omega Company's bonds have been effectively retired. Thus, the difference between the $1,057,466 payment and the January 1, 2023, carrying amount of the liability must be recognized in the consolidated statements as a gain or loss. The carrying amount for the debt on that date depends on the amortization process. Exhibit 6.5 shows the bond amortization schedule for January 1, 2021, through December 31, 2024.[8]

As seen in Exhibit 6.5, the carrying amount of Omega Company's bonds has increased to $946,651 as of December 31, 2022, the date immediately before the day that Alpha Company acquired the bonds.

Because Alpha paid $110,815 in excess of the recorded liability ($1,057,466 − $946,651), the consolidated entity must recognize a loss of this amount. After the loss has been acknowledged, the bond is considered to be retired, and no further reporting is necessary by the *business combination* after January 1, 2023.

Despite the simplicity of this approach for consolidation, neither company separately accounts for the event in this manner. Omega retains the $1 million debt balance within its separate financial records and amortizes the remaining discount each year. Annual cash interest payments of $90,000 (9 percent) continue to be made. At the same time, Alpha records the investment at the historical cost of $1,057,466, an amount that also requires periodic

EXHIBIT 6.5
Omega Company Bond Issue Amortization Schedule

Date	Face Value	Unamortized Discount	Carrying Amount	Effective Interest	Cash Interest	Discount Amortized
01/01/21	$1,000,000	$61,445	$938,555			
12/31/21	1,000,000	57,590	942,410	$93,855	$90,000	$3,855
12/31/22	1,000,000	53,349	946,651	94,241	90,000	4,241
12/31/23	1,000,000	48,684	951,316	94,665	90,000	4,665
12/31/24	1,000,000	43,552	956,448	95,132	90,000	5,132

[8] The effective rate method of amortization is demonstrated here because this approach is theoretically preferable. However, the straight-line method can be applied if the resulting balances are not materially different from the figures computed using the effective rate method.

amortization. Furthermore, as the owner of these bonds, Alpha receives the $90,000 interest payments made by Omega.

To organize the accountant's approach to this consolidation, we analyze the subsequent financial records for each company. Omega records only two journal entries during 2023, assuming that interest is paid each December 31:

	Omega Company's Financial Records		
12/31/23	Interest Expense	90,000	
	Cash		90,000
	To record payment of annual cash interest on $1 million, 9 percent bonds payable.		
12/31/23	Interest Expense	4,665	
	Discount on Bonds Payable		4,665
	To adjust interest expense to effective rate based on original yield rate of 10 percent ($946,651 carrying amount for 2023 × 10% = $94,665). Carrying amount increases to $951,316.		

Concurrently, Alpha journalizes entries to record its ownership of this investment:

	Alpha Company's Financial Records		
1/1/23	Investment in Omega Company Bonds	1,057,466	
	Cash		1,057,466
	To record acquisition of $1,000,000 in Omega Company bonds paying 9 percent cash interest, acquired to yield an effective rate of 8 percent.		
12/31/23	Cash	90,000	
	Interest Income		90,000
	To record receipt of cash interest from Omega Company bonds ($1,000,000 × 9%).		
12/31/23	Interest Income	5,403	
	Investment in Omega Company Bonds		5,403
	To reduce $90,000 interest income to effective rate based on original yield rate of 8 percent ($1,057,466 carrying amount for 2023 × 8% = $84,597). Carrying amount decreases to $1,052,063.		

Even a brief review of these entries indicates that the reciprocal accounts to be eliminated within the consolidation process do not agree in amount. You can see the dollar amounts appearing in each set of financial records in Exhibit 6.6. Despite the presence of these recorded balances, none of the four intra-entity accounts (the bond liability, investment,

EXHIBIT 6.6

ALPHA COMPANY AND OMEGA COMPANY Effects of Intra-Entity Debt Transaction 2023		
	Omega Company Reported Debt	**Alpha Company Investment**
2023 interest expense*	$ 94,665	$ –0–
2023 interest income[†]	–0–	(84,597)
Bonds payable.	(1,000,000)	–0–
Discount on bonds payable*	48,684	–0–
Investment in bonds, 12/31/23[†]	–0–	1,052,063
Loss on retirement	–0–	–0–

Note: Parentheses indicate a credit balance.
*Company total is adjusted for 2023 amortization of $4,665 (see journal entry).
[†]Adjusted for 2023 amortization of $5,403 (see journal entry).

interest expense, and interest revenue) appear in the consolidated financial statements. *The only figure that the business combination reports is the $110,815 loss created by the effective extinguishment of this debt.*

Effects on Consolidation Process

As previous discussions indicated, consolidation procedures convert information generated by the individual accounting systems to the perspective of a single economic entity. A worksheet entry is therefore required on December 31, 2023, to eliminate the intra-entity balances shown in Exhibit 6.6 and to recognize the loss resulting from the effective retirement. Mechanically, the differences in the liability and investment balances as well as the interest expense and interest income accounts stem from the $110,815 difference between the purchase price of the investment and the carrying amount of the liability. Recognition of this loss, in effect, bridges the gap between the divergent figures.

Consolidation Entry B (December 31, 2023)		
Bonds Payable	1,000,000	
Interest Income	84,597	
Loss on Retirement of Bonds	110,815	
Discount on Bond Payable		48,684
Investment in Omega Company Bonds		1,052,063
Interest Expense		94,665
To eliminate intra-entity bonds and related interest accounts and to recognize loss on effective retirement. (Labeled **B** in reference to bonds.)		

The preceding entry successfully transforms the separate financial reporting of Alpha and Omega to that appropriate for the business combination. The objective of the consolidation process has been met: The statements present the bonds as having been retired on January 1, 2023. The debt and the corresponding investment are eliminated along with both interest accounts. Only the loss now appears on the worksheet to be reported within the consolidated financial statements.

Assignment of Retirement Gain or Loss

An issue in accounting for intra-entity debt repurchases concerns the assignment of any retirement gains or losses. Should the $110,815 loss just reported be attributed to Alpha or to Omega? From a practical perspective, this assignment affects only the consolidated net income allocation to the controlling and noncontrolling interests. In the absence of FASB guidance on the assignment of retirement gain or loss, all income effects in this textbook relating to intra-entity debt transactions are assigned solely to the parent company. Such treatment is consistent with the perspective that the parent company ultimately controls the repurchase decision.

Intra-Entity Debt Transactions—Years Subsequent to Effective Retirement

Even though the preceding Entry **B** correctly eliminates Omega's bonds in the year of retirement for consolidation purposes, the debt remains within the financial accounts of both companies until maturity. Therefore, in each succeeding time period, all balances must again be consolidated so that the liability is always reported as having been extinguished on January 1, 2023. Unfortunately, a simple repetition of Entry **B** is not possible. Developing the appropriate worksheet entry is complicated by the amortization process that produces continual change in the various account balances. Thus, as a preliminary step in each subsequent consolidation, current carrying amounts, as reported by the two parties, must be identified.

? Discussion Question

WHO LOST THIS $300,000?

Several years ago, Penston Company purchased 90 percent of the outstanding shares of Swansan Corporation. Penston made the acquisition because Swansan produced a vital component used in Penston's manufacturing process. Penston wanted to ensure an adequate supply of this item at a reasonable price. The former owner, James Swansan, retained the remaining 10 percent of Swansan's stock and agreed to continue managing this organization. He was given responsibility for the subsidiary's daily manufacturing operations but not for any financial decisions.

Swansan's takeover has proven to be a successful undertaking for Penston. The subsidiary has managed to supply all of the parent's inventory needs and distribute a variety of items to outside customers.

At a recent meeting, Penston's president and the company's chief financial officer began discussing Swansan's debt position. The subsidiary had a debt-to-equity ratio that seemed unreasonably high considering the significant amount of cash flows being generated by both companies. Payment of the interest expense, especially on the subsidiary's outstanding bonds, was a major cost, one that the corporate officials hoped to reduce. However, the bond indenture specified that Swansan could retire this debt prior to maturity only by paying 107 percent of face value.

This premium was considered prohibitive. Thus, to avoid contractual problems, Penston acquired a large portion of Swansan's liability in the open market for 101 percent of face value. Penston's purchase created an effective loss of $300,000 on the debt, the excess of the price over the carrying amount of the debt, as reported on Swansan's books.

Company accountants currently are computing the noncontrolling interest's share of consolidated net income to be reported for the current year. They are unsure about the impact of this $300,000 loss. The subsidiary's debt was retired, but officials of the parent company made the decision. Who lost this $300,000?

To illustrate, the 2024 journal entries for Alpha and Omega follow. Exhibit 6.7 shows the resulting account balances as of the end of that year.

EXHIBIT 6.7

ALPHA COMPANY AND OMEGA COMPANY Effects of Intra-Entity Debt Transactions 2024		
	Omega Company Reported Debt	Alpha Company Investment
2024 interest expense*........................	$ 95,132	$ –0–
2024 interest income†.........................	–0–	(84,165)
Bonds payable................................	(1,000,000)	–0–
Discount on bonds payable*..................	43,552	–0–
Investment in bonds, 12/31/24†..............	–0–	1,046,228
Income effect within retained earnings, 1/1/24‡.....	94,665	(84,597)

Note: Parentheses indicate a credit balance.
*Company total is adjusted for 2024 amortization of $5,132 (see journal entry).
† Adjusted for 2024 amortization of $5,835 (see journal entry).
‡ The balance shown for the Retained Earnings account of each company represents the 2023 reported interest figures.

Omega Company's Financial Records—December 31, 2024		
Interest Expense	90,000	
Cash		90,000
To record payment of annual cash interest on $1 million, 9 percent bonds payable.		
Interest Expense	5,132	
Discount on Bonds Payable		5,132
To adjust interest expense to effective rate based on an original yield rate of 10 percent ($951,316 carrying amount for 2024 × 10% = $95,132). Carrying amount increases to $956,448.		

Alpha Company's Financial Records—December 31, 2024		
Cash	90,000	
Interest Income		90,000
To record receipt of cash interest from Omega Company bonds.		
Interest Expense	5,835	
Investment in Omega Company Bonds		5,835
To reduce $90,000 interest income to effective rate based on an original yield rate of 8 percent ($1,052,063 carrying amount for 2024 × 8% = $84,165). Carrying amount decreases to $1,046,228.		

After assembling the information in Exhibit 6.7, the necessary December 31, 2024, consolidation entry is prepared. We first assume that the parent applies either the initial value or the partial equity method to its Investment in Omega account. We then show this final consolidation entry assuming the parent applies the equity method.

Parent Applies the Initial Value or Partial Equity Method

To recognize the January 1, 2023, effective retirement on the December 31, 2024, consolidated financial statements, the individual affiliate's balances for the intra-entity bonds and interest income and expense must be removed. Because neither the initial value nor the partial equity method recognizes the retirement loss, the parent's retained earnings will fail to reflect the prior year effective retirement loss. However, retained earnings will reflect past interest income and expense to the extent of any discount or premium amortization.[9] A worksheet adjustment therefore reduces Alpha's January 1, 2024, retained earnings by $110,815 to reflect the original loss net of the prior year's discount and premium amortizations.

Consolidation Entry *B, When Parent Uses the Initial Value or Partial Equity Method (December 31, 2024)		
Bonds Payable	1,000,000	
Interest Income	84,165	
Retained Earnings—Alpha	100,747	
Discount on Bond Payable		43,552
Investment in Omega Company Bonds		1,046,228
Interest Expense		95,132
To eliminate intra-entity bond and related interest accounts and to adjust Alpha's Retained Earnings from $10,068 (currently recorded net debit balance) to $110,815. (Labeled *B in reference to prior year bond transaction.)		

Analysis of this latest consolidation entry should emphasize several important factors:

1. The individual account balances change during the present fiscal period so that the current consolidation entry differs from Entry **B.** These alterations are a result of the amortization

---

[9] If there is no discount or premium amortization, interest revenue will simply offset interest expense, leaving no net effect on retained earnings.

process. To ensure the accuracy of the worksheet entry, the adjusted balances are isolated in Exhibit 6.7.

2. As indicated previously, all income effects arising from intra-entity debt transactions are assigned to the parent company. For this reason, the adjustment to beginning Retained Earnings in Entry *B is attributed to Alpha, as is the $10,967 increase in current income ($95,132 interest expense elimination less the $84,165 interest revenue elimination).[10] Consequently, the noncontrolling interest balances are not altered by Entry *B.

3. The 2024 reduction to beginning Retained Earnings in Entry *B ($100,747) does not agree with the original $110,815 retirement loss. The individual companies have recorded a net deficit balance of $10,068 (the amount by which previous interest expense exceeds interest revenue) at the start of 2024. To achieve the proper consolidated total, an adjustment of only $100,747 is required ($110,815 − $10,068).

Retained earnings balance—consolidation perspective (loss on retirement of debt)...............................		$110,815
Individual retained earnings balances, 1/1/24:		
Omega Company (interest expense—2023)................	$ 94,665	
Alpha Company (interest income—2023)	(84,597)	10,068
Adjustment to consolidated retained earnings, 1/1/24		$100,747

Note: Parentheses indicate a credit balance

The periodic amortization of both the bond payable discount and the premium on the investment impacts the interest expense and revenue recorded by the two companies. As this schedule shows, these two interest accounts do not offset exactly; a $10,068 net residual amount remains in Retained Earnings after the first year. Because this balance continues to increase each year, the subsequent consolidation adjustments to record the loss decrease to $100,747 in 2024 and constantly lesser thereafter. *Over the life of the bond, the amortization process gradually brings the totals in the individual Retained Earnings accounts into agreement with the consolidated balance.*

Parent Applies the Equity Method

Entry *B as shown is appropriate for consolidations in which the parent has applied either the initial value or the partial equity method. However, a deviation is required if the parent uses the equity method for internal reporting purposes. Properly applying the equity method ensures that the parent's income and, hence, its retained earnings are correctly stated prior to consolidation. Alpha would have already recognized the loss in accounting for this investment. Consequently, when the parent applies the equity method, no adjustment to Retained Earnings is needed. In this one case, the $100,747 debit in Entry *B is made to the Investment in Omega Company (instead of Retained Earnings) because the loss has become a component of that account.

Consolidation Entry *B, When Parent Uses the Equity Method (December 31, 2024)		
Bonds Payable...	1,000,000	
Interest Income	84,165	
Investment in Omega.....................................	100,747	
Discount on Bond Payable.............................		43,552
Investment in Omega Company Bonds		1,046,228
Interest Expense....................................		95,132
To eliminate intra-entity bond and related interest accounts and to adjust the Investment in Omega from $10,068 (currently recorded net debit balance) to $110,815. (Labeled "*B" in reference to prior year bond transaction.)		

[10] Had the effects of the retirement been attributed solely to the original issuer of the bonds, the $10,967 addition to current income would have been assigned to Omega (the subsidiary), thus creating a change in the noncontrolling interest computations.

The Entry *B debit to the Investment in Omega account then serves as part of the investment account elimination sequence.

LO 6-4

Understand that subsidiary preferred stock not owned by the parent is a component of the noncontrolling interest and is initially measured at acquisition–date fair value.

Subsidiary Preferred Stock

Although both small and large corporations routinely issue preferred shares, their presence within a subsidiary's equity structure adds a new dimension to the consolidation process. What accounting should be made of a subsidiary's preferred stock and the parent's payments that are made to acquire these shares?

Recall that preferred shares, although typically nonvoting, possess other "preferences" over common shares such as a cumulative dividend preference or participation rights. Some preferred shares even offer limited voting rights. Regardless, preferred shares are part of the subsidiary's stockholders' equity and are treated as such in consolidated financial reports.

The existence of subsidiary preferred shares does little to complicate the consolidation process. The acquisition method measures all business acquisitions (whether 100 percent or less than 100 percent acquired) at their full fair values. In accounting for the acquisition of a subsidiary with preferred stock, the essential process of determining the acquisition-date business fair value of the subsidiary remains intact. Any preferred shares not owned by the parent simply become a component of the noncontrolling interest and are included in the subsidiary business fair-value calculation. The acquisition-date fair value for any subsidiary common and/or preferred shares owned by outsiders becomes the basis for the noncontrolling interest valuation in the parent's consolidated financial reports.

To illustrate, assume that on January 1, 2023, High Company acquires control over Low Company by purchasing 80 percent of its outstanding common stock and 60 percent of its nonvoting, cumulative, preferred stock. Low owns land undervalued in its records by $100,000, but all other assets and liabilities have fair values equal to their book values. High paid $1 million for the common shares and $62,400 for the preferred shares. On the acquisition date, the 20 percent noncontrolling interest in the common shares had a fair value of $250,000, and the 40 percent preferred stock noncontrolling interest had a fair value of $41,600.

Low's capital structure immediately prior to the acquisition is as follows:

Common stock, $20 par value (20,000 shares outstanding)	$ 400,000
Preferred stock, 6% cumulative with a par value of $100	
(1,000 shares outstanding)	100,000
Additional paid-in capital	200,000
Retained earnings	516,000
Total stockholders' equity (book value)	$1,216,000

Exhibit 6.8 shows High's calculation of the acquisition-date fair value of Low and the allocation of the difference between the fair and book values to land and goodwill.

As seen in Exhibit 6.8, the subsidiary's ownership structure (i.e., comprising both preferred and common shares) does not affect the fair-value principle for determining the basis for consolidating the subsidiary. Moreover, the acquisition method follows the same procedure for calculating business fair value regardless of the various preferences the preferred shares may possess. Any cumulative or participating preferences (or other rights) attributed to the preferred shares are assumed to be captured by the acquisition-date fair value of the shares and thus automatically incorporated into the subsidiary's valuation basis for consolidation.

By utilizing the preceding information, we next construct a basic worksheet entry as of January 1, 2023 (the acquisition date). In the presence of both common and preferred subsidiary shares, combining the customary consolidation entries S and A avoids an unnecessary allocation of the subsidiary's retained earnings across these equity shares. The combined

EXHIBIT 6.8

LOW COMPANY **Acquisition-Date Fair Value** **January 1, 2023**	
Consideration transferred for 80% interest in Low's common stock	$1,000,000
Consideration transferred for 60% interest in Low's preferred stock	62,400
Noncontrolling interest in Low's common stock (20%)	250,000
Noncontrolling interest in Low's preferred stock (40%)	41,600
Total fair value of Low on 1/1/23	$1,354,000

HIGH'S ACQUISITION OF LOW **Excess Fair Value Over Book Value Allocation** **January 1, 2023**		
Low Company business fair value		$1,354,000
Low Company book value		1,216,000
Excess acquisition-date fair value over book value		$ 138,000
Assigned to land	$100,000	
Assigned to goodwill	38,000	138,000
		$ –0–

consolidation entry also recognizes the allocations made to the undervalued land and goodwill. No other consolidation entries are needed because no time has passed since the acquisition took place.

Consolidation Entries S and A (combined)		
Common Stock (Low)	400,000	
Preferred Stock (Low)	100,000	
Additional Paid-In Capital (Low)	200,000	
Retained Earnings (Low)	516,000	
Land	100,000	
Goodwill	38,000	
Investment in Low's Common Stock		1,000,000
Investment in Low's Preferred Stock		62,400
Noncontrolling Interest		291,600
To eliminate the subsidiary's common and preferred shares, recognize the fair values of the subsidiary's assets, and recognize the outside ownership.		

The preceding combined consolidation entry recognizes the noncontrolling interest as the total of acquisition-date fair values of $250,000 for the common stock and $41,600 for the preferred shares. Consistent with previous consolidation illustrations throughout the text, the entire subsidiary's stockholders' equity section is eliminated along with the parent's investment accounts—in this case, for both the common and preferred shares.

Allocation of Subsidiary Income

The final factor influencing a consolidation that includes subsidiary preferred shares is the allocation of the company's income between the two types of stock. A division must be made for every period subsequent to the takeover (1) to compute the noncontrolling interest's share and (2) for the parent's own recognition purposes. For a cumulative nonparticipating preferred stock such as the one presently being examined, only the specified annual dividend is attributed to the preferred stock with all remaining income assigned to common stock. Consequently, if we assume that Low reports earnings of $100,000 in 2023 while declaring and paying the annual $6,000 dividend on its preferred stock, we allocate income for consolidation purposes as follows:

	Income
Subsidiary total	$100,000
Preferred stock (6% dividend × $100,000 par value of the stock)	$ 6,000
Common stock (residual amount).	94,000

During 2023, High Company, as the parent, is entitled to $3,600 in dividends ($6,000 × 60%) from Low's preferred stock because of its 60 percent ownership. In addition, High holds 80 percent of Low's common stock so that another $75,200 of the income ($94,000 × 80%) is attributed to the parent. The noncontrolling interest in consolidated net income can be calculated in a similar fashion:

		Percentage Outside Ownership	Noncontrolling Interest
Preferred stock dividend.	$ 6,000	40%	$ 2,400
Income attributed to common stock	94,000	20	18,800
Noncontrolling interest in consolidated net income			$21,200

LO 6-5

Prepare a consolidated statement of cash flows.

Consolidated Statement of Cash Flows

Current accounting standards require that companies include a statement of cash flows among their consolidated financial reports. The main purpose of the statement of cash flows is to provide information about the entity's cash receipts and cash payments during a period. The statement is also designed to show why an entity's net income is different from its operating cash flows. For a consolidated entity, the cash flows relate to the entire business combination, including the parent and all of its subsidiaries.

The statement of cash flows allocates the consolidated entity's overall change in cash during a period to three separate categories:

1. Cash flows from operating activities.
2. Cash flows from investing activities.
3. Cash flows from financing activities.

The cash flows from operating activities can be shown using either the indirect method or the direct method. The indirect method begins with consolidated net income and then adds and subtracts various items to adjust the accrual number to a cash flow amount. The direct method examines cash flows directly from distinct sources that typically include revenues, purchases of inventory, and cash payments of other expenses. However, firms using the direct method must also supplement the statement with the calculation of cash flows from operating activities using the indirect method.

The consolidated statement of cash flows is not prepared from the individual cash flow statements of the separate companies. Instead, the consolidated income statements and balance sheets are first brought together on the worksheet. The cash flows statement is then based on the resulting consolidated figures. Thus, this statement is not actually produced by a consolidation worksheet but is created from numbers generated by the process. Because special accounting procedures are needed in the period when the parent acquires a subsidiary, we first discuss preparation of the consolidated statement of cash flows for periods in which an acquisition takes place, followed by statement preparation in periods subsequent to acquisition.

Acquisition Period Statement of Cash Flows

If a business combination occurs during a particular reporting period, the consolidated cash flow statement must properly reflect several considerations. For many business combinations, the following issues frequently are present.

Business Acquisitions in Exchange for Cash

Cash purchases of businesses are an investing activity. The *net cash outflow* (cash paid less subsidiary cash acquired) is reported as the amount paid in a business acquisition.[11]

Operating Cash Flow Adjustments

Keeping in mind that the focus is on the consolidated entity's cash flows (not just the parent's), consolidated net income is the starting point for the indirect calculation of consolidated operating cash flows. Recall that consolidated net income includes only postacquisition subsidiary revenues and expenses. Therefore, the adjustment to the accrual-based income number must also reflect only postacquisition amounts for the subsidiary. One important category of adjustments to consolidated net income to arrive at cash flows from operations involves changes in current operating accounts (e.g., accounts receivable, accounts payable, etc.).

For example, an increase in an accounts receivable balance typically indicates that a firm's accrual-based sales exceed the actual cash collections for sales during a period. Therefore, in computing operating cash flows, the increase in accounts receivable are deducted from the sales amount (direct method) or the net income (indirect method). However, when an acquisition takes place, the change in accounts receivable will often include amounts from the newly acquired subsidiary. Because the consolidated entity recognizes only postacquisition subsidiary revenues, such acquired receivables do not reflect sales that have been made by the consolidated entity. Therefore, any subsidiary acquisition-date current operating account balances must be removed before calculating the change in accounts receivable.

In fact, any changes in operating balance sheet accounts (accounts receivable, inventory, accounts payable, etc.) must be computed net of the amounts acquired in the combination. Use of the direct method of presenting operating cash flows also reports the separate computations of cash collected from customers and cash paid for inventory net of acquisition-date balances of newly acquired businesses.

Excess Fair-Value Amortizations

Any adjustments arising from the subsidiary's revenues or expenses (e.g., depreciation, amortization) must reflect only postacquisition amounts. Closing the subsidiary's books at the date of acquisition facilitates the determination of the appropriate current-year postacquisition subsidiary effects on the consolidated entity's cash flows.

Subsidiary Dividends Paid

The cash outflow from subsidiary dividends only leaves the consolidated entity when paid to the noncontrolling interest. Thus, dividends paid by a subsidiary to its parent do not appear as financing outflows. However, subsidiary dividends paid to the noncontrolling interest are a component of cash outflows from financing activities.

Intra-Entity Transfers

A significant volume of transfers between affiliated companies comprising a business combination often occurs. The resulting effects of intra-entity activities are eliminated in the preparation of consolidated statements. Likewise, the consolidated statement of cash flows does not include the impact of these transfers. Intra-entity sales and purchases do not change the amount of cash held by the business combination when viewed as a whole. Because the statement of cash flows is derived from the consolidated balance sheet and income statement, the impact of all transfers is already removed. Therefore, the proper presentation of cash flows

---

[11] For acquisitions that do not involve cash, or only partially involve cash, the details of the acquisitions should be provided in a supplemental disclosure to the statement of cash flows for "significant noncash investing and financing activities."

requires no special adjustments for intra-entity transfers. The worksheet entries produce correct balances for the consolidated statement of cash flows.

Consolidated Statement of Cash Flows Illustration

Assume that on July 1, 2023, Pinto Company acquires 90 percent of Salida Company's outstanding stock for $774,000 in cash. At the acquisition date, the 10 percent noncontrolling interest has a fair value of $86,000. Exhibit 6.9 shows book and fair values of Salida's assets and liabilities and Pinto's acquisition-date fair-value allocation schedule.

At the end of 2020, the following comparative balance sheets and consolidated income statement are available:

PINTO COMPANY AND SUBSIDIARY SALIDA COMPANY
Comparative Balance Sheets

	Pinto Co. January 1, 2023	Consolidated December 31, 2023
Cash	$ 170,000	$ 431,000
Accounts receivable (net)	118,000	319,000
Inventory	310,000	395,000
Land	250,000	370,000
Buildings (net)	350,000	426,000
Equipment (net)	1,145,000	1,380,000
Database	–0–	49,000
Total assets	$2,343,000	$3,370,000
Accounts payable	$ 50,000	$ 45,000
Long-term liabilities	18,000	522,000
Common stock	1,500,000	1,500,000
Noncontrolling interest	–0–	98,250
Retained earnings	775,000	1,204,750
Total liabilities and equities	$2,343,000	$3,370,000

PINTO COMPANY AND SUBSIDIARY SALIDA COMPANY
Consolidated Income Statement (partial presentation)
For the Year Ended December 31, 2023

Revenues		$1,255,000
Cost of goods sold	$600,000	
Depreciation	124,000	
Database amortization	1,000	
Interest and other expenses	35,500	760,500
Consolidated net income		$ 494,500

Additional Information for 2023

- The consolidated income statement totals include Salida's postacquisition revenues and expenses.
- During the year, Pinto paid $50,000 in dividends. On August 1, Salida paid a $25,000 dividend.
- During the year, Pinto issued $504,000 in long-term debt at par value.
- No asset purchases or dispositions occurred during the year other than Pinto's acquisition of Salida.

In preparing the consolidated statement of cash flows, note that each adjustment derives from the consolidated income statement or changes from Pinto's January 1, 2023, balance sheet to the consolidated balance sheet at December 31, 2023.

EXHIBIT 6.9

SALIDA COMPANY		
Book and Fair Values		
July 1, 2023		
Account	**Book Value**	**Fair Value**
Cash	$ 35,000	$ 35,000
Accounts receivable	145,000	145,000
Inventory	90,000	90,000
Land	100,000	120,000
Buildings	136,000	136,000
Equipment	259,000	299,000
Database	–0–	50,000
Accounts payable	(15,000)	(15,000)
Net book value	$750,000	$860,000

PINTO'S ACQUISITION OF SALIDA		
Excess Fair-Value over Book-Value Allocation		
July 1, 2023		
Consideration transferred by Pinto		$774,000
Noncontrolling interest fair value		86,000
Salida's total fair value		$860,000
Salida's book value		750,000
Excess fair over book value		$110,000
To land	$ 20,000	
To equipment (5-year remaining life)	40,000	
To database (25-year remaining life)	50,000	110,000
		$ –0–

Depreciation and Amortization

These expenses do not represent current operating cash outflows and thus are added back to convert accrual basis income to cash provided by operating activities.

Increases in Accounts Receivable, Inventory, and Accounts Payable (net of acquisition)

Changes in balance sheet accounts affecting operating cash flows must take into account amounts acquired in business acquisitions. In this case, note that the changes in Accounts Receivable, Inventory, and Accounts Payable are computed as follows:

	Accounts Receivable	Inventory	Accounts Payable
Pinto's balance, 1/1/23	$118,000	$310,000	$50,000
Increase from Salida acquisition	145,000	90,000	15,000
Adjusted beginning balance	263,000	400,000	65,000
Consolidated balance, 12/31/23	319,000	395,000	45,000
Operating cash flow adjustment	$ 56,000	$ 5,000	$20,000

Acquisition of Salida Company

The Investing Activities section of the cash flow statement shows increases and decreases in assets purchased or sold involving cash. The cash outflow from the acquisition of Salida Company is determined as follows:

Cash paid for 90% interest in Salida	$774,000
Cash acquired	(35,000)
Net cash paid for Salida investment	$739,000

Note here that although Pinto acquires only 90 percent of Salida, 100 percent of Salida's cash is offset against the cash consideration paid in the acquisition in determining the investing cash outflow. Ownership divisions between the noncontrolling and controlling interests do not affect reporting for the entity's investing cash flows.

Issue of Long-Term Debt

Pinto Company's issuance of long-term debt represents a cash inflow from financing activities.

Dividends

The dividends paid to Pinto Company owners ($50,000) combined with the dividends paid to the noncontrolling interest ($2,500) represent cash outflows from financing activities.

Based on the consolidated totals from the comparative balance sheets and the consolidated income statement, the following consolidated statement of cash flows is then prepared. Pinto chooses to use the indirect method of reporting cash flows from operating activities.

PINTO COMPANY AND SUBSIDIARY SALIDA COMPANY
Consolidated Statement of Cash Flows (partial presentation)
For the Year Ended December 31, 2023

Consolidated net income		$ 494,500
Depreciation expense	$ 124,000	
Amortization expense	1,000	
Increase in accounts receivable (net of acquisition effects)	(56,000)	
Decrease in inventory (net of acquisition effects)	5,000	
Decrease in accounts payable (net of acquisition effects)	(20,000)	54,000
Net cash provided by operating activities		$ 548,500
Purchase of Salida Company (net of cash acquired)		
Net cash used in investing activities	$(739,000)	(739,000)
Issue long-term debt	$ 504,000	
Dividends	(52,500)	
Net cash provided by financing activities		451,500
Increase in Cash, 1/1/23 to 12/31/23		**$261,000**

Statement of Cash Flows in Periods Subsequent to Acquisition

Preparing a consolidated statement of cash flows during periods of no acquisition is relatively uncomplicated. As before, consolidated net income is the starting point for the indirect calculation of consolidated operating cash flows. If the operating accounts (e.g., accounts receivable, accounts payable, etc.) do not include amounts acquired in a business combination, then no further special adjustments are required. Because the consolidation process eliminates intra-entity balances, preparation of the operating activity section of the statement of cash flows typically proceeds in a straightforward manner using the already available consolidated income statement and balance sheet amounts. Finally, subsidiary dividends paid to the noncontrolling interest are shown as a component of cash outflows from financing activities.

LO 6-6

Compute basic and diluted earnings per share for a business combination.

Consolidated Earnings per Share

The consolidation process affects one other intermediate accounting topic, the computation of earnings per share (EPS). Publicly held companies must disclose EPS each period.

The following steps calculate such figures:

- Determine basic EPS by dividing the parent's share of consolidated net income (after reduction for preferred stock dividends)[12] by the weighted-average number of common stock shares outstanding for the period. If the reporting entity has no dilutive options, warrants, or other convertible items, only basic EPS is presented on the face of the income statement. However, diluted EPS also must be presented if any dilutive convertibles are present.

---

[12] Earnings per share is actually earning per *common* share; thus the reduction of consolidated net income for preferred dividends.

- Compute diluted EPS by combining the effects of *any dilutive securities* with basic earnings per share. Stock options, stock warrants, convertible debt, and convertible preferred stock often qualify as dilutive securities.[13]

In most instances, the computation of EPS for a business combination follows the same general pattern. Consolidated net income attributable to the parent company owners, along with the number of outstanding parent shares, provides the basis for calculating basic EPS. Any convertibles, warrants, or options for the parent's stock that can possibly dilute the reported figure must be included as described earlier in determining diluted EPS.

However, a problem arises if warrants, options, or convertibles that can dilute the subsidiary's earnings are outstanding. Although the parent company is not directly affected, the potential impact of these items on its share of consolidated net income must be given weight in computing diluted EPS for the consolidated income statement. Because of possible conversion, the subsidiary earnings figure included in consolidated net income is not necessarily applicable to the diluted EPS computation.

Moreover, the number of subsidiary shares assumed outstanding can change from the assumed conversion to common shares. The larger number of potential subsidiary common shares can affect the parent's percentage ownership and thus its share of subsidiary income. *Accordingly, the accountant must separately determine the parent's share of subsidiary income in computing consolidated diluted EPS.*

Finally, the focus is on earnings per share for the parent company stockholders, even in the presence of a noncontrolling interest. As stated in FASB ASC (para. 260-10-45-11A):

> For purposes of computing EPS in consolidated financial statements (both basic and diluted),
> if one or more less-than-wholly-owned subsidiaries are included in the consolidated group,
> income from continuing operations and net income shall exclude the income attributable to the
> noncontrolling interest in subsidiaries.

Thus, consolidated income attributable to the parent's interest forms the basis for the numerator in all EPS calculations for consolidated financial reporting.

Earnings per Share Illustration

Assume Parka Corporation has 100,000 shares of its common stock outstanding during the current year. The company also has issued 15,000 shares of nonvoting preferred stock, paying an annual cumulative preferred dividend of $4 per share ($60,000 total). Each of these preferred shares is convertible into two shares of Parka's common stock.

Parka owns 80 percent of Snow Company's common stock. Annual excess fair-value amortization is $13,000, related to various intangibles. Parka is preparing its 2023 EPS computations. During the year, Parka reported separate income of $524,000, and Snow earned $98,000. A simplified calculation below indicates consolidated net income attributable to Parka of $592,000:

Parka's separate income		$524,000
Snow's separate income	$ 98,000	
Amortization expense resulting from original fair-value allocation	(13,000)	
Snow's income after excess fair-value amortization		85,000
Consolidated net income		$609,000
Noncontrolling interest in consolidated net income (20% × $85,000)		(17,000)
Net income attributable to Parka (parent)		$592,000

---

[13] Complete coverage of the EPS computation can be found in virtually any intermediate accounting textbook. To adequately understand this process, a number of complex procedures must be mastered, including calculating the weighted-average number of common shares outstanding and understanding the method of including stock rights, convertible debt, and convertible preferred stock within the computation of diluted EPS.

Snow has 20,000 shares of common stock and $200,000 in convertible bonds outstanding that were originally issued at face value. This debt has both a cash and an effective interest rate of 5 percent ($10,000 per year) and can be converted by the owners into 5,000 shares of Snow's common stock. Parka owns none of these bonds. Snow's tax rate is 25 percent.

To better visualize these factors, the convertible items are scheduled as follows:

Company	Item	Dividend or Interest	Conversion to Common Stock	Parka Owns
Parka	Convertible preferred stock	$60,000/year	32,000 shares	Not applicable
Snow	Convertible bonds	7,500/year*	5,000 shares	–0–

*Interest on the bonds is shown net of the 25 percent tax effect ($10,000 interest less $2,500 tax savings).

Because the subsidiary has a convertible item that can affect the company's outstanding shares and net income, Snow's separate diluted earnings per share must be derived *before* Parka's diluted EPS can be determined. As shown in Exhibit 6.10, Snow's diluted EPS equals $3.70. Four aspects of this schedule should be noted:

- Because the earnings in the schedule will be used to compute consolidated EPS, subsidiary earnings are presented net of excess fair-value amortizations.
- Both Snow's earnings and number of shares change as a result of the potential dilution from the assumed conversion of the convertible bonds to common shares. These diluted figures will be used in the computation of the parent's diluted EPS.
- The individual impact of the convertible bonds ($1.50) did not raise the EPS figures above the $4.25 basic EPS. Thus, the bonds are not antidilutive, and are properly included in these computations.
- Absent the presence of the subsidiary's convertible bonds, the parent's share of consolidated net income would form the basis for computing EPS.

As shown in Exhibit 6.10, Snow's income is $92,500 for diluted EPS. The issue then becomes how much of this amount should be included in computing the parent's diluted EPS. This allocation is based on the percentage of shares controlled by the parent. Note that if the subsidiary's bonds are converted into common shares, Parka's ownership falls from 80 to 64 percent. Consequently, Parka's 64 percent ownership (16,000/25,000) becomes the basis for allocating the subsidiary's $92,500 income to the parent for computing diluted EPS.

Supporting Calculations for Diluted Earnings per Share

	Snow Company Shares	Parka's Percentage	Parka's Ownership
Common stock	20,000	80%	16,000
Possible new shares—convertible bonds	5,000	–0–	–0–
Total	25,000		16,000

Parka's ownership (diluted): 16,000/25,000 = 64%
Income assigned to Parka (diluted earnings per share computation): $92,500 × 64% = $59,200

EXHIBIT 6.10
Subsidiary's Diluted Earnings per Share

SNOW COMPANY Basic and Diluted Earnings per Common Share For Year Ending December 31, 2023			
	Earnings	Shares	Per share
Basic EPS	$85,000	20,000	$4.25
Effect of possible bond conversion:			
Interest saved (net of taxes)	$ 7,500	5,000	$1.50 impact
Diluted EPS	$92,500	25,000	$3.70

EXHIBIT 6.11

PARKA COMPANY AND CONSOLIDATED SUBSIDIARY		
Basic Earnings per Common Share		
For Year Ending December 31, 2023		
	Earnings	Shares
Consolidated net income (to Parka) . .	$592,000	
Parka's shares outstanding		100,000
Preferred stock dividends (Parka) . . .	(60,000)	
Basic EPS	$532,000	100,000 $5.32

Diluted Earnings per Common Share		
For Year Ending December 31, 2023		
	Earnings	Shares
Computed below	$583,200*	
Parka's shares outstanding		100,000
Preferred stock dividends (Parka) . . .	(60,000)	
Effect of possible preferred		
stock (Parka) conversion:		
Dividends saved	60,000 New shares	30,000 $2.00 impact
Diluted EPS	$583,200	130,000 $4.49 (rounded)

*Net income for diluted EPS computation:

Parka's separate income	$524,000
Portion of Snow's income assigned to diluted	
earnings per share calculation	59,200 (computed in supporting calculations)
Earnings of the business combination applicable	
to diluted earnings per share	$583,200

We can now determine Parka Company's EPS. Note that Parka includes only $59,200 of subsidiary income in computing diluted EPS. Because separate income figures are utilized, Exhibit 6.11 above shows separate basic and diluted EPS calculations. Consequently, Parka Company reports basic EPS of $5.32 and diluted earnings per share of $4.49 (rounded) as part of its consolidated income statement.

LO 6-7

Demonstrate the accounting effects of subsidiary stock transactions on the parent's financial records and consolidated financial statements.

Subsidiary Stock Transactions

A note to the financial statements of Gerber Products Company disclosed a transaction carried out by one of the organization's subsidiaries: "The Company's wholly owned Mexican subsidiary sold previously unissued shares of common stock to Grupo Coral, S.A., a Mexican food company, at a price in excess of the shares' net book value." The note added that Gerber had increased consolidated Additional Paid-In Capital by $432,000 as a result of this stock sale.

As this illustration shows, subsidiary stock transactions can alter the level of parent ownership. A subsidiary, for example, can decide to sell previously unissued stock to raise needed capital. Although the parent company can acquire a portion or even all of these new shares, such issues frequently are marketed entirely to outsiders. A subsidiary could also be legally forced to sell additional shares of its stock. As an example, companies holding control over foreign subsidiaries occasionally encounter this problem because of laws in the individual localities. Regulations requiring a certain percentage of local ownership as a prerequisite for operating within a country can mandate issuance of new shares. Of course, changes in the level of parent ownership do not result solely from stock sales: A subsidiary also can repurchase its own stock. The acquisition, as well as the possible retirement, of such treasury shares serves as a means of reducing the percentage of outside ownership.

Changes in Subsidiary Value—Stock Transactions

When a subsidiary subsequently buys or sells its own stock, a nonoperational increase or decrease occurs in the company's fair and book value. Because the transaction need not involve the parent, the parent's investment account does not automatically reflect the effect of this change. However, the parent's percentage ownership of the subsidiary may change. *Thus, a separate adjustment must be recorded to maintain reciprocity between the subsidiary's stockholders' equity accounts and the parent's investment balance.* The accountant measures the impact the stock transaction has on the parent to ensure that this effect is appropriately recorded in the parent's investment account and then reflected in the consolidation process.

An overall perspective of accounting for subsidiary stock transactions follows from the fundamental notion that the parent establishes the subsidiary's valuation basis at fair value as of the acquisition date. Over time, the parent adjusts this initial fair value for subsidiary income less excess amortization and subsidiary dividends. If the subsidiary issues (or buys) any of its own stock subsequent to acquisition, the effect on the parent will depend on whether the price received (or paid) is greater or less than the per-share subsidiary adjusted fair value at that point in time.

An example demonstrates the mechanics of this issue. Assume that on January 1, 2023, Giant Company acquires in the open market 60,000 of Small Company's outstanding 80,000 shares and prepares the following fair-value allocation schedule:

Consideration transferred by Giant	$480,000	
Noncontrolling interest fair value	160,000	
Small Company acquisition-date fair value		$640,000
Small Company acquisition-date book value		
Common stock (80,000 shares outstanding)	$ 80,000	
Additional paid-in capital	200,000	
Retained earnings, 1/1/23	260,000	540,000
Excess fair value assigned to trademark (10-year remaining life)		$100,000

Assuming Small reports earnings of $50,000 in 2023 and pays no dividends, Giant prepares the following routine consolidation entries for the December 31, 2023, worksheet. Giant uses the equity method to account for its 75 percent interest in Small.

December 31, 2023, Consolidation Worksheet Entries

Consolidation Entry S

Common Stock (Small Company)	80,000	
Additional Paid-In Capital (Small Company)	200,000	
Retained Earnings, 1/1/23 (Small Company)	260,000	
Investment in Small Company (75%)		405,000
Noncontrolling Interest in Small Company (25%)		135,000

To eliminate subsidiary's stockholders' equity accounts and recognize noncontrolling interest beginning balance in Small's book value.

Consolidation Entry A

Trademark	100,000	
Investment in Small Company (75%)		75,000
Noncontrolling Interest in Small Company (25%)		25,000

To recognize the excess acquisition-date fair value assigned to Small's trademark with allocations to the controlling and noncontrolling interest.

Consolidation Entry I

Equity in Small's Earnings	30,000	
Investment in Small Company		30,000

To eliminate Giant's equity in Small's earnings [75% × ($50,000 less $10,000 trademark excess amortization)].

Consolidation Entry E

Amortization Expense	10,000	
Trademark		10,000

To recognize the excess trademark amortization ($100,000 ÷ 10 years).

We now introduce a subsidiary stock transaction to demonstrate the effect created on the consolidation process. Assume that on January 1, 2024, Giant announces plans for expansion of Small's operations. To help finance the expansion, Small sells 20,000 previously unissued shares of its common stock to outside parties for $10 per share. After the stock issue, Small's book value is as follows:

Common stock ($1.00 par value with 100,000 shares issued and outstanding)	$100,000
Additional paid-in capital	380,000
Retained earnings, 1/1/24	310,000
Total stockholders' equity, 1/1/24	$790,000

Note that the common stock and additional paid-in capital balances reflect increases from the new stock issue. Retained earnings have also increased from Small's $50,000 income in 2023 (no dividends). Although Small's book value is now $790,000, its valuation for the consolidated entity is derived from its acquisition-date fair value as adjusted through time as follows:

Consideration transferred	$480,000
Noncontrolling interest acquisition-date fair value	160,000
2023 Small income less excess amortization	40,000
Adjusted subsidiary value, 1/1/24	$680,000
Stock issue proceeds ($10 × 20,000 shares)	200,000
Subsidiary valuation basis, 1/1/24	$880,000

Because of Small's stock issue, Giant no longer possesses a 75 percent interest. Instead, the parent now holds 60 percent (60,000 shares of a total of 100,000 shares) of Small Company. The effect on the parent's ownership can be computed as follows:

Small's valuation basis, 1/1/24 (above)	$880,000
Giant's post-issue ownership (60,000 shares ÷ 100,000 shares)	60%
Giant's post, stock issue ownership balance	$528,000
Giant's equity-adjusted investment account [$480,000 + (75% × $40,000)]	510,000
Required adjustment—increase in Giant's additional paid-in capital	$ 18,000

Independent of any action by the parent company, the assigned fair-value equivalency of this investment has risen from $510,000 to $528,000. Small's ability to sell shares of stock at more than the per-share consolidated subsidiary value ($680,000 ÷ 80,000 shares = $8.50 per share) created an increased value for the parent. Therefore, Giant records the $18,000 increment as an adjustment to both its investment account (because the underlying value of the subsidiary has increased) and additional paid-in capital:

Giant Company's Financial Records—January 1, 2024		
Investment in Small Company	18,000	
Additional Paid-In Capital (Giant Company).		18,000
To recognize change in equity of business combination created by Small Company issuing 20,000 additional shares of common stock at above the previously assigned fair value.		

Note that the parent reports a change in stockholders' equity (i.e., Additional Paid-In Capital) for effects from subsidiary stock transactions. GAAP literature states that

> [c]hanges in a parent's ownership interest while the parent retains its controlling financial interest in its subsidiary shall be accounted for as equity transactions (investments by owners and distributions to owners acting in their capacity as owners). Therefore, no gain or loss shall be recognized in consolidated net income or comprehensive income. The carrying amount of the noncontrolling interest shall be adjusted to reflect the change in its ownership interest in the subsidiary. Any difference between the fair value of the consideration received or paid and the amount by which the noncontrolling interest is adjusted shall be recognized in equity attributable to the parent. (FASB ASC [para. 810-10-45-23])

Consistent with this view, this textbook treats the effects from subsidiary stock transactions on the consolidated entity as adjustments to Additional Paid-In Capital.

After the change in the parent's records has been made, the consolidation process can proceed in a normal fashion. Assuming Small reports earnings of $85,000 in 2024 and pays no dividends, Giant prepares the following routine consolidation entries for the December 31, 2024, worksheet. *Although the investment and subsidiary equity accounts are removed here, the change recorded earlier in Giant's Additional Paid-In Capital remains within the consolidated figures.*

December 31, 2024, Consolidation Worksheet Entries

Consolidation Entry S		
Common Stock (Small Company).	100,000	
Additional Paid-In Capital (Small Company).	380,000	
Retained Earnings (Small Company)	310,000	
Investment in Small Company (60%).		474,000
Noncontrolling Interest in Small Company (40%)		316,000
To eliminate subsidiary's stockholders' equity accounts and recognize noncontrolling interest book value beginning balance. Small's capital accounts have been updated to reflect the issuance of 20,000 shares of $1 par value common stock at $10 per share.		

Consolidation Entry A		
Trademark	90,000	
Investment in Small Company (60%).		54,000
Noncontrolling Interest in Small Company (40%)		36,000
To recognize the unamortized excess acquisition-date fair value assigned to Small's trademark as of the beginning of the period with allocations to the controlling and noncontrolling interests' adjusted ownership percentages.		

Consolidation Entry I

Equity in Small's Earnings	45,000	
Investment in Small Company		45,000
To eliminate Giant's equity in Small's earnings [60% ×($85,000 −$10,000 trademark excess amortization)].		

Consolidation Entry E

Amortization Expense	10,000	
Trademark		10,000
To recognize the excess trademark amortization ($100,000 ÷ 10 years).		

The noncontrolling interest now stands at 40 percent ownership. Because these 40 percent owners will share in the profits generated by the subsidiary's trademark, they are allocated a 40 percent share to their overall equity balance in the consolidated financial statements. The noncontrolling interest is also assigned 40 percent of the excess fair-value trademark amortization.

Subsidiary Stock Transactions—Illustrated

No single example can demonstrate the many possible variations that different types of subsidiary stock transactions could create. To provide a working knowledge of this process, we analyze four additional cases briefly, each based on the following scenario.

Assume that Antioch Company acquires 90 percent of the common stock of Westminster Company on January 1, 2023, in exchange for $1,350,000 cash. The acquisition-date fair value of the 10 percent noncontrolling interest is $150,000. At that date, Westminster has the following stockholders' equity accounts:

Common stock—100,000 shares outstanding	$ 200,000
Additional paid-in capital	450,000
Retained earnings, 1/1/23...	750,000
Total stockholders' equity..	$1,400,000

The $100,000 excess acquisition-date fair over book value was allocated to a customer list with a five-year remaining life. In 2023, Westminster reports $190,000 in earnings and declares a $30,000 dividend. Antioch accrues its share of Westminster's income (less excess fair-value amortization related to the customer list) through application of the equity method. Antioch's equity method balance for its investment in Westminster is computed as follows:

Consideration transferred for 90% of Westminster.........................	$1,350,000
Equity earnings of Westminster [90% × ($190,000 − $20,000 excess amortization)]	153,000
Dividends from Westminster (90% × $30,000)	(27,000)
Equity method balance, 12/31/23....................................	$1,476,000

View each of the following cases as an independent situation.

Case 1

Assume that on January 1, 2024, Westminster Company sells 25,000 shares of previously unissued common stock to outside parties for $14.40 per share. This stock issue changes both the parent's percentage interest in the subsidiary and the subsidiary's consolidated valuation basis. The parent's percentage ownership declines to 72 percent (90,000 shares ÷ 125,000 total shares). The subsidiary's valuation basis for consolidation becomes the following:

Consideration transferred	$1,350,000
Noncontrolling interest acquisition-date fair value	150,000
2023 Westminster income less excess amortization.	170,000
Westminster dividends.	(30,000)
Stock issue proceeds ($14.40 × 25,000 shares)	360,000
Subsidiary valuation basis, 1/1/24.	$2,000,000

Next, the effect on the parent's ownership can be computed as follows:

Westminster's valuation basis, 1/1/24 (above)	$2,000,000
Antioch's post–stock issue ownership (90,000 shares ÷ 125,000 shares)	72%
Antioch's post–stock issue ownership balance	$1,440,000
Antioch's pre–stock issue equity-adjusted investment account (above)	1,476,000
Required adjustment—decrease in Antioch's additional paid-in capital.	$ 36,000

To reflect this effect of the stock issue change on its valuation of the subsidiary, the parent makes the following journal entry on its financial records.

Antioch Company's Financial Records		
Additional Paid-In Capital (Antioch Company)	36,000	
Investment in Westminster Company		36,000
To recognize change in equity of business combination created by issuance of 25,000 additional shares of Westminster's common stock.		

Case 2

Assume that on January 1, 2024, Westminster issues 20,000 new shares of common stock for $16 per share. Of this total, Antioch acquires 18,000 shares to maintain its 90 percent level of ownership. Antioch pays a total of $288,000 (18,000 shares × $16) for this additional stock. Outside parties buy the remaining shares.

Under these circumstances, the stock transaction alters the consolidated valuation basis of the subsidiary but not the percentage owned by the parent. Thus, only the subsidiary value must be updated prior to determining the necessity of an equity revaluation:

Consideration transferred	$1,350,000
Noncontrolling interest acquisition-date fair value	150,000
2023 Westminster income less excess amortization.	170,000
Westminster dividends.	(30,000)
Stock issue proceeds ($16 × 20,000 shares)	320,000
Subsidiary valuation basis 1/1/24	$1,960,000

The effect on the parent's ownership is computed as follows:

Westminster's valuation basis 1/1/24 (above)		$1,960,000
Antioch's post–stock issue ownership (108,000 shares ÷ 120,000 shares)		90%
Antioch's post–stock issue ownership balance		$1,764,000
Antioch's equity-adjusted investment account before stock purchase	$1,476,000	
Additional payment for 18,000 shares of Westminster	288,000	1,764,000
Required adjustment		$ –0–

This case requires no adjustment because Antioch's underlying interest remains aligned with the subsidiary's consolidated valuation basis. Any purchase of new stock by the parent in the same ratio as previous ownership does not affect consolidated Additional Paid-In Capital. The transaction creates no proportionate increase or decrease.

Case 3

Assume that instead of issuing new stock, on January 1, 2024, Westminster reacquires all 10,000 shares owned by the noncontrolling interest. It pays $16 per share for this treasury stock.

This illustration presents another type of subsidiary stock transaction: the acquisition of treasury stock. In this case, the effect on the parent can be computed by reference to the amount of noncontrolling interest that must be reduced to zero in the consolidated financial statements.

Noncontrolling interest (NCI) acquisition-date fair value	$ 150,000
NCI share of 2023 Westminster income less excess amortization ($170,000 × 10%)	17,000
NCI share of Westminster dividends ($30,000 × 10%)	(3,000)
Noncontrolling interest valuation basis at 1/1/24	$ 164,000
Treasury stock purchase ($16 × 10,000 shares)	(160,000)
Required adjustment—increase in Antioch's additional paid-in capital	$ 4,000

The consolidated entity paid $160,000 to reduce a $164,000 owners' equity interest (the noncontrolling interest) to zero, thus increasing its own equity by $4,000. As usual, the increase in equity is attributed to additional paid-in capital and is recorded on the parent's records.

Antioch Company's Financial Records		
Investment in Westminster Company	4,000	
Additional Paid-In Capital (Antioch Company)		4,000
To recognize change in equity of business combination created by acquisition of 10,000 treasury shares by Westminster.		

This third illustration represents a newly introduced subsidiary stock transaction, the purchase of treasury stock. Therefore, display of consolidation Entries **S** and **A** are also presented. These entries demonstrate the worksheet eliminations required when the subsidiary holds treasury shares:

Consolidation Entry S		
Common Stock (Westminster Company)	200,000	
Additional Paid-In Capital (Westminster Company)	450,000	
Retained Earnings, 1/1/24 (Westminster Company)	910,000	
Treasury Stock		160,000
Investment in Westminster Company		1,400,000
To eliminate equity accounts of Westminster Company.		

Consolidation Entry A		
Customer List	80,000	
Investment in Westminster Company		80,000
To recognize the beginning-of-year unamortized excess acquisition-date fair value allocated to the customer list.		

Note first the absence of a noncontrolling interest entry. Also note that the sum of the credits to the Investment in Westminster account is $1,480,000, which is the pretreasury stock purchase equity method balance of $1,476,000 plus the $4,000 addition from the acquisition of the noncontrolling interest.

Case 4

Assume that on January 1, 2024, Westminster issues a 10 percent stock dividend (10,000 new shares) to its owners when the stock's fair value is $15 per share.

This final case illustrates another example of a subsidiary stock transaction producing no effect on the parent's records. Stock dividends, whether large or small, capitalize a portion of the issuing company's retained earnings without altering total book value. Shareholders recognize the receipt of a stock dividend as a change in the per share value rather than as an adjustment to the investment balance. Because neither party perceives a net effect, the consolidation process proceeds in a routine fashion. Therefore, a subsidiary stock dividend requires no special treatment prior to development of a worksheet.

Consideration transferred	$1,350,000
Noncontrolling interest acquisition-date fair value	150,000
2023 Westminster income less excess amortization	170,000
Westminster dividends	(30,000)
Subsidiary valuation basis, 1/1/24	$1,640,000
Antioch's ownership (adjusted for 10% stock dividend 99,000 ÷ 110,000 shares)	90%
Antioch's post–stock dividend ownership interest	$1,476,000
Antioch's equity-adjusted investment account	1,476,000
Adjustment required by stock dividend	$ –0–

The consolidation Entries **S** and **A** made just after the stock dividend follow. The $1,404,000 component of the investment account is offset against the stockholders' equity of the subsidiary. Although the stock dividend did not affect the parent's investment, the equity accounts of the subsidiary have been realigned in recognition of the $150,000 stock dividend (10,000 shares of $2 par value stock valued at $15 per share):

Consolidation Entry S

Common Stock (Westminster Company)	220,000	
Additional Paid-In Capital (Westminster Company)	580,000	
Retained Earnings, 1/1/24 (Westminster Company)	760,000	
Investment in Westminster Company (90%)		1,404,000
Noncontrolling Interest (10%)		156,000

Consolidation Entry A

Customer List	80,000	
Investment in Westminster Company		72,000
Noncontrolling Interest		8,000
To recognize the beginning-of-year unamortized excess fair value attributable to the customer list.		

Note here that the sum of the credits to the Investment in Westminster account is $1,476,000, which equals the pre–stock dividend equity method balance.

Summary

1. Variable interest entities (VIEs) typically take the form of a trust, partnership, joint venture, or corporation. In most cases, a sponsoring firm creates these entities to engage in a limited and well-defined set of business activities. Control of VIEs, by design, often does not rest with their equity holders. Instead, control is exercised through contractual arrangements with the sponsoring firm that becomes the entity's "primary beneficiary." These contracts can take the form of leases, participation rights, guarantees, or other residual interests. Through contracting, the primary beneficiary bears a significant portion of the risks and receives a significant portion of the rewards of the entity, often without owning any voting shares. Current accounting standards require a business that has a controlling financial interest in a VIE to consolidate the financial statements of the VIE with its own.

2. In periods after the primary beneficiary gains control over a VIE, consolidation procedures follow a similar process as if the entity were controlled by voting interests. All intra-entity transactions between the primary beneficiary and the VIE must be eliminated in consolidation. The consolidated net income distribution to the noncontrolling interest, however, must be based on the contractual agreement with the primary beneficiary, rather than voting interests.

3. If one member of a business combination acquires an affiliate's debt instrument (e.g., a bond or note) from an outside party, the purchase price usually differs from the carrying amount of the liability. Thus, a gain or loss has been incurred from the perspective of the business combination. However, both the debt and investment remain in the individual financial accounts of the two companies, but the gain or loss goes unrecorded. The consolidation process must adjust all balances to reflect the effective retirement of the debt.

4. Following a related party's acquisition of a company's debt, Interest Income and Expense are recognized. Because these accounts result from intra-entity transactions, they also must be removed in every subsequent consolidation along with the debt and investment figures. Retained Earnings also requires adjustment in each year after the purchase to record the impact of the gain or loss.

5. Amortization of intra-entity debt/investment balances often is necessary because of discounts and/or premiums. Consequently, the Interest Income and Interest Expense figures reported by the two parties will not agree. The closing of these two accounts into Retained Earnings each year gradually reduces the consolidation adjustment that must be made to this equity account.

6. When acquired, many subsidiaries have preferred stock outstanding as well as common stock. The existence of subsidiary preferred shares does little to complicate the consolidation process. The acquisition method values all business acquisitions at their full fair values. If a subsidiary has preferred stock, the essential process of determining its acquisition-date business fair value remains intact. Any preferred shares not owned by the parent simply become a component of the noncontrolling interest and are included in the acquisition-date measure of subsidiary fair value.

7. Every business combination must prepare a statement of cash flows. This statement is not created by consolidating the individual cash flows of the separate companies. Instead, both a consolidated income statement and balance sheet are produced, and the cash flows statement is developed from these figures. Dividends paid to the noncontrolling interest are listed as a financing activity.

8. For most business combinations, the determination of earnings per share (EPS) follows the normal pattern presented in intermediate accounting textbooks. However, if the subsidiary has potentially dilutive items outstanding (stock warrants, convertible preferred stock, convertible bonds, etc.), a different process must be followed. The subsidiary's own diluted EPS is computed as a preliminary procedure. The parent and the outside owners then allocate the earnings used in each of these calculations based on the ownership levels of the subsidiary's shares and the dilutive items. The determination of the EPS figures to be reported for the business combination is based on the portion of consolidated net income assigned to the parent.

9. After the combination is created, a subsidiary may enter into stock transactions such as issuing additional shares or acquiring treasury stock. Such actions normally create a proportional increase or decrease in the subsidiary's equity when compared with the parent's investment. The change is measured and then reflected in the consolidated statements through the Additional Paid-In Capital account. To achieve the appropriate accounting, the parent adjusts the Investment in Subsidiary account as well as its own Additional Paid-In Capital. Because the worksheet does not eliminate this equity balance, the required increase or decrease carries over to the consolidated figures.

Comprehensive Illustration

(*Estimated Time: 35 to 45 Minutes*) Pop, Inc., acquires 90 percent of the 20,000 shares of Son Company's outstanding common stock on December 31, 2022. Of the acquisition-date fair value, it allocates $80,000 to trademarks, a figure amortized at the rate of $2,000 per year. Comparative consolidated balance sheets for 2024 and 2023 are as follows:

Problem: Consolidated Statement of Cash Flows and Earnings per Share

	2024	2023
Cash	$ 210,000	$ 130,000
Accounts receivable	350,000	220,000
Inventory	320,000	278,000
Land, buildings, and equipment (net)	1,090,000	1,120,000
Trademarks	78,000	80,000
Total assets	$2,048,000	$1,828,000
Accounts payable	$ 290,000	$ 296,000
Long-term liabilities	650,000	550,000
Noncontrolling interest	37,800	34,000
Preferred stock (10% cumulative)	100,000	100,000
Common stock (26,000 shares outstanding)	520,000	520,000
Retained earnings, 12/31	450,200	328,000
Total liabilities and stockholders' equity	$2,048,000	$1,828,000

Additional Information for 2024

- Consolidated net income (after adjustments for all intra-entity items) was $178,000.
- Consolidated depreciation and amortization equaled $52,000.
- On April 10, Son sold a building with a $40,000 book value, receiving cash of $50,000. Later that month, Pop borrowed $100,000 from a local bank and purchased equipment for $60,000. These transactions were all with outside parties.
- During the year, Pop declared and paid $40,000 dividends on its common stock and $10,000 on its preferred stock, and Son declared and paid a $20,000 dividend on its common stock.
- Son has long-term convertible debt of $180,000 outstanding included in consolidated liabilities. It recognized interest expense of $16,000 (net of taxes) on this debt during the year. This debt can be exchanged for 10,000 shares of the subsidiary's common stock. Pop owns none of this debt.
- Son recorded $60,000 net income from its own operations. Noncontrolling interest in consolidated net income was $5,800.
- Pop recorded $4,000 in profits on sales of goods to Son. These goods remain in Son's warehouse at December 31.
- Pop applies the equity method to account for its investment in Son. On its own books, Pop recognized $48,200 equity in earnings from Son [90% × ($60,000 less $2,000 amortization) and $4,000 intra-entity gross profit in inventory from its sales to Son].

Required

a. Prepare a consolidated statement of cash flows for Pop, Inc., and Son Company for the year ending December 31, 2024. Use the indirect method for determining the amount of cash provided from operations.[14]

b. Compute basic earnings per share and diluted earnings per share for Pop, Inc.

---

[14] Prior to attempting this problem, a review of an intermediate accounting textbook might be useful to obtain a complete overview of the production of a statement of cash flows.

Solution

a. **Consolidated Statement of Cash Flows**

The problem specifies that the indirect method should be used in preparing the consolidated statement of cash flows. Therefore, all items that do not represent cash flows from operations must be removed from the $178,000 consolidated net income. For example, both the depreciation and amortization are eliminated (noncash items) as well as the gain on the sale of the building (a nonoperational item). In addition, each of the changes in consolidated Accounts Receivable, Inventory, and Accounts Payable produces a noncash impact on net income. The increase in Accounts Receivable, for example, indicates that the sales figure for the period was larger than the amount of cash collected so that adjustment is required in producing this statement.

From the information given, several nonoperational changes in cash can be determined: the bank loan, the acquisition of equipment, the sale of a building, the dividend paid by Son to the noncontrolling interest, and the dividend paid by the parent. Each of these transactions is included in the consolidated statement of cash flows shown in Exhibit 6.12, which explains the $80,000 increase in cash experienced by the entity during 2024.

b. **Earnings per Share**

The subsidiary's convertible debt has a potentially dilutive effect on earnings per share. Therefore, diluted EPS cannot be determined for the business combination directly from consolidated net income. First, the diluted EPS figure must be calculated for the subsidiary. This information is then used in the computations made by the consolidated entity.

Diluted EPS of $2.47 for the subsidiary is determined as follows:

Son Company—Diluted Earnings per Share

	Earnings		Shares	
As reported less excess amortization.....	$58,000		20,000	$2.90
Effect of possible debt conversion:				
Interest saved (net of taxes)	16,000	New shares	10,000	$1.60 impact
				(16,000/10,000)
Diluted EPS............................	$74,000		30,000	$2.47 (rounded)

EXHIBIT 6.12

POP, INC., AND SON COMPANY
Consolidated Statement of Cash Flows
Year Ending December 31, 2024

Cash flows from operating activities		
Consolidated net income		$178,000
Adjustments to reconcile consolidated net income to net cash provided by operating activities:		
Depreciation and amortization..........................	$ 52,000	
Gain on sale of building................................	(10,000)	
Increase in accounts receivable	(130,000)	
Increase in inventory	(42,000)	
Decrease in accounts payable..........................	(6,000)	(136,000)
Net cash provided from operations......................		$ 42,000
Cash flows from investing activities		
Purchase of equipment.................................	$ (60,000)	
Sale of building	50,000	
Net cash used in investing activities.....................		(10,000)
Cash flows from financing activities		
Payment of cash dividends—Pop	$ (50,000)	
Payment of cash dividend to noncontrolling owners of Son ...	(2,000)	
Borrowed from bank	100,000	
Net cash provided by financing activities.................		48,000
Net increase in cash....................................		$ 80,000
Cash, January 1, 2024..................................		130,000
Cash, December 31, 2024		$210,000

EXHIBIT 6.13

POP, INC., AND SON COMPANY
Earnings per Share Year Ending
December 31, 2024

	Earnings	Shares	
Basic Earnings per Share			
Pop's share of consolidated net income	$172,200		
Preferred dividend declared by Pop.............................	(10,000)		
Basic EPS	162,200	26,000	$6.24 (rounded)
Diluted Earnings per Share			
Pop's share of consolidated net income	$172,200		
Remove equity income	(48,200)		
Remove intra-entity gross profit................................	(4,000)		
Preferred stock dividend......................................	(10,000)		
Common shares outstanding (Pop, Inc.)...........................		26,000	
Common stock income—Pop (for EPS computations)	$110,000		
Income of Son (for diluted EPS)	44,400		
Diluted EPS...	$154,400	26,000	$5.94 (rounded)

The parent owns none of the convertible debt included in computing diluted EPS. Pop holds only 18,000 (90 percent of the outstanding common stock) of the 30,000 shares used in this EPS calculation. Consequently, in determining diluted EPS for the parent company, only $44,400 of the subsidiary's income is applicable:

$$\$74,000 \times 18,000/30,000 = \$44,400$$

Exhibit 6.13 reveals basic EPS of $6.24 and diluted EPS of $5.94. Because the subsidiary's earnings figure is included separately in the computation of diluted EPS, the parent's individual income must be identified in the same manner. Thus, the effect of the equity income and intra-entity (downstream) transactions are taken into account in arriving at the parent's separate earnings.

Questions

1. What is a variable interest entity (VIE)?

2. What are variable interests in an entity, and how might they provide financial control over an entity?

3. When is a firm required to consolidate the financial statements of a VIE with its own financial statements?

4. A parent company acquires from a third party bonds that had been issued originally by one of its subsidiaries. What accounting problems are created by this purchase?

5. In Question 4, why is the consolidation process simpler if the bonds had been acquired directly from the subsidiary than from a third party?

6. When a company acquires an affiliated company's debt instruments from a third party, how is the gain or loss on extinguishment of the debt calculated? When should this balance be recognized?

7. Several years ago, Bennett, Inc., bought a portion of the outstanding bonds of Smith Corporation, a subsidiary organization. The acquisition was made from an outside party. In the current year, how should these intra-entity bonds be accounted for within the consolidation process?

8. One company purchases the outstanding debt instruments of an affiliated company on the open market. This transaction creates a gain that is appropriately recognized in the consolidated financial statements of that year. Thereafter, a worksheet adjustment is required to correct the beginning balance of consolidated Retained Earnings (or the parent's Investment in Subsidiary account when the equity method is employed). Why is the amount of this adjustment reduced from year to year?

9. A parent acquires the outstanding bonds of a subsidiary company directly from an outside third party. For consolidation purposes, this transaction creates a gain of $45,000. Should this gain be allocated to the parent or the subsidiary? Why?

10. Perkins Company acquires 90 percent of the outstanding common stock of the Butterfly Corporation as well as 55 percent of its preferred stock. How should these preferred shares be accounted for within the consolidation process?

11. The income statement and the balance sheet are produced using a worksheet, but a consolidated statement of cash flows is not. What process is followed in preparing a consolidated statement of cash flows?

12. How do noncontrolling interest balances affect the consolidated statement of cash flows?

13. In many cases, EPS is computed based on the parent's portion of consolidated net income and parent company shares and convertibles. However, a different process must be used for some business combinations. When is this alternative approach required?

14. A subsidiary has (1) a convertible preferred stock and (2) a convertible bond. How are these items factored into the computation of earnings per share for the parent company?

15. Why might a subsidiary decide to issue new shares of common stock to parties outside the business combination?

16. Washburn Company owns 75 percent of Metcalf Company's outstanding common stock. During the current year, Metcalf issues additional shares to outside parties at a price more than its per share consolidated value. How does this transaction affect the business combination? How is this impact recorded within the consolidated statements?

17. Assume the same information as in Question 16 except that Metcalf issues a 10 percent stock dividend instead of selling new shares of stock. How does this transaction affect the business combination?

Problems

LO 6-1

1. An enterprise that holds a variable interest in a variable interest entity (VIE) is required to consolidate the assets, liabilities, revenues, expenses, and noncontrolling interest of that entity if
   a. The VIE has issued no voting stock.
   b. The variable interest held by the enterprise involves a lease.
   c. The enterprise has a controlling financial interest in the VIE.
   d. Other equity interests in the VIE have the obligation to absorb the expected losses of the VIE.

LO 6-2

2. Porter Corporation is a primary beneficiary for Vince Company, a variable interest entity. When Porter obtained financial control over Vince, any excess fair value over Vince's book value was attributed solely to in-process research and development with an indefinite life. Porter owns 15 percent of Vince Company's common stock and participation rights that entitle it to an additional 40 percent of Vince's net income. In the current year, Porter reports $400,000 of net income before consideration of its investment in Vince. Vince Company reports net income of $100,000. What amount of consolidated net income is attributable to the noncontrolling interest?
   a. $15,000
   b. $45,000
   c. $60,000
   d. $85,000

LO 6-3

3. A parent company buys bonds on the open market that had been previously issued by its subsidiary. The price paid by the parent is less than the carrying amount of the bonds on the subsidiary's records. How should the parent report the difference between the price paid and the carrying amount of the bonds on its consolidated financial statements?
   a. As a loss on retirement of the bonds.
   b. As a gain on retirement of the bonds.
   c. As an increase to interest expense over the remaining life of the bonds.
   d. Because the bonds now represent intra-entity debt, the difference is not reported.

LO 6-3

4. A subsidiary has a debt outstanding that was originally issued at a discount. At the beginning of the current year, the parent company acquired the debt at a slight premium from outside parties. Which of the following statements is true?
   a. Whether the balances agree or not, both the subsequent interest income and interest expense should be reported in a consolidated income statement.
   b. The interest income and interest expense will agree in amount and should be offset for consolidation purposes.
   c. In computing any noncontrolling interest allocation, the interest income should be included but not the interest expense.
   d. Although subsequent interest income and interest expense will not agree in amount, both balances should be eliminated for consolidation purposes.

LO 6-4

5. The parent company acquires all of a subsidiary's common stock but only 70 percent of its preferred shares. This preferred stock pays a 7 percent annual cumulative dividend. No dividends are in arrears at the current time. How is the noncontrolling interest's share of the subsidiary's income computed?

   a. As 30 percent of the subsidiary's preferred dividend.

   b. No allocation is made because the dividends have been paid.

   c. As 30 percent of the subsidiary's income after all dividends have been subtracted.

   d. Income is assigned to the preferred stock based on total par value, and 30 percent of that amount is allocated to the noncontrolling interest.

LO 6-5

6. Aceton Corporation owns 80 percent of the outstanding stock of Voctax, Inc. During the current year, Voctax made $140,000 in sales to Aceton. How does this transfer affect the consolidated statement of cash flows?

   a. The transaction should be included if payment has been made.

   b. Only 80 percent of the transfers should be included because the subsidiary made the sales.

   c. Because the transfers were from a subsidiary organization, the cash flows are reported as investing activities.

   d. Because of the intra-entity nature of the transfers, the amount is not reported in the consolidated cash flow statement.

Problems 7 and 8 are based on the following information:

Comparative consolidated balance sheet data for Iverson, Inc., and its 80 percent–owned subsidiary Oakley Co. follow:

	2024	2023
Cash	$ 7,000	$ 20,000
Accounts receivable (net)	55,000	38,000
Merchandise inventory	85,000	45,000
Buildings and equipment (net)	95,000	105,000
Trademark	85,000	100,000
Totals	$327,000	$308,000
Accounts payable	$ 75,000	$ 63,000
Notes payable, long-term	–0–	25,000
Noncontrolling interest	39,000	35,000
Common stock, $10 par	200,000	200,000
Retained earnings (deficit)	13,000	(15,000)
Totals	$327,000	$308,000

Additional Information for Fiscal Year 2024

- Iverson and Oakley's consolidated net income was $45,000.
- Oakley paid $5,000 in dividends during the year. Iverson paid $12,000 in dividends.
- Oakley sold $11,000 worth of merchandise to Iverson during the year.
- There were no purchases or sales of long-term assets during the year.

In the 2024 consolidated statement of cash flows for Iverson Company:

LO 6-5

7. Net cash flows from operating activities were

   a. $12,000.

   b. $20,000.

   c. $24,000.

   d. $25,000.

LO 6-5

8. Net cash flows from financing activities were

   a. $(25,000).

   b. $(37,000).

   c. $(38,000).

   d. $(42,000).

LO 6-6

9. Bensman Corporation is computing EPS. One of its subsidiaries has stock warrants outstanding. How do these convertible items affect Bensman's EPS computation?

  a. No effect is created because the stock warrants were for the subsidiary company's shares.

  b. The stock warrants are not included in the computation unless they are antidilutive.

  c. The effect of the stock warrants must be computed in deriving the amount of subsidiary income to be included in making the diluted EPS calculation.

  d. The stock warrants are included only in basic EPS but never in diluted EPS.

LO 6-7

10. Arcola, Inc., acquires all 40,000 shares of Tuscola Company for $725,000. A year later, when Arcola's equity-adjusted balance in its investment in Tuscola equals $800,000, Tuscola issues an additional 10,000 shares to outside investors for $25 per share. Which of the following best describes the effect of Tuscola's stock issue on Arcola's investment account?

  a. There is no effect because the shares were all sold to outside parties.

  b. The investment account is reduced because Arcola now owns a smaller percentage of Tuscola.

  c. The investment account is increased because Arcola's share of Tuscola's value has increased.

  d. There is no effect because Arcola maintains control over Tuscola despite the new stock issue.

LO 6-3

11. Dane, Inc., owns Carlton Corporation. For the current year, Dane reports net income (without consideration of its investment in Carlton) of $185,000, and the subsidiary reports $105,000. The parent had a bond payable outstanding on January 1, with a carrying amount of $209,000. The subsidiary acquired the bond on that date for $196,000. During the current year, Dane reported interest expense of $18,000 while Carlton reported interest income of $19,000, both related to the intra-entity bond payable. What is consolidated net income?

  a. $289,000

  b. $291,000

  c. $302,000

  d. $304,000

LO 6-6

12. Mattoon, Inc., owns 80 percent of Effingham Company. For the current year, this combined entity reported consolidated net income of $500,000. Of this amount, $465,000 was attributable to Mattoon's controlling interest while the remaining $35,000 was attributable to the noncontrolling interest. Mattoon has 100,000 shares of common stock outstanding, and Effingham has 25,000 shares outstanding. Neither company has issued preferred shares or has any convertible securities outstanding. On the face of the consolidated income statement, how much should be reported as Mattoon's earnings per share?

  a. $5.00

  b. $4.65

  c. $4.00

  d. $3.88

LO 6-3

13. Ayer Company's books show current earnings of $430,000 and $46,000 in cash dividends. Zane Company earns $164,000 in net income and declares $11,500 in dividends. Ayer has held a 70 percent interest in Zane for several years, an investment with an acquisition-date excess fair over book value attributable solely to indefinite-lived trademarks. Ayer uses the initial value method to account for these shares and includes dividend income in its internal earnings reports.

  On January 1 of the current year, Zane acquired in the open market $64,400 of Ayer's 8 percent bonds. The bonds had originally been issued several years ago at 92, reflecting a 10 percent effective interest rate. On the date of purchase, the carrying amount of the bonds payable was $60,200. Zane paid $56,000 based on a 12 percent effective interest rate over the remaining life of the bonds.

  What is consolidated net income for this year?

  a. $598,900

  b. $589,450

  c. $438,050

  d. $590,850

LO 6-3

14. Perry Company reports current earnings of $420,000 while declaring $52,000 in cash dividends. Swen Company earns $147,000 in net income and declares $13,000 in dividends. Perry has held a 70 percent interest in Swen for several years, an investment with an acquisition-date excess fair over book value attributable solely to an indefinite-lived intangible.

On January 1 of the current year, Swen acquired in the open market $51,600 of Perry's 8 percent bonds. The bonds had originally been issued several years ago at 92, reflecting a 10 percent effective interest rate. On the date of purchase, the carrying amount of the bonds payable was $50,400. Swen paid $49,200 based on a 12 percent effective interest rate over the remaining life of the bonds. What is the noncontrolling interest's share of consolidated net income?

  a. $40,200
  b. $44,100
  c. $40,560
  d. $44,460

LO 6-3

15. Pesto Company possesses 80 percent of Salerno Company's outstanding voting stock. Pesto uses the initial value method to account for this investment. On January 1, 2020, Pesto sold 9 percent bonds payable with a $10 million face value (maturing in 20 years) on the open market at a premium of $600,000. On January 1, 2023, Salerno acquired 40 percent of these same bonds from an outside party at 96.6 percent of face value. Both companies use the straight-line method of amortization. For a 2024 consolidation, what adjustment should be made to Pesto's beginning Retained Earnings as a result of this bond acquisition?

  a. $320,000 increase
  b. $326,000 increase
  c. $331,000 increase
  d. $340,000 increase

LO 6-4

16. On January 1, Tesco Company spent a total of $4,384,000 to acquire control over Blondel Company. This price was based on paying $424,000 for 20 percent of Blondel's preferred stock and $3,960,000 for 90 percent of its outstanding common stock. At the acquisition date, the fair value of the 10 percent noncontrolling interest in Blondel's common stock was $440,000. The fair value of the 80 percent of Blondel's preferred shares not owned by Tesco was $1,696,000. Blondel's stockholders' equity accounts at January 1 were as follows:

Preferred stock—9%, $100 par value, cumulative and participating; 10,000 shares outstanding.	$1,000,000
Common stock—$50 par value; 40,000 shares outstanding.	2,000,000
Retained earnings.	3,000,000
Total stockholders' equity.	$6,000,000

Tesco believes that all of Blondel's accounts approximate their fair values within the company's financial statements. What amount of consolidated goodwill should be recognized?

  a. $ 300,000
  b. $ 316,000
  c. $ 364,000
  d. $ 520,000

LO 6-5

17. Premier Company owns 90 percent of the voting shares of Stanton, Inc. Premier reports sales of $480,000 during the current year, and Stanton reports $264,000. Stanton sold inventory costing $28,800 to Premier (upstream) during the year for $57,600. Of this amount, 25 percent is still in ending inventory at year-end. Total receivables on the consolidated balance sheet were $81,800 at the first of the year and $119,100 at year-end. No intra-entity debt existed at the beginning or end of the year. Using the direct method, what is the consolidated amount of cash collected by the business combination from its customers?

  a. $706,700
  b. $649,100
  c. $686,400
  d. $744,000

LO 6-7

18. Aaron owns 100 percent of the 12,000 shares of Veritable, Inc. The Investment in Veritable account has a balance of $588,000, corresponding to the subsidiary's unamortized acquisition-date fair value of $49 per share. Veritable issues 3,000 new shares to the public for $50 per share. How does this transaction affect the Investment in Veritable account?

  a. It is not affected because the shares were sold to outside parties.
  b. It should be increased by $2,400.

   c. It should be increased by $3,000.

   d. It should be decreased by $117,600.

LO 6-7

19. Poseidon Company purchases 80 percent of the common stock of Stuart Company on January 1, 2020, when Stuart has the following stockholders' equity accounts:

Common stock—40,000 shares outstanding	$100,000
Additional paid-in capital	75,000
Retained earnings, 1/1/20	540,000
Total stockholders' equity	$715,000

   To acquire this interest in Stuart, Poseidon pays a total of $592,000. The acquisition-date fair value of the 20 percent noncontrolling interest was $148,000. Any excess fair value was allocated to an indefinite-lived intangible, which has not experienced any impairment.

   On January 1, 2021, Stuart reports retained earnings of $620,000. Poseidon has accrued the increase in Stuart's retained earnings through application of the equity method.

   View the following requirements as independent situations:

   a. On January 1, 2024, Stuart issues 10,000 additional shares of common stock for $25 per share. Poseidon acquires 8,000 of these shares. Describe the effect of this transaction on the parent company's Additional Paid-In Capital account.

   b. On January 1, 2024, Stuart issues 10,000 additional shares of common stock for $15 per share. Poseidon does not acquire any of this newly issued stock. Compute the effect of this transaction on the parent company's Additional Paid-In Capital account.

   c. On January 1, 2024, Stuart reacquires 8,000 of the outstanding shares of its own common stock for $24 per share. None of these shares belonged to Poseidon. Compute the effect of this transaction on the parent company's Additional Paid-In Capital account.

LO 6-1

20. Paige Clothing Company (Paige) helped form Apparel Media LLC, a company that will conduct e-commerce sales for Paige through a dedicated internet site. Two outside investors contributed $50,000 in start-up capital to Apparel Media as the sole owners of the company. Apparel Media's governing contract stipulates the following:

   • Paige is to be Apparel Media's sole client, and Paige must approve any expenditures by Apparel Media.

   • Apparel Media will receive a fee of 5 percent of all sales revenue generated through its e-commerce internet site up to a maximum fee of $30,000 per year. The maximum fee will increase by 4 percent per year.

   • Paige and Apparel Media will pay 50 percent of the costs to maintain the internet site. However, if Apparel Media's fees are insufficient to cover its 50 percent share of the costs, Paige will reimburse Apparel Media for the loss.

   Explain whether Apparel Media qualifies as a variable interest entity. Explain whether Paige should consolidate Apparel Media.

LO 6-1

21. The following describes a set of arrangements between TecPC Company and a variable interest entity (VIE) as of December 31, 2023. TecPC agrees to design and construct a new research and development (R&D) facility. The VIE's sole purpose is to finance and own the R&D facility and lease it to TecPC Company after construction is completed. Payments under the operating lease are expected to begin in the first quarter of 2025.

   The VIE has financing commitments sufficient for the construction project from equity and debt participants (investors) of $4 million and $42 million, respectively. TecPC, in its role as the VIE's construction agent, is responsible for completing construction by December 31, 2023. TecPC has guaranteed a portion of the VIE's obligations during the construction and post-construction periods.

   TecPC agrees to lease the R&D facility for five years with multiple extension options. The lease is a variable rate obligation indexed to a three-month market rate. As market interest rates increase or decrease, the payments under this operating lease also increase or decrease, sufficient to provide a return to the investors. If all extension options are exercised, the total lease term is 35 years.

   At the end of the first five-year lease term or any extension, TecPC may choose one of the following:

   • Renew the lease at fair value subject to investor approval.

   • Purchase the facility at its original construction cost.

- Sell the facility on the VIE's behalf to an independent third party. If TecPC sells the project and the proceeds from the sale are insufficient to repay the investors their original cost, TecPC may be required to pay the VIE up to 85 percent of the project's cost.

a. What is the purpose of reporting consolidated statements for a company and the entities that it controls?

b. When should a VIE's financial statements be consolidated with those of another company?

c. Identify the risks of ownership of the R&D facility that (1) TecPC has effectively shifted to the VIE's owners and (2) remain with TecPC.

d. What characteristics of a primary beneficiary does TecPC possess?

22. On December 31, 2023, Petra Company invests $20,000 in Valery, a variable interest entity. In contractual agreements completed on that date, Petra established itself as the primary beneficiary of Valery. Previously, Petra had no equity interest in Valery. Immediately after Petra's investment, Valery presents the following balance sheet:

Cash	$ 20,000	Long-term debt	$120,000
Marketing software	140,000	Noncontrolling interest	60,000
Computer equipment	40,000	Petra equity interest	20,000
Total assets	$200,000	Total liabilities and equity	$200,000

Each of the amounts represents an assessed fair value at December 31, 2023, except for the marketing software. The December 31 business fair value of Valery is assessed at $80,000.

a. If the carrying amount of the marketing software was undervalued by $25,000, what amounts for Valery would appear in Petra's December 31, 2023, consolidated financial statements?

b. If the carrying amount of the marketing software was overvalued by $25,000, what amounts for Valery would appear in Petra's December 31, 2023, consolidated financial statements?

23. On January 1, 2024, Platform Company exchanged $1,000,000 for 40 percent of the outstanding voting stock of Vector Company. Especially attractive to Platform was a research project underway at Vector that would enhance both the speed and quantity of client-accessible data. Although not recorded in Vector's financial records, the fair value of the research project was considered to be $1,960,000. Also Vector possessed unpatented technology with a fair value of $376,000.

In contractual agreements with the sole owner of the remaining 60 percent of Vector, Platform was granted (1) various decision-making rights over Vector's operating decisions and (2) special service purchase provisions at below-market rates. As a result of these contractual agreements, Platform established itself as the primary beneficiary of Vector. Immediately after the purchase, Platform and Vector presented the following balance sheets:

	Platform	Vector
Cash	$ 61,000	$ 41,000
Investment in Vector	1,000,000	
Capitalized software	981,000	156,000
Computer equipment	1,066,000	56,000
Communications equipment	916,000	336,000
Patent		191,000
Total assets	$ 4,024,000	$ 780,000
Long-term debt	(941,000)	(616,000)
Common stock—Platform	(2,660,000)	
Common stock—Vector		(41,000)
Retained earnings	(423,000)	(123,000)
Total liabilities and equity	$(4,024,000)	$(780,000)

Each of the above amounts represents a fair value at January 1, 2024. The fair value of the 60 percent of Vector shares not owned by Platform was estimated at $1,500,000.

Prepare an acquisition-date consolidation worksheet for Platform and its variable interest entity.

24. On January 1, 2024, Pikes Corporation loaned Venti Company $300,000 and agreed to guarantee all of Venti's long-term debt in exchange for (1) decision-making authority over all of Venti's

activities and (2) an annual management fee of 25 percent of Venti's annual revenues. As a result of the agreement, Pikes becomes the primary beneficiary of Venti (now a variable interest entity). Pikes's loan to Venti stipulated a 7 percent (market) rate of interest to be paid annually with principal due in 10 years.

On January 1, 2024, Pikes estimated that the fair value of Venti's equity shares equaled $75,000 while Venti's book value was $55,000. Any excess fair over book value at that date was attributed to Venti's trademark with an indefinite life. Because Pikes owns no equity in Venti, all of the acquisition-date excess fair over book value is allocated to the noncontrolling interest.

Venti paid Pikes 25 percent of its 2024 revenues at the end of the year and recorded the payment in other operating expenses. Venti also paid the interest to Pikes for the loan. On December 31, 2024, Pikes and Venti submitted the following statements for consolidation. (Parentheses indicate credit balances.)

	Pikes	Venti
Revenues	(792,000)	(216,000)
Management fee	(54,000)	–0–
Cost of good sold	621,000	89,000
Other operating expenses	76,000	64,000
Interest income	(21,000)	–0–
Interest expense	–0–	39,000
Net income	(170,000)	(24,000)
Retained earnings, 1/1	(1,380,000)	(40,000)
Net income	(170,000)	(24,000)
Dividends declared	75,000	–0–
Retained earnings, 12/31	(1,475,000)	(64,000)
Current assets	360,000	73,000
Loan receivable from Venti	300,000	–0–
Equipment (net)	895,000	527,000
Trademark	–0–	125,000
Total assets	1,555,000	725,000
Current liabilities	(30,000)	(92,000)
Loan payable to Pikes	–0–	(300,000)
Other long-term debt	–0–	(254,000)
Common stock	(50,000)	(15,000)
Retained earnings, 12/31	(1,475,000)	(64,000)
Total liabilities and equity	(1,555,000)	(725,000)

Prepare the December 31, 2024, consolidation worksheet for Pikes and its variable interest entity Venti.

LO 6-3

25. Cairns owns 75 percent of the voting stock of Hamilton, Inc. The parent's interest was acquired several years ago on the date that the subsidiary was formed. Consequently, no goodwill or other allocation was recorded in connection with the acquisition. Cairns uses the equity method in its internal records to account for its investment in Hamilton.

On January 1, 2020, Hamilton sold $1,000,000 in 10-year bonds to the public at 105. The bonds had a cash interest rate of 9 percent payable every December 31. Cairns acquired 40 percent of these bonds at 96 percent of face value on January 1, 2022. Both companies utilize the straight-line method of amortization. Prepare the consolidation worksheet entries to recognize the effects of the intra-entity bonds at each of the following dates.

 a. December 31, 2022

 b. December 31, 2023

 c. December 31, 2024

LO 6-3

26. Highlight, Inc., owns all outstanding stock of Kiort Corporation. The two companies report the following balances for the year ending December 31, 2023:

	Highlight	Kiort
Revenues and interest income.	$(670,000)	$(390,000)
Operating and interest expense	540,000	221,000
Other gains and losses	(120,000)	(32,000)
Net income.	$(250,000)	$(201,000)

On January 1, 2023, Highlight acquired on the open market bonds for $108,000 originally issued by Kiort. This investment had an effective rate of 8 percent. The bonds had a face value of $100,000 and a cash interest rate of 9 percent. At the date of acquisition, these bonds were shown as liabilities by Kiort with a carrying amount of $84,000 (based on an effective rate of 11 percent). Determine the balances that should appear on a consolidated income statement for 2023.

LO 6-3

27. Several years ago, Brant, Inc., sold $900,000 in bonds to the public. Annual cash interest of 9 percent ($81,000) was to be paid on this debt. The bonds were issued at a discount to yield 12 percent. At the beginning of 2019, Zack Corporation (a wholly owned subsidiary of Brant) purchased $180,000 of these bonds on the open market for $201,000, a price based on an effective interest rate of 7 percent. The bond liability had a carrying amount on that date of $760,000. Assume Brant uses the equity method to account internally for its investment in Zack.

   a. What consolidation entry would be required for these bonds on December 31, 2022?

   b. What consolidation entry would be required for these bonds on December 31, 2024?

LO 6-3

28. Paulina, Incorporated, owns 90 percent of Southport Company. On January 1, 2024, Paulina acquires half of Southport's $500,000 outstanding 13-year bonds. These bonds had been sold on the open market on January 1, 2021, at a 12 percent effective rate. The bonds pay a cash interest rate of 10 percent every December 31 and are scheduled to come due on December 31, 2033. Southport issued this debt originally for $435,765. Paulina paid $283,550 for this investment, indicating an 8 percent effective yield.

   a. Assuming that both parties use the effective rate method, what gain or loss from the retirement of this debt should be reported on the consolidated income statement for 2023?

   b. Assuming that both parties use the effective rate method, what balances should appear in the Investment in Southport Bonds account on Paulina's records and the Bonds Payable account of Southport as of December 31, 2024?

   c. Assuming that both parties use the straight-line method, what consolidation entry would be required on December 31, 2024, because of these bonds? Assume that the parent is not applying the equity method.

LO 6-4

29. Hepner Corporation has the following stockholders' equity accounts:

Preferred stock (6% cumulative dividend)	$500,000
Common stock	750,000
Additional paid-in capital	300,000
Retained earnings	950,000

The preferred stock is participating. Wasatch Corporation buys 80 percent of this common stock for $1,600,000 and 70 percent of the preferred stock for $630,000. The acquisition-date fair value of the noncontrolling interest in the common shares was $400,000 and was $270,000 for the preferred shares. All of the subsidiary's assets and liabilities are viewed as having fair values equal to their book values. What amount is attributed to goodwill on the date of acquisition?

LO 6-4

30. Smith, Inc., has the following stockholders' equity accounts as of January 1, 2024:

Preferred stock—$100 par, nonvoting and nonparticipating, 8% cumulative dividend	$2,000,000
Common stock—$20 par value	4,000,000
Retained earnings	10,000,000

Haried Company purchases all of Smith's common stock on January 1, 2024, for $14,040,000. The preferred stock remains in the hands of outside parties. Any excess acquisition-date fair value will be assigned to franchise contracts with a 40-year remaining life.

During 2024, Smith reports earning $450,000 in net income and declares $360,000 in cash dividends. Haried applies the equity method to this investment.

a. What is the noncontrolling interest's share of consolidated net income for this period?

b. What is the balance in the Investment in Smith account as of December 31, 2024?

c. What consolidation entries are needed for 2024?

LO 6-5

31. The following information has been taken from the consolidation worksheet of Peak and its 90 percent–owned subsidiary, Valley:

- Peak reports a $12,000 gain on the sale of a building. The building had a book value of $32,000 but was sold for $44,000 cash.
- Intra-entity inventory transfers of $129,000 occurred during the current period.
- Valley declared and paid a $30,000 dividend during the year, with $27,000 of this amount going to Peak.
- Amortization of an intangible asset recognized by Peak's worksheet was $16,000 for the current period.
- Consolidated accounts payable decreased by $11,000 during the year.

Indicate how to reflect each of these events on a consolidated statement of cash flows.

LO 6-5

32. Alford Company and its 80 percent–owned subsidiary, Knight, have the following income statements for 2024:

	Alford	Knight
Revenues	$(500,000)	$(230,000)
Cost of goods sold	300,000	140,000
Depreciation and amortization	40,000	10,000
Other expenses	20,000	20,000
Gain on sale of equipment	(30,000)	–0–
Equity in earnings of Knight	(36,200)	–0–
Net income	$(206,200)	$ (60,000)

Additional Information for 2024

- Intra-entity inventory transfers during the year amounted to $90,000. All intra-entity transfers were downstream from Alford to Knight.
- Intra-entity gross profits in inventory at January 1 were $6,000, but at December 31 they are $9,000.
- Annual excess amortization expense resulting from the acquisition is $11,000.
- Knight paid dividends totaling $20,000.
- The noncontrolling interest's share of the subsidiary's income is $9,800.
- During the year, consolidated inventory rose by $11,000 while accounts receivable and accounts payable declined by $8,000 and $6,000, respectively.

Using either the direct or indirect method, compute net cash flows from operating activities during the period for the business combination.

LO 6-6

33. Porter Corporation owns all 30,000 shares of the common stock of Street, Inc. Porter has 60,000 shares of its own common stock outstanding. During the current year, Porter earns net income (without any consideration of its investment in Street) of $150,000 while Street reports $130,000. Annual amortization of $10,000 is recognized each year on the consolidation worksheet based on acquisition-date fair-value allocations. Both companies have convertible bonds outstanding. During the current year, bond-related interest expense (net of taxes) is $32,000 for Porter and $24,000 for Street. Porter's bonds can be converted into 8,000 shares of common stock; Street's bonds can be converted into 10,000 shares. Porter owns none of these bonds. What are the earnings per share amounts that Porter should report in its current year consolidated income statement?

LO 6-6

34. Primus, Inc., owns all outstanding stock of Sonston, Inc. For the current year, Primus reports net income (exclusive of any investment income) of $600,000. Primus has 100,000 shares of common stock outstanding. Sonston reports net income of $200,000 for the period, with 40,000 shares of common stock outstanding. Sonston also has 10,000 stock warrants outstanding that allow the holder to acquire shares at $10 per share. The value of this stock was $20 per share throughout the year. Primus owns 2,000 of these warrants. What amount should Primus report for diluted earnings per share?

LO 6-6

35. Bravo, Inc., owns all of the stock of Echo, Inc. For 2024, Bravo reports income (exclusive of any investment income) of $480,000. Bravo has 80,000 shares of common stock outstanding. It also has 5,000 shares of preferred stock outstanding that pay a dividend of $15,000 per year. Echo reports net income of $290,000 for the period with 80,000 shares of common stock outstanding. Echo also has a liability from its 10,000, $100 bonds that pay annual interest of $8 per bond. Each of these bonds can be converted into two shares of common stock. Bravo owns none of these bonds. Assume a tax rate of 21 percent. What amount should Bravo report as diluted earnings per share?

LO 6-7

36. DeMilo, Inc., owns 100 percent of the 40,000 outstanding shares of Ricardo, Inc. DeMilo currently carries the Investment in Ricardo account at $490,000 using the equity method.

    Ricardo issues 10,000 new shares to the public for $15.75 per share. How does this transaction affect the Investment in Ricardo account that appears on DeMilo's financial records?

LO 6-7

37. Albuquerque, Inc., acquired 16,000 shares of Marmon Company several years ago for $600,000. At the acquisition date, Marmon reported a book value of $710,000, and Albuquerque assessed the fair value of the noncontrolling interest at $150,000. Any excess of acquisition-date fair value over book value was assigned to broadcast licenses with indefinite lives. Since the acquisition date and until this point, Marmon has issued no additional shares. No impairment has been recognized for the broadcast licenses.

    At the present time, Marmon reports $800,000 as total stockholders' equity, which is broken down as follows:

Common stock ($10 par value)	$200,000
Additional paid-in capital	230,000
Retained earnings	370,000
Total	$800,000

    View the following as independent situations:

    a. Marmon sells 5,000 shares of previously unissued common stock to the public for $47 per share. Albuquerque purchased none of this stock. What journal entry should Albuquerque make to recognize the impact of this stock transaction?

    b. Marmon sells 4,000 shares of previously unissued common stock to the public for $33 per share. Albuquerque purchased none of this stock. What journal entry should Albuquerque make to recognize the impact of this stock transaction?

LO 6-7

38. On January 1, 2022, Aronsen Company acquired 90 percent of Siedel Company's outstanding shares. Siedel had a net book value on that date of $480,000: common stock ($10 par value) of $200,000 and retained earnings of $280,000.

    Aronsen paid $584,100 for this investment. The acquisition-date fair value of the 10 percent noncontrolling interest was $64,900. The excess fair value over book value associated with the acquisition was used to increase land by $89,000 and to recognize copyrights (16-year remaining life) at $80,000. Subsequent to the acquisition, Aronsen applied the initial value method to its investment account.

    In the 2022–2023 period, the subsidiary's retained earnings increased by $100,000. During 2024, Siedel earned income of $80,000 while declaring $20,000 in dividends. Also, at the beginning of 2024, Siedel issued 4,000 new shares of common stock for $38 per share to finance the expansion of its corporate facilities. Aronsen purchased none of these additional shares and therefore recorded no entry. Prepare the appropriate 2024 consolidation entries for these two companies.

LO 6-3

39. Pavin acquires all of Stabler's outstanding shares on January 1, 2021, for $460,000 in cash. Of this amount, $30,000 was attributed to equipment with a 10-year remaining life and $40,000 was assigned to trademarks expensed over a 20-year period. Pavin applies the partial equity method so that income is accrued each period based solely on the earnings reported by the subsidiary.

    On January 1, 2024, Pavin reports $300,000 in bonds outstanding with a carrying amount of $282,000. Stabler purchases half of these bonds on the open market for $145,500.

    During 2024, Pavin begins to sell merchandise to Stabler. During that year, inventory costing $80,000 was transferred at a price of $100,000. All but $10,000 (at sales price) of these goods were resold to outside parties by year-end. Stabler still owes $33,000 for inventory shipped from Pavin during December.

    The following financial figures are for the two companies for the year ending December 31, 2024. Dividends were both declared and paid during the current year. Prepare a worksheet to produce consolidated balances. (Credits are indicated by parentheses.)

	Pavin	Stabler
Revenues	$ (740,000)	$(505,000)
Cost of goods sold	455,000	240,000
Expenses	125,000	158,500
Interest expense—bonds.	36,000	–0–
Interest income—bond investment	–0–	(16,500)
Loss on extinguishment of bonds	–0–	–0–
Equity in Stabler's income	(123,000)	–0–
Net income.	$ (247,000)	$(123,000)
Retained earnings, 1/1/24.	$ (345,000)	$(361,000)
Net income (above)	(247,000)	(123,000)
Dividends declared.	155,000	61,000
Retained earnings, 12/31/24	$ (437,000)	$(423,000)
Cash and receivables.	$ 217,000	$ 35,000
Inventory.	175,000	87,000
Investment in Stabler	613,000	–0–
Investment in Pavin bonds	–0–	147,000
Land, buildings, and equipment (net)	245,000	541,000
Trademarks	–0–	–0–
Total assets	$ 1,250,000	$ 810,000
Accounts payable	$ (225,000)	$(167,000)
Bonds payable.	(300,000)	(100,000)
Discount on bonds	12,000	–0–
Common stock	(300,000)	(120,000)
Retained earnings (above).	(437,000)	(423,000)
Total liabilities and stockholders' equity.	$(1,250,000)	$(810,000)

LO 6-3

40. Paiton, Inc., and Sandra Corporation formed a business combination on January 1, 2022, when Paiton acquired a 60 percent interest in Sandra's common stock for $312,000 in cash. The book value of Sandra's assets and liabilities on that day totaled $300,000, and the fair value of the non-controlling interest was $208,000. Patents being held by Sandra (with a 12-year remaining life) were undervalued by $90,000 within the company's financial records, and a trademark (10-year life) worth $130,000 was also recognized as part of the acquisition-date fair value.

  Intra-entity inventory transfers occur regularly between the two companies. Merchandise carried over from one year to the next is always sold in the subsequent period.

Year	Original Cost to Sandra	Transfer Price to Paiton	Ending Balance at Transfer Price
2022	$ 80,000	$100,000	$20,000
2023	100,000	125,000	40,000
2024	90,000	120,000	30,000

  Paiton had not paid for half of the 2024 inventory transfers by year-end.

  On January 1, 2023, Paiton sold $15,000 in land to Sandra for $22,000. Sandra is still holding this land.

  On January 1, 2024, Sandra acquired $20,000 (face value) of Paiton's bonds in the open market. These bonds had an 8 percent cash interest rate. On the date of repurchase, the liability was shown within Paiton's records at $21,386, indicating an effective yield of 6 percent. Sandra's acquisition price was $18,732 based on an effective interest rate of 10 percent.

  Sandra indicated earning a net income of $25,000 within its 2024 financial statements. The subsidiary also reported a beginning Retained Earnings balance of $300,000, dividends of $4,000, and common stock of $100,000. Sandra has not issued any additional common stock since its takeover. The parent company has applied the equity method to record its investment in Sandra.

a. Prepare consolidation worksheet adjustments for 2024.

b. Calculate the amount of consolidated net income attributable to the noncontrolling interest for 2024. In addition, determine the ending 2024 balance for noncontrolling interest in the consolidated balance sheet.

c. Determine the consolidation worksheet adjustments needed in 2025 in connection with the intra-entity bonds.

LO 6-3, 6-4

41. On January 1, 2023, Mona, Inc., acquired 80 percent of Lisa Company's common stock as well as 60 percent of its preferred shares. Mona paid $65,000 in cash for the preferred stock, with a call value of 110 percent of the $50 per share par value. The remaining 40 percent of the preferred shares traded at a $34,000 fair value. Mona paid $552,800 for the common stock. At the acquisition date, the noncontrolling interest in the common stock had a fair value of $138,200. The excess fair value over Lisa's book value was attributed to franchise contracts of $40,000. This intangible asset is being amortized over a 40-year period. Lisa pays all preferred stock dividends (a total of $8,000 per year) on an annual basis. During 2023, Lisa's book value increased by $50,000.

On January 2, 2023, Mona acquired one-half of Lisa's outstanding bonds payable to reduce the business combination's debt position. Lisa's bonds had a face value of $100,000 and paid cash interest of 10 percent per year. These bonds had been issued to the public to yield 14 percent. Interest is paid each December 31. On January 2, 2023, these bonds had a total $88,350 carrying amount. Mona paid $53,310, indicating an effective interest rate of 8 percent.

On January 3, 2023, Mona sold Lisa fixed assets that had originally cost $100,000 but had accumulated depreciation of $60,000 when transferred. The transfer was made at a price of $120,000. These assets were estimated to have a remaining useful life of 10 years.

The individual financial statements for these two companies for the year ending December 31, 2024, are as follows:

	Mona, Inc.	Lisa Company
Sales and other revenues	$ (500,000)	$ (200,000)
Expenses	220,000	120,000
Dividend income—Lisa common stock	(8,000)	–0–
Dividend income—Lisa preferred stock	(4,800)	–0–
Net income	$ (292,800)	$ (80,000)
Retained earnings, 1/1/24	$ (700,000)	$ (500,000)
Net income (above)	(292,800)	(80,000)
Dividends declared—common stock	92,800	10,000
Dividends declared—preferred stock	–0–	8,000
Retained earnings, 12/31/24	$ (900,000)	$ (562,000)
Current assets	$ 130,419	$ 500,000
Investment in Lisa—common stock	552,800	–0–
Investment in Lisa—preferred stock	65,000	–0–
Investment in Lisa—bonds	51,781	–0–
Fixed assets	1,100,000	800,000
Accumulated depreciation	(300,000)	(200,000)
Total assets	$ 1,600,000	$ 1,100,000
Accounts payable	$ (400,000)	$ (144,580)
Bonds payable	–0–	(100,000)
Discount on bonds payable	–0–	6,580
Common stock	(300,000)	(200,000)
Preferred stock	–0–	(100,000)
Retained earnings, 12/31/24	(900,000)	(562,000)
Total liabilities and equities	$(1,600,000)	$(1,100,000)

a. What consolidation worksheet adjustments would have been required as of January 1, 2023, to eliminate the subsidiary's common and preferred stocks?

b. What consolidation worksheet adjustments would have been required as of December 31, 2023, to account for Mona's purchase of Lisa's bonds?

c. What consolidation worksheet adjustments would have been required as of December 31, 2023, to account for the intra-entity sale of fixed assets?

d. Assume that consolidated financial statements are being prepared for the year ending December 31, 2024. Calculate the consolidated balance for each of the following accounts:

Franchises
Fixed Assets
Accumulated Depreciation
Expenses

LO 6-5

42. Bolero Company holds 80 percent of the common stock of Rivera, Inc., and 40 percent of this subsidiary's convertible bonds. The following consolidated financial statements are for 2023 and 2024 (credit balances indicated by parentheses):

Bolero Company and Consolidated Subsidiary Rivera		
	2023	**2024**
Revenues	$ (900,000)	$(1,030,000)
Cost of goods sold	610,000	650,000
Depreciation and amortization	100,000	120,000
Gain on sale of building	–0–	(30,000)
Interest expense	40,000	40,000
Consolidated net income	(150,000)	(250,000)
to noncontrolling interest	19,000	21,000
to parent company	$ (131,000)	$ (229,000)
Retained earnings, 1/1	$ (310,000)	$ (381,000)
Net income	(131,000)	(229,000)
Dividends declared	60,000	110,000
Retained earnings, 12/31	$ (381,000)	$ (500,000)
Cash	$ 90,000	$ 180,000
Accounts receivable	170,000	150,000
Inventory	210,000	360,000
Buildings and equipment (net)	650,000	710,000
Databases	170,000	155,000
Total assets	$1,290,000	$ 1,555,000
Accounts payable	$ (160,000)	$ (110,000)
Bonds payable	(410,000)	(520,000)
Noncontrolling interest in Rivera	(42,000)	(61,000)
Common stock	(110,000)	(140,000)
Additional paid-in capital	(187,000)	(224,000)
Retained earnings	(381,000)	(500,000)
Total liabilities and equities	$(1,290,000)	$(1,555,000)

Additional Information for 2024

- The parent issued bonds during the year for cash.
- Amortization of databases amounts to $15,000 per year.
- The parent sold a building with a cost of $80,000 but a $40,000 book value for cash on May 11.
- The subsidiary purchased equipment on July 23 for $205,000 in cash.
- Late in November, the parent issued stock for cash.

- During the year, the subsidiary paid dividends of $10,000. Both parent and subsidiary pay dividends in the same year as declared.

  Prepare a consolidated statement of cash flows for this business combination for the year ending December 31, 2024. Use the indirect method to compute cash flow from operating activities.

LO 6-6

43. Following are separate income statements for Amarillo, Inc., and its 80 percent–owned subsidiary, Saltillo Corporation as well as a consolidated statement for the business combination as a whole (credit balances indicated by parentheses).

	Amarillo	Saltillo	Consolidated
Revenues	$(700,000)	$(500,000)	$(1,200,000)
Cost of goods sold	400,000	300,000	700,000
Operating expenses	100,000	70,000	195,000
Equity in earnings of Saltillo	(84,000)		
Individual company net income	$(284,000)	$(130,000)	
Consolidated net income			$ (305,000)
Noncontrolling interest in consolidated net income			(21,000)
Consolidated net income attributable to Amarillo			$ (284,000)

Additional Information

- Annual excess fair over book value amortization of $25,000 resulted from the acquisition.
- The parent applies the equity method to this investment.
- Amarillo has 50,000 shares of common stock and 10,000 shares of preferred stock outstanding. Owners of the preferred stock are paid an annual dividend of $40,000, and each share can be exchanged for two shares of common stock.
- Saltillo has 30,000 shares of common stock outstanding.
- Saltillo has convertible bonds outstanding, none of which Amarillo owned. During the current year, total interest expense (net of taxes) was $22,000. These bonds can be exchanged for 10,000 shares of the subsidiary's common stock.

  Determine Amarillo's basic and diluted EPS.

LO 6-5

44. On June 30, 2024, Plaster, Inc., paid $916,000 for 80 percent of Stucco Company's outstanding stock. Plaster assessed the acquisition-date fair value of the 20 percent noncontrolling interest at $229,000. At acquisition date, Stucco reported the following book values for its assets and liabilities:

Cash	$ 60,000
Accounts receivable	127,000
Inventory	203,000
Land	65,000
Buildings	175,000
Equipment	300,000
Accounts payable	(35,000)

On June 30, Plaster allocated the excess acquisition-date fair value over book value to Stucco's assets as follows:

Equipment (3-year remaining life)	$ 75,000
Database (10-year remaining life)	175,000

At the end of 2024, the following comparative (2023 and 2024) balance sheets and consolidated income statement were available:

	Plaster, Inc. December 31, 2023	Consolidated December 31, 2024
Cash	$ 43,000	$ 242,850
Accounts receivable (net)	362,000	485,400
Inventory.	415,000	720,000
Land.	300,000	365,000
Buildings (net)	245,000	370,000
Equipment (net)	1,800,000	2,037,500
Database	–0–	166,250
Total assets	$3,165,000	$4,387,000
Accounts payable.	$ 80,000	$ 107,000
Long-term liabilities.	400,000	1,200,000
Common stock	1,800,000	1,800,000
Noncontrolling interest.	–0–	255,500
Retained earnings.	885,000	1,024,500
Total liabilities and equities.	$3,165,000	$4,387,000

PLASTER, INC., AND SUBSIDIARY STUCCO COMPANY
Consolidated Income Statement
For the Year Ended December 31, 2024

Revenues		$1,217,500
Cost of goods sold	$737,500	
Depreciation	187,500	
Database amortization.	8,750	
Interest and other expenses.	9,750	943,500
Consolidated net income		$ 274,000

Additional Information for 2024

- On December 1, Stucco paid a $40,000 dividend. During the year, Plaster paid $100,000 in dividends.
- During the year, Plaster issued $800,000 in long-term debt at par.
- Plaster reported no asset purchases or dispositions other than the acquisition of Stucco.

  Prepare a 2024 consolidated statement of cash flows for Plaster and Stucco. Use the indirect method of reporting cash flows from operating activities.

Develop Your Skills

EXCEL CASE: INTRA-ENTITY BONDS—ANALYSIS OF ALTERNATIVE YIELD RATES AND PRICES

Place Company owns a majority voting interest in Sassano, Inc. On January 1, 2022, Place issued $1,000,000 of 11 percent 10-year bonds at $943,497.77 to yield 12 percent. On January 1, 2024, Sassano purchased all of these bonds in the open market at a price of $904,024.59 with an effective yield of 13 percent.

Required

Using an Excel spreadsheet, do the following:

1. Prepare amortization schedules for the Place Company bonds payable and the Investment in Place Bonds for Sassano, Inc.

2. Using the values from the amortization schedules, compute the worksheet adjustment for a December 31, 2024, consolidation of Place and Sassano to reflect the effective retirement of the Place bonds. Formulate your solution to be able to accommodate various yield rates (and therefore prices) on the repurchase of the bonds.

Hints

Present value of $1 = 1/(1 + r)n$

Present value of an annuity of $1 = [1 - 1/(1 + r)n]/r$

Where r = effective yield and n = years remaining to maturity

RESEARCH CASE: STATEMENT OF CASH FLOWS

CPA
skills

Download a recent copy of Pfizer's annual report (search Pfizer Investor Relations). Locate the firm's consolidated statement of cash flows and answer the following:

- Does the firm employ the direct or indirect method of accounting for operating cash flows?
- Why does the firm account for the changes in balances in operating accounts (e.g., accounts receivable, inventory, accounts payable) in determining operating cash flows as net of acquisitions and divestitures?
- Describe the accounting for cash paid for business acquisitions in the statement of cash flows.
- Describe the accounting for any noncontrolling subsidiary interest and any other business combination–related items in the consolidated statement of cash flows.

FINANCIAL REPORTING RESEARCH AND ANALYSIS CASE

CPA
skills

The FASB ASC Subtopic "Variable Interest Entities" affects thousands of business enterprises that now, as primary beneficiaries, consolidate entities that qualify as controlled VIEs. Retrieve a recent annual report of one or more of the following companies (or any others you may find) that consolidate VIEs:

- The Walt Disney Company.
- General Electric.
- Harley-Davidson.

Required

Write a brief report that describes

1. The reasons for consolidation of the company's VIE(s).
2. The effect of the consolidation of the VIE(s) on the company's financial statements.

Foreign Currency Transactions and Hedging Foreign Exchange Risk

Today, international business transactions such as export sales and import purchases are a regular occurrence. In its 2020 annual report, Lockheed Martin Corporation reported export sales of $16 billion, representing 25 percent of total sales. Some businesses are even more significantly involved in making sales to foreign customers. In 2020, Apple Inc., disclosed that 60 percent of its sales (approximately $165 billion) were made to customers located outside of the United States, which was down slightly from 61 percent in 2019, and 63 percent in 2018.

Collections from export sales or payments for imported items might not be made in U.S. dollars but in pesos, pounds, yen, and the like, depending on the negotiated terms of the transaction. As foreign currency exchange rates fluctuate, so does the U.S. dollar value of these export sales and import purchases. Companies often find it necessary to engage in some form of hedging activity to reduce losses arising from fluctuating exchange rates. At the end of fiscal year 2020, in conjunction with foreign currency hedging activities, Lockheed Martin reported having outstanding foreign currency hedges with a notional value of $3.4 billion, while Apple had outstanding foreign exchange contracts with a notional value of $146.0 billion.

This chapter covers accounting issues related to foreign currency transactions and foreign currency hedging activities. To provide a background for subsequent discussions of the accounting issues, this chapter begins by describing foreign exchange markets. This chapter then discusses accounting for foreign currency–denominated import and export transactions, followed by coverage of various hedging techniques. Because they are most popular, the discussion concentrates on foreign currency forward contracts and foreign currency options. Understanding how to account for these items is important for any company engaged in international transactions.

Learning Objectives

After studying this chapter, you should be able to:

LO 7-1 Understand concepts related to foreign currency, exchange rates, and foreign exchange risk.

LO 7-2 Account for foreign currency transactions using the two-transaction perspective, accrual approach.

LO 7-3 Account for foreign currency borrowings.

LO 7-4 Understand the different types of foreign exchange risk that can be hedged and how foreign currency forward contracts and foreign currency options can be used to hedge those risks.

LO 7-5 Understand the accounting guidelines for derivative financial instruments.

LO 7-6 Understand the basic concepts of hedge accounting.

LO 7-7 Account for forward contracts and options used as hedges of foreign currency–denominated assets and liabilities.

LO 7-8 Account for forward contracts and options used as hedges of foreign currency firm commitments.

LO 7-9 Account for forward contracts and options used as hedges of forecasted foreign currency transactions.

LO 7-1

Understand concepts related to foreign currency, exchange rates, and foreign exchange risk.

Foreign Exchange Markets

Each country (or group of countries) uses its own currency as the unit of value for the purchase and sale of goods and services. The currency used in the United States is the U.S. dollar, the currency used in Mexico is the Mexican peso, the currency used by a subset of European Union countries is the euro, and so on. If a U.S. citizen travels to Mexico and wishes to purchase local goods, Mexican merchants require payment to be made in Mexican pesos. To make a purchase in Mexico, a U.S. citizen would need to acquire pesos using U.S. dollars. The foreign currency *exchange rate* is the price at which the foreign currency can be acquired (or sold). A variety of factors determine the exchange rate between two currencies; unfortunately for those engaged in international business, the exchange rate can fluctuate over time.[1]

Exchange Rate Mechanisms

Exchange rates have not always fluctuated. During the period 1945–1973, countries fixed the value of their currency in terms of the U.S. dollar, and the value of the U.S. dollar was fixed in terms of gold. In March 1973, most countries allowed their currencies to float in value. Today, several different currency arrangements exist. Some of the more important ones and the countries affected follow:

1. *Independent float:* The value of the currency is allowed to fluctuate freely according to market forces with little or no intervention from the central bank (example countries include Australia, Brazil, Canada, Japan, Sweden, Switzerland, the United Kingdom, and the United States).

2. *Pegged to another currency:* The value of the currency is fixed (pegged) in terms of a particular foreign currency, and the central bank intervenes as necessary to maintain the fixed value. For example, Bahrain, Hong Kong, Panama, and Saudi Arabia peg their currency to the U.S. dollar.

3. *European Monetary System (euro):* In 1998, those European Union countries comprising the European Monetary System adopted a common currency called the *euro* and established a European Central Bank.[2] On January 1, 2002, local currencies (such as the French franc, German mark, and Spanish peseta) disappeared, and the euro became the currency in 12 European Union countries. Today, 19 countries are part of the euro zone. The value of the euro floats freely against other currencies such as the Swiss franc, British pound, Japanese yen, and U.S. dollar.

Foreign Exchange Rates

Exchange rates between the U.S. dollar and many foreign currencies are readily available online at websites such as www.oanda.com and www.x-rates.com. To illustrate exchange rates and the foreign currency market, next we take a look at exchange rates for selected currencies reported for September 15 and 16, 2021, as shown in Exhibit 7.1.

The exchange rates shown in Exhibit 7.1 are for trades between banks; that is, these are *interbank* or wholesale prices. Prices charged by banks to retail customers, such as companies engaged in international business, are higher. Exhibit 7.1 shows *ask* rates at which banks will *sell* currency to one another. The prices at which banks are willing to buy foreign currency (bid rates) are somewhat less than the selling rates. The difference between the buying and selling rates is the spread through which banks earn a profit on foreign exchange trades. For example, the September 15, 2021, U.S. dollar selling (ask) rate for the British pound was $1.3828, while the the buying (bid) rate was $1.3826 (not shown). On that date, banks were

---

[1] Several theories attempt to explain exchange rate fluctuations but with little success, at least in the short term. An understanding of the causes of exchange rate changes is not necessary to comprehend the concepts underlying the accounting for changes in exchange rates.

[2] Most longtime members of the European Union (EU) are "euro zone" countries. The major exception is Denmark, which elected not to participate. Switzerland is another economically important European country not part of the euro zone because it is not a member of the EU.

EXHIBIT 7.1
U.S. Dollar (USD) Exchange Rates for Selected Currencies (September 15–16, 2021)

Currency	September 15, 2021		September 16, 2021	
	Direct*	Indirect†	Direct*	Indirect†
Euro (EUR).	1.1814	0.8465	1.1780	0.8489
British pound (GBP)	1.3828	0.7232	1.3812	0.7240
Canadian dollar (CAD).	0.7896	1.2665	0.7902	1.2655
Brazilian real (BRL).	0.1908	5.2411	0.1909	5.2383
Saudi Arabian riyal (SAR)	0.2670	3.7453	0.2670	3.7453

Source: https://www.oanda.com/fx-for-business/historical-rates.
*www.oanda.com/fx-for-business/historical-rates.
†Indirect quotes have been calculated by the author and rounded to four digits behind the decimal point.

willing to buy British pounds (GBP) for $1.3826 and sell them for $1.3828, earning a profit of $0.0002 per GBP.

Two columns of information are shown for each day's exchange rates. The first column reports *direct quotes,* which indicate the number of U.S. dollars needed to purchase one unit of foreign currency. The direct quote for the Brazilian real (BRL) on September 15 was $0.1908; in other words, 1.0 Brazilian real could be purchased for $0.1908. The second column reports *indirect quotes,* which indicate the number of foreign currency units that could be purchased with one U.S. dollar. These rates are simply the inverse of direct quotes (indirect quote = 1 ÷ direct quote). If one BRL can be purchased with $0.1908, then 5.2411 BRL can be purchased with $1.00. To avoid confusion, *direct quotes are used exclusively in this chapter.*

The third and fourth columns in Exhibit 7.1 show exchange rates for September 16, 2021. Two of the currencies shown increased in U.S. dollar price (appreciated) from September 15 to September 16, namely the Canadian dollar and Brazilian real. For example, the Canadian dollar (CAD) increased in price by $0.0006 (from $0.7896 to $0.7902) from one day to the next. As a result, the purchase of 100,000 CAD on September 16, 2021, would have cost $60 more than on the previous day. In contrast, the U.S. dollar price for two currencies decreased (depreciated) from one day to the next, namely the euro and British pound. The Saudi riyal did not change in U.S. dollar value from one day to the next because this currency was effectively pegged to the U.S. dollar.

Foreign Currency Forward Contracts

Foreign currency trades can be executed on a spot or forward basis. The *spot rate* is the price at which a foreign currency can be purchased or sold today. In contrast, the *forward rate* is the price available today at which foreign currency can be purchased or sold sometime in the future. Because many international business transactions take some time to be completed, the ability to lock in a price today at which foreign currency can be purchased or sold at some future date has definite advantages.

A *foreign currency forward contract* can be negotiated by a firm with its bank to exchange foreign currency for U.S. dollars, or vice versa, on a specified future date at a predetermined exchange rate. A forward contract can be written for whatever currency and for whatever future date is required. Entering into a forward contract has no up-front cost; the firm and its bank simply agree today to exchange foreign currency for U.S. dollars at the forward rate on a future date. Similar to how banks make a profit in the spot market, there is a spread between the buying and selling rates in the forward market. For example, on February 1, a bank might agree to buy 500,000 British pounds in three months from one customer at a forward rate of $1.30 per British pound and simultaneously agree to sell 500,000 British pounds in three months to another customer at a rate of $1.31 per British pound. In this way, the bank generates a profit of $5,000 ($0.01 × 500,000 British pounds) from entering into these two forward contracts.

The difference between the forward rate and the spot rate for a currency on a given date is referred to as *forward points,* which can be either positive or negative. When the forward rate exceeds the spot rate on a given date, positive forward points exist and the foreign currency is said to be selling at a *premium* in the forward market. When the forward rate is less than the spot rate, negative forward points exist and the currency is selling at a *discount.* Currencies sell at a premium or a discount in the forward market because of differences in interest rates between two countries. When the interest rate in the foreign country exceeds the domestic interest rate, the foreign currency sells at a discount in the forward market. Conversely, if the foreign interest rate is less than the domestic rate, the foreign currency sells at a premium.[3]

The forward exchange rate for a specific future settlement date will change over time due to changes in the spot exchange rate and/or changes in the differential interest rates between two countries. For example, assume on April 15 the U.S. dollar (USD) per Mexican peso (MXN) spot rate is $0.051 and the forward rate for a forward contract to be settled on June 15 is $0.046. In this case, the peso is selling at a discount of $0.005 in the two-month forward market due to a higher interest rate in Mexico than in the United States. If the USD/MXN spot rate decreases to $0.044 on May 15, the forward rate for a June 15 settlement-date forward contract also will decrease, to an amount less than $0.044. The peso will continue to sell at a discount in the one-month forward market because of the higher interest rate in Mexico.

Foreign Currency Options

To provide companies more flexibility than exists with a forward contract, a market for *foreign currency options* was created. A foreign currency option gives the holder of the option *the right but not the obligation* to trade foreign currency in the future. A *put* option is for the sale of foreign currency by the holder of the option; a *call* option is for the purchase of foreign currency by the holder of the option. The *strike price* is the exchange rate at which the option will be executed if the option holder decides to exercise the option. The strike price is similar to a forward rate. There are generally several strike prices to choose from on a particular date. Foreign currency options can be purchased on the Philadelphia Stock Exchange or the Chicago Mercantile Exchange, but most foreign currency options are purchased directly from a bank in the so-called over-the-counter (OTC) market. Options purchased in the OTC market usually have a strike price that is equal to the spot rate on that date. These options are said to be "at the money."

Unlike a forward contract, for which banks earn their profit through the spread between buying and selling rates, options are purchased by paying an *option premium,* which is a function of two components: intrinsic value and time value. An option's *intrinsic value* is equal to the gain that could be realized by exercising the option immediately. For example, if the spot rate for the euro is $1.18, a *call* option (to purchase euros) with a strike price of $1.16 has an intrinsic value of $0.02 per euro. Euros can be purchased for $1.16 and sold for $1.18, generating a gain of $0.02 per euro. On the other hand, when the spot rate for the euro is $1.18, a *put* option (to sell euros) with a strike price of $1.16 has an intrinsic value of zero. An option with a positive intrinsic value is said to be "in-the-money." The *time value* of an option relates to the fact that the spot rate can change over time and cause the option's intrinsic value to increase. Even though a call option (to purchase euros) with a strike price of $1.18 has zero intrinsic value when the spot rate is $1.18, it has a positive time value because there is a chance that the spot rate could increase over the next 90 days and bring the option into the money. As time passes, the time value of an option decreases because there is less time remaining for the option to increase in intrinsic value. On the option's expiration date, the time value is zero because there is no time remaining for the option to become more valuable. It is important to remember that the *fair value of a foreign currency option on a specific date is the sum of its intrinsic and time values on that date, and the time value of the option decreases to zero over the life of the option.*

The fair value of a foreign currency option can be determined by applying an adaptation of the Black-Scholes option pricing formula. This formula is discussed in detail in international finance books. In very general terms, the value of an option is a function of several factors: the difference between the current spot rate and strike price, the difference between domestic and foreign interest rates, the length of time to expiration, and the potential volatility of changes in the spot rate. For purposes of this book, the premium originally paid for a foreign currency option and its subsequent fair value up to the date of expiration derived from applying the option pricing formula will be given.

---

[3] This relationship is based on the theory of interest rate parity that indicates the difference in national interest rates should be equal to, but opposite in sign to, the forward rate discount or premium. This topic is covered in detail in international finance textbooks.

Account for foreign currency transactions using the two-transaction perspective, accrual approach.

Foreign Currency Transactions

Export sales and import purchases are international transactions; they are components of what is called *international trade.* When two parties from different countries enter into a transaction, they must decide which of the two countries' currencies to use to settle the transaction. For example, if a U.S. computer manufacturer sells to a customer in Japan, the parties must decide whether the transaction will be denominated (payment will be made) in U.S. dollars or in Japanese yen.

Assume that a U.S.-based trading company (Eximco) sells goods to a British customer that will pay in British pounds (£). In this situation, Eximco has entered into a foreign currency transaction. It must restate the British pound amount that it actually will receive into U.S. dollars to account for this transaction. This is necessary because Eximco keeps its books and prepares financial statements in U.S. dollars. Although the British customer has entered into an international transaction, it does not have a foreign currency transaction (payment will be made in its currency), and no restatement is necessary.

Assume that, as is customary in its industry, Eximco does not require immediate payment and allows its British customer 30 days to pay for its purchases. By doing this, Eximco runs the risk that the British pound might depreciate (decrease in value) against the U.S. dollar between the sale date and the date of payment. If so, the sale would generate fewer U.S. dollars than it would have had the British pound not decreased in value, and the sale is less profitable because it was made on a credit basis. In this situation, Eximco is said to have an *exposure to foreign exchange risk.* Specifically, Eximco has a foreign currency *transaction exposure* that can be summarized as follows:

- *Export sale:* A foreign currency transaction exposure exists when the exporter *allows the buyer to pay in a foreign currency* and *allows the buyer to pay sometime after the sale has been made.* The exporter is exposed to the risk that the foreign currency might depreciate (decrease in value) between the date of sale and the date payment is received, thereby decreasing the U.S. dollars ultimately collected.
  - Note that there is no exposure to foreign exchange risk if the exporter requires the foreign customer to make payment on the date of sale. In that case, the exporter would receive foreign currency and immediately convert it into U.S. dollars at the spot rate on the date of sale.
- *Import purchase:* A foreign currency transaction exposure exists when the importer *is required to pay in foreign currency* and *is allowed to pay sometime after the purchase has been made.* The importer is exposed to the risk that the foreign currency might appreciate (increase in price) between the date of purchase and the date of payment, thereby increasing the U.S. dollars that have to be paid for the imported goods.
  - Note that there is no exposure to foreign exchange risk if the importer makes payment in foreign currency on the date of purchase. In that case, the importer converts U.S. dollars into foreign currency at the spot rate on the date of purchase and immediately makes payment.

Accounting Issue

The major issue in accounting for foreign currency transactions is how to deal with the change in U.S. dollar value of the sales revenue and account receivable resulting from the export sale when the foreign currency changes in value. (The corollary issue is how to deal with the change in the U.S. dollar value of the account payable and goods acquired in an import purchase.) For example, assume that Eximco, a U.S. company, sells goods to a British customer at a price of 1 million British pounds (£) when the spot exchange rate is $1.300 per pound. If payment were received at the sale date, Eximco could have converted £1,000,000 into $1,300,000; this amount clearly would be the amount at which the sales revenue would be recognized. Instead, Eximco allows the British customer 30 days to pay for its purchase. At the end of 30 days, the British pound has depreciated to $1.285, and Eximco is able to convert

£1,000,000 received on that date into only $1,285,000. How should Eximco account for this $15,000 decrease in value?

FASB ASC 830-20 Foreign Currency Matters–Foreign Currency Transactions requires companies to use what can be referred to as a *two-transaction perspective* in accounting for foreign currency transactions. This perspective treats the export sale and the subsequent collection of cash as two separate transactions. Because management has made two decisions: (1) to make the export sale and (2) to extend credit in foreign currency to the customer, the company should report the income effect from each of these decisions separately. The U.S. dollar value of the sale is recorded at the date the sale occurs. At that point, the sale has been completed; there are no subsequent adjustments to the Sales account. Any difference between the number of U.S. dollars that could have been received at the date of sale and the number of U.S. dollars actually received at the date of collection due to fluctuations in the exchange rate is a result of the decision to extend foreign currency credit to the customer. This difference is recognized in a Foreign Exchange Gain or Loss account that is reported separately from Sales in the income statement.

Similarly, an import purchase denominated in a foreign currency and the subsequent payment of cash must be accounted for separately. The U.S. dollar value of the goods purchased is recorded at the date of purchase, with no subsequent adjustments to the Cost of Goods Sold account. Any difference between the number of U.S. dollars that could have been paid on the date of purchase and the actual number of U.S. dollars that is paid on the payment date due to a change in the exchange rate is recognized in a separate Foreign Exchange Gain or Loss account.

Using the two-transaction perspective to account for its export sale to the British customer, Eximco would make the following journal entries (in $):

Date of Sale:	Accounts Receivable (£).........................	1,300,000	
	Sales......................................		1,300,000
	To record the sale and £1,000,000 receivable at the spot rate of $1.300.		
Date of Collection:	Foreign Exchange Gain or Loss...................	15,000	
	Accounts Receivable (£)		15,000
	To adjust the value of the £1,000,000 receivable to the new spot rate of $1.285 and recognize a foreign exchange loss resulting from the depreciation in the £.		
	Cash	1,285,000	
	Accounts Receivable (£)		1,285,000
	To record the receipt of £1,000,000 and conversion into U.S. dollars at the spot rate of $1.285.		

Sales are reported in net income at the amount that would have been received if the customer had not been given 30 days to pay £1,000,000—that is, $1,300,000. A separate foreign exchange loss of $15,000 is reported in net income to indicate that because of the decision to extend foreign currency credit to the British customer and because the British pound decreased in value, Eximco actually received fewer U.S. dollars.[4]

Note that Eximco creates an "Accounts Receivable (£)" account, which is separate from its U.S. dollar accounts receivables. Companies engaged in international trade need to keep separate receivable and payable accounts in each of the currencies in which they have transactions. Each foreign currency receivable and payable should have a separate account number in the company's chart of accounts.

The loss on the foreign currency account receivable is recorded in a Foreign Exchange Gain or Loss account, which will have either a debit (net loss) or credit (net gain) balance at the end of each accounting period. If the British pound had appreciated against the U.S. dollar from the date of sale to the date of collection, Eximco would have made a credit to the Foreign Exchange Gain or Loss account to recognize the gain.

---

[4] Note that the foreign exchange loss results because the customer is allowed to pay in foreign currency and is given 30 days to pay. If the transaction were denominated in U.S. dollars, no loss would result, nor would there be a loss if the foreign currency had been received at the date the sale was made.

We can summarize the relationship between fluctuations in exchange rates and foreign exchange gains and losses as follows:

		Foreign Currency (FC)	
Transaction	Type of Exposure	Appreciates	Depreciates
Export sale	Asset (receivable)	Gain	Loss
Import purchase	Liability (payable)	Loss	Gain

A foreign currency receivable arising from an export sale creates an *asset exposure* to foreign exchange risk. If the foreign currency appreciates, the foreign currency asset increases in U.S. dollar value and a foreign exchange gain arises; depreciation of the foreign currency causes a foreign exchange loss. A foreign currency payable arising from an import purchase creates a *liability exposure* to foreign exchange risk. If the foreign currency appreciates, the foreign currency liability increases in U.S. dollar value and a foreign exchange loss results; depreciation of the currency results in a foreign exchange gain.

Balance Sheet Date before Date of Payment

The question arises as to what adjustments should be made if a balance sheet date falls between the date of sale (or purchase) and the date of collection (or payment). For example, assume that Eximco shipped goods to its British customer on December 1, 2023, with payment to be received on March 1, 2024. Assume that at December 1, the spot rate for the British pound was $1.300, but by December 31, the pound has depreciated to $1.285. Is any adjustment needed at December 31, 2023, when the books are closed, to account for the fact that the foreign currency receivable has changed in U.S. dollar value since December 1?

Authoritative accounting literature requires foreign currency balances such as a foreign currency receivable or a foreign currency payable to be revalued at the balance sheet date to account for the change in exchange rates. Under the two-transaction perspective, this means that a foreign exchange gain or loss arises at the balance sheet date. The next question then is what should be done with these foreign exchange gains and losses that have not yet been realized in cash. Should they be included in net income?

U.S. GAAP requires unrealized foreign exchange gains and losses to be reported in net income in the period in which the exchange rate changes. This is consistent with accrual accounting as it results in reporting the effect of a rate change that will have an impact on cash flow in the period when the event causing the impact takes place. Thus, any change in the exchange rate from the date of sale to the balance sheet date results in a foreign exchange gain or loss to be reported in net income in that period. Any change in the exchange rate from the balance sheet date to the date of collection results in a second foreign exchange gain or loss that is reported in net income in the second accounting period. Eximco makes the following journal entries under this approach:

12/1/23	Accounts Receivable (£)............................	1,300,000	
	Sales...		1,300,000
	To record the sale and £1,000,000 receivable at the spot rate of $1.300.		
12/31/23	Foreign Exchange Gain or Loss......................	15,000	
	Accounts Receivable (£).......................		15,000
	To adjust the value of the £1,000,000 receivable to the new spot rate of $1.285 and record a foreign exchange loss in 2023 net income resulting from the depreciation in the £ since December 1.		
3/1/24	Foreign Exchange Gain or Loss......................	13,000	
	Accounts Receivable (£).......................		13,000
	To adjust the value of the £1,000,000 receivable to the new spot rate of $1.272 and record a foreign exchange loss in 2024 net income resulting from the depreciation in the £ since December 31.		

(*continued*)

(continued)

Cash	1,272,000	
Accounts Receivable (£)		1,272,000
To record the receipt of £1,000,000 and conversion at the spot rate of $1.272.		

The net impact on income in 2023 is a sale of $1,300,000 and a foreign exchange loss of $15,000; in 2024, Eximco records a foreign exchange loss of $13,000. This results in a net increase of $1,272,000 in Retained Earnings that is balanced by an equal increase in Cash over the two-year period. Over the two-year period, Eximco recognizes a net foreign exchange loss of $28,000.

Restatement at the balance sheet date is required for all foreign currency assets and liabilities carried on a company's books. In addition to foreign currency payables and receivables arising from import and export transactions, companies might have dividends receivable from foreign subsidiaries, loans payable to foreign lenders, or lease payments receivable from foreign customers that are denominated in a foreign currency and therefore must be restated at the balance sheet date. Each of these foreign currency–denominated assets and liabilities is exposed to foreign exchange risk; therefore, fluctuation in exchange rates result in foreign exchange gains and losses on all foreign currency–denominated assets and liabilities.

FASB ASC Topic 830 requires companies to either present in the financial statements or disclose in the notes thereto the aggregate foreign currency transaction gain or loss included in determining net income for the year. Many U.S. companies include foreign exchange gains and losses in an income statement line item often titled "Other income (expense)." Companies that follow this approach must disclose in the notes to the financial statements the amount included in this line item as foreign exchange gains and losses. Merck & Co, Inc., provides an example of this in its 2020 Form 10-K. Merck's income statement for that year included the line item "Other (Income) Expense, Net" with total positive other income of $886 million. In Note 14 to the financial statements, Merck disclosed that other income of $886 million was determined after subtracting a net foreign exchange loss of $145 million.

International Accounting Standard 21—The Effects of Changes in Foreign Exchange Rates

Similar to U.S. GAAP, *IAS 21,* "The Effects of Changes in Foreign Exchange Rates," also requires the use of a two-transaction perspective in accounting for foreign currency transactions with unrealized foreign exchange gains and losses accrued in net income in the period of exchange rate change. There are no substantive differences between IFRS and U.S. GAAP in the accounting for foreign currency transactions.

LO 7-3

Account for foreign currency borrowings.

Foreign Currency Borrowing

In addition to the receivables and payables that arise from import and export activities, companies often must account for foreign currency borrowings, another type of foreign currency transaction. Companies borrow foreign currency from foreign lenders either to finance foreign operations or perhaps to take advantage of more favorable interest rates. The facts that both the principal and interest are denominated in foreign currency and both create an exposure to foreign exchange risk complicate accounting for a foreign currency borrowing.

To demonstrate the accounting for foreign currency debt, assume that on July 1, 2023, Multicorp International borrowed 1 billion Japanese yen (¥) on a one-year note at an interest rate of 5 percent per annum. Interest is payable and the note comes due on July 1, 2024. The following exchange rates apply:

Date	U.S. Dollars per Japanese Yen Spot Rate
July 1, 2023	$0.00921
December 31, 2023	0.00932
July 1, 2024	0.00937

On July 1, 2023, Multicorp borrows ¥1 billion and converts it into $9,210,000 in the spot market. On December 31, 2023, Multicorp must revalue the Japanese yen note payable with an offsetting foreign exchange gain or loss reported in income and must accrue interest expense and interest payable. Interest is calculated by multiplying the loan principal in yen by the relevant interest rate. The amount of interest payable in yen is then translated to U.S. dollars at the spot rate to record the accrual journal entry. On July 1, 2024, any difference between the amount of interest accrued at year-end and the actual U.S. dollar amount that must be spent to pay the accrued interest is recognized as a foreign exchange gain or loss. These journal entries account for this foreign currency borrowing:

7/1/23	Cash		9,210,000	
	Note Payable (¥)			9,210,000
	To record the ¥ note payable at the spot rate of $0.00921 and the conversion of ¥1 billion into U.S. dollars.			
12/31/23	Interest Expense		233,000	
	Accrued Interest Payable (¥)			233,000
	To accrue interest for the period July 1–December 31: ¥1 billion × 5% × ½ year = ¥25 million × $0.00932 = $233,000.			
	Foreign Exchange Gain or Loss		110,000	
	Note Payable (¥)			110,000
	To revalue the ¥ note payable at the spot rate of $0.00932 and record a foreign exchange loss of $110,000 [¥1 billion × ($0.00932 − $0.00921)].			
7/1/24	Interest Expense		234,250	
	Accrued Interest Payable (¥)			234,250
	To accrue interest for the period January 1–July 1: ¥1 billion × 5% × ½ year = ¥25 million × $0.00937 = $234,250.			
	Foreign Exchange Gain or Loss		1,250	
	Accrued Interest Payable (¥)			1,250
	To revalue the ¥ interest payable accrued on December 31 at the current spot rate of $0.00937 and record a foreign exchange loss of $1,250 [¥25 million × ($0.00937 − $0.00932)].			
	Accrued Interest Payable (¥)		468,500	
	Cash			468,500
	To record the cash interest payment of $468,500 [¥50 million × spot rate of $0.00937] and remove the ¥ accrued interest payable from the books.			
	Foreign Exchange Gain or Loss		50,000	
	Note Payable (¥)			50,000
	To revalue the ¥ note payable at the spot rate of $0.00937 and record a foreign exchange loss of $50,000 [¥1 billion × ($0.00937 − $0.00932)].			
	Note Payable (¥)		9,370,000	
	Cash			9,370,000
	To record repayment of the ¥1 billion note through purchase of ¥1 billion at the spot rate of $0.00937 and remove the ¥ note payable from the books.			

The total U.S. dollar borrowing cost on the 1 billion Japanese yen note payable is equal to the difference between the U.S. dollar cash outflows and cash inflow: $9,370,000 + $468,500 − $9,210,000 = $628,500. This borrowing cost is reflected in Multicorp's financial statements as a combination of interest expense ($467,250) and foreign exchange loss ($161,250). Taking the exchange rate effect on the cost of borrowing into consideration results in an "effective borrowing rate" of 6.8 percent ($628,500/$9,210,000), even though the stated interest rate is only 5 percent.

Foreign Currency Loan

At times, companies lend foreign currency to related parties, creating the opposite situation from a foreign currency borrowing. The accounting involves keeping track of a note receivable and related interest receivable, both of which are denominated in foreign currency. Fluctuations in the U.S. dollar value of the principal and interest generally give rise to foreign exchange gains and losses that would be included in net income. An exception arises when the foreign currency loan is made on a long-term basis to a foreign branch, subsidiary, or equity method affiliate. Foreign exchange gains and losses on "intra-entity foreign currency transactions that are of a long-term investment nature (that is, settlement is not planned or anticipated in the foreseeable future)" are deferred in accumulated other comprehensive income until the loan is repaid.[5] Only the foreign exchange gains and losses related to the interest receivable are recorded currently in net income.

Hedges of Foreign Exchange Risk

LO 7-4

Understand the different types of foreign exchange risk that can be hedged and how foreign currency forward contracts and foreign currency options can be used to hedge those risks.

In the example provided in the earlier section on foreign currency transactions, Eximco has an asset exposure in British pounds when it sells goods to the U.K. customer and allows the customer three months to pay for its purchase. If the British pound depreciates over the next three months, Eximco will incur a net foreign exchange loss. For many companies, the uncertainty of not knowing exactly how many U.S. dollars an export sale will generate is of great concern. (Similarly, not knowing exactly how many U.S. dollars a foreign currency–denominated import purchase will cost is also of concern.) To avoid this uncertainty, companies often use derivative financial instruments to hedge against the effect of unfavorable changes in the value of foreign currencies. A derivative financial instrument, or simply derivative, derives its value from some "underlying." In the case of foreign currency derivatives, the underlying is the currency exchange rate. The two most common derivatives used to hedge foreign exchange risk are *foreign currency forward contracts* and *foreign currency options*.

In our example, Eximco will receive British pounds in three months when it collects the receivable, and it will need to sell those pounds at that time. Through a forward contract, Eximco can lock in the price at which it will sell the pounds it receives in three months. Alternatively, an option establishes a price at which Eximco will be able, but is not required, to sell the pounds it receives in three months. If Eximco enters into a forward contract or purchases a put option on the date the sale is made, the derivative is being used as a *hedge of a recognized foreign currency–denominated asset* (the British pound account receivable).

Companies engaged in foreign currency activities often enter into hedging arrangements as soon as they receive a noncancelable sales order or place a noncancelable purchase order. A noncancelable order that specifies the foreign currency price and date of delivery is known as a *foreign currency firm commitment*. Assume that on June 1, Eximco accepts an order to sell parts to a customer in South Korea at a price of 5 million Korean won. The parts will be delivered and payment will be received on August 15. On June 1, when the order is accepted but before the sale has been made, Eximco enters into a forward contract to sell 5 million Korean won on August 15. In this case, Eximco is using a foreign currency derivative as a *hedge of an unrecognized foreign currency firm commitment*.

Some companies have foreign currency transactions that occur on a regular basis and can be reliably forecasted. For example, Eximco regularly purchases materials from a supplier in Hong Kong for which it pays in Hong Kong dollars. Even if Eximco has no contract to make future purchases, it has an exposure to foreign currency risk if it plans to continue making purchases from the Hong Kong supplier. Assume that on October 1, Eximco forecasts that it will make a purchase from the Hong Kong supplier in three months. To hedge against a possible increase in the price of the Hong Kong dollar, Eximco acquires a call option on October 1 to

---

[5] FASB ASC (para. 830-20-35-3b).

purchase Hong Kong dollars in three months. The foreign currency option represents a *hedge of a forecasted foreign currency–denominated transaction*.

To summarize, there are three points in time at which a company might choose to initiate a hedge of the foreign exchange risk associated with a foreign currency transaction, resulting in these three types of hedges:

1. Hedge of a recognized foreign currency–denominated asset or liability.
2. Hedge of an unrecognized foreign currency firm commitment.
3. Hedge of a forecasted foreign currency transaction.

The following timeline illustrates how these hedges differ in terms of timing.

Timeline for Possible Hedges Related to an Import Purchase

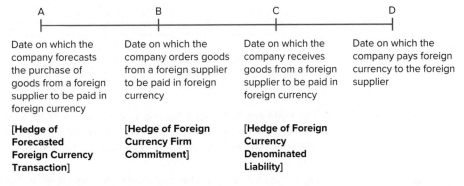

The company can enter into a hedge at any of the dates A, B, or C.

<table>
<tr><td></td></tr>
</table>

Derivatives Accounting

LO 7-5

Understand the accounting guidelines for derivative financial instruments.

FASB ASC Topic 815, "Derivatives and Hedging," governs the accounting for derivatives, including those used to hedge foreign exchange risk. This authoritative literature provides guidance for hedges of the following sources of foreign exchange risk:

1. Recognized foreign currency–denominated assets and liabilities.
2. Unrecognized foreign currency–denominated firm commitments.
3. Foreign currency–denominated forecasted transactions.
4. Net investments in foreign operations.

Different accounting applies to each type of foreign currency hedge. This chapter demonstrates the accounting for the first three types of hedges. The next chapter covers hedges of net investments in foreign operations.

Fundamental Requirement of Derivatives Accounting

The fundamental requirement of FASB ASC 815 is that companies carry all derivatives on the balance sheet at their fair value. Derivatives are reported on the balance sheet as assets when they have a positive fair value and as liabilities when they have a negative fair value. The first issue in accounting for derivatives is the determination of fair value.

The fair value of derivatives can change over time, causing adjustments to be made to the carrying values of the assets and liabilities. The second issue in accounting for derivatives is the treatment of the gains and losses that arise from these fair value changes.

Determination of Fair Value of Derivatives

Foreign Currency Forward Contract

The *fair value of a foreign currency forward contract* is determined by reference to changes in the forward rate over the life of the contract (discounted to present value).

Three pieces of information are needed to determine the fair value of a forward contract at any point in time:

1. The forward rate when the forward contract was entered into.
2. The current forward rate for a contract that matures on the same date as the forward contract entered into.
3. A discount rate—typically, the company's incremental borrowing rate.

Assume that International Company enters into a forward contract with its bank on December 1 to sell 1 million Mexican pesos (MXN) on March 1 at a forward rate of $0.055 per peso, or a total of $55,000. International Company incurs no cost to enter into the forward contract, and the forward contract has no value on December 1.

U.S. dollar (USD) per MXN exchange rates over the life of the forward contract are as follows:

Date	Spot Rate	Forward Rate to March 1
December 1	$0.0560	$0.055
December 31	$0.0535	$0.052
March 1	$0.0518	n/a

The USD per MXN spot rate on December 1 is $0.056, so the peso sold at a forward discount. The forward points component of the forward contract is negative $1,000 [MXN 1,000,000 × ($0.056 − $0.055)]. In other words, this forward contract includes a discount of $1,000.

On December 31, when International Company closes its books to prepare financial statements, the forward rate to sell Mexican pesos on March 1 has changed to $0.052. On that date, a forward contract for the delivery of MXN 1 million could be signed, resulting in a cash inflow of only $52,000 on March 1. This represents a favorable change in the value of International Company's forward contract of $3,000 ($55,000 − $52,000), because International Company has contracted to sell pesos for $55,000. (Note that the spot rate on December 31 is irrelevant in determining the value of the forward contract.)

The undiscounted fair value of the forward contract on December 31 is $3,000. Assuming that the company's incremental borrowing rate is 4 percent per annum, the undiscounted fair value of the forward contract should be discounted at 0.3333 percent per month for two months (from the current date of December 31 to the settlement date of March 1). The fair value of the forward contract at December 31 is $2,980.10 ($3,000 × 0.993367).[6] Thus, the change in fair value since December 1 also is $2,980.10, because the fair value on December 1 was $0.

Authoritative literature indicates that the fair value of a derivative should be measured on a discounted (present value) basis. However, in a low interest rate environment, the difference between measuring a derivative on a discounted or undiscounted basis can be immaterial. For simplicity, examples presented later in this chapter recognize the fair value of derivatives at undiscounted amounts. Discounting to present value is ignored.

Foreign Currency Option

As noted earlier in this chapter, the fair value of a foreign currency option is composed of two components: intrinsic value and time value. The manner in which the *fair value of a foreign currency option* is determined depends on whether the option is traded on an exchange or has been acquired in the over-the-counter market. The fair value of an exchange-traded foreign currency option is its current market price quoted on the exchange. For over-the-counter options, fair value usually can be determined by obtaining a price quote from the option dealer. If dealer price quotes are unavailable, the company can estimate the value of an option using the modified Black-Scholes option pricing model (briefly mentioned earlier). Regardless of who does the calculation, principles similar to those of the Black-Scholes pricing model can be used to determine the fair value of the option.

---

[6] The present value factor for two months at 0.3333 percent per month is calculated as $1/1.003333^2$, or 0.993367.

Accounting for Changes in the Fair Value of Derivatives

Changes in the fair value of derivatives must be included in *comprehensive income,* which consists of two components: *Net Income* and *Other Comprehensive Income.* Other Comprehensive Income (OCI) consists of income items that authoritative accounting literature requires to be deferred in stockholders' equity such as unrealized gains and losses on available-for-sale debt securities. OCI is accumulated and closed to a separate line in the stockholders' equity section of the balance sheet titled *Accumulated Other Comprehensive Income* (AOCI). (In contrast, Net Income is closed to Retained Earnings.)

In accordance with U.S. GAAP, gains and losses arising from changes in the fair value of derivatives are recognized initially either (1) in Net Income (closed to Retained Earnings on the balance sheet) or (2) in Other Comprehensive Income (reflected on the balance sheet in Accumulated Other Comprehensive Income). Recognition treatment depends partly on whether a derivative is used for hedging or for speculation.

Using derivatives for speculation is not commonly done by companies other than financial institutions. Financial institutions might acquire derivative financial instruments as investments for speculative purposes. For example, assume that the three-month U.S. dollar–euro forward exchange rate is $1.12, and a speculator believes the U.S. dollar–euro spot rate in three months will be $1.10. In that case, the speculator would enter into a three-month forward contract to sell euros. At the future date, the speculator purchases euros at the spot rate of $1.10 and sells them at the contracted forward rate of $1.12, realizing a gain of $0.02 per euro. Of course, such an investment might just as easily generate a loss if the spot rate does not move in the expected direction. For speculative derivatives, the change in the fair value of the derivative must be recognized immediately as a foreign exchange gain or loss in net income.[7]

The accounting for changes in the fair value of derivatives used for hedging depends on a variety of factors, including whether the derivative qualifies for *hedge accounting.*

LO 7-6

Understand the basic concepts of hedge accounting.

Hedge Accounting

Companies enter into hedging relationships to minimize the adverse effect that changes in exchange rates have on cash flows and net income. As such, companies would like to account for hedges in a way that recognizes the gain or loss from the hedging instrument in net income in the same period as the loss or gain on the risk being hedged. This approach is known as *hedge accounting.* U.S. GAAP allows hedge accounting for foreign currency derivatives only if three conditions are satisfied:

1. The derivative is used to hedge either a cash flow exposure or a fair value exposure to foreign exchange risk.
2. The derivative is highly effective in offsetting changes in the cash flows or fair value related to the hedged item.
3. The derivative is properly documented as a hedge.

Each of these conditions is discussed in turn.[8]

Nature of the Hedged Risk

Derivatives for which companies wish to use hedge accounting must be designated as either a *cash flow hedge* or a *fair value hedge.* For hedges of recognized foreign currency–denominated assets and liabilities and hedges of foreign currency–denominated firm commitments, companies may choose between the two types of designation. Hedges of forecasted foreign currency–denominated transactions can qualify only as cash flow hedges. Accounting procedures differ for the two types of hedges. In general, gains and losses on cash flow hedges are included in other comprehensive income (and deferred on the balance sheet in

---

[7] In the next section, we will see that the change in fair value of a derivative designated as the fair value hedge of a foreign currency–denominated asset or liability also is recognized immediately in net income.

[8] The requirements to qualify for hedge accounting are rigorous, and companies must expend resources to meet them. Not all hedges that are effective in minimizing risk will qualify for hedge accounting and, in some cases, companies might decide not to pursue hedge accounting because the cost to do so exceeds the benefit.

Accumulated Other Comprehensive Income), and gains and losses on fair value hedges are recognized immediately in net income (and closed to Retained Earnings).

A *fair value exposure* exists if changes in exchange rates can affect the fair value of an asset or liability reported on the balance sheet. To qualify for hedge accounting, the fair value risk must have the potential to affect net income if it is not hedged. For example, a fair value risk is associated with a recognized foreign currency account receivable. If the foreign currency depreciates, the receivable must be written down with an offsetting loss recognized in net income. Authoritative literature has determined that a fair value exposure also exists for unrecognized foreign currency firm commitments.

A *cash flow exposure* exists if changes in exchange rates can affect the amount of cash flow to be realized from a foreign currency transaction with changes in cash flow reflected in net income. A foreign currency account receivable, for example, has both a fair value exposure and a cash flow exposure. A cash flow exposure exists for (1) recognized foreign currency assets and liabilities, (2) unrecognized foreign currency firm commitments, and (3) forecasted foreign currency transactions.

Hedge Effectiveness

For hedge accounting to be used initially, the derivative hedging instrument must be expected to be *highly effective* in mitigating foreign exchange risk related to the fair value or cash flow of the item being hedged. To continue to apply hedge accounting over the life of the derivative, the derivative instrument's effectiveness must be evaluated at each subsequent balance sheet date (including when interim financial statements are prepared). If a derivative instrument is deemed no longer to be highly effective at a subsequent balance sheet date, hedge accounting must be discontinued and the instrument's change in fair value is recognized immediately in net income.

At inception, a foreign currency derivative can be considered to be highly effective as a hedge if the *critical terms* of the hedging instrument match those of the hedged item. Critical terms include the currency type, currency amount, and settlement date. For example, a forward contract to purchase 100,000 Canadian dollars in one year would be a highly effective hedge of a 100,000 Canadian dollar liability that is payable in one year.

In practice, assessing hedge effectiveness for many derivative hedging instruments can be rather complicated, and could include the use of regression analysis or other quantitative methods. The FASB allows firms to avoid quantitative analysis of effectiveness when a derivative is perfectly effective—that is, the critical terms of the hedging instrument are exactly the same as the hedged item.

Exclusion of Components from Hedge Effectiveness Assessment

In general terms, the assessment of hedge effectiveness involves comparing the change in fair value of the hedging instrument with the change in fair value of the item being hedged. Accounting guidelines allow a reporting entity to exclude these components of the hedging instrument from the assessment of hedge effectiveness:

- Forward points (discount or premium)—when a forward contract is the hedging instrument.
- Time value—when an option is the hedging instrument.

In other words, an entity may choose to designate only the spot component of a forward contract as the hedging instrument, and may choose to designate only the intrinsic value of an option as the hedging instrument. When this choice is made, the excluded components (forward points, time value) must be recognized in net income using one of two approaches:

- The initial value of the excluded component is amortized to net income using a systematic and rationale method (such as straight-line) over the life of the hedging instrument.
- The change in fair value of the excluded component is recognized currently in net income.

Under either approach, the total amount of the excluded component will be recognized in net income over the life of the hedging instrument; only the pattern of income recognition will differ between the two approaches.

Conceptually, excluding forward points and time value from the hedging instrument and then allocating the excluded element to net income over its life is analogous to treating the hedging instrument as an insurance contract.

When a foreign currency option is purchased "at the money" (strike price equals spot rate), the option's purchase price is solely attributable to time value (intrinsic value is zero). Thus, the original time value of the option is the amount paid for "insurance." The cost of normal insurance, such as fire insurance, is recognized as insurance expense over the life of the insurance contract. Allocating the cost of a foreign currency option over its life to net income is analogous to treating the option as insurance. A similar conceptual argument can be made for allocating the forward points on a forward contract to net income over the life of the forward contract.

The only difference between the accounting for normal insurance and allocating the excluded component to net income is that the FASB requires the amortization of the derivative instrument's excluded component to be recognized in the same line item in the income statement as the item that is being hedged. For example, if a *forecasted* foreign currency export sale is being hedged, the amortization of the derivative instrument's excluded component must be reported in Sales. Similarly, if a *forecasted* foreign currency import purchase of inventory is being hedged, the amortization of the derivative instrument's excluded component must be reported in Cost of Goods Sold. Conversely, when a recognized foreign currency–denominated asset or liability is being hedged, the excluded component is allocated to the Foreign Exchange Gain or Loss line item in net income.

Hedge Documentation

For hedge accounting to be applied, U.S. GAAP requires formal documentation of the hedging relationship at the inception of the hedge (i.e., on the date a foreign currency forward contract is entered into or a foreign currency option is acquired). The hedging company must prepare a document that identifies the hedged item (for example, a 100,000 Canadian dollar liability), the hedging instrument (a forward contract to purchase 100,000 Canadian dollars), the nature of the risk being hedged (a cash flow exposure), how the hedging instrument's effectiveness will be assessed (through comparison of critical terms), and the risk management objective and strategy for undertaking the hedge (to minimize risk associated with a possible Canadian dollar appreciation).

Hedging Combinations

The specific accounting procedures followed and journal entries needed to account for a foreign currency hedging relationship are determined by a combination of the following factors:

1. The type of foreign currency item being hedged:
   a. Foreign currency–denominated asset or liability.
   b. Foreign currency–denominated firm commitment.
   c. Forecasted foreign currency–denominated transaction.

2. The nature of the risk exposure being hedged:
   a. Fair value exposure.
   b. Cash flow exposure.

3. The nature of the foreign currency item being hedged:
   a. Asset (or future sale).
   b. Liability (or future purchase).

4. The type of derivative hedging instrument used:
   a. Forward contract.
   b. Option.

5. The component(s) of the derivative identified as the hedging instrument:
   a. Forward contract—spot component only or spot and forward components.
   b. Option—intrinsic value component only or intrinsic and time value components.

In the next several sections in this chapter, we discuss the accounting for hedges of (1) recognized foreign currency assets and liabilities, (2) unrecognized foreign currency firm commitments, and (3) forecasted foreign currency transactions. We demonstrate through examples the use of both forward contracts and options to hedge these items, and we selectively demonstrate the accounting for both cash flow and fair value hedges. For simplicity, we focus on examples in which only the spot component (forward contract) or intrinsic value component (option) has been identified as the hedging instrument. Also, for simplicity, we ignore discounting to present value in determining the fair value of forward contracts and firm commitments.

We focus on hedges entered into by an exporter that has a current or future foreign currency asset (receivable) that is exposed to foreign exchange risk. The comprehensive illustration at the end of this chapter demonstrates the accounting for hedges entered into by an importer that has an existing or future foreign currency liability (payable).

Exhibit 7.2 provides an overall summary of the procedures followed in accounting for hedges of foreign exchange risk for those combinations presented in this chapter. By examining this exhibit, the similarities and differences in the procedures followed and accounting entries prepared to account for each hedge combination can be discerned.

LO 7-7

Account for forward contracts and options used as hedges of foreign currency–denominated assets and liabilities.

Hedges of Foreign Currency–Denominated Assets and Liabilities

Hedges of foreign currency–denominated assets and liabilities, such as accounts receivable and accounts payable, can qualify as either *cash flow hedges* or *fair value hedges*. To qualify as a cash flow hedge, the hedging instrument must completely offset the variability in the cash flows associated with the foreign currency receivable or payable. If the hedging instrument does not qualify as a cash flow hedge or if the company elects not to designate the hedging instrument as a cash flow hedge, the hedge is designated as a fair value hedge. The following summarizes the basic accounting for the two types of hedges of foreign currency–denominated assets and liabilities, assuming that forward points (forward contract) and time value (option) are excluded in assessing hedge effectiveness.

Cash Flow Hedge

At each balance sheet date, the following procedures are required:

1. The hedged asset (foreign currency account receivable) or liability (foreign currency account payable) is adjusted to fair value based on changes in the spot exchange rate, and a foreign exchange gain or loss is recognized in net income (Cash Flow Hedge Step B.1 in Exhibit 7.2).

2. To comply with the fundamental requirement of derivatives accounting, the derivative hedging instrument (forward contract or option) is adjusted to fair value (resulting in an asset or liability reported on the balance sheet) with the counterpart recognized as a change in other comprehensive income (OCI) (Cash Flow Hedge Step B.2 in Exhibit 7.2).

3. To achieve hedge accounting, a foreign exchange gain or loss related to the hedging instrument is recognized to offset the foreign exchange loss or gain on the hedged asset or liability, with the counterpart recorded in OCI (Cash Flow Hedge Step B.3 in Exhibit 7.2).

4. An additional foreign exchange loss is recognized in net income (with the counterpart in OCI) to reflect (a) the current period's amortization of the original discount or premium on the forward contract (if a forward contract is the hedging instrument) or (b) the change in the *time value* of the option (if an option is the hedging instrument) (Cash Flow Hedge Step B.4 in Exhibit 7.2).

Fair Value Hedge

At each balance sheet date, the following procedures are required:

1. Adjust the hedged asset or liability to fair value based on changes in the spot exchange rate and recognize a foreign exchange gain or loss in net income (Fair Value Hedge Step B.1 in Exhibit 7.2).

2. Adjust the derivative hedging instrument to fair value (resulting in an asset or liability reported on the balance sheet) and recognize the counterpart as a foreign exchange gain or loss in net income (Fair Value Hedge Step B.2 in Exhibit 7.2).

EXHIBIT 7.2 Summary of Accounting for Hedges of Foreign Exchange Risk

| | Hedge of a Foreign Currency–Denominated Asset or Liability | | | | Hedge of a Foreign Currency Firm Commitment | | Hedge of a Forecasted Foreign Currency Transaction | |
| | Cash Flow Hedge | | Fair Value Hedge | | Fair Value Hedge | | Cash Flow Hedge | |
Date	Forward Contract	Option	Forward Contract	Option	Forward Contract	Option	Forward Contract	Option
A. Initiation Date	1. Recognize the transaction (sale or purchase) and foreign currency–denominated asset or liability 2. No entry related to forward contract (zero fair value)	1. Recognize the transaction (sale or purchase) and foreign currency–denominated asset or liability 2. Recognize option as an asset (purchase price is fair value)	1. Recognize the transaction (sale or purchase) and foreign currency–denominated asset or liability 2. No entry related to forward contract (zero fair value)	1. Recognize the transaction (sale or purchase) and foreign currency–denominated asset or liability 2. Recognize option as an asset (purchase price is fair value)	1. No entry related to the firm commitment (zero value) 2. No entry related to forward contract (zero fair value)	1. No entry related to the firm commitment 2. Recognize option as an asset (purchase price is fair value)	1. No entry related to the forecasted transaction 2. No entry related to forward contract (zero fair value)	1. No entry related to the forecasted transaction 2. Recognize option as an asset (purchase price is fair value)
B. Balance Sheet Date	1. Adjust hedged asset or liability to fair value, with counterpart (change in fair value) reported as foreign exchange gain or loss in net income 2. Adjust forward contract to fair value (either an asset or a liability), with counterpart (change in fair value) reported in OCI	1. Adjust hedged asset or liability to fair value, with counterpart (change in fair value) reported as foreign exchange gain or loss in net income 2. Adjust option to fair value (either an asset or zero value), with counterpart (change in fair value) reported in OCI	1. Adjust hedged asset or liability to fair value, with counterpart (change in fair value) reported as foreign exchange gain or loss in net income 2. Adjust forward contract to fair value (either an asset or a liability), with counterpart (change in fair value) reported as foreign exchange gain or loss in net income	1. Adjust hedged asset or liability to fair value, with counterpart (change in fair value) reported as foreign exchange gain or loss in net income 2. Adjust option to fair value (either an asset or zero value), with counterpart (change in fair value) reported as foreign exchange gain or loss in net income	1. Adjust forward contract to fair value (either an asset or a liability), with counterpart (change in fair value) reported as foreign exchange gain or loss in net income 2. Adjust firm commitment to fair value (based on change in forward rate), with counterpart (change in fair value) reported as foreign exchange gain or loss in net income	1. Adjust option to fair value (either an asset or zero value), with counterpart (change in fair value) reported as foreign exchange gain or loss in net income 2. Adjust firm commitment to fair value (based on change in spot rate), with counterpart (change in fair value) reported as foreign exchange gain or loss in net income	1. N/A 2. Adjust forward contract to fair value (either an asset or a liability), with counterpart (change in fair value) reported in OCI	1. N/A 2. Adjust option to fair value (either an asset or zero value), with counterpart (change in fair value) reported in OCI

(continued)

EXHIBIT 7.2 (Continued)

Date	Hedge of a Foreign Currency–Denominated Asset or Liability				Hedge of a Foreign Currency Firm Commitment		Hedge of a Forecasted Foreign Currency Transaction	
	Cash Flow Hedge		Fair Value Hedge		Fair Value Hedge		Cash Flow Hedge	
	Forward Contract	Option	Forward Contract	Option	Forward Contract	Option	Forward Contract	Option
	3. Recognize a loss or gain related to the hedging instrument (with counterpart reported in OCI) to offset the foreign exchange gain or loss on the hedged item recognized in B.1	3. Recognize a loss or gain related to the hedging instrument (with counterpart reported in OCI) to offset the foreign exchange gain or loss on the hedged item recognized in B.1	3. N/A	3. N/A	3. N/A	3. N/A	3. N/A	3. N/A
	4. Recognize a portion of the forward points (discount or premium) in net income with the counterpart reported in OCI	4. Recognize a portion of the time value of the option in net income with the counterpart reported in OCI	4. Adjust the already recognized net foreign exchange gain or loss to reflect the current period's allocation of forward points in net income, with the counterpart reported in OCI	4. Adjust the already recognized net foreign exchange gain or loss to reflect the current period's allocation of option time value in net income, with the counterpart reported in OCI (this step is needed only when the option has no intrinsic value)	4. N/A	4. N/A	4. Recognize a portion of the forward points (discount or premium) in net income with counterpart reported in OCI	4. Recognize a portion of the time value of the option in net income with counterpart reported in OCI

(continued)

EXHIBIT 7.2 (Continued)

| | Hedge of a Foreign Currency–Denominated Asset or Liability | | | | Hedge of a Foreign Currency Firm Commitment | | Hedge of a Forecasted Foreign Currency Transaction | |
| | Cash Flow Hedge | | Fair Value Hedge | | Fair Value Hedge | | Cash Flow Hedge | |
Date	Forward Contract	Option	Forward Contract	Option	Forward Contract	Option	Forward Contract	Option
C. Settlement Date	1–4. Repeat steps B.1–B.4 5. Recognize settlement of the foreign currency–denominated asset or liability 6. Recognize settlement of the forward contract[*]	1–4. Repeat steps B.1–B.4 5. Recognize settlement of the foreign currency 6. Recognize exercise (or expiration) of the option[*]	1–2. Repeat steps B.1 and B.2 3. Transfer the amount in AOCI (as a result of step B.4) to net income to reflect the current period's allocation of forward points 4. Recognize settlement of the foreign currency–denominated asset or liability 5. Recognize settlement of the forward contract[†]	1–2. Repeat steps B.1 and B.2 3. Transfer the amount in AOCI (as a result of step B.4) to net income to reflect the current period's allocation of option time value 4. Recognize settlement of the foreign currency–denominated asset or liability 5. Recognize exercise (or expiration) of the option[†]	1–2. Repeat steps B.1 and B.2 3. Recognize the transaction (sale or purchase) 4. Recognize settlement of the forward contract[#] 5. Close the balance in the firm commitment account as an adjustment to net income	1–2. Repeat steps B.1 and B.2 3. Recognize the transaction (sale or purchase) 4. Recognize exercise (or expiration) of the option[#] 5. Close the balance in the firm commitment account as an adjustment to net income	1–2. Repeat steps B.2 and B.4 3. Recognize the transaction (sale or purchase) 4. Recognize settlement of the forward contract[#] 5. Close the balance in AOCI related to the forward contract as an adjustment to net income	1–2. Repeat steps B.2 and B.4 3. Recognize the transaction (sale or purchase) 4. Recognize exercise (or expiration) of the option[#] 5. Close the balance in AOCI related to the option as an adjustment to net income

[*]Step 6 precedes step 5 in the case of a foreign currency–denominated liability.
[†]Step 4 precedes step 3 in the case of a foreign currency–denominated liability.
[#]Step 4 precedes step 3 in the case of a foreign currency purchase transaction.

3. Adjust the net foreign exchange gain or loss thus far recognized to properly reflect (a) the current period's amortization of the original discount or premium on the forward contract (if a forward contract is the hedging instrument) or (b) the change in the *time value* of the option (if an option is the hedging instrument) (Fair Value Hedge Step B.4 in Exhibit 7.2). *Note: If an option is the hedging instrument, this procedure is only needed if the option has zero intrinsic value at the balance sheet date. If the option has a positive intrinsic value at the balance sheet date, this procedure is unnecessary. In that case, procedures 1. and 2. (Fair Value Hedge Steps B.1 and B2 in Exhibit 7.2) will automatically result in the net foreign exchange gain or loss being equal to the change in the time value of the option.*

Forward Contract Hedge of a Foreign Currency–Denominated Asset

We now return to the Eximco example in which the company has a foreign currency account receivable to demonstrate the accounting for a hedge of a recognized foreign currency–denominated asset.[9] In the preceding example, Eximco has an asset exposure in British pounds when it sells goods to the U.K. customer and allows the customer three months to pay for its purchase. To hedge its exposure to a possible decline in the U.S. dollar value of the British pound, Eximco enters into a forward contract.

Assume that on December 1, 2023, the three-month forward rate for British pounds is $1.288 and Eximco signs a contract with New World Bank to deliver 1 million British pounds in three months in exchange for $1,288,000. No cash changes hands on December 1, 2023. Because the spot rate on December 1 is $1.300, the British pound (£) is selling at a discount in the three-month forward market (the forward rate is less than the spot rate). Because the British pound is selling at a discount of $0.012 ($1.300 – $1.288) per pound, Eximco receives $12,000 less than it would have if payment had been received at the date the goods are delivered ($1,288,000 versus $1,300,000). This $12,000 can be viewed as the "insurance" that Eximco pays to avoid the risk that the British pound could depreciate over the next three months. The $12,000 reduction in cash flow also is the cost of extending foreign currency credit to the foreign customer.[10] Conceptually, this cost is similar to the transaction loss that arises on the export sale. It exists only because the transaction is denominated in a foreign currency. The major difference is that Eximco knows the exact amount of the loss at the date of sale, whereas when it is left unhedged, the company does not know the size of the transaction loss until three months pass. (In fact, it is possible that the unhedged receivable could result in a transaction gain rather than a transaction loss.)

Because the future spot rate turns out to be only $1.272, selling British pounds at a forward rate of $1.288 is better than leaving the British pound receivable unhedged: Eximco will receive $16,000 more as a result of the hedge. This can be viewed as an economic gain resulting from the use of the forward contract. Unlike the discount loss, however, the exact size of this gain is not known until three months pass. (In fact, it is possible that use of the forward contract could result in an additional loss. This would occur if the spot rate on March 1, 2024, is higher than the forward rate of $1.288.)

Eximco must account for its foreign currency transaction and the related forward contract simultaneously but separately. The process can be better understood by referring to the steps involving the three parties—Eximco, the British customer, and New World Bank—shown in Exhibit 7.3.

Because the critical terms (currency type, currency amount, and settlement date) of the forward contract match the corresponding terms of the account receivable, the hedge is assessed as being highly effective. If Eximco properly designates the forward contract as a hedge of its British pound account receivable position, it may apply hedge accounting. Because it completely offsets the variability in the cash flows related to the account receivable, Eximco may

---

[9] The comprehensive illustration at the end of this chapter demonstrates the accounting for the hedge of a foreign currency–denominated liability.

[10] This should not be confused with the cost associated with normal credit risk—that is, the risk that the customer will not pay for its purchase. That is a separate issue unrelated to the currency in which the transaction is denominated.

EXHIBIT 7.3
Hedge of a Foreign Currency Account Receivable with a Forward Contract

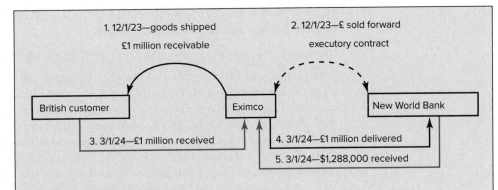

Steps on December 1, 2023

1. Eximco ships goods to the British customer, thereby creating an Account Receivable of £1 million.
2. Eximco then sells £1 million three months forward to New World Bank, creating an executory contract to pay £1 million and receive $1,288,000.

Steps on March 1, 2024

3. The British customer remits £1 million to Eximco—the £ Account Receivable has been received and Eximco has £1 million reflected in an account titled Foreign Currency (£).
4. Eximco delivers £1 million to New World Bank.
5. New World Bank pays Eximco $1,288,000.

designate the forward contract as a cash flow hedge. Alternatively, because changes in the spot rate affect not only the cash flows but also the fair value of the foreign currency receivable, Eximco may elect to account for this forward contract as a fair value hedge.

In either case, Eximco determines the fair value of the forward contract by referring to the change in the forward rate for a contract maturing on March 1, 2024. The relevant exchange rates, U.S. dollar value of the British pound receivable, and fair value of the forward contract are determined as follows:

| | | Account Receivable (£) | | Forward | Forward Contract | |
| | | U.S. Dollar | Change in U.S. | Rate to | | Change in |
Date	Spot Rate	Value	Dollar Value	3/1/24	Fair Value	Fair Value
12/1/23	$1.300	$1,300,000	$ –0–	$1.288	$ –0–	$ –0–
12/31/23	1.285	1,285,000	–15,000	1.278	10,000*	+10,000
3/1/24	1.272	1,272,000	–13,000	1.272 (spot)	16,000†	+ 6,000

*$1,288,000 − $1,278,000 = $10,000. For simplicity, discounting to present value is ignored.
†$1,288,000 − $1,272,000 = $16,000.

Eximco pays nothing to enter into the forward contract at December 1, 2023, and the forward contract has a fair value of zero on that date. The original discount on the forward contract is $12,000, determined by the difference in the British pound spot rate and three-month forward rate on December 1, 2023 [($1.300 − $1.288) × £1 million]. At December 31, 2023, the forward rate for a contract to deliver British pounds on March 1, 2024, is $1.278. Eximco could enter into a forward contract on December 31, 2023, to sell 1 million British pounds for $1,278,000 on March 1, 2024. Because Eximco has contracted to sell 1 million British pounds for $1,288,000, the value of the forward contract is $10,000.[11] Because the fair value is positive, the forward contract is recognized as an asset on December 31, 2023. On March 1, 2024, the forward rate to sell British pounds on that date is, by definition, the spot rate of $1.272. At that rate, Eximco could sell 1 million British pounds for $1,272,000. Because Eximco has a contract to sell British pounds for $1,288,000, the fair value of the forward contract on

[11] Conceptually, the undiscounted value of the forward contract should be discounted to its present value. However, in the current low-interest environment, the difference between the discounted and undiscounted values is immaterial. For simplicity, we ignore discounting in determining the fair value of a forward contract.

March 1, 2024, is $16,000. From December 31, 2023, to March 1, 2024, the fair value of the forward contract asset has increased by $6,000.

Forward Contract Designated as Cash Flow Hedge

Assume that Eximco designates the forward contract as a *cash flow hedge* of a foreign currency–denominated asset. Furthermore, the company elects to exclude the forward points component of the forward contract in assessing hedge effectiveness. In this case, Eximco must allocate the $12,000 original forward contract discount as a loss to net income over the life of the contract using either an amortization method or by referring to changes in the fair value of the forward points. For simplicity, the company chooses to amortize the forward discount to net income using a straight-line method on a monthly basis, as follows:

2023: $12,000 × ⅓ = $4,000 (one month of amortization)

2024: $12,000 × ⅔ = $8,000 (two months of amortization)

The company prepares the following journal entries to account for the foreign currency transaction and the related forward contract:

2023 Journal Entries—Forward Contract Designated as a Cash Flow Hedge

12/1/23	Accounts Receivable (£).............................	1,300,000	
	Sales.......................................		1,300,000
	To record the sale and £1 million account receivable at the spot rate of $1.300 (Cash Flow Hedge Step A.1 in Exhibit 7.2).		
	The company makes no formal entry for the forward contract because it is an executory contract (no cash changes hands) and has a fair value of zero (Cash Flow Hedge Step A.2 in Exhibit 7.2).		

Eximco prepares a memorandum designating the forward contract as a hedge of the risk of changes in the cash flow to be received on the foreign currency account receivable resulting from changes in the U.S. dollar–British pound exchange rate. Following steps B.1–B.4 in accounting for a cash flow hedge presented in Exhibit 7.2, the company prepares the following journal entries on December 31:

12/31/23	Foreign Exchange Gain or Loss.......................	15,000	
	Accounts Receivable (£).........................		15,000
	To adjust the value of the £ receivable to the new spot rate of $1.285 and recognize a foreign exchange loss resulting from the depreciation of the £ since December 1 (Cash Flow Hedge Step B.1 in Exhibit 7.2).		
	Forward Contract....................................	10,000	
	Other Comprehensive Income (OCI)...............		10,000
	To record the forward contract as an asset at its fair value of $10,000 with a corresponding credit to OCI (Cash Flow Hedge Step B.2 in Exhibit 7.2).		
	Other Comprehensive Income (OCI)....................	15,000	
	Foreign Exchange Gain or Loss....................		15,000
	To record a foreign exchange gain related to the forward contract to offset the foreign exchange loss on the account receivable with a corresponding debit to OCI (Cash Flow Hedge Step B.3 in Exhibit 7.2).		
	Foreign Exchange Gain or Loss.......................	4,000	
	Other Comprehensive Income (OCI)...............		4,000
	To amortize the forward contract discount to net income over the life of the contract using the straight-line method with a corresponding credit to OCI (Cash Flow Hedge Step B.4 in Exhibit 7.2).		

The first entry at December 31, 2023, serves to revalue the foreign currency account receivable and recognize a foreign exchange loss of $15,000 in net income. Because the forward contract has a positive fair value of $10,000, it must be recognized on the balance sheet as an asset. Thus, the second entry makes a debit of $10,000 to Forward Contract (an asset account). Under cash flow hedge accounting, the change in the fair value of the forward contract, which has gone from $0 to $10,000, is not recognized immediately in net income, but instead is recognized in Other Comprehensive Income (OCI), which is subsequently closed to Accumulated Other Comprehensive Income (AOCI) in stockholders' equity.

The third entry achieves the objective of hedge accounting by recognizing a $15,000 foreign exchange gain on the forward contract with the counterpart reported in OCI. As a result of this entry, the foreign exchange gain on forward contract of $15,000 and the foreign exchange loss on the account receivable of $15,000 exactly offset one another, and the impact on net income is zero. The gain on forward contract and loss on account receivable are both recorded in the Foreign Exchange Gain or Loss account, which will have either a debit (net loss), credit (net gain), or zero balance at the end of the period.

The last entry uses the straight-line method to amortize a portion of the $12,000 forward contract discount to net income (Foreign Exchange Gain or Loss). By making the credit in this entry to OCI, the correct amounts are reported in net income and on the balance sheet, and the balance sheet remains in balance.

The impact on net income for the year 2023 follows:

Sales	$1,300,000
Net foreign exchange gain (loss)	(4,000)
Impact on net income	$1,296,000

The impact on net income is closed to Retained Earnings and the debit balance of $1,000 in OCI is closed to AOCI. The overall impact on the December 31, 2023, balance sheet is as follows:

Assets		**Liabilities and Stockholders' Equity**	
Accounts receivable (£)	$1,285,000	Retained earnings	$1,296,000
Forward contract	10,000	AOCI	(1,000)
	$1,295,000		$1,295,000

2024 Journal Entries—Forward Contract Designated as Cash Flow Hedge

From December 31, 2023, to March 1, 2024, the British pound account receivable decreases in value by $13,000 and the forward contract increases in value by $6,000. In addition, on March 1, 2024, the remaining discount on forward contract must be amortized to net income. The company prepares the following journal entries on March 1, 2024, to reflect these changes:

3/1/24	Foreign Exchange Gain or Loss	13,000	
	Accounts Receivable (£)		13,000
	To adjust the value of the £ receivable to the new spot rate of $1.272 and recognize a foreign exchange loss resulting from the depreciation of the £ since December 31 (Cash Flow Hedge Step C.1 in Exhibit 7.2).		
	Forward Contract	6,000	
	Other Comprehensive Income (OCI)		6,000
	To adjust the carrying value of the forward contract to its current fair value of $16,000 with a corresponding credit to OCI (Cash Flow Hedge Step C.2 in Exhibit 7.2).		

(*continued*)

(*continued*)

Other Comprehensive Income (OCI).....................	13,000
Foreign Exchange Gain or Loss....................	13,000
To record a foreign exchange gain on forward contract to offset the foreign exchange loss on account receivable with a corresponding debit to OCI (Cash Flow Hedge Step C.3 in Exhibit 7.2).	
Foreign Exchange Gain or Loss........................	8,000
Other Comprehensive Income (OCI)................	8,000
To amortize the remaining forward contract discount to net income with a corresponding credit to OCI (Cash Flow Hedge Step C.4 in Exhibit 7.2).	

This series of journal entries results in a net credit to OCI of $1,000 in 2024. Once this net credit to OCI is closed to AOCI, the balance in AOCI is reduced to zero.

The next two journal entries record the receipt of British pounds from the customer, close out the British pound account receivable, and record the settlement of the forward contract.

3/1/24	Foreign Currency (£)...............................	1,272,000
	Accounts Receivable (£).........................	1,272,000
	To record receipt of £1 million from the British customer as an asset (Foreign Currency) at the spot rate of $1.272 (Cash Flow Hedge Step C.5 in Exhibit 7.2).	
	Cash	1,288,000
	Foreign Currency (£)............................	1,272,000
	Forward Contract	16,000
	To record settlement of the forward contract (i.e., record receipt of $1,288,000 in exchange for delivery of £1 million) and remove the forward contract from the accounts (Cash Flow Hedge Step C.6 in Exhibit 7.2).	

The impact on net income for the year 2024 follows:

Net foreign exchange gain (loss).....................	$(8,000)
Impact on net income	$(8,000)

The net foreign exchange loss of $8,000 in 2024 is solely attributable to the current period's amortization of the forward contract discount.

Over the two accounting periods, Eximco reports sales of $1,300,000 and a cumulative net foreign exchange loss of $12,000. The net foreign exchange loss is equal to the original forward contract discount and reflects the cost of extending credit to the British customer. It also reflects the amount of cost the company incurred as "insurance" to hedge the foreign exchange risk associated with a foreign currency receivable. The net effect on the balance sheet over the two years is an increase in Cash of $1,288,000 with a corresponding increase in Retained Earnings of $1,288,000 ($1,296,000 − $8,000).

The net benefit from entering into the forward contract is $16,000. This "gain" is not directly reflected in net income. However, it can be calculated as the fair value of the forward contract immediately prior to its settlement.

Forward Contract Premium

What if the forward rate on December 1, 2023, had been $1.306 rather than $1.288 (i.e., the British pound was selling at a premium in the forward market)? In that case, Eximco would receive $6,000 more through the forward sale of British pounds ($1,306,000) than if it had received the British pounds at the date of sale ($1,300,000). Eximco would allocate the forward contract premium as an increase in net income at the rate of $2,000 per month: $2,000 at December 31, 2023, and $4,000 at March 1, 2024.

Forward Contract Designated as Fair Value Hedge

Now assume that Eximco designates the forward contract as a fair value hedge rather than as a cash flow hedge. In that case, the company recognizes the change in fair value of the forward contract as a foreign exchange gain or loss directly in net income. Eximco chooses to exclude the forward component in assessing hedge effectiveness and to recognize the forward discount in net income on a straight-line basis. However, the company does not need to make a separate entry to amortize the original discount on the forward contract. Instead, the company will make an adjustment to the net foreign exchange gain or loss otherwise recognized to properly recognize a discount loss.

2023 Journal Entries—Forward Contract Designated as a Fair Value Hedge

12/1/23	Accounts Receivable (£).............................	1,300,000	
	Sales...		1,300,000
	To record the sale and £1 million account receivable at the spot rate of $1.30 (Fair Value Hedge Step A.1 in Exhibit 7.2).		

The forward contract requires no formal entry (Fair Value Hedge Step A.2 in Exhibit 7.2). A memorandum designates the forward contract as a hedge of the risk of changes in the fair value of the foreign currency account receivable resulting from changes in the U.S. dollar–British pound exchange rate.

Following the two steps in accounting for a fair value hedge presented in Exhibit 7.2, the company prepares the following entries on December 31:

12/31/23	Foreign Exchange Gain or Loss.........................	15,000	
	Accounts Receivable (£)		15,000
	To adjust the value of the £ receivable to the new spot rate of $1.285 and record a foreign exchange loss resulting from the depreciation of the £ since December 1 (Fair Value Hedge Step B.1 in Exhibit 7.2).		
	Forward Contract	10,000	
	Foreign Exchange Gain or Loss.....................		10,000
	To record the forward contract as an asset at its fair value of $10,000 and recognize a forward contract gain for the change in the fair value of the forward contract since December 1 (Fair Value Hedge Step B.2 in Exhibit 7.2).		

The first entry at December 31, 2023, serves to revalue the foreign currency account receivable and recognize a foreign exchange loss of $15,000. The second entry recognizes the forward contract as an asset of $10,000 on the balance sheet. At this point, the company has recognized a net foreign exchange loss of $5,000. The current period's amortization of forward contract discount is only $4,000 ($12,000 × ⅓), so the following adjustment must be made:

12/31/23	Other Comprehensive Income (OCI).....................	1,000	
	Foreign Exchange Gain or Loss.....................		1,000
	To adjust the amount recognized as foreign exchange loss to reflect the current period's amortization of the forward contract discount in net income with a corresponding debit to OCI (Fair Value Hedge Step B.4 in Exhibit 7.2).		

As a result of this entry, a net foreign exchange loss of $4,000 ($5,000 − $1,000), equal to the current period's amortization of forward contract discount, is reported in net income.

The impact on net income for the year 2023 is as follows:

Sales	$1,300,000
Net foreign exchange gain (loss)	(4,000)
Impact on net income	$1,296,000

Once net income and OCI are closed to Retained Earnings and AOCI, respectively, the effect on the December 31, 2023, balance sheet is as follows:

Assets		**Liabilities and Stockholders' Equity**	
Accounts receivable (£)	$1,285,000	Retained earnings	$1,296,000
Forward contract	10,000	AOCI	(1,000)
	$1,295,000		$1,295,000

2024 Journal Entries—Forward Contract Designated as a Fair Value Hedge

The company prepares the following entries on March 1:

3/1/24	Foreign Exchange Gain or Loss	13,000	
	Accounts Receivable (£)		13,000
	To adjust the value of the £ receivable to the new spot rate of $1.272 and record a foreign exchange loss resulting from the depreciation of the £ since December 31 (Fair Value Hedge Step C.1 in Exhibit 7.2).		
	Forward Contract	6,000	
	Foreign Exchange Gain or Loss		6,000
	To adjust the carrying value of the forward contract to its current fair value of $16,000 and record a forward contract gain for the change in the fair value since December 31 (Fair Value Hedge Step C.2 in Exhibit 7.2).		
	Foreign Exchange Gain or Loss	1,000	
	Accumulated Other Comprehensive Income (AOCI)		1,000
	To transfer the amount deferred in AOCI to net income to accurately reflect the current period's amortization of forward contract discount (Fair Value Hedge Step C.3. in Exhibit 7.2).		
	Foreign Currency (£)	1,272,000	
	Accounts Receivable (£)		1,272,000
	To record receipt of £1 million from the German customer as an asset at the spot rate of $1.272 (Fair Value Hedge Step C.4. in Exhibit 7.2).		
	Cash	1,288,000	
	Foreign Currency (£)		1,272,000
	Forward Contract		16,000
	To record settlement of the forward contract (i.e., record receipt of $1,288,000 in exchange for delivery of £1 million) and remove the forward contract from the accounts (Fair Value Hedge Step C.5. in Exhibit 7.2).		

The first three entries result in the recognition of a net foreign exchange loss of $8,000 ($13,000 − $6,000 + $1,000), which is equal to the current period's amortization of forward contract discount.

The impact on net income for the year 2024 follows:

Net foreign exchange gain (loss)	$(8,000)
Impact on net income	$(8,000)

? Discussion Question

DO WE HAVE A GAIN OR WHAT?

Ahnuld Corporation, a health juice producer, recently expanded its sales through exports to foreign markets. Earlier this year, the company negotiated the sale of several thousand cases of turnip juice to a retailer in the country of Tcheckia. The customer is unwilling to assume the risk of having to pay in U.S. dollars. Desperate to enter the Tcheckian market, the vice president for international sales agrees to denominate the sale in tchecks, the national currency of Tcheckia. The current exchange rate for 1 tcheck is $2.00. In addition, the customer indicates that it cannot pay until it sells all of the juice. Payment of 100,000 tchecks is scheduled for six months from the date of sale.

Fearful that the tcheck might depreciate in value over the next six months, the head of the risk management department at Ahnuld Corporation enters into a forward contract to sell tchecks in six months at a forward rate of $1.80. The forward contract is designated as a fair value hedge of the tcheck receivable. Six months later, when Ahnuld receives payment from the Tcheckian customer, the exchange rate for the tcheck is $1.70. The corporate treasurer calls the head of the risk management department in for a meeting.

Treasurer: I see that your decision to hedge our foreign currency position on that sale to Tcheckia was a bad one.

Department head: What do you mean? We have a gain on that forward contract. We're $10,000 better off from having entered into that hedge.

Treasurer: That's not what the books say. The accountants have recorded a net loss of $20,000 on that particular deal. I'm afraid I'm not going to be able to pay you a bonus this year. Another bad deal like this one and I'm going to have to demote you back to the interest rate swap department.

Department head: Those bean counters have messed up again. I told the folks in international sales that selling to customers in Tcheckia was risky, but at least by hedging our exposure, we managed to receive a reasonable amount of cash on that deal. In fact, we ended up with a gain of $10,000 on the hedge. Tell the accountants to check their debits and credits again. I'm sure they just put a debit in the wrong place or some accounting thing like that.

Have the accountants made a mistake? Does the company have a loss, a gain, or both from this forward contract?

Over the two periods, Eximco has recognized a total net foreign exchange loss of $12,000, which is equal to the original discount on forward contract, and accurately reflects the cost of extending credit to the British customer. (The company receives only $1,288,000 in cash rather than $1,300,000 if it had received payment on the date of sale.)

The net effect on the balance sheet for the two periods is an increase in Cash of $1,288,000 with a corresponding increase in Retained Earnings of $1,288,000 ($1,296,000 in 2023 less $8,000 in 2024). The fair value of the forward contract of $16,000 reflects the net benefit (increase in cash inflow) from Eximco's decision to hedge the British pound receivable. (The company receives $1,288,000 from entering into a forward contract rather than $1,272,000 if it had not hedged the British pound account receivable.)

Companies often cannot (or do not bother to) designate as hedges the forward contracts they use to hedge foreign currency–denominated assets and liabilities. In those cases, the company accounts for the forward contract as if it were a speculative investment. The company reports an undesignated forward contract on the balance sheet at fair value as an asset or liability and immediately recognizes changes in the fair value of the forward contract in net income. This accounting treatment is the same as if the forward contract had been designated as a fair value hedge. However, there would be no adjustment to Foreign Exchange Gain or Loss to reflect the current period's amortization of forward contract discount. Therefore, the only difference between a forward contract designated as a fair value hedge of a foreign currency–denominated asset or liability and an undesignated (speculative) forward contract is the pattern in which the company recognizes the original forward discount in net income.

Option Hedge of a Foreign Currency–Denominated Asset

As an alternative to a forward contract, Eximco could hedge its exposure to foreign exchange risk arising from the British pound account receivable by purchasing a foreign currency put option. A put option would give Eximco the right but not the obligation to sell 1 million British pounds on March 1, 2024, at a predetermined strike price. Assume that on December 1, 2023, Eximco purchases an over-the-counter option from its bank with a strike price of $1.300 when the spot rate is $1.300 and pays a premium of $0.020 per British pound.[12] Thus, the purchase price for the option is $20,000 ($0.020 × £1 million).

Because the strike price and spot rate are the same, no intrinsic value is associated with this option. The premium is based solely on time value; that is, it is possible that the British pound will depreciate and the spot rate on March 1, 2024, will be less than $1.300, in which case the option will be "in the money." If the spot rate for British pounds on March 1, 2024, is less than the strike price of $1.300, Eximco will exercise its option and sell its 1 million British pounds at the strike price of $1.300. Conversely, if the spot rate for British pounds in three months is more than the strike price of $1.300, Eximco will not exercise its option but will sell the British pounds it receives at the higher spot rate. By purchasing this option, Eximco is guaranteed a minimum cash flow from the export sale of $1,280,000 ($1,300,000 from exercising the option less the $20,000 cost of the option). There is no limit to the maximum number of U.S. dollars that Eximco could receive.

As is true for other derivative financial instruments, authoritative accounting literature requires foreign currency options to be reported on the balance sheet at fair value. The fair value of a foreign currency option at the balance sheet date is determined by reference to the premium quoted by banks on that date for an option with a similar expiration date. Banks (and other sellers of options) determine the current premium by incorporating relevant variables at the balance sheet date into the modified Black-Scholes option pricing model. Changes in value for the British pound account receivable and the foreign currency option are summarized as follows:

Date	Spot Rate	Account Receivable (£)		Option Premium for 3/1/24	Foreign Currency Option	
		U.S. Dollar Value	Change in U.S. Dollar Value		Fair Value	Change in Fair Value
12/1/23	$1.300	$1,300,000	$ –0–	$0.0200	$20,000	$ –0–
12/31/23	1.285	1,285,000	−15,000	0.0245	24,500	+4,500
3/1/24	1.272	1,272,000	−13,000	N/A	28,000	+3,500

The fair value of the foreign currency put option at December 1 is its cost of $20,000. The spot rate for the British pound decreases during December, which causes an increase in the fair value of the put option; the right to sell British pounds at $1.300 is of more value when the spot rate is $1.285 (on December 31) than when the spot rate was $1.300 (on December 1). The bank determines the fair value of the option at December 31 to be $24,500. By March 1, the British pound spot rate has decreased to $1.272. By exercising its option on March 1 at the

---

[12] The seller of the option determined the price of the option (the premium) by using a variation of the Black-Scholes option pricing formula.

strike price of $1.300, Eximco will receive $1,300,000 from its export sale, rather than only $1,272,000 if it were required to sell British pounds in the spot market on March 1. Thus, the option has a fair value of $28,000 on March 1.

We can decompose the fair value of the foreign currency option into its intrinsic value and time value components as follows:

Date	Fair Value	Intrinsic Value	Time Value	Change in Time Value
12/1/23	$20,000	$ –0–	$20,000	$ –0–
12/31/23	24,500	15,000	9,500	–10,500
3/1/24	28,000	28,000	–0–	–9,500

Because the option strike price of $1.300 is higher than the spot rate of $1.285 on December 31, the option has an intrinsic value of $15,000 on that date. The time value of the option decreases from $20,000 on December 1 to $9,500 on December 31. On March 1, the date of expiration, no time value remains, and the entire amount of fair value for the option is attributable to intrinsic value.

Option Designated as Cash Flow Hedge

Assume that Eximco designates the foreign currency option as a *cash flow hedge* of a foreign currency–denominated asset. Eximco has elected to exclude the time value of the option from the assessment of hedge effectiveness. Furthermore, the company has chosen to recognize the change in the option's time value in net income (rather than apply straight-line amortization). The company prepares the following journal entries to account for the foreign currency transaction and the related foreign currency option:

2023 Journal Entries—Option Designated as a Cash Flow Hedge

12/1/23	Accounts Receivable (£).............................	1,300,000	
	Sales..		1,300,000
	To record the sale and £1 million account receivable at the spot rate of $1.300 (Cash Flow Hedge Step A.1 in Exhibit 7.2).		
	Foreign Currency Option.............................	20,000	
	Cash...		20,000
	To record the purchase of the foreign currency option as an asset at its fair value of $20,000 (Cash Flow Hedge Step A.2 in Exhibit 7.2).		

From December 1 to December 31, the British pound account receivable decreases in value by $15,000, and the option increases in value by $4,500. The company prepares the following journal entries on December 31 to reflect these changes:

12/31/23	Foreign Exchange Gain or Loss.........................	15,000	
	Accounts Receivable (£)		15,000
	To adjust the value of the £ receivable to the new spot rate of $1.285 and recognize a foreign exchange loss resulting from the depreciation of the £ since December 1 (Cash Flow Hedge Step B.1 in Exhibit 7.2).		
	Foreign Currency Option	4,500	
	Other Comprehensive Income (OCI).................		4,500
	To adjust the fair value of the option from $20,000 to $24,500 and recognize the change in fair value in OCI (Cash Flow Hedge Step B.2 in Exhibit 7.2).		

(continued)

(*continued*)

Other Comprehensive Income (OCI)......................	15,000	
Foreign Exchange Gain or Loss.....................		15,000
To record a foreign exchange gain on the foreign currency option (to offset the foreign exchange loss on the account receivable) with a corresponding debit to OCI (Cash Flow Hedge Step B.3 in Exhibit 7.2).		
Foreign Exchange Gain or Loss.........................	10,500	
Other Comprehensive Income (OCI)................		10,500
To recognize the change in the time value of the option as a decrease in net income with a corresponding credit to OCI (Cash Flow Hedge Step B.4 in Exhibit 7.2).		

The first three journal entries prepared on December 31 result in the British pound account receivable and the foreign currency option being reported on the balance sheet at fair value with a net foreign exchange gain (loss) of zero reflected in net income, which is consistent with the concept of hedge accounting. The final entry serves to recognize a portion of the option cost in net income, in the same line item in which changes in the $ value of the account receivable are recognized.

The impact on net income for the year 2023 follows:

Sales	$1,300,000
Net foreign exchange gain (loss)..............	(10,500)
Impact on net income	$1,289,500

The effect on the December 31, 2023, balance sheet is as follows:

Assets		**Liabilities and Stockholders' Equity**	
Cash	$ (20,000)	Retained earnings...........	$1,289,500
Accounts receivable (£)	1,285,000		
Foreign currency option	24,500		
	$1,289,500		$1,289,500

At March 1, 2024, the option has increased in fair value by $3,500—intrinsic value increases by $13,000 and time value decreases by $9,500. The accounting entries made in 2024 are presented next.

2024 Journal Entries—Option Designated as a Cash Flow Hedge

3/1/24	Foreign Exchange Gain or Loss.........................	13,000	
	Accounts Receivable (£)		13,000
	To adjust the value of the £ receivable to the spot rate of $1.272 and recognize a foreign exchange loss resulting from the depreciation of the £ since December 31 (Cash Flow Hedge Step C.1 in Exhibit 7.2).		
	Foreign Currency Option.............................	3,500	
	Other Comprehensive Income (OCI)................		3,500
	To adjust the fair value of the option from $24,500 to $28,000 and recognize the change in fair value in OCI (Cash Flow Hedge Step C.2 in Exhibit 7.2).		
	Other Comprehensive Income (OCI)....................	13,000	
	Foreign Exchange Gain or Loss....................		13,000
	To record a foreign exchange gain on the foreign currency option (to offset the foreign exchange loss on the account receivable) with a corresponding debit to OCI (Cash Flow Hedge Step C.3 in Exhibit 7.2).		

(*continued*)

(continued)

	Foreign Exchange Gain or Loss............................	9,500	
	Other Comprehensive Income (OCI)................		9,500
	To recognize the change in the time value of the option as a decrease in net income with a corresponding credit to OCI (Cash Flow Hedge Step C.4 in Exhibit 7.2).		

The first three entries on March 1 result in the British pound account receivable and the foreign currency option being reported at their fair values, with a net gain (loss) of zero. The fourth entry serves to recognize the remaining cost of the option in net income.

The next two journal entries recognize the receipt of British pounds from the customer, close out the British pound account receivable, and record the exercise of the foreign currency option.

3/1/24	Foreign Currency (£)...................................	1,272,000	
	Accounts Receivable (£)		1,272,000
	To record receipt of £1 million as an asset at the spot rate of $1.300 (Cash Flow Hedge Step C.5 in Exhibit 7.2).		
	Cash	1,300,000	
	Foreign Currency (£)...............................		1,272,000
	Foreign Currency Option		28,000
	To record exercise of the option (i.e., record receipt of $1,300,000 in exchange for delivery of £1 million) and remove the foreign currency option from the accounts (Cash Flow Hedge Step C.6 in Exhibit 7.2).		

The impact on net income for the year 2024 is

Net foreign exchange gain (loss)....................	$(9,500)
Impact on net income	$(9,500)

Over the two accounting periods, Eximco reports sales of $1,300,000 and a cumulative net foreign exchange loss of $20,000. The net foreign exchange loss is equal to the original cost of the foreign currency option. The net effect on the balance sheet is an increase in Cash of $1,280,000 ($1,300,000 – $20,000) with a corresponding increase in Retained Earnings.

The net benefit from having acquired the option is $8,000. This is the difference between the net amount Eximco received from executing the option ($1,280,000) and the amount Eximco would have received if it had not acquired the option ($1,272,000). This "gain" is equal to the increase in fair value of the option over its life, and is not directly reflected in net income.

Option Designated as Fair Value Hedge

Assume that Eximco decides not to designate the foreign currency option as a cash flow hedge but to treat it as a fair value hedge. In that case, the company recognizes the change in fair value of the option directly to net income. Furthermore, the company excludes the time value of the option in assessing hedge effectiveness and recognizes each period's change in time value in net income. The journal entries for 2023 are shown next.

2023 Journal Entries—Option Designated as a Fair Value Hedge

12/1/23	Accounts Receivable (£)................................	1,300,000	
	Sales..		1,300,000
	To record the sale and £1 million account receivable at the spot rate of $1.300 (Fair Value Hedge Step A.1 in Exhibit 7.2).		

(continued)

(continued)

	Foreign Currency Option..............................	20,000	
	Cash		20,000
	To record the purchase of the foreign currency option as an asset at its fair value of $20,000 (Fair Value Hedge Step A.2 in Exhibit 7.2).		
12/31/23	Foreign Exchange Gain or Loss........................	15,000	
	Accounts Receivable (£)		15,000
	To adjust the value of the £ receivable to the new spot rate of $1.285 and recognize a foreign exchange loss resulting from the depreciation of the £ since December 1 (Fair Value Hedge Step B.1 in Exhibit 7.2).		
	Foreign Currency Option..............................	4,500	
	Foreign Exchange Gain or Loss....................		4,500
	To adjust the fair value of the option from $20,000 to $24,500 and recognize the change in fair value of the option since December 1 as a gain (Fair Value Hedge Step B.2 in Exhibit 7.2).		
	Note that because the option has a positive intrinsic value, Fair Value Hedge Step B.4 in Exhibit 7.2 is unnecessary.		

The two journal entries on December 31, 2023, serve to (a) measure the foreign currency account receivable and foreign currency option at their fair values, and (b) simultaneously recognize the change in the time value of the option in net income. The net foreign exchange loss recognized in 2023 is $10,500 ($15,000 − $4,500), which equals the change in the time value of the option for that year. There is no need to record any additional journal entries.

The impact on net income for the year 2023 follows:

Sales	$1,300,000
Net foreign exchange gain (loss)	(10,500)
Impact on net income	$1,289,500

2024 Journal Entries—Option Designated as a Fair Value Hedge

3/1/24	Foreign Exchange Gain or Loss........................	13,000	
	Accounts Receivable (£)		13,000
	To adjust the value of the £ receivable to the new spot rate of $1.272 and recognize a foreign exchange loss resulting from the depreciation of the £ since December 31 (Fair Value Hedge Step C.1 in Exhibit 7.2).		
	Foreign Currency Option..............................	3,500	
	Foreign Exchange Gain or Loss....................		3,500
	To adjust the fair value of the option from $24,500 to $28,000 and recognize the change in fair value of the option since December 31 as a gain (Fair Value Hedge Step C.2 in Exhibit 7.2).		
	Foreign Currency (£).................................	1,272,000	
	Accounts Receivable (£)		1,272,000
	To record receipt of £1 million as an asset at the spot rate of $1.272 (Fair Value Hedge Step C.3 in Exhibit 7.2).		
	Cash	1,300,000	
	Foreign Currency (£)................................		1,272,000
	Foreign Currency Option		28,000
	To record exercise of the option (i.e., record receipt of $1,300,000 in exchange for delivery of £1 million) and remove the foreign currency option from the accounts (Fair Value Hedge Step C.4 in Exhibit 7.2).		

The impact on net income for the year 2024 is

Net foreign exchange gain (loss)	$(9,500)
Impact on net income	$(9,500)

Over the two accounting periods, Eximco reports sales of $1,300,000 and a cumulative net foreign exchange loss of $20,000 ($10,500 in 2023 and $9,500 in 2024). The net effect on the balance sheet is an increase in Cash of $1,280,000 ($1,300,000 − $20,000) with a corresponding increase in Retained Earnings.

The accounting for an option used as a fair value hedge of a foreign currency–denominated asset or liability is the same as if the option had been considered a speculative derivative. The only possible advantage to designating the option as a fair value hedge would relate to the disclosures made in the notes to the financial statements explaining the hedging relationship.

Spot Rate Exceeds Strike Price

If the spot rate on March 1, 2024, had turned out to be $1.302 (i.e., higher than the strike price of $1.300), Eximco would allow its option to expire unexercised. Instead it would sell the foreign currency (£) it receives on March 1, 2024, at the spot rate on that date. In this case, the company will realize a net cash inflow of $1,282,000 ($1,302,000 less $20,000 for the option). The fair value of the foreign currency option on March 1, 2024, would be zero. The journal entries for 2023 to reflect this scenario would be the same as the preceding ones. The option would be reported as an asset on the December 31, 2023, balance sheet at $24,500, and the £ receivable would have a carrying value of $1,285,000. The entries on March 1, 2024, assuming a spot rate on that date of $1.302 (rather than $1.272), would be as follows:

3/1/24	Accounts Receivable (£).	17,000	
	Foreign Exchange Gain or Loss.		17,000
	To adjust the value of the £ receivable to the new spot rate of $1.302 and record a foreign exchange gain resulting from the appreciation of the £ since December 31 (Fair Value Hedge Step C.1. in Exhibit 7.2).		
	Foreign Exchange Gain or Loss.	24,500	
	Foreign Currency Option		24,500
	To adjust the fair value of the option from $24,500 to $0 and recognize a loss for the change in fair value since December 31 (Fair Value Hedge Step C.2. in Exhibit 7.2).		

The above two entries result in a net foreign exchange loss of $7,500 recognized in 2024, which results in a cumulative net loss of $18,000 since December 1, 2023. This accurately measures the net cost of extending credit to the British customer ($1,282,000 in net cash inflow versus $1,300,000). There is no need to adjust the net foreign exchange loss to reflect the current period's change in the time value of the option.

The next two journal entries recognize the receipt of British pounds from the customer, close out the British pound account receivable, and record the sale of British pounds at the current spot rate.

	Foreign Currency (£).	1,302,000	
	Accounts Receivable (£)		1,302,000
	To record receipt of £1 million as an asset at the spot rate of $1.302 (Fair Value Hedge Step C.3 in Exhibit 7.2).		
	Cash	1,302,000	
	Foreign Currency (£).		1,302,000
	To record the sale of £1 million at the spot rate of $1.302 (Fair Value Hedge Step C.4 in Exhibit 7.2).		

The overall impact on net income for the year 2024 is:

Net foreign exchange gain (loss)	$(7,500)
Impact on net income.	$(7,500)

In this situation, over the two accounting periods, Eximco reports Sales of $1,300,000 and a cumulative net foreign exchange loss of $18,000 ($10,500 in 2023 and $7,500 in 2024). The net effect on the balance sheet is an increase in Cash of $1,282,000 ($1,302,000 − $20,000) with a corresponding increase in Retained Earnings.

LO 7-8

Account for forward contracts and options used as hedges of foreign currency firm commitments.

Hedge of Unrecognized Foreign Currency Firm Commitment

In the examples thus far, Eximco does not enter into a hedge of its export sale until it actually makes the sale. Assume now that on December 1, 2023, Eximco receives and accepts an order from a British customer to deliver goods on March 1, 2024, at a price of 1 million British pounds. Assume further that under the terms of the sale agreement, Eximco will ship the goods to the British customer on March 1, 2024, and will receive immediate payment on delivery. Although Eximco will not make the sale until March 1, 2024, it has a firm commitment to make the sale and receive 1 million British pounds in three months. This creates a British pound asset exposure to foreign exchange risk as of December 1, 2023. On that date, Eximco wants to hedge against an adverse change in the value of the British pound over the next three months. This is known as a *hedge of a foreign currency–denominated firm commitment.* U.S. GAAP allows hedges of firm commitments to be designated either as cash flow or fair value hedges. However, because the results of fair value hedge accounting are intuitively more appealing, we do not cover cash flow hedge accounting for firm commitments.

A firm commitment is an executory contract; the company has not delivered goods nor has the customer paid for them. Normally, executory contracts are not recognized in financial statements. However, when a firm commitment is hedged using a derivative financial instrument, hedge accounting requires explicit recognition on the balance sheet at fair value of both the derivative financial instrument (forward contract or option) and the firm commitment. The change in fair value of the firm commitment results in a gain or loss that offsets the loss or gain on the hedging instrument (forward contract or option), thus achieving the goal of hedge accounting. This raises the conceptual question of how to measure the fair value of the firm commitment. When a forward contract is used as the hedging instrument, the fair value of the firm commitment is determined through reference to changes in the forward exchange rate. Changes in the spot exchange rate are used to determine the fair value of the firm commitment when a foreign currency option is the hedging instrument.

Forward Contract Fair Value Hedge of a Firm Commitment

To hedge its firm commitment exposure to a decline in the U.S. dollar value of the British pound, Eximco decides to enter into a forward contract on December 1, 2023. As in previous examples, assume that on that date, the spot rate for British pounds is $1.300 and the three-month forward rate is $1.288. Eximco signs a contract with New World Bank to deliver 1 million British pounds in three months in exchange for $1,288,000. No cash changes hands on December 1, 2023. Eximco measures the fair value of the firm commitment through changes in the forward exchange rate. Because the fair value of the forward contract also is measured using changes in the forward rate, the gains and losses on the firm commitment and forward contract exactly offset. The fair value of the forward contract and firm commitment are determined as follows:

Date	Forward Rate to 3/1/24	Forward Contract		Firm Commitment	
		Fair Value	Change in Fair Value	Fair Value	Change in Fair Value
12/1/23	$1.288	$ –0–	$ –0–	$ –0–	$ –0–
12/31/23	1.278	10,000*	+10,000	(10,000)*	−10,000
3/1/24	1.272 (spot)	16,000†	+ 6,000	(16,000)†	− 6,000

*$1,288,000 − $1,278,000 = $10,000. Discounting to present value is ignored for simplicity.
†$1,288,000 − $1,272,000 = $16,000.

Eximco pays nothing to enter into the forward contract on December 1, 2023. Both the forward contract and the firm commitment have a fair value of zero on that date. As a result, there are no journal entries needed on December 1, 2023. On December 31, 2023, the forward rate for a contract to deliver British pounds on March 1, 2024, is $1.278. A forward contract could be entered into on December 31, 2023, to sell 1 million British pounds for $1,278,000 on March 1, 2024. Because Eximco is committed to sell 1 million British pounds for $1,288,000, the value of the forward contract is $10,000. The fair value of the firm commitment is also measured through reference to changes in the forward rate. On December 31, 2023, the firm commitment is a liability of $(10,000). To apply the steps in accounting for a fair value hedge of a firm commitment at the balance sheet date, on December 31, 2023, Eximco will

1. Adjust the forward contract to fair value, which results in the recognition of an asset of $10,000, and recognize the counterpart as a foreign exchange loss in net income (Fair Value Hedge Step B.1 in Exhibit 7.2).
2. Adjust the firm commitment to fair value, which results in the recognition of a liability of $10,000, and recognize the counterpart as a foreign exchange gain in net income (Fair Value Hedge Step B.2 in Exhibit 7.2).

Because changes in the fair value of the firm commitment are measured using changes in the forward exchange rate, the original forward points may not be excluded from the assessment of hedge effectiveness. Thus, the *forward contract discount is not separately amortized to net income.*

The journal entries in 2023 to account for the forward contract fair value hedge of a foreign currency firm commitment are as follows.

2023 Journal Entries—Forward Contract Fair Value Hedge of Firm Commitment

12/1/23	There is no entry to record either the sales agreement or the forward contract because both are executory contracts.		
	A memorandum designates the forward contract as a hedge of the risk of changes in the fair value of the firm commitment resulting from changes in the U.S. dollar–British pound forward exchange rate (Fair Value Hedge Steps A.1 and A.2 in Exhibit 7.2).		
12/31/23	Forward Contract	10,000	
	Foreign Exchange Gain or Loss		10,000
	To record the forward contract as an asset at its fair value of $10,000 and recognize the change in fair value since December 1 as a gain (Fair Value Hedge Step B.1 in Exhibit 7.2).		
	Foreign Exchange Gain or Loss	10,000	
	Firm Commitment		10,000
	To record the firm commitment as a liability at fair value of $10,000 and recognize the change in fair value since December 1 as a loss (Fair Value Hedge Step B.2 in Exhibit 7.2).		

Eximco reports the forward contract as an asset and reports the firm commitment as a liability on the December 31, 2023, balance sheet. Consistent with the objective of hedge accounting, the loss on the firm commitment offsets the gain on the forward contract such that the impact on net income is zero.

On March 1, 2024, the forward rate to sell British pounds on that date, by definition, is the spot rate, $1.272. At that rate, Eximco could sell 1 million British pounds for $1,272,000. Because Eximco has a contract to sell British pounds for $1,282,000, the fair value of the forward contract on March 1, 2024, is $16,000. The firm commitment has a value of $(16,000).

On March 1, 2024, Eximco recognizes changes in the fair value of the forward contract and firm commitment since December 31. The company then records the sale and the settlement of the forward contract. Finally, the balance in the firm commitment account is closed to net income (as an adjustment to Sales). The required journal entries are as follows.

2024 Journal Entries—Forward Contract Fair Value Hedge of Firm Commitment

3/1/24	Forward Contract	6,000	
	Foreign Exchange Gain or Loss		6,000
	To adjust the fair value of the forward contract asset from $10,000 to $16,000 and recognize the change in fair value since December 31 as a gain (Fair Value Hedge Step C.1 in Exhibit 7.2).		
	Foreign Exchange Gain or Loss	6,000	
	Firm Commitment		6,000
	To adjust the fair value of the firm commitment liability from $10,000 to $16,000 and recognize the change in fair value since December 31 as a loss (Fair Value Hedge Step C.2 in Exhibit 7.2).		
	Foreign Currency (£)	1,272,000	
	Sales		1,272,000
	To record the sale and the receipt of €1 million as an asset at the spot rate of $1.30 (Fair Value Hedge Step C.3 in Exhibit 7.2).		
	Cash	1,288,000	
	Foreign Currency (£)		1,272,000
	Forward Contract		16,000
	To record settlement of the forward contract (receipt of $1,288,000 in exchange for delivery of £1 million) and remove the forward contract asset from the accounts (Fair Value Hedge Step C.4 in Exhibit 7.2).		
	Firm Commitment	16,000	
	Sales		16,000
	To transfer the balance in the firm commitment account to net income (as an adjustment to Sales) (Fair Value Hedge Step C.5 in Exhibit 7.2).		

As a result of these entries, Sales are effectively recognized at the forward exchange rate ($1.288 forward rate × £1 million = $1,288,000), which is exactly equal to the increase in Cash resulting from the export sale. Once again, the gain on forward contract and the loss on firm commitment offset. The original forward contract discount has not been separately recognized in net income.

Option Fair Value Hedge of Firm Commitment

Now assume that to hedge its firm commitment exposure to a decline in the U.S. dollar value of the British pound, Eximco purchases a put option to sell 1 million British pounds on March 1, 2024, at a strike price of $1.300. The premium for such an option on December 1, 2023, is $0.020 per British pound. With this option, Eximco is guaranteed a minimum cash flow from the export sale of $1,280,000 ($1,300,000 from option exercise less $20,000 cost of the option).

In this case, Eximco measures the fair value of the firm commitment by referring to changes in the U.S. dollar–British pound spot rate. The fair value and changes in fair value for the foreign currency option and firm commitment are summarized here:

| Date | Option Premium for 3/1/24 | Foreign Currency Option | | Spot Rate | Firm Commitment | |
		Fair Value	Change in Fair Value		Fair Value	Change in Fair Value
12/1/23	$0.0200	$20,000	$ –0–	$1.300	$ –0–	$ –0–
12/31/23	0.0245	24,500	+4,500	1.285	(15,000)*	−15,000
3/1/24	0.0280	28,000	+3,500	1.272	(28,000)†	−13,000

*$1,300,000 − $1,285,000 = $15,000. Discounting to present value is ignored for simplicity.
†$1,300,000 − $1,272,000 = $28,000.

On December 1, 2023, given the spot rate of $1.300, the firm commitment to receive 1 million British pounds in three months would generate a cash flow of $1,300,000. On December 31, 2023, the cash flow that the firm commitment could generate decreases by $15,000 to $1,285,000. Therefore, the fair value of the firm commitment on December 31, 2023, is $(15,000). On March 1, 2024, when the spot rate is $1.272, the fair value of the firm commitment is $(28,000), a further reduction in fair value since December 31 of $13,000.

Because changes in the fair value of the firm commitment are measured using changes in the spot exchange rate, the time value of the option may be excluded from the assessment of hedge effectiveness. Through the process of revaluing the option and firm commitment over time, and as long as the option has a positive intrinsic value, the company will automatically recognize the change in the option's time value in net income. There is no need to record an additional entry related to the excluded component. However, an additional entry to adjust the net amount recognized as foreign exchange loss is necessary when the intrinsic value of the option is zero.

The journal entries to account for the foreign currency option and related foreign currency firm commitment are discussed next.

2023 Journal Entries—Option Fair Value Hedge of Firm Commitment

12/1/23	Foreign Currency Option.	20,000	
	Cash		20,000
	To record the purchase of the foreign currency option as an asset (Fair Value Hedge Step A.2 in Exhibit 7.2).		
	There is no entry to record the sales agreement because it is an executory contract (Fair Value Hedge Step A.1 in Exhibit 7.2). Eximco prepares a memorandum to designate the option as a hedge of the risk of changes in the fair value of the firm commitment resulting from changes in the spot exchange rate.		

12/31/23	Foreign Currency Option.	4,500	
	Foreign Exchange Gain or Loss.		4,500
	To adjust the fair value of the option from $20,000 to $24,500 and record the change in the value of the option since December 1 as a foreign exchange gain (Fair Value Hedge Step B.1 in Exhibit 7.2).		
	Foreign Exchange Gain or Loss.	15,000	
	Firm Commitment.		15,000
	To record the firm commitment as a liability at its fair value of $(15,000) and record the change in fair value of the firm commitment since December 1 as a foreign exchange loss (Fair Value Hedge Step B.2 in Exhibit 7.2).		

Because the fair value of the firm commitment is based on changes in the spot rate, whereas the fair value of the option is based on a variety of factors, the loss on the firm commitment and gain on the option do not exactly offset. The difference between the gain and the loss is

$10,500, which effectively recognizes the current period's change in time value of the option in net income. No additional entry is needed.

The impact on net income for the year 2023 is as follows:

Net foreign exchange gain (loss)	$(10,500)
Impact on net income	$(10,500)

The effect on the December 31, 2023, balance sheet follows:

Assets		Liabilities and Stockholders' Equity	
Cash	$(20,000)	Firm commitment.	$ 15,000
Foreign currency option	24,500	Retained earnings.	(10,500)
	$ 4,500		$ 4,500

On March 1, 2024, following fair value hedge accounting procedures, Eximco first recognizes changes in the fair value of the option and the fair value of the firm commitment since December 31. The company then records the sale and the exercise of the option. Finally, the $28,000 balance in the firm commitment account is closed to net income (as an adjustment to Sales). The required journal entries are as follows.

2024 Journal Entries—Option Fair Value Hedge of Firm Commitment

3/1/24	Foreign Currency Option.	3,500	
	Foreign Exchange Gain or Loss.		3,500
	To adjust the fair value of the foreign currency option from $24,500 to $28,000 and recognize the change in fair value since December 31 as a foreign exchange gain (Fair Value Hedge Step C.1 in Exhibit 7.2).		
	Foreign Exchange Gain or Loss.	13,000	
	Firm Commitment.		13,000
	To adjust the fair value of the firm commitment from $(15,000) to $(28,000) and recognize the change in fair value since December 31 as a foreign exchange loss (Fair Value Hedge Step C.2 in Exhibit 7.2).		
	Foreign Currency (£).	1,272,000	
	Sales.		1,272,000
	To record the sale and the receipt of £1 million as an asset at the spot rate of $1.272 (Fair Value Hedge Step C.3 in Exhibit 7.2).		
	Cash	1,300,000	
	Foreign Currency (£).		1,272,000
	Foreign Currency Option		28,000
	To record exercise of the foreign currency option (receipt of $1,300,000 in exchange for delivery of £1 million) and remove the foreign currency option from the accounts (Fair Value Hedge Step C.4 in Exhibit 7.2).		
	Firm Commitment	28,000	
	Sales.		28,000
	To close the firm commitment to net income (as an adjustment to Sales) (Fair Value Hedge Step C.5 in Exhibit 7.2).		

As a result of these entries, Sales are effectively recognized at the strike price on the option ($1.30 strike price × £1 million = $1,300,000). The difference ($9,500) between the gain on the option and the loss on the firm commitment serves to recognize the current period's change in time value of the option in net income. The following is the impact on net income for the year 2024:

Sales	$1,300,000
Net foreign exchange gain (loss)	(9,500)
Impact on net income	$1,290,500

The net increase in net income over the two accounting periods is $1,280,000 ($1,290,500 increase in 2024 less $10,500 decrease in 2023), which exactly equals the net cash flow realized on the export sale ($1,300,000 from exercising the option less $20,000 to purchase the option).

Hedge of Forecasted Foreign Currency Transaction

Cash flow hedge accounting also is used for foreign currency derivatives used to hedge the cash flow risk associated with a forecasted foreign currency transaction. For hedge accounting to apply, the forecasted transaction must be probable (likely to occur), the hedge must be highly effective in offsetting fluctuations in the cash flow associated with the foreign currency risk, and the hedging relationship must be properly documented.

Accounting for a hedge of a forecasted transaction differs from accounting for a hedge of a foreign currency firm commitment in two ways:

1. Unlike the accounting for a firm commitment, there is no recognition of the forecasted transaction or gains and losses on the forecasted transaction. (Because there is no recognition of an asset or liability, there is no fair value exposure to foreign exchange risk. Thus, fair value hedge accounting is not appropriate for hedges of forecasted transactions.)

2. The company reports the hedging instrument (forward contract or option) at fair value and recognizes changes in the fair value of the hedging instrument in other comprehensive income. On the projected date of the forecasted transaction, the company transfers the cumulative change in the fair value of the hedging instrument from accumulated other comprehensive income (balance sheet) to net income (income statement). The impact on net income is reported in the same line item in which the income effect of the forecasted transaction is reflected.

Forward Contract Cash Flow Hedge of a Forecasted Transaction

To demonstrate the accounting for a hedge of a forecasted foreign currency transaction, assume that Eximco has a long-term relationship with its British customer and can reliably forecast that the customer will require delivery of goods costing 1 million British pounds in March 2024. Confident that it will receive 1 million British pounds on March 1, 2024, Eximco enters into a forward contract on December 1, 2023, to sell 1 million British pounds on March 1, 2024, at a forward rate of $1.288. The facts are essentially the same as those for the hedge of a firm commitment except that Eximco does not receive a sales order from the British customer until late February 2024. Relevant exchange rates and the fair value of the forward contract are as follows:

| | | Forward Contract | |
Date	Forward Rate to 3/1/24	Fair Value	Change in Fair Value
12/1/23	$1.288	$ –0–	$ –0–
12/31/23	1.278	10,000*	+10,000
3/1/24	1.272 (spot)	16,000†	+ 6,000

*$1,288,000 − $1,278,000 = $10,000. Discounting to present value is ignored for simplicity.
†$1,288,000 − $1,272,000 = $16,000.

The company elects to exclude the forward points from assessment of hedge effectiveness, and chooses to amortize the forward contract discount using the straight-line method on a monthly basis. The original discount on the forward contract is determined by the difference in the £ spot rate and the three-month forward rate on December 1, 2023: ($1.300 − $1.288) × £1 million = $12,000. The discount will be amortized at the rate of $4,000 per month.

2023 Journal Entries—Forward Contract Hedge of a Forecasted Transaction

12/1/23	There is no entry to record either the forecasted sale or the forward contract.		
	A memorandum designates the spot component of the forward contract as a hedge of the risk of changes in the cash flows related to the forecasted sale, and indicates that the forward component of the forward contract will be systematically amortized to net income (Cash Flow Hedge Steps A.1 and A.2 in Exhibit 7.2).		

On December 31, the forward contract is recognized as an asset at its fair value, with the counterpart reflected in other comprehensive income (OCI). The forward contract discount is amortized to net income (as an adjustment to Sales), with the counterpart also reflected in OCI. The necessary journal entries are as follows:

12/31/23	Forward Contract	10,000	
	Other Comprehensive Income (OCI)................		10,000
	To record the forward contract as an asset at its fair value of $10,000 with a corresponding credit to OCI (Cash Flow Hedge Step B.2 in Exhibit 7.2).		
	Sales	4,000	
	Other Comprehensive Income (OCI)................		4,000
	To record straight-line amortization of the forward contract discount: $12,000 × ⅓ = $4,000 (Cash Flow Hedge Step B.4 in Exhibit 7.2).		

The debit to Sales reduces 2023 net income by $4,000. After net income is closed to Retained Earnings and OCI is closed to Accumulated Other Comprehensive Income (AOCI), the impact on the December 31, 2023, balance sheet is as follows:

Assets		Liabilities and Stockholders' Equity	
Forward contract...............	$10,000	Retained earnings..............	$ (4,000)
	$10,000	AOCI	14,000
			$10,000

On March 1, 2024, the carrying value of the forward contract asset is adjusted to fair value, and the forward contract discount is amortized to net income (as an adjustment to Sales). Then the sale and the settlement of the forward contract are recorded. Finally, the balance in AOCI related to the hedge of the forecasted transaction is closed as an adjustment to net income (Sales). The following entries are required:

2024 Journal Entries—Forward Contract Hedge of a Forecasted Transaction

3/1/24	Forward Contract	6,000	
	Other Comprehensive Income (OCI)................		6,000
	To adjust the carrying value of the forward contract to its current fair value of $16,000 with a corresponding credit to OCI (Cash Flow Hedge Step C.1 in Exhibit 7.2).		
3/1/24	Sales	8,000	
	Other Comprehensive Income (OCI)................		8,000
	To record straight-line amortization of the forward contract discount: $12,000 × ⅔ = $8,000 (Cash Flow Hedge Step C.2 in Exhibit 7.2).		

(continued)

(continued)

Foreign Currency (£)	1,272,000	
Sales		1,272,000
To record the sale and the receipt of £1 million as an asset at the spot rate of $1.272 (Cash Flow Hedge Step C.3 in Exhibit 7.2).		
Cash	1,288,000	
Foreign Currency (£)		1,272,000
Forward Contract		16,000
To record settlement of the forward contract (receipt of $1,288,000 in exchange for delivery of £1 million) and remove the forward contract from the accounts (Cash Flow Hedge Step C.4 in Exhibit 7.2).		
Accumulated Other Comprehensive Income (AOCI)	28,000	
Sales		28,000
To close AOCI as an adjustment to net income (Cash Flow Hedge Step C.5 in Exhibit 7.2).		

Note that prior to the final entry on March 1, 2024, OCI was closed to AOCI, which then had a credit balance of $28,000 ($14,000 in 2023 plus $14,000 in 2024).

As a result of these entries, the forward contract asset has been reduced to zero, as has been the balance in AOCI related to this forward contract.

The impact on net income for the year 2024 follows:

Sales	$1,292,000
Impact on net income	$1,292,000

Over the two accounting periods, $1,288,000 has been recognized in Sales, which equals the amount of net cash inflow realized from the sale.

Option Cash Flow Hedge of a Forecasted Transaction

Now assume that Eximco hedges its forecasted foreign currency transaction by purchasing a 1 million British pound put option on December 1, 2023. The option, which expires on March 1, 2024, has a strike price of $1.30 and a premium of $0.020 per British pound. The fair value of the option at relevant dates is as follows (same as in previous examples):

Date	Option Premium for 3/1/24	Foreign Currency Option				
		Fair Value	Change in Fair Value	Intrinsic Value	Time Value	Change in Time Value
12/1/23	$0.0200	$20,000	$ –0–	$ –0–	$20,000	$ –0–
12/31/23	0.0245	24,500	+ 4,500	15,000	9,500	−10,500
3/1/24	0.0280	28,000	+ 3,500	28,000	–0–	− 9,500

2023 Journal Entries—Option Hedge of a Forecasted Transaction

12/1/23	Foreign Currency Option	20,000	
	Cash		20,000
	To record the purchase of the foreign currency option as an asset (Cash Flow Hedge Step A.2 in Exhibit 7.2).		
	There is no entry to record the forecasted sale. A memorandum designates the foreign currency option as a hedge of the risk of changes in the cash flows related to the forecasted sale and indicates that changes in the option's time value will be recognized in net income (Cash Flow Hedge Step A.1 in Exhibit 7.2).		

At December 31, the carrying value of the option is increased for the change in fair value since December 1, and the change in the time value of the option since December 1 is recognized in net income (as an adjustment to Sales). The required journal entries are as follows:

12/31/23	Foreign Currency Option...............................	4,500	
	Other Comprehensive Income (OCI).................		4,500
	To adjust the carrying value of the option to its fair value with a corresponding credit to OCI (Cash Flow Hedge Step B.2. in Exhibit 7.2).		
	Sales...	10,500	
	Other Comprehensive Income (OCI)................		10,500
	To recognize the change in the time value of the option as a decrease in net income with a corresponding credit to OCI (Cash Flow Hedge Step B.4 in Exhibit 7.2).		

The impact on net income for the year 2023 follows:

Sales.......................................	$(10,500)
Impact on net income	$(10,500)

On the December 31, 2023, balance sheet, Cash is decreased by $20,000 and Foreign Currency Option is reported as $24,500, for a net increase in assets of $4,500. Retained Earnings is decreased by $10,500, while AOCI is increased by $15,000, for a net increase in stockholders' equity of $4,500.

On March 1, 2024, first, the carrying value of the option is adjusted to fair value, and the change in the time value of the option is recognized in net income (as an adjustment to Sales). Then the sale and the exercise of the foreign currency option are recorded. Finally, the balance in AOCI related to the hedge of the forecasted transaction is closed to net income (as an adjustment to Sales). The following entries are required:

2024 Journal Entries—Option Hedge of a Forecasted Transaction

3/1/24	Foreign Currency Option............................	3,500	
	Other Comprehensive Income (OCI)...............		3,500
	To adjust the carrying value of the option to its fair value with a corresponding credit to OCI (Cash Flow Hedge Step C.1 in Exhibit 7.2).		
	Sales...	9,500	
	Other Comprehensive Income (OCI)................		9,500
	To recognize the change in the time value of the option as a decrease in net income with a corresponding credit to AOCI (Cash Flow Hedge Step C.2 in Exhibit 7.2).		
	Foreign Currency (£)................................	1,272,000	
	Sales...		1,272,000
	To record the sale and the receipt of £1 million as an asset at the spot rate of $1.272 (Cash Flow Hedge Step C.3 in Exhibit 7.2).		
	Cash	1,300,000	
	Foreign Currency (£).............................		1,272,000
	Foreign Currency Option		28,000
	To record the exercise of the foreign currency option (receipt of $1,300,000 in exchange for delivery of £1 million) and remove the foreign currency option from the accounts (Cash Flow Hedge Step C.4 in Exhibit 7.2).		
	Accumulated Other Comprehensive Income (AOCI)	28,000	
	Sales...		28,000
	To close AOCI as an adjustment to net income (Cash Flow Hedge Step C.5 in Exhibit 7.2).		

Note that prior to the final entry on March 1, 2024, AOCI had a credit balance of $28,000 ($15,000 beginning credit balance from 2023 plus $13,000 from closing OCI in 2024).

As a result of these entries, the net amount recognized as Sales over the two periods is $1,280,000 ($1,290,500 net credit in 2024 less $10,500 debit in 2023), which is equal to the net increase in Cash realized from the export sale ($1,300,000 from exercising the option less $20,000 for the cost of the option).

Use of Hedging Instruments

There are probably as many different corporate strategies regarding hedging foreign exchange risk as there are companies exposed to that risk. Some companies require hedges of all foreign currency transactions. Others require the use of a forward contract hedge when the forward rate results in a larger cash inflow or smaller cash outflow than with the spot rate. Still other companies have proportional hedging policies that require hedging on some predetermined percentage (e.g., 50 percent, 60 percent, or 70 percent) of transaction exposure.

Companies are required to provide information on the use of derivative financial instruments to hedge foreign exchange risk in the notes to financial statements. Exhibit 7.4 presents disclosures made by Abbott Laboratories in its 2020 annual report. Abbott uses forward contracts to hedge foreign exchange risk associated with anticipated foreign currency transactions, foreign currency–denominated payables and receivables, and foreign currency-denominated intercompany loans. Much of its hedging activity relates to intra-entity (intercompany) transactions involving foreign subsidiaries. The table in Exhibit 7.4 discloses that (1) Abbott's forward contracts primarily are to sell foreign currencies to receive U.S. dollars; (2) 40 percent of Abbott's $19,140 million in forward contracts at December 31, 2020, was in euros; and (3) the net fair value of all the company's forward contracts was negative and reported on the balance sheet as a liability (payable).

EXHIBIT 7.4   Disclosures Related to Hedging Foreign Exchange Risk in Abbott Laboratories' 2020 Annual Report

Excerpt from Foreign Currency Sensitive Financial Instruments

Certain Abbott foreign subsidiaries enter into foreign currency forward exchange contracts to manage exposures to changes in foreign exchange rates for anticipated intercompany purchases by those subsidiaries whose functional currencies are not the U.S. dollar. These contracts are designated as cash flow hedges of the variability of the cash flows due to changes in foreign exchange rates and are marked-to-market with the resulting gains or losses reflected in Accumulated other comprehensive income (loss). Gains or losses will be included in Cost of products sold at the time the products are sold, generally within the next 12 to 18 months. At December 31, 2020 and 2019, Abbott held $8.1 billion and $6.8 billion, respectively, of such contracts. Contracts held on December 31, 2020, will mature in 2021 or 2022 depending on the contract. Contracts held on December 31, 2019, matured in 2020 or will mature in 2021, depending upon the contract.

Abbott enters into foreign currency forward exchange contracts to manage its exposure to foreign currency–denominated intercompany loans and trade payables and third-party trade payables and receivables. The contracts are marked-to-market, and resulting gains or losses are reflected in income and are generally offset by losses or gains on the foreign currency exposure being managed. On December 31, 2020, and 2019, Abbott held $11.0 billion and $9.1 billion, respectively, of such contracts, which generally mature in the next 13 months.

The following table reflects the total foreign currency forward contracts outstanding on December 31, 2020.

(dollars in millions)	Contract Amount	Weighted Average Exchange Rate	Fair and Carrying Value Receivable/ (Payable)
Receive primarily U.S. dollars in exchange for the following currencies:			
Euro	$ 7,781	1.1821	$ (91)
Chinese yuan	2,401	6.4900	(99)
Japanese yen	1,589	115.3861	(20)
All other currencies	7,369	n/a	(198)
Total	$19,140		$(408)

Source: Abbott Laboratories, 2020 Annual Report, page 61.

? Discussion Question

IS BITCOIN A FOREIGN CURRENCY?

The following conversation took place among the president, sales vice president (VP), and chief financial officer (CFO) of Copanema Manufacturing Company in the company's executive offices.

President: Hi, thanks for coming to my office. I just got off the phone with the CEO and CFO at Motonaka Corporation, that new computer chip manufacturer. They would like to order 10,000 shaft collars from us, but Motonaka's CFO is proposing that they pay us with Bitcoin, which I'm not so sure about. We could deliver product to them tomorrow and, based on today's market price for Bitcoin, they would transfer 10 Bitcoins to us two weeks later.

Sales VP: Well, I certainly would be interested in having Motonaka as a customer, and building a reputation among chip makers would be a very good thing. I understand that Bitcoin is a so-called cryptocurrency and that it has increased in price significantly in the last couple of years, but that's about all I know about it.

CFO: This is good news. I have been thinking recently about investing some of our idle cash in one of the various cryptocurrencies, like Bitcoin, with the hope that we could then resell it and earn a decent gain in a short period of time. Rather than figuring out how to buy Bitcoins ourselves, I like the idea of Motonaka sending us some in two weeks. We then would hang on to them for a while until we can sell them at a higher price.

President: So, if we do this deal, we will need to account for Bitcoin in some way. I assume that cryptocurrency is just another type of foreign currency and we would use foreign currency accounting rules to account for it.

Sales VP: Well, I'm obviously not an accountant, but it seems to me that Bitcoin is a financial instrument, like a share of stock, and we would account for it similarly. I am sure there must be special rules for accounting for financial instruments that we could follow. What does our CFO think?

CFO: That's an interesting question. At first blush, I would think that Bitcoin is an intangible asset, and an indefinite-lived one at that. It certainly has no physical substance. It doesn't exist in the form of paper certificates or metal coins, but only as zeros and ones on a debit card or in a digital wallet. Maybe I should call our accounting department and get them to figure it out before we say yes to this transaction.

Is Bitcoin (or any other cryptocurrency) a foreign currency, or some other kind of asset? How should a sale and account receivable denominated in Bitcoin be accounted for? How should a subsequent investment in Bitcoin be accounted for?

Abbott Laboratories uses forward contracts exclusively to manage its foreign exchange risk, whereas Thermo Fisher Scientific, Inc., uses both foreign currency forward contracts and foreign currency options to hedge exposures resulting from changes in currency exchange rates. In contrast, The Coca-Cola Company employs a combination of forward contracts, currency options, and collars[13] in its foreign exchange risk-hedging strategy.

International Financial Reporting Standard 9— Financial Instruments

IFRS 9, "Financial Instruments," provides guidance on the accounting for hedging instruments, including those used to hedge foreign exchange risk. Rules and procedures in *IFRS 9* related to foreign currency hedge accounting generally are consistent with U.S. GAAP.

---

[13] A foreign currency collar is created by simultaneously purchasing a call option and selling a put option in a foreign currency to fix a range of prices at which the foreign currency can be purchased at a predetermined future date.

Similar to current U.S. standards, *IFRS 9* allows hedge accounting for foreign currency–denominated assets and liabilities, firm commitments, and forecasted transactions when documentation requirements and effectiveness tests are met and requires hedges to be designated as cash flow or fair value hedges. While the hedge accounting models in U.S. GAAP and IFRS generally are based on similar principles, numerous differences exist in the application guidance provided by the two sets of standards.

One difference between the two sets of standards relates to the type of financial instrument that can be designated as a hedge. U.S. GAAP generally does not permit a nonderivative financial instrument to be used as a hedging instrument. In contrast, under IFRS, nonderivative financial instruments classified at fair value through profit or loss are permitted to be used as hedging instruments for all types of risks.

Summary

1. Several exchange rate systems are used around the world. Most national currencies fluctuate in value against other currencies over time. However, some countries have pegged their national currency to the U.S. dollar.

2. Exposure to foreign exchange risk exists when a payment to be made or to be received is denominated (stated) in terms of a foreign currency. Appreciation in a foreign currency results in a foreign exchange gain when the foreign currency is to be received, and it results in a foreign exchange loss when the foreign currency is to be paid. Conversely, a decrease in the value of a foreign currency results in a foreign exchange loss when the foreign currency is to be received, and it results in a foreign exchange gain when the foreign currency is to be paid.

3. Companies must revalue foreign currency assets and liabilities to their current U.S. dollar value using current exchange rates when financial statements are prepared. The change in U.S. dollar value of foreign currency balances is recognized as a foreign exchange gain or loss in net income in the period in which the exchange rate change occurs. This is known as the two-transaction perspective, accrual approach.

4. Borrowing foreign currency creates two exposures to foreign exchange risk. Foreign exchange gains and losses both on the foreign currency note payable and on the accrued foreign currency interest payable are recognized in net income over the life of the debt.

5. IFRS rules related to the accounting for foreign currency transactions generally are consistent with U.S. GAAP. *IAS 21* requires a two-transaction, accrual approach in accounting for foreign currency transactions.

6. Exposure to foreign exchange risk can be eliminated through hedging. Hedging involves establishing a price today at which a foreign currency to be received in the future can be sold in the future or at which a foreign currency to be paid in the future can be purchased in the future.

7. The two most popular derivative financial instruments for hedging foreign exchange risk are foreign currency forward contracts and foreign currency options. A *forward contract* is a binding agreement to exchange currencies at a predetermined rate. An *option* gives the buyer the right, but not the obligation, to exchange currencies at a predetermined rate.

8. Hedge accounting is appropriate when three criteria are met: (a) the derivative is used to hedge either a fair value exposure or cash flow exposure to foreign exchange risk, (b) the derivative is highly effective in offsetting changes in the fair value or cash flows related to the hedged item, and (c) the derivative is properly documented as a hedge. Hedge accounting requires reporting gains and losses on the hedging instrument in net income in the same period as gains and losses on the item being hedged.

9. In assessing hedge effectiveness, companies may elect to exclude the forward points on a forward contract or the time value on an option from the hedging instrument. When this choice is made, the excluded component should be recognized in net income over the life of the derivative financial instrument.

10. Companies must report all derivatives, including forward contracts and options, on the balance sheet at their fair value. Changes in fair value are included in other comprehensive income if the derivative is designated as a cash flow hedge and in net income if it is designated as a fair value hedge.

11. Authoritative accounting literature provides guidance for hedges of (a) recognized foreign currency–denominated assets and liabilities, (b) unrecognized foreign currency–denominated firm commitments, and (c) forecasted foreign currency–denominated transactions. Cash flow hedge accounting can be used for all three types of hedges; fair value hedge accounting can be used only for (a) and (b).

12. If a company hedges a foreign currency firm commitment and designates the hedging instrument as a fair value hedge, it should recognize gains and losses on the hedging instrument as well as on

the underlying firm commitment in net income. The firm commitment account created to offset the gain or loss on firm commitment is treated as an adjustment to the underlying transaction when it takes place.

13. If a company hedges a forecasted transaction, it must designate the hedging instrument as a cash flow hedge and report changes in the fair value of the hedging instrument in other comprehensive income. The cumulative change in fair value reported in other comprehensive income is included in net income in the period in which the forecasted transaction was originally anticipated to take place.

14. Similar to U.S. GAAP, *IFRS 9* allows hedge accounting for hedges of foreign currency assets and liabilities, firm commitments, and forecasted transactions, provided that the hedge is properly documented and is effective. Foreign currency hedging instruments are designated either as a cash flow or a fair value hedge; in either case, the hedging instrument must be reported at fair value.

Comprehensive Illustration

(*Estimated Time: 90 to 120 Minutes*) Felix Toy Company (Felix) is a U.S.-based company that sells toys through its online store in the United States. Felix regularly purchases inventory from a supplier located in Xiamen, China, and makes payment in Chinese yuan. The following spot exchange rates, forward exchange rates, and call option premia for Chinese yuan exist during the period August to October.

Problem

	U.S. Dollar (USD) per Chinese Yuan (CNY)		
Date	Spot Rate	Forward Rate to October 31	Call Option Premium for October 31 (strike price $0.143)
August 1	$0.143	$0.148	$0.0081
September 30	0.149	0.151	0.0123
October 31	0.154	0.154 (spot)	N/A

Part A

On August 1, Felix imports inventory from its Chinese supplier at a price of 1 million Chinese yuan. It receives the inventory on August 1 but does not pay for it until October 31. On August 1, Felix enters into a forward contract to purchase 1 million yuan on October 31. It appropriately designates the forward contract as a *cash flow hedge* of the Chinese yuan liability exposure. Because the critical terms of the hedging instrument match those of the hedged item, the forward contract is a highly effective hedge. Felix excludes the forward points from the assessment of hedge effectiveness, and uses a straight-line method on a monthly basis to amortize the forward premium to net income. The inventory is sold in November.

Part B

The facts are the same as in Part A with the exception that Felix designates the forward contract as a *fair value hedge* of the Chinese yuan liability exposure.

Part C

On August 1, Felix imports inventory from its Chinese supplier at a price of 1 million Chinese yuan. It receives the inventory on August 1 but does not pay for it until October 31. On August 1, Felix purchases a three-month call option on 1 million Chinese yuan with a strike price of $0.143. The option is appropriately designated as a *cash flow hedge* of the Chinese yuan liability exposure. Because the critical terms of the hedging instrument match those of the hedged item, the option is a highly effective hedge. Felix excludes the time value of the option from the assessment of hedge effectiveness and recognizes the change in option time value in net income. The inventory is sold in November.

Part D

On August 1, Felix orders inventory from its Chinese supplier at a price of 1 million Chinese yuan. On that date, Felix enters into a forward contract to purchase 1 million yuan on October 31. The company designates the forward contract as a *fair value hedge* of the Chinese yuan firm commitment exposure.

Because the critical terms of the hedging instrument match those of the hedged item, the forward contract is a highly effective hedge. Felix measures the fair value of the foreign currency firm commitment using forward exchange rates. As a result, the forward points may not be excluded from the assessment of hedge effectiveness, and therefore are not amortized to net income. Felix receives the inventory and pays for it on October 31. The inventory is sold in November.

Part E

On August 1, Felix orders inventory from its Chinese supplier at a price of 1 million Chinese yuan. On that date, Felix purchases a three-month call option on 1 million Chinese yuan with a strike price of $0.143. The company designates the option as a *fair value hedge* of the Chinese yuan firm commitment exposure. Because the critical terms of the hedging instrument match those of the hedged item, the option is a highly effective hedge. Felix excludes the time value of the option from the assessment of hedge effectiveness and recognizes the change in option time value in net income. Felix measures the fair value of the firm commitment using spot exchange rates. The company receives the inventory and pays for it on October 31. The inventory is sold in November.

Part F

Felix anticipates that it will import inventory from its Chinese supplier in the near future. On August 1, Felix purchases a three-month call option on 1 million Chinese yuan with a strike price of $0.143. The company appropriately designates the option as a *cash flow hedge* of a forecasted Chinese yuan transaction. Because the critical terms of the hedging instrument match those of the hedged item, the option is a highly effective hedge. Felix excludes the time value of the option from the assessment of hedge effectiveness and recognizes the change in option time value in net income. Felix receives the inventory and pays for it on October 31. The inventory is sold in November.

Required

Prepare journal entries for each of these independent situations in accordance with U.S. GAAP, and determine the impact each situation has on the third-quarter (September 30) and year-end (December 31) trial balances. Ignore any discounting to present values.

Solution

Part A. Forward Contract Cash Flow Hedge of a Recognized Foreign Currency Liability

8/1	Inventory	143,000	
	Accounts Payable (CNY)		143,000
	To record the purchase of inventory and a CNY account payable at the spot rate of $0.143.		

The forward contract requires no formal entry. Felix prepares a memorandum to designate the forward contract as a hedge of the risk of changes in the cash flow to be paid on the foreign currency payable resulting from changes in the U.S. dollar–Chinese yuan exchange rate, indicating that the forward points are excluded from hedge effectiveness, and will be amortized to net income on a straight-line basis.

9/30	Foreign Exchange Gain or Loss	6,000	
	Accounts Payable (CNY)		6,000
	To adjust the value of the CNY account payable to the new spot rate of $0.149 and record a foreign exchange loss resulting from the appreciation of the yuan since August 1.		
	Forward Contract	3,000	
	Other Comprehensive Income (OCI)		3,000
	To record the forward contract as an asset at its fair value of $3,000 with a corresponding credit to OCI.		

Felix determines the fair value of the forward contract by referring to the change in the forward rate for a contract that settles on October 31: ($0.151 − $0.148) × CNY 1 million = $3,000. The difference in the undiscounted and discounted fair value is immaterial; therefore, for simplicity, discounting to present value is ignored.

9/30	Other Comprehensive Income (OCI).................	6,000	
	Foreign Exchange Gain or Loss.................		6,000
	To record a gain on forward contract to offset the foreign exchange loss on account payable with a corresponding debit to OCI.		
	Foreign Exchange Gain or Loss......................	3,333	
	Other Comprehensive Income (OCI).............		3,333
	To allocate the forward contract premium to net income over the life of the contract using a straight-line method on a monthly basis ($5,000 × ⅔ = $3,333).		

The original premium on the forward contract is determined by the difference in the U.S. dollar–Chinese yuan three-month forward rate and the spot rate on August 1: ($0.148 − $0.143) × CNY 1 million = $5,000.

Trial Balance—September 30	Debit	Credit
Inventory...	$143,000	$ –0–
Forward Contract (asset)	3,000	–0–
Accounts Payable (CNY)	–0–	149,000
AOCI		333
Foreign exchange gain (loss)	3,333	–0–
Total	$149,333	$149,333

10/31	Foreign Exchange Gain or Loss......................	5,000	
	Accounts Payable (CNY)		5,000
	To adjust the value of the CNY account payable to the new spot rate of $0.154 and record a foreign exchange loss resulting from the appreciation of the CNY since September 30.		
	Forward Contract	3,000	
	Other Comprehensive Income (OCI).............		3,000
	To adjust the carrying value of the forward contract to its current fair value of $6,000 with a corresponding credit to OCI.		

The current fair value of the forward contract is determined by referring to the difference in the spot rate on October 31 and the original forward rate: ($0.154 − $0.148) × CNY 1 million = $6,000. The forward contract adjustment on October 31 is calculated as the difference in the current fair value and the carrying value at September 30: $6,000 − $3,000 = $3,000.

10/31	Other Comprehensive Income (OCI).................	5,000	
	Foreign Exchange Gain or Loss.................		5,000
	To record a foreign exchange gain on forward contract to offset the foreign exchange loss on account payable with a corresponding debit to OCI.		
	Foreign Exchange Gain or Loss......................	1,667	
	Other Comprehensive Income (OCI).............		1,667
	To allocate the forward contract premium to income over the life of the contract using a straight-line method on a monthly basis ($5,000 × ⅓ = $1,667).		
	Foreign Currency (CNY)............................	154,000	
	Cash		148,000
	Forward Contract		6,000

(*continued*)

(continued)

To record settlement of the forward contract: Record payment of $148,000 in exchange for CNY 1 million, record the receipt of CNY 1 million as an asset at the spot rate of $0.154, and remove the forward contract from the accounts.

Accounts Payable (CNY)	154,000	
Foreign Currency (CNY)........................		154,000

To record remittance of CNY 1 million to the Chinese supplier.

11/30	Cost of Goods Sold	143,000	
	Inventory.......................................		143,000

To transfer the carrying value of inventory to cost of goods sold (at the time inventory is sold).

Trial Balance—December 31	Debit	Credit
Cash	$ –0–	$148,000
Retained earnings, 9/30	3,333	–0–
Cost of goods sold	143,000	–0–
Foreign exchange gain (loss)	1,667	–0–
Total	$148,000	$148,000

Part B. Forward Contract Fair Value Hedge of a Recognized Foreign Currency Liability

8/1	Inventory..	143,000	
	Accounts Payable (CNY)		143,000

To record the purchase of inventory and a CNY account payable at the spot rate of $0.143.

The forward contract requires no formal entry. Felix prepares a memorandum to designate the forward contract as a hedge of the risk of changes in the cash flow to be paid on the foreign currency payable resulting from changes in the U.S. dollar–Chinese yuan exchange rate, indicating that the forward points are excluded from hedge effectiveness and will be amortized to net income on a straight-line basis.

9/30	Foreign Exchange Gain or Loss......................	6,000	
	Accounts Payable (CNY)		6,000

To adjust the value of the CNY payable to the new spot rate of $0.149 and record a foreign exchange loss resulting from the appreciation of the CNY since August 1.

	Forward Contract	3,000	
	Foreign Exchange Gain or Loss..................		3,000

To record the forward contract as an asset at its fair value of $3,000 and record a forward contract gain for the change in the fair value of the forward contract since August 1.

	Foreign Exchange Gain or Loss......................	333	
	Other Comprehensive Income (OCI)..............		333

To adjust the amount recognized as the current period's amortization of the forward contract discount in net income with a corresponding debit to OCI (which is subsequently closed to AOCI).

As a result of the third entry, a net foreign exchange loss of $3,333 is reported in third-quarter net income, which equals the current period's amortization of forward contract premium ($5,000 × ⅔ = $3,333).

Trial Balance—September 30	Debit	Credit
Inventory	$143,000	$ –0–
Forward contract (asset)	3,000	–0–
Accounts payable (CNY)		149,000
Accumulated other comprehensive income (AOCI)	–0–	333
Foreign exchange gain (loss)	3,333	–0–
Total	$149,333	$149,333

			Debit	Credit
10/31	Foreign Exchange Gain or Loss		5,000	
		Accounts Payable (CNY)		5,000
	To adjust the value of the CNY account payable to the new spot rate of $0.154 and record a foreign exchange loss resulting from the appreciation of the CNY since September 30.			
	Forward Contract		3,000	
		Foreign Exchange Gain or Loss		3,000
	To adjust the carrying value of the forward contract to its current fair value of $6,000 and record a foreign exchange gain for the change in fair value since September 30.			
	Accumulated Other Comprehensive Income (AOCI)		333	
		Foreign Exchange Gain or Loss		333
	To adjust the amount recognized as the current period's amortization of the forward contract discount by transferring the credit balance in AOCI to net income.			
	Foreign Currency (CNY)		154,000	
		Cash		148,000
		Forward Contract		6,000
	To record settlement of the forward contract: Record payment of $154,000 in exchange for CNY 1 million, record the receipt of CNY 1 million as an asset at the spot rate of $0.154, and remove the forward contract from the accounts.			
	Accounts Payable (CNY)		154,000	
		Foreign Currency (CNY)		154,000
	To record remittance of CNY 1 million to the Chinese supplier.			
11/30	Cost of Goods Sold		143,000	
		Inventory		143,000
	To transfer the carrying value of inventory to cost of goods sold (at the time inventory is sold).			

Trial Balance—December 31	Debit	Credit
Cash	$ –0–	$148,000
Retained earnings, 9/30	3,333	–0–
Cost of goods sold	143,000	–0–
Foreign exchange gain (loss)	1,667	–0–
Total	$148,000	$148,000

Part C. Option Cash Flow Hedge of a Recognized Foreign Currency Liability

The following schedule summarizes the changes in the components of the fair value of the Chinese yuan call option with a strike price of $0.143:

Date	Spot Rate	Option Premium	Fair Value	Change in Fair Value	Intrinsic Value	Time Value	Change in Time Value
8/1	$0.143	$0.0081	$ 8,100	$ –0–	$ –0–	$8,100*	$ –0–
9/30	0.149	0.0123	12,300	+4,200	6,000†	6,300†	–1,800
10/31	0.154	N/A	11,000	–1,300	11,000	–0–‡	–6,300

*Because the strike price and spot rate are the same, the option has no intrinsic value. Fair value is attributable solely to the time value of the option.

†With a spot rate of $0.149 and a strike price of $0.143, the option has an intrinsic value of $6,000. The remaining $6,300 of fair value is attributable to time value.

‡The time value of the option at maturity is zero.

8/1	Inventory...		143,000	
	Accounts Payable (CNY).........................			143,000

To record the purchase of inventory and a CNY account payable at the spot rate of $0.143.

Foreign Currency Option.............................   8,100

   Cash   8,100

To record the purchase of a foreign currency option as an asset.

9/30   Foreign Exchange Gain or Loss......................   6,000

   Accounts Payable (CNY).........................   6,000

To adjust the value of the CNY account payable to the new spot rate of $0.149 and record a foreign exchange loss resulting from the appreciation of the CNY since August 1.

Foreign Currency Option.............................   4,200

   Other Comprehensive Income (OCI)...............   4,200

To adjust the fair value of the option from $8,100 to $12,300 with a corresponding credit to OCI.

Other Comprehensive Income (OCI)...................   6,000

   Foreign Exchange Gain or Loss..................   6,000

To record a foreign exchange gain on foreign currency option to offset the foreign exchange loss on account payable with a corresponding debit to OCI.

Foreign Exchange Gain or Loss......................   1,800

   Other Comprehensive Income (OCI)...............   1,800

To recognize the change in the time value of the foreign currency option since August 1 as an adjustment to net income with a corresponding credit to OCI.

Trial Balance—September 30	Debit	Credit
Cash	$ –0–	$ 8,100
Inventory...	143,000	–0–
Foreign currency option (asset)	12,300	–0–
Accounts payable (CNY)	–0–	149,000
Foreign exchange gain (loss)	1,800	–0–
Total	$157,100	$157,100

10/31   Foreign Exchange Gain or Loss......................   5,000

   Accounts Payable (CNY).........................   5,000

To adjust the value of the CNY account payable to the new spot rate of $0.154 and record a foreign exchange loss resulting from the appreciation of the CNY since September 30.

(*continued*)

(continued)

		Debit	Credit
Other Comprehensive Income (OCI)................		1,300	
Foreign Currency Option			1,300

To adjust the carrying value of the foreign currency option to its current fair value of $11,000 with a corresponding credit to OCI.

Other Comprehensive Income (OCI)................		5,000	
Foreign Exchange Gain or Loss................			5,000

To record a foreign exchange gain on foreign currency option to offset the foreign exchange loss on account payable with a corresponding debit to OCI.

Foreign Exchange Gain or Loss....................		6,300	
Other Comprehensive Income (OCI).............			6,300

To recognize the change in the time value of the foreign currency option since September 30 in net income with a corresponding credit to OCI.

Foreign Currency (CNY)...........................		154,000	
Cash			143,000
Foreign Currency Option			11,000

To record exercise of the foreign currency option: Record payment of $143,000 in exchange for CNY 1 million, record the receipt of CNY 1 million as an asset at the spot rate of $0.154, and remove the option from the accounts.

Accounts Payable (CNY)		154,000	
Foreign Currency (CNY).......................			154,000

To record remittance of CNY 1 million to the Chinese supplier.

11/30	Cost of Goods Sold	143,000	
	Inventory..		143,000

To transfer the carrying value of inventory to cost of goods sold (at the time inventory is sold).

Trial Balance—December 31	Debit	Credit
Cash ($5,200 credit balance + $143,000 credit)...............	$ –0–	$151,100
Retained earnings, 9/30	1,800	–0–
Cost of goods sold	143,000	–0–
Foreign exchange gain (loss)	6,300	–0–
Total	$151,100	$151,100

Part D. Forward Contract Fair Value Hedge of a Foreign Currency Firm Commitment

		Debit	Credit
8/1	There is no entry to record either the purchase order or the forward contract because both are executory contracts.		
	A memorandum designates the forward contract as a fair value hedge of the risk of changes in the fair value of the firm commitment resulting from changes in the U.S. dollar–Chinese yuan forward exchange rate, and indicates that the firm commitment will be measured using forward exchange rates.		
9/30	Forward Contract	3,000	
	Foreign Exchange Gain or Loss.................		3,000

(continued)

(*continued*)

To record the forward contract as an asset at its fair value of $3,000 and record a forward exchange gain for the change in the fair value of the forward contract since August 1.

Foreign Exchange Gain or Loss.....................	3,000	
Firm Commitment................................		3,000

To record the firm commitment as a liability at its fair value of $3,000 based on changes in the forward rate and record a foreign exchange loss on firm commitment for the change in fair value since August 1.

Trial Balance—September 30	Debit	Credit
Forward contract (asset)..	$3,000	$ –0–
Firm commitment (liability).....................................	–0–	3,000
Total	$3,000	$3,000

10/31	Forward Contract	3,000	
	Foreign Exchange Gain or Loss..................		3,000

To adjust the carrying value of the forward contract to its current fair value of $6,000 and record a foreign exchange gain for the change in fair value since September 30.

	Foreign Exchange Gain or Loss.....................	3,000	
	Firm Commitment...............................		3,000

To adjust the carrying value of the firm commitment to $6,000 based on changes in the forward rate and record a foreign exchange loss for the change in fair value since September 30.

	Foreign Currency (CNY)...........................	154,000	
	Cash		148,000
	Forward Contract		6,000

To record settlement of the forward contract: Record payment of $148,000 in exchange for CNY 1 million, record the receipt of CNY 1 million as an asset at the spot rate of $0.154, and remove the forward contract from the accounts.

	Inventory..	154,000	
	Foreign Currency (CNY)........................		154,000

To record the purchase of inventory through the payment of CNY 1 million to the Chinese supplier.

11/30	Cost of Goods Sold	154,000	
	Inventory......................................		154,000

To transfer the carrying value of inventory to cost of goods sold (at the time inventory is sold).

	Firm Commitment	6,000	
	Cost of Goods Sold		6,000

To close the firm commitment account to net income (as an adjustment to cost of goods sold).

(*Note:* The final entry to close the Firm Commitment account to Cost of Goods sold is made *only* in the period in which Inventory affects net income through Cost of Goods Sold. The Firm Commitment account remains on the books as a liability until that point in time.)

Trial Balance—December 31	Debit	Credit
Cash	$ –0–	$148,000
Cost of goods sold	148,000	–0–
Total	$148,000	$148,000

Part E. Option Fair Value Hedge of a Foreign Currency Firm Commitment

			Debit	Credit
8/1	Foreign Currency Option.		8,100	
	Cash			8,100
	To record the purchase of a foreign currency option as an asset.			
9/30	Foreign Currency Option.		4,200	
	Foreign Exchange Gain or Loss.			4,200
	To adjust the fair value of the option from $8,100 to $12,300 and record a foreign exchange gain on option for the change in fair value since August 1.			
	Foreign Exchange Gain or Loss.		6,000	
	Firm Commitment			6,000
	To record the firm commitment as a liability at its fair value of $6,000 based on changes in the spot rate and record a foreign exchange loss on firm commitment for the change in fair value since August 1.			

The fair value of the firm commitment on September 30 is determined by referring to changes in the spot rate from August 1 to September 30: ($0.143 − $0.149) × CNY 1 million = $(6,000).

Trial Balance—September 30	Debit	Credit
Cash	$ –0–	$ 8,100
Foreign currency option (asset)	12,300	–0–
Firm commitment (liability)	–0–	6,000
Foreign exchange gain (loss)	1,800	–0–
Total	$14,100	$14,100

			Debit	Credit
10/31	Foreign Exchange Gain or Loss.		1,300	
	Foreign Currency Option			1,300
	To adjust fair value of the foreign currency option from $12,300 to $11,000 and record a foreign exchange loss for the change in fair value since September 30.			
	Foreign Exchange Gain or Loss.		5,000	
	Firm Commitment			5,000
	To adjust the fair value of the firm commitment liability from $6,000 to $11,000 and record a foreign exchange loss for the change in fair value since September 30.			

The fair value of the firm commitment is determined by referring to changes in the spot rate from August 1 to October 31: ($0.143 − $0.154) × CNY 1 million = $(11,000).

			Debit	Credit
10/31	Foreign Currency (CNY).		154,000	
	Cash			143,000
	Foreign Currency Option			11,000
	To record exercise of the foreign currency option: Record payment of $143,000 in exchange for CNY 1 million, record the receipt of CNY 1 million as an asset at the spot rate of $0.154, and remove the option from the accounts.			

(continued)

(continued)

	Debit	Credit
Inventory..	154,000	
Foreign Currency (CNY).......................		154,000
To record the purchase of inventory through the payment of CNY 1 million to the Chinese supplier.		

11/30	Cost of Goods Sold	154,000	
	Inventory.......................................		154,000
	To transfer the carrying value of inventory to cost of goods sold (at the time inventory is sold).		
	Firm Commitment	11,000	
	Cost of Goods Sold		11,000
	To close the firm commitment account to net income (as an adjustment to cost of goods sold).		

(*Note:* The final entry to close the Firm Commitment to Cost of Goods Sold is made *only* in the period in which Inventory affects net income through Cost of Goods Sold. The Firm Commitment account remains on the books as a liability until that point in time.)

Trial Balance—December 31	**Debit**	**Credit**
Cash ($8,100 credit balance + $143,000 credit)...............	$ –0–	$151,100
Retained earnings, 9/30	1,800	–0–
Cost of goods sold...	143,000	–0–
Foreign exchange gain (loss)	6,300	–0–
Total	$151,100	$151,100

Part F. Option Cash Flow Hedge of a Forecasted Foreign Currency Transaction

8/1	Foreign Currency Option............................	8,100	
	Cash		8,100
	To record the purchase of a foreign currency option as an asset.		
9/30	Foreign Currency Option............................	4,200	
	Other Comprehensive Income (OCI)..............		4,200
	To adjust the fair value of the option from $5,200 to $9,500 with a corresponding adjustment to OCI.		
	Cost of Goods Sold	1,800	
	Other Comprehensive Income (OCI)..............		1,800
	To recognize the change in the time value of the foreign currency option in net income (in the same line item that will be affected by the import purchase—i.e., cost of goods sold) with a corresponding credit to OCI.		

Trial Balance—September 30	**Debit**	**Credit**
Cash	$ –0–	$ 8,100
Foreign currency option (asset)	12,300	–0–
Accumulated other comprehensive income (AOCI).............	–0–	6,000
Cost of goods sold..	1,800	–0–
Total..	$14,100	$14,100

10/31	Other Comprehensive Income (OCI)..................	1,300	
	Foreign Currency Option		1,300
	To adjust the fair value of the foreign currency option asset from $12,300 to $11,000 with a corresponding adjustment to OCI.		

(continued)

(continued)

	Debit	Credit
Cost of Goods Sold	6,300	
Other Comprehensive Income (OCI).		6,300

To recognize the change in the time value of the foreign currency option in net income with a corresponding credit to OCI.

	Debit	Credit
Foreign Currency (CNY).	154,000	
Cash		143,000
Foreign Currency Option		11,000

To record exercise of the foreign currency option: Record payment of $143,000 in exchange for CNY 1 million, record the receipt of CNY 1 million as an asset at the spot rate of $0.154, and remove the option from the accounts.

	Debit	Credit
Inventory.	154,000	
Foreign Currency (CNY).		154,000

To record the purchase of inventory through the payment of CNY 1 million to the Chinese supplier.

	Debit	Credit
Accumulated Other Comprehensive Income (AOCI)	11,000	
Cost of Goods Sold		11,000

To close the balance in AOCI (after closing the current period's OCI) to net income (as an adjustment to cost of goods sold).

		Debit	Credit
11/30	Cost of Goods Sold	154,000	
	Inventory.		154,000

To transfer the carrying value of inventory to cost of goods sold (at the time inventory is sold).

(*Note:* The entry to close AOCI to Cost of Goods Sold is made at the date that the forecasted transaction was expected to occur, regardless of when the inventory affects net income.)

Trial Balance—December 31	Debit	Credit
Cash ($8,100 credit balance + $143,000 credit).	$ –0–	$151,100
Retained earnings, 9/30	1,800	–0–
Cost of goods sold	149,300	–0–
Total	$151,100	$151,100

Questions

1. What concept underlies the two-transaction perspective in accounting for foreign currency transactions?

2. A company makes an export sale denominated in a foreign currency and allows the customer one month to pay. Under the two-transaction perspective, accrual approach, how does the company account for fluctuations in the exchange rate for the foreign currency?

3. What factors create a foreign exchange gain on a foreign currency transaction? What factors create a foreign exchange loss?

4. In what way is the accounting for a foreign currency borrowing more complicated than the accounting for a foreign currency account payable?

5. What does the term *hedging* mean? Why do companies elect to follow this strategy?

6. How does a foreign currency option differ from a foreign currency forward contract?

7. How does the timing of hedges of (*a*) foreign currency–denominated assets and liabilities, (*b*) foreign currency firm commitments, and (*c*) forecasted foreign currency transactions differ?

8. Why would a company prefer a foreign currency option over a forward contract in hedging a foreign currency firm commitment? Why would a company prefer a forward contract over an option in hedging a foreign currency asset or liability?

9. How do companies report foreign currency derivatives, such as forward contracts and options, on the balance sheet?

10. How does a company determine the fair value of a foreign currency forward contract? How does it determine the fair value of an option?

11. What is hedge accounting?

12. Under what conditions can companies use hedge accounting to account for a foreign currency option used to hedge a forecasted foreign currency transaction?

13. Under what conditions can a foreign currency derivative be considered "highly effective" as a hedge without conducting a quantitative assessment?

14. What are the differences in accounting for a forward contract used as (*a*) a cash flow hedge and (*b*) a fair value hedge of a foreign currency–denominated asset or liability?

15. How does the accounting for a hedge of a foreign currency firm commitment affect assets and liabilities reported on the balance sheet differently from the accounting for a hedge of a forecasted foreign currency transaction?

16. How are changes in the fair value of an option accounted for in a cash flow hedge? In a fair value hedge?

Problems

LO 7-1

1. Which of the following combinations correctly describes the relationship between foreign currency transactions, exchange rate changes, and foreign exchange gains and losses?

Type of Transaction	Foreign Currency	Foreign Exchange Gain or Loss
a. Export sale	Appreciates	Loss
b. Import purchase	Appreciates	Gain
c. Import purchase	Depreciates	Gain
d. Export sale	Depreciates	Gain

LO 7-2

2. In accounting for foreign currency transactions, which of the following approaches is used in the United States?

   a. One-transaction perspective; accrue foreign exchange gains and losses

   b. One-transaction perspective; defer foreign exchange gains and losses

   c. Two-transaction perspective; defer foreign exchange gains and losses

   d. Two-transaction perspective; accrue foreign exchange gains and losses

LO 7-2

3. On October 1, Tile Co., a U.S. company, purchased products from Azulejo, a Portuguese company, with payment due on December 1. If Tile's operating income included no foreign exchange gain or loss, the transaction could have

   a. Been denominated in U.S. dollars.

   b. Resulted in an unusual gain.

   c. Generated a foreign exchange gain to be reported in accumulated other comprehensive income on the balance sheet.

   d. Generated a foreign exchange loss to be reported as a separate component of stockholders' equity.

LO 7-2

4. Brief, Inc., had a receivable from a foreign customer that is payable in the customer's local currency. On December 31, 2023, Brief correctly included this receivable for 200,000 local currency units (LCU) in its balance sheet at $110,000. When Brief collected the receivable on February 15, 2024, the U.S. dollar equivalent was $120,000. In Brief's 2024 consolidated income statement, how much should it report as a foreign exchange gain?

   a. $–0–

   b. $10,000

   c. $15,000

   d. $25,000

LO 7-2, 7-3

5. On July 1, 2023, Mifflin Company borrowed 200,000 euros from a foreign lender, evidenced by an interest-bearing note due on July 1, 2024. The note is denominated in euros. The U.S. dollar equivalent of the note principal is as follows:

Date	Amount
July 1, 2023 (date borrowed)	$225,000
December 31, 2023 (Mifflin's year-end)	220,000
July 1, 2024 (date repaid)	210,000

In its 2024 income statement, what amount should Mifflin include as a foreign exchange gain or loss on the note?

a. $15,000 gain

b. $15,000 loss

c. $10,000 gain

d. $10,000 loss

LO 7-1, 7-2

6. Grace Co. had a Chinese yuan payable resulting from imports from China and a Mexican peso receivable resulting from exports to Mexico. Grace recorded foreign exchange losses related to both its yuan payable and peso receivable. Did the foreign currencies increase or decrease in dollar value from the date of the transaction to the settlement date?

	Yuan	Peso
a.	Increase	Increase
b.	Increase	Decrease
c.	Decrease	Increase
d.	Decrease	Decrease

LO 7-2, 7-3

7. Matthias Corp. had the following foreign currency transactions during 2024:

- Purchased merchandise from a foreign supplier on January 20 for the U.S. dollar equivalent of $60,000 and paid the invoice on April 20 at the U.S. dollar equivalent of $50,000.

- On September 1, borrowed the U.S. dollar equivalent of $300,000, evidenced by a note that is payable in the lender's local currency in one year. On December 31, the U.S. dollar equivalent of the principal amount was $320,000.

In Matthias's 2024 income statement, what amount should be included as a net foreign exchange gain or loss?

a. $10,000 gain

b. $10,000 loss

c. $20,000 gain

d. $30,000 loss

LO 7-7

8. A U.S. exporter has a Thai baht account receivable resulting from an export sale on June 1 to a customer in Thailand. The exporter signed a forward contract on June 1 to sell Thai baht and designated it as a cash flow hedge of a recognized Thai baht receivable. The spot rate was $0.022 on that date, and the forward rate was $0.021. Forward points are excluded from the assessment of hedge effectiveness. Which of the following is true with respect to the forward points on this contract? The forward points are a

a. Forward contract discount that is recognized in net income as a foreign exchange loss.

b. Forward contract discount that is recognized in net income as a foreign exchange gain.

c. Forward contract premium that is recognized in net income as a foreign exchange loss.

d. Forward contract premium that is recognized in net income as a foreign exchange gain.

LO 7-3

9. A company borrows foreign currency on a two-year note at an interest rate of 4 percent per annum. Which of the following items is not an item that might be included in net income related to this foreign currency borrowing?

a. Interest income

b. Interest expense

c. Foreign exchange gain or loss on the note payable

d. Foreign exchange gain or loss on accrued interest payable

LO 7-4

10. On which of the following dates would a company enter into a hedge of a forecasted foreign currency import purchase?

a. Date on which the company receives goods from a foreign supplier

b. Date on which the company orders goods from a foreign supplier

c. Date on which the company forecasts the purchase of goods from a foreign supplier

d. Date on which the company pays for goods received from a foreign supplier

LO 7-6

11. Which of the following is not one of the three conditions that must be satisfied in order for a foreign currency forward contract to be accounted for as a hedge, that is, using hedge accounting?

    a. The forward contract is used to hedge a cash flow exposure to foreign exchange risk.

    b. The forward contract is highly effective in offsetting changes in the cash flows related to the hedged item.

    c. The forward contract is properly documented as a hedge.

    d. The forward contract is purchased in an officially recognized foreign currency market.

LO 7-6

12. Which of the following components may be excluded from a hedging instrument in assessing its effectiveness as a hedge?

    a. Time value in a foreign currency forward contract

    b. Time value in a foreign currency option

    c. Intrinsic value in a foreign currency forward contract

    d. Intrinsic value in a foreign currency option

LO 7-6

13. In the document formally designating a foreign currency forward contract as a hedge for hedge accounting purposes, a company must do all of the following except

    a. Identify the item that is being hedged.

    b. Name the financial institution that is party to the forward contract.

    c. Specify the nature of the foreign exchange risk that is being hedged.

    d. Disclose the risk management objective and strategy for undertaking the hedge.

LO 7-7

14. What is the appropriate accounting treatment for the discount on a foreign currency forward contract when forward points are excluded from the forward contract in assessing its effectiveness as a hedge? The forward contract discount should be

    a. Recognized immediately in net income as a foreign exchange gain or loss.

    b. Recognized immediately in net income as an adjustment to interest expense.

    c. Amortized to net income as a foreign exchange gain or loss over the life of the forward contract.

    d. Amortized to net income as an adjustment to interest expense over the life of the forward contract.

LO 7-8

15. Monument Company (a U.S.-based company) ordered a machine costing €100,000 from a foreign supplier on January 15, when the spot rate was $1.20 per €. A one-month forward contract was signed on that date to purchase €100,000 at a forward rate of $1.23. The forward contract is properly designated as a fair value hedge of the €100,000 firm commitment. On February 15, when the company receives the machine, the spot rate is $1.22.

    Determine the amount at which Monument Company should capitalize the machine on its books.

LO 7-5

16. On December 1, 2023, Venice Company (a U.S.-based company) entered into a three-month forward contract to purchase 1,000,000 pesos on March 1, 2024. The following U.S. dollar per peso exchange rates apply:

Date	Spot Rate	Forward Rate (to March 1, 2024)
December 1, 2023	$0.088	$0.094
December 31, 2023	0.095	0.098
March 1, 2024	0.105	N/A

Ignoring present values, determine whether Venice Company should report the forward contract as an asset or as a liability on its December 31, 2023, balance sheet, and at what amount.

LO 7-2, 7-7

17. Brandt Corp. (a U.S.-based company) sold parts to a South Korean customer on December 1, 2023, with payment of 10 million South Korean won to be received on March 31, 2024. The following exchange rates apply:

Date	Spot Rate	Forward Rate (to March 31, 2024)
December 1, 2023	$0.0035	$0.0034
December 31, 2023	0.0033	0.0032
March 31, 2024	0.0038	N/A

a. Assuming that Brandt did not hedge its foreign exchange risk, determine how much foreign exchange gain or loss the company should report on its 2023 income statement with regard to this transaction.

b. Assuming that Brandt entered into a forward contract to sell 10 million South Korean won on December 1, 2023, as a fair value hedge of a foreign currency receivable, determine the net impact on net income in 2023 resulting from a fluctuation in the value of the won. Brandt amortizes forward points on a monthly basis using a straight-line method. Ignore present values.

LO 7-9

18. On March 1, Derby Corporation (a U.S.-based company) expects to order merchandise from a supplier in Norway in three months. On March 1, when the spot rate is $0.10 per Norwegian krone, Derby enters into a forward contract to purchase 500,000 Norwegian kroner at a three-month forward rate of $0.12. Forward points are excluded in assessing the forward contract's effectiveness as a hedge, and are amortized to net income on a straight-line basis. At the end of three months, when the spot rate is $0.115 per Norwegian krone, Derby orders and receives the merchandise, paying 500,000 kroner. The merchandise is sold within 30 days.

Prepare all journal entries for Derby Corporation related to this transaction and hedge, and answer the following questions:

a. What amount should Derby Corporation report in the current year's net income as cost of goods sold?

b. What amount should Derby Corporation report in the current year's net income as foreign exchange gain or loss?

LO 7-9

19. Shandra Corporation (a U.S.-based company) expects to order goods from a foreign supplier at a price of 100,000 pounds, with delivery and payment to be made on June 15. On April 15, when the spot rate is $1.00 per pound, Shandra purchases a two-month call option on 100,000 pounds and designates this option as a cash flow hedge of a forecasted foreign currency transaction. The time value of the option is excluded in assessing hedge effectiveness; the change in time value is recognized in net income over the life of the option. The option has a strike price of $1.00 per pound and costs $1,000. The goods are received and paid for on June 15. Shandra sells the imported goods in the local market immediately. The spot rate for pounds is $1.025 on June 15.

Prepare all journal entries for Shandra Corporation related to this transaction and hedge, and answer the following questions:

a. What amount should Shandra Corporation report in net income as cost of goods sold for the quarter ending June 30?

b. What amount should Shandra Corporation report in net income as foreign exchange gain or loss for the quarter ending June 30?

LO 7-8

20. On September 1, 2023, Stone Company received an order to sell a machine to a customer in Australia at a price of 100,000 Australian dollars. Stone shipped the machine and received payment on March 1, 2024. On September 1, 2023, Stone purchased a put option giving it the right to sell 100,000 Australian dollars on March 1, 2024, at a price of $80,000. Stone properly designated the option as a fair value hedge of the Australian dollar firm commitment. The option's time value is excluded in assessing hedge effectiveness, and the change in time value is recognized in net income over the life of the option. The option cost $2,000 and had a fair value of $2,300 on December 31, 2023. The fair value of the firm commitment was measured by referring to changes in the spot rate (discounting to present value is ignored). The following spot exchange rates apply:

Date	U.S. Dollar per Australian Dollar (AUD)
September 1, 2023	$0.80
December 31, 2023	0.79
March 1, 2024	0.77

Prepare all journal entries for Stone Company related to this transaction and hedge, and answer the following questions:

a. What is the net impact on Stone Company's 2023 income as a result of this fair value hedge of a firm commitment?

b. What is the net impact on Stone Company's 2024 income as a result of this fair value hedge of a firm commitment and export sale?

c. What is Stone Company's net increase or decrease in cash flow from having purchased the foreign currency option to hedge this exposure to foreign exchange risk?

LO 7-8

21. On June 1, Munchkin Corp. received an order for finished goods from a Turkish customer at a price of 500,000 Turkish lira with a delivery date of July 31. On June 1, when the U.S. dollar–Turkish lira spot rate is $0.230, Munchkin Corp. entered into a two-month forward contract to sell 500,000 lira at a forward rate of $0.240 per lira. Munchkin designates the forward contract as a fair value hedge of the firm commitment to receive lira. The fair value of the firm commitment is measured by referring to changes in the lira forward rate, so forward points must be included in assessing hedge effectiveness of the forward contract. Munchkin delivers the goods and receives payment on July 31, when the U.S. dollar–Turkish lira spot rate is $0.236. On June 30, the Turkish lira spot rate is $0.246, and the forward contract has a fair value of $2,400.

    Prepare all journal entries for Munchkin Corp. related to this transaction and hedge, and answer the following questions:

    a. What is the net impact on Munchkin Corp.'s net income for the quarter ended June 30, as a result of this forward contract hedge of a firm commitment?

    b. What is the net impact on Munchkin Corp.'s net income for the quarter ended September 30, as a result of this forward contract hedge of a firm commitment?

    c. What is Munchkin Corp.'s net increase or decrease in cash flow from having entered into this forward contract hedge?

LO 7-9

22. On November 1, 2023, Good Life Company forecasts the purchase of raw materials from a Chilean supplier on February 1, 2024, at a price of 20,000,000 Chilean pesos. On November 1, 2023, Good Life pays $1,500 for a three-month call option on 20,000,000 pesos with a strike price of $0.0015 per peso. On December 31, 2023, the option has a fair value of $1,100. The following spot exchange rates apply:

Date	U.S. Dollar per Chilean Peso (CLP)
November 1, 2023	$0.0015
December 31, 2023	0.0013
February 1, 2024	0.0016

Good Life properly designates the option as a cash flow hedge of a forecasted foreign currency transaction. The time value of the option is excluded from the assessment of hedge effectiveness, and the change in time value is recognized in net income over the life of the option. Raw materials are received and paid for on February 1, 2024, and the finished goods into which the materials are incorporated are sold by March 30, 2024.

    Prepare all journal entries for Good Life Company related to this transaction and hedge, and answer the following questions:

    a. What is the net impact on Good Life Company's 2023 net income as a result of this hedge of a forecasted foreign currency transaction?

    b. What is the net impact on Good Life Company's 2024 net income as a result of this hedge of a forecasted foreign currency transaction and import purchase? Assume that the raw materials are consumed and become a part of the cost of goods sold in 2024.

LO 7-2

23. Bento Corporation (a U.S.-based company) acquired merchandise on account from a foreign supplier on November 1, 2023, for 100,000 crowns. It paid the foreign currency account payable on January 15, 2024. The following exchange rates are relevant:

Date	U.S. Dollar per Crown
November 1, 2023	$0.754
December 31, 2023	0.742
January 15, 2024	0.747

    a. How does the fluctuation in the U.S. dollar per crown exchange rate affect Bento's 2023 income statement?

    b. How does the fluctuation in the U.S. dollar per crown exchange rate affect Bento's 2024 income statement?

LO 7-2

24. On December 20, 2023, Momeier Company (a U.S.-based company) sold parts to a foreign customer at a price of 50,000 rials. Payment is received on January 10, 2024. Currency exchange rates are as follows:

Date	U.S. Dollar per Rial
December 20, 2023	$1.05
December 31, 2023	1.02
January 10, 2024	0.98

a. How does the fluctuation in the U.S. dollar per rial exchange rate affect Momeier's 2023 income statement?

b. How does the fluctuation in the U.S. dollar per rial exchange rate affect Momeier's 2024 income statement?

LO 7-2

25. Peerless Corporation (a U.S.-based company) made a sale to a foreign customer on September 15, for 100,000 crowns. It received payment on October 15. The following exchange rates for 1 crown apply:

Date	U.S. Dollar per Crown
September 15	$0.60
September 30	0.66
October 15	0.62

Prepare all journal entries for Peerless Corporation in connection with this export sale, assuming that the company closes its books on September 30 to prepare interim financial statements.

LO 7-2

26. On December 15, 2023, Lisbeth, Inc. (a U.S.-based company), purchases merchandise inventory from a foreign supplier for 50,000 schillings. Lisbeth agrees to pay in 45 days, after it sells the merchandise. Lisbeth makes sales rather quickly and pays the entire obligation on January 25, 2024. Currency exchange rates for 1 schilling are as follows:

Date	U.S. Dollar per Schilling
December 15, 2023	$0.28
December 31, 2023	0.30
January 25, 2024	0.33
January 31, 2024	0.34

Prepare all journal entries for Lisbeth Company in connection with this purchase and payment.

LO 7-2

27. Voltac Corporation (a U.S.-based company) has the following import/export transactions denominated in Mexican pesos in 2024:

March 1	Bought inventory costing 100,000 pesos on credit.
May 1	Sold 60 percent of the inventory for 80,000 pesos on credit.
August 1	Collected 70,000 pesos from customers.
September 1	Paid 60,000 pesos to suppliers.

Currency exchange rates for 1 peso for 2024 are as follows:

Date	U.S. Dollar per Peso
March 1	$0.10
May 1	0.12
August 1	0.13
September 1	0.14
December 31	0.15

For each of the following accounts, what amount will Voltac report on its 2024 financial statements?

a. Inventory

b. Cost of Goods Sold

c. Sales

d. Accounts Receivable

e. Accounts Payable

f. Cash

LO 7-3

28. On April 1, 2023, Mendoza Company (a U.S.-based company) borrowed 500,000 euros for one year at an interest rate of 5 percent per annum. Mendoza must make its first interest payment on the loan on October 1, 2023, and will make a second interest payment on March 31, 2024, when the loan is repaid. Mendoza prepares U.S. dollar financial statements and has a December 31 year-end. Prepare all journal entries related to this foreign currency borrowing, assuming the following exchange rates for 1 euro:

Date	U.S. Dollar per Euro
April 1, 2023	$1.10
October 1, 2023	1.20
December 31, 2023	1.24
March 31, 2024	1.28

LO 7-2

29. Spindler, Inc. (a U.S.-based company), imports surfboards from a supplier in Brazil and sells them in the United States. Purchases are denominated in terms of the Brazilian real (BRL). During 2023, Spindler acquires 200 surfboards at a price of BRL 1,600 per surfboard, for a total of BRL 320,000. Spindler will pay for the surfboards when it sells them. Relevant exchange rates are as follows:

Date	U.S. Dollar per Brazilian Real (BRL)
September 1, 2023	$0.230
December 1, 2023	0.220
December 31, 2023	0.240
March 1, 2024	0.225

a. Assume that Spindler acquired the surfboards on September 1, 2023, and made payment on December 1, 2023. What is the effect of the exchange rate fluctuations on reported income in 2023?

b. Assume that Spindler acquired the surfboards on December 1, 2023, and made payment on March 1, 2024. What is the effect of the exchange rate fluctuations on reported income in 2023 and 2024?

c. Assume that Spindler acquired the surfboards on September 1, 2023, and made payment on March 1, 2024. What is the effect of the exchange rate fluctuations on reported income in 2023 and in 2024?

LO 7-3

30. On September 30, 2023, Peace Frog International (PFI) (a U.S.-based company) negotiated a two-year, 1,000,000 Chinese yuan loan from a Chinese bank at an interest rate of 2 percent per year. The company makes interest payments annually on September 30 and will repay the principal on September 30, 2025. PFI prepares U.S. dollar financial statements and has a December 31 year-end. Relevant exchange rates are as follows:

Date	U.S. Dollar per Chinese Yuan (CNY)
September 30, 2023	$0.100
December 31, 2023	0.105
September 30, 2024	0.120
December 31, 2024	0.125
September 30, 2025	0.150

a. Prepare all journal entries related to this foreign currency borrowing.

b. Taking the exchange rate effect on the cost of borrowing into consideration, determine the U.S. dollar "effective borrowing rate" on the loan in each of the three years 2023, 2024, and 2025.

LO 7-7

31. Icebreaker Company (a U.S.-based company) sells parts to a foreign customer on December 1, 2023, with payment of 16,000 dinars to be received on March 1, 2024. Icebreaker enters into a forward contract on December 1, 2023, to sell 16,000 dinars on March 1, 2024. The forward points on the forward contract are excluded in assessing hedge effectiveness and are amortized to net income using a straight-line method on a monthly basis. Relevant exchange rates for the dinar on various dates are as follows:

Date	Spot Rate	Forward Rate (to March 1, 2024)
December 1, 2023	$2.70	$2.775
December 31, 2023	2.80	2.900
March 1, 2024	2.95	N/A

Icebreaker must close its books and prepare financial statements at December 31.

a. Assuming that Icebreaker designates the forward contract as a cash flow hedge of a foreign currency receivable, prepare journal entries for the sale and foreign currency forward contract in U.S. dollars. What is the impact on 2023 net income? What is the impact on 2024 net income? What is the impact on net income over the two accounting periods?

b. Assuming that Icebreaker designates the forward contract as a fair value hedge of a foreign currency receivable, prepare journal entries for the sale and foreign currency forward contract in U.S. dollars. What is the impact on 2023 net income? What is the impact on 2024 net income? What is the impact on net income over the two accounting periods?

LO 7-7

32. Use the same facts as in Problem 31 except that Icebreaker Company purchases materials from a foreign supplier on December 1, 2023, with payment of 16,000 dinars to be made on March 1, 2024. The materials are consumed immediately and recognized as cost of goods sold at the date of purchase. On December 1, 2023, Icebreaker enters into a forward contract to purchase 16,000 dinars on March 1, 2024.

a. Assuming that Icebreaker designates the forward contract as a cash flow hedge of a foreign currency payable, prepare journal entries for the import purchase and foreign currency forward contract in U.S. dollars. What is the impact on 2023 net income? What is the impact on 2024 net income? What is the impact on net income over the two accounting periods?

b. Assuming that Icebreaker designates the forward contract as a fair value hedge of a foreign currency payable, prepare journal entries for the import purchase and foreign currency forward contract in U.S. dollars. What is the impact on net income in 2023 and in 2024? What is the impact on net income over the two accounting periods?

LO 7-7

33. On June 1, Maxwell Corporation (a U.S.-based company) sold goods to a foreign customer at a price of 1,000,000 pesos and will receive payment in three months on September 1. On June 1, Maxwell acquired an option to sell 1,000,000 pesos in three months at a strike price of $0.062. The time value of the option is excluded from the assessment of hedge effectiveness, and the change in time value is recognized in net income over the life of the option. Relevant exchange rates and option premia for the peso are as follows:

Date	Spot Rate	Put Option Premium for September 1 (strike price $0.062)
June 1	$0.062	$0.0025
June 30	0.061	0.0022
September 1	0.060	N/A

Maxwell must close its books and prepare its second-quarter financial statements on June 30.

a. Assuming that Maxwell designates the foreign currency option as a cash flow hedge of a foreign currency receivable, prepare journal entries for the export sale and related hedge in U.S. dollars. What is the impact on net income over the two accounting periods?

b. Assuming that Maxwell designates the foreign currency option as a fair value hedge of a foreign currency receivable, prepare journal entries for the export sale and related hedge in U.S. dollars. What is the impact on net income over the two accounting periods?

LO 7-7

34. On September 1, Westbrook Corporation purchased goods from a foreign supplier at a price of 1,000,000 francs and will make payment in three months on December 1. On September 1, Westbrook acquired an option to purchase 1,000,000 francs in three months at a strike price of $0.852. The time value of the option is excluded from the assessment of hedge effectiveness, and the change in time value is recognized in net income over the life of the option. Relevant exchange rates and option premia for the franc are as follows:

Date	Spot Rate	Call Option Premium for December 1 (strike price $0.852)
September 1	$0.852	$0.0020
September 30	0.858	0.0075
December 1	0.870	N/A

Westbrook must close its books and prepare its third-quarter financial statements on September 30. The goods purchased on September 1 are sold in December.

a. Assuming that Westbrook designates the foreign currency option as a cash flow hedge of a foreign currency payable, prepare journal entries for the import purchase and related hedge in U.S. dollars. What is the impact on net income over the two accounting periods?

b. Assuming that Westbrook designates the foreign currency option as a fair value hedge of a foreign currency payable, prepare journal entries for the import purchase and related hedge in U.S. dollars. What is the impact on net income over the two accounting periods?

LO 7-7

35. On November 1, 2023, Cheng Company (a U.S.-based company) forecasts the purchase of goods from a foreign supplier for 100,000 yuan. Cheng expects to receive the goods on April 30, 2024, and make immediate payment. On November 1, 2023, Cheng enters into a six-month forward contract to buy 100,000 yuan. The company properly designates the forward contract as a cash flow hedge of a forecasted foreign currency transaction. Forward points are excluded in assessing hedge effectiveness and are amortized to net income using a straight-line method on a monthly basis over the life of the contract. The following U.S. dollar–yuan exchange rates apply:

Date	Spot Rate	Forward Rate (to April 30, 2024)
November 1, 2023	$0.21	$0.195
December 31, 2023	0.19	0.170
April 30, 2024	0.18	N/A

As expected, Cheng receives goods from the foreign supplier on April 30, 2024, and pays 100,000 yuan immediately. Cheng sells the imported goods in the local market in May 2024.

a. Prepare all journal entries, including December 31 adjusting entries, to record the foreign currency forward contract and import purchase.

b. What is the impact on net income in 2023?

c. What is the impact on net income in 2024?

LO 7-7

36. On November 30, 2023, Raval Corporation (a U.S.-based company) forecasts the sale of equipment to a foreign customer at a price of 500,000 crowns. The equipment is expected to be delivered on January 31, 2024, with payment received upon delivery. Also on November 30, 2023, Raval pays $3,000 for an option to sell 500,000 crowns on January 31, 2024, at a strike price of $0.52. Raval properly designates its foreign currency option as a cash flow hedge of a forecasted foreign currency transaction. The time value of the option is excluded in assessing hedge effectiveness, and

the change in time value is recognized in net income over the life of the option. The following U.S. dollar–crown exchange rates apply:

Date	Spot Rate	Put Option Premium for January 31, 2024 (strike price $0.52)
November 30, 2023	$0.53	$0.006
December 31, 2023	0.50	0.024
January 31, 2024	0.49	N/A

Raval Corporation delivers the equipment to the foreign customer on January 31, 2024, and immediately receives 500,000 crowns.

a. Prepare all journal entries, including December 31 adjusting entries, to record the foreign currency option and export sale.

b. What is the impact on net income in 2023?

c. What is the impact on net income in 2024?

LO 7-7, 7-8

37. On October 1, 2023, Mertag Company (a U.S.-based company) receives an order from a customer in Poland to deliver goods on January 31, 2024, for a price of 1,000,000 Polish zlotys (PLN). Mertag enters into a forward contract on October 1, 2023, to sell PLN 1,000,000 in four months (on January 31, 2024). U.S. dollar–Polish zloty exchange rates are as follows:

Date	Spot Rate	Forward Rate (to January 31, 2024)
October 1, 2023	$0.25	$0.29
December 31, 2023	0.28	0.31
January 31, 2024	0.30	N/A

Mertag designates the forward contract as a fair value hedge of a foreign currency firm commitment. The fair value of the firm commitment is measured by referring to changes in the forward rate and, therefore, forward points are included in assessing hedge effectiveness. Mertag must close its books and prepare financial statements on December 31. Discounting to present value can be ignored.

a. Prepare journal entries for the foreign currency forward contract, foreign currency firm commitment, and export sale.

b. Determine the net benefit, if any, realized by Mertag from entering into the forward contract.

LO 7-8

38. On August 1, Pure Joy Corporation (a U.S.-based importer) placed an order to purchase merchandise from a foreign supplier at a price of 400,000 pounds. Pure Joy will receive and make payment for the merchandise in three months on October 31. On August 1, Pure Joy entered into a forward contract to purchase 400,000 pounds in three months at a forward rate of $0.60 per pound. The company properly designates the forward contract as a fair value hedge of a foreign currency firm commitment. The fair value of the firm commitment is measured by referring to changes in the forward rate and, therefore, forward points are included in assessing hedge effectiveness. Relevant U.S. dollar exchange rates for the pound are as follows:

Date	Spot Rate	Forward Rate (to October 31)
August 1	$0.60	$0.60
September 30	0.63	0.66
October 31	0.68	N/A

Pure Joy must close its books and prepare its third-quarter financial statements on September 30. The merchandise is received and paid for on October 31 and sold to local customers in November. Discounting to present value can be ignored.

    a. Prepare journal entries for the foreign currency forward contract, foreign currency firm commitment, and import purchase.

    b. What is the impact on net income over the two accounting periods?

    c. What is the amount of net cash outflow resulting from the purchase of merchandise from the foreign supplier?

LO 7-8

39. On June 1, Parker-Mae Corporation (a U.S.-based company) received an order to sell goods to a foreign customer at a price of 100,000 francs. Parker-Mae will ship the goods and receive payment in three months, on September 1. On June 1, Parker-Mae purchased an option to sell 100,000 francs in three months at a strike price of $1.00. The company designated the option as a fair value hedge of a foreign currency firm commitment. The option's time value is excluded in assessing hedge effectiveness, and the change in time value is recognized in net income. The fair value of the firm commitment is measured by referring to changes in the spot rate (discounting to present value is ignored). Relevant exchange rates and option premiums for the franc are as follows:

Date	Spot Rate	Put Option Premium for September 1 (strike price $1.00)
June 1	$1.00	$0.020
June 30	0.94	0.072
September 1	0.90	N/A

Parker-Mae Corporation must close its books and prepare its second-quarter financial statements on June 30.

    a. Prepare journal entries for the foreign currency option, foreign currency firm commitment, and export sale.

    b. What is the impact on net income in each of the two accounting periods?

    c. What is the amount of net cash inflow resulting from the sale of goods to the foreign customer?

LO 7-8

40. Amaretta Company (a U.S.-based company) ordered merchandise from a foreign supplier on November 20 at a price of 1,000,000 rupees when the spot rate was $0.050 per rupee. Delivery and payment were scheduled for December 20. On November 20, Amaretta acquired a call option on 1,000,000 rupees at a strike price of $0.050, paying a premium of $0.001 per rupee. The company designates the option as a fair value hedge of a foreign currency firm commitment. The fair value of the firm commitment is measured by referring to changes in the spot rate. The option's time value is excluded from the assessment of hedge effectiveness, and the change in time value is recognized in net income. The merchandise arrives, and Amaretta makes payment according to schedule. Amaretta sells the merchandise by December 31, when it closes its books.

    a. Assuming a spot rate of $0.053 per rupee on December 20, prepare all journal entries to account for the foreign currency option, foreign currency firm commitment, and purchase of inventory.

    b. Assuming a spot rate of $0.048 per rupee on December 20, prepare all journal entries to account for the foreign currency option, foreign currency firm commitment, and purchase of inventory.

LO 7-9

41. Based on past experience, Maas Corp. (a U.S.-based company) expects to purchase raw materials from a foreign supplier at a cost of 1,000,000 francs on March 15, 2024. To hedge this forecasted transaction, on December 15, 2023, the company acquires a call option to purchase 1,000,000 francs in three months. Maas selects a strike price of $0.58 per franc when the spot rate is $0.58 and pays a premium of $0.005 per franc. The spot rate increases to $0.584 at December 31, 2023, causing the fair value of the option to increase to $7,500. By March 15, 2024, when the raw materials are purchased, the spot rate has climbed to $0.59, resulting in a fair value for the option of $10,000. The raw materials are used in assembling finished products, which are sold by December 31, 2024, when Maas prepares its annual financial statements.

    a. Prepare all journal entries for the option hedge of a forecasted transaction and for the purchase of raw materials.

    b. What is the overall impact on net income over the two accounting periods?

    c. What is the net cash outflow to acquire the raw materials?

LO 7-2, 7-7, 7-8

42. Pacifico Company, a U.S.-based importer of beer and wine, purchased 1,000 cases of Oktoberfest-style beer from a German supplier for 50,000 euros. Relevant U.S. dollar exchange rates for the euro are as follows:

Date	Spot Rate	Forward Rate to October 15	Call Option Premium for October 15 (strike price $1.10)
August 15	$1.10	$1.16	$0.05
September 30	1.15	1.19	0.06
October 15	1.18	1.18 (spot)	N/A

The company closes its books and prepares third-quarter financial statements on September 30.

a. Assume that the beer arrived on August 15, and the company made payment on October 15. There was no attempt to hedge the exposure to foreign exchange risk. Prepare journal entries to account for this import purchase.

b. Assume that the beer arrived on August 15, and the company made payment on October 15. On August 15, the company entered into a two-month forward contract to purchase 50,000 euros. The company designated the forward contract as a cash flow hedge of a foreign currency payable. Forward points are excluded in assessing hedge effectiveness and amortized to net income using a straight-line method on a monthly basis. Prepare journal entries to account for the import purchase and foreign currency forward contract.

c. Assume that the company ordered the beer on August 15. The beer arrived and the company paid for it on October 15. On August 15, the company entered into a two-month forward contract to purchase 50,000 euros. The company designated the forward contract as a fair value hedge of a foreign currency firm commitment. The fair value of the firm commitment is measured by referring to changes in the forward rate. Forward points are not excluded in assessing hedge effectiveness. Prepare journal entries to account for the foreign currency forward contract, foreign currency firm commitment, and import purchase.

d. Assume that the company ordered the beer on August 15. The beer arrived and the company paid for it on October 15. On August 15, the company purchased a two-month call option on 50,000 euros. The company designated the option as a fair value hedge of a foreign currency firm commitment. The fair value of the firm commitment is measured by referring to changes in the spot rate. The time value of the option is excluded from the assessment of hedge effectiveness, and the change in time value is recognized in net income over the life of the option. Prepare journal entries to account for the foreign currency option, foreign currency firm commitment, and import purchase.

e. Assume that, on August 15, the company forecasted the purchase of beer on October 15. On August 15, the company acquired a two-month call option on 50,000 euros. The company designated the option as a cash value hedge of a forecasted foreign currency transaction. The time value of the option is excluded from the assessment of hedge effectiveness, and the change in time value is recognized in net income over the life of the option. Prepare journal entries to account for the foreign currency option and import purchase.

Develop Your Skills

RESEARCH CASE—INTERNATIONAL FLAVORS AND FRAGRANCES

Many companies make annual reports available on their corporate website, sometimes under SEC Filings on Form 10-K.

Access the most recent annual report for International Flavors and Fragrances, Inc. (IFF), to complete the following requirements.

Required

1. Identify the location(s) in the annual report where IFF provides disclosures related to its management of foreign exchange risk.

2. Determine the types of hedging instruments the company uses and the types of hedges in which it engages.

3. Determine the manner in which the company discloses the fact that its foreign exchange hedges are effective in offsetting gains and losses on the underlying items being hedged.

ACCOUNTING STANDARDS CASE—FORECASTED TRANSACTIONS

Fergusson Corporation, a U.S. company, manufactures components for the automobile industry. In the past, Fergusson purchased actuators used in its products from a supplier in the United States. The company plans to shift its purchases to a supplier in Portugal. Fergusson's CFO expects to place an order with the Portuguese supplier in the amount of 200,000 euros in three months. In contemplation of this future import, the CFO purchased a euro call option to hedge the cash flow risk that the euro might appreciate against the U.S. dollar over the next three months. The CFO is aware that a foreign currency option used to hedge the cash flow risk associated with a forecasted foreign currency transaction may be designated as a hedge for accounting purposes only if the forecasted transaction is probable. However, the CFO is unsure how to demonstrate that the anticipated import purchase from Portugal is likely to occur, and wonders whether management's intention to make the purchase is sufficient.

Required

Search current U.S. authoritative accounting literature to determine whether management's intent is sufficient to assess that a forecasted foreign currency transaction is likely to occur. If not, what additional evidence must be considered? Identify the FASB ASC guidance for answering these questions.

ANALYSIS CASE—CASH FLOW HEDGE

On February 1, when the spot rate was $1.00 per Swiss franc, Blue Bogey Company (BBC) forecasted the purchase of component parts on May 1, at a price of 100,000 Swiss francs. On that date, BBC entered into a forward contract to purchase 100,000 Swiss francs on May 1, and designated the forward contract as a cash flow hedge of the forecasted transaction. The forward points are excluded from the assessment of hedge effectiveness and are straight-line amortized on a monthly basis. On May 1, the forward contract was settled, and the component parts were received and paid for. The parts were used in the assembly of finished goods that were sold by June 30.

BBC's trial balance at March 31 (end of the first quarter) reported the following amounts related to this cash flow hedge (credit balance in parentheses):

Trial Balance	March 31
Forward contract (asset)	$ 2,000
Cost of goods sold	6,000
Other comprehensive income (OCI)	(8,000)
Total	$ –0–

Required

Answer the following questions:

1. On February 1, was the Swiss franc selling at a discount or at a premium in the three-month forward market?
2. On February 1, what was the U.S. dollar per Swiss franc forward rate to May 1?
3. On March 31, what was the U.S. dollar per Swiss franc forward rate to May 1?
4. What amount did BBC recognize as Cost of Goods Sold in the second quarter ended June 30?

INTERNET CASE—HISTORICAL EXCHANGE RATES

The Diez Mil Company (DMC), a U.S. company, made credit sales to four customers in Asia on September 6, 2021, and received payment on October 6, 2021. Information related to these sales is as follows:

Customer	Location	Invoice Price
Boroda Ltd.	Vadodara, India	3,655,000 Indian rupees (INR)
Thai Group	Nonthaburi, Thailand	1,625,000 Thai baht (THB)
Thai Group	Nagoya, Japan	5,494,000 Japanese yen (JPY)
Mainan Syarikat	Skudai, Malaysia	207,400 Malaysian ringgits (MYR)

DMC's fiscal year ends September 30.

Required

1. Use historical exchange rate information available on the Internet at www.x-rates.com, Historical Lookup, to find exchange rates between the U.S. dollar and each foreign currency for September 6, September 30, and October 6, 2021.

2. Determine the foreign exchange gains and losses that DMC would have recognized in net income in the fiscal years ended September 30, 2021, and September 30, 2022, and the overall foreign exchange gain or loss for each transaction. Determine for which transaction, if any, it would have been important for DMC to hedge its foreign exchange risk.

3. DMC could have acquired a one-month put option on September 6, 2021, to hedge the foreign exchange risk associated with each of the four export sales. In each case, the put option would have cost $500 with the strike price equal to the September 6, 2021, spot rate. Determine for which hedges, if any, DMC would have realized a net cash flow benefit from the foreign currency option.

COMMUNICATION CASE—FORWARD CONTRACTS AND OPTIONS

Palmetto Bug Extermination Corporation (PBEC), a U.S. company, regularly purchases chemicals from a supplier in Switzerland with the invoice price denominated in Swiss francs. PBEC has experienced several foreign exchange losses in the past year due to increases in the U.S. dollar price of the Swiss currency. As a result, PBEC's CEO has asked you to investigate the possibility of using derivative financial instruments, specifically foreign currency forward contracts and foreign currency options, to hedge the company's exposure to foreign exchange risk.

Required

Draft a memo to PBEC's CEO comparing the advantages and disadvantages of using forward contracts and options to hedge foreign exchange risk. Recommend the type of hedging instrument you believe the company should employ, and justify your recommendation.

Translation of Foreign Currency Financial Statements

In 2021, U.S.-based digital payments company Square, Inc., agreed to acquire Australia's buy-now-pay-later (BNPL) company Afterpay Limited for $29 billion. A few days later, Swedish cloud services firm Sinch AB announced its plan to acquire Texas-based email delivery provider Pathwire for $1.9 billion. In 2020, personal care products manufacturer Kimberly-Clark Corporation indicated it had purchased diaper maker Softex Indonesia for approximately $1.2 billion. Also that year, Seven & i Holdings Co. Ltd., the Japanese owner of 7-Eleven stores, agreed to purchase Speedway gas stations in the United States for $21 billion.

These are only a few of the many recent transactions in which one company acquired another company located in a foreign country. Companies establish operations in foreign countries for a variety of reasons including to develop new markets, take advantage of potential synergies, or gain access to new technology. Some multinational companies have reached a stage in their development in which domestic operations are no longer considered to be of higher priority than international operations. For example, in 2020, New York–headquartered International Flavors and Fragrances, Inc., had operations in 47 countries and generated 78 percent of its net sales outside the United States, while pharmaceutical giant Merck & Co., Inc., generated 56 percent of its sales and had 41 percent of its property, plant, and equipment outside of the United States.

Foreign operations create numerous managerial problems for the parent company that do not exist for domestic operations. Some of these problems arise from cultural differences between the home and foreign countries. Other problems exist because foreign operations generally are required to comply with the laws and regulations of the foreign country. For example, most countries require companies to prepare financial statements in the local currency using local accounting rules.

To prepare worldwide consolidated financial statements, a U.S. parent company must (1) convert the foreign GAAP financial statements of its foreign operations into U.S. GAAP and (2) translate the financial statements from the foreign currency into U.S. dollars. This conversion and translation process must be carried out regardless of whether the foreign operation is a branch, joint venture, majority-owned subsidiary, or affiliate accounted for under the equity method. This chapter deals with the issue of translating foreign currency financial statements into the parent's reporting currency.

Two major theoretical issues are related to the translation process: (1) which *translation method* should be used (the current rate method or the

Learning Objectives

After studying this chapter, you should be able to:

LO 8-1 Explain the theoretical underpinnings and the limitations of the current rate and temporal methods.

LO 8-2 Describe guidelines for determining a foreign subsidiary's functional currency and when foreign currency financial statements are to be translated using the current rate method and when they are to be remeasured using the temporal method.

LO 8-3 Translate a foreign subsidiary's financial statements into its parent's reporting currency using the current rate method and calculate the related translation adjustment.

LO 8-4 Remeasure a foreign subsidiary's financial statements using the temporal method and calculate the associated remeasurement gain or loss.

LO 8-5 Understand the rationale for hedging balance sheet exposure to foreign exchange risk and describe the treatment of gains and losses on hedges used for this purpose.

LO 8-6 Prepare a consolidation worksheet for a parent and its foreign subsidiary.

temporal method) and (2) where the resulting *translation adjustment* should be reported in the consolidated financial statements (as a translation gain/loss in net income or as a component of accumulated other comprehensive income in equity). In this chapter, these two issues are examined first from a conceptual perspective and second by the manner in which the FASB in the United States has resolved these issues. This chapter also discusses IFRS on this topic.

Exchange Rates Used in Translation

Two methods currently are used in the United States and most other countries to translate foreign currency financial statements into the parent company's reporting currency, and *two types of exchange rates* are used in applying these methods:

1. *Historical exchange rate:* the exchange rate that existed when a transaction occurred.
2. *Current exchange rate:* the exchange rate that exists at the balance sheet date.

Translation methods differ as to which balance sheet and income statement accounts are translated at historical exchange rates and which are translated at current exchange rates. Before continuing on to the next paragraph, please read the Discussion Question: How Do We Report This?

Assume that the company described in the Discussion Question began operations in Gualos on December 31, 2023, when the exchange rate was $0.20 per vilsek. When Southwestern Corporation prepared its consolidated balance sheet at December 31, 2023, it had no choice about the exchange rate used to translate the Land account into U.S. dollars. It translated the Land account carried on the foreign subsidiary's books at 150,000 vilseks at an exchange rate of $0.20; $0.20 was both the *historical* and *current* exchange rate for the Land account at December 31, 2023.

Consolidated Balance Sheet: 12/31/23	
Land (150,000 vilseks × $0.20)...............	$30,000

During the first quarter of 2024, the vilsek appreciates relative to the U.S. dollar by 15 percent; the exchange rate at March 31, 2024, is $0.23 per vilsek. In preparing its balance sheet at the end of the first quarter of 2024, Southwestern must decide whether the Land account carried on the subsidiary's balance sheet at 150,000 vilseks should be translated into dollars using the *historical exchange rate* of $0.20 or the *current exchange rate* of $0.23.

If the historical exchange rate is used on March 31, 2024, Land continues to be carried on the consolidated balance sheet at $30,000 with no change from December 31, 2023.

Historical Rate—Consolidated Balance Sheet: 3/31/24	
Land (150,000 vilseks × $0.20)...............	$30,000

If the current exchange rate is used, Land is carried on the consolidated balance sheet at $34,500, an increase of $4,500 from December 31, 2023.

Current Rate—Consolidated Balance Sheet: 3/31/24	
Land (150,000 vilseks × $0.23)...............	$34,500

Translation Adjustments

To keep the accounting equation (A = L + SE) in balance, the increase of $4,500 in the Land account on the asset (A) side of the consolidated balance sheet when the current exchange rate

Discussion Question

HOW DO WE REPORT THIS?

Southwestern Corporation operates throughout Texas, buying and selling widgets. To expand into more profitable markets, the company recently decided to open a small subsidiary in the country of Gualos. The currency in Gualos is the vilsek. For some time, the government of that country held the exchange rate constant: 1 vilsek equaled $0.20 (or 5 vilseks equaled $1.00). Initially, Southwestern invested cash in this new operation; its $90,000 was converted into 450,000 vilseks ($90,000 × 5). Southwestern used one-third of this cash (150,000 vilseks, or $30,000) to purchase land to hold for the possible construction of a plant, spent one-third in acquiring inventory for future resale, and invested one-third in short-term marketable securities.

Shortly thereafter, the Gualos government officially revalued the currency so that 1 vilsek was worth $0.23. Because of the strength of the local economy, the vilsek gained buying power in relation to the U.S. dollar. The vilsek then was considered more valuable than in the past. Southwestern's accountants realized that a change had occurred; each of the assets (land, inventory, and marketable securities) was now worth more in U.S. dollars than the original $30,000 investment: 150,000 vilseks × $0.23 = $34,500. Two of the company's top officers met to determine the appropriate method for reporting this change in currency values.

Controller: Nothing has changed. Our cost is still $30,000 for each item. That's what we spent. Accounting uses historical cost wherever possible. Thus, we should do nothing.

Finance director: Yes, but the old exchange rates are meaningless now. We would be foolish to report figures based on a rate that no longer exists. The cost is still 150,000 vilseks for each item. You are right, the cost has not changed. However, the vilsek is now worth $0.23, so our reported value must change.

Controller: The new rate affects us only if we take money out of the country. We don't plan to do that for many years. The rate will probably change 20 more times before we remove money from Gualos. We've got to stick to our $30,000 historical cost. That's our cost, and that's good, basic accounting.

Finance director: You mean that for the next 20 years we will be translating balances for external reporting purposes using an exchange rate that has not existed for years? That doesn't make sense. I have a real problem using an antiquated rate for the inventory and marketable securities. They will be sold for cash when a new exchange rate is in effect. These balances no longer have any relation to the original exchange rate.

Controller: You misunderstand the impact of an exchange rate fluctuation. Within Gualos, no impact occurs. One vilsek is still one vilsek. The effect is realized only when an actual conversion takes place into U.S. dollars at a new rate. At that point, we will properly measure and report the gain or loss. That is when realization takes place. Until then, our cost has not changed.

Finance director: I simply see no value at all in producing financial information based entirely on an exchange rate that does not exist any more. I don't care when realization takes place.

Controller: You've got to stick with historical cost; believe me. The exchange rate today isn't important unless we actually convert vilseks into dollars.

How should Southwestern report each of these three assets on its current balance sheet? Does the company have a gain because the value of the vilsek has increased relative to the U.S. dollar?

is used must be offset by an equal $4,500 *increase* in stockholders' equity (SE) on the other side of the balance sheet. The increase in stockholders' equity is called a *positive translation adjustment*. It has a *credit* balance.

The increase in dollar value of the Land due to the vilsek's appreciation creates a positive translation adjustment. This is true for any asset on the Gualos subsidiary's balance sheet that is translated at the *current* exchange rate. *Assets translated at the current exchange rate when the foreign currency has appreciated generate a positive (credit) translation adjustment.*

Liabilities on the Gualos subsidiary's balance sheet that are translated at the current exchange rate also increase in dollar value when the vilsek appreciates. For example, Southwestern would report Notes Payable of 10,000 vilseks at $2,000 on the December 31, 2023, balance sheet and at $2,300 on the March 31, 2024, balance sheet. To keep the accounting equation in balance, the increase in liabilities (L) must be offset by a *decrease* in stockholders' equity (SE), giving rise to a *negative translation adjustment*. This has a *debit* balance. *Liabilities translated at the current exchange rate when the foreign currency has appreciated generate a negative (debit) translation adjustment.*

Balance Sheet Exposure

Balance sheet items (assets and liabilities) translated at the *current* exchange rate change in dollar value from balance sheet to balance sheet as a result of the change in exchange rate. These items are *exposed* to translation adjustment. Balance sheet items translated at *historical* exchange rates do not change in dollar value from one balance sheet to the next. These items are *not* exposed to translation adjustment. Exposure to translation adjustment is referred to as *balance sheet, translation,* or *accounting exposure. Transaction exposure,* discussed in the previous chapter, arises when a company has foreign currency receivables and payables and can be contrasted with *balance sheet exposure* in the following way: *Transaction exposure gives rise to foreign exchange gains and losses that are ultimately realized in cash; translation adjustments arising from balance sheet exposure do not directly result in cash inflows or outflows.*

Each item translated at the current exchange rate is exposed to translation adjustment. In effect, a separate translation adjustment exists for each of these exposed items. However, negative translation adjustments on liabilities offset positive translation adjustments on assets when the foreign currency appreciates. If total exposed assets equal total exposed liabilities throughout the year, the translation adjustments (although perhaps significant on an individual basis) net to a zero balance. The *net* translation adjustment needed to keep the consolidated balance sheet in balance is based solely on the *net asset* or *net liability* balance sheet exposure.

A foreign operation has a *net asset balance sheet exposure* when assets translated at the current exchange rate are higher in amount than liabilities translated at the current exchange rate. A *net liability balance sheet exposure* exists when liabilities translated at the current exchange rate are higher than assets translated at the current exchange rate. The following summarizes the relationship between exchange rate fluctuations, balance sheet exposure, and translation adjustments:

Balance Sheet Exposure	Foreign Currency (FC)	
	Appreciates	**Depreciates**
Net asset	Positive translation adjustment	Negative translation adjustment
Net liability	Negative translation adjustment	Positive translation adjustment

Exactly how to handle the translation adjustment in the consolidated financial statements is a matter of some debate. The major issue is whether the translation adjustment should be treated as a *translation gain or loss reported in net income* (and then closed to retained earnings) or whether it should be treated as a *translation adjustment in other comprehensive income* (OCI) (and then closed to accumulated other comprehensive income (AOCI)). We consider this issue in more detail later, after examining methods of translation.

Explain the theoretical under-pinnings and the limitations of the current rate and temporal methods.

Translation Methods

Two major translation methods are currently used: (1) the current rate method and (2) the temporal method. (Although standard setters do not specifically use these names in their authoritative guidance, *current rate method* and *temporal method* provide a useful shorthand for describing the procedures required.) In this section, we discuss the concepts and basic procedures of each method from the perspective of a U.S.-based multinational company translating foreign currency financial statements into U.S. dollars.

Current Rate Method

The basic assumption underlying the *current rate method* is that a company's *net investment* in a foreign operation is *exposed* to foreign exchange risk. In other words, a foreign operation represents a foreign currency net asset, and if the foreign currency *decreases* in value against the U.S. dollar, a *decrease in the U.S. dollar value of the foreign currency net asset* occurs. This decrease in U.S. dollar value of the net investment will be reflected by reporting a *negative* (debit balance) translation adjustment in the consolidated financial statements. If the foreign currency *increases* in value, an *increase in the U.S. dollar value of the net asset* occurs and will be reflected through a *positive* (credit balance) translation adjustment.

To measure the net investment's exposure to foreign exchange risk, *all assets and all liabilities* of the foreign operation are translated at the *current* exchange rate. Stockholders' equity items are translated at historical exchange rates. *The balance sheet exposure under the current rate method is equal to the foreign operation's net asset (total assets minus total liabilities) position.*[1]

$$\text{Total assets} > \text{Total liabilities} \rightarrow \text{Net asset exposure}$$

A positive translation adjustment arises when the foreign currency appreciates, and a negative translation adjustment arises when the foreign currency depreciates.

To reiterate, assets and liabilities are translated at the current rate and stockholders' equity accounts are translated at historical rates to reflect the fact that the current rate method assumes that the company's net investment in a foreign operation is exposed to foreign exchange risk; net investment is equal to stockholders' equity.

Another reason to translate equity accounts at historical rates is so that the translated amount for the subsidiary's equity accounts will be equal to the original amount of the investment in subsidiary on the parent's balance sheet. Otherwise, the parent will not be able to exactly eliminate the investment in subsidiary account against the subsidiary's stockholders' equity accounts on the consolidation worksheet.

As mentioned, the major difference between the translation adjustment and a foreign exchange gain or loss is that the translation adjustment is not necessarily realized through inflows and outflows of cash. The translation adjustment that arises when using the current rate method is unrealized. It can become a realized gain or loss only if the foreign operation is sold (for its book value) and the foreign currency proceeds from the sale are converted into U.S. dollars.

The current rate method requires translation of all income statement items at the exchange rate in effect at the date of accounting recognition. For example, January 1 sales revenue should be translated at the January 1 exchange rate, January 2 sales at the January 2 exchange rate, and so on. With so many transactions, this would be overly burdensome. Thus, in many cases, an assumption can be made that the revenue or expense is incurred evenly throughout the accounting period and a weighted average-for-the-period exchange rate can be used for translation. However, when an income account, such as a gain or loss, occurs at a specific point in time, the exchange rate at that date should be used for translation.

Temporal Method

The basic objective underlying the *temporal method* of translation is to produce a set of U.S. dollar–translated financial statements as if the foreign subsidiary had actually used U.S.

---

[1] In rare cases, a foreign subsidiary could have liabilities higher than assets (negative stockholders' equity). In those cases, a net liability exposure exists under the current rate method.

dollars in conducting its operations. Continuing with the Gualos subsidiary example, Southwestern, the U.S. parent, should report the Land account on the consolidated balance sheet at the amount of U.S. dollars that it would have spent if it had sent dollars to the subsidiary to purchase land. Because the land cost 150,000 vilseks at a time when one vilsek could be acquired with $0.20, the parent would have sent $30,000 to the subsidiary to acquire the land; this is the land's historical cost *in U.S. dollar terms*. The following rule is consistent with the temporal method's underlying objective:

1. Assets and liabilities carried on the foreign operation's balance sheet at *historical cost* are translated at *historical* exchange rates to yield an equivalent historical cost in U.S. dollars.
2. Conversely, assets and liabilities carried at a *current or future value* are translated at the *current* exchange rate to yield an equivalent current value in U.S. dollars.

Application of this rule maintains the underlying valuation method (current value or historical cost) that the foreign subsidiary uses in accounting for its assets and liabilities. In addition, stockholders' equity accounts are translated at historical exchange rates. Similar to the current rate method, this ensures that the translated amount of subsidiary's stockholders' equity is equal to the original amount of the investment in subsidiary on the parent's balance sheet.

Cash, marketable securities, receivables, and most liabilities are carried at current or future value and translated at the *current* exchange rate under the temporal method.[2] The temporal method generates either a net asset or a net liability balance sheet exposure, depending on whether cash plus marketable securities plus receivables are more than or less than liabilities.

> Cash + Marketable securities + Receivables > Liabilities → Net asset exposure
> Cash + Marketable securities + Receivables < Liabilities → Net liability exposure

Because the amount of liabilities (current plus long term) translated at the current exchange rate usually exceeds the amount of assets translated at the current exchange rate, *a net liability exposure generally exists when the temporal method is used.*

One way to understand the concept of exposure underlying the temporal method is to suppose that the parent actually carries on its balance sheet the foreign operation's cash, marketable securities, receivables, and payables. For example, consider the Japanese subsidiary of a U.S. parent company. The Japanese subsidiary's yen receivables that result from sales in Japan may be thought of as Japanese yen receivables of the U.S. parent that result from export sales to Japan. If the U.S. parent had yen receivables on its balance sheet, a decrease in the yen's value would result in a *foreign exchange loss.* A foreign exchange loss also occurs on the Japanese yen held in cash by the U.S. parent and on the Japanese yen–denominated marketable securities. A foreign exchange gain on the parent's Japanese yen payables resulting from foreign purchases would offset these foreign exchange losses. Whether a net gain or a net loss exists depends on the relative amount of yen cash, marketable securities, and receivables versus yen payables. Under the temporal method, the translation adjustment measures the "net foreign exchange gain or loss" on the foreign operation's cash, marketable securities, receivables, and payables, *as if those items were actually carried on the parent's books.*

Again, the major difference between the translation adjustment resulting from the use of the temporal method and a foreign exchange gain or loss is that the translation adjustment is not necessarily realized through inflows or outflows of cash. The U.S. dollar translation adjustment in this case *is realized* only if (1) the parent sends U.S. dollars to the Japanese subsidiary to pay all of its yen liabilities, and (2) the subsidiary converts its yen receivables and marketable securities into yen cash and then sends this amount plus the amount in its yen cash account to the U.S. parent, which converts it into U.S. dollars.

The temporal method translates income statement items at exchange rates that exist when the revenue is generated or the expense is incurred. For most items, an assumption can be

---

[2] Under current authoritative literature, all marketable equity securities and marketable debt securities that are classified as "trading" or "available for sale" are carried at fair value. Marketable debt securities classified as "held to maturity" are carried at amortized cost. Throughout the remainder of this chapter, we will assume that all marketable securities are reported at fair value.

made that the revenue or expense is incurred evenly throughout the accounting period and an average-for-the-period exchange rate can be used for translation. However, some expenses are related to assets carried at historical cost—for example, cost of goods sold, depreciation of property, plant, and equipment, and amortization of intangibles. Because the related assets are translated at historical exchange rates, these expenses must be translated at historical rates as well.

The current rate method and temporal method are the two methods currently used in the United States and in all countries that have adopted International Financial Reporting Standards as their local GAAP. A summary of the appropriate exchange rates for selected financial statement items under these two methods is presented in Exhibit 8.1.

Translation of Retained Earnings

Stockholders' equity items are translated at historical exchange rates under both the current rate and temporal methods. This creates somewhat of a problem in translating retained earnings. Retained earnings is an accumulation of all of the net income less dividends declared by a company since its inception. At the end of the first year of a company's operations, foreign currency (FC) retained earnings (R/E) is translated as follows:

Net income in FC	[translated per method used to translate income statement items]	=	Net income in $
− Dividends in FC	× historical exchange rate when declared	=	−Dividends in $
Ending R/E in FC			Ending R/E in $

EXHIBIT 8.1
Exchange Rates for Selected Financial Statement Items

	Temporal Method Exchange Rate	Current Rate Method Exchange Rate
	Balance Sheet	**Balance Sheet**
Assets		
Cash and receivables	Current	Current
Marketable securities	Current*	Current
Inventory at net realizable value	Current	Current
Inventory at cost	Historical	Current
Prepaid expenses	Historical	Current
Property, plant, and equipment	Historical	Current
Intangible assets	Historical	Current
Liabilities		
Current liabilities	Current	Current
Deferred income	Historical	Current
Long-term debt	Current	Current
Stockholders' equity		
Capital stock	Historical	Historical
Additional paid-in capital	Historical	Historical
Retained earnings	Composite	Composite
Dividends	Historical	Historical
	Income Statement	**Income Statement**
Revenues	Average	Average
Most expenses	Average	Average
Cost of goods sold	Historical	Average
Depreciation of property, plant, and equipment	Historical	Average
Amortization of intangibles	Historical	Average

*Marketable debt securities classified as held to maturity are carried at amortized cost and translated at the historical exchange rate under the temporal method.

The ending dollar amount of retained earnings in Year 1 becomes the beginning dollar retained earnings for Year 2, and the translated retained earnings in Year 2 (and subsequent years) are then determined as follows:

Beginning R/E in FC	(carried forward from last year's translation)	=	Beginning R/E in $
+ Net income in FC	[translated per method used to translate income statement items]	=	+ Net income in $
− Dividends in FC	× historical exchange rate when declared	=	− Dividends in $
Ending R/E in FC			Ending R/E in $

The same approach translates retained earnings under both the current rate and the temporal methods. The only difference is that translation of the current period net income is calculated differently under the two methods.

Complicating Aspects of the Temporal Method

Under the temporal method, keeping a record of the acquisition date exchange rates is necessary when translating inventory, prepaid expenses, property, plant, and equipment, and intangible assets because these assets, carried at historical cost, are translated at historical exchange rates. Keeping track of the historical rates for these assets is not necessary under the current rate method. Translating these assets at historical rates makes the application of the temporal method more complicated than the current rate method.

Calculation of Cost of Goods Sold

Under the *current rate method,* the account Cost of Goods Sold (COGS) in foreign currency (FC) is simply translated using the average-for-the-period exchange rate (ER):

$$\text{COGS in FC} \times \text{Average ER} = \text{COGS in \$}$$

Under the *temporal method,* no single exchange rate can be used to directly translate COGS in FC into COGS in $. Instead, COGS must be decomposed into beginning inventory, purchases, and ending inventory, and each component of COGS must then be translated at its appropriate historical rate. For example, if a company acquires beginning inventory (FIFO basis) in the year 2024 evenly throughout the fourth quarter of 2023, then it uses the average exchange rate in the fourth quarter of 2023 to translate beginning inventory. Likewise, it uses the fourth-quarter (4thQ) 2024 exchange rate to translate ending inventory. When purchases can be assumed to have been made evenly throughout 2024, the average 2024 exchange rate is used to translate purchases:

Beginning inventory in FC	×	Historical ER (4thQ 2023)	=	Beginning inventory in $
+ Purchases in FC	×	Average ER (2024)	=	+ Purchases in $
− Ending inventory in FC	×	Historical ER (4thQ 2024)	=	− Ending inventory in $
COGS in FC				COGS in $

Application of the Lower-of-Cost-or-Net-Realizable-Value Rule

Under the *current rate method,* the ending inventory reported on the foreign currency balance sheet is translated at the current exchange rate regardless of whether it is carried at cost or a lower net realizable value. Application of the *temporal method* requires the inventory's foreign currency cost to be translated into U.S. dollars at the historical exchange rate and foreign currency net realizable value to be translated into U.S. dollars at the current exchange rate. The *lower of the dollar cost and dollar net realizable value* is reported on the consolidated balance sheet. As a result, inventory can be carried at foreign currency cost on the foreign currency balance sheet and at U.S. dollar–translated net realizable value on the U.S. dollar consolidated balance sheet, and vice versa.

Property, Plant, and Equipment, Depreciation, and Accumulated Depreciation

The *temporal method* requires translating property, plant, and equipment acquired at different times at different (historical) exchange rates. The same is true for depreciation of property, plant, and equipment and accumulated depreciation related to property, plant, and equipment.

For example, assume that a company purchases a piece of equipment on January 1, 2022, for FC 1,000 when the exchange rate is $1.00 per FC. It purchases another item of equipment one year later on January 1, 2023, for FC 5,000 when the exchange rate is $1.20 per FC. Both pieces of equipment have a five-year useful life. The temporal method reports the amount of the equipment on the consolidated balance sheet on December 31, 2024, when the exchange rate is $1.50 per FC, as follows:

$$
\begin{array}{rll}
\text{FC } 1,000 \times \$1.00 = & \$1,000 \\
5,000 \times 1.20 = & \underline{6,000} \\
\hline
\text{FC } 6,000 & \$7,000 \\
\end{array}
$$

Depreciation expense for 2024 under the temporal method is calculated as shown here:

$$
\begin{array}{rll}
\text{FC } 200 \times \$1.00 = & \$200 \\
1,000 \times 1.20 = & \underline{1,200} \\
\hline
\text{FC } 1,200 & \$1,400 \\
\end{array}
$$

Accumulated depreciation under the temporal method is calculated as shown:

$$
\begin{array}{rll}
\text{FC } 600 \times \$1.00 = & \$600 \\
2,000 \times 1.20 = & \underline{2,400} \\
\hline
\text{FC } 2,600 & \$3,000 \\
\end{array}
$$

Similar procedures apply for intangible assets as well.

The *current rate method* reports equipment on the December 31, 2024, balance sheet at $9,000 (FC 6,000 × $1.50). Depreciation expense is translated at the average exchange rate of $1.40 to be $1,680 (FC 1,200 × $1.40), and accumulated depreciation is $3,900 (FC 2,600 × $1.50 = $3,900).

In this example, the foreign subsidiary has only two pieces of equipment requiring translation. In comparison with the current rate method, the temporal method can require substantial additional work for subsidiaries that own hundreds and thousands of items of property, plant, and equipment.

Gain or Loss on the Sale of an Asset

Assume that a foreign subsidiary sells land that cost FC 1,000 at a selling price of FC 1,200. The subsidiary reports an FC 200 gain on the sale of land on its income statement. It acquired the land when the exchange rate was $1.00 per FC; it made the sale when the exchange rate was $1.20 per FC; and the exchange rate at the balance sheet date is $1.50 per FC. How should the gain on the sale of an asset be translated into U.S. dollars?

The *current rate method* translates the gain on sale of land at the exchange rate in effect at the date of sale:

$$
\text{FC } 200 \times \$1.20 = \$240
$$

The *temporal method* cannot translate the gain on the sale of land directly. Instead, it requires translating the cash received and the cost of the land sold into U.S. dollars separately, with the difference being the U.S. dollar value of the gain. In accordance with the rules of the temporal method, the Cash account is translated at the exchange rate on the date of sale, and the Land account is translated at the historical rate:

Cash	FC1,200 × $1.20 =	$1,440
Land	1,000 × 1.00 =	1,000
Gain	FC 200	$ 440

Treatment of Translation Adjustment

The *first issue* related to the translation of foreign currency financial statements is selecting the appropriate method. The *second issue* in financial statement translation relates to deciding *where to report the resulting translation adjustment in the consolidated financial statements.* There are two prevailing schools of thought with regard to this second issue:

1. *Translation gain or loss:* This treatment considers the translation adjustment to be a gain or loss analogous to the gains and losses arising from foreign currency transactions and reports it in net income in the period in which the fluctuation in the exchange rate occurs. At the end of the accounting period, the translation gain or loss is closed to Retained Earnings along with all other income items.

The first of two conceptual problems with treating translation adjustments as gains or losses in income is that the gain or loss is unrealized; that is, no cash inflow or outflow accompanies it. The second problem is that the gain or loss could be inconsistent with economic reality. For example, the depreciation of a foreign currency can have a *positive* impact on the foreign operation's export sales and income, but the particular translation method used gives rise to a translation *loss.*

2. *Cumulative translation adjustment in other comprehensive income:* The alternative to reporting the translation adjustment as a gain or loss in net income is to include it in other comprehensive income. In effect, this treatment defers the gain or loss in stockholders' equity (Accumulated Other Comprehensive Income, or AOCI) until it is realized in some way. As a balance sheet account, the cumulative translation adjustment (CTA) is not closed at the end of an accounting period and fluctuates in amount over time. Moreover, it can have a positive (credit) balance or a negative (debit) balance.

The two major translation methods and the two possible treatments for the translation adjustment give rise to these four possible combinations:

Combination	Translation Method	Treatment of Translation Adjustment
A	Temporal	Gain or loss in Net Income
B	Temporal	CTA in Accumulated Other Comprehensive Income
C	Current rate	Gain or loss in Net Income
D	Current rate	CTA in Accumulated Other Comprehensive Income

Authoritative Guidance

Prior to 1975, the United States had no authoritative guidance on which translation method to use or where to report the translation adjustment in the consolidated financial statements. Different companies used different combinations. As an indication of the importance of this particular accounting issue, the first official pronouncement issued by the newly created FASB in 1974 was *SFAS 1,* "Disclosure of Foreign Currency Translation Information." It did not express a preference for any particular combination but simply required disclosure of the method used and the treatment of the translation adjustment.

The use of different combinations by different companies created a lack of comparability across companies. To eliminate this noncomparability, in 1975 the FASB issued *SFAS 8,* "Accounting for the Translation of Foreign Currency Transactions and Foreign Currency Financial Statements." It mandated use of the *temporal method* with all companies reporting *translation gains or losses* in net income for all foreign operations.

U.S. multinational companies (MNCs) strongly opposed *SFAS 8.* Specifically, they considered reporting translation gains and losses in income to be inappropriate because they are unrealized. Moreover, because currency fluctuations often reversed themselves in subsequent quarters, artificial volatility in quarterly earnings resulted.

After releasing two exposure drafts proposing new translation rules, the FASB finally issued *SFAS 52,* "Foreign Currency Translation," in 1981. This resulted in a complete overhaul of U.S. GAAP with regard to foreign currency translation. A narrow four-to-three vote of the board approving *SFAS 52* indicates how contentious the issue of foreign currency translation has been. Despite the narrow vote, *SFAS 52* has stood the test of time and was incorporated into the FASB *Accounting Standards Codification®* (ASC) in 2009 as part of Topic 830, "Foreign Currency Matters."

Determining the Appropriate Translation Method

LO 8-2

Describe guidelines for determining a foreign subsidiary's functional currency and when foreign currency financial statements are to be translated using the current rate method and when they are to be remeasured using the temporal method.

Implicit in the *temporal method* is the assumption that foreign subsidiaries of U.S. MNCs have very close ties to their parent companies and that they would actually carry out their day-to-day operations and keep their books in the U.S. dollar if they could. To reflect the integrated nature of the foreign subsidiary with its U.S. parent, the translation process should create a set of U.S. dollar–translated financial statements as if the foreign subsidiary had actually used the dollar in carrying out its activities. This is the *U.S. dollar perspective* to translation.

In developing the current authoritative guidance, the FASB recognized two types of foreign entities. First, some foreign entities are so closely integrated with their parents that they conduct much of their business in U.S. dollars. *Second, other foreign entities are relatively self-contained and integrated with the local economy; primarily, they use a foreign currency in their daily operations.* For the first type of entity, the FASB determined that the U.S. dollar perspective still applies, and, therefore, use of the *temporal method* with translation gains and losses reported in *net income* (and closed to retained earnings) is still relevant.

For the second relatively independent type of entity, a *local currency perspective* to translation is applicable. For this type of entity, the FASB determined that a different translation methodology, namely the *current rate method,* should be used for translation. Furthermore, translation adjustments should be reported in *other comprehensive income* and then closed out to *accumulated other comprehensive income* on the balance sheet.

Functional Currency

To determine whether a specific foreign operation is integrated with its parent or self-contained and integrated with the local economy, the FASB created the concept of the *functional currency.* The functional currency is defined as the currency of the foreign entity's primary economic operating environment. It can be either the parent's currency (U.S. dollar for a U.S.-based company) or a foreign currency (generally the local currency). The functional currency orientation results in the following rule:

Functional Currency	Translation Method	Translation Adjustment
U.S. dollar	Temporal method	Gain (loss) in Net Income (closed to Retained Earnings)
Foreign currency	Current rate method	Separate component of Other Comprehensive Income (closed to Accumulated Other Comprehensive Income)

In addition to introducing the concept of the *functional currency,* the FASB introduced some new terminology. The *reporting currency* is the currency in which the entity prepares its financial statements. For U.S.-based corporations, this is the U.S. dollar. If a foreign operation's functional currency is the U.S. dollar, foreign currency balances must be *remeasured* into U.S. dollars using the temporal method with translation adjustments reported as *remeasurement gains and losses* in net income (and closed to retained earnings). When a foreign currency is the functional currency, foreign currency balances are *translated* using the current rate method, and a *translation adjustment* is reported in other comprehensive income (and closed to AOCI).

The functional currency is essentially a matter of fact. However, in some cases, the facts will not clearly indicate a single functional currency. Management's judgment is essential in assessing the facts to determine a foreign entity's functional currency. Indicators provided by the FASB to guide parent company management in its determination of a foreign entity's functional currency are presented in Exhibit 8.2. ASC 830-10-55-5 states that these indicators, "and possibly others, should be considered individually and collectively when determining the functional currency." However, the FASB provides no guidance as to how to weight these indicators in determining the functional currency. Leaving the decision about identifying the functional currency up to management allows some flexibility in this process.

Highly Inflationary Economies

Multinationals do not need to determine the functional currency of those foreign entities located in a *highly inflationary economy*. In those cases, entities must use the *temporal method with remeasurement gains or losses reported in net income.*

A country is defined as having a *highly inflationary economy* when its cumulative three-year inflation exceeds 100 percent. With compounding, this equates to an average of approximately 26 percent per year for three years in a row. Countries that have met this definition at some time include Argentina, Brazil, Israel, Mexico, and Turkey. In any given year, a country may or may not be classified as highly inflationary, depending on its most recent three-year experience with inflation.

One reason for this rule is to avoid a "disappearing plant problem" caused by using the current rate method in a country with high inflation. Remember that under the current rate method, all assets (including land) are translated at the current exchange rate. To see the problem this creates in a highly inflationary economy, consider the following hypothetical example.

The Brazilian subsidiary of a U.S. parent purchased land at the end of 1984 for 10,000,000 cruzeiros (Cr$) when the exchange rate was $0.001 per Cr$. Under the *current rate method,* Land is reported in the parent's consolidated balance sheet (B.S.) at $10,000:

	Historical Cost		Current ER		Consolidated B.S.
1984	Cr$ 10,000,000	×	$0.001	=	$10,000

In 1985, Brazil experienced roughly 200 percent inflation. Accordingly, with the forces of purchasing power parity at work, the cruzeiro plummeted against the U.S. dollar to a value of

EXHIBIT 8.2
Indicators for Determining the Functional Currency

Indicator	Indication That Functional Currency Is the:	
	Foreign Currency	**Parent's Currency**
Cash flow	Primarily in foreign currency and does not affect parent's cash flows	Directly impacts parent's cash flows on a current basis
Sales price	Not affected on short-term basis by changes in exchange rate	Affected on short-term basis by changes in exchange rate
Sales market	Active local sales market	Sales market mostly in parent's country or sales denominated in parent's currency
Expenses	Primarily local costs	Primarily costs for components obtained from parent's country
Financing	Primarily denominated in foreign currency and foreign currency cash flows are adequate to service obligations	Primarily from parent or denominated in parent currency or FC cash flows not adequate to service obligations
Intra-entity transactions	Low volume of intra-entity transactions, not extensive interrelationship with parent's operations	High volume of intra-entity transactions and extensive interrelationship with parent's operations

$0.00025 at the end of 1985. Under the current rate method, the parent's consolidated balance sheet now reports Land at $2,500, and a negative translation adjustment of $7,500 results:

	Historical Cost		Current ER		Consolidated B.S.
1985	Cr$ 10,000,000	×	$0.00025	=	$2,500

Using the current rate method, 75 percent of the Land's U.S. dollar value "disappeared" in one year—and land is not even a depreciable asset!

In the exposure draft that led to the current authoritative guidance on translation, the FASB proposed requiring companies with operations in highly inflationary countries to first *restate* the foreign financial statements for inflation and then *translate* all financial statement accounts using the current exchange rate. For example, with 200 percent inflation in 1985, the Land account would have been written up to Cr$ 40,000,000 and then translated at the current exchange rate of $0.00025, producing a U.S. dollar–translated amount of $10,000, the same as in 1984.

Companies objected to making inflation adjustments, however, because of a lack of reliable inflation indices in many countries. The FASB backed off from requiring the *restate/translate* approach; instead, it requires using the temporal method in highly inflationary countries. In the previous example, under the *temporal method,* a firm uses the historical rate of $0.001 to translate the land value year after year. The firm carries land on the consolidated balance sheet at $10,000 each year, thereby avoiding the disappearing plant problem.

Once a country is classified as highly inflationary, a decrease in the cumulative three-year inflation rate below 100 percent is not necessarily sufficient to remove it from this classification. FASB ASC 830-10-55-25 and the SEC staff suggest that if there is no evidence to suggest that the drop below 100 percent is "other than temporary," the country should continue to be viewed as highly inflationary. The magnitude of the decrease below 100 percent, the length of time the rate is less than 100 percent, and the country's current economic conditions should be taken into account in the "other than temporary" analysis.

The FASB does not identify which specific countries a company should treat as hyperinflationary. The International Practices Task Force (IPTF) of the Center for Audit Quality (CAQ) monitors the inflationary status of countries in order to assist companies in complying with U.S. GAAP. In November 2020, the IPTF identified these seven countries as having a three-year cumulative inflation rate exceeding 100 percent: Argentina, Iran, Lebanon, South Sudan, Sudan, Venezuela, and Zimbabwe. The IPTF determined that the rate of inflation in Venezuela for 2019 was 9,500%, with a three-year cumulative inflation rate exceeding 120,000%! In contrast, Argentina had a 2019 inflation rate of 54%, and a three-year cumulative rate of 183%.[3]

Appropriate Exchange Rate

In some countries, such as Venezuela, there is more than one rate at which the local currency can be converted into foreign currency. Often there is an "official rate" that is available from the Central Bank, and a "parallel rate" that is available in the open (sometimes illegal) market. Or in some countries there is one rate for certain types of transactions and another rate for other transactions. For example, in January 2010, in conjunction with an official devaluation of the local currency, the Venezuelan government established an exchange rate of 2.6 bolivar fuertes (BsF) per one U.S. dollar for *essential* imports (such as food and medicine), and an exchange rate of BsF 4.3 per U.S. dollar for the import of *nonessential* goods. The existence of multiple exchange rates raises the question of which exchange rate to use in the financial statement translation process.

When the *temporal method* is used, ASC 830-20-30-3 indicates that the appropriate rate to use is the applicable rate at which a transaction could be settled, which is a matter for

---

[3] Center for Audit Quality, International Practices Task Force, *Document for Discussion: Monitoring Inflation in Certain Countries,* November 10, 2020, available at www.thecaq.org (accessed December 1, 2021).

management judgment. In the case of Venezuela, for example, the Center for Audit Quality's IPTF determined that while Venezuelan law generally requires foreign currency transactions to be settled at the official exchange rate, because some transactions denominated in U.S. dollars may be settled using the parallel rate of exchange, either exchange rate might be appropriate for the translation of U.S. dollar–denominated assets and liabilities.

In contrast, when the *current rate method* is used, ASC 830-30-45-6 states that the exchange rate applicable for converting dividend remittances into U.S. dollars should be used to translate financial statements. Generally, this will be the official exchange rate established by the Central Bank or other governmental authority.

International Accounting Standard 21—The Effects of Changes in Foreign Exchange Rates

IAS 21, "The Effects of Changes in Foreign Exchange Rates," provides guidance in IFRS with respect to the translation of foreign currency financial statements. *IAS 21* generally follows the functional currency approach introduced by the FASB. Under *IAS 21,* as is true under U.S. GAAP, a foreign subsidiary's financial statements are translated using the current rate method when a foreign currency is the functional currency and are remeasured using the temporal method when the parent company's currency is the functional currency. Significant differences between IFRS and U.S. GAAP relate to (1) the hierarchy of factors used to determine the functional currency and (2) the method used to translate the foreign currency statements of a subsidiary located in a hyperinflationary country.

Although stated differently, the factors to be considered in determining the functional currency of a foreign subsidiary in *IAS 21* generally are consistent with U.S. GAAP functional currency indicators. Specifically, *IAS 21* indicates that the *primary* factors to be considered are the following:

1. The currency that influences the foreign subsidiary's sales prices, which typically is the currency in which prices are stated.
2. The currency of the country whose competitive forces and regulations determine the foreign subsidiary's sales prices.
3. The currency that influences the foreign subsidiary's cost of providing goods and services.

Other factors to be considered are the following:

1. The currency in which the foreign subsidiary generates cash inflows from financing activities.
2. The currency in which the foreign subsidiary receives cash inflows from operating activities.
3. Whether the foreign subsidiary is an extension of the parent or operates with a significant amount of autonomy.
4. The volume of transactions between the foreign subsidiary and its parent.
5. Whether cash flows of the foreign subsidiary directly affect cash flows of the parent.
6. Whether the foreign subsidiary generates sufficient cash flows to service its debt.

IAS 21 states that when the preceding indicators are mixed and the functional currency is not obvious, the parent must give priority to the primary indicators in determining the foreign entity's functional currency.

As noted earlier, U.S. GAAP is silent with respect to weights to be assigned to various indicators to determine the functional currency, and there is no hierarchy provided. Because of this difference in the functional currency determination process, it is possible that a foreign subsidiary could be determined to have a functional currency under IFRS that would be different from the functional currency determined under U.S. GAAP.

Under *IAS 21,* the financial statements of a foreign subsidiary located in a hyperinflationary economy are translated into the parent's currency using a two-step process. First, the financial statements are restated for local inflation in accordance with *IAS 29,* "Financial Reporting in Hyperinflationary Economies." Second, each financial statement line item, which has now been restated for local inflation, is translated using the current exchange rate. In effect, neither the temporal method nor the current rate method is used when the subsidiary is located in a country experiencing hyperinflation. Because all balance sheet accounts, including stockholders' equity, are translated at the current exchange rate, a translation adjustment does not exist. Unlike U.S. GAAP, IFRS does not provide a bright-line threshold to identify a hyperinflationary economy. Instead, *IAS 29* provides a list of characteristics that indicate hyperinflation, including (1) the general population prefers to keep its wealth in a relatively stable foreign currency; (2) interest rates, wages, and other prices are linked to a price index; and (3) the cumulative rate of inflation over three years is approaching, or exceeds, 100 percent. As noted earlier in this chapter, under current U.S. GAAP, the financial statements of a foreign subsidiary located in a highly inflationary economy must be translated using the temporal method, and high inflation is defined as a cumulative three-year inflation of 100 percent or more.

The Translation Process Illustrated

To provide a basis for demonstrating the translation and remeasurement procedures prescribed by current authoritative literature, assume that USCO (a U.S.-based company) forms a wholly owned subsidiary in Switzerland (SWISSCO) on December 31, 2023. On that date, USCO invested $500,000 in exchange for all of the subsidiary's common stock. Given the exchange rate of $1.00 per Swiss franc (CHF), the initial capital investment was CHF 500,000, of which CHF 150,000 was immediately invested in inventory and the remainder held in cash. Thus, SWISSCO began operations on January 1, 2024, with stockholders' equity (net assets) of CHF 500,000 and net monetary assets of CHF 350,000. (Recall that monetary assets consist primarily of cash, receivables, and marketable securities.)

SWISSCO
Opening Balance Sheet
January 1, 2024

Assets	CHF	Liabilities and Equity	CHF
Cash	350,000	Common stock	100,000
Inventory	150,000	Additional paid-in capital	400,000
	500,000		500,000

During 2024, SWISSCO purchased property, plant, and equipment, acquired a patent, and purchased additional inventory, primarily on account. It negotiated a five-year loan to help finance the purchase of equipment. It sold goods, primarily on account, and incurred expenses. It generated income after taxes of CHF 470,000 and declared dividends of CHF 150,000 on October 1, 2024.

As a company incorporated in Switzerland, SWISSCO accounts for its activities using IFRS, which differs from U.S. GAAP in many respects. As noted in the introduction to this chapter, to prepare consolidated financial statements, USCO must first convert SWISSCO's financial statements to a U.S. GAAP basis. SWISSCO's U.S. GAAP financial statements for the year 2024 in Swiss francs appear in Exhibit 8.3.

To properly translate the Swiss franc financial statements into U.S. dollars, USCO must gather exchange rates between the Swiss franc and U.S. dollar at various points in time. Relevant exchange rates (in U.S. dollars) are as follows:

January 1, 2024	$1.00
Rate when property, plant, and equipment was acquired and long-term debt was incurred, March 15, 2024	1.01
Rate when patent was acquired, April 10, 2024	1.02
Average 2024	1.05
Rate when dividends were declared, October 1, 2024	1.07
Average fourth quarter 2024	1.08
December 31, 2024	1.10

EXHIBIT 8.3
Foreign Currency Financial Statements

SWISSCO
Income Statement
For Year Ending December 31, 2024

	CHF
Sales	4,000,000
Cost of goods sold	(3,000,000)
Gross profit	1,000,000
Depreciation expense	(100,000)
Amortization expense	(10,000)
Other expenses	(220,000)
Income before income taxes	670,000
Income taxes	(200,000)
Net income	470,000

Statement of Retained Earnings
For Year Ending December 31, 2024

	CHF
Retained earnings, 1/1/24	–0–
Net income, 2024	470,000
Less: Dividends, 10/1/24	(150,000)
Retained earnings, 12/31/24	320,000

Balance Sheet December 31, 2024

Assets	CHF	Liabilities and Equity	CHF
Cash	130,000	Accounts payable	600,000
Accounts receivable	200,000	Total current liabilities	600,000
Inventory*	400,000	Long-term debt	250,000
Total current assets	730,000	Total liabilities	850,000
Property, plant, and equipment	1,000,000	Common stock	100,000
Accumulated depreciation	(100,000)	Additional paid-in capital	400,000
Patents, net	40,000	Retained earnings	320,000
Total assets	1,670,000	Total equity	820,000
		Total liabilities and equity	1,670,000

*Inventory is valued at FIFO cost under the lower-of-cost-or-net-realizable-value rule; ending inventory was acquired evenly throughout the fourth quarter.

Statement of Cash Flows
For Year Ending December 31, 2024

	CHF
Operating activities:	
Net income	470,000
Add: Depreciation expense	100,000
Amortization expense	10,000
Increase in accounts receivable	(200,000)
Increase in inventory	(250,000)
Increase in accounts payable	600,000
Net cash from operations	730,000
Investing activities:	
Purchase of property, plant, and equipment	(1,000,000)
Acquisition of patent	(50,000)
Net cash from investing activities	(1,050,000)

(continued)

(*continued*)

Statement of Cash Flows For Year Ending December 31, 2024	
Financing activities:	
Proceeds from long-term debt	250,000
Payment of dividends	(150,000)
Net cash from financing activities	100,000
Decrease in cash	(220,000)
Cash at 12/31/23	350,000
Cash at 12/31/24	130,000

The Swiss franc steadily appreciated against the U.S. dollar during the year, from a value of $1.00 on January 1 to $1.10 on December 31.

Translation of Financial Statements—Current Rate Method

LO 8-3

Translate a foreign subsidiary's financial statements into its parent's reporting currency using the current rate method and calculate the related translation adjustment.

The first step in translating foreign currency financial statements is to determine the functional currency. Assuming that the Swiss franc is the functional currency, the current rate method must be used with the cumulative translation adjustment reported in a separate component of stockholders' equity on the balance sheet. The amount of the cumulative translation adjustment can be determined indirectly as the amount that is needed to keep the translated balance sheet in balance. Translating the income statement first, followed by the statement of retained earnings, and then the balance sheet, facilitates the translation adjustment being reported in the balance sheet. (Conversely, the balance sheet is remeasured first when the temporal method is used.) Translation of the income statement and statement of retained earnings into U.S. dollars using the current rate method is shown in Exhibit 8.4.

All revenues and expenses are translated at the exchange rate in effect at the date of accounting recognition. We utilize the weighted average exchange rate for 2024 here because each revenue and expense in this illustration would have been recognized evenly throughout the year. However, when an income account, such as a gain or loss, occurs at a specific point in time, the exchange rate as of that date is applied. Depreciation and amortization expenses also are translated at the average rate for the year. These expenses accrue evenly throughout the year even though the journal entry to recognize them might not have been made until year-end for convenience.

The translated amount of net income for 2024 is brought down from the income statement into the statement of retained earnings. Dividends are translated at the exchange rate on the date of declaration.

Translation of the Balance Sheet

Looking at SWISSCO's translated balance sheet in Exhibit 8.5, note that all assets and liabilities are translated at the current exchange rate. Common stock and additional paid-in capital are translated at the exchange rate on the day the common stock was originally acquired by the parent company. Retained earnings at December 31, 2024, is brought down from the statement of retained earnings. Application of these procedures results in total assets of $1,837,000 and total liabilities and equities of $1,768,000. The balance sheet is brought into balance by creating a positive translation adjustment of $69,000 that is treated as an increase in stockholders' equity.

Note that the translation adjustment for 2024 is a *positive* $69,000 (credit balance). The sign of the translation adjustment (positive or negative) is a function of two factors: (1) the nature of the balance sheet exposure (asset or liability) and (2) the change in the exchange rate (appreciation or depreciation). In this illustration, SWISSCO has a *net asset exposure* (total assets translated at the current exchange rate are more than total liabilities translated at the current exchange rate), and the Swiss franc has *appreciated,* creating a *positive translation adjustment.*

EXHIBIT 8.4
Translation of Income Statement and Statement of Retained Earnings—Current Rate Method

SWISSCO
Income Statement
For Year Ending December 31, 2024

	CHF	Translation Rate*	U.S.$
Sales	CHF 4,000,000	1.05 A	$ 4,200,000
Cost of goods sold	(3,000,000)	1.05 A	(3,150,000)
Gross profit	1,000,000		1,050,000
Depreciation expense	(100,000)	1.05 A	(105,000)
Amortization expense	(10,000)	1.05 A	(10,500)
Other expenses	(220,000)	1.05 A	(231,000)
Income before income taxes	670,000		703,500
Income taxes	(200,000)	1.05 A	(210,000)
Net income	CHF 470,000		$ 493,500

Statement of Retained Earnings
For Year Ending December 31, 2024

	CHF	Translation Rate*	U.S.$
Retained earnings, 1/1/24	CHF –0–		$ –0–
Net income, 2024	470,000	From income statement	493,500
Dividends, 10/1/24	(150,000)	1.07 H	(160,500)
Retained earnings, 12/31/24	CHF 320,000		$ 333,000

*Indicates the exchange rate used and whether the rate is the current (C), average (A), or historical (H) rate.

EXHIBIT 8.5
Translation of Balance Sheet—Current Rate Method

SWISSCO
Balance Sheet
December 31, 2024

	CHF	Translation Rate	U.S.$
Assets			
Cash	CHF 130,000	1.10 C	$ 143,000
Accounts receivable	200,000	1.10 C	220,000
Inventory	400,000	1.10 C	440,000
Total current assets	730,000		803,000
Property, plant, and equipment	1,000,000	1.10 C	1,100,000
Less: Accumulated depreciation	(100,000)	1.10 C	(110,000)
Patents, net	40,000	1.10 C	44,000
Total assets	CHF 1,670,000		$1,837,000
Liabilities and Equities			
Accounts payable	CHF 600,000	1.10 C	$ 660,000
Total current liabilities	600,000		660,000
Long-term debt	250,000	1.10 C	275,000
Total liabilities	850,000		935,000
Common stock	100,000	1.00 H	100,000
Additional paid-in capital	400,000	1.00 H	400,000
Retained earnings	320,000	From statement of R/E	333,000
Cumulative translation adjustment		To balance	69,000
Total equity	820,000		902,000
Total liabilities and equity	CHF 1,670,000		$1,837,000

The translation adjustment can be derived as the amount needed to bring the balance sheet back into balance. The translation adjustment also can be calculated by considering the impact of exchange rate changes on the beginning balance and subsequent changes in the net asset position, summarized as follows:

1. Translate the net asset balance of the subsidiary at the beginning of the year at the exchange rate in effect on that date (*a*).
2. Translate individual increases and decreases in the net asset balance during the year at the rates in effect when those increases and decreases occurred (*b*). Only a few events, such as net income, dividends, stock issuance, and the acquisition of treasury stock, actually change net assets. Transactions such as the acquisition of equipment or the payment of a liability have no effect on total net assets.
3. Combine the translated beginning net asset balance (*a*) and the translated value of the individual changes (*b*) to arrive at the relative value of the net assets being held prior to the impact of any exchange rate fluctuations during the year (*c*).
4. Translate the ending net asset balance at the current exchange rate to determine the reported value after all exchange rate changes have occurred (*d*).
5. Compare the translated value of the net assets prior to any rate changes (*c*) with the ending translated value (*d*). The difference is the result of exchange rate changes during the period. If (*c*) is higher than (*d*), a negative (debit) translation adjustment arises. If (*d*) is higher than (*c*), a positive (credit) translation adjustment results.

Computation of Translation Adjustment

Based on the process just described, the translation adjustment for SWISSCO in this example is calculated as follows:

Net asset balance, 1/1/24	CHF 500,000 × 1.00 =	$500,000	(*a*)
Change in net assets:			
Net income, 2024	470,000 × 1.05 =	493,500	(*b*)
Dividends declared, 10/1/24	(150,000) × 1.07 =	(160,500)	(*b*)
Net asset balance, 12/31/24	CHF 820,000	$833,000	(*c*)
Net asset balance, 12/31/24 at current exchange rate	CHF 820,000 × 1.10 =	902,000	(*d*)
Translation adjustment, 2024 (positive)		$ (69,000)	

The process just described and demonstrated is used to calculate the current period's translation adjustment. Because SWISSCO began operations at the beginning of the current year, the $69,000 translation adjustment is the only amount that will be needed to keep the U.S. dollar consolidated balance sheet in balance. In subsequent years, a cumulative translation adjustment comprising the current year's translation adjustment plus translation adjustments from prior years will be included in stockholders' equity on the U.S. dollar consolidated balance sheet. Companies report the *cumulative translation adjustment* in Accumulated Other Comprehensive Income (AOCI), along with unrealized foreign exchange gains and losses, gains and losses on cash flow hedges, unrealized gains and losses on available-for-sale marketable debt securities, and adjustments for pension accounting.

The cumulative translation adjustment (CTA) remains within AOCI only until the foreign operation is sold or liquidated. In the period in which sale or liquidation occurs, the CTA related to the particular foreign entity is removed from AOCI and included as part of the gain or loss on the sale of the investment. In effect, the accumulated unrealized foreign exchange gain or loss that has been deferred in AOCI becomes realized when the entity is disposed of.

Translation of the Statement of Cash Flows

The current rate method requires translating all operating items in the statement of cash flows at the average-for-the-period exchange rate (see Exhibit 8.6). This is the same rate used for

EXHIBIT 8.6
Translated Statement of Cash Flows—Current Rate Method

SWISSCO
Statement of Cash Flows
For Year Ending December 31, 2024

	CHF	Translation Rate	U.S.$
Operating activities:			
Net income.	CHF 470,000	1.05 A	$ 493,500
Add: Depreciation.	100,000	1.05 A	105,000
Amortization.	10,000	1.05 A	10,500
Increase in accounts receivable	(200,000)	1.05 A	(210,000)
Increase in inventory	(250,000)	1.05 A	(262,500)
Increase in accounts payable.	600,000	1.05 A	630,000
Net cash from operations	730,000		766,500
Investing activities:			
Purchase of property, plant, and equipment	(1,000,000)	1.01 H	(1,010,000)
Acquisition of patent	(50,000)	1.02 H	(51,000)
Net cash from investing activities	(1,050,000)		(1,061,000)
Financing activities:			
Proceeds from long-term debt.	250,000	1.01 H	252,500
Payment of dividends.	(150,000)	1.07 H	(160,500)
Net cash from financing activities	100,000		92,000
Decrease in cash	(220,000)		(202,500)
Effect of exchange rate change on cash		To balance	(4,500)
Cash at December 31, 2023	CHF 350,000	1.00 H	350,000
Cash at December 31, 2024	CHF130,000	1.10 C	$ 143,000

translating income statement items. Although the ending balances in Accounts Receivable, Inventory, and Accounts Payable on the balance sheet are translated at the current exchange rate, the average rate is used for the *changes* in these accounts because those changes are caused by operating activities (such as sales and purchases) that are translated at the average rate.

Investing and financing activities are translated at the exchange rate on the day the activity took place. Although long-term debt is translated in the balance sheet at the current rate, in the statement of cash flows, it is translated at the historical rate when the debt was incurred.

The $(4,500) "effect of exchange rate change on cash" is a part of the overall translation adjustment of $69,000. It represents that part of the translation adjustment attributable to a decrease in Cash and is derived as a balancing amount.

LO 8-4

Remeasure a foreign subsidiary's financial statements using the temporal method and calculate the associated remeasurement gain or loss.

Remeasurement of Financial Statements— Temporal Method

Now assume that a careful examination of the functional currency indicators in Exhibit 8.2 leads USCO's management to conclude that SWISSCO's functional currency is the U.S. dollar. In that case, the Swiss franc financial statements must be remeasured into U.S. dollars using the temporal method, and the remeasurement gain or loss must be reported in income. To ensure that the remeasurement gain or loss is reported in income, it is easiest to remeasure the balance sheet first (as shown in Exhibit 8.7).

According to the procedures outlined in Exhibit 8.1, the temporal method remeasures cash, receivables, and liabilities into U.S. dollars using the current exchange rate of $1.10. Inventory (carried at FIFO cost); property, plant, and equipment; patents; and contributed capital (common stock and additional paid-in capital) are remeasured at historical rates. These procedures result in total assets of $1,744,800, total liabilities of $935,000, and contributed capital of $500,000. To balance the balance sheet, retained earnings must total $309,800. We verify the accuracy of this amount later.

EXHIBIT 8.7
Remeasurement of Balance Sheet—Temporal Method

SWISSCO
Balance Sheet
December 31, 2024

	CHF	Remeasurement Rate	U.S.$
Assets			
Cash	CHF 130,000	1.10 C	$ 143,000
Accounts receivable.	200,000	1.10 C	220,000
Inventory.	400,000	1.08 H	432,000
Total current assets	730,000		795,000
Property, plant, and equipment	1,000,000	1.01 H	1,010,000
Less: Accumulated depreciation	(100,000)	1.01 H	(101,000)
Patents, net	40,000	1.02 H	40,800
Total assets	CHF 1,670,000		$1,744,800
Liabilities and Equities			
Accounts payable.	CHF 600,000	1.10 C	$ 660,000
Total current liabilities	600,000		660,000
Long-term debt	250,000	1.10 C	275,000
Total liabilities	850,000		935,000
Common stock	100,000	1.00 H	100,000
Additional paid-in capital.	400,000	1.00 H	400,000
Retained earnings.	320,000	To balance	309,800
Total equity	820,000		809,800
Total liabilities and equity	CHF 1,670,000		$1,744,800

Remeasurement of the Income Statement

Exhibit 8.8 shows the remeasurement of SWISSCO's income statement and statement of retained earnings. Revenues and expenses incurred evenly throughout the year (sales, other expenses, and income taxes) are remeasured at the average exchange rate of $1.05 Expenses related to assets remeasured at historical exchange rates (depreciation expense and amortization expense) are remeasured at relevant historical rates.

The following procedure remeasures cost of goods sold at historical exchange rates. Beginning inventory acquired on January 1 is remeasured at the exchange rate on that date ($1.00). Purchases made evenly throughout the year are remeasured at the average rate for the year ($1.05). Ending inventory (at FIFO cost) is purchased evenly throughout the fourth quarter of 2024, and the average exchange rate for the quarter ($1.08) is used to remeasure that component of cost of goods sold. These procedures result in cost of goods sold of $3,130,500, calculated as follows:

Beginning inventory, 1/1/24	CHF 150,000 × 1.00 =	$ 150,000
Plus: Purchases, 2024	3,250,000 × 1.05 =	3,412,500
Less: Ending inventory, 12/31/24	(400,000) × 1.08 =	(432,000)
Cost of goods sold, 2024	CHF 3,000,000	$3,130,500

The ending balances in retained earnings on the balance sheet and on the statement of retained earnings must reconcile with one another. Because dividends are remeasured into a U.S. dollar equivalent of $160,500 and the ending balance in retained earnings on the balance sheet is $309,800, net income must be $470,300.

Reconciling the amount of income reported in the statement of retained earnings and in the income statement requires a remeasurement loss of $47,000 in calculating net income. Without this remeasurement loss, the income statement, statement of retained earnings, and balance sheet are not consistent with one another.

The remeasurement loss can be calculated by considering the impact of exchange rate changes on the subsidiary's balance sheet exposure. Under the temporal method, SWISSCO's balance

EXHIBIT 8.8
Remeasurement of Income Statement and Statement of Retained Earnings— Temporal Method

SWISSCO
Income Statement
For Year Ending December 31, 2024

	CHF	Remeasurement Rate	U.S.$
Sales	CHF 4,000,000	1.05 A	$4,200,000
Cost of goods sold	(3,000,000)	Calculation	(3,130,500)
Gross profit	1,000,000		1,069,500
Depreciation expense	(100,000)	1.01 H	(101,000)
Amortization expense	(10,000)	1.02 H	(10,200)
Other expenses	(220,000)	1.05 A	(231,000)
Income before income taxes	670,000		727,300
Income taxes	(200,000)	1.05 A	(210,000)
Income before remeasurement loss	470,000		517,300
Remeasurement loss	–0–	To balance	(47,000)
Net income	CHF 470,000	Below	$ 470,300

Statement of Retained Earnings
For Year Ending December 31, 2024

	CHF	Remeasurement Rate	U.S.$
Retained earnings, 1/1/24	CHF –0–		$ –0–
Net income, 2024	470,000	To balance	470,300
Dividends	(150,000)	1.07 H	(160,500)
Retained earnings, 12/31/24	CHF 320,000	Above	$ 309,800

sheet exposure is defined by its net monetary asset or net monetary liability position. SWISSCO began 2024 with net monetary assets (cash) of CHF 350,000. During the year, however, expenditures of cash and the incurrence of liabilities caused monetary liabilities (accounts payable + long-term debt = CHF 850,000) to exceed monetary assets (cash + accounts receivable = CHF 330,000). A net monetary liability position of CHF 520,000 exists at December 31, 2024. The remeasurement loss is computed by translating the beginning net monetary asset position and subsequent changes in monetary items at appropriate exchange rates and then comparing this with the dollar value of net monetary liabilities at year-end based on the current exchange rate:

Computation of Remeasurement Loss

Net monetary assets, 1/1/24	CHF 350,000 × 1.00 =	$ 350,000
Increase in monetary assets:		
Sales, 2024	4,000,000 × 1.05 =	4,200,000
Decreases in monetary assets and increases in monetary liabilities:		
Purchases, 2024	(3,250,000) × 1.05 =	(3,412,500)
Other expenses, 2024	(220,000) × 1.05 =	(231,000)
Income taxes, 2024	(200,000) × 1.05 =	(210,000)
Purchase of property, plant, and equipment, 3/15/20	(1,000,000) × 1.01 =	(1,010,000)
Acquisition of patent, 4/10/24	(50,000) × 1.02 =	(51,000)
Dividends, 10/1/24	(150,000) × 1.07 =	(160,500)
Net monetary liabilities, 12/31/24	CHF (520,000)	$ (525,000)
Net monetary liabilities, 12/31/24 at the current exchange rate	CHF (520,000) × 1.10 =	(572,000)
Remeasurement loss		$ 47,000

Had SWISSCO maintained its net monetary asset position of CHF 350,000 for the entire year, a $35,000 remeasurement gain would have resulted. The CHF held in cash was worth $350,000 (CHF 350,000 × $1.00) at the beginning of the year and $385,000 (CHF 350,000 × $1.10) at year-end. However, the net monetary asset position is not maintained because of changes during the year in monetary items other than the original cash balance. Indeed, a net monetary liability position arises over the course of the year. The foreign currency *appreciation* coupled with an increase in *net monetary liabilities* generates a *remeasurement loss* for the year.

Remeasurement of the Statement of Cash Flows

In remeasuring the statement of cash flows (shown in Exhibit 8.9), the U.S. dollar value for net income comes directly from the remeasured income statement. Depreciation and amortization are remeasured at the rates used in the income statement, and the remeasurement loss is added back to net income because it is a noncash item. The increases in accounts receivable and accounts payable relate to sales and purchases and therefore are remeasured at the average rate. The U.S. dollar value for the increase in inventory is determined by referring to the remeasurement of the cost of goods sold.

The resulting U.S. dollar amount of "net cash from operations" ($766,500) is exactly the same as when the current rate method was used in translation. In addition, the investing and financing activities are translated in the same manner under both methods. This makes sense; the amount of cash inflows and outflows is a matter of fact and is not affected by the particular translation methodology employed.

Nonlocal Currency Balances

One additional issue related to the translation of foreign currency financial statements needs to be considered. How should a company deal with nonlocal currency balances in the foreign

EXHIBIT 8.9
Remeasurement of Statement of Cash Flows— Temporal Method

SWISSCO Statement of Cash Flows For Year Ending December 31, 2024			
	CHF	**Remeasurement Rate**	**U.S.$**
Operating activities:			
Net income	CHF 470,000	From I/S	$ 470,300
Add: Depreciation expense	100,000	1.01 H	101,000
Amortization expense	10,000	1.02 H	10,200
Remeasurement loss		From I/S	47,000
Increase in accounts receivable	(200,000)	1.05 A	(210,000)
Increase in inventory	(250,000)	*	(282,000)
Increase in accounts payable	600,000	1.05 A	630,000
Net cash from operations	730,000		766,500
Investing activities:			
Purchase of property and equipment	(1,000,000)	1.01 H	(1,010,000)
Acquisition of patent	(50,000)	1.02 H	(51,000)
Net cash from investing activities	(1,050,000)		(1,061,000)
Financing activities:			
Proceeds from long-term debt	250,000	1.01 H	252,500
Payment of dividends	(150,000)	1.07 H	(160,500)
Net cash from financing activities	100,000		92,000
Decrease in cash	(220,000)		(202,500)
Effect of exchange rate changes on cash		To balance	(4,500)
Cash at December 31, 2023	CHF 350,000	1.00 H	$ 350,000
Cash at December 31, 2024	CHF 130,000	1.10 C	$ 143,000

*In remeasuring cost of goods sold earlier, beginning inventory was remeasured as $150,000, and ending inventory was remeasured as $432,000: an increase of $282,000.

currency financial statements of their foreign operations? For example, if any of the accounts of the Swiss subsidiary are denominated in a currency other than the Swiss franc, those balances would first have to be restated into francs in accordance with the rules discussed in the previous chapter. Both the foreign currency balance and any related foreign exchange gain or loss would then be translated (or remeasured) into U.S. dollars.

For example, assume that SWISSCO borrows 100,000 euros on January 1, 2024. Exchange rates in 2024 between the Swiss franc (CHF) and euro (€) and between the CHF and U.S. dollar ($) are as follows:

	CHF per €	$ per CHF
January 1, 2024	CHF 1.15	$1.00
Average, 2024	CHF 1.18	$1.05
December 31, 2024	CHF 1.20	$1.10

On December 31, 2024, SWISSCO remeasures the €100,000 note payable into CHF using the current rate as follows: €100,000 × CHF 1.20 = CHF 120,000. SWISSCO also recognizes a CHF 5,000 [€100,000 × (CHF 1.20 − CHF 1.15)] foreign exchange loss. To consolidate Swissco's CHF financial statements with those of its parent, the note payable remeasured in CHF is then translated into U.S. dollars using the current exchange rate, and the related foreign exchange loss in CHF is translated into U.S. dollars using the average exchange rate, as follows:

Note payable	CHF 120,000 × $1.10 C = $132,000
Foreign exchange loss	CHF 5,000 × $1.05 A = $5,250

A note payable of $132,000 will be reported on the consolidated balance sheet, and a loss of $5,250 will be reflected in the measurement of consolidated net income.

The comprehensive illustration at the end of this chapter further demonstrates how nonlocal currency balances of a foreign entity are treated in the preparation of consolidated financial statements.

Comparison of the Results from Applying the Two Different Methods

The determination of the foreign subsidiary's functional currency (and the use of different translation methods) can have a significant impact on consolidated financial statements. The following chart shows differences for SWISSCO in several key items under the two different translation methods:

Item	Translation Method		Difference
	Current Rate	Temporal	
Net income (NI)	$ 493,500	$ 470,300	+ 4.7%
Total assets (TA)	1,837,000	1,744,800	+ 5.0%
Total equity (TE)	902,000	809,800	+10.2%
Return on equity (NI/TE)	54.7%	58.1%	− 6.1%

In this illustration, if the Swiss franc is determined to be SWISSCO's functional currency (and the current rate method is applied), net income reported in the consolidated income statement would be 4.7 percent more than if the U.S. dollar is the functional currency (and the temporal method is applied). In addition, total assets would be 5.0 percent more and total equity would be 10.2 percent more using the current rate method. Because of the larger amount of equity, return on equity (net income/total equity) using the current rate method is 6.1 percent less.

Note that the current rate method does not always result in higher net income and a higher amount of equity than the temporal method. For example, had SWISSCO maintained its net monetary asset position, it would have computed a remeasurement gain under the temporal method, leading to higher income than under the current rate method. Moreover, if the Swiss franc had depreciated during 2024, the temporal method would have resulted in higher net income.

The important point is that determining the functional currency and resulting translation method can have a significant impact on the amounts a parent company reports in its consolidated financial statements. Different functional currencies selected by different companies in the same industry could have a significant impact on the comparability of financial statements within that industry. Indeed, one concern that those FASB members dissenting on the current standard raised was that the functional currency rules might not result in similar accounting for similar situations.

In addition to differences in amounts reported in the consolidated financial statements, the results of the SWISSCO illustration demonstrate several conceptual differences between the two translation methods.

Underlying Valuation Method

Using the temporal method, SWISSCO remeasured its property, plant, and equipment as follows:

$$\text{Property, plant, and equipment CHF } 1,000,000 \times \$1.01 \text{ H} = \$1,010,000$$

By multiplying the historical cost in Swiss francs by the historical exchange rate, $1,010,000 represents the U.S. dollar–equivalent historical cost of this asset. It is the amount of U.S. dollars that the parent company would have had to pay to acquire assets having a cost of CHF 1,000,000 when the exchange rate was $1.01 per Swiss franc.

Property, plant, and equipment was translated under the current rate method as follows:

$$\text{Property, plant, and equipment CHF } 1,000,000 \times \$1.10 \text{ C} = \$1,100,000$$

The $1,100,000 amount is not readily interpretable. It does not represent the U.S. dollar–equivalent historical cost of the asset; that amount is $1,010,000. Nor does it represent the U.S. dollar–equivalent fair value of the asset because CHF 1,000,000 is not the fair value of the asset in Switzerland. The $1,100,000 amount is simply the product of multiplying two numbers together!

Underlying Relationships

The following table reports the values for selected financial ratios calculated from the original foreign currency financial statements and from the U.S. dollar–translated statements using the two different translation methods:

Ratio	CHF	U.S.$ Current Rate	U.S.$ Temporal
Current ratio (current assets/current liabilities)	1.22	1.22	1.20
Debt/equity ratio (total liabilities/total equities)	1.04	1.04	1.15
Gross profit ratio (gross profit/sales)	25.0%	25.0%	25.5%
Return on equity (net income/total equity)	57.3%	54.7%	58.1%

The temporal method distorts all of the ratios measured in the foreign currency. The subsidiary appears to be less liquid, more highly leveraged, and more profitable than it does in Swiss franc terms.

The current rate method maintains the first three ratios but distorts return on equity. The distortion occurs because income was translated at the average-for-the-period exchange rate, whereas total equity was translated at the current exchange rate. In fact, the use of the average rate for income and the current rate for assets and liabilities distorts any ratio combining balance sheet and income statement figures, such as turnover ratios.

LO 8-5

Understand the rationale for hedging balance sheet exposure to foreign exchange risk and describe the treatment of gains and losses on hedges used for this purpose.

Hedging Balance Sheet Exposure

When the U.S. dollar is the functional currency (or when a foreign operation is located in a highly inflationary economy), remeasurement gains and losses are reported in net income. Management of U.S. multinational companies could wish to avoid reporting remeasurement losses in net income because of the perceived negative impact this has on the company's stock price. Likewise, when the foreign currency is the functional currency, management could wish to avoid negative translation adjustments because of the adverse impact these have on the debt-to-equity ratio.

Translation adjustments and remeasurement gains or losses are functions of two factors: (1) changes in the exchange rate and (2) balance sheet exposure. Although a company can do little if anything to influence exchange rates, parent companies can use several techniques to hedge the balance sheet exposures of their foreign operations.

Parent companies can hedge balance sheet exposure by using a derivative financial instrument, such as a forward contract or a foreign currency option, or a nonderivative hedging instrument, such as a foreign currency borrowing. To illustrate the latter, assume that SWISSCO's functional currency is the Swiss franc, which means that the current rate method will be used to translate the Swiss franc financial statements; this creates a net asset balance sheet exposure. USCO believes that the Swiss franc will depreciate against the U.S. dollar over the course of the coming year, thereby generating a negative translation adjustment that will reduce USCO's consolidated stockholders' equity. USCO could hedge this Swiss franc net asset balance sheet exposure by borrowing Swiss francs for a period of time, thus creating an offsetting Swiss franc liability exposure. As the Swiss franc depreciates, the U.S. dollar value of the Swiss franc borrowing decreases, and USCO will be able to repay the Swiss franc borrowing using fewer U.S. dollars. This generates a foreign exchange gain, which offsets the negative translation adjustment arising from the translation of SWISSCO's financial statements.

As an alternative to the Swiss franc borrowing, USCO might have acquired a Swiss franc put option to hedge its Swiss franc net asset balance sheet exposure. A put option gives the company the right to sell Swiss francs at a predetermined strike price, creating a potential Swiss franc liability. As the Swiss franc depreciates, the fair value of the put option increases, resulting in a gain, which offsets the negative translation adjustment.

The paradox of hedging a balance sheet exposure is that in the process of avoiding an unrealized negative translation adjustment (or unrealized remeasurement loss), realized foreign exchange gains and losses can result. Consider USCO's foreign currency borrowing to hedge a Swiss franc net asset balance sheet exposure. At the initiation of the loan, USCO converts the borrowed Swiss francs into U.S. dollars at the spot exchange rate. When the liability matures, USCO purchases Swiss francs at the spot rate prevailing at that date to repay the loan. The change in the U.S. dollar/Swiss franc exchange rate over the life of the loan generates a *realized* gain or loss. If the Swiss franc depreciates as expected, a realized foreign exchange gain that offsets the negative translation adjustment reported in AOCI results. Although the net effect on AOCI is zero, a net increase in cash occurs as a result of the hedge. If the Swiss franc unexpectedly appreciates, a realized foreign exchange loss occurs. This is offset by a positive translation adjustment in AOCI, but a net decrease in cash exists. While a hedge of a balance sheet exposure eliminates the possibility of reporting a negative translation adjustment in AOCI, gains and losses realized in cash can result.

Accounting for Hedges of Remeasurement-Related Balance Sheet Exposure

When a foreign entity's financial statements are remeasured using the temporal method, a net liability balance sheet exposure normally exists. A foreign currency borrowing, which creates an additional foreign currency liability, would not be effective in hedging this type of balance sheet exposure. However, either a forward contract or an option to *purchase* foreign currency in the future creates a foreign currency asset exposure and would act as a hedge against the remeasurement-based net liability balance sheet exposure.

Following the proper accounting for derivative financial instruments, the gain/loss on a foreign currency option or forward contract is reported in net income and offsets the remeasurement loss/gain that also is reported in net income. Thus, there is no need for the FASB to allow hedge accounting to be applied in accounting for hedges of remeasurement-related balance sheet exposure.

Accounting for Hedges of Translation-Related Balance Sheet Exposure

When a foreign entity's financial statements are translated using the current rate method, the resulting translation adjustment is reported in AOCI. Normally, the gain or loss on a financial instrument is reflected in net income. However, when such a financial instrument is effective and properly designated as a hedge of translation-related balance sheet exposure, ASC 815-35-35 indicates that hedge accounting applies. In this case, the gain or loss on the hedging instrument should be reported in the same manner as the translation adjustment being hedged—that is, in AOCI. The FASB describes this type of hedge as a *hedge of the net investment in a foreign operation.*

Thus, returning to the hedge of SWISSCO's translation-related balance sheet exposure described earlier, the foreign exchange gain on the Swiss franc borrowing (or the gain on the foreign currency option) would be included in AOCI along with the negative translation adjustment arising from the translation of SWISSCO's financial statements.

To demonstrate the accounting for a hedge of a net investment, assume that SWISSCO has net assets of CHF 820,000 on January 1, 2025, when the exchange rate is $1.10 per CHF. USCO is concerned that the Swiss franc will depreciate against the U.S. dollar and wishes to hedge against reporting a negative translation adjustment in the quarter ending March 31, 2025. On January 1, 2025, USCO negotiates a 5 percent, 90-day note payable for CHF 820,000 with its bank and properly designates this borrowing as a hedge of a net investment. The journal entry to record this foreign currency borrowing is as follows:

1/1/25	Cash	902,000	
	Note Payable (CHF)		902,000
	To record the Swiss franc note payable at the spot rate of $1.10 and the conversion of CHF 820,000 into U.S. dollars.		

Assuming that SWISSCO maintains net assets of CHF 820,000 during the first quarter of 2025, the negative translation adjustment for that time period resulting from the decrease in value of the Swiss franc is calculated as follows:

Net assets × Exchange rate at 3/31/25	CHF 820,000 × $1.04 = $852,800
Less: Net assets × Exchange rate at 1/1/25	CHF 820,000 × $1.10 = 902,000
Translation adjustment (negative − debit)	$ (49,200)

The summary entry to recognize the first quarter 2025 translation adjustment on USCO's books is as follows:

3/31/25	Translation Adjustment (AOCI)	49,200	
	Net Investment in SWISSCO		49,200
	To record the negative translation adjustment resulting from a decrease in U.S. dollar value of the Swiss franc.		

On March 31, 2025, USCO purchases CHF 820,000 at the spot of $1.04 for $852,800 and delivers them to the bank to extinguish the note payable. On that date, USCO acquires an additional CHF 10,250 for $10,660 to cover the accrued interest on the loan. The entries related to the foreign currency borrowing used as a net investment hedge are the following:

3/31/25	Foreign Currency (CHF)	863,460	
	Cash		863,460
	To record the purchase of CHF 830,250 at the spot rate of $1.04.		
	Note Payable (CHF)	902,000	
	Foreign Currency (CHF)		852,800
	Translation Adjustment (AOCI)		49,200
	To record payment of CHF 820,000 to extinguish the CHF note payable, and recognize the resulting transaction gain as an adjustment to the translation adjustment component of AOCI.		
	Interest Expense	10,660	
	Foreign Currency (CHF)		10,660
	To record the cash interest payment of CHF 10,250 and recognize interest expense.		

As a result of the net investment hedge, the net translation adjustment reflected in AOCI is zero ($49,200 − $49,200). However, avoiding the recognition of a negative translation adjustment in the first quarter of 2025 cost USCO a total of $10,660 in cash interest paid.

Many U.S. companies regularly hedge their net investments in foreign operations. For example, McDonald's Corporation disclosed in its 2020 annual report that the company primarily uses foreign currency–denominated debt to hedge its net investments in certain foreign subsidiaries. In contrast, Hewlett Packard Enterprises Company reported in its 2020 Form 10-K that it uses forward contracts to hedge net investments in selected foreign subsidiaries.

International Financial Reporting Standard 9–Financial Instruments

As noted in the previous chapter, there is considerable similarity between IFRS and U.S. GAAP with respect to the accounting for derivative financial instruments used to hedge foreign exchange risk. Similar to U.S. GAAP, *IFRS 9* also allows hedge accounting for hedges of net investments in a foreign operation. The gain or loss on the hedging instrument is recognized in Accumulated Other Comprehensive Income (AOCI), along with the translation adjustment that is being hedged. Under both IFRS and U.S. GAAP, the cumulative translation adjustment and cumulative net gain or loss on the net investment hedge are transferred from AOCI to net income when the foreign subsidiary is sold or otherwise disposed of.

Disclosures Related to Translation

Current authoritative standards require firms to present an analysis of the change in the cumulative translation adjustment account in the financial statements or notes thereto. Many companies comply with this requirement directly in their statement of comprehensive income. Other companies provide separate disclosure in the notes. Exhibit 8.10 provides an example of note disclosure for Mondelēz International, Inc.

That exhibit shows that the company's cumulative translation adjustment account had a negative (debit) balance of $7,714 million on January 1, 2018, which increased to negative $8,622 million on December 31, 2018. The negative balance in this account decreased to $8,320 million by the end of 2019, and then increased to negative $8,655 million on

EXHIBIT 8.10
Mondelēz International, Inc., Analysis of Change in Cumulative Translation Adjustment

Excerpt from Note 15. Reclassifications from Accumulated Other Comprehensive Income
The following table summarizes the changes in the accumulated balances of each component of accumulated other comprehensive earnings/(losses) attributable to Mondelēz International.

	For the Years Ended December 31,		
	2020	**2019**	**2018**
Currency Translation Adjustments:		(in millions)	
Balance at beginning of period	$(8,320)	$(8,622)	$(7,714)
Currency translation adjustments	(398)	251	(743)
Reclassification to earnings related to:			
Equity method investment transactions	29	-	6
Tax (expense)/benefit	47	49	(173)
Other comprehensive earnings/(losses)	(322)	300	(910)
Less: Other comprehensive (earnings)/loss attributable to noncontrolling interests	(13)	2	2
Balance at end of period	$(8,655)	$(8,320)	$(8,622)

Source: Mondelēz International, Inc., 2020 Form 10-K, page 120.

December 31, 2020. An analysis of the *Currency translation adjustments* row in Exhibit 8.10 indicates negative translation adjustments of $743 million and $398 million in 2018 and 2020, respectively, and a positive translation adjustment of $251 million in 2019. From the signs of these translation adjustments, one can infer that, in aggregate, the foreign currencies in which Mondelēz has operations decreased in value against the U.S. dollar in both 2018 and 2020, with a much larger decrease in value in 2018, and appreciated in value against the U.S. dollar in 2019.

Although not specifically required to do so, many companies describe their translation procedures in their "summary of significant accounting policies" in the notes to the financial statements. The following excerpt from International Business Machines (IBM) Corporation's 2020 annual report (page 82) illustrates this type of disclosure.

> **Translation of Non-U.S. Currency Amounts**—Assets and liabilities of non-U.S. subsidiaries that have a local functional currency are translated to U.S. dollars at year-end exchange rates. Translation adjustments are recorded in OCI. Income and expense items are translated at weighted-average rates of exchange prevailing during the year.
>
> Inventories, property, plant and equipment—net and other non-monetary assets and liabilities of non-U.S. subsidiaries and branches that operate in U.S. dollars are translated at the approximate exchange rates prevailing when the company acquired the assets or liabilities. All other assets and liabilities denominated in a currency other than U.S. dollars are translated at year-end exchange rates with the transaction gain or loss recognized in other (income) and expense. Income and expense items are translated at the weighted-average rates of exchange prevailing during the year. These translation gains and losses are included in net income for the period in which exchange rates change.

Note that IBM uses the terms translated and translation gains and losses (rather than remeasured and remeasurment gains and losses) in describing its accounting policy with regard to foreign entities that operate in U.S. dollars.

LO 8-6

Prepare a consolidation worksheet for a parent company and its foreign subsidiary.

Consolidation of a Foreign Subsidiary

This section of the chapter demonstrates the procedures used to consolidate a foreign subsidiary's financial statements with those of its parent. The treatment of the excess of fair value over book value requires special attention. As an item denominated in foreign currency, translation of the excess gives rise to a translation adjustment recorded on the consolidation worksheet.

On January 1, 2023, Altman, Inc., a U.S.-based manufacturing firm, acquired 100 percent of Bradford Ltd. in Great Britain. Altman paid 25 million British pounds (£25,000,000), which was equal to Bradford's fair value. Bradford's balance sheet on January 1, 2023, which reflects a book value of £22,700,000, showed the following totals:

Cash	£ 925,000	Accounts payable	£ 675,000
Accounts receivable	1,400,000	Long-term debt	4,000,000
Inventory	6,050,000	Common stock	20,000,000
Property, plant and equipment (net)	19,000,000	Retained earnings	2,700,000
Total	£27,375,000	Total	£27,375,000

The £2,300,000 excess of fair value over book value resulted from undervalued land (part of Property, plant, and equipment) and therefore is not subject to amortization. Altman uses the equity method to account for its investment in Bradford.

On December 31, 2024, two years after the acquisition date, Bradford submitted the following trial balance for consolidation (credit balances are in parentheses):

Cash	£ 600,000
Accounts receivable	2,700,000
Inventory	9,000,000
Property, plant, and equipment (net)	17,200,000
Accounts payable	(500,000)
Long-term debt	(2,000,000)
Common stock	(20,000,000)
Retained earnings, 1/1/24	(3,800,000)
Sales	(13,900,000)
Cost of goods sold	8,100,000
Depreciation expense	900,000
Other expenses	950,000
Dividends declared, 6/30/24	750,000
	£ –0–

Although Bradford generated net income of £1,100,000 in 2023, it neither declared nor paid dividends that year. Other than the payment of dividends in 2024, no intra-entity transactions occurred between the two affiliates. Altman has determined the British pound to be Bradford's functional currency.

Relevant exchange rates for the British pound were as follows:

	January 1	June 30	December 31	Average
2023	$1.51	N/A	$1.56	$1.54
2024	1.56	$1.58	1.53	1.55

Translation of Foreign Subsidiary Trial Balance

The initial step in consolidating the foreign subsidiary is to translate its trial balance from British pounds into U.S. dollars. Because the British pound has been determined to be the functional currency, this translation uses the current rate method. The historical exchange rate for translating Bradford's common stock and January 1, 2023, retained earnings is the exchange rate that existed at the acquisition date—$1.51.

	British Pounds	Rate	U.S. Dollars
Cash	£ 600,000	1.53 C	$ 918,000
Accounts receivable	2,700,000	1.53 C	4,131,000
Inventory	9,000,000	1.53 C	13,770,000
Property, plant, and equipment (net)	17,200,000	1.53 C	26,316,000
Accounts payable	(500,000)	1.53 C	(765,000)
Long-term debt	(2,000,000)	1.53 C	(3,060,000)
Common stock	(20,000,000)	1.51 H	(30,200,000)
Retained earnings, 1/1/24	(3,800,000)	*	(5,771,000)
Sales	(13,900,000)	1.55 A	(21,545,000)
Cost of goods sold	8,100,000	1.55 A	12,555,000
Depreciation expense	900,000	1.55 A	1,395,000
Other expenses	950,000	1.55 A	1,472,500
Dividends declared, 6/30/24	750,000	1.58 H	1,185,000
Cumulative translation adjustment			(401,500)
	£ –0–		$ –0–
*Retained Earnings, 1/1/23	£ 2,700,000	1.51 H	$ 4,077,000
Net Income, 2023	1,100,000	1.54 A	1,694,000
Retained Earnings, 12/31/23	£ 3,800,000		$ 5,771,000

A positive (credit balance) cumulative translation adjustment of $401,500 is required to make the trial balance actually balance. The cumulative translation adjustment is calculated as follows:

Net assets, 1/1/23	£22,700,000	1.51 H	$34,277,000
Change in net assets, 2023			
Net income, 2023................	1,100,000	1.54 A	1,694,000
Net assets, 12/31/23	£23,800,000		$35,971,000
Net assets, 12/31/23, at current exchange rate	£23,800,000	1.56 C	37,128,000
Translation adjustment, 2023 (positive)			$(1,157,000)
Net assets, 1/1/24	£23,800,000	1.56 H	$37,128,000
Change in net assets, 2024			
Net income, 2024................	3,950,000	1.55 A	6,122,500
Dividends, 6/30/24................	(750,000)	1.58 H	(1,185,000)
Net assets, 12/31/24	£27,000,000		$42,065,500
Net assets, 12/31/24, at current exchange rate	£27,000,000	1.53 C	$41,310,000
Translation adjustment, 2024 (negative)			755,500
Cumulative translation adjustment, 12/31/24 (positive)			$ (401,500)

The translation adjustment in 2023 is positive because the British pound appreciated against the U.S. dollar that year; the translation adjustment in 2024 is negative because the British pound depreciated against the U.S. dollar that year.

Determination of Balance in Investment Account—Equity Method

The original value of the investment in Bradford, the net income earned by Bradford, and the dividends paid by Bradford are all denominated in British pounds. Relevant amounts must be translated from pounds into U.S. dollars so Altman can account for its investment in Bradford under the equity method. In addition, the translation adjustment calculated each year is included in the Investment in Bradford account to update the foreign currency investment to its U.S. dollar equivalent. The counterpart is recorded as a translation adjustment on Altman's books:

12/31/23	Investment in Bradford	1,157,000	
	Cumulative Translation Adjustment		1,157,000
	To record the positive translation adjustment related to the investment in a British subsidiary when the British pound appreciated.		
12/31/24	Cumulative Translation Adjustment	755,500	
	Investment in Bradford		755,500
	To record the negative translation adjustment related to the investment in a British subsidiary when the British pound depreciated.		

As a result of these two journal entries, Altman has a cumulative translation adjustment of $401,500 on its separate balance sheet.

The carrying value of the investment account in U.S. dollar terms on December 31, 2024, is determined as follows:

Investment in Bradford	British Pounds	Exchange Rate	U.S. Dollars
Original value.	£25,000,000	1.51 H	$37,750,000
Bradford net income, 2023.	1,100,000	1.54 A	1,694,000
Translation adjustment, 2023.			1,157,000
Balance, 12/31/23	£26,100,000		$40,601,000
Bradford net income, 2024.	3,950,000	1.55 A	6,122,500
Bradford dividends, 6/30/24.	(750,000)	1.58 H	(1,185,000)
Translation adjustment, 2024.			(755,500)
Balance, 12/31/24	£29,300,000		$44,783,000

In addition to Altman's $44,783,000 investment in Bradford, it has equity income on its December 31, 2024, trial balance in the amount of $6,122,500.

Consolidation Worksheet

Once the subsidiary's trial balance has been translated into dollars and the carrying value of the investment is known, the consolidation worksheet on December 31, 2024, can be prepared. As is true in the consolidation of domestic subsidiaries, the investment account, the subsidiary's equity accounts, and the effects of intra-entity transactions must be eliminated. The excess of fair value over book value at the date of acquisition also must be allocated to the appropriate accounts (in this example, Property, plant, and equipment).

Unique to the consolidation of foreign subsidiaries is the fact that the excess of fair value over book value, denominated in foreign currency, also must be translated into the parent's reporting currency. When the foreign currency is the functional currency, the excess is translated at the current exchange rate with a resulting translation adjustment. The excess is not carried on either the parent's or the subsidiary's books, but is recognized only in the consolidation worksheet. *Neither the parent nor the subsidiary has recorded the translation adjustment related to the excess, and it also must be entered in the consolidation worksheet.* Exhibit 8.11 presents the consolidation worksheet of Altman and Bradford at December 31, 2024.

Explanation of Consolidation Entries

S—Eliminates the subsidiary's stockholders' equity accounts as of the beginning of the current year along with the equivalent book value component within the original value of the Investment in Bradford account.

EXHIBIT 8.11   **Consolidation Worksheet—Parent and Foreign Subsidiary**

ALTMAN, INC., AND BRADFORD LTD.
Consolidation Worksheet
For Year Ending December 31, 2024

Accounts	Altman	Bradford	Consolidation Entries Debits	Consolidation Entries Credits	Consolidated Totals
Income Statement					
Sales	$ (32,489,000)	$(21,545,000)			$ (54,034,000)
Cost of goods sold	16,000,000	12,555,000			28,555,000
Depreciation expense	9,700,000	1,395,000			11,095,000
Other expenses	2,900,000	1,472,500			4,372,500
Equity income	(6,122,500)		(I) $ 6,122,500		–0–
Net income	$ (10,011,500)	$ (6,122,500)			$ (10,011,500)
Statement of Retained Earnings					
Retained earnings, 1/1/24	$ (25,194,000)	$ (5,771,000)	(S) 5,771,000		$ (25,194,000)
Net income (above)	(10,011,500)	(6,122,500)			(10,011,500)
Dividends	1,500,000	1,185,000		(D) $ 1,185,000	1,500,000
Retained earnings, 12/31/24	$ (33,705,500)	$(10,708,500)			$ (33,705,500)
Balance Sheet					
Cash	$ 3,649,800	$918,000			$ 4,567,800
Accounts receivable	3,100,000	4,131,000			7,231,000
Inventory	11,410,000	13,770,000			25,180,000
Investment in Bradford	44,783,000			(S) 35,971,000	–0–
				(A) 3,473,000	
			(D) 1,185,000	(I) 6,122,500	
				(T) 401,500	
Property, plant, and equipment (net)	39,500,000	26,316,000	(A) 3,473,000		69,335,000
			(E) 46,000		
Total assets	$ 102,442,800	$ 45,135,000			$ 106,313,800
Accounts payable	$ (2,500,000)	$(765,000)			$ (3,265,000)
Long-term debt	(22,728,800)	(3,060,000)			(25,788,800)
Common stock	(43,107,000)	(30,200,000)	(S) 30,200,000		(43,107,000)
Retained earnings, 12/31/24 (above)	(33,705,500)	(10,708,500)			(33,705,500)
Cumulative translation adjustment	(401,500)	(401,500)	(T) 401,500	(E) 46,000	(447,500)
Total liabilities and equities	$(102,422,800)	$(45,135,000)	$47,199,000	$47,199,000	$(106,313,800)

A—Allocates the excess of fair value over book value at the date of acquisition to land (Property, plant, and equipment) and eliminates that amount within the original value of the Investment in Bradford account.

I—Eliminates the amount of equity income recognized by the parent in the current year and included in the Investment in Bradford account under the equity method.

D—Eliminates the subsidiary's dividend payment that was a reduction in the Investment in Bradford account under the equity method.

T—Eliminates the cumulative translation adjustment included in the Investment in Bradford account under the equity method and the cumulative translation adjustment on the subsidiary's translated books.

E—Revalues the excess of fair value over book value for the change in exchange rate since the date of acquisition with the counterpart recognized as an increase in the consolidated cumulative translation adjustment. The revaluation is calculated as follows:

Excess of Fair Value over Book Value			
U.S. dollar equivalent at 12/3124	£2,300,000 × $1.53	=	$3,519,000
U.S. dollar equivalent at 1/1/23	2,300,000 × $1.51	=	3,473,000
Cumulative translation adjustment related to excess, 12/31/24			$ 46,000

Summary

1. Because many companies have significant financial involvement in foreign countries, the process by which foreign currency financial statements are translated into U.S. dollars has special accounting importance. The two major issues related to the translation process are (a) which method to use and (b) where to report the resulting translation adjustment in the consolidated financial statements.

2. Translation methods differ on the basis of which accounts are translated at the current exchange rate and which are translated at historical rates. Accounts translated at the current exchange rate are exposed to translation adjustment. Different translation methods give rise to different concepts of balance sheet exposure and translation adjustments of differing signs and magnitude.

3. The temporal method translates assets carried at current value (cash, marketable securities, receivables) and liabilities at the current exchange rate. This method translates assets carried at historical cost and stockholders' equity at historical exchange rates. When liabilities are more than the sum of cash, marketable securities, and receivables, a net liability balance sheet exposure exists. Foreign currency appreciation results in a negative translation adjustment (remeasurement loss). Foreign currency depreciation results in a positive translation adjustment (remeasurement gain). By translating assets carried at historical cost at historical exchange rates, the temporal method maintains the underlying valuation method used by the foreign operation but distorts relationships in the foreign currency financial statements.

4. The current rate method translates all assets and liabilities at the current exchange rate, giving rise to a net asset balance sheet exposure. Foreign currency appreciation results in a positive translation adjustment. Foreign currency depreciation results in a negative translation adjustment. By translating assets carried at historical cost at the current exchange rate, the current rate method maintains relationships in the foreign currency financial statements but distorts the underlying valuation method used by the foreign operation.

5. Current U.S. accounting procedures require two separate procedures for translating foreign currency financial statements into the parent's reporting currency. *Translation* through use of the current rate method is appropriate when the foreign operation's functional currency is a foreign currency. In this case, the translation adjustment is reported in the Accumulated Other Comprehensive Income (AOCI) account and reflected on the balance sheet as a separate component of stockholders' equity. *Remeasurement* by using the temporal method is appropriate when the operation's functional currency is the U.S. dollar. Remeasurement also is applied when the operation is in a country with a highly inflationary economy. In these situations, the translation adjustment is treated as a remeasurement gain or loss in net income.

6. IFRS and U.S. GAAP have broadly similar rules with regard to the translation of foreign currency financial statements. Differences exist with respect to the determination of functional currency, with *IAS 21* establishing a hierarchy of functional currency indicators, and in translating financial statements of foreign entities located in high-inflation countries. For these entities, *IAS 21* requires financial statements to first be restated for local inflation and then be translated into the parent's currency using the current exchange rate for all financial statement items.

7. Some companies hedge their balance sheet exposures to avoid reporting remeasurement losses in net income and/or negative translation adjustments in stockholders' equity. When a remeasurement-related balance sheet exposure is hedged, both the gain/loss on the hedging instrument and the remeasurement gain/loss are reported in net income. When a translation-related balance sheet exposure is hedged (referred to by the FASB as a *hedge of a net investment in a foreign operation*), hedge accounting is appropriate and the gain/loss on the hedging instrument is reported in AOCI along with the translation adjustment being hedged.

Comprehensive Illustration

(*Estimated Time: 55 to 65 Minutes*) Arlington Company is a U.S.-based organization with numerous foreign subsidiaries. As a preliminary step in preparing consolidated financial statements for 2024, it must translate the financial information from each foreign operation into its reporting currency, the U.S. dollar.

Arlington owns a Swedish subsidiary that has been in business for several years. On December 31, 2023, this entity's balance sheet was translated from Swedish kroner (SEK), its functional currency, into U.S. dollars as prescribed by U.S. GAAP. Equity accounts at that date follow (all credit balances):

Common stock	SEK 110,000 = $21,000
Retained earnings	194,800 = 36,100
Cumulative translation adjustment	3,860

At the end of 2024, the Swedish subsidiary produced the following trial balance. These amounts include all of the entity's transactions for the year except for the results of several transactions related to sales made to a Chinese customer. A separate ledger has been maintained for these transactions denominated in Chinese renminbi (RMB). This ledger follows the company's trial balance.

Trial Balance—Swedish Subsidiary
December 31, 2024

	Debit	Credit
Cash	SEK 41,000	
Accounts receivable	126,000	
Inventory	128,000	
Property, plant, and equipment	388,000	
Accumulated depreciation		SEK 98,100
Accounts payable		39,000
Notes payable		56,000
Bonds payable		125,000
Common stock		110,000
Retained earnings, 1/1/24		194,800
Sales		350,000
Cost of goods sold	165,000	
Depreciation expense	10,900	
Salary expense	36,000	
Rent expense	12,000	
Interest expense	10,000	
Other expenses	31,000	
Dividends, 7/1/24	25,000	
Totals	SEK 972,900	SEK 972,900

Ledger—Transactions in Chinese Renminbi
December 31, 2024

	Debit	Credit
Cash	RMB 10,000	
Accounts receivable	28,000	
Property, plant, and equipment	20,000	
Accumulated depreciation		RMB 4,000
Notes payable		15,000
Sales		44,000
Depreciation expense	4,000	
Interest expense	1,000	
Totals	RMB 63,000	RMB 63,000

Additional Information

- The Swedish subsidiary began selling to the Chinese customer at the beginning of the current year. At that time, it borrowed 20,000 RMB to acquire a truck for delivery purposes. It paid one-fourth of that debt before the end of the year. The subsidiary made sales to China evenly during the period.

- The U.S. dollar exchange rates for 1 SEK are as follows:

January 1, 2024	$0.200 = 1.00 SEK
Weighted average rate for 2024	0.192 = 1.00
July 1, 2024	0.190 = 1.00
December 31, 2024	0.182 = 1.00

- The exchange rates applicable for the remeasurement of 1 RMB into Swedish kroner are as follows:

January 1, 2024	1.25 SEK = 1.00 RMB
Weighted average rate for 2024	1.16 = 1.00
December 1, 2024	1.101 = 1.00
December 31, 2024	1.04 = 1.00

- The Swedish subsidiary expended SEK 10,000 during the year on development activities. In accordance with IFRS, this cost has been capitalized within the Property, plant, and equipment account. This expenditure had no effect on the depreciation recognized for the year.

Required

a. Prepare the Swedish kroner trial balance for the Swedish subsidiary for the year ending December 31, 2024. Verify, through separate calculation, the amount of remeasurement gain/loss derived as a plug figure in the trial balance.

b. Translate the Swedish kroner trial balance into U.S. dollars to facilitate Arlington Company's preparation of consolidated financial statements. Verify, through separate calculation, the amount of cumulative translation adjustment derived as a plug figure in the trial balance.

Solution

Part A

A portion of the Swedish subsidiary's operating results is presently stated in Chinese renminbi. These balances must be remeasured into the functional currency, the Swedish krona, before the translation process can begin. In remeasuring these accounts using the temporal method, the krona value of the monetary assets and liabilities is determined by using the current (C) exchange rate (1.04 SEK per RMB), whereas all other accounts are remeasured at historical (H) or average (A) exchange rates.

Remeasurement of Foreign Currency Balances

	Renminbi Debit	Renminbi Credit	Rate			Kroner Debit	Kroner Credit
Cash	10,000		×	1.04 C	=	10,400	
Accounts receivable	28,000		×	1.04 C	=	29,120	
Property, plant, and equipment	20,000		×	1.25 H	=	25,000	
Accumulated depreciation		4,000	×	1.25 H	=		5,000
Notes payable		15,000	×	1.04 C	=		15,600
Sales		44,000	×	1.16 A	=		51,040
Depreciation expense	4,000		×	1.25 H	=	5,000	
Interest expense	1,000		×	1.16 A	=	1,160	
	63,000	63,000				70,680	71,640
Remeasurement loss						960	
Total						71,640	71,640

Remeasurement Loss for 2024

Net monetary asset balance, 1/1/24	–0–			–0–
Increases in net monetary items:				
Operations (sales less interest expense)	RMB 43,000	× 1.16 A	=	SEK 49,880
Decreases in net monetary items:				
Purchased truck, 1/1/24	(20,000)	× 1.25 H	=	(25,000)
Net monetary assets, 12/31/24	RMB 23,000			SEK 24,880
Net monetary assets, 12/31/24, at current exchange rate	RMB 23,000	× 1.04 C	=	SEK 23,920
Remeasurement loss (gain)				SEK 960

The net monetary asset exposure (cash and accounts receivable > notes payable) and depreciation of the Chinese renminbi create a remeasurement loss of SEK 960.

The remeasured amounts from the Chinese operation must be combined in some manner with the subsidiary's trial balance denominated in Swedish kroner. For example, a year-end adjustment can be recorded in the Swedish subsidiary's accounting system to add the remeasured balances for financial reporting purposes, as follows:

	Kroner	
12/31/24 Adjustment	**Debit**	**Credit**
Cash	10,400	
Accounts Receivable	29,120	
Property, Plant, and Equipment	25,000	
Depreciation Expense	5,000	
Interest Expense	1,160	
Remeasurement Loss	960	
Accumulated Depreciation		5,000
Notes Payable		15,600
Sales		51,040
To record in Swedish kroner the foreign currency transactions originally denominated in Chinese renminbi.		

One more adjustment is necessary before translating the subsidiary's Swedish krona financial statements into the parent's reporting currency. The development costs incurred by the Swedish entity should be reclassified as an expense as required by U.S. authoritative literature. After this adjustment, the Swedish subsidiary's statements conform with U.S. GAAP.

	Kroner	
12/31/24 Adjustment	**Debit**	**Credit**
Other Expenses	10,000	
Property, Plant, and Equipment		10,000
To adjust property, plant, and equipment and expenses in Swedish kroner to be in compliance with U.S. GAAP.		

Alternatively, the results from remeasuring the Chinese renminbi balances into Swedish kroner and reclassification of development costs can be added to the Swedish subsidiary's unadjusted trial balance as follows:

Preparation of Adjusted Trial Balance in Swedish Kroner

	Unadjusted		Adjustments		Adjusted	
	Debit	**Credit**	**Debit**	**Credit**	**Debit**	**Credit**
Cash	41,000		10,400		51,400	
Accounts receivable	126,000		29,120		155,120	
Inventory	128,000				128,000	
Property, plant, and equipment	388,000		25,000	10,000	403,000	
Accumulated depreciation		98,100		5,000		103,100
Accounts payable		39,000				39,000
Notes payable		56,000		15,600		71,600
Bonds payable		125,000				125,000
Common stock		110,000				110,000
Retained earnings, 1/1/24		194,800				194,800
Sales		350,000		51,040		401,040
Cost of goods sold	165,000				165,000	
Depreciation expense	10,900		5,000		15,900	
Salary expense	36,000				36,000	
Rent expense	12,000				12,000	
Interest expense	10,000		1,160		11,160	

(*continued*)

Chapter 8

(*continued*)

	Unadjusted		Adjustments		Adjusted	
	Debit	**Credit**	**Debit**	**Credit**	**Debit**	**Credit**
Other expenses	31,000		10,000		41,000	
Remeasurement loss			960		960	
Dividends, 7/1/24	25,000				25,000	
Total	972,900	972,900	81,640	81,640	1,044,540	1,044,540

Having established all account balances in the functional currency (Swedish kroner), the subsidiary's trial balance now can be translated into U.S. dollars. Under the current rate method, the dollar values to be reported for income statement items are based on the average exchange rate for the current year. All assets and liabilities are translated at the current exchange rate at the balance sheet date, and equity accounts are translated at historical rates in effect at the date of accounting recognition.

Part B

Translation of Swedish Kroner Trial Balance into U.S. Dollars

	Swedish Kroner		Rate			U.S. Dollars	
	Debit	**Credit**				**Debit**	**Credit**
Cash	51,400		× 0.182	C	=	9,354.80	
Accounts receivable	155,120		× 0.182	C	=	28,231.84	
Inventory	128,000		× 0.182	C	=	23,296.00	
Property, plant, and equipment	403,000		× 0.182	C	=	73,346.00	
Accumulated depreciation		103,100	× 0.182	C	=		18,764.20
Accounts payable		39,000	× 0.182	C	=		7,098.00
Notes payable		71,600	× 0.182	C	=		13,031.20
Bonds payable		125,000	× 0.182	C	=		22,750.00
Common stock		110,000	**Given**				21,000.00
Retained earnings, 1/1/24		194,800	**Given**				36,100.00
Sales		401,040	× 0.192	A	=		76,999.68
Cost of goods sold	165,000		× 0.192	A	=	31,680.00	
Depreciation expense	15,900		× 0.192	A	=	3,052.80	
Salary expense	36,000		× 0.192	A	=	6,912.00	
Rent expense	12,000		× 0.192	A	=	2,304.00	
Interest expense	11,160		× 0.192	A	=	2,142.72	
Other expenses	41,000		× 0.192	A	=	7,872.00	
Remeasurement loss	960		× 0.192	A	=	184.32	
Dividends, 7/1/24	25,000		× 0.190	H	=	4,750.00	
Total	1,044,540	1,044,540				193,126.48	195,743.08
Cumulative translation adjustment						2,616.60	
Total						195,743.08	195,743.08

The cumulative translation adjustment at 12/31/24 comprises the beginning balance (given) plus the translation adjustment for the current year:

Cumulative Translation Adjustment	
Balance, 1/1/24	$ 3,860.00
Translation adjustment for 2024	(6,476.60)
Balance, 12/31/24	$(2,616.60)

The negative translation adjustment for 2024 of $6,476.60 is calculated by considering the effect of exchange rate changes on net assets:

Translation Adjustment for 2024					
Net assets, 1/1/24	SEK 304,800*	×	0.200 C	=	$60,960.00
Increase in net assets:					
Net income, 2024...................	119,020	×	0.192 A	=	22,851.84
Decrease in net assets:					
Dividends, 7/1/24...................	(25,000)	×	0.190 H	=	(4,750.00)
Net assets, 12/31/4	SEK 398,820†				$79,061.84
Net assets, 12/31/24, at current					
exchange rate......................	SEK 398,820	×	0.182 C	=	72,585.24
Translation adjustment, 2024—					
negative					$ 6,476.60

*Indicated by January 1, 2024, stockholders' equity balances—Common Stock, SEK 110,000; Retained Earnings, SEK 194,800.

† Indicated by December 31, 2024, stockholders' equity balances—Common Stock, SEK 110,000; Retained Earnings, SEK 288,820.

Questions

1. What are the two major issues related to the translation of foreign currency financial statements?

2. What causes balance sheet exposure to foreign exchange risk? How does balance sheet exposure compare with transaction exposure?

3. What concept underlies the current rate method of translation? What concept underlies the temporal method of translation? How does balance sheet exposure differ under these two methods?

4. What are the major procedural differences in applying the current rate and temporal methods of translation?

5. In translating the financial statements of a foreign subsidiary, why is the value assigned to retained earnings especially difficult to determine? How is this problem normally resolved?

6. Clarke Company has a subsidiary operating in a foreign country. In relation to this subsidiary, what does the term *functional currency* mean? How is the functional currency determined?

7. When is remeasurement rather than translation appropriate? How does remeasurement differ from translation?

8. A translation adjustment must be calculated and disclosed when financial statements of a foreign subsidiary are translated into the parent's reporting currency. How is this translation adjustment computed, and where is the amount reported in the financial statements?

9. Which translation method does U.S. GAAP require for operations in highly inflationary countries? What is the rationale for mandating use of this method?

10. In what ways does IFRS differ from U.S. GAAP with respect to the translation of foreign currency financial statements?

11. Why might a company want to hedge its balance sheet exposure? What is the paradox associated with hedging balance sheet exposure?

12. How are gains and losses on financial instruments used to hedge the balance sheet exposure of a foreign operation reported in the consolidated financial statements?

13. In preparing the consolidation worksheet for a parent company and its foreign subsidiary, what consolidation entries are made related to the cumulative translation adjustment?

Problems

LO 8-2

LO 8-3, 8-4

1. Which of the following best describes a foreign subsidiary's functional currency?
   a. The parent's reporting currency
   b. The currency used by the parent to acquire the subsidiary
   c. The currency in which the entity primarily generates and expends cash
   d. Always the currency of the country in which the company has its headquarters

2. In comparing the current rate and temporal methods of translation, which of the following is true?
   a. The reported balance of accounts receivable is normally the same under both methods.
   b. The reported balance of inventory is normally the same under both methods.

c. The reported balance of equipment is normally the same under both methods.

d. The reported balance of depreciation expense is normally the same under both methods.

LO 8-3

3. Which of the following statements is true for the translation process using the current rate method?

a. A translation adjustment can affect consolidated net income.

b. Equipment is translated at the historical exchange rate in effect at the date of its purchase.

c. A translation adjustment is created by the change in the relative value of a subsidiary's monetary assets and monetary liabilities caused by exchange rate fluctuations.

d. A translation adjustment is created by the change in the relative value of a subsidiary's net assets caused by exchange rate fluctuations.

LO 8-2, 8-3

4. A foreign subsidiary of Thun Corporation has one asset (inventory) and no liabilities. The functional currency for this subsidiary is the yuan. The inventory was acquired for 100,000 yuan when the exchange rate was $0.16 = 1 yuan. Consolidated statements are to be produced, and the current exchange rate is $0.12 = 1 yuan. Which of the following statements is true for the consolidated financial statements?

a. A remeasurement gain must be reported.

b. A positive translation adjustment must be reported.

c. A negative translation adjustment must be reported.

d. A remeasurement loss must be reported.

LO 8-3

5. At what rates should the following balance sheet accounts in foreign statements be translated (using the current rate method) into U.S. dollars?

	Equipment	Accumulated Depreciation—Equipment
a.	Current	Current
b.	Current	Average for year
c.	Historical	Current
d.	Historical	Historical

Problems 6 and 7 are based on the following information.

Certain balance sheet accounts of a foreign subsidiary of Orchid Company have been stated in U.S. dollars as follows:

	Stated at	
	Current Rates	Historical Rates
Accounts receivable, current	$200,000	$220,000
Accounts receivable, long term	100,000	110,000
Land	50,000	55,000
Patents	80,000	85,000
	$430,000	$470,000

LO 8-2, 8-3

6. This subsidiary's functional currency is a foreign currency. What total should Orchid's balance sheet include for the preceding items?

a. $430,000

b. $435,000

c. $440,000

d. $450,000

LO 8-2, 8-4

7. This subsidiary's functional currency is the U.S. dollar. What total should Orchid's balance sheet include for the preceding items?

a. $430,000

b. $435,000

c. $440,000

d. $450,000

Problems 8 and 9 are based on the following information:

Navarro, Inc., whose reporting currency is the U.S. dollar, has a subsidiary in Argentina, whose functional currency also is the U.S. dollar. The subsidiary acquires inventory on credit on November 1,

2023, for 100,000 pesos that is sold on January 17, 2024, for 130,000 pesos. The subsidiary pays for the inventory on January 31, 2024. Currency exchange rates are as follows:

November 1, 2023	$0.16 = 1 peso
December 31, 2023	0.17 = 1
January 17, 2024	0.18 = 1
January 31, 2024	0.19 = 1

LO 8-2, 8-4

8. What amount does Navarro's consolidated balance sheet report for this inventory on December 31, 2023?
   a. $16,000
   b. $17,000
   c. $18,000
   d. $19,000

LO 8-2, 8-4

9. What amount does Navarro's consolidated income statement report for cost of goods sold for the year ending December 31, 2024?
   a. $16,000
   b. $17,000
   c. $18,000
   d. $19,000

Problems 10 and 11 are based on the following information:

A Katz Corporation subsidiary buys marketable equity securities and inventory on April 1, 2024, for 100,000 won each. It pays for both items on June 1, 2024, and they are still on hand at year-end. Inventory is carried at cost under the lower-of-cost-or-net realizable rule. Currency exchange rates in 2024 follow:

January 1	$0.15 = 1 won
April 1	0.16 = 1
June 1	0.17 = 1
December 31	0.19 = 1

LO 8-2, 8-3

10. Assume that the won is the subsidiary's functional currency. What balances does a consolidated balance sheet report as of December 31, 2024?
    a. Marketable equity securities = $16,000 and Inventory = $16,000
    b. Marketable equity securities = $17,000 and Inventory = $17,000
    c. Marketable equity securities = $19,000 and Inventory = $16,000
    d. Marketable equity securities = $19,000 and Inventory = $19,000

LO 8-2, 8-4

11. Assume that the U.S. dollar is the subsidiary's functional currency. What balances does a consolidated balance sheet report as of December 31, 2024?
    a. Marketable equity securities = $16,000 and Inventory = $16,000
    b. Marketable equity securities = $17,000 and Inventory = $17,000
    c. Marketable equity securities = $19,000 and Inventory = $16,000
    d. Marketable equity securities = $19,000 and Inventory = $19,000

LO 8-1

12. In the translated financial statements, which method of translation maintains the underlying valuation methods used in preparing the foreign currency financial statements?
    a. Current rate method; income statement translated at average exchange rate for the year
    b. Current rate method; income statement translated at exchange rate at the balance sheet date
    c. Temporal method
    d. Monetary/nonmonetary method

LO 8-4

13. Which of the following items is remeasured using the current exchange rate under the temporal method?
    a. Bonds payable
    b. Dividends declared
    c. Additional paid-in capital
    d. Amortization of intangibles

LO 8-2

14. In accordance with U.S. GAAP, which translation combination is appropriate for a foreign operation whose functional currency is the U.S. dollar?

	Method	Treatment of Translation Adjustment
a.	Current rate	Other comprehensive income
b.	Current rate	Gain or loss in net income
c.	Temporal	Other comprehensive income
d.	Temporal	Gain or loss in net income

LO 8-3

15. A foreign subsidiary's functional currency is its local currency, which has not experienced significant inflation. The current exchange rate at the balance sheet date is the appropriate exchange rate for translating which of the following?

	Insurance Expense	Prepaid Insurance
a.	Yes	Yes
b.	Yes	No
c.	No	Yes
d.	No	No

LO 8-5

16. The functional currency of Bertrand, Inc.'s Irish subsidiary is the euro. Bertrand borrowed euros as a partial hedge of its investment in the subsidiary. Since then, the euro has decreased in value. Bertrand's negative translation adjustment on its investment in the subsidiary exceeded its foreign exchange gain on its euro borrowing. How should Bertrand report the effects of the negative translation adjustment and foreign exchange gain in its consolidated financial statements?

   a. Report the translation adjustment in accumulated other comprehensive income on the balance sheet and the foreign exchange gain as a gain on the income statement.

   b. Report the translation adjustment in the income statement and defer the foreign exchange gain in accumulated other comprehensive income on the balance sheet.

   c. Report the translation adjustment less the foreign exchange gain in accumulated other comprehensive income on the balance sheet.

   d. Report the translation adjustment less the foreign exchange gain in the income statement.

LO 8-2

17. Which of the following is an indicator that a foreign currency is the functional currency of a foreign subsidiary?

   a. Cash flows of the foreign subsidiary directly impact the cash flows of the parent company.

   b. The foreign subsidiary's sales market primarily is in the parent company's country.

   c. The foreign subsidiary primarily obtains its financing in a foreign currency.

   d. There is a high volume of transactions between the foreign subsidiary and the parent company.

LO 8-2, 8-4

18. A U.S. company's foreign subsidiary had these amounts in local currency units (LCU) in 2024:

Cost of goods sold	LCU 5,000,000
Beginning inventory	500,000
Ending inventory	600,000

   The average exchange rate during 2024 was $1.00 = LCU 1. The beginning inventory was acquired when the exchange rate was $0.80 = LCU 1. Ending inventory was acquired when the exchange rate was $1.10 = LCU 1. The exchange rate on December 31, 2024, was $1.15 = LCU 1.

   Assuming that the foreign country is highly inflationary, determine the amount at which the foreign subsidiary's cost of goods sold should be reflected in the U.S. dollar income statement.

LO 8-3

19. Yang Corporation starts a foreign subsidiary on January 1 by investing 20,000 rand. Yang owns all of the shares of the subsidiary's common stock. The foreign subsidiary generates 40,000 rand of net income throughout the year and pays no dividends. The rand is the foreign subsidiary's functional currency. Currency exchange rates for 1 rand are as follows:

January 1	$0.25 = 1 rand
Average for the year	0.28 = 1
December 31	0.31 = 1

   In preparing consolidated financial statements, determine the translation adjustment that Yang Corporation will report at the end of the current year.

LO 8-4

20. Charleston Corporation owns a branch in a foreign country. Although this branch operates in euros, the U.S. dollar is its functional currency. Thus, a remeasurement is necessary to produce financial information for external reporting purposes. The branch began the year with 500,000 euros in cash and no other assets or liabilities. However, the branch immediately used 300,000 euros to acquire a warehouse. On May 1, it purchased inventory costing 100,000 euros for cash that it sold on July 1 for 160,000 euros cash. The branch transferred 10,000 euros to the parent on October 1 and recorded depreciation on the warehouse of 10,000 euros for the year. U.S dollar exchange rates for 1 euro follow:

January 1	$1.14 = 1 euro
May 1	1.18 = 1
July 1	1.20 = 1
October 1	1.18 = 1
December 31	1.16 = 1
Average for the year	1.19 = 1

Calculate the remeasurement gain or loss to be recognized in the consolidated income statement.

LO 8-4

21. McCarthy, Inc.'s Brazilian subsidiary borrowed 100,000 euros on January 1, 2024. Exchange rates between the Brazilian real (BRL) and euro (€) and between the U.S. dollar ($) and BRL are as follows:

	BRL per €	US$ per BRL
January 1, 2024	BRL 4.2	$0.28
Average, 2024	BRL 4.3	$0.25
December 31, 2024	BRL 4.6	$0.20

a. Determine the amount at which the Brazilian subsidiary's euro note payable should be reported on McCarthy's December 31, 2024, consolidated balance sheet.

b. Determine the amount of foreign exchange gain or loss that should be reflected in McCarthy's 2024 consolidated net income.

LO 8-3

22. On January 1, Narnevik Corporation formed a subsidiary in a foreign country. On April 1, the subsidiary purchased inventory on account at a cost of 250,000 local currency units (LCU). One-fifth of this inventory remained unsold on December 31, while 30 percent of the accounts payable had not yet been paid. The U.S. dollar–per-LCU exchange rates were as follows:

January 1	$0.60
April 1	0.58
Average for the current year	0.56
December 31	0.54

At what amounts should the December 31 balances in inventory and accounts payable be translated into U.S. dollars using the current rate method?

LO 8-3, 8-4

23. The following accounts are denominated in rubles as of December 31, 2024. For reporting purposes, these accounts need to be stated in U.S. dollars. For each account, indicate the exchange rate that would be used to translate the ruble balance into U.S. dollars under the current rate method. Then, again for each account, indicate the exchange rate that would be used to remeasure the ruble balance to U.S. dollars using the temporal method. The company was started in 2019. The buildings were acquired in 2020 and the patents in 2021.

	Translation	Remeasurement
Accounts payable		
Accounts receivable		
Accumulated depreciation—buildings		
Advertising expense		
Amortization expense (patents)		
Buildings		
Cash		
Common stock		
Depreciation expense		
Dividends (10/1/24)		
Notes payable—due in 2027		
Patents (net)		
Salary expense		
Sales		

Exchange rates for 1 ruble are as follows:

2019	1 ruble = $0.28
2020	1 = 0.26
2021	1 = 0.25
January 1, 2024	1 = 0.24
April 1, 2024	1 = 0.23
July 1, 2024	1 = 0.22
October 1, 2024	1 = 0.20
December 31, 2024	1 = 0.16
Average for 2024	1 = 0.19

LO 8-1, 8-3, 8-4

24. On December 18, 2024, Stephkado Corporation acquired 100 percent of a Swiss company for 4.0 million Swiss francs (CHF), which is indicative of book and fair value. At the acquisition date, the exchange rate was $1.00 = CHF 1. On December 18, 2024, the book and fair values of the subsidiary's assets and liabilities were as follows:

Cash	CHF 800,000
Inventory	1,300,000
Property, plant, and equipment	4,000,000
Notes payable	(2,100,000)

Stephkado prepares consolidated financial statements on December 31, 2024. By that date, the Swiss franc has appreciated to $1.10 = CHF 1. Because of the year-end holidays, no transactions took place prior to consolidation. Property, plant, and equipment is depreciated using a units-of-production method, so no depreciation is required from December 18 to December 31. The Swiss subsidiary has no revenues and no expenses from December 18 to December 31, and its book value is unchanged from December 18 to December 31.

a. Determine the translation adjustment to be reported on Stephkado's December 31, 2024, consolidated balance sheet, assuming that the Swiss franc is the Swiss subsidiary's functional currency. What is the economic relevance of this translation adjustment?

b. Determine the remeasurement gain or loss to be reported in Stephkado's 2024 consolidated net income, assuming that the U.S. dollar is the functional currency. What is the economic relevance of this remeasurement gain or loss?

LO 8-3, 8-4

25. The Isle of Palms Company (IOP), a U.S.-based entity, has a wholly owned subsidiary in Israel that has been determined as having the Israeli shekel (ILS) as its functional currency. On October 1, 2023, the Israeli subsidiary borrowed 500,000 Swiss francs (CHF) from a bank in Geneva for two years at an interest rate of 5 percent per year. The note payable and accrued interest are payable at the date of maturity. On December 31, 2024, the Israeli subsidiary has the following foreign currency balances on its books:

Interest expense	CHF 25,000
Interest payable	CHF 31,250
Note payable	CHF 500,000

Relevant exchange rates between the Israeli shekel (ILS) and Swiss franc (CHF), and between the U.S. dollar (USD) and Israeli shekel (ILS) follow:

	ILS per CHF	USD per ILS
October 1, 2023	3.86	0.30
January 1, 2024	3.91	0.29
Average for 2024	3.95	0.27
December 31, 2024	4.02	0.25

a. Determine the Israeli shekel amounts at which the Swiss franc balances should be reported on the Israel subsidiary's December 31, 2024, trial balance.

b. Determine the U.S. dollar amounts at which the Swiss franc balances should be included in IOP's 2024 consolidated financial statements.

LO 8-3

26. Sullivan's Island Company began operating a subsidiary in a foreign country on January 1, 2024, by investing capital in the amount of 60,000 pounds. The subsidiary immediately borrowed 140,000 pounds on a five-year note with 10 percent interest payable annually beginning on January 1, 2025. The subsidiary then purchased for 200,000 pounds a building that had a 10-year expected life and no salvage value and is to be depreciated using the straight-line method. Also on January 1, 2024, the subsidiary rented the building for three years to a group of local attorneys for 8,000 pounds per month. By year-end, rent payments totaling 80,000 pounds had been received, and 16,000 pounds was in accounts receivable. On October 1, 2024, 4,000 pounds was paid for a repair made to the building. The subsidiary transferred a cash dividend of 12,000 pounds back to Sullivan's Island Company on December 31, 2024. The functional currency for the subsidiary is the pound. Currency exchange rates for 1 pound follow:

January 1, 2024	$2.00 = 1 pound
October 1, 2024	2.05 = 1
December 31, 2024	2.08 = 1
Average for 2024	2.04 = 1

Prepare an income statement, statement of retained earnings, and balance sheet for this subsidiary in pounds, and then translate these amounts into U.S. dollars.

LO 8-3

27. Refer to the information in Problem 26. Prepare a statement of cash flows in pounds for Sullivan's Island Company's foreign subsidiary, and then translate this statement into U.S. dollars.

LO 8-3, 8-4

28. Rolfe Company (a U.S.-based company) has a subsidiary in Nigeria, where the local currency unit is the naira (NGN). On December 31, 2023, the subsidiary had the following balance sheet (amounts are in thousands [000s]):

Cash	NGN 16,000	Note payable	NGN 20,000
Inventory....................	10,000	Common stock	20,000
Land........................	4,000	Retained earnings	10,000
Building.....................	40,000		
Accumulated depreciation	(20,000)		
	NGN 50,000		NGN 50,000

The subsidiary issued the common stock in 2015, and acquired the land and building in 2016. It acquired the inventory on August 1, 2023. During 2024, the following transactions took place:

2024	
Feb. 1	Paid 8,000,000 NGN on the note payable.
May 1	Sold entire inventory for 16,000,000 NGN on account.
June 1	Sold land for 6,000,000 NGN cash.
Aug. 1	Collected all accounts receivable.
Sept. 1	Signed long-term note to receive 8,000,000 NGN cash.
Oct. 1	Bought inventory for 20,000,000 NGN cash.
Nov. 1	Bought land for 3,000,000 NGN on account.
Dec. 1	Declared and paid 3,000,000 NGN cash dividend to parent.
Dec. 31	Recorded depreciation for the entire year of 2,000,000 NGN.

The U.S dollar ($) exchange rates for 1 NGN are as follows:

2015	NGN1 = $0.0048
2016	1 = 0.0042
August 1, 2023	1 = 0.0062
December 31, 2023...............	1 = 0.0064
February 1, 2024	1 = 0.0066
May 1, 2024....................	1 = 0.0068
June 1, 2024....................	1 = 0.0070
August 1, 2024	1 = 0.0074
September 1, 2024	1 = 0.0076
October 1, 2024	1 = 0.0078
November 1, 2024...............	1 = 0.0080
December 1, 2024...............	1 = 0.0082
December 31, 2024...............	1 = 0.0084
Average for 2024................	1 = 0.0074

a. Assuming the NGN is the subsidiary's functional currency, what is the translation adjustment determined solely for 2024?

b. Assuming the U.S. dollar is the subsidiary's functional currency, what is the remeasurement gain or loss determined solely for 2024?

LO 8-3, 8-4

29. Zugar Company is domiciled in a country whose currency is the dinar. Zugar begins 2024 with three assets: Cash of 20,000 dinars, Accounts receivable of 80,000 dinars, and Land that cost 200,000 dinars when acquired on April 1, 2023. On January 1, 2024, Zugar has a 150,000 dinar Note payable, and no other liabilities. On May 1, 2024, Zugar renders services to a customer for 120,000 dinars, which was immediately paid in cash. On June 1, 2024, Zugar incurred a 100,000 dinar operating expense, which was immediately paid in cash. No other transactions occurred during the year. Currency exchange rates for 1 dinar follow:

April 1, 2023	$0.33 = 1 dinar
January 1, 2024	0.36 = 1
May 1, 2024	0.37 = 1
June 1, 2024	0.39 = 1
December 31, 2024	0.41 = 1

a. Assume that Zugar is a foreign subsidiary of a U.S. multinational company that uses the U.S. dollar as its reporting currency. Assume also that the dinar is the subsidiary's functional currency. What is the translation adjustment for this subsidiary for the year 2024?

b. Assume that Zugar is a foreign subsidiary of a U.S. multinational company that uses the U.S. dollar as its reporting currency. Assume also that the U.S. dollar is the subsidiary's functional currency. What is the remeasurement gain or loss for 2024?

c. Assume that Zugar is a foreign subsidiary of a U.S. multinational company. On the December 31, 2024, balance sheet, what is the *translated* value of the Land account? On the December 31, 2024, balance sheet, what is the *remeasured* value of the Land account?

LO 8-3, 8-4

30. Compte, Inc. (a U.S.-based company), establishes a subsidiary in Croatia on January 1, 2023. The following account balances for the year ending December 31, 2024, are stated in kuna (K), the local currency:

Sales	K 200,000
Inventory (bought on 3/1/24)	100,000
Equipment (bought on 1/1/23)	80,000
Rent expense	10,000
Dividends (declared on 10/1/24)	20,000
Notes receivable (to be collected in 2027)	30,000
Accumulated depreciation—equipment	24,000
Salary payable	5,000
Depreciation expense	8,000

The following U.S. dollar per kuna exchange rates are applicable:

January 1, 2023	$0.13
Average for 2023	0.14
January 1, 2024	0.18
March 1, 2024	0.19
October 1, 2024	0.21
December 31, 2024	0.22
Average for 2024	0.20

Compte is preparing account balances to produce consolidated financial statements.

a. Assuming that the kuna is the functional currency, what exchange rate would be used to report each of these accounts in U.S. dollar consolidated financial statements?

b. Assuming that the U.S. dollar is the functional currency, what exchange rate would be used to report each of these accounts in U.S. dollar consolidated financial statements?

LO 8-3, 8-5

31. Stilton Company (a U.S.-based company) has a subsidiary in Canada that began operations at the start of 2024 with assets of 132,000 Canadian dollars (CAD) and liabilities of CAD 54,000. During

this initial year of operation, the subsidiary reported a profit of CAD 26,000. It distributed two dividends, each for CAD 5,000 with one dividend declared on March 1 and the other on October 1. Applicable U.S. dollar ($) exchange rates for 1 Canadian dollar follow:

January 1, 2024 (start of business)	$0.80
March 1, 2024	0.78
Weighted average rate for 2024	0.77
October 1, 2024	0.76
December 31, 2024	0.75

a. Assume that the Canadian dollar is this subsidiary's functional currency. What translation adjustment would the company report for the year 2024?

b. Assume that on October 1, 2024, Stilton entered into a forward exchange contract to hedge the net investment in this subsidiary. On that date, the company agreed to sell CAD 400,000 in three months at a forward exchange rate of $0.76/CAD 1. Prepare the journal entries required by this forward contract.

c. Compute the net translation adjustment the company will report in accumulated other comprehensive income for the year 2024 under this second set of circumstances.

LO 8-3, 8-4

32. Aguilar Company establishes a subsidiary operation in a foreign country on January 1, 2024. The country's currency is the rial (R). To start this business, Aguilar invests 10,000 rials. Of this amount, it spends 3,000 rials immediately to acquire equipment. Later, on April 1, 2024, it also purchases land. All subsidiary operational activities occur at an even rate throughout the year. Aguilar uses the U.S. dollar as its reporting currency. The U.S. dollar ($) exchange rates for the rial for 2024 follow:

January 1	$1.71
April 1	1.59
June 1	1.66
Weighted average	1.64
December 31	1.62

As of December 31, 2024, the subsidiary reports the following trial balance:

	Debits	Credits
Cash	R 8,000	
Accounts receivable	9,000	
Equipment	3,000	
Accumulated depreciation		R 600
Land	5,000	
Accounts payable		3,000
Notes payable (due 2032)		5,000
Common stock		10,000
Dividends declared (6/1/24)	4,000	
Sales		25,000
Salary expense	5,000	
Depreciation expense	600	
Miscellaneous expenses	9,000	
Totals	R 43,600	R 43,600

a. Assume that the subsidiary's functional currency is the rial (R). Prepare a trial balance for it in U.S. dollars so that 2024 consolidated financial statements can be prepared.

b. Assume that the subsidiary's functional currency is the U.S. dollar. Prepare a trial balance for it in U.S. dollars so that 2024 consolidated financial statements can be prepared.

LO 8-3

33. Livingston Company is a wholly owned subsidiary of Rose Corporation. Livingston operates in a foreign country with financial statements recorded in pounds (P), the company's functional currency. Financial statements for the year 2024 are as follows:

Income Statement
for Year Ending December 31, 2024

Sales	P 270,000
Cost of goods sold	(155,000)
Gross profit	115,000
Less: Operating expenses	(54,000)
Gain on sale of equipment	10,000
Net income	P 71,000

Statement of Retained Earnings
for Year Ending December 31, 2024

Retained earnings, 1/1/24	P 216,000
Net income	71,000
Less: Dividends	(26,000)
Retained earnings, 12/31/24	P 261,000

Balance Sheet
December 31, 2024

Assets

Cash	P 44,000
Receivables	116,000
Inventory	58,000
Property, plant, and equipment (net)	339,000
Total assets	P 557,000

Liabilities and Equities

Liabilities	P 176,000
Common stock	120,000
Retained earnings, 12/31/24	261,000
Total liabilities and equities	P 557,000

Additional Information

- The common stock was issued in 2017 when the exchange rate was $2.08 per pound; property, plant, and equipment was acquired in 2018 when the exchange rate was $2.00 per pound.
- As of January 1, 2024, the retained earnings balance was translated as $396,520.
- The U.S. dollar–per-pound exchange rates for 2024 follow:

January 1	$1.67
April 1	1.61
September 1	1.72
December 31	1.54
Weighted average	1.59

- Inventory was acquired evenly throughout the year.
- The December 31, 2023, balance sheet reported a translation adjustment with a debit balance of $85,000.
- Dividends were declared on April 1, 2024, and a piece of equipment was sold on September 1, 2024.

    Assume that the pound is Livingston Company's functional currency. Translate the 2024 foreign currency financial statements into the parent's reporting currency, the U.S. dollar.

LO 8-3, 8-4

34. The following account balances are for the Agee Company as of January 1, 2024, and December 31, 2024. All amounts are denominated in kroner (Kr).

	January 1, 2024	December 31, 2024
Accounts payable	(15,000)	(25,000)
Accounts receivable	54,000	104,000
Accumulated depreciation—buildings	(45,000)	(50,000)
Accumulated depreciation—equipment	–0–	(7,500)
Bonds payable—due 2027	(64,000)	(64,000)
Buildings	134,000	105,000
Cash	60,000	10,500
Common stock	(69,000)	(82,000)
Depreciation expense	–0–	40,000
Dividends (10/1/24)	–0–	57,000
Equipment	–0–	64,000
Gain on sale of building	–0–	(8,500)
Rent expense	–0–	21,500
Retained earnings	(55,000)	(55,000)
Salary expense	–0–	45,000
Sales	–0–	(162,000)
Utilities expense	–0–	7,000

Additional Information

- Agee issued additional shares of common stock during the year on April 1, 2024. Common stock on January 1, 2024, was sold at the start of operations in 2017.
- Agee purchased buildings in 2018 and sold one building with a book value of Kr 1,500 on July 1 of the current year.
- Equipment was acquired on April 1, 2024.

  Relevant exchange rates for 1 Kr were as follows:

2017	$2.90
2018	2.70
January 1, 2024	3.00
April 1, 2024	3.10
July 1, 2024	3.30
October 1, 2024	3.40
December 31, 2024	3.50
Average for 2024	3.20

a. Assuming the U.S. dollar is the functional currency, what is the remeasurement gain or loss for 2024? The December 31, 2023, U.S. dollar–translated balance sheet reported retained earnings of $145,200, which included a remeasurement loss of $28,300.

b. Assuming the foreign currency is the functional currency, what is the translation adjustment for 2024? The December 31, 2023, U.S. dollar–translated balance sheet reported retained earnings of $162,250 and a cumulative translation adjustment of $9,650 (credit balance).

LO 8-3, 8-4

35. Sendelbach Corporation is a U.S.-based organization with operations throughout the world. One of its subsidiaries is headquartered in Toronto, Canada. Although this wholly owned subsidiary operates primarily in Canada, it engages in some transactions through a branch in Mexico. Therefore, the subsidiary maintains a ledger denominated in Mexican pesos (Ps) and a general ledger in Canadian dollars (C$). As of December 31, 2024, the subsidiary is preparing financial statements in anticipation of consolidation with the U.S. parent corporation. Both ledgers for the subsidiary are as follows:

Main Operation—Canada

	Debit	Credit
Accounts payable		C$ 35,000
Accumulated depreciation		27,000
Buildings and equipment	C$167,000	
Cash	26,000	
Common stock		50,000
Cost of goods sold	203,000	
Depreciation expense	8,000	
Dividends, 4/1/24	28,000	
Gain on sale of equipment, 6/1/24		5,000
Inventory	98,000	
Notes payable—due in 2027		76,000
Receivables	68,000	
Retained earnings, 1/1/24		135,530
Salary expense	26,000	
Sales		312,000
Utility expense	9,000	
Branch operation	7,530	
Totals	C$640,530	C$640,530

Branch Operation—Mexico

	Debit	Credit
Accounts payable		Ps 49,000
Accumulated depreciation		19,000
Building and equipment	Ps 40,000	
Cash	59,000	
Depreciation expense	2,000	
Inventory (beginning—income statement)	23,000	
Inventory (ending—income statement)		28,000
Inventory (ending—balance sheet)	28,000	
Purchases	68,000	
Receivables	21,000	
Salary expense	9,000	
Sales		124,000
Main office		30,000
Totals	Ps 250,000	Ps 250,000

Additional Information

- The Canadian subsidiary's functional currency is the Canadian dollar, and Sendelbach's reporting currency is the U.S. dollar. The Canadian and Mexican operations are not viewed as separate accounting entities.
- The building and equipment used in the Mexican operation were acquired in 2014 when the currency exchange rate was C$0.25 = Ps 1.
- Purchases of inventory were made evenly throughout the fiscal year.
- Beginning inventory was acquired evenly throughout 2023; ending inventory was acquired evenly throughout 2024.
- The Main Office account on the Mexican records should be considered an equity account. This balance was remeasured into C$7,530 on December 31, 2024.
- Currency exchange rates for 1 Ps applicable to the Mexican operation follow:

Weighted average rate for 2023	C$0.30
January 1, 2024	0.32
Weighted average rate for 2024	0.34
December 31, 2024	0.35

- The December 31, 2023, consolidated balance sheet reported a cumulative translation adjustment with a $36,950 credit (positive) balance.
- The subsidiary's common stock was issued in 2011 when the exchange rate was $0.45 = C$1.
- The subsidiary's December 31, 2023, retained earnings balance was C$135,530, an amount that has been translated into US$70,421.
- The applicable currency exchange rates for 1 C$ for translation purposes are as follows:

January 1, 2024	US$0.70
April 1, 2024	0.69
June 1, 2024	0.68
Weighted average rate for 2024	0.67
December 31, 2024	0.65

a. Remeasure the Mexican operation's account balances into Canadian dollars. (Note: Back into the beginning net monetary asset or liability position.)

b. Prepare financial statements (income statement, statement of retained earnings, and balance sheet) for the Canadian subsidiary in its functional currency, Canadian dollars.

c. Translate the Canadian dollar functional currency financial statements into U.S. dollars so that Sendelbach can prepare consolidated financial statements.

LO 8-3, 8-6

36. On January 1, 2023, Cayce Corporation acquired 100 percent of Simbel Company for consideration transferred with a fair value of $126,000. Cayce is a U.S.-based company headquartered in Buffalo, New York, and Simbel is in Cairo, Egypt. Cayce accounts for its investment in Simbel under the initial value method. Any excess of fair value of consideration transferred over book value is attributable to undervalued land on Simbel's books. Simbel had no retained earnings at the date of acquisition. The following are the 2024 financial statements for the two operations. Information for Cayce and for Simbel is in U.S. dollars ($) and Egyptian pounds (£E), respectively.

	Cayce Corporation	Simbel Company
Sales	$200,000	£E 800,000
Cost of goods sold	(93,800)	(420,000)
Salary expense	(19,000)	(74,000)
Rent expense	(7,000)	(46,000)
Other expenses	(21,000)	(59,000)
Dividend income—from Simbel	13,750	–0–
Gain on sale of building, 10/1/24	–0–	30,000
Net income	$ 72,950	£E 231,000
Retained earnings, 1/1/24	$318,000	£E 133,000
Net income	72,950	231,000
Dividends	(24,000)	(50,000)
Retained earnings, 12/31/24	$366,950	£E 314,000
Cash and receivables	$110,750	£E 146,000
Inventory	98,000	297,000
Prepaid expenses	30,000	–0–
Investment in Simbel (initial value)	126,000	–0–
Property, plant, and equipment (net)	398,000	455,000
Total assets	$762,750	£E 898,000
Accounts payable	$ 60,800	£E 54,000
Notes payable—due in 2027	132,000	140,000
Common stock	120,000	240,000
Additional paid-in capital	83,000	150,000
Retained earnings, 12/31/24	366,950	314,000
Total liabilities and equities	$762,750	£E 898,000

Additional Information

- During 2023, the first year of joint operation, Simbel reported income of £E 163,000 earned evenly throughout the year. Simbel declared a dividend of £E 30,000 to Cayce on June 1 of that year. Simbel also declared the 2024 dividend on June 1.

- On December 9, 2024, Simbel classified a £E 10,000 expenditure as a rent expense, although this payment related to prepayment of rent for the first few months of 2025.

- The exchange rates for 1 £E are as follows:

January 1, 2023	$0.300
June 1, 2023	0.290
Weighted average rate for 2023	0.288
December 31, 2023	0.280
June 1, 2024	0.275
October 1, 2024	0.273
Weighted average rate for 2024	0.274
December 31, 2024	0.270

Translate Simbel's 2024 financial statements into U.S. dollars and prepare a consolidation worksheet for Cayce and its Egyptian subsidiary. Assume that the Egyptian pound is the subsidiary's functional currency.

LO 8-1, 8-3, 8-4

37. Dieckmann Company, a U.S.-based company, acquired a 100 percent interest in Rakona A.S. in the Czech Republic on January 1, 2023, when the exchange rate for the Czech koruna (Kčs) was $0.05. Rakona's financial statements as of December 31, 2024, two years later, follow:

Balance Sheet
December 31, 2024

Assets

Cash	Kčs 2,000,000
Accounts receivable (net)	3,300,000
Inventory	8,500,000
Equipment	25,000,000
Less: Accumulated depreciation	(8,500,000)
Buildings	72,000,000
Less: Accumulated depreciation	(30,300,000)
Land	6,000,000
Total assets	Kčs 78,000,000

Liabilities and Stockholders' Equity

Accounts payable	Kčs 2,500,000
Long-term debt	50,000,000
Common stock	5,000,000
Additional paid-in capital	15,000,000
Retained earnings	5,500,000
Total liabilities and stockholders' equity	Kčs 78,000,000

Income Statement
For Year Ending December 31, 2024

Sales	Kčs 25,000,000
Cost of goods sold	(12,000,000)
Depreciation expense—equipment	(2,500,000)
Depreciation expense—buildings	(1,800,000)
Research and development expense	(1,200,000)
Other expenses (including taxes)	(1,000,000)
Net income	Kčs 6,500,000
Plus: Retained earnings, 1/1/24	500,000
Less: Dividends, 2024	(1,500,000)
Retained earnings, 12/31/24	Kčs 5,500,000

Additional Information

- The January 1, 2024, beginning inventory of Kčs 6,000,000 was acquired on December 18, 2023, when the exchange rate was $0.043. Purchases of inventory were acquired uniformly during 2024. The December 31, 2024, ending inventory of Kčs 8,500,000 was acquired in the latter part of 2024 when the exchange rate was $0.032. All depreciable assets (equipment and buildings) were on the books when the subsidiary was acquired—except for Kčs 5,000,000 of equipment acquired on January 3, 2024, when the exchange rate was $0.036, and Kčs 12,000,000 in buildings acquired on March 5, 2024, when the exchange rate was $0.034. Straight-line depreciation is 10 years for equipment and 40 years for buildings. A full year's depreciation is taken in the year of acquisition.

- Dividends were declared and paid on December 15, 2024, when the exchange rate was $0.031.

- Other exchange rates for 1 Kčs follow:

January 1, 2024	$0.040
Weighted average rate for 2024	0.035
December 31, 2024	0.030

Part I. Translate the Czech koruna financial statements on December 31, 2024, in the following three situations:

- *a.* The Czech koruna is the functional currency. The December 31, 2023, U.S. dollar–translated balance sheet reported retained earnings of $22,500. The December 31, 2023, cumulative translation adjustment was negative $202,500 (debit balance).

- *b.* The U.S. dollar is the functional currency. The December 31, 2023, U.S. dollar–remeasured balance sheet reported retained earnings (including a 2023 remeasurement gain) of $353,000.

- *c.* The U.S. dollar is the functional currency. Rakona has no long-term debt. Instead, it has common stock of Kčs 20,000,000 and additional paid-in capital of Kčs 50,000,000. The December 31, 2023, U.S. dollar–remeasured balance sheet reported a negative balance in retained earnings of $147,000 (including a 2023 remeasurement loss).

Part II. Explain the positive or negative sign of the translation adjustment in Part I(*a*), and explain why a remeasurement gain or loss exists in Parts I(*b*) and I(*c*).

LO 8-3, 8-4

38. Millager Company is a U.S.-based multinational corporation with the U.S. dollar (USD) as its reporting currency. To prepare consolidated financial statements for 2024, the company must translate the accounts of its subsidiary in Mexico, Cadengo S.A. On December 31, 2023, Cadengo's balance sheet was translated from Mexican pesos (MXN) (its functional currency) into U.S. dollars as prescribed by U.S. GAAP. Equity accounts at that date follow:

December 31, 2023	MXN	USD
Common stock	12,000,000	1,000,000
Retained earnings	2,500,000	200,000
Cumulative translation adjustment (debit balance)		(40,000)

Early in 2024, Cadengo negotiated a 5,000 Brazilian real (BRL) loan from a bank in Rio de Janeiro and established a sales office in Brazil.

At the end of 2024, Cadengo provided Millager a trial balance that includes all of Cadengo's Mexican peso–denominated transactions for the year. A separate ledger has been maintained for transactions carried out by the Brazilian sales office that are denominated in BRL. A trial balance for the Brazilian real–denominated transactions follows Cadengo's MXN trial balance.

CADENGO S.A.
Trial Balance
December 31, 2024

	Debit	Credit
Cash	MXN 1,000,000	
Accounts receivable	3,000,000	
Inventory	5,000,000	
Land	2,000,000	
Machinery and equipment	15,000,000	
Accumulated depreciation		MXN 6,000,000
Accounts payable		1,500,000
Notes payable		4,000,000
Common stock		12,000,000
Retained earnings, 1/1/24		2,500,000
Sales		34,000,000
Cost of goods sold	28,000,000	
Depreciation expense	600,000	
Rent expense	3,000,000	
Interest expense	400,000	
Dividends, 7/1/24	2,000,000	
Total	MXN 60,000,000	MXN 60,000,000

BRAZILIAN SALES OFFICE
Trial Balance
December 31, 2024

	Debit	Credit
Cash	BRL 5,500	
Accounts receivable	28,000	
Notes payable		BRL 5,000
Sales		35,000
Rent expense	6,000	
Interest expense	500	
Total	BRL 40,000	BRL 40,000

Additional Information

The Mexican peso exchange rate for 1 Brazilian real (MXN/BRL) and the U.S. dollar exchange rate for 1 Mexican peso (USD/MXN) during 2024 follow:

Date	MXN/BRL	USD/MXN
January 1, 2024	6.00	0.080
Weighted average rate for 2024	6.20	0.075
July 1, 2024	6.28	0.073
December 31, 2024	6.30	0.072

a. Using an electronic spreadsheet, prepare the Mexican peso trial balance for Cadengo S.A. for the year ending December 31, 2024. Verify the amount of remeasurement gain/loss derived as a plug figure in the spreadsheet through separate calculation.

b. Using a second electronic worksheet, translate Cadengo S.A.'s Mexican peso trial balance into U.S. dollars to facilitate Millager Company's preparation of consolidated financial statements. Verify the amount of cumulative translation adjustment derived as a plug figure in the spreadsheet through separate calculation. Note: An additional row must be inserted in the trial balance for the remeasurement gain/loss calculated in part (a).

Develop Your Skills

RESEARCH CASE 1—FOREIGN CURRENCY TRANSLATION AND HEDGING DISCLOSURES

CPA
skills

Many companies make annual reports (sometimes on Form 10-K) available on their corporate website. Access the most recent annual report for a U.S.-based multinational company with which you are familiar to complete the following requirements.

Required

a. Identify the location(s) in the annual report that provides disclosures related to the translation of foreign currency financial statements and foreign currency hedging.

b. Determine whether the company's foreign operations have a predominant functional currency.

c. List the amount of translation adjustment, if any, reported in other comprehensive income in each of the three most recent years. Explain the sign (positive or negative) of the translation adjustment in each of the three most recent years.

d. Determine whether the company hedges net investments in foreign operations. If so, determine the type(s) of hedging instrument used.

RESEARCH CASE 2—FOREIGN CURRENCY TRANSLATION AND HEDGING DISCLOSURES

CPA
skills

Many companies make annual reports (sometimes on Form 10-K) available on their corporate website. Access the annual report indicated for each of the following U.S.-based multinational corporations to complete the requirements:

International Business Machines Corporation, 2020 Annual Report.
Oracle Corporation, Form 10-K for the Fiscal Year Ended May 31, 2021.

Required

a. Identify the location(s) in the annual report that provides disclosures related to foreign currency translation and foreign currency hedging.

b. Determine whether the company's foreign operations have a predominant functional currency.

c. List the amount of translation adjustment, if any, reported in other comprehensive income in each of the three most recent years. Explain the sign (positive or negative) of the translation adjustment in each of the three most recent years.

d. Determine whether each company hedges net investments in foreign operations. If so, determine the type(s) of hedging instrument used.

ACCOUNTING STANDARDS CASE 1—MORE THAN ONE FUNCTIONAL CURRENCY

CPA
skills

Lynch Corporation has a wholly owned subsidiary in Mexico (Lynmex) with two distinct and unrelated lines of business. Lynmex's Small Appliance Division manufactures small household appliances such as toasters and coffeemakers at a factory in Monterrey, Nuevo Leon, and sells them directly to retailers such as Gigantes throughout Mexico. Lynmex's Electronics Division imports finished products produced by Lynch Corporation in the United States and sells them to a network of distributors operating throughout Mexico.

Lynch's CFO believes that the two divisions have different functional currencies. The functional currency of the Small Appliance Division is the Mexican peso, whereas the functional currency of the Electronics Division is the U.S. dollar. The CFO is unsure whether to designate the Mexican peso or the U.S. dollar as Lynmex's functional currency, or whether the subsidiary can be treated as two separate foreign operations with different functional currencies.

Required

Search current U.S. authoritative accounting literature to determine how the functional currency should be determined for a foreign entity that has more than one distinct and separable operation. Identify the source of guidance for answering this question.

ACCOUNTING STANDARDS CASE 2—CHANGE IN FUNCTIONAL CURRENCY

Kang, Inc., has a wholly owned subsidiary in Canada that previously had been determined as having the Canadian dollar as its functional currency. Due to a recent restructuring, Kang, Inc.'s CFO believes that the functional currency of the Canadian company has changed to the U.S. dollar. A large cumulative translation adjustment related to the Canadian subsidiary is included in accumulated other comprehensive income on Kang, Inc.'s balance sheet. The CFO is unsure whether the cumulative translation adjustment should be removed from equity, and if so, to what other account it should be transferred. He also questions whether the change in functional currency qualifies as a change in accounting principle, which would require retrospective application of the temporal method in translating the Canadian subsidiary's financial statements. He wonders, for example, whether the Canadian subsidiary's nonmonetary assets need to be restated as if the temporal method had been applied in previous years.

Required

Search current U.S. authoritative accounting literature for guidance on how to handle a change in functional currency from a foreign currency to the U.S. dollar. Summarize that guidance to answer the CFO's questions. Identify the source of guidance for answering these questions.

EXCEL CASE—TRANSLATING FOREIGN CURRENCY FINANCIAL STATEMENTS

Banda Company established a subsidiary in a foreign country on January 1, 2024, by investing FC 3,200,000 when the exchange rate was $0.50/FC. Banda negotiated a bank loan of FC 3,000,000 on January 5, 2024, and purchased plant and equipment in the amount of FC 6,000,000 on January 8, 2024. It depreciated plant and equipment on a straight-line basis over a 10-year useful life. It purchased its beginning inventory of FC 1,000,000 on January 10, 2024, and acquired additional inventory of FC 4,000,000 at three points in time during the year at an average exchange rate of $0.43/FC. It uses the first-in, first-out (FIFO) method to determine cost of goods sold. Additional exchange rates per FC 1 during the year 2024 follow:

January 1–31, 2024	$0.50
Weighted average rate for 2024	0.45
December 31, 2024	0.38

The foreign subsidiary's income statement for 2024 and balance sheet at December 31, 2024, follow:

INCOME STATEMENT For the Year Ended December 31, 2024 FC (in thousands)	
Sales	FC 5,000
Cost of goods sold	3,000
Gross profit	2,000
Selling expense	400
Depreciation expense	600
Income before tax	1,000
Income taxes	300
Net income	700
Retained earnings, 1/1/24	–0–
Retained earnings, 12/31/24	FC 700

BALANCE SHEET
At December 31, 2024
FC (in thousands)

Cash	FC 1,000
Inventory	2,000
Property, plant, and equipment	6,000
Less: Accumulated depreciation	(600)
Total assets	FC 8,400
Current liabilities	FC 1,500
Long-term debt	3,000
Contributed capital	3,200
Retained earnings	700
Total liabilities and stockholders' equity	FC 8,400

As the controller for Banda Company, you have evaluated the characteristics of the foreign subsidiary to determine that the FC is the subsidiary's functional currency.

Required

a. Use Excel to translate the foreign subsidiary's FC financial statements into U.S. dollars at December 31, 2024, in accordance with U.S. GAAP. Insert a row in the spreadsheet after retained earnings and before total liabilities and stockholders' equity for the cumulative translation adjustment. Calculate the translation adjustment separately to verify the amount obtained as a balancing figure in the translation worksheet.

b. Use Excel to remeasure the foreign subsidiary's FC financial statements in U.S. dollars on December 31, 2024, assuming that the U.S. dollar is the subsidiary's functional currency. Insert a row in the spreadsheet after depreciation expense and before income before taxes for the remeasurement gain (loss).

c. Prepare a report for Banda Company's CEO summarizing the differences that will be reported in the company's 2024 consolidated financial statements because the FC, rather than the U.S. dollar, is the foreign subsidiary's functional currency. In your report, discuss the relations between the current ratio, the debt-to-equity ratio, profit margin, return on equity, and inventory turnover calculated from the FC financial statements and from the translated U.S. dollar financial statements. Also discuss the meaning of the translated U.S. dollar amounts for inventory and for fixed assets.

COMMUNICATION CASE—FUNCTIONAL CURRENCY OF A FOREIGN SUBSIDIARY

Earlier this year, Alltime Company (headquartered in Kansas City, Missouri) acquired a small watch manufacturer in Berlin, Germany, that keeps its books in euros. (This is the first foreign direct investment made by Alltime.) The end of the fiscal year is approaching, and Alltime's CFO is beginning to plan for the financial statement consolidation of the German subsidiary. The CFO has heard that Alltime must determine the "functional currency" of the foreign subsidiary to be able to comply with U.S. GAAP. The CFO has asked you to provide answers to the following questions.

1. What is the functional currency of a foreign subsidiary?
2. Why must the functional currency of a foreign subsidiary be determined?
3. How is the functional currency of a foreign subsidiary determined?

Required

Draft a memorandum to the company's CFO, answering the preceding questions.

EXCEL AND ANALYSIS CASE—CONSOLIDATION OF A FOREIGN SUBSIDIARY

On January 1, 2023, Parker, Inc., a U.S.-based firm, acquired 100 percent of Suffolk PLC located in Great Britain for consideration paid of 52,000,000 British pounds (£), which was equal to fair value. The excess of fair value over book value is attributable to land (part of Property, plant, and equipment) and is not subject to depreciation. Parker accounts for its investment in Suffolk at cost. On January 1, 2023, Suffolk reported the following balance sheet:

Cash	£ 2,000,000	Accounts payable	£ 1,000,000
Accounts receivable	3,000,000	Long-term debt	8,000,000
Inventory	14,000,000	Common stock	44,000,000
Property, plant,		Retained earnings	6,000,000
and equipment (net)	40,000,000		
	£59,000,000		£59,000,000

Suffolk's 2023 income was recorded at £2,000,000. It declared and paid no dividends in 2023.

On December 31, 2024, two years after the date of acquisition, Suffolk submitted the following trial balance to Parker for consolidation:

Cash	£ 1,500,000
Accounts Receivable	5,200,000
Inventory	18,000,000
Property, Plant, and Equipment (net)	36,000,000
Accounts Payable	(1,450,000)
Long-Term Debt	(5,000,000)
Common Stock	(44,000,000)
Retained Earnings, 1/1/24	(8,000,000)
Sales	(28,000,000)
Cost of Goods Sold	16,000,000
Depreciation	2,000,000
Other Expenses	6,000,000
Dividends, 1/30/24	1,750,000
	£ —0—

Other than paying dividends, no intra-entity transactions occurred between the two companies. Relevant U.S. dollar exchange rates for the British pound follow:

	January 1	January 30	Average	December 31
2023	$1.60	$1.61	$1.62	$1.64
2024	1.64	1.65	1.66	1.68

The December 31, 2024, financial statements (before consolidation with Suffolk) follow. Dividend income is the U.S. dollar amount of dividends received from Suffolk translated at the $1.65/£ exchange rate on January 30, 2024. The amounts listed for dividend income and all affected accounts (i.e., net income, December 31 retained earnings, and cash) reflect the $1.65/£ exchange rate on January 30, 2024. Credit balances are in parentheses.

Parker	
Sales	$ (70,000,000)
Cost of goods sold	34,000,000
Depreciation	20,000,000
Other expenses	6,000,000
Dividend income	(2,887,500)
Net income	$ (12,887,500)
Retained earnings, 1/1/24	$ (48,000,000)
Net income, 2024	(12,887,500)
Dividends, 1/30/24	4,500,000
Retained earnings, 12/31/24	$ (56,387,500)
Cash	$ 3,687,500
Accounts receivable	10,000,000
Inventory	30,000,000
Investment in Suffolk	83,200,000
Plant and equipment (net)	105,000,000
Accounts payable	(25,500,000)
Long-term debt	(50,000,000)
Common stock	(100,000,000)
Retained earnings, 12/31/24	(56,387,500)
	$ –0–

Parker's chief financial officer (CFO) wishes to determine the effect that a change in the value of the British pound would have on consolidated net income and consolidated stockholders' equity. To help assess the foreign currency exposure associated with the investment in Suffolk, the CFO requests assistance in comparing consolidated results under actual exchange rate fluctuations with results that would have occurred had the dollar value of the pound remained constant or declined during the first two years of Parker's ownership.

Required

Use Excel to complete the following four parts:

Part I. Given the relevant exchange rates presented,

a. Translate Suffolk's December 31, 2024, trial balance from British pounds to U.S. dollars. The British pound is Suffolk's functional currency.
b. Prepare a schedule that details the change in Suffolk's cumulative translation adjustment (beginning net assets, income, dividends, etc.) for 2023 and 2024.
c. Prepare the December 31, 2024, consolidation worksheet for Parker and Suffolk.
d. Prepare the 2024 consolidated income statement and the December 31, 2024, consolidated balance sheet.

Note: Worksheets should possess the following qualities:

- Each spreadsheet should be programmed so that all relevant amounts adjust appropriately when different values of exchange rates (subsequent to January 1, 2023) are entered into it.
- Be sure to program Parker's dividend income, cash, and retained earnings to reflect the dollar value of alternative January 30, 2024, exchange rates.

Part II. Repeat tasks (*a*), (*b*), (*c*), and (*d*) from Part I to determine consolidated net income and consolidated stockholders' equity if the exchange rate had remained at $1.60/£ over the period 2023 to 2024.
Part III. Repeat tasks (*a*), (*b*), (*c*), and (*d*) from Part I to determine consolidated net income and consolidated stockholders' equity if the following exchange rates had existed:

	January 1	January 30	Average	December 31
2023	$1.60	$1.59	$1.58	$1.56
2024	1.56	1.55	1.54	1.52

Part IV. Prepare a report that provides Parker's CFO the risk assessments requested. Focus on profitability, cash flow, and the debt-to-equity ratio.

Partnerships: Formation and Operation

A reader of college accounting textbooks might well conclude that business activity is carried out exclusively by corporations. Because most large companies are legally incorporated, a vast majority of textbook references and illustrations concern corporate organizations. Contrary to the perception being relayed, partnerships (as well as sole proprietorships) make up a vital element of the business community. The Internal Revenue Service projects that by 2025, more than 4.7 million partnership income tax returns will be filed (as compared to over 7.5 million projected corporation income tax returns).[1]

The partnership form serves a wide range of business activities, from small local operations to worldwide enterprises. The following examples exist in the U.S. economy:

· Individual proprietors often join together to form a partnership as a way to reduce expenses, expand services, and add increased expertise. As will be discussed, partnerships also provide important tax benefits.

· A partnership is a common means by which friends and relatives can easily create and organize a business endeavor.

· Historically, doctors, lawyers, and other professionals have formed partnerships because of legal prohibitions against the incorporation of their practices. Although most states now permit alternative forms for such organizations, operating as a partnership or sole proprietorship is still necessary in many areas.

Over the years, some partnerships have grown to enormous sizes. The professional services firm of PricewaterhouseCoopers, a partnership, recently reported revenues of more than $45 billion.[2] In 2021, Deloitte indicated operations in more than 150 countries,[3] and Ernst & Young reported having more than 300,000 employees around the world.[4]

Learning Objectives

After studying this chapter, you should be able to:

LO 9-1 Explain the advantages and disadvantages of the partnership versus the corporate form of business.

LO 9-2 Describe the purpose of the articles of partnership and list specific items that should be included in this agreement.

LO 9-3 Prepare the journal entry to record the initial capital investment made by a partner.

LO 9-4 Use both the bonus method and the goodwill method to record a partner's capital investment.

LO 9-5 Demonstrate the impact that the allocation of partnership income has on the partners' individual capital balances.

LO 9-6 Allocate income to partners when interest and/or salary factors are included.

LO 9-7 Explain the meaning of partnership dissolution and understand that a dissolution will often have little or no effect on the operations of the partnership business.

LO 9-8 Prepare journal entries to record the acquisition by a new partner of either all or a portion of a current partner's interest.

LO 9-9 Prepare journal entries to record a new partner's admission by a contribution made directly to the partnership.

LO 9-10 Prepare journal entries to record the withdrawal of a current partner.

[1] Internal Revenue Service, Publication 6292 (Rev. 8-2018), *Fiscal Year Return Projections for the United States: 2018–2025,* Washington, D.C. 20224.

[2] "Global Annual Review 2021," pwc.com.

[3] "Deloitte 2021 Global Impact Report," deloitte.com.

[4] "EY Building a Better Working World," ey.com.

LO 9-1

Explain the advantages and disadvantages of the partnership versus the corporate form of business.

Partnerships—Advantages and Disadvantages

The popularity of partnerships derives from several advantages inherent to this type of organization. An analysis of these attributes explains why millions of enterprises in the United States are partnerships rather than corporations.

One of the most common motives is the ease of formation. Only an oral agreement is necessary to create a legally binding partnership. In contrast, depending on specific state laws, incorporation requires filing a formal application and completing various other forms and documents. Operators of small businesses may find the convenience and reduced cost involved in creating a partnership to be an especially appealing characteristic. Tax advantages also can be found in the partnership form of business. As articulated by the American Bar Association:

> The principal advantage of partnerships is the ability to make virtually any arrangements defining their relationship to each other that the partners desire. There is no necessity, as there is in a corporation, to have the ownership interest in capital and profits proportionate to the investment made; and losses can be allocated on a different basis from profits. It is also generally much easier to achieve a desirable format for control of the business in a partnership than in a corporation, since the control of a corporation, which is based on ownership of voting stock, is much more difficult to alter . . .
>
> Partnerships are taxed on a conduit or flow-through basis under subchapter K of the Internal Revenue Code. This means that the partnership itself does not pay any taxes. Instead the net income and various deductions and tax credits from the partnership are passed through to the partners based on their respective percentage interest in the profits and losses of the partnership, and the partners include the income and deductions in their individual tax returns.[5]

Thus, partnership revenue and expense items (as defined by the tax laws) must be assigned directly each year to the individual partners who pay the income taxes. Passing income balances through to the partners in this manner avoids double taxation of the profits that are earned by a business and then distributed to its owners. A corporation's income is taxed twice: when earned and again when conveyed as a dividend. A partnership's income is taxed only at the time that the business initially earns it.

For example, assume that a business earns $100. After paying any income taxes, the remainder is immediately conveyed to its owners. An income tax rate of 25 percent (combined federal and state) is assumed for corporations and individuals. The tax rate on corporate dividends is assumed to be 15 percent.[6] As the following table shows, if this business is a partnership rather than a corporation, the owners have $11.25 more expendable income, which is 11.25 percent of the business income. Although potentially significant in amount, this difference narrows as tax rates are lowered.

	Partnership	Corporation
Income before income taxes	$100.00	$100.00
Income taxes paid by business (25%)	–0–	(25.00)
Income distributed to owners	$100.00	$ 75.00
Income taxes paid by owners*	(25.00)	(11.25)
Expendable income	$ 75.00	$ 63.75

*25 percent assumed rate on ordinary income; 15 percent assumed rate on dividend income.

Historically, another tax advantage has long been associated with partnerships. Because income is taxable to the partners as the business earns it, any operating losses can be used to reduce their personal taxable income directly. In contrast, a corporation is viewed as legally

[5] American Bar Association, Division for Public Education, *ABA Guide to Family Law,* July 16, 2020.

[6] Corporate dividends paid to shareholders are taxed either 0 percent, 15 percent, or 20 percent depending on their overall earnings level.

separate from its owners, so losses cannot be passed through to them. A corporation has the ability to carry forward indefinitely operating losses to decrease future taxable income (up to a maximum of 80 percent in any particular year). However, if a corporation is newly formed or has not been profitable, operating losses provide no immediate benefit to a corporation or its owners as losses do for a partnership.

The tax advantage of deducting partnership losses is limited, however. For tax purposes, ownership of a partnership is labeled as a passive activity unless the partner materially participates in the actual business activities. Passive activity losses thus serve only to offset other passive activity profits. In most cases, these partnership losses cannot be used to reduce earned income such as salaries. Thus, unless a taxpayer has significant passive activity income (from rents, for example), losses reported by a partnership create little or no tax advantage unless the partner materially participates in the actual business activity.

Another partnership tax advantage was created by the 2017 Tax Cuts and Jobs Act.[7] Eligible taxpayers, including those with partnership income, may be entitled to a deduction of up to 20 percent of qualified income from domestic "pass-through" businesses. Partnerships (along with other tax entities) must be considered a qualified trade or business for their owners to benefit from the 20 percent deduction. Even though many partnerships will be unable to qualify (e.g., health, law, accounting, financial services, etc.), others may qualify and thus entitle their partners to the 20 percent deduction for pass-through businesses.

The partnership form of business also has certain significant disadvantages. Perhaps the most severe problem is the unlimited liability that each partner automatically incurs. Partnership law specifies that any partner can be held personally liable for *all* debts of the business. The potential risk is especially significant when coupled with the concept of *mutual agency*. This legal term refers to the right that each partner has to incur liabilities in the name of the partnership. Consequently, partners acting within the normal scope of the business have the power to obligate the company for any amount. If the partnership fails to pay these debts, creditors can seek satisfactory remuneration from any partner that they choose.

Such legal concepts as unlimited liability and mutual agency describe partnership characteristics that have been defined and interpreted over a number of years. To provide consistent application across state lines in regard to these terms as well as many other legal aspects of a partnership, the Uniform Partnership Act (UPA) was created. This act, which was first proposed in 1914 (and revised in 1997), now has been adopted by all states in some form. It establishes uniform standards in such areas as the nature of a partnership, the relationship of the partners to outside parties, and the dissolution of the partnership. For example, Section 6 of the act provides the most common legal definition of a partnership: "an association of two or more persons to carry on a business as co-owners for profit."

Alternative Legal Forms

Because of the possible owner liability, partnerships often experience difficulty in attracting large amounts of capital. Potential partners frequently prefer to avoid the risk that is a basic characteristic of a partnership. However, the tax benefits of avoiding double taxation still provide a strong pull toward the partnership form. Hence, in recent years, a number of alternative types of organizations have been developed. The availability of these legal forms depends on state laws as well as applicable tax laws. In each case, however, the purpose is to limit the owners' personal liability while providing the tax benefits of a partnership.[8]

---

[7] *Tax Cuts and Jobs Act, Provision 11011 Section 199A—Qualified Business Income Deduction FAQs,* www.irs.gov.

[8] Many factors should be considered in choosing a specific legal form for an organization. The information shown here is merely an overview. For more information, consult a tax guide or a business law textbook. Also see Hopson and Hopson, "Making the Right Choice of Business Entity," *CPA Journal,* October 2014, pp. 42–47.

Subchapter S Corporation

A Subchapter S corporation (often referred to as an *S corporation*) is created as a corporation and, therefore, has all of the legal characteristics of that form.[9] According to U.S. tax laws, if the corporation meets certain regulations, it will be taxed in virtually the same way as a partnership. Thus, the Subchapter S corporation pays no income taxes, although any income (and losses) pass directly through to the taxable income of the individual owners. This form avoids double taxation, and the owners do not face unlimited liability. To qualify, the business can have only one class of stock and is limited to 100 stockholders. All owners must be individuals, estates, certain tax-exempt entities, or certain types of trusts. The most significant problem associated with this business form is that its growth potential is limited because of the restriction on the number and type of owners.

Limited Partnerships (LPs)

A *limited partnership* is a type of investment designed primarily for individuals who want the tax benefits of a partnership but who do not wish to work in a partnership or have unlimited liability. In such organizations, a number of limited partners invest money as owners but are not allowed to participate in the company's management. These partners can still incur a loss on their investment, but the amount is restricted to what has been contributed. To protect the creditors of a limited partnership, one or more general partners must be designated to assume responsibility for all obligations created in the name of the business.

Bloomberg, L.P., Enterprise Products, and the Blackstone Group are examples of limited partnerships of which the latter two are public companies. Private equity companies widely employ both general and limited partners for their investment funds.

Many limited partnerships were originally formed as tax shelters to create immediate losses (to reduce the taxable income of the partners) with profits spread out into the future. As mentioned earlier, tax laws limit the deduction of passive activity losses, and this significantly reduced the formation of limited partnerships.

Limited Liability Partnerships (LLPs)

The *limited liability partnership* has most of the characteristics of a general partnership except that it significantly reduces the partners' liability. Partners may lose their investment in the business and are responsible for the contractual debts of the business. The advantage here is created in connection with any liability resulting from damages. In such cases, the partners are responsible for only their own acts or omissions plus the acts and omissions of individuals under their supervision.

As Section 306(c) of the Uniform Partnership Act notes,

> An obligation of a partnership incurred while the partnership is a limited liability partnership, whether arising in contract, tort, or otherwise, is solely the obligation of the partnership. A partner is not personally liable, directly or indirectly, by way of contribution or otherwise, for such an obligation solely by reason of being or so acting as a partner.

Thus, a partner in the Houston office of a public accounting firm would probably not be held liable for a poor audit performed by that firm's San Francisco office. Not surprisingly, limited liability partnerships have become very popular with professional service organizations that have multiple offices. For example, all of the four largest accounting firms are LLPs.

Limited Liability Companies (LLCs)

The limited liability company was first seen in the United States in 1977. By 1996, all 50 states had LLC statutes approved. Currently, it is estimated that two-thirds of all new companies in the United States are LLCs.[10] An LLC is classified as a partnership for tax purposes and court purposes. However, depending on state laws, the owners risk only their own investments. Thus, similar to a Subchapter S entity, the LLC provides liability protection for its owners and managers. In contrast to a Subchapter S corporation, the number of owners is not usually restricted, so growth may be easier to accomplish.

---

[9] Unless a corporation qualifies as a Subchapter S corporation or some other legal variation, it is referred to as a *Subchapter C corporation.* Therefore, a vast majority of all businesses are C corporations.

[10] "The History of LLCS," *IncNow,* January 18, 2018.

Partnership Accounting—Capital Accounts

Despite legal distinctions, questions should be raised as to the need for an entirely separate study of partnership accounting:

- Does an association of two or more persons require accounting procedures significantly different from those of a corporation?
- Does proper accounting depend on the legal form of an organization?

The answers to these questions are both yes and no. Accounting procedures are normally standardized for assets, liabilities, revenues, and expenses, regardless of the legal form of a business. *Partnership accounting, though, does exhibit unique aspects that warrant study, but they lie primarily in the handling of the partners' capital accounts.*

The stockholders' equity accounts of a corporation do not correspond directly with the capital balances found in a partnership's financial records. The various equity accounts reported by an incorporated enterprise display a greater range of information. This characteristic reflects the wide variety of equity transactions that can occur in a corporation as well as the influence of state and federal laws. Government regulation has had an enormous effect on the accounting for corporate equity transactions in that extensive disclosure is required to protect stockholders and other outside parties such as potential investors.

To provide adequate information and to meet legal requirements, corporate accounting must provide details about a variety of equity transactions and account balances. For example, the amount of a corporation's paid-in capital is shown separately from earned capital (retained earnings) and accumulated other comprehensive income; the par value of each class of stock is disclosed; treasury stock, stock options, stock dividends, and other capital transactions are reported based on prescribed accounting principles.

In contrast, partnerships provide only limited equity disclosures primarily in the form of individual capital accounts that are accumulated for every partner or every class of partners. These balances measure each partner's or group's interest in the book value of the net assets of the business. Thus, the equity section of a partnership balance sheet is composed solely of capital accounts that can be affected by many different events: contributions from partners as well as distributions to them, earnings, and any other equity transactions.

However, partnership accounting does not differentiate between the various sources of ownership capital. Disclosing the composition of the partners' capital balances has not been judged necessary because partnerships have historically tended to be small with equity transactions that were rarely complex. Additionally, absentee ownership is not common, a factor that minimizes both the need for government regulation and outside interest in detailed information about the capital balances.

Articles of Partnership

LO 9-2

Describe the purpose of the articles of partnership and list specific items that should be included in this agreement.

Because the demand for information about capital balances is limited, accounting principles specific to partnerships are based primarily on traditional approaches that have evolved over the years rather than on official pronouncements. These procedures attempt to mirror the relationship between the partners and their business, especially as defined by the partnership agreement. This legal covenant, which may be either oral or written, is often referred to as the *articles of partnership* and forms the central governance for a partnership's operation. The financial arrangements spelled out in this contract establish guidelines for the various capital transactions. Therefore, the articles of partnership, rather than either laws or official rules, provide much of the underlying basis for partnership accounting.

Because the articles of partnership are a negotiated agreement that the partners create, an unlimited number of variations can be encountered in practice. Partners' rights and responsibilities frequently differ from business to business. Consequently, firms often hire accountants in an advisory capacity to participate in creating this document to ensure the equitable treatment of all parties. Although the articles of partnership may contain a number of provisions, an explicit understanding should always be reached in regards to the following:

- Name and address of each partner.
- Business location.

? Discussion Question

WHAT KIND OF BUSINESS IS THIS?

After graduating from college, Shelley Williams held several different jobs but found that she did not enjoy working for other people. Finally, she and Yvonne Hargrove, her college roommate, decided to start a business of their own. They rented a small building and opened a florist shop selling cut flowers such as roses and chrysanthemums that they bought from a local greenhouse.

Williams and Hargrove agreed orally to share profits and losses equally, although they also decided to take no money from the operation for at least four months. No other arrangements were made, but the business did reasonably well, and after the first four months had passed, each began to draw out $500 in cash every week.

At year-end, they took their financial records to a local accountant so that they could get their income tax returns completed. He informed them that they had been operating as a partnership and that they should draw up formal articles of partnership agreement or consider incorporation or some other legal form of organization. They confessed that they had never really considered the issue and asked for his advice on the matter.

What advice should the accountant give to these clients?

- Description of the nature of the business.
- Rights and responsibilities of each partner.
- Initial contribution to be made by each partner and the method to be used for valuation.
- Specific method by which profits and losses are to be allocated.
- Periodic withdrawal of assets by each partner.
- Procedure for admitting new partners.
- Method for arbitrating partnership disputes.
- Life insurance provisions enabling remaining partners to acquire the interest of any deceased partner.
- Method for settling a partner's share in the business upon withdrawal, retirement, or death.

Accounting for Capital Contributions

LO 9-3

Prepare the journal entry to record the initial capital investment made by a partner.

Several types of capital transactions occur in a partnership: allocation of profits and losses, retirement of a current partner, admission of a new partner, and so on. The initial transaction, however, is the contribution the original partners make to begin the business. In the simplest situation, the partners invest only cash amounts. For example, assume that Carter and Green form a business to be operated as a partnership. Carter contributes $50,000 in cash, and Green invests $20,000. The initial journal entry to record the creation of this partnership follows:

Cash	70,000	
Carter, Capital		50,000
Green, Capital		20,000
To record cash contributed to start new partnership.		

The assumption that the partners invested only cash avoids complications in this first illustration. Often, though, one or more of the partners transfers noncash assets such as inventory, land, equipment, or a building to the business. Although partnerships record asset contributions at fair value, a case could be developed for initially valuing any contributed asset at the partner's current book value. According to the concept of unlimited liability (as well as present tax laws), a partnership does not exist as an entity apart from its owners. A logical extension of the idea is that the investment of an asset is not a transaction occurring between two independent parties such as would warrant revaluation. This contention holds that the semblance of an arm's-length transaction is necessary to justify a change in the book value of any account.

Although retaining the recorded value for assets contributed to a partnership may seem reasonable, this method of valuation proves to be inequitable to any partner investing appreciated property. A $50,000 capital balance always results from a cash investment of that amount, but recording other assets depends entirely on the original book value.

For example, should a partner who contributes a building having a recorded value of $18,000 but a fair value of $50,000 be credited with only an $18,000 interest in the partnership? Because $50,000 in cash and $50,000 in appreciated property are equivalent contributions, a $32,000 difference in the partners' capital balances cannot be justified. To prevent such inequities, each item transferred to a partnership is initially recorded for external reporting purposes at current value.[11]

Requiring revaluation of contributed assets can, however, be advocated for reasons other than just the fair treatment of all partners. Despite some evidence to the contrary, a partnership can be viewed legitimately as an entity standing apart from its owners. As an example, a partnership maintains legal ownership of its assets and (depending on state law) can initiate lawsuits. For this reason, accounting practice traditionally has held that the contribution of assets (and liabilities) to a partnership is an exchange between two separately identifiable parties that should be recorded based on fair values.

Determining an appropriate valuation for each capital balance is more than just an accounting exercise. Over the life of a partnership, these figures serve in a number of important capacities:

1. The totals in the individual capital accounts often influence the assignment of profits and losses to the partners.
2. The capital account balance is usually one factor in determining the final distribution that will be received by a partner at the time of withdrawal or retirement.
3. Ending capital balances indicate the allocation to be made of any assets that remain following the liquidation of a partnership.

To demonstrate, assume that Carter invests $50,000 in cash to begin the previously discussed partnership and Green contributes the following assets:

	Book Value to Green	Fair Value
Inventory	$ 9,000	$10,000
Land	14,000	11,000
Building	32,000	46,000
Totals	$55,000	$67,000

As an added factor, Green's building is encumbered by a $23,600 mortgage that the partnership has agreed to assume.

Green's net investment is equal to $43,400 ($67,000 − $23,600). The following journal entry records the formation of the partnership created by these contributions:

Cash	50,000	
Inventory	10,000	
Land	11,000	
Building	46,000	
Mortgage Payable		23,600
Carter, Capital		50,000
Green, Capital		43,400
To record properties contributed to start partnership. Assets and liabilities are recorded at fair value.		

[11] For federal income tax purposes, the $18,000 book value is retained as the basis for this building, even after transfer to the partnership. Within the tax laws, no difference is seen between partners and their partnership, so no adjustment to fair value is warranted.

We should make one additional point before leaving this illustration. Although having contributed inventory, land, and a building, Green holds no further right to these individual assets; they now belong to the partnership. The $43,400 capital balance represents an ownership interest in the business as a whole but does not constitute a specific claim to any asset. Having transferred title to the partnership, Green has no more right to these assets than does Carter.

LO 9-4

Use both the bonus method and the goodwill method to record a partner's capital investment.

Intangible Contributions

In forming a partnership, the contributions made by one or more of the partners may go beyond assets and liabilities. A doctor, for example, can bring a particular line of expertise to a partnership, and a practicing dentist might have already developed an established patient list. These attributes, as well as many others, are frequently as valuable to a partnership as cash and fixed assets. *Hence, formal accounting recognition of such special contributions may be appropriately included as a provision of any partnership agreement.*

To illustrate, assume that James and Joyce plan to open an advertising agency, and they decide to organize the endeavor as a partnership. James contributes cash of $70,000, and Joyce invests only $10,000. Joyce, however, is an accomplished graphic artist, a skill that is considered especially valuable to this business. Therefore, in producing the articles of partnership, the partners agree to start the business with equal capital balances. Often such decisions result only after long, and sometimes heated, negotiations. Because the value assigned to an intangible contribution such as artistic talent is arbitrary at best, proper reporting depends on the partners' ability to arrive at an equitable arrangement.

In recording this agreement, James and Joyce have two options: (1) the bonus method and (2) the goodwill method. Each of these approaches achieves the desired result of establishing equal capital account balances. Recorded figures can vary significantly, however, depending on the procedure selected. Thus, the partners should reach an understanding prior to beginning business operations as to the method to be used. The accountant can help avoid conflicts by assisting the partners in evaluating the impact created by each of these alternatives.

The Bonus Method The bonus method assumes that a specialization such as Joyce's artistic abilities does *not* constitute a recordable partnership asset with a measurable cost. Hence, this approach recognizes only the assets that are physically transferred to the business (such as cash, patents, and inventory). Although these contributions determine total partnership capital, the establishment of specific capital balances is viewed as an independent process based solely on the partners' agreement. Because the initial equity figures result from negotiation, they do not need to correspond directly with the individual investments.

James and Joyce have contributed a total of $80,000 in identifiable assets to their partnership and have decided on equal capital balances. According to the bonus method, this agreement is fulfilled simply by splitting the $80,000 capital evenly between the two partners. The following entry records the formation of this partnership under this assumption:

Cash	80,000	
James, Capital		40,000
Joyce, Capital		40,000
To record cash contributions with bonus to Joyce because of artistic abilities.		

Joyce received a *capital bonus* here of $30,000 (the $40,000 recorded capital balance in excess of the $10,000 cash contribution) from James in recognition of the artistic abilities she brought into the business.

The Goodwill Method The goodwill method is based on the assumption that an implied value can be calculated mathematically and recorded for any intangible contribution made by a partner. In the present illustration, Joyce invested $60,000 less cash than James but receives an equal amount of capital according to the partnership agreement. Proponents of the goodwill method argue that Joyce's artistic talent has an apparent value of $60,000, a figure that should be included as part of this partner's capital investment. If not recorded, Joyce's primary contribution to the business is ignored completely within the accounting records.

Cash	80,000	
Goodwill	60,000	
James, Capital		70,000
Joyce, Capital		70,000
To record cash contributions with goodwill attributed to Joyce in recognition of artistic abilities.		

Comparison of Methods   Both approaches achieve the intent of the partnership agreement: to record equal capital balances despite a difference in the partners' cash contributions. The bonus method allocates the $80,000 invested capital according to the percentages designated by the partners, whereas the goodwill method capitalizes the implied value of Joyce's intangible contribution.

Although nothing prohibits the use of either technique, the recognition of goodwill poses definite theoretical problems. In previous discussions of both the equity method (Chapter 1) and business combinations (Chapter 2), goodwill was recognized but only as a result of an acquisition made by the reporting entity. Consequently, this asset had a historical cost in the traditional accounting sense. Partnership goodwill has no such cost; the business recognizes an asset even though no funds have been spent.

The partnership of James and Joyce, for example, is able to record $60,000 in goodwill without any expenditure. Furthermore, the value attributed to this asset is based solely on a negotiated agreement between the partners; the $60,000 balance has no objectively verifiable basis. Thus, although partnership goodwill is sometimes encountered in actual practice, this "asset" should be viewed with a strong degree of professional skepticism.

Additional Capital Contributions and Withdrawals

Subsequent to forming a partnership, the owners may choose to contribute additional capital amounts during the life of the business. These investments can be made to stimulate expansion or to assist the business in overcoming working capital shortages or other problems. Regardless of the reason, the contribution is again recorded as an increment in the partner's capital account based on fair value. For example, in the previous illustration, assume that James decides to invest another $5,000 cash in the partnership to help finance the purchase of new office furnishings. The partner's capital account balance is immediately increased by this amount to reflect the transfer to the partnership.[12]

In many instances, the articles of partnership allow withdrawals on a regular periodic basis as a reward for ownership or as compensation for work performed for the business. Often such distributions are recorded initially in a separate drawing account that is closed into the individual partner's capital account at year-end. Assume for illustration purposes that James and Joyce take out $1,200 and $1,500, respectively, from their business. The journal entry to record these payments is as follows:

James, Drawing	1,200	
Joyce, Drawing	1,500	
Cash		2,700
To record withdrawal of cash by partners.		

Larger amounts might also be withdrawn from a partnership on occasion. A partner may have a special need for money or just desire to reduce the basic investment that has been made in the business. Such transactions are usually sporadic occurrences and entail amounts significantly higher than the partner's periodic drawing. The articles of partnership may require prior approval by the other partners.

---

[12] The partners also may reverse this process by withdrawing assets from the business for their own personal use. To protect the interests of the other partners, the articles of partnership should clearly specify the amount and timing of such withdrawals.

? Discussion Question

HOW WILL THE PROFITS BE SPLIT?

James J. Dewars has been the sole owner of a small CPA firm for the past 20 years. Now 52 years old, Dewars is concerned about the continuation of his practice after he retires. He would like to begin taking more time off now although he wants to remain active in the firm for at least another 8 to 10 years. He has worked hard over the decades to build up the practice so that he presently makes a profit of $180,000 annually.

Lewis Huffman has been working for Dewars for the past four years. He now earns a salary of $68,000 per year. He is a very dedicated employee who generally works 44 to 60 hours per week. In the past, Dewars has been in charge of the larger, more profitable audit clients, whereas Huffman, with less experience, worked with the smaller clients. Both Dewars and Huffman do some tax work although that segment of the business has never been emphasized.

Sally Scriba has been employed for the past seven years with another CPA firm as a tax specialist. She has no auditing experience but has a great reputation in tax planning and preparation. She currently earns an annual salary of $80,000.

Dewars, Huffman, and Scriba are negotiating the creation of a new CPA firm as a partnership. Dewars plans to reduce his time in this firm, although he will continue to work with many of the clients that he has served for the past two decades. Huffman will begin to take over some of the major audit jobs. Scriba will start to develop an extensive tax practice for the firm.

Because of the changes in the firm, the three potential partners anticipate earning a total net income in the first year of operations of between $130,000 and $260,000. Thereafter, they hope that profits will increase at the rate of 10 to 20 percent annually for the next five years or so.

How should this new partnership allocate its future net income among these partners?

LO 9-5

Demonstrate the impact that the allocation of partnership income has on the partners' individual capital balances.

Allocation of Income

At the end of each fiscal period, partnership revenues and expenses are closed out, accompanied by an allocation of the resulting net income or loss to the partners' capital accounts. Because a separate capital balance is maintained for each partner, a method must be devised for this assignment of annual income. Because of the importance of the process, the articles of partnership should always stipulate the procedure the partners established. If no arrangement has been specified, state partnership law normally holds that all partners receive an equal allocation of any income or loss earned by the business. If the partnership agreement specifies only the division of profits, then losses must be divided in the same manner as directed for profit allocation.

The profit allocation pattern can be important to the success of any organization because it can help emphasize and reward outstanding performance. Therefore, many partner compensation plans recognize contributions to revenue, growth, time spent with the firm, management skill development, or any other attribute the partnership deems important. Profit allocation plans can thus become complex in attempting to recognize and reward the various elements of each partner's contributions to the firm's success. Alternatively, partnerships can avoid all complications by assigning net income on an equal basis among all partners.

As an initial illustration, assume that Tinker, Evers, and Chance form a partnership by investing cash of $120,000, $90,000, and $75,000, respectively. The articles of partnership agreement specifies that Evers will be allotted 40 percent of all profits and losses because of previous business experience. Tinker and Chance are to divide the remaining 60 percent equally. This agreement also stipulates that each partner is allowed to withdraw $10,000 in cash annually from the business. The amount of this withdrawal does not directly depend on the method utilized for income allocation. *From an accounting perspective, the assignment of income and the setting of withdrawal limits are two separate decisions.*

At the end of the first year of operations, the partnership reports net income of $60,000. To reflect the changes made in the partners' capital balances, the closing process consists of the following two journal entries. The assumption is made here that each partner has taken the allowed amount of drawing during the year. In addition, for convenience, all revenues and expenses already have been closed into the Income Summary account.

Tinker, Capital	10,000	
Evers, Capital	10,000	
Chance, Capital	10,000	
Tinker, Drawing		10,000
Evers, Drawing		10,000
Chance, Drawing		10,000
To close out drawing accounts recording payments made to the three partners.		

Income Summary	60,000	
Tinker, Capital (30%)		18,000
Evers, Capital (40%)		24,000
Chance, Capital (30%)		18,000
To allocate net income based on provisions of partnership agreement.		

Statement of Partners' Capital

Because a partnership does not separately disclose a retained earnings balance, the statement of retained earnings usually reported by a corporation is replaced by a statement of partners' capital. The following financial statement is based on the data presented for the partnership of Tinker, Evers, and Chance. The changes made during the year in the individual capital accounts are outlined along with totals representing the partnership as a whole:

TINKER, EVERS, AND CHANCE
Statement of Partners' Capital
For Year Ending December 31, Year 1

	Tinker, Capital	Evers, Capital	Chance, Capital	Totals
Capital balances beginning of year.	$120,000	$ 90,000	$75,000	$285,000
Allocation of net income	18,000	24,000	18,000	60,000
Drawings.	(10,000)	(10,000)	(10,000)	(30,000)
Capital balances end of year	$128,000	$104,000	$83,000	$315,000

LO 9-6

Allocate income to partners when interest and/or salary factors are included.

Alternative Allocation Techniques—Example 1

Assigning net income based on a ratio may be simple, but this approach is not necessarily equitable to all partners. For example, assume that Tinker does not participate in the partnership's operations but is the contributor of the highest amount of capital. Evers and Chance both work full time in the business, but Evers has considerably more experience in this line of work.

Under these circumstances, no single ratio is likely to reflect properly the various contributions made by each partner. Indeed, an unlimited number of alternative allocation plans could be devised in hopes of achieving fair treatment for all parties. For example, because of the different levels of capital investments, consideration should be given to including interest within the allocation process to reward the contributions. A compensation allowance is also a possibility, usually in an amount corresponding to the number of hours worked or the level of a partner's business expertise.

To demonstrate one possible option, assume that Tinker, Evers, and Chance begin their partnership based on the original facts except that they arrive at a more detailed method of allocating profits and losses. After considerable negotiation, an articles of partnership agreement credits each partner annually for interest in an amount equal to 10 percent of that partner's beginning capital balance for the year. Evers and Chance also will be allotted $15,000 each as a compensation allowance in recognition of their participation in daily operations. Any remaining profit or loss will be split 3:4:3, with the largest share going to Evers because of the work experience that this partner brings to the business. As with any appropriate allocation, this pattern attempts to provide fair treatment for all three partners.

Under this arrangement, the $60,000 net income earned by the partnership in the first year of operation would be allocated as follows. The sequential alignment of the various provisions is irrelevant except that the ratio, which is used to assign the remaining profit or loss, must be calculated last.

Allocation of Partnership Net Income	Tinker	Evers	Chance	Total
Net Income				$ 60,000
Interest (10% of beginning capital)	$12,000	$9,000	$7,500	(28,500)
Net income remaining after interest				$ 31,500
Compensation allowance	–0–	15,000	15,000	(30,000)
Net income remaining after interest and compensation				$ 1,500
Remaining income distribution	450 (30%)	600 (40%)	450 (30%)	(1,500)
Net income allocation totals	$12,450	$24,600	$22,950	$ –0–

Importantly, the schedule computing the division of income must be completed prior to determining the final capital balances for the partners. For the Tinker, Evers, and Chance partnership, the allocations just calculated lead to the following year-end closing entry:

Income Summary	60,000	
Tinker, Capital		12,450
Evers, Capital		24,600
Chance, Capital		22,950
To allocate income for the year to the individual partners' capital accounts based on partnership agreement.		

Alternative Allocation Techniques—Example 2

As the preceding illustration indicates, the assignment process is no more than a series of mechanical steps reflecting the change in each partner's capital balance resulting from the provisions of the partnership agreement. The number of different allocation procedures that could be employed is limited solely by the partners' imagination. Although interest, compensation allowances, and various ratios are the predominant factors encountered in practice, other possibilities exist. Therefore, another approach to the allocation process is presented to further illustrate some of the variations that can be utilized. A two-person partnership is used here to simplify the computations.

Assume that Webber and Rice formed a partnership several years ago to operate a coffee shop. Webber contributed the initial capital, and Rice manages the business. With the assistance of their accountant, they wrote an articles of partnership agreement that contains the following provisions:

1. Each partner is allowed to draw $1,000 in cash from the business every month. Any withdrawal in excess of that figure will be accounted for as a direct reduction to the partner's capital balance.
2. Partnership profits and losses will be allocated each year according to the following plan:
   a. Each partner will earn 15 percent interest based on the monthly average capital balance for the year (calculated without regard for normal drawings or current income).

b. As a reward for operating the business, Rice is to receive credit for a bonus equal to 20 percent of the year's net income. However, no bonus is earned if the partnership reports a net loss.

c. The two partners will divide any remaining profit or loss equally.

Assume that Webber and Rice subsequently begin the current year with capital balances of $150,000 and $30,000, respectively. On April 1 of the current year, Webber invests an additional $8,000 cash in the business, and on July 1, Rice withdraws $6,000 in excess of the specified drawing allowance. Assume further that the partnership reports income of $30,000 for the current year.

Because the interest factor established in this allocation plan is based on a monthly average figure, the specific amount to be credited to each partner is determined by means of a preliminary calculation:

Webber—Interest Allocation

Beginning balance...	$150,000 × 3 months =	$ 450,000
Balance, April 1......	$158,000 × 9 months =	1,422,000
		1,872,000
		× ½
Monthly average capital balance		156,000
Interest rate.........................		× 15%
Interest credited to Webber		$ 23,400

Rice—Interest Allocation

Beginning balance...	$30,000 × 6 months =	$180,000
Balance, July 1	$24,000 × 6 months =	144,000
		324,000
		× ½
Monthly average capital balance		27,000
Interest rate.........................		× 15%
Interest credited to Rice		$ 4,050

Following this initial computation, the actual income assignment can proceed according to the provisions specified in the articles of partnership. The stipulations drawn by Webber and Rice must be followed exactly, even though the business's $30,000 profit for the current year is not sufficient to cover both the interest and the bonus. Income allocation is a mechanical process that should always be carried out as stated in the articles of partnership without regard to the specific level of income or loss.

Based on the plan that was created, Webber's capital increases by $21,675 during the current year, but Rice's account increases by only $8,325:

Allocation of Partnership Net Income	Weber	Rice	Total
Net Income			$ 30,000
Interest (above).............................	$23,400	$4,050	(27,450)
Net income remaining after interest.............			$ 2,550
Bonus to Rice (20% × $30,000)	0	6,000	(6,000)
Net income (loss) remaining after interest and bonus....................................			(3,450)
Remaining income (loss) distribution	(1,725) (50%)	(1,725) (50%)	$ 3,450
Net income allocation totals	$21,675	$8,325	$ -0-

As discussed earlier, the interest and bonus allocations sum to $33,450 and thus exceed the available net income of $30,000. The remaining overallocation of $3,450 is then treated as a loss in allocating the partnership's income to the individual partners.

LO 9-7

Explain the meaning of partnership dissolution and understand that a dissolution will often have little or no effect on the operations of the partnership business.

Accounting for Partnership Dissolution

Many partnerships limit capital transactions almost exclusively to contributions, drawings, and profit and loss allocations. Normally, though, over any extended period, changes in the members who make up a partnership occur. Employees may be promoted into the partnership or new owners brought in from outside the organization to add capital or expertise to the business. Current partners eventually retire, die, or simply elect to leave the partnership. Large operations may even experience such changes on a routine basis.

Regardless of the nature or the frequency of the event, any alteration in the specific individuals composing a partnership automatically leads to legal dissolution. In many instances, the breakup is merely a prerequisite to the formation of a new partnership. For example, if Abernethy and Chapman decide to allow Miller to become a partner in their business, the legally recognized partnership of Abernethy and Chapman has to be dissolved first. The business property as well as the right to future profits can then be conveyed to the newly formed partnership of Abernethy, Chapman, and Miller. The change is a legal one. Actual operations of the business would probably continue unimpeded by this alteration in ownership.

Conversely, should the partners so choose, dissolution can be a preliminary step in the termination and liquidation of the business. The death of a partner, lack of sufficient profits, or internal management differences can lead the partners to break up the partnership business. Under this circumstance, the partnership sells properties, pays debts, and distributes any remaining assets to the individual partners. Thus, in liquidations (which are analyzed in detail in the next chapter), both the partnership and the business cease to exist.

Dissolution—Admission of a New Partner

One of the most prevalent changes in the makeup of a partnership is the addition of a new partner. An employee may have worked for years to gain this opportunity, or a prospective partner might offer the new investment capital or business experience necessary for future business success. An individual can gain admittance to a partnership in one of two ways: (1) by purchasing an ownership interest from a current partner or (2) by contributing assets directly to the business.

In recording either type of transaction, the accountant has the option, once again, to retain the book value of all partnership assets and liabilities (as exemplified by the bonus method) or revalue these accounts to their present fair values (the goodwill method). The decision as to a theoretical preference between the bonus and goodwill methods hinges on one single question: *Should the dissolved partnership and the newly formed partnership be viewed as two separate reporting entities?*

If the new partnership is merely an extension of the old, no basis exists for restatement. The transfer of ownership is a change only in a legal sense and has no direct impact on business assets and liabilities. However, if the continuation of the business represents a legitimate transfer of property from one partnership to another, revaluation of all accounts and recognition of goodwill can be justified.

Because both approaches are encountered in practice, this textbook presents each. However, the concerns previously discussed in connection with partnership goodwill still exist: Recognition is not based on historical cost, and no objective verification of the capitalized amount can be made. One alternative revaluation approach that attempts to circumvent the problems involved with partnership goodwill has been devised. This hybrid method revalues all partnership assets and liabilities to fair value without making any corresponding recognition of goodwill.

LO 9-8

Prepare journal entries to record the acquisition by a new partner of either all or a portion of a current partner's interest.

Admission through Purchase of a Current Interest

As mentioned, one method of gaining admittance to a partnership is by the purchase of a current interest. One or more partners can choose to sell their portion of the business to an outside party. This type of transaction is most common in operations that rely primarily on monetary capital rather than on the business expertise of the partners.

In making a transfer of ownership, a partner can actually convey only three rights:

1. *The right of co-ownership in the business property.* This right justifies the partner's periodic drawings from the business as well as the distribution settlement paid at liquidation or at the time of a partner's withdrawal.

2. *The right to share in profits and losses as specified in the articles of partnership.*

3. *The right to participate in the management of the business.*

Unless restricted by the articles of partnership, every partner has the power to sell or assign the first two of these rights at any time. Their transfer poses no threat of financial harm to the remaining partners. In contrast, partnership law states that the right to participate in the management of the business can be conveyed only with the consent of all partners. This particular right is considered essential to the future earning power of the enterprise as well as the maintenance of business assets. Therefore, current partners are protected from the intrusion of parties who might be considered detrimental to the management of the company.

As an illustration, assume that Scott, Thompson, and York formed a partnership several years ago. Subsequently, York decides to leave the partnership and offers to sell his interest to Morgan. Although York may transfer the right of property ownership as well as the specified share of future profits and losses, the partnership does not automatically admit Morgan. York legally remains a partner until such time as both Scott and Thompson agree to allow Morgan to participate in the management of the business.

To demonstrate the accounting procedures applicable to the transfer of a partnership interest, assume that the following information is available relating to the partnership of Scott, Thompson, and York:

Partner	Capital Balance	Profit and Loss Ratio
Scott	$ 50,000	20%
Thompson	30,000	50
York	20,000	30
Total capital	$100,000	

As often happens, the relationship of the capital accounts to one another does not correspond with the partners' profit and loss ratio. Capital balances are historical cost figures. They result from contributions and withdrawals made throughout the life of the business as well as from the allocation of partnership income. Therefore, any correlation between a partner's recorded capital at a particular point in time and the profit and loss percentage would probably be coincidental. Scott, for example, has 50 percent of the current partnership capital ($50,000/$100,000) but is entitled to only a 20 percent allocation of income.

Instead of York selling his interest to Morgan, assume that each of these three partners elects to transfer a 20 percent interest to Morgan for a total payment of $30,000. According to the sales contract, *the money is to be paid directly to the owners.*

One approach to recording this transaction is that, because Morgan's purchase is carried out between the individual parties, the acquisition has no impact on partnership assets and liabilities. Because the business is not involved directly, the transfer of ownership requires a simple capital reclassification without any accompanying revaluation. This approach is similar to the bonus method; only a legal change in ownership is occurring so that revaluation of neither assets or liabilities nor goodwill is appropriate.

Book Value Method

Scott, Capital (20% of capital balance)	10,000	
Thompson, Capital (20%)	6,000	
York, Capital (20%)	4,000	
Morgan, Capital (20% of total)		20,000
To reclassify capital to reflect Morgan's acquisition. Money is paid directly to partners.		

An alternative for recording Morgan's acquisition relies on a different perspective of the new partner's admission. Legally, the partnership of Scott, Thompson, and York is transferring all assets and liabilities to the partnership of Scott, Thompson, York, and Morgan.

Therefore, according to the logic underlying the goodwill method, a transaction is occurring between two separate reporting entities, an event that necessitates the complete revaluation of all assets and liabilities.

Because Morgan is paying $30,000 for a 20 percent interest in the partnership, the implied value of the business as a whole is $150,000 ($30,000/20%). However, the book value is only $100,000; thus, a $50,000 upward revaluation is indicated. This adjustment is reflected by restating specific partnership asset and liability accounts to fair value with any remaining balance recorded as goodwill.

Goodwill (Revaluation) Method

Goodwill (or specific accounts)	50,000	
Scott, Capital (20% of goodwill)		10,000
Thompson, Capital (50%)		25,000
York, Capital (30%)		15,000
To recognize goodwill and revaluation of assets and liabilities based on value of business implied by Morgan's purchase price.		

Note that this entry credits the $50,000 revaluation to the original partners based on the profit and loss ratio rather than on capital percentages. Recognition of goodwill (or an increase in the book value of specific accounts) indicates that unrecorded gains have accrued to the business during previous years of operation. Therefore, the equitable treatment is to allocate this increment among the partners according to their profit and loss percentages. After the implied value of the partnership is established, the reclassification of ownership can be recorded based on the new capital balances as follows:

Scott, Capital (20% × new $60,000 capital balance)	12,000	
Thompson, Capital (20% × $55,000)	11,000	
York, Capital (20% × $35,000)	7,000	
Morgan, Capital (20% × $150,000 new total)		30,000
To reclassify capital to reflect Morgan's acquisition. Money is paid directly to partners.		

LO 9-9

Prepare journal entries to record a new partner's admission by a contribution made directly to the partnership.

Admission by a Contribution Made to the Partnership

Entrance into a partnership is not limited solely to the purchase of a current partner's interest. An outsider may be admitted to the ownership by contributing cash or other assets directly to the business rather than to the partners. For example, assume that King and Wilson maintain a partnership and presently report capital balances of $80,000 and $20,000, respectively. According to the articles of partnership, King is entitled to 60 percent of all profits and losses with the remaining 40 percent credited each year to Wilson. By agreement of the partners, Goldman is allowed to enter the partnership for a payment of $20,000 *with this money going into the business.* Based on negotiations that preceded the acquisition, all parties have agreed that Goldman receives an initial 10 percent interest in the net assets of the partnership.

Bonus Credited to Original Partners   The bonus (or no revaluation) method maintains the same recorded value for all partnership assets and liabilities despite Goldman's admittance. The capital balance for this new partner is simply set at the appropriate 10 percent level based on the total net assets of the partnership after the payment is recorded. Because $20,000 is invested, total reported capital increases to $120,000. Thus, Goldman's 10 percent interest is computed as $12,000. *The $8,000 difference between the amount contributed and this allotted capital balance is viewed as a bonus.* Because Goldman is willing to accept a capital balance that is less than his investment, this bonus is attributed to the original partners (again based on their profit and loss ratio). As a result of the nature of the transaction, no need exists to recognize goodwill or revalue any of the assets or liabilities.

Cash	20,000	
Goldman, Capital (10% of total capital)		12,000
King, Capital (60% of bonus)		4,800
Wilson, Capital (40% of bonus)		3,200
To record Goldman's entrance into partnership with $8,000 extra payment recorded as a bonus to the original partners.		

Goodwill Credited to Original Partners   The goodwill method views Goldman's payment as evidence that the partnership as a whole possesses an actual value of $200,000 ($20,000/10%). Because—even with the new partner's investment—only $120,000 in net assets is reported, a valuation adjustment of $80,000 is implied.[13] Over the previous years, unrecorded gains have apparently accrued to the business. This $80,000 figure might reflect the need to revalue specific accounts such as inventory or equipment, although the entire amount, or some portion of it, may simply be recorded as goodwill.

Goodwill (or specific accounts)	80,000	
King, Capital (60% of goodwill)		48,000
Wilson, Capital (40%)		32,000
To recognize goodwill based on Goldman's purchase price.		
Cash	20,000	
Goldman, Capital		20,000
To record Goldman's admission into partnership.		

Comparison of Bonus Method and Goodwill Method   Completely different capital balances as well as asset and liability figures result from these two approaches. In both cases, however, the new partner is credited with the appropriate 10 percent of total partnership capital.

	Bonus Method	Goodwill Method
Assets less liabilities (as reported)	$100,000	$100,000
Goldman's contribution	20,000	20,000
Goodwill	–0–	80,000
Total	$120,000	$200,000
Goldman's capital	$ 12,000	$ 20,000

Because Goldman contributed an amount more than 10 percent of the partnership's resulting book value, this business is perceived as being worth more than the recorded accounts indicate. Therefore, the bonus in the first instance and the goodwill in the second were both assumed as accruing to the two original partners. Such a presumption is not unusual in an established business, especially if profitable operations have developed over a number of years.

Hybrid Method of Recording Admission of New Partner   One other approach to Goldman's admission can be devised. Assume that the assets and liabilities of the King and Wilson partnership have a book value of $100,000, as stated earlier. Also assume that a piece of land held by the business is actually worth $30,000 more than its currently recorded book value. Thus, the identifiable assets of the partnership are worth $130,000. Goldman pays $20,000 for a 10 percent interest.

[13] In this example, because $20,000 is invested in the business, total capital to be used in the goodwill computation has increased to $120,000. If, as in the previous illustration, payment had been made directly to the partners, the original capital of $100,000 is retained in determining goodwill.

In this approach, the identifiable assets (such as land) are revalued, but no goodwill is recognized.

Land	30,000	
King, Capital (60% of revaluation)		18,000
Wilson, Capital (40%)		12,000
To record current fair value of land in preparation for admission of new partner.		

The admission of Goldman and the payment of $20,000 bring the total capital balance to $150,000. Because Goldman is acquiring a 10 percent interest, a capital balance of $15,000 is recorded. The extra $5,000 payment ($20,000 − $15,000) is attributed as a bonus to the original partners. In this way, asset revaluation and a capital bonus are both used to align the accounts.

Cash	20,000	
Goldman, Capital (10% of total capital)		15,000
King, Capital (60% of bonus)		3,000
Wilson, Capital (40% of bonus)		2,000
To record entrance of Goldman into partnership and bonus assigned to original partners.		

Bonus or Goodwill Credited to New Partner As previously discussed, Goldman also may be contributing some attribute other than tangible assets to this partnership. Therefore, the articles of partnership may be written to credit the new partner, rather than the original partners, with either a bonus or goodwill. Because of an excellent professional reputation, valuable business contacts, or myriad other possible factors, Goldman might be able to negotiate a beginning capital balance in excess of the $20,000 cash contribution. This same circumstance may also result if the business is desperate for new capital and is willing to offer favorable terms as an enticement to the potential partner.

To illustrate, assume that Goldman receives a 20 percent interest in the partnership (rather than the originally stated 10 percent) in exchange for the $20,000 cash investment. The specific rationale for the higher ownership percentage need not be identified.

The bonus method sets Goldman's initial capital at $24,000 (20 percent of the $120,000 book value). To achieve this balance, a capital bonus of $4,000 must be credited to Goldman and taken from the present partners:

Cash	20,000	
King, Capital (60% of bonus)	2,400	
Wilson, Capital (40% of bonus)	1,600	
Goldman, Capital		24,000
To record Goldman's entrance into partnership with reduced payment reported as a bonus from original partners.		

If goodwill rather than a bonus is attributed to the *entering partner,* a mathematical problem arises in determining the implicit value of the business as a whole. In the current illustration, Goldman paid $20,000 for a 20 percent interest. Therefore, the value of the company is calculated as only $100,000 ($20,000/20%), a figure that is less than the $120,000 in net assets reported after the new contribution. Negative goodwill appears to exist. One possibility is that individual partnership assets are overvalued and require reduction. As an alternative, the cash contribution might not be an accurate representation of the new partner's investment. Goldman could be bringing an intangible contribution (goodwill) to the business along with the $20,000. This additional amount must be determined algebraically:

$$\text{Goldman's capital} = 20\% \text{ of partnership capital}$$

Therefore:

$$\$20,000 + \text{Goodwill} = 0.20 \,(\$100,000 + \$20,000 + \text{Goodwill})$$
$$\$20,000 + \text{Goodwill} = \$20,000 + \$4,000 + 0.20 \text{ Goodwill}$$
$$0.80 \text{ Goodwill} = \$4,000$$
$$\text{Goodwill} = \$5,000$$

If the partners determine that Goldman is, indeed, making an intangible contribution (a particular skill, for example, or a loyal clientele), Goldman should be credited with a $25,000 capital investment: $20,000 cash and $5,000 goodwill. When added to the original $100,000 in net assets reported by the partnership, this contribution raises the total capital for the business to $125,000. As the articles of partnership specified, Goldman's interest now represents a 20 percent share of the partnership ($25,000/$125,000).

Recognizing $5,000 in goodwill has established the proper relationship between the new partner and the partnership. Therefore, the following journal entry reflects this transaction:

Cash	20,000	
Goodwill	5,000	
Goldman, Capital		25,000
To record Goldman's entrance into partnership with goodwill attributed to this new partner.		

Dissolution—Withdrawal of a Partner

LO 9-10

Prepare journal entries to record the withdrawal of a current partner.

Admission of a new partner is not the only method by which a partnership can undergo a change in composition. Over the life of the business, partners might leave the organization. Death or retirement can occur, or a partner may simply elect to withdraw from the partnership. The articles of partnership also can allow for the expulsion of a partner under certain conditions. Again, any change in membership legally dissolves the partnership, although its operations usually continue uninterrupted under the remaining partners' ownership.

Regardless of the reason for dissolution, some method of establishing an equitable settlement of the withdrawing partner's interest in the business is necessary. Often, the partner (or the partner's estate) may simply sell the interest to an outside party, with approval, or to one or more of the remaining partners. As an alternative, the business can distribute cash or other assets as a means of settling a partner's right of co-ownership. Consequently, many partnerships hold life insurance policies solely to provide adequate cash to liquidate a partner's interest upon death.

Whether death or some other reason caused the withdrawal, a final distribution will not necessarily equal the book value of the partner's capital account. A capital balance is only a recording of historical transactions and rarely represents the true value inherent in a business. Instead, payment is frequently based on the value of the partner's interest as ascertained by either negotiation or appraisal. Because a settlement determination can be derived in many ways, the articles of partnership should contain exact provisions regulating this procedure.

The withdrawal of an individual partner and the resulting distribution of partnership property can, as before, be accounted for by either the bonus (no revaluation) method or the goodwill (revaluation) method. Again, a hybrid option is also available.

As in earlier illustrations, if a bonus is recorded, the amount can be attributed to either of the parties involved: the withdrawing partner or the remaining partners. Conversely, any revaluation of partnership property (as well as the establishment of a goodwill balance) is allocated among all partners to recognize possible unrecorded gains. The hybrid approach restates assets and liabilities to fair value but does not record goodwill. This last alternative reflects the legal change in ownership but avoids the theoretical problems associated with partnership goodwill.

Accounting for the Withdrawal of a Partner

To demonstrate the various approaches that can be taken to account for a partner's withdrawal, assume that the partnership of Duncan, Smith, and Windsor has existed for a number of years. At the present time, the partners have the following capital balances as well as the indicated profit and loss percentages:

Partner	Capital Balance	Profit and Loss Ratio
Duncan	$ 70,000	50%
Smith	20,000	30
Windsor	10,000	20
Total capital	$100,000	

Windsor decides to withdraw from the partnership, but Duncan and Smith plan to continue operating the business. As per the original partnership agreement, a final settlement distribution for any withdrawing partner is computed based on the following specified provisions:

- An independent expert will appraise the business to determine its estimated fair value.
- Any individual who leaves the partnership will receive cash or other assets equal to that partner's current capital balance after including an appropriate share of any adjustment indicated by the previous valuation. The allocation of unrecorded gains and losses is based on the normal profit and loss ratio.

Following Windsor's decision to withdraw from the partnership, its property is immediately appraised. Total fair value is estimated at $180,000, a figure $80,000 in excess of book value. According to this valuation, land held by the partnership is currently worth $50,000 more than its original cost. In addition, $30,000 in goodwill is attributed to the partnership based on its value as a going concern. *Therefore, Windsor receives $26,000 on leaving the partnership: the original $10,000 capital balance plus a 20 percent share of this $80,000 increment.* The amount of payment is not in dispute, but the method of recording the withdrawal is.

Bonus Method Applied If the partnership used the bonus method to record this transaction, the extra $16,000 paid to Windsor is simply assigned as a decrease in the remaining partners' capital accounts. Historically, Duncan and Smith have been credited with 50 percent and 30 percent of all profits and losses, respectively. This same relative ratio is used now to allocate the reduction between these two remaining partners on a ⅝ and ⅜ basis:

Bonus Method		
Windsor, Capital (to remove account balance)	10,000	
Duncan, Capital (⅝ of excess distribution)	10,000	
Smith, Capital (⅜ of excess distribution)	6,000	
Cash		26,000
To record Windsor's withdrawal with $16,000 excess distribution taken from remaining partners.		

Goodwill Method Applied This same transaction can also be accounted for by means of the goodwill (or revaluation) approach. The appraisal indicates that land is undervalued on the partnership's records by $50,000 and that goodwill of $30,000 has apparently accrued to the business over the years. The first two of the following entries recognize these valuations. The adjustments properly equate Windsor's capital balance with the $26,000 cash amount to be distributed. Windsor's equity balance is merely removed in the final entry at the time of payment.

Land Revaluation

Land	50,000	
Duncan, Capital (50%)		25,000
Smith, Capital (30%)		15,000
Windsor, Capital (20%)		10,000
To recognize land value as a preliminary step to Windsor's withdrawal.		

Goodwill Recognition

Goodwill	30,000	
Duncan, Capital (50%)		15,000
Smith, Capital (30%)		9,000
Windsor, Capital (20%)		6,000
To recognize goodwill at the time of ownership change.		
Windsor, Capital (to remove account balance)	26,000	
Cash		26,000
To distribute cash to Windsor in settlement of partnership interest.		

After the land revaluation, Windsor's recorded capital balance increases to $20,000. The remaining unrecorded increase in partnership value is then assigned to the intangible asset goodwill. Goodwill represents an asset that captures the intangible increase in partnership value attributable to the past efforts of the individual partners.[14] Upon withdrawal, a partner is entitled to share in any unrecorded increase in partnership value based on his or her profit and loss ratio. The extra $6,000 paid to Windsor (beyond the $20,000 adjusted capital balance) thus is consistent with the $30,000 overall recognition of partnership goodwill: ($6,000 ÷ 20%) = $30,000.

The implied value of a partnership as a whole, however, cannot be determined directly from the amount distributed to a withdrawing partner. For example, paying Windsor $26,000 did not indicate that total capital should be $130,000 ($26,000 ÷ 20%). This computation is appropriate only when (1) a new partner is admitted or (2) the percentage of capital is the same as the profit and loss ratio. Here, an outside valuation of the business indicated that it was worth $80,000 more than book value. As a 20 percent owner, Windsor was entitled to $16,000 of that amount, raising the partner's capital account from $10,000 to $26,000, the amount of the final payment.

Hybrid Method Applied   As indicated previously, a hybrid approach also can be adopted to record a partner's withdrawal. It also recognizes asset and liability revaluations but ignores goodwill. A bonus must then be recorded to reconcile the partner's adjusted capital balance with the final distribution.

The following journal entry, for example, does not record goodwill. However, the book value of the land is increased by $50,000 in recognition of present worth. This adjustment increases Windsor's capital balance to $20,000, a figure that is still less than the $26,000 distribution. The $6,000 difference is recorded as a bonus taken from the remaining two partners according to their relative profit and loss ratio.

Hybrid Method

Land	50,000	
Duncan, Capital (50%)		25,000
Smith, Capital (30%)		15,000
Windsor, Capital (20%)		10,000
To adjust Land account to fair value as a preliminary step in Windsor's withdrawal.		

(continued)

---

[14] The value of many partnerships derives overwhelmingly from intangibles such as professional reputation and expertise. Because increases in intangible partnership value are difficult to quantify on an ongoing basis, they typically go unrecorded until a change in partnership ownership forces a reckoning.

(continued)

Windsor, Capital (to remove account balance)	20,000	
Duncan, Capital (⅝ of bonus)...	3,750	
Smith, Capital (⅜ of bonus)	2,250	
Cash		26,000
To record final distribution to Windsor with $6,000 bonus taken from remaining partners.		

Summary

1. A partnership is defined as "an association of two or more persons to carry on a business as co-owners for profit." This form of business organization exists throughout the U.S. economy ranging in size from small, part-time operations to international enterprises. The partnership format is popular for many reasons, including the ease of creation and the avoidance of the double taxation that is inherent in corporate ownership. However, the unlimited liability incurred by each general partner normally restricts the growth potential of most partnerships. Thus, although the number of partnerships in the United States is large, the size of each tends to be small.

2. Over the years, a number of different types of organizations have been developed to take advantage of both the single taxation of partnerships and the limited liability afforded to corporate stockholders. Such legal forms include S corporations, limited partnerships, limited liability partnerships, and limited liability companies.

3. The unique elements of partnership accounting are found primarily in the capital accounts accumulated for each partner. The basis for recording these balances is the articles of partnership, a document that should be established as a prerequisite to the formation of any partnership. One of the principal provisions of this agreement is each partner's initial investment. Noncash contributions such as inventory or land are entered into the partnership's accounting records at fair value.

4. In forming a partnership, the partners' contributions need not be limited to tangible assets. A particular line of expertise possessed by a partner and an established clientele are attributes that can have a significant value to a partnership. Two methods of recording this type of investment are found in practice. The bonus method recognizes only identifiable assets. The capital accounts are then aligned to indicate the balances negotiated by the partners. According to the goodwill approach, all contributions (even those of a nebulous nature such as expertise) are valued and recorded, often as goodwill.

5. Another accounting issue to be resolved in forming a partnership is the allocation of annual net income. In closing out the revenue and expense accounts at the end of each period, some assignment must be made to the individual capital balances. Although an equal division can be used to allocate any profit or loss, partners frequently devise unique plans in an attempt to be equitable. Such factors as time worked, expertise, and invested capital should be considered in creating an allocation procedure.

6. Over time, changes occur in the makeup of a partnership because of death or retirement or because of the admission of new partners. Such changes dissolve the existing partnership, although the business frequently continues uninterrupted through a newly formed partnership. If, for example, a new partner is admitted by the acquisition of a present interest, the capital balances can simply be reclassified to reflect the change in ownership. As an alternative, the purchase price may be viewed as evidence of the underlying value of the organization as a whole. Based on this calculation, asset and liability balances are adjusted to fair value, and any residual goodwill is recognized.

7. Admission into an existing partnership also can be achieved by a direct capital contribution from the new partner. Because of the parties' negotiations, the amount invested will not always agree with the beginning capital balance attributed to the new partner. The bonus method resolves this conflict by simply reclassifying the various capital accounts to align the balances with specified totals and percentages. No revaluation is carried out under this approach. Conversely, according to the goodwill method, all asset and liability accounts are adjusted first to fair value. The price the new partner paid is used to compute an implied value for the partnership, and any excess over fair value is recorded as goodwill.

8. The composition of a partnership also can undergo changes because of the death or retirement of a partner. Individuals may decide to withdraw. Such changes legally dissolve the partnership, although business operations frequently continue under the remaining partners' ownership. In compensating the departing partner, the final asset distribution may differ from the ending capital balance. This disparity can, again, be accounted for by means of the bonus method, which adjusts the remaining capital accounts to absorb the bonus. The goodwill approach by which all assets and liabilities are restated to fair value with any goodwill being recognized also can be applied. Finally, a hybrid method revalues the assets and liabilities but ignores goodwill. Under this last approach, any amount paid to the departing partner in excess of the newly adjusted capital balance is accounted for by means of the bonus method.

Comprehensive Illustration

(*Estimated Time: 30 to 55 Minutes*) Heyman and Mullins begin a partnership on January 1, 2023. Heyman invests $40,000 cash and inventory costing $15,000 but with a current appraised value of only $12,000. Mullins contributes a building with a $40,000 book value and a $48,000 fair value. The partnership also accepts responsibility for a $10,000 note payable owed in connection with this building.

Problem

The partners agree to begin operations with equal capital balances. The articles of partnership also provide that at each year-end, profits and losses are allocated as follows:

1. For managing the business, Heyman is credited with a bonus of 10 percent of partnership income after subtracting the bonus. No bonus is accrued if the partnership records a loss.
2. Both partners are entitled to interest equal to 10 percent of the average monthly capital balance for the year without regard for the income or drawings of that year.
3. Any remaining profit or loss is divided 60 percent to Heyman and 40 percent to Mullins.
4. Each partner is allowed to withdraw $800 per month in cash from the business.

On October 1, 2023, Heyman invested an additional $12,000 cash in the business. For 2023, the partnership reported income of $33,000.

Lewis, an employee, is allowed to join the partnership on January 1, 2024. The new partner invests $66,000 directly into the business for a one-third interest in the partnership property. The revised partnership agreement still allows for both the bonus to Heyman and the 10 percent interest, but all remaining profits and losses are now split 40 percent each to Heyman and Lewis with the remaining 20 percent to Mullins. Lewis is also entitled to $800 per month in drawings.

Mullins chooses to withdraw from the partnership a few years later. After negotiations, all parties agree that Mullins should be paid a $90,000 settlement. The capital balances on that date were as follows:

Heyman, Capital	$88,000
Mullins, Capital	78,000
Lewis, Capital	72,000

Required

a. Assuming that this partnership uses the bonus method exclusively, make all necessary journal entries. Entries for the monthly drawings of the partners are not required.

b. Assuming that this partnership uses the goodwill method exclusively, make all necessary journal entries. Again, entries for the monthly drawings are not required.

Solution

a. **Bonus Method**
2023

Jan. 1 All contributed property is recorded at fair value. Under the bonus method, total capital is then divided as specified between the partners.

Cash	40,000	
Inventory	12,000	
Building	48,000	
Note Payable		10,000
Heyman, Capital (50%)		45,000
Mullins, Capital (50%)		45,000
To record initial contributions to partnership along with equal capital balances.		

Oct. 1

Cash	12,000	
Heyman, Capital		12,000
To record additional investment by partner.		

Dec. 31 Both the bonus assigned to Heyman and the interest accrual must be computed as preliminary steps in the income allocation process. Because the bonus is based on income after subtracting the bonus, the amount must be calculated algebraically:

$$
\begin{aligned}
\text{Bonus} &= 0.10\,(\$33,000 - \text{Bonus}) \\
\text{Bonus} &= \$3,300 - 0.10\,\text{Bonus} \\
1.10\,\text{Bonus} &= \$3,300 \\
\text{Bonus} &= \$3,000
\end{aligned}
$$

According to the articles of partnership, the interest allocation is based on a monthly average figure. Mullins's capital balance of $45,000 did not change during the year; therefore, $4,500 (10 percent) is the appropriate interest accrual for that partner. However, because of the October 1, 2023, contribution, Heyman's interest must be determined as follows:

Beginning balance	$45,000 × 9 months =	$405,000
New balance	$57,000 × 3 months =	171,000
		576,000
		× $\frac{1}{12}$
Monthly average—capital balance		48,000
Interest rate		× 10%
Interest credited to Heyman.		$ 4,800

Following the bonus and interest computations, the $33,000 income earned by the business is allocated according to the previously specified arrangement:

	Heyman	Mullins	Totals
Net Income.			$ 33,000
Bonus to Heyman	3,000		(3,000)
Income remaining after bonus			$ 30,000
Interest on monthly average capital balance. . . .	4,800	4,500	(9,300)
Income remaining after bonus and interest			$ 20,700
Remaining income allocation	12,420 (60%)	8,280 (40%)	(20,700)
Net income allocation total	$20,220	$12,780	$ 0

The partnership's closing entries for the year would be recorded as follows:

Heyman, Capital	9,600	
Mullins, Capital.	9,600	
Heyman, Drawing.		9,600
Mullins, Drawing		9,600
To close out $800 per month drawing accounts for the year.		
Income Summary	33,000	
Heyman, Capital		20,220
Mullins, Capital		12,780
To close out profit for year to capital accounts as computed above.		

At the end of this initial year of operation, the partners' capital accounts hold these balances:

	Heyman	Mullins	Totals
Beginning balance	$45,000	$45,000	$ 90,000
Additional investment.	12,000	–0–	12,000
Drawing.	(9,600)	(9,600)	(19,200)
Net income (above)	20,220	12,780	33,000
Total capital	$67,620	$48,180	$115,800

2024

Jan. 1   Lewis contributed $66,000 to the business for a one-third interest in the partnership property. Combined with the $115,800 balance previously computed, the partnership now has total capital of $181,800. Because no revaluation is recorded under the bonus approach, a one-third interest in the partnership equals $60,600 ($181,800 × ⅓). Lewis has invested $5,400 in excess of this amount, a balance viewed as a bonus accruing to the original partners:

Cash	66,000	
Lewis, Capital		60,600
Heyman, Capital (60% of bonus)		3,240
Mullins, Capital (40% of bonus)........................		2,160

To record Lewis's entrance into partnership with bonus to original partners.

Several years later   The final event in this illustration is Mullins's withdrawal from the partnership. Although this partner's capital balance reports only $78,000, the final distribution is set at $90,000. The extra $12,000 payment represents a bonus assigned to Mullins, an amount that decreases the capital of the remaining two partners. Because Heyman and Lewis have previously accrued equal 40 percent shares of all profits and losses, the reduction is split evenly between the two.

Mullins, Capital..	78,000	
Heyman, Capital (½ of bonus payment)	6,000	
Lewis, Capital (½ of bonus payment)...................	6,000	
Cash		90,000

To record withdrawal of Mullins with a bonus from remaining partners.

b. Goodwill Method

2023

Jan. 1   The fair value of Heyman's contribution is $52,000, whereas Mullins is investing only a net $38,000 (the value of the building less the accompanying debt). Because the capital accounts are initially to be equal, Mullins is presumed to be contributing goodwill of $14,000.

Cash	40,000	
Inventory...	12,000	
Building..	48,000	
Goodwill	14,000	
Note payable.......................................		10,000
Heyman, Capital		52,000
Mullins, Capital		52,000

Creation of partnership with goodwill attributed to Mullins.

Oct. 1

Cash	12,000	
Heyman, Capital		12,000

To record additional contribution by partner.

Dec. 31   Although Heyman's bonus is still $3,000 as derived in requirement part (*a*), the interest accruals must be recalculated because the capital balances are different. Mullins's capital for the entire year was $52,000; thus, interest of $5,200 (10 percent) is appropriate. However, Heyman's balance changed during the year, so a monthly average must be determined as a basis for computing interest:

Beginning balance	$52,000 × 9 months =	$468,000
New balance	$64,000 × 3 months =	192,000
		660,000
		× ¹⁄₁₂
Monthly average—capital balance		55,000
Interest rate		× 10%
Interest credited to Heyman............................		$ 5,500

The $33,000 partnership income is allocated as follows:

	Heyman	Mullins	Totals
Net Income.			$33,000
Bonus to Heyman	$ 3,000		(3,000)
Income remaining after bonus			$30,000
Interest on monthly average capital balance.	5,500	5,200	(10,700)
Income remaining after bonus and interest			$19,300
Remaining income allocation	11,580 (60%)	7,720 (40%)	(19,300)
Net income allocation total	$20,080	$12,920	$ –0–

The closing entries made under the goodwill approach would be as follows:

Heyman, Capital	9,600	
Mullins, Capital.	9,600	
Heyman, Drawing		9,600
Mullins, Drawing		9,600
To close out drawing accounts for the year.		
Income Summary	33,000	
Heyman, Capital		20,080
Mullins, Capital		12,920
To assign profits per allocation schedule.		

After the closing process, the capital balances are composed of the following items:

	Heyman	Mullins	Totals
Beginning balance	$52,000	$52,000	$104,000
Additional investment.	12,000	–0–	12,000
Drawing.	(9,600)	(9,600)	(19,200)
Net income.	20,080	12,920	33,000
Total capital	$74,480	$55,320	$129,800

2024

Jan. 1   Lewis's investment of $66,000 for a one-third interest in the partnership property implies that the business as a whole is worth $198,000 ($66,000 ÷ ⅓). After adding Lewis's contribution to the present capital balance of $129,800, the business reports total net assets of only $195,800. Thus, a $2,200 increase in value ($198,000 − $195,800) is indicated and will be recognized at this time. Under the assumption that all partnership assets and liabilities are valued appropriately, this entire balance is attributed to goodwill.

Goodwill	2,200	
Heyman, Capital (60%).		1,320
Mullins, Capital (40%)		880
To recognize goodwill based on Lewis's acquisition price.		
Cash	66,000	
Lewis, Capital		66,000
To admit Lewis to the partnership.		

Several years later   To conclude this illustration, Mullins's withdrawal must be recorded. This partner is to receive a distribution that is $12,000 more than the corresponding capital balance of $78,000. Because Mullins is entitled to a 20 percent share of profits and losses, the additional $12,000 payment indicates that the partnership as a whole is undervalued by $60,000 ($12,000/20%). Only in that circumstance would the extra payment to Mullins be justified. Therefore, once again, goodwill is recognized and is followed by the final distribution.

Goodwill	60,000	
Heyman, Capital (40%).		24,000
Mullins, Capital (20%)		12,000
Lewis, Capital (40%)		24,000
Recognition of goodwill based on withdrawal amount paid to		
Mullins.		
Mullins, Capital.	90,000	
Cash		90,000
To distribute money to partner.		

Questions

1. What are the advantages of operating a business as a partnership rather than as a corporation? What are the disadvantages?
2. How does partnership accounting differ from corporate accounting?
3. What information do the capital accounts found in partnership accounting convey?
4. Describe the differences between a Subchapter S corporation and a Subchapter C corporation.
5. A company is being created, and the owners are trying to decide whether to form a general partnership, a limited liability partnership, or a limited liability company. What are the advantages and disadvantages of each of these legal forms?
6. What is an articles of partnership agreement, and what information should this document contain?
7. What valuation should be recorded for noncash assets transferred to a partnership by one of the partners?
8. If a partner is contributing attributes to a partnership such as an established clientele or a particular expertise, what two methods can be used to record the contribution? Describe each method.
9. What is the purpose of a drawing account in a partnership's financial records?
10. At what point in the accounting process does the allocation of partnership income become significant?
11. What provisions in a partnership agreement can be used to establish an equitable allocation of income among all partners?
12. If no agreement exists in a partnership as to the allocation of income, what method is appropriate?
13. What is a partnership dissolution? Does dissolution automatically necessitate the cessation of business and the liquidation of partnership assets?
14. By what methods can a new partner gain admittance into a partnership?
15. When a partner sells an ownership interest in a partnership, what rights are conveyed to the new owner?
16. A new partner enters a partnership, and goodwill is calculated and credited to the original partners. How is the specific amount of goodwill assigned to these partners?
17. Under what circumstance might goodwill be allocated to a new partner entering a partnership?
18. When a partner withdraws from a partnership, why is the final distribution often based on the appraised value of the business rather than on the book value of the capital account balance?

Problems

1. Which of the following is *not* a reason for the popularity of partnerships as a legal form for businesses?

   LO 9-1
   a. Partnerships may be formed merely by an oral agreement.
   b. Partnerships can more easily generate significant amounts of capital.
   c. Partnerships avoid the double taxation of income that is found in corporations.
   d. In some cases, losses may be used to offset gains for tax purposes.

2. How does partnership accounting differ from corporate accounting?

   LO 9-1
   a. The matching principle is not considered appropriate for partnership accounting.
   b. Revenues are recognized at a different time by a partnership than is appropriate for a corporation.
   c. Individual capital accounts replace the contributed capital and retained earnings balances found in corporate accounting.
   d. Partnerships report all assets at fair value as of the latest balance sheet date.

LO 9-2

3. Which of the following best describes the articles of partnership agreement?

   a. The purpose of the partnership and partners' rights and responsibilities are required elements of the articles of partnership.

   b. The articles of partnership are a legal covenant and must be expressed in writing to be valid.

   c. The articles of partnership are an agreement that limits partners' liability to partnership assets.

   d. The articles of partnership are a legal covenant that may be expressed orally or in writing, and form the central governance for a partnership's operations.

LO 9-9

4. Pat, Jean Lou, and Diane are partners with capital balances of $50,000, $30,000, and $20,000, respectively. These three partners share profits and losses equally. For an investment of $50,000 cash (paid to the business), MaryAnn will be admitted as a partner with a one-fourth interest in capital and profits. Based on this information, which of the following best justifies the amount of MaryAnn's investment?

   a. MaryAnn will receive a bonus from the other partners upon her admission to the partnership.

   b. Assets of the partnership were overvalued immediately prior to MaryAnn's investment.

   c. The book value of the partnership's net assets was less than the fair value immediately prior to MaryAnn's investment.

   d. MaryAnn is apparently bringing goodwill into the partnership, and her capital account will be credited for the appropriate amount.

LO 9-10

5. A partnership has the following capital balances with partners' profit and loss percentages indicated parenthetically:

Henry (50%)	$135,000
Thomas (30%)	85,000
Catherine (20%).	80,000

Anne is going to invest $125,000 into the business to acquire a 40 percent ownership interest. Goodwill is to be recorded. What will be Anne's beginning capital balance?

   a. $125,000

   b. $170,000

   c. $200,000

   d. $245,000

LO 9-8

6. A partnership has the following capital balances with partners' profit and loss percentages indicated parenthetically:

Burks (35%).	$280,000
Donovan (40%)	300,000
Watkins (25%).	170,000

Ranzilla agrees to pay a total of $245,000 directly to these three partners to acquire a 25 percent ownership interest from each. The partnership will record goodwill based on the new partner's payment. What is Donovan's capital balance after the transaction?

   a. $225,000

   b. $294,000

   c. $392,000

   d. $398,000

LO 9-9

7. The capital balance for Maxwell is $110,000 and for Russell is $40,000. These two partners share profits and losses 70 percent (Maxwell) and 30 percent (Russell). Evan invests $50,000 in cash into the partnership for a 30 percent ownership. The bonus method will be used. What is Russell's capital balance after Evan's investment?

   a. $35,000

   b. $37,000

   c. $40,000

   d. $43,000

LO 9-9

8. Patrick has a capital balance of $120,000 in a local partnership, and Caitlin has a $90,000 balance. These two partners share profits and losses by a ratio of 60 percent to Patrick and 40 percent to Caitlin. Camille invests $60,000 in cash in the partnership for a 20 percent ownership. The goodwill method will be used. What is Caitlin's capital balance after this new investment?

   a. $99,600

   b. $102,000

   c. $112,000

   d. $126,000

LO 9-9

9. The capital balance for Messalina is $210,000 and for Romulus is $140,000. These two partners share profits and losses of 60 percent (Messalina) and 40 percent (Romulus). Claudius invests $100,000 in cash in the partnership for a 20 percent ownership. The bonus method will be used. What are the capital balances for Messalina, Romulus, and Claudius after this investment is recorded?

   a. $216,000, $144,000, $90,000
   b. $218,000, $142,000, $88,000
   c. $222,000, $148,000, $80,000
   d. $240,000, $160,000, $100,000

LO 9-6

10. A partnership begins its first year with the following capital balances:

Alexander, Capital.	$ 90,000
Bertrand, Capital	100,000
Coloma, Capital.	160,000

The articles of partnership stipulate that profits and losses be assigned in the following manner:

- Each partner is allocated interest equal to 5 percent of the beginning capital balance.
- Bertrand is allocated compensation of $45,000 per year.
- Any remaining profits and losses are allocated on a 3:3:4 basis, respectively.
- Each partner is allowed to withdraw up to $25,000 cash per year.

Assuming that the net income is $115,000 and that each partner withdraws the maximum amount allowed, what is the balance in Coloma's capital account at the end of the year?

   a. $143,000
   b. $135,000
   c. $168,000
   d. $164,000

LO 9-5, 9-6

11. A partnership begins its first year of operations with the following capital balances:

Allegan, Capital	$110,000
Berrien, Capital	80,000
Kent, Capital.	110,000

According to the articles of partnership, all profits will be assigned as follows:

- Allegan will be awarded an annual salary of $20,000 with $10,000 assigned to Kent.
- The partners will be attributed interest equal to 10 percent of the capital balance as of the first day of the year.
- The remainder will be assigned on a 5:2:3 basis, respectively.
- Each partner is allowed to withdraw up to $10,000 per year.

The net loss for the first year of operations is $20,000, and net income for the subsequent year is $40,000. Each partner withdraws the maximum amount from the business each period.

   Prepare schedules that compute the balances in each partner's capital account at the end of each of the first two years of partnership operations.

LO 9-10

12. A partnership has the following capital balances:

Artur, Capital	$60,000
Bella, Capital	30,000
Callo, Capital	90,000

Profits and losses are split as follows: Artur (20 percent), Bella (30 percent), and Callo (50 percent). Callo wants to leave the partnership and is paid $100,000 from the business based on provisions in the articles of partnership.

   Assuming the partnership uses the bonus method, compute the balance of Bella's capital account after Callo withdraws.

Problems 13 and 14 are *independent* problems based on the following scenario:

At year-end, the Queen City partnership has the following capital balances:

Isabella, Capital	$130,000
Catherine, Capital	110,000
Elizabeth, Capital.	80,000
Victoria, Capital	70,000

Profits and losses are split on a 3:3:2:2 basis, respectively. Elizabeth decides to leave the partnership and is paid $90,000 from the business based on the original contractual agreement.

LO 9-10

13. The payment made to Elizabeth beyond her capital account was for Elizabeth's share of previously unrecognized goodwill. After recognizing partnership goodwill, compute Isabella's capital balance after Elizabeth withdraws.

LO 9-10

14. If instead the partnership uses the bonus method, compute the balance of Isabella's capital account after Elizabeth withdraws.

Problems 15 and 16 are *independent* problems based on the following capital account balances and profit and loss percentages (indicated parenthetically):

Alden (40%)	$220,000
Boyd (40%)	160,000
Carmel (20%)	110,000

LO 9-8

15. Del Mar invests $270,000 in cash for a 30 percent ownership interest. The money goes to the original partners. Goodwill is to be recorded.

   a. Compute the amount of goodwill to be recorded upon Del Mar's investment.

   b. Del Mar's beginning capital balance.

LO 9-9

16. Del Mar invests $250,000 in cash for a 30 percent ownership interest. The money goes to the business. No goodwill or other revaluation is to be recorded. After the transaction, compute Boyd's capital balance.

LO 9-9

17. Lear is to become a partner in the WS partnership by paying $80,000 in cash to the business. At present, the capital balance for Hamlet is $70,000 and for MacBeth is $40,000. Hamlet and MacBeth share profits on a 7:3 basis. Lear is acquiring 40 percent of the new partnership.

   a. If the goodwill method is applied, what will the three capital balances be following the payment by Lear?

   b. If the bonus method is applied, what will the three capital balances be following the payment by Lear?

LO 9-9

18. The Distance Plus partnership has the following capital balances at the beginning of the current year along with respective profit and loss percentages:

Tiger (50%)	$85,000
Phil (30%)	60,000
Ernie (20%)	55,000

Each of the following questions should be viewed independently.

   a. If Sergio invests $100,000 in cash in the business for a 25 percent interest, what journal entry is recorded? Assume that the bonus method is used.

   b. If Sergio invests $60,000 in cash in the business for a 25 percent interest, what journal entry is recorded? Assume that the bonus method is used.

   c. If Sergio invests $72,000 in cash in the business for a 25 percent interest, what journal entry is recorded? Assume that the goodwill method is used.

LO 9-9

19. A partnership has the following account balances: Cash, $50,000; Other Assets, $600,000; Liabilities, $240,000; Nixon, Capital (50 percent of profits and losses), $200,000; Hoover, Capital (20 percent), $120,000; and Polk, Capital (30 percent), $90,000. Each of the following questions should be viewed as an independent situation:

   a. Grant invests $80,000 in the partnership for an 18 percent capital interest. Goodwill is to be recognized. What are the capital accounts thereafter?

   b. Grant invests $100,000 in the partnership to get a 20 percent capital balance. Goodwill is not to be recorded. What are the capital accounts thereafter?

LO 9-5, 9-6, 9-9

20. The Prince-Robbins partnership has the following capital account balances on January 1, 2024:

Prince, Capital	$70,000
Robbins, Capital	60,000

Prince is allocated 80 percent of all profits and losses with the remaining 20 percent assigned to Robbins after interest of 10 percent is given to each partner based on beginning capital balances.

On January 2, 2024, Jeffrey invests $37,000 cash for a 20 percent interest in the partnership. This transaction is recorded by the goodwill method. After this transaction, 10 percent interest is still to go to each partner. Profits and losses will then be split as follows: Prince (50 percent), Robbins (30 percent), and Jeffrey (20 percent). In 2024, the partnership reports a net income of $15,000.

   a. Prepare the journal entry to record Jeffrey's entrance into the partnership on January 2, 2024.

   b. Prepare a schedule showing how the 2024 net income allocation to the partners should be determined.

LO 9-6

21. The partnership agreement of Jones, King, and Lane provides for the annual allocation of the business's profit or loss in the following sequence:

- Jones, the managing partner, receives a bonus equal to 20 percent of the business's profit.
- Each partner receives 15 percent interest on average capital investment.
- Any residual profit or loss is divided equally.

The average capital investments for 2024 were as follows:

Jones	$100,000
King	200,000
Lane	300,000

The partnership earned $90,000 net income for 2024. Prepare a schedule showing how the 2024 net income should be allocated to the partners.

LO 9-4, 9-5, 9-6

22. Alford, Beeson, and Carlton have operated a coffee shop for a number of years as a partnership. At the beginning of 2024, capital balances were as follows:

Alford	$60,000
Beeson	40,000
Carlton	20,000

Due to a cash shortage, Alford invests an additional $8,000 in the business on April 1, 2024.
   Each partner is allowed to withdraw $1,000 cash each month.
   The partners have used the same method of allocating profits and losses since the business's inception:

- Each partner is given the following compensation allowance for work done in the business: Alford, $18,000; Beeson, $25,000; and Carlton, $8,000.
- Each partner is credited with interest equal to 10 percent of the average monthly capital balance for the year without regard for normal drawings.
- Any remaining profit or loss is allocated 4:2:4 to Alford, Beeson, and Carlton, respectively. The net income for 2024 is $23,600. Each partner withdraws the allotted amount each month.

Prepare a schedule showing calculations for the partners' 2024 ending capital balances.

LO 9-4, 9-5, 9-6

23. On January 1, 2023, the dental partnership of Angela, Diaz, and Krause was formed when the partners contributed $30,000, $58,000, and $60,000, respectively. Over the next three years, the business reported net income and (loss) as follows:

2023	$70,000
2024	42,000
2025	(25,000)

During this period, each partner withdrew cash of $15,000 per year. Krause invested an additional $5,000 in cash on February 9, 2024.
   At the time that the partnership was created, the three partners agreed to allocate all profits and losses according to a specified plan written as follows:

- Each partner is entitled to interest computed at the rate of 10 percent per year based on the individual capital balances at the beginning of that year.
- Because of prior work experience, Angela is entitled to an annual salary allowance of $12,000 per year, and Diaz is entitled to an annual salary allowance of $9,000 per year.
- Any remaining profit will be split as follows: Angela, 20 percent; Diaz, 40 percent; and Krause, 40 percent. If a net loss remains after the initial allocations to the partners, the balance will be allocated: Angela, 30 percent; Diaz, 50 percent; and Krause, 20 percent.

Prepare a schedule that determines the ending capital balance for each partner as of the end of each of these three years.

LO 9-10

24. The E.N.D. partnership has the following capital balances as of the end of the current year:

Pineda....................................	$230,000
Adams.....................................	190,000
Fergie	160,000
Gomez.....................................	140,000
Total capital	$720,000

Answer each of the following *independent* questions:

a. Assume that the partners share profits and losses 3:3:2:2, respectively. Fergie retires and is paid $190,000 based on the terms of the original partnership agreement. If the goodwill method is used, what is the capital balance of the remaining three partners?

b. Assume that the partners share profits and losses 4:3:2:1, respectively. Pineda retires and is paid $280,000 based on the terms of the original partnership agreement. If the bonus method is used, what is the capital balance of the remaining three partners?

LO 9-10

25. The partnership of Matteson, Richton, and O'Toole has existed for a number of years. At the present time, the partners have the following capital balances and profit and loss sharing percentages:

Partner	Capital Balance	Profit and Loss Percentage
Matteson	$ 90,000	30%
Richton	150,000	50
O'Toole	100,000	20

O'Toole elects to withdraw from the partnership, leaving Matteson and Richton to operate the business. Following the original partnership agreement, when a partner withdraws, the partnership and all of its individual assets are to be reassessed to current fair values by an independent appraiser. The withdrawing partner will receive cash or other assets equal to that partner's current capital balance after including an appropriate share of any adjustment indicated by the appraisal. Gains and losses indicated by the appraisal are allocated using the regular profit and loss percentages.

An independent appraiser is hired and estimates that the partnership as a whole is worth $600,000. Regarding the individual assets, the appraiser finds that a building with a book value of $180,000 has a fair value of $220,000. The book values for all other identifiable assets and liabilities are the same as their appraised fair values.

Accordingly, the partnership agrees to pay O'Toole $120,000 upon withdrawal. Matteson and Richton, however, do not wish to record any goodwill in connection with the change in ownership. Prepare the journal entry to record O'Toole's withdrawal from the partnership.

LO 9-2, 9-4, 9-6, 9-9

26. In the early part of 2024, the partners of Hugh, Jacobs, and Thomas sought assistance from a local accountant. They had begun a new business in 2023 but had never used an accountant's services.

Hugh and Jacobs began the partnership by contributing $150,000 and $100,000 in cash, respectively. Hugh was to work occasionally at the business, and Jacobs was to be employed full-time. They decided that year-end profits and losses should be assigned as follows:

- Each partner was to be allocated 10 percent interest computed on the beginning capital balances for the period.
- A compensation allowance of $5,000 was to go to Hugh with a $25,000 amount assigned to Jacobs.
- Any remaining income would be split on a 4:6 basis to Hugh and Jacobs, respectively.

In 2023, revenues totaled $175,000, and expenses were $146,000 (not including the partners' compensation allowance). Hugh withdrew cash of $9,000 during the year, and Jacobs took out $14,000. In addition, the business paid $7,500 for repairs made to Hugh's home and charged it to repair expense.

On January 1, 2024, the partnership sold a 15 percent interest to Thomas for $64,000 cash. This money was contributed to the business with the bonus method used for accounting purposes.

Answer the following questions:

a. Why was the original profit and loss allocation, as just outlined, designed by the partners?

b. Why did the drawings for 2023 not agree with the compensation allowances provided for in the partnership agreement?

  c. What journal entries should the partnership have recorded on December 31, 2023?

  d. What journal entry should the partnership have recorded on January 1, 2024?

27. The following is the current balance sheet for a local partnership of doctors:

Cash and current assets	$ 30,000	Liabilities	$ 40,000
Land	180,000	A, Capital	20,000
Building and equipment (net)	100,000	B, Capital	40,000
		C, Capital	90,000
		D, Capital	120,000
Totals	$310,000	Totals	$310,000

The following questions represent *independent* situations:

 a. E is going to invest enough money in this partnership to receive a 25 percent interest. No goodwill or bonus is to be recorded. How much should E invest?

 b. E contributes $36,000 in cash to the business to receive a 10 percent interest in the partnership. Goodwill is to be recorded. Profits and losses have previously been split according to the following percentages: A, 30 percent; B, 10 percent; C, 40 percent; and D, 20 percent. After E makes this investment, what are the individual capital balances?

 c. E contributes $42,000 in cash to the business to receive a 20 percent interest in the partnership. Goodwill is to be recorded. The four original partners share all profits and losses equally. After E makes this investment, what are the individual capital balances?

 d. E contributes $55,000 in cash to the business to receive a 20 percent interest in the partnership. No goodwill or other asset revaluation is to be recorded. Profits and losses have previously been split according to the following percentages: A, 10 percent; B, 30 percent; C, 20 percent; and D, 40 percent. After E makes this investment, what are the individual capital balances?

 e. C retires from the partnership and, as per the original partnership agreement, is to receive cash equal to 125 percent of her final capital balance. No goodwill or other asset revaluation is to be recognized. All partners share profits and losses equally. After the withdrawal, what are the individual capital balances of the remaining partners?

28. Gorman and Morton form a partnership on May 1, 2022. Gorman contributes cash of $50,000; Morton conveys title to the following properties to the partnership:

	Book Value	Fair Value
Equipment	$15,000	$28,000
Licensing agreements	35,000	36,000

The partners agree to start their partnership with equal capital balances. No goodwill is to be recognized.

According to the articles of partnership written by the partners, profits and losses are allocated based on the following formula:

- Gorman receives a compensation allowance of $1,000 per month.
- All remaining profits and losses are split 40:60 between Gorman and Morton, respectively.
- Each partner can make annual cash drawings of $25,000 beginning in 2023.

Net income of $11,000 is earned by the business during 2022.

Steele is invited to join the partnership on January 1, 2023. Because of her business reputation and financial expertise, she is given a 40 percent interest for $54,000 cash. The bonus approach is used to record this investment, made directly to the business. The articles of partnership are amended to give Steele a $2,000 compensation allowance per month and an annual cash drawing of $20,000. Remaining profits are now allocated:

Gorman	12%
Morton	48
Steele	40

All drawings are taken by the partners during 2023. At year-end, the partnership reports net income of $86,000.

On January 1, 2024, Frank (previously a partnership employee) is admitted into the partnership. Each partner transfers 10 percent to Frank, who makes the following payments directly to the partners:

Gorman.	$5,216
Morton.	4,724
Steele	9,560

Once again, the articles of partnership must be amended to allow for the entrance of the new partner. This change entitles Frank to a compensation allowance of $800 per month and an annual drawing of $14,000. Profits and losses are now assigned as follows:

Gorman.	13.5%
Morton.	40.5
Steele	36.0
Frank	10.0

For the year of 2024, the partnership earned a profit of $40,000, and each partner withdrew the allowed amount of cash.

Prepare schedules that determine the capital balances for the individual partners as of the end of each year 2022 through 2024.

LO 9-4, 9-5, 9-6, 9-9

29. Kimble, Sykes, and Gerard open an accounting practice on January 1, 2022, in Chicago, Illinois, to be operated as a partnership. Kimble and Sykes will serve as the senior partners because of their years of experience. To establish the business, Kimble, Sykes, and Gerard contribute cash and other properties valued at $208,000, $180,000, and $92,000, respectively. An articles of partnership agreement is drawn up stipulating the following:

- Personal drawings are allowed annually up to an amount equal to 10 percent of the partner's beginning capital balance for the year.
- Profits and losses are allocated according to the following plan:

  1. Each partner receives an annual salary allowance of $55 per billable hours worked.
  2. Interest is credited to the partners' capital accounts at the rate of 12 percent of the beginning capital balance for the year.
  3. Kimble and Sykes are eligible for an annual bonus of 10 percent of net income after subtracting the bonus, salary allowance, and interest. The agreement also states that there will be no bonus if there is a net loss or if salary and interest result in a negative remainder of net income to be distributed.
  4. Any remaining partnership profit or loss is to be divided evenly among all partners.

On January 1, 2023, the partners admit Nichols to the partnership. Nichols contributes cash directly to the business in an amount equal to a 25 percent interest in the book value of the partnership property subsequent to this contribution. The partnership profit and loss sharing agreement is not altered upon Nichols's entrance into the firm; the general provisions continue to be applicable.

The billable hours for the partners during the first three years of operation follow:

	2022	2023	2024
Kimble	1,700	1,800	1,880
Sykes	1,440	1,500	1,620
Gerard	1,300	1,380	1,310
Nichols	–0–	1,560	1,550

The partnership reports net income (loss) for 2022 through 2024 as follows:

2022	$282,000
2023	(12,400)
2024	477,000

Each partner withdraws the maximum allowable amount each year.

a. Prepare schedules that allocate each year's net income to the partners (to the nearest dollar).

b. Prepare in appropriate form a statement of partners' capital for the year ending December 31, 2024.

LO 9-8, 9-9, 9-10

30. A partnership of attorneys in the St. Louis, Missouri, area has the following balance sheet accounts as of January 1, 2024:

Assets	$320,000	Liabilities.	$120,000
		Athos, capital	80,000
		Porthos, capital	70,000
		Aramis, capital	50,000

According to the articles of partnership, Athos is to receive an allocation of 50 percent of all partnership profits and losses, while Porthos receives 30 percent, and Aramis, 20 percent. The book value of each asset and liability should be considered an accurate representation of fair value.

For each of the following *independent* situations, prepare the journal entry or entries to be recorded by the partnership. (Round to nearest dollar.)

a. Porthos, with permission of the other partners, decides to sell half of his partnership interest to D'Artagnan for $50,000 in cash. No asset revaluation or goodwill is to be recorded by the partnership.

b. All three of the present partners agree to sell 10 percent of each partnership interest to D'Artagnan for a total cash payment of $25,000. Each partner receives a negotiated portion of this amount. Goodwill is recorded as a result of the transaction.

c. D'Artagnan is allowed to become a partner with a 10 percent ownership interest by contributing $30,000 in cash directly into the business. The bonus method is used to record this admission.

d. Use the same facts as in requirement part (c) except that the entrance into the partnership is recorded by the goodwill method.

e. D'Artagnan is allowed to become a partner with a 10 percent ownership interest by contributing $12,222 in cash directly to the business. The goodwill method is used to record this transaction.

f. Aramis decides to retire and leave the partnership. An independent appraisal of the business and its assets indicates a current fair value of $280,000. Goodwill is to be recorded. Aramis will then be given the exact amount of cash that will close out his capital account.

LO 9-2, 9-3, 9-5, 9-6, 9-8, 9-10

31. Steve Reese is a well-known interior designer in Fort Worth, Texas. He wants to start his own business and convinces Rob O'Donnell, a local merchant, to contribute the capital to form a partnership. On January 1, 2022, O'Donnell invests a building worth $52,000 and equipment valued at $16,000 as well as $12,000 in cash. Although Reese makes no tangible contribution to the partnership, he will operate the business and be an equal partner in the beginning capital balances.

To entice O'Donnell to join this partnership, Reese draws up the following profit and loss agreement:

- O'Donnell will be credited annually with interest equal to 20 percent of the beginning capital balance for the year.

- O'Donnell will also have added to his capital account 15 percent of partnership income each year (without regard for the preceding interest figure) or $4,000, whichever is larger. All remaining income is credited to Reese.

- Neither partner is allowed to withdraw funds from the partnership during 2022. Thereafter, each can draw $5,000 annually or 20 percent of the beginning capital balance for the year, whichever is larger.

The partnership reported a net loss of $10,000 during the first year of its operation. On January 1, 2023, Terri Dunn becomes a third partner in this business by contributing $15,000 cash to the partnership. Dunn receives a 20 percent share of the business's capital. The profit and loss agreement is altered as follows:

- O'Donnell is still entitled to (1) interest on his beginning capital balance as well as (2) his share of partnership income as specified above.

- Any remaining profit or loss will be split on a 6:4 basis between Reese and Dunn, respectively.

Partnership income for 2023 is reported as $44,000. Each partner withdraws the full amount that is allowed.

On January 1, 2024, Dunn becomes ill and sells her interest in the partnership (with the consent of the other two partners) to Judy Postner. Postner pays $46,000 directly to Dunn. Net income for 2024 is $61,000 with the partners again taking their full drawing allowance.

On January 1, 2025, Postner withdraws from the business for personal reasons. The articles of partnership state that any partner may leave the partnership at any time and is entitled to receive cash in an amount equal to the recorded capital balance at that time plus 10 percent.

(Round all amounts to the nearest dollar.)

a. Prepare journal entries to record the preceding transactions on the assumption that the bonus (or no revaluation) method is used. Drawings need not be recorded, although the balances should be included in the closing entries.

b. Prepare journal entries to record the previous transactions on the assumption that the goodwill (or revaluation) method is used. Drawings need not be recorded, although the balances should be included in the closing entries.

Develop Your Skills

RESEARCH CASE

CPA *skills*

Go to the Enterprise Products Partners, L.P., website where forms filed with the SEC are available through the Investors tab. Find Enterprise Products's recent annual financial statements in their 10–K report for the partnership.

Required

Review the financial statements of Enterprise Products Partners as well as the accompanying notes. List and briefly discuss information included for this partnership that would typically not appear in financial statements produced for a corporation.

ANALYSIS CASE

CPA *skills*

Erin Carson, Megyn Delaney, and Caitlin Erikson form a partnership as a first step in creating a business. Carson invests most of the capital but does not plan to be actively involved in the day-to-day operations. Delaney has had some experience and is expected to do a majority of the daily work. Erikson has been in this line of business for some time and has many connections. Therefore, she will devote a majority of her time to getting new clients.

Required

Write a memo to these three partners suggesting at least two different ways in which the profits of the partnership can be allocated each year in order to be fair to all parties.

COMMUNICATION CASE 1

CPA *skills*

Kelly Fernandez and Michael Webster have decided to create a business. They have financing available and have a well-developed business plan. However, they have not yet decided which type of legal business structure would be best for them.

Required

Write a report for these two individuals outlining the types of situations in which the corporate form of legal structure would be the best choice.

COMMUNICATION CASE 2

CPA *skills*

Use the information in Communication Case 1.

Required

Write a report for these two individuals outlining the types of situations in which the partnership form of legal structure would be the best choice.

EXCEL CASE

CPA
skills

The Ace and Deuce partnership has been created to operate a law firm. The partners are attempting to devise a fair system to allocate profits and losses. Ace plans to work more billable hours each year than Deuce. However, Deuce has more experience and can charge a higher hourly rate. Ace expects to invest more money in the business than Deuce.

Required

Build a spreadsheet that can be used to allocate profits and losses to these two partners each year. The spreadsheet should be constructed so that the following variables can be entered:

Net income for the year.

Number of billable hours for each partner.

Hourly rate for each partner.

Capital investment by each partner.

Interest rate on capital investment.

Profit and loss ratio.

Use this spreadsheet to determine the allocation if partnership net income for the current year is $200,000, the number of billable hours is 2,000 for Ace and 1,500 for Deuce, the hourly rate for Ace is $20 and for Deuce is $30, and investment by Ace is $80,000 and by Deuce is $50,000. Interest on capital will be accrued each year at 10 percent of the beginning balance. Any remaining income amount will be split 50–50.

Use the spreadsheet a second time but make these changes: Deuce reports 1,700 billable hours, Ace invests $100,000, and interest will be recognized at a 12 percent annual rate. How do these three changes impact the allocation of the $200,000?

Partnerships: Termination and Liquidation

Partnerships can be rather fragile organizations. Termination of business activities followed by the liquidation of partnership property can take place for a variety of reasons, both legal and personal. Although a business organized as a partnership can exist indefinitely through periodic changes within the ownership, the actual cessation of operations is not an uncommon occurrence. Eventually, most partnerships will come to an end. Possible causes include one partner dying, retiring, or deciding to get into a different line of business; the partners becoming incompatible and choosing to cease working with one another; or profits failing to reach projected levels and the partners decide to terminate their partnership and move on to other business opportunities.

The termination of a partnership occurs when business operations are discontinued. The subsequent liquidation of a partnership generally involves three important steps:

1. Noncash partnership assets are sold for cash. Gains and losses on the asset sales are allocated to the capital accounts of individual partners on the basis of their profit and loss ratios.
2. Partnership liabilities and expenses incurred during the liquidation are paid from the partnership's available cash. Liquidation expenses are allocated to partners' capital accounts on the basis of profit and loss ratios.
3. Any partnership cash remaining after paying liabilities and liquidation expenses is distributed to the individual partners on the basis of their respective capital balances.

The accountant can summarize and keep track of these steps in a *statement of partnership liquidation.*

The liquidation of a partnership becomes more complicated when

- One or more partners has a negative (deficit) capital balance. A deficit (debit) capital balance can exist either at the beginning of the liquidation process or can arise during the liquidation as partners' capital balances absorb losses from noncash asset sales and liquidation expenses. In some cases, a partner with a deficit capital balance will have sufficient personal assets to be able to make a contribution to the partnership to offset the deficit. In other cases, a partner will be personally insolvent, and the other partners will have to absorb the deficit through reductions in their capital accounts.

- The liquidation takes place over an extended period of time. In this case, the partners are likely to request that cash be distributed to them as it

Learning Objectives

After studying this chapter, you should be able to:

LO 10-1 Determine amounts to be paid to partners in a liquidation.

LO 10-2 Prepare journal entries to record the transactions incurred in the liquidation of a partnership.

LO 10-3 Prepare a statement of partnership liquidation that summarizes transactions occurring during the liquidation of a partnership.

LO 10-4 Determine the distribution of available cash when one or more partners have a deficit capital balance.

LO 10-5 Calculate the safe payments that can be made to individual partners from cash that becomes available prior to final liquidation.

LO 10-6 Prepare a proposed schedule of liquidation to determine an equitable preliminary distribution of available partnership assets.

LO 10-7 Develop a predistribution plan to guide the distribution of cash in a partnership liquidation.

becomes available through the liquidation of partnership assets. The accountant can facilitate the distribution of cash in installments by calculating the *safe payments* that can be made without running the risk that an individual partner will incur a deficit capital balance, and then by preparing a series of *proposed statements of liquidation* based on those calculations. Or the accountant might choose to prepare a cash *predistribution plan* in advance of any sales of noncash assets to guide the distribution of installment payments during the course of the partnership liquidation.

Termination and Liquidation—Protecting the Interests of All Parties

As the chapter on bankruptcy discussed, accounting for the termination and liquidation of a business can prove to be a delicate task. Beyond the goal of merely reporting transactions, the accountant must work to ensure the equitable treatment of all parties involved in the liquidation. The accounting records are the basis for allocating available assets to creditors and to the individual partners. If assets are limited, the accountant also might have to make recommendations as to the appropriate method for distributing any remaining funds. Protecting the interests of partnership creditors is an especially significant duty because the Uniform Partnership Act specifies that they have first priority to the assets held by the business at dissolution.

Not only the creditors but also the partners themselves have a great interest in the financial data produced during the period of liquidation. They must be concerned with the possibility of incurring substantial monetary losses. The potential for loss is especially significant because of the unlimited liability to which the partners are exposed.

As long as a partnership can meet all of its obligations, the risk to partners is normally no more than that of corporate stockholders; the most they can lose is their capital investment. However, should the partnership become insolvent (that is, have insufficient cash to pay its obligations), *each* partner faces the possibility of having to satisfy *all* remaining partnership obligations personally. Although any partner suffering more than a proportionate share of these losses can seek legal remedy from the other partners, this process is not always effective. The other partners may themselves be personally insolvent, or anticipated legal costs might discourage the damaged partner from seeking recovery. Therefore, each partner usually has a keen interest in monitoring the progress of a liquidation as it transpires.

LO 10-1

Determine amounts to be paid to partners in a liquidation.

Partnership Liquidation Procedures

The procedures involved in terminating and liquidating a partnership are basically mechanical. Partnership assets are converted into cash that is then used to pay partnership liabilities as well as any liquidation expenses. *Any remaining cash is distributed to the individual partners based on their final capital balances.* Once all cash has been distributed, the partnership's books are permanently closed. If each partner has a capital balance large enough to absorb all liquidation losses and expenses, the accountant should experience little difficulty in recording this series of transactions.

To illustrate a simple liquidation process, assume that Morgan and Houseman have been operating an art gallery as a partnership for a number of years. Morgan and Houseman allocate all profits and losses on a 60%:40% basis, respectively. On May 1, the partners decide to terminate business activities, liquidate all noncash assets, and dissolve their partnership. Although they give no specific explanation for this action, any number of reasons could exist. The partners, for example, could have come to a disagreement so that they no longer believe they can work together. Another possibility is that business profits have become inadequate to warrant the continuing investment of their time and capital.

The following is a balance sheet for the partnership of Morgan and Houseman as of the termination date (that is, the date the partners close the art gallery). The partnership has $75,000 of noncash assets to be liquidated. The revenue, expense, and partner's drawing accounts have been closed as a preliminary step in terminating the business. A separate reporting of the gains and losses that occur during the liquidation process will subsequently be made.

MORGAN AND HOUSEMAN
Balance Sheet
Termination Date (May 1)

Assets		Liabilities and Capital	
Cash	$ 45,000	Liabilities.	$ 32,000
Accounts receivable.	12,000	Morgan, capital	50,000
Inventory.	22,000	Houseman, capital	38,000
Land, building, and			
equipment (net).	41,000		
Total assets	$120,000	Total liabilities and capital.	$120,000

The liquidation of Morgan and Houseman proceeds in an orderly fashion through the following events:

June 1	The inventory is sold at auction for $15,000.
June 15	Of the total accounts receivable, the partnership collected $9,000 and wrote off the remainder as being uncollectible.
July 1	The land, building, and equipment are sold for a total of $29,000.
July 5	All partnership liabilities are paid.
July 10	A total of $3,000 in liquidation expenses is paid to cover accounting and legal fees as well as the sales commissions incurred in disposing of partnership property.
July 12	All remaining cash is distributed to the owners based on their final capital account balances.

The partnership of Morgan and Houseman incurred a number of losses in liquidating its assets. Losses often are expected because the need for immediate sale usually holds a high priority in a liquidation. Furthermore, a portion of the assets used by any business, such as its equipment and buildings, could have value that is strictly limited to a particular type of operation. If the assets are not easily adaptable for other uses, disposal at any reasonable price often proves to be difficult.

LO 10-2

Prepare journal entries to record the transactions incurred in the liquidation of a partnership.

To record the liquidation of Morgan and Houseman, the following journal entries would be made. Rather than report specific income and expense balances, gains and losses are recorded directly to the partners' capital accounts, allocated on the basis of the partners' profit and loss ratio. Because operations have ceased, determination of a separate net income figure for this period is unnecessary, as it would provide little informational value. *Instead, a primary concern of the parties involved in any liquidation is keeping track of the continuing changes in each partner's capital balance.*

6/1	Cash	15,000	
	Morgan, Capital (60% of loss)	4,200	
	Houseman, Capital (40% of loss)	2,800	
	Inventory.		22,000
	To record sale of partnership inventory at a $7,000 loss.		

(continued)

(continued)

6/15	Cash	9,000	
	Morgan, Capital	1,800	
	Houseman, Capital	1,200	
	Accounts Receivable		12,000
	To record collection of accounts receivable with write-off of remaining $3,000 in accounts as being uncollectible.		
7/1	Cash	29,000	
	Morgan, Capital	7,200	
	Houseman, Capital	4,800	
	Land, Building, and Equipment (net)		41,000
	To record sale of land, building, and equipment and allocation of $12,000 loss.		
7/5	Liabilities	32,000	
	Cash		32,000
	To record payment made to settle the liabilities of the partnership.		
7/10	Morgan, Capital	1,800	
	Houseman, Capital	1,200	
	Cash		3,000
	To record payment of liquidation expenses with the amounts recorded as direct reductions to the partners' capital accounts.		

After liquidating the partnership assets, paying all partnership liabilities, and paying liquidation expenses, the $63,000 cash that remains can be distributed to Morgan and Houseman on the basis of their capital balances. The following schedule determines the partners' ending capital account balances and, thus, the appropriate distribution of the final cash balance.

Cash and Capital Account Balances

	Cash	Morgan, Capital	Houseman, Capital
Beginning balances*	$45,000	$50,000	$38,000
Sold inventory	15,000	(4,200)	(2,800)
Collected accounts receivable	9,000	(1,800)	(1,200)
Sold fixed assets	29,000	(7,200)	(4,800)
Paid liabilities	(32,000)	–0–	–0–
Paid liquidation expenses	(3,000)	(1,800)	(1,200)
Final balances	$63,000	$35,000	$28,000

*Because of the presence of other assets as well as liabilities, the beginning balances in Cash and in the capital accounts are not equal.

After the final capital balances have been calculated, the remaining cash can be distributed to the partners to close out the financial records of the partnership:

7/12	Morgan, Capital	35,000	
	Houseman, Capital	28,000	
	Cash		63,000
	To record distribution of cash to partners in accordance with final capital balances.		

LO 10-3

Prepare a statement of partnership liquidation that summarizes transactions occurring during the liquidation of a partnership.

Statement of Partnership Liquidation

Liquidation can take a considerable length of time to complete. Because the various parties involved seek continually updated financial information, the accountant should produce frequent reports summarizing transactions as they occur. Consequently, a statement (often referred to as a *statement of partnership liquidation*) can be prepared at periodic intervals to reflect:

- Transactions to date.
- Assets still held by the partnership.
- Liabilities remaining to be paid.
- Current cash and capital balances.

Although the preceding Morgan and Houseman example has been condensed into a few events occurring during a relatively brief period of time, partnership liquidations usually require numerous transactions that transpire over months and, perhaps, even years. By receiving frequent statements of partnership liquidation, both the creditors and the partners are able to stay apprised of the results of this lengthy process.

Exhibit 10.1 shows the final statement of partnership liquidation for the partnership of Morgan and Houseman. The accountant should have distributed previous statements at each important juncture of this liquidation to meet the informational needs of the parties involved. Exhibit 10.1 demonstrates the stair-step approach incorporated in preparing a statement of liquidation. The effects of each transaction (or group of transactions) are outlined in a horizontal fashion so that current account balances and all prior transactions are evident. This structuring also facilitates the preparation of future statements: A new layer summarizing recent events can simply be added at the bottom each time a new statement is to be produced.

Deficit Capital Balances

LO 10-4

Determine the distribution of available cash when one or more partners have a deficit capital balance.

During the liquidation process, one or more partners could have a negative (deficit) balance in their capital account. Such deficits are most likely to occur when the partnership has incurred significant operating losses that have negatively affected partners' capital balances or when the sale of noncash assets during the liquidation process results in material losses.

In some cases, partners with deficit capital balances will make a cash contribution to the partnership to offset their deficit. When a deficit partner lacks sufficient cash (is insolvent) or is simply unwilling to make a contribution, remaining partners must absorb that partner's

EXHIBIT 10.1

		Noncash		Morgan, Capital	Houseman, Capital
MORGAN AND HOUSEMAN Statement of Partnership Liquidation					
	Cash	Assets	Liabilities	(60%)	(40%)
Beginning balances, 5/1	$ 45,000	$ 75,000	$ 32,000	$ 50,000	$ 38,000
Sold inventory, 6/1	15,000	(22,000)	–0–	(4,200)	(2,800)
Updated balances	60,000	53,000	32,000	45,800	35,200
Collected receivables, 6/15	9,000	(12,000)	–0–	(1,800)	(1,200)
Updated balances	69,000	41,000	32,000	44,000	34,000
Sold land, building, and equipment, 7/1	29,000	(41,000)	–0–	(7,200)	(4,800)
Updated balances	98,000	–0–	32,000	36,800	29,200
Paid liabilities, 7/5	(32,000)		(32,000)	– 0–	–0–
Updated balances	66,000	–0–	–0–	36,800	29,200
Paid liquidation expenses, 7/10	(3,000)			(1,800)	(1,200)
Updated balances	63,000	–0–	–0–	35,000	28,000
Distributed remaining cash, 7/12	(63,000)			(35,000)	(28,000)
Closing balances...........................	$ –0–	$ –0–	$ –0–	$ –0–	$ –0–

Discussion Question

WHAT HAPPENS IF A PARTNER BECOMES INSOLVENT?

Three dentists—Menchaca, Nguyen, and St. Clair—formed a partnership to open a practice in New Braunfels, Texas. The partnership's primary purpose was to reduce expenses by sharing building and equipment costs, supplies, and the services of clerical staff. Each partner contributed $100,000 in cash and, with the help of a bank loan, constructed a building and acquired furniture, fixtures, and equipment. Because the partners maintained their own separate clients, annual net income was allocated as follows: Each partner received the specific amount of revenues that they generated less one-third of all expenses. From the beginning, the partners did not anticipate expansion of the practice; consequently, they agreed to be able to withdraw cash each year up to 90 percent of their share of income for the period.

The partnership was profitable since its creation. Over the years, St. Clair invested heavily in real estate in the local area. After several years, St. Clair was spending less time with the dental practice to be able to concentrate on real estate investments. Unfortunately, a number of these real estate deals proved to be bad decisions, and St. Clair incurred significant personal losses. A week ago, St. Clair's personal creditors filed a $143,000 claim against the partnership's assets. Unbeknownst to Menchaca and Nguyen, St. Clair had become personally insolvent.

Menchaca and Nguyen hurriedly met to discuss the problem because St. Clair could not be located. St. Clair's capital account had a balance of $120,000, but the partnership had only $38,000 in cash. The partners knew that St. Clair's dental equipment could be sold for relatively little. In contrast, the building had appreciated in value, and St. Clair's creditors' claims could be satisfied by selling the property. However, this action would have a tremendously disruptive impact on the dental practice of the remaining two partners.

What alternatives are available to Menchaca and Nguyen to deal with this situation, and what are the advantages and disadvantages of each alternative?

deficit as losses to their capital accounts. This section demonstrates the procedures for dealing with three different scenarios:

1. One partner has a deficit capital balance; that partner makes a contribution to the partnership to offset the deficit.
2. One partner has a deficit capital balance; other partners absorb that deficit as a loss.
3. Two partners have deficit capital balances; only one partner makes a contribution to offset the deficit.

Recognize that these are only three of an infinite number of possible situations involving deficit capital balances.

Partner with Deficit—Contribution to Partnership

To illustrate the situation in which a partner with a deficit capital balance makes a cash contribution to the partnership, assume that the partnership of Kozel, Petroff, and Zeman was terminated at the beginning of the current year. Business activities ceased and all noncash assets were subsequently converted into cash. During the liquidation process, the partnership incurred a number of large losses that have been allocated to the partners' capital accounts on a 4:4:2 basis, respectively. A portion of the resulting cash is then used to pay all partnership liabilities and liquidation expenses.

Following these transactions, only the following four account balances remain open within the partnership's records:

Cash	$20,000	Kozel, capital 40%	$ (6,000)	
		Petroff, capital 40%	15,000	
		Zeman, capital 20%	11,000	
		Total	$20,000	

Kozel has a negative capital balance of $6,000; the share of partnership losses allocated to Kozel has exceeded this partner's capital balance at the date the partnership terminated. Kozel is personally solvent and agrees to contribute $6,000 to the partnership to offset the negative capital balance. This contribution raises the cash balance to $26,000, which allows a complete distribution of cash to be made to Petroff ($15,000) and Zeman ($11,000) based on their capital account balances. The journal entries for these final payments close out the partnership records:

Cash	6,000	
Kozel, Capital..		6,000
To record contribution made by Kozel to extinguish negative capital balance.		
Petroff, Capital...	15,000	
Zeman, Capital..	11,000	
Cash		26,000
To record distribution of remaining cash to partners in accordance with their ending capital balances.		

Partner with Deficit—Loss to Remaining Partners

An alternative scenario could easily arise for the previous partnership liquidation. Assume that although Kozel's capital account shows a $6,000 deficit balance, this partner is personally insolvent and is unable to make a cash contribution.

In this case, Petroff and Zeman must absorb a $6,000 loss on the basis of their relative profit and loss ratio (4:2, or ⅔:⅓). This is reflected in the following journal entry:

Petroff, Capital (⅔ of loss)	4,000	
Zeman, Capital (⅓ of loss)	2,000	
Kozel, Capital..		6,000
To record allocation of deficit capital balance of insolvent partner.		

After posting this entry to the accounts, Petroff has a capital balance of $11,000 ($15,000 − $4,000) and Zeman has a capital balance of $9,000 ($11,000 − $2,000). One final entry records the distribution of the $20,000 ending cash balance to the remaining partners and serves to close out the partnership books.

Petroff, Capital...	11,000	
Zeman, Capital..	9,000	
Cash		20,000
To record distribution of remaining cash to partners in accordance with their ending capital balances.		

Two Partners with Deficit Capital Balances

Now we consider a different partnership in which two partners have negative ending capital balances. The following balance sheet is presented for the medical practice partnership of Agarwal, Garza, Mochi, and Watt and indicates the applicable profit and loss percentages.

Cash	$ 10,000	Liabilities	$ 70,000
Noncash assets	140,000	Agarwal, capital (40%)	15,000
		Garza, capital (20%)	10,000
		Mochi, capital (20%)	23,000
		Watt, capital (20%)	32,000
Total assets	$150,000	Total liabilities and capital	$150,000

Both Agarwal and Watt are personally insolvent. Agarwal's personal creditors have brought an $8,000 claim against the partnership's assets, and Watt's creditors are seeking $15,000. These claims have forced the partnership to terminate operations so that the business property can be liquidated and the insolvent partners can settle their personal obligations. The question arises as to how much cash each partner is entitled to as a result of the liquidation.

Assume that the partnership sells the noncash assets for a total of $80,000, creating a $60,000 loss, and pays all its liabilities. The partnership records these two events as follows:

Cash	80,000	
Agarwal, Capital (40% of loss)	24,000	
Garza, Capital (20% of loss)	12,000	
Mochi, Capital (20% of loss)	12,000	
Watt, Capital (20% of loss)	12,000	
Noncash Assets		140,000
To record sale of noncash assets and allocation of resulting $60,000 loss.		
Liabilities	70,000	
Cash		70,000
To record payment of partnership liabilities.		

As a result of these two transactions, the partnership's cash balance has increased from $10,000 to $20,000.

After allocation of the loss on the sale of the noncash assets, the capital accounts for Agarwal and Garza have deficit balances of $9,000 ($15,000 − $24,000) and $2,000 ($10,000 − $12,000), respectively. Although Garza is personally solvent and therefore will make a cash contribution to the partnership, Agarwal's personal financial condition does not allow for any further contribution. Therefore, Garza, Mochi, and Watt must absorb Agarwal's $9,000 deficit. Because each of these three partners has a 20 percent share of partnership profits and losses, they share this deficit equally:

Garza, Capital (⅓ of loss)	3,000	
Mochi, Capital (⅓ of loss)	3,000	
Watt, Capital (⅓ of loss)	3,000	
Agarwal, Capital		9,000
To record write-off of deficit capital balance of insolvent partner.		

This allocation increases Garza's deficit to a $5,000 balance ($2,000 + $3,000), an amount that this partner now contributes to the partnership.

Cash	5,000	
Garza, Capital		5,000
To record contribution from solvent partner necessitated by negative capital balance.		

Exhibit 10.2 presents the statement of partnership liquidation summarizing the series of transactions that takes place in the liquidation of this partnership.

EXHIBIT 10.2

	Cash	Noncash Assets	Liabilities	Agarwal, Capital (40%)	Garza, Capital (20%)	Mochi, Capital (20%)	Watt, Capital (20%)
AGARWAL, GARZA, MOCHI, AND WATT PARTNERSHIP **Statement of Partnership Liquidation**							
Beginning balances	$10,000	$140,000	$(70,000)	$15,000	$10,000	$23,000	$32,000
Sold noncash assets.	80,000	(140,000)	–0–	(24,000)	(12,000)	(12,000)	(12,000)
Updated balances	90,000	–0–	(70,000)	(9,000)	(2,000)	11,000	20,000
Paid liabilities	(70,000)	–0–	70,000	–0–	–0–	–0–	–0–
Updated balances	20,000	–0–	–0–	(9,000)	(2,000)	11,000	20,000
Default by Agarwal	–0–	–0–	–0–	9,000	(3,000)	(3,000)	(3,000)
Updated balances	20,000	–0–	–0–	–0–	(5,000)	8,000	17,000
Contribution by Garza	5,000	–0–	–0–	–0–	5,000	–0–	–0–
Updated balances	25,000	–0–	–0–	–0–	–0–	8,000	17,000
Distribute remaining cash	(25,000)	–0–	–0–	–0–	–0–	(8,000)	(17,000)
Closing balances.	$ –0–	$ –0–	$ –0–	$ –0–	$ –0–	$ –0–	$ –0–

The journal entry to close this partnership's books is as follows:

Mochi, Capital	8,000	
Watt, Capital.	17,000	
Cash		25,000
To record distribution of remaining cash based upon final capital account balances.		

Although $8,000 of the partnership's remaining cash is paid directly to Mochi, the $17,000 attributed to Watt is first subjected to the claims of the partner's personal creditors. Because of their claims, $15,000 of this amount must be used to satisfy these obligations, with only the final $2,000 actually being paid directly to Watt. Because Agarwal receives no distribution of cash from the partnership, no assets become available to settle claims of this partner's personal creditors.

LO 10-5

Calculate the safe payments that can be made to individual partners from cash that becomes available prior to final liquidation.

Safe Payments to Partners

In the earlier scenarios in which one of the partners in the law firm of Kozel, Petroff, and Zeman had a deficit capital balance, no cash was distributed to any partner until the deficit capital balance had been resolved—either by Kozel making a contribution to the partnership or by the other partners absorbing Kozel's deficit. Recall that the partnership had the following balances after liquidation of noncash assets and payment of liabilities and expenses:

Cash	$20,000	Kozel, capital	$ (6,000)
		Petroff, capital	15,000
		Zeman, capital.	11,000
		Total	$20,000

While awaiting the final resolution of Kozel's capital deficit, no compelling reason exists for the partnership to continue holding $20,000 in cash. These funds eventually will be paid to Petroff and Zeman regardless of whether Kozel makes a contribution or not. An immediate transfer of cash should be made to these two partners to allow them the use of their money. However, because Petroff has a $15,000 capital account balance and Zeman currently has

$11,000, a complete distribution to close their capital accounts is not possible. A method must be devised, therefore, to allow for a fair allocation of the available $20,000.

To ensure the equitable treatment of all parties, this initial distribution is based on the assumption that the $6,000 deficit capital balance will prove to be a total loss to the partnership. By making this conservative presumption, the accountant is able to calculate the lowest possible amounts (or *safe capital balances*) that Petroff and Zeman must retain in their capital accounts to be able to absorb all future losses. Based upon these safe capital balances, the accountant can determine the amount of *safe payments* that can be made to Petroff and Zeman without running the risk that future losses will cause either of these partners to have a deficit capital balance.

Calculation of Safe Payments

Should Kozel's $6,000 deficit (or any portion of it) prove uncollectible, the loss will be written off against the capital accounts of Petroff and Zeman based on their relative profit and loss ratio. Petroff and Zeman are credited with 40 percent and 20 percent of partnership income, respectively, which equates to ⅔:⅓ split between the two of them. Thus, if no part of the $6,000 deficit balance is ever recovered from Kozel, $4,000 (two-thirds) of the loss will be assigned to Petroff and $2,000 (one-third) to Zeman:

Petroff	⅔ of $(6,000) = $(4,000)
Zeman	⅓ of $(6,000) = $(2,000)

These amounts represent the maximum potential reductions that could be allocated to the two remaining partners' capital accounts. These balances must therefore remain in the respective capital accounts until Kozel's deficit is resolved. Therefore, a safe payment of $11,000 may be made to Petroff at the present time; this distribution reduces that partner's capital account from $15,000 to the safe capital balance of $4,000. Likewise, a safe payment of $9,000 may be made to Zeman, which decreases this partner's $11,000 capital account to the $2,000 safe balance. Thus, $11,000 and $9,000 are the safe payments that can be distributed to the partners at the present time without fear of creating new deficits in the future:

Petroff, Capital...	11,000	
Zeman, Capital...	9,000	
Cash		20,000
To record distribution of safe payments of cash to Petroff and Zeman based on the assumption that Kozel will not contribute further to the partnership.		

After this $20,000 cash distribution, only a few other events can occur during the remaining life of the partnership. Kozel could contribute the entire $6,000 needed to offset the capital deficit. In this case, the cash contributed should be immediately distributed to Petroff ($4,000) and Zeman ($2,000) based on their remaining capital balances. This final distribution effectively closes the partnership records.

A second possibility is that Petroff and Zeman could be unable to recover any part of the deficit from Kozel. These two remaining partners must then absorb the $6,000 loss themselves. Because adequate capital balances have been maintained, recording a complete default by Kozel serves to close out the partnership books:

Petroff, Capital (⅔ of loss)	4,000	
Zeman, Capital (⅓ of loss)	2,000	
Kozel, Capital..		6,000
To record allocation of deficit capital balance of insolvent partner.		

Partial Contribution to Partnership

One other ending to this partnership liquidation is possible. The partnership could recover a portion of the $6,000 from Kozel, but the remainder could prove to be uncollectible. Kozel could become bankrupt, or the other partners could simply give up trying to collect from Kozel. The partners could also negotiate a partial settlement to avoid protracted legal actions.

To illustrate, assume that Kozel manages to contribute $3,600 to the partnership but subsequently files for relief under the provisions of bankruptcy law. In a later legal arrangement, Kozel makes an additional $1,000 cash payment to the partnership, but the final $1,400 will never be collected. This series of events creates the following effects within the liquidation process:

1. The $3,600 contribution made by Kozel is distributed to Petroff and Zeman based on a new calculation of safe payments.
2. The $1,400 default is charged against the two positive capital balances in accordance with their relative profit and loss ratio.
3. The final $1,000 contribution made by Kozel is then paid to Petroff and Zeman in amounts equal to their ending capital balances, a transaction that closes the partnership's financial records.

The distribution of the $3,600 contribution made by Kozel depends on a recalculation of the minimum capital balances that Petroff and Zeman must maintain to absorb all potential losses. At this point, the potential remaining loss is $2,400 ($6,000 deficit − $3,600 contribution). Petroff and Zeman absorb this loss in a 40:20 (⅔:⅓) ratio, respectively. This approach guarantees that these two partners will continue to report sufficient capital until the liquidation is ultimately resolved.

	Current Capital		Allocation of Potential Loss		Safe Payments
Petroff	$4,000	−	⅔ of $(2,400) = $(1,600)	=	$2,400
Zeman	$2,000	−	⅓ of $(2,400) = $ (800)	=	$1,200

Petroff and Zeman must maintain capital balances of $1,600 and $800, respectively, to absorb a potential default by Kozel on the remaining $2,400. The $3,600 in cash that is now available is distributed immediately to Petroff and Zeman as safe payments. These two entries record Kozel's contribution and the subsequent safe payments made to Petroff and Zeman:

Cash	3,600	
Kozel, Capital.		3,600
To record a cash contribution by Kozel.		
Petroff, Capital.	2,400	
Zeman, Capital.	1,200	
Cash		3,600
To record safe payments to Petroff and Zeman.		

After recording this $3,600 contribution from Kozel and the subsequent disbursement to Petroff and Zeman, the partnership's capital accounts stay open, registering the following balances:

Kozel, Capital (deficit).	$(2,400)
Petroff, Capital.	1,600
Zeman, Capital.	800

These accounts continue to remain on the partnership books until the final resolution of Kozel's deficit capital balance.

In this illustration, the $1,000 legal settlement and the remaining $1,400 loss ultimately allow the parties to close out the records:

Cash	1,000	
Petroff, Capital (⅔ of loss)	933	
Zeman, Capital (⅓ of loss)	467	
Kozel, Capital.		2,400
To record final $1,000 cash settlement of Kozel's interest and resulting $1,400 loss.		
Petroff, Capital.	667	
Zeman, Capital.	333	
Cash		1,000
To record distribution of final cash balance based upon remaining capital account totals.		

LO 10-6

Prepare a proposed schedule of liquidation to determine an equitable preliminary distribution of available partnership assets.

Preliminary Distribution of Partnership Assets

As previously mentioned, a liquidation can take an extended time to complete. During this lengthy process, the partnership need not retain any assets that eventually will be disbursed to the partners. Partnerships often have a sufficient cash balance at the date of termination that some amount of cash can be paid out to individual partners even before noncash assets are sold. If the business is solvent (that is, cash exceeds liabilities plus estimated liquidation expenses), waiting until all affairs have been settled before transferring cash to the owners is not warranted. The partners should be allowed to receive cash to which they are entitled at the earliest possible time.

Examples presented earlier in this chapter have shown how to calculate safe payments that can be made to individual partners prior to the completion of all liquidation transactions. Indeed, in some cases, cash can be distributed to partners at the date of partnership termination before any liquidation transactions have taken place. The accountant can determine a *preliminary distribution of partnership assets* at the beginning of the liquidation process. The accountant can facilitate such an early distribution of cash by preparing a *proposed schedule of liquidation.*

The objective in making any type of preliminary distribution is to ensure that the partnership maintains enough capital to absorb all future losses. To determine safe payments that can be made to partners at any time, the accountant *assumes* that all subsequent events will result in maximum losses: No cash will be received in liquidating remaining noncash assets, and each partner is personally insolvent. Any positive capital balances that remain even after the inclusion of all potential losses can be paid to partners without delay. Although the assumption that no further funds will be generated could be unrealistic, it does ensure that negative capital balances cannot arise as a result of premature payments being made to any of the partners.

Preliminary Distribution Illustrated

Assume the partnership of Ahn, Bayu, and Chaniago has decided to terminate operations and liquidate the business. The partnership reports the following balance sheet at the date of termination:

Cash	$ 60,000		Liabilities..........................	$ 40,000
Noncash assets..........	140,000		Ahn, loan..........................	20,000
			Ahn, capital (50%)	60,000
			Bayu, capital (30%)	30,000
			Chaniago, capital (20%)	50,000
Total assets	$200,000		Total liabilities and capital........	$200,000

Assume also that the partners estimate that $6,000 will be the maximum expense incurred in carrying out this liquidation. Consequently, the partnership needs $46,000 to meet all obligations: $40,000 to satisfy partnership liabilities and $6,000 for liquidation expenses. Because the partnership holds $60,000 in cash, it can transfer the extra $14,000 to the partners immediately without fear of injuring any participants in the liquidation. However, the appropriate allocation of this money is not readily apparent; safe capital balances must be computed to guide the actual distribution of safe payments.

Before demonstrating the allocation of this $14,000, we examine the appropriate handling of a partner's loan balance. According to the balance sheet, Ahn has lent $20,000 to the business at some point in the past, an amount that was considered a loan rather than additional capital. Perhaps the partnership was in desperate need of funds and Ahn was willing to contribute only if the contribution was structured as a loan. Regardless of the reason, the question as to the status of this account remains: Is the $20,000 to be viewed as a liability to the partnership or as a part of the partner's capital balance? The answer becomes especially significant during the liquidation process because available funds often are limited. In this regard, the Uniform Partnership Act (UPA) (Section 807[a]) indicates that the assets of the partnership must be applied to pay obligations to creditors, including partners who are creditors; any surplus is distributed to partners based on their capital balances.

Although the UPA indicates that the debt to Ahn should be repaid entirely before any distribution of capital can be made to the other partners, actual accounting practice takes a different view. Accountants normally offset partners' loans against partners' capital accounts when making preliminary distributions of partnership assets.[1] In other words, the loan is merged with the partner's capital account balance at the beginning of liquidation. Thus, accounting practice and the UPA seem to differ in the handling of a loan from a partner. To follow common practice, this textbook accounts for a loan from a partner in liquidation as if the loan were a component of the partner's capital. By this offset, the accountant can reduce the amount accumulated as a negative capital balance for any insolvent partner. Any such loan can be transferred into the corresponding capital account at the start of the liquidation process. Similarly, any loans *due from* a partner should be shown as a reduction in the partner's capital account balance.

Proposed Schedule of Liquidation

Returning to the current illustration, the accountant needs to determine an equitable distribution of the $14,000 cash currently available. To structure this computation, a proposed schedule of liquidation is developed *based on the underlying assumption that all future events will result in total losses.* Exhibit 10.3 presents this statement for the Ahn, Bayu, and Chaniago partnership. To expedite procedures, in accordance with common accounting practice, the $20,000 loan has already been transferred into Ahn's capital account. Thus, regardless of whether this partner ends up with a positive or negative capital account balance, the loan amount already has been included.

The preparation of Exhibit 10.3 forecasts complete losses ($140,000) in connection with the disposition of all noncash assets and anticipates liquidation expenses at maximum amounts ($6,000). Following the projected payment of liabilities, any partner reporting a negative capital balance is assumed to be personally insolvent. These potential deficit balances are written off, and the losses are assigned to the remaining solvent partners based on their relative profit and loss ratio. Bayu, with a negative capital balance of $13,800, is eliminated first. This allocation creates a deficit of $2,857 for Ahn, an amount that Chaniago alone must absorb. After this series of maximum losses is simulated, Chaniago is the only partner with a positive capital balance.

Exhibit 10.3 indicates that only Chaniago has a large enough capital balance at the present time to absorb all possible future losses. Thus, the entire $14,000 can be safely distributed to Chaniago with no fear that this partner's capital account will ever result in a deficit balance. Based on current practice, Ahn, despite having made a $20,000 loan to the partnership, is entitled to no part of this initial distribution. The loan is of insufficient size to prevent potential deficits from occurring in Ahn's capital account.

---

[1] Robert E. Whitis and Jeffrey R. Pittman, "Inconsistencies between Accounting Practices and Statutory Law in Partnership Liquidations," *Accounting Educators' Journal*, Fall 1996, p. 99.

EXHIBIT 10.3

		Noncash		Ahn, Capital and	Bayu, Capital	Chaniago, Capital
	Cash	Assets	Liabilities	Loan (50%)	(30%)	(20%)

AHN, BAYU, AND CHANIAGO
Proposed Schedule of Liquidation—Initial Safe Payments

	Cash	Noncash Assets	Liabilities	Ahn, Capital and Loan (50%)	Bayu, Capital (30%)	Chaniago, Capital (20%)
Beginning balances	$60,000	$140,000	$40,000	$80,000	$30,000	$50,000
Maximum loss on noncash assets	–0–	(140,000)	–0–	(70,000)	(42,000)	(28,000)
Maximum liquidation expenses	(6,000)	–0–	–0–	(3,000)	(1,800)	(1,200)
Payment of liabilities.	(40,000)	–0–	(40,000)	–0–	–0–	–0–
Subtotal (potential balances).	14,000	–0–	–0–	7,000	(13,800)	20,800
Allocation of Bayu's deficit						
capital balance	–0–	–0–	–0–	(9,857) (5/7)	13,800	(3,943) 2/7
Subtotal (potential balances).	14,000	–0–	–0–	(2,857)	–0–	16,857
Allocation of Ahn's deficit						
capital balance	–0–	–0–	–0–	2,857	–0–	(2,857)
Initial safe payments.	$14,000	$ –0–	$ –0–	$ –0–	$ –0–	$14,000

One series of computations found in this proposed schedule of liquidation merits additional attention. The simulated losses initially create a $13,800 negative balance in Bayu's capital account while the other two partners continue to report positive balances. Ahn and Chaniago must then absorb Bayu's projected deficit according to their relative profit and loss percentages. Previously, Ahn was allocated 50 percent of net income with 20 percent recorded to Chaniago. These figures equate to a $50/70:20/70$ or a 5/7 : 2/7 ratio. Based on this realigned relationship, the $13,800 potential deficit is allocated between Ahn (5/7 or $9,857) and Chaniago (2/7 or $3,943), reducing Ahn's own capital account to a negative balance as shown in Exhibit 10.3.

Liquidation in Installments

In reality, complete losses are not likely to occur in the liquidation of any business. Thus, at various points during this process, additional cash amounts can become available as partnership property is sold. If the assets are disposed of in a piecemeal fashion, cash can actually flow into the company on a regular basis for an extended period of time. As needed, additional proposed schedules of liquidation can be developed to determine the distribution of newly available funds. Because numerous cash distributions could be required, this process is often referred to as a *liquidation made in installments*.

To illustrate, assume that the partnership of Ahn, Bayu, and Chaniago undergoes the following *actual* events in connection with its liquidation:

- As the proposed schedule of liquidation in Exhibit 10.3 indicates, Chaniago receives $14,000 in cash as a preliminary capital distribution based on the calculation of *initial* safe payments.
- Noncash assets with a book value of $50,000 are sold for $20,000.
- All $40,000 in liabilities are paid in cash.
- Liquidation expenses of $2,000 are paid; the partners now believe that only an additional $3,000 of expenses will be incurred. The original estimation of $6,000 apparently was too high.

As a result of these transactions, the partnership has an additional $21,000 in cash now available to safely distribute to the partners: $20,000 received from the sale of noncash assets and another $1,000 because of the reduced estimation of liquidation expenses. Once again, the accountant must assume maximum future losses as a means of determining the appropriate distribution of these funds. The accountant produces a second proposed schedule of liquidation to determine *subsequent* safe payments. This schedule, shown in Exhibit 10.4, indicates that $12,143 of the additional $21,000 should go to Ahn with the remaining $8,857

EXHIBIT 10.4

AHN, BAYU, AND CHANIAGO
Proposed Schedule of Liquidation—Subsequent Safe Payments

	Cash	Noncash Assets	Liabilities	Ahn, Capital Loan (50%)	Bayu, Capital (30%)	Chaniago, Capital (20%)
Beginning balances	$60,000	$140,000	$40,000	$80,000	$30,000	$50,000
Cash distribution—initial safe payments*	(14,000)	–0–	–0–	–0–	–0–	(14,000)
Disposal of noncash assets.	20,000	(50,000)	–0–	(15,000)	(9,000)	(6,000)
Liabilities paid	(40,000)	–0–	(40,000)	–0–	–0–	–0–
Liquidation expenses.	(2,000)	–0–	–0–	(1,000)	(600)	(400)
Subtotal (actual balances)	24,000	90,000	–0–	64,000	20,400	29,600
Maximum loss on remaining noncash assets	–0–	(90,000)	–0–	(45,000)	(27,000)	(18,000)
Maximum liquidation expenses	(3,000)	–0–	–0–	(1,500)	(900)	(600)
Subtotal (potential balances).	21,000	–0–	–0–	17,500	(7,500)	11,000
Allocation of Bayu's deficit capital balance	–0–	–0–	–0–	(5,357) [5/7]	7,500	(2,143) [2/7]
Subsequent safe payments	$21,000	$ –0–	$ –0–	$12,143	$ –0–	$8,857

*Based upon the determination of initial safe payments in Exhibit 10.3.

to Chaniago. To facilitate a better visual understanding, actual transactions are recorded first on this schedule, followed by the assumed losses. *A dotted line separates the real from the potential transactions.*

LO 10-7

Develop a predistribution plan to guide the distribution of cash in a partnership liquidation.

Predistribution Plan

The liquidation of a partnership can require numerous transactions occurring over a lengthy period of time. The continual production of proposed schedules of liquidation could become a burdensome chore. The previous illustration already has required two separate proposed schedules of liquidation, and the partnership still holds $90,000 in noncash assets that could be converted to cash. *Therefore, at the start of a liquidation, accountants often produce a single predistribution plan to serve as a guide for all future payments.* Thereafter, whenever cash becomes available, this plan indicates the appropriate distribution of cash without the necessity of drawing up ever-changing proposed schedules of liquidation.

A predistribution plan is developed by simulating a series of losses, each of which is just large enough to eliminate, one at a time, all of the partners' claims to partnership property. This approach recognizes that the individual capital accounts exhibit differing degrees of sensitivity to losses. Capital accounts possess varying balances and could be charged with losses at different rates. Consequently, a predistribution plan is based on calculating the losses (the "maximum loss that can be absorbed") that would eliminate each of these capital balances in a sequential pattern. This series of absorbed losses then forms the basis for the predistribution plan.

To demonstrate the creation of a predistribution plan, assume that the Onifade, Folgar, and Khan partnership is to be liquidated. The partnership's balance sheet at the date of termination follows:

Cash	$ –0–	Liabilities.	$100,000
Noncash assets.	221,000	Onifade, capital (50%).	30,000
		Folgar, capital (20%)	40,000
		Khan, capital (30%)	51,000
Total assets	$221,000	Total liabilities and capital	$221,000

The partnership's capital totals $121,000. However, the individual partners' capital balances range from $30,000 to $51,000, and profits and losses are assigned according to three different percentages (50%, 20%, 30%). Thus, differing losses would reduce each partner's current capital balance to zero. *As a prerequisite to developing a predistribution plan, the sensitivity to losses exhibited by each of these capital accounts must be measured:*

Partner	Capital Balance/ Loss Allocation	Maximum Loss That Can Be Absorbed
Onifade..............................	$30,000/50%	$ 60,000 ✓
Folgar	40,000/20%	200,000
Khan	51,000/30%	170,000

According to this initial computation, Onifade is the partner in the most vulnerable position at the present time. Based on a 50 percent share of profit and loss, a loss of only $60,000 would reduce this partner's capital account to a zero balance. If the partnership incurs a loss of this amount, Onifade will not receive any funds from the liquidation process. The following schedule simulates the potential effects of this loss (referred to as a *Step 1 loss*):

	Onifade, Capital	Folgar, Capital	Khan, Capital
Beginning balances	$ 30,000	$ 40,000	$ 51,000
Assumed $60,000 loss	(30,000) (50%)	(12,000) (20%)	(18,000) (30%)
Step 1 balances	$ –0–	$ 28,000	$ 33,000

As previously discussed, the predistribution plan is based on describing the series of losses that would eliminate each partner's capital in turn and, thus, all claims to cash. In the previous Step 1 schedule, the $60,000 loss reduced Onifade's capital account to zero. Assuming, as a precautionary step, that Onifade is personally insolvent, all further losses would have to be allocated between Folgar and Khan. Because these two partners have previously shared partnership profits and losses on a 20 percent and 30 percent basis, a $20/50:30/50$ (or 40%:60%) relationship exists between them. Therefore, these realigned percentages must now be utilized in calculating a *Step 2 loss,* the amount just large enough to exclude another of the remaining partners from sharing in any future cash distributions:

Partner	Capital Balance/ Loss Allocation	Maximum Loss That Can Be Absorbed
Folgar	$28,000/40%	$70,000
Khan	33,000/60%	55,000 ✓

Because Onifade's capital balance already has been eliminated, Khan is now in the most vulnerable position: Only a $55,000 Step 2 loss is required to reduce this partner's capital balance to zero.

	Onifade, Capital	Folgar, Capital	Khan, Capital
Beginning balances	$ 30,000	$ 40,000	$ 51,000
Assumed $60,000 loss	(30,000) (50%)	(12,000) (20%)	(18,000) (30%)
Step 1 balances	$–0–	$ 28,000	33,000
Assumed $55,000 loss	–0–	(22,000) (40%)	(33,000) (60%)
Step 2 balances	$ –0–	$ 6,000	$ –0–

According to this second schedule, a total loss of $115,000 ($60,000 from Step 1 plus $55,000 from Step 2) leaves capital of only $6,000, a balance attributed entirely to Folgar. At this final point in the simulation, an additional loss of this amount also ends Folgar's right to receive any funds from the liquidation process. Having the sole positive capital balance remaining, this partner would have to absorb the entire amount of the final loss.

	Onifade, Capital	Folgar, Capital	Khan, Capital
Beginning balances	$ 30,000	$ 40,000	$ 51,000
Assumed $60,000 loss	(30,000) (50%)	(12,000) (20%)	(18,000) (30%)
Step 1 balances	$ –0–	$ 28,000	$ 33,000
Assumed $55,000 loss	–0–	(22,000) (40%)	(33,000) (60%)
Step 2 balances	–0–	6,000	–0–
Assumed $6,000 loss	–0–	(6,000) (100%)	–0–
Final balances	$ –0–	$ –0–	$ –0–

Once this series of simulated losses has reduced each partner's capital account to a zero balance, a predistribution plan for the liquidation can be devised. *This procedure requires working backward through the preceding final schedule to determine the effects that will result if the assumed losses do not occur.* Without these losses, cash becomes available for the partners; therefore, a direct relationship exists between the volume of losses and the distribution pattern. For example, Folgar will entirely absorb the last $6,000 loss. Should that loss fail to materialize, Folgar is left with a positive safe capital balance of this amount. Thus, as cash becomes available, the first $6,000 received (in excess of partnership obligations and anticipated liquidation expenses) should be distributed solely to Folgar.

Similarly, the preceding $55,000 Step 2 loss was divided between Folgar and Khan on a 4:6 basis. Again, if such losses do not occur, these balances need not be retained to protect the partners against deficit capital balances. Therefore, after Folgar has received the initial $6,000, additional cash that becomes available (up to $55,000) will be split between Folgar (40 percent) and Khan (60 percent). For example, if the partnership holds exactly $61,000 in cash in excess of liabilities and possible liquidation expenses, this distribution should be made:

	Onifade	Folgar	Khan	Total
First $6,000	$–0–	$ 6,000	$ –0–	$ 6,000
Next $55,000	–0–	22,000 (40%)	33,000 (60%)	55,000
Cash distribution	$–0–	$28,000	$33,000	$61,000

The predistribution plan can be completed by including the Step 1 loss, an amount that was to be absorbed by the partners on a 5:2:3 basis. All cash that becomes available to the partners after the initial $61,000 should be distributed to the partners according to the original profit and loss ratio. At this point in the liquidation, enough cash would have been generated to ensure that each partner has a safe capital balance: No possibility exists that a future deficit can occur. Any additional increases in the projected capital balances will be allocated on a 5:2:3 basis. *Once all partners begin to receive a portion of the cash disbursements, any remaining funds are divided based on the original profit and loss percentages.*

To inform all parties of the pattern by which available cash will be disbursed, the predistribution plan should be formally prepared in a schedule format prior to beginning the liquidation. The following is the predistribution plan for the partnership of Onifade, Folgar, and Khan. To complete this illustration, liquidation expenses of $12,000 have been estimated. Because these expenses have the same effect on the capital accounts as losses, they do not change the sequential pattern by which cash eventually will be distributed.

ONIFADE, FOLGAR, AND KHAN PARTNERSHIP
Predistribution Plan

Available Cash		Recipient
First	$112,000	Creditors ($100,000) and liquidation expenses (estimated at $12,000)
Next.	6,000	Folgar
Next.	55,000	Folgar (40%) and Khan (60%)
All further cash		Onifade (50%), Folgar (20%), and Khan (30%)

To demonstrate how this predistribution plan is used, assume that the partnership of Onifade, Folgar, and Khan converts some of its noncash assets into $130,000 of cash. According to the predistribution plan, this amount would be distributed as follows:

First, $112,000 is held to pay creditors and liquidation expenses; $18,000 is available for payment to partners.
Next, $6,000 is paid to Folgar.
The remaining $12,000 is paid to Folgar (40% = $4,800) and Khan (60% = $7,200).

Thus, Folgar would receive $10,800 and Khan would receive $7,200 from the first $130,000 of cash that becomes available.

Summary

1. Termination of a partnership's business activities and liquidation of partnership assets can take place for a number of reasons. Because of the risk that the partnership will incur large losses during liquidation, all parties usually seek frequent and timely information describing ongoing liquidation developments. The accountant is expected to furnish these data while also working to ensure the equitable treatment of all parties.

2. Liquidation procedures include (a) selling partnership assets for cash, (b) paying partnership liabilities and liquidation expenses, and (c) distributing remaining cash to the partners based on their capital account balances. As a means of reporting these transactions, a statement of partnership liquidation should be produced at periodic intervals. This statement discloses all recent transactions, the assets and liabilities still being held, and the current capital balances. Distribution of this statement on a regular basis allows the various parties involved in the liquidation to monitor the progress being made.

3. During a liquidation, negative (deficit) capital balances can arise for one or more of the partners, especially if the partnership incurs significant losses in disposing of its property. In such cases, the specific partner or partners should contribute enough cash to the partnership to offset their deficits. If a deficit partner is unable or unwilling to make such a contribution, the remaining partners absorb the deficit based on their relative profit and loss ratio.

4. Each time cash becomes available during the partnership liquidation process, the accountant can calculate the amount of safe payments that can be made to individual partners from the available cash. Safe payments are the amounts that can be distributed to partners immediately without running the risk that future losses will cause any partner to have a deficit capital balance.

5. Partnerships often have a sufficient cash balance at the date of termination that a preliminary distribution of cash can be paid to individual partners even before noncash assets are sold. A proposed schedule of liquidation can be created as a guide for such cash distributions. This schedule is based on a simulated series of transactions: sale of all noncash assets, payment of liquidation expenses, and so on. At every point, maximum losses are assumed: Noncash assets have no resale value, liquidation expenses are set at the maximum level, and all partners are personally insolvent. The proposed schedule of liquidation formally presents the calculation of safe payments that may be made to partners.

6. Because a partnership liquidation can require numerous transactions over a lengthy time period, the accountant could discover that the continual production of proposed schedules of liquidation becomes burdensome. For this reason, at the start of the liquidation process, the accountant often produces a single predistribution plan that serves as a guide for all payments to be made to the partners. To create this plan, the accountant simulates a series of losses with each loss, in turn, exactly eliminating a partner's capital balance. After these assumed losses have reduced all capital balances to zero, the accountant devises the predistribution plan by working backward through the series of simulated losses. In effect, the accountant is measuring the cash that will become available if such losses do not occur.

Comprehensive Illustration

Problem

(*Estimated Time: 30 to 40 Minutes*) For the past several years, the Ali, Ito, Russo, and Suwan partnership has operated a local department store. Based on the provisions of the original articles of partnership, all profits and losses have been allocated on a 4:3:2:1 ratio, respectively. As a brick-and-mortar establishment, the store has not been profitable for the past two years. More recently, both Ito and Russo have undergone personal financial problems and, as a result, are now personally insolvent. Ito's creditors have filed a $20,000 claim against the partnership's assets, and $22,000 of partnership assets is being sought by creditors to cover Russo's personal debts. To satisfy these legal obligations and exit a no longer profitable enterprise, the partners have agree to terminate operations and liquidate assets. The partners estimate that they will incur $12,000 in expenses to liquidate all noncash assets.

At the time that active operations terminate and the liquidation begins, the following partnership balance sheet is produced.

Cash	$ 20,000	Liabilities	$140,000
Noncash assets	280,000	Ito, loan (to partnership)	10,000
		Ali, capital (40%)	76,000
		Ito, capital (30%)	14,000
		Russo, capital (20%)	51,000
		Suwan, capital (10%)	9,000
Total assets	$300,000	Total liabilities and capital	$300,000

During the lengthy liquidation process, the following transactions take place:

- Sale of noncash assets with a book value of $190,000 for $140,000 cash.
- Payment of $14,000 liquidation expenses. No further expenses are expected.
- Distribution of safe payments to the partners.
- Payment of all business liabilities.
- Sale of the remaining noncash assets for $10,000.
- Negative capital balances of any insolvent partners written off as uncollectible.
- Cash contribution received from any solvent partner with negative capital balance.
- Distribution of ending cash balance.

Required

a. Using the information available prior to the start of the liquidation process, develop a predistribution plan for this partnership.

b. Prepare journal entries to record the actual liquidation transactions.

Solution

a. This partnership begins the liquidation process with capital totaling $160,000. This includes the $10,000 loan from Ito added to Ito's capital balance for a total of $24,000. Therefore, the predistribution plan is based on the assumption that $160,000 in losses will be incurred, entirely eliminating all partnership capital. Simulated losses are arranged in a series so that each capital balance is sequentially reduced to zero. At the start of the liquidation, Ito's capital position is the most vulnerable.

Partner	Capital Balance/Loss Allocation	Maximum Loss That Can Be Absorbed
Ali	$76,000/40%	$190,000
Ito	24,000/30%	80,000 ✓
Russo	51,000/20%	255,000
Suwan	9,000/10%	90,000

As the schedule indicates, an $80,000 loss would eliminate Ito's $14,000 capital balance and $10,000 loan to the partnership. Therefore, to start the development of a predistribution plan, a loss of $80,000 is assumed to have occurred.

	Ali, Capital	Ito, Capital and Loan	Russo, Capital	Suwan, Capital
Beginning balances	$ 76,000	$24,000	$ 51,000	$ 9,000
Assumed $80,000 loss	(32,000) (40%)	(24,000) (30%)	(16,000) (20%)	(8,000) (10%)
Step 1 balances	$ 44,000	$ –0–	$ 35,000	$ 1,000

With Ito's capital balance eliminated, further losses are to be split among the remaining partners in the ratio of 4:2:1 (or $4/7:2/7:1/7$). Because only an additional $7,000 loss (the preceding $1,000 Step 1 capital balance divided by $1/7$) is now needed to reduce Suwan's balance to zero, this partner is in the second most vulnerable position. A simulated loss of $7,000 eliminates Suwan's capital balance.

	Ali	Ito	Russo	Suwan
Step 1 balances (above)	$44,000	$–0–	$35,000	$ 1,000
Assumed $7,000 loss	(4,000) (4/7)	–0–	(2,000) (2/7)	(1,000) (1/7)
Step 2 balances	$40,000	$–0–	$33,000	$ –0–

Following these two simulated losses, only Ali and Russo continue to report positive capital balances. Thus, they divide any additional losses on a 4:2 basis, or $2/3:1/3$. Based on these realigned percentages, Ali's position has become the more vulnerable. An additional loss of $60,000 ($40,000/$2/3$) reduces this partner's remaining capital balance to zero, whereas a $99,000 loss ($33,000/$1/3$) is required to eliminate Russo's capital balance. Step 3 assumes a $60,000 loss.

	Ali	Ito	Russo	Suwan
Step 2 balances	$ 40,000	$–0–	$ 33,000	$–0–
Assumed $60,000 loss	(40,000) (2/3)	–0–	(20,000) (1/3)	–0–
Step 3 balances	$ –0–	$–0–	$ 13,000	$–0–

After this simulated loss, Russo has a capital balance of $13,000; an additional loss of this amount would reduce this partner's capital account to zero. Based on the results of this series of simulated losses, the accountant can create a predistribution plan. The first $152,000 of available cash must be held to cover the $140,000 in liabilities owed by the partnership, and $12,000 of anticipated liquidation expenses. The complete predistribution plan is as follows:

ALI, ITO, RUSSO, AND SUWAN
Predistribution Plan

Available Cash		Recipient
First	$152,000	Creditors and anticipated liquidation expenses
Next......................	13,000	Russo (100%)
Next......................	60,000	Ali (2/3) and Russo (1/3)
Next......................	7,000	Ali (4/7), Russo (2/7), and and Suwan (1/7)
All further cash		Ali (40%), Ito (30%), Russo (20%), and Suwan (10%)

b. Journal entries for the liquidation:

Ito, Loan	10,000	
Ito, Capital		10,000
To record offset of loan to capital balance in anticipation of liquidation.		

(continued)

(*continued*)

Cash	140,000	
Ali, Capital (40%)	20,000	
Ito, Capital (30%)	15,000	
Russo, Capital (20%)	10,000	
Suwan, Capital (10%)	5,000	
Noncash Assets		190,000
To record sale of noncash assets and allocation of $50,000 loss.		
Ali, Capital (40%)	5,600	
Ito, Capital (30%)	4,200	
Russo, Capital (20%)	2,800	
Suwan, Capital (10%)	1,400	
Cash		14,000
To record payment of liquidation expenses.		

- The partnership now holds $146,000 in cash, $6,000 more than is needed to satisfy all liabilities. According to the predistribution plan drawn up in requirement (*a*), this entire amount can be safely distributed to Russo (or to Russo's creditors).

Russo, Capital	6,000	
Cash		6,000
To record distribution of safe payments of available cash.		
Liabilities	140,000	
Cash		140,000
To record extinguishment of all partnership debts.		
Cash	10,000	
Ali, Capital (40% of loss)	32,000	
Ito, Capital (30% of loss)	24,000	
Russo, Capital (20% of loss)	16,000	
Suwan, Capital (10% of loss)	8,000	
Noncash Assets		90,000
To record sale of remaining noncash assets and allocation of $80,000 loss.		

- At this point in the liquidation, only the cash and the capital accounts remain open on the partnership books.

	Cash	Ali, Capital	Ito, Capital	Russo, Capital	Suwan, Capital
Beginning balances	$ 20,000	$76,000	$ 14,000	$51,000	$ 9,000
Loan offset	–0–	–0–	10,000	–0–	–0–
Sale of noncash assets	140,000	(20,000)	(15,000)	(10,000)	(5,000)
Liquidation expenses	(14,000)	(5,600)	(4,200)	(2,800)	(1,400)
Cash distribution	(6,000)	–0–	–0–	(6,000)	–0–
Payment of liabilities	(140,000)	–0–	–0–	–0–	–0–
Sale of noncash assets	10,000	(32,000)	(24,000)	(16,000)	(8,000)
Current balances	$ 10,000	$ 18,400	$(19,200)	$16,200	$(5,400)

Because Ito is personally insolvent, the $19,200 deficit balance will not be repaid, and the remaining three partners must absorb it on a 4:2:1 basis.

Ali, Capital (4/7 of loss)	10,971	
Russo, Capital (2/7 of loss)	5,486	
Suwan, Capital (1/7 of loss)	2,743	
Ito, Capital		19,200
To record write-off of deficit capital balance of insolvent partner.		

- This allocation decreases Suwan's capital account to a negative balance of $8,143. Suwan contributes this amount to the partnership to cover the deficit.

Cash	8,143	
Suwan, Capital...		8,143
To record contribution made to eliminate deficit capital balance.		

- Suwan's contribution brings the final cash total for the partnership to $18,143. This amount is distributed to the two partners who continue to maintain positive capital balances: Ali and Russo (or Russo's creditors).

	Ali, Capital	Russo, Capital
Balances above...	$ 18,400	$16,200
Ito deficit...	(10,971)	(5,486)
Final balances	$ 7,429	$10,714

Ali, Capital..	7,429	
Russo, Capital	10,714	
Cash		18,143
To record distribution of remaining cash according to final capital balances.		

Questions

1. What is the difference between the termination of a partnership and the liquidation of partnership property?
2. Why would the members of a partnership elect to terminate business operations and liquidate all noncash assets?
3. Why are liquidation gains and losses usually recorded as direct adjustments to the partners' capital accounts?
4. After liquidating all property and paying partnership obligations, what is the basis for allocating remaining cash among the partners?
5. What is the purpose of a statement of partnership liquidation? What information does it convey to its readers?
6. How are safe payments to partners calculated when cash becomes available for distribution?
7. How do loans from partners affect the distribution of assets in a partnership liquidation?
8. What is the purpose of a proposed schedule of liquidation, and how is it developed?
9. How is a predistribution plan created for a partnership liquidation?

Problems

LO 10-1

1. When a partnership is liquidated, how is the final distribution of partnership cash made to the partners?
   a. Equally
   b. According to the profit and loss ratio
   c. According to the final capital account balances
   d. According to the initial investment made by each of the partners

LO 10-1

2. Which of the following statements is true concerning the accounting for a partnership going through liquidation?
   a. Gains and losses are reported directly as increases and decreases in the appropriate capital account.
   b. A separate income statement is created to measure only the profit or loss generated during liquidation.
   c. Because gains and losses rarely occur during liquidation, no special accounting treatment is warranted.
   d. Within a liquidation, all gains and losses are divided equally among the partners.

LO 10-4

3. During a liquidation, if a partner's capital account balance drops below zero, what *should* happen?
   a. The other partners file a legal suit against the partner with the deficit balance.
   b. The partner with the highest capital balance contributes sufficient assets to eliminate the deficit.
   c. The deficit balance is removed from the accounting records with only the remaining partners sharing in future gains and losses.
   d. The partner with a deficit contributes enough assets to offset the deficit balance.

LO 10-7

4. What is a predistribution plan?
   a. A list of the procedures to be performed during a liquidation
   b. A guide for the cash distributions to partners during a liquidation
   c. A determination of the final cash distribution to the partners on the settlement date
   d. A detailed list of the transactions that will transpire in the reorganization of a partnership

LO 10-4

5. A local partnership is liquidating and is currently reporting the following capital balances:

Barley, capital (50% share of all profits and losses)	$ 44,000
Carter, capital (30%)	32,000
Desai, capital (20%)	(24,000)

   Desai has indicated that a forthcoming contribution will cover the $24,000 deficit. However, the two remaining partners have asked to receive the $52,000 in cash that is currently available. How much of this money should each of the partners receive?
   a. Barley, $22,000; Carter, $30,000
   b. Barley, $32,000; Carter, $20,000
   c. Barley, $29,000; Carter, $23,000
   d. Barley, $32,500; Carter, $19,500

LO 10-4

6. A partnership is considering possible liquidation because one of the partners (Bell) is personally insolvent. Profits and losses are divided on a 4:3:2:1 basis, respectively. Capital balances at the current time are

Bell, capital	$ 50,000
Hardy, capital	56,000
Dennard, capital	14,000
Suddath, capital	80,000

   Bell's creditors have filed a $21,000 claim against the partnership's assets. The partnership currently holds assets of $300,000 and liabilities of $100,000. An independent appraiser indicates that the assets can be sold for $190,000.
   Prepare a statement of partnership liquidation to determine the amount of cash that Bell would receive from the sale of partnership assets.

LO 10-3

7. A partnership has the following balance sheet prior to liquidation (partners' profit and loss ratios are in parentheses):

Cash	$ 33,000	Liabilities		$ 50,000
Other assets	100,000	Playa, capital (40%)		24,000
		Bahia, capital (30%)		29,000
		Arco, capital (30%)		30,000
Total	$133,000	Total		$133,000

   During liquidation, other assets are sold for $80,000, liabilities are paid in full, and $15,000 in liquidation expenses are paid.
   Prepare a statement of partnership liquidation to determine the amount of cash each partner receives as a result of this liquidation.

LO 10-1, 10-4, 10-5

8. A partnership has the following capital balances: X (50 percent of profits and losses) = $150,000; Y (30 percent of profits and losses) = $120,000; Z (20 percent of profits and losses) = $80,000. The partnership is being liquidated.
   Calculate the safe payments that can be made to each partner assuming that $30,000 in cash becomes immediately available.

LO 10-7

9. A partnership is currently holding $400,000 in assets and $234,000 in liabilities. The partnership is to be liquidated, and $20,000 is the best estimation of the expenses that will be incurred during this process. The four partners share profits and losses as shown. Capital balances at the start of the liquidation follow:

Berzina, capital (40%)	$59,000
Horvath, capital (30%)	39,000
Markov, capital (10%)	34,000
Petronis, capital (20%)	34,000

Prepare a predistribution plan to determine which partner will be the first to receive cash from the liquidation and what amount that partner will receive before other partners receive any cash.

LO 10-7

10. Chen, Korhonen, Lebuca, and Swid are partners who share profits and losses on a 4:3:2:1 basis, respectively. They are beginning to liquidate the business. At the start of this process, capital balances are

Chen, capital	$60,000
Korhonen, capital	27,000
Lebuca, capital	43,000
Swid, capital	20,000

Prepare a predistribution plan to determine which partner will be the first to receive cash from the liquidation and what amount that partner will receive before other partners receive any cash.

LO 10-4, 10-5

11. A partnership has gone through liquidation and now reports the following account balances:

Cash	$16,000
Loan from Molina	3,000
Ashman, capital	(2,000) (deficit)
Molina, capital	(5,000) (deficit)
Pinckney, capital	13,000
Diaz, capital	7,000

Profits and losses are allocated on the following basis: Ashman, 30 percent; Molina, 20 percent; Pinckney, 30 percent; and Diaz, 20 percent.

Calculate the safe payments that can be made to individual partners.

LO 10-3

12. A partnership has the following account balances at the date of termination: Cash, $80,000; Noncash Assets, $660,000; Liabilities, $320,000; Alonso, capital (50 percent of profits and losses), $200,000; Mann, capital (30 percent), $120,000; Suzuki, capital (20 percent), $100,000. The following transactions occur during liquidation:

- Noncash assets with a book value of $500,000 are sold for $400,000 in cash.
- A creditor reduces his claim against the partnership from $120,000 to $100,000, and this amount is paid in cash.
- The remaining noncash assets are sold for $130,000 in cash.
- The remaining liabilities of $200,000 are paid in full.
- Liquidation expenses of $24,000 are paid in cash.
- Cash remaining after the above transactions have occurred is distributed to the partners.

Prepare a statement of partnership liquidation to determine how much cash each partner receives from the liquidation of the partnership.

LO 10-1, 10-4

13. A local partnership is liquidating and has only two assets (cash of $10,000 and land with a cost of $35,000). All partnership liabilities have been paid. All partners are personally insolvent. The partners have capital balances and share profits and losses as follows:

Ortega, capital (40%)	$25,000
Borek, capital (30%)	15,000
Stone, capital (30%)	5,000

a. If the land is sold for $25,000, how much cash does each partner receive in a final settlement?
b. If the land is sold for $15,000, how much cash does each partner receive in a final settlement?
c. If the land is sold for $5,000, how much cash does each partner receive in a final settlement?

LO 10-4

14. A local dental partnership has been liquidated and the final capital balances are

Abbas, capital (40% of all profits and losses)...............	$ 70,000
Baptiste, capital (30%)	30,000
Krishna, capital (20%)	(42,000)
Urias, capital (10%)	(58,000)

If Urias contributes cash of $20,000 to the partnership, how would this amount be distributed to the other partners?

LO 10-5

15. The partnership of Kumar, Correa, Getz, and Pham currently holds three assets: Cash, $10,000; Land, $35,000; and Building, $50,000. The partnership has no liabilities. The partners anticipate that expenses required to liquidate their partnership will amount to $5,000. Capital balances are as follows:

Kumar, capital	$25,000
Correa, capital...............................	28,000
Getz, capital.................................	20,000
Pham, capital	22,000

The partners share profits and losses as follows: Kumar (30 percent), Correa (30 percent), Getz (20 percent), and Pham (20 percent). If a preliminary distribution of cash is to be made, what is the amount of safe payment that can be made to each partner?

LO 10-6

16. The following condensed balance sheet is for the partnership of Gulian, Singh, and Zahiri, who share profits and losses in the ratio of 4:3:3, respectively:

Cash	$ 90,000	Accounts payable..................	$210,000
Other assets............	820,000	Zahiri, loan	40,000
Gulian, loan	30,000	Gulian, capital	300,000
		Singh, capital	200,000
		Zahiri, capital	190,000
Total assets	$940,000	Total liabilities and capital.........	$940,000

The partners decide to liquidate the partnership. Forty percent of the other assets are sold for $200,000. Prepare a proposed schedule of liquidation at this point in time.

LO 10-5

17. The following condensed balance sheet is for the partnership of Ludolf, Sambal, and Urad, who share profits and losses in the ratio of 6:2:2, respectively:

Cash	$ 50,000	Liabilities............................	$ 42,000
Other assets............	150,000	Ludolf, capital.......................	69,000
		Sambal, capital	69,000
		Urad, capital........................	20,000
Total assets	$200,000	Total liabilities and capital..........	$200,000

Assuming no liquidation expenses, calculate the safe payments that can be made to partners at this point in time. For how much money must the other assets be sold so that each partner receives some amount of cash in a liquidation?

LO 10-5

18. The balance sheet for the Delphine, Xavier, and Olivier partnership follows:

Cash	$ 60,000	Liabilities............................	$ 40,000
Noncash assets.........	100,000	Delphine, capital....................	60,000
		Xavier, capital	40,000
		Olivier, capital	20,000
Total assets	$160,000	Total liabilities and capital..........	$160,000

Delphine, Xavier, and Olivier share profits and losses in the ratio of 4:4:2, respectively. The partners have agreed to terminate the business and estimate that $12,000 in liquidation expenses will be incurred.

a. What is the amount of cash that safely can be paid to partners prior to liquidation of noncash assets?

b. Calculate the amount of safe payment that can be made to each partner prior to liquidation of noncash assets.

LO 10-4

19. A partnership has liquidated all assets but still reports the following account balances for its partners:

Beck, loan.	$ 8,000
Cisneros, capital (40%).	5,000
Beck, capital (20%)	(12,000) (deficit)
Sadak, capital (10%)	(8,000) (deficit)
Emerson, capital (20%).	13,000
Page, capital (10%)	(6,000) (deficit)

The partners split profits and losses as follows: Cisneros, 40 percent; Beck, 20 percent; Sadak, 10 percent; Emerson, 20 percent; and Page, 10 percent.

Assuming that Cisneros, Beck, and Page are personally insolvent, how much cash must Sadak now contribute to this partnership?

LO 10-6

20. The following balance sheet is for a partnership in which the partners have decided to terminate operations and liquidate assets. The partners estimate liquidation expenses will be $10,000.

Cash	$130,000	Liabilities.	$ 50,000
Noncash assets.	230,000	Arch, capital (40%).	120,000
		Bibb, capital (20%).	60,000
		Dao, capital (40%)	130,000
Total assets	$360,000	Total liabilities and capital.	$360,000

Prepare a proposed schedule of liquidation to carry out a preliminary distribution of partnership assets at the date of termination.

LO 10-2, 10-3, 10-5

21. Alex and Bess have been in partnership for many years. The partners, who share profits and losses on a 60:40 basis, respectively, wish to retire and have agreed to liquidate the business. Liquidation expenses are estimated to be $5,000. At the date the partnership ceases operations, the balance sheet is as follows:

Cash	$ 50,000	Liabilities.	$ 40,000
Noncash assets.	150,000	Alex, capital	90,000
Total assets	$200,000	Bess, capital.	70,000
		Total liabilities and capital.	$200,000

Part A
Prepare journal entries for the following transactions that occurred in chronological order:

a. Distributed safe cash payments to the partners.

b. Paid $30,000 of the partnership's liabilities.

c. Sold noncash assets for $160,000.

d. Distributed safe cash payments to the partners.

e. Paid remaining partnership liabilities of $10,000.

f. Paid $4,000 in liquidation expenses; no further expenses will be incurred.

g. Distributed remaining cash held by the business to the partners.

Part B
Prepare a final statement of partnership liquidation.

LO 10-7

22. The partnership of Larson, Rojas, Spencer, and Tran has decided to terminate operations and liquidate all business property. During this process, the partners expect to incur $8,000 in liquidation expenses. All partners are currently solvent.

The balance sheet reported by this partnership at the time that the liquidation commenced follows. The percentages indicate the allocation of profits and losses to each of the four partners.

Cash	$ 28,250	Liabilities	$ 47,000
Accounts receivable	44,000	Larson, capital (20%)	15,000
Inventory	39,000	Rojas, capital (30%)	60,000
Land and buildings	23,000	Spencer, capital (20%)	75,000
Equipment	104,000	Tran, capital (30%)	41,250
Total assets	$238,250	Total liabilities and capital	$238,250

Based on the information provided, prepare a predistribution plan for liquidating this partnership.

LO 10-7

23. The Drysdale, Koufax, and Marichal partnership has the following balance sheet immediately prior to liquidation:

Cash	$ 36,000	Liabilities	$50,000
Noncash assets	204,000	Drysdale, loan	10,000
		Drysdale, capital (50%)	70,000
		Koufax, capital (30%)	60,000
		Marichal, capital (20%)	50,000
Total assets	$240,000	Total liabilities and capital	$240,000

a. Liquidation expenses are estimated to be $15,000. Prepare a predistribution schedule to guide the distribution of cash.

b. Assume that assets costing $74,000 are sold for $60,000. How is the available cash to be divided?

LO 10-7

24. The Bui, Clemente, Devian, and Toussaint partnership has terminated operations and is undergoing liquidation. Sales commissions and other liquidation expenses are expected to total $19,000. The partnership's balance sheet prior to the commencement of liquidation is as follows:

Cash	$ 27,000	Liabilities	$ 40,000
Noncash assets	254,000	Bui, capital (20%)	18,000
		Clemente, capital (40%)	40,000
		Devian, capital (20%)	48,000
		Toussaint, capital (20%)	135,000
Total assets	$281,000	Total liabilities and capital	$281,000

Prepare a predistribution plan for this partnership.

LO 10-4

25. The partnership of Guerin, Moradi, and Veloso has the following account balances:

Cash	$ 50,000	Liabilities	$ 30,000
Noncash assets	135,000	Guerin, capital	100,000
		Moradi, capital	70,000
		Veloso, capital	(15,000)

This partnership is being liquidated. Guerin and Moradi are each entitled to 40 percent of all profits and losses with the remaining 20 percent going to Veloso.

a. What is the maximum amount that Veloso might have to contribute to this partnership because of the deficit capital balance?

b. How should the $20,000 cash that is presently available in excess of liabilities be distributed?

c. If the noncash assets are sold for a total of $50,000, what is the minimum amount of cash that Guerin could receive?

LO 10-4

26. The partnership of Ramos, Rios, Safar, and Wong is being liquidated. It currently holds cash of $20,000 but no other assets. Liabilities amount to $30,000. The capital balances are

Ramos (40% of profits and losses)	$ 20,000
Rios (30%)	12,000
Safar (20%)	(17,000) (deficit)
Wong (10%)	(25,000) (deficit)

a. If both Safar and Wong are personally insolvent, how much money must Rios contribute to the partnership?

b. If only Wong is personally insolvent, how much money must Safar contribute to the partnership? How will these funds be distributed?

c. If only Safar is personally insolvent, how much money should Ramos receive from the liquidation?

LO 10-2

27. Agarwal, Bergeron, and Cishek have been in partnership for a number of years. The partners allocate all profits and losses on a 2:3:1 basis, respectively. Recently, each partner has become personally insolvent and, thus, the partners have decided to liquidate the business in hopes of remedying their personal financial problems. As of September 1, the partnership's balance sheet is as follows:

Cash	$ 11,000	Liabilities..................	$ 61,000
Accounts receivable................	84,000	Agarwal, capital............	25,000
Inventory.........................	74,000	Bergeron, capital...........	75,000
Land, building, and equipment (net)....	38,000	Cishek capital	46,000
Total assets	$207,000	Total liabilities and capital ...	$207,000

Prepare journal entries for the following transactions:
a. Sold all inventory for $56,000 cash.
b. Paid $7,500 in liquidation expenses.
c. Paid $40,000 of the partnership's liabilities.
d. Collected $45,000 of the accounts receivable.
e. Distributed safe payments of cash; the partners anticipate no further liquidation expenses.
f. Sold remaining accounts receivable for 30 percent of face value.
g. Sold land, building, and equipment for $17,000.
h. Paid all remaining liabilities of the partnership.
i. Distributed cash held by the business to the partners.

LO 10-7

28. The partnership of Winn, Xie, Yang, and Zed has the following balance sheet:

Cash	$ 40,000	Liabilities..................................	$ 66,000
Other assets.......	300,000	Winn, capital (50% of profits and losses)......	100,000
		Xie, capital (30%).........................	84,000
		Yang, capital (10%).......................	50,000
		Zed, capital (10%)........................	40,000

Zed is personally insolvent, and one of Zed's creditors is considering suing the partnership for the $10,000 that is currently owed. The creditor realizes that this litigation could result in partnership liquidation and does not wish to force such an extreme action unless Zed is reasonably sure of obtaining at least $10,000 from the liquidation.

Prepare a predistribution plan to determine the amount for which the partnership must sell the other assets to ensure that Zed receives $10,000 from the liquidation. Liquidation expenses are expected to be $30,000.

LO 10-6

29. On January 1, the partners of Mori, Lux, and Khan (who share profits and losses in the ratio of 5:3:2, respectively) decide to terminate operations and liquidate their partnership. The trial balance at this date follows:

	Debit	Credit
Cash	$ 28,000	
Accounts receivable..	86,000	
Inventory...	72,000	
Machinery and equipment, net...............................	209,000	
Mori, loan	50,000	
Accounts payable..		$ 93,000
Lux, loan..		40,000
Mori, capital		128,000
Lux, capital		100,000
Khan, capital..		84,000
Totals...	$445,000	$445,000

The partners plan a program of piecemeal conversion of the partnership's assets to minimize liquidation losses. All available cash, less an amount retained to provide for future expenses, is to be distributed to the partners at the end of each month. A summary of the liquidation transactions follows:

January Collected $51,000 of the accounts receivable; the balance is deemed uncollectible.
    Received $48,000 for the entire inventory.
    Paid $4,000 in liquidation expenses.
    Paid $88,000 to the outside creditors after offsetting a $5,000 credit memorandum received by the partnership on January 11.
    Retained $20,000 cash in the business at the end of January to cover liquidation expenses. The remainder is distributed to the partners.
February Paid $5,000 in liquidation expenses.
    Retained $8,000 cash in the business at the end of the month to cover additional liquidation expenses.
March Received $156,000 on the sale of all machinery and equipment.
    Paid $7,000 in final liquidation expenses.
    Retained no cash in the business.

Prepare proposed schedules of liquidation on January 31, February 28, and March 31 to determine the safe payments made to the partners at the end of each of these three months.

LO 10-1, 10-4

30. Following is a series of *independent cases*. In each situation, indicate the cash distribution to be made to partners at the end of the liquidation process. *Unless otherwise stated, assume that all solvent partners will reimburse the partnership for their deficit capital balances.*

Part A
The Buarque, Monte, and Vinicius partnership reports the following accounts. Vinicius is personally insolvent and can contribute only an additional $9,000 to the partnership.

Cash	$130,000
Liabilities	35,000
Monte, loan	20,000
Buarque, capital (50% of profits and losses)	50,000
Monte, capital (25%)	40,000
Vinicius, capital (25%)	(15,000) (deficit)

Part B
Drawdy, Langston, and Pearl operate a local accounting firm as a partnership. After working together for several years, they have decided to liquidate the partnership's property. The partners have prepared the following balance sheet:

Cash	$ 20,000	Liabilities	$ 40,000
Drawdy, loan	5,000	Langston, loan	8,000
Noncash assets	150,000	Drawdy, capital (40%)	65,000
		Langston, capital (30%)	50,000
		Pearl, capital (30%)	12,000
Total assets	$175,000	Total liabilities and capital	$175,000

The firm sells the noncash assets for $120,000; it will use $15,000 of this amount to pay liquidation expenses. All three of these partners are personally insolvent.

Part C
Use the same information as in Part B, but assume that the profits and losses are split 2:4:4 to Drawdy, Langston, and Pearl, respectively, and that liquidation expenses are only $6,000.

Part D
Following the liquidation of all noncash assets, the partnership of Krups, Lindau, Riedel, and Schnee has the following account balances. Krups is personally insolvent.

Liabilities..	$ 9,000
Krups, loan...	6,000
Krups, capital (30% of profits and losses)................	(20,000) deficit
Lindau, capital (30%)....................................	(30,000) deficit
Riedel, capital (20%)....................................	15,000
Schnee, capital (20%)....................................	20,000

LO 10-2, 10-3, 10-7

31. The partnership of Bauer, Ohtani, and Souza has elected to cease all operations and liquidate its business property. A balance sheet drawn up at this time shows the following account balances:

Cash	$ 60,000	Liabilities.........................	$ 40,000
Noncash assets........	219,000	Bauer, capital (60%)	129,000
		Ohtani, capital (20%)..............	35,000
		Souza, capital (20%)	75,000
Total assets	$279,000	Total liabilities and capital........	$279,000

Part A
Prepare a predistribution plan for this partnership.

Part B
The following transactions occur in liquidating this business:

1. Distributed safe payments of cash immediately to the partners. Liquidation expenses of $8,000 are estimated as a basis for this computation.
2. Sold noncash assets with a book value of $94,000 for $60,000.
3. Paid all liabilities.
4. Distributed safe payments of cash again.
5. Sold remaining noncash assets for $51,000.
6. Paid actual liquidation expenses of $6,000 only.
7. Distributed remaining cash to the partners and closed the financial records of the business permanently.

Prepare a final statement of liquidation for this partnership using the predistribution plan to determine payments of cash to partners.

Part C
Prepare journal entries to record the liquidation transactions reflected in the final statement of liquidation.

LO 10-2, 10-7

32. The partnership of Wing, Mehta, Rodgers, and Yan was formed several years ago as a local architectural firm. Several partners have recently undergone personal financial problems and have decided to terminate operations and liquidate the business. The following balance sheet is drawn up as a guideline for this process:

Cash	$ 15,000	Liabilities......................	$ 74,000
Accounts receivable............	82,000	Rodgers, loan..................	35,000
Inventory.....................	101,000	Wing, capital (30%)	120,000
Land.........................	85,000	Mehta, capital (10%)	88,000
Building and		Rodgers, capital (20%)	74,000
equipment (net)..............	168,000	Yan, capital (40%)	60,000
Total assets	$451,000	Total liabilities and capital.....	$451,000

When the liquidation commenced, liquidation expenses of $16,000 were anticipated as being necessary to dispose of all property.

Part A
Prepare a predistribution plan for this partnership.

Part B

The following transactions transpire during the liquidation of the Wing, Mehta, Rodgers, and Yan partnership:

1. Collected 80 percent of the total accounts receivable with the rest judged to be uncollectible.
2. Sold the land, building, and equipment for $150,000.
3. Distributed safe payments of cash.
4. Learned that Yan, who has become personally insolvent, will make no further contributions.
5. Paid all liabilities.
6. Sold all inventory for $71,000.
7. Distributed safe payments of cash again.
8. Paid actual liquidation expenses of $11,000 only.
9. Made final cash disbursements to the partners based on the assumption that all partners other than Yan are personally solvent.

Prepare journal entries to record these liquidation transactions.

LO 10-2, 10-7

33. The partnership of Garcia, Iglesias, and Kassabian was formed several years ago as a local tax preparation firm. Two partners have reached retirement age, and the partners have decided to terminate operations and liquidate the business. Liquidation expenses of $34,000 are expected. The partnership balance sheet at the start of liquidation is as follows:

Cash	$ 30,000	Liabilities	$170,000
Accounts receivable	60,000	Garcia, loan	30,000
Office equipment (net)	50,000	Garcia, capital (25%)	50,000
Building (net)	110,000	Iglesias, capital (25%)	30,000
Land	100,000	Kassabian, capital (50%)	70,000
Total assets	$350,000	Total liabilities and capital	$350,000

Part A

Prepare a predistribution plan for this partnership.

Part B

The following transactions transpire in chronological order during the liquidation of the partnership:

1. Collected 90 percent of the accounts receivable and wrote the remainder off as uncollectible.
2. Sold the office equipment for $20,000, the building for $80,000, and the land for $120,000.
3. Distributed safe payments of cash.
4. Paid all liabilities in full.
5. Paid actual liquidation expenses of $30,000 only.
6. Made final cash distributions to the partners.

Prepare journal entries to record these liquidation transactions.

Develop Your Skills

ANALYSIS CASE

CPA *skills*

Go to the website ir.cedarfair.com and click on "Investor Information" to locate "SEC Filings." Download Cedar Fair, L.P.'s annual report on Form 10-K filed with the SEC on 02/19/2021.

Review the financial statements and the accompanying notes contained in this annual report, especially any that discuss the partnership form of organization.

Assume that an investor is considering investing in this partnership and has downloaded this report for analysis.

Required

1. Briefly describe Cedar Fair's business and major properties.
2. Summarize the major differences that exist between Cedar Fair's financial statements and those of a corporation.
3. Assume that the investor is not aware of the potential implications of investing in a partnership rather than a corporation. What information is available in Cedar Fair's annual report that relates to unique characteristics of investing in a partnership?

COMMUNICATION CASE 1

CPA
skills

One of your colleagues has been hired by the Kim, Ozkan, and Samuels partnership to guide it through the liquidation process. The partnership currently has cash in a bank account that exceeds the amount it owes creditors, and has other assets consisting of equipment, land, and a building. Each partner has a positive balance in their capital account. Your colleague has asked your opinion with respect to two questions: (1) Would it be appropriate to distribute some cash to the partners even before the other assets have been sold and creditors have been paid, and if so, (2) should each partner receive an equal amount of cash?

Required

Write a memorandum to your colleague providing your opinion with regard to questions (1) and (2).

COMMUNICATION CASE 2

CPA
skills

You have been engaged to do the accounting for the termination and liquidation of the Devi, Smith, and Tavares partnership. Devi has requested an immediate distribution of cash from the partnership that is being questioned by the other partners. Although Devi's capital account currently has a positive balance, Smith and Tavares are concerned that this might change as the liquidation process unfolds. They argue that Devi should wait before receiving a cash distribution. All of the partners would like you to explain how it is possible that they might develop a deficit in their capital account during the liquidation process.

Required

Write a memorandum to Devi, Smith, and Tavares explaining how a positive capital account balance could develop into a deficit balance during the partnership liquidation process.

Accounting for State and Local Governments (Part 1)

Financial statements prepared by state and local governments in conformity with generally accepted accounting principles provide citizens and taxpayers, legislative and oversight bodies, municipal bond analysts, and others with information they need to evaluate the financial health of governments, make decisions, and assess accountability. This information is intended, among other things, to assist these users of financial statements in assessing (1) whether a government's current-year revenues were sufficient to pay for current-year services (known as *interperiod equity*), (2) whether a government complied with all finance-related legal and contractual obligations, (3) where a government's financial resources come from and how it uses them, and (4) a government's financial position and economic condition and how they have changed over time.[1]

To even a seasoned veteran of accounting, the financial statements produced by a state or local government can appear to be written in a complex foreign language.

- Financial statements for the State of North Dakota include several "other financing sources (uses)" for the state's governmental funds for the year ended June 30, 2020, that disclose $563 million from transfers in and $1.004 billion for transfers out.

- The June 30, 2020, balance sheet for the governmental funds of Portland, Maine, reports total fund balances of $173.3 million. Of that amount, non-expendable permanent funds made up $7.5 million, whereas another $9.8 million was committed to capital improvements.

- The 2020 annual comprehensive financial report (ACFR) for Phoenix, Arizona, contains more than 330 pages of data—including the dollar amounts of expenditures made in connection with public safety ($1.075 billion), community enrichment ($234.4 million), and environmental services ($31.3 million).

- Greensboro, North Carolina, reports two complete and distinct sets of financial statements. The first discloses that the city's governmental activities owed $669.0 million in liabilities as of June 30, 2020, whereas the second indicates that, at the same point in time, the city's governmental funds owed a mere $39.4 million in liabilities.

- The June 30, 2020, statement of net position for the Metropolitan Government of Nashville and Davidson County, Tennessee, reports total deferred outflows of resources of $854.1 million along with total deferred inflows of resources of $2.175 billion.

[1] GASB Statement 77, *Tax Abatement Disclosures*, August 2015.

Learning Objectives

After studying this chapter, you should be able to:

LO 11-1 Explain the rationale for the unique characteristics used in creating the financial statements produced for state and local governments.

LO 11-2 Differentiate between the two sets of financial statements prepared by state and local governments.

LO 11-3 Understand the reason that fund accounting has traditionally been a prominent factor in the internal recording of state and local governments.

LO 11-4 Identify the three fund types and the individual fund categories within each of these fund types.

LO 11-5 Understand the basic structure of both government-wide financial statements and fund financial statements (as produced for the governmental funds).

LO 11-6 Record the passage of a budget by a state or local government and the subsequent recording of encumbrances and expenditures.

LO 11-7 Explain the reporting of capital assets, supplies, and prepaid expenses by a state or local government.

LO 11-8 Determine the proper timing for the recognition of revenues generated by various types of nonexchange transactions.

LO 11-9 Account for the issuance of long-term bonds.

LO 11-10 Account for special assessment projects.

LO 11-11 Record the various types of monetary transfers that occur within the funds maintained by a state or local government.

Even a perfunctory examination of such information illustrates the fundamental differences between state and local government accounting and the reporting associated with the financial statements created for a for-profit entity. These differences are not accidental. Financial statements produced by state and local governments are unique for many specific reasons. This chapter and the next present the principles and practices that underlie state and local government accounting and analyze the logic that forms the foundation for their application.

These chapters explain a wide variety of unique state and local government reporting procedures. They also introduce the evolution that has led these governments to produce financial statements that are markedly different from those published by for-profit entities.

LO 11-1

Explain the rationale for the unique characteristics used in creating the financial statements produced for state and local governments.

Introduction to the Financial Reporting for State and Local Governments

In the United States, thousands of state and local governments touch the lives of the citizenry on a daily basis. In addition to the federal and 50 state governments, 90,075 local governments existed as of the most recent census of governments in 2017. Of these, 38,779 were general-purpose local governments—3,031 county governments and 35,748 subcounty governments (19,495 municipal governments and 16,253 township governments). The remainder, which comprised more than half of the total, were special purpose local governments that performed only one function or a very limited number of functions: 12,754 independent school districts and 38,542 special district governments.[2]

Actions of one or more governments affect virtually every citizen each day. Income and sales taxes are collected, property taxes are assessed, schools provide education, police and fire departments maintain public safety, garbage is collected, and roads are paved. Nearly 14.7 million people are employed by state and local governments and they earn more than $80 billion annually.[3]

When seeking to understand the financial reporting for state and local governments, the question should be addressed as to whether a complete set of specialized accounting principles is necessary. Could the financial information of a state or local government be presented fairly by applying the same rules and procedures used by a for-profit entity such as Microsoft or Coca-Cola? In response to that basic question, the Governmental Accounting Standards Board (GASB) has identified several major differences in the reporting needs of these governments.

> The primary purpose of governments is to enhance or maintain the well-being of citizens by providing services in accordance with public policy goals. In contrast, business enterprises focus primarily on wealth creation, interacting principally with those segments of society that fulfill their mission of generating a financial return on investment for shareholders.

GASB goes on to cite several crucial differences that justify the unique presentations and principles encountered in a study of state and local government accounting.

- Governments serve a broader group of stakeholders, including taxpayers, citizens, elected representatives, oversight groups, bondholders, and others in the financial community.
- Most government revenues are raised through involuntary taxes rather than a willing exchange of comparable value between two parties in a typical business transaction.
- Monitoring actual compliance with budgeted public policy priorities is central to government public accountability reporting.
- Governments exist longer than for-profit businesses and are not typically subject to bankruptcy and dissolution.[4]

---

[2] U.S. Census Bureau, 2017 Census of Governments—Organizations, Table 2, www.census.gov/topics /public-sector/government-organization/data/tables.html.

[3] U.S. Census Bureau, 2017 ASPEP Datasets & Tables, State and Local Government Employment Data, www.census.gov/data/tables/2017/econ/apes/annual-apes.html.

[4] "Users of Governmental Financial Reports Require Substantially Different Information than Users of Business Financial Reports," News Release, March 16, 2006, http://www.gasb.org/cs/ContentServer?pagen ame=GASB%2FGASBContent_C%2FGASBNewsPage&cid=1176156736250.

Accounting for state and local governments is not merely the determination of when a performance obligation is satisfied and an expense incurred in order to calculate reported net income. The setting of tax rates and allocation of limited financial resources among many worthy causes such as education, police protection, welfare, health care, and the environment create heated debates throughout the world. Without a profit motive, what type of financial reporting is appropriate for a government? Who are the potential users of the information? Historically, to enable the public to stay properly informed, the traditional focus of government reporting has been on identifying the sources of current financial resources and the uses made of those resources. In other words, where did the government get its money, and how did the government use that money?

Indeed, this approach is appropriate for the short-term decisions necessitated by the government's need to gather and spend current financial resources each year to carry out public policy. However, during the last two decades, a much broader view has been taken of government financial reporting. For the longer term, information to reflect the overall financial stability of the government is also essential, especially for creditors who often provide funding through the acquisition of government-issued bonds.

Hence, state and local government officials face a number of unique financial reporting challenges. Those issues are addressed by GASB, which was created in 1984 to serve as the public-sector counterpart of the Financial Accounting Standards Board (FASB). GASB holds the primary responsibility in the United States for setting authoritative accounting standards for state and local government units.[5] In the same manner as FASB, GASB is an independent body functioning under the oversight of the Financial Accounting Foundation.

"Each of the final Statements of Governmental Accounting Standards issued by the GASB since its establishment in 1984 is designed to provide taxpayers, legislators, municipal bond analysts, and others with information that is useful to their decision-making process regarding governmental entities."[6] The following pronouncements are available for download at www.gasb.org:

- Statements of Governmental Accounting Standards
- Concepts Statements
- GASB Interpretations
- GASB Technical Bulletins
- GASB Implementation Guides

GASB is only in charge of the financial reporting for state and local governments. Financial reporting for the U.S. federal government has evolved over a different path. In 1990, the Director of the Office of Management and Budget, the Secretary of the Treasury, and the Comptroller General created the Federal Accounting Standards Advisory Board (FASAB). FASAB recommends accounting principles and standards for the U.S. federal government and its agencies. Although those rules are beyond the coverage of this textbook, additional information about FASAB is available on its website at www.fasab.gov.

Governmental Accounting—User Needs

Much of this chapter and the next reflect the efforts by GASB to provide relevant information to a wide array of individuals and groups interested in assessing both resource allocation decisions and the financial health of a state or local government.

The unique aspects of any accounting and reporting system should be a direct result of the needs of the people who read and study the financial statements. Identifying those users and their informational requirements is a logical first step in the study of state and local government accounting.

[5] The National Committee on Municipal Accounting held the authority for state and local government accounting from 1934 until 1941. The National Committee on Governmental Accounting, a quasi-independent agency of the Government Finance Officers Association, established government accounting principles from 1949 through 1954 and again from 1967 until 1983, when GASB was formed. During several time periods, no group held primary responsibility for the development of governmental accounting. For an overview of the work of GASB, see Terry K. Patton and Robert J. Freeman, "The GASB Turns 25: A Retrospective," *Government Finance Review,* April 2009.

[6] Governmental Accounting Standards Board, "Standards & Guidance," https://www.gasb.org/jsp/GASB/Page/GASBLandingPage&cid=1176160042327.

Early in its tenure, GASB addressed this challenge by describing several distinct groups of primary users of external state and local governmental financial reports:

> The Board believes there are three groups of primary users of external state and local governmental financial reports. They are (a) those to whom government is primarily accountable (the citizenry), (b) those who directly represent the citizens (legislative and oversight bodies), and (c) those who lend or who participate in the lending process (investors and creditors). . . . The citizenry group includes citizens (whether they are classified as taxpayers, voters, or service recipients), the media, advocate groups, and public finance researchers. The legislative and oversight officials group includes members of state legislatures, county commissions, city councils, boards of trustees, and school boards, and those executive branch officials with oversight responsibility over other levels of government. Investors and creditors include individual and institutional investors and creditors, municipal security underwriters, bond rating agencies, bond insurers, and financial institutions.[7]

Thus, the quest for useful government reporting encounters a significant obstacle. User needs are so broad that no one set of financial statements or accounting principles can satisfy all expectations. How can voters, bondholders, administrative officials, and all of the other users of the financial statements produced by state and local governments receive the information they need for decision-making purposes? How can statements that are prepared for citizens also be sufficient for the needs of creditors and investors? That conflict has always been at the heart of state and local government accounting.

Two Sets of Financial Statements

LO 11-2

Differentiate between the two sets of financial statements prepared by state and local governments.

Eventually, the desire to provide such a wide variety of information that could satisfy such broad user demands led GASB to require state and local governments to report two separate sets of financial statements, each with its own unique principles and objectives. For a complete understanding of state and local government accounting, nothing is more essential than recognizing the need for creating and distributing two sets of statements.

1. **Fund financial statements** provide portraits of the ongoing activities of the various aspects of a government. At least for a portion of the government, these statements report the current period revenues earned and expenditures incurred by individual government functions. These statements also focus on disclosing restrictions that have been placed on the use of the government's financial resources. Citizens interested in the operating efficiency of a government's functions, especially in comparison to approved budgets, are likely to study fund financial statements.

2. **Government-wide financial statements** have a longer-term focus with reporting centered on the government as a whole. These statements report all revenues and all costs as well as all assets and liabilities. Creditors, especially bondholders, are likely to be most interested in government-wide financial statements as they assess the likelihood of being paid when obligations come due, possibly years into the future. Citizens also study these statements to evaluate the chance of future deficits or surpluses.

Fund Financial Statements

Preparation of fund statements has long been the traditional reporting approach for state and local governments because the information focuses on the transactions of individual government functions. These statements present the amount of financial resources allocated by officials to various activities. Fund statements also report the use made of those resources. Citizens are able to assess the government's fiscal efficiency and accountability in raising and spending money. Fund financial statements report the amounts actually collected during the current year from various taxes and borrowings and the amounts spent on services such as public safety, education, health, sanitation, and the construction of new roads. For many users, especially the local citizens, this information can be extremely valuable.

---

[7] Government Accounting Standards Board, Codification of Governmental Accounting and Financial Reporting Standards as of June 30, 2021, Concepts Statement No. 1, "Objectives of Financial Reporting," paras. 30–31.

Fund financial statements exhibit flexibility. As will be described later in this chapter, different methods of accounting are applied to different activities. The **primary measurement focus** for public service activities such as the police department is the sources and uses of *current financial resources,* assets that eventually will be spent such as cash and receivables. For these public service activities, the **timing of recognition** is based on a system known as *modified accrual accounting.* This approach recognizes (1) revenues when the resulting current financial resources are both measurable and available to be used and (2) expenditures when the net amount of current financial resources is reduced.

When applying modified accrual accounting, identifying the moment when financial resources are available to be used is an important decision because it guides the timing of revenue recognition. The term "available to be used" means that current financial resources will be received soon enough in the future so that they can be used to pay for expenditures made in the current period. The determination of what is meant by "soon enough in the future" is at the discretion of the reporting government.

For example, in its 2020 financial statements, the City of Norfolk, Virginia, disclosed that "the City generally considers revenues, except for grant revenues, to be available if collected within 45 days of the end of the fiscal year."* Therefore, according to modified accrual accounting, a 2020 revenue collected by the City of Norfolk within the first 45 days of 2021 is recognized in 2020 because the resulting money is considered available to pay 2020 expenditures. In contrast, the City of Richmond, Virginia, applies a policy of two months, whereas the City of Raleigh, North Carolina, uses 90 days. As shown by these cities, the definition of "available to be used" often varies from one government to the next. The one exception for modified accrual accounting as designated by GASB is the recognition of property taxes, where a 60-day maximum period is mandated.

Government-Wide Financial Statements

GASB created government-wide financial statements more than two decades ago to provide information about a government's financial affairs as a whole. These statements provide readers with a method of assessing operational accountability, the government's ability to meet its operating objectives. This information helps users make evaluations of the financial decisions and long-term stability of the government by allowing them to

- Determine whether the government's overall financial position improved or deteriorated during the reporting period.
- Understand the cost of providing services to the citizenry.
- Gain insight into how the government finances its programs.
- Understand the extent to which the government has invested in capital assets such as roads, bridges, and other infrastructure assets.

This information has become especially relevant in recent years as a number of governments have declared bankruptcy (such as San Bernardino, California; Stockton, California; Central Falls, Rhode Island; Jefferson County, Alabama; and Detroit, Michigan) while others face daunting financial difficulties.[8] The need to assess the risk of overall financial instability is becoming an ever more important aspect of state and local government accounting. The financial stress of the COVID-19 pandemic adds another layer of financial burden on governments.

To achieve these reporting goals, the government-wide financial statements' measurement focus is on *all economic resources* (not just current financial resources). For timing purposes, these statements apply *accrual accounting* much like a for-profit entity. Consequently, government-wide statements report all assets and liabilities (and deferred inflows and outflows of resources) and recognize revenues and expenses in a way that is comparable to business-type accounting.

---

[8] A fascinating picture of a government in financial crisis can be found at http://www.npr.org/blogs/money/2012/03/23/149057880/how-a-city-goes-broke, which details the difficulties of governing Harrisburg, Pennsylvania, as it fights through a series of bad financial decisions.

* The City of Norfolk, Virginia, 2020.

The Evolution to Reporting Two Sets of Financial Statements

The goal of making a government and its officials accountable to the public is one aspect of financial reporting that has remained constant over many decades. Because of the essential role of democracy within U.S. society, the creators of accounting principles have always sought to provide the information needed for evaluating governmental actions. Citizens should be able to ascertain the techniques officials use to raise money and then the allocation made of those scarce financial resources.

Most citizens are both voters and taxpayers. They have a special interest in the results obtained from their involuntary contributions to the government in the form of taxes, tolls, and other fees. Traditionally, because elected and appointed officials hold authority over the public's money, governmental reporting has stressed this stewardship responsibility.

> Accountability is the cornerstone of all financial reporting in government. . . . Accountability requires governments to answer to the citizenry—to justify the raising of public resources and the purposes for which they are used. Governmental accountability is based on the belief that the citizenry has a "right to know," a right to receive openly declared facts that may lead to public debate by the citizens and their elected representatives.[9]

To promote transparency, governmental reporting has historically been directed toward measuring and identifying the current financial resources generated and expended by the various government functions. As in decades past, the fund financial statements of today allow readers to focus on individual government activities. In connection with public services, such as the police department and public library, fund statements answer three relevant questions:

- How did a particular part of the government generate current financial resources?
- Where was use made of the current financial resources?
- What amount of the current financial resources is held presently?

The term *current financial resources* normally encompasses the monetary assets available for officials to spend to meet the government's needs during the present budget period. When accounting for current financial resources, a government is primarily monitoring cash, investments, and receivables as well as any current claims to those resources. In this reporting, virtually no emphasis is placed on accounts such as Buildings, Equipment, and Long-Term Debts because they have no direct impact on current financial resources.

Stressing accountability by monitoring the inflows and outflows of current financial resources is not an approach that will meet all user needs. Prior to the creation of government-wide financial statements, many conventional reporting objectives were ignored. For example, does the government have too much debt to service? As a result, investors and creditors were frequently sharp critics of governmental accounting. "When cities get into financial trouble, few citizens know about it until the day the interest can't be met or the teachers paid. . . . Had the books been kept like any decent corporation's that could never have happened."[10]

Consequently, in 1998, GASB mandated that separate government-wide financial statements be included along with fund financial statements in the general-purpose financial reporting for a state or local government. This second set of statements has a different purpose. It reports all assets and other resources at the disposal of government officials. It reports all liabilities that must eventually be paid. Revenues and expenses are recognized according to accrual accounting. When compared to fund financial statements, government-wide statements provide a completely different perspective of a government's financial affairs.

With two sets of financial statements, all users (whether citizen, creditor, or other interested party) can select the information considered to be the most relevant to their needs. Of course, not everyone believes that this additional data will always be helpful. "One of the tougher challenges of the current information age is sorting out the information most relevant for decision making from the vast amounts of data generated by today's state-of-the-art

---

[9] GASB, *Codification,* as of June 30, 2021, Concepts Statement No. 1, "Objectives of Financial Reporting," para. 56.

[10] Richard Greene, "You Can't Fight City Hall—If You Can't Understand It," *Forbes,* March 3, 1980, p. 92.

information systems. Financial reports cannot simply keep growing in size indefinitely to encompass every new type of information that becomes available."[11]

	Fund Financial Statements*	Government-Wide Financial Statements
Emphasis	Individual activities (during current period).	Government as a whole.
Measurement focus	Current financial resources (cash, investments, and receivables and claims to those assets).	All economic resources (all assets, liabilities, and other resources).
General information	Inflows and outflows of current financial resources.	Overall financial health.
Timing of recognition	Modified accrual accounting.	Accrual accounting.

*The guidance provided here for fund financial statements only applies to public service activities such as public safety, infrastructure construction, and education. As will be discussed shortly, other activities in fund financial statements (business-type activities and fiduciary responsibilities) are reported more in keeping with government-wide financial statements.

LO 11-3

Understand the reason that fund accounting has traditionally been a prominent factor in the internal recording of state and local governments.

Internal Recordkeeping—Fund Accounting

In gathering financial information, state and local governments have always faced the challenge of reporting a diverse array of activities financed from numerous sources. Accountability and control become special concerns for governments that are composed of a multitude of relatively independent departments and functions. How does a government account for its police department separately from parks and recreation? For the internal monitoring of these individual activities, most governments maintain a separate quasi-independent bookkeeping system referred to as a *fund* with its own complete set of accounts. One fund records the transactions and maintains account balances for the police department while a separate fund records them for parks and recreation. In this way, information can be accumulated and organized for every activity.

Internal information gathered in this manner serves as the foundation for fund financial statements. An underlying assumption of government reporting has long been that most citizens want to see information segregated by function in order to assess each activity individually. How much money did the fire department receive? What was done with that money? By using fund accounting, the accounting records can provide that information. The resulting figures are the basis for the fund financial statements prepared for external distribution.

Because no common profit motive exists to tie various government functions and services together, consolidated balances were historically not presented. Combining financial results from the city zoo, fire department, water system, print shop, and a wide variety of other operations provides figures of questionable utility, especially if accountability and control over the usage of current financial resources are primary goals. Fund financial reporting was designed to provide information about individual activities, not the government as a whole.

The addition of government-wide statements has no direct effect on fund accounting. Consequently, the separate funds monitored by each state and local government still serve as the foundation for internal reporting. Although a single list of identifiable functions is not possible, the following are routinely performed by many governments. Many of these are departments, cost centers, or agencies reported within the government's general fund. Some, though, are monitored within separate funds for control purposes or because the operational nature is different from a typical government activity:

Public safety	Judicial system
Highway maintenance	Debt repayment
Sanitation	Bridge construction
Health	Water and sewer system
Welfare	Municipal swimming pool
Culture and recreation	Data processing center
Education	Endowment funds
Parks	Employee pensions

[11] Jeffrey L. Esser, "Standard Setting—How Much Is Enough?" *Government Finance Review,* April 2005, p. 3.

The number of funds in use depends on the extent of services that a particular government provides and the grouping of related activities. For example, two separate funds might be established to account for a high school and its athletic programs, or these activities may be combined into a single fund.

> Only the minimum number of funds consistent with legal and operating requirements should be established, however, because unnecessary funds result in inflexibility, undue complexity, and inefficient financial administration.[12]

The requirement that government-wide financial statements be reported along with fund financial statements was a radical advancement designed to better communicate the overall financial health of the government. One significant outcome was that governments had to begin tracking information (the total cost of roads, for example) that had never been accumulated previously because fund accounting for public service activities focuses on changes in current financial resources. Financial statements that report all economic resources force the government to gather a considerable amount of additional information.

LO 11-4

Identify the three fund types and the individual fund categories within each of these fund types.

Fund Accounting Classifications

For internal recordkeeping, each individual fund (whether it accounts for the police department, the municipal golf course, or some other activity) is identified within one of three distinct categories. This classification system provides clearer reporting of the government's various activities. Furthermore, dividing funds into separate groups allows unique accounting principles to be applied to each.

- *Governmental funds*—this category includes all activities a government carries out to provide citizens with services that are financed primarily through taxes and other general revenue sources. Fire departments, police departments, and school systems are a few of the many activities reported within the governmental funds.
- *Proprietary funds*—this category accounts for a government's ongoing activities that are similar to those conducted by a for-profit entity. This fund type reports operations that assess a user charge so that determining profitability or cost recovery is relevant. A transit system, a municipal golf course, and a toll road are all typically reported within the proprietary funds because the service is provided for a fee.
- *Fiduciary funds*—this category monitors monies held by the government in a trustee capacity. Such assets must be maintained for others and cannot be used by officials for government programs. One common example is the monitoring of assets held in a pension plan for government employees such as teachers, fire fighters, or sanitation workers.

Governmental Funds

In many state and municipal accounting systems, governmental funds tend to dominate because governments usually have a service orientation. The internal accounting system maintains individual funds for every distinct service function: public safety, libraries, construction of a town hall, and so on.

Each of these governmental funds accumulates and expends current financial resources to achieve one or more desired public goals. Modified accrual accounting is applied for timing purposes. To provide clearer information, governmental funds are subdivided into five fund types: the general fund, special revenue funds, capital projects funds, debt service funds, and permanent funds. This classification system provides an overall structure for the financial reporting of the governmental funds.

The General Fund   GASB's definition of the general fund appears to be somewhat understated: "to account for and report all financial resources not accounted for and reported in another fund."[13] This description seems to imply that the general fund records only miscellaneous revenues and expenditures when, in actuality, it reports many of a government's most

---

[12] GASB, *Codification*, as of June 30, 2021, Sec. 1100.104.
[13] GASB, *Codification*, as of June 30, 2021, Sec. 1300.104.

important ongoing functions. The 2020 fund financial statements for the City of Baltimore, Maryland, disclosed 12 major areas of current expenditures within its general fund:

General government	Recreation and culture
Public safety and regulations	Highways and streets
Conservation of health	Sanitation and waste removal
Social services	Public service
Education	Economic development
Public library	Debt service

Expenditures for these general fund categories were in excess of $1.94 billion and comprised more than 77 percent of the total for all of Baltimore's governmental funds for the year ended June 30, 2020.

Special Revenue Funds Special revenue funds account for current financial resources restricted or committed for a specific purpose (other than debt payments or capital projects). Because of donor stipulations or legislative mandates, these government resources must be spent according to the designated fashion. Saint Paul, Minnesota, for example, maintained 18 individual special revenue funds during the 2019 fiscal year. Sources of those restricted monies were as diverse as the rental use of Lowertown Ball Park, administration fees from charitable gambling, and revenues collected from solid waste and recycling programs.

The special revenue funds category records these monies because legal or donor restrictions require that expenditure be limited to specific operating purposes. According to Saint Paul's annual comprehensive financial report, a special revenue fund designated for "Street Lighting Districts" accounts "for levied assessments used to operate above standard (ornamental) street lighting systems in various areas of the city, installed at the request of adjacent property owners."* In the same manner, the City of Charlotte, North Carolina, maintains a special revenue fund to account for money from a room occupancy tax and from private contributions that must support the NASCAR Hall of Fame. Using a special revenue fund helps to ensure that the city will spend this money as required.

Capital Projects Funds As the title implies, this fund type accounts for financial resources restricted, committed, or assigned for capital outlays such as acquiring or constructing bridges, high schools, roads, or municipal office buildings. Funding for these projects can come from a number of sources such as grants, the sale of bonds, or transfers from general revenue. The actual capital asset is not reported here. Only the money to finance construction or acquisition is monitored in a capital projects fund. For example, the Lexington-Fayette Urban County Government in Kentucky reported, as of June 30, 2020, that it held a total of more than $39.5 million of current financial resources in 15 different capital projects funds. This money had to be used in a variety of projects such as the acquisition or construction of a performing arts and exhibit facility, fire trucks, park projects, and improvements to the public libraries.

Debt Service Funds These funds record financial resources accumulated to pay long-term liabilities and interest as they come due. However, this fund type does not monitor a government's long-term debt. Governments establish debt service funds to account for monetary balances that are restricted, committed, or assigned to make the eventual payments needed to satisfy long-term liabilities. For example, on June 30, 2020, the City of Birmingham, Alabama, reported holding approximately $58.2 million of cash and investments in its debt service funds to pay long-term debt and interest. For the year then ended, more than $11.4 million in principal payments were made from this fund and $13.6 million in interest payments.

Permanent Funds The permanent funds category accounts for financial resources restricted by external donor, contract, or legislation with the stipulation that the principal can never be spent. Nevertheless, the government can use resulting income, often for a specified public program. The City of Dallas, Texas, reported holding $10.3 million in its permanent funds as of September 30, 2020. This money came from private donations. Subsequent income

---

* Saint Paul's Annual Comprehensive Financial Report, 2016.

was designated by the donors to maintain four different local parks and to help finance other municipal projects. Such gifts are frequently referred to as *endowments*.

Proprietary Funds

The proprietary funds category accounts for activities of a government, such as a bus system, toll road, or subway line, that assess a user charge. As in the business world, customers pay and then receive a service in return. Because the user charge helps the government make a profit or at least recover a portion of its cost, the accounting process for proprietary funds resembles that of a for-profit activity. Accrual basis accounting is used with a focus on reporting all economic resources and not just current financial resources. In contrast to governmental funds, proprietary funds are reported in much the same way on both the fund financial statements and the government-wide financial statements.

To facilitate financial reporting, proprietary funds are divided into two fund types: enterprise funds and internal service funds.

Enterprise Funds   Any government operation that is open to the public and financed, at least in part, by user charges is likely to be classified as an enterprise fund. A municipality, for example, might generate revenues from the use of a public swimming pool, golf course, airport, water and sewage service, and the like. The City of Houston, Texas, generated approximately $1.6 billion in revenue during the year ending June 30, 2020, from operating three enterprise funds: the city's airport system, utility system, and the convention and entertainment facilities.

The number of enterprise funds across the country has increased in recent years as government officials attempt to expand services without raising taxes. Thus, citizens utilizing a particular service might have to absorb a higher percentage of its costs. "Enterprise funds have become an attractive alternative revenue source for local governments to recover all or part of the cost of goods or services from those directly benefiting from them."[14]

A practical question arises as to how much revenue an activity must generate before the government should view it as an enterprise fund. For example, if a city wants to promote mass transit and charges only a nickel to ride its bus line, should that service be viewed as an enterprise fund (a business-type activity) or within the general fund (a governmental activity)?

A government may classify any activity that charges a user fee as an enterprise fund. However, this designation is *required* if the activity meets any one of the following criteria. At that point, the government would likely view the amount of revenue as significant to its operation.

- The activity generates revenues that provide the sole security for the debts of the activity.
- Laws or regulations require recovering the activity's costs (including depreciation and debt service) through fees or charges.
- Fees and charges are set at prices intended to recover costs including depreciation and debt service.[15]

Internal Service Funds   This second proprietary fund type accounts for any activity that provides services to another department or agency within the government for a fee. As with enterprise funds, internal service funds are accounted for much like for-profit operations in the private sector.

The City of Lincoln, Nebraska, lists six operations in its 2020 financial statements that are accounted for as individual internal service funds:

Information services fund—to account for the cost of operating a central data processing facility.

Transportation & utilities revolving fund—to account for the cost of operating a central pool to charge engineering and right of way operating costs and transportation and utilities administrative costs.

---

[14] Jeffrey Molinari and Charlie Tyer, "Local Government Enterprise Fund Activity: Trends and Implications," *Public Administration Quarterly,* Fall 2003, p. 369.

[15] GASB, *Codification,* as of June 30, 2021, Sec. 1300.109.

Insurance revolving fund—to account for the cost of providing several types of self-insurance programs.

Fleet services fund—to account for the operations of a centralized maintenance facility for city equipment.

Police garage fund—to account for the operation of a maintenance facility for police and other government vehicles.

Municipal services center fund—to account for the purchase, improvement, and operation of a facility to provide a location for various government functions.

Fiduciary Funds

The final classification, fiduciary funds, accounts for assets held in a trustee capacity for external parties. This designation indicates that the money or other resources cannot be used to support the government's programs. The government controls these assets but cannot use them. Like proprietary funds, fiduciary funds follow the economic resources measurement focus and accrual accounting for the timing of revenues and expenses. Because these assets are not available for the benefit of the government, fiduciary funds are omitted entirely from government-wide financial statements. Separate statements are included within the fund financial statements.

Four different fund types are identified within the fiduciary funds category.

Investment Trust Funds   The first fiduciary fund type accounts for the outside portion of investment pools. This category is necessary when a government accumulates financial resources from other governments in order to have a large sum of money to invest so that a higher rate of return can potentially be earned by all parties. The State of Texas held approximately $30.6 billion at August 31, 2021, in external investment trust funds identified as TexPool and TexPool Prime.

Private-Purpose Trust Funds   The second fiduciary fund type accounts for monies held in a trustee capacity for the benefit of specifically designated external parties such as individuals, private organizations, or other governments. The Commonwealth of Virginia has four private-purpose trust funds with a total in 2020 of $5.4 billion in investments. These trust funds include Invest529, a program offered by the Virginia College Savings Plan.

Pension (and Other Postemployment Benefit) Trust Funds   The third fiduciary fund type accounts for assets held to pay employee pension (and other postemployment) benefits. Because of the need to provide adequate money for retired government workers (for a period of time that might last many years), this fund type can grow quite large. The City of Philadelphia, Pennsylvania, for example, reported assets of more than $6.9 billion in its pension trust funds as of June 30, 2020. As will be discussed, many users of government financial statements have expressed concern in the past that long-term pension responsibilities were not properly reported. Consequently, GASB has mandated the reporting of the size of any unfunded pension obligation.

Custodial Funds   The fourth fund type records any resources a government holds in a fiduciary capacity that does not fall under one of the other three categories. For example, a state government could collect taxes and tolls on behalf of a county or city government. Money often passes through custodial funds quickly. To ensure safety and control, custodial funds are used to maintain this money until physically transferred to the proper authority.

Overview of State and Local Government Financial Statements

LO 11-5

Understand the basic structure of both government-wide financial statements and fund financial statements (as produced for the governmental funds).

A complete analysis of the financial statements created by a state or local government is presented in the subsequent chapter. Nevertheless, an overview of four basic financial statements will be presented at this point to help (1) illustrate the reporting of basic government events, (2) demonstrate the two separate sets of financial statements issued by these governments, and (3) show the use of individual funds. Although these examples cover only a few transactions, they should create a basic understanding of the reporting process used in governmental accounting.

Government-Wide Financial Statements

Only two financial statements make up the government-wide financial statements: *the statement of net position* and *the statement of activities.* In each of these statements, the reporting is separated into governmental activities (all governmental funds and most internal service funds) and business-type activities (all enterprise funds and any remaining internal service funds).[16] As mentioned earlier, government-wide financial statements do not include transactions and account balances of fiduciary funds because those resources are not available for the benefit of the reporting government. Fiduciary funds are only reported in their own separate fund financial statements.

Exhibit 11.1 outlines the basic structure of a statement of net position. Because government-wide financial statements use the economic resources measurement focus, all assets and liabilities are reported. In addition, as will be discussed later, GASB has identified several balances that relate to future periods of time but do not qualify as either assets or liabilities. As can be seen in Exhibit 11.1, these amounts are shown as deferred outflows or deferred inflows of resources. The government reporting of these balances has no direct correspondence in the financial accounting for a for-profit entity.

The final section of this statement, the net position category, indicates several separate figures that serve to balance the statement: (1) the amount of capital assets reported less related debt, (2) legal or external restrictions on the use of any reported assets or resources, and (3) the total unrestricted amount available for use by government officials. For example, in Exhibit 11.1, the Governmental Activities hold $80 that is unrestricted, whereas the

EXHIBIT 11.1
Statement of Net Position
Government-Wide
Financial Statements

	Governmental Activities	Business-Type Activities	Total
Assets			
Cash	$ 100	$ 130	$ 230
Investments	900	40	940
Receivables	600	400	1,000
Internal amounts due	50	(50)	–0–
Supplies and materials.	30	40	70
Capital assets (net of depreciation)	2,950	2,750	5,700
Total assets	$4,630	$3,310	$7,940
Deferred Outflows of Resources			
Unamortized cost of debt refunding	$ 200	$ 40	$ 240
Liabilities			
Accounts payable.	$ 750	$ 230	$ 980
Noncurrent liabilities.	2,300	920	3,220
Total liabilities	$3,050	$1,150	$4,200
Deferred Inflows of Resources			
Unavailable property tax collections.	$ 100	$ –0–	$ 100
Net Position			
Net investment in capital assets.	$1,410	$2,110	$3,520
Restricted for:			
Capital projects.	50	–0–	50
Debt service.	140	60	200
Unrestricted	80	30	110
Total net position	$1,680	$2,200	$3,880

[16] Government-wide financial statements report internal service funds as governmental activities if their primary purpose is to serve the governmental funds. Conversely, internal service funds are included with business-type activities if they mainly exist to help one or more enterprise funds. For example, a print shop (an internal service fund) should be reported within the governmental activities if its work is primarily for the benefit of a governmental fund such as the public library. If its work is to service a bus line (or some other enterprise fund), the print shop is classified within the business-type activities.

Business-Type Activities reports only $30. Government officials can make use of that money and resources as they believe is best.

The statement of activities in Exhibit 11.2 provides details about revenues and expenses, again separated into governmental activities and business-type activities. This statement is usually read horizontally first and then vertically. Direct expenses and program revenues are shown for each government function (such as the general government and public safety). Program revenues include fines, fees, grants, and the like that a specific activity generates. Thus, a single net revenue or net expense figure is determined for each function to indicate the financial burden or financial benefit to the government and its citizens.

For example, at Point A in this statement, a reader can see that maintaining public safety (probably through a police department, a fire department, and maybe an ambulance service) has a net cost to the government of $8,820. Direct expenses of $9,700 are partially offset by program revenues of $880 (possibly generated by fines, fees, or other charges). A taxpayer can judge the wisdom of incurring that cost to help ensure public safety, a figure that is greater than the $8,100 net cost of education as shown two lines farther down.

The net expense and net revenue for all governmental activities are then summed vertically to arrive at the total cost of operating the government, an amount that is offset by general revenues such as property taxes and sales taxes. As can be seen, governmental activities had a net cost of $20,720 (Point B), whereas the business-type activities generated a net financial benefit of $1,940 (Point C). At Point D, the statement shows that the government generated property tax revenues of $20,400 to cover virtually all of the cost of providing governmental activities. Investment earnings and transfers more than made up the difference so that the net position of the governmental activities increased by $700 this year (Point E). The net position of the business-type activities increased by $1,410 (Point F).

Fund Financial Statements

Most state or local governments produce quite a number of fund financial statements because of all the diverse functions that are normally performed. At this introductory stage, only the

EXHIBIT 11.2   Statement of Activities—Government-Wide Financial Statements

Function	Expenses	Program Revenues	Net (Expense) Revenue Governmental Activities	Net (Expense) Revenue Business-Type Activities	Total
Governmental activities					
General government	$ 3,200	$ 1,400	$ (1,800)	n/a	$ (1,800)
Public safety.	9,700	880	(8,820) Ⓐ	n/a	(8,820)
Public works.	2,600	600	(2,000)	n/a	(2,000)
Education	8,400	300	(8,100)	n/a	(8,100)
Total governmental activities	$23,900	$ 3,180	$(20,720)	n/a	$(20,720)
Business-type activities					
Water.	$ 3,600	$ 4,030	n/a	$ 430	$ 430
Sewer	4,920	5,610	n/a	690	690
Airport.	2,300	3,120	n/a	820	820
Total business-type activities	$10,820	$12,760	n/a	$1,940	$ 1,940
Total government	$34,720	$15,940	$(20,720) Ⓑ	$1,940 Ⓒ	$(18,780)
General revenues:					
Property taxes.			$ 20,400 Ⓓ	$ –0–	$ 20,400
Investment earnings.			420	70	490
Transfers.			600	(600)	–0–
Total general revenues and transfers.			$ 21,420	$ (530)	$ 20,890
Change in net position.			$ 700 Ⓔ	$1,410 Ⓕ	$ 2,110
Beginning net position.			980	790	1,770
Ending net position.			$ 1,680	$2,200	$ 3,880

two fundamental statements that most parallel the two government-wide statements will be examined. Exhibit 11.3 shows *a balance sheet* for the governmental funds, and Exhibit 11.4 presents *a statement of revenues, expenditures, and changes in fund balances* for the same governmental funds. The balance sheet reports only the current financial resources (assets) held by the various funds and the claims to those resources (liabilities).

In studying Exhibit 11.4, a reader can see that three separate categories are present in this fund financial statement. They will each be discussed in detail throughout the remainder of this chapter and the next:

Revenues

Expenditures

Other Financing Sources (Uses)

Note that the figures found for the governmental funds in the fund financial statements will not be the same as those presented for the governmental activities in the government-wide statements. For example, the asset total reported for the governmental activities in Exhibit 11.1 is $4,630, whereas the asset total for all governmental funds in Exhibit 11.3 is only $1,560. These differences can be quite large and confusing. They result primarily for three reasons:

1. For government-wide statements, internal service funds are grouped with the funds that they primarily benefit. Internal service funds are reported within the governmental activities if they assist governmental funds and within business-type activities if they assist enterprise funds. In fund financial statements, all internal service funds are reported as proprietary funds and not as governmental funds. *Reported totals will vary because internal service funds are not governmental funds in the fund statements but, in some cases, can be included within the governmental activities in the government-wide financial statements.*

EXHIBIT 11.3 **Balance Sheet—Governmental Funds—Fund Financial Statements**

	General Fund	Library Program	Other Governmental Funds	Total Governmental Funds
Assets				
Cash	$ 40	$ 10	$ 50	$ 100
Investments	580	120	200	900
Receivables	120	200	210	530
Supplies and materials	10	10	10	30
Total assets	$750	$340	$470	$1,560
Liabilities				
Accounts payable	$230	$170	$110	$ 510
Notes payable—current	200	–0–	100	300
Total liabilities	$430	$170	$210	$ 810
Deferred Inflows of Resources				
Unavailable property tax collections	$100	$–0–	$–0–	$ 100
Fund Balances				
Nonspendable	$ 10	$ 10	$ 10	$ 30
Restricted	100	90	60	250
Committed	30	50	100	180
Assigned	20	20	90	130
Unassigned	60	–0–	–0–	60
Total fund balances	$220	$170	$260	$ 650
Total liabilities, deferred inflows, and fund balances	$750	$340	$470	$1,560

EXHIBIT 11.4 Statement of Revenues, Expenditures, and Other Changes in Fund Balances—Governmental Funds—Fund Financial Statements

	General Fund	Library Program	Other Governmental Funds	Total Governmental Funds
Revenues				
Property taxes	$17,200	$ 900	$2,300	$20,400
Investment earnings	100	200	180	480
Program revenues.	500	100	2,500	3,100
Total revenues.	$17,800	$1,200	$4,980	$23,980
Expenditures				
Current:				
General government.	$ 3,400	$ –0–	$ 100	$ 3,500
Public safety	5,100	–0–	400	5,500
Education	6,700	800	–0–	7,500
Debt service:				
Principal.	–0–	–0–	1,000	1,000
Interest.	–0–	–0–	600	600
Capital outlay	1,100	300	3,300	4,700
Total expenditures	$16,300	$1,100	$5,400	$22,800
Excess (deficiency) of revenues over expenditures.	$ 1,500	$ 100	$ (420)	$ 1,180
Other Financing Sources (Uses)				
Bond proceeds.	$ –0–	$ –0–	$1,000	$ 1,000
Transfers in	–0–	20	580	600
Transfers out.	(1,300)	–0–	(1,000)	(2,300)
Total other financing sources and uses	$ (1,300)	$ 20	$ 580	$ (700)
Change in fund balances	$ 200	$ 120	$ 160	$ 480
Fund balances—beginning	20	50	100	170
Fund balances—ending	$ 220	$ 170	$ 260	$ 650

2. In government-wide statements, governmental activities apply the economic resources measurement focus so that all assets and liabilities are reported. In contrast, in the fund statements, the governmental funds use the current financial resources measurement focus and report only current financial resources and and claims against those resources. *The two sets of statements report different assets and liabilities.*

3. Governmental activities use accrual accounting in creating government-wide statements. However, modified accrual accounting is used in preparing fund financial statements for the governmental funds. *The timing of recognition is different.*

Because of these differences, reconciliations must be reported between the totals presented in Exhibits 11.1 and 11.3 and between Exhibits 11.2 and 11.4. Those reconciliations are discussed in detail in the following chapter.

Major Funds

In both of the fund financial statements presented in Exhibits 11.3 and 11.4, the general fund is shown in a separate column as is every other individual fund that qualifies as major. The assumption here is that the Library Program (probably one of this government's special revenue funds if financed by a designated tax levy) is the only individual fund outside the general fund that is considered major. Information for all "other governmental funds" is then grouped into a single nonmajor column. Consequently, identification of a major fund is quite important for disclosure purposes because it will be reported in its own separate column. A major fund is identified as follows:

The reporting government's main operating fund (the general fund or its equivalent) should always be reported as a major fund. Other individual governmental and enterprise funds should be reported in separate columns as major funds based on these criteria:

a. The total of assets and deferred outflows of resources, the total of liabilities and deferred inflows of resources, revenues, or expenditures/expenses of that individual governmental or enterprise fund are at least 10 percent of the corresponding element(s) total (total assets and deferred outflows of resources, total liabilities and deferred inflows of resources, and so forth) for all funds of that category or type (that is, total governmental or total enterprise funds), *and*

b. The same element(s) that met the 10 percent criterion in (a) is at least 5 percent of the corresponding element(s) total for all governmental and enterprise funds combined.

In addition to funds that meet the major fund criteria, any other governmental or enterprise fund that the government's officials believe is particularly important to financial statement users (for example, because of public interest or consistency) may be reported as a major fund.[17]

Fund Balances

One other unique characteristic of the fund financial statements created for the governmental funds should be noted. Because state or local governments have no owners, the balance sheet does not need a stockholders' equity section to report contributed capital, retained earnings, and the like. Instead, a variety of "fund balance" accounts, as shown in Exhibit 11.3, indicate the net current financial resources held by each fund and what use can be made of those resources.

Fund balance accounts have long been reported in governmental accounting in a rather generic fashion to balance the balance sheet. Official rules now standardize the reporting of fund balances within five categories discussed in this section. These designations aid financial statement readers in understanding the use that can be made of each fund's net current financial resources. Often, because of legal or external restrictions, a portion of the current financial resources cannot be used by government officials as they please. "The fund balance classifications are GASB's response to credit market participants who sought general information about the availability of reported fund balances."[18]

In Exhibit 11.3, the general fund reports assets of $750, and liabilities and deferred inflows of $430 and $100, indicating a net fund balance of $220. From a reporting perspective, the most significant question to be addressed in connection with this amount is: What use can government officials make of the excess $220? The purpose of the fund balance classifications is to indicate restrictions (both external and internal) that limit the ability of officials to spend these resources as they wish. For example, at June 30, 2020, the City of Las Vegas, Nevada, reported total fund balances for its governmental funds of $624.8 million. In this statement, the city's assets exceeded its liabilities and deferred inflows by that amount. What use can be made of this excess? How much discretion do government officials have with these resources?

Fund Balance—Nonspendable   As the name implies, this figure shows the amount of the fund's current financial resources that cannot be spent. This restricted classification is normally necessary for one of two reasons. First, assets such as supplies and prepaid expenses are not in a spendable form. Second, financial resources may be received that cannot be used because of externally imposed limitations. A cash gift, for example, falls within this category if the donor stipulates that only the future income generated from this balance can be spent for a specific purpose. This fund balance designation indicates that assets are held but are not available for government spending. As of June 30, 2020, the City of Las Vegas, reported a fund balance—nonspendable within its governmental funds totaling $3.5 million. That reporting was necessary because the governmental funds held $1.5 million in inventory and

---

[17] GASB, *Codification*, as of June 21, 2021, Sec. 2200.159.

[18] Paul A. Copley, *Essentials of Accounting for Governmental and Not-for-Profit Organizations,* 13th ed. (McGraw Hill Education, 2018), p. 57.

prepaid expenses that could not be spent and another $2.0 million in assets were to generate income for the perpetual care of a local cemetery.

Fund Balance—Restricted   This figure indicates the amount of net assets held by the government that must be spent in a manner designated by an external party. For example, a grant from another government for a specified purpose such as classroom teachers or playground equipment creates an increase in this category, as does a bond covenant that requires the debt proceeds to be used in a particular manner. The City of Las Vegas reported a $171.1 million fund balance—restricted as of June 30, 2020. Separate disclosure information indicates the restrictions apply to a wide range of projects including economic development and assistance, public safety (fire and safety), and public works for roads and flooding.

Fund Balance—Committed   Here, assets have been designated for a particular purpose, not by an outside party but rather by the highest level of decision-making authority within the government. For example, a state legislature might vote to set aside $700 million for road construction. On the government's balance sheet, that decision is disclosed by an increase in the amount reported as the "fund balance—committed." Of course, the legislature holds the power to reverse this decision so the commitment is not necessarily binding. The City of Las Vegas reports its fund balance—committed as $157.4 million at June 30, 2020. More specifically, this amount has been committed for general government, parks projects, and several other government functions. The reporting is explained in a note to the city's financial statements as representing amounts that "can be used only for specific purposes pursuant to constraints imposed by a formal action of the the Mayor and City Council, the City's highest level of decision-making authority."*

Fund Balance—Assigned   Frequently, in the regular operations of a government, money is designated for a specific purpose without any formal action taken by the highest level of decision-making authority. These are often larger amounts held for a particular purpose. The head of the government's finance committee might designate cash of $1 million to be used in a few months to pay the current installment of a bond. However, if necessary, that money could be switched to some other purpose in the interim. At June 30, 2020, the City of Las Vegas reports a fund balance—assigned of $121.2 million for its governmental funds. Of that total, $19.5 million was assigned for debt service.

Fund Balance—Unassigned   This category is normally found only in the general fund and reflects any amount of financial resources where no use has yet been designated either externally or internally. This amount is available to government officials for any purpose viewed as appropriate. On the June 30, 2020, balance sheet for the City of Las Vegas, the fund balance—unassigned was $171.6 million. That money is available for use by city officials.

To illustrate, note how each of the following events affects the balance sheet within the fund financial statements for the governmental funds.

- *Cash of $30,000 is held by the government that can be spent for any purpose. On the last day of the fiscal year, the money is spent to buy supplies for a variety of public activities. Assume, as will be discussed shortly, government officials choose to apply the consumption method.* The supplies are shown initially as an asset with an equal decrease in cash. The "fund balance--unassigned" must be reclassified as a "fund balance—nonspendable." The $30,000 is no longer available to be spent as the government chooses.

- *A citizen dies and leaves investments valued at $3 million to the city with the requirement that the government expend these resources solely for park beautification.* Officials have no discretion in the use. In reporting these investments, the government must also show a "fund balance—restricted" on its balance sheet equal to $3 million. The use of the investments is limited to the designated purpose.

- *The highest level of decision makers for the city (perhaps the city council or the mayor) officially decides to set aside $110,000 in previously unassigned cash to beautify several local parks that are in need of maintenance.* No asset account is affected because nothing happens to the money. Nevertheless, the amount shown on the balance sheet as "fund

---

* The City of Las Vegas.

balance—unassigned" decreases $110,000, and the "fund balance—committed" increases by the same amount. No one within the government can overrule the decision.

- *The director of finance for the city sets aside $12,000 in previously unassigned cash to be used to buy new benches for the city's parks. The city council is the highest level of decision making in the government.* Because the decision was not made at the highest level of decision making, the "fund balance—unassigned" goes down while the "fund balance—assigned" increases. The decision, as well as the authority level of the decision, is shown in this way. Although the decision is made, it can be changed by a higher level of decision makers.

- *The city government receives property tax revenues of $1.4 million.* Officials might eventually choose to use some or all of this money to complete specific projects such as the beautification of local parks. However, no such decision has yet been made. In the general fund, the government reports the asset along with a "fund balance—unassigned" amount. This reporting allows readers of the financial statements to see that the money is available for use by government officials.

Accounting for Governmental Funds

LO 11-6

Record the passage of a budget by a state or local government and the subsequent recording of encumbrances and expenditures.

The remainder of this chapter examines many of the important accounting procedures used within the five governmental funds: the general fund, special revenue funds, capital projects funds, debt service funds, and permanent funds. The distinct approach that marks governmental accounting as unique can best be seen in these individual funds. Because of the dual nature of the financial reporting model, most procedures will be demonstrated twice, once for the government-wide financial statements and a second time for the governmental fund financial statements.

The reporting applied to proprietary funds and to fiduciary funds (as well as to the government-wide financial statements as a whole) is more likely to resemble the accounting used by for-profit businesses. It is less unique. Thus, the emphasis here is on accounting for the individual governmental funds.

One preliminary question to address is whether governments should establish two separate sets of internal financial records (one for fund statements and another for government-wide statements)? Or, should governments maintain only one set for fund accounting that must be adjusted rather significantly at the end of each year to create government-wide financial statements?

> Most governments have not changed their day-to-day accounting at all from basic fund accounting. They continue to record their routine transactions, like tax collections and grant reimbursements, on a cash basis. Then, at year end when government-wide statements are to be produced, the government records the full accrual amounts as required by GASB. Given the nature of control environments in most governments, they find it easier to record full accrual only at year end.[19]

From an educational perspective, this textbook could follow the lead established in practice of the government reporting each event based on the fund financial statement model. Then, the government makes a one-time conversion at the end of the year to convert those fund financial statements into government-wide statements. Or, the textbook could simultaneously examine each event from both a fund financial statement and a government-wide perspective.

The second approach is adopted here because it allows a clearer comparison of the two distinct methods of financial reporting. This textbook analyzes significant transactions from both a fund and a government-wide perspective. Examining the two ways of reporting side by side should be a more understandable process than learning fund financial reporting and later converting the resulting balances into a completely different set of figures based on the government-wide model. However, students need to understand that many state and local governments make only fund financial statement journal entries for internal reporting. The resulting balances are adjusted at a later time to enable the preparation of government-wide financial statements.

[19] From Jack Reagan, partner with UHY LLP, December 5, 2021.

The Importance of Budgets and the Recording of Budgetary Entries

Many believe the budget is the most significant financial document produced by a governmental entity. The budget has been defined as a plan for the coordination of revenues and expenditures or as the amount of money that is available for, required for, or assigned to a particular purpose.[20]

A budget is a legally approved plan for operations. To enhance accountability, government officials are usually required to adopt an annual budget for each separate activity to anticipate the inflow of financial resources and establish approved expenditure levels. In a chronological sense, the recording of budgetary entries is the first significant accounting procedure carried out by a state or locality.

The budget serves several important purposes:

1. *Expresses public policy.* If, for example, more money is budgeted for child care and less for the environment, both positive and negative consequences are likely to occur. Through the budget, citizens are made aware of decisions made by government officials as to the allocation of limited financial resources.
2. *Serves as an expression of financial intent for the upcoming fiscal year.* The budget presents the government's financial plan for the current period.
3. *Provides control because it establishes spending limitations for each activity.* Officials typically cannot spend more for a particular activity than has been legally budgeted without passage of a special authorization allowing them to do so.
4. *Offers a means of evaluating performance.* The budget allows a comparison to be made between the authorized level that has been set and approved and the actual financial results for each period.
5. *Indicates whether the government anticipates having sufficient revenues to pay for all of the approved expenditures.* In the current economic climate, when many governments face declining revenue totals, the amount and handling of proposed deficits should be of interest to every citizen.

GASB states that "financial reports are used primarily to compare actual financial results with the legally adopted budget."[21]

After a government enacts its budget into law, formal accounting recognition is frequently required as a means of enhancing the informational benefits. The public is given the opportunity to review the amounts of current financial resources expected to be received and expended. By entering budget figures into the accounting records at the start of each fiscal year, comparisons can be drawn between actual and budgeted amounts at any point in time. At the end of the year, because the budget entries have served their purpose, they are reversed to remove the balances from the accounting records.

In the formal reporting process, at a minimum budget information must be disclosed for the general fund and each major fund that exists within the special revenue funds. For these funds, governments provide comparisons between (1) the original budget, (2) the final budget, and (3) the actual figures for the period. This information appears as required supplementary information located after the notes to the financial statements. As an allowed alternative, the government can include a separate statement within the fund financial statements to compare the budget and actual figures.

To illustrate, assume that officials for the City of West enact a motel excise tax with the resulting revenue to be spent to promote tourism and conventions. Because these receipts are legally restricted for a specified purpose, the city must utilize a special revenue fund. Assume that for the 2024 fiscal year, the tax is expected to generate $490,000 in revenues.

Based on this projection, the city council passes a budget to authorize specific expenditures during the current year (referred to as *appropriations*): $420,000 for promotional programs,

[20] GASB, *Codification,* as of June 30, 2021, Appendix B, Concepts Statement No. 1, "Objectives of Financial Reporting," para. 19.

[21] Ibid., para. 77.

$200,000 for salaries, $30,000 for utilities, $80,000 for advertising, and $110,000 for supplies. The $70,000 difference between the anticipated revenue and the appropriation total is a projected budget surplus. It might be set up by the government for future use or in case actual revenue amounts prove to be too small to support approved expenditures.

To acknowledge the council's action, the accounting records of this fund include the following journal entry. No similar budget entry is made within the government-wide financial statements.

Fund Financial Statements—Budgetary Entry

Special Revenue Fund—Tourism and Convention Promotions		
Estimated Revenues—Motel Tax Levy	490,000	
Appropriations—Salaries		200,000
Appropriations—Utilities		30,000
Appropriations—Advertising		80,000
Appropriations—Supplies		110,000
Budgetary Fund Balance		70,000
To record current annual budget for tourism and convention promotions. Funding is to come from the government's motel excise tax.		

This entry reveals the expected level of funding and its origin (the motel tax levy). It also shows the authorized amount for each type of expenditure. Unless officially changed, each of these figures remains in the records of the special revenue fund for the entire year to allow for planning, disclosure, and control. The Budgetary Fund Balance account indicates an anticipated surplus (or, in some cases, a shortfall) projected for the period. Here, the current financial resources for this activity are expected to increase by $70,000 during the year.

In this way, budgetary entries reflect a government's *interperiod equity*. This term refers to the alignment of revenues and spending during a fiscal period and the possible shift of payments to future generations. If a government projects revenues as $10 million but approves expenditures of $11 million, the extra $1 million must be financed in some manner, often by the issuance of debt to be repaid in the future. The benefits of the additional expenditures are enjoyed today, but citizens of a later time will bear the cost.

Final appropriations are not always identical to the original budget because of later amendments formally made during the year. Officials can vote to change appropriation levels if more or less money becomes available than had been anticipated or government needs suddenly change. For the year ended June 30, 2020, the City of Greensboro, North Carolina, reported that $30,750,615 had originally been appropriated for culture and recreation. During the year, officials increased that amount to a final budget of $31,293,854, but only $28,815,526 was actually spent. A perusal of the budgetary data shows how close individual functions within the culture and recreation category came to their budgeted amounts.

To continue with the earlier illustration, assume that officials for the City of West who are in charge of tourism make an appeal to the city council for an additional $50,000 to create a special advertising campaign. If approved, the original budgetary entry is updated.

Fund Financial Statements—Budget Amendment

Special Revenue Fund—Tourism and Convention Promotions		
Budgetary Fund Balance	50,000	
Appropriations—Advertising		50,000
To record an additional appropriation for advertising.		

Now assume that the City of West actually receives $488,000 from the motel tax levy during the year and spends $457,000 as follows:

Salaries.............................	$196,000
Utilities.............................	29,000
Advertising.........................	125,000
Supplies	107,000

This information is disclosed as follows. The variance column is recommended but not required.

TOURISM AND CONVENTION PROMOTIONS
CITY OF WEST
Year Ended December 31, 2024
Budget Comparison Schedule

	Budgeted Amounts		Actual Amounts	Variance from Final Budget to Actual Amounts— Positive Impact on Fund Balance (negative)
	Original	Final		
Resources (inflows):				
Motel tax levy.........................	$490,000	$490,000	$488,000	$ (2,000)
Charges to appropriations (outflows):				
Salaries................................	$200,000	$200,000	$196,000	$ 4,000
Utilities	30,000	30,000	29,000	1,000
Advertising...........................	80,000	130,000	125,000	5,000
Supplies	110,000	110,000	107,000	3,000
Total charges..........................	$420,000	$470,000	$457,000	$13,000
Change in fund balance	$ 70,000	$ 20,000	$ 31,000	$11,000

Encumbrances

One additional budgetary procedure that has historically played a central role in state and local government accounting is the recording of financial commitments referred to as *encumbrances*. In contrast to for-profit accounting, purchase commitments and contracts are often recorded within governmental funds prior to any recognition of an actual liability. The recording of encumbrances provides an efficient method for monitoring financial commitments so that officials do not accidentally overspend a fund's approved appropriations. GASB states that "encumbrances should be recorded for budgetary control purposes, especially in general and special revenue funds." Information on both expended and committed amounts is then available to aid officials as they manage the government's financial resources.

To illustrate, assume that the police department for the City of West orders $18,000 in equipment from an approved vendor. The various items will take several weeks to reach the city and its police department. As an ongoing service function, the police department is accounted for within the general fund. When the commitment is made, the following entry is made to help ensure that the government stays within legal budgetary constraints. In contrast, no formal recording of the commitment is made for government-wide financial statements because they are reported much like for-profit business activities.

Fund Financial Statements—Commitment Created by Governmental Fund Activity

General Fund—Police Department		
Encumbrances—Equipment	18,000	
Encumbrances Outstanding		18,000
To record a purchase order for equipment.		

When the equipment is received by the City of West, a legal liability replaces the commitment. First, the encumbrance is removed from the accounting records, and, second, an

Expenditures account is recognized to reflect the reduction in current financial resources. Often—as a result of transportation charges, discounts, or other price adjustments—the actual cost will differ from the original estimate. The recorded expenditure will not necessarily agree with the corresponding encumbrance.

Because of the current financial resource focus found in the fund financial statements (for the governmental funds), no equipment account entry is recorded for this long-lived asset. Instead, the Expenditures account balance identifies the reason for the reduction in current financial resources. In the fund financial statements, readers are told where the current financial resources went during the fiscal year.

To illustrate, assume the equipment has a total cost of $18,160 by the time it arrives.

Fund Financial Statements—Equipment Order Received by Governmental Fund Activity

General Fund		
Encumbrances Outstanding	18,000	
Encumbrances—Equipment		18,000
To remove encumbrance for equipment that has now been received.		
Expenditures—Equipment	18,160	
Vouchers (or Accounts) Payable		18,160
To record the receipt of equipment and the accompanying liability for its cost.		

In accounting for the government-wide financial statements, the only entry for the ordering and receiving of this equipment is an increase in the asset and related liability when the order is filled. The commitment is not recorded but is disclosed in the notes to the financial statements.

At the end of the fiscal year, any commitments that remain outstanding are removed from the fund accounting records by reversing the original entry because no transaction has yet occurred. The recording of encumbrances is to help prevent the government from spending more money than the amount authorized for the period.

Assuming that the commitment will still be honored in the subsequent period, what reporting is needed in fund financial statements on the year-end balance sheet? If the fund balance has already been reclassified as restricted, committed, or assigned in recognition of the eventual expenditure, then no further change is needed. The labeling of the fund balance reflects the decision to use that part of the fund's financial resources to meet this commitment. If no fund balance has yet been reported as restricted, committed, or assigned, then a portion of the fund balance—unassigned should be reclassified as either committed (designated by the highest level of decision-making authority) or assigned (designated by a party other than the highest level of decision-making authority) for the anticipated amount to denote the expected use of the fund's current financial resources.[22]

To illustrate, assume that the general fund of the City of West that ordered the $18,000 in equipment reports assets and deferred outflows of $600,000 and liabilities and deferred inflows of $500,000. On the balance sheet, the fund balance accounts are shown as $100,000 unassigned. At the end of the fiscal year, the $18,000 encumbrance is still unfulfilled. It is removed from the records because it is no longer a commitment of current financial resources for the period. Assume that city officials decide that the government will accept and pay for the equipment when it arrives in the following year. No liability yet exists but, based on that decision, the reporting of the fund balance figures on the balance sheet is affected.

The fund balance—unassigned is reduced by the $18,000 commitment, and fund balance—assigned (or possibly committed depending on the level of the decision makers who agreed to acquire the equipment) is increased. The reported assets and liabilities are not affected

[22] The restricted designation is used to indicate that external parties or applicable laws created the restriction. A fund balance—unassigned cannot be internally restricted.

because the equipment has not yet been received, but the fund balance is shown as assigned (or committed) to indicate that $18,000 of the fund's current financial resources are not freely available to government officials. "Encumbered amounts for specific purposes for which amounts have not been previously restricted, committed, or assigned should not be classified as unassigned but, rather, should be included within committed or assigned fund balance, as appropriate."[23]

LO 11-7

Explain the reporting of capital assets, supplies, and prepaid expenses by a state or local government.

Recognition of Expenditures and Revenues

Although budgetary and encumbrance entries are unique, their impact on the accounting process is limited. They do not directly affect a fund's current financial results for the period. Their purpose is to prevent overspending.

Conversely, the method by which a state or locality records the receipt and disbursement of its current financial resources can alter the presented data. Because a primary emphasis in reporting the fund financial statements of the governmental funds is on explaining all changes in current financial resources, *neither expenses nor capital assets are recorded.* Probably no more significant distinction exists between the fund financial statements and the government-wide statements.

As shown in the previous purchase of equipment, governmental funds report an Expenditures account in the fund statements. This balance reflects decreases in current financial resources from the acquisition of a good or service. The reduction of these resources is recorded as an expenditure, whether it is for rent, a fire truck, salaries, a computer, or the like. In each case, a good or service is acquired. The statement of revenues, expenditures, and other changes in fund balances (Exhibit 11.4) allows the reader to see the use made of an activity's current financial resources. The fire department spending $1,000 for electricity for the past three months is an expenditure of current financial resources in exactly the same way as buying a $70,000 ambulance.

Fund Financial Statements—Expenditures for Expense and Capital Asset by Governmental Fund Activity

General Fund		
Expenditures—Electricity	1,000	
Vouchers (or Accounts) Payable		1,000
To record charges covering the past three months.		
Expenditures—Ambulance	70,000	
Vouchers (or Accounts) Payable		70,000
To record acquisition of ambulance.		

Within the fund financial statements for the governmental funds, the timing of the recognition of expenditures and revenues follows the *modified accrual basis of accounting.* Under modified accrual accounting, expenditures are recognized at the time that the government incurs a liability that creates a claim against current financial resources.

Government accountants must check to determine whether transactions at the end of a year affect the budget of the earlier year or the later. If a claim is established in one period to be settled in the subsequent period, the expenditure and liability are typically recorded in the initial year. However, as discussed earlier, the maximum length of time for the payment of current financial resources to occur—often selected by governments as 60 days into the subsequent period—should be disclosed. Thus, for example, if equipment is received on the last day of one year and payment is to be made within just a few days, the expenditure and liability are reported in the first year. In contrast, if payment will not be made until many weeks later, the recording of the expenditure and liability is based on what the government has formally adopted as the recognition period.

[23] GASB, *Codification,* as of June 30, 2021, Sec. 1800.184.

In fund financial statements, a governmental fund records both operating costs such as salaries and utilities and the entire cost of all buildings, machines, and other capital assets as expenditures to show the use made of current financial resources. Furthermore, depreciation has no effect on current financial resources so its recognition is omitted entirely. Without the recording of expenses, net income is neither calculated nor reported in the fund statements for the governmental funds.

Government-wide financial statements are different. All economic resources are measured. Consequently, the previous transactions for electricity and an ambulance are recorded for this second set of statements when the liability is created. Depreciation is subsequently recorded for the ambulance as time passes.

Government-Wide Financial Statements—Recording Expense and Acquisition of Capital Asset

Utilities Expense	1,000	
Vouchers (or Accounts) Payable		1,000
To record electricity charges for the past three months.		
Ambulance	70,000	
Vouchers (or Accounts) Payable		70,000
To record acquisition of new ambulance.		

Reporting Capital Assets and Infrastructure

One result of recording only expenditures within the fund statements for the governmental funds is that virtually no assets are reported other than current financial resources such as cash, receivables, and investments. The cost of a capital asset is recorded as expenditures at the time of acquisition with that balance closed out at the end of each fiscal period. Note that the balance sheet in Exhibit 11.3 reflects no buildings, school facilities, computers, trucks, or other equipment as assets.

Prior to the creation of government-wide financial statements, only a minimum amount of information was available about the capital assets controlled by a state or local government. A listing was included in the financial statements for informational purposes. Even then, the inclusion of infrastructure items (roads, sidewalks, bridges, and the like that are normally stationary and can be preserved for a significant period of time) was optional. A bridge, for example, with proper care might last more than 100 years. To save time and energy, many governments simply did not maintain records of such infrastructure items after the original expenditure. The eventual requirement that government-wide financial statements be created to include all economic resources meant that capital assets (including infrastructure items) had to be recorded and, where applicable, depreciation had to be included. As will be discussed in the following chapter, depreciation of infrastructure can still be avoided under certain circumstances.

Thus, today, the fund financial statements report the amount expended each period by the governmental funds for capital assets, whereas the government-wide financial statements report those capital assets as well as all infrastructure items.

Supplies and Prepaid Items

In gathering information for government-wide financial statements, the acquisition of supplies and prepaid costs such as rent or insurance is not particularly complicated. An asset is recorded at the time of acquisition and subsequently reclassified to expense as the asset's utility is consumed by use or time. The City and County of Denver, Colorado, reported $37.6 million for prepaid items and other assets in its government-wide statements as of December 31, 2020.

However, reporting prepaid costs and supplies by the governmental funds within the fund financial statements is not so straightforward. These assets have a relatively short life, but they are not current financial resources that can be spent. Should the cost of prepaid expenses

? Discussion Question

IS IT AN ASSET OR A LIABILITY?

During the long evolution of state and local government accounting, many scholars have discussed its unique features. In the August 1989 issue of the *Journal of Accountancy,* R. K. Mautz described the reporting needs of governments and not-for-profit organizations (such as charities) in his essay "Not-For-Profit Financial Reporting: Another View."

To illustrate the governmental accounting challenges, Mautz examined the method by which a city should record a newly constructed high school building. Conventional business wisdom would say that such a property is an asset owned by the government. Thus, the cost should be capitalized and then depreciated over an estimated useful life. However, Mautz pointed to paragraph 26 of FASB *Concepts Statement No. 6,* which asserted that an essential characteristic of an asset is "a probable future benefit . . . to contribute directly or indirectly to future net cash inflows."

Mautz reasoned that the school building cannot be considered an asset because it provides no net contribution to cash inflows. In truth, a high school requires the government to make significant cash outflows for maintenance, repairs, utilities, salaries, and the like. Public educational facilities (as well as many of the other properties of a government, such as a fire station or municipal building) are acquired with the understanding that net cash outflows will result for years to come.

Consequently, Mautz then considered whether the construction of a high school is not actually the establishment of a liability because the government is taking on an obligation that will necessitate future cash payments. He also rejects this idea, once again based on the guidance of *Concepts Statement No. 6* (para. 36), because a probable future transfer or use of assets is not required at a "specified or determinable date, on occurrence of a specified event, or on demand."

Is a high school building an asset or is it a liability? If it is neither, how should the cost be recorded? How is a high school reported in fund financial statements? How is the same high school reported in government-wide financial statements? Which of these two approaches best portrays the decision to acquire or construct this structure? Does providing two different approaches for the same building provide the information decision makers need?

and supplies be reported as an asset until consumed or recorded directly as an expenditure at the time of acquisition?

Traditionally, governmental funds have used the *purchases method,* which records prepaid expenses and supplies as expenditures at the point that a claim to current financial resources is created. No asset of this type is recognized when acquired. Thus, in its 2020 statements, the City of Kansas City, Missouri, explains that the "Governmental funds record an expenditure at the time of the purchase of the inventory item." For informational purposes, though, any supplies or prepaid items (such as insurance or rent) remaining at year end are entered into the accounting records as assets as a step in the production of financial statements. At that time, the asset is recorded along with an offsetting amount in fund balance—nonspendable so the reader is aware that these assets are held but they are not current financial resources available for spending by the government.

The *purchases method* reflects modified accrual accounting because the entire cost is recognized as an expenditure when current financial resources are reduced. However, some governments have chosen an accepted alternative known as the *consumption method* for the reporting of supplies and prepaid items acquired by their governmental funds.

The consumption method parallels the process utilized in creating government-wide financial statements. Supplies or prepayments are recorded as assets when acquired. As the utility is consumed by usage or time, the governmental funds reclassify the cost into an expenditures account. As explained in 2020 by the City of Birmingham, "Inventory consists of expendable supplies held in the General Fund for consumption. The cost is recorded as an expenditure at the time individual inventory items are used (consumption method)."[*] Under this approach, the expenditure is recognized in the period of usage. Because these assets cannot be spent for government programs or other needs, an equal portion of the Fund Balance account should be reclassified as nonspendable as shown in the balance sheet in Exhibit 11.3.

To illustrate, assume that the City of West purchases $20,000 in supplies and prepaid items for various general fund activities. During the remainder of the fiscal period, $18,000 of this amount is consumed so that only $2,000 remains at year-end. These events could be recorded through either of the following sets of entries. Notice that, depending on the approach, the expenditures will increase by either $20,000 or $18,000 in the year of purchase. Because of budgeting limitations, that can be an important difference.

Fund Financial Statements—Supplies and Prepaid Expenses—Governmental Funds

Purchases Method

Expenditures—Supplies and Prepayments	20,000	
Vouchers (or Accounts) Payable		20,000
To record purchase of supplies for various ongoing activities. Entry is made when claim is created.		
Supplies and Prepayments	2,000	
Fund Balance—Nonspendable		2,000
At year's end, entry to establish balance for supplies and prepaid items remaining.		

Consumption Method

Supplies and Prepayments	20,000	
Vouchers (or Accounts) Payable		20,000
To record purchase of supplies and prepayments for various ongoing activities. Entry is made when claim is created.		
Expenditures—Supplies and Prepayments	18,000	
Supplies and Prepayments		18,000
To record consumption of supplies and prepayments during the current period. Because an asset that cannot be spent remains on the balance sheet, a $2,000 portion of the Fund Balance is also reclassified from unassigned to nonspendable. This reclassification is normally done in creating the statements and not through an adjusting entry.		

LO 11-8

Determine the proper timing for the recognition of revenues generated by various types of nonexchange transactions.

Recognition of Revenues—Overview

The reporting of certain revenues has always posed theoretical issues in governmental accounting. Revenues such as property taxes, income taxes, and many grants do not have the same type of exchange process as is found in for-profit entities. Governments impose taxes, fines, and the like on citizens to support its operations rather than provide a specific good or service in return for payment. Consequently, these revenues are referred to as nonexchange transactions.

To assist in the timing of such revenue recognition, GASB has created a comprehensive set of guidelines. These rules do not apply to revenues such as interest or rents for which a true exchange does exist. Instead, they focus on nonexchange transactions, including most taxes,

---

[*] The City of Birmingham, Alabama, 2020.

fines, grants, gifts, and the like for which the government does not provide a direct and equal benefit for the amount collected.

> In a nonexchange transaction, a government (including the federal government, as a provider) either gives value (benefit) to another party without directly receiving equal value in exchange or receives value (benefit) from another party without directly giving equal value in exchange.[24]

For organizational purposes, GASB separates nonexchange transactions into four distinct classifications, each with its own rules as to proper recognition:

1. *Derived tax revenues.* Some tax assessments occur when an underlying exchange takes place. Income taxes and sales taxes are common examples of derived tax revenues. A citizen earns income and a tax is incurred. A business makes a sale and a tax is charged. A derived tax is tied to an event.

2. *Imposed nonexchange revenues.* Property taxes, fines, and penalties are classified as imposed nonexchange revenues. The government makes an assessment, but no underlying exchange occurs. With a property tax, for example, the government taxes ownership rather than a specific event or transaction.

3. *Government-mandated nonexchange transactions.* This category includes monies, such as grants conveyed from one government to another, to help cover the cost of a required program. For example, assume that the state government specifies that the City of West must create a homeless shelter and then the state provides a grant of $900,000 to help defray the cost. The city records this inflow of money as a government-mandated nonexchange transaction. The state government required construction of the shelter and provided a portion of the funding. City officials did not make the decision.

4. *Voluntary nonexchange transactions.* In this classification, money is conveyed willingly to the state or local government by an individual, another government, or an organization, usually for a particular purpose. For example, the state government might grant the City of West $1.3 million to help improve reading programs in local schools. Unless the state had mandated an enhancement in these reading programs, this grant is accounted for as a voluntary nonexchange transaction. The money will provide an important benefit, but no separate government requirement led the state to make the conveyance.

Reporting Derived Tax Revenues Such as Income Taxes and Sales Taxes

Accounting for derived tax revenues is relatively straightforward. These revenues are normally recognized in government-wide financial statements when the underlying transaction occurs. When an individual taxpayer earns income, the government records the resulting income tax revenue. Likewise, when a business makes a sale to a customer, the government should recognize the related sales tax revenue.

Assume, for example, that sales made by businesses operating within the City of West amount to $100 million for the current year and the government assesses a 4 percent sales tax. In the period in which the sales are made, the following entry is required. However, the amount should be reported net of any estimated refunds or balances that cannot be collected.

Government-Wide Financial Statements—Derived Tax Revenues

Receivable—Sales Taxes..	4,000,000	
Revenue—Sales Taxes...		4,000,000
To recognize sales tax that will be collected in connection with sales during the current period.		

For fund financial statements, the preceding rules also apply, except for one additional requirement. In reporting governmental funds, as mentioned previously, current financial

---

[24] GASB, *Codification,* as of June 30, 2021, Sec. N50.104.

resources must be "available" before revenue can be recognized. "Available" means that the amounts must be received during the present year or soon enough thereafter so that the money can be used to satisfy current claims. For example, if the City of West defines available as a 60-day period, then the amount expected by the end of the first 60 days of the subsequent year will still be recognized in the first year. The remainder is not reported until the following year.

Reporting Imposed Nonexchange Revenues Such as Property Taxes and Fines

Accounting for imposed nonexchange revenues is more complicated because no underlying transaction exists to guide the timing of the revenue recognition. Interestingly, GASB set up separate rules here for recognizing the asset and the related revenue.

- The receivable is recorded as soon as the government has an enforceable legal claim as defined in that particular jurisdiction. If a prepayment is made before the claim is enforceable, cash is recorded rather than the receivable.
- For the revenue side of the transaction, recognition is reported in the time period when the resulting resources are required to be used or in the first period in which use is permitted.

To illustrate, assume that on October 1, Year 1, property tax assessments to finance the government during Year 2 are mailed by the City of West. The total amount is $530,000. Assume that, according to applicable state law, the city has no enforceable claim until January 1, Year 2 (often referred to as the *lien date*). To encourage early payment, the city offers a 5 percent discount on any amount received by December 31, Year 1.

No entry is recorded on October 1, Year 1. Although the assessments have been delivered, no enforceable legal claim yet exists, and the proceeds from the tax cannot be used until Year 2.

Assume that $30,000 of these assessments are collected from citizens during the final three months of Year 1. After reduction for the 5 percent discount, the cash collection is $28,500.

Government-Wide Financial Statements and Fund Financial Statements—Property Taxes Prepaid in Year 1 for Year 2

Year 1		
Cash	28,500	
Unavailable Property Tax Collections.		28,500
To record collection of property tax prior to the start of the levy year after reduction for 5 percent discount.		

The collection of prepaid taxes does not create a liability because no type of payment or service is required. Nevertheless, because the money cannot be spent until Year 2, it is not yet reported as a revenue. That creates a reporting challenge as to the placement of the "Unavailable Property Tax Collections." As shown in Exhibits 11.1 and 11.3, this balance represents a *deferred inflow of resources* on the statement of net position (government-wide statements) and the balance sheet (fund financial statements for the governmental funds). The deferred inflow is grouped with liabilities but is clearly a separate type of account. A revenue will be recognized for the amount received but that has not yet occurred.

Moving into Year 2, assume that city officials expect to collect 96 percent of the remaining $500,000 in assessments, or $480,000. At the beginning of Year 2, both this receivable and the related revenue are recognized.

- The receivable is reported at that time because an enforceable claim comes into existence.
- For government-wide statements, the revenue is reported in Year 2 because that is the period in which the money can first be used.

Note here that the revenue is reduced directly by the $20,000 estimate of taxes expected to be uncollectible. In addition, the previously collected $28,500 is now recognized in Year 2 as revenue because, once again, this is the period for which use is allowed.

Government-Wide Financial Statement—Property Taxes for Year 2

January 1, Year 2		
Property Tax Receivable	500,000	
Allowance for Uncollectible Taxes		20,000
Revenues—Property Taxes		480,000
To recognize property tax assessment for Year 2.		
Unavailable Property Tax Collections	28,500	
Revenues—Property Taxes		28,500
To recognize property tax proceeds for Year 2 collected during Year 1.		

The preceding recording is the same for the fund financial statements unless some portion of the $480,000 future cash collection is viewed as not being available to be used this period. Because property taxes are such a significant source of revenue for many governments, a specific 60-day maximum period for recognition has been standardized rather than allowing a government to choose a longer period as a way of increasing the amount of revenue recognized.

To illustrate, assume that records kept by the City of West for the past several years indicate that $400,000 of this anticipated $480,000 will be collected during Year 2, another $50,000 in the first 60 days of Year 3, and the final $30,000 in the months beyond 60 days into Year 3. For fund-based statements, this last $30,000 is not viewed as available to pay for Year 2 expenditures. For that amount, recognition is delayed until Year 3. Only $450,000 of the financial resources is expected to be available for Year 2 expenditures. Once again, the unavailable property tax collections amount ($30,000 in this case) is shown as a deferred inflow of resources for the governmental fund. The receivable is recognized but this $30,000 will not be available until Year 3.

Fund Financial Statements—Property Taxes for Year 2—Governmental Funds

January 1, Year 2		
Property Tax Receivable	500,000	
Allowance for Uncollectible Taxes		20,000
Revenues—Property Taxes		450,000
Unavailable Property Tax Collections		30,000
To record amount of property taxes measurable and available to be used for Year 2 expenditures. Final $30,000 is not expected until after 60 days into Year 3.		
Unavailable Property Tax Collections	28,500	
Revenues—Property Taxes		28,500
To recognize property tax proceeds for Year 2 collected during Year 1.		

Reporting Government-Mandated Nonexchange Transactions and Voluntary Nonexchange Transactions

Although these two sources of revenues are identified separately by GASB, timing of accounting recognition is the same, so they are discussed here together. Governments recognize these types of revenue (often coming in the form of a grant) when all eligibility requirements have been met. Until eligibility is established, the existence of some degree of uncertainty precludes recognition. Thus, revenue is reported at the time of eligibility even if money was received earlier.

Eligibility requirements are divided into four general classifications. All applicable requirements must be met before revenue can be recorded for either government-mandated nonexchange transactions or voluntary nonexchange transactions.

1. *Required characteristics of the recipients.* Governments must often attain specific standards in order to qualify for the receipt of funding. To illustrate, assume that a not-for-profit foundation awards a grant to the City of West to finance improved reading education for all kindergarten children in the school system. Assume also that state law has been changed to mandate that all kindergarten teachers must gain proper certification within the next five years. Consequently, the foundation states that it will only convey the grant to the city when all kindergarten teachers have met this standard. The city must conform to the law to qualify for the money. Because of this eligibility requirement, recognition of grant revenue is delayed until all kindergarten teachers are certified.

2. *Time requirements.* The parties providing the funding can specify when the money is to be used. The time becomes an eligibility requirement. For example, assume that in April, a state government provides a grant to the City of West to buy milk for each child during the subsequent school year starting in September. The grant should be recognized as revenue in the period of use or in the period when the use of the funds is first permitted. Here, the money cannot be used in April so it is not yet revenue. Recognition begins in September.

3. *Reimbursement.* Many grants and other forms of similar support are designed to reimburse a state or local government for amounts spent according to specified guidelines. These arrangements are often called *expenditure-driven programs.* Assume that a state informs the City of West that it will reimburse the government for money paid to provide books to schoolchildren who could not otherwise afford them. In such cases, proper spending is the eligibility requirement. The city recognizes no revenue until it spends its own money for these books.

4. *Contingencies.* In voluntary nonexchange transactions (but not in government-mandated nonexchange transactions), funding may be withheld until a specified procurement action has been taken. A grant might be given to the City of West to buy park equipment, for example, but the money is only available after an appropriate piece of land has been acquired on which to build the park. Until land is obtained (or other required action is taken), the revenue should not be recognized.

For most of these events, a liability is recognized in the government-wide statements if money is received before the eligibility requirements are met. The liability is necessary because the government is obligated to act in some manner. Nevertheless, if only a time restriction exists, then a deferred inflow of resources is reported (rather than a liability or revenue) because no further action is required of the government—only the passage of time. In fund financial statements, if the cash is received but eligibility requirements have not yet been met, a deferred inflow of resources is reported.

LO 11-9

Account for the issuance of long-term bonds.

Issuance of Bonds

The issuance of bonds serves as a major source of financing for many, if not most, state and local governments. The amounts can be staggering. "According to data from the U.S. Census Bureau, total state and local government debt was $3.17 trillion in 2019 or about $9,700 per person."[25] Money received from the issuance of these debts is used for many purposes, including general financing and a wide variety of construction projects such as roads, bridges, and airports. As of June 30, 2020, the City and County of San Francisco, California, reported noncurrent bonds, loans, capital leases, and other liabilities outstanding of approximately $19.5 billion. Of that total, the governmental activities owed $3.8 billion and the business-type activities owed $15.7 billion.

Because the proceeds of a long-term bond must be repaid, the government recognizes no revenues under either method of financial reporting. The reporting process for the government-wide financial statements is straightforward. Both the cash and the debt are increased to reflect the issuance just as is normally reported in a for-profit business.

In fund financial statements for the governmental funds, the accounting process is more complicated. Cash is received, but the debt is not a claim on current financial resources. It will

---

[25] Marco Csokasi, "State and Local Governments With the Most Debt Per Capita," September 30, 2021, https://www.governing.com/finance/state-and-local-governments-with-the-most-debt-per-capita.

not be settled for years into the future. From a governmental fund perspective, the inflow of current financial resources cannot be reported as a long-term liability. Furthermore, it is not a revenue because the money must be repaid.

Assume, for example, that the City of West issues $21 million in general obligation bonds at face value due in 12 years to finance the construction of a new school building. Because of the intended use for the proceeds, the town establishes a capital projects fund to monitor the receipt and spending of the cash. To emphasize that the money is not derived from a revenue, the City of West will use a special designation, *Other Financing Sources*. Note in Exhibit 11.4 the placement of Other Financing Sources (Uses) at the bottom of the statement of revenues, expenditures, and other changes in fund balance. This balance identifies changes in the current financial resources held by the governmental funds as a result of transactions other than revenues and expenditures. The issuance of a bond is a primary example.

The following journal entry reflects the issuance of these bonds as recorded in fund financial statements.

Fund Financial Statements—Issuance of Bonds—Governmental Funds

Capital Projects Fund—School Building		
Cash...	21,000,000	
Other Financing Sources—Bond Proceeds		21,000,000
To record issuance of bonds to finance school construction project.		

Once again, the reporting of the governmental funds stresses accountability for the inflows and outflows of current financial resources. Although an inflow of cash has taken place, it was not generated by a revenue. The money came from a loan but one that will not be repaid for many years. This increase in current financial resources is reflected by the Other Financing Sources balance, a measurement account that is closed out at each year-end. The $21 million bond liability is not reported by the capital projects fund because it is not yet a claim to current financial resources.

Recognition of long-term debts has traditionally been ignored in the reporting of governmental funds. For example, the balance sheet in Exhibit 11.3 shows no noncurrent liabilities for the governmental funds, only claims to current financial resources. A reader of the financial statements who wants to see the complete record of the government's debts must examine the statement of net position in the government-wide financial statements (see Exhibit 11.1).

Because state and local governments often issue significant amounts of debts, related costs can be quite large. GASB requires any debt issuance cost to be recognized as an expense/expenditure when incurred rather than being capitalized.

In addition, if available interest rates subsequently fall, a government will sometimes reacquire its bonds so that new financing can be arranged at a lower cost. In fund statements, the debt is not reported so the payment is merely an expenditure. However, in government-wide statements, the debt is reported. The difference between the amount paid to retire the original debt and its net carrying amount is not recorded immediately as a gain or loss. Instead, the difference is reported on the statement of net position as a deferred outflow of resources (if more than the net carrying amount is paid) or a deferred inflow of resources (if less than the net carrying amount is paid) (see Exhibit 11.1). Because the refunding arrangement was set up to reduce the cost of interest, this deferred amount is amortized over time against interest expense.

For example, at June 30, 2020, the State of Florida reported an "amount deferred on refunding of debt" as a deferred outflow of resources (just below the reported assets) of $114.3 million while showing the exact same account title as a deferred inflow of resources (just below the liabilities) of $116.3 million. Apparently, several debts were refunded by the state in recent years, sometimes for more than the face value of the debt and sometimes for less than the face value.

Payment of Noncurrent Liabilities

The payment of noncurrent liabilities by one of the governmental funds again demonstrates the fundamental differences between the two sets of financial statements.

- For government-wide statements, the payment of principal and interest is recorded in the same manner as that used by a for-profit organization. The liability is removed at the time of payment and interest expense is recognized as time passes.
- On fund financial statements, an expenditure is recognized for settlement of the debt and also for the related interest when it becomes a claim on current financial resources. Both payments are often made directly from a debt service fund if the government has set aside the money.

As an illustration, assume that the City of West makes a $500,000 bond payment along with three months of interest amounting to $10,000. Government officials have previously transferred sufficient cash into a debt service fund to satisfy this obligation.

Government-Wide Financial Statements—Bond and Interest Payments

Bond Payable...	500,000	
Interest Expense..	10,000	
Cash..		510,000
To record payment of bond and related interest.		

Fund Financial Statements—Bond and Interest Payments—Governmental Funds

Debt Service Funds		
Expenditure—Bond Principal	500,000	
Expenditure—Interest..	10,000	
Cash..		510,000
To record payment of bond and related interest.		

Tax Anticipation Notes

Governments do record one type of debt in the same manner on both government-wide and fund financial statements. States and localities often issue short-term debts to provide financing until revenue sources such as property taxes are collected. If tax receipts are expected at a particular point in time, the government might need to borrow money to finance operations until that date. These short-term liabilities are often referred to as *tax anticipation notes* because they are outstanding only until a sufficient amount of tax money is collected.

As short-term liabilities, these debts are a claim on current financial resources. For that reason, in fund financial statements, the issuance is not recorded as another financing source but as a liability in the same manner as in the government-wide financial statements. Amounts paid for interest, though, are still recorded as an expenditure in producing fund statements, but as an expense on the government-wide financial statements.

To illustrate, assume the City of West borrows $700,000 on a 60-day note on January 1 and agrees to pay back $712,000 on March 1. City officials expect to repay the debt with receipts from property tax assessments. In creating both sets of financial statements, cash and the related liability are increased at the time of issuance.

At repayment, however, different entries are required.

Fund Financial Statements—Payment of Tax Anticipation Notes by Governmental Funds

General Fund		
Tax Anticipation Note Payable...	700,000	
Expenditure—Interest..	12,000	
Cash..		712,000
To record payment of short-term debt and interest for two months.		

Government-Wide Financial Statements—Payment of Tax Anticipation Notes

Tax Anticipation Note Payable...	700,000	
Interest Expense...	12,000	
Cash...		712,000
To record payment of short-term debt and interest for two months.		

Special Assessments

LO 11-10

Account for special assessment projects.

Governments can provide improvements or services that directly benefit a particular property and then assess the costs (in whole or in part) to the owner. In some cases, owners petition the government to initiate such projects to enhance their property values. Paving streets, installing water and sewage lines, adding street lights, and constructing curbs and sidewalks are typical examples. The government usually issues debt to finance the work and places a lien on the property being improved to ensure eventual reimbursement. The amounts are not necessarily small. The City of Fargo, North Dakota, reported special assessment receivables of more than $461 million as of December 31, 2020. This balance represents the second biggest asset listed by Fargo in its government-wide statements, with only the city's infrastructure (bridges, roads, and the like) reporting a larger balance.

Government-wide financial statements handle the debt issuance and the subsequent cost of the construction work in the same manner as for-profit enterprises. The government records the debt balance as well as the cost of the asset. Assessments are then made and collected. Receipts from the property owners are used to settle the debt.

For example, assume that a sidewalk is to be built throughout a neighborhood in the City of West at an approximate cost of $600,000. The city issues bonds to finance construction with repayment to be made using money subsequently collected from the owners of the neighborhood property. Total interest of $30,000 is expected. The assessment to the owners is set at $630,000 to cover all costs, both for the construction and the interest.

Government-Wide Financial Statements—Special Assessment Project

Cash..	600,000	
Bond Payable—Special Assessment................................		600,000
To record debt issued to finance sidewalk construction.		
Infrastructure Asset—Sidewalk...	600,000	
Cash...		600,000
To record payment to contractor for the cost of building new sidewalk.		
Taxes Receivable—Special Assessment.................................	630,000	
Revenue—Special Assessment......................................		630,000
To record citizens' charges for special assessment project.		
Cash..	630,000	
Taxes Receivable—Special Assessment.............................		630,000
To record collection of money from assessment of citizens for sidewalk construction.		
Bond Payable—Special Assessment.....................................	600,000	
Interest Expense...	30,000	
Cash...		630,000
To record payment of debt on special assessment bonds.		

In the fund financial statements for government funds, this same series of transactions has a completely different appearance. Because the current financial resources measurement basis is used, neither the infrastructure asset nor the long-term debt is recorded.

Fund Financial Statements—Special Assessment Project—Governmental Funds

Capital Projects Fund—Special Assessment Project		
Cash	600,000	
Other Financing Sources—Bond Proceeds		600,000
To record issuance of bonds to finance sidewalk construction with payment to be made from a special assessment levy.		
Expenditures—Sidewalk	600,000	
Cash		600,000
To record payment to contractor for the cost of constructing sidewalk.		

Debt Service Fund—Special Assessment Project		
Taxes Receivable—Special Assessment	630,000	
Revenue—Special Assessment		630,000
To record assessment that will be used to pay bond principal and related interest.		
Cash	630,000	
Taxes Receivable—Special Assessment		630,000
To record collection of assessment paid by citizens to extinguish bond and interest incurred in construction of sidewalk.		
Expenditure—Special Assessment Bond	600,000	
Expenditure—Interest	30,000	
Cash		630,000
To record payment of bonds payable and interest incurred in construction of sidewalk.		

One alternative for the reporting of special assessment projects does exist. In some cases, the government may facilitate a project but accept no legal obligation. The government assumes no liability (either primary or secondary) for the debt or the construction. The money goes from the citizens to the government and then directly to the contractors. The government serves merely as a conduit.

If the government has no liability for defaults, overruns, or other related problems, the recording of special assessment assets, liabilities, revenues, expenses, other financing sources, and expenditures is not relevant to the government and its resources. In that situation, all transactions are recorded in a custodial fund as increases and decreases in (1) cash, (2) amounts due from citizens, and (3) amounts due to contractors. No other balances are needed. Because all recording is within a fiduciary fund, no dollar amounts appear in the government-wide statements.

Interfund Transactions

LO 11-11

Record the various types of monetary transfers that occur within the funds maintained by a state or local government.

Interfund transactions are common within governments as a way to direct sufficient resources to activities and functions as needed. Monetary transfers made from the general fund are prevalent because general tax revenues are initially accumulated in this fund. For example, in fund financial statements for the year ended June 30, 2020, the City of Houston indicated that $438.8 million was transferred out of the city's general fund to other funds (a significant amount of that total went to the debt service fund) while only $64.8 million was transferred in to the general fund from other funds.

Transfers into and out of a fund are not offset in the reporting of fund financial statements. The two amounts are not netted to arrive at a single transfer amount. More information is available by showing both balances.

In contrast, the government-wide financial statements do not report most transfers because they frequently occur solely within the governmental activities. For example, a transfer from the general fund to a debt service fund is reported in both funds on fund financial statements.

Nevertheless, it creates no net impact in the government-wide financial statements because both funds are classified within the governmental activities. The increase and decrease offset.

For government-wide financial reporting, the following distinctions are drawn for transfers:

- *Intra-activity transactions* occur between two governmental funds (so that the net totals reported for the governmental activities are not affected) or between two enterprise funds (so that the net totals reported for business-type activities are not affected). Transfers between governmental funds and many of the internal service funds are also included in this category because, as discussed previously, governments often identify internal service funds as governmental activities. Intra-activity transactions are not reported in government-wide financial statements. No overall change results for either the governmental activities or the business-type activities.

- *Interactivity transactions* occur between governmental funds and enterprise funds. They affect the total amount of resources reported by both governmental activities and business-type activities. One increases as the other decreases. Consequently, governments do report interactivity transactions in their government-wide financial statements. For example, in Exhibit 11.1, internal amounts due ($50) at year-end are reported as both a positive and a negative within the asset section of the statement of net position and then offset in arriving at overall totals. Likewise, in Exhibit 11.2, transfers ($600) occurring between the two classifications during the year appear at the bottom of the general revenues section. Once again, individual totals are shown and then offset so that no amount appears for the government as a whole. Although most transfers are intra-activity, interactivity transactions are not uncommon. In its June 30, 2020, the government-wide statement of net position for the City of St. Louis, Missouri, reported (and then eliminated) internal balances of $8.4 million. These amounts appeared in the asset section of that statement. On the statement of activities, the city shows offsetting transfers of $14.2 million between its governmental activities and its business-type activities.

Consequently, governments only report interfund transactions in their government-wide statements when it involves an interactivity transaction.

Monetary Transfers Illustrated

The most common interfund transactions are transfers within the governmental funds to ensure adequate financing of budgeted expenditures. For example, assume the city council for the City of West votes to transfer $2 million from the general fund to a capital projects fund to cover a portion of the construction cost of a new school building.

Because this transfer is an intra-activity transaction, no reporting appears in the government-wide financial statements. Financial resources are simply shifted within the governmental activities with no net effect. In contrast, because two different fund types are involved, reporting for the fund financial statements is necessary.

Fund Financial Statements—Intra-Activity Transaction

General Fund

Other Financing Uses—Transfers Out—Capital Projects Fund...............	2,000,000	
Due to Capital Projects Fund (a payable).............................		2,000,000
To record authorization of transfer for school construction.		

Capital Projects Fund—School Building

Due from General Fund (a receivable).....................................	2,000,000	
Other Financing Sources—Transfers In—General Fund................		2,000,000
To record authorization of transfer for school construction.		

The *Other Financing Uses/Sources* designations are appropriate here. Financial resources are moved into and out of these two governmental funds and neither is a revenue nor an expenditure. As Exhibit 11.4 shows, these sources and uses are reported in the statement of revenues, expenditures, and other changes in fund balances. The figures are shown but not offset in any way. Both accounts are then closed out at the end of the current year.

In contrast, the *Due to/Due from* accounts in these entries are interfund payable and receivable balances. They appear on the balance sheet for the governmental funds. Again, no elimination is made in arriving at total figures.

Not all monetary transfers are for annual operating purposes. Governments can also make nonrecurring or nonroutine transfers. For example, City of West officials might transfer money from the general fund to create or expand an enterprise fund such as a bus system or a toll road. To illustrate, assume the city internally transfers $20 million of previously unassigned money to help permanently finance a new subway system that will be open to the public. For convenience, this transaction is recorded as if cash is transferred immediately so that no receivable or payable is necessary. The enterprise fund for the subway will increase cash and likely increase some type of "contributed capital" account.

Fund Financial Statements—Interactivity Transaction

General Fund		
Other Financing Uses—Transfers Out—Subway System.	20,000,000	
Cash		20,000,000
To record transfer to help finance subway system.		

This transfer is an interactivity transaction (between governmental activities and business-type activities) so entries are also made for the government-wide financial statements. The transfer reduces the assets of the governmental activities but increases the assets held by the business-type activities. These two transfer balances are shown but will be offset in arriving at totals for the government as a whole (as can be seen in Exhibit 11.2).

Government-Wide Financial Statements—Interactivity Transaction

Governmental Activities		
Transfers Out—Subway System.	20,000,000	
Cash		20,000,000
To record transfer to help finance subway system.		

Business-Type Activities		
Cash	20,000,000	
Transfers In—General Fund		20,000,000
To record receipt of transfer from unrestricted funds.		

Internal Exchange Transactions

Some payments made within a government are not transfers but are actually the same as transactions with an outside party. For example, a city will likely compensate its own print shop (or other internal service fund or enterprise fund) for services or materials acquired as if an outside vendor performed the work. To avoid confusion in reporting the work being done, such transfers are recorded as revenues and as expenditures or expenses. These transactions are not the equivalent of a transfer. Payments are made for work done or materials acquired. They are not designed to shift financial resources from one fund to another.

Fund financial statements record and report all such internal exchange transactions. However, as previously discussed, most internal service funds appear within governmental activities on the government-wide statements. Exchanges between a governmental fund and one of these internal service funds will have no net effect on government-wide figures. The increases and decreases offset. Therefore, those balances are omitted.

To illustrate, assume that the City of West pays its print shop (an internal service fund) $15,000 for work done for the police department. In addition, the government pays another $6,000 to a toll road (operated as an enterprise fund) to allow police department vehicles to ride on the highway without having to make individual payments.

Fund Financial Statements—Internal Exchange Transaction

General Fund		
Expenditures—Printing..	15,000	
Expenditures—Toll Road Privileges......................................	6,000	
Cash		21,000
To record payment for printing supplies for use by police department and for use of a toll road by fire department.		

Internal Service Fund—Print Shop		
Cash	15,000	
Revenues...		15,000
To record collection of money paid by the police department for printed materials.		

Enterprise Fund—Toll Road		
Cash	6,000	
Revenues...		6,000
To record collection of money from government for fire department vehicular use of toll roads.		

Government-wide financial statements will not reflect the $15,000 transaction with the print shop if this internal service fund is classified within the governmental activities. In that case, the transfer is the equivalent of an intra-activity transaction. However, the $6,000 payment made by the police department (a governmental activity) to the toll road (an enterprise fund and, thus, a business-type activity) is the same as an interactivity transfer. It is reported through the following entries.

Government-Wide Financial Statements—Internal Exchange Transaction

Governmental Activities		
Expenses—Toll Road Privileges..	6,000	
Cash		6,000
To record payment for use of toll road by fire department's vehicles.		

Business-Type Activities		
Cash	6,000	
Revenues...		6,000
To record collection of money from government for the police department vehicular use of toll roads.		

Summary

1. Readers of state and local government financial statements desire a wide variety of information. No single set of financial statements is capable of meeting all user needs, a factor that has led to the requirement that two sets of statements be reported. Accountability of government officials and control over public spending have been essential elements of traditional government accounting. By requiring two sets of financial statements, GASB is able to keep those priorities in place while also broadening the scope of the government's financial reporting.

2. A state or local government prepares fund financial statements to report the various transactions of individual funds. In this system, activities are classified into three broad categories (governmental, proprietary, and fiduciary). Governmental funds account for service activities. Proprietary funds account for activities for which a user charge is assessed. Fiduciary funds account for resources that the government holds as a trustee for an external party.

3. Governmental funds are further divided into five fund types: the general fund, special revenue funds, capital projects funds, debt service funds, and permanent funds. Proprietary funds are composed of enterprise funds and internal service funds. Fiduciary funds are composed of pension trust funds, investment trust funds, private-purpose trust funds, and custodial funds.

4. Government-wide financial statements are made up of (a) a statement of net position and (b) a statement of activities. Government-wide statements separately report governmental activities (the governmental funds and most internal service funds) and business-type activities (enterprise funds and occasionally an internal service fund). These statements measure all economic resources. The timing of recognition is guided by accrual accounting. Fiduciary funds are not included because the government does not control those resources.

5. Fund financial statements include a number of financial statements. This chapter focuses on (a) the balance sheet for the governmental funds and (b) the statement of revenues, expenditures, and other changes in fund balances for the governmental funds. These statements separately report the general fund and any other individual fund that qualifies as major. For the governmental funds, these statements report current financial resources (mostly cash, receivables, and investments and claims on those current financial resources). Modified accrual accounting guides the timing of recognition.

6. Within the governmental funds, "fund balance" figures reflect the net amount of resources held by a particular fund type. To indicate the government's level of control over these resources, fund financial statements identify the fund balance as nonspendable (a specific resource cannot be spent), restricted (use has been designated by a party outside the government), committed (use has been approved by the highest level of authority within the government), assigned (use has been set by the government but not by the highest level of authority), and unassigned (use has not been designated so it is at the discretion of government officials). In this way, readers of fund financial statements are made aware of the amount of money over which government officials have some power.

7. To aid in control over financial resources and also to disclose government allocation decisions, the approved budgets for several of the governmental funds are recorded and reported each year. The initial budget, a final amended budget, and actual figures for the period are reported as required supplementary information along with the financial statements or as a separate statement within the fund financial statements.

8. Monetary commitments for purchase orders and contracts are recorded in the individual governmental funds by recognizing encumbrances. These balances are recorded when the commitment is made and removed when an actual claim to current financial resources comes into existence. This recording helps government officials avoid spending more than the amounts properly appropriated in the budget process.

9. Fund financial statements for governmental funds recognize expenditures for capital outlay, long-term debt payment, and expense-type costs (but only when a claim to current financial resources is created). In contrast, government-wide financial statements capitalize capital outlay, reduce liabilities for debt payments, and record expenses.

10. Accounting for nonexchange transactions such as sales taxes and property taxes is based on a classification system. The timing and method of revenue recognition depend on whether the transaction is a derived tax revenue, imposed nonexchange revenue, government-mandated nonexchange transaction, or voluntary nonexchange transaction.

11. The cash received from the issuance of long-term bonds is recorded as an "other financing source" by the governmental funds because no claim to current financial resources is created and the financial resource inflow is not a revenue. In contrast, the same event is reported as an increase in long-term liabilities both in the proprietary funds and in the government-wide financial statements as a whole.

12. Transfers between funds are normally reported as an "other financing source" and "other financing use" within the fund financial statements. To show the separate effect on each fund type, these balances are not eliminated or offset. The government-wide statements do not report such transactions if they are totally within the governmental activities or within the business-type activities. Transfers between governmental activities and business-type activities are shown. If reported, these amounts are offset in arriving at totals for the government as a whole.

13. For internal exchange transactions in which payment is made from one activity of the government to another for a good or service, the fund statements recognize a revenue and an expenditure or expense. Government-wide financial statements normally do not reflect internal exchange transfers unless they occur between an enterprise fund and a governmental fund.

Comprehensive Illustration

Problem

(*Estimated Time: 50 Minutes*) The Town of Drexel has the following financial transactions.

1. The town council adopts an annual budget for the general fund with estimated general revenues of $1.7 million, approved expenditures of $1.5 million, and approved transfers out of $120,000.

2. The town levies property taxes of $1.3 million. It expects to collect all but 3 percent of these taxes during the current year. Of the collected amount, the government estimates that it will receive $40,000 next year but only after more than 60 days into that year.

3. The town orders two new police cars at an approximate cost of $150,000.

4. A transfer of $50,000 is made from the general fund to the debt service fund.

5. The town makes a payment on a bond payable of $40,000 along with $10,000 of interest using the money previously set aside.

6. The Town of Drexel issues a $2 million bond at face value to finance the acquisition of a building to convert into a high school.

7. The two police cars are received with an invoice price of $152,000. An official has approved the voucher but the government will not pay it for three weeks.

8. The town purchases the building mentioned earlier to use as a high school for $2 million in cash and immediately begins the renovation.

9. Depreciation on the new police cars is computed as $30,000 for the period.

10. The town borrows $100,000 on a 30-day tax anticipation note.

11. The Town of Drexel begins a special assessment curbing project at the request of property owners. The government issues $800,000 in notes at face value to finance the work. The town guarantees the debt if a sufficient amount of money is not collected from the property owners.

12. A contractor completes the curbing project and is paid the entire $800,000 as agreed.

13. The town assesses citizens $850,000 for the completed curbing project.

14. The town collects the special assessments of $850,000 in full and repays the debt plus $50,000 in interest.

15. The town receives a $10,000 cash grant from a regional charity to beautify a local park. According to terms of the grant, the money must be used to cover the specific costs incurred by the town.

16. The town spends the first $4,000 to beautify the park.

Required

a. Prepare journal entries in anticipation of preparing fund financial statements.

b. Prepare journal entries in anticipation of preparing government-wide financial statements.

Solution

a. *Fund Financial Statements*

1. **General Fund**

Estimated Revenues	1,700,000	
Appropriations		1,500,000
Estimated Other Financing Uses		120,000
Budgetary Fund Balance		80,000

2. **General Fund**

Property Tax Receivable	1,300,000	
Allowance for Uncollectible Taxes		39,000
Unavailable Property Tax Revenues		40,000
Revenues—Property Taxes		1,221,000

3. **General Fund**

Encumbrances—Police Cars	150,000	
Encumbrances Outstanding		150,000

4.

General Fund

Other Financing Uses—Transfers Out	50,000	
Cash		50,000

Debt Service Funds

Cash	50,000	
Other Financing Sources—Transfers In		50,000

5.

Debt Service Funds

Expenditures—Principal	40,000	
Expenditures—Interest	10,000	
Cash		50,000

6.

Capital Projects Funds

Cash	2,000,000	
Other Financing Sources—Bond Proceeds		2,000,000

7.

General Fund

Encumbrances Outstanding	150,000	
Encumbrances—Police Cars		150,000
Expenditures—Police Cars	152,000	
Vouchers Payable		152,000

8.

Capital Projects Funds

Expenditures—Building	2,000,000	
Cash		2,000,000

9. No entry is recorded. Expenditures rather than expenses are recorded by the governmental funds. Depreciation is not an expenditure.

10.

General Fund

Cash	100,000	
Tax Anticipation Note Payable		100,000

11.

Capital Projects Funds

Cash	800,000	
Other Financing Sources—Special Assessments Note		800,000

12.

Capital Projects Funds

Expenditures—Curbing	800,000	
Cash		800,000

13.

Debt Service Funds

Taxes Receivable—Special Assessment	850,000	
Revenues—Special Assessment		850,000

14.

Debt Service Funds

Cash	850,000	
Taxes Receivable—Special Assessment		850,000
Expenditures—Principal	800,000	
Expenditures—Interest	50,000	
Cash		850,000

15. **Special Revenue Funds**

Cash..	10,000	
Grant Collected in Advance		10,000

16. **Special Revenue Funds**

Expenditures—Park Beautification	4,000	
Cash...		4,000
Grant Collected in Advance	4,000	
Revenues—Grants		4,000

b. *Government-Wide Financial Statements*

1. Budgetary entries are not reported within the government-wide financial statements. Budgets are recorded in the individual funds and are then shown as required supplementary information or in a separate fund financial statement.

2. **Governmental Activities**

Property Tax Receivable	1,300,000	
Allowance for Uncollectible Taxes		39,000
Revenues—Property Taxes...............................		1,261,000

3. Commitments are not reported in government-wide financial statements.

4. This transfer was entirely within the governmental funds and, therefore, creates no net effect on the governmental activities. It is an intra-activity transaction. No journal entry is needed for government-wide statements.

5. **Governmental Activities**

Bonds Payable...	40,000	
Interest Expense	10,000	
Cash		50,000

6. **Governmental Activities**

Cash	2,000,000	
Bonds Payable		2,000,000

7. **Governmental Activities**

Police Cars (or Vehicles)	152,000	
Vouchers (or Accounts) Payable		152,000

8. **Governmental Activities**

Building..	2,000,000	
Cash		2,000,000

9. **Governmental Activities**

Depreciation Expense	30,000	
Accumulated Depreciation		30,000

10. **Governmental Activities**

Cash	100,000	
Tax Anticipation Note Payable...........................		100,000

11. | **Governmental Activities** | | |
|---|---|---|
| Cash .... | 800,000 | |
| Special Assessment Notes Payable .... | | 800,000 |

12. | **Governmental Activities** | | |
|---|---|---|
| Infrastructure Assets—Curbing............................. | 800,000 | |
| Cash .... | | 800,000 |

13. | **Governmental Activities** | | |
|---|---|---|
| Taxes Receivable—Special Assessment .... | 850,000 | |
| Revenues—Special Assessment .... | | 850,000 |

14. | **Governmental Activities** | | |
|---|---|---|
| Cash .... | 850,000 | |
| Taxes Receivable—Special Assessment .... | | 850,000 |
| Special Assessment Notes Payable .... | 800,000 | |
| Interest Expense....................................... | 50,000 | |
| Cash .... | | 850,000 |

15. | **Governmental Activities** | | |
|---|---|---|
| Cash .... | 10,000 | |
| Grant Collected in Advance .... | | 10,000 |

16. | **Governmental Activities** | | |
|---|---|---|
| Expenses—Park Beautification............................ | 4,000 | |
| Cash .... | | 4,000 |
| Grant Collected in Advance .... | 4,000 | |
| Revenues—Grants .... | | 4,000 |

Questions

1. How have users' needs affected the development of accounting principles for the reporting of state and local government units?

2. Why have accountability and control been so important in the traditional accounting for state and local government units?

3. How has the dual system of financial statements affected the financial reporting of state and local governments?

4. What are the basic financial statements that a state or local government now produces?

5. What measurement focus is used in fund financial statements for governmental funds? What system is applied to determine the timing of revenue and expenditure recognition?

6. What measurement focus is used in government-wide financial statements? What system is applied to determine the timing of revenue and expense recognition?

7. What assets are viewed as current financial resources?

8. In applying the current financial resources measurement focus, when are liabilities recognized in fund financial statements for the governmental funds?

9. What are the three categories of funds? What funds are included in each of these three categories?

10. What are the five fund types within the governmental funds? What events do each of these five fund types report?

11. What are the two fund types within the proprietary funds? What types of events does each report?

12. What are the four fund types within the fiduciary funds? What types of events does each report?

13. What are the two major divisions reported in government-wide financial statements? What funds are *not* reported in these financial statements?

14. Fund financial statements have separate columns for each activity. Which activities are reported individually in this manner?

15. The general fund of a city reports assets of $300,000 and liabilities of $200,000 in fund financial statements. Explain what is meant by each of the following balances: fund balance—nonspendable of $40,000, fund balance—restricted of $28,000, fund balance—committed of $17,000, fund balance—assigned of $4,000, and fund balance—unassigned of $11,000.

16. Why are budgetary entries recorded in several of the individual funds of a state or local government?

17. How are budget results shown in the financial reporting of a state or local government?

18. What is an encumbrance? When is an encumbrance recorded? What happens to this balance? How are encumbrances reported in government-wide financial statements?

19. What costs necessitate the reporting of an expenditure by a governmental fund?

20. At what point does a governmental fund report an expenditure?

21. How do governmental funds report capital outlay in fund financial statements? How do government-wide financial statements report capital expenditures?

22. What are the two different ways that a state or local government can report the cost and use of supplies and prepaid items on fund financial statements for governmental funds?

23. What are the four classifications of nonexchange revenues that a state or local government can report? In each case, when are revenues normally recognized?

24. When does a government recognize a receivable for property tax assessments? When is the associated revenue recognized?

25. How is the issuance of a long-term bond reported on fund financial statements for a governmental fund? How is the issuance of a long-term bond reported on government-wide financial statements?

26. What is a special assessment project? Describe the reporting of a special assessment project.

27. How does a state or local government report interfund transfers in the fund financial statements for the governmental funds?

28. In government-wide financial statements, how do intra-activity and interactivity transactions differ? How does a state or local government report each type of transaction?

29. What is an internal exchange transaction, and how is it reported?

Problems

LO 11-4

1. Which of the following is *not* a governmental fund?
   a. Special revenue fund
   b. Internal service fund
   c. Capital projects fund
   d. Debt service fund

LO 11-4

2. What is the purpose of a special revenue fund?
   a. To account for revenues legally or externally restricted as an operating expenditure
   b. To account for ongoing activities
   c. To account for gifts when only subsequently earned income can be expended
   d. To account for the cost of long-lived assets bought with designated funds

LO 11-4

3. What is the purpose of enterprise funds?
   a. To account for operations that provide services to other departments within a government
   b. To account for asset transfers
   c. To account for ongoing activities such as the police and fire departments
   d. To account for operations financed in whole or in part by outside user charges

LO 11-4

4. Which of the following statements is true?
   a. There are three different types of proprietary funds.
   b. There are three different types of fiduciary funds.
   c. There are five different types of fiduciary funds.
   d. There are five different types of governmental funds.

LO 11-1, 11-6

5. A government expects to receive revenues of $400,000 but has approved expenditures of $430,000. The anticipated shortage will have an impact on which of the following?

   a. Interperiod equity
   b. Modified accrual accounting
   c. Consumption accounting
   d. Account groups

LO 11-4

6. A citizen donates investments valued at $22,000 to the City of Townsend. The citizen stipulates that the investments be held. Any resulting income must be used to help maintain the city's cemetery. In which fund should the city report this investment?

   a. Special revenue funds
   b. Capital projects funds
   c. Permanent funds
   d. General fund

LO 11-2

7. Which of the following statements is correct about the reporting of governmental funds?

   a. Fund financial statements measure only economic resources.
   b. Government-wide financial statements measure only current financial resources.
   c. Fund financial statements measure both economic resources and current financial resources.
   d. Government-wide financial statements measure economic resources.

LO 11-2

8. Which of the following statements is correct about the reporting of governmental funds?

   a. Fund financial statements measure revenues and expenditures based on modified accrual accounting.
   b. Government-wide financial statements measure revenues and expenses based on modified accrual accounting.
   c. Fund financial statements measure revenues and expenses based on accrual accounting.
   d. Government-wide financial statements measure revenues and expenditures based on accrual accounting.

LO 11-2, 11-7

9. During the current year, the City of West buys land for $80,000. Which of the following is *not* a possibility?

   a. The land could be reported as an asset by the business-type activities in the government-wide financial statements.
   b. The land could be reported as an asset by the governmental activities in the government-wide financial statements.
   c. The land could be reported as an asset by the proprietary funds in the fund financial statements.
   d. The land could be reported as an asset by the governmental funds in the fund financial statements.

LO 11-5

10. The City of Bagranoff holds $90,000 in cash that will be used to make a bond payment when the debt comes due early next year. The assistant treasurer initially made the decision to set this money aside for this purpose. Just before the end of the current year, the city council formally approved using the money in this way. The city council is the highest level of decision-making authority for this government. What impact does the council's action have on the reporting of fund financial statements?

    a. Fund balance—unassigned goes down and fund balance—restricted goes up.
    b. Fund balance—assigned goes down and fund balance—committed goes up.
    c. Fund balance—unassigned goes down and fund balance—assigned goes up.
    d. Fund balance—assigned goes down and fund balance—restricted goes up.

LO 11-6

11. Which of the following statements is true concerning the recording of a budget?

    a. At the beginning of the year, a debit is made to Appropriations.
    b. A debit to the Budgetary Fund Balance account indicates an expected surplus for the period.
    c. At the beginning of the year, a debit is made to Estimated Revenues.
    d. At the end of the year, a credit is made to Appropriations.

LO 11-1, 11-2, 11-7

12. The general fund pays rent for two months. Which of the following is *not* correct?

    a. Rent expense should be reported in the government-wide financial statements.
    b. Rent expense should be reported in the fund financial statements.
    c. An expenditure should eventually be reported in the fund financial statements.
    d. If one month of rent is in the first year with the other month in the next year, either the purchases method or the consumption method can be used in fund financial statements.

LO 11-6, 11-7

13. A purchase order for $3,000 is recorded in the general fund for the purchase of a new computer. The computer is received, but the actual cost is $3,020 because of a sales tax. Which of the following statements is correct for fund financial statements?
    a. Machinery is increased by $3,020.
    b. An encumbrance account is reduced by $3,020.
    c. An expenditure is increased by $3,020.
    d. An expenditure is recorded for the additional $20.

LO 11-5

14. At the end of the current year, a government reports $9,000 as a fund balance—assigned in connection with an encumbrance. What information does this balance convey?
    a. A donor has given the government $9,000 that must be used in a specified fashion.
    b. The government has made $9,000 in commitments in one year that will be honored in the subsequent year.
    c. Encumbrances exceeded expenditures by $9,000 during the current year.
    d. The government spent $9,000 less during the year than was appropriated.

LO 11-2, 11-3, 11-7

15. A government buys equipment for its police department at a cost of $54,000. Which of the following is *not* true?
    a. Equipment will increase by $54,000 in the government-wide financial statements.
    b. Depreciation in connection with this equipment will be reported in the fund financial statements.
    c. The equipment will not appear within the reported assets in the fund financial statements.
    d. An expenditure for $54,000 will be reported in the fund financial statements.

LO 11-3, 11-7

16. A city acquires supplies for its fire department and uses the consumption method of accounting. Which of the following statements is true for the fund financial statements?
    a. An expenditures account is debited at the time of receipt.
    b. An expense is recorded as the supplies are consumed.
    c. An inventory account is debited at the time of the acquisition.
    d. The supplies are recorded within the General Fixed Assets Account Group.

LO 11-8

17. An income tax is an example of which of the following?
    a. Derived tax revenue
    b. Imposed nonexchange revenue
    c. Government-mandated nonexchange revenue
    d. Voluntary nonexchange transaction

LO 11-8

18. The state government passes a law requiring all localities to upgrade their water treatment facilities. The state then awards a grant of $500,000 to the Town of Midlothian to help pay for the resulting cost. What type of revenue is this grant?
    a. Derived tax revenue
    b. Imposed nonexchange revenue
    c. Government-mandated nonexchange revenue
    d. Voluntary nonexchange transaction

LO 11-8

19. The state awards a grant of $50,000 to the Town of Glenville. The state will pay the grant money to the town but only as a reimbursement for money spent on road repair. At the time of the grant, the state pays $8,000 in advance. During the first year of this program, the town spent $14,000 and applies for reimbursement. What amount of revenue should be recognized this year?
    a. $–0–
    b. $8,000
    c. $14,000
    d. $50,000

LO 11-5, 11-9

20. A city issues a 60-day tax anticipation note to fund operations until the collection of sufficient tax money. How does the city record this liability?
    a. The liability should be reported in the government-wide financial statements, whereas an other financing source should be shown in the fund financial statements.
    b. A liability should be reported in both the government-wide financial statements and the fund financial statements.

c. An other financing source should be shown in both the government-wide financial statements and the fund financial statements.

d. An other financing source should be shown in the government-wide financial statements, whereas a liability is reported in the fund financial statements.

LO 11-5, 11-9

21. A city issues five-year bonds payable to finance construction of a new school. What recording should be made?

a. Report the liability in the government-wide financial statements. Show an other financing source in the fund financial statements.

b. Report a liability in both the government-wide financial statements and the fund financial statements.

c. Show an other financing source in both the government-wide financial statements and the fund financial statements.

d. Show an other financing source in the government-wide financial statements. Report a liability in the fund financial statements.

LO 11-9

22. The City of Dylan issues a 10-year bond payable of $1 million at face value on the first day of Year 1. Debt issuance costs of $10,000 are paid on that day. For government-wide financial statements, how is this debt issuance cost reported?

a. $1,000 is recorded as an expense, and $9,000 is recorded as an asset.

b. $1,000 is recorded as an expense, and $9,000 is recorded as a deferred outflow of resources.

c. $10,000 is recorded as an expense.

d. $10,000 is recorded as an asset.

LO 11-9

23. The City of Frost has a 20-year debt outstanding. On the last day of the current year, this debt has an outstanding balance of $4.8 million, and five years remain until it comes due. On the current date, the debt is paid off early for $5 million. A new debt is issued (with a lower interest rate) for $5.4 million. How is the $200,000 difference between the amount paid and the outstanding balance of $4.8 million reported on government-wide financial statements?

a. As an expense

b. As a reduction in liabilities

c. As a deferred outflow of resources on the statement of net position

d. As an asset on the statement of net position

LO 11-2, 11-9

24. A $110,000 payment is made on a long-term liability. Of this amount, $10,000 represents interest. Which of the following is *not* true for the recording of this transaction?

a. Reduce liabilities by $100,000 in the government-wide financial statements.

b. Record a $110,000 expenditure in the fund financial statements.

c. Reduce liabilities by $100,000 in the fund financial statements.

d. Recognize $10,000 interest expense in the government-wide financial statements.

LO 11-1, 11-10

25. A city constructs a special assessment project (a sidewalk) for which it is secondarily liable. The city issues bonds of $90,000. It authorizes another $10,000 transferred out of the general fund. The sidewalk is built for $100,000, and payment is made. The citizens are billed for $90,000. They pay this amount, and the debt is paid off. Where is the $100,000 expenditure for construction recorded?

a. It is not recorded by the city.

b. It is recorded in a custodial fund.

c. It is recorded in the general fund.

d. It is recorded in a capital projects fund.

LO 11-4, 11-10

26. A city constructs curbing in a new neighborhood and finances it as a special assessment. Under what condition should these transactions be recorded in a custodial fund?

a. Never; the work is reported in a capital projects fund.

b. Only if the city is secondarily liable for any debt incurred to finance construction costs.

c. Only if the city is in no way liable for the costs of the construction.

d. In all cases.

LO 11-11

27. Which of the following is an example of an interactivity transaction?

a. A city transfers money from the general fund to a debt service fund.

b. A city transfers money from a capital projects fund to the general fund.

c. A city transfers money from a special revenue fund to a debt service fund.

d. A city transfers money from the general fund to an enterprise fund.

LO 11-5, 11-11

28. A town transfers cash of $60,000 from its general fund to a debt service fund. What does the town report in its government-wide financial statements?
    a. No reporting is made.
    b. Other Financing Sources increase by $60,000. Other Financing Uses increase by $60,000.
    c. Revenues increase by $60,000. Expenditures increase by $60,000.
    d. Revenues increase by $60,000. Expenses increase by $60,000.

LO 11-5, 11-11

29. A county transfers cash of $60,000 from its general fund to a debt service fund. What is reported on the county's fund financial statements?
    a. No reporting is made.
    b. Other Financing Sources increase by $60,000. Other Financing Uses increase by $60,000.
    c. Revenues increase by $60,000. Expenditures increase by $60,000.
    d. Revenues increase by $60,000. Expenses increase by $60,000.

LO 11-5, 11-11

30. A city transfers cash of $20,000 from its general fund to an enterprise fund to pay for work performed by the enterprise fund for the school system. How does the city report this transfer on its government-wide financial statements?
    a. No reporting is made.
    b. Other Financing Sources increase by $20,000. Other Financing Uses increase by $20,000.
    c. Revenues increase by $20,000. Expenditures increase by $20,000.
    d. Revenues increase by $20,000. Expenses increase by $20,000.

LO 11-5, 11-11

31. A city transfers cash of $20,000 from its general fund to an enterprise fund to pay for work done by the enterprise fund for the school system. What is reported on the city's fund financial statements?
    a. No reporting is made.
    b. Other Financing Sources increase by $20,000. Other Financing Uses increase by $20,000.
    c. Revenues increase by $20,000. Expenditures increase by $20,000.
    d. Revenues increase by $20,000. Expenses increase by $20,000.

LO 11-3, 11-6

32. The board of commissioners of the City of Hartmoore adopts a general fund budget for the year ending June 30, 2024. It includes revenues of $1,000,000, bond proceeds of $400,000, appropriations of $900,000, and operating transfers out of $300,000. If this budget is formally integrated into the accounting records, what journal entry is required at the beginning of the year? What later entry is required?

LO 11-2, 11-6, 11-7

33. A city orders a new computer for its police department that is recorded within its general fund. The computer has an anticipated cost of $88,000. Its actual cost when received is $89,400. Payment is subsequently made. Prepare all required journal entries for both fund and government-wide financial statements. What information is found on the fund financial statements? What information is found on the government-wide financial statements?

LO 11-1, 11-2, 11-7

34. A city transfers cash of $90,000 from its general fund to start construction on a police station. The city issues a bond at its $1.8 million face value. The police station is built for a total cost of $1.89 million. Prepare all necessary journal entries for these transactions for both fund and government-wide financial statements. Assume that the city does not record the commitment for this construction. What information is found on the fund financial statements? What information is found on the government-wide financial statements?

LO 11-5

35. The governmental funds of the City of Westchester report $445,000 in assets and $140,000 in liabilities. The following are some of the assets that the government reports.
    - Prepaid items—$7,000
    - Cash from a bond issuance that must be spent within the school system according to the bond indenture—$80,000
    - Supplies—$5,000
    - Investments given by a citizen that will be sold soon with the proceeds used to beautify a public park—$33,000
    - Cash that the assistant director of finance designated for use in upgrading the local roads—$40,000
    - Cash from a state grant that must be spent to supplement the pay of local kindergarten teachers—$53,000
    - Cash that the city council (the highest level of decision-making authority in the government) voted to use in renovating a school gymnasium—$62,000

On a balance sheet for the governmental funds, what fund balance amounts should the City of Westchester report?

LO 11-5

36. Government officials of Hampstead County ordered a computer near the end of the current fiscal year for $6,400 to be used by the police department. It failed to arrive prior to the end of the year. At its final meeting of the year, the city council (the highest decision-making authority for the government) agreed to pay for the computer when delivered in the subsequent year. In preparing a set of government-wide financial statements and a set of fund financial statements for the current year, how will this purchase be reported?

LO 11-2, 11-5, 11-11

37. A local government has the following transactions during the current fiscal period. Prepare journal entries without dollar amounts, first for fund financial statements and then for government-wide financial statements.

   a. The budget for the police department, ambulance service, and other ongoing activities is passed. Funding is from property taxes, transfers, and bond proceeds. All monetary outflows will be for expenses and fixed assets. A deficit is projected.

   b. A bond is issued at face value to fund the construction of a new municipal building.

   c. The government orders a computer for the tax department.

   d. The computer is received.

   e. The invoice for the computer is paid.

   f. The city council agrees to transfer money from the general fund as partial payment for a special assessments construction project, but the funds have not yet been transferred. The city will be secondarily liable for any money borrowed to finance this construction.

   g. The city council creates a motor pool to service all government vehicles. Money is transferred from the general fund to permanently finance this facility.

   h. Property taxes are levied. Although officials believe that most of these taxes will be collected during the current period, they anticipate that a small percentage will be uncollectible.

   i. The city collects grant money from the state that must be spent to supplement the salaries of the police force. The city has not yet made any journal entry. Appropriate payment of the supplement is viewed as an eligibility requirement.

   j. A portion of the grant money in (i) is properly spent.

LO 11-2, 11-4, 11-7, 11-8, 11-11

38. Prepare journal entries for the City of Pudding's governmental funds to record the following transactions, first for fund financial statements and then for government-wide financial statements.

   a. A new truck for the sanitation department was ordered at a cost of $94,000.

   b. The city print shop did $1,200 worth of work for the school system (but has not yet been paid).

   c. An $11 million bond was issued at face value to build a new road.

   d. The city transfers cash of $140,000 from its general fund to provide permanent financing for a municipal swimming pool that will be maintained as an enterprise fund.

   e. The truck ordered in (a) is received but at an actual cost of $96,000. Payment is not made at this time.

   f. The city transfers cash of $32,000 from its general fund to a capital projects fund.

   g. The city receives a state grant of $30,000 that must be spent to promote recycling by the citizens.

   h. The first $5,000 of the state grant received in (g) is expended as intended.

LO 11-2, 11-5, 11-7, 11-8, 11-9, 11-11

39. Prepare journal entries for a local government to record the following transactions, first for fund financial statements and then for government-wide financial statements.

   a. The government sells $900,000 in bonds at face value to finance the construction of a new warehouse.

   b. A $1.1 million contract is signed for construction of the warehouse. The commitment is reported, if allowed.

   c. The government transfers cash of $130,000 in unrestricted funds for the eventual payment of the debt in (a).

   d. The government receives equipment for the fire department with a cost of $12,000. When ordered, an anticipated cost of $11,800 was recorded.

   e. Supplies to be used in the schools are bought for $2,000 cash. The consumption method is used.

   f. The state awards a grant of $90,000 to supplement police salaries. The money will be paid to reimburse the government but only after the supplement payments have been made.

   g. The government mails property tax assessments to its citizens. The total assessment is $600,000, although officials anticipate that 4 percent will never be collected. The government holds an enforceable legal claim to this money. It can be spent immediately.

LO 11-4, 11-5, 11-6, 11-7, 11-8, 11-9, 11-10, 11-11

40. The following unadjusted trial balances are for the governmental funds of the City of Copeland.

General Fund	Debit	Credit
Cash	$ 19,000	
Taxes Receivable	202,000	
Allowance for Uncollectible Taxes		$ 2,000
Vouchers Payable		24,000
Due to Debt Service Fund		10,000
Unavailable Revenues		16,000
Encumbrances Outstanding		9,000
Fund Balance—Unassigned		103,000
Revenues		176,000
Expenditures	110,000	
Encumbrances	9,000	
Estimated Revenues	190,000	
Appropriations		171,000
Budgetary Fund Balance		19,000
Totals	$530,000	$530,000

Debt Service Fund	Debit	Credit
Cash	$ 8,000	
Investments	51,000	
Taxes Receivable	11,000	
Due from General Fund	10,000	
Fund Balance—Committed		$ 45,000
Revenues		20,000
Other Financing Sources—Operating Transfers In		90,000
Expenditures	75,000	
Totals	$155,000	$155,000

Capital Projects Fund	Debit	Credit
Cash	$ 70,000	
Special Assessments Receivable	90,000	
Contracts Payable		$ 50,000
Unavailable Revenues		90,000
Encumbrances Outstanding		16,000
Fund Balance—Unassigned		–0–
Other Financing Sources		150,000
Expenditures	130,000	
Encumbrances	16,000	
Estimated Other Financing Sources	150,000	
Appropriations		150,000
Totals	$456,000	$456,000

Special Revenue Fund	Debit	Credit
Cash	$ 14,000	
Taxes Receivable	41,000	
Inventory of Supplies	4,000	
Vouchers Payable		$ 25,000
Grant Revenues Collected in Advance		3,000
Fund Balance—Nonspendable		4,000

(continued)

(continued)

Special Revenue Fund	Debit	Credit
Encumbrances Outstanding		3,000
Fund Balance—Unassigned		19,000
Revenues		56,000
Expenditures	48,000	
Encumbrances.	3,000	
Estimated Revenues.	75,000	
Appropriations.		60,000
Budgetary Fund Balance.		15,000
Totals.	$185,000	$185,000

Based on the information presented for each of these governmental funds, answer the following questions:

a. How much more money can city officials expend or commit from the general fund during the remainder of the current year without amending the budget?

b. Why does the capital projects fund have no construction or capital asset accounts?

c. What does the $150,000 Appropriations balance found in the capital projects fund represent?

d. Several funds have balances for Encumbrances and Encumbrances Outstanding. How will these amounts be accounted for at the end of the fiscal year?

e. Why does the Fund Balance—Unassigned account in the capital projects fund have a zero balance?

f. What are possible explanations for the $150,000 Other Financing Sources balance found in the capital projects fund?

g. What does the $75,000 balance in the Expenditures account of the debt service fund represent?

h. What is the purpose of the Special Assessments Receivable found in the capital projects fund?

i. In the special revenue fund, what is the purpose of the Fund Balance—Nonspendable account?

j. Why does the debt service fund not have budgetary account balances?

LO 11-2, 11-3, 11-4, 11-5, 11-6, 11-7, 11-8, 11-9, 11-11

41. Following are descriptions of transactions and other financial events for the City of Tetris for the year ending December 2024. Not all transactions have been included here. Only the general fund formally records a budget. No encumbrances were carried over from 2023.

Paid salary for police officers	$ 21,000
Received government grant to pay ambulance drivers.	40,000
Estimated revenues	232,000
Received invoices for rent on equipment used by fire department during last four months of the year	3,000
Paid for newly constructed city hall.	1,044,000
Made commitment to acquire ambulance	111,000
Received cash from bonds sold for construction purposes	300,000
Placed order for new sanitation truck	154,000
Paid salary to ambulance drivers—money derived from state government grant given for that purpose	24,000
Paid for supplies for school system.	16,000
Made transfer from General Fund to eventually pay off a long-term debt.	33,000
Received but did not pay for new ambulance.	120,000
Levied property tax receivables for 2024. City officials anticipate that 95% ($190,000) will be collected during the year and 5% will prove to be uncollectible.	200,000
Acquired and paid for new school bus.	40,000
Received cash from business licenses and parking meters (not previously accrued)	14,000
Approved appropriations.	225,000

The following questions are *independent* although each is based on the preceding information. Assume that the government is preparing information for its fund financial statements.

a. What is the balance in the Budgetary Fund Balance account for the budget for the year? Is it a debit or credit?

b. Assume that 60 percent of the school supplies are used during the year so that 40 percent remain. If the consumption method is being applied, how is this recorded?

c. The sanitation truck that was ordered was not received before the end of the year. The commitment will be honored in the subsequent year when the truck arrives. What reporting is made at the end of 2024?

d. Assume that a new ambulance was received on December 31, 2024. Provide all necessary journal entries on that date.

e. Prepare all journal entries that should have been made when the $33,000 transfer was made for the eventual payment of a long-term debt.

f. What amount of revenue should the city recognize for the period? Explain the composition of this total.

g. What are the total expenditures? Explain the makeup of this total. Include response to (b) here.

h. What journal entry or entries did the city prepare for the issuance of the bonds?

LO 11-2, 11-3, 11-4, 11-5, 11-6, 11-7, 11-8, 11-9, 11-11

42. Chesterfield County had the following transactions. Prepare the entries first for fund financial statements and then for government-wide financial statements.

a. A budget is passed for all ongoing activities. Revenue is anticipated to be $834,000, with approved spending of $540,000 and operating transfers out of $242,000.

b. A contract is signed with a construction company to build a new central office building for the government at a cost of $8 million. The county previously recorded the budget for this project.

c. Bonds are issued for $8 million (face value) to finance construction of the new office building.

d. The new building is completed. An invoice for $8 million is received by the county and paid.

e. Previously unrestricted cash of $1 million is set aside by county officials to begin paying the bonds issued in (c).

f. A portion of the bonds comes due, and $1 million is paid. Of this total, $100,000 represents interest. The interest had not been previously accrued.

g. Property tax levies are assessed. Total billing for this tax is $800,000. On this date, the assessment is a legally enforceable claim according to the laws of the state. All money to be received is designated for the current period, and 90 percent is assumed to be collectible in this period. Receipt of an additional 6 percent is not expected until the subsequent period but in time to be available to pay current period claims. The remaining amount is viewed as uncollectible.

h. The county collects cash of $120,000 from a toll road. The money is restricted for highway maintenance.

i. The county receives stock investments valued at $300,000 as a donation from a grateful citizen. The investments are to be held permanently, but any income from these investments must be used to beautify local parks.

LO 11-5

43. The following trial balance is taken from the General Fund of the City of Jennings for the year ending December 31, 2024. Prepare a condensed statement of revenues, expenditures, and other changes in fund balance. Also prepare a condensed balance sheet.

	Debit	Credit
Accounts Payable.		$ 90,000
Cash	$ 30,000	
Contracts Payable.		90,000
Unavailable Revenues.		40,000
Due from Capital Projects Funds	60,000	
Due to Debt Service Funds.		40,000
Expenditures	530,000	
Fund Balance—Unassigned		170,000
Investments	410,000	
Revenues		760,000
Other Financing Sources—Bond Proceeds		300,000
Other Financing Sources—Transfers In		50,000
Other Financing Uses—Transfers Out.	470,000	
Taxes Receivable	220,000	
Vouchers Payable.		180,000
Totals.	$1,720,000	$1,720,000

LO 11-2, 11-5, 11-6, 11-7, 11-8, 11-9

44. A city has only one activity, its school system. The school system is accounted for within the general fund. For convenience, assume that, at the start of 2024, the school system and the city have no assets. During the year, the city assesses property taxes of $400,000. Of this amount, it collects $320,000 during the year, collects $50,000 within a few weeks after the end of the year, and expects the remainder to be collected about six months later. The city makes the following payments during 2024: salary expense, $100,000; rent expense, $70,000; equipment (received on January 1 with a five-year life and no salvage value), $50,000; land, $30,000; and maintenance expense, $20,000.

In addition, on the last day of the year, the city purchases a $200,000 building by signing a long-term note payable. The building has a 20-year life and no salvage value, and the liability accrues interest at a 10 percent annual rate. The city also buys two computers on the last day of the year for $4,000 each. One will be paid for in 30 days and the other in 90 days. The computers should last four years and have no expected residual value. During the year, the school system charges students $3,000 for school fees and collects the entire amount. The city determines depreciation using the straight-line method.

a. Produce a statement of net position and a statement of activities for this city's government-wide financial statements.

b. Produce a balance sheet and a statement of revenues, expenditures, and changes in fund balance for the fund financial statements. Assume that *available* is defined by the city as anything to be received within 60 days.

LO 11-2, 11-4, 11-6, 11-7, 11-8, 11-10

45. The fiscal year for the City of Havisham ends December 31, Year 5. If the city were to produce financial statements before any adjustments, the following figures would be included:

- Governmental activities: Assets = $800,000, Liabilities = $300,000, and Change in Net Position for the period = increase of $100,000

- Business-type activities: Assets = $500,000, Liabilities = $200,000, and Change in Net Position for the period = increase of $60,000

- Governmental funds: Assets = $300,000, Liabilities = $100,000, and Change in Fund Balances = increase of $40,000

- Proprietary funds: Assets = $700,000, Liabilities = $300,000, and Change in Net Assets for the period = increase of $70,000

Other information: The city council is the highest level of decision-making authority for the government. Where applicable, current financial resources are viewed by the government as available if collected within 75 days.

For each of the following, indicate whether the overall statement is true or false. Assume that each situation is independent of all others.

a. In the information provided about the city, an error has apparently been made because the amount of proprietary fund assets ($700,000) cannot be greater than the amount of business-type activity assets ($500,000).

b. Assume that a separate governmental fund (such as one recording money designated for the construction of Highway 61) reports total assets of $32,000. Based on that information alone, this fund must be reported separately as a major fund.

c. The city starts a bus system to help eliminate traffic congestion. To encourage ridership, passengers are charged only a nickel for each trip, although that fee will not come close to covering the cost of the bus system or pay for its debts. The bus system must be reported as a part of the general fund rather than as a separate enterprise fund.

d. The city council passes an annual budget for all general fund activities. Revenues are expected to be $1 million, and approved expenditures are $900,000. These budgetary amounts are recorded through a journal entry at the beginning of the year (an entry that is removed at the end of the year). In recording this budget, an estimated revenue account is debited for $1 million.

e. The city council passes an annual budget for all general fund activities. Revenues are expected to be $1 million, and approved expenditures are $900,000. These budgetary amounts are recorded through a journal entry at the beginning of the year (that entry is removed at the end of the year). In recording this budget, an expenditures account is debited for $900,000.

f. The government paid for a standard three-year insurance policy on January 1, Year 5, for its school system. If the government applies the purchases method, the amount of expenditures reported by the city is larger for that year than if the consumption method had been used.

g. The city receives money from an income tax. It is classified as a derived tax revenue.

h. After the provided figures were determined, officials learned that the city was entitled to an additional $100,000 in taxes on income earned during Year 5. Starting on January 1, Year 6, the city will collect $1,000 per day of this amount for the next 98 days (the final $2,000 is expected to be uncollectible). As a result of this discovery, the reported change in net position for the governmental activities in government-wide statements for Year 5 will go up by $98,000.

i. The city police department orders equipment on October 17, Year 5, for $43,000. The equipment is received on December 29, Year 5, but at an actual cost of $44,000. In the general fund, the encumbrance account will be credited $44,000 and the expenditure account debited $44,000 to indicate the switch from a monetary commitment to liability.

j. The police department orders equipment on October 17, Year 5, for $43,000. The equipment is not received prior to the end of Year 5. The police chief authorizes the department to accept and pay for the equipment when it arrived in Year 6. In reporting fund financial statements at the end of Year 5, a fund balance—committed balance of $43,000 should be reported on the balance sheet for the governmental funds.

k. The city transfers cash of $32,000 from the general fund to a capital projects fund. On the statement of activities, for the government-wide financial statements, this transaction is shown as both a transfer in and a transfer out.

LO 11-5, 11-8, 11-10, 11-11

46. The City of Gargery has a fiscal year ending December 31, Year 5. If the city were to produce financial statements without any further adjustment, the following figures would be included:

    - Governmental activities: Assets = $800,000, Liabilities = $300,000, and Change in Net Position for the period = increase of $100,000.
    - Business-type activities: Assets = $500,000, Liabilities = $200,000, and Change in Net Position for the period = increase of $60,000.
    - Governmental funds: Assets = $300,000, Liabilities = $100,000, and Change in Fund Balances = increase of $40,000.
    - Proprietary funds: Assets = $700,000, Liabilities = $300,000, and Change in Net Assets for the period = increase of $70,000.

    Other information: The city council is the highest level of decision-making authority for the government. Where applicable, current financial resources are viewed as available if collected within 75 days.

    For each of the following, indicate whether the overall statement is true or false. Assume that each situation is independent of all others.

    a. The city transfers cash of $19,000 from the general fund to an internal service fund to pay for work that was done by the city's print shop for the school system. On the statement of revenues, expenditures, and other changes in fund balances for the Governmental Funds (in the fund financial statements), this resource outflow is reported as an other financing use.

    b. After the provided figures were determined, city officials learned that $100,000 in property taxes had been assessed but not recorded on December 29, Year 5. Per legal requirements, these taxes were solely to finance government operations in Year 6. Starting on January 1, Year 6, the city will collect $1,000 per day for the next 98 days (the final $2,000 is expected to be uncollectible). The change in net position for the governmental activities in the government-wide statements reported for Year 5 should be increased by $98,000.

    c. Assume that after the provided figures were determined, city officials learned that $100,000 in property taxes had been assessed but not recorded on December 29, Year 5. Per legal requirements, these taxes were solely to finance government operations in Year 6. Starting on January 1, Year 6, the city will collect $1,000 per day for the next 98 days (the final $2,000 is expected to be uncollectible). The change in fund balances for the Governmental Funds reported for Year 5 should be increased by $60,000.

    d. Assume that after the provided figures were determined, city officials learned that $100,000 in property taxes had been assessed but not recorded on December 29, Year 5. As per legal requirements, these taxes were solely to finance government operations in Year 6. The government collected $5,000 on December 30, Year 5, but the rest will not be collected until June of Year 6. On fund financial statements for the Governmental Funds as of December 31, Year 5, the total liability balance will be increased by $5,000.

    e. Investments (bonds and stocks) with a value of $5 million are given to the city by a donor. All income earned from these investments must be used to construct a small library in one of the local neighborhoods, but the investments must be held forever. In Year 5, income of $480,000 was received from these investments. However, none of this money has yet been spent for the library. On fund financial statements, the year-end balance sheet for the Governmental Funds must show a "fund balance—restricted" of $5 million and a "fund balance—committed" of $480,000.

f. The State of Virginia requires the City of Gargery to buy equipment to monitor local air quality. The state awards the city $100,000 to help pay for the equipment. This grant is known as a voluntary nonexchange transaction so that revenue is not recognized until all eligibility requirements are met.

g. The city constructs curbing for a neighborhood in a special assessment project. The individuals whose property benefits from the curbs will pay for all of the work. The city has no legal responsibility for this work, so it is recorded in a custodial fund. The money eventually collected should be reported as revenue on the statement of activities in the government-wide financial statements.

h. On January 1, Year 5, the city receives a grant for $130,000 to supplement the salaries of police and fire department employees. The city will receive no money until after the salaries are paid. On December 30, Year 5, all $130,000 is distributed to the appropriate workers and the city applies for reimbursement. The city will receive the money within the next month. The $130,000 revenue is recognized in the government-wide financial statements in Year 5 but not in the fund financial statements for Year 5.

LO 11-5, 11-7, 11-8, 11-9, 11-11

47. The following transactions relate to the general fund of the City of Lost Angels for the year ending December 31, 2024. Prepare a statement of revenues, expenditures, and other changes in fund balance for the general fund for the period to be included in the fund financial statements. Assume that the fund balance at the beginning of the year was $180,000. Assume also that the city applies the purchases method to supplies. Receipt within 60 days serves as the definition of available resources.

a. Collects property tax revenue of $700,000. A remaining assessment of $100,000 will be collected in the subsequent period. Half of that amount should be received within 30 days, and the remainder approximately five months after the end of the year.

b. Spends $200,000 on three new police cars with 10-year lives. The anticipated price was $207,000 when the cars were ordered. The city calculates all depreciation using the straight-line method with no expected residual value. The city applies the half-year convention.

c. Transfers $90,000 of unrestricted cash to a debt service fund.

d. Issues a long-term bond for its $200,000 face value on July 1. Interest at a 10 percent annual rate will be paid each year starting on June 30, 2025.

e. Orders a new computer with a five-year life for $40,000.

f. Pays salaries of $30,000. Another $10,000 is owed to employees at the end of the year but will not be paid for 30 days.

g. Receives the new computer near the end of 2024. The actual cost is $41,000. Payment is to be made in 45 days.

h. Buys supplies for $10,000 in cash.

i. Uses $8,000 of the supplies bought in (h).

LO 11-7, 11-8, 11-9, 11-11

48. Use the transactions in Problem 47, but prepare a statement of net position for the government-wide financial statements. Assume that the general fund held $180,000 in cash on the first day of the year and no other assets or liabilities. No amount of the cash was restricted, committed, or assigned.

LO 11-1, 11-6

49. Government officials of the City of Johnson expect to receive general fund revenues of $400,000 in 2024 but approve spending only $380,000. Later in the year, as they receive more information, they increase the revenue projection to $420,000. Officials also approve the spending of an additional $15,000. For each of the following, indicate whether the statement is true or false and, if false, explain why.

a. In recording this budget, appropriations are credited initially for $380,000.

b. The city must disclose this budgetary data within the required supplemental information section reported after the notes to the financial statements.

c. When reporting budgetary information for the year, three figures should be reported: amended budget, initial budget, and actual figures.

d. In making the budgetary entry, a debit must be made to some type of Fund Balance account to indicate the projected surplus and its effect on the future size of the fund.

e. The reporting of the budget is presented in the government-wide financial statements.

LO 11-8

50. On December 1, 2024, a state government awards a city government a grant of $1 million to be used specifically to provide hot lunches for all schoolchildren. No money is received until June 1, 2025. For each of the following, indicate whether the statement is true or false and, if false, explain why.

a. Because the government receives no money until June 1, 2025, no amount of revenue can be recognized in 2024 on the government-wide financial statements.

b. If this grant has no eligibility requirements and the money is properly spent in September 2025 for the hot lunches, the revenue should be recognized during that September.

c. Because this money came from the state government and because that government specified its use, this is a government-mandated nonexchange transaction.

d. If the government had received the money on December 1, 2024, but eligibility reimbursement requirements had not been met, unearned revenue of $1 million would have been recognized on the government-wide financial statements.

LO 11-7, 11-8, 11-9, 11-11

51. The following are transactions of the City of Grayson. Indicate how each of the following transactions affects the fund balance of the general fund, and its classifications, for fund financial statements. Then describe the effect each transaction has on the net position balance of the Government Activities on the government-wide financial statements.

a. Issues a five-year bond for its face value of $6 million to finance general operations.

b. Pays cash of $149,000 for a truck to be used by the police department.

c. The city's fire department pays $17,000 to a government motor pool that services vehicles owned by the police and fire departments. Work was done on several department vehicles.

d. Levies property taxes of $75,000 for the current year that will not be collected until four months into the subsequent year.

e. Receives a grant for $7,000 from a charity that must be returned unless the money is spent according to the stipulations of the conveyance. Those actions are expected to happen in the future.

f. Local businesses make sales of $20 million during the current year. The government assesses a 5 percent sales tax. Half of this amount is to be collected 10 days after the end of the current year with the remainder to be collected 14 weeks later. "Available" has been defined by this government as 75 days.

g. Orders a computer for the school system at an anticipated cost of $23,000.

h. A cash transfer of $18,000 is approved from the general fund to a capital projects fund.

LO 11-4, 11-5, 11-11

52. Inside the City of Patience, Fund A transfers $20,000 in cash to Fund B. For each of the following, indicate whether the statement is true or false and, if false, explain why.

a. If Fund A is the general fund and Fund B is an enterprise fund, nothing is shown for this transfer on the statement of activities within the government-wide financial statements.

b. If Fund A is the general fund and Fund B is a debt service fund, nothing is shown for this transfer on the statement of activities within the government-wide financial statements.

c. If Fund A is the general fund and Fund B is an enterprise fund, a $20,000 reduction is reported on the statement of revenues, expenditures, and other changes in fund balance for the governmental funds within the fund financial statements.

d. If Fund A is the general fund and Fund B is a special revenue fund (which is not considered a major fund), no changes are shown on the statement of revenues, expenditures, and other changes in fund balance within the fund financial statements.

e. If Fund A is the general fund and Fund B is an internal service fund and this transfer is to pay for work done, the general fund will report an expense of $20,000 within the fund financial statements.

Use the following information for Problems 53–59:
Assume that the City of Coyote has produced its financial statements for December 31, 2024, and the year then ended. The city's general fund was only used to monitor education and parks. Its capital projects funds worked in connection with each of these functions at times during the current year. The city also maintained an enterprise fund to account for its art museum.

The government-wide financial statements provide the following figures:

- Education reports net expenses of $600,000.
- Parks reports net expenses of $100,000.
- Art museum reports net revenues of $50,000.
- General government revenues for the year were $800,000 with an overall increase in the city's net position of $150,000.

The fund financial statements provide the following for the entire year:

- The general fund reports a $30,000 increase in its fund balance.
- The capital projects fund reports a $40,000 increase in its fund balance.
- The enterprise fund reports a $60,000 increase in its net position.

The city asks the CPA firm of Abernethy and Chapman to examine several transactions that occurred during 2024 and indicate how to correct any erroneous reporting. Officials also want to know the effect of each error. View each of the following situations as independent.

LO 11-2, 11-5, 11-10

53. During 2024, the City of Coyote contracts to build a bus stop for schoolchildren costing $10,000 as a special assessments project. The city collects $10,000 from directly affected citizens. The government has no obligation in connection with this project. The city records both a $10,000 revenue and a $10,000 expenditure in the capital projects fund. In preparing government-wide financial statements, the city records an asset and a general revenue for $10,000.

    a. In the general information, the capital projects fund reports a $40,000 increase in its fund balance for the year. What was the correct change in the capital projects fund balance during 2024?

    b. In the general information, a $150,000 overall increase in the city's net position was found on the government-wide financial statements. What was the correct overall change in the city's net position on the government-wide financial statements?

LO 11-9

54. On December 30, 2024, the City of Coyote borrows $20,000 for the general fund on a 60-day note. In that fund, the city records Cash and Other Financing Sources. In the general information, this city reports a $30,000 overall increase in the fund balance of the general fund. What was the correct change in the fund balance of the general fund for 2024?

LO 11-2, 11-4, 11-5

55. The City of Coyote records an art display within its general fund. The display generates revenues of $9,000 this year as well as expenditures of $45,000 ($15,000 in expenses and $30,000 to buy land for the display). The CPA firm determines that the city should report this program as an enterprise fund activity because of its association with the city's art museum.

    a. Based on the information provided, what was the correct change in the fund balance for the general fund for 2024?

    b. What was the correct overall change in the city's net position on government-wide financial statements?

    c. What was the correct change in the net position of the enterprise fund on the fund financial statements?

LO 11-2, 11-5, 11-8

56. The City of Coyote mails property tax bills for 2025 to its citizens during August 2024. Property owners could make payments early to receive a discount. The levy becomes legally enforceable on February 15, 2025. All money received by the city must be spent during 2025 or later. The total assessment is $300,000. Of that amount, the city collects 40 percent, less a 10 percent discount, in 2024. The city expects to receive all of the remaining money during 2025 with no discount. During 2024, the government increases cash as well as revenue for the amount received. No change was made in creating government-wide financial statements.

    a. What is the correct overall change in the city's net position as should be shown on the government-wide financial statements?

    b. What is the correct change for 2024 in the fund balance reported for the city's general fund?

LO 11-2, 11-5, 11-8

57. The City of Coyote mails property tax bills for 2025 to its citizens during August 2024. Payments could be made early to receive a discount. The levy becomes legally enforceable on February 15, 2025. All money the government receives must be spent during 2025 or later. The total assessment is $300,000, and the city collects 40 percent of that amount in 2024 less a 10 percent discount. The city expects to receive all remaining money during 2025 with no discount. During 2024, the government increases cash and a revenue for the amount received. In addition, a receivable and an unavailable revenue for $180,000 are recognized.

    a. In the general information, an overall increase in the city's net position of $150,000 was found on the government-wide financial statements. What is the correct overall change in the city's net position as reported on the government-wide financial statements?

    b. In the general information, an overall increase of $30,000 is reported in the fund balance for the general fund. What was the correct change during 2024?

LO 11-2, 11-5, 11-7, 11-8

58. In 2024, the City of Coyote receives a $320,000 cash grant from the state to reduce air pollution. Although a special revenue fund could have been set up, the money remains in the general fund. The cash was received immediately but will have to be returned if the city does not lower its air pollution by 25 percent by 2028. On December 31, 2024, Coyote spends $210,000 of the money for a large machine to help begin the process of reducing air pollution. City officials expect the machine to last for five years. The city recorded the cost as an expenditure in the general fund but as an asset on the government-wide financial statements, where it was depreciated based on the straight-line method and the half-year convention. Because the city received the money, it recorded all $320,000 as a revenue on both the fund and the government-wide financial statements.

> *a.* What was the correct change for 2024 in the total fund balance reported by the general fund?
>
> *b.* What was the correct overall change in the net position reported on the government-wide financial statements?

LO 11-2

59. During 2024, the City of Coyote received $10,000, which was recorded as a general revenue in the general fund. It was actually a program revenue earned by the city's park program.

> *a.* What was the correct overall change for 2024 in the net position reported on the government-wide financial statements?
>
> *b.* In the general information, the parks program reported net expenses for the period of $100,000. What was the correct amount of net expenses that should have been reported by the parks program?

Develop Your Skills

RESEARCH CASE 1

CPA *skills*

The City of Hampshore is currently preparing financial statements for the past fiscal year. The city manager is concerned because the city encountered some unusual transactions during the current fiscal period and is unsure as to their handling.

Required

Locate a copy (either in hard copy or online) of GASB's *Codification of Governmental Accounting and Reporting Standards.* Either through an online search or a review of the index, answer each of the following questions.

1. For government accounting, what is the definition of an *extraordinary item*?
2. For government accounting, what is the definition of a *special item*?
3. On government-wide financial statements, how should extraordinary items and special items be reported?

RESEARCH CASE 2

CPA *skills*

The City of Danmark is preparing financial statements. Officials are currently working on the statement of activities within the government-wide financial statements. A question has arisen as to whether a particular revenue should be identified on government-wide statements as a program revenue or a general revenue.

Required

Locate a copy (either in hard copy or online) of GASB's *Codification of Governmental Accounting and Reporting Standards.* Either through an online search or a review of the index, answer each of the following questions.

1. How is a program revenue defined?
2. What are common examples of program revenues?
3. How is a general revenue defined?
4. What are common examples of general revenues?

ANALYSIS CASE

CPA *skills*

Search the internet for the official website of one or more state or local governments. Determine whether the government's latest annual comprehensive financial report (ACFR) is available on the site. For example, the most recent ACFR for the City of Raleigh can be found at https://raleighnc.gov/services /government/annual-comprehensive-financial-report. Use the financial statements that you locate (for Raleigh or some other state or local government) to answer the following questions.

Required

1. How does the audit opinion rendered on the financial statements of government by its independent auditors differ from the audit opinion rendered on the financial statements for a for-profit business?

2. A reconciliation should be presented to explain the difference between the net changes in fund balances for the governmental funds (fund financial statements, the statement of revenues, expenditures, and other changes in fund balances) and the change in net position for the governmental activities (government-wide financial statements: the statement of activities). What were several of the largest reasons for the difference?

3. What were the city's largest sources of general revenues?

4. What was the total amount of expenditures recorded by the general fund during the period? How were those expenditures classified?

5. What assets are reported for the general fund?

6. Review the notes to the financial statements and then determine the number of days the government uses to define the end-of-year financial resources that are viewed as currently available.

7. Did the size of the general fund balance increase or decrease during the most recent year and by how much?

COMMUNICATION CASE 1

CPA skills

Go to the website www.gasb.org and click on "Projects" included in the list that runs across the top of the page. Then click on "Current Projects & Pre-Agenda Research." Click on either the "Conceptual Framework," "Comprehensive Projects," or "Practice Issues." Then, click on the name of one of the current projects that is listed. At that point, a list of informational sites are provided, including "Project Description," "Background," "Accounting and Financial Reporting Issues," "Project History," "Current Developments," "Work Plan," and more.

Required

Using the information provided on the GASB website, write a memo to explain the reason that this particular issue has been chosen for study by GASB. Describe the progress that has been made to date as well as the potential effect that a change in reporting rules might have on state and local government accounting.

COMMUNICATION CASE 2

CPA skills

Go to www.accountingfoundation.org/strategicplan. At that address, you should find the *Strategic Plan* (as of April 2015) for the Financial Accounting Foundation, the Financial Accounting Standards Board, and the Governmental Accounting Standards Board. Within this 16-page document, read the sections titled "Mission," "Vision," and "Core Values."

Required

Assume that a financial analyst with whom you are working is interested in knowing more about the role that FASB and GASB play in setting authoritative accounting standards. Write a short memo explaining the work of this bodies based on its vision, mission, core values, and goals.

COMMUNICATION CASE 3

CPA skills

Go to www.gasb.org. Click on "Standards & Guidance" and then click on "Pronouncements." Click on "Statements of Governmental Accounting Standards." Click on "26-50" and then click on "GASB Statement 34." Click on "Full Text" and read paragraphs 239 through 277.

Required

Write a report describing alternatives in *Statement 34* that GASB considered when creating the dual reporting model (fund financial statements separate from government-wide financial statements). Indicate the alternative that you would have viewed as most appropriate, and describe why the GASB did not choose it.

COMMUNICATION CASE 4

Search the internet for the official website of one or more state or local governments. On this website, determine whether the latest annual comprehensive financial report (ACFR) is available. For example, a recent annual comprehensive financial report for the City of Winston-Salem can be found at https://www.cityofws.org/Departments/Finance. Read the Management's Discussion & Analysis (MD&A) that should be located near the beginning of the annual report. For the ACFR for Winston-Salem for the year ended June 30, 2021, the MD&A begins on page 36.

Required

Write a memo to explain four or five of the most interesting pieces of information that the Management's Discussion and Analysis provides.

EXCEL CASE

The City of Bainland has been undergoing financial difficulties because of a decrease in its tax base caused by corporations leaving the area. On January 1, 2024, the city has a fund balance of only $400,000 in its governmental funds. At that year, the city had revenues of $1.4 million and expenditures of $1.48 million. The city's treasurer has forecast that, unless something is done, revenues will decrease at 2 percent per year while expenditures will increase at 3 percent per year.

Required

1. Create a spreadsheet to predict in what year the government will have a zero fund balance.
2. One proposal is that the city slash its expenditures by laying off government workers. That will lead to a 3 percent decrease in expenditures each year rather than a 3 percent increase. However, because of the unemployment, the city will receive less tax revenue. Thus, instead of a 2 percent decrease in revenues, the city expects a 5 percent decrease per year. Adapt the spreadsheet created in requirement (1) to predict what year the government will have a zero fund balance if this option is taken.
3. Another proposal is to increase spending to draw new businesses to the area. This action will lead to a 7 percent increase in expenditures every year, but revenues are expected to rise by 4 percent per year. Adapt the spreadsheet created in requirement (1) to predict what year the government will have a zero fund balance under this option.

Accounting for State and Local Governments (Part 2)

T he previous chapter introduced many unique aspects of the financial reporting applicable for state and local governments. Fund account- ing, budgets, encumbrances, expenditures, revenue recognition, transfers, the issuance of bonds, and the like were all described in connection with both traditional fund financial statements and government-wide financial statements. The coverage explained the rationale underlying the accounting designed for these government entities, especially the differences caused by the dual nature of the financial reporting process.

The current chapter carries this analysis further, first by delving into more complex financial situations. Many state and local government units are large and encounter numerous transactions as complicated as any faced by for-profit businesses. Topics such as tax abatements, solid waste land- fills, defined benefit pension plans, donated artworks, and depreciation of infrastructure assets are discussed here to broaden the reader's understand- ing of state and local government accounting. This chapter also introduces standards developed by GASB to report lease arrangements, rules that have several interesting differences from the lease accounting procedures estab- lished by FASB for business entities. A student of accounting might well consider whether GASB or FASB has done a better job in creating financial reporting for leases.

Second, this chapter discusses the overall financial reporting model for state and local governments. Within this coverage, the composition of a reporting entity is examined. Because of the wide variety of agencies, departments, and other activities often connected to a government, deter- mining inclusion within a set of financial statements is not as easy as with a for-profit business, where ownership of more than 50 percent of voting stock is the primary criterion.

The Hierarchy of U.S. Generally Accepted Accounting Principles (GAAP) for State and Local Governments

State and local governments often face complex reporting issues. Governmental financial events can be as unusual and complex as those encountered in large for-profit entities. Officials in cities like Chicago and Boston manage billion-dollar budgets that include a wide array of monetary resources and costs. Those accounting issues rival anything companies like Coca-Cola and Proctor & Gamble must solve.

Learning Objectives

After studying this chapter, you should be able to:

LO 12-1   Understand how the hierarchy of U.S. generally accepted accounting principles for state and local governments can be used to resolve financial reporting issues.

LO 12-2   Explain the informational benefit derived from required disclosure of tax abatements reported by state and local governments.

LO 12-3   Explain the meaning of a net pension liability resulting from a defined benefit pension plan provided to employees by a state or local government.

LO 12-4   Report leased assets from the perspective of the government as lessee and then from the perspective of the government as lessor.

LO 12-5   Recognize the liability caused by the anticipated closure and postclosure costs of operating a solid waste landfill.

LO 12-6   Record the receipt of donated and acquired works of art and historical treasures by a state or local government.

LO 12-7   Explain the reporting and possible depreciation of infrastructure assets by state and local governments.

LO 12-8   Understand the composition of a state or local government's annual comprehensive financial report (ACFR).

LO 12-9   Explain the makeup of a primary government and its relationship to component units and related organizations.

LO 12-10   Describe the physical structure of a complete set of government-wide financial statements and a complete set of fund financial statements.

LO 12-11   Understand the construction and presentation of financial statements for a public college or university.

LO 12-1

Understand how the hierarchy of U.S. generally accepted accounting principles for state and local governments can be used to resolve financial reporting issues.

For a vast majority of transactions, appropriate application of U.S. GAAP is not a serious question. Most government events such as tax collections and bond issuances occur with regularity so that standard reporting has become widely understood and accepted. For example, the accounting procedures discussed in the previous chapter are all well established through official pronouncements or long-term practical use.

Nevertheless, events can arise that do not lend themselves to easy reporting solutions. Perhaps a new type of transaction is undertaken with an unusual nature or a particular twist that seems unique. To complicate the reporting, different rules can sometimes provide guidance that seems to be contradictory. For financial statements to be in conformity with U.S. GAAP, state and local government accountants must be able to establish the validity of the suggested reporting. The same challenge is true for independent auditors (CPAs) who are hired to examine and certify that the information is presented fairly, in all material respects, in accordance with the accounting principles generally accepted in the United States.

When faced with a new or unusual transaction, how do accountants and auditors determine what accounting is consistent with U.S. GAAP? When a variety of sources indicate different possible reporting resolutions, which guidance should be followed? For accountants, answers to these practical questions are essential.

In 2015, the Governmental Accounting Standards Board (GASB) issued its Statement No. 76, *The Hierarchy of Generally Accepted Accounting Principles for State and Local Governments*. GASB created this pronouncement to provide reporting guidance whenever the question of establishing conformity with U.S. GAAP arises. According to this standard, all sources of authoritative U.S. GAAP for state and local governments can be divided into two categories, with Category A having more authority than Category B.

Category A: This first level of authoritative rules is composed of official GASB statements. Those statements are available on the Board's website (www.gasb.org). In addition, prior to the release of Statement No. 76, GASB occasionally issued interpretations to help clarify, explain, or provide more detailed information about various GASB statements. Over the years, the Board issued only a few interpretations and has discontinued further usage. The Board now uses other methods (see Category B) to provide this type of guidance about U.S. GAAP. However, Category A does include any previously released interpretations that remain in effect.

Category B: The second level is made up of GASB Technical Bulletins, GASB Implementation Guides, and any literature of the American Institute of Certified Public Accountants (AICPA) that has been cleared by GASB. Again, specific listings of these resources can be found on GASB's website.

- GASB releases technical bulletins as needed to serve much the same function as the interpretations described previously. Technical bulletins can be issued in a relatively short period of time to provide practical solutions for pressing reporting problems. Technical bulletins have not been used frequently, but can be created to indicate that a majority of the Board does not object to a proposed method of reporting. For example, in June 2020, GASB Technical Bulletin No. 2020-1 was issued with the explanatory title, *Accounting and Financial Reporting Issues Related to the Coronavirus Aid, Relief, and Economic Security Act (CARES Act) and Coronavirus Diseases*.

- Implementation guides clarify, explain, or elaborate on existing U.S. GAAP for state and local governments. In contrast to technical bulletins, they do not go beyond that function. Therefore, they do not establish the acceptability of new approaches to specific reporting issues. Because implementation guides tend to have a broader effect and less urgency, a period of public exposure provides a chance for feedback that can highlight potential problems before the guide is issued. Like technical bulletins, they indicate that a majority of the Board does not object to the guidance given. For example, in April 2020, GASB Implementation Guide No. 2020-1 was issued. In a question-and-answer format, it provided guidance on numerous topics ranging from leases to fiduciary activities.

To establish the validity of a proposed reporting treatment, accountants and auditors look first to sources within Category A. If no answer is found, they then move on to guidance found in Category B.

What happens if a satisfactory answer cannot be found in either Category A or Category B? No set of generally accepted accounting principles can ever anticipate all of the wide variety of reporting issues that might be faced by a government. At that point, reasoned judgment becomes essential. "If specific guidance cannot be found in either category, financial statement preparers and auditors are to consider guidance for similar transactions or events."[1]

Is official guidance available that is similar enough to be considered applicable? For example, if a rule on the reporting of the cost of a highway is provided in a GASB statement, can the same logic be used in accounting for a parking lot? Ultimately, the reporting of complex transactions in governmental accounting (as well as that used with for-profit entities) requires accountants and auditors to have a strong understanding of the purpose of the reporting process and the principles on which it is founded.

As additional help, GASB also provides a list of nonauthoritative sources that can be considered in determining the method of reporting that is most consistent with generally accepted accounting principles: GASB Concepts Statements, pronouncements of other accounting bodies such as FASB and the IASB, practices that are prevalent in state and local governments, published literature of professional associations and regulatory agencies, and accounting textbooks and articles.

No function performed by an accountant or auditor is more significant than the determination of how a reporting entity accounts for a unique transaction or event so as to be in conformity with U.S. GAAP. That decision requires both deep technical knowledge and sound judgment. The nature of the event must be understood completely and then compared to rules that have been established over many decades. With Statement 76, GASB has specified which of these rules (and other sources of guidance) should be analyzed and which has the most authority.

Tax Abatement Disclosure

LO 12-2

Explain the informational benefit derived from required disclosure of tax abatements provided by state and local governments.

For years, taxpayers have questioned whether the estimated $70 billion in subsidies governments shower on the free enterprise system each year are savvy investments or corporate welfare run amok. Soon, they will have more information to make that call. This month, the Governmental Accounting Standards Board—the Norwalk, Connecticut, body that oversees government accounting rules—said it will require governments to disclose how much tax revenue they are foregoing because of incentives provided to businesses. State and local governments, as well as school districts, also will have to disclose the jobs promises and other commitments businesses make in order to avoid paying taxes.[2]

Government decisions to provide tax abatements have come under increased scrutiny in recent years. Resistance to Amazon's original decision to build an additional headquarters in the New York City area focused at least in part on the size of the tax reductions and other government benefits provided to the company. While many citizens argued that the offer was a wise economic move for the region, others viewed it as a sign of acquiescence to corporate greed.

Accounting rules are not always limited to specifying the correct debits and credits that will properly reflect a transaction. Disclosure issues can be as challenging as the reporting of an actual event. One question stands at the center of any disclosure discussion: What information will create a representative financial picture for interested parties without requiring so much data that (1) readers become overwhelmed and (2) unnecessary costs are incurred by the reporting company? Financial statements should enlighten outside parties and not confuse them with excessive amounts of information. In any accounting debate, reporting entities usually argue for less disclosure, whereas decision makers typically call for more.

Governments often make agreements with outside organizations to forego tax revenues for a period of time in exchange for a specific action. For example, "Nevada promised to provide Tesla Motors $1.3 billion in tax incentive packages to build the Tesla Gigafactory in that state."[3] GASB has ruled (in GASB Statement No. 77, *Tax Abatement Disclosures)* that

---

[1] Stephen J. Gauthier, "New Guidance on the GAAP Hierarchy," *Government Finance* Review, December 2015, pp. 47–48.

[2] Len Boselovic, "Pittsburgh Post-Gazette Len Boselovic's Heard Off the Street Column," *McClatchy Tribune Business News,* August 30, 2015.

[3] Anthony Billings, Jeanette A. Boles, and Kyungjin Kim, "Tax Abatement Under GASB Statement 77," *CPA Journal,* April 2018.

information about such tax abatement programs is beneficial and worth the associated cost of disclosure. Disclosure becomes necessary as soon as an agreement is reached between the government and the outside organization.[4]

In its ACFR as of September 30, 2020, and the year then ended, the City of Fort Worth, Texas, describes its three tax abatement programs: Tax Abatement Agreements, Neighborhood Empowerment Zones, and Economic Development Program Grant Agreements. The first two of these programs allow a recipient a reduction of up to 100 percent of annual property taxes depending on the specifics of the agreement. The third program allows a recipient a reduction of up to 100 percent of annual property, sales, and hotel occupancy taxes. The tax revenues for the City of Fort Worth were reduced by a total of $3.6 million by the first two programs and by more than $28.1 million by the third program. On the same date, the City of San Antonio, Texas, had 59 tax abatement agreements that were active.

These abatement programs represent exchanged promises. The city reduces or eliminates an organization's taxes for a period of time. In return, the business or other entity agrees to a defined action such as keeping operations in the city or the construction of a new facility.

In a traditional sense, tax abatements create no transaction to report. The choice to forego the collection of taxes is not easy to reflect in a journal entry that would be meaningful. However, the financial effect of such agreements can be quite significant. Is a company's promise to create 50 jobs and invest $1.5 million in construction worth a government's loss of real estate tax collections for 10 years? If government officials make such a decision, citizens need to be aware of the financial ramifications.

GASB now requires state and local governments to disclose information about tax abatements in their financial statements.

> Tax abatement has been a common carrot that communities use to attract development. To date, however, cities and other tax-abating governments haven't shared much information about the accumulated financial consequences of those tax breaks. Now, because of an edict from the board that oversees government accounting, they will. That means that the counties, cities and public authorities in seven counties in Northeast Ohio will have to provide details about the roughly $1.4 billion in taxes that are passed up annually. . . . "I'm going to be the happy recipient of more information," said Tim Offtermatt, an investment banker with the Cleveland office of Stifel Financial Corp. who specializes in public finance. "It helps us put together a comprehensive credit package for credit analysts."[5]

As a result of GASB's pronouncement, a state or local government must disclose significant information about abatement agreements including:

- The purpose of the tax abatement program.
- The type of tax being abated.
- Dollar amount of taxes abated.
- The type of commitments made by the tax abatement recipients.
- Any commitments made by the government (or other parties), for example, agreeing to construct infrastructure assets such as roads.

Because of the importance of reported information, few accounting rules manage to escape without some amount of questioning. Here, GASB has been criticized for not requiring governments to identify the companies receiving the abatements. Additional criticism was levied by parties who want to know more about the long-term financial effect of these abatement decisions.

- "Critics disagree, arguing that governments should at least be required to disclose the names of the largest recipients. One reason for this is that many believe subsidies don't generally help small, homegrown businesses flourish."[6]

---

[4] A list of state tax abatement programs can be found at https://mf.freddiemac.com/docs/approved_tax_abatement_programs.pdf.

[5] Jay Miller, "GASB Ruling Will Make Tax Breaks More Transparent," *Crain's Cleveland Business*, September 7, 2015, p. 3.

[6] Liz Farmer, "3 Things the New Tax Incentive Disclosures Rules Won't Reveal," *McClatchy Business News*, November 24, 2015.

- "Policy Matters Ohio's Schiller questioned the lack of long-term cost projections—a key element in the pension fund crisis. 'It's hard to figure why (GASB) didn't approve any kind of forward-looking cost of this,' Schiller said. 'From (a municipal bond) investor's standpoint, isn't your biggest concern not what they paid last year, but what they have to pay in the future?'"[7]

Defined Benefit Pension Plans

LO 12-3

Explain the meaning of a net pension liability resulting from a defined benefit pension plan provided to employees by a state or local government.

Sanitation workers, firefighters, teachers and other state and local government employees have performed their duties in the public sector for decades with the understanding that their often lackluster salaries were propped up by excellent benefits, including an ironclad pension. But Moody's Investors Service recently estimated that public pensions are underfunded by $4.4 trillion. That amount, which is equivalent to the economy of Germany, accounts for one-fifth of national debt. It's a significant concern for public employees who were banking on a fully funded retirement to get them through their golden years.[8]

State and local governments often provide pension plans for many of their employees. An educator in the public schools, for example, might be eligible to retire with full benefits after a specified length of service (such as 30 years). Because businesses have been moving for many years into defined contribution pension plans, government employees are more likely than for-profit business employees to have defined benefit pension plans. In 2014, 30 percent of employees in the private sector were covered by defined benefit pension plans whereas 90 percent of public-sector employees had those type of pension plans.[9]

Pension requirements create a huge financial obligation for many governments across the United States. Retirees are usually entitled to benefits based on a contractually set formula. "Future pension obligations of both companies and state governments collectively amount to trillions of dollars; obligations of numerous pension plans can be measured individually in billions of dollars. Public-sector pension obligations generally dwarf those in the private sector."[10]

Many state and local governments establish pension trust funds to (1) accumulate and invest monetary resources and (2) pay out pension benefits. Because the money is held for retirees, these pension trusts are classified as fiduciary funds and, thus, are not included in reporting government-wide financial statements. A question has long been raised as to the amount of pension obligation a government should include in its overall financial reporting, especially considering the potential size of these obligations. Historically, as long as all legal funding requirements were met in a timely manner, governments reported no pension liability. Because these requirements did not necessarily cover the expected amount of the eventual pension payments, financial analysts argued that the financial position of many state and local governments was considerably more precarious than was being reported.

GASB's Statement No. 68, *Accounting and Financial Reporting for Pensions,* now requires a more extensive reporting of pension liabilities. Because virtually all of these payments will take place well beyond the current fiscal period, this reporting applies almost exclusively to government-wide financial statements (and to fund financial statements for proprietary funds). GASB also created similar requirements for postemployment benefit plans other than

---

[7] Jay Miller, "GASB Ruling Will Make Tax Breaks More Transparent," *Crain's Cleveland Business,* September 7, 2015, p. 3.

[8] Olivia Mitchell and Leora Friedberg, "The Time Bomb Inside Public Pension Plans," August 23, 2018, on the Knowledge @ Wharton website, http://knowledge.wharton.upenn.edu/article/the-time-bomb-inside-public-pension-plans/.

[9] Craig Foltin, Dale L. Flesher, Gary J. Previts, and Mary S. Stone, "State and Local Government Pensions at the Crossroads," *CPA Journal,* April 2017, p. 44.

[10] Kathryn E. Easterday and Tim V. Eaton, "Defined Benefit Pension Plans," *CPA Journal,* September 1, 2012, p. 22.

pension plans (such as medical coverage) to reflect more completely each government's total obligation to its retired employees.

For pensions, this authoritative guidance establishes several steps in the reporting of a government's liability.

- First, an actuary estimates the total pension payments that will ultimately be required.
- Second, the government determines the portion of those payments attributable to past periods of employee service. This figure reflects the amount of their pension earned to date by employees.
- Third, the government calculates the present value of the payments relating to those past amounts to arrive at its obligation at the current time.
- Fourth, if that liability is larger than the net asset position held in the pension trust fund, the excess is shown in the government-wide financial statements as a net pension liability. It reflects the shortfall between what is owed and the amount held at present to settle that obligation. Conversely, if the net position of the pension trust fund is larger than the present value of the pension benefits earned by employees to date, the government reports a net pension asset. This net liability or net asset appears on the statement of net position as either a governmental activity or a business-type activity, depending on the nature of the function responsible for the payments. Pensions for educators, firefighters, sanitation workers, and the like fall under governmental activities. As of June 30, 2020, the City of Boston, Massachusetts, reported on its statement of net position for its governmental activities a net pension liability of approximately $1.8 billion and an other postemployment benefits obligation of $2.3 billion. Those two liabilities together made up more than 60 percent of the reported liability total for the City of Boston.

To illustrate, assume that a city has maintained a pension plan for several decades to cover all of the teachers in its school system who remain employed for a minimum of three years. Years ago, the city began a pension trust fund that now holds $1 billion in cash and investments. No payments are currently due to retirees. Assume that an actuary calculates the total amount of expected pension payments for current and retired teachers to be $10 billion. To date, those individuals have earned only 80 percent of that amount, or $8 billion. Assume that these future cash payments have a present value of $3 billion. On government-wide financial statements, the city must report $2 billion as its net pension liability. The $1 billion held in the pension trust fund is subtracted from the $3 billion present value of the future $8 billion in payments to arrive at the $2 billion unfunded portion of the obligation. Because the school system is responsible for these eventual pension payments, the city reports the debt on its government-wide financial statements within the governmental activities.

Accountants must deal with a number of complex challenges in applying this reporting standard. Although many of these problems are beyond the scope of this textbook, students should be aware of several key issues.

- In any present-value computation, the question of an appropriate discount rate is essential. The size of the rate is inversely related to the size of the reported liability. The higher the rate, the more interest is assigned to future cash flows, leaving a smaller liability balance to report currently. GASB specifies that, in most cases, the government should calculate the present value of the future pension obligation using the estimated long-term investment yield for the plan's assets.

  The choice of this rate has proven controversial. Because the expected rate of return on investments is normally higher than other possible discount rates, the remaining pension liability to be reported is smaller. The average rate used in 2014 was 7.3 percent. Had 4 percent been used for the entire liability, "The unfunded liability to be reported would increase from $900 billion to $3.41 trillion."[11] The higher rate decreases the liability and reduces the apparent cost that taxpayers will have to bear in the future for these pension plans.[12]

---

[11] Ibid., p. 46.

[12] "The Not-So-Great GASB," *Economist,* Buttonwood's Notebook, May 2, 2013, www.economist.com/blogs/buttonwood/2013/05/pensions.

Financial economists have recommended for decades that governments calculate pension liabilities using so-called "risk-free" rates pegged to high-grade municipal bonds or long-term Treasurys. . . . However, GASB let governments stick with their desired, or, expected rate of return, which is typically about 8 percent. Public pension funds have returned 5.7 percent on average since 2000. Achieving much higher returns over the long run would require markets to perform as well as they did in the 1980s and '90s. Would that be true. Governments have resisted climbing down from Fantasyland because using lower discount rates would explode their liabilities.[13]

- The government must identify the components of pension expense that are recognized immediately. GASB lists those as (1) the service cost for the current period, (2) interest expense on the total pension liability, and (3) projected earnings on plan investments. Any increases or decreases in the liability caused by changes in benefit terms are also included in pension expense immediately rather than being amortized over time as is the case with for-profit enterprises.

- Numerous assumptions (such as the life expectancy of retirees) are necessary to arrive at the total pension liability figure. The effect of periodic changes in these assumptions and differences between the assumptions and actual experience are not included immediately by the government as pension expense. Instead, those amounts are recorded as either deferred outflows of resources or deferred inflows of resources and then amortized to pension expense over the average expected remaining service lives of the employees in the pension plan. As an example, at June 30, 2020, because of having multiple pension arrangement with various employee groups, Nashville and Davidson County, Tennessee, reports both a $147.7 million deferred outflow of resources and a $167.9 million deferred inflow of resources on its statement of net position. Such balances are explained as, "The amounts for pensions relate to certain differences between projected and actual actuarial results and certain differences between projected and actual investment earnings."

Elements similar to the reporting used by for-profit organizations can be seen throughout these government pension rules. Nevertheless, GASB created several unique aspects in the reporting of defined benefit pension plans administered by state and local government entities. Decision makers could certainly debate whether FASB or GASB has invented a better approach for the reporting of these extremely large obligations.

LO 12-4

Report leased assets from the perspective of the government as lessee and then from the perspective of the government as lessor.

Lease Accounting

In its ACFR for September 30, 2020, and the year then ended, the City of San Antonio, Texas, disclosed that machinery and equipment with a cost of more than $45 million had been obtained through capital leases. The city's financial statements also indicated that the "Total rental revenue from operating leases received for the fiscal year-ended September 30, 2020, was $11,391,000 for Governmental Activities and $39,970,000 for Business-Type Activities." These two examples show how financially involved state and local governments can be in lease contracts. The monetary amounts are frequently substantial whether the government is the lessee or the lessor.

In February 2016, FASB issued Accounting Standards Update 2016-02, *Leases.* It provided new authoritative guidance for both lessees and lessors. Then, in June 2017, GASB issued Statement No. 87, *Leases,* for much the same purpose. The first pronouncement standardized financial reporting for business entities and private not-for-profit entities. The second standardized reporting for state and local government entities. Comparison of these two official approaches to account for contractual lease arrangements is inevitable. The underlying transactions are the same and these two standards provide many similar methods of reporting. However, fascinating differences do exist.[14]

---

[13] "Pension Accounting for Dummies: New Government Reporting Rules Are No Better than the Old Ones," *Wall Street Journal* (online), July 11, 2012.

[14] Extensive coverage of FASB's ASU 2016-02 can be found in any current intermediate accounting textbook. Hence, discussion is limited primarily to points of comparison with Statement No. 87.

The Lessee—According to FASB FASB ASU 2016-02 establishes five criteria to distinguish financing leases from operating leases. Nevertheless, for a lessee, the accounting for these categories is not markedly different. In either situation, the lessee records both an intangible (right-of-use) asset and liability at the present value of the payments based on the lessee's incremental borrowing rate (unless the lessee knows the implicit interest rate built into the payments by the lessor). If the contract qualifies as a financing lease, according to FASB, the lessee recognizes interest expense by multiplying the liability balance for the current period by the applicable rate. The lessee also reports amortization to assign the cost of the leased asset to expense over the period of its use.

According to FASB, the significant difference for the lessee between reporting a financing lease and an operating lease is in the computation of amortization expense. In a financing lease, the lessee applies the straight-line or some other appropriate method. Interest and amortization are determined independently.

In contrast, for an operating lease, the lessee first calculates a single expense balance for the current period as if the total of all payments was spread evenly over the asset's useful life. This figure is the periodic lease expense that the lessee reports. Interest expense is then determined by the previous calculation. The liability balance is multiplied by the appropriate rate. Amortization of the asset is merely the amount that increases this interest balance to the total lease expense figure determined by the lessee. Hence, for an operating lease, the lessee does not compute amortization based on either the reported cost of the asset or its expected life. Amortization is simply the number to be recognized to arrive at a consistent annual lease expense.

To illustrate an operating lease under FASB's new rules, assume that a city pays $100,000 to lease a truck over the next five years (an average of $20,000 per year). If the government computes interest for the first year as $12,000, it automatically recognizes amortization for that period as $8,000. On the lessee's income statement, the government combines these two figures to report a single lease expense of $20,000.

For any lease contract that cannot be extended beyond one year and does not contain a bargain purchase option, FASB makes a short-term alternative available. In this optional approach, the lessee merely recognizes lease expense as time passes. Other than prepaid rent, the entity reports neither an asset nor a liability.

The Lessee—According to GASB GASB takes a different approach to lease accounting. No criteria exist. Unless the maximum life is one year or less, all leases are the equivalent of financing leases. The split identified by FASB between operating and financing leases is not viewed as relevant. As the Summary to Statement No. 87 explains, GASB "Establishes a single model for lease accounting based on the foundational principle that leases are financings of the right to use an underlying asset. Under this Statement, a lessee is required to recognize a lease liability and an intangible right-to-use lease asset."

To illustrate, assume on December 31, Year 0, that the City of North leases a large truck with a 20-year life for four years to use during a construction project. After the contract ends, the city must return the truck to the lessor but has not guaranteed any residual value. The lease requires four annual payments of $30,000 per year beginning immediately. Because the city does not know the implicit interest rate the lessor is charging, the lessee applies its own incremental borrowing rate of 10 percent per year. The present value of a $30,000 annuity due for four years at an annual interest rate of 10 percent is $104,604 (rounded). In government-wide financial statements, the City of North records the first two years of this lease contract as follows.

Government-Wide Financial Statements

December 31, Year 0		
Right-of-Use Asset—Truck..	104,604	
Lease Payable...		74,604
Cash		30,000
To record city's four-year lease of truck at the present value of the payments. The first payment is made immediately.		

(continued)

(*continued*)

December 31, Year 1		
Interest Expense	7,460	
Lease Payable		7,460
To record interest for the year as 10 percent of the $74,604 liability.		
Amortization Expense	26,151	
Right-of-Use Asset—Truck		26,151
Cost of the leased asset is amortized over four years using straight-line method ($104,604/4 years).		
Lease Payable	30,000	
Cash		30,000
To record payment at end of Year 1.		
December 31, Year 2		
Interest Expense	5,206	
Lease Payable		5,206
To record interest as 10 percent of liability, which is now $74,604 less $30,000 plus $7,460, or $52,064.		
Amortization Expense	26,151	
Right-of-Use Asset—Truck		26,151
To record annual amortization of leased asset.		
Lease Payable	30,000	
Cash		30,000
To record payment at end of Year 2.		

If this lease had been for a maximum of one year or less, the lessee could have recorded the payment as a prepaid asset and then assigned that balance to rent or lease expense over the time of the asset's use.

Returning to the original example, in fund financial statements for any one of the governmental funds, the City of North reports neither a right-of-use asset nor a lease liability. Signing the contract does not affect current financial resources. Instead, the city records expenditures and other financing sources for the present value of the payments.

Fund Financial Statements—Governmental Funds

December 31, Year 0		
Expenditure—Lease Contract	104,604	
Other Financing Sources—Lease Contract		104,604
Contract is signed that will require four annual payments of $30,000 per year with a present value of $104,604.		
Expenditure—Leased Truck	30,000	
Cash		30,000
To record first lease payment.		
December 31, Year 1		
Expenditure—Leased Truck	30,000	
Cash		30,000
To record second lease payment.		

For a short-term lease of one year or less, the entries for the fund financial statements are the same except that the initial recording is not necessary.

The Lessor—According to FASB The difference between an operating lease and a financing lease becomes more significant under FASB's lease rules. If the contract meets one or more of the five criteria, the lessor records a lease receivable at its present value and removes the asset from its records. If the present value is equal to the cost of the asset, the lessor reports no immediate profit. Interest revenue constitutes the only profit. The lessor recognizes that interest over the length of the contract based on multiplying the receivable balance for each period times the implicit interest rate.

If the present value of the cash inflows is higher than the cost of the asset, the contract is a sales-type lease that contains a selling profit. The lessor records sales revenue for the present value of the lease (same as the initial receivable balance) but also records cost of goods sold for the cost of the asset. The difference between the revenue and cost of goods sold is an immediate increase in net income. Subsequently, the lessor recognizes interest revenue over time based on the receivable balance and the implicit interest rate.

In contrast, if the contract meets none of the five criteria, the lease is an operating lease. To report an operating lease, the entries are entirely different. The lessor reports the cash collected and recognizes a deferred lease revenue (a liability balance). As time passes, the lessor reclassifies the deferred lease revenue as lease revenue. For the lessor, moving between an operating lease and a financing-/sales-type lease has a dramatic effect on the reported figures.

The Lessor—According to GASB   Again, for government-wide financial statements, GASB does not recognize separate categories for lease contracts. Unless the lease is for a maximum of one year or less, the lessor has only one option. Initially, the lessor records both the receivable and a deferred lease revenue at present value. This deferral is not a liability but rather a deferred inflow of resources. It appears below the government's liabilities on the statement of net position to indicate that this balance is not a debt. Regardless of the length of the contract, the asset is reported within the financial records of the lessor.

The lessor reports no immediate profit. Instead, over time, the lessor reclassifies the deferred lease revenue as lease revenue in a systematic and rational manner. Concurrently, interest revenue is calculated and recognized on the receivable balance for each period. Because the asset is still present in the accounting records, the lessor also reports periodic depreciation expense.

Through this system, the lessor reports a portion of the lease revenue each period, along with interest revenue on the receivable and amortization expense on the asset. To illustrate, assume that the City of North holds a truck with a net book value of $120,000. The city no longer has a need for the truck and leases it to a nearby county government for eight years, the entire remaining life. Officials do not anticipate any residual value. Based on an implicit interest rate of 10 percent per year, annual payments starting on December 31, Year 0, are computed as $20,448 (rounded). Because the lessor computes these payments based on a 10 percent annual interest rate and the asset's net book value, the initial present value is also $120,000.

The city makes the following entries.

December 31, Year 0		
Lease Receivable	120,000	
Deferred Lease Revenue.		120,000
To record lease of truck for eight years with payments based on a 10 percent annual interest rate, the implicit rate built into the contract.		
Cash.	20,448	
Lease Receivable		20,448
To record collection of first lease payment.		
December 31, Year 1		
Lease Receivable	9,955	
Interest Revenue.		9,955
To record interest on lease receivable. Balance for Year 1 was the original balance of $120,000 less first payment of $20,448 or $99,552. Interest is 10 percent of that figure.		
Deferred Lease Revenue.	15,000	
Lease Revenue		15,000
To reclassify deferred lease revenue to lease revenue. Straight-line method is used ($120,000/8 years) although GASB allows any systematic and rational approach.		

(continued)

(continued)

Depreciation Expense.	15,000	
Accumulated Depreciation		15,000
Depreciation is recorded on remaining net book value over the asset's useful life ($120,000/8 years). City did not remove truck after signing lease contract.		

Notice here that the lease revenue and depreciation expense offset each year so that only the interest revenue affects net income. If the lease is not for the entire life of the asset or if expected residual values or bargain purchase options are present, the revenue and the depreciation expense will not necessarily be the same amounts. In that case, some amount of reported profit results each year.

Furthermore, if the lease is for a maximum of one year or less, GASB simplifies the process by recognizing deferred lease revenue as the government collects payments. This deferral becomes lease revenue as time passes. In fund financial statements for governmental funds, the entries for a lessor are virtually identical except that the asset is not present within the financial records so depreciation is not appropriate.

LO 12-5

Recognize the liability caused by the anticipated closure and post-closure costs of operating a solid waste landfill.

Solid Waste Landfill

As of June 30, 2020, the City of Greensboro, North Carolina, reported a $500,000 current liability in its statement of net position as an accrued landfill liability. Within its noncurrent liabilities, the city reported an additional obligation of approximately $27.2 million with the same account title. As an enterprise fund, the city identifies both balances as business-type activities. What information is conveyed by these account balances that total $27.7 million?

Many communities operate landfills. These sites often create large environmental liabilities that might not be finalized for decades. The notes to the financial statements of the City of Greensboro, as of June 30, 2020, explain the reporting of its landfill debt.

> The City owns and operates a regional landfill site located in the northeast portion of the City. State and federal laws require the City to place a final cover on its White Street landfill site and to perform certain maintenance and monitoring functions at the site for thirty years after closure. The City reports a portion of these closure and postclosure care costs as an operating expense in each period based on landfill capacity used as of each June 30. The $27,654,593 reported as landfill closure and postclosure care liability at June 30, 2020, is based on 100% use of the estimated capacity of Phase II and Phase III, Cells 1 and 2. Phase III, Cell 3, is estimated at 58.2% of capacity. . . .
>
> The estimated liability amounts are based on what it would cost to perform all closure and postclosure care in the current year. Actual cost may be higher due to inflation, changes in technology, or changes in regulations. At June 30, 2020, the City had expended $3,876,035 to complete closure for the White Street facility, Phase II and $2,535,980 to begin closure activities at the construction and demolition site located on top of the municipal waste filled space. The balance of closure costs, estimated at $14,194,163, and an estimated $13,460,230 for postclosure care will be funded over the remaining life of the landfill estimated to be 20 to 25 years.

Similar to Greensboro, thousands of state and local governments operate solid waste landfills to provide a place for citizens and local companies to dispose of trash and other forms of refuse. Governments frequently report landfill operations within their enterprise funds if these facilities charge a user fee. Other landfills are open to the public for free so that reporting within the general fund is appropriate.

Regardless of the type of fund utilized for reporting, solid waste landfills can create huge liabilities for these governments. The U.S. Environmental Protection Agency has strict rules on closure requirements as well as groundwater monitoring and other postclosure activities. Satisfying such requirements can be costly. The operation of a landfill can ultimately necessitate large payments to ensure that the facility is closed properly and then monitored and maintained for an extended period. The relevant accounting question has always been how to report these eventual costs while the landfill is still in operation.

To illustrate, assume that the City of North opens a landfill in Year 1 that is expected to take 10 years to fill. To determine the annual amount to be reported, the city must estimate the current costs required to close the landfill. Such costs include the amount to be paid to cover the area and for all postclosure maintenance. As mentioned in the City of Greensboro disclosure, the government uses current—rather than an estimate of future—closure and post-closure costs as a measure of the present obligation. Such amounts must then be adjusted each period for factors such as inflation, technology, and regulation changes.

Assume in this example that the current cost for closure for a landfill of this size is esti-mated at $10 million and for postclosure maintenance at $4 million for a total obligation of $14 million. Assume that during Year 1 the city makes an initial payment of $300,000 toward these closure costs. At the end of this first year, city engineers determine that 16 percent of the available space is now filled.

Landfills—Government-Wide Financial Statements

Regardless of whether the City of North reports this solid waste landfill as a governmental activity (within the general fund) or as a business-type activity (within an enterprise fund), closure and postclosure costs in government-wide statements must be based on accrual accounting and the economic resources measurement basis. The government anticipates that the total current cost of closure and cleanup is $14 million. Because the landfill is 16 percent filled, the city should accrue $2,240,000 at the end of the first year ($14 million × 16%). The initial $300,000 payment reduces the liability being reported.

Government-Wide Financial Statements—Estimated Landfill Closure Costs

Year 1		
Expense—Landfill Closure......................................	2,240,000	
Landfill Closure Liability.....................................		2,240,000
To recognize the Year 1 portion of total costs (16 percent) for eventual closure of landfill.		
Landfill Closure Liability.......................................	300,000	
Cash		300,000
To record first payment of costs necessitated by eventual closure of landfill.		

To complete this example, assume that the landfill is judged to be 27 percent filled at the end of Year 2 and the city makes another $300,000 payment toward future closure costs. Because of inflation and recent changes in technology, the city now believes that current clo-sure costs are $11 million, with postclosure costs of $5 million. The current cost of the total landfill obligation has jumped from $14 million to $16 million.

Based on this newly revised information, the City of North will report an estimated total cost of $4,320,000 at the end of Year 2 ($16 million × 27%). Because the city recog-nized $2,240,000 in Year 1, it accrues an additional $2,080,000 in Year 2 ($4,320,000 − $2,240,000).

Government-Wide Financial Statements—Estimated Landfill Closure Costs

Year 2		
Expense—Landfill Closure......................................	2,080,000	
Landfill Closure Liability.....................................		2,080,000
To recognize Year 2 portion of costs for eventual closure of landfill.		
Landfill Closure Liability.......................................	300,000	
Cash		300,000
To record second payment necessitated by eventual closure of the landfill.		

Consequently, the City of North reports the following information in its Year 2 government-wide financial statements, regardless of whether the landfill is part of the general fund (a governmental activity) or as an enterprise fund (a business-type activity):

Expense—Landfill closure	$2,080,000
Landfill closure liability ($2,240,000 + 2,080,000 − 300,000 − 300,000)	$3,720,000

Landfills—Fund Financial Statements

When a solid waste landfill is maintained as an enterprise fund, reporting in the fund financial statements is the same as is shown for government-wide statements. All economic resources are again measured based on accrual accounting.

If the landfill is recorded in the general fund because the facility charges little or no user fee, the City of North reports only the actual change in current financial resources. Despite the huge eventual liability, the reduction in current financial resources is limited to the annual payment of $300,000. The remaining liability is too far into the future to necessitate reporting. Clearly, for governmental funds, fund financial statements and government-wide financial statements serve radically different purposes.

When fund financial statements are prepared, the only entry required each year is as follows:

Fund Financial Statements—Payment toward Landfill Closure Costs—Governmental Funds

Year 1 and Year 2 General Fund		
Expenditures—Closure Costs	300,000	
Cash		300,000
To record annual payment toward the eventual closure costs of the city's solid waste landfill.		

LO 12-6

Record the receipt of donated and acquired works of art and historical treasures by a state or local government.

Works of Art and Historical Treasures

Interested parties have long debated the proper reporting by private not-for-profit entities of artworks and other museum pieces whether bought or received by gift. State and local governments can face the same issue. How should works of art, historical artifacts, and other such treasures be reported by these governments in their financial statements? These properties have value, but are they really assets in an accounting sense?

Assume, for example, that the City of North maintains a museum in a building formerly used as a high school. Officials created the museum to display documents, maps, paintings, and other works that depict the history of the area. Admission is free. Consequently, the museum generates no revenue.

The government bought a number of the items that are now on display. Local citizens donated the remaining pieces. Several paintings and pieces of furniture are quite valuable.

GASB has made the basic rule in accounting for such items quite clear. Other than a few specific exceptions, "governments should capitalize works of art, historical treasures, and similar assets at their historical cost or acquisition value whether they are held as individual items or in a collection."[15]

Thus, an antique map bought by the City of North for $5,000 appears in the government-wide statement of net position as an asset at that cost. A similar map received as a gift is also shown as a $5,000 asset if that is the value when acquired. Such donations qualify as voluntary nonexchange transactions. In recording the gift, the city recognizes revenue for the value

---

[15] Governmental Accounting Standards Board, *Codification of Governmental Accounting and Financial Reporting Standards,* as of June 30, 2021, Sec. 1400.109.

of the map but only when all eligibility requirements are met. Until that time, the government reports a liability.[16]

In preparing fund financial statements, if an entrance fee is charged, the City of North might designate the museum as an enterprise fund. If that decision is made, the reporting of these two assets simply follows the same pattern as in government-wide statements.

If the city views the museum as a governmental fund, it reports any such acquisition as an expenditure (rather than as an asset) to reflect the decrease in current financial resources. If obtained by gift, no entry is made within the governmental funds because the amount of current financial resources remains unchanged. The city spent no money or other resources to acquire these maps.

In government-wide financial statements, a theoretical problem arises as to the recognition of such properties, regardless of whether by purchase or by gift. Despite their value, do such items qualify as assets to be reported by a government? A museum will display historical maps, artistic paintings, and the like for the public to view but often does not expect to generate any direct cash inflows or other economic benefit. Does that satisfy the characteristics of an asset? Is a painting by Picasso a reported asset if it merely hangs on a wall so that it can be appreciated by visitors who paid nothing for the privilege?

In response to that question, GASB encourages capitalization of all artworks, historical treasures, and the like as assets. Nevertheless, if all three of the following criteria are met, the recording of such a property as an asset is optional:

1. It is held for public exhibition, education, or research in furtherance of public service rather than for financial gain.
2. It is protected, kept unencumbered, cared for, and preserved.
3. It is subject to an organizational policy that requires the proceeds from sales of collection items to be used to acquire other items for collections.[17] This last requirement ensures that the work is not held for investment purposes.

If these guidelines are met, the artwork or historical treasure provide no direct economic benefit to the government. Although recording the transaction is necessary, recognition of an asset is not required. If this option is taken, the government records an expense in the government-wide statements rather than an asset whether the item is obtained by purchase or by gift. In government-wide statements, the artwork, museum piece, or the like is shown as either an asset or as an expense if these three requirements are met.

In its 2020 government-wide financial statements, the City of Chicago reports works of art and historical collections as assets with a reported value of $48.6 million, although other items of this type are not capitalized. A footnote explains the reporting of these properties.

> The City has a collection of artwork and historical treasures presented for public exhibition and education that are being preserved for future generations. The proceeds from sales of any pieces of the collection are used to purchase other acquisitions. A portion of this collection is not capitalized or depreciated as part of capital assets.

GASB's handling of artwork and historical treasures closely parallels rules established by FASB for private not-for-profit entities. Nevertheless, differences do remain.

One related issue needs to be addressed: the recording of depreciation. Does the map on display in the museum actually depreciate in value over time? Does the *Mona Lisa* have a finite life? The Lascaux cave paintings in France are estimated to be 20,000 years old and are still beautiful.

For works of art or museum artifacts reported as assets, a state or local government records depreciation but only if it deems the asset as "exhaustible"—that is, if its utility will be consumed by display, education, or research. The recording of depreciation is not necessary if the item is judged to be inexhaustible. If properly maintained, many such properties can be considered as inexhaustible assets so that depreciation is allowed but not required.

---

[16] A deferred inflow of resources is recorded rather than a liability if all eligibility requirements have been met except for a time requirement.

[17] GASB, *Codification,* as of June 30, 2021, Sec. 1400.109.

Explain the reporting and possible depreciation of infrastructure assets by state and local governments.

Infrastructure Assets and Depreciation

Governments frequently hold a significant number of infrastructure assets. As mentioned in the previous chapter, infrastructure is a general term for long-lived capital assets that normally are stationary in nature and can be preserved for a significantly greater number of years than most other capital assets. Common examples include roads, bridges, tunnels, lighting systems, curbing, and sidewalks.

At one time in government accounting, the recording of infrastructure items was an optional practice because these properties did not generate revenue in any traditional sense. Now, though, infrastructure costs are recorded as assets in government-wide statements. As of June 30, 2020, the City of Cincinnati, Ohio, listed infrastructure assets, net of accumulated depreciation, of $681.3 million on its government-wide statements. In contrast, for governmental funds, these costs continue to be recorded as expenditures in fund financial statements because both acquisition and construction creates a reduction in current financial resources.

As discussed previously, depreciation is required for all capital assets (such as buildings) that have a finite life. Governments must also record depreciation for capitalized artworks and historical treasures that are deemed to be exhaustible. GASB has debated the need for depreciating infrastructure assets in government-wide financial statements. Is depreciation appropriate for this type of asset? When originally debated, "The responses to the Statement's exposure draft included arguments that infrastructure assets should not be depreciated because they are intended to be preserved in perpetuity."[18]

For example, construction of the Brooklyn Bridge was finished in 1883 at a cost of about $15 million. That piece of infrastructure has operated now for approximately 140 years and, with proper maintenance, might well continue to carry traffic for another 140 years. Much the same can be said of many roads, sidewalks, and the like. With appropriate repair and maintenance, such assets could have lives that are almost indefinite. What expected life should New York City use to depreciate the cost incurred in constructing a street such as Fifth Avenue?

GASB eventually determined that depreciation of infrastructure items was appropriate in government-wide financial statements. Not surprisingly, governments tend to depreciate many infrastructure items over extended periods. The City of Portland, Oregon, with approximately $4.8 billion in infrastructure ($700 million in governmental activities and $4.1 billion in business-type activities), uses lives that range from 20 to 100 years. The City of Portland, Maine, with $266 million in infrastructure ($143 million in governmental activities and $123 million in business-type activities), depreciates this cost over periods from 30 to 67 years.

Because of the questionable need for depreciation for such long-lived assets, GASB did provide a unique alternative to depreciating the cost of eligible infrastructure assets such as the Brooklyn Bridge or Fifth Avenue. This method, known as the *modified approach,* eliminates the need for depreciating infrastructure assets. If specified guidelines are met, a government can choose to expense all maintenance costs each year in lieu of recording depreciation. Additions and improvements must be capitalized, but the cost of maintaining the infrastructure in proper working condition is expensed. Thus, if applied, New York City would expense the amount spent on the repair and other maintenance of Fifth Avenue so that no depreciation of the street's capitalized cost need be recorded. Effectively, proper maintenance of infrastructure assets can extend their lives indefinitely.

Use of the modified approach requires the government to accumulate information about all infrastructure assets that are classified within either a network or a subsystem of a network. For example, all roads could be deemed a network while state roads, rural roads, and interstate highways might make up three separate subsystems of that network. To qualify for the modified approach, the government takes specific steps.

---

[18] Charlotte A. Pryor, "Local Governments and the Modified Approach to Reporting the Cost of Infrastructure," *Government Accountants Journal,* April 1, 2013.

- For eligible assets, the government must establish a minimum acceptable condition level and then documents that this minimum level is being met.
- The government must also have an asset management system in place to monitor the eligible assets. This system assesses the ongoing condition to ensure that the eligible assets are, indeed, operating at the predetermined level. The maintenance system in place keeps the network or subsystem operating adequately.

The City of Los Angeles, California, has adopted the modified approach in reporting all of its bridges. In its annual comprehensive financial report for 2020, the system used by that government is explained as follows. This description does indicate that the city has properly followed the preceding rules.

> The modified approach is used in reporting the City's bridges infrastructure system. A comprehensive bridge database system, the Bridges and Tunnels System, enables the City to track the entire bridge inventory, the structural condition of various bridge elements, and bridge sufficiency ratings. Condition assessments of these structures are completed in a three-year cycle. The latest assessment report was as of December 31, 2019. A system of letter grades identifies the condition of each structure. Letter grades "A" through "D" represent the condition of the structure as Very Good, Good to Fair, Fair to Poor, and Very Poor. "F" rating symbolizes a failed condition where replacement of the structure is necessary. These letter grades are based on sufficiency ratings, or the overall condition of the structure based on the last inspection. It is the City's policy that at least 70% of the bridges are rated "B" or better and that no bridge shall be rated worse than "D." The City performs regular inspection and maintenance of the various structural elements for any defects. Funds for annual estimated inspection, maintenance and repair costs are provided in the City's budget. *Bridges are excluded in the determination of depreciation provisions for capital assets, while preservation and maintenance costs are charged to expense.* [Emphasis added.]

The modified approach provides a method by which governments can avoid depreciating infrastructure assets such as the Brooklyn Bridge that have virtually an unlimited life. The issue is: How many governments will be like the City of Los Angeles and go to the trouble of creating the standards and documentation required by this approach simply to avoid recording depreciation expense? According to one expert in the field, "There are relatively few governmental entities that have adopted the modified approach. Airports, transportation authorities and large transportation departments are really the only ones that I've seen that follow the modified approach."[19]

Annual Comprehensive Financial Report (ACFR)

LO 12-8
Understand the composition of a state or local government's annual comprehensive financial report (ACFR).

Government-wide financial statements and fund financial statements are most often presented to the public by a state or local government as part of its annual comprehensive financial report (ACFR). The ACFR is not limited to these two sets of financial statements. It includes an extensive amount of information about the reporting government. As an example, the ACFR for the City of Orlando, Florida, as of September 30, 2020, reported total assets of $4.0 billion within a document that was approximately 300 pages in length. For comparison, the financial statements for Walmart as of January 31, 2021, showed more than $252 billion in assets but contained only about 30 pages (although the entire Form 10-K that Walmart filed with the SEC for that year was about 100 pages).

The length of the ACFR indicates an attempt to provide a broad range of information to a wide assortment of interested parties. As stated previously, bond investors and taxpayers both want information but not necessarily the same information.

The ACFR for most state and local governments can be found on the internet through a search of the government name along with "ACFR." The document is composed of three broad sections:

1. *Introductory section*—includes a letter of transmittal from appropriate government officials, an organization chart, and a list of principal officers.

[19] Jack Reagan, partner, UHY LLP, Washington, DC, December 28, 2021.

2. *Financial section*—presents the general purpose external financial statements (both government-wide and fund financial statements) and reproduces the independent auditor's report. The ACFR also includes the management's discussion and analysis (MD&A) and other required supplementary information.

3. *Statistical section*—discloses a wide range of data about the government encompassing both financial and nonfinancial information. The statistical facts can be fascinating. In its 2020 ACFR, the City of Buffalo, New York, reports the following for that year (along with considerable other data): number of police officers (746), number of firefighters (724), traffic violations assessed (28,713), recyclables collected (54 tons per day), fire stations (20), fire hydrants (7,994), streetlights (31,935), traffic signals (671), acreage for parks (1,853), street resurfacing (506,304 square yards), and materials used to fill potholes (1,043 tons).

The financial section of a state or local government's ACFR is composed of three distinct sections:

1. Management's discussion and analysis. The MD&A is required supplemental information that "should provide an objective and easily readable analysis of the government's financial activities based on currently known facts, decisions, or conditions. . . . MD&A provides financial managers with the opportunity to present both a short- and a long-term analysis of the government's activities."[20]

2. Financial statements:
   a. Government-wide financial statements.
   b. Fund financial statements.
   c. Notes to the financial statements.

3. Required supplementary information (other than the MD&A). This section includes information required by U.S. GAAP that does not fall within the financial statements or accompanying notes. For example, the City of Orlando presents a comparison of budgetary figures for the city with actual results for each major fund, although a separate statement within the fund financial statements could also have been used for this purpose. Orlando also includes required supplementary information about pensions and postemployment benefits that it provides to former employees. The city presents a schedule of employer contributions, a schedule of investment returns, and a schedule of changes in the net pension liability. That is not required as footnote disclosure but is important to understand the government's pension obligation.

For many readers, one of the most interesting aspects of the financial section is the MD&A because it provides a relatively clear description of the past, future, and present of the government's financial situation and operations. As an illustration, the ACFR for the fiscal year ending June 30, 2021, for the City of Raleigh, North Carolina, includes a 16-page management's discussion and analysis that contains information such as the following:

- "The current year revenue increase was driven primarily by strong sales tax collections and development user fees activity, which more than offset the decline in parks and recreation revenues. Current year expenses increased moderately and are in-line with expected operating increases."
- "Those who directly benefited from governmental service-fee based programs, such as ones involving parks, recreation and cultural resources and development and inspection related fees, paid $39.3 million in charges for those services."
- "The largest business-type operation is the City's water and sewer utility. Water and sewer utility operations are supported by financial models to ensure both operational and capital infrastructure needs are maintained and properly funded. Water and sewer operating revenue of $271.0 million in 2020–21 reflects an increase of 2.7% from the prior year."

[20] GASB, *Codification*, as of June 30, 2021, Sec. 2200.106.

The Primary Government and Component Units

Primary Government

It always should be possible in the public sector to trace financial accountability to elected officials. Consistent with this presumption of the ultimate financial accountability of elected officials, a typical state or local government financial report is built around the core of a single government with an elected governing body, known as the primary government.[21]

Each state and local government prepares and distributes an ACFR if it qualifies as a reporting entity. Officials must identify the exact composition of that reporting entity because it is not always easy to discern. The process begins with a primary government such as a town, city, county, or state. A primary government has (1) separate legal status, (2) an elected governing board, and (3) fiscal independence. Beyond that, each reporting entity also includes all organizations, agencies, offices, departments, and the like that are not legally separate from the primary government.

Complications can arise because many of the activities that interact closely with a primary government are legally separate. For example, an agency to provide job training might have its own incorporation but still be within the purview of city officials. Should a primary government include such outside functions as part of the reporting entity and, therefore, as a part of its financial statements? With a for-profit entity, that question is less complicated. Except in unusual cases, a business enterprise such as IBM or PepsiCo consolidates all separate entities over which it holds control through majority ownership. Control is not as clearly delineated in state and local governmental accounting. Should an outside activity be included within an ACFR even if it is legally separate from the primary government, and if so, what reporting is appropriate?

The almost unlimited number of functions that can be connected to a primary government raises problems for accountants who are attempting to outline the parameters of the entity being reported. Organizations such as turnpike commissions, port authorities, public housing boards, and downtown development commissions are commonplace for many cities and counties. Such operations are usually established to focus attention on specific issues or problems. The primary government might well have created many of these activities but structured them as legally separate organizations.

As an example, notes to the financial statements in the 2020 ACFR for the City of Boston identify four discretely presented component units (Boston Planning & Development Agency, Economic Development Industrial Corporation, Boston Public Health Commission, and Trustees of the Public Library of the City of Boston) and three blended component units (the Boston Retirement System as well as the Dudley Square Realty Corporation and Ferdinand Building Development Corporation). The city also acknowledges three related organizations (Boston Housing Authority, Boston Industrial Development Finance Authority, and Boston Water and Sewer Commission).

- Discretely presented component units?
- Blended component units?
- Related organizations?

How do each of these separate entities relate to the primary government (the City of Boston), and what effect do they have on the financial reporting for the city?

Identifying Component Units

In the June 30, 2020, Management's Discussion and Analysis section of the ACFR for the City of Atlanta, Georgia, the composition of the reporting entity is clearly described as follows.

"The government-wide financial statements include not only the City itself (known as the primary government), but also the legally separate Atlanta Fulton County Recreation Authority and the Atlanta Development Authority (doing business as Invest Atlanta), both of which the

---

[21] Stephen J. Gauthier, *Governmental Accounting, Auditing, and Financial Reporting* (Chicago: Government Finance Officers Association, 2012), p. 73.

City is financially accountable. Financial information for these component units is reported separately from the financial information presented for the primary government. The Atlanta Housing Opportunity, Inc. is presented as a component unit, however their financial statements are blended with the primary government. Other blended component units of the City include Atlanta Public Safety, Judicial Facilities Authority and Solid Waste Management Authority."

When producing an ACFR, the major requirement for inclusion as a component unit is the financial accountability of the primary government. "Financial reporting based on accountability should enable the financial statement reader to focus on the body of organizations that are related by a common thread of accountability to the constituent citizenry."[22] When elected officials of a primary government are financially accountable for an outside organization, it is labeled a component unit. Such legally separate activities are so closely connected to the primary government that omission from the financial statements cannot be justified. They are "related by a common thread of accountability."

For that reason, the ACFR for the City of Atlanta includes the Atlanta Fulton County Recreation Authority and those other separate activities. They qualify as component units. They are not part of the primary government but are still reported in the ACFR to reflect the City of Atlanta's financial accountability.

Because of the potential effect on the financial statements of a primary government, the determination of component units is of significant importance. GASB established two sets of criteria to indicate the presence of financial accountability. If an activity meets either one, it qualifies as a component unit to be reported within the ACFR of the primary government. Furthermore, a government has the right to include a legally separate entity in this way, even if neither criteria is met, if officials believe exclusion will be misleading to the users of the financial statements.

Criterion 1 for Financial Accountability

An outside entity (such as the Atlanta Fulton County Recreation Authority) qualifies as a component unit if it fiscally depends on the primary government (the City of Atlanta). *Fiscal dependency* means that the separate entity cannot do one or more of the following without approval of the primary government:

- adopt its own budget,
- levy taxes or set rates, or
- issue bonded debt.

This criterion also requires that the primary government and the component unit must be financially interdependent (a relationship exists that creates a potential financial benefit or burden between the two).

Criterion 2 for Financial Accountability

Two separate connections are necessary to establish this criterion for financial accountability. First, officials of the primary government must appoint a voting majority of the governing board of the separate organization. Second, either the primary government must be able to impose its will on this governing board or the separate organization provides a financial benefit or imposes a financial burden on the primary government.

Because of the importance of this identification process, aspects of these criteria need to be explained in more depth to ensure proper application.

Voting Majority of the Governing Board The primary government's authority to elect a voting majority of the separate entity must be substantive. If, for example, the primary government simply confirms choices made by other parties, then financial accountability is not present. Likewise, financial accountability does not result when the primary government merely selects the governing board from a limited slate of candidates (such as picking three individuals from an approved slate of five). To meet this provision of the second criterion, officials of the primary government must have actual responsibility for appointing a voting majority of the board.

---

[22] GASB, *Codification*, as of June 30, 2021, Sec. 2100.102.

Imposition of the Primary Government's Will on the Governing Board   Such power exists if the primary government can significantly influence programs, projects, activities, or the level of services the separate organization provides. This degree of influence is present if the primary government is able to remove an appointed board member at will, modify or approve budgets, override decisions of the board, modify or approve rate or fee changes, or hire or dismiss individuals responsible for day-to-day operations. Such power shows the primary government's true level of authority.

Financial Benefit or Financial Burden on the Primary Government   This level of financial connection exists between the primary government and any outside organization if the government is entitled to the organization's resources, the government is legally obligated to finance any deficits or provide support, or the government is responsible for the organization's debts.

Reporting Component Units

After being identified, component units are reported by a primary government in one of two ways:

- discretely presented or
- blended.

If discretely presented, financial information about the component units is presented on the far right side of the government-wide statements. For example, as of June 30, 2020, the government-wide statements in the ACFR for the City of Detroit, Michigan, show that the primary government holds total assets and deferred outflows of resources of more than $6.2 billion. The city's discretely presented component units appearing just to the right of the primary government report similar accounts totaling $1.8 billion.

According to the notes to Detroit's financial statements, these component unit figures were gathered from 14 separate organizations:

- Detroit Brownfield Redevelopment Authority.
- Detroit Public Library.
- Detroit Transportation Corporation.
- Detroit Housing Commission.
- Downtown Development Authority.
- Eastern Market Corporation.
- Economic Development Corporation.
- Local Development Finance Authority.
- Museum of African American History.
- Detroit Land Bank Authority.
- Eight Mile/Woodward Corridor Improvement Authority.
- Detroit Employment Solutions Corporation.
- Community Education Commission.
- Joint Employment and Procurement Advisory Board.

GASB allows an alternative placement for component units within the ACFR. A primary government can include a component unit as an actual part of the reporting government as if it were another fund. This process is referred to as *blending*. Although legally separate, a component unit can be so intertwined with the primary government that inclusion is necessary to present the financial information for the local or state government in an appropriate fashion.

The blending of a component unit is usually at the discretion of government officials but the process is required if the separate entity's debt will be repaid entirely, or almost entirely, from resources of the primary government. Beyond the discretely presented units previously listed, the City of Detroit blends three of its component units: the Detroit Building Authority, the Greater Detroit Resource Recovery Authority, and the Public Lighting Authority. This inclusion with the primary government is justified in the city's ACFR, "Blended component

? Discussion Question

IS IT PART OF THE COUNTY?

Harland County is in a financially distressed area within the state of Missouri. In hopes of enticing new business to the county, the state legislature appropriates $3 million to start an industrial development commission. The federal government provides an additional $1 million. The state appoints 15 individuals to a board to oversee the operations of this commission. Harland County officials name 5 additional members. The commission begins operations by raising funds from local citizens and businesses. During the past 12 months, it received $700,000 in donations and pledges. The county government provides clerical assistance and allows the commission to use one wing of a county office building for its headquarters. The Harland County government must approve the commission's annual operating budget. The county will also cover any deficits that might occur.

During the current period, the commission spent $2.4 million and achieved notable success. Several large companies recently began to explore the possibility of opening manufacturing plants in the county.

Harland County is currently preparing its annual comprehensive financial report. Should the county's ACFR include the revenues, expenditures, assets, expenses, and liabilities of the industrial development commission? Is it a fund within the county's primary government, a component unit, or a related organization?

Is the industrial development commission a component unit of the State of Missouri? How should its activities be presented in the state's annual comprehensive financial report?

units, although legally separate entities, are, in substance, part of the City's operations. Thus, blended component units are appropriately presented as funds of the City."

The City of Detroit also lists several related organizations. They are not closely tied to the primary government so less reporting is necessary. The primary government is accountable only because it appoints a voting majority of the outside organization's governing board. Fiscal dependency is not present. The primary government cannot impose its will on the board and does not gather financial benefits or burdens from the relationship. Consequently, the separate organization is not a component unit. For a related organization, the primary government must still identify the nature of the relationship. The City of Detroit discloses two related organizations: the Detroit Historical Society and the Detroit Zoological Society.

Special-Purpose Governments

Most individuals think of primary governments in terms of general-purpose governments such as states, cities, counties, towns, and the like. Nevertheless, numerous special-purpose governments also exist around the country. As noted at the beginning of the previous chapter, more than 50,000 school systems and other special-purpose districts exist across the United States. Their qualifications as primary governments can be seen in a note to the 2020 ACFR for the Atlanta Independent School System.

> The Atlanta Independent School System (School System or the District) was established by the Georgia State Legislature and is composed of nine publicly elected members serving four-year terms. The School System has the authority to approve its own budget and to provide for the levy of taxes to cover the cost of operations and maintenance and to cover debt service payments. Additionally, the School System has decision-making authority, the power to approve selection of management personnel, the ability to significantly influence operations, and primary accountability for fiscal matters. Accordingly, the School System is a primary government and consists of all the organizations that compose its legal entity.

Special-purpose governments carry out only a single function or a limited number of functions. Common examples include public school districts, colleges and universities, water utilities, hospitals, transit authorities, and library services. In deciding the appropriate method of reporting, officials must address one central question: Is the operation truly a special-purpose government or merely a part of a larger government (such as a city or county) so that it should be reported as a fund or a component unit? Or, perhaps, it is not a government entity at all but rather a nongovernmental not-for-profit organization with accounting rules that will be explained in the subsequent chapter.

As shown by the note in the ACFR for the Atlanta Independent School System, an activity or function is deemed a special-purpose government if it meets the following criteria:

1. Has a separately elected governing body.
2. Is legally independent, which can be demonstrated by having corporate powers such as the right to sue and be sued as well as the right to buy, sell, and lease property in its own name.
3. Is fiscally independent of any state or local government. As mentioned previously, an activity is normally considered to be fiscally independent if its leadership can determine its operating budget, levy taxes or set rates, or issue bonded debt without having to seek approval of an outside party.

A school system or other activity that satisfies all three of these requirements is reported as a special-purpose government that produces its own ACFR. If an activity fails to meet any one of these criteria, its financial affairs are likely to be maintained within the general fund or special revenue funds of a state or municipal government.

Acquisitions, Mergers, and Transfers of Operations

LO 12-9

Explain the makeup of a primary government and its relationship to component units and related organizations.

With so many general-purpose governments, special-purpose governments, component units, and related organizations, combinations and realignment transactions are common.

- A city government might take over operations of a homeless shelter from a not-for-profit entity.
- A toll road operated as a special-purpose government might be acquired by a local county.
- Two independent school systems might be brought together to create more efficient operations.

After voters approved a ballot question last month approving the consolidation of the Atwood-Hammond and Arthur school districts, school officials, teachers and students have begun the process of merging the two districts into a single entity. Atwood-Hammond Superintendent Kenny Schwengel said the two school districts will spend the 2013–14 school year getting ready for the merger, which takes effect on July 1, 2014.[23]

In accounting for state and local governments, a combination can be reported as either a merger or an acquisition.

- GASB views a combination as a *merger* if two legally separate entities are brought together to form a new entity and no significant consideration is exchanged. The combination is still a merger even if one of these entities ceases to exist while the other continues to function. The combination of two agencies or two school systems might meet this criterion. In a merger, because of the lack of paid consideration, the net carrying values for all assets, deferred outflows of resources, liabilities, and deferred inflows of resources are simply combined. Account balances are not changed or updated. Additional accounts are neither created nor recognized as a result of this type of combination. Account balances are literally merged.
- Reporting an *acquisition* is quite different. In an acquisition, consideration is exchanged. For example, the cash purchase of a special-purpose government toll road by a county government is an acquisition if the toll road ceases to exist as a separate entity and becomes

[23] Tim Mitchell, "School Districts Prepare for Merger," *News-Gazette,* May 20, 2013.

part of the county government. In government-wide financial statements, the acquiring government records all acquired assets, deferred outflows of resources, liabilities, and deferred inflows of resources at acquisition value (other than a few specific exceptions such as landfills). GASB defines acquisition value as the market-based entry price—the amount that the government would pay to acquire or discharge each item through individual transactions.

As with for-profit transactions, an acquiring entity often must pay more than the total acquisition values assigned to the various assets, liabilities, and deferrals. In for-profit accounting—as discussed in prior chapters of this textbook—any excess payment is reported as the asset "goodwill."

On government-wide financial statements, any consideration paid in excess of acquisition value is reported initially as a deferred outflow of resources on the statement of net position. The balance is then written off to expense over a period of time based on factors such as the service life of capital assets, technology available, and contracts acquired.

When an acquisition takes place, fund financial statements for the governmental funds record any acquired current financial resources and the claims against those resources. That approach is in line with the usual reporting of those funds. Once again, acquisition value is applied to each balance. The government also records any reduction in current financial resources caused by the payment to create the acquisition. Fund balances are adjusted to reflect the net change.

To illustrate, assume cash of $4 million is paid by a large city to acquire an outside employment agency that holds (1) current financial resources with a total acquisition value of $1 million and (2) capital assets with a total acquisition fair value of $2 million.

In government-wide financial statements, current assets are reported by the city as $1 million, capital assets are reported as $2 million, and deferred outflow of resources is recognized at the $1 million difference. Cash is reduced as a result of the payment.

In fund financial statements, cash is reduced by $4 million with the acquired current financial resources recorded at $1 million. Capital assets are not reported on fund statements for governmental funds. To reflect the $3 million difference, the government reduces the fund balance for the acquiring fund.

Occasionally, an entity will convey one of its activities to another entity but not the entire operation. A government might transfer the operations of a soup kitchen to a local charity. A not-for-profit entity might transfer a homeless shelter to the local city. If a government receives an operation purely by transfer, all assets, deferred outflows of resources, liabilities, and deferred inflows of resources are recorded at the previous net carrying amounts. Conversely, if a state or local government is turning over an activity to another party, a gain or loss on disposal is reported depending on whether any resources are received in return.

<table>
<tr><td>**LO 12-10**</td></tr>
<tr><td>Describe the physical structure of a complete set of government-wide financial statements and a complete set of fund financial statements.</td></tr>
</table>

Government-Wide and Fund Financial Statements Illustrated

General-purpose financial statements are at the core of a governmental reporting entity's ACFR. These statements consist of government-wide financial statements and fund financial statements.

- Government-wide statements present financial information for both governmental activities and business-type activities (and often discretely presented component units). These statements measure economic resources and utilize accrual accounting.

- In contrast, separate fund financial statements are created for (1) the governmental funds, (2) the proprietary funds, and (3) the fiduciary funds. No fund financial statement reflects the government as a whole. The measurement focus and timing of recognition depend on the fund in question. For governmental funds, the current financial resources measurement focus is used with modified accrual accounting. Both proprietary funds and fiduciary funds apply accrual accounting to report all economic resources.

Four of these statements were outlined briefly in the previous chapter to introduce their basic structure. Now that a deeper understanding of state and local government accounting has been established, government-wide and fund financial statements can be examined in more detail.[24]

Statement of Net Position—Government-Wide Financial Statements

Exhibit 12.1 presents a hypothetical version of the June 30, 2024, statement of net position for the City of Eastern South. As a government-wide financial statement, it reports the economic resources of the government as a whole (except for the fiduciary funds, which are not included because the resources must be used for a purpose outside the government).

Please note several aspects of the statement of net position:

- The measurement focus is on the economic resources controlled by the government. Thus, all assets, including capital assets, are reported. Noncurrent liabilities are presented for the same reason.

- Capital assets (other than land, inexhaustible works of art, construction in progress, and infrastructure assets if the modified approach is applied) are reported net of accumulated depreciation. Other than these exceptions, depreciation of capital assets is recognized in the government-wide statements. (See Point A.)

- As discussed in the previous chapter, categories titled Deferred Outflows of Resources and Deferred Inflows of Resources are included on this statement. These sections provide a location to report balances that do not qualify as either assets or liabilities in state and local government accounting.

- The primary government is divided into governmental activities and business-type activities. Governmental funds are reported as governmental activities, whereas enterprise funds comprise most, if not all, of the business-type activities. Even though recorded as proprietary funds, internal service funds are frequently classified within the governmental activities. That is appropriate when those services are primarily for the benefit of activities within the governmental funds. For example, if a vehicle maintenance facility works mainly for the local school system, it is a proprietary fund that would be included in governmental activities. A vehicle maintenance facility that serves an enterprise fund such as a bus line is still a proprietary fund but should be reported within the business-type activities.

- The internal balances shown in the asset section (Point B) reflect receivables and payables between the governmental activities and the business-type activities. These internal balances have no financial effect outside the government and are offset so that no change results in the totals reported for the primary government.

- Discretely presented component units are grouped and shown to the far right side of the statement (Point C) so that their reported amounts do not affect the primary government figures. In contrast, any blended component units are included within either the governmental activities or the business-type activities as if they were individual funds of the government. As seen in the final column of Exhibit 12.1, this city has one discretely presented component unit: the Eastern South Regional Art Space. The government might also have blended component units, but readers must check the disclosure notes to ascertain their presence.

- As the Net Position section shows, several monetary amounts have been restricted for capital projects, debt service, and the like. Restrictions are identified in this manner only if usage of those resources has been designated (1) by external parties such as creditors, grantors, or other external party; or (2) as a result of laws that have been passed through constitutional provisions or enabling legislation.

Statement of Activities—Government-Wide Financial Statements

The statement of activities presents a wide array of information about the various functions of a state or local government. As shown in the statement for the City of Eastern South in

---

[24] The examples presented here illustrate the government-wide financial statements and the fund financial statements for both governmental funds and proprietary funds. Because fund financial statements for the fiduciary funds are more specialized, they have been omitted.

EXHIBIT 12.1 **Government-Wide Financial Statements—Statement of Net Position**

CITY OF EASTERN SOUTH
Statement of Net Position
June 30, 2024
(in thousands)

	Primary Government			Component Unit—Eastern South Regional Art Space ©
	Governmental Activities	Business-Type Activities	Total	
Assets				
Cash and investments	$ 232,450	$ 149,333	$ 381,783	$ 25,735
Receivables, net	219,435	59,812	279,247	–0–
Internal balances Ⓑ	23,876	(23,876)	–0–	–0–
Inventories and supplies	11,654	12,922	24,576	2,159
Prepaid items	5,075	2,117	7,192	822
Land and other capital assets not depreciated	250,883	165,873	416,756	1,451
Other capital assets, net of depreciation Ⓐ	821,490	688,523	1,510,013	11,434
Total assets	$1,564,863	$1,054,704	$2,619,567	$41,601
Deferred outflows of resources				
Unamortized excess cost of entity acquisition	$ 59,447	$ –0–	$ 59,447	$ –0–
Liabilities				
Accounts payable	$ 23,775	$ 14,315	$ 38,090	$ 5,076
Other liabilities and unearned revenue	30,766	5,225	35,991	432
Bonds payable—current	87,922	12,885	100,807	3,124
Landfill closure obligation	–0–	9,078	9,078	–0–
Bonds payable—noncurrent	289,217	221,441	510,658	6,780
Net pension liability	111,000	–0–	111,000	–0–
Lease payable—noncurrent	24,548	21,669	46,217	2,277
Total liabilities	$ 567,228	$ 284,613	$ 851,841	$17,689
Deferred inflows of resources				
Unavailable property tax collections	$ 26,500	$ –0–	$ 26,500	$ –0–
Net Position				
Invested in capital assets, net of related debt	$ 811,487	$ 723,656	$1,535,143	$ 872
Restricted for:				
Capital projects	125,769	19,774	145,543	5,045
Debt service	2,355	1,056	3,411	84
Other	29,267	–0–	29,267	–0–
Unrestricted	61,704	25,605	87,309	17,911
Total net position	$1,030,582 Ⓨ	$ 770,091	$1,800,673	$23,912

Exhibit 12.2, the same general classification system of governmental activities, business-type activities, and component units used in Exhibit 12.1 forms the structural basis for reporting. Nevertheless, the format here is more complex and requires close analysis. It is often studied from left to right and then from top to bottom.

- The government presents its operating expenses in the first column (Point D). The balances are not classified according to individual causes such as salaries, rent, depreciation, or insurance. Instead, expenses are shown by function: general government, police, fire, general services, and the like. This approach is likely to be more relevant to the needs of the people reading the statements. "As a minimum, governments should report direct

EXHIBIT 12.2 Government-Wide Financial Statements—Statement of Activities

CITY OF EASTERN SOUTH
Statement of Activities
For the Fiscal Year Ended June 30, 2024
(in thousands)

Functions/Programs	Operating Expenses Ⓓ	Program Revenues ⒻCharge for Services	Program Revenues ⒻOperating Grants and Contributions	Program Revenues ⒻCapital Grants and Contributions	Net (Expenses) Revenues and Changes in Net PositionPrimary GovernmentGovernmental Activities	Net (Expenses) Revenues and Changes in Net PositionPrimary GovernmentBusiness-type Activities	Net (Expenses) Revenues and Changes in Net PositionPrimary GovernmentTotal	Net (Expenses) Revenues and Changes in Net PositionComponent Unit—Eastern South Regional Art Space Total
Primary government:								
Governmental activities								
General government	$ (28,055)	$ 6,554	$ 5,472	$ 2,384	$ (13,645)		$ (13,645)	
Police	(103,465)	17,980	13,256	6,747	(65,482) Ⓗ		(65,482)	
Fire	(97,687)	5,306	19,821	23,063	(49,497)		(49,497)	
Transportation	(96,088)	31,365	355	16,984 Ⓖ	(47,384)		(47,384)	
Economic development	(5,563)	898	143	1,875	(2,647)		(2,647)	
Parks and recreation	(64,725)	17,168	16,778	4,221	(26,558)		(26,558)	
Neighborhood services	(3,965)	649	132	2,993	(191)		(191)	
Library	(17,744)	5,365	2,784	2,257	(7,338)		(7,338)	
Interest on noncurrent debt	(23,550) Ⓔ	–0–	–0–	–0–	(23,550)		(23,550)	
Total governmental activities	$ (440,842)	$ 85,285	$ 58,741	$60,524	$(236,292) Ⓘ		$(236,292)	
Business-type activities								
Water	$ (39,273)	$ 50,877	$ 121	$ 6,339		$18,064 Ⓙ	$ 18,064	
Sewer	(12,868)	11,836	488	2,451		1,907	1,907	
Parking	(11,776)	25,990	1,342	844		16,400	16,400	
Others	(8,074)	795	5,434	6,009		4,164	4,164	
Total business-type activities	(71,991)	89,498	7,385	15,643		40,535 Ⓚ	40,535	
Total primary government	$(512,833)	$174,783	$66,126	$76,167	$(236,292)	$40,535	$(195,757)	
Component unit:								
Eastern South Regional Art Space	$ (8,128)	$ 2,896	$ 1,676	$ –0–				$(3,556) Ⓛ

EXHIBIT 12.2 (Continued)

CITY OF EASTERN SOUTH
Statement of Activities
For the Fiscal Year Ended June 30, 2024
(in thousands)

Functions/Programs	Program Revenues (F)				Net (Expenses) Revenues and Changes in Net Position			
					Primary Government			Component Unit—Eastern South Regional Art Space Total
	Operating Expenses (D)	Charge for Services	Operating Grants and Contributions	Capital Grants and Contributions	Governmental Activities	Business-type Activities	Total	
General revenues								
Property taxes					$ 111,762 (M)	$ –0–	$ 111,762	
Income taxes					49,079	–0–	49,079	
Sales taxes					43,809	–0–	43,809	
Unrestricted grants					17,227	–0–	17,227	
Gain on sale of capital asset					–0–	556	556	
Investment earnings					13,244	3,101	16,345	$ 279
Transfers					18,633	(18,633)	–0– (N)	
Total general revenues, transfers, and others					$ 253,754	$ (14,976)	$ 238,778	$ 279
Change in net position					$ 17,462 (T)	$ 25,559	$ 43,021	$ (3,277)
Net position, beginning of year					$1,013,120	$744,532	$1,757,652	$27,189
Net position, end of year					$1,030,582	$770,091	$1,800,673	$23,912

expenses for each function. Direct expenses are those that are specifically associated with a service, program, or department and, thus, are clearly identifiable to a particular function."[25] Expenses are shown in this statement for governmental activities, business-type activities, and discretely presented component units.

- Interest expense on general long-term debt is normally considered an indirect expense because borrowed money can benefit many government activities. Nevertheless, it is often a large monetary amount with significant informational value. Furthermore, it can be difficult to allocate in a logical way among different activities. For these reasons, state and local governments can report interest expense as shown in this example (Point E) as a separate "function."

- After operating expenses have been reported in the first column, related program revenues are listed in the next three columns (Point F). Program revenues are derived by the function itself or from outsiders (through grants or gifts) seeking to reduce the government's cost for providing a service or benefit. Program revenues are different from general government revenues (such as property and sales taxes) that are reported near the bottom of the statement. As shown in Exhibit 12.2, program revenues are usually classified within three categories:

  1. *Charges for services.* For example, a monthly charge is normally assessed for water service. Therefore, this first business-type activity shows earning nearly $50.9 million in program revenues. In contrast, because of their public service nature, most government functions generate only small amounts of revenue from sources such as parking meter fees, fines for speeding tickets, concessions at parks, and the like.

  2. *Operating grants and contributions.* This column reports resources received from outside grants and similar sources designated for some type of operating purpose. For example, the police department is shown here as having approximately $13.3 million in operating grants and contributions during the year. That money might have been specified for officers' salaries.

  3. *Capital grants and contributions.* This column presents outside grants and similar sources designated by the donor for capital asset additions (rather than operations). As an example for the City of Eastern South, more than $16.9 million in capital grants and contributions came in to support the transportation function (Point G). Perhaps the city received grant funding to assist in the acquisition of electric busses.

- After operating expenses have been assigned along with related program revenues, the statement of activities shows a net (expense) or revenue for each function. This figure is an important measure of the financial cost (or benefit) of each of the various government functions. For example, in Exhibit 12.2, the police incurred $103.5 million in operating expenses but also generated enough charges, grants, and contributions so that (at Point H) taxpayers only had to bear a financial burden of roughly $65.5 million for police protection. That cost is significant information for citizens. Are they satisfied with that level of service? Do they wish that some of that money had been spent in other ways? In contrast, the water system reported operating expenses of $39.3 million. Because of user charges, grants, and contributions, this business-type activity generated net revenues of approximately $18.1 million (see Point I) as a financial benefit for the government.

- All governmental activities are combined to report net expenses of $236.3 million (Point J). In contrast, business-type activities generated total net revenues of approximately $40.5 million (Point K). The one component unit reports net expenses for the year of $3.6 million (Point L). The financial cost or benefit from each government function is evident. Such information enables citizens to be informed about the cost of operating the government and the allocation of financial resources.

- Reading down the statement, general revenues are reported next as additions to either the governmental activities, business-type activities, or component units. All taxes are general revenues because they do not reflect a direct charge for services. The government obtains this money from the population as a whole. Property taxes of nearly $112 million are shown (Point M) as the largest revenue source. Citizens pay that money in order for the

---

[25] GASB, *Codification,* as of June 30, 2021, Sec. 2200.129.

government to cover the costs of the various benefits and activities provided by the City of Eastern South. Significant amounts were also collected as income taxes and sales taxes.

- Transfers of $18.6 million between governmental activities and business-type activities are also shown within the general revenues because they affect both groups. Nevertheless, these inflows and outflows are offset to indicate that no financial effect is created on the total figures reported for the primary government (Point N).

Balance Sheet—Governmental Funds—Fund Financial Statements

Switching now to the fund financial statements reported by the City of Eastern South, Exhibit 12.3 presents the balance sheet for the governmental funds. This statement reports only current financial resources (along with supplies and prepaid items) and claims to those current financial resources. It was prepared using modified accrual accounting for timing purposes. This fund-based statement reflects just the governmental funds. No proprietary funds, discretely presented component units, or fiduciary funds are included. Several parts of this statement should be noted.

- Separate columns are shown for the general fund and any other fund that qualifies as major. The city identifies two other funds as major. The Highway 61 Construction Fund is a major capital projects fund. The Educational Services Fund is a major special revenue fund. Remaining governmental funds that are not considered major are combined to be reported as Other Governmental Funds.
- The balance sheet reports no capital assets or long-term debts simply because they are neither current financial resources nor claims to current financial resources.
- The Fund Balances figures (Point O) indicate the amount of current financial resources that are nonspendable, restricted, committed, assigned, and unassigned. The meaning of these categories was discussed in the previous chapter.
- The Total Fund Balances figure for the governmental funds of $319.2 million (Point P) is significantly different from the $1.0 billion total net position (Point Y) reported for governmental activities in the statement of net position (Exhibit 12.1). To explain that large disparity, the government presents a reconciliation along with the balance sheet. This reconciliation starts with the total fund balance figure (Point P) and describes individual differences with the total net position amount (Point Y). For example, this reconciliation might look something like the following for the City of Eastern South. Note the reason for each line item and consider whether this inclusion should have been anticipated. Any direct comparison of the two statements is difficult because of the inclusion of the internal service funds within the governmental activities. The accounts of the internal service fund can affect virtually every balance in the governmental activities.

Reconciliation of the Balance Sheet **Governmental Funds to the Governmental** **Activities in the Statement of Net Position** **June 30, 2024** **(in thousands)**	
Total fund balance for governmental funds, June 30, 2020, as reported on balance sheet	$ 319,200
Capital assets reported by governmental activities but not reported in governmental funds.	1,021,800
Bonds payable reported by governmental activities but not reported in governmental funds.	(422,650)
Other assets and liabilities reported by governmental activities but not reported in governmental funds	(43,866)
Revenues reported by governmental activities but not reported in governmental funds because they are not available	32,845
Internal service funds reported by governmental activities but not reported in governmental funds	123,253
Total net position, governmental activities, June 30, 2020, as reported in statement of net position.	$1,030,582

EXHIBIT 12.3 Fund Financial Statements—Balance Sheet for the Governmental Funds

CITY OF EASTERN SOUTH
Governmental Funds
Balance Sheet
June 30, 2024
(in thousands)

	General Fund	Highway 61 Construction	Educational Services	Other Governmental Funds	Total Governmental Funds
Assets:					
Cash and investments	$111,673	$87,056	$11,908	$10,905	$221,542
Receivables, net					
Taxes	53,875	–0–	17,854	–0–	71,729
Accounts	108,654	–0–	–0–	–0–	108,654
Inventory of supplies	3,222	2,076	3,112	2,175	10,585
Prepaid Items	887	1,015	1,322	556	3,780
Total assets	$278,311	$90,147	$34,196	$13,636	$416,290
Liabilities:					
Accounts payable	$ 21,659	$ 776	$ 452	$ 298	$ 23,185
Accrued liabilities	7,174	323	2,572	1,963	12,032
Other claims to financial resources	1,128	1,733	–0–	312	3,173
Bonds currently due	25,000	–0–	7,200	–0–	32,200
Total liabilities	$ 54,961	$ 2,832	$10,224	$ 2,573	$ 70,590
Deferred inflows of resources:					
Unavailable property tax collections	$ 26,500	$ –0–	$ –0–	$ –0–	$ 26,500
Total liabilities and deferred inflows of resources	$ 81,461	$ 2,832	$10,224	$ 2,573	$ 97,090
Fund balances: Ⓒ					
Nonspendable	$ 11,465	$ 3,091	$ 4,434	$ 2,989	$ 21,979
Restricted	46,717	–0–	19,538	875	67,130
Committed	2,044	1,159	–0–	993	4,196
Assigned	35,009	83,065	–0–	6,206	124,280
Unassigned	101,615	–0–	–0–	–0–	101,615
Total fund balances	$196,850	$87,315	$23,972	$11,063	$319,200 Ⓟ
Total liabilities, deferred inflows of resources, and fund balances	$278,311	$90,147	$34,196	$13,636	$416,290

Statement of Revenues, Expenditures, and Other Changes in Fund Balances—Governmental Funds—Fund Financial Statements

Exhibit 12.4 presents the statement of revenues, expenditures, and other changes in fund balances for the governmental funds of the City of Eastern South. Once again, details for the general fund appear in a separate column along with each of the other major funds previously identified. Figures for all remaining nonmajor funds are accumulated and shown together.

In examining Exhibit 12.4, note the following:

- Because the government focuses here on measuring current financial resources, expenditures (Point Q) rather than expenses are reported. For example, Capital Outlay is presented as a reduction in resources rather than as the acquisition of an asset. Similarly, Debt Service—Principal is an expenditure instead of a decrease in long-term liabilities.
- The government applies the modified accrual method of accounting for timing purposes. Thus, reported amounts will be different from those previously shown under accrual accounting. For example, property taxes are reported here as $107.2 million but as $111.8 million in Exhibit 12.2.
- At Point R, Exhibit 12.4 presents other financing sources and uses to reflect the financial effect of the issuance of long-term debt and transfers made between the funds. In those cases, the amount of current financial resources change but no revenues or expenditures take place. Because the fund financial statements focus on individual activities rather than government-wide figures, no elimination of the transfers is made. They do affect the individual funds.

Another reconciliation is needed to explain the difference that exists between the amounts reported in the statement of revenues, expenditures, and other changes in fund balances and the statement of activities. At Point S, Exhibit 12.4 indicates that the fund balances for the governmental funds increased during the period by more than $24.8 million. In Exhibit 12.2, Point T reports an increase in the net position of the governmental activities by only $17.5 million. A $7.3 million difference exists between two figures that sound alike. To avoid confusion, the government must present a reconciliation.

Although not included here, this reconciliation begins with the change in the total fund balances and makes all necessary adjustments to arrive at the reported change in net position. Those changes often include

- The acquisition of capital assets during the period that will decrease the fund balance because current financial resources are used but not the government's net position.
- The recording of depreciation that decreases the city's net position but has no effect on current financial resources.
- The recording of any revenues and expenses that do not affect current financial resources but do change the net position of the government.
- The issuance of long-term debt that increases the city's current financial resources but not its net position.
- The inclusion of any internal service funds within the governmental activities although they are proprietary funds and not governmental funds.

Statement of Net Position—Proprietary Funds—Fund Financial Statements

The assets and liabilities of the City of Eastern South's proprietary funds, as reported in the fund financial statements, are presented in Exhibit 12.5. This statement shows individual information about three major enterprise funds, with a single column for the summation of all other enterprise funds. The statement then provides a combined total for the enterprise funds as a whole. Because of their size, specific information is made available here for the water fund, sewer fund, and parking fund.

In examining Exhibit 12.5, note several important features:

- This fund financial statement combines and exhibits all internal service funds (Point U) because they are classified as proprietary funds. In the government-wide financial

EXHIBIT 12.4   Fund Financial Statements—Statement of Revenues, Expenditures, and Other Changes in Fund Balances

CITY OF EASTERN SOUTH
Governmental Funds
Statement of Revenues, Expenditures, and Other Changes in Fund Balance
For the Fiscal Year Ended June 30, 2024 (in thousands)

	General Fund	Highway 61 Construction	Educational Services	Other Governmental Funds	Total Governmental Funds
Revenues:					
Property taxes	$ 99,737	$ –0–	$ 7,500	$ –0–	$ 107,237
Income taxes	43,556	–0–	–0–	–0–	43,556
Sales taxes	38,760	5,000	–0–	–0–	43,760
Charges for services	61,223	–0–	3,327	1,196	65,746
Fines and penalties	2,657	–0–	–0–	312	2,969
Grants and contributions	87,332	17,901	9,448	1,323	116,004
Investment earnings and miscellaneous	20,775	3,989	2,887	624	28,275
Total revenues	$354,040	$26,890	$23,162	$ 3,455	$407,547
Expenditures: Ⓠ					
Current:					
General government	$ 23,909	$ –0–	$ –0–	$ –0–	$ 23,909
Police	79,565	–0–	–0–	–0–	79,565
Fire	81,100	–0–	–0–	–0–	81,100
Transportation	76,826	8,554	–0–	–0–	85,380
Economic development	5,129	–0–	–0–	656	5,785
Parks and recreation	53,119	–0–	547	134	53,800
Neighborhood services	1,445	–0–	1,389	–0–	2,834
Library	6,022	–0–	10,083	–0–	16,105
Capital outlay	42,459	17,809	8,220	2,500	70,988
Debt service:					
Principal	5,334	–0–	2,108	–0–	7,442
Interest	3,989	–0–	434	–0–	4,423
Total expenditures	$378,897	$26,363	$22,781	$ 3,290	$431,331
Excess (deficiency) of revenues over (under) expenditures	$ (24,857)	$ 527	$ 381	$ 165	$ (23,784)
Other financing sources (uses): Ⓡ					
Transfers in	$ 16,157	$ 442	$ 2,331	$11,090	$ 30,020
Transfers out	(30,050)	–0–	–0–	(6,552)	(36,602)
Issuance of long-term debt	45,000	8,112	2,090	–0–	55,202
Total other financing sources (uses)	$ 31,107	$ 8,554	$ 4,421	$ 4,538	$ 48,620
Net change in fund balances	$ 6,250	$ 9,081	$ 4,802	$ 4,703	$ 24,836 Ⓢ
Fund balance, beginning of year	$190,600	$78,234	$19,170	$ 6,360	$294,364
Fund balance, end of year	$196,850	$87,315	$23,972	$11,063	$319,200

EXHIBIT 12.5 Fund Financial Statements—Statement of Net Position for Proprietary Funds

CITY OF EASTERN SOUTH
Proprietary Funds
Statement of Net Position
June 30, 2024
(in thousands)

	Water	Sewer	Parking	Other Enterprise Funds	Total Enterprise Funds	Internal Service Funds ①
Assets						
Current assets						
Cash and equivalents	$ 18,400	$ 16,150	$ 17,100	$ 9,225	$ 60,875	$ 5,000
Investments	35,045	12,285	25,803	15,325	88,458	8,882
Receivables, net						
Accounts	22,943	9,076	7,577	3,782	43,378	2,178
Other	8,435	3,081	2,290	2,628	16,434	3,006
Due from other funds	–0–	–0–	366	43	409	9,092
Inventories and supplies	3,642	1,810	1,708	5,762	12,922	722
Prepaid items	461	226	824	606	2,117	658
Total current assets	$ 88,926	$ 42,628	$ 55,668	$ 37,371	$ 224,593	$29,538
Noncurrent assets						
Capital assets						
Land	$ 62,981	$ 55,773	$ 29,100	$ 18,019	$ 165,873	$ 9,817
Buildings	388,278	206,149	72,925	45,785	713,137	12,713
Leased property	3,672	8,179	10,433	7,734	30,018	2,058
Vehicles	33,012	26,567	37,007	18,633	115,219	3,118
Equipment	34,227	15,995	4,303	7,883	62,408	5,004
Less: Accumulated depreciation	(83,445)	(77,881)	(41,642)	(29,291)	(232,259)	(11,886)
Total noncurrent assets	$438,725	$234,782	$112,126	$ 68,763	$ 854,396	$20,824
Total assets	$527,651	$277,410	$167,794	$106,134	$1,078,989	$50,362

(*continued*)

EXHIBIT 12.5 (Continued)

CITY OF EASTERN SOUTH
Proprietary Funds
Statement of Net Position
June 30, 2024
(in thousands)

	Water	Sewer	Parking	Other Enterprise Funds	Total Enterprise Funds	Internal Service Funds ①
Liabilities						
Current liabilities						
Accounts payable and other accrued expenses	$ 9,260	$ 3,065	$ 2,084	$ 1,696	$ 16,105	$ 983
Due to other funds	11,522	8,044	4,088	631	24,285	375
Unearned revenue	1,418	883	316	154	2,771	310
Lease payable, current	327	125	98	114	664	55
Bonds and notes payable, current	5,837	3,992	1,760	1,296	12,885	100
Total current liabilities	$ 28,364	$ 16,109	$ 8,346	$ 3,891	$ 56,710	$ 1,823
Noncurrent liabilities						
Liability for landfill closure	$ –0–	$ –0–	$ –0–	$ 9,078	$ 9,078	$ –0–
Capital lease payable, long-term	3,607	7,503	8,291	2,268	21,669	1,323
Bonds and notes payable, long-term	96,048	47,155	26,121	52,117	221,441	19,880
Total noncurrent liabilities	99,655	54,658	34,412	63,463	252,188	21,203
Total liabilities	$128,019	$ 70,767	$ 42,758	$ 67,354	$308,898	$23,026
Net Position						
Invested in capital assets, net of related debt	$389,145	$215,103	$ 92,771	$ 26,637	$ 723,656	$10,831
Restricted for:						
Capital projects	4,083	11,092	415	4,184	19,774	–0–
Debt service	227	284	432	113	1,056	–0–
Unrestricted	6,177	(19,836)	31,418	7,846	25,605	16,505
Total Net Position	$399,632	$206,643	$125,036	$ 38,780	$ 770,091	$27,336

statements, these same internal service funds are frequently reported within governmental activities. As explained previously, that reporting is appropriate when the activity provides services primarily for functions within the governmental funds.

- Because the proprietary funds apply accrual accounting to measure economic resources, the totals for the enterprise funds in Exhibit 12.5 agree in most ways with the total figures included in Exhibit 12.1. The amount of detail, however, is more extensive in the fund financial statements. For example, the statement in Exhibit 12.1 uses only two accounts to describe capital assets, whereas Exhibit 12.5 uses five.

Statement of Revenues, Expenses, and Other Changes in Net Position—Proprietary Funds—Fund Financial Statements

Just as the statement of net position in Exhibit 12.5 provides individual information about specific enterprise funds (and totals for internal service funds), the statement of revenues, expenses, and changes in net position in Exhibit 12.6 gives the revenues, expenses, nonoperating items, and transfers for those same proprietary funds.

As an example, in Exhibit 12.2, operating expenses are listed for each of the business-type activities (water, sewer, parking, and community center). Here, in Exhibit 12.6 (Point V), operating expenses are listed based on the type of expense for each of the proprietary funds: employee services, services and supplies, depreciation and amortization, utilities, maintenance and repairs, and others. A reader of the ACFR can find most information that is desired but must know where to look.

Statement of Cash Flows—Proprietary Funds—Fund Financial Statements

One of the most unique aspects of the fund financial statements is the statement of cash flows for the proprietary funds (Exhibit 12.7). Because a proprietary fund operates in a manner similar to a for-profit business, GASB views information about cash flows as vital as it is in a financial analysis for Intel or Coca-Cola. Nevertheless, the physical structure is not entirely the same.

One of the main differences is that the statement of cash flows shown for the proprietary funds has four sections rather than the three required of for-profit entities (operating activities, investing activities, and financing activities). For proprietary funds, cash flows are classified as follows:

1. Cash flows from operating activities.
2. Cash flows from noncapital financing activities.
3. Cash flows from capital and related financing activities.
4. Cash flows from investing activities.

- The presentation of cash flows from operating activities (Point W) is similar to that prepared by a for-profit business. However, the direct method of reporting is required rather than being merely an allowed option as in for-profit accounting. The indirect method that is almost universally applied by for-profit businesses is not allowed for state and local governments.
- Cash flows from noncapital financing activities include (1) proceeds and payments on debt *not* attributable to the acquisition or construction of capital assets and (2) grants and subsidies *not* restricted for either capital purposes or operating activities.
- As the title implies, cash flows from capital and related financing activities focus on the amounts spent on capital assets and the source of that funding. Exhibit 12.7 shows typical examples (Point X): proceeds from issuance of debt for the construction and acquisition of capital assets, acquisition and construction of capital assets, and proceeds from disposition of capital assets.
- Cash flows from investing activities disclose amounts paid and received from investments, a much narrower category than used in a for-profit business.
- The government should also provide a reconciliation of operating income to operating cash flows. That information has been omitted here because of space considerations.

EXHIBIT 12.6 Fund Financial Statements—Statement of Changes in Revenues, Expenses, and Other Changes in Net Position for the Proprietary Funds

CITY OF EASTERN SOUTH
Proprietary Funds
Statement of Revenues, Expenses, and Other Changes in Net Position
For the Fiscal Year Ended June 30, 2024
(in thousands)

	Water	Sewer	Parking	Other Enterprise Funds	Total Enterprise Funds	Internal Service Funds ①
Operating revenues:						
Charges for services	$ 50,877	$ 11,836	$ 25,990	$ 795	$ 89,498	$ 9,044
Miscellaneous	3,776	2,189	772	290	7,027	112
Total operating revenues	$ 54,653	$ 14,025	$ 26,762	$ 1,085	$ 96,525	$ 9,156
Operating expenses: Ⓥ						
Employee services	$ 16,118	$ 5,017	$ 3,982	$ 1,298	$ 26,415	$ 3,372
Services and supplies	3,109	812	971	618	5,510	611
Depreciation and amortization	6,271	1,219	1,311	294	9,095	476
Utilities	7,216	1,315	2,045	416	10,992	1,342
Maintenance and repairs	3,894	2,119	3,183	1,220	10,416	682
Others	2,665	2,386	284	4,228	9,563	525
Total operating expenses	$ 39,273	$ 12,868	$ 11,776	$ 8,074	$ 71,991	$ 7,008
Total operating income (loss)	$ 15,380	$ 1,157	$ 14,986	$ (6,989)	$ 24,534	$ 2,148
Nonoperating revenues and expenses:						
Grant revenue	$ 2,684	$ 750	$ 1,414	$11,153	$ 16,001	$ 447
Investment earnings	704	525	1,561	311	3,101	29
Gain on disposal of capital asset	400	–0–	156	–0–	556	–0–
Total nonoperating revenues and expenses	$ 3,788	$ 1,275	$ 3,131	$11,464	$ 19,658	$ 476
Income (loss) before transfers	$ 19,168	$ 2,432	$ 18,117	$ 4,475	$ 44,192	$ 2,624
Transfers to governmental and fiduciary funds	(8,703)	(454)	(9,000)	(476)	(18,633)	–0–
Change in net position	$ 10,465	$ 1,978	$ 9,117	$ 3,999	$ 25,559	$ 2,624
Net position, beginning of year	389,167	204,665	115,919	34,781	744,532	24,712
Net position, end of year	$399,632	$206,643	$125,036	$38,780	$770,091	$27,336

EXHIBIT 12.7 Fund Financial Statements—Statement of Cash Flows for Proprietary Funds

CITY OF EASTERN SOUTH
Proprietary Funds
Statement of Cash Flows
For the Fiscal Year Ended June 30, 2024
(in thousands)

	Water	Sewer	Parking	Other Enterprise Funds	Total Enterprise Funds	Internal Service Funds
Cash flows from operating activities: Ⓦ						
Receipts from customers	$49,772	$12,816	$25,045	$ 996	$88,629	$8,961
Payments to employees	(16,553)	(4,849)	(3,717)	(1,011)	(26,130)	(3,402)
Payments to suppliers	(2,816)	(785)	(963)	(580)	(5,144)	(529)
Payments on operating expenses	(13,287)	(6,612)	(5,030)	(6,016)	(30,945)	(1,873)
Receipts from operating grants	3,178	2,985	1,040	8,211	15,414	–0–
Net cash provided by operating activities	$ 20,294	$ 3,555	$16,375	$ 1,600	$ 41,824	$ 3,157
Cash flows from noncapital financing activities:						
Issuance of revenue anticipation notes	$ 5,000	$ –0–	$ 800	$ –0–	$ 5,800	$ –0–
Transfers	(8,703)	(454)	(9,000)	(476)	(18,633)	–0–
Net cash provided by (used for) noncapital financing activities Ⓧ	$ (3,703)	$ (454)	$ (8,200)	$ (476)	$(12,833)	$ –0–
Cash flows from capital and related financing activities: Ⓧ						
Proceeds from bonds issued for construction and acquisition of capital assets	$ 27,500	$ 8,100	$10,500	$ –0–	$ 46,100	$ 2,316
Receipt of capital grants	2,375	–0–	1,100	–0–	3,475	–0–
Received from sale of capital assets	1,980	–0–	753	–0–	2,733	–0–
Paid to acquire capital assets	(28,900)	(17,446)	(2,545)	(5,667)	(54,558)	(1,895)
Paid on bonds issued for construction	(2,300)	(540)	(1,508)	(944)	(5,292)	(135)
Paid interest on bonds issued for construction	(1,122)	(665)	(513)	(1,029)	(3,329)	(271)
Net cash provided by (used for) capital and related financing activities	$ (467)	$(10,551)	$ 7,787	$(7,640)	$(10,871)	$ 15
Cash flows from investing activities:						
Purchase of investments	$(41,200)	$(19,884)	$(19,936)	$(2,415)	$(83,435)	$(6,552)
Received from sale and maturity of investments	35,375	20,900	16,650	7,000	79,925	7,255
Received from investment earnings	704	500	1,510	300	3,014	29
Net cash provided by (used for) investing activities:	$ (5,121)	$ 1,516	$ (1,776)	$ 4,885	$ (496)	$ 732
Net increase (decrease) in cash and cash equivalents	$ 11,003	$ (5,934)	$14,186	$(1,631)	$ 17,624	$ 3,904
Cash and cash equivalents, beginning of year	7,397	22,084	2,914	10,856	43,251	1,096
Cash and cash equivalents, end of year	$ 18,400	$ 16,150	$17,100	$ 9,225	$ 60,875	$ 5,000

On the Horizon

FINANCIAL REPORTING MODEL

Probably no official accounting pronouncement of any type has had more of an overall effect than GASB's Statement No. 34, "Basic Financial Statements—and Management's Discussion and Analysis—for State and Local Governments." Issued in June 1999, it dramatically altered the financial reporting for these governments. Although significant elements of the fund financial statements were changed, the primary effect was the creation of government-wide financial statements. Because of this one authoritative statement, state and local governments moved from a single fund-based set of financial statements to the dual reporting system described in the previous and current chapters.

To better understand the impact of Statement No. 34, go to the following URL for the City and County of San Francisco, California: https://sfcontroller.org/annual-comprehensive-financial-report-acfr.

Then, click on the government's 1999 annual report and study the financial statements on pages 3–12. Next, go to the 2002 annual report and look at the financial statements on pages 21–37. The differences that occur in this government's financial statements in such a short period of time are hard to overstate. Those changes resulted from Statement No. 34. The City and County of San Francisco, as well as the readers of the financial statements, had to adjust to an entirely new approach to the entire reporting process.

After using this reporting model for two decades, GASB is now examining possible improvements that should be made. Based on years of practical experience with the dual system, GASB first began research on needed changes in 2013. Those deliberations are still ongoing with no final pronouncements expected before 2023 if not later. Items being studied include possible eliminations and additions to Management's Discussion and Analysis to improve its usefulness. GASB is also considering better ways to report comparisons between actual figures and budgetary balances.

The improvements being considered are wide-ranging but will certainly not have the drastic effect created in 1999 when Statement No. 34 was issued. Nevertheless, U.S. GAAP does evolve over time as rules are modified and updated to improve the information being provided to decision makers.

LO 12-11

Understand the construction and presentation of financial statements for a public college or university.

Reporting Public Colleges and Universities

Private not-for-profit schools such as Harvard, Duke, and Stanford follow FASB's *Accounting Standards Codification®*. Authoritative accounting literature provides a significant amount of official guidance for these private institutions on issues such as reporting contributions and the proper form of financial statements. Generally accepted accounting principles developed for private not-for-profit organizations have progressed greatly over the years.

In contrast, GASB retains primary authority over the reporting of public colleges and universities. For decades, interested parties have had theoretical discussions as to whether financial statements prepared for public colleges and universities (such as the University of Virginia and the University of Kansas) should resemble those of private schools. Generally, the operations of public colleges and universities differ in at least two important ways from private schools. Are those differences significant enough to warrant a separate set of reporting standards?

- State and other governments directly provide a significant amount of funding, lessening the reliance on tuition and fees. For example, the statement of revenues, expenses, and changes in net position for the University of Alabama for the year ended September 30, 2020, disclosed federal grants and contracts of $61.1 million, state and local grants and contracts of $31.2 million, local grants and contracts of $1.2 million, and private grants and contracts of $4.6 million.

- Because of the ongoing support from the government, public schools have traditionally accumulated a smaller amount of endowment funds than private colleges and universities. Private schools try to build a large endowment to help ensure financial security. This need is less urgent for public schools that are backed by the state or another government. For example, at June 30, 2021, Princeton University, a private school, held investments with a fair value of approximately $37 billion, an amount (roughly equal to $4.7 million per student) that is nearly beyond the comprehension of officials at most public colleges. On that same date, the University of Georgia (along with its component units) reported approximately $2 billion in investments (about $50,000 per student).

Do these and other differences necessitate the creation of unique financial statements for public colleges and universities? In many ways, public and private schools are much alike. They both educate students, charge tuition and other fees, conduct scholarly research, maintain libraries and sports teams, operate cafeterias and museums, and the like. What should be the measurement basis and form of the financial statements to reflect the financial activity and position of colleges and universities?

Over the years, at least three alternatives have been suggested for constructing the financial statements that public colleges and universities prepare and distribute:

1. Adopt FASB's requirements so that all colleges and universities (public and private) prepare comparable financial statements. The private school reporting model is relatively well developed. However, some parties believe this suggestion presents potential problems. Over the decades, FASB has not had to deal with the intricacies of governmental entities and might fail to comprehend the unique aspects of public schools. Specific reporting needs associated with such institutions might fail to be addressed.

2. Apply a traditional model focusing on fund financial statements to highlight the wide variety of funds that such schools often have to maintain. However, both private not-for-profit organizations and governmental entities have abandoned (at least in part) the reporting of individual funds. For public schools to rely solely on a fund-based approach seems somewhat outdated.

3. Adopt for public schools the same reporting model that has been created for state and local governments. Because a large amount of funding for public schools comes directly from governments, the financial statement format used by a city or county government could be applied.

GASB has selected the third option by specifying that public colleges and universities are special-purpose governments. "Public universities, hospitals, utilities, and other business-type activities may operate similar to businesses but they are nonetheless governments—and therefore are accountable to the citizenry," said GASB Chairman Robert H. Attmore.[26] This decision creates a standard reporting model for public schools such as the University of Tennessee and Michigan State University.

Nevertheless, a review of public college and university financial statements shows that many do not prepare both government-wide and fund financial statements like a city or county. Such schools can logically be viewed as large enterprise funds. They have a user charge (tuition and fees), and they are open to the public. As has been discussed, the accounting for enterprise funds is very similar in government-wide statements and fund financial statements. Thus, having two sets of almost identical statements was viewed by GASB as redundant. For this reason, many public schools prepare a single set of statements equivalent to those of an enterprise fund (similar to the previous examples shown in this chapter for the proprietary funds of the City of Eastern South).

[26] "GASB Publishes New User Guide on Business-Type Activities," *Business Wire*, March 12, 2013.

Consequently, Note 1 to the June 30, 2020, financial statements for Middle Tennessee State University (a public school) provides a common rationale for the method by which the statements are structured.

For financial statement purposes, the university is considered a special-purpose government entity engaged *only in business-type activities.* Accordingly, the financial statements have been prepared using the economic resources measurement focus and the accrual basis of accounting. Revenues are recorded when earned and expenses are recorded when a liability is incurred, regardless of the timing of related cash flows. Grants and similar items are recognized as revenue as soon as all eligibility requirements imposed by the provider have been met. [Emphasis added.]

Exhibit 12.8 presents financial statements for a hypothetical public school, the University of Western North, for illustration purposes. Because of space considerations, accompanying notes have not been created. Note, as expected, that these statements are quite similar to the fund financial statements presented earlier in this chapter for the proprietary funds of the City of Eastern South (Exhibits 12.5, 12.6, and 12.7).

EXHIBIT 12.8

University of Western North Statement of Net Position As of June 30, 2024		
	University of Western North	Component Unit Foundation for University
ASSETS		
Current assets:		
Cash and cash equivalents	$ 182,400,000	$ 12,000,000
Short-term investments.	27,100,000	–0–
Accounts receivable (net of allowance for doubtful accounts of $900,000 and $45,000).	12,300,000	600,000
Contributions receivable (net of allowance for doubtful accounts of $410,000)	–0–	7,300,000
Due from state government.	4,800,000	1,200,000
Prepaid expenses	7,800,000	1,500,000
Inventory and other current assets.	1,100,000	400,000
Total current assets.	$ 235,500,000	$ 23,000,000
Noncurrent assets:		
Restricted cash and cash equivalents	$ 35,400,000	–0–
Endowment investments	46,700,000	$ 51,800,000
Contributions receivable (net of allowance for doubtful accounts of $1,600,000)	–0–	44,200,000
Nondepreciable capital assets	171,900,000	5,400,000
Depreciable capital assets, net.	919,600,000	14,700,000
Other assets	26,000,000	4,300,000
Total noncurrent assets	$1,199,600,000	$ 120,400,000
Total assets.	$1,435,100,000	$ 143,400,000
DEFERRED OUTFLOWS OF RESOURCES		
Loss on refunding of debt	$ 3,900,000	–0–
Related to pension and other post-employment benefits	42,100,000	–0–
Total deferred outflows of resources.	$ 46,000,000	–0–
Total assets and deferred outflows of resources	$1,481,100,000	$ 143,400,000

(continued)

EXHIBIT 12.8
(Continued)

	University of Western North	Component Unit Foundation for University
LIABILITIES		
Current liabilities:		
Accounts payable and accrued expenses	$ 64,800,000	$ 3,600,000
Unearned revenue	25,400,000	1,300,000
Deposits held in custody for others	11,700,000	–0–
Long-term liabilities – current portion	39,800,000	2,700,000
Other liabilities	3,400,000	2,200,000
Total current liabilities.	$145,100,000	$ 9,800,000
Noncurrent liabilities:		
Long-term liabilities for capital assets	$137,300,000	$ 10,500,000
Other notes and long-term liabili	290,000,000	13,000,000
Liabilities for pensions and other post-employment benefits.	245,100,000	6,400,000
Total noncurrent liabilities	$672,400,000	$ 29,900,000
Total liabilities.	$817,500,000	$ 39,700,000
DEFERRED INFLOWS OF RESOURCES		
Related to pensions and other post-employment benefits	$ 51,100,000	–0–
Total deferred inflows of resources	$ 51,100,000	–0–
Total liabilities and deferred inflows of resources	$868,600,000	$ 39,700,000
NET POSITION		
Net investment in capital assets	$554,200,000	$ 9,600,000
Restricted for:		
Nonexpendable.		
Scholarships and fellowships	13,700,000	–0–
Permanently restricted	–0–	43,500,000
Expendable:		
Scholarships and fellowships	3,200,000	–0–
Research.	1,300,000	5,900,000
Capital projects	14,900,000	29,300,000
Other	–0–	2,400,000
Unrestricted	25,200,000	13,000,000
Total net position.	$612,500,000	$103,700,000

University of Western North
Statement of Revenues, Expenses, and Changes in Net Position
For the year ended June 30, 2024

	University of Western North	Component Unit Foundation for University
Operating revenues:		
Student tuition and fees (net of scholarship allowances of $33,900,000)	$226,800,000	–0–
Gifts and contributions	–0–	$21,500,000
Federal grants and contracts.	14,100,000	–0–

(continued)

EXHIBIT 12.8
(Continued)

University of Western North
Statement of Revenues, Expenses, and Changes in Net Position
For the year ended June 30, 2024

	University of Western North	Component Unit Foundation for University
State grants and contracts	10,400,000	–0–
Nongovernmental grants and contracts	4,700,000	–0–
Sponsored research	–0–	13,000,000
Auxiliary enterprises (net of scholarship allowances of $19,600,000)	161,300,000	–0–
Other operating revenues	4,200,000	1,200,000
Total operating revenues	$421,500,000	$ 35,700,000
Operating expenses:		
Instruction	$169,700,000	$ 300,000
Research	18,200,000	–0–
Public service	4,500,000	700,000
Academic support	49,100,000	1,200,000
Student services	18,200,000	–0–
Institutional support	43,900,000	6,900,000
Operation and maintenance—plant	55,000,000	11,300,000
Depreciation	39,800,000	–0–
Student aid	37,700,000	5,400,000
Auxiliary activities	122,100,000	–0–
Total operating expenses	$558,200,000	$ 25,800,000
Operating income/(loss)	($136,700,000)	$ 9,900,000
Nonoperating revenues/(expenses):		
State appropriations	$155,600,000	–0–
Grants and contracts	31,300,000	–0–
Gifts	4,000,000	–0–
Investment income (net of investment expenses of $200,000 and $700,000)	6,800,000	17,500,000
Other nonoperating revenues	1,400,000	–0–
Other nonoperating expenses	(500,000)	–0–
Interest on capital asset – related debt	(4,600,000)	–0–
Payments to the state government	(2,100,000)	–0–
Net nonoperating revenues/(expenses)	$191,900,000	$ 17,500,000
Income before other revenues, expenses, gains, and losses	$ 55,200,000	$ 27,400,000
Capital appropriations and contributions	$ 27,800,000	–0–
Capital gifts	1,000,000	–0–
Loss on disposal of capital asset	(900,000)	–0–
Contribution to permanent endowments	–0–	$ 3,900,000
Total other revenues, expenses, gains, and losses	$ 27,900,000	$ 3,900,000
Increase in net position	$ 83,100,000	$ 31,300,000
Net position – beginning of year	529,400,000	72,400,000
Net position – end of year	$612,500,000	$103,700,000

(continued)

EXHIBIT 12.8
(Continued)

University of Western North
Statement of Revenues, Expenses, and Changes in Net Position
For the year ended June 30, 2024

Cash flows from operating activities:	
Student tuition and fees	$212,500,000
Grants and contracts	27,200,000
Auxiliary enterprises	48,400,000
Payments for compensation and benefits	(388,400,000)
Payments for services, supplies, and utilities	(9,200,000)
Payments for scholarships and fellowships	(38,600,000)
Payments for noncapitalized plant improvements and equipment	(32,700,000)
Collections of loans from students	600,000
Net cash used by operating activities	($180,200,000)
Cash flows from noncapital financing activities:	
State appropriations	$152,800,000
Nonoperating grants and contracts	31,500,000
Payment to the state government	(2,100,000)
Gifts and grants for other than capital purposes	3,600,000
Custodial receipts	2,700,000
Custodial payments	(1,500,000)
Net cash provided by noncapital financing activities	$187,000,000
Cash flows from capital and related financing activities	
Capital appropriations and contributions	$ 27,800,000
Proceeds from capital debt	64,900,000
Proceeds from sale of capital assets	2,900,000
Capital gifts	63,600,000
Purchase of capital assets	(35,700,000)
Principal paid on capital debt, leases, and installments	(17,600,000)
Interest paid on capital debt, leases, and installments	(36,700,000)
Net cash provided by capital and related financing activities	$ 69,200,000
Cash flows from investing activities:	
Interest and dividends on investments	$ 6,700,000
Proceeds from sale of investments	15,200,000
Purchase of investments	(31,900,000)
Net cash used by investing activities	($10,000,000)
Net increase in cash	$ 66,000,000
Cash and cash equivalents — beginning of the year	151,800,000
Cash and cash equivalents — end of the year	$217,800,000

A component unit is included here that is assumed to be a legally separate foundation created by the university to raise funds and promote the achievements and aims of the university. As an example, the 2021 financial statements for the Georgia Institute of Technology includes several component units including the Georgia Tech Foundation which is described in the notes to the statements as follows.

The Georgia Tech Foundation (Foundation) is a legally separate, not-for-profit corporation under the laws of the state of Georgia. The purposes of the Foundation are to promote higher education in the state of Georgia, to raise and receive funds for the support and enhancement of the Institute, and to aid the Institute in its development as a leading educational institution.

Interestingly, most public universities are also reported as component units of their state government. The interconnection between public schools and governments is demonstrated by that reporting.

Notice here that the assets and liabilities of the university appear much like those seen in for-profit entities. Nevertheless, the deferred outflows and inflows of resources have no direct comparisons in for-profit financial reporting. The same is true of the Net Position section of the statement of net position. The information is quite different from that seen in traditional for-profit accounting.

Summary

1. GASB has established a hierarchy for the generally accepted accounting principles that should be applied by state and local governments. Two categories of authoritative U.S. GAAP are listed. Category A is most important and includes GASB's official statements. Category B is composed of GASB Technical Bulletins, GASB Implementation Guides, and literature of the AICPA cleared by GASB. Sources of nonauthoritative accounting literature include GASB Concepts Statements and pronouncements and other literature of the Financial Accounting Standards Board, Federal Accounting Standards Advisory Board, and International Accounting Standards Board.

2. Governments often give tax breaks to entice desired actions by businesses and other taxpayers. These abatements limit the government's ability to collect tax money. To provide citizens and other interested parties with pertinent information about the actions of government officials, disclosure is required for tax abatements. This information should indicate the type of commitment that was made and the benefit expected by the government in return.

3. State and local governments often have significant obligations for defined benefit pension plans and other postemployment plans. The governments must determine the amounts to be reported for these obligations. Future benefits that have been earned to date are estimated and the present value calculated. If the resulting obligation is greater than the net position held by a related pension trust fund, the excess is shown in government-wide statements as the net pension liability.

4. For a state or local government involved in a lease contract, a single accounting model is used whether the government is a lessee or a lessor (unless the contract has a maximum life of one year or less). In government-wide financial statements, a government lessee records a right-of-use asset and associated liability at the present value of the cash payments. As time passes, the lessee reports interest on the liability and amortization expense on the cost of the asset. In contrast, a government lessor continues to report the asset while also recognizing a receivable and a deferred inflow of resources. The lessor then depreciates the asset and also records interest revenue on the receivable. At the same time, the deferred inflow of resources is reclassified as lease revenue on a systematic and rational basis. On fund financial statements for governmental funds, the lessee initially records both an expenditure and an other financing source for the present value of the payments. Subsequent payments are shown as additional expenditures. The lessor initially records a receivable and a deferred inflow of resources, both for present value. Over time, collection is made to reduce and remove the receivable. The deferred inflow of resources is reclassified as lease revenue.

5. Solid waste landfills create potentially large debts for a government because of eventual closure and postclosure costs. Government-wide statements accrue a liability each period based on (a) the latest current cost estimations and (b) the portion of the property filled to date. Fund financial statements report no expenditures until a claim to current financial resources is made.

6. A state or local government that obtains a work of art or historical treasure normally records it as a capital asset on government-wide financial statements. If specified guidelines are met, an expense can replace recognition of the asset. Whether recorded as expense or asset, a state or local government that receives such a work of art or historical treasure as a donation must still recognize revenue according to the rules established for voluntary nonexchange transactions. Fund financial statements for the governmental funds report no capital assets and, therefore, do not recognize these items except as expenditures if purchased.

7. Depreciation must be recorded each period for works of art and historical treasures that are capitalized unless they are judged to be inexhaustible.

8. Infrastructure assets such as bridges and roads are capitalized on government-wide financial statements. Governments then record depreciation over time unless they apply the modified approach. Under this method, the government must create a monitoring system to ensure that each network of infrastructure is maintained at a predetermined condition. When the modified approach is applied, the cost of upkeep is expensed as incurred by the government in lieu of recording depreciation.

9. A state or local government must include a management's discussion and analysis (MD&A) as part of its general-purpose external financial reporting. As with for-profit businesses, this MD&A provides a verbal explanation of the government's operations and financial position.

10. A primary government produces an annual comprehensive financial report (ACFR). Both general-purpose governments (such as states, cities, towns, counties, and the like) and special-purpose governments (such as some school systems and transit systems) that meet defined provisions are viewed as primary governments. A component unit is any function that is legally separate from a primary government but where financial accountability still exists. In government-wide statements, component units are either discretely presented to the right of the primary government or blended within the actual funds of the primary government.

11. A statement of net position and a statement of activities are prepared as government-wide financial statements based on the economic resources measurement focus and accrual accounting. These statements separate governmental activities from business-type activities. Internal service funds are often included within the governmental activities based on the activities they serve. The statement of activities reports expenses by function along with related program revenues to determine the net expense or revenue resulting from each function. The various general revenues are then listed by the government to indicate the method used to finance the net expenses incurred by the various functions.

12. In creating fund financial statements for governmental funds, the general fund and any other major fund are reported in separate columns. These statements are based on measuring current financial resources using modified accrual accounting. Additional separate statements are presented for proprietary funds and also for fiduciary funds.

13. Financial statements prepared by public colleges and universities must follow the same reporting guidelines as those created for state and local government units. Those statements differ in several ways from the statements produced by private schools that follow FASB guidelines. In practice, public schools are normally viewed as special-purpose governments that are engaged only in business-type activities like an enterprise fund. Thus, such schools only need to present fund financial statements as a proprietary fund.

Comprehensive Illustration

(*Estimated Time: 40 Minutes*) The following is a series of transactions for a city. Indicate how the city reports each transaction within government-wide financial statements and then on fund financial statements. Assume the city follows a policy of considering resources as available if they will be received within 60 days. Incurred liabilities are assumed to be claims to current resources if they will be paid within 60 days.

Problem

1. Borrows money by issuing 20-year bonds for a total of $3 million, the face value. The city plans to use the money to construct a highway around its perimeter.

2. Transfers cash of $100,000 from the general fund to the debt service funds to make the first payment of principal and interest on the bonds in (1).

3. Pays the cash in (2) on the bonds. Of this total, $70,000 represents interest. The remainder reduces the principal of the bonds.

4. Completes construction of the highway and pays the entire $3 million construction costs.

5. The highway in (4) is expected to last 30 years. The government qualifies to use the modified approach, which it has adopted for its system of highways. The government incurs a $350,000 cost during the year to maintain the highway at an appropriate, predetermined condition. Of this amount, $290,000 was paid immediately. The other $60,000 will not be paid until the sixth month of the subsequent year.

6. Receives lights for the new highway donated from a local business. The lights are valued at $200,000 and should last 20 years. The modified approach is not used for this network of infrastructure. The city applies straight-line depreciation using the half-year convention.

7. Agrees to stop collecting property taxes from the Acme Company for eight years in exchange for the promise that the company will build a small manufacturing plant within the city to generate capital investment and 60 new job opportunities.

8. Records cash revenues of $2 million from the local subway system. Makes salary expense payments of $300,000 to its employees.

9. At the start of the year, the city leases a new firetruck for seven years by agreeing to pay $40,000 per year starting immediately. The city does not know the implicit interest rate used by the lessor. The city has an incremental annual borrowing rate of 6 percent. The present value of an annuity due of $1 at 6 percent interest over seven years is 5.91732.

10. Opens a solid waste landfill at the beginning of the year that will be used for 20 years. This year the city fills an estimated 4 percent of the capacity. Officials anticipate closure, and postclosure requirements will be $2 million based on current cost figures although no costs have been incurred to date.

Solution

1. *Government-wide financial statements.* On the statement of net position under the governmental activities column, both cash and noncurrent liabilities increase by $3 million.

   Fund financial statements. The cash balance increases on the balance sheet by $3 million. Other financing sources increases by the same amount on the statement of revenues, expenditures, and changes in fund balances. These amounts will be shown in the other governmental funds column unless officials judge that this particular capital projects fund is major. If so, a separate column is used.

2. *Government-wide financial statements.* No recording of this transfer is shown because the amount is an intra-activity transaction entirely carried out within the governmental activities. For the governmental activities no net financial change occurs.

   Fund financial statements. The cash balance of the general fund on the balance sheet decreases while the cash listed for the debt service fund (or the other governmental funds) increases. On the statement of revenues, expenditures, and other changes in fund balances, the general fund shows an other financing use of $100,000, whereas the debt service funds (or other governmental funds) report an other financing source. These balances will not be offset in arriving at total figures.

3. *Government-wide financial statements.* On the statement of net position, cash reported by the governmental activities decreases by $100,000 and the total reported for noncurrent liabilities drops $30,000 to reflect the principal payment. The statement of activities then recognizes $70,000 in interest expense as a governmental activity.

   Fund financial statements. First, cash decreases by $100,000 on the balance sheet under the debt service funds (or other governmental funds) column. Second, the statement of revenues, expenditures, and changes in fund balances reports a $30,000 principal expenditure and a $70,000 interest expenditure. These amounts are shown within the debt service funds (or other governmental funds).

4. *Government-wide financial statements.* Under the governmental activities on the statement of net position, cash decreases $3 million, and capital assets increases by the same amount. Governments capitalize infrastructure costs.

   Fund financial statements. On the balance sheet, cash reported for other governmental funds decreases. Again, if this particular capital projects fund qualifies as major, the effects are shown in a separate column rather than in the other governmental funds column. The statement of revenues, expenditures, and changes in fund balances reports a $3 million expenditure as a capital outlay.

5. *Government-wide financial statements.* The statement of net position reports a $290,000 decrease in cash under governmental activities and a $60,000 increase in a current liability. The statement of activities includes the $350,000 expense within an appropriate function such as public works. Because the government applies the modified approach, maintenance expense is recognized instead of depreciation expense.

   Fund financial statements. Because the $60,000 liability will not require the use of current financial resources (it will not be paid within 60 days of the end of the year), no recording is made at this time at the fund level. Thus, the balance sheet reports only a $290,000 drop in cash, probably under the general fund. This $290,000 expenditure appears on the statement of revenues, expenditures, and changes in fund balances for public works.

6. *Government-wide financial statements.* The lights do not qualify as works of art or historical treasures and must be reported as capital assets on the statement of net position at their $200,000 value. Based on an expected life of 20 years and use of the half-year convention, $5,000 ($200,000/20 years × 0.5 year) in accumulated depreciation reduces the reported net balance to $195,000. For the statement of activities, a $200,000 revenue is appropriate unless eligibility requirements connected to the donation have not yet been fulfilled. This revenue should be shown as a program revenue (capital grants and contributions) to offset the expenses reported for public works. Depreciation of $5,000 should also be included as an expense for public works.

Fund financial statements. No reporting is required because current financial resources were not affected by the gift or subsequent depreciation.

7. *Government-wide financial statements and fund financial statements.* Tax abatement information should be disclosed. It includes the purpose of the tax abatement program, the tax being abated, dollar amount of taxes abated, the type of commitments made by the tax abatement recipients, and other commitments made by the government such as agreeing to build infrastructure assets like roads or sewer systems.

8. *Government-wide financial statements.* Cash reported on the statement of net position increases under the business-type activities by $1.7 million. The statement of activities reports expenses for the subway system as $300,000 while the related program revenues for charges for services increase by $2 million. The net revenue resulting from this business-type activity is $1.7 million.

   Fund financial statements. The statement of net position for the proprietary funds (see Exhibit 12.5) should include a separate column for the subway system, assuming that it qualifies as a major fund. Cash in this column increases by $1.7 million. Likewise, the statement of revenues, expenses, and changes in net position for the proprietary funds (see Exhibit 12.6) reports operating revenues of $2 million for the subway system. The operating expenses will include personnel services of $300,000. The statement of cash flows (see Exhibit 12.7) also reports both the inflow and outflow of cash under cash flows from operating activities.

9. *Government-wide financial statements.* Under the governmental activities on the statement of net position, the city reports this right-of-use asset at the present value of the cash flows or $236,693 (rounded). The computed amount is $40,000 × 5.91732. That amount is later reduced by $33,813 (rounded) by the annual amortization ($236,693/7). Cash drops $40,000 because of the first payment. The lease liability begins as $236,693 but decreases immediately by the $40,000 payment to $196,693. At the end of the year, interest expense of $11,802 is recognized ($196,693 times 6 percent interest). The interest is compounded and increases the liability balance to $208,495. On the statement of activities, the amortization and interest expenses are reported under governmental activities.

   Fund financial statements. When the city signs this agreement, it recognizes expenditures—lease contract for the present value of the obligation or $236,693 and also other financing sources—lease contract for the same amount. Both figures appear on the statement of revenues, expenditures, and other changes in fund balances for the governmental funds. When the $40,000 payment is made, then expenditures—firetruck is also shown for that amount, along with a reduction in cash on the balance sheet for the governmental funds.

10. *Government-wide financial statements.* The landfill is 4 percent filled. This is its first year of operations. That portion of the anticipated $2 million cost ($80,000) is recognized. The statement of net position shows this $80,000 amount as a noncurrent liability. The balance is presented as either a governmental activity or a business-type activity, depending on the landfill's classification. Likewise, the statement of activities reports the same $80,000 figure as an expense.

    Fund financial statements. This liability does not require the use of current financial resources and is not reported if the landfill is considered a governmental fund. If the landfill is an enterprise fund, the separate statements prepared for the proprietary funds include both the $80,000 expense and liability (see Exhibits 12.5 and 12.6).

Questions

1. Authoritative U.S. GAAP for state and local governments is divided into two categories, with the first category having more authority than the second. What sources of U.S. GAAP are found in both of these categories?

2. The accountants for a city government are attempting to determine the appropriate method of reporting a series of unique financial transactions. They review all of the authoritative sources of U.S. GAAP but have not located an answer. What action should they take next?

3. Officials for the city of Winfield have agreed to forgo real estate taxes normally charged to Jamieson Corporation for the subsequent 10 years. In exchange, Jamieson agrees to build a distribution facility that is expected to hire 500 new employees. What information must the city provide in its financial statements to inform taxpayers and other interested parties about the nature of this tax abatement?

4. A teacher employed by the City of Lights qualifies for a defined benefit pension plan. The city sets up a pension trust fund to monitor the resources held for these future payments. How is the amount of net pension liability to be reported in the government-wide financial statements determined?

5. The City of Ronchester has a defined benefit pension plan for its firefighters. How is the amount of pension expense determined that the city should recognize in the current year?

6. At the start of Year 1, the City of Peacock leases 30 computers for use by various officials in school administration and public safety at a total cost of $90,000 per year. The first lease payment is made immediately. The contracts are for five years, the expected life of the computers. After that period, the city will return them to the lessor. What reporting is appropriate for the city for the first year? Assume the city has an annual incremental borrowing rate of 8 percent.

7. Pittston County has an empty school building with a net book value of $700,000 and a remaining life of 10 years with no expected residual value. The building is leased to the City of Lincoln at the start of the current year for 10 years. Annual payments are set at $103,565 to reflect Pittston's implicit interest rate of 10 percent per year. This rate is known by both parties. The first payment is made immediately. What revenue and expense does Pittston report in the first year on government-wide statements? What expense does Lincoln report in the first year on government-wide statements?

8. Why does the operation of a solid waste landfill create significant reporting concerns for many local governments?

9. A city believes its new landfill will fill to capacity gradually over a 10-year period. At the end of the first year of operations, the landfill is 7 percent filled. How much liability for closure and post-closure costs should be recognized on government-wide financial statements? How much liability should be recognized on fund financial statements, assuming the landfill is recorded in an enterprise fund? How much liability should be recognized on fund financial statements, assuming the landfill is recorded in the general fund?

10. The City of VanHesse operates a solid waste landfill. This facility is 11 percent filled after the first year of operation and 24 percent after the second year. How much expense should be recognized on the government-wide financial statements in the second year because of its obligation for closure costs? Assuming that the landfill is reported in the general fund, what expenditure should be recognized in the second year on the fund financial statements?

11. A local citizen gives the City of Salem a painting by Picasso to display in city hall. Under what condition will the city *not* report this painting as a capital asset on its government-wide financial statements? If the city does report the painting as a capital asset, must the city report depreciation?

12. Assume in Question 11 that the city does not choose to report the painting on the government-wide financial statements as a capital asset. Must the city report a revenue as a result of the gift?

13. Under what condition is the modified approach applied by a state or local government?

14. What effect does application of the modified approach have on reporting within government-wide financial statements?

15. What does a state or local government normally include in its management's discussion and analysis (MD&A)? Where does a state or local government present this information?

16. What does an annual comprehensive financial report (known as the ACFR) include?

17. A primary government can be either a general-purpose government or a special-purpose government. What is the difference in these two? How does an activity qualify as a special-purpose government?

18. The Willingham Museum qualifies as a component unit of the City of Willingham. How does an activity or function meet the requirements to be deemed a component unit of a primary government?

19. What is the difference between a blended component unit and a discretely presented component unit?

20. What are the two government-wide financial statements? What does each normally present?

21. What are the two fund financial statements for governmental funds? What information does each normally present?

22. For a state or local government, what is the difference between program revenues and general revenues? Why is that distinction important?

23. Why does a government determine the net expenses or net revenues for each of the functions within its statement of activities?

24. How are internal service funds reported on government-wide financial statements?

25. In governmental accounting, what is the difference between an acquisition and a merger? What differences exist between the accounting for an acquisition and for a merger?

26. A general-purpose government takes over a special-purpose government in an acquisition. The consideration is larger than the acquisition value of all assets and liabilities. How is the excess reported?

27. What are some of the major differences that exist between private colleges and universities and public colleges and universities that affect financial reporting?

28. What is the most common form used in creating the financial statements prepared by public colleges and universities?

Problems

LO 12-1

1. Which of the following has the least amount of official authority for the financial reporting of state and local governments?

   a. GASB Technical Bulletins

   b. GASB Statements of Governmental Accounting Standards

   c. GASB Concepts Statements

   d. GASB Implementation Guides

LO 12-1

2. City government officials are analyzing a complicated financial transaction. A GASB Implementation Guide seems to provide one reporting answer. A GASB Concepts Statement seems to provide a different answer. What reporting is most appropriate?

   a. The government can use either method and still be in conformity with U.S. GAAP.

   b. Government officials should follow the guidance provided by the GASB Implementation Guide.

   c. The city's financial statements must be in conformity with the GASB Concepts Statement.

   d. The city's accountants should seek some type of compromise that takes both of these pronouncements into consideration.

LO 12-1

3. The accountants for a city are attempting to determine the proper reporting for a new transaction so that financial statements will be in conformity with U.S. GAAP. They are unable to find any authoritative answer. What should happen next?

   a. The city will receive a qualified audit report on its financial statements.

   b. The accountants can report the transaction in the way that they believe is best.

   c. The accountants should study other nonauthoritative sources such as GASB Concepts Statements and the official standards produced by FASB.

   d. The city will separate the transaction and report it separately in such a way as to draw attention to the method of reporting that was followed.

LO 12-2

4. A city agrees to allow the Jones Company to operate within its geographical boundaries without having to pay real estate taxes for the next 10 years. In exchange, Jones agrees to continue employing at least 120 people at all times during this period. For this tax abatement, which of the following does the city not have to disclose?

   a. The party receiving the tax abatement

   b. The purpose of the tax abatement program

   c. Dollar amount of taxes abated

   d. The tax being abated

LO 12-2

5. City officials provide a tax abatement to a local business so that it can avoid paying real estate taxes for the next five years. In exchange, the business agrees to construct a new facility and hire 50 or more individuals. How does the city report this decision?

   a. Only on the government-wide financial statements

   b. Only on the fund financial statements

   c. On both the government-wide and fund financial statements

   d. Only as a footnote disclosure

LO 12-3

6. The City of Nomanchester has a defined benefit pension plan for a number of its employees. A pension trust fund has been set up that currently has a net position of $32.7 million because quite a number of investments are being held. An actuary estimates that city employees will eventually receive $99.7 million as a result of this pension. However, only $72.4 million of that amount is for work already provided. The present value of the $72.4 million in payments is $49.8 million. On its government-wide financial statements, what amount of net pension liability should be reported?

   a. $—0—

   b. $17.1 million

   c. $39.7 million

   d. $67.0 million

LO 12-3

7. The City of Huble has a defined benefit pension plan for a significant number of its employees. Which of the following does the city not include immediately in the determination of pension expense in its government-wide financial statements?

   a. Service cost

   b. Interest on total pension liability

   c. Changes in pension liability as a result of a change in benefit terms

   d. Changes in pension liability as a result of a change in economic or demographic assumptions

LO 12-4

8. Reynolds County has three large trucks with a total net book value of $600,000 and remaining lives of six years with no expected residual value. County officials lease the trucks to the City of Webster on January 1, Year Three, for six years. Based on a negotiated annual implicit interest rate of 5 percent, the parties agree on annual payments of $112,581 beginning immediately and each January 1 thereafter. For both governments, the trucks relate to activities maintained with the General Fund. What is the total expense Webster reports on government-wide financial statements for Year Three?
   a. $112,581
   b. $124,371
   c. $130,000
   d. $142,581

LO 12-4

9. Use the same information as in Problem 8. What liability balance will Webster report on its government-wide financial statements on December 31, Year Three?
   a. $463,048
   b. $487,419
   c. $511,790
   d. $517,419

LO 12-4

10. Use the same information as in Problem 8. What is the total amount of expenditures that Webster will report on its fund financial statements for the governmental funds for Year Three?
   a. $112,581
   b. $136,954
   c. $600,000
   d. $712,581

LO 12-4

11. Use the same information as in Problem 8. What amount of depreciation expense will Reynolds report in its government-wide financial statements for Year Three?
   a. $–0–
   b. $52,581
   c. $100,000
   d. $112,581

LO 12-4

12. Use the same information as in Problem 8. What amount of deferred lease revenue will Reynolds report on its statement of net position as of December 31, Year Three, assuming that the county recognizes revenue on a straight-line method?
   a. $–0–
   b. $487,419
   c. $500,000
   d. $511,790

LO 12-5

13. A city creates a solid waste landfill. It assesses a charge to every individual or company that uses the landfill based on the amount of materials added. In which of the following will the landfill probably be recorded?
   a. General fund
   b. Special revenues funds
   c. Internal service funds
   d. Enterprise fund

Use the following information for Problems 14, 15, and 16.

A city opens a solid waste landfill that it expects to fill to capacity gradually over a 10-year period. At the end of Year One, it is 8 percent filled. At the end of Year Two, it is 19 percent filled. Currently, the cost of closure and postclosure is estimated at $1 million. None of this amount will be paid until the landfill has reached 90 percent of its capacity.

LO 12-5

14. Which of the following is true for the Year 2 government-wide financial statements?
   a. Both expense and liability will be zero.
   b. Both expense and liability will be $110,000.
   c. Expense will be $110,000, and liability will be $190,000.
   d. Expense will be $100,000, and liability will be $200,000.

LO 12-5

15. If this landfill is judged to be a proprietary fund, what liability will the city report at the end of Year Two on its fund financial statements?

 a. $–0–
 b. $110,000
 c. $190,000
 d. $200,000

LO 12-5

16. If this landfill is judged to be a governmental fund, what liability will the city report at the end of Year Two on fund financial statements?

 a. $–0–
 b. $110,000
 c. $190,000
 d. $200,000

LO 12-6

17. The City of Wilson receives a large sculpture valued at $240,000 as a gift to be placed in front of the municipal building. Which of the following is true for reporting the gift within the government-wide financial statements?

 a. A capital asset of $240,000 must be reported.
 b. The city will not report a capital asset.
 c. If conditions are met, recording the sculpture as a capital asset is optional.
 d. The city will record the sculpture but only for the amount it had to pay.

LO 12-6

18. In Problem 17, which of the following statements is true about reporting a revenue in connection with this gift?

 a. A revenue will be reported.
 b. Revenue is reported but only if the asset is reported.
 c. If the asset is not capitalized, the city recognizes no revenue.
 d. As a gift, no revenue is ever reported.

LO 12-6

19. Assume in Problem 17 that the city reports the work as a capital asset. Which of the following is true?

 a. Depreciation is not recorded because the city has no cost.
 b. Depreciation is not required if the asset is viewed as inexhaustible.
 c. Depreciation must be recognized because the asset is capitalized.
 d. Because the city received the property as a gift, recognition of depreciation is optional.

LO 12-7

20. A city builds sidewalks throughout various neighborhoods at a cost of $2.1 million. Which of the following statements is *not* true?

 a. Because the sidewalks qualify as infrastructure, the asset is viewed in the same way as land so that no depreciation is recorded.
 b. Depreciation is required unless the city uses the modified approach.
 c. The modified approach recognizes maintenance expense in lieu of depreciation expense for qualifying infrastructure assets.
 d. The modified approach is allowed but only if the city maintains the network of sidewalks at least at a predetermined condition.

LO 12-7

21. Which of the following statements is true about use of the modified approach?

 a. It can be applied to all capital assets of a state or local government.
 b. It is used to adjust depreciation expense either up or down based on conditions for the period.
 c. It is required for infrastructure assets.
 d. For qualified assets, it eliminates the recording of depreciation.

LO 12-8

22. Which of the following is true about the management's discussion and analysis (MD&A)?

 a. It is an optional addition to the comprehensive annual financial report, but GASB encourages its inclusion.
 b. It adds a verbal explanation for the numbers and trends presented in the financial statements.
 c. It appears at the very end of a government's annual comprehensive financial report.
 d. It replaces a portion of the fund financial statements traditionally presented by state and local governments.

LO 12-9

23. Which of the following is *not* necessary for a special-purpose local government to be viewed as a primary government for reporting purposes?
    a. It must have a separately elected governing body.
    b. It must have specifically defined geographic boundaries.
    c. It must be fiscally independent.
    d. It must have corporate powers to prove that it is legally independent.

LO 12-9

24. An accountant is trying to determine whether the school system of the City of Abraham is fiscally independent. Which of the following is *not* a requirement for the school system to be judged as fiscally independent?
    a. Holding property in its own name
    b. Issuing bonded debt without outside approval
    c. Passing its own budget without outside approval
    d. Setting taxes or rates without outside approval

LO 12-9

25. An employment agency for individuals with disabilities works closely with the City of Hanover. The employment agency is legally separate from the city but still depends on the city for financial support. This support creates a potential financial burden for the city. How should Hanover report the employment agency in its comprehensive annual financial report?
    a. Not at all because the agency is legally separate
    b. As a part of the general fund
    c. As a component unit
    d. As a related organization

LO 12-9

26. The City of Bacon is located in the County of Pork. The city has a school system that reports buildings at a net $3.6 million although they are actually worth $4.2 million. The county has a separate school system that reports buildings at a net $5.2 million although they are actually worth $5.6 million. Both school systems qualify as special-purpose governments. If the school systems are combined in a merger, what balance should be reported for the buildings?
    a. $8.6 million
    b. $8.8 million
    c. $9.4 million
    d. $9.8 million

LO 12-9

27. For component units, what is the difference between *discrete presentation* and *blending*?
    a. A blended component unit is shown to the left of the statements; a discretely presented component unit is shown to the right.
    b. A blended component unit is shown at the bottom of the statements; a discretely presented component unit is shown within the statements, like a fund.
    c. A blended component unit is shown within the statements, like a fund; a discretely presented component unit is shown to the right.
    d. A blended component unit is shown to the right of the statements; a discretely presented component unit is shown in completely separate statements.

LO 12-10

28. A government reports that its public safety function had expenses of $900,000 last year and program revenues of $200,000 so that its net expenses were $700,000. On which financial statement is this information presented?
    a. Statement of activities
    b. Statement of cash flows
    c. Statement of revenues and expenditures
    d. Statement of net position

LO 12-10

29. Government-wide financial statements make a distinction between program revenues and general revenues. How is that difference shown?
    a. Program revenues are offset against the expenses of a specific function; general revenues are assigned to governmental activities and business-type activities in general.
    b. General revenues are shown at the top of the statement of revenues and expenditures; program revenues are shown at the bottom.
    c. General revenues are labeled as operating revenues; program revenues are shown as miscellaneous income.
    d. General revenues are broken down by type; program revenues are reported as a single figure for the government.

LO 12-10

30. Which of the following is true about the statement of cash flows for the proprietary funds of a state or local government?
    a. The indirect method of reporting cash flows from operating activities is allowed, although the direct method is recommended.
    b. The structure of the statement is virtually identical to that of a for-profit business.
    c. The statement is divided into four separate sections of cash flows.
    d. Amounts spent on capital assets are reported in a separate section from amounts raised to finance those capital assets.

LO 12-11

31. Which of the following is most likely to be true about the financial reporting of a public college or university?
    a. It resembles the financial reporting of private colleges and universities.
    b. It will continue to use its own unique style of financial reporting.
    c. It resembles the financial reporting made by a proprietary fund within the fund financial statements for a state or local government.
    d. It will soon be reported using a financial statement format unique to the needs of public colleges and universities.

LO 12-3

32. The City of Columbus has approximately 2,000 employees. For the past three decades, the city has provided employees with a defined benefit pension plan. The plan contract calls for specific payment amounts to be made to each retiree based on a set formula. The city transfers money periodically to a pension trust fund where it is invested so that eventual payments can be made.
    a. Describe how the city determines the amount (if any) of a net pension liability that should be reported within government-wide financial statements.
    b. Describe how the city determines the amount (if any) of pension expense that should be reported within government-wide financial statements.
    c. How is the pension reported in fund financial statements for the governmental funds?

LO 12-4

33. The City of Leonard decides to lease school desks for its school system rather than buy them because the lessor will do all scheduled maintenance. On January 1, 2024, the school system leases 5,000 school desks for four years. After that, they will be returned to the manufacturer. Payment will be $20 per desk per year with payments on January 1, beginning on January 1, 2024. The city does not know how the lessor determined the annual charge. The city has an annual incremental borrowing rate of 8 percent. The present value of an annuity due of $1 at an 8 percent annual rate for four periods is 3.5771.
    a. Make the journal entries for the City of Leonard for 2024 and 2025 in preparing government-wide financial statements.
    b. Make the journal entries for the City of Leonard for 2024 and 2025 in preparing fund financial statements for its governmental funds.

LO 12-4

34. The City of Raylan has a rather large warehouse that it no longer needs. The city had previously used the warehouse to store supplies and equipment for the school system, police department, and other public service functions. It has a remaining expected life of 18 years with no expected residual value. On January 1, 2024, the warehouse has a net book value of $1.4 million. On that date, city officials agree to lease the property to Acme International for its remaining life. Both parties agree to an implicit interest rate of 12 percent. The first payment is to be made immediately and on each subsequent January 1. The straight-line method is used where an allocation method is required.
    a. Assume that the present value of an annuity due of $1 at a 12 percent annual rate for 18 periods is 8.11963. Based on that assumption, what amount does the City of Raylan charge Acme each period?
    b. Assume the annual payments are properly calculated as $172,400 based on the information provided. What journal entries does the City of Raylan make for this lease for the year 2024 in preparing government-wide financial statements? Assume the city reports these transactions within the governmental activities.
    c. Assume the annual payments are properly calculated as $172,400 based on the information provided. What journal entries does the City of Raylan make for this lease for the year 2024 in preparing fund financial statements? Assume the city reports these transactions within the general fund.

LO 12-5

35. On January 1, 2024, the City of Hastings creates a solid waste landfill that it expects to reach capacity gradually over the next 20 years. If the landfill were to be closed at the current time, closure costs would be approximately $1.2 million plus an additional $700,000 for postclosure work. Of these totals, the city must pay $50,000 on December 31 of each year for preliminary closure work.

At the end of 2024, the landfill reaches 3 percent of capacity. At the end of 2025, the landfill reaches 9 percent of capacity. At the end of 2025, a reassessment is made. Experts determine total closure costs will be $1.4 million rather than $1.2 million.

a. Assume the city views the landfill as an enterprise fund. What journal entries should the city make in 2024 and 2025 in preparing government-wide financial statements?

b. Assume the city views the landfill as being within the general fund. What journal entries should the city make in 2024 and 2025 in preparing government-wide financial statements?

c. Assume the city views the landfill as an enterprise fund. What journal entries should the city make in 2024 and 2025 in preparing fund financial statements?

d. Assume the city views the landfill as being within the general fund. What journal entries should the city make in 2024 and 2025 in preparing fund financial statements?

LO 12-4

36. The City of Lawrence opens a solid waste landfill in 2024 that is at 54 percent of capacity on December 31, 2024. City officials had initially anticipated closure costs of $2 million but later that year decided that closure costs would actually be $2.4 million. None of these costs will be incurred until 2028, when the landfill is scheduled to be closed.

a. What appears on the government-wide financial statements for this landfill for the year ended December 31, 2024?

b. Assuming that the landfill is recorded within the general fund, what appears on the fund financial statements for this landfill for the year ended December 31, 2024?

LO 12-6

37. On January 1, 2024, a rich citizen of the Town of Ristoni donates a painting valued at $300,000 to be displayed to the public in a government building. Although this painting meets the three criteria to qualify as an artwork, town officials choose to record it as an asset. The gift has no eligibility requirements. These officials judge the painting to be inexhaustible so that depreciation will not be reported.

a. For the year ended December 31, 2024, what does the town report on its government-wide financial statements in connection with this gift?

b. How does the answer to part (a) change if the government decides to depreciate this asset over a 10-year period using straight-line depreciation?

c. How does the answer to part (a) change if the government decides not to capitalize the asset?

LO 12-6

38. On January 1, 2024, the City of Graf pays $60,000 for a work of art to display in the local library. The city will take appropriate measures to protect and preserve the piece. However, if the work is ever sold, the money received will go into unrestricted funds. Officials view the work as inexhaustible, but they have opted to depreciate the cost over 20 years (using the straight-line method).

a. How is this work reported on government-wide financial statements for the year ended December 31, 2024?

b. How is this work reported in fund financial statements for the governmental funds for the year ended December 31, 2024?

LO 12-7

39. A city government adds streetlights within its boundaries at a total cost of $300,000. These lights should burn for at least 10 years but can last significantly longer if maintained properly. The city develops a system to monitor these lights with the goal that 97 percent will be working at any one time. During the year, the city spends $48,000 to clean and repair the lights so that they are working according to the specified conditions. The city also spends another $78,000 to construct lights for several new streets.

Describe the various ways these costs could be reported on government-wide financial statements.

LO 12-8

40. The City of Francois, Texas, is in the process of producing its current annual comprehensive financial report (ACFR). Several organizations that operate within the city are related in various ways to the primary government. Officials are attempting to determine how the city should report each of these organizations in the reporting process.

a. What is the major criterion for inclusion in a government's ACFR?

b. How does an activity or function qualify as a special-purpose government?

c. How is the legal separation of a special-purpose government evaluated?

d. How is the fiscal independence of a special-purpose government evaluated?

e. What is a component unit, and how does a government normally report it on government-wide financial statements?

f. How does a primary government prove that it can impose its will on a component unit?

g. What is meant by the blending of a component unit?

LO 12-5

41. The County of Maxnell decides to create a waste management department and offer its services to the public for a fee. As a result, county officials plan to account for this activity as an enterprise fund. Prepare journal entries for this operation for the following 2024 transactions. Also prepare any necessary adjusting entries at the end of the year. Assume the information is gathered so that the county can prepare fund financial statements. Only entries for the waste management department are required here:

January 1—Receive unrestricted funds of $160,000 from the general fund as permanent financing.

February 1—Borrow an additional $130,000 from a local bank at a 12 percent annual interest rate.

March 1—Order a truck at an expected cost of $108,000.

April 1—Receive the truck and make full payment. The actual cost including transportation was $110,000. The truck has a 10-year life and no residual value. The county uses straight-line depreciation.

May 1—Receive a $20,000 cash grant from the state to help supplement the pay of the department workers. According to the grant, the money must be used for that purpose.

June 1—Rent a garage for the truck at a cost of $1,000 per month. The county pays 12 months of rent in advance. The contract has no provisions for extensions or purchases.

July 1—Charge citizens $13,000 for services. Of this amount, $11,000 is collected.

August 1—Make a $10,000 cash payment on the 12 percent note of February 1. This payment covers both interest and principal.

September 1—Pay salaries of $18,000 using the grant money received on May 1.

October 1—Pay truck maintenance costs of $1,000.

November 1—Pay additional salaries of $10,000, first using the rest of the grant money received May 1.

December 31—Send invoices totaling $19,000 to customers for services during the past six months. Collect $3,000 of the cash immediately.

December 31—A new government landfill opened this year. At the end of the year, it is 12 percent filled. The estimated current cost for the eventual closure of this facility is $4 million, although no payments will be made for approximately nine years.

LO 12-6, 12-8, 12-10

42. The following information pertains to the City of Williamson for 2024, its first year of legal existence. For convenience, assume that all transactions are for the general fund, which has three separate functions: general government, public safety, and health and sanitation.

Receipts:	
Property taxes	$320,000
Franchise taxes	42,000
Charges for general government services	5,000
Charges for public safety services	3,000
Charges for health and sanitation services	42,000
Issued long-term note payable	200,000
Receivables at end of year:	
Property taxes (90% estimated to be collectible)	90,000
Payments:	
Salary:	
General government	66,000
Public safety	39,000
Health and sanitation	22,000
Rent:	
General government	11,000
Public safety	18,000
Health and sanitation	3,000
Maintenance:	
General government	21,000
Public safety	5,000
Health and sanitation	9,000

(continued)

(continued)

Insurance:	
General government	8,000
Public safety ($2,000 still prepaid at end of year)	11,000
Health and sanitation	12,000
Interest on debt	16,000
Principal payment on debt	4,000
Storage shed	120,000
Equipment	80,000
Supplies (20% still held) (public safety)	15,000
Investments	90,000
Ordered but not received:	
Equipment	12,000
Liabilities, all of which are due in one month at end of year:	
Salaries:	
General government	4,000
Public safety	7,000
Health and sanitation	8,000

Compensated absences (such as vacations and sick days) legally owed to general government workers at year-end total $13,000. These amounts will not be taken by the employees until so late in 2025 that the payment is not viewed as requiring 2024 current financial resources.

The city received a piece of art this year as a donation. It is valued at $14,000. The city plans to use it for general government purposes. The gift has no eligibility requirements. The city chose not to capitalize this property.

General government activities use the storage shed that was acquired this year. It is depreciated over a 10-year period using the straight-line method with no residual value. The city uses the equipment for health and sanitation and depreciates it using the straight-line method over five years with no residual value.

The investments are valued at $103,000 at the end of the year.

For the equipment that was ordered but not yet received, the city council (the highest decision-making body in the government) voted to honor the commitment when the equipment eventually arrives.

a. Prepare a statement of activities and a statement of net position for governmental activities in government-wide financial statements for December 31, 2024, and the year then ended.

b. Prepare a statement of revenues, expenditures, and other changes in fund balances and a balance sheet for the general fund in fund financial statements as of December 31, 2024, and the year then ended. Assume that the city applies the consumption method.

LO 12-2, 12-3, 12-9, 12-11 43. The City of Bernard starts the year of 2024 with the following unrestricted amounts in its general fund: cash of $20,000 and investments of $70,000. In addition, it holds a small building bought on January 1, 2023, for general government purposes for $300,000 and a related long-term debt of $240,000. The building is depreciated on the straight-line method over 10 years. The annual interest rate on the debt is 10 percent. The general fund has four separate functions: general government, public safety, public works, and health and sanitation. Other information includes the following:

Receipts:	
Property taxes	$510,000
Sales taxes	99,000
Dividend income	20,000
Charges for general government services	15,000
Charges for public safety services	8,000
Charges for public works	4,000
Charges for health and sanitation services	31,000
Charges for landfill	8,000
Grant to be used for salaries for health workers (no eligibility requirements)	25,000
Issued long-term note payable	200,000
Sold investments (mentioned above)	84,000

(continued)

(*continued*)

Receivables at year-end:
    Property taxes ($10,000 is expected to be uncollectible) 130,000
Payments:
  Salary:
    General government 90,000
    Public safety.. 94,000
    Public works.. 69,000
    Health and sanitation (all from grant)................. 22,000
  Utilities:
    General government 9,000
    Public safety.. 16,000
    Public works.. 13,000
    Health and sanitation.................................... 4,000
  Insurance:
    General government 25,000
    Public safety.. 12,000
    Public works (all prepaid as of the end of the year)................... 6,000
    Health and sanitation.................................... 4,000
  Miscellaneous:
    General government 12,000
    Public safety.. 10,000
    Public works.. 9,000
    Health and sanitation.................................... 7,000
  Interest on previous debt 24,000
  Principal payment on previous debt...................... 10,000
  Interest on new debt 18,000
  Building (public works).................................... 210,000
  Equipment (public safety) 90,000
  Public works supplies (30% still held) 20,000
  Investments 111,000
Ordered but not received:
    Equipment 24,000
    Supplies 7,000
Due at end of year:
  Salaries:
    General government 14,000
    Public safety.. 17,000
    Public works.. 5,000

On the last day of the year, the city borrows $64,000 from a local bank and uses the money to buy a truck. The first payment on the loan (plus interest) will be made at the end of the next year.

The city opens a landfill this year that it records within its general fund. It is a public works function. Closure costs today are estimated as $260,000 although officials do not expect the landfill to be filled for nine more years. The city has incurred no costs to date. The landfill is now 15 percent filled.

For the equipment and supplies that were ordered but not yet received, the city council (the highest decision-making body in the government) has voted to honor the commitment when the items arrive.

The new building is depreciated over 20 years using the straight-line method and no residual value. Depreciation of the equipment is similar except that its life is only 10 years. Assume the city records a full year's depreciation in the year of acquisition.

The investments have a market value of $116,000 at year-end.

a. Prepare a statement of activities and a statement of net position for governmental activities in government-wide financial statements for December 31, 2024, and the year then ended.

b. Prepare a statement of revenues, expenditures, and other changes in fund balances and a balance sheet for the general fund in fund financial statements as of December 31, 2024, and the year then ended. Assume the purchases method is applied.

LO 12-7, 12-8, 12-9, 12-11

44. The City of Pfeiffer starts the year of 2024 with the general fund and an enterprise fund. The general fund has two activities: education and parks/recreation. For convenience, assume that the general fund holds $123,000 cash and a new school building costing $1 million. The city utilizes straight-line depreciation. The building has a 20-year life and no residual value. The enterprise fund has $62,000 cash and a new $600,000 civic auditorium with a 30-year life and no residual value. The enterprise fund monitors one activity, the rental of the civic auditorium for entertainment and other cultural affairs.

   The following transactions for the city take place during 2024. Assume that the city's fiscal year ends on December 31.

   a. Decides to build a municipal park and transfers cash of $70,000 into a capital projects fund. Both the creation of this fund and the transfer were made by the highest level of government authority. The city immediately expends $20,000 to acquire three acres of land.

   b. Borrows $110,000 cash on a long-term bond for use in creating the new municipal park.

   c. Assesses property taxes on the first day of the year. The assessment, which is immediately enforceable, totals $600,000. Of this amount, $510,000 will be collected during 2024. Officials expect another $50,000 during the first month of 2025. They anticipate the remainder halfway through 2025.

   d. Constructs a covered building in the new municipal park for $80,000 cash so that local citizens can play basketball when it rains. The building is put into service on July 1. It should last 10 years with no expected residual value.

   e. Builds a sidewalk through the new park for $10,000 cash and puts it into service on July 1. The sidewalk should normally last for 10 years, but the city plans to keep it fixed up to a predetermined quality level so that it can last almost indefinitely.

   f. Opens the park and charges an entrance fee of only a token amount. The city reports the park within its general fund. Collections during the first year of operations total $8,000.

   g. Buys a new parking deck for $200,000, paying $20,000 cash and signing a long-term note for the rest. The parking deck, which goes into operation on July 1, is across the street from the civic auditorium and is considered part of that activity. It has a 20-year life and no residual value.

   h. Receives a $100,000 cash grant for the city school system that must be spent for school lunches for children in low-income families. Officials view the appropriate spending of these funds as an eligibility requirement of this grant. During the current year, $37,000 of the amount received was spent for the intended purpose.

   i. Charges students in the school system a total fee of $6,000 for books and the like. Of this amount, 90 percent is collected during 2024 with the remainder expected to be collected in the first few weeks of 2025.

   j. Buys school supplies for $22,000 cash and uses $17,000 of them. The general fund applies the purchases method.

   k. Receives a painting by a local artist to be displayed in the local school. It qualifies as a work of art, and officials have chosen not to capitalize it. The painting has a value of $80,000. Officials have set up security precautions so that the painting will be viewed as inexhaustible.

   l. Transfers $20,000 cash from the general fund to the enterprise fund as a capital contribution.

   m. Orders a school bus for $99,000.

   n. Receives the school bus and pays an actual cost of $102,000, including transportation and other necessary costs. The bus goes into operation on October 1. It should last for five years with no residual value.

   o. Pays salaries of $240,000 to school teachers. In addition, owes and will pay $30,000 during the first two weeks of 2025. Vacations worth $23,000 have also been earned by the teachers but will not be taken until July 2025.

   p. Pays salaries of $42,000 to city auditorium workers. In addition, owes and will pay $3,000 in the first two weeks of 2025. Vacations worth $5,000 have also been earned by the workers but will not be taken until July 2025.

   q. Charges customers $130,000 for short-term rental of the civic auditorium. Of this balance, collects $110,000 in cash and will collect the remainder in April 2025.

   r. Pays $9,000 maintenance charges for the building and sidewalk in (d) and (e).

   s. Pays $14,000 on the bond in part (b) on the last day of 2024: $5,000 principal and $9,000 interest.

t. Accrues interest of $13,000 on the note in part (*g*) as of the end of 2024, an amount the city will pay in June 2025.

u. Assumes a museum operating within the city is a component unit that will be discretely presented. The museum reports to city officials that it incurred $42,000 of direct expenses this past year and earned $50,000 in revenues from admission charges. The only assets held at year-end were cash of $24,000, building (net of depreciation) of $300,000, and a long-term liability of $210,000.

Prepare the 2024 government-wide financial statements for this city. Assume the use of the modified approach.

LO 12-7, 12-8, 12-9, 12-11

45. Use the information in Problem 44 to prepare the 2024 fund financial statements for (a) the governmental funds and (b) the proprietary funds. A statement of cash flows is not required. Assume the city defines "available" as within 60 days and that all funds qualify as major. Assume that major funds are labeled as "Special Revenue Fund" and "Capital Projects Fund." The general fund is used for debt repayment.

LO 12-3, 12-4, 12-6, 12-9, 12-11

46. Indicate whether each of the following statements is true or false, and include a brief explanation for your answer.

a. A pension trust fund appears in the government-wide financial statements but not in the fund financial statements.

b. Permanent funds are included as one of the governmental funds.

c. A fire department places orders of $20,000 for equipment. Later, the equipment is received but at a total cost of $20,800. In compliance with requirements for fund financial statements, an encumbrance of $20,000 was recorded when the government placed the order, and recorded an expenditure of $20,800 when the equipment arrived.

d. A city reports a landfill as an enterprise fund. At the end of Year 1, the government estimated that the landfill will cost $800,000 to clean up when it is eventually full. At that time, it was 12 percent filled. At the end of Year 2, it is 20 percent filled, and the estimated cost of the cleanup was changed to $860,000. No payments are due for several years. Fund financial statements for Year 2 should report a $76,000 expense.

e. A city reports a landfill in the general fund. At the end of Year 1, the government estimated the landfill will cost $900,000 to clean up when it is eventually full. At that time, it was 11 percent filled. At the end of Year 2, it is 20 percent filled, and the estimated cost of the cleanup was changed to $850,000. No payments are due for several years. Government-wide financial statements for Year 2 should report a $71,000 expense.

f. A custodial fund has neither revenues nor expenditures but reports expenses.

g. A city leases several ambulances to use for 5 years although they have an expected life of 10 years. The city must determine whether this is an operating lease or a financing lease.

h. A city has an old school building that it leases to a hospital for its entire remaining life. The city must remove the school building from its government-wide financial statements.

i. A city leases several large trucks to use by its fire department for the next eight years. Total payments will be $260,000. The present value of those payments at an appropriate interest rate is $173,000. On the date of signing, the city immediately records an expenditure and another financing source of $173,000 for its fund financial statements.

For Problems 47 through 50, use the following introductory information:

The City of Wolfe issues its financial statements for Year 4 (assume that the city uses a calendar year). The city's general fund is composed of two functions: (1) education and (2) parks. The city also utilizes capital projects funds for ongoing construction and an enterprise fund to account for an art museum. The city also has one discretely presented component unit.

The government-wide financial statements indicate the following Year 4 totals.

Education had net expenses of $710,000.

Parks had net expenses of $130,000.

Art museum had net revenues of $80,000.

General revenues were $900,000. The overall increase in net position for the city was $140,000.

The fund financial statements for Year 4 indicate the following:

The general fund had an increase of $30,000 in its fund balance.

The capital projects fund had an increase of $40,000 in its fund balance.

The enterprise fund had an increase of $60,000 in its net position balance.

Officials for the City of Wolfe define "available" as current financial resources to be paid or collected within 60 days.

LO 12-6

47. On the first day of Year 4, the city receives a painting as a gift that qualifies as a work of art. It has an expected life of 30 years, is worth $15,000, and is displayed by the city at one of the local parks. The accountant accidentally capitalizes and depreciates it although officials wanted to use the allowed alternative.

Respond to the following questions:

a. According to the information provided, the general fund reported a $30,000 increase in its fund balance. If the accountant had used the allowed alternative, what would the city report as the change in fund balance for the general fund for the year?

b. According to the information provided, the parks reported net expenses of $130,000. If the accountant had used the allowed alternative, what would the city report as the correct net expense for parks for the year?

c. Assume the same information except that the art was given to the art museum but then not recorded at all. What should have been the overall change in net position for Year 4 on government-wide financial statements, assuming that officials still preferred the allowed alternative?

LO 12-9

48. Assume that the one component unit had program revenues of $30,000 and expenses of $42,000 and spent $10,000 for land during Year 4. However, it should have been handled as a blended component unit, not as a discretely presented component unit. According to the information provided, the overall increase in net position reported was $140,000. What was the correct overall change in the net position in the government-wide financial statements?

LO 12-5

49. The city maintains a landfill and records it within its parks. The landfill generates program revenues of $4,000 in Year 4 and cash expenses of $15,000. It also pays $3,000 cash for a piece of land. These transactions were recorded as would have been anticipated, but no other recording was made this year. The city assumes that it will have to pay $200,000 to clean up the landfill when it is closed in several years. The landfill was 18 percent filled at the end of Year 3 and is 26 percent filled at the end of Year 4. No payments will be necessary for several more years. For convenience, assume that the entries in all previous years were correctly handled regardless of the situation.

a. The city believes that the landfill was included appropriately in all previous years as one of the enterprise funds. According to the information provided, the overall increase in net position was $140,000. What is the correct overall change in the net position in the government-wide financial statements?

b. The city believes that the landfill was included appropriately in all previous years in one of the enterprise funds. According to the information provided, the enterprise fund reports an increase in its net position of $60,000. What is the correct change in the net position of the enterprise fund in fund financial statements?

c. The city believes that the landfill was included appropriately in all previous years within the general fund. What is the correct change in the fund balance of the general fund?

LO 12-8, 12-10

50. On the first day of the year, the City of Wolfe buys $20,000 of equipment with a five-year life and no residual value for its school system. This cost was capitalized. No other entries were ever made. The city maintained the equipment using the modified approach.

a. Based on the information provided, what was the correct overall change in the net position in the government-wide financial statements?

b. What was the correct amount of net expenses for education in the government-wide statements?

LO 12-5

51. A city maintains a solid waste landfill that was 12 percent filled at the end of Year 1 and 26 percent filled at the end of Year 2. During those periods, the government estimated that total closure costs would be $2 million. It pays $50,000 to an environmental company on July 1 of each of these two years to begin some of the restoration process. Such payments will continue for years to come. Indicate whether each of the following *independent* statements is true or false and briefly explain each answer. The city has a December 31 year-end.

a. The government-wide financial statements will show a $230,000 expense in Year 2 but only if reported in an enterprise fund.

b. Fund financial statements will show a $50,000 liability in Year 2 if this landfill is reported in the general fund.

c. Fund financial statements will show a $50,000 liability at the end of Year 2 if this landfill is reported in an enterprise fund.

d. If the city reports this landfill in an enterprise fund, government-wide financial statements and fund financial statements will have the same basic reporting.

e. Government-wide financial statements will show a $420,000 liability at the end of Year 2.

f. Assume the city reports the landfill in the general fund. Over the landfill's entire life, the amount of expense recognized in government-wide financial statements will be the same as the amount of expenditures recognized in fund financial statements.

LO 12-5

52. Use the same information as in Problem 51, except that, by the end of Year 3, the landfill is 40 percent filled. The city now realizes that the total closure costs will be $3 million. Indicate whether each of the following *independent* statements is true or false and briefly explain each answer.

a. Assume the city reports the landfill as an enterprise fund. If the city had estimated the costs as $3 million from the beginning, the reporting on the fund financial statements would have been different in the past years.

b. Assume the city reports the landfill in the general fund. A liability will be reported for the governmental activities in the government-wide financial statements at the end of Year 3.

c. A $680,000 expense should be recognized in Year 3 in the government-wide financial statements.

d. Because the closure costs reflect a future flow of cash, any liability reported in the government-wide financial statements must be reported at present value.

LO 12-6

53. A city receives a copy of its original charter from the year 1799 as a gift from a citizen. The document is put under protective glass and displayed in the city hall for all to see. The city estimates its fair value at $10,000. Indicate whether each of the following *independent* statements is true or false, and briefly explain each answer.

a. Assume the city government does not have a policy for handling any proceeds if it ever sells the document. The city must report a $10,000 asset within its government-wide financial statements.

b. Assume this gift qualifies for optional handling and the city chooses to report it as an asset. For government-wide financial statements, depreciation is required.

c. Assume this gift qualifies for optional handling and the document is deemed to be exhaustible. The city must report an immediate expense of $10,000 in government-wide financial statements.

d. Assume this gift qualifies for optional handling. The city must make a decision as to whether to recognize a revenue of $10,000 in government-wide financial statements.

e. Assume this gift qualifies for optional handling. The city can choose to report the gift in the statement of net activities for government-wide financial statements in a way so that no overall net effect is reported.

LO 12-9

54. A city starts a public library that has separate incorporation and receives some of its operating money from the state and some from private donations. Indicate whether each of the following *independent* statements is true or false, and briefly explain each answer.

a. If the city appoints 9 of the 10 directors, the city must report the library as a component unit.

b. If the library qualifies as a component unit and its financial results are shown as part of the city's governmental activities, it is a blended component unit.

c. If the library appoints its own board but the city must approve its annual budget, the city must report the library as a blended component unit.

LO 12-6, 12-7, 12-9, 12-10

55. The City of Dickens has a fiscal year ending December 31, Year 5. The city council is the highest level of decision-making authority for the government. For each of the following, indicate whether the overall statement is true or false. Assume that each situation is independent of all others.

a. On December 30, Year 5, the city spends $900,000 on a sidewalk project that is not a special assessment. On the Year 5 financial statements, a reconciliation is presented that starts with the total change in fund balances for the governmental funds and works down to end with the total change in net position for the governmental activities. As a result of this acquisition, this $900,000 must be subtracted as part of this reconciliation.

b. The city appoints all members of the board of directors for a nature museum. This fact alone qualifies this nature museum a component unit of the city.

c. The city appoints none of the governing board of a parks commission. This fact alone prohibits this parks commission from being a component unit of the city.

d. The city has a school system with a separately elected governing board (elected by the public). This fact alone makes the school system a special-purpose government with its own required financial reporting.

e. The modified approach applies only to infrastructure assets.

f. The modified approach has become widely used in state and local government accounting over the most recent few years.

g. The city's school system charges students a $10 per person fee each year. In the statement of activities, this fee should be shown as miscellaneous revenue directly under general revenues.

h. The city receives a work of art worth $100,000 as a gift and also spends $70,000 in cash to buy a second artwork. Both artworks will be exhibited publicly and properly protected and preserved. The city council passes a resolution that if either item is ever sold the proceeds must be used to buy replacement art works. Both of the artworks are viewed as inexhaustible. The city has the option to report both of these pieces of art as expenses rather than as assets in government-wide financial statements.

i. Assume that the city issues 30-day revenue anticipation notes on December 30, Year 5, to finance the government until it collects new taxes. These notes are issued at their face value of $500,000. On the Year 5 financial statements, a reconciliation is presented that starts with the total change in fund balances for the governmental funds and works down to end with the total change in the net position for the governmental activities. As a result of the note issuance, this $500,000 must be subtracted as part of this reconciliation.

Develop Your Skills

RESEARCH CASE 1

The accountant for the City of Abernethy calls the local CPA firm that audits the city's financial statements with a question:

> At the start of the current year, city officials signed a contract to lease a new police car for seven years, its entire useful life. We drove a hard bargain. The annual payments are only $18,000 per year so the liability has a present value of $98,031. I realize the city has to report the initial liability at that amount. Nevertheless, the car has a fair value of $114,000. We know that based on its sales price. Can we report the asset at $114,000 even if we have to report the liability at $98,031?

Required

Go to www.gasb.org. Click on "Standards & Guidance." Under "Pronouncements," click on "More" to expand. Scroll down to "View GASB Pronouncements" and click on "76-100." Scroll down to GASB Statement No. 87. Click on "Full Text." Scroll to the Contents page for this pronouncement. Locate "Appendix B: Basis for Conclusions." This section explains what options GASB considered and what decisions were made. Locate and read paragraphs B47 through B50. Based on that discussion, write a memo to officials for the City of Abernethy answering the question posed by the accountant.

RESEARCH CASE 2

Officials for the City of Anderson, West Virginia, recently formed a transit authority to create a public transportation system for the community. These same officials are now preparing the city's ACFR for the most recent year. The transit authority is projected to lose a considerable amount of money at least for the next few years. Officials are interested in its financial reporting and whether it qualifies as a component unit of the city.

Following are several articles written about the reporting of component units by a state or local government:

"Changes in Component Units," *Government Finance Review,* February 2011.

"GASB Issues Guidance on Financial Reporting Entity, Component Units," *Accounting Policy & Practice Report,* January 7, 2011.

"Financial Reporting for Affiliated Organizations," *Journal of Government Financial Management,* Winter 2003.

"How to Implement GASB *Statement No. 34*," *Journal of Accountancy,* November 2001.

"GASB Issues Guidance on Blending Certain Component Units into Financial Statements," *Investment Weekly News,* February 27, 2016.

"Accounting for Affiliated Organizations," *Government Finance Review,* December 2002.

"Component Unit Reporting in the New Reporting Model," *CPA Journal,* October 2001.

Required

Read one or more of the preceding articles and any others that you may discover about component units. Write a memo to city officials providing as much detailed information as you can about component units and their reporting to help these individuals understand the challenges and difficulties of the required reporting.

ANALYSIS CASE 1

Read the following journal articles: "25 Years of State and Local Governmental Financial Reporting— An Accounting Standards Perspective," *Government Accountants Journal,* Fall 1992; "The GASB Turns 25: A Retrospective," *Government Finance Review,* April 2009; and "GASB at 35, A Look Back, A Look Forward," *CPA Journal,* April 2020.

Next, go to https://pittsburghpa.gov/controller/annualreport for the City of Pittsburgh, Pennsylvania, and pick an ACFR (formerly referred to as a CAFR) that is more than 25 years old (perhaps 1995, for example). Compare the financial information presented in that report to the ACFR for Pittsburgh for the most recent year.

Required

Accounting for state and local governments has changed considerably over the years. Write a report to highlight some of the most significant differences you noted between the reporting process used by these governments before 2000 and the process presented in this textbook.

ANALYSIS CASE 2

Go to www.phoenix.gov, and do a search for the term "ACFR." Those results should lead to the latest ACFR for the City of Phoenix, Arizona. The financial statements for a state and local government must include a management's discussion and analysis of the information being reported. Read this section of the Phoenix ACFR. It should only be about 10–12 pages in length, but should contain much interesting financial information for the government.

Required

Write a report indicating the types of information found in this government's MD&A.

COMMUNICATION CASE 1

Read the following articles and any other papers that are available on setting governmental accounting standards:

"The Governmental Accounting Standards Board: Factors Influencing Its Operation and Initial Technical Agenda," *Government Accountants Journal,* Spring 2000.

"Governmental Accounting Standards Come of Age: Highlights from the First 20 Years," *Government Finance Review,* April 2005.

"A Valuable Opportunity to Improve Government Accounting—and Accountability," *CPA Journal,* April 2018.

"Forward-Looking Information: What It Is and Why It Matters," *Government Accountants Journal,* December 1, 2010.

"GASB Simplifies GAAP Hierarchy for State and Local Governments," *Business Wire,* June 29, 2015.

"A Century of Governmental Accounting and Financial Reporting Leadership," *Government Finance Review,* April 2006.

"The GASB Turns 25: A Retrospective," *Government Finance Review,* April 2009.

"GASB at 35, A Look Back, A Look Forward," *CPA Journal,* April 2020.

"Envisioning the Future of Government Reporting," *CPA Journal,* November 2020.

Required

Write a short paper discussing the evolution of financial reporting for state and local governments over the years.

COMMUNICATION CASE 2

CPA *skills*

The City of Larissa recently opened a solid waste landfill to serve the area's citizens and businesses. The city's accountant has gone to city officials for guidance as to whether to record the landfill within the general fund or as a separate enterprise fund. Officials have asked for guidance on how to make that decision and how the answer will impact the government's financial reporting.

Required

Write a memo to the government officials describing the factors that should influence the decision as to the fund in which to report the landfill. Describe the impact that this decision will have on the city's future comprehensive annual financial reports.

EXCEL CASE

CPA *skills*

Prior to the creation of government-wide financial statements, the City of Loveland did not report the cost of its infrastructure assets. Now city officials are attempting to determine reported values for major infrastructure assets that were constructed prior to the passage of the current rules for reporting. The chief concern is determining a value for the city's hundreds of miles of roads that were built at various times over the past several decades. The city assumes each road will last for 50 years (depreciation is 2 percent per year).

As of December 31, 2024, city engineers believed that one mile of new road would cost $2.3 million. For convenience, each road is assumed to have been acquired as of January 1 of the year in which it was put into operation. Officials have done some investigation and believe that the cost of constructing a mile of road has increased by 8 percent each year over the past 30 years.

Required

Build a spreadsheet to determine the value that should now be reported for each mile of road depending on the year it was put into operation. For example, what reported value should be disclosed in the government-wide financial statements for 10 miles of roads put into operation on January 1, 1999?

Index